Consumer Behavior

Building Marketing Strategy

THIRTEENTH EDITION

David L. Mothersbaugh
University of Alabama

Del I. Hawkins
University of Oregon

Contributing Authors

Linda L. Mothersbaugh
Integrated Solutions, LLC

Gail Tom
California State University, Sacramento

CONSUMER BEHAVIOR: BUILDING MARKETING STRATEGY, THIRTEENTH EDITION

Published by McGraw-Hill Education, 2 Penn Plaza, New York, NY 10121.

Some ancillaries, including electronic and print components, may not be available to customers outside the United States.

This book is printed on acid-free paper.

3 4 5 6 7 8 9 LWI 21 20 19 18 17

ISBN 978-1-259-23254-1
MHID 1-259-23254-9

Senior Vice President, Products & Markets: *Kurt L. Strand*
Vice President, General Manager, Products & Markets: *Michael Ryan*
Vice President, Content Design & Delivery: *Kimberly Meriwether David*
Managing Director: *Susan Gouijnstook*
Director: *Michael Ablassmeir*
Brand Manager: *Kim Leistner*
Director, Product Development: *Meghan Campbell*
Product Developer: *Heather Darr*
Director, Content Design & Delivery: *Terri Schiesl*
Executive Program Manager: *Faye M. Herrig*
Content Project Managers: *Jessica Portz, Danielle Clement, Judi David*
Buyer: *Susan K. Culbertson*
Design: *Tara McDermott*
Content Licensing Specialist: *Keri Johnson*
Cover Image: © *Frederic Cirou/PhotoAlto/Corbis*
Compositor: SPi Global
Printer: *LSC Communications*

All credits appearing on page or at the end of the book are considered to be an extension of the copyright page.

Library of Congress Cataloging-in-Publication Data

Hawkins, Del I.
Consumer behavior : building marketing strategy / David L. Mothersbaugh, University of Alabama, Del I. Hawkins, University of Oregon.—Thirteenth edition.
pages cm
Hawkins's name appears first on earlier editions.
ISBN 978-1-259-23254-1 (alk. paper)
1. Consumer behavior—United States. 2. Market surveys—United States. 3. Consumer behavior—United States—Case studies. I. Mothersbaugh, David L. II. Title.
HF5415.33.U6H38 2016
658.8'3420973—dc23
2015003823

www.mhhe.com

Preface

Marketing attempts to influence the way consumers behave. These attempts have implications for the organizations making them, the consumers they are trying to influence, and the society in which these attempts occur. We are all consumers and we are all members of society, so consumer behavior, and attempts to influence it, is critical to all of us. This text is designed to provide an understanding of consumer behavior. This understanding can make us better consumers, better marketers, and better citizens.

MARKETING CAREERS AND CONSUMER BEHAVIOR

A primary purpose of this text is to provide the student with a usable, managerial understanding of consumer behavior. Most students in consumer behavior courses aspire to careers in marketing management, sales, or advertising. They hope to acquire knowledge and skills that will be useful to them in these careers. Unfortunately, some may be seeking the type of knowledge gained in introductory accounting classes; that is, a set of relatively invariant rules that can be applied across a variety of situations to achieve a fixed solution that is known to be correct. For these students, the uncertainty and lack of closure involved in dealing with living, breathing, changing, stubborn consumers can be very frustrating. However, if they can accept dealing with endless uncertainty, utilizing an understanding of consumer behavior in developing marketing strategy will become tremendously exciting.

It is our view that the utilization of knowledge of consumer behavior in the development of marketing strategy is an art. This is not to suggest that scientific principles and procedures are not applicable; rather, it means that the successful application of these principles to particular situations requires human judgment that we are not able to reduce to a fixed set of rules.

Let us consider the analogy with art in some detail. Suppose you want to become an expert artist. You would study known principles of the visual effects of blending various colors, of perspective, and so forth. Then you would practice applying these principles until you developed the ability to produce acceptable paintings. If you had certain natural talents, the right teacher, and the right topic, you might even produce a masterpiece. The same approach should be taken by one wishing to become a marketing manager, a salesperson, or an advertising director. The various factors or principles that influence consumer behavior should be thoroughly studied. Then, one should practice applying these principles until acceptable marketing strategies result. However, while knowledge and practice can in general produce acceptable strategies, great marketing strategies, like masterpieces, require special talents, effort, timing, and some degree of luck (what if Mona Lisa had not wanted her portrait painted?).

The art analogy is useful for another reason. All of us, professors and students alike, tend to ask, "How can I use the concept of, say, social class to develop a successful marketing strategy?" This makes as much sense as an artist asking, "How can I use blue to create a great picture?" Obviously, blue alone will seldom be sufficient for a great work of art. Instead, to be successful, the artist must understand when and how to use blue in conjunction with other elements in the picture. Likewise, the marketing manager must understand when and how to use a knowledge of social class in conjunction with a knowledge of other factors in designing a successful marketing strategy.

This book is based on the belief that knowledge of the factors that influence consumer behavior can, with practice, be used to develop sound marketing strategy. With this in mind, we have attempted to do three things. First, we present a reasonably comprehensive description of the various behavioral concepts and theories that have been found useful for understanding consumer behavior. This is generally done at the beginning of each chapter or at the beginning of major subsections in each chapter. We believe that a person must have a thorough understanding of a concept in order to successfully apply that concept across different situations.

Second, we present examples of how these concepts have been utilized in the development of marketing strategy. We have tried to make clear that these examples are not "how you use this concept." Rather, they are presented as "how one organization facing a particular marketing situation used this concept."

Third, at the end of each chapter and each major section, we present a number of questions, activities, or cases that require the student to apply the concepts.

CONSUMING AND CONSUMER BEHAVIOR

The authors of this book are consumers, as is everyone reading this text. Most of us spend more time buying and consuming than we do working or sleeping. We consume products such as cars and fuel, services such as haircuts and home repairs, and entertainment such as television and concerts. Given the time and energy we devote to consuming, we should strive to be good at it. A knowledge of consumer behavior can be used to enhance our ability to consume wisely.

Marketers spend billions of dollars attempting to influence what, when, and how you and I consume. Marketers not only spend billions attempting to influence our behavior but also spend hundreds of millions of dollars studying our behavior. With a knowledge of consumer behavior and an understanding of how marketers use this knowledge, we can study marketers. A television commercial can be an annoying interruption of a favorite program. However, it can also be a fascinating opportunity to speculate on the commercial's objective, its target audience, and the underlying behavior assumptions. Indeed, given the ubiquitous nature of commercials, an understanding of how they are attempting to influence us or others is essential to understand our environment.

Throughout the text, we present examples that illustrate the objectives of specific marketing activities. By studying these examples and the principles on which they are based, one can develop the ability to discern the underlying logic of the marketing activities encountered daily.

SOCIAL RESPONSIBILITY AND CONSUMER BEHAVIOR

What are the costs and benefits of regulating the marketing of food to children? How much more needs to be done to protect the online privacy of children? Of adults? What is the appropriate type and size of warning label for cigarettes that should be mandated by the federal government? These issues are currently being debated by industry leaders and consumer advocacy groups. As educated citizens, we have a responsibility to take part in these sorts of debates and work toward positive solutions. However, developing sound positions on these issues requires an understanding of such factors as information processing as it relates to advertising—an important part of our understanding of consumer behavior.

The debates described above are just a few of the many that require an understanding of consumer behavior. We present a number of these topics throughout the text. The objective is to develop the ability to apply consumer behavior knowledge to social and regulatory issues as well as to business and personal issues.

FEATURES OF THE THIRTEENTH EDITION

Marketing and consumer behavior, like the rest of the world, are changing at a rapid pace. Both the way consumers behave and the practices of studying that behavior continue to evolve. In order to keep up with this dynamic environment, the thirteenth edition includes a number of important features.

Internet, Mobile, and Social Media

The Internet, mobile marketing, and social media are dramatically changing the way in which consumers shop and buy. This edition integrates the latest research, practices, and examples concerning technology throughout the text and the cases.

Global Marketing

Previous editions have included a wealth of global material, and this edition is no exception. Most chapters contain multiple global examples woven into the text. In addition, Chapter 2 and several of the cases are devoted to global issues.

Ethnic Subcultures

This edition continues our emphasis on the exciting issues surrounding marketing to ethnic subcultures. Ethnic diversity is increasing and we draw in the latest research and emerging trends to shed light on this important topic.

Strategic Application

This edition continues our emphasis on the application of consumer behavior concepts and theory to exciting marketing problems and important emerging trends. We do this through our heavy emphasis on segmentation schemes, as well as opening examples, featured consumer insights, and cases. This edition contains many segmentation schemes that provide insights into the development of marketing strategy. The opening examples, in-text examples, and consumer insights provide additional strategic insight by showing how specific companies utilize various consumer behavior concepts in developing effective marketing strategies. Finally, cases provide an opportunity to apply consumer behavior concepts to real-world problems.

Walkthrough

Chapter Features

Each chapter contains a variety of features designed to enhance students' understanding of the material as well as to make the material more fun.

chapter

2 Cross-Cultural Varia In Consumer Behav

Learning Objectives

We are dedicated to making this text a valuable learning and teaching resource. We believe the learning objectives aid both students and instructors. Each chapter starts with a set of learning objectives linked to key learning outcomes that are then integrated throughout the text and in other learning and teaching resources.

LEARNING OBJECTIVES

LO1 Define the concept of culture.

LO2 Describe core values that vary across culture and influence behaviors.

LO3 Understand cross-cultural variations in non-verbal communications.

LO4 Summarize key aspects of the global youth culture.

LO5 Understand the role of global demographics

LO6 List the key dimensions in deciding to enter a foreign market.

- Areas in the chapter that deal with a learning objective are tagged for easy reference.
- The summary section in the end-of-chapter material is organized around the learning objectives to provide additional clarity.
- The student quizzes on the student online learning center (Student OLC) are tagged by these learning objectives.

CHANGES IN AMERICAN CULTURAL VALUES

LO1 Observable shifts in behavior, including consumption behavior, often reflect shifts in **cultural values,** *widely held beliefs that affirm what is desirable.* Therefore, it is necessary to understand the underlying value shifts to understand current and future consumer behavior. Although we discuss American values as though every American has the same values, in fact there is substantial variance in values across individuals and groups. In addition, changes in values tend to occur slowly and unevenly across individuals and groups. While traumatic events such as the 9/11 attacks and the recent major recession can produce value shifts, a slow evolution is more common. Caution should be used in assuming that short-term behavioral or attitudinal changes in response to such events represent long-lasting value shifts.

Figure 3–1 presents our estimate of how American values are changing. These are the same values used to describe different cultures in Chapter 2. It must be emphasized that Figure 3–1 is based on the authors' subjective interpretation of the American society. You should feel free, indeed compelled, to challenge these judgments.

Opening Vignettes

Each chapter begins with a practical example that introduces the material in the chapter. These involve situations in which businesses, government units, or nonprofit organizations have used or misused consumer behavior principles. Many of the opening vignettes are new to the thirteenth edition.

LEARNING OBJECTIVES

LO1 Define the concept of culture.

LO2 Describe core values that vary across culture and influence behaviors.

LO3 Understand cross-cultural variations in nonverbal communications.

LO4 Summarize key aspects of the global youth culture.

LO5 Understand the role of global demographics

LO6 List the key dimensions in deciding to enter a foreign market.

Firms often aspire to be global. The benefits can be significant, but the challenges are staggering. The adaptations, adjustments, and considerations necessary when doing business across country and cultural borders are numerous. The following examples (Target, Bunnies, and Apple) illustrate the branding and logo issues created by global trademark law.

Target: United States versus Australia— Target, the 1,800-store Minneapolis-based retailer, recently established its first non-U.S. stores in Canada.[1] Although this is Target's first venture beyond its American borders, since 1968 there have been Target department stores in Australia. Target Australia (300 stores, $3.8 B annual revenue) bears an uncanny resemblance to the U.S. Target, with the same (a) "Target" name in the same font; (b) red and white bulls'-eye logo on its storefront, website, and ads; (c) tagline "Expect more, Pay less"; as well as a mix of products that consumers likely would find indistinguishable from those offered in Target U.S.

The explanation for this seemingly odd occurrence can be found in trademark law and the historical development of regional and local brands at a time when globalization was less prevalent. Trademarks for the most part can be established only in one country at a time. A company doing business in multiple countries must obtain trademarks for its name separately for each country (Target U.S. did so in 1966–67; Target Australia did so in 1968). Why Target U.S. would have allowed this is speculative, but one expert suggests:

> . . . the two Targets [likely] had some sort of informal, handshake agreement. Fifty years ago, retail was primarily a local business and there were very few, if any, truly global brands. The idea that Target U.S. and Target Australia would somehow cross paths seemed remote at best.

Currently, Target U.S. and Target Australia are not directly competing. But the globalized nature of consumer buying, the permeability of country boundaries provided by Internet access, and Target U.S.'s desire to grow beyond its borders paints a scenario that could create challenges and conflict moving forward.

Pink Bunnies: Energizer versus Duracell— The localized nature of trademark laws also explains the existence of two battery bunnies, the Energizer Bunny in the United States and Canada and the Duracell Bunnies in Europe and Australia. In 1973, Duracell created the Duracell Bunny to personify the long life of its batteries. In a worldwide advertisement campaign from 1973 to 1980, the drum-beating bunny powered by Duracell batteries outlasted

37

Four-Color Illustrations

Print ads, web pages, storyboards, and photos of point-of-purchase displays and packages appear throughout the text. Each is directly linked to the text material both by text references to each illustration and by the descriptive comments that accompany each illustration. These illustrations, which we've continued to update with the thirteenth edition, provide vivid examples and applications of the concepts and theories presented in the text.

ILLUSTRATION 2-7

This ad campaign uses a global youth appeal to target style leaders around the world.

Integrated Coverage of Ethical/Social Issues

Marketers face numerous ethical issues as they apply their understanding of consumer behavior in the marketplace. We describe and discuss many of these issues. These discussions are highlighted in the text via an "ethics" icon in the margin. In addition, Chapter 20 is devoted to social and regulation issues relating to marketing practice. Several of the cases are also focused on ethical or regulatory issues, including all of the cases following Part Six.

- Global agnostics (9 percent)—Don't base decisions on global brand name; evaluate as they would local brands; don't see global brands as special. Higher in the United States and South Africa. Lower in Japan, Indonesia, China, and Turkey.

Corporate responsibility and ethical issues can span from labor policies to influences on consumption of products linked to negative consequences. One example is American tobacco companies, which are aggressively marketing their products in the developing countries of Asia, Latin America, Africa, and Eastern Europe. Smoking-related deaths are now a leading killer in Asia, where increases in female smoking are a major concern.[8] As one World Health Organization (WHO) official notes:

Tables

Cultural Values of Relevance to Consumer Behavior — TABLE 2-1
Other-Oriented Values
• *Individual/Collective.* Are individual activity and initiative valued more highly than collective activity and conformity?
• *Youth/Age.* Is family life organized to meet the needs of the children or the adults? Are younger or older people viewed as leaders and role models?
• *Extended/Limited family.* To what extent does one have a lifelong obligation to numerous family members?
• *Masculine/Feminine.* To what extent does social power automatically go to males?
• *Competitive/Cooperative.* Does one obtain success by excelling over others or by cooperating with them?
• *Diversity/Uniformity.* Does the culture embrace variation in religious belief, ethnic background, political views, and other important behaviors and attitudes?
Environment-Oriented Values
• *Cleanliness.* To what extent is cleanliness pursued beyond the minimum needed for health?
• *Performance/Status.* Is the culture's reward system based on performance or on inherited factors such as family or class?
• *Tradition/Change.* Are existing patterns of behavior considered to be inherently superior to new patterns of behavior?
• *Risk taking/Security.* Are those who risk their established positions to overcome obstacles or achieve high goals admired more than those who do not?
• *Problem solving/Fatalistic.* Are people encouraged to overcome all problems, or do they take a "what will be, will be" attitude?
• *Nature.* Is nature regarded as something to be admired or overcome?
Self-Oriented Values
• *Active/Passive.* Is a physically active approach to life valued more highly than a less active orientation?
• *Sensual gratification/Abstinence.* To what extent is it acceptable to enjoy sensual pleasures such as food, drink, and sex?
• *Material/Nonmaterial.* How much importance is attached to the acquisition of material wealth?
• *Hard work/Leisure.* Is a person who works harder than economically necessary admired more than one who does not?
• *Postponed gratification/Immediate gratification.* Are people encouraged to "save for a rainy day" or to "live for today"?
• *Religious/Secular.* To what extent ar

Consumer Insights

These boxed discussions provide an in-depth look at a particularly interesting consumer study or marketing practice. Each has several questions within it that are designed to encourage critical thinking by the students. Many of the consumer insights are new to the thirteenth edition.

CONSUMER INSIGHT 2-1

Unilever Adapts to Sell Laundry Products Globally

Unilever is highly successful in marketing its laundry products outside of the United States. The reason is it continually adapts to existing and emerging factors both within and across the countries where it does business. A stunning statistic is that "[e]very half hour 7 million people in the world wash their cloths with Unilever products, and 6 million of them do so by hand." Below we touch on each of the seven global considerations as they relate to Unilever's global strategy.[138]

- ***Cultural Homogeneity.*** In the global laundry market, heterogeneity, even within a country, can occur. For example, Brazil's Northeast and Southeast regions are very different. One difference is that in the poorer Northeast region, most laundry is done by hand and more bar soap than powder is used. In the more affluent Southeast region, most laundry is done in a washing machine and more powder detergent is used than bar soap in the process.
- ***Needs.*** Hand washing versus machine washing leads to different laundry product needs. In addition, in developing countries that are an important focus for Unilever, products must be adapted to meet strength of cleaning needs related to removing sweat, odors, and tough stains due to physical labor.
- ***Affordability.*** Clearly affordability is a component in pricing the laundry detergents themselves to be competitive. However, Unilever also faces the situation that a transition from hand washing to washing machines depends in large part on the economic prosperity of a country or region, as this determines the affordability of washing machines. Adoption of washing machines, in turn, changes the type and amounts of laundry products used, as we saw earlier.
- ***Relevant Values.*** One source indicates that cleanliness, convenience, and sustainability are key value aspects in laundry products that vary across cultures. In many countries where Unilever operates, there are segments of kids dubbed "Nintendo Kids" who don't tend to go outside and play and thus don't get dirty. A core strategy for a number of their brands in these markets is the "dirt is good" campaign that stresses that playing and getting dirty are part of a healthy child's development and "let Unilever worry about getting their clothes clean."
- ***Infrastructure.*** A broad infrastructure issue in laundry is access to hot water. Many in developing countries don't have access to hot water or large quantities of water. Unilever responded in India with Surf Excel Quick Wash, an enzyme-based product that uses less water and works under lower water temperatures.
- ***Communication.*** Europeans have traditionally cleaned their clothes in much hotter water with the logic being that "boiling clothes" is the only real way to get them clean and kill germs. This trend is reversing as Unilever pushes more environmental-friendly products and as Europeans have begun to wash in cooler temperatures to save energy. An interesting consequence of the shift is that antibacterial additives are now demanded by European customers to kill the germs.
- ***Ethical Implications.*** While conversion of the world's consumers to fully automated washing machines would help standardize Unilever's approach, it has major implications for water usage. This is because compared to hand washing, machine washing can, depending critically on the number of rinse cycles needed, use more water. Continued innovation in products toward lower water use will be a key ethical and performance issue for Unilever moving forward.

As you can see, Unilever has and must continue to innovate and adjust as its target markets evolve along these critical dimensions.

Critical Thinking Questions

1. How might generational influences affect the adoption of washing machines even after economic conditions make them affordable?
2. What other features beyond price and form (bar versus powder) do you think Unilever has had to adjust to meet different needs/wants/preferences across different markets?
3. Which core value is related to sustainability and green marketing? Does this value vary across countries and cultures?

67

End of Chapter Material

Summary

The summary section integrates material organized around the learning objectives to provide additional clarity.

SUMMARY

LO1: Define the concept of culture

Culture is defined as the complex whole that includes knowledge, beliefs, art, law, morals, customs, and any other capabilities acquired by humans as members of society. It includes almost everything that influences an individual's thought processes and behaviors. Culture operates primarily by setting boundaries for individual behavior and by influencing the functioning of such institutions as the family and mass media. The boundaries, or *norms,* are derived from *cultural values.* Values are widely held beliefs that affirm what is desirable.

LO2: Describe core values that vary across culture and influence behaviors

Cultural values are classified into three categories: other, environment, and self. *Other-oriented values* reflect a society's view of the appropriate relationships between individuals and groups within that society. Relevant values of this nature include *individual/collective, youth/age, extended/limited family, masculine/feminine, competitive/cooperative,* and *diversity/uniformity. Environment-oriented values* prescribe a society's relationships with its economic, technical, and physical environments. Examples of environment values are *cleanliness, performance/status, tradition/change, risk taking/security, problem solving/fatalistic,* and *nature. Self-oriented values* reflect the objectives and approaches to life that individual members of society find desirable. These include *active/passive, sensual gratification/abstinence, material/nonmaterial, hard work/leisure, postponed gratification/immediate gratification,* and *religious/secular.*

LO3: Understand cross-cultural variations in nonverbal communications

Nonverbal communication systems are the arbitrary meanings a culture assigns actions, events, and things other than words. Major examples of nonverbal communication variables that affect marketers are *time, space, symbols, relationships, agreements, things,* and *etiquette.*

SMARTBOOK

Key Terms

KEY TERMS

Review Questions

The review questions at the end of each chapter allow students or the instructor to test the acquisition of the facts contained in the chapter. The questions require memorization, which we believe is an important, though insufficient, part of learning.

REVIEW QUESTIONS

1. What are some of the ethical issues involved in cross-cultural marketing?
2. What is meant by the term *culture?*
3. What does the statement "Culture sets boundaries on behaviors" mean?
4. What is a *norm?* From what are norms derived?
5. What is a *cultural value?*
6. What is a *sanction?*
7. Cultural values can be classified as affecting one of three types of relationships—other, environment, or self. Describe each of these, and differentiate each one from the others.
8. How does the first of the following paired orientations differ from the second?
   a. Individual/Collective
   b. Performance/Status
   c. Tradition/Change
   d. Limited/Extended family
   e. Active/Passive
   f. Material/Nonmaterial
   g. Hard work/Leisure
   h. Risk taking/Security
   i. Masculine/Feminine
   j. Competitive/Cooperative
   k. Youth/Age
   l. Problem solving/Fatalistic
   m. Diversity/Uniformity
   n. Postponed gratification/Immediate gratification
   o. Sensual gratification/Abstinence
   p. Religious/Secular
9. What is meant by *nonverbal communications?* Why is this a difficult area to adjust to?

DISCUSSION QUESTIONS

19. Why should we study foreign cultures if we do not plan to engage in international or export marketing?
20. Is a country's culture more likely to be reflected in its art museums or its television commercials? Why?
21. Are the cultures of the world becoming more similar or more distinct?
22. Why do values differ across cultures?
23. The text lists 18 cultural values (in three categories) of relevance to marketing practice.
   d. Fast food
   e. Luxury cars
   f. Cell phones
27. Why is materialism higher in Korea than in the United States, where given their collectivist culture one might expect materialism to be lower?
28. What values underlie the differences between Fiji Island and U.S. children in terms of the strategies they use to influence their parents' decisions? What marketing implications emerge?

Discussion Questions

These questions can be used to help develop or test the students' understanding of the material in the chapter. Answering these questions requires the student to utilize the material in the chapter to reach a recommendation or solution. However, they can generally be answered without external activities such as customer interviews; therefore, they can be assigned as in-class activities.

Application Activities

The final learning aid at the end of each chapter is a set of application exercises. These require the students to utilize the material in the chapter in conjunction with external activities such as visiting stores to observe point-of-purchase displays, interviewing customers or managers, or evaluating television ads. They range in complexity from short evening assignments to term projects.

APPLICATION ACTIVITIES

42. Interview two students from two different cultures. Determine the extent to which the following are used in those cultures and the variations in the values of those cultures that relate to the use of these products:
    a. Gift cards
    b. Energy drinks (like Red Bull)
    c. Fast-food restaurants
    d. Exercise equipment
    e. Music
    f. Internet

46. Interview two st
regarding their p
and conspicuous
their responses r
traditional value
countries.

47. Imagine you are
state's or provinc
been asked to ad
promotional ther

OTHER LEARNING AIDS IN THE TEXT

Three useful sets of learning material are presented outside the chapter format—cases, an overview of consumer research methods, and a format for a consumer behavior audit.

Cases

There are cases at the end of each major section of the text except the first. Many of the cases are new to the 13e. Many of the cases can be read in class and used to generate discussion of a particular topic. Students like this approach, and many instructors find it a useful way to motivate class discussion.

Other cases are more complex and data intense. They require several hours of effort to analyze. Still others can serve as the basis for a term project. We have used several cases in this manner with success (the assignment is to develop a marketing plan clearly identifying the consumer behavior constructs that underlie the plan).

Each case can be approached from a variety of angles. A number of discussion questions are provided with each case. However, many other questions can be used. In fact, while the cases are placed at the end of the major sections, most lend themselves to discussion at other points in the text as well.

Consumer Research Methods Overview

Appendix A provides a brief overview of the more commonly used research methods in consumer behavior. While not a substitute for a course or text in marketing research, it is a useful review for students who have completed a research course. It can also serve to provide students who have not had such a course with relevant terminology and a very basic understanding of the process and major techniques involved in consumer research.

Consumer Behavior Audit

Appendix B provides a format for doing a consumer behavior audit for a proposed marketing strategy. This audit is basically a list of key consumer behavior questions that should be answered for every proposed marketing strategy. Many students have found it particularly useful if a term project relating consumer behavior to a firm's actual or proposed strategy is required.

Instructor Features

Connect Marketing

Less Managing. More Teaching. Greater Learning.

Connect® Marketing is McGraw-Hill's web-based assignment and assessment platform that connects you and your students to the coursework. Interactive applications provided for each chapter of the textbook allow instructors to assign application-focused interactive activities, engage students to "do" marketing, stimulate critical thinking, and reinforce key concepts. Students apply what they've learned and receive immediate feedback. Instructors can customize these activities and monitor student progress. Connect Marketing for Consumer Behavior includes:

Simple Assignment Management and Grading

With Connect Marketing, creating assignments is easier than ever, so you can spend more time teaching and less time managing. The assignment management function enables you to:

- Create and deliver assignments easily with selectable test bank items.
- Streamline lesson planning, student progress reporting, and assignment grading to make classroom management more efficient than ever.
- Go paperless with the eBook and online submission and grading of student assignments.

New! LearnSmart and SmartBook™

LearnSmart is an adaptive study tool proven to strengthen memory recall, increase class retention, and boost grades. Students are able to study more efficiently because they are made aware of what they know and don't know. Real-time reports quickly identify the concepts that require more attention from individual students—or the entire class. SmartBook is the first and only adaptive reading experience designed to change the way students read and learn. It creates a personalized reading experience by highlighting the most impactful concepts a student needs to learn at that moment in time. As a student engages with SmartBook, the reading experience continuously adapts by highlighting content based on what the student knows and doesn't know. This ensures that the focus is on the content he or she needs to learn, while simultaneously promoting long-term retention of material. Use SmartBook's real-time reports to quickly identify the concepts that require more attention from individual students—or the entire class. The end result? Students are more engaged with course content, can better prioritize their time, and come to class ready to participate.

Instructor Library

The Connect Marketing Instructor Library is your repository for additional resources to improve student engagement in and out of class. You can select and use any asset that enhances your lecture. The Connect Marketing Instructor Library includes:

- ***The Instructor's Manual***
- ***Test Bank***
- ***PowerPoint***
- ***Video Cases***—A set of video cases are available to adopters. These videos describe firm strategies or activities that relate to material in the text. A guide for teaching from the videos is contained in the Instructor's manual.
- ***Searchable Video Links Database***—This database, is organized by chapter and searchable by topic. It contains links and classroom discussion guides for commercials and concept-based news items found in such locations as YouTube and ABC News online. This video links database provides instructors with a powerful set of teaching materials that can be used to customize PPT lectures quickly and easily.
- ***Searchable CB Press Highlights Database***—This database, is organized by chapter and searchable by topic. CB Press Highlights provide short summaries of a current concept, company situation, regulatory issue, and so forth. These short summaries are accompanied by an in-class discussion guide. CB Press Highlights are an excellent and easy way for instructors to add value to the classroom experience with examples that are not in the text. Or instructors can assign the articles to students prior to class to generate in-class discussion.

Responding to Learning Needs

CREATE

Instructors can now tailor their teaching resources to match the way they teach! With McGraw-Hill Create, **www.mcgrawhillcreate.com,** instructors can easily rearrange chapters, combine material from other content sources, and quickly upload and integrate their own content, like course syllabi or teaching notes. Find the right content in Create by searching through thousands of leading McGraw-Hill textbooks. Arrange the material to fit your teaching style. Order a Create book and receive a complimentary print review copy in three to five business days or a complimentary electronic review copy via e-mail within one hour. Go to **www.mcgrawhillcreate.com** today and register.

TEGRITY CAMPUS

Tegrity makes class time available 24/7 by automatically capturing every lecture in a searchable format for students to review when they study and complete assignments. With a simple one-click start-and-stop process, you capture all computer screens and corresponding audio. Students can replay any part of any class with easy-to-use browser-based viewing on a PC or Mac. Educators know that the more students can see, hear, and experience class resources, the better they learn. In fact, studies prove it. With patented Tegrity "search anything" technology, students instantly recall key class moments for replay online, or on iPods and mobile devices. Instructors can help turn all their students' study time into learning moments immediately supported by their lecture. To learn more about Tegrity, watch a two-minute Flash demo at **http://tegritycampus.mhhe.com.**

BLACKBOARD® PARTNERSHIP

McGraw-Hill Education and Blackboard have teamed up to simplify your life. Now you and your students can access *Connect* and Create right from within your Blackboard course—all with one single sign-on. The grade books are seamless, so when a student completes an integrated *Connect* assignment, the grade for that assignment automatically (and instantly) feeds your Blackboard grade center. Learn more at **www.domorenow.com.**

MCGRAW-HILL CAMPUS™

McGraw-Hill Campus is a new one-stop teaching and learning experience available to users of any learning management system. This institutional service allows faculty and students to enjoy single sign-on (SSO) access to all McGraw-Hill Higher Education materials, including the award-winning McGraw-Hill *Connect* platform, from directly within the institution's website. With McGraw-Hill Campus, faculty receive instant access to teaching materials (e.g., eBooks, test banks, PowerPoint slides, animations, learning objects), allowing them to browse, search, and use any instructor ancillary content in our vast library at no additional cost to instructor or students.

ASSURANCE OF LEARNING READY

Many educational institutions today focus on the notion of *assurance of learning,* an important element of some accreditation standards. *Consumer Behavior: Building Marketing Strategy* is designed specifically to support instructors' assurance of learning initiatives with a simple yet powerful solution. Each test bank question maps to a specific chapter learning objective listed in the text. Instructors can use our test bank software, EZ Test and EZ Test Online, to easily query for learning objectives that directly relate to the learning outcomes for their course. Instructors can then use the reporting features of EZ Test to aggregate student results in similar fashion, making the collection and presentation of assurance of learning data simple and easy.

AACSB TAGGING

McGraw-Hill Education is a proud corporate member of AACSB International. Understanding the importance and value of AACSB accreditation, *Consumer Behavior: Building Marketing Strategy* recognizes the curricula guidelines detailed in the AACSB standards for business accreditation by connecting selected questions in the text and the test bank to the six general knowledge and skill guidelines in the AACSB standards. The statements contained in *Consumer Behavior: Building Marketing Strategy* are provided only as a guide for the users of this textbook. The AACSB leaves content coverage and assessment within the purview of individual schools, the mission of the school, and the faculty. While the *Consumer Behavior: Building Marketing Strategy* teaching package makes no claim of any specific AACSB qualification or evaluation, we have labeled selected questions according to the six general knowledge and skills areas.

MCGRAW-HILL CUSTOMER EXPERIENCE GROUP CONTACT INFORMATION

At McGraw-Hill Education, we understand that getting the most from new technology can be challenging. That's why our services don't stop after you purchase our products. You can e-mail our Product Specialists 24 hours a day to get product training online. Or you can search our knowledge bank of Frequently Asked Questions on our support website. For Customer Support, call **800-331-5094** or visit **www.mhhe.com/support.** One of our Technical Support Analysts will be able to assist you in a timely fashion.

Acknowledgments

We enjoy studying, teaching, consulting, and writing about consumer behavior. Most of the faculty we know feel the same. As with every edition of this book, our goal for the thirteenth edition has been to make a book that students enjoy reading and that excites them about a fascinating topic.

Numerous individuals and organizations helped us in the task of writing this edition. We are grateful for their assistance. At the risk of not thanking all who deserve credit, we would like to thank Martin Horn at DDB, Tom Spencer at Claritas, Sucharita Mulpuru and Becky Anzalone at Forrester Research, Dr. Sijun Wang at Loyola Marymount University, Dr. Junwu Dong at Guangdong University, Matt Bailey at Site Logic, Ted Hornbein at Richco China, Inc., and Hyunju Shin and Woojung Chang at The University of Alabama. Thanks also to Polly Ricketts and Rachel Minor at The University of Alabama for their research assistance.

We would also like to thank the many members of the McGraw-Hill Higher Education team, including Kim Leistner, brand manager; Heather Darr, product developer; Laura Vogel, marketing manager; Jessica Portz, content project manager; Tara McDermott, designer; DeAnna Dausener, content licensing specialist, Keri Johnson, lead photo researcher.

Finally, to our colleagues at Alabama and Oregon—Thanks for your ongoing support, encouragement, and friendship.

David L. Mothersbaugh
Del I. Hawkins

Brief Contents

Contents

Consumer Behavior

part I

INTRODUCTION

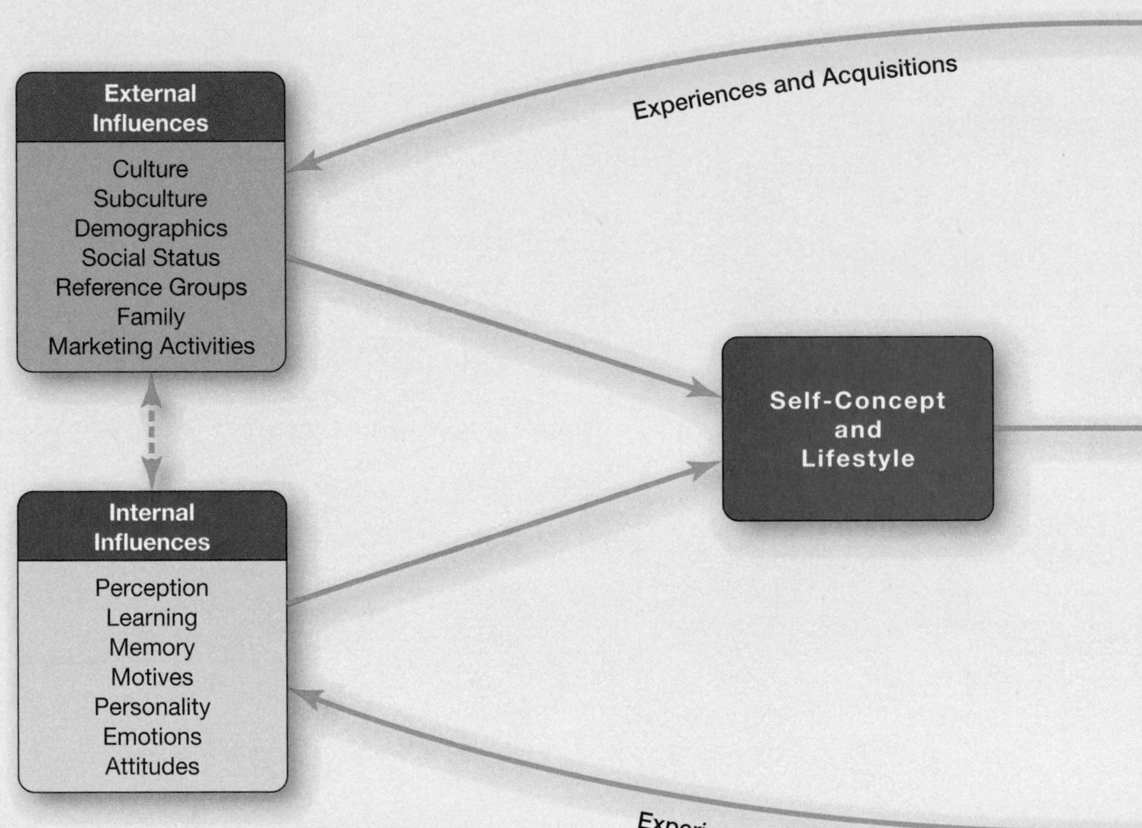

What is consumer behavior? Why should we study it? Do marketing managers, regulators, and consumer advocates actually use knowledge about consumer behavior to develop strategies and policy? How? Will a sound knowledge of consumer behavior help you in your career? Will it enable you to be a better citizen? How does consumer behavior impact the quality of all of our lives and of the environment? How can we organize our knowledge of consumer behavior to understand and use it more effectively?

Chapter 1 addresses these and a number of other interesting questions, describes the importance and usefulness of the material to be covered in this text, and provides an overview of the text. Chapter 1 also explains the logic of the model of consumer behavior shown below, which is presented again in Figure 1–3 and discussed toward the end of the chapter.

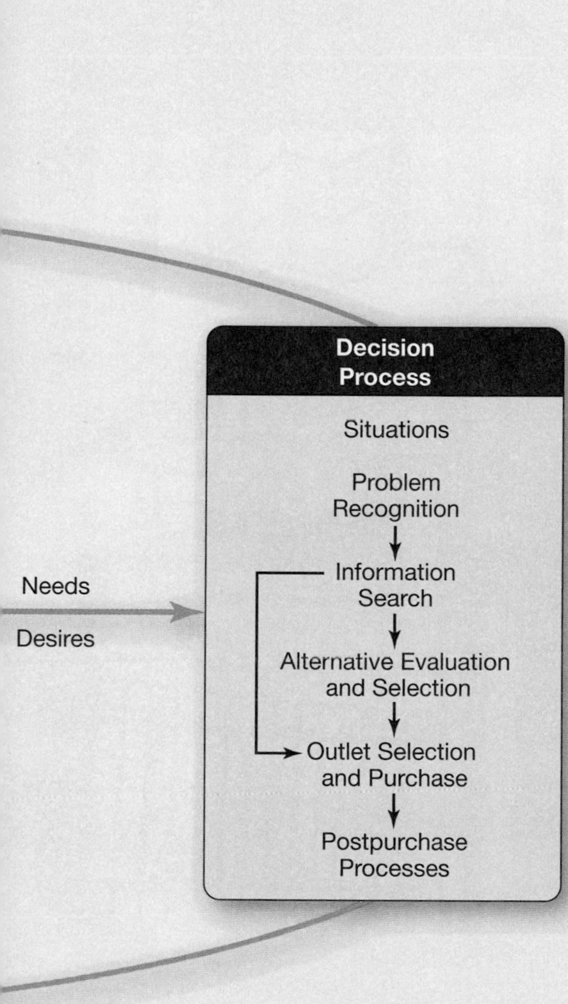

chapter

1 Consumer Behavior and Marketing Strategy

LEARNING OBJECTIVES

LO1 **Define consumer behavior.**

LO2 **Summarize the applications of consumer behavior.**

LO3 **Explain how consumer behavior can be used to develop marketing strategy.**

LO4 **Explain the components that constitute a conceptual model of consumer behavior.**

LO5 **Discuss issues involving consumption meanings and firm attempts to influence them.**

Marketers face exciting and daunting challenges as the forces that drive and shape consumer behavior rapidly evolve. Here are just a few examples.

Evolution of Marketing and Customer Experience—Marketers offer different ways for consumers to get their cup of coffee. Consumers can buy coffee beans and make a cup of coffee. They can buy a package of ground coffee and make a cup of coffee. They can opt to go to a coffee shop and buy a cup of coffee. Or they can go to Starbucks and buy a cup of coffee. Which option do you think is more expensive? Likely you would say that the first option is the least expensive and the final option the most expensive—and generally you would be correct! But why is that so? The answer lies in the layers of value that marketers can add to "commodity-like" products. These layers include services and experiences that consumers have indicated are of value to them. Thus, as products move from being a commodity to a good to a service to an experience, consumers are likely to pay more. The success of Starbucks attests to consumer willingness to pay more for a cup of coffee from Starbucks that layers the core product with service and experience. And Starbucks is going further. For example, it recently opened a store in New Orleans that is one of its portfolios of "local relevancy" stores. These *hyper local* stores are designed to provide intense experiential aspects that reflect the historical and cultural ambience of the store's locale.[1] A Starbucks in Philadelphia pictured at the beginning of this chapter is another example of this hyper local approach.

Marketing 2 Consumers versus Marketing 4 Consumers—Marketing has evolved not only in its offerings, but also in its relationship to consumers. A power shift away from marketers to consumers has changed the landscape. Succinctly stated, Marketing 2 Consumers has shifted to Marketing 4 Consumers. Marketing 2 Consumers used mass marketing, a scattered approach to reach as many consumers as possible including unavoidably wasting resources on consumers who have no interest in the product offering. Marketing 2 Consumers saturated consumers with advertisements, repeatedly and frequently, in an effort to gain consumer attention. In contrast, Marketing 4 Consumers uses a more targeted approach in an effort more likely to reach only the consumers who want the marketer's offering. Marketing 4 Consumers recognizes that consumers have the power to choose whether or not they will allow marketers' permission (say with a click on the Internet) to start a dialog. Product creation is no longer exclusively in the hands of marketers. Consumers can initiate and participate in product innovation by pitching an idea and/or funding a pitch (e.g., Kickstarter, Etsy). Consumers can verify marketers' promises of competitive prices for all nature of things from air fare (e.g., Kayak) to products (e.g., Fat Wallet). And consumers do not have to take marketers at their word because they can easily access customer reviews (e.g., Amazon.com).[2]

Social Media—The power shift from marketers to consumers has been further amplified by the rise of social media—Facebook, Pinterest, Tumblr, Twitter—which place user-generated, consumer-to-consumer(s) communication outside of the direct control and influence of marketers. A humorous example is the more than 8,000 Tweets (on Twitter) reporting the abnormally long receipts CVS gives its customers. Tweets show photos of consumers holding up CVS receipts that stretch above their heads and wrap around their waists. The motivation behind these long receipts is big data. CVS collects data on each customer purchase via the customer's CVS card. When customers check out, the cash register prints out on each consumer's receipt custom coupons mined from the history of previous purchases. CVS was both fortunate and savvy. They noticed the trend (social media allow for this to be done quickly and efficiently), noted the negativity (consumers' perception of waste and lack of environmental concern), and are reacting (moving more of their coupons and rewards direct to consumer cards). Such "real-time" trend tracking was simply not possible in most cases prior to social and digital media.

This shift in power from Marketing 2 Consumers to Marketing 4 Consumers and the rise of social media have made it all the more crucial for marketers to understand consumer behavior. Marketers' use of crowdsourcing to give voice to their consumers' needs and wants exemplifies marketers' understanding of the need to place consumers at the center of marketing. Examples of online crowdsourcing include Nike's Nikeidea, Nokia's Betalabs, and Dell's Ideastorm. These examples show how valuable it can be when marketers talk "with" their customers rather than simply talk "to" them.[3]

L01

The field of **consumer behavior** is *the study of individuals, groups, or organizations and the processes they use to select, secure, use, and dispose of products, services, experiences, or ideas to satisfy needs and the impacts that these processes have on the consumer and society.* This view of consumer behavior is broader than the traditional one, which focused more narrowly on the buyer and the immediate antecedents and consequences of the purchasing process. Our broader view will lead us to examine more indirect influences on consumption decisions as well as far-reaching consequences that involve more than just the purchaser and the seller.

The opening examples above summarize some attempts to apply an understanding of consumer behavior in a rapidly evolving environment that includes changes in technology and how consumers interact and communicate with firms. Throughout this text, we will explore the factors and trends shaping consumer behavior and the ways marketers and regulators can use this information. Four key aspects regarding consumer behavior are highlighted in this text.

- *Consumer behavior is a complex, multidimensional process.* Consumer decisions often involve numerous steps and are influenced by a host of factors including demographics, lifestyle, and cultural values. Consumer decisions are further complicated when the needs and wants of multiple individuals or groups are considered, as when families must make decisions about where to eat for dinner or where to go on vacation.

ILLUSTRATION 1-1

These advertisements are targeting the same consumers with very similar products, yet they use two very different approaches. Why? They are based on different assumptions about consumer behavior and how to influence it.

- *Successful marketing decisions by firms, nonprofit organizations, and regulatory agencies require an understanding of the processes underlying consumer behavior.* This relates to understanding theories about when and why consumers act in certain ways. Whether they realize it or not, organizations are making decisions every day based on explicit or implicit assumptions about what processes drive consumer behavior. Examine Illustration 1–1. *What assumptions about consumer behavior underlie each ad? Which approach is best? Why?*
- *Successful marketing decisions require organizations to collect information about the specific consumers involved in the marketing decision at hand.* Consumer decisions are heavily influenced by situation and product category. Thus, consumer research is necessary to understand how specific consumers will behave in a specific situation for a given product category. Appendix A examines various consumer research approaches.
- *Marketing practices designed to influence consumer behavior involve ethical issues that affect the firm, the individual, and society.* The issues are not always obvious and many times involve trade-offs at different levels. The fast-food industry is currently dealing with such issues. While their products are highly desirable to many consumers in terms of taste and affordability, they also tend to be high in calories, fat, and sodium. These health-related issues have gotten the attention of government and consumer groups.

Sufficient knowledge of consumer behavior exists to provide usable guidelines. However, applying these guidelines effectively requires monitoring the environment for changes and factoring those changes into marketing decisions. It also requires practice. We provide a variety of such opportunities in the form of (a) questions and exercises at the end of each chapter, (b) short cases at the end of each main part of the text, and (c) a consumer behavior audit for developing marketing strategy (Appendix B) at the end of the text.

APPLICATIONS OF CONSUMER BEHAVIOR

Marketing Strategy

LO2

Marketing decisions based on explicit consumer behavior theory, assumptions, and research are more likely to be successful than those based on hunches or intuition, and thus create a competitive advantage. An accurate understanding of consumer behavior can greatly reduce the odds of failures such as:

> S.C. Johnson pulled the plug on its Ziploc TableTops, a line of semi-disposable plates. TableTops was one of the company's most expensive launches with $65 million spent on marketing. A number of factors appear to have contributed to the failure including relatively high prices (which made consumers less likely to throw them away) and the fact that the products really weren't all that disposable. As one retailer explained, "There are no repeat purchases. The things last forever."[4]

Thus, a primary goal of this book is to help you obtain a usable managerial understanding of consumer behavior to help you become a more effective marketing manager. Before we take a look at marketing strategy and consumer behavior, let's examine regulatory policy, social marketing, and the importance of being an informed individual.

Regulatory Policy

Various regulatory bodies exist to develop, interpret, and/or implement policies designed to protect and aid consumers. For example, the Food and Drug Administration (FDA) administers the Nutrition Labeling and Education Act (NLEA). Among other things, NLEA requires that packaged foods prominently display nutrition information in the form of the Nutrition Facts panel.

Has NLEA succeeded? A recent study suggests that it depends. For example, the Nutrition Facts panel is of most benefit to highly motivated consumers who are low in nutritional knowledge. Demonstrating such benefits is important in light of the estimated $2 billion in compliance costs. However, such cost–benefit comparisons are complicated since placing a dollar value on individual and societal benefits is often difficult.[5]

Clearly, effective regulation of many marketing practices requires an extensive knowledge of consumer behavior. We will discuss this issue throughout the text and provide a detailed treatment in Chapter 20.

Social Marketing

Social marketing is *the application of marketing strategies and tactics to alter or create behaviors that have a positive effect on the targeted individuals or society as a whole.*[6] Social marketing has been used in attempts to reduce smoking, to increase the percentage of children receiving their vaccinations in a timely manner, to encourage environmentally sound behaviors such as recycling, to reduce behaviors potentially leading to AIDS, to enhance support of charities, to reduce drug use, and to support many other important causes.

Just as for commercial marketing strategy, successful social marketing strategy requires a sound understanding of consumer behavior. For example, Oakley's "For Strength: Not Surrender" campaign (see Illustration 1–2) uses an emotional-based appeal. In Chapter 11, we will analyze the conditions under which such campaigns are likely to succeed.

ILLUSTRATION 1-2

Nonprofits as well as commercial firms such as Oakley as shown here attempt to influence consumption patterns. Both types of organizations must base their efforts on knowledge of consumer behavior to maximize their chances of success.

Informed Individuals

Most economically developed societies are legitimately referred to as consumption societies. Most individuals in these societies spend more time engaged in consumption than in any other activity, including work or sleep (both of which also involve consumption). In addition, marketers spend billions to influence consumer decisions. These attempts occur in ads, in websites, on packages, as product features, in sales pitches, and in store environments. They also occur in the content of many TV shows, in the brands that are used in movies, and in the materials presented to children in schools.

It is important that consumers accurately understand the strategies and tactics being used so they can be more effective consumers. It is equally important that, as citizens, we understand the consumer behavior basis of these strategies so we can set appropriate limits when required. That is, an understanding of consumer behavior can establish a foundation for reasoned business ethics.

MARKETING STRATEGY AND CONSUMER BEHAVIOR

L03

The applications of consumer behavior involve the development, regulation, and effects of marketing strategy. We now examine marketing strategy in more depth.

Marketing strategy, as described in Figure 1–1, is conceptually very simple. It begins with an analysis of the market the organization is considering. On the basis of the consumer analysis undertaken in this step, the organization identifies groups of individuals, households, or

FIGURE 1-1 Marketing Strategy and Consumer Behavior

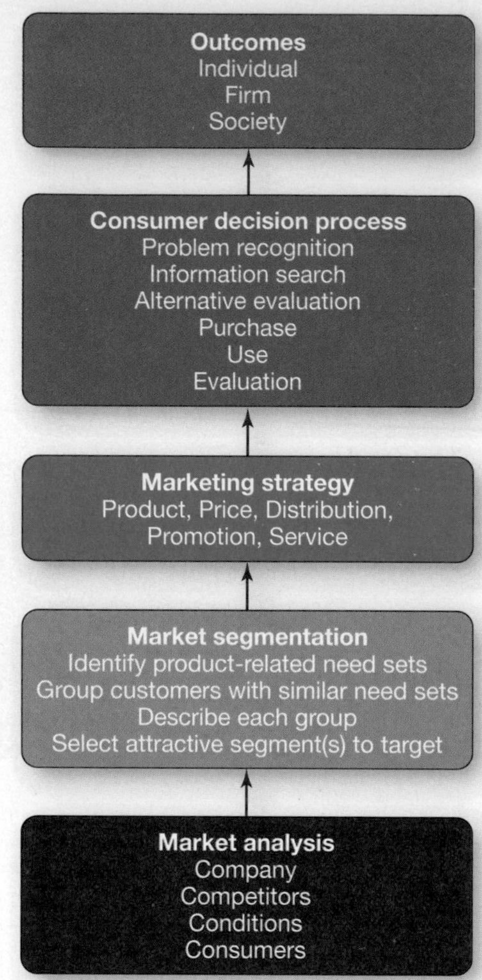

firms with similar needs. These market segments are described in terms of demographics, media preferences, geographic location, and so forth. Management then selects one or more of these segments as target markets on the basis of the firm's capabilities relative to those of its competition (given current and forecasted economic and technological conditions).

Next, marketing strategy is formulated. To survive in a competitive environment, an organization must provide its target customers more value than is provided to them by its competitors. **Customer value** is *the difference between all the benefits derived from a total product and all the costs of acquiring those benefits.* It is critical that a firm consider value *from the customer's perspective.* Ziploc's TableTops failed because consumers felt the benefit of being semi-disposable did not outweigh the cost of the product itself or the guilt they felt about eventually throwing it away. Thus, marketing strategy seeks to provide the customer with more value than the competition while still producing a profit for the firm.

Marketing strategy is formulated in terms of the marketing mix; that is, it involves determining the product features, price, communications, distribution, and services that will provide customers with superior value. This entire set of characteristics is often

ILLUSTRATION 1-3

What do you buy when you go to a restaurant or coffee shop? The experience is the product as much as or more than the actual food and beverage.

referred to as the **total product.** The total product is presented to the target market, which is consistently engaged in processing information and making decisions designed to maintain or enhance its lifestyle (individuals and households) or performance (businesses and other organizations).

Look at Illustration 1–3. What is the total product? Clearly, it is much more than food and beverages. It also involves an experience. Increasingly, marketers sell experiences as much as or more than actual products and services. An "experience" occurs when a company intentionally creates a memorable event for customers. While products and services are to a large extent external to the customer, an experience is largely internal to each customer. The experience exists in the mind of an individual who has been engaged on an emotional, physical, intellectual, or even spiritual level.

Outcomes based on the execution of a marketing strategy occur for the firm, thc individual, and society. Firms expect to establish an image or position in the marketplace among target customers, generate sales, and ultimately create satisfied customers who are the key to long-term profits. For the individual, the process results in some level of need satisfaction, financial expenditure, attitude creation or change, and/or behavioral changes. Note that some of these behaviors may involve injurious consumption. For society, the cumulative effect of the marketing process affects economic growth, pollution, and social welfare, the latter of which creates many ethical implications.

We detail each phase of Figure 1–1 next.

MARKET ANALYSIS COMPONENTS

Market analysis requires a thorough understanding of the consumption process of potential customers; the organization's own capabilities; the capabilities of current and future competitors; and the economic, physical, and technological environment in which these elements will interact.

The Consumers

It is not possible to anticipate and react to customers' needs and desires without a complete understanding of consumer behavior. Discovering customers' needs is a complex process, but it can often be accomplished by marketing research. For example, Target wanted to tap into the $210 billion college market. In particular, Target was looking at the furnishings and accessories market and was interested in the specific needs and motivations of students making the transition from home to college dorm life. Jump Associates conducted the research for Target and took a unique approach:

> [Jump Associates] sponsored a series of "game nights" at high school grads' homes, inviting incoming college freshmen as well as students with a year of dorm living under their belts. To get teens talking about dorm life, Jump devised a board game that involved issues associated with going to college. The game naturally led to informal conversations—and questions—about college life. Jump researchers were on the sidelines to observe, while a video camera recorded the proceedings.

On the basis of this research (which is a variation of focus groups—see Appendix A), Target successfully launched the Todd Oldham Dorm Room line, which included such products as Kitchen in a Box and Bath in a Box—all-in-one assortments of the types of products needed by college freshmen.[7] Target continues to appeal to the college market with logo merchandise and other dorm products.

Knowing the consumer requires understanding the behavioral principles that guide consumption behaviors. These principles are covered in depth in the remainder of this text.

The Company

A firm must fully understand its own ability to meet customer needs. This involves evaluating all aspects of the firm, including its financial condition, general managerial skills, production capabilities, research and development capabilities, technological sophistication, reputation, and marketing skills. Marketing skills would include new-product development capabilities, channel strength, advertising abilities, service capabilities, marketing research abilities, market and consumer knowledge, and so forth.

Failure to fully understand strengths and weaknesses can cause serious problems. IBM's first attempt to enter the home computer market, with the PC Jr., was a failure in part for that reason. Although IBM had an excellent reputation with large business customers and a very strong direct sales force for serving them, these strengths were not relevant to the household consumer market. Its more recent move into high-end business consulting, through IBM Global Business Services, has been a major success and, interestingly, moves IBM back to a focus on its earlier core strengths.

The Competitors

It is not possible to consistently do a better job than the competition of meeting customer needs without a thorough understanding of the competition's capabilities and strategies. This understanding requires the same level of knowledge of a firm's key competitors that is required of one's own firm. In addition, for any significant marketing action, the following questions must be answered:

1. If we are successful, which firms will be hurt (lose sales or sales opportunities)?
2. Of those firms that are injured, which have the capability (financial resources, marketing strengths) to respond?
3. How are they likely to respond (reduce prices, increase advertising, introduce a new product)?
4. Is our strategy (planned action) robust enough to withstand the likely actions of our competitors, or do we need additional contingency plans?

The Conditions

The state of the economy, the physical environment, government regulations, and technological developments affect consumer needs and expectations as well as company and competitor capabilities. The deterioration of the physical environment has produced not only consumer demand for environmentally sound products but also government regulations affecting product design and manufacturing.

International agreements such as NAFTA (North American Free Trade Agreement) have greatly reduced international trade barriers and raised the level of both competition and consumer expectations for many products. And technology is changing the way people live, work, deal with disease, and so on. Corporate websites, social media such as Twitter and Facebook, and mobile apps are just some of the ways technology is changing the way consumers communicate and access media.

Clearly, a firm cannot develop a sound marketing strategy without anticipating the conditions under which that strategy will be implemented.

MARKET SEGMENTATION

Perhaps the most important marketing decision a firm makes is the selection of one or more market segments on which to focus. A **market segment** is *a portion of a larger market whose needs differ somewhat from the larger market.* Since a market segment has unique needs, a firm that develops a total product focused solely on the needs of that segment will be able to meet the segment's desires better than a firm whose product or service attempts to meet the needs of multiple segments.

To be viable, a segment must be large enough to be served profitably. However, it should be noted that technology advances such as flexible manufacturing and customized media are allowing for mass customization such that firms can target smaller segments and even individuals profitably. *Behavioral targeting,* in which consumers' online activity is tracked and specific banner ads are delivered based on that activity, is another example of how technology is making individualized communication increasingly cost-effective.

Market segmentation involves four steps:

1. Identifying product-related need sets.
2. Grouping customers with similar need sets.
3. Describing each group.
4. Selecting an attractive segment(s) to serve.

ILLUSTRATION 1-4

Both the Lumi Nox and Tudor ads are for the same basic product. Yet, as these ads show, the products are designed to meet different sets of needs beyond their basic function.

Product-Related Need Sets

Organizations approach market segmentation with a set of current and potential capabilities. These capabilities may be a reputation, an existing product, a technology, or some other skill set. The first task of the firm is to identify need sets that the organization is capable, or could become capable, of meeting. The term **need set** is used to reflect the fact that most products in developed economies satisfy more than one need. Thus, a watch can meet more needs than just telling time. Some customers purchase watches to meet status needs, while others purchase them to meet style needs, and so on. Illustration 1–4 shows two watch ads; one for Lumi Nox, the other for Tudor. Even though these ads are for the same general product, *what needs are these different ads appealing to?*

Identifying the various need sets that the firm's current or potential product might satisfy typically involves consumer research, particularly focus groups and depth interviews, as well as logic and intuition. These need sets are often associated with other variables such as age, stage in the household life cycle, gender, social class, ethnic group, or lifestyle, and many firms start the segmentation process focusing first on one or more of the groups defined by one of these variables. Thus, a firm might start by identifying various ethnic groups and then attempt to discover similarities and differences in consumption-related needs across these groups. While better-defined segments will generally be discovered by focusing first on needs and then on consumer characteristics associated with those needs, both approaches are used in practice and both provide a useful basis for segmentation.

Need sets exist for products and services and can include needs related to various shopping venues. Consumer Insight 1–1 examines the need sets of mall and factory outlet shoppers.

CONSUMER INSIGHT 1-1

Need Sets of Mall and Factory Outlet Shoppers

What do you look for in a retail experience? Entertainment? Branded merchandise? Convenient parking? It turns out that all of these are important, but not all of them are important to every consumer. Thus, retailers must know what need sets exist and what segments exist around those need sets. One research study that gives some insight into this found four basic need sets for traditional malls and factory outlets:[8]

1. ***Mall Essentials***—*basic requirements including*
   - Cleanliness
   - Décor
   - Employee service and friendliness
   - Safety and security
   - Parking
2. ***Entertainment***—*fun extras such as*
   - Fast food
   - Movie theatres
   - Other services such as banks and hair specialists
   - Friends who shop the retailer
3. ***Convenience***—*factors that make shopping easier including*
   - Close to work and/or home
   - Accessible to home and/or work
4. ***Brand-name Merchandise***—*brand availability as follows:*
   - Brand-name stores
   - Current fashions
   - New products
   - More stores

As you can see, each need set represents a related cluster of characteristics. In addition, however, consumers can be grouped (segmented) in terms of their similarity regarding the importance they place on the different need sets. For example, there is the "Basic" shopper segment that only cares about mall essentials; an "Enthusiast" shopper segment that cares about all the need sets, with a particularly high emphasis on entertainment; a "serious shopper" who cares about brand-name merchandise and convenience; a "Destination" shopper who cares about mall essentials and brand-name merchandise; and a "Brand" shopper who only cares about brand-name merchandise. Clearly all shoppers are not the same, and retailers must work hard to adapt to the differing need sets of different shopper segments.

Critical Thinking Questions

1. Think of various retailers you are aware of. Can you match these different retailers to the different shopper segments?
2. Can you characterize the different shopper segments in terms of various demographic traits such as age, gender, income, family role, and so on?
3. What do you think the need sets are for online retailers?

Customers with Similar Need Sets

The next step is to group consumers with similar need sets. For example, the need for moderately priced, fun, sporty automobiles appears to exist in many young single individuals, young couples with no children, and middle-aged couples whose children have left home. These consumers can be grouped into one segment as far as product features and perhaps even product image are concerned despite sharply different demographics. Consumer Insight 1–1 provides an additional example of "clustering" or grouping consumers with similar need sets. For example, those who are basic shoppers are all similar in that their most critical need set is mall essentials.

This step generally involves consumer research, including focus group interviews, surveys, and product concept tests (see Appendix A). It could also involve an analysis of current consumption patterns.

Description of Each Group

Once consumers with similar need sets are identified, they should be described in terms of their demographics, lifestyles, and media usage. Designing an effective marketing program requires having a complete understanding of the potential customers. It is only with such a complete understanding that we can be sure we have correctly identified the need set. In addition, we cannot communicate effectively with our customers if we do not understand the context in which our product is purchased and consumed, how it is thought about by our customers, and the language they use to describe it. Thus, while many young single individuals, young couples with no children, and middle-aged couples whose children have left home may want the same features in an automobile, the media required to reach each group and the appropriate language and themes to use with each group would likely differ.

Attractive Segment(s) to Serve

Once we are sure we have a thorough understanding of each segment, we must select our **target market**—*the segment(s) of the larger market on which we will focus our marketing effort.* This decision is based on our ability to provide the selected segment(s) with superior customer value at a profit. Thus, the size and growth of the segment, the intensity of the current and anticipated competition, the cost of providing the superior value, and so forth are important considerations. Table 1–1 provides a simple worksheet for use in evaluating and comparing the attractiveness of various market segments.

As Table 1–1 indicates, segments that are sizable and growing are likely to appear attractive. However, profitability cannot be ignored. After all, a large unprofitable segment is still

TABLE 1-1 Market Segment Attractiveness Worksheet

Criterion	Score*
Segment size	________
Segment growth rate	________
Competitor strength	________
Customer satisfaction with existing products	________
Fit with company image	________
Fit with company objectives	________
Fit with company resources	________
Distribution available	________
Investment required	________
Stability/predictability	________
Cost to serve	________
Sustainable advantage available	________
Communications channels available	________
Risk	________
Segment profitability	________
Other (______)	________

*Score on a 1–10 scale, with 10 being most favorable.

unprofitable. Finding profitable segments means identifying a maximal fit between customer needs and the firm's offerings. This means that some customers and segments will be unprofitable to serve and may need to be "fired." While firing customers may be difficult, it can lead to greater profits, as ING Direct has found. ING Direct is a bare-bones bank. It has limited offerings (no checking) and does most of its transactions online. ING Direct wants "low-maintenance" customers who are attracted by its higher interest rates. As their CEO notes:

> The difference between ING Direct and the rest of the financial industry is like the difference between take-out food and a sit-down restaurant. The business isn't based on relationships; it's based on a commodity product that's high-volume and low-margin. We need to keep expenses down, which doesn't work when customers want a lot of empathetic contact.[9]

ING Direct keeps costs lower and profits higher by identifying high-cost customers and (nicely) letting them go by suggesting they might be better served by a "high-touch" community bank. *Can you think of any potential risks of "firing" customers?*

It is important to remember that each market segment requires its own marketing strategy. Each element of the marketing mix should be examined to determine if changes are required from one segment to another. Sometimes each segment will require a completely different marketing mix, including the product. At other times, only the advertising message or retail outlets may need to differ.

MARKETING STRATEGY

It is not possible to select target markets without simultaneously formulating a general marketing strategy for each segment. A decisive criterion in selecting target markets is the ability to provide superior value to those market segments. Because customer value is delivered by the marketing strategy, the firm must develop its general marketing strategy as it evaluates potential target markets.

Marketing strategy is basically the answer to the question, *How will we provide superior customer value to our target market?* The answer to this question requires the formulation of a consistent marketing mix. The **marketing mix** is *the product, price, communications, distribution, and services provided to the target market.* It is the combination of these elements that meets customer needs and provides customer value. For example, in the chapter opener, we see that Starbucks creates value through a combination of products, service, and a superior experience.

The Product

A **product** is *anything a consumer acquires or might acquire to meet a perceived need.* Consumers are generally buying need satisfaction, not physical product attributes.[10] As the former head of Revlon said, "in the factory we make cosmetics, in the store we sell hope." Thus, consumers don't purchase quarter-inch drill bits but the ability to create quarter-inch holes. Federal Express lost much of its overnight letter delivery business not to UPS or Airborne but to fax machines and the Internet because these technologies could meet the same consumer needs faster, cheaper, or more conveniently.

We use the term *product* to refer to physical products and primary or core services. Thus, an automobile is a product, as is a transmission overhaul or a ride in a taxi. Packaged goods alone (food, beverages, pet products, household products) account for over 30,000 new product introductions each year.[11] Obviously, many of these will not succeed. To be successful, a product must meet the needs of the target market better than the competition's product does.

Product-related decisions also include issues of packaging, branding, and logos, which have functional and symbolic dimensions. When Starbucks changed its logo by eliminating the words "Starbucks Coffee" and the circle around their emblematic "Siren," there was some consumer backlash on social media against this new logo. *Do you think Starbucks' new logo is effective? What factors underlie your judgment?*

Communications

Marketing communications include *advertising, the sales force, public relations, packaging, and any other signal that the firm provides about itself and its products.* An effective communications strategy requires answers to the following questions:

1. *With whom, exactly, do we want to communicate?* While most messages are aimed at the target-market members, others are focused on channel members, or those who influence the target-market members. For example, pediatric nurses are often asked for advice concerning diapers and other nonmedical infant care items. A firm marketing such items would be wise to communicate directly with the nurses.

   Often it is necessary to determine who within the target market should receive the marketing message. For a children's breakfast cereal, should the communications be aimed at the children or the parents, or both? The answer depends on the target market and varies by country.
2. *What effect do we want our communications to have on the target audience?* Often a manager will state that the purpose of advertising and other marketing communications is to increase sales. While this may be the ultimate objective, the behavioral objective for most marketing communications is often much more immediate. That is, it may seek to have the audience learn something about the product, seek more information about the product, like the product, recommend the product to others, feel good about having bought the product, or a host of other communications effects.
3. *What message will achieve the desired effect on our audience?* What words, pictures, and symbols should we use to capture attention and produce the desired effect? Marketing messages can range from purely factual statements to pure symbolism. The best approach depends on the situation at hand. Developing an effective message requires a thorough understanding of the meanings the target audience attaches to words and symbols, as well as knowledge of the perception process. Consider Illustration 1–5. Many older consumers may not relate to the approach of this ad. However, it communicates clearly to its intended youth market.
4. *What means and media should we use to reach the target audience?* Should we use personal sales to provide information? Can we rely on the package to provide needed information? Should we advertise in mass media, use direct mail, or rely on consumers to find us on the Internet? If we advertise in mass media, which media (television, radio, magazines, newspapers, Internet) and which specific vehicles (television programs, specific magazines, websites, banner ads, and so forth) should we use? Is it necessary or desirable to adjust the language used? With respect to the media and language issues, MasterCard's approach is instructive. They indicate that

   > Hispanics are the largest and fastest growing ethnic group in the U.S. . . . As we continue to bring value to Hispanic consumers, it is important for MasterCard to be speaking their language in the channels that are relevant to them.[12]

5. *When should we communicate with the target audience?* Should we concentrate our communications near the time that purchases tend to be made or evenly throughout

ILLUSTRATION 1-5

All aspects of the marketing mix should be designed around the needs and characteristics of the target audience. Many segments would not appreciate this ad, but it works with the targeted segment.

the week, month, or year? Do consumers seek information shortly before purchasing our product? If so, where? Answering these questions requires knowledge of the decision process used by the target market for this product.

Price

Price is *the amount of money one must pay to obtain the right to use the product.* One can buy ownership of a product or, for many products, limited usage rights (i.e., one can rent or lease the product, as with a video). Economists often assume that lower prices for the same product will result in more sales than higher prices. However, price sometimes serves as a signal of quality. A product priced "too low" might be perceived as having low quality. Owning expensive items also provides information about the owner. If nothing else, it indicates that the owner can afford the expensive item. This is a desirable feature to some consumers. Starbucks charges relatively high prices for its coffee. Yet it understands that the Starbucks brand allows consumers to "trade up" to a desired image and lifestyle without breaking the bank. Therefore, setting a price requires a thorough understanding of the symbolic role that price plays for the product and target market in question.

It is important to note that the price of a product is not the same as the cost of the product to the customer. **Consumer cost** is *everything the consumer must surrender in order to receive the benefits of owning/using the product.* As described earlier, the cost of owning/

using an automobile includes insurance, gasoline, maintenance, finance charges, license fees, parking fees, time and discomfort while shopping for the car, and perhaps even discomfort about increasing pollution, in addition to the purchase price. One of the ways firms seek to provide customer value is to reduce the nonprice costs of owning or operating a product. If successful, the total cost to the customer decreases while the revenue to the marketer stays the same or even increases.

Distribution

Distribution, *having the product available where target customers can buy it,* is essential to success. Only in rare cases will customers go to much trouble to secure a particular brand. Obviously, good channel decisions require a sound knowledge of where target customers shop for the product in question. Today's distribution decisions also require an understanding of cross-channel options. Savvy retailers are figuring out ways to let each distribution channel (e.g., online versus offline) do what it does best. For example, retailers are often challenged to balance appropriate types and levels of in-store inventory with internet kiosks. Obviously, retailers who adopt this approach have to choose an appropriate merchandising strategy where fast-moving, high-profit, seasonal items are in-store to attract customers while other merchandise is available online.[13] Finally, retailer characteristics such as those examined in Consumer Insight 1–1 need to be understood and delivered upon. Disney is in the process of renovating its stores to be more interactive, and this has driven increased store visits and sales. The remodel seems to focus on entertainment that is especially appropriate in light of their brand and customer. Specifically

> [t]he new [Disney] retail format sports more features to entertain shoppers, such as a table where kids can assemble cars from the popular Disney-Pixar "Cars" movie to a two-story princess castle that kids can enter.[14]

Service

Earlier, we defined *product* to include primary or core services such as haircuts, car repairs, and medical treatments. Here, **service** refers to *auxiliary or peripheral activities that are performed to enhance the primary product or primary service.* Thus, we would consider car repair to be a product (primary service), while free pickup and delivery of the car would be an auxiliary service. Although many texts do not treat service as a separate component of the marketing mix, we do because of the critical role it plays in determining market share and relative price in competitive markets. A firm that does not explicitly manage its auxiliary services is at a competitive disadvantage.

Auxiliary services cost money to provide. Therefore, it is essential that the firm furnish only those services that provide value to the target customers. Providing services that customers do not value can result in high costs and high prices without a corresponding increase in customer value.

CONSUMER DECISIONS

As Figure 1–1 illustrated, the consumer decision process intervenes between the marketing strategy (as implemented in the marketing mix) and the outcomes. That is, the outcomes of the firm's marketing strategy are determined by its interaction with the

ILLUSTRATION 1-6

This ad positions the brand as fun.

consumer decision process. The firm can succeed only if consumers see a need that its product can solve, become aware of the product and its capabilities, decide that it is the best available solution, proceed to buy it, and become satisfied with the results of the purchase. A significant part of this text is devoted to the understanding of the consumer decision process.

OUTCOMES

Firm Outcomes

Product Position The most basic outcome of a firm's marketing strategy is its **product position**—*an image of the product or brand in the consumer's mind relative to competing products and brands.* This image consists of a set of beliefs, pictorial representations, and feelings about the product or brand. It does not require purchase or use for it to develop. It is determined by communications about the brand from the firm and other sources, as well as by direct experience with it. Most marketing firms specify the product position they want their brands to have and measure these positions on an ongoing basis. This is because a brand whose position matches the desired position of a target market is likely to be purchased when a need for that product arises.

The ad in Illustration 1–6 is positioning the brand as a fun brand. This image and personality are facilitated and enhanced by the color and imagery used.

Sales and Profits Sales and profits are critical outcomes, as they are necessary for the firm to continue in business. Therefore, virtually all firms evaluate the success of their marketing programs in terms of sales revenues and profits. As we have seen, sales and profits are likely to occur only if the initial consumer analysis was correct and if the marketing mix matches the consumer decision process.

FIGURE 1-2 Creating Satisfied Customers

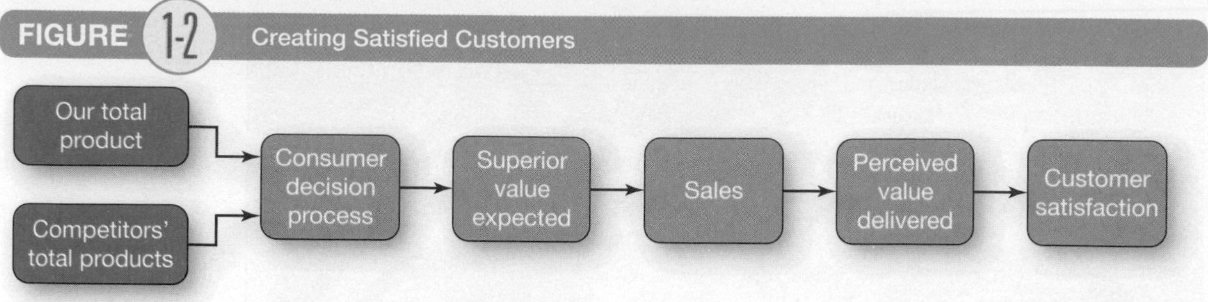

Customer Satisfaction Marketers have discovered that it is generally more profitable to maintain existing customers than to replace them with new customers. Retaining current customers requires that they be satisfied with their purchase and use of the product. Thus, **customer satisfaction** is a major concern of marketers.

As Figure 1–2 indicates, convincing consumers that your brand offers superior value is necessary in order to make the initial sale. Obviously, one must have a thorough understanding of the potential consumers' needs and of their information acquisition processes to succeed at this task. However, *creating satisfied customers,* and thus future sales, requires that customers continue to believe that your brand meets their needs and offers superior value *after they have used it.* You must deliver as much or more value than your customers initially expected, and it must be enough to satisfy their needs. Doing so requires an even greater understanding of consumer behavior.

Individual Outcomes

Need Satisfaction The most obvious outcome of the consumption process for an individual, whether or not a purchase is made, is some level of satisfaction of the need that initiated the consumption process. This can range from no satisfaction (or even a negative level if a purchase increases the need rather than reduces it) to complete satisfaction. Two key processes are involved: the actual need fulfillment and the perceived need fulfillment. These two processes are closely related and are often identical. However, at times they differ. For example, people might take food supplements because they believe the supplements are enhancing their health, while in reality they could have no direct health effects or even negative effects. One objective of government regulation and a frequent goal of consumer groups is to ensure that consumers can adequately judge the extent to which products are meeting their needs.

Injurious Consumption Although we tend to focus on the benefits of consumption, we must remain aware that consumer behavior has a dark side. **Injurious consumption** occurs *when individuals or groups make consumption decisions that have negative consequences for their long-run well-being.* Examples can include (a) overspending due to aggressive marketing efforts and cheap credit; (b) consumption of products that are not healthy including fast foods, cigarettes, alcohol, and so on; and (c) engaging in activities such as gambling that can have devastating financial consequences for some.

One product that caught the attention of the FDA was caffeinated alcohol beverages. They tend to be large in volume and also contain high levels of alcohol and caffeine. It is estimated that one can of these new caffeinated alcohol beverages has the same impact on people as drinking five to six beers. These beverages also increase the chances that people engage in dangerous behaviors such as driving under the influence, in part because the caffeine causes them to misgauge how intoxicated they are.[15]

Although these are issues we should be concerned with, and we will address them throughout this text, we should also note that alcohol consumption seems to have arisen simultaneously with civilization and evidence of gambling is nearly as old. Consumers smoked and chewed tobacco long before mass media or advertising as we know it existed, and illegal drug consumption continues to grow worldwide despite the absence of large-scale marketing, or at least advertising. Thus, though marketing activities based on knowledge of consumer behavior undoubtedly exacerbate some forms of injurious consumption, they are not the sole cause and, as we will see shortly, such activities may be part of the cure.

Society Outcomes

Economic Outcomes The cumulative impact of consumers' purchase decisions, including the decision to forgo consumption, is a major determinant of the state of a given country's economy. Consumers' decisions on whether to buy or to save affect economic growth, the availability and cost of capital, employment levels, and so forth. The types of products and brands purchased influence the balance of payments, industry growth rates, and wage levels. Decisions made in one society—particularly large, wealthy societies such as those of the United States, Western Europe, and Japan—have a major impact on the economic health of many other countries.

Physical Environment Outcomes Consumers make decisions that have a major impact on the physical environments of both their own and other societies. The cumulative effect of U.S. consumers' decisions to rely on relatively large private cars rather than mass transit results in significant air pollution in American cities as well as the consumption of nonrenewable resources from other countries. The decisions of people in most developed and in many developing economies to consume meat as a primary source of protein result in the clearing of rain forests for grazing land; the pollution of many watersheds due to large-scale feedlots; and an inefficient use of grain, water, and energy to produce protein. It also appears to produce health problems for many consumers. Similar effects are being seen as ethanol (made from corn, sugar cane, or rice) becomes a more popular alternative to oil as a source of fuel for automobiles. The high cost of fuel, along with the diversion of grain from food to fuel, is driving up food costs and threatens to increase poverty levels around the world.[16] Such outcomes attract substantial negative publicity. However, these resources are being used because of consumer demand, and consumer demand consists of the decisions you and I and our families and our friends make!

As we will see in Chapter 3, many consumers now recognize the indirect effects of consumption on the environment and are altering their behavior to minimize environmental harm.

Social Welfare Consumer decisions affect the general social welfare of a society. Decisions concerning how much to spend for private goods (personal purchases) rather than public goods (support for public education, parks, health care, and the like) are generally made indirectly by consumers' elected representatives. These decisions have a major impact on the overall quality of life in a society.

Injurious consumption, as described above, affects society as well as the individuals involved. The social costs of smoking-induced illnesses, alcoholism, and drug abuse are staggering. To the extent that marketing activities increase or decrease injurious consumption, they have a major impact on the social welfare of a society. Consider the following:

According to the U.S. Public Health Service, of the 10 leading causes of death in the United States, at least 7 could be reduced substantially if people at risk would change just 5 behaviors: compliance (e.g., use of antihypertensive medication), diet, smoking, lack of exercise, and alcohol and drug abuse. Each of these behaviors is inextricably linked with marketing efforts and the reactions of consumers to marketing campaigns. The link between consumer choices and social problems is clear.[17]

However, the same authors conclude: "Although these problems appear daunting, they are all problems that are solvable through altruistic [social] marketing." Thus, marketing and consumer behavior can both aggravate and reduce serious social problems.

THE NATURE OF CONSUMER BEHAVIOR

LO4

Figure 1–3 shows the model that we use to capture the general structure and process of consumer behavior and to organize this text. It is a **conceptual model.** It does not contain sufficient detail to predict particular behaviors; however, it does reflect our beliefs about the general nature of consumer behavior. Individuals develop self-concepts (their view of themselves) and subsequent lifestyles (how they live) based on a variety of internal (mainly psychological and physical) and external (mainly sociological and demographic) influences. These self-concepts and lifestyles produce needs and desires, many of which require consumption decisions to satisfy. As individuals encounter relevant situations, the consumer decision process is activated. This process and the experiences and acquisitions it produces in turn influence the consumers' self-concept and lifestyle by affecting their internal and external characteristics.

Of course, life is rarely so structured as Figure 1–3 and our discussion of it so far may seem to suggest. Consumer behavior is hardly ever so simple, structured, conscious, mechanical, or linear. A quick analysis of your own behavior and that of your friends will reveal that, on the contrary, consumer behavior is frequently complex, disorganized, nonconscious, organic, and circular. Remember—Figure 1–3 is only a model, a starting point for our analysis. It is meant to aid you in thinking about consumer behavior. As you look at the model and read the following chapters based on this model, continually relate the descriptions in the text to the rich world of consumer behavior that is all around you.

The factors shown in Figure 1–3 are given detailed treatment in the subsequent chapters of this book. Here we provide a brief overview so that you can initially see how they work and fit together. Our discussion here and in the following chapters moves through the model from left to right.

External Influences (Part II)

Dividing the factors that influence consumers into categories is somewhat arbitrary. For example, we treat learning as an internal influence despite the fact that much human learning involves interaction with, or imitation of, other individuals. Thus, learning could also be considered a group process. In Figure 1–3, the two-directional arrow connecting internal and external influences indicates that each set interacts with the other.

We organize our discussion of external influences from large-scale macrogroups to smaller, more microgroup influences. *Culture* is perhaps the most pervasive influence on consumer behavior. We begin our consideration of culture in Chapter 2 by examining

Overall Model of Consumer Behavior FIGURE 1-3

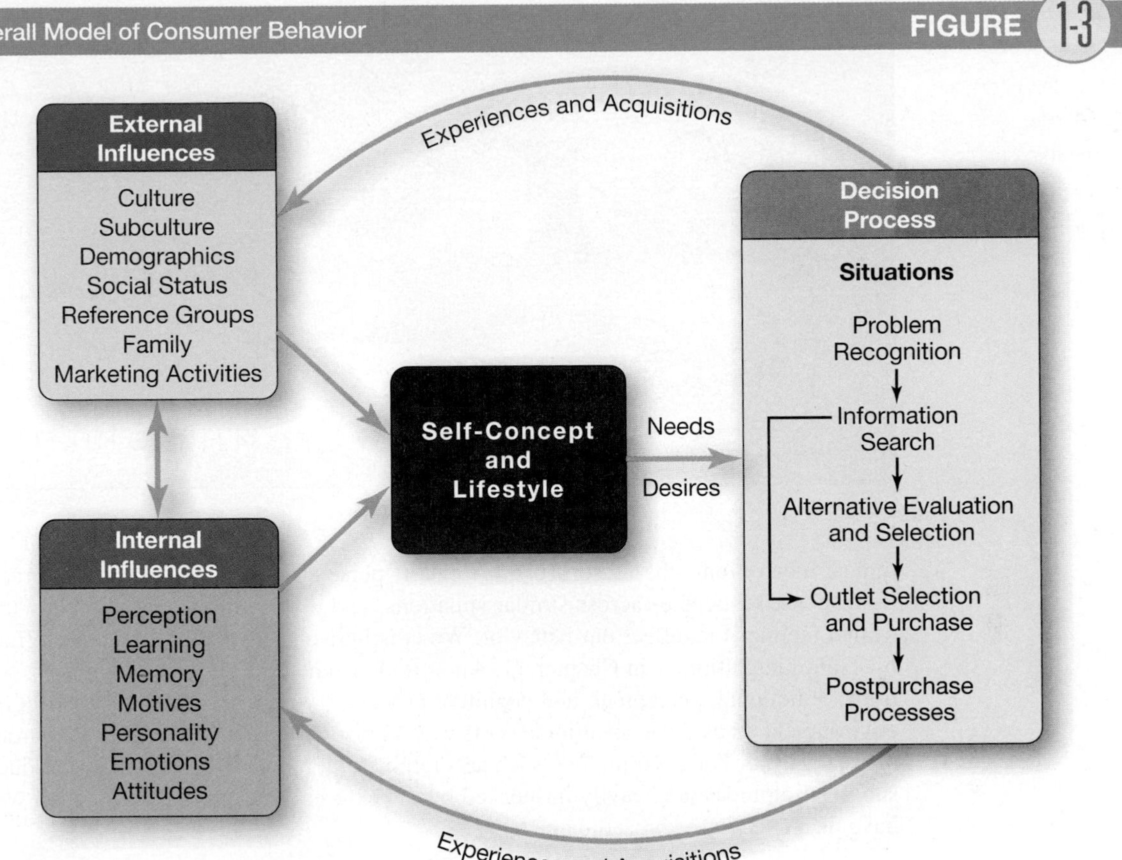

differences in consumption patterns across cultures. In Chapters 3 through 7, we focus on American culture in detail. In Chapter 3, we examine cultural values. As we will see, while Americans share many values and consumption behaviors, there are also rich diversity and ongoing change in this society that create both marketing opportunities and unique social energy. Illustration 1–7 shows how marketers are embracing this diversity in their advertisements.

Chapter 4 continues our examination of American society by analyzing its demographics (the number, education, age, income, occupation, and location of individuals in a society) and social stratification. Chapter 5 considers ethnic, religious, and regional subcultures. Chapter 6 analyzes families, households, and household decision making. Finally, in Chapter 7, we look at the processes by which groups influence consumer behavior and group communication, including the role of groups in the acceptance of new products and technologies. Taken together, Chapters 2 through 7 provide a means of comparing and contrasting the various external factors that influence consumer behavior in America—and around the world. Cross-cultural variations are highlighted when possible throughout the text.

Internal Influences (Part III)

Internal influences begin with perception, the process by which individuals receive and assign meaning to stimuli (Chapter 8). This is followed by learning—changes in the content or structure of long-term memory (Chapter 9). Chapter 10 covers three closely related

ILLUSTRATION 1-7

America is increasingly diverse. Ads such as this one reflect and embrace such diversity.

topics: motivation—the reason for a behavior; personality—an individual's characteristic response tendencies across similar situations; and emotion—strong, relatively uncontrolled feelings that affect our behavior. We conclude our coverage of internal influences by examining attitudes in Chapter 11. An attitude is an enduring organization of motivational, emotional, perceptual, and cognitive processes with respect to some aspect of our environment. In essence, an attitude is the way a person thinks, feels, and acts toward some aspect of his or her environment, such as a retail store, television program, or product. As such, our attitudes are heavily influenced by the external and internal factors that we will have discussed in the preceding chapters.

Self-Concept and Lifestyle

Chapter 12 concludes Part III with a detailed discussion of the key concepts of self-concept and lifestyle around which our model revolves. As a result of the interaction of the internal and external variables described earlier, individuals develop a self-concept that is reflected in a lifestyle. **Self-concept** is *the totality of an individual's thoughts and feelings about him- or herself.* **Lifestyle** is, quite simply, *how one lives,* including the products one buys, how one uses them, what one thinks about them, and how one feels about them. Lifestyle is the manifestation of the individual's self-concept, the total image the person has of him- or herself as a result of the culture he or she lives in and the individual situations and experiences that comprise his or her daily existence. It is the sum of the person's past decisions and future plans.

Both individuals and families exhibit distinct lifestyles. We often hear of "career-oriented individuals," "outdoor families," or "devoted parents." One's lifestyle is determined by both conscious and unconscious decisions. Often we make choices with full awareness of their impact on our lifestyle, but generally we are unaware of the extent to which our decisions are influenced by our current or desired lifestyle. Our model shows that consumers' self-concepts and lifestyles produce needs and desires that interact with the situations in which consumers find themselves to trigger the consumer decision process.

We do not mean to imply that consumers think in terms of lifestyle. None of us consciously think, "I'll have an Evian bottled water in order to enhance my lifestyle." Rather, we make decisions consistent with our lifestyles without deliberately considering lifestyle.

Most consumer decisions involve very little effort or thought on the part of the consumer. They are what we call *low-involvement decisions.* Feelings and emotions are as important in many consumer decisions as logical analysis or physical product attributes. Nonetheless, most consumer purchases involve at least a modest amount of decision making, and most are influenced by the purchaser's current and desired lifestyle.

Consumer Decision Process (Part IV)

Consumer decisions result from perceived problems ("I'm thirsty") and opportunities ("That looks like it would be fun to try"). We will use the term *problem* to refer both to problems and to opportunities. Consumer problems arise in specific situations and the nature of the situation influences the resulting consumer behavior. Therefore, we provide a detailed discussion of situational influences on the consumer decision process in Chapter 13.

As Figure 1–3 indicates, a consumer's needs/desires may trigger one or more levels of the consumer decision process. It is important to note that for most purchases, consumers devote very little effort to this process, and emotions and feelings often have as much or more influence on the outcome as do facts and product features. Despite the limited effort that consumers often devote to the decision process, the results have important effects on the individual consumer, the firm, and the larger society. Therefore, we provide detailed coverage of each stage of the process: problem recognition (Chapter 14); information search (Chapter 15); alternative evaluation and selection (Chapter 16); outlet selection and purchase (Chapter 17); and use, disposition, and purchase evaluation (Chapter 18). The increasing role of technology, particularly the Internet, in consumer decision making is highlighted throughout these chapters.

Organizations (Part V) and Regulation (Part VI)

Organizations or businesses can also be consumers as when Mercedes-Benz purchases dashboard subcomponents from a supplier. This type of marketing is often termed business-to-business (B2B) marketing to differentiate it from business-to-consumer (B2C) marketing that is the focus of much of this text. The special nature of organizations and how they behave warrant special attention. In Chapter 19, we show how our model of individual and household consumer behavior can be modified to help understand the consumer behavior of organizations.

Regulation is an aspect of consumer behavior that permeates marketer actions relating to all parts of our model and it warrants special attention as well. Chapter 20 focuses our attention on the regulation of marketing activities, especially those targeting children. We pay particular attention to the role that knowledge of consumer behavior plays or could play in regulation.

THE MEANING OF CONSUMPTION

As we proceed through this text, we will describe the results of studies of consumer behavior, discuss theories about consumer behavior, and present examples of marketing programs designed to influence consumer behavior. While reading this material, however, do not lose sight of the fact that consumer behavior is not just a topic of study or a basis for developing marketing or regulatory strategy. Consumption frequently has deep meaning for the consumer.[18] LO5

CONSUMER INSIGHT 1-2

Consumption Meaning and Motivation

Consumer behavior is the study of why consumers buy. Understanding consumer behavior is at the heart of marketing strategy and a major focus of this text. Government agencies must "sell" ideas and services (e.g., The Affordable Care Act, tax increases) to citizens. Nonprofits must convince consumers to contribute to their organizations (e.g., Salvation Army). Companies must persuade consumers to buy their products and services. Some products and services are essential. However, much of consumption is not need-based, at least in a functional sense. Many companies spend considerable money and effort convincing consumers to buy products, services, or brands they don't really need. And consumers often want products and services they cannot afford, which, if acted on, can lead to negative financial consequences such as crushing credit card debt. In this insight we explore some of the factors driving consumer purchases that drive at the deeper meaning of consumption beyond mere function and necessity.

Meaning in the mundane—Sometimes consumers know what they want—from simple and relatively inexpensive everyday things like milk, bread, and socks, which require little decision effort, to more expensive items such as cars, TVs, and homes, which require considerable decision effort. Even in these situations where products meet basic needs, there can be far more meaning in the objects purchased than might meet the eye. Cars and homes can take on important meanings over time when they are associated with major events such as a first date, a child's first step, and so on. Even truly mundane products can attain heightened meaning if associated with important events or people in one's life. Chapter 12 deals with this idea of products becoming a part of the extended self and as a consequence taking on much deeper meanings than might initially seem possible.

Meaning in avoidance—Consumers often know what they don't want—at least at the broadest level—and make consumption choices accordingly. Consumers don't want fear of physical harm in their lives—so they buy cars with safety enhancements and products such as smoke alarms and carbon monoxide detectors to reduce physical risk. Consumers don't want financial risk in their lives—so they buy insurance and extended warranties, and hire financial planners. Risk and risk avoidance are an important part of consumer behavior and decision making, as discussed in Chapter 3 and Chapter 16.

Meaning in innovative brands—The iPhone is unquestionably a marketing success. It has helped to make Apple one of the most profitable companies in the

Consider the example of a man named Andre. Andre, just escaping homelessness, proudly states that he was able to save for and buy a pair of Nikes. He could undoubtedly have purchased a different brand that would have met his physical needs just as well as the Nikes for much less money. Although Andre does not state why he bought the more expensive Nikes, a reasonable interpretation is that they serve as a visible symbol that Andre is back as a successful member of society. In fact, Nike is sometimes criticized for creating, through its marketing activities, symbols of success or status that are unduly expensive. *Consider this issue as you read about the various meanings and motives underlying Consumer Insight 1–2.*[19]

As you read the chapters that follow, keep in mind that the decisions consumers make are the result of a complex set of forces, often reflecting meaning and motivations that are powerful, nuanced, and beyond mere function.

world.[20] Consumers willingly wait in long lines for hours to have the chance to buy a new version of the iPhone. And yet, consumers didn't know they wanted that product until it already existed. The iPhone is clearly more than just a phone. It has many meanings to consumers—including innovative, cutting-edge, sophisticated, intellectual—that consumers buy as much or more than the phone. In fact, a brand's personality can be as much a driver of purchase as how well it meets functional requirements, as discussed in Chapter 10.

The more radical the innovation, the more marketers must be able to see the match between customer core needs and the possibilities created by emerging technology. Below are a few quotes about the challenges of *innovating ahead of the customer.*

> You can't just ask customers what they want and then try to give that to them. By the time you get it built, they'll want something new.[21]
>
> —Steve Jobs

> It's really hard to design products by focus groups. A lot of times, people don't know what they want until you show it to them.[22]
>
> —Steve Jobs

The iPhone is a marketer's dream. However, most new products do not succeed. Why this is so and how marketers can adapt their strategies is a key aspect of Chapter 7.

Meaning beyond function—Women's hair removal is highly popular in the United States and has led to a thriving industry including razors, chemical depilatories, and electrolysis. However, women in other parts of the world—France, Italy, China—do not shave.[23] Crest's introduction of "Whitestrips" in 2001 created a new over-the-counter product to whiten teeth that has since grown to a multimillion-dollar market.[24] Such examples highlight the fact that "needs" come in various forms. While being hair-free under one's arms or having whiter teeth may not improve one's physical well-being, in many countries and cultures, such attributes are related to the need to belong or to be respected, as discussed in Chapter 10. Some consumer groups argue that marketers create unnecessary needs on the part of the consumer and worry about their consequences for both the individual and society, as discussed in Chapter 20.

Critical Thinking Questions

1. How and why do you think products acquire meaning to consumers?
2. Can you see any potential negative consequences to marketing attempts to encourage purchases of products consumers don't need?
3. Do marketers create needs?

SUMMARY

SMARTBOOK™

LO1: Define consumer behavior.

The field of *consumer behavior* is the study of individuals, groups, or organizations and the processes they use to select, secure, use, and dispose of products, services, experiences, or ideas to satisfy needs and the impacts that these processes have on the consumer and society.

LO2: Summarize the applications of consumer behavior.

Consumer behavior can be applied in four areas: (a) marketing strategy, (b) regulatory policy, (c) social marketing, and (d) creation of informed individuals. Developing marketing strategy involves setting levels of the marketing mix based on an understanding of the market and segments involved to create desirable outcomes. Developing regulatory guidelines involves developing policies, guidelines, and laws to protect and aid consumers. *Social marketing* is the application of marketing strategies and tactics to alter or create behaviors that have a positive effect on the targeted individuals or society as a whole. Creating more informed individuals involves educating consumers about their own consumption behaviors as well as marketers' efforts to influence them in such a way as to create a more sound citizenship, effective purchasing behavior, and reasoned business ethics.

LO3: Explain how consumer behavior can be used to develop marketing strategy.

The interplay between consumer behavior and marketing strategy involves five stages. First is market analysis, which involves gathering data and tracking trends related to the company, competitors, conditions, and consumers. Second is market segmentation. A *market segment* is a portion of a larger market whose needs differ somewhat from the larger market. Firms segment their markets and choose a segment or segments that best fit their capabilities and market conditions. Third is marketing strategy, which involves setting appropriate levels for the marketing mix as a function of the segments being targeted and the market conditions that exist. Fourth is the consumer decision process, which is a series of steps starting with problem recognition and moving through information search, alternative evaluation, purchase, use, and post-purchase evaluation. Marketing efforts can be targeted to these different stages. Fifth is outcomes at the individual, firm, and societal levels. And while profit maximization is often a goal at the firm level, possible adverse effects at the individual and societal level are of importance to firms, government organizations, and regulators. An understanding of consumer behavior theory and concepts is critical at each stage as marketers gather information, develop marketing strategies to influence consumer decisions, and evaluate the effects of their marketing efforts.

LO4: Explain the components that constitute a conceptual model of consumer behavior.

The conceptual model of consumer behavior developed here can be broken into four interrelated parts. External and internal influences affect the consumer's self-concept and lifestyle, which, in turn, affects the decision process. External influences (Part II of the text) include culture, reference groups, demographics, and marketing activities. Internal influences (Part III) include perception, emotions, attitudes, and personality. *Self-concept* is the totality of an individual's thoughts and feelings about him- or herself. *Lifestyle* is, quite simply, how one lives, including the products one buys, how one uses them, what one thinks about them, and how one feels about them. External and internal factors operate to influence self-concept and lifestyle, which, in turn, influences the decision process (Part IV). Overlaying these basic components is organizations (Part V) and regulation (Part VI). Organizations or businesses can also be consumers, as when Mercedes-Benz purchases dashboard subcomponents from a supplier. This type of marketing is often termed business-to-business (B2B) marketing to differentiate it from business-to-consumer (B2C) marketing, which is the focus of much of this text. The special nature of organizations and how they behave warrant special attention. Regulation is an aspect of consumer behavior that permeates marketer actions relating to all parts of our model and it warrants special attention as well.

LO5: Discuss issues involving consumption meanings and firm attempts to influence them.

Consumption has meaning beyond the satisfaction of minimum or basic consumer needs. Thus, consumers might purchase Nike sneakers not only to satisfy the functional needs associated with safety and support, but also for symbolic needs associated with status, identity, and group acceptance. Some criticize marketers for their attempts to instill in, or amplify, consumer desires for products beyond minimum functional aspects. And while this criticism may hold true, it also seems likely that such desires and symbolic meanings are naturally assigned to objects even in the relative absence of marketing. Nonetheless, the ethical implications of marketers' actions in this regard are important to consider.

KEY TERMS

Conceptual model 24
Consumer behavior 6
Consumer cost 19
Customer satisfaction 22
Customer value 10
Distribution 20
Injurious consumption 22
Lifestyle 26
Marketing communications 18
Marketing mix 17
Marketing strategy 17
Market segment 13
Need set 14
Price 19
Product 17
Product position 21
Self-concept 26
Service 20
Social marketing 8
Target market 16
Total product 11

REVIEW QUESTIONS

1. How is the field of consumer behavior defined?
2. What conclusions can be drawn from the examples at the beginning of this chapter?
3. What are the four major uses or applications of an understanding of consumer behavior?
4. What is *social marketing?*
5. What is *customer value,* and why is it important to marketers?
6. What is required to provide superior customer value?
7. What is a *total product?*
8. What is involved in the *consumer* analysis phase of market analysis in Figure 1–1?
9. What is involved in the *company* analysis phase of market analysis in Figure 1–1?
10. What is involved in the *competitor* analysis phase of market analysis in Figure 1–1?
11. What is involved in the *conditions* analysis phase of market analysis in Figure 1–1?
12. Describe the process of *market segmentation.*
13. What is *marketing strategy?*
14. What is a *marketing mix?*
15. What is a *product?*
16. What does an effective communications strategy require?
17. What is a *price?* How does the price of a product differ from the *cost of the product to the consumer?*
18. How is *service* defined in the text?
19. What is involved in creating satisfied customers?
20. What are the major outcomes for the firm of the marketing process and consumers' responses to it?
21. What are the major outcomes for the individual of the marketing process and consumers' responses to it?
22. What are the major outcomes for society of the marketing process and consumers' responses to it?
23. What is *product position?*
24. What is meant by *injurious consumption?*
25. What is meant by *consumer lifestyle?*
26. Describe the consumer decision process.

DISCUSSION QUESTIONS

27. Why would someone shop on the Internet? Buy an iPod? Eat at TGI Friday's frequently?
    a. Why would someone else not make those purchases?
    b. How would you choose one outlet, brand, or model over the others? Would others make the same choice in the same way?
28. Respond to the questions in Consumer Insight 1–1.
29. Of what use, if any, are models such as the one in Figure 1–3 to managers?
30. What changes would you suggest in the model in Figure 1–3? Why?
31. Describe your lifestyle. How does it differ from your parents' lifestyle?
32. Do you anticipate any changes in your lifestyle in the next five years? What will cause these changes? What new products or brands will you consume because of these changes?
33. Describe a recent purchase you made. To what extent did you follow the consumer decision-making process described in this chapter? How would you explain any differences?
34. Describe several *total products* that are more than their direct physical features.
35. Describe the needs that the following items might satisfy and the total cost to the consumer of obtaining the benefits of the total product.
    a. Digital video recorder (e.g., TiVo)
    b. Lasik eye surgery
    c. Motorcycle
    d. SUV
36. How would you define the product that the Hard Rock Cafe provides? What needs does it meet?
37. To what extent, if any, are marketers responsible for injurious consumption involving their products?

38. How could social marketing help alleviate some of society's problems?
39. Respond to the questions in Consumer Insight 1–2.

40. Is the criticism of Nike for creating a shoe that is symbolic of success to some groups valid? Why or why not?
41. Robert's American gourmet snack foods produces herbal-based snacks such as Spirulina Spirals and St. John's Wort Tortilla Chips. According to the company president, "We're selling like crazy. We don't do research. We react as sort of a karma thing."[25] How would you explain the firm's success? What are the advantages and risks of this approach?

APPLICATION ACTIVITIES

42. Interview the manager or marketing manager of a retail firm. Determine how this individual develops the marketing strategy. Compare this person's process with the approach described in the text.
43. Interview the managers of a local charity. Determine what their assumptions about the consumer behavior of their supporters are. To what extent do they use marketing strategy to increase support for the organization or compliance with its objectives?
44. Interview five students. Have them describe the last three restaurant meals they consumed and the situations in which they were consumed. What can you conclude about the impact of the situation on consumer behavior? What can you conclude about the impact of the individual on consumer behavior?
45. Visit one or more stores that sell the following items. Report on the sales techniques used (point-of-purchase displays, store design, salesperson comments, and so forth). What beliefs concerning consumer behavior appear to underlie these techniques? It is often worthwhile for a male and a female student to visit the same store and talk to the same salesperson at different times. The variation in salesperson behavior is sometimes quite revealing.
    a. Books and magazines
    b. Cellular phones
    c. Pet supplies
    d Expensive art
    e. Expensive jewelry
    f. Personal computers
46. Interview individuals who sell the items listed below. Try to discover their personal models of consumer behavior for their products.
    a. Expensive jewelry
    b. Pets
    c. Golfing equipment
    d. Plants and garden supplies
    e. Flowers
    f. Car insurance
47. Interview three individuals who recently made a major purchase and three others who made a minor purchase. In what ways were their decision processes similar? How were they different?

REFERENCES

1. Sources for "Evolution of Marketing" section: J. B. Pine and J. H. Gilmore, *The Experience Economy* (Boston, MA: Harvard Business Press, 1999); and M. Rhodes, "Starbucks Channels Old-World Mysticism in New Big Easy Store," *FastCompany.com,* December 13, 2013, www.fastcodesign.com, accessed July 13, 2014.
2. Sources for "Marketing 2 Consumers" section: S. Godin, *Permission Marketing* (New York: Simon & Schuster, 1999); P. Fuller and K. Hein, "A Two-Way Conversation," *Brandweek,* February 24, 2002, pp. 20–28.
3. Sources for the "Social Media" section: J. Howe, "The Rise of Crowdsourcing," *Wired Magazine,* June 2006, http://archive.wired.com/wired/archive/14.06/crowds.html, accessed July 13, 2014; J. Howe, *Crowdsourcing* (New York: Three Rivers Press, 2008); T. Smith, "The Social Media Revolution," *International Journal of Market Research* 51, no. 4 (2009), pp. 559–61; H. Simula, A. Tollinen, and H. Karjaluoto, "Crowdsourcing in the Social Media Era," *Journal of Marketing Development and Competitiveness,* May 2013, pp. 122–37; T. Luna, "Long CVS Receipts Spark Social Media Sensation," *The Boston Globe,* August 31, 2013, www.bostonglobe.com, accessed July 13, 2014.
4. J. Neff, "S.C. Johnson Likely to Bag Ziploc TableTops," *Advertising Age,* November 25, 2002, p. 3; and J. Neff, "S.C. Johnson Faces a Clean-up Job," *Advertising Age,* November 29, 2004, p. 8.
5. See W. I. Ghani and N. M. Childs, "Wealth Effects of the Passage of the Nutrition Labeling and Education Act of 1990 for Large U.S. Multinational Food Corporations," *Journal of Public Policy and Marketing,* Fall 1999, pp. 147–58; and

S. K. Balasubramanian and C. Cole, "Consumers' Search and Use of Nutrition Information," *Journal of Marketing,* July 2002, pp. 112–27.

6. See A. R. Andreasen, "Social Marketing," *Journal of Public Policy & Marketing,* Spring 1994, pp. 108–14; and P. Kotler, N. Roberto, and N. Lee, *Social Marketing* (Thousand Oaks, CA: Sage, 2002).
7. A. S. Wellner, "The New Science of Focus Groups," *American Demographics,* March 2003, pp. 29–33.
8. Insight based on K. E. Reynolds, J. Ganesh, and M. Luckett, "Traditional Malls vs. Factory Outlets," *Journal of Business Research,* 55 (2002), pp. 687–96.
9. E. Esfahani, "How to . . . Get Tough with Bad Customers," *Business 2.0,* October 2004, p. 52.
10. T. F. McMahon, "What Buyers Buy and Sellers Sell," *Journal of Professional Services Marketing,* 2 (1996), pp. 3–16.
11. "'Build a Better Mousetrap': 2004 New Product Innovations of the Year," *Productscan Online* (press release), December 27, 2004 (www.productscan.com).
12. "MasterCard Launches Marketing, Education Campaign for Hispanics," *Payment News,* May 18, 2009.
13. See, e.g., J. Weber and A. T. Palmer, "How the Net Is Remaking the Mall," *BusinessWeek Online,* May 9, 2005.
14. "Disney Hits New Markets with Retail Makeover," *Reuters,* January 11, 2011.
15. P. Wingert, "Why It's So Risky," *Newsweek,* November 22, 2010, p. 14.
16. "Price Rises Threaten Progress on Poverty," *Financial Times,* April 10, 2008, p. 8.
17. R. E. Petty and J. T. Cacioppo, "Addressing Disturbing and Disturbed Consumer Behavior," *Journal of Marketing Research,* February 1996, pp. 1–8.
18. See M. L. Richins, "Special Possessions and the Expression of Material Values," *Journal of Consumer Research,* December 1994, pp. 522–33.
19. C. Miller, "The Have-Nots," *Marketing News,* August 1, 1994, pp. 1–2; P. Mergenhagen, "What Can Minimum Wage Buy?," *American Demographics,* January 1996, pp. 32–36; and A. Hank, "Hank Finds Two Families," *StreetWise,* May 16–31, 1996, p. 7. See also R. P. Hill, "Disadvantaged Consumers," *Journal of Business Ethics* 80 (2008), pp. 77–83.
20. "Apple Becomes Most Valuable Company Ever," *CBS News (online),* August 20, 2012, www.cbsnews.com/news/apple-becomes-most-valuable-company-ever/, accessed July 21, 2014.
21. B. Burlingham and G. Gendron, "The Entrepreneur of the Decade," *Inc. Magazine,* April 1, 1989, www.inc.com/magazine/19890401/5602.html/7, accessed July 21, 2014.
22. A. Reinhart, "Steve Jobs on Apple's Resurgence," *BusinessWeek,* May 25, 1998, www.businessweek.com/bwdaily/dnflash/may1998/nf80512d.htm, accessed July 21, 2014.
23. C. Hope, "Caucasian Female Body Hair and American Culture," *Journal of American Culture,* Spring 1982, pp. 93–99.
24. K. Higgins, "P&G Reinvents Itself," *Marketing Management,* November/December 2002, pp. 12–15; A. Dutra, J. Frary, and R. Wise, "Higher-Order Needs Drive New Growth in Mature Consumer Markets," *The Journal of Business Strategy*, 25, no. 5 (2004), pp. 26–34.
25. M. W. Fellman, "New Age Dawns for Product Niche," *Marketing News,* April 27, 1998, p. 1.

part

II EXTERNAL INFLUENCES

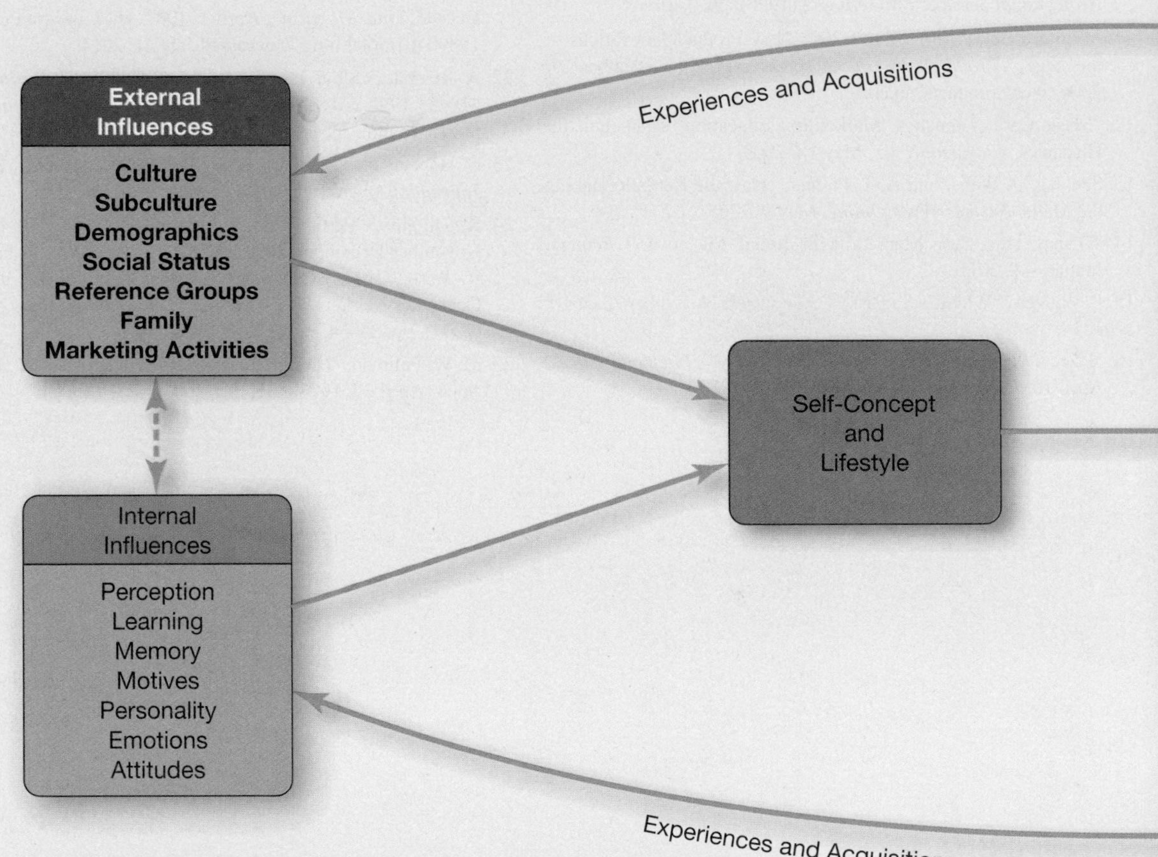

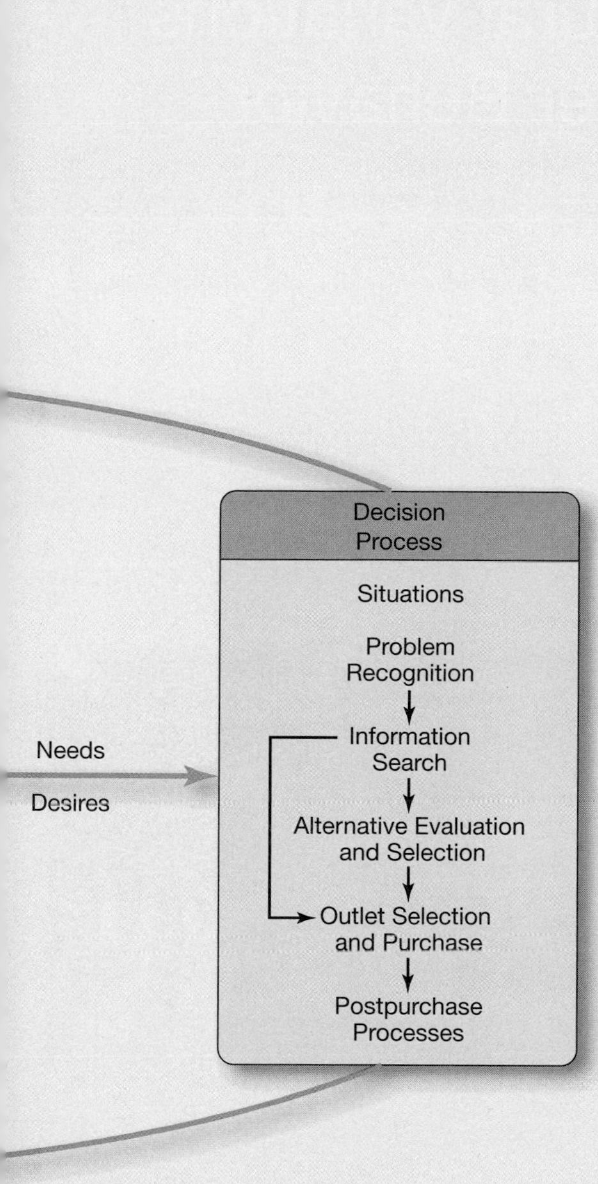

The external influence area of our model shown at the left is the focal point of this part of the text. Any division of the factors that influence consumer behavior into separate and distinct categories is somewhat arbitrary. For example, we will consider learning in Part III of the text, which focuses on internal influences. However, a substantial amount of learning involves interaction with, or imitation of, other individuals. Thus, learning clearly involves external influences such as family and peers. Our focus in this part is on the functioning of the various external groups, not the processes by which individuals react to these groups.

In this part, we begin with large-scale, macrogroup influences and move to smaller, more microgroup influences. As we progress, the nature of the influence exerted changes from general guidelines to explicit expectations for specific behaviors. In Chapter 2, we examine how cultures cause differing behaviors across countries and other cultural units. Chapters 3 through 6 focus primarily on the American society, examining its values, demographics, social stratification, subcultures, and family structure. Chapter 7 examines the mechanisms by which groups influence consumer behaviors. In combination, these chapters allow for a comparison and contrast of how external influences operate in America and around the world.

chapter

2 Cross-Cultural Variations In Consumer Behavior

LEARNING OBJECTIVES

- **LO1** **Define the concept of culture.**
- **LO2** **Describe core values that vary across culture and influence behaviors.**
- **LO3** **Understand cross-cultural variations in nonverbal communications.**
- **LO4** **Summarize key aspects of the global youth culture.**
- **LO5** **Understand the role of global demographics**
- **LO6** **List the key dimensions in deciding to enter a foreign market.**

Firms often aspire to be global. The benefits can be significant, but the challenges are staggering. The adaptations, adjustments, and considerations necessary when doing business across country and cultural borders are numerous. The following examples (Target, Bunnies, and Apple) illustrate the branding and logo issues created by global trademark law.

Target: United States versus Australia—Target, the 1,800-store Minneapolis-based retailer, recently established its first non-U.S. stores in Canada.[1] Although this is Target's first venture beyond its American borders, since 1968 there have been Target department stores in Australia. Target Australia (300 stores, $3.8 B annual revenue) bears an uncanny resemblance to the U.S. Target, with the same (a) "Target" name in the same font; (b) red and white bulls'-eye logo on its storefront, website, and ads; (c) tagline "Expect more, Pay less"; as well as a mix of products that consumers likely would find indistinguishable from those offered in Target U.S.

The explanation for this seemingly odd occurrence can be found in trademark law and the historical development of regional and local brands at a time when globalization was less prevalent. Trademarks for the most part can be established only in one country at a time. A company doing business in multiple countries must obtain trademarks for its name separately for each country (Target U.S. did so in 1966–67; Target Australia did so in 1968). Why Target U.S. would have allowed this is speculative, but one expert suggests:

> . . . the two Targets [likely] had some sort of informal, handshake agreement. Fifty years ago, retail was primarily a local business and there were very few, if any, truly global brands. The idea that Target U.S. and Target Australia would somehow cross paths seemed remote at best.

Currently, Target U.S. and Target Australia are not directly competing. But the globalized nature of consumer buying, the permeability of country boundaries provided by Internet access, and Target U.S.'s desire to grow beyond its borders paints a scenario that could create challenges and conflict moving forward.

Pink Bunnies: Energizer versus Duracell—The localized nature of trademark laws also explains the existence of two battery bunnies, the Energizer Bunny in the United States and Canada and the Duracell Bunnies in Europe and Australia. In 1973, Duracell created the Duracell Bunny to personify the long life of its batteries. In a worldwide advertisement campaign from 1973 to 1980, the drum-beating bunny powered by Duracell batteries outlasted all the drum-beating bunnies powered by rival batteries. However, in 1987 when Duracell failed to renew its trademark Duracell Bunny in the United States, Energizer seized the lapse to trademark its Energizer Bunny, sporting sunglasses and wearing flip-flop sandals with a noticeably brighter shade of pink fur, beating on a noticeably larger drum. Today, consumers in the United States and Canada are familiar with the fuzzy, pink-furred, sunglass-wearing, drum-beating Energizer Bunny that "keeps on going and going" while an equally iconic fuzzy, pink-furred "copper-top" Duracell Bunny exists only in Europe and Australia.[2]

Apple: Computers and Music—Apple computer, now known as Apple, Inc., is at the apex of the technology world as well as an iconic global brand. Apple Corporation is the holding company for the Beatles. Both Apple Computer and Apple Corporation have an apple as their logo, and as long as the two companies excelled in their own separate realms (computers versus music), the two companies were able to work out their trademark differences. However, things became murky when Apple Computer entered the realm of music via iTunes. In 2006, the courts ruled in favor of Apple Computers and the two companies reached a licensing agreement in 2007.[3]

As we will see throughout this chapter and the remainder of the text, names, signs, and symbols generate imagery, beliefs, and attitudes about brands that are important drivers of consumer behavior. The local and global laws governing how brand names and logos operate across country borders is critical in light of how important the embodied meaning of such names and symbols is to the consumers who buy those brands.

As the opening vignette suggests, marketing across country and cultural boundaries is difficult and challenging. As Figure 2–1 indicates, cultures (and countries) may differ in demographics, language, nonverbal communications, and values. The success of global marketers depends on how well they understand and adapt to these differences.

FIGURE 2-1 Cultural Factors Affect Consumer Behavior and Marketing Strategy

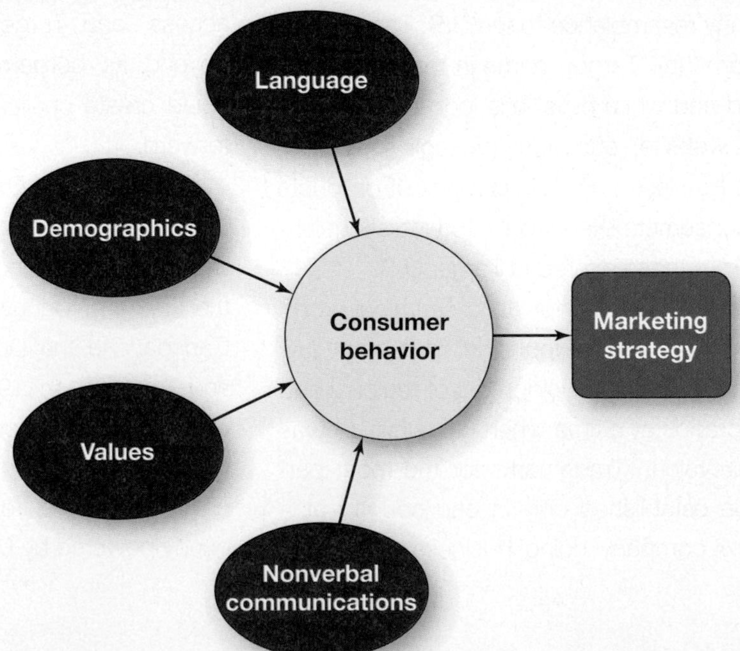

In this chapter, we focus on cultural variations in *values* and *nonverbal communications.* In addition, we briefly describe how *demographic variations* across countries and cultures influence consumption patterns.

Before dealing with specifics, we must consider the broader issues of cross-cultural marketing, including globalization, attitudes toward multinational brands, and ethical considerations. Globalization means more than product exports and imports. Globalization can involve exporting and importing values, lifestyles, and attitudes. Historically, such influence has been thought of as primarily going one way—that is, large American and other Western multinational companies and brands influencing the values and lifestyles of the countries they enter. And, no doubt, such effects occur. For example, television advertising in countries such as China and India is extensive and reflects many Western values, such as individualism and an emphasis on youth. Over time, such advertising would be expected to influence not only how many Chinese and Indians choose to live (lifestyle) but also what they value and how they think and feel.[4]

Increasingly, however, globalization means mutual influence as products, brands, cultures, and values move back and forth across the world. So, while Western brands such as Mercedes still have cachet as luxury symbols in Eastern countries such as Japan, Eastern brands such as Japan's Lexus now have developed similar luxury status in Western countries such as the United States. Additional examples include:[5]

- Soccer is being imported into the United States particularly as symbolized by U.K. star David Beckham, while American-style football (termed *olive ball*) is being exported to China.
- Harajuku, a broad term for the "street" fashion developed by style-conscious Japanese youth, which often incorporates elements of Western style but in unique and creative ways, has become popular around the world, as shown in Illustration 2–1.
- Brazilian products and fashion became all the rage in London as "Brazilian chic" was marketed through department stores, cultural events, and positive media coverage. Similar trends are occurring not only in the United States but also all over the world.

Although globalization can influence cultural values, it would be a mistake to think that all cultures are becoming homogenized. While younger generations of consumers appear to be more similar, modern, and, in some cases Western, older consumers in those same

ILLUSTRATION 2-1

Harajuku style is popular all over the world with its creative combination of traditional Japanese influences with more modern Western style.

markets cling to traditional values that must be respected. For example, China appeared to eagerly (and profitably) copy TV contest shows like *American Idol* (*Supergirl* is a Chinese version). However, lawmakers there have clamped down with regulations to make the contestants act more conservatively and to keep the judges from embarrassing the contestants. According to one expert:

> The authorities are reacting against the sensationalistic, slightly rebellious nature of the contest programs, which promote individualism and personal achievement. The winners become idols with extreme influence on Chinese citizens. "Supergirl" also introduced Chinese to the concept of voting.[6]

Beyond elders and authorities attempting to maintain traditional cultural values, consumers across the globe often hold strong pride in their local heritage and sometimes mistrust or resent international brands, seeing them as irresponsible and hurtful to local culture and business. Indeed, a recent study indicates that regardless of country, there are four basic types of world citizens:[7]

- Global citizens (55 percent)—Positive toward international brands and view them as a signal of higher quality; most concerned about corporate responsibility to the local country. Prominent in Brazil, China, and Indonesia. Rare in the United States and the United Kingdom.
- Global dreamers (23 percent)—Positive toward international brands and buy into their positive symbolic aspects; less concerned about corporate responsibility to the local country. Equally distributed across countries.
- Antiglobals (13 percent)—Negative toward international brands; don't like brands that preach American values; don't trust multinationals. Higher in the United Kingdom and China. Lower in Egypt and South Africa.
- Global agnostics (9 percent)—Don't base decisions on global brand name; evaluate as they would local brands; don't see global brands as special. Higher in the United States and South Africa. Lower in Japan, Indonesia, China, and Turkey.

Corporate responsibility and ethical issues can span from labor policies to influences on consumption of products linked to negative consequences. One example is American tobacco companies, which are aggressively marketing their products in the developing countries of Asia, Latin America, Africa, and Eastern Europe. Smoking-related deaths are now a leading killer in Asia, where increases in female smoking are a major concern.[8] As one World Health Organization (WHO) official notes:

> Here in Japan we see Western cigarette brands marketed as a kind of liberation tool. We see cigarette companies calling on young Japanese women to assert themselves, shed their inhibitions and smoke.[9]

Clearly, there are both subtle and direct ethical issues involved in international marketing.

THE CONCEPT OF CULTURE

Culture is *the complex whole that includes knowledge, belief, art, law, morals, customs, and any other capabilities and habits acquired by humans as members of society.*

Several aspects of culture require elaboration. First, culture is a comprehensive concept. It includes almost everything that influences an individual's thought processes and behaviors. Although culture does not determine the nature or frequency of biological drives such as hunger or sex, it does influence if, when, and how these drives will be gratified. It influences not only our preferences but how we make decisions[10] and even how we perceive the world around us. Second, culture is acquired. It does not include inherited responses and predispositions. However, because much of human behavior is learned rather than innate, culture does affect a wide array of behaviors.

Third, the complexity of modern societies is such that culture seldom provides detailed prescriptions for appropriate behavior. Instead, in most industrial societies, culture supplies boundaries within which most individuals think and act. Finally, the nature of cultural influences is such that we are seldom aware of them. One behaves, thinks, and feels in a manner consistent with that of other members of the same culture because it seems "natural" or "right" to do so.

Imagine sweet corn. Most Americans think of it as a hot side dish. However, uses vary by country. Consider the following:

> Instead of being eaten as a hot side dish, the French add it to salad and eat it cold. In Britain, corn is used as a sandwich and pizza topping. In Japan, school children gobble down canned corn as an after-school treat. And in Korea, the sweet corn is sprinkled over ice cream.[11]

Some of these uses probably seem strange or disgusting to you but are perfectly natural to members of other cultures. This is the nature of culture. We don't think about the fact that many of our preferences are strongly influenced by our culture.

Culture operates primarily by setting rather loose boundaries for individual behavior and by influencing the functioning of such institutions as the family and mass media. Thus, culture provides the framework within which individual and household lifestyles evolve.

The boundaries that culture sets on behavior are called **norms,** which are simply *rules that specify or prohibit certain behaviors in specific situations.* Norms are derived from **cultural values,** or *widely held beliefs that affirm what is desirable.* Violation of cultural norms results in **sanctions,** or *penalties ranging from mild social disapproval to banishment from the group.* Thus, as Figure 2–2 indicates, cultural values give rise to norms and associated sanctions, which in turn influence consumption patterns.

The preceding discussion may leave the impression that people are aware of cultural values and norms and that violating any given norm carries a precise and known sanction. This is seldom the case. We tend to "obey" cultural norms without thinking because to do otherwise would seem unnatural. For example, we are seldom aware of how close we stand to other individuals while conducting business. Yet this distance is well defined and adhered to, even though it varies from culture to culture.

Values, Norms, Sanctions, and Consumption Patterns FIGURE 2-2

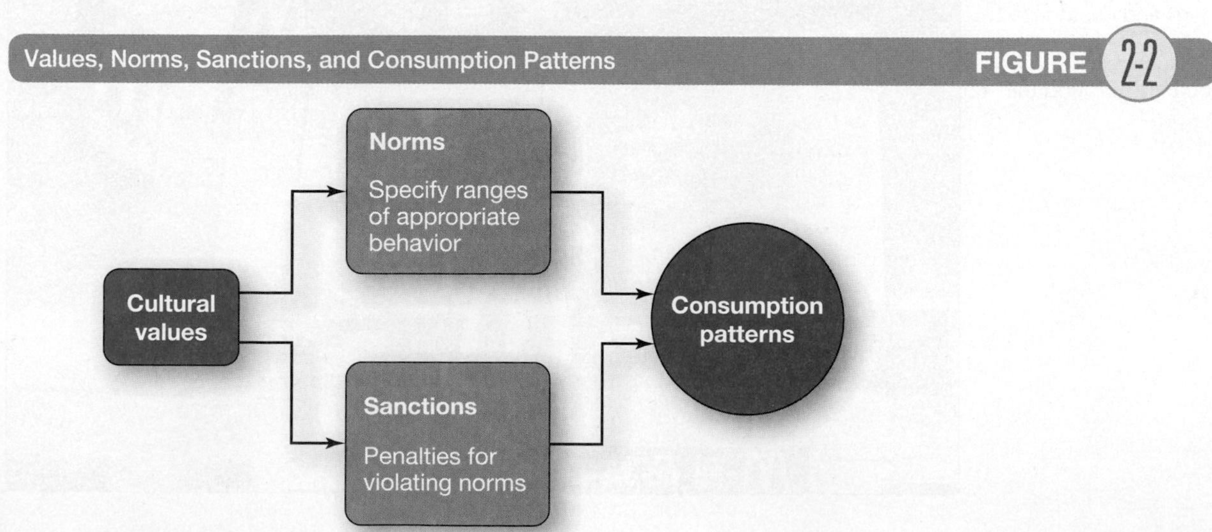

Cultures are not static. They typically evolve and change slowly over time. Marketing managers must understand both the existing cultural values and the emerging cultural values of the societies they serve. A failure to understand cultural differences can produce negative consequences, such as the following:

- An Indian entrepreneur flew in the Washington Redskin's cheerleaders for a cricket game. In a sexually conservative culture such as India's, this did not translate in a positive fashion. Lawmakers pressured the team and it switched to a band of local drummers. Their view was the cheerleaders were "lewd and not appropriate for India's traditional culture."[12]
- A U.S. electronics firm landed a major contract with a Japanese buyer. The U.S. firm's president flew to Tokyo to sign the contract. The head of the Japanese firm read the contract intently for an extraordinary length of time. At last, the U.S. executive offered a price discount. The Japanese executive was surprised but didn't object. The U.S. executive's mistake was assuming that the long scrutiny was an attempt to reopen negotiations. Instead, the Japanese executive was demonstrating his concern and authority by closely and slowly examining the document.
- Lipton created a line of instant meals named *Side Dishes.* The meals sold well in the United States but not in Latin America, a large market that Lipton had hoped would fuel growth for the line. Latin American housewives, with more traditional views of their family role, felt that "instant" meals implied they were lazy or poor caretakers for their families.[13]

Starbucks' CEO offers this cautionary note for American businesses going global: "The biggest lesson is not to assume that the market or the consumers are just like Americans, even if they speak English or otherwise behave as if they were."[14] However, with appropriate strategies and an eye toward the needs and wants of local consumers, sophisticated retailers and manufacturers can and do succeed throughout the world, as shown in Illustration 2–2.

ILLUSTRATION 2-2

Many companies offer a mix of standard and customized products in their locations around the world.

VARIATIONS IN CULTURAL VALUES

L02

Cultural values are widely held beliefs that affirm what is desirable. These values affect behavior through norms, which specify an acceptable range of responses to specific situations. A useful approach to understanding cultural variations in behavior is to understand the values embraced by different cultures.

Numerous values vary across cultures and affect consumption. We will present a classification scheme consisting of three broad forms of cultural values: *other-oriented, environment-oriented,* and *self-oriented.* The cultural values that have the most impact on consumer behavior can be classified in one of these three general categories.

Other-oriented values reflect a society's view of the appropriate relationships *between individuals and groups* within that society. These relationships have a major influence on marketing practice. For example, if the society values collective activity, consumers will look toward others for guidance in purchase decisions and will not respond favorably to promotional appeals to "be an individual."

Environment-oriented values prescribe a society's relationship *to its economic and technical as well as its physical environment.* As a manager, you would develop a very different marketing program for a society that stressed a problem-solving, risk-taking, performance-oriented approach to its environment than you would for a fatalistic, security- and status-oriented society.

Self-oriented values reflect the objectives and approaches to life *that the individual members of society find desirable.* Again, these values have strong implications for marketing management. For instance, the acceptance and use of credit is very much determined by a society's position on the value of postponed versus immediate gratification.

Table 2-1 provides a list of 18 values that are important in most cultures. Most of the values are shown as dichotomies (e.g., materialistic versus nonmaterialistic). However,

Cultural Values of Relevance to Consumer Behavior

TABLE 

Other-Oriented Values

- *Individual/Collective.* Are individual activity and initiative valued more highly than collective activity and conformity?
- *Youth/Age.* Is family life organized to meet the needs of the children or the adults? Are younger or older people viewed as leaders and role models?
- *Extended/Limited family.* To what extent does one have a lifelong obligation to numerous family members?
- *Masculine/Feminine.* To what extent does social power automatically go to males?
- *Competitive/Cooperative.* Does one obtain success by excelling over others or by cooperating with them?
- *Diversity/Uniformity.* Does the culture embrace variation in religious belief, ethnic background, political views, and other important behaviors and attitudes?

Environment-Oriented Values

- *Cleanliness.* To what extent is cleanliness pursued beyond the minimum needed for health?
- *Performance/Status.* Is the culture's reward system based on performance or on inherited factors such as family or class?
- *Tradition/Change.* Are existing patterns of behavior considered to be inherently superior to new patterns of behavior?
- *Risk taking/Security.* Are those who risk their established positions to overcome obstacles or achieve high goals admired more than those who do not?
- *Problem solving/Fatalistic.* Are people encouraged to overcome all problems, or do they take a "what will be, will be" attitude?
- *Nature.* Is nature regarded as something to be admired or overcome?

Self-Oriented Values

- *Active/Passive.* Is a physically active approach to life valued more highly than a less active orientation?
- *Sensual gratification/Abstinence.* To what extent is it acceptable to enjoy sensual pleasures such as food, drink, and sex?
- *Material/Nonmaterial.* How much importance is attached to the acquisition of material wealth?
- *Hard work/Leisure.* Is a person who works harder than economically necessary admired more than one who does not?
- *Postponed gratification/Immediate gratification.* Are people encouraged to "save for a rainy day" or to "live for today"?
- *Religious/Secular.* To what extent are behaviors and attitudes based on the rules specified by a religious doctrine?

this is not meant to represent an either/or situation but a continuum. For example, two societies can each value tradition, but one may value it more than the other. For several of the values, a natural dichotomy does not seem to exist. For a society to place a low value on cleanliness does not imply that it places a high value on dirtiness. These 18 values are described in the following paragraphs.

Other-Oriented Values

Individual/Collective Does the culture emphasize and reward individual initiative, or are cooperation with and conformity to a group more highly valued? Are individual differences appreciated or condemned? Are rewards and status given to individuals or to groups? Answers to these questions reveal the individual or collective orientation of a culture. Individualism is a defining characteristic of American culture. Australia, the United Kingdom, Canada, New Zealand, and Sweden are also relatively individualistic. Taiwan, Korea, Hong Kong, Mexico, Japan, India, and Russia are more collective in their orientation.[15]

This value is a key factor differentiating cultures, and it heavily influences the self-concept of individuals. Not surprisingly, consumers from cultures that differ on this value differ in their reactions to foreign products,[16] advertising,[17] and the Internet.[18] Examples include:

- Consumers in more collectivist countries care more about how they are treated in terms of respect and concern after a service failure than do consumers in more individualistic countries.[19]
- Consumers from more collectivist countries tend to be more imitative and less innovative in their purchases than those from individualistic cultures.[20] Thus, ad themes such as "be yourself" and "stand out" are often effective in the United States but generally not in Japan, Korea, or China.
- Advertising in collectivist countries such as Korea contains more celebrity appeals than does advertising in individualistic countries such as the United States.[21]

Interestingly, you might expect luxury items to be less important in collectivist cultures. However, they are quite important, but for different reasons. In individualistic cultures, luxury items are purchased as a means of self-expression or to stand out.[22] This is often not the case in more collectivist Asian societies. As one expert describes:

> Brands take on roles as symbols that extend well beyond the intrinsic features of the category. One is not buying a watch, or even a status brand, one is buying club membership, or an "I am just like you" (symbol).[23]

Similarly, the notion of conspicuous consumption is often associated with individualistic societies. However, a recent study finds that brand reputation influences decisions more for conspicuously consumed products in collectivist countries.[24] Another study finds that concern for appearance is 40 percent higher for those in collectivist countries. One explanation is that a given behavior is used for different reasons in different cultures. As one expert notes:

> Dressing well . . . might convey a sense of individuality in individualist cultures. However, it might be interpreted by collectivist-culture consumers as a way to demonstrate their in-group identity, show their concerns with in-group norms, follow in-group trends and avoid loss of face in front of in-group members.[25]

As useful as such generalizations are, it is important to realize that cultural values can and do evolve. This is particularly true among young, urban consumers in the developed and developing countries of Asia, where individualism is on the rise.[26] For example, 26 percent of Chinese teens consider individuality an important trait, more than double the rate of older Chinese.[27] Although this number is substantially lower than that of Western cultures, it represents an important shift. Consider the following description of the new young single woman in Japan:

> [T]he young single woman in Japan is now on an odyssey. The stereotyped office lady of the 80s was a junior office clerk. Today, though, Japanese women are climbing higher up the corporate career ladder, which is in turn bringing out a more independent streak. Women now are going out and finding their own path in life . . . and more are saying, "I don't want to follow the trend all the time, I can find my own way."[28]

In the face of such changes, traditional appeals may not work as they once did. For example, in the late 1980s, Shiseido Co. launched its very successful Perky Jean makeup line with the theme, "Everyone is buying it." "That would never work now," says a company executive.

The different values held by younger and older Asian consumers illustrate that few cultures are completely homogeneous. Marketers must be aware of differences both *between* cultures and *within* cultures.[29]

Youth/Age To what extent do the primary family activities focus on the needs of the children instead of those of the adults? What role, if any, do children play in family decisions? What role do they play in decisions that primarily affect the child? Are prestige, rank, and important social roles assigned to younger or older members of society? Are the behavior, dress, and mannerisms of the younger or older members of a society imitated by the rest of the society?

While American society is clearly youth oriented, many Asian cultures have traditionally valued the wisdom that comes with age. Thus, mature spokespersons would tend to be more successful in these cultures than would younger ones. However, some Asian cultures are becoming increasingly youth oriented with increases in youth-oriented ads designed to target them.[30] Consider the following description of Taiwan:

> Taiwan is very, very youth-oriented, and it is a very hip culture. . . . You have a consumer-based economy that is quite potent, and pitching to the youth is a good way of ensuring that your products are going to be bought.[31]

Illustration 2–3 demonstrates 7-Up's use of a youth theme in China. These unique outdoor "light pole" signs are common in China's major cities.

This youth trend can also be seen in Arab countries. One study of Arab consumers from Saudi Arabia, Bahrain, Kuwait, and the United Arab Emirates shows the rapid emergence of several youth segments. The largest (35 percent) consists of younger, more liberal, individualistic married couples living in nuclear (versus communal) families in which women are more likely to work outside the home and thus demand a greater voice in family decisions.[32] This youth trend may explain why recent research finds numerous similarities in values such as independence and respect for the elderly reflected in Arab and American television ads.[33]

Children's influence on purchases and the tactics they use vary according to the youth-versus-age value and this has implications for marketers.[34] For example, one study compared the tactics used by children in the Fiji Islands with those used in the United States. The Fiji Islands (and other Pacific Island nations) can be characterized as less individualistic and higher in respect for authority and seniority. As a consequence, Fiji children were more likely to "request" than "demand" and Fiji parents responded more favorably

ILLUSTRATION 2-3

This outdoor signage for 7-Up in China demonstrates the youth trend that is emerging in Asian cultures, which have historically been quite traditional with a high value placed on age and wisdom.

(i.e., bought the item) to "requests." In contrast, American children were more likely to demand than to request, and American parents responded more positively to demands.[35]

China's policy of limiting families to one child has produced a strong focus on the child, a shift toward youth, and increasing Westernization of children's commercials. In fact, many Chinese children receive so much attention that they are known in Asia as "little emperors."[36] Consider the following description of the Zhou family and their 10-year-old daughter Bella, who live in Shanghai:

> Under traditional Confucian teachings, respecting and obeying one's elders were paramount. In today's urban China, it is increasingly children who guide their parents through a fast-changing world. When the Zhous bought a new television set last year, Bella chose the brand. When they go out to eat, Bella insists on Pizza Hut.[37]

Obviously, while changes to traditional cultures such as those in Asia and the Gulf are occurring, it is important to remember that traditional segments and values still remain and that marketers must adapt not only across but within cultures.

Extended/Limited Family The family unit is the basis for virtually all societies. Nonetheless, the definition of the family and the rights and obligations of family members vary widely across cultures. As we will see in Chapter 6, our families have a lifelong impact on us, both genetically and through our early socialization, no matter what culture we come from. However, cultures differ widely in the obligations one owes to other family members at various stages of life as well as who is considered to be a member of the family.

In the United States, the family is defined fairly narrowly and is less important than in many other cultures. In general, strong obligations are felt only to immediate family members, and these diminish as family members establish new families. In many other countries and regions, including South America, Fiji, Israel, and Asia, the role of the family is much stronger. Families, and obligations, often extend to cousins, nieces, nephews, and beyond. The following description indicates the complexity and extent of the extended Chinese family:

> The family is critically important in all aspects of Chinese life and there is a distrust of nonfamily members. In response to this, the Chinese have developed family-like links to a greater extent than almost any other culture. It stretches to the furthest horizons, from close family, to slightly distant, to more distant, embracing people who are not really family but are connected to someone in one's family and to all their families. As such, the family is really a system of contacts, rather than purely an emotional unit as in the west.[38]

Clearly, marketers need to understand the role of families in the cultures they serve and adapt accordingly. For example:

- Adolescents and young adults in Mexico and Thailand (compared to the United States) are more influenced by parents and family in terms of consumption values and purchases.[39]
- Because Indian consumers tend to shop in groups and with their families, Biyani (a large discounter similar to Walmart) has U- and C-shaped aisles to provide private corners where families can discuss their purchase decisions.[40]

Masculine/Feminine Are rank, prestige, and important social roles assigned primarily to men? Can a female's life pattern be predicted at birth with a high degree of accuracy? Does the husband, wife, or both make important family decisions? Basically, we live in a masculine-oriented world, yet the degree of masculine orientation varies widely, even across the relatively homogeneous countries of Western Europe.

This value dimension influences both obvious and subtle aspects of marketing. For example, the roles and manner in which one would portray women in ads in Muslim countries would differ from those in the United States.[41] Indeed, when the U.S. military worked recently with an Afghan agency to create ads featuring pictures of babies that were designed to promote Afghan pride and discourage suicide bombings, they found that ". . . the babies all had to be boys, and the ad copy focused on males."[42]

However, roles of women are changing and expanding throughout much of the world.[43] This is creating new opportunities as well as challenges for marketers.[44] For example, the increasing percentage of Japanese women who continue to work after marriage has led to increased demand for time-saving products as well as other products targeted at the working woman. And during a recent U.K. election cycle, the major parties heavily targeted educated women through Mumsnet, the largest online parenting site in the United Kingdom, with 1.2 million users who are predominantly higher-income, college-educated women.[45]

Participation in sports and exercise is another aspect strongly influenced by the masculinity dimension. There tends to be a wide disparity between men and women participation rates (men higher) in countries and cultures high in masculine orientation such as South Korea, Mexico, Brazil, and France. However, as always, modern trends must be considered. In Mexico, for example, a strong masculine orientation toward sports is slowly giving way among younger Mexican women. One recent example is runner Ana Guevara, whose TV viewer numbers have sometimes been higher than those of men's soccer—something unheard of in the history of Mexican sports. One expert points to the "changing status of women in Mexico."[46] And women from South Korea and China are now a dominant force in women's professional golf, winning six of the LPGA's last 12 major titles. Illustration 2–4 shows the changing role of women as represented by their ever-increasing participation in professional sports.

ILLUSTRATION 2-4

The changing role of women around the world creates new marketing opportunities. The popularity and participation of women in sports is increasing in many cultures.

Again, it is important to remember that traditional segments and values certainly do still remain and that marketers must adapt not only across but within cultures. For example, a recent study of women in mainland China found both traditionalist and modern segments.[47] In Hong Kong, however, the traditional values are not necessarily giving way when economic and social independence are gained. Instead, the conflict is internalized, as indicated by the following quote:

> Women in Hong Kong, who are faced with both traditional Chinese culture and western culture, are at a crossroads of modernism and traditionalism. On one hand, they are having increasing amount of financial and decision power within the family and in the society. On the other hand, they are still under the pressure of traditional expectations on females as being a good wife and mother.[48]

For marketers, this conflict creates challenges in some cases to segment consumers into modern and traditional markets. In other cases the challenge is to help consumers (through products, positioning, advertising, and so on) deal with tensions between traditional and modern values.

Competitive/Cooperative Is the path to success found by outdoing other individuals or groups, or is success achieved by forming alliances with other individuals or groups? Does everyone admire a winner? Cultures with more masculine and individualistic orientations, such as the United Kingdom, the United States, and Australia, tend to value competitiveness and demonstrate it openly. Collectivist cultures, even if high in masculinity (e.g., Japan), tend to find *openly* competitive gestures offensive as they cause others to "lose face."[49]

Variations on this value can be seen in the ways different cultures react to comparative advertisements. For example, the United States encourages them, while their use in other cultures can lead to consumer (and even legal) backlash. As one would expect, the more collectivist Japanese have historically found comparative ads to be distasteful, as do the Chinese, although Pepsi found Japanese youth somewhat more receptive if comparisons are done in a frank and funny way.[50] As a rule, comparative ads should be used with care and only after considerable testing.

Diversity/Uniformity Do members of the culture embrace variety in terms of religions, ethnic backgrounds, political beliefs, and other important behaviors and attitudes? A culture that values diversity not only will accept a wide array of personal behaviors and attitudes but is also likely to welcome variety in terms of food, dress, and other products and services. In contrast, a society valuing uniformity is unlikely to accept a wide array of tastes and product preferences, though such a society may be subject to fads, fashions, and other changes over time.

Collectivist cultures tend to place a strong value on uniformity and conformity,[51] whereas more individualistic cultures tend to value diversity. For example, "in-group" influence (e.g., wanting to see the same movies as everyone else) tends to be higher in China and Japan than in the United Kingdom and the United States.[52] Obviously, however, economic and social changes associated with the youth movement in many collectivist societies mean relatively more acceptance of diversity than has been traditionally found, even if absolute levels trend lower than in their individualistic counterparts.

Environment-Oriented Values

Cleanliness Is cleanliness next to godliness, or is it a rather minor matter? Are homes, offices, and public spaces expected to be clean beyond reasonable health requirements? In the United States, a high value is placed on cleanliness, where germ-fighting liquid soaps alone are a multi-billion-dollar market.[53] In fact, people from many other cultures consider Americans to be paranoid on the subject of personal hygiene.

Although there are differences in the value placed on cleanliness among the economically developed cultures, the largest differences are between these cultures and those of many of the underdeveloped nations. In many poorer countries, cleanliness is not valued at a level sufficient to produce a healthy environment. This is true even in large parts of rapidly developing countries such as China and India, where a lack of basic hygiene still causes significant health problems.[54] While often criticized for having a negative impact on local cultures, McDonald's has been credited with introducing more hygienic food preparation and toilets in several East Asian markets, including China.[55]

Performance/Status Are opportunities, rewards, and prestige based on an individual's performance or on the status associated with the person's family, position, or class? Do all people have an equal opportunity economically, socially, and politically at the start of life, or are certain groups given special privileges? Are products and brands valued for their ability to accomplish a task or for the reputation or status of the brand?

A status-oriented society is more likely to prefer "quality" or established and prestigious brand names and high-priced items to functionally equivalent items with unknown brand names or lower prices (e.g., private label or store brands).[56] As a result, compared with that in the United States, advertising in Japan, China, and India tends to involve more appeals to status or wealth.[57] According to a Levi's executive in charge of their new global dENiZEN™ brand targeting emerging markets:

> We've realized a new consumer has emerged, status-seekers in rapidly emerging middle classes. This is primarily a developing-market phenomenon—they exist outside the U.S. in markets like China, India, Indonesia, Mexico, and Brazil.[58]

Performance/status is closely related to the concept of **power distance,** which refers to *the degree to which people accept inequality in power, authority, status, and wealth as* *natural or inherent in society.*[59] India, China, Brazil, Mexico, France, Hong Kong, and Japan are relatively high in their acceptance of power. Austria, Denmark, New Zealand, Sweden, and the United States are relatively low. Expert sources in ads have a greater impact in a high-power distance country than in a low one.[60] In addition, consumers in high-power distance countries are more likely to seek the opinions of others in making decisions.[61]

How power is used may depend on other cultural factors, however. In the United States, power is seen in terms of coercion and in Japan as relational. As a consequence, in negotiations where the buyer has more power, buyers are more likely to use that power to extract higher prices and profits in the United States, whereas that is not true in Japan. Marketers need to understand such nuances when negotiating with partners in other countries.[62]

Tradition/Change Is tradition valued simply for the sake of tradition? Is change or "progress" an acceptable reason for altering established patterns? Compared with Americans, Korean and Chinese consumers have traditionally been much less comfortable dealing with new situations or ways of thinking.[63] Britain, too, has a culture laden with tradition. This value is reflected in their advertising, where, compared to ads in America, those in Britain and China are more likely to emphasize tradition and history.[64]

It is important to note once again that change can and does live alongside traditional values. For example, both the Korean and Chinese cultures are now enthusiastically embracing change. In China, "modernness" (often symbolized by a Western name) is an important product attribute, particularly among younger, urban Chinese. A recent study found that advertisers in China segment their advertising depending on audience. For the mainstream audiences targeted by television, traditional appeals are used more often. In magazines targeted at younger Chinese (e.g., *Elle, Cosmopolitan,* and *Sanlian*), modern appeals focusing on technology, fashion, and leisure are used more often.[65] Younger urban Korean, Japanese, and more recently Chinese consumers often lead the way in technology adoption and usage and are highly demanding.[66] Vodafone found out just how much after their market share in Japan plummeted when they failed to innovate and stay on the cutting edge.[67]

Risk Taking/Security Do the "heroes" of the culture meet and overcome obstacles? Is the person who risks established position or wealth on a new venture admired or considered foolhardy? This value relates to tolerance for ambiguity and uncertainty avoidance. It has a strong influence on entrepreneurship and economic development as well as new-product acceptance. A society that does not admire risk taking is unlikely to develop enough entrepreneurs to achieve economic change and growth. New-product introductions, new channels of distribution, advertising themes, and reliance on brand name are affected by this value.[68]

Problem Solving/Fatalistic Do people react to obstacles and disasters as challenges to be overcome, or do they take a "what will be, will be" attitude? Is there an optimistic, "we can do it" orientation? Fatalists tend to feel they don't have control over the outcome of events. This has been shown to reduce consumer expectations of quality and decrease the likelihood that consumers make formal complaints when faced with an unsatisfactory purchase.[69]

Western Europe and the United States tend to fall toward the problem-solving end of the continuum, whereas Mexico and most Middle Eastern countries fall toward the fatalistic end. As with many of the values we have discussed, traditional and modern approaches can live along side each other. Consider the following examples:[70]

Traditional: In the Asia-Pacific region, supernatural beliefs traditionally are believed to have a strong influence on product sales performance. In particular, name giving . . . has a strong perceived connection to fate. In more than 50 percent of the [brand names] we studied, the creation . . . was based, in part, on a "lucky" number of total strokes drawn in the creation of the characters that spelled out the brand name. [And lucky names] were more common in high-uncertain than low-uncertain market environments.

Modern: Tiger leadership is a new leadership style prowling around Southeast Asia which combines the brashness of a Western entrepreneurial style with a tireless Asian work ethic.

Nature Is nature assigned a positive value, or is it viewed as something to be overcome, conquered, or tamed? Americans historically considered nature as something to be overcome or improved. Most northern European countries place a high value on the environment. Packaging and other environmental regulations are stronger in these countries than in America. In fact, a British company recently developed a zero-emissions motorcycle that runs on hydrogen. They worry, however, because it also makes no sound! *Would you want a motorcycle that didn't growl when you revved it up?*[71]

In turn, Americans and Canadians appear to place a higher value on the environment than the southern European countries and most developing countries, though this may reflect variations in the financial ability to act on this value rather than the value itself. These differences in attitudes are reflected in consumers' purchase decisions, consumption practices, and recycling efforts.[72]

As with all the values we are discussing, there are wide ranges within as well as between countries, which create market opportunities. For example, overall, China does not have a strong environmental orientation. However, there are segments of the country that do have such an orientation and the means to buy products and services that reflect this focus.[73]

Self-Oriented Values

Active/Passive Are people expected to take a physically active approach to work and play? Are physical skills and feats valued more highly than nonphysical performances? Is emphasis placed on doing? Americans are much more prone to engage in physical activities and to take an action-oriented approach to problems. "Don't just stand there; do something" is a common response to problems in America. Participation in active exercise varies widely across countries, especially for women, as discussed earlier. While this obviously limits the market for exercise equipment in certain countries, it also affects advertising themes and formats. For example, an exercise or sports theme for bottled water would not be appropriate in a country such as Japan, where two-thirds of the men and three-fourths of the women exercise less than twice a year.

Sensual Gratification/Abstinence Is it acceptable to pamper oneself, to satisfy one's desires for food, drink, or sex beyond the minimum requirement? Is one who forgoes such gratification considered virtuous or strange? Muslim cultures are extremely conservative on this value, as are many Asian cultures, including Hong Kong and India. A full 37 percent of Saudis indicated modesty is important, compared with 9 percent in the United States.[74] Perhaps not surprisingly, compared with U.S. and Australian ads, ads in Hong Kong and India contain fewer sex appeals.[75] And China has put legal restrictions on the use of sex appeals in ads.[76]

In Arab countries, advertisements, packaging, and products must carefully conform to Muslim standards. Polaroid's instant cameras gained rapid acceptance because they

ILLUSTRATION 2-5

Cultures differ in their acceptance of sensual gratification. This ad for Radox would work well in some cultures but would not be appropriate in cultures that place a high value on abstinence.

allowed Arab men to photograph their wives and daughters without fear that a stranger in a film laboratory would see the women unveiled.

In contrast, Brazilian and European advertisements contain nudity and blatant (by U.S. standards) appeals to sensual gratification. The Radox ad shown in Illustration 2-5 provides a great example of how marketers make use of sensuality. While quite appropriate for some cultures, it would not be successful in a culture that did not accept sensual gratification.

Material/Nonmaterial Is the accumulation of material wealth a positive good in its own right? Does material wealth bring more status than family ties, knowledge, or other activities?

There are two types of materialism. **Instrumental materialism** is *the acquisition of things to enable one to do something.* Skis can be acquired to allow one to ski. **Terminal materialism** is *the acquisition of items for the sake of owning the item itself.* Art is generally acquired for the pleasure of owning it rather than as a means to another goal. Cultures differ markedly in their relative emphasis on these two types of materialism.[77]

Increased wealth, exposure to international media and brands, and modernization appear to be increasing materialism in places generally thought to be less materialistic. For example, in more collectivist China, where family and relationships might be thought to trump possessions, Chinese youth now demonstrate greater materialism than their U.S. counterparts.[78] Beyond the youth trend, there are also subtle differences in the types of materialism across cultures. For example, while U.S. consumers place a higher value on the importance of obtaining possessions (called the centrality dimension of materialism), Korean consumers place a higher value on possessions as a means for demonstrating success (the success dimension) because it is seen as uplifting the family unit.[79]

Hard Work/Leisure Is work valued for itself, independent of external rewards, or is work merely a means to an end? Will individuals continue to work hard even when their minimum economic needs are satisfied, or will they opt for more leisure time? For example, in parts of Latin America, work has traditionally been viewed as a necessary evil. However, generational gaps exist. For example, in Mexico, 100 percent of the older generation agreed with the statement "Today's emphasis on work is a bad thing," compared with only 28 percent of the younger generation. The trend was just the opposite in the United Kingdom, Netherlands, France, Canada, and Australia, where agreement by the older generation was around 55 percent, while agreement by the younger generation was around 80 percent. In the United States and Hong Kong, younger and older generations were roughly the same (about 50 percent agreeing) on this value.[80]

These attitudes do not necessarily reflect *actual* work patterns. For example, hours worked per week are highest in Hong Kong (48.6 hours) and Mexico (41.6) and lowest in France (34.1) and Canada (34.8).[81] Nonetheless, this value has important consequences for lifestyle and demand for leisure activities.

Postponed Gratification/Immediate Gratification Is one encouraged to "save for a rainy day," or should one "live for today"? Is it better to secure immediate benefits and pleasures, or is it better to suffer in the short run for benefits in the future, or in the hereafter, or for future generations? The United States, the United Kingdom, and Australia tend to have short-term orientations, while India, Hungary, Brazil, Hong Kong, and China have long-term orientations. This value has implications for business strategies, efforts to encourage savings, and the use of credit. For example, valued business goals in short-term cultures tend to include "this year's profits," while those in long-term cultures included "profits 10 years from now."[82] In addition, use of credit is lower in long-term–oriented cultures, where cash and debit card usage are more common.[83]

Religious/Secular To what extent are daily activities determined by religious doctrine? The United States is relatively secular. Many Islamic cultures as well as some Catholic cultures are much more religiously oriented.[84] In contrast, religion plays a very small role in Chinese culture. However, even in a country such as China, where few are actively involved with a formal religion, many of the culture's values were formed in part by historical religious influences. The same is true for the secular nations of the West. Understanding the extent and type of religious influences operating in a culture is essential for effectively designing all elements of the marketing mix.[85]

Clearly, the preceding discussion has not covered all the values operating in the various cultures. However, it should suffice to provide a feel for the importance of cultural values and how cultures differ along value dimensions.

CULTURAL VARIATIONS IN NONVERBAL COMMUNICATIONS

LO3

Differences in **verbal communication systems** (languages) are immediately obvious to anyone entering a foreign culture. An American traveling in Britain or Australia will be able to communicate, but differences in pronunciation, timing, and meaning will still occur. For example, Dogpile, a U.S.-based metasearch engine (www.dogpile.com), changed its name in Europe to WebFetch after realizing that in the United Kingdom "pile" refers to hemorrhoids or the result of a dog relieving itself![86]

Attempts to translate marketing communications from one language to another can result in ineffective communications, as shown in Table 2-2.

The problems of literal translations and slang expressions are compounded by symbolic meanings associated with words, the absence of some words from various languages, and the difficulty of pronouncing certain words:[87]

- In Japan, a global soft-drink company wanted to introduce a product with the attribute "creaminess." However, research showed that there was no corresponding word in Japan for this attribute, so the company had to find something comparable, which turned out to be "milk feel."[88]
- Mars addressed the problem of making the M&M's name pronounceable in France, where neither ampersands nor the apostrophe "s" plural form exists, by advertising extensively that M&M's should be pronounced "aimainaimze."
- To market its Ziploc food storage bags in Brazil, Dow Chemical had to use extensive advertising to actually create the word *zipar,* meaning "to zip," because there was no such term in Portuguese.

Additional communication factors that can cause problems include humor, style, and pace, for which preferences vary across cultures, even those speaking the same basic

TABLE 2-2 Translation Problems in International Marketing

- Colgate's Cue toothpaste had problems in France, as *cue* is a crude term for "butt" in French.
- Parker Pen mistook *embarazar* (to impregnate) to mean to embarrass and ran an ad in Mexico stating, "it won't leak in your pocket and make you pregnant."
- Pet milk encountered difficulties in French-speaking countries where *pet* means, among other things, "to break wind."
- Kellogg's Bran Buds translates to "burned farmer" in Swedish.
- United Airlines' in-flight magazine cover for its Pacific Rim routes showed Australian actor Paul Hogan in the outback. The caption stated, "Paul Hogan Camps It Up." "Camps it up" is Australian slang for "flaunts his homosexuality."
- China attempted to export Pansy brand men's underwear to America.
- American Airlines introduced its new leather first-class seats in Mexico with the theme "Fly in Leather," which, when translated, literally read, "Fly Naked."

language.[89] Nonetheless, verbal language translations generally do not present major problems as long as we are careful. What many of us fail to recognize, however, is that each culture also has nonverbal communication systems or languages that, like verbal languages, are specific to each culture. **Nonverbal communication systems** are *the arbitrary meanings a culture assigns actions, events, and things other than words.*

The following discussion examines the seven variables shown in Figure 2–3, all of which influence nonverbal communications: time, space, symbols, relationships, agreements, things, and etiquette.

Time

The meaning of time varies between cultures in two major ways. First is what we call time perspective, that is, a culture's overall orientation toward time.[90] The second is the interpretations assigned to specific uses of time.

Time Perspective Most Americans, Canadians, Western Europeans, and Australians tend to view time as inescapable, linear, and fixed in nature. It is a road reaching into the

FIGURE 2-3 Factors Influencing Nonverbal Communications

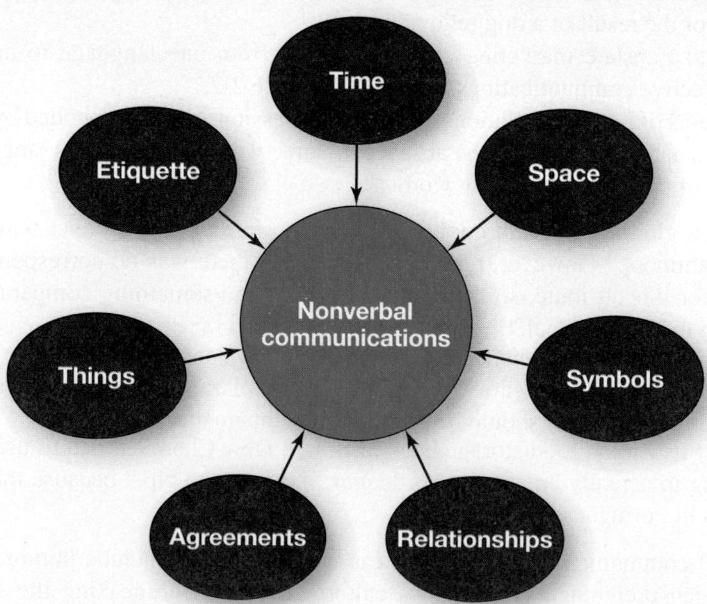

future with distinct, separate sections (hours, days, weeks, and so on). Time is seen almost as a physical object; we can schedule it, waste it, lose it, and so forth. Believing that a person does one thing at a time, we have a strong orientation toward the present and the short-term future. This is known as a **monochronic time perspective.**

Most Latin Americans, Asians, and Indians tend to view time as being less discrete and less subject to scheduling. They view simultaneous involvement in many activities as natural. People and relationships take priority over schedules, and activities occur at their own pace rather than according to a predetermined timetable. Such cultures have an orientation toward the present and the past. This is known as a **polychronic time perspective.**

Some important differences between individuals with a monochronic perspective and those with a polychronic perspective are listed below.[91]

Individuals in a Monochronic Culture	Individuals in a Polychronic Culture
Do one thing at a time	Do many things at once
Concentrate on the job	Are highly distractible and subject to interruptions
Take deadlines and schedules seriously	Consider deadlines and schedules secondary
Are committed to the job or task	Are committed to people and relationships
Emphasize promptness	Base promptness on the relationship
Are accustomed to short-term relationships	Prefer long-term relationships

How would marketing activities vary between monochronic and polychronic cultures? Personal selling and negotiation styles and strategies would need to differ, as would many advertising themes. Contests and sales with deadlines would generally be more effective in monochronic than in polychronic cultures. Convenience foods frequently fail when positioned in terms of time saving and convenience in polychronic cultures, where "saving time" is not part of the cultural thought processes. For example, in countries like Argentina with more polychronic views, fast-food restaurants are often seen as more expensive and modern and as representing modern and liberated value systems. The time-saving aspect is not as prominent there as it is in countries like the United States that are more monochronic.[92]

Interestingly, even within a culture, time perspectives can vary by age and by situation. For example, in Japan, work is approached in terms of monochronic time whereas leisure is approached, as their culture might suggest, in terms of polychronic time.[93] Also, while Americans have tended to be monochronic, younger consumers appear to demonstrate elements of polychronic time. This so-called MTV generation seems to have no attention span and may simultaneously be found doing homework, watching TV, and surfing the net! Not surprisingly, U.S. advertisers find it hard to capture and hold the attention of this audience.

Meanings in the Use of Time Specific uses of time have varying meanings in different cultures. In much of the world, the time required for a decision is proportional to the importance of the decision. Americans, by being well prepared with ready answers, may adversely downplay the importance of the business being discussed. Likewise, both Japanese and Middle Eastern executives are put off by Americans' insistence on coming to the point directly and quickly in business transactions.

Promptness is considered very important in America and Japan. Furthermore, promptness is defined as being on time for appointments, whether you are the person making the call or the person receiving the caller. According to one expert:

> Time is money and a symbol of status and responsibility. To be kept waiting is offensive in monochronic cultures, it is perceived as a message. It is not in polychronic cultures.[94]

What is meant by "being kept waiting" also varies substantially by culture. Thirty minutes might seem like an eternity in the United States, but it may seem like very little time in other countries, such as those in the Middle East. As you can see, understanding such differences *prior* to doing business in a given country is critical.

Space

The use people make of space and the meanings they assign to their use of space constitute a second form of nonverbal communication.[95] In America, "bigger is better." Thus, office space in corporations generally is allocated according to rank or prestige rather than need. The president will have the largest office, followed by the executive vice president, and so on.

A second major use of space is **personal space.** It is the nearest that others can come to you in various situations without your feeling uncomfortable. In the United States, normal business conversations occur at distances of 3 to 5 feet and highly personal business from 18 inches to 3 feet. In parts of northern Europe, the distances are slightly longer; in most of Latin America, they are substantially shorter.

An American businessperson in Latin America will tend to back away from a Latin American counterpart in order to maintain his or her preferred personal distance. In turn, the host will tend to advance toward the American in order to maintain his or her personal space. The resulting "chase" would be comical if it were not for the results. Both parties generally are unaware of their actions or the reasons for them. Furthermore, each assigns a meaning to the other's actions according to what the action means in his or her own culture. Thus, the North American considers the Latin American to be pushy and aggressive. The Latin American, in turn, considers the North American to be cold, aloof, and snobbish.

Symbols

An American seeing a baby wearing a pink outfit would most likely assume the child to be female. If the outfit were blue, the assumed gender would be male. These assumptions would be accurate most of the time in the United States but not in many other parts of the world, such as Holland. Colors, animals, shapes, numbers, and music have varying meanings across cultures. Failure to recognize the meaning assigned to a symbol can cause serious problems:

- AT&T had to change its "thumbs-up" ads in Russia and Poland, where showing the palm of the hand in this manner has an offensive meaning. The change was simple. The thumbs-up sign was given showing the back of the hand.
- Mont Blanc has a white marking on the end of its pens, meant to represent the snow-capped Alpine mountain peaks. However, Arab consumers reacted negatively because it looked like the "Star of David," which is Israel's national symbol. Mont Blanc worked to clear up the misunderstanding.[96]
- In the United States, blond hair color in women is often perceived as a symbol of beauty. In a study of seven European cities, the hair color most symbolic of beauty varied from dark brown (Madrid, Paris, and London), to black (Milan), to blond (Hamburg).[97]

Table 2-3 presents additional illustrations of varying meanings assigned to symbols across cultures.[98] Despite frequent cultural differences in symbols, many symbols work well across a wide range of cultures. Kellogg's Tony the Tiger works in the United States, China (see Illustration 2–6), and many other cultures.

The Meaning of Numbers, Colors, and Other Symbols

TABLE 

• White	Symbol for mourning or death in the Far East; purity in the United States
• Purple	Associated with death in many Latin American countries
• Blue	Connotation of femininity in Holland; masculinity in Sweden, the United States
• Red	Unlucky or negative in Chad, Nigeria, Germany; positive in Denmark, Rumania, Argentina
• Yellow flowers	Sign of death in Mexico; infidelity in France
• White lilies	Suggestion of death in England
• 7	Unlucky number in Ghana, Kenya, Singapore; lucky in Morocco, India, Czechoslovakia, Nicaragua, the United States
• Triangle	Negative in Hong Kong, Korea, Taiwan; positive in Colombia
• Owl	Wisdom in United States; bad luck in India
• Deer	Speed, grace in United States; homosexuality in Brazil

Relationships

The rights and obligations imposed by relationships and friendship are another nonverbal cultural variable. Americans, more so than those in most other cultures, form relationships and make friends quickly and easily and drop them easily also. In large part, this may be because America has always had a great deal of both social and geographic mobility. People who move every few years must be able to form friendships in a short time period and depart from them with a minimum of pain. In many other parts of the world, relationships and friendships are formed slowly and carefully because they imply deep and lasting

ILLUSTRATION 2-6

Kellogg's tiger is an effective symbol in many cultures.

obligations. As the following quote indicates, friendship and business are deeply intertwined in many cultures around the globe including Latin America and Asia.

> In many cultures, the written word is used simply to satisfy legalities. In their eyes, emotion and personal relations are more important than cold facts.[99]

In addition, long-run success in many cultures involves more than just "getting to know" someone in the Western sense of the expression. For example, Chinese relationships are complex and described under the concept of ***guanxi:***

> *Guanxi* is literally translated as personal connections/relationships on which an individual can draw to secure resources or advantages when doing business as well as in the course of social life. Its main characteristics are (1) the notion of a continuing reciprocal relationship over an indefinite period of time, (2) favors are banked, (3) it extends beyond the relationship between two parties to include other parties within the social network (it can be transferred), (4) the relationship network is built among individuals not organizations, (5) status matters—relationships with a senior will extend to his subordinates but not vice versa, and (6) the social relationship is prior to and a prerequisite to the business relationship.[100]

It should be quickly noted, however, that in an increasingly intertwined, modern, and global setting, even traditional notions like *guanxi* are being challenged. The following excerpt suggests the tensions felt by modern professionals in China:

> It is a bit strange but even as we almost act the part of the dynamic, modern, assertive business person, we still—underneath—still look for something deeper—far deeper—a more traditional and emotionally driven sense of trust, respect and guanxi—but we realize that in today's fast paced living (environment), it is often not possible to achieve this deeper level of relationship formation in a business climate—but to us, underneath it all, this is still the ultimate.[101]

One expert suggests that different approaches may therefore be necessary depending on the depth and length of relationship desired.

Agreements

Americans rely on an extensive and, generally, highly efficient legal system for ensuring that business obligations are honored and for resolving disagreements. Many other cultures have not developed such a system and rely instead on relationships, friendship, and kinship; local moral principles; or informal customs to guide business conduct. For example, the Chinese "tend to pay more attention to relationships than contracts."[102] Under the American system, we would examine a proposed contract closely. Under the Chinese system, we would examine the character of a potential trading partner closely. In the words of an American CEO based in China:

> Relationships are everything in China, more so than in the United States, which is more focused on business. The Chinese want to know and understand you before they buy from you.[103]

Americans generally assume that, in almost all instances, prices are uniform for all buyers, related to the service rendered, and reasonably close to the going rate. We order many products such as taxi rides without inquiring in advance about the cost. In many Latin American, Asian, and Middle East countries, the procedure is different. Virtually all prices are negotiated prior to the sale, including those for industrial products.[104]

Things

The cultural meaning of things leads to purchase patterns that one would not otherwise predict. One observer noted a strong demand for expensive, status brands whose absolute cost was not too high among those Russians beginning to gain economically under capitalism. He concluded:

> They may stick to their locally produced toothpaste, but they want the Levi's, the Mont Blanc pens, the Moët & Chandon champagne to establish their self-esteem and their class position.[105]

The differing meanings that cultures attach to things, including products, make gift giving a particularly difficult task.[106] For example, giving a Chinese business customer or distributor a nice desk clock—a common gift in many countries—would be inappropriate. Why? In China, the word for *clock* is similar to the word for *funeral,* making clocks inappropriate gifts. When does receipt of a gift "require" a gift in return? In China this depends on the closeness of the relationship between the parties—the closer the relationship, the less a return gift is required.[107]

The business and social situations that call for a gift, and the items that are appropriate gifts, vary widely. For example, a gift of cutlery is generally inappropriate in Russia, Japan, Taiwan, and Germany. In Japan, small gifts are required in many business situations, yet in China they are less appropriate. In China, gifts should be presented privately, but in Arab countries, they should be given in front of others.

Etiquette

Etiquette represents generally accepted ways of behaving in social situations. Assume that an American is preparing a commercial that shows people eating an evening meal, with one person about to take a bite of food from a fork. The person will have the fork in the right hand, and the left hand will be out of sight under the table. To an American audience this will seem natural. However, in many European cultures, a well-mannered individual would have the fork in the left hand and the right hand on the table.

Behaviors considered rude or obnoxious in one culture may be quite acceptable in another. The common and acceptable American habit, for males, of crossing one's legs while sitting, such that the sole of a shoe shows, is extremely insulting in many Eastern cultures. In these cultures, the sole of the foot or shoe should never be exposed to view. While most Americans are not hesitant to voice dissatisfaction with a service encounter, many Asians are. This also appears to be true of the British, who have traditionally been characterized by their reserved nature. Such factors can lead U.S. managers to misjudge customer response to their services abroad.[108]

Normal voice tone, pitch, and speed of speech differ among cultures and languages, as does the use of gestures. Westerners often mistake the seemingly loud, volatile speech of some Asian cultures as signifying anger or emotional distress (which it would if it were being used by a Westerner) when it is normal speech for the occasion.

As American trade with Japan increases, we continue to learn more of the subtle aspects of Japanese business etiquette. For example, a Japanese executive will seldom say "no" directly during negotiations; doing so would be considered impolite. Instead, he might say, "That will be very difficult," which would mean "no." A Japanese responding "yes" to a request often means, "Yes, I understand the request," not "Yes, I agree to the request." Many Japanese find the American tendency to look straight into another's eyes when talking to be aggressive and rude.

Another aspect of Japanese business etiquette is *meishi,* epitomized by "A man without a *meishi* has no identity in Japan." The exchange of *meishi* is the most basic of social rituals in a nation where social ritual matters very much. The act of exchanging *meishi* is weighted with meaning. Once the social minuet is completed, the two know where they stand in relation to each other and their respective statures within the hierarchy of corporate or government bureaucracy. What is *meishi?* It is the exchange of business cards when two people meet! A fairly common, simple activity in America, it is an essential, complex social exchange in Japan.

Other cultures also find it necessary to learn about the subtleties of doing business with Westerners. Business leaders in China are developing training programs to help sensitize Chinese businesspeople to other cultures. According to Jack Ma, who runs one such program:

> Chinese businessmen are shrewd, but they need to learn to be more polished. At a World Economic Forum held in Bejing, Mr. Ma was depressed at how many conducted themselves, noting—Many smoked constantly and held loud cellphone conversations, even during meetings.[109]

The importance of proper, culture-specific etiquette is obvious. Although people recognize that etiquette varies from culture to culture, there is still a strong emotional feeling that "our way is natural and right."

Conclusions on Nonverbal Communications

Can you imagine yourself becoming upset or surprised because people in a different culture spoke to you in their native language, say Spanish or German, instead of English? Of course not. We all recognize that verbal languages vary around the world. Yet we generally feel that our nonverbal languages are natural or innate. Therefore, we misinterpret what is being "said" to us because we think we are hearing English when in reality it is Japanese, Italian, or Russian. It is this error that marketers can and must avoid.

GLOBAL CULTURES

An important issue facing marketers is the extent to which one or more global consumer cultures or segments are emerging. Evidence suggests that there is indeed movement in this direction.[110] Such a culture would have a shared set of consumption-related symbols with common meaning and desirability among members. One such proposed global culture is that portion of local cultures that view themselves as cosmopolitan, knowledgeable, and modern. Such individuals share many values and consumption-related behaviors with similar individuals across a range of national cultures.

Such cultures are being created by the globalization of mass media, work, education, and travel. Some product categories (cell phones, Internet) and brands (Sony, Nike) have become symbolically related to this culture. This does not imply that these brands use the same advertising globally but rather that the underlying theme and symbolism may be the same. Thus, a combined shampoo and conditioner could be positioned as a time-saver for the time-pressured modern career woman. The advertisement might portray the shampoo being used in the context of a gym in the United States or Germany, where many females exercise, but in a home context in Japan, where few women visit gyms. Philips Electronic is one firm that has developed a global positioning strategy based on such a global culture.[111]

Perhaps the closest thing to a global culture today is urban youth, which we examine next.

A Global Youth Culture?

LO4

> Consider _____, a 19-year-old hip-hop music producer scouting for a new pair of Air Force 1 sneakers at the Nike shop. . . . _____, who prefers to be addressed by his street name, "Jerzy King"—moved to _____ three years ago. . . . A music school dropout who has never set foot outside of _____, he totes a mini-disc player loaded with Eminem, Puff Daddy, and Fabolous. On this particular day he's looking phat in a blue-and-white fleece jacket bearing the logo of the Toronto Maple Leafs.[112]

Can you fill in the blanks with any degree of confidence? The young man is Wang Qi and he lives in Beijing. However, many of his behaviors and possessions echo those of millions of other teenagers in Europe, North and South America, and Asia. And as we discussed earlier, it is incorrect to think of the youth influence as a one-way street from America to the rest of the world with entities like Levi's, Coke, and Lady Gaga leading the way:

> Now it's a two-way street. Americans are learning Bollywood dance steps at their local health clubs. M.I.A., an up-and-coming pop singer who has Sri Lankan roots and was brought up in London, intermingles hip-hop, reggae, and South Asian influences. And Japanese *anime* has swept the globe.[113]

Similarities and convergence of lifestyles, values, and purchases make this global youth market compelling for companies, particularly given its large size. For example, a recent survey of global youth (age 14–29) across six countries found that 86 percent believe that products help to define and communicate their personality. It also found compelling similarities in the top three spending categories, as follows:[114]

	First Category	Second Category	Third Category
Amsterdam	Going out	Clothing	Food
Hong Kong	Clothing	Food	Transportation
Malaysia	Transportation	Food	Going out
Singapore	Food	Clothing	Entertainment
South Korea	Food	Clothing	Entertainment
United Kingdom	Going out	Clothing	Phone
United States	Clothing	Food	Music

What is causing this convergence? The largest single influence is worldwide mass media, including the Internet, and, more recently, mobile devices. Music, sports, and fashion appear to be major points of convergence, although the convergence often goes far beyond this to underlying values such as independence and risk taking. Marketers are using the similarities among youth across cultures to launch global brands or to reposition current brands to appeal to this large market. Levi's, reacting to the growing online trend among global teens, launched an online campaign in Asia targeted at "young, tech-savvy trendsetters." The website played heavily on Western music and style to promote its Levi's re-cut 501 Re-Born jeans. The theme emphasized that the jeans have been re-cut for today, with one page showing a teen being "reborn" or transformed by the new Levi's jeans.[115] Illustration 2–7 provides another example of an ad using a global youth appeal.

Several recent trends in the global youth market are critical for global marketers to understand. These include the following:[116]

- *Technology is mainstream.* Wired teens are a global phenomenon not restricted to developed countries. Fifty-six percent of teens globally are "superconnectors," meaning they use two or more electronic devices (e.g., cell phone and the Internet) daily.

ILLUSTRATION 2-7

This ad campaign uses a global youth appeal to target style leaders around the world.

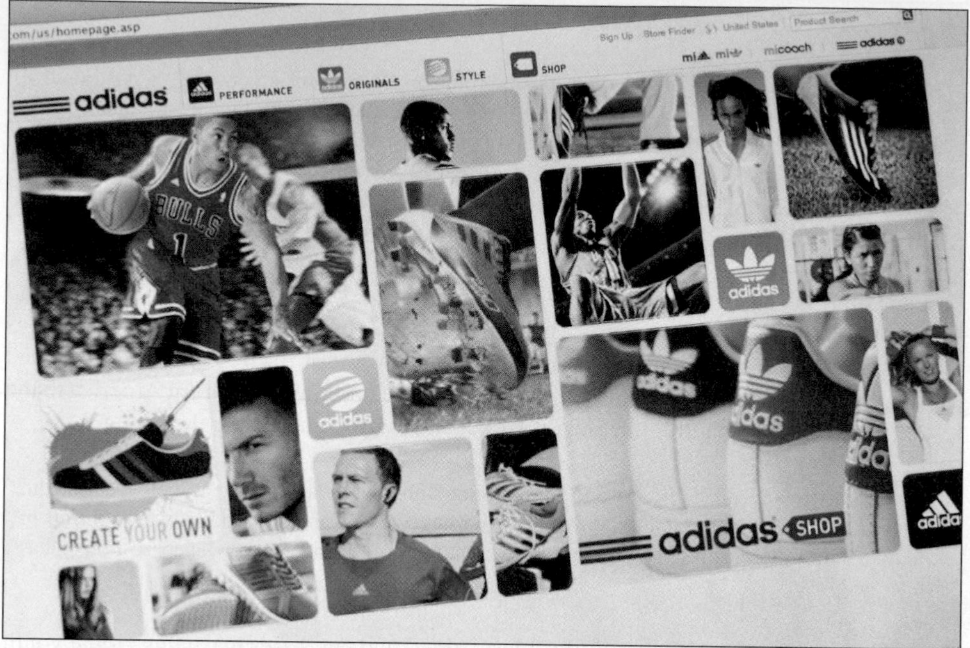

- *U.S. teens no longer lead the way.* Now it's more about mind-set and the "creatives" are leading the way. Creatives are most prevalent in Europe (not the United States), are open to new ideas, and like expressing themselves in various ways, including personal web pages and art.
- *U.S. brands are not currently the leaders.* U.S. brands used to be the leaders among global teens. Now the top three are Sony (Japan), Nokia (Finland), and Adidas (Germany).

As the global youth culture moves increasingly away from U.S. influence and brands, marketers in the United States must find ways to understand and connect with the trends and trendsetters across the globe. In addition, it is critical to understand that global youth also have a great many culturally unique behaviors, attitudes, and values. As one expert states, "European teens resent being thought of as Americans with an accent."[117] Also, the similarities described above are most noticeable among middle-class teens living in urban areas. Poorer, rural teens often conform more closely to their society's traditional culture. For example, Coke distinguishes between major urban centers and smaller cities and towns in China. Consider the following:

> In the smaller cities and towns Coke uses a famous Chinese actor traveling the countryside in a hot bus and stresses taste and price. In China's largest markets its TV spot "features a hip Taiwanese VJ . . . who shows off his dance moves as he pretends his Coke can magnetically draw him to an attractive lady across the street." According to a Coke executive, "The (urban TV) ad is aimed at young adults who want to do things their own way, as opposed to following a famous actor as in the bus spot."[118]

The distinction between rural and urban markets is one aspect of demographics discussed next.

GLOBAL DEMOGRAPHICS

LO5 Economies such as India and China have seen rapid growth, which has led to increased personal disposable income and strong and growing middle classes that are the envy of marketers worldwide.[119] Concerns about the extent to which economic growth in these and other countries will continue at current rates are beginning to appear due to rising fuel and food costs.[120] To the extent that growth continues at a relatively rapid pace, such expansion not only creates opportunities, but can also present challenges.

Examine Illustration 2–8. The rapid increase in ownership of automobiles as replacements for bicycles in China has provided many with the freedom to travel greater distances. However, elevated emissions and traffic congestion have also become areas of concern.[121]

ILLUSTRATION 2-8

The rapid growth in personal income in China has led to an explosion in car ownership. This has resulted in increased personal freedom but also concerns about congestion and emissions.

Disposable income is one aspect of demographics. **Demographics** *describe a population in terms of its size, structure, and distribution. Size* refers to the number of individuals in the society. *Structure* describes the society in terms of age, income, education, and occupation. *Distribution* refers to the physical location of individuals in terms of geographic region and rural, suburban, and urban location.

Demographics are both a result and a cause of cultural values. Densely populated societies are likely to have more of a collective orientation than an individualistic one because a collective orientation helps such societies function smoothly. Cultures that value hard work and the acquisition of material wealth are likely to advance economically, which alters their demographics both directly (income) and indirectly (families in economically advanced countries tend to be smaller).

A critical aspect of demographics for marketers is income, particularly the distribution of income. One country with a relatively low average income can have a sizable middle-income segment, while another country with the same average income may have most of the wealth in the hands of a few individuals. As shown below, Brazil's average per capita income is slightly higher than Romania's.[122] However, the distribution of that income differs sharply. Forty-five percent of the income generated in Brazil goes to just 10 percent of the population. In contrast, the top 10 percent of households in Romania command only 21 percent of that country's income. *How will these and the other differences shown below affect consumption?*

	Per Capita Income	Percent of Total Income to Top 10 Percent of Population	Per Capita PPP
Brazil	$ 4,791	45	$ 8,596
Canada	35,133	25	35,078
Chile	7,305	45	12,262
China	1,721	35	4,091
Egypt	1,412	30	5,049
France	34,008	25	29,644
India	707	31	2,126
Japan	35,604	22	30,290
Kenya	531	37	1,395
Mexico	7,401	37	11,317
Romania	4,575	21	9,374
United Kingdom	37,266	29	31,580
United States	41,674	30	41,674

Source: Per Capita Income and Per Capita PPP: *2005 International Comparison Program* (International Bank for Reconstruction and Development/The World Bank, 2008); Percent of Total Income to Top 10 Percent of Population: *The World Factbook* (Washington, DC: Central Intelligence Agency, 2008).

Marketers increasingly use **purchasing power parity (PPP)** rather than average or median income to evaluate markets. PPP is based on the cost of a standard market basket of products bought in each country. An average household in one country may have a lower income in U.S. dollars. However, that household may be able to buy *more* than a household in other countries with higher income in U.S. dollars because of a lower local cost structure, government-provided health care, and so forth. The World Bank describes all countries in terms of PPP in its annual World Bank Atlas.[123] Notice how Brazil's purchasing power is substantially higher than its per capita income would suggest. *How might an understanding of PPP change marketer decisions about such things as market potential and entry?*

The estimated age distributions of the United States, the Philippines, Japan, and Canada are shown below.[124] Note that over 40 percent of the populations of the Philippines and of India are under 20, compared with around one-fourth for the United States and Canada, and about one-fifth for Japan. In the Middle East, a massive baby boom is under way, with two-thirds of the population under 25, fueling the youth movement in this region, which we discussed earlier.[125] *What product opportunities do this and the other age differences among these countries suggest?*

Age	United States (%)	Philippines (%)	Japan (%)	Canada (%)	India (%)
Under 10	14.1	22.7	8.7	11.3	23.3
10–19	14.5	20.7	9.4	13.3	21.9
20–29	13.6	17.8	11.3	13.8	16.9
30–39	15.4	13.8	14.4	14.5	14.1
40–49	15.1	10.8	12.9	16.6	10.0
50–59	11.0	7.4	13.2	13.0	6.3
60 and over	16.3	6.8	30.1	17.7	7.5

CROSS-CULTURAL MARKETING STRATEGY

As we have seen throughout the chapter, cross-cultural variations in such factors as values and demographics may make it necessary to adapt products and services to local considerations. One term for this adaptation is **glocalization,** which is generally taken to mean *global localization.*[126] There is continuing controversy over the *degree* to which cross-cultural marketing strategies should be standardized versus customized.[127] Standardized strategies can result in substantial cost savings. Maybelline's Manhattan line of cosmetics designed for the Asian market used one ad campaign in China, Taiwan, Hong Kong, Thailand, and Singapore. The ads featured an attractive Asian model in a low-cut, short dress against the Manhattan skyline at night. This combination of appeals to youth, beauty, and sophistication could be used in many other countries, though this ad would be inappropriate, and probably banned, in most Islamic countries.

Uniformity is sometimes possible, but companies must often adapt to cultural differences. We saw this earlier in the case of KFC in Malaysia. Consider McDonald's:

> McDonald's used to strive for uniformity around the Globe. Now it adapts its products as appropriate—adding fried eggs to burgers in Japan and offering Samurai Pork Burgers with a sweet barbecue sauce in Thailand. However, its most dramatic changes were made when it entered India for the first time. So, instead of the all-beef Big Macs, the menu featured the mutton [lamb] Maharaja Mac.[128]

McDonald's also adapts its store layout. As shown in Illustration 2–9, separate sections for families and singles are provided in Muslim countries.

In addition to values and demographics, attitudes toward international brands can influence the need to customize offerings. For example, higher levels of patriotism and

ILLUSTRATION 2-9

McDonald's offers both family and singles sections in Muslim countries to accommodate the cultural norms governing interactions between men and women. The singles section is for single men only.

ethnocentrism appear to drive more negative views of international brands and may require more extreme forms of local customization.[129] Miller beer uses such customization to develop what they call "local intimacy" by creating specific local brands of beer for very specific markets. For example, in Peru:

> . . . bottles of its Cusquena brand feature replica stones of an Incan wall that pay tribute to the elite standard of Inca craftsmanship that continues to this day in every bottle.[130]

Alternatively, higher levels of internationalism and cosmopolitanism appear to drive more positive views of international brands and thus allow for more standardization. In general, most companies will blend standardization and customization and a critical success factor in achieving the right balance.

Considerations in Approaching a Foreign Market

LO6

There are seven key considerations for each geographic market that a firm is contemplating. An analysis of these seven variables provides the background necessary for deciding whether or not to enter the market and to what extent, if any, an individualized marketing strategy is required. A small sample of experts, preferably native to the market under consideration, often will be able to furnish sufficient information on each variable.

Is the Geographic Area Homogeneous or Heterogeneous with Respect to Culture? Marketing efforts are generally directed at defined geographic areas, primarily political and economic entities. Legal requirements and existing distribution channels often encourage this approach. However, it is also supported by the implicit assumption that geographical or political boundaries coincide with cultural boundaries. As we have seen, country boundaries represent general tendencies, but differences *within* a given country are also critical to consider. For example, research suggests that strategies in Latin America need to consider not only cross-country (e.g., Brazil vs. Chile) but also within-country (e.g., regional; urban vs. rural) differences.[131]

Likewise, China has strong regional cultures, urban and rural cultures, as well as sharp differences associated with income, age, and education.[132] Thus, marketing campaigns must be developed for cultural and demographic groups, not just countries.

What Needs Can This Product or a Version of It Fill in This Culture? Most firms examine a new market with an existing product or product technology in mind. The question they must answer is what needs their existing or modified product can fill in the culture involved. For example, bicycles and motorcycles serve primarily recreational needs in the United States, but they provide basic transportation in many other countries.

Can Enough of the People Needing the Product Afford the Product? An initial demographic analysis is required to determine the number of individuals or households that might need the product and who can actually afford it. For example, although China has over 1.3 billion consumers, the effective market for most Western goods is estimated to be considerably smaller than this total.[133] Future economic expansion in countries like China and India is expected to enhance their market potential in coming years. In addition, the possibilities of establishing credit, obtaining a government subsidy, or making a less expensive version should be considered. This latter approach is being used by P&G in China, where a tiered pricing system was designed to help reach consumers with relatively low incomes.[134] Indeed, many marketers are seeing growth in lower-middle-class markets. For example, Brazil's "Class C" customer, who earns $600 to $2,600 per month, is now their largest segment, and car sales to this customer increased 50 percent in 2009![135]

What Values or Patterns of Values Are Relevant to the Purchase and Use of This Product? The first section of this chapter focused on values and their role in consumer behavior. The value system should be investigated for influences on purchasing the product, owning the product, using the product, and disposing of the product. Much of the marketing strategy will be based on this analysis.

What Are the Distribution, Political, and Legal Structures for the Product? The legal structure of a country can have an impact on each aspect of a firm's marketing mix. China recently banned sex appeals during family view time and is tightening regulations on the opening of new Internet cafes. The United Kingdom recently banned junk-food ads targeted at kids under the age of 16 and has tightened regulations on paid tweets. And Brazil has put laws in place that limit the amount of alcohol advertising.[136] Such legal restrictions limit the ability of companies to use standardized approaches to their marketing efforts. *What effect would China's ban on sex appeals have on Maybelline's advertising in Asia for its Manhattan line?*

Distribution challenges also exist. Companies like GM, Nike, and Procter & Gamble are finding this out as they move into so-called second-tier cities in China such as Chanchun. Here, distribution practices are different and require adaptation compared to first-tier cities like Bejing.[137]

In What Ways Can We Communicate about the Product? This question requires an investigation into (1) available media and who attends to each type, (2) the needs the product fills, (3) values associated with the product and its use, and (4) the verbal and nonverbal communications systems in the culture(s). All aspects of the firm's promotional mix—including packaging, nonfunctional product design features, personal selling techniques, and advertising—should be based on these four factors.

CONSUMER INSIGHT 2-1

Unilever Adapts to Sell Laundry Products Globally

Unilever is highly successful in marketing its laundry products outside of the United States. The reason is it continually adapts to existing and emerging factors both within and across the countries where it does business. A stunning statistic is that "[e]very half hour 7 million people in the world wash their cloths with Unilever products, and 6 million of them do so by hand." Below we touch on each of the seven global considerations as they relate to Unilever's global strategy.[138]

- ***Cultural Homogeneity.*** In the global laundry market, heterogeneity, even within a country, can occur. For example, Brazil's Northeast and Southeast regions are very different. One difference is that in the poorer Northeast region, most laundry is done by hand and more bar soap than powder is used. In the more affluent Southeast region, most laundry is done in a washing machine and more powder detergent is used than bar soap in the process.
- ***Needs.*** Hand washing versus machine washing leads to different laundry product needs. In addition, in developing countries that are an important focus for Unilever, products must be adapted to meet strength of cleaning needs related to removing sweat, odors, and tough stains due to physical labor.
- ***Affordability.*** Clearly affordability is a component in pricing the laundry detergents themselves to be competitive. However, Unilever also faces the situation that a transition from hand washing to washing machines depends in large part on the economic prosperity of a country or region, as this determines the affordability of washing machines. Adoption of washing machines, in turn, changes the type and amounts of laundry products used, as we saw earlier.
- ***Relevant Values.*** One source indicates that cleanliness, convenience, and sustainability are key value aspects in laundry products that vary across cultures. In many countries where Unilever operates, there are segments of kids dubbed "Nintendo Kids" who don't tend to go outside and play and thus don't get dirty. A core strategy for a number of their brands in these markets is the "dirt is good" campaign that stresses that playing and getting dirty are part of a healthy child's development and "let Unilever worry about getting their clothes clean."
- ***Infrastructure.*** A broad infrastructure issue in laundry is access to hot water. Many in developing countries don't have access to hot water or large quantities of water. Unilever responded in India with Surf Excel Quick Wash, an enzyme-based product that uses less water and works under lower water temperatures.
- ***Communication.*** Europeans have traditionally cleaned their clothes in much hotter water with the logic being that "boiling clothes" is the only real way to get them clean and kill germs. This trend is reversing as Unilever pushes more environmental-friendly products and as Europeans have begun to wash in cooler temperatures to save energy. An interesting consequence of the shift is that antibacterial additives are now demanded by European customers to kill the germs.
- ***Ethical Implications.*** While conversion of the world's consumers to fully automated washing machines would help standardize Unilever's approach, it has major implications for water usage. This is because compared to hand washing, machine washing can, depending critically on the number of rinse cycles needed, use more water. Continued innovation in products toward lower water use will be a key ethical and performance issue for Unilever moving forward.

As you can see, Unilever has and must continue to innovate and adjust as its target markets evolve along these critical dimensions.

Critical Thinking Questions

1. How might generational influences affect the adoption of washing machines even after economic conditions make them affordable?
2. What other features beyond price and form (bar versus powder) do you think Unilever has had to adjust to meet different needs/wants/preferences across different markets?
3. Which core value is related to sustainability and green marketing? Does this value vary across countries and cultures?

The Internet seems like a natural media through which to communicate to consumers. However, Internet access varies widely across countries as does the percentage of consumers who will actually buy online. Moreover, tailoring websites to specific countries is critical to online marketing success because of cultural variations in website dimensions driving purchase and loyalty.[139]

What Are the Ethical Implications of Marketing This Product in This Country? All marketing programs should be evaluated on ethical as well as financial dimensions. As discussed at the beginning of the chapter, international marketing activities raise many ethical issues. The ethical dimension is particularly important and complex in marketing to third world and developing countries. Consider Kellogg's attempt to introduce cold cereal as a breakfast food in a developing country. An ethical analysis would consider various factors, including the following:

If we succeed, will the average nutrition level be increased or decreased?

If we succeed, will the funds spent on cereal be diverted from other uses with more beneficial long-term impacts for the individuals or society?

If we succeed, what impact will this have on the local producers of currently consumed breakfast products?

Such an ethical analysis not only is the right thing to do but also may head off conflicts with local governments or economic interests. Understanding and acting on ethical considerations in international marketing is a difficult task. However, it is also a necessary one.

Consumer Insight 2–1 provides an illustration of how Unilever has dealt with a number of these considerations in marketing its laundry products globally.

SUMMARY

LO1: Define the concept of culture

Culture is defined as the complex whole that includes knowledge, beliefs, art, law, morals, customs, and any other capabilities acquired by humans as members of society. It includes almost everything that influences an individual's thought processes and behaviors. Culture operates primarily by setting boundaries for individual behavior and by influencing the functioning of such institutions as the family and mass media. The boundaries, or *norms,* are derived from *cultural values.* Values are widely held beliefs that affirm what is desirable.

LO2: Describe core values that vary across culture and influence behaviors

Cultural values are classified into three categories: other, environment, and self. *Other-oriented values* reflect a society's view of the appropriate relationships between individuals and groups within that society. Relevant values of this nature include *individual/collective, youth/age, extended/limited family, masculine/feminine, competitive/cooperative,* and *diversity/uniformity. Environment-oriented values* prescribe a society's relationships with its economic, technical, and physical environments. Examples of environment values are *cleanliness, performance/status, tradition/change, risk taking/security, problem solving/fatalistic,* and *nature. Self-oriented values* reflect the objectives and approaches to life that individual members of society find desirable. These include *active/passive, sensual gratification/abstinence, material/nonmaterial, hard work/leisure, postponed gratification/immediate gratification,* and *religious/secular.*

LO3: Understand cross-cultural variations in nonverbal communications

Nonverbal communication systems are the arbitrary meanings a culture assigns actions, events, and things other than words. Major examples of nonverbal communication variables that affect marketers are *time, space, symbols, relationships, agreements, things,* and *etiquette.*

SMARTBOOK™

LO4: Summarize key aspects of the global youth culture

There is evidence that urban youth around the world share at least some aspects of a common culture. This culture is driven by worldwide mass media and common music and sports stars. Emerging aspects include the importance of technology and the fact that U.S. teens and brands are no longer leading the way.

LO5: Understand the role of global demographics

Demographics describe a population in terms of its size, structure, and distribution. Demographics differ widely across cultures and influence cultural values (and are influenced by them) as well as consumption patterns.

LO6: List the key dimensions in deciding to enter a foreign market

Seven questions are relevant for developing a cross-cultural marketing strategy: (1) Is the geographic area homogeneous or heterogeneous with respect to culture? (2) What needs can this product fill in this culture? (3) Can enough of the people needing the product afford the product? (4) What values or patterns of values are relevant to the purchase and use of this product? (5) What are the distribution, political, and legal structures for the product? (6) In what ways can we communicate about the product? (7) What are the ethical implications of marketing this product in this country?

KEY TERMS

REVIEW QUESTIONS

1. What are some of the ethical issues involved in cross-cultural marketing?
2. What is meant by the term *culture?*
3. What does the statement "Culture sets boundaries on behaviors" mean?
4. What is a *norm?* From what are norms derived?
5. What is a *cultural value?*
6. What is a *sanction?*
7. Cultural values can be classified as affecting one of three types of relationships—other, environment, or self. Describe each of these, and differentiate each one from the others.
8. How does the first of the following paired orientations differ from the second?
   a. Individual/Collective
   b. Performance/Status
   c. Tradition/Change
   d. Limited/Extended family
   e. Active/Passive
   f. Material/Nonmaterial
   g. Hard work/Leisure
   h. Risk taking/Security
   i. Masculine/Feminine
   j. Competitive/Cooperative
   k. Youth/Age
   l. Problem solving/Fatalistic
   m. Diversity/Uniformity
   n. Postponed gratification/Immediate gratification
   o. Sensual gratification/Abstinence
   p. Religious/Secular
9. What is meant by *nonverbal communications?* Why is this a difficult area to adjust to?

10. What is meant by each of the following as a form of nonverbal communication?
    a. Time
    b. Space
    c. Symbols
    d. Relationships
    e. Agreements
    f. Things
    g. Etiquette
11. What is *guanxi?*
12. What is the difference between *instrumental* and *terminal* materialism?
13. What are the differences between a *monochronic* time perspective and a *polychronic* time perspective?
14. What forces seem to be creating a global youth culture?
15. What are *demographics?* Why are they important to international marketers?
16. What is *purchasing power parity?*
17. What is *glocalization?* What factors affect the need to adapt to local considerations?
18. What are the seven key considerations in deciding whether or not to enter a given international market?

DISCUSSION QUESTIONS

19. Why should we study foreign cultures if we do not plan to engage in international or export marketing?
20. Is a country's culture more likely to be reflected in its art museums or its television commercials? Why?
21. Are the cultures of the world becoming more similar or more distinct?
22. Why do values differ across cultures?
23. The text lists 18 cultural values (in three categories) of relevance to marketing practice. Describe and place into one of the three categories two additional cultural values that have some relevance to marketing practice.
24. Select two cultural values from each of the three categories. Describe the boundaries (norms) relevant to that value in your society and the sanctions for violating those norms.
25. What are the most relevant cultural values affecting the consumption of each of the following? Describe how and why these values are particularly important.
    a. Internet
    b. MP3 player
    c. Milk
    d. Fast food
    e. Luxury cars
    f. Cell phones
26. What variations between the United States and other societies, *other than cultural variations,* may affect the relative level of usage of the following?
    a. Internet
    b. MP3 player
    c. Milk
    d. Fast food
    e. Luxury cars
    f. Cell phones
27. Why is materialism higher in Korea than in the United States, where given their collectivist culture one might expect materialism to be lower?
28. What values underlie the differences between Fiji Island and U.S. children in terms of the strategies they use to influence their parents' decisions? What marketing implications emerge?
29. What are the marketing implications of the differences in the *masculine/feminine orientation* across countries?
30. Respond to the questions in Consumer Insight 2–1.
31. Why do nonverbal communication systems vary across cultures?
32. Which, if any, nonverbal communication factors might be relevant in the marketing of the following?
    a. Watches
    b. Jewelry
    c. Facial tissue
    d. Laundry detergent
    e. Lip balm
    f. Women's clothing
33. What are the implications of *guanxi* for a Western firm entering the Chinese market?
34. To what extent do you think youth are truly becoming a single, global culture?
35. Will today's youth still be a "global culture" when they are 40? Why or why not?
36. How do demographics affect a culture's values? How do a culture's values affect its demographics?

37. What causes the differences between purchasing power parity and income, as shown in the text?
38. The text provides a seven-step procedure for analyzing a foreign market. Using this procedure, analyze your country as a market for
    a. Laptop computers from Japan.
    b. Automobiles from Korea.
    c. Sunglasses from Italy.
    d. Wine from Chile.
39. What are the major ethical issues in introducing prepared foods such as fast foods to developing countries? 
40. Should U.S. tobacco firms be allowed to market cigarettes in developing countries? Why or why not?
41. How can developing countries keep their cultures from being overly Westernized or Americanized?

APPLICATION ACTIVITIES

42. Interview two students from two different cultures. Determine the extent to which the following are used in those cultures and the variations in the values of those cultures that relate to the use of these products:
    a. Gift cards
    b. Energy drinks (like Red Bull)
    c. Fast-food restaurants
    d. Exercise equipment
    e. Music
    f. Internet
43. Interview two students from two different foreign cultures. Report any differences in nonverbal communications they are aware of between their culture and your culture.
44. Interview two students from two different foreign cultures. Report their perceptions of the major differences in cultural values between their culture and your culture.
45. Interview a student from India. Report on the advice that the student would give an American firm marketing consumer products in India.
46. Interview two students from Southeast Asia regarding their perceptions of materialism and conspicuous consumption. Report on how their responses reinforce or conflict with the traditional value systems found in their countries.
47. Imagine you are a consultant working with your state's or province's tourism agency. You have been asked to advise the agency on the best promotional themes to use to attract foreign tourists. What would you recommend if Germany and Australia were the two target markets?
48. Analyze a foreign culture of your choice, and recommend a marketing program for a brand of one of the following made in your country:
    a. Automobile
    b. Beer
    c. MP3 player
    d. Discount retailer
    e. Movies
    f. Cosmetics

REFERENCES

1. T. Lee, "Target Has a Twin in Australia, but They're Not Related," *Star Tribune,* August 24, 2013, www.startribune.com/business/220867991.html, accessed August 24, 2014; as well as company websites at (Target U.S.) www.target.com/ and (Target Australia) www.target.com.au/#!.
2. K. Kovalchik, "Easter with . . . the Duracell Bunny?," *Mentalfloss.com,* http://mentalfloss.com/article/24372/easter-duracell-bunny, accessed August 24, 2014; and "Duracell Bunny vs. Energizer Bunny," blog post on September 30, 2013, at www.budgetbatteries.co.uk/blog/?p=23, accessed August 24, 2014.
3. I. Paul, "The Beatles and iTunes: A Complicated History," *PC World,* September 9, 2009; S. Tibken, "Apple Now Officially Owns Beatles' Apple Corps Logo," *cnet news,* October 25, 2012, http://news.cnet.com/8301-13579_3-57540017-37/apple-now-officially-owns-beatles-apple-corps-logo/, accessed August 24, 2014; and S. Crawford, "Why Weren't The Beatles on iTunes?," *electronics.howstuffworks.com,* http://electronics.howstuffworks.com/beatles-itunes2.htm, accessed August 24, 2014.
4. See, e.g., M. Fielding, "Special Delivery," *Marketing News,* February 1, 2007, pp. 13–14; and T. Sangkhawasi and L. M. Johri, "Impact of Status Brand Strategy on Materialism in Thailand," *Journal of Consumer Marketing,* 24, no. 5 (2007), pp. 275–82.
5. Examples from G. Burton, "Brazilian Lessons on Coolness and Imagination," *Brazzil,* April 2005, accessed April 27, 2008;

N. Madden, "How the NFL Intends to Push 'Olive Ball' in China," *Advertising Age,* October 2, 2006, p. 45; I. Rowley, "Lexus," *BusinessWeek,* March 31, 2008, p. 72; and P. Cloud, "Tokyo Style—Harajuku Streets," *McClatchy-Tribune Business News,* February 1, 2010.

6. N. Madden, "China Cracks Down on TV Talent Competitions," *Advertising Age,* April 3, 2006, p. 14.
7. D. Holt, J. A. Quelch, and E. L. Taylor, "How Global Brands Compete," *Harvard Business Review,* September 2004, pp. 1–8.
8. See S. Mulley, "Young Women's Smoking Crisis Declared in Asia," *Medical Post,* January 11, 2000, p. 68; J. Mackay and M. Eriksen, *The Tobacco Atlas* (Brighton, U.K.: World Health Organization, 2002), pp. 31 and 89; M. E. Goldberg and H. Baumgartner, "Cross-Country Attraction as a Motivation for Product Consumption," *Journal of Business Research,* 55 (2002), pp. 901–906; and http://tobaccoatlas.org/consumption.html, accessed January 29, 2011.
9. Mulley, "Young Women's Smoking Crisis Declared in Asia."
10. See, e.g., J. L. Aaker and J. Sengupta, "Additivity versus Attenuation," *Journal of Consumer Psychology,* 2 (2000), pp. 67–82; and D. A. Briley, M. W. Morris, and I. Simonson, "Reasons as Carriers of Culture," *Journal of Consumer Research,* September 2000, pp. 157–77.
11. T. Parker-Pope, "Custom-Made," *The Wall Street Journal,* September 26, 1996, p. R22; see also M. Fielding, "Walk the Line," *Marketing News,* September 1, 2006, pp. 8–10.
12. "At Cricket Event, U.S. Cheerleaders Shake India's Conservative Values," *SI.com,* April 30, 2008, www.si.com, accessed April 30, 2008.
13. For this and other global missteps, see M. D. White, *A Short Course in International Marketing Blunders* (Petaluma: World Trade Press, 2002).
14. "It's a Grande-Latte World," *The Wall Street Journal,* December 15, 2003, p. B1.
15. G. Hofstede, *Culture's Consequences,* 2nd ed. (Thousand Oaks, CA: Sage, 2001).
16. Z. Gurhan-Canli and D. Maheswaran, "Cultural Variations in Country of Origin Effects," *Journal of Marketing Research,* August 2000, pp. 309–17.
17. C. Pornpitakpan and J. N. P. Francis, "The Effect of Cultural Differences, Source Expertise, and Argument Strength on Persuasion," *Journal of International Consumer Marketing,* 1 (2001), pp. 77–101.
18. H. Ko, M. S. Roberts, and C. Cho, "Cross-Cultural Differences in Motivations and Perceived Interactivity," *Journal of Current Issues and Research in Advertising,* Fall 2006, pp. 93–104.
19. K. Schoefer, "Cultural Moderation in the Formation of Recovery Satisfaction Judgments," *Journal of Service Research,* 13, no. 1 (2010), pp. 52–64.
20. J. E. M. Steenkamp, F. Ter Hofstede, and M. Wedel, "A Cross-National Investigation into the Individual and National Cultural Antecedents of Consumer Innovativeness," *Journal of Marketing,* April 1999, pp. 55–69; and I. S. Yaveroglu and N. Donthu, "Cultural Differences on the Diffusion of New Products," *Journal of International Consumer Marketing,* 14, no. 4 (2002), pp. 49–63.
21. S. M. Choi, W. Lee, and H. Kim, "Lessons from the Rich and Famous," *Journal of Advertising,* Summer 2005, pp. 85–98.
22. N. Y. Wong and A. C. Ahuvia, "Personal Taste and Family Face," *Psychology & Marketing,* August 1998, pp. 423–41.
23. C. Robinson, "Asian Culture," *Journal of the Market Research Society,* January 1996, pp. 55–62.
24. T. Erdem, J. Swait, and A. Valenzuala, "Brands as Signals," *Journal of Marketing,* January 2006, pp. 34–49.
25. T. Sun, M. Horn, and D. Merritt, "Values and Lifestyles of Individualists and Collectivists," *Journal of Consumer Marketing,* 21, no. 5 (2004), pp. 318–31.
26. See, e.g., J. Zhang and S. Shavitt, "Cultural Values in Advertisements to the Chinese X-Generation," *Journal of Advertising,* 32, no. 1 (2003), pp. 23–33.
27. "Global Teen Culture," *Brand Strategy,* January 2003, pp. 37–38.
28. J. Bowman, "Asian Women Put on a New Face," *Media,* April 17, 2008, p. 22.
29. See, e.g., K. C. C. Yang, "The Effects of Allocentrism and Idiocentrism on Consumers' Product Attribute Evaluation," *Journal of International Consumer Marketing,* 16, no. 4 (2004), pp. 63–84.
30. B. Barak et al., "Perceptions of Age-Identity," *Psychology & Marketing,* October 2001, pp. 1003–29; C. A. Lin, "Cultural Values Reflected in Chinese and American Television Advertising," *Journal of Advertising,* Winter 2001, pp. 83–94; and D. H. Z. Khairullah and Z. Y. Khairullah, "Dominant Cultural Values," *Journal of Global Marketing,* 16, no. 1/2 (2002), pp. 47–70.
31. P. L. Andruss, "Groups Make Fruits Apple of Taiwan's Eye," *Marketing News,* December 4, 2000, p. 5.
32. H. Fattah, "The New Arab Consumer," *American Demographics,* September 2002, p. 58.
33. M. Kalliny and L. Gentry, "Cultural Values Reflected in Arab and American Television Advertising," *Journal of Current Issues and Research in Advertising,* Spring 2007, pp. 15–32.
34. A. Shoham and V. Dalakas, "Family Consumer Decision Making in Israel," *Journal of Consumer Marketing*, 20, no. 3 (2003), pp. 238–51; and M. Laroche et al., "How Culture Matters in Children's Purchase Influence," *Journal of the Academy of Marketing Science,* 35 (2007), pp. 113–26.
35. J. S. Wimalasiri, "A Comparison of Children's Purchase Influence and Parental Response in Fiji and the United States," *Journal of International Consumer Marketing,* 4 (2000), pp. 55–73. See also J. S. Wimalasiri, "A Cross-National Study on Children's Purchasing Behavior and Parental Response," *Journal of Consumer Marketing,* 21, no. 4 (2004), pp. 274–84.
36. M. F. Ji and J. U. McNeal, "How Chinese Children's Commercials Differ from Those of the United States," *Journal of Advertising,* Fall 2001, pp. 79–92; K. Chan and J. U. McNeal, "Parent–Child Communications about Consumption and Advertising in China," *Journal of Consumer Marketing*, 20, no. 4 (2003), pp. 317–34; and "Little Emperors," *Fortune,* October 4, 2004, pp. 138–50.
37. L. Chang, "The New Stresses of Chinese Society Shape a Girl's Life," *The Wall Street Journal,* December 4, 2003, pp. A1, A13.
38. P. Kotler, S. W. Ang, and C. T. Tan, *Marketing Management: An Asian Perspective* (Singapore: Prentice Hall Pergamon, 1996), p. 524. But see M. Liu, "China's Empty Nest," *Newsweek,* March 10, 2008, p. 41, for evidence of how this is changing among younger generations of Chinese.

39. M. Viswanathan, T. L. Childers, and E. S. Moore, "The Measurement of Intergenerational Communication and Influence on Consumption," *Journal of the Academy of Marketing Science,* Summer 2000, pp. 406–24.

40. M. Kripalani, "Here Come the Wal-Mart Wannabes," *BusinessWeek,* April 4, 2005, p. 56.

41. See F. S. Al-Olayan and K. Karande, "A Content Analysis of Magazine Advertisements from the United States and the Arab World," *Journal of Advertising,* Fall 2000, pp. 69–82.

42. L. Wentz, "U.S. Military Goes Native in Afghanistan Ad Push," *Advertising Age,* April 12, 2010, pp. 1 and 20.

43. S. M. Sidin et al., "The Effects of Sex Role Orientation on Family Purchase Decision Making in Malaysia," *Journal of Consumer Marketing,* 21, no. 6 (2004), pp. 381–90; and "Rate of Chinese Businesswomen Higher Than World Average," *China Daily,* March 20, 2005, www.chinadaily.com.

44. L. M. Milner and J. M. Collins, "Sex-Role Portrayals and the Gender of Nations," *Journal of Advertising,* Spring 2000, pp. 67–78; and G. Fowler, "China Cracks Down on Commercials," *The Wall Street Journal,* February 19, 2004, p. B7.

45. E. Hall, "U.K. Politicians Court Mommy Bloggers," *Advertising Age,* February 18, 2010.

46. K. Simon, "A Rare Mexican Mania over a Female Sporting Icon Ana Guevara May Like to Be Seen as an Inspiration to Girls Back Home," *Financial Times,* September 21, 2002, p. 24.

47. L. Y. Sin and O. H. Yau, "Female Role Orientation and Consumption Values," *Journal of International Consumer Marketing,* 13, no. 2 (2001), pp. 49–75.

48. L. Y. M. Sin and O. H. M. Yau, "Female Role Orientation of Chinese Women," *Psychology & Marketing,* December 2004, pp. 1033–58.

49. For a related discussion, see M. de Mooij, *Global Marketing and Advertising* (Thousand Oaks, CA: Sage, 1998), pp. 252–53.

50. See K. L. Miller, "You Just Can't Talk to These Kids," *BusinessWeek,* April 19, 1993, pp. 104–106; P. Sellers, "Pepsi Opens a Second Front," *Fortune,* August 8, 1994, pp. 70–76; and N. Donthu, "A Cross-Country Investigation of Recall of and Attitude toward Comparative Advertising," *Journal of Advertising,* Summer 1998, pp. 111–22.

51. See M. de Mooij, *Consumer Behavior and Culture* (Thousand Oaks, CA: Sage, 2004), pp. 162–64. For a discussion of how language can influence accessibility of cultural values, see D. A. Briley, M. W. Morris, and I. Simonson, "Cultural Chameleons," *Journal of Consumer Psychology,* 15, no. 4 (2005), pp. 351–62.

52. Sun, Horn, and Merritt, "Values and Lifestyles of Individualists and Collectivists."

53. L. Shannahan, "Bugging Out over Germs," *Brandweek,* November 22, 2004, p. 17.

54. See, e.g., V. Kurian, "'Hand Wash' Campaign in Kerala Raises a Stink," *Businessline,* November 6, 2002, p. 1.

55. J. L. Watson, *Golden Arches East* (Stanford, CA: Stanford University Press, 1997).

56. R. Mandhachitara, R. M. Shannon, and C. Hadjicharalambous, "Why Private Label Grocery Brands Have Not Succeeded in Asia," *Journal of Global Marketing,* 20, no. 2/3 (2007), pp. 71–87.

57. Lin, "Cultural Values Reflected in Chinese and American Television Advertising"; Khairullah and Khairullah, "Dominant Cultural Values"; S. Okazaki and B. Mueller, "An Analysis of Advertising Appeals Employed in Japanese and American Print Advertising—Revisited," *Working Paper,* San Diego State University (San Diego, 2008); and S. Biswas, M. Hussain, and K. O'Donnel, "Celebrity Endorsements in Advertisements and Consumer Perceptions," *Journal of Global Marketing,* 22 (2009), pp. 121–37.

58. N. Madden, "In China, Multinationals Forgo Adaptation for New-Brand Creation," *Advertising Age,* January 17, 2011.

59. For a related dimension, see S. Shavitt et al., "The Horizontal/Vertical Distinction in Cross-Cultural Consumer Research, *Journal of Consumer Psychology,* 16, no. 4 (2006), pp. 325–56.

60. Pornpitakpan and Francis, "The Effect of Cultural Differences, Source Expertise, and Argument Strength on Persuasion"; see also B. R. Barnes et al., "Investigating the Impact of International Cosmetics Advertising in China," *International Journal of Advertising,* 23 (2004), pp. 361–87.

61. C. Pornpitakpan, "Factors Associated with Opinion Seeking," *Journal of Global Marketing,* 17, no. 2/3 (2004), pp. 91–113.

62. N. R. Buchan, R. T. A. Croson, and E. J. Johnson, "When Do Fair Beliefs Influence Bargaining Behavior?," *Journal of Consumer Research,* June 2004, pp. 181–90.

63. D. Kim, Y. Pan, and H. S. Park, "High- versus Low-Context Culture," *Psychology & Marketing,* September 1998, pp. 507–21.

64. Z. Caillat and B. Mueller, "The Influence of Culture on American and British Advertising," *Journal of Advertising Research,* May–June 1996, pp. 79–88; and Lin, "Cultural Values Reflected in Chinese and American Television Advertising."

65. Zhang and Shavitt, "Cultural Values in Advertisements to the Chinese X-Generation."

66. C. Riegner, "Wired China," *Journal of Advertising Research,* December 2008, pp. 496–505.

67. G. Parker, "Going Global Can Hit Snags," *The Wall Street Journal,* June 16, 2004, p. B1.

68. Steenkamp, Ter Hofstede, and Wedel, "A Cross-National Investigation into the Individual and National Cultural Antecedents of Consumer Innovativeness"; Pornpitakpan and Francis, "The Effect of Cultural Differences, Source Expertise, and Argument Strength on Persuasion"; J. M. Jung and J. J. Kellaris, "Cross-National Differences in Proneness to Scarcity Effects," *Psychology & Marketing,* September 2004, pp. 739–53; and Erdem, Swait, and Valenzuala, "Brands as Signals."

69. See, e.g., P. Raven and D. H. B. Welsh, "An Exploratory Study of Influences on Retail Service Quality," *Journal of Services Marketing,* 18, no. 3 (2004), pp. 198–214.

70. W. L. Chang and P. Lii, "Luck of the Draw," *Journal of Advertising Research,* December 2008, pp. 523–30; and E. Coggins, "The New Asian Tiger Leadership Style," *suite101.com,* accessed February 5, 2011.

71. "Quiet Motorcycle Seeks Added Vroom," *CNN.com,* March 17, 2005, www.cnn.com.

72. T. S. Chan, "Concerns for Environmental Issues," *Journal of International Consumer Marketing,* 1 (1996), pp. 43–55.

73. R. Y. K. Chan, "Determinants of Chinese Consumers' Green Purchase Behavior," *Psychology & Marketing,* April 2001, pp. 389–413; and K. Lee, "Gender Differences in Hong Kong Adolescent Consumers' Green Purchase Behavior," *Journal of Consumer Marketing,* 26, no. 2 (2009), pp. 87–96.

74. "Saudis and Americans," *NOP World* (New York: United Business Media), January 6, 2003, www.nopworld.com.

75. S. L. M. So, "A Comparative Content Analysis of Women's Magazine Advertisements from Hong Kong and Australia on Advertising Expressions," *Journal of Current Issues and Research in Advertising,* Spring 2004, pp. 47–58; and Khairullah and Khairullah, "Dominant Cultural Values."

76. K. Chen and L. Chang, "China Takes Aim at Racy, Violent TV Shows," *The Wall Street Journal,* May 24, 2004, p. B1.

77. C. Webster and R. C. Beatty, "Nationality, Materialism, and Possession Importance," *in Advances in Consumer Research,* vol. 24, ed. M. Brucks and D. J. MacInnis (Provo, UT: Association for Consumer Research, 1997), pp. 204–10.

78. K. Chan and G. P. Prendergast, "Social Comparison, Imitation of Celebrity Models and Materialism among Chinese Youth," *International Journal of Advertising* 27, no. 5 (2008), pp. 799–826; and J. S. Podoshen, L. Li, and J. Zhang, "Materialism and Conspicuous Consumption in China," *International Journal of Consumer Studies,* 35 (2011), pp. 17–25.

79. J. E. Workman and S. H. Lee, "Materialism, Fashion Consumers, and Gender," *International Journal of Consumer Studies*, 35 (2011), pp. 50–57.

80. P. Paul, "Global Generation Gap," *American Demographics,* March 2002, pp. 18–19.

81. "Work Hard? Play Hard? It's Not the Countries You Might Think," *NOP World* (New York: United Business Media), November 8, 2004, www.nopworld.com.

82. G. Hofstede et al., "What Goals Do Business Leaders Pursue?," *Journal of International Business Studies*, 33, no. 4 (2002), pp. 785–803.

83. M. de Mooij and G. Hofstede, "Convergence and Divergence in Consumer Behavior: Implications for International Retailing," *Journal of Retailing,* 78 (2002), pp. 61–69.

84. See S. S. Al-Makaty, "Attitudes toward Advertising in Islam," *Journal of Advertising Research,* May–June 1996, pp. 16–25; and "Saudis and Americans."

85. See, e.g., D. S. Waller, K. S. Fam, and B. Z. Erdogan, "Advertising of Controversial Products," *The Journal of Consumer Marketing,* 22, no. 1 (2005), pp. 6–18.

86. "Dogpile," *Kwintessential,* www.kwintessential.co.uk/translation/articles/cross-cultural-issues.htm, accessed March 20, 2005.

87. See S. Zhang and B. H. Schmitt, "Creating Local Brands in Multilingual International Markets," *Journal of Marketing Research,* August 2001, pp. 313–25.

88. D. L. Vence, "Proper Message, Design in Global Markets Require Tests," *Marketing News,* September 1, 2006, pp. 18, 24.

89. See M. F. Toncar, "The Use of Humor in Television Advertising," *International Journal of Advertising,* 20 (2001), pp. 521–39.

90. See N. Spears, X. Lin, and J. C. Mowen, "Time Orientation in the United States, China, and Mexico," *Journal of International Consumer Marketing,* 1 (2001), pp. 57–75.

91. L. A. Manrai and A. K. Manrai, "Effect of Cultural-Context, Gender, and Acculturation on Perceptions of Work versus Social/Leisure Time Usage," *Journal of Business Research,* February 1995, pp. 115–28; J. D. Lindquist and C. F. Kaufman-Scarborough, "Polychronic Tendency Analysis," *Journal of Consumer Marketing* 21, no. 5 (2004), pp. 332–42; and G. H. Brodowsky et al., "If Time is Money Is It a Common Currency?," *Journal of Global Marketing,* 21, no. 4 (2008), pp. 245–57.

92. M. Lee and F. M. Ulgado, "Consumer Evaluations of Fast-Food Services," *Journal of Services Marketing,* 1 (1997), pp. 39–52; and G. H. Brodowsky and B. B. Anderson, "A Cross-Cultural Study of Consumer Attitudes toward Time," *Journal of Global Marketing*, 3 (2000), pp. 93–109.

93. de Mooij, *Global Marketing and Advertising.*

94. Ibid., p. 71.

95. See M. Chapman and A. Jamal, "Acculturation," *in Advances in Consumer Research,* vol. 24, ed. M. Brucks and D. J. MacInnis (Provo, UT Association for Consumer Research, 1997), pp. 138–44.

96. From White, *A Short Course in International Marketing Blunders,* p. 39.

97. R. Bjerke and R. Polegato, "How Well Do Advertising Images of Health and Beauty Travel across Cultures?," *Psychology & Marketing,* October 2006, pp. 865–84.

98. See also de Mooij, *Global Marketing and Advertising;* and T. J. Madden, K. Hewett, and M. S. Roth, "Managing Images in Different Cultures," *Journal of International Marketing,* 8, no. 4 (2000), pp. 90–107.

99. P. A. Herbig and H. E. Kramer, "Do's and Don'ts of Cross-Cultural Negotiations," *Industrial Marketing Management,* 4 (1992), p. 293; see also P. Fan and Z. Zigang, "Cross-Cultural Challenges When Doing Business in China," *Singapore Management Review,* 26, no. 1 (2004), pp. 81–90.

100. M. Ewing, A. Caruana, and H. Wong, "Some Consequences of *Guanxi,*" *Journal of International Consumer Marketing,* 4 (2000), p. 77. See also F. Balfour, "You Say *Guanxi,* I Say Schmoozing," *BusinessWeek,* November 19, 2007, pp. 84–85.

101. M. Willis, "Tradition versus Change," *Journal of Global Marketing,* 22 (2009), pp. 67–89. See also F. F. Gu, K. Hung, and D. K. Tse, "When Does *Guanxi* Matter?," *Journal of Marketing,* July 2008, pp. 12–28.

102. Fan and Zigang, "Cross-Cultural Challenges When Doing Business in China," p. 85; and N. J. White and J. Lee, "Dispute Resolution in the Korean and U.S. Markets," *Mid-American Journal of Business,* 19, no. 2 (2004), pp. 23–30.

103. G. Brewer, "An American in Shanghai," *Sales and Marketing Management,* November 1997, p. 42.

104. See H. McDonald, P. Darbyshire, and C. Jevons, "Shop Often, Buy Little," *Journal of Global Marketing,* 4 (2000), pp. 53–72; and A. G. Abdul-Muhmin, "The Effect of Perceived Seller Reservation Prices on Buyers' Bargaining Behavior in a Flexible-Price Market," *Journal of International Consumer Marketing,* 3 (2001), pp. 29–45.

105. C. Miller, "Not Quite Global," *Marketing News,* July 3, 1995, p. 9.

106. S. Y. Park, "A Comparison of Korean and American Gift-Giving Behaviors," *Psychology & Marketing,* September 1998, pp. 577–93.

107. A. Joy, "Gift Giving in Hong Kong and the Continuum of Social Ties," *Journal of Consumer Research,* September 2001, pp. 239–54. See also J. Wang, F. Piron, and M. V. Xuan, "Faring One Thousand Miles to Give Goose Feathers," *in Advances in*

Consumer Research, vol. 28, ed. M. C. Gilly and J. Meyers-Levy (Provo, UT: Association for Consumer Research, 2001), pp. 58–63.

108. M. K. Hui and K. Au, "Justice Perceptions of Complaint Handling," *Journal of Business Research* 52 (2001), pp. 161–73; and C. A. Voss et al., "A Tale of Two Countries' Conservatism, Service Quality, and Feedback on Customer Satisfaction," *Journal of Service Research,* February 2004, pp. 212–30.
109. M. Fong, "Chinese Charm School," *The Wall Street Journal,* January 13, 2004, pp. B1, B6.
110. B. D. Keillor, M. D'Amico, and V. Horton, "Global Consumer Tendencies," *Psychology & Marketing,* January 2000, pp. 1–19; and F. Ter Hofstede, M. Wedel, and J. E. M. Steenkamp, "Identifying Spacial Segments in International Markets," *Marketing Science,* Spring 2002, pp. 160–77.
111. C. Edy, "The Olympics of Marketing," *American Demographics,* June 1999, pp. 47–48.
112. "Little Emperors," p. 143.
113. S. Hamm, "Children of the Web," *BusinessWeek,* July 2, 2007, pp. 50–58.
114. "Global Youth Panel," *NGT,* www.nextgreatthing.com, accessed May 5, 2008.
115. N. Madden, "Levi's Enjoys 'Rebirth' on the Web in Asia," *Advertising Age,* April 19, 2004, p. N-10.
116. C. Walker, "Six Seismic Shifts in Global Teen Culture," *Chief Marketer,* www.chiefmarketer.com, accessed February 6, 2011.
117. L. Bertagnoli, "Continental Spendthrifts," *Marketing News,* October 22, 2001, p. 15.
118. N. Madden, "Coke Targets Second Cities," *Advertising Age,* August 16, 2004, p. 22.
119. See, e.g., L. Tong, "Consumerism Sweeps the Mainland," *Marketing Management,* Winter 1998, pp. 32–35; J. Slater, "In India, a Market Unleashed," *The Wall Street Journal,* March 12, 2004, p. A13; and N. Madden, "China Passes Japan as Second-Largest Economy," *Advertising Age,* August 25, 2010.
120. "Picturing a World of Want," *Newsweek,* May 5, 2008, p. 7.
121. J. L. Lee, "China Senses Need for Cleaner Fuel," *The Wall Street Journal,* December 11, 2003, p. A16.
122. *The World Factbook* (Washington, DC: Central Intelligence Agency, 2008).
123. *2005 International Comparison Program* (International Bank for Reconstruction and Development/The World Bank, 2008), www.worldbank.org/data/quickreferences (per capita income in U.S. dollars; per capita PPP in international dollars).
124. *Statistical Abstract of the United States* (2010), www.census.gov; *2010 Philippine Statistical Yearbook* (Makati City: National Statistical Information Center, 2010), p. 1.18; *Statistics Canada* (2004), www.statcan.ca; *Japan Statistical Yearbook* (2009), www.stat.go.jp; Census of India 2001.
125. H. Fattah, "The Middle East Baby Boom," *American Demographics,* September 2002, pp. 55–60.
126. A. Esser, "The Transnationalization of European Television," *Journal of European Area Studies,* 10, no. 1 (2002), pp. 13–29.
127. See, e.g., de Mooij and Hofstede, "Convergence and Divergence in Consumer Behavior"; and A. Kanso and R. A. Nelson, "Advertising Localization Overshadows Standardization," *Journal of Advertising Research,* January–February 2002, pp. 79–89.
128. "When in Rome . . . ," *Businessline,* April 15, 2004, p. 1.
129. I. Vida and J. Reardon, "Domestic Consumption," *Journal of Consumer Marketing,* 25, no. 1 (2008), pp. 34–44; L. Dong and K. Tian, "The Use of Western Brands in Asserting Chinese National Identity," *Journal of Consumer Research,* October 2009, pp. 504–23; M. O. Lwin, A. Stanaland, and J. D. Williams, "Exporting America," *International Journal of Advertising,* 29, no. 2 (2010), pp. 245–77; and A. A. Maher, P. Clark, and A. Maher, "International Consumer Admiration and the Persistence of Animosity," *Journal of Consumer Marketing,* 27, no. 5 (2010), pp. 415–24.
130. E. J. Schultz, "MillerCoors Thinks Globally, but Gets 'Intimate' Locally," *Advertising Age,* October 4, 2010, pp. 1 and 19.
131. C. Rubel, "Survey," *Marketing News,* July 15, 1996, p. 5; and D. Barros, "Create Unique Strategy for Each Brazilian Culture," *Marketing News,* September 1, 2004, pp. 17–18.
132. G. Cui, "Segmenting China's Consumer Market," *Journal of International Consumer Marketing,* 1 (1999), pp. 55–76; and T. Sun and G. Wu, "Consumption Patterns of Chinese Urban and Rural Consumers," *Journal of Consumer Marketing,* 21, no. 4 (2004), pp. 245–53.
133. P. L. Andruss, "Slow Boat to China," *Marketing News,* September 10, 2001, p. 11.
134. N. Madden and J. Neff, "P&G Adapts Attitude toward Local Markets," *Advertising Age,* February 23, 2004, p. 28.
135. C. Penteado, "Emerging Lower Middle Class Fires Up Marketers in Brazil," *Advertising Age,* June 14, 2010, p. 12.
136. Examples come from Chen and Chang, "China Takes Aim at Racy, Violent TV Shows"; G. A. Fowler, "China Cracks Down on Commercials," *The Wall Street Journal,* February 19, 2004, p. B7; "Molson Airs Ad under New Rules," *Advertising Age,* February 23, 2004, p. 12; "China Bans Opening New Internet Cafes," *CNN.com,* March 2006, www.cnn.com; E. Hall, "In Europe, the Clash over Junk-Food Ads Heats Up," *Advertising Age,* March 5, 2007, p. 32; and E. Hall, "U.K. to Tighten Regulations for Paid Tweets, Sponsored Posts," *Advertising Age,* January 13, 2011.
137. N. Madden, "Lower-Tier Cities Offer Most Growth," *Advertising Age,* June 23, 2010.
138. Sources include "Unilever in Brazil (1997–2007): Marketing Strategies for Low-Income Consumers," *Insead,* (2007); E. Wong, "Unilever's True Grit," *Adweek,* 50, no. 21 (May 24, 2009), p. AM8; C. Challener, "Developing and Industrialized Nations Present Diverse Opportunities for Innovation and Growth in Laundry Products," *ICIS Chemical Business,* June 18, 2008; K. Capell, "Unilever's Laundry Biz Is Greener and Growing," *BusinessWeek Online,* December 29, 2008; J. Neff, "The Dirt on Laundry Trends around the World," *Advertising Age,* June 14, 2010, p. 8; and Unilever's corporate website, www.unilever.com.
139. P. D. Lynch, R. J. Kent, and S. S. Srinivasan, "The Global Internet Shopper," *Journal of Advertising Research,* May–June 2001, pp. 15–23.

chapter

3 The Changing American Society: Values

LEARNING OBJECTIVES

LO1 **Understand core American cultural values.**

LO2 **Summarize changes in self, environment, and other-oriented values.**

LO3 **Discuss values as they relate to green marketing.**

LO4 **Discuss values as they relate to cause-related marketing.**

LO5 **Discuss values as they relate to marketing to gay and lesbian consumers.**

LO6 **Discuss values as they relate to gender-based marketing.**

Gender roles continue to evolve in the United States with more women taking on traditionally male-oriented tasks and more men taking on traditionally female-oriented tasks.[1] One area that has recently gotten the attention of marketers is grocery shopping. A recent Yahoo! study finds that 51 percent of adult men in the United States report being the primary grocery shopper for their home. And, while men may be inflating their participation, other research supports the fact that men, indeed, are involved in the grocery shopping task more than ever before. You might wonder what has caused this shift. Many factors are likely to be involved, a few of which are discussed next. First, generational shifts are occurring, where younger women are now more educated than their male counterparts. This is changing career and family dynamics and causing couples to revisit how household duties should be divided up. Second is economic. Nearly three out of every four jobs lost in the most recent recession were those of men, another dynamic that has led couples to revisit household duties. A third aspect is the masculine/feminine value itself. This value appears to be shifting in the United States away from the traditional masculine-dominated value to a more balanced masculine/feminine value. As this shift has occurred, role differentiation between men and women has reduced. Consider the following excerpt:

> In masculine cultures, household work is less shared between husband and wife than in feminine cultures. Men also do more household shopping in the feminine cultures. Data from Eurostat . . . show that low masculinity explains 52% of variance of the proportion of men who spend time on shopping activities.

Given the increased participation by men in the grocery shopping task, several marketing factors become critical. First is to understand differences in how men and women shop. A recent RIVET survey indicates the following differences:

> MEN are (a) more likely to stick to brand names they recognize, (b) less likely to shop with a list, and (c) less likely to look for in-store bargains.
>
> WOMEN are (a) more likely to change brands for the sake of variety, (b) more likely to make unplanned purchases, and (c) more likely to shop every aisle.

Such differences have implications for retailers ranging from the role of coupons (probably less pronounced for men) to the appeal of store brands (probably more pronounced for women). Understanding such differences for grocery retailers is critical. A second critical marketing factor is adjusting numerous aspects of grocery retailing toward men. This may include a range of issues including store layout, in-store promotions, and advertising for grocery products. For example, "themed events" catering to men's interests such as beer-tasting nights may help make the grocery shopping task more engaging. Providing free samples may also be effective because it is a major factor cited by men in terms of influencing them to switch brands. Finally, appropriate inclusion of male-oriented themes in advertising is critical. Only a quarter of men currently feel that ads in the grocery category are designed to speak to them.

Chapter 2 discussed how variations in values influence consumption patterns *across* cultures. Here, we describe how changes in values *within* culture over time influence consumption patterns, with a specific focus on the United States. The changing role of men and women in American society, highlighted in the chapter opener, reflects changes in the "masculine/feminine" value described in Chapter 2. As this example makes clear, cultural values are not constant. Rather, they evolve over time.[2] We begin by examining the evolution of American values in general. Next, we examine four marketing trends that have evolved in response to changing values: green marketing, cause-related marketing, marketing to gay and lesbian consumers, and gender-based marketing.

CHANGES IN AMERICAN CULTURAL VALUES

LO1 Observable shifts in behavior, including consumption behavior, often reflect shifts in **cultural values,** *widely held beliefs that affirm what is desirable.* Therefore, it is necessary to understand the underlying value shifts to understand current and future consumer behavior. Although we discuss American values as though every American has the same values, in fact there is substantial variance in values across individuals and groups. In addition, changes in values tend to occur slowly and unevenly across individuals and groups. While traumatic events such as the 9/11 attacks and the recent major recession can produce value shifts, a slow evolution is more common. Caution should be used in assuming that short-term behavioral or attitudinal changes in response to such events represent long-lasting value shifts.

Figure 3–1 presents our estimate of how American values are changing. These are the same values used to describe different cultures in Chapter 2. It must be emphasized that Figure 3–1 is based on the authors' subjective interpretation of the American society. You should feel free, indeed compelled, to challenge these judgments.

Self-Oriented Values

LO2 Traditionally, Americans have been active, materialistic, hardworking, religious people inclined toward abstinence and postponed gratification. Beginning after the end of World War II and accelerating rapidly during the 1970s and early 1980s, Americans placed increased emphasis on leisure, immediate gratification, and sensual gratification. While these changes have remained relatively intact, we discuss what role, if any, the most recent recession (dubbed by some as the Great Recession) has had on specific values such as materialism and immediate gratification.

Traditional, Current and Emerging American Values

FIGURE 3-1

	Self-Oriented	
Religious	T EC	Secular
Sensual gratification	E C T	Abstinence
Postponed gratification	T C E	Immediate gratification
Material	T C E	Nonmaterial
Hard work	T C E	Leisure
Active	ECT*	Passive
	Environment-Oriented	
Maximum cleanliness	TC E	Minimum cleanliness
Tradition	EC T	Change
Risk taking	T E C	Security
Problem solving	T CE	Fatalistic
Admire nature	E C T	Overcome nature
Performance	T E C	Status
	Other-Oriented	
Individual	T CE	Collective
Diversity	E C T	Uniformity
Limited family	TEC	Extended family
Youth	T C E	Age
Competition	T C E	Cooperation
Masculine	T C E	Feminine

*T = Traditional, E = Emerging, and C = Current.

Religious/Secular America is basically a secular society. A religious group does not control the educational system, government, or political process, and most people's daily behaviors are not guided by strict religious guidelines. Nonetheless, roughly 82 percent of American adults claim a religious affiliation, 30 percent claim to attend a religious service at least once a week, and 54 percent state that religion is very important in their lives.[3]

While Americans often profess to be more religious than their behaviors would suggest, religious-based beliefs do influence decisions.[4] Many Americans for whom religion is especially important are conservative in their beliefs. They are quite active politically and as consumers. Their political activism involves attempts to regulate various marketing activities, including products (particularly "sin" products such as liquor, gambling, and pornography) and advertising.[5] Their consumption patterns include both positive consumption (purchasing religious objects and books) and negative consumption (avoiding or boycotting products and companies).

Although conservative religious groups generate substantial publicity and have considerable political power, the culture remains relatively secular. Indeed, increasing secularism is cited as one reason for the increase in interfaith marriages.[6] However, it is estimated that the devoutly religious make up 25 percent of the U.S. population.[7] And advertising to this group requires a nuanced approach—advertisers can't simply put a religious symbol on all products and think that it will have a positive effect. Only when there is a product-religion match (e.g., a counseling center) does the inclusion of a religious symbol such as a

ILLUSTRATION 3-1

American culture values sensual gratification. Products and ads based on this appeal such as TBD4Men are generally well received but can cause problems when they go too far.

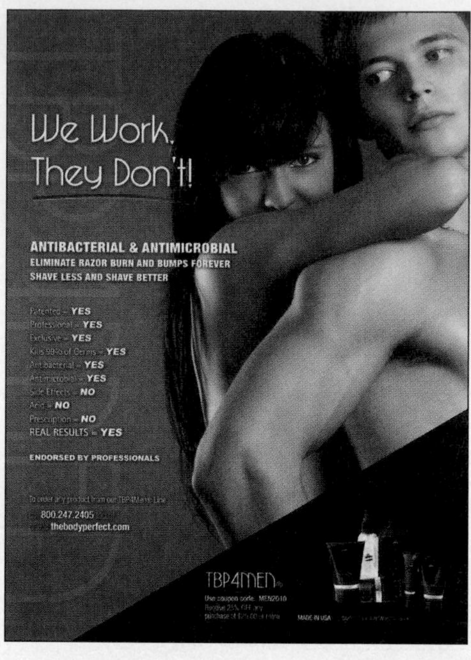

cross have a positive influence on purchasing. When there is a perceived lack of fit (e.g., alcohol), the inclusion of a religious symbol has a negative effect. In addition, the more religious a person is, the more pronounced these effects are.[8] We treat religion and its impact on our society in considerable depth in Chapter 5 when we discuss subcultures.

Sensual Gratification/Abstinence Closely tied to America's traditional religious orientation was a belief in the virtue of abstinence. As American society became more secular, sensual gratification became more acceptable. This trend appears to remain strong, even as consumer and government agencies have tried to push back and curb violence, indecency, and nudity in such venues as ads, movies, and video games.[9] For example, Axe body spray is the number one brand in its category and relies heavily on sex appeals targeting young men. And while the United States is not the highest in its use of nudity in ads, it outranked Brazil, China, South Korea, and Thailand in a recent study. However, the effectiveness of sexual appeals in ads depends on viewer gender. Men tend to react more positively than women to sex appeals involving female nudity. However, women with more liberal attitudes toward sex view sexually explicit ads just as positively as men.[10]

Other evidence of the greater value placed on sensual gratification comes from a recent study showing that one of the biggest value shifts in the United States is in the greater importance placed on fun and excitement. That is, people today, more than ever, want to lead a "pleasurable, happy life; to experience stimulation and thrills."[11] The food industry certainly relies on consumer desires for sensual gratification by selling the pleasure, happiness, and thrills that various foods can deliver. According to one Pepperidge Farm executive, their premium cookies offer a "small indulgence anytime, anywhere."[12]

Illustration 3–1 shows an ad for TBP4Men, that appeals to sensual gratification. How do you feel this ad would be received by men? By women?

Postponed/Immediate Gratification In line with the value they generally place on sensual gratification, Americans seem unwilling to delay pleasures, even in the face of discomfort over spending levels and debt. For a time, there was hope that the Great Recession would usher in a new frugality among consumers and a willingness to postpone gratification by delaying or eliminating purchases. And, to some degree, it has. Americans are now saving more and paying down debt. However, recently these trends have begun to recede as once again U.S. consumers get back to "spending as usual." Consider the following quote:

> The truth is that spending may be hard to contain. Entire generations of consumers have grown up with the idea of instant gratification and the credit culture that comes with it.[13]

It is really quite difficult, therefore, to say whether U.S. consumer values relating to instant gratification have truly been affected (it does appear that they have somewhat, as represented in Figure 3–1), or whether the behavioral changes related to spending and saving had more to do with the economic constraints imposed by the recession. As a consequence, we show an emerging trend back toward instant gratification more in line with pre-recession levels moving forward.

Material/Nonmaterial Americans have maintained a strong material orientation. An outcome of America's focus on materialism is a consumption-driven society. As we will see, Americans are working longer hours, in part, to afford material possessions. That is, Americans are trading time and energy for things and services such as cars and travel. One factor found to influence materialism is television. As one group of researchers note:

> Television is a powerful medium . . . consumers often use information from television to construct perceptions of social reality including the prevalence of affluence. Heavier viewers tend to believe luxury products and services to be more commonplace than they actually are.[14]

As we have seen, the recent recession has curtailed spending to some degree. However, at least some of that frugality appears to have been more economically than value-related. Indeed, one expert notes that consumers are going through "frugality fatigue," which suggests that consumers are acting due to an external constraint more than an internal value change. And, consider the following quote from a young woman who simply got fed up with trying to save and began spending again, which led to her eviction and caused her to have to move back in with her parents:

> After awhile, I just decided, "Screw it. I need some new clothes. I'm going to get them." My mamma's not happy, but I don't care. You stop spending and you stop living.[15]

While materialism appears to be the norm, a movement away from materialism in the United States is occurring among a select group of consumers. Role overload, burnout, and emotional exhaustion are causing some to rethink priorities and simplify their lives. Consider the following:

> I had all the stuff that was supposed to make me successful—my car and my clothes, the house in the right neighborhood and belonging to the right health club. All the external framework was excellent and inside I kind of had this pit eating away at me.[16]

Consumers' efforts to reduce their reliance on consumption and material possessions have been termed **voluntary simplicity.** Voluntary simplicity can span a continuum from minor life adjustments and reduced spending to drastic lifestyle adjustments, including downsized jobs, incomes, houses, and spending. The key is that it is a conscious and voluntary decision, not one brought on by economic necessity. Major factors in the decision to simplify appear to be reduced stress and increased life satisfaction, although other motivations, including environmentalism, can be involved. While the voluntary simplicity movement appears to represent a relatively small proportion of the U.S. population, its growth certainly holds economic and marketing consequences, including the market for secondhand products and green products.[17]

Hard Work/Leisure Americans continue their strong tradition of hard work, leading much of the industrialized world in hours worked. Average weekly hours worked is around 40 for full-time workers, with 24 percent of workers clocking more than 40 hours per week. The percentage of married women who work outside the home for wages has increased almost 50 percent since 1970, from 41 to 61 percent of all married women.[18] Americans work long hours for many reasons. One is clearly their material orientation. Americans work to have such things as a large home, two cars, and a nice vacation. Others work long hours because they lack the skills or job opportunities to provide even a moderate lifestyle without doing so. However, Americans also work long and hard because work is meaningful and valuable to them, in part because of the self-esteem and respect they gain from the work they do.[19]

Partly in response to the increase in work hours, the value placed on work relative to leisure has dropped over the past several decades. Clearly work is still important, and higher unemployment during the recent recession has put this into even greater perspective. However, a recent study finds that for working women with children, the percentage who indicated that full-time work was ideal for them has decreased by 11 percent since 1997, while the percentage who indicated part-time work was ideal for them has increased by 12 percent.[20] And yet, over two-thirds of married women with children work outside the home for wages. Together, these statistics suggest such factors as time pressures and role conflict associated with the fact that work competes with other important aspects of one's life. This opens up opportunities for marketers who can deliver convenience. Still, we can't seem to get away from work. One study finds that between 51 and 65 percent of U.S. workers with work e-mail check it during off hours including nights, weekends, and while on vacation.[21] Thus, we have a situation in which hard work and leisure are both valued (often by the same people) and commingled in people's lives.

Active/Passive Americans continue to value an active approach to life. Although less than half of all American adults exercise regularly, most Americans take an active approach to both leisure and problem-solving activities. Television viewing as a primary form of entertainment has dropped sharply from its peak in the mid-1980s (young men [18 to 24 years of age] seem to be moving away from TV faster than any other group).[22] Alternative activities, including surfing the net, sports, cooking, and gardening, are popular. And the amount of time children spend in scheduled activities continues to increase.[23] The following quote illustrates that Americans differ on this value, but most would agree more with the second speaker than the first.

> My idea of a vacation is a nice oceanfront resort, a beach chair, and a piña colada.
>
> Mine too. For a day or two. Then I'd go bug spit. I'd feel like I was in prison. I'd *do* something.[24]

Illustration 3–2 describes how Club Med has 71 worldwide resorts designed for active leisure.

Environment-Oriented Values

LO2 Environment-oriented values prescribe a society's relationship with its economic, technical, and physical environments. Americans have traditionally admired cleanliness, change, performance, risk taking, problem solving, and the conquest of nature. While this cluster of values remains basically intact, there are some important shifts occurring.

Cleanliness Americans have long valued cleanliness. This strong focus seems to be declining somewhat, particularly in terms of our homes. Likely due to increased time

ILLUSTRATION 3-2

This Club Med ad is consistent with American values for leisure, activeness, sensual gratification, and risk taking.

demands caused by work, messier homes are more acceptable.[25] However, such shifts don't appear to suggest major changes. The popularity of TV shows like *Mission: Organization* on HGTV suggests that while Americans may accept messier homes, they are not happy about them. This obviously presents marketing opportunities.[26] For example, the development of robotic vacuum cleaners such as iRobot's Roomba taps the desire for cleanliness while offering much-needed convenience and time savings.

Personal hygiene, another aspect of cleanliness, remains very important to most Americans. One study shows that antibacterial hand sanitizers such as Purell are an important part of the arsenal of products carried around by mothers.[27] Illustration 3–3 demonstrates how Clorox emphasizes cleanliness which is in line with the importance that Americans place on personal hygiene.

Tradition/Change Americans have always been very receptive to change. *New* has traditionally been taken to mean *improved.* While still very appreciative of change, Americans are now less receptive to change for its own sake. New-product recalls, the expense and the failure of various government programs, and the energy required to keep pace with rapid technological changes are some of the reasons for this shift. Another reason is the aging of the American population. As we will see in the next chapter, the average age of the population is increasing, and people generally become somewhat less accepting of change as they age. Still, much of America continues to embrace change, as evidenced by a growing segment of workers that one expert calls the *creative class.* The creative class includes those who work in such professions as architecture, science, engineering, and health care as well as business and who generate new ideas and technologies for a living or engage in

ILLUSTRATION 3-3

Americans continue to place a high value on cleanliness, as this Clorox ad demonstrates.

complex problem solving. This group now constitutes about 33 percent of the workforce, compared with just 10 percent in 1900. Fiat, in re-launching its brand in the United States, indicated that they were targeting the creative class with a campaign heavy on digital, viral, and event-marketing approaches they felt would work best with this segment.[28]

Risk Taking/Security Americans' risk-taking orientation seems to have changed somewhat over time. There was an increased emphasis on security during the period from 1930 through the mid-1980s. This attitude was a response to the tremendous upheavals and uncertainties caused by the Depression, World War II, and the cold war. However, risk taking remains highly valued and is gaining appreciation as Americans look to entrepreneurs for economic growth and to smaller firms and self-employment to obtain desired lifestyles. Figure 3–1 indicates that there seems to currently be a greater emphasis on security, driven at least in part by the recent economic recession. However, a long-term study of the importance that Americans place on security shows that the desire for security has seen one of the largest declines over the last several decades. This suggests that the short-term focus on security may give way once again to risk taking as the economy recovers.[29]

Problem Solving/Fatalistic Americans take great pride in being problem solvers, and as we saw earlier, as a percentage of the workforce, problem solvers and creative types are on the increase. By and large, Americans believe that virtually anything can be fixed given sufficient time and effort. For example, even in the midst of the recent recession, nearly two-thirds of Americans agreed that "[a]s Americans, we can always find ways to solve problems."[30] Marketers introduce thousands of new products each year with the theme that they will solve a problem better than existing products will. We will examine the results of this value later in this chapter in the sections on green marketing and cause marketing.

Admire/Overcome Nature Traditionally, nature was viewed as an obstacle. Americans attempted to bend nature to fit their desires without realizing the negative consequences this could have for both nature and humanity. However, this attitude has shifted dramatically over the past 30 years.

Experts have been concerned that environmentalism is dead. Some cite the fact that the percentage of Americans who call themselves environmentalists dropped from 73 to 47 percent between 1990 and 2000. Part of the decline may be real, but part of the decline may simply be in how people define *environmentalism.* For example, a recent Gallop Poll shows that 80 percent of Americans are active or sympathetic to environmentalism (21 percent "active"; 49 percent "sympathetic" but not active). This puts active participation up by five percentage points since 2000. Here are other indications that concern for the environment among Americans remains strong and may be on the rise:

- Eighty-three percent report changing their lifestyle to protect the environment.
- Recycling (89 percent), energy reduction (85 percent), and environmentally friendly purchases (70 percent) remain strong.
- Sixty-seven percent say that "even in rough economic times, it is important to purchase products with social and environmental benefits."
- Fifty-one percent report being willing to pay more for products with environmental benefits.[31]

Table 3–1 shows eight segments, identified by IRI/TNS, based on consumer attitudes and behaviors toward the environment.[32]

Firms that convince environmentally concerned consumers that their products are environmentally sound can reap huge rewards. Such an approach has been termed **enviropreneurial marketing.** Enviropreneurial marketing is *environmentally friendly marketing practices, strategies, and tactics initiated by a firm to achieve a competitive differentiation.* Research shows that such a marketing approach can lead to increased new-product success and increased market share.[33]

We describe the marketing response to this value in the section of this chapter on green marketing.

Performance/Status Americans are shifting back to a focus on performance rather than status. Although consumers are still willing to purchase "status" brands, these

Shades of Green Segmentation™ Scheme by IRI/TNS — TABLE 3-1
Eco-Centrists (16 percent): Highly committed to and concerned about environment. Beliefs reflected in their consumption behaviors across a wide range of products will pay more for eco-friendly products. Cynical about corporate green efforts—viewed as merely marketing tactics. High education and income; Urban South and West.
Respectful Stewards (7 percent): Most highly concerned about environment. Beliefs reflected in their consumption behaviors. Will pay more for eco-friendly products. Not cynical about corporate green marketing efforts. Focused on community and culture. Lower education and income; Hispanic; Urban.
Proud Traditionalists (14 percent): Environmental efforts focused on keeping home running efficiently and effectively (insulation and water-efficient products). Focused on family and hard work. Rural Midwest.
Frugal Earth Mothers (18 percent): Environmental efforts focused on running a more efficient home to save money (buy used, wash in cold water, air-dry clothes). Focused on practicality and lowering day-to-day costs. Lower income; Rural; Female.
Skeptical Individuals (13 percent): Believe in environmental issues like global warming and carbon emission concerns. Skeptical of corporate green efforts. Very high income and education; Urban coasts; Male.
Eco-Chic (14 percent): Environmentally concerned, but actions don't match beliefs. More interested in appearing to be green to "ride the wave of environmental consciousness." May try eco-friendly products but tend to return to their favorite nongreen brands. Young adults.
Green Naives (11 percent): Environmental issues have not registered with this group in terms of beliefs or actions. Sedentary; Lower income.
Eco-Villians (7 percent): Highly dismissive of environmental concerns. Don't believe global warming exists. Highly negative of corporate green efforts—seen as marketing ploys. Middle income; Male, Smaller metro areas.

brands must provide style and functionality in addition to the prestige of the name. This has led to substantial increases in sales at stores that combine price, service, and quality, such as Walmart and Target stores, and for quality retailer private-label brands such as those offered by Albertson's, Target, and Walmart. In contrast, outlets with inappropriate cost structures or images, such as The Gap, Kmart, and Montgomery Ward, have struggled or failed.[34]

Other-Oriented Values

LO2 Other-oriented values reflect a society's view of the appropriate relationships between individuals and groups within that society. Historically, American society has been oriented toward individualism, competitiveness, masculinity, youth, limited families, and uniformity. However, several aspects of this orientation are undergoing change.

Individual/Collective A strong emphasis on individualism is one of the defining characteristics of American society. Watch any American hit movie. The leading character will virtually always behave as an individual, often despite pressures to conform to the group. Americans believe in "doing your own thing." Even the "uniforms" that each generation of teenagers invents for itself allow ample room for individual expression. This value affects incentive systems for salespeople, advertising themes, product design, and customer complaining behavior.[35] For example, consumers higher in individualism are more likely to complain, switch, or engage in negative word-of-mouth when faced with poor service performance.[36] Individualism is also evident in the customization craze for cars, trucks, and motorcycles, a market worth over $2 billion a year. Discovery Channel and CMT have tapped into this trend with shows such as *American Chopper* and *Trick My Truck,* which attract the highly elusive younger male audience.[37]

Diversity/Uniformity While American culture has always valued individualism, it has also valued a degree of uniformity, particularly with respect to groups. America was founded in part by people seeking religious freedom or fleeing from various forms of persecution. The Constitution and many laws seek to protect diverse religions, political beliefs, and so forth. Nonetheless, Americans historically insisted that immigrants quickly adopt the language, dress, values, and many other aspects of the majority. Those who did not were often subject to various forms of discrimination. This was particularly true for racial and some religious minorities.

Since World War II, Americans have increasingly valued diversity. Consider the following:

> Hallmark markets a collection of greeting cards called "Common Threads," whose messages reflect a variety of world cultures, emphasizing global community and diverse cultural expression.[38]

Researchers speculate that the market for products such as "Common Threads" is "*cultural creatives,*" the "26% of adult Americans who are concerned with self-actualization, spirituality, and self-expression and who like things that are foreign and exotic."[39] Cultural creatives, regardless of ethnicity, are more likely to cross traditional ethnic boundaries in seeking out products.

Although far from being free of racial, religious, ethnic, or class prejudice, American culture is evolving toward valuing diversity more than uniformity, as reflected in Illustration 3–4. And a recent study shows that 61 percent of Americans think that the increased racial and

ILLUSTRATION 3-4

Americans increasingly value diversity. As a result, a diversity approach is used in many ads.

ethnic diversity "has been a change for the better." This percentage is higher for younger generations.[40] We examine one aspect of America's increasing acceptance of diversity—marketing to gay and lesbian consumers—later in this chapter.

Limited/Extended Family America was settled by immigrants, people who left their extended families behind. As the nation grew, the western movement produced a similar phenomenon. Even today, frequent geographic moves as well as differential rates of social mobility mean that few children grow up in close interaction with aunts, uncles, cousins, nieces, or nephews.[41] It is also common for children to leave their hometowns and parents once they begin their own careers. The physical separation of traditional family members often reduces the sense of family among those members. This, in turn, reduces the impact that the family has on the individual.

This is not to say that Americans do not love their family members or that how an American is raised does not influence the person for life. Rather, it means that a 35-year-old American is unlikely to have a cousin who would feel obligated to respond positively to a loan request (this is not the case in many other cultures). Likewise, this 35-year-old would be unlikely to have one or more cousins, aunts, or nephews live with him or her for an extended time period. The role of families in the American culture is covered in depth in Chapter 6.

Youth/Age Traditionally, older people were considered wiser than young people and were, therefore, looked to as models and leaders in almost all cultures. This has never been as true in American culture, probably because transforming a wilderness into a new type of producing nation required characteristics such as physical strength, stamina, youthful vigor, and imagination. The value on youth continued as America became an industrial nation.

Since World War II, it has increased to such an extent that products such as cars, clothing, cosmetics, and hairstyles seem designed for and sold only to the young. For example, youth appeals in American advertising still appear to outstrip appeals to age and tradition.[42]

But a slow reversal of this value on youth seems to be occurring. Because of their increasing numbers and disposable income, older citizens have developed political and economic clout and are beginning to use it. Cosmetics, medicines, and hair care products are being marketed specifically to older consumers, and ads for these products increasingly feature older models, such as Julianne Moore, who are closer in age to the target audience. However, most of these products still have either a direct or indirect appeal of creating a younger appearance.

Age portrayal in advertising is a difficult issue. Since people often feel younger than their actual age, ads using younger models might generate a more positive reaction. In addition, for youth-oriented or conspicuously consumed products, using older models in ads may alienate younger consumers. These two factors help explain the overrepresentation of younger models in ads.[43] There is the worry, however, that at some point older consumers may feel ignored by ads that portray overly young users. Clearly, marketers have a lot to learn in this area.

Competition/Cooperation America has long been a competitive society, and this value remains firmly entrenched. It is reflected in our social, political, and economic systems. We reward particularly successful competitors in business, entertainment, and sports with staggering levels of financial compensation. Although the focus on cooperation and teamwork in schools and businesses has increased, teamwork is generally instituted so that the team or group can outperform some other team or group. It is no wonder that America was one of the first countries to allow comparative advertising.

Masculine/Feminine American society, like most others, has reflected a masculine orientation for a long time. But as indicated by this chapter's opening vignette, this orientation is changing, as are gender roles. Although American society is becoming less masculine oriented, it still leans clearly in that direction. For example, 37 percent of parents indicate that they would prefer a boy if they could have only one child, compared with 28 percent who would opt for a girl.[44] And textbooks aimed at children still depict physical activity more often for boys (65 percent) than for girls (35 percent).[45] Still, there is a shift taking place in this value. For example, preference for male bosses continues to decline while preference for female bosses continues to increase.[46] The marketing implications resulting from evolving gender roles are discussed later in this chapter.

MARKETING STRATEGY AND VALUES

We have examined a number of marketing implications of American values and changes in these values. It is critical that all aspects of the firm's marketing mix be consistent with the value system of its target market. We will now examine marketing responses to four evolving American values: green marketing, cause-related marketing, marketing to gay and lesbian consumers, and gender-based marketing.

Green Marketing

LO3 Marketers have responded to Americans' increasing concern for the environment with an approach called **green marketing.**[47] Green marketing generally involves (1) developing products whose production, use, or disposal is less harmful to the environment than the traditional versions of the product; (2) developing products that have a positive impact on the environment; or (3) tying the purchase of a product to an environmental organization or event. For example:[48]

- Levi's launched its Levi's Eco line of 100 percent organic cotton jeans.
- CBS created the "EcoAd" program whereby 10 percent of a company's ad buy goes to local environmental causes. Participation is signaled with a "green-leaf" eco-ad logo.
- Office Depot offers Recycled Enviro-Copy printer and copier paper, which contains 35 percent postconsumer, recycled fibers, with green-colored packaging and the name "Office Depot Green" to emphasize the environment.

ILLUSTRATION 3-5

Environmentally friendly products such as the Audi TDI diesel must also provide consumer benefits to be successful.

Environmental concerns don't guarantee purchase of green products. Even among those who are environmentally concerned, negative perceptions are on the rise including beliefs that green products are too expensive, of lower quality, and not better for the environment, and that green claims can't be trusted.[49] Overcoming these obstacles is critical to the success of green marketing (see the Audi TDI Clean Diesel ad in Illustration 3–5). For example, Honda discontinued its Accord hybrid in 2007. Poor sales were likely due to the fact that highway mileage for the hybrid was only 1 mpg higher than the gas-only Accord, but it cost nearly $15,000 more![50]

The FTC shares consumer skepticism about green claims. Amid substantial increases in green marketing and green claims by companies, the FTC has made the first modifications in over a decade to its voluntary guidelines called the "Green Guides." The Green Guides provide guidance on acceptable and unacceptable practices relating to environmental claims. Several issues motivated the FTC to make the modifications:[51]

- First, terms such as *eco-friendly* appear to be misleading to consumers who believe that such products have "far-reaching benefits in almost all environmental areas without having any substantial drawbacks." According to the FTC, few products can live up to the perceptions that consumers have of them.
- Second is a practice termed **greenwashing** whereby a firm promotes environmental benefits that are unsubstantiated and on which they don't deliver.

Prominent among the modifications to the Green Guides are (a) a focus on qualifying claims so that it is clear in what way the product is environmentally friendly and (b) a crackdown on third-party certifications and seals. This crackdown reflects the fact that some companies have created their own seals or utilize third-party vendors that don't do anything to substantiate the claims being made (to learn more about Green Guides, visit www.ftc.gov).[52]

Cause-Related Marketing

The term *cause marketing* is sometimes used interchangeably with *social marketing*. However, the two are different. As noted in Chapter 1, social marketing is marketing done to enhance the welfare of individuals or society without direct benefit to a firm. In contrast,

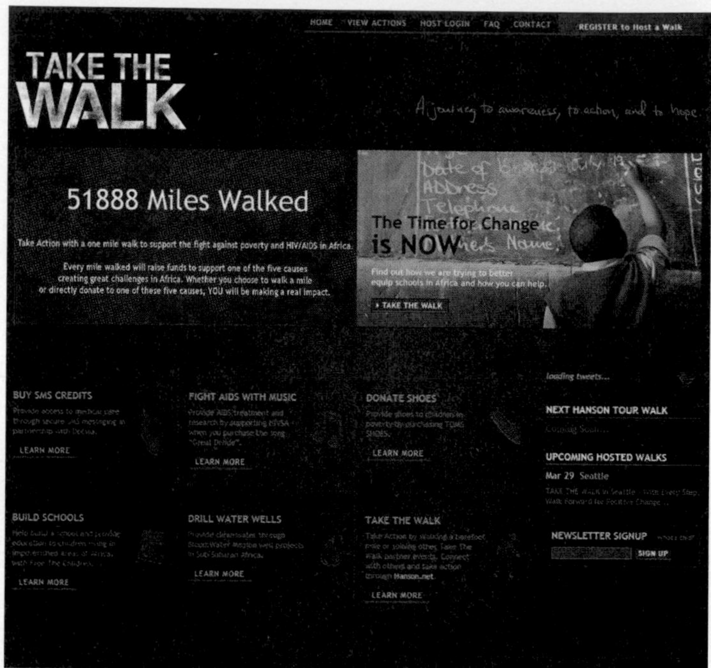

ILLUSTRATION 3-6

The Take the Walk ad on the left promotes a benefit to the world community without advancing the profits or image of a commercial firm. That ad is an example of social marketing. The Secret Mean Stinks ad on the right represents cause-related marketing. It not only benefits a cause but also enhances the image and sales of a commercial firm.

cause marketing, or **cause-related marketing (CRM),** is *marketing that ties a company and its products to an issue or cause with the goal of improving sales or corporate image while providing benefits to the cause.*[53] Companies associate with causes to create long-term relationships with their customers, building corporate and brand equity that should eventually lead to increased sales. A good example of CRM is Secret's "Mean Stinks" anti-bullying campaign.

Examine the two ads in Illustration 3–6. The ad on the left in Illustration 3–6 is an example of social marketing; it promotes a benefit to the world community without advancing the profits or image of a commercial firm. The ad on the right in Illustration 3–6 is an example of cause-related marketing; it attempts to benefit a cause *and* to enhance the image and sales of a commercial firm.

The foundation of CRM is marketing to consumers' values, and it can be very effective. Cause-related marketing is often effective because it is consistent with strongly held American values.[54] For example, a common theme in most CRM programs taps America's problem-solving orientation by presenting a problem, such as breast cancer, AIDS, or pollution, and an action that individuals can take to help solve the problem. Thus, consumer expectations, acceptance of CRM, and response to CRM have increased dramatically over the past decade.

Research shows that many consumers will travel out of their way to find stores and brands that support the causes they care about and also pay more for those products. In addition:

- Seventy-one percent have purchased a cause-related brand.
- Eighty-eight percent think companies should try to accomplish their business goals while simultaneously working to improve society.

- Seventy-four percent claim that a company's commitment to a social issue is important when deciding which products and services to recommend to other people.
- Eighty-six percent are likely to switch brands based on CRM when price and quality are equal.[55]

Given consumer receptivity to CRM, it is not surprising that corporate spending on it is on the rise. One area of spending, cause-related sponsorship, has grown from $120 million in 1990 to $1.5 billion, which represents the third-largest area of corporate sponsorship![56] Consumer skepticism and apathy remain a challenge. When consumers feel that the company is engaged in CRM due to positive values (they feel morally obligated), corporate trust is enhanced, which increases word-of-mouth and purchases. Alternatively, when consumers feel the company is engaged in CRM simply to enhance their own image or because stockholders expect it, corporate trust is reduced, which decreases positive word-of-mouth and purchases.[57] CRM skepticism and apathy are demonstrated in the following descriptions and quotes of four consumer types based on their responses to CRM:[58]

Skeptic (doubts sincerity or effectiveness of CRM): "I think those are fake, most of them. Because what they give is so little it doesn't amount to anything."

Balancer (believes in CRM but generally doesn't act accordingly): "I hate to say this, but, as far as grocery stores, I go to the one that is closest to me. It makes me feel better . . . about Food Lion that they were willing to do this (participate in CRM) . . . but, sometimes I don't put out that extra effort, but I guess I really should."

Attribution-oriented (concerned about motives behind CRM): "I always approach them with a skeptical eye, but I try and use good judgment and common sense based on who they are, what they're doing and try to see the end result."

Socially concerned (driven by desire to help): "I mean, as long as they're doing it, the motives can be questionable as far as I'm concerned. . . . Even if there's questionable motives, it's that much more important to support companies who do those things. Just to reinforce that good behavior."

An emerging consensus is that a "fit" between the company and the cause can improve results.[59] For example, ConAgra (a food marketing company) launched *Feeding Children Better* to combat child hunger while Crest and the Boys and Girls Club of America partnered to form *Healthy Smiles 2010* to teach kids about oral hygiene. In both cases there is a business–cause fit.[60]

Beyond fit, a unique approach to cause-related marketing is being used with success by Toms Shoes, as discussed in Consumer Insight 3–1. *Do you think their approach overcomes some of the challenges faced by cause-related marketing?*

Marketing to Gay and Lesbian Consumers

As Americans in general are shifting to valuing diversity, they are increasingly embracing ethnic, religious, and racial diversity. Another group gaining increased public acceptance is the gay and lesbian community (we follow business press convention and refer to gay and lesbian consumers as the gay market). Overall, 52 percent of Americans feel that gay and lesbian relations are morally acceptable, up from 40 percent in 2001. The strongest support comes from younger men (62 percent) and women (59 percent), supporting our earlier observation that shifts on the diversity value appear to be strongest among LO5

CONSUMER INSIGHT 3-1

Cause Marketing "Baked into the Brand" at Toms Shoes

A Target store popped up on Times Square in New York City, one of the most expensive pieces of real estate in the country. The store interior was blanketed in a sea of pink products—pink bicycles, sweaters, flip-flops, tee shirts. Outside a coffee cart served pink donuts. All proceeds during the store's short one-month existence went to the Breast Cancer Research Foundation.[61] For every home Habitat for Humanity builds for the homeless in North America, Whirlpool donates a range and a refrigerator.[62] Hand in hand with the Red Cross, P&G Tide's "Loads of Hope" provides mobile laundromats to victims of natural disasters (e.g., New Orleans after Hurricane Katrina).[63]

These cause-marketing campaigns establish a partnership between a corporation and a nonprofit and often result in "doing well by doing good." Marketers increase their bottom line amid a halo of goodwill, while nonprofits receive needed contributions and public attention, and consumers purchase goods for themselves and thus contribute to a worthy cause. Despite the benefits of a win-win-win, critics have pointed out the downside of cause marketing. Corporations may come to lose consumer trust if consumers perceive the corporate–cause relationship as exploitation of the charity. Rather than contribute directly to nonprofits, cause marketing may be teaching consumers to contribute only when they receive something in return and at no cost to themselves. Unlike the unfettered contributions received directly from the public, the contributions charities receive in partnership with corporations may come with strings and obligations.[64]

However, the success of Toms Shoes puts a new twist to cause marketing. Toms Shoes does not partner with a nonprofit or charity. Rather, Toms Shoes is a "for profit" company with the cause "one for one" *baked into the brand.* For each pair of Toms shoes consumers buy, the company donates a pair of Toms shoes to children who need shoes but cannot afford them. In spring 2013 Toms Shoes donated 13 million pairs of shoes in 59 countries. It is now expanding its efforts to eyeglasses in 15 countries. The "baked in brand" strategy of Toms Shoes has been described as a metastory—story telling through action. The consumer act of buying Toms shoes tells the story about the brand and the consumer. The story came first. The "for profit" status of the firm makes doing the right thing sustainable.[65]

Critical Thinking Questions

1. Should marketers, whose primary motivation is to increase the bottom line, deserve the goodwill and burnished reputation that arise through partnerships with nonprofit organizations?
2. Cause marketing teaches consumers that they can improve the world by their consumption, to contribute only when they receive something in return and at no additional cost. Do you agree with that statement?
3. Do the concerns that surround cause marketing apply to the new form of cause marketing such as Toms Shoes?

younger generations.[66] Interestingly, the value that Americans place on individual rights and protection appears to transcend personal opinions about lifestyle. For example, over 70 percent support hate-crime protection laws and same-sex couple rights such as hospital visitation, and 60 percent favor allowing gays and lesbians to serve openly in the military. These numbers are even stronger among younger consumers.[67] The emergence and popularity of TV shows with openly gay or lesbian characters, such as *Modern Family* and *The L Word,* are additional evidence of increased public acceptance.

State and federal actions have also increased in the direction of protecting and expanding the rights of gays and lesbians on a number of fronts including open service in the military and rights as couples, including legalizing gay marriage. In addition, nearly nine out of ten Fortune 500 companies protect workers based on sexual orientation.[68]

Before we begin, it is important to emphasize that gay consumers, like heterosexuals, vary in terms of ethnicity, geographic region, occupation, and age. These and other factors influence their behavior and, in most instances, play a much larger role in their consumption process than does their sexual orientation.

The gay market is substantial in both size and purchase power. The size of the gay market is estimated to be about 7 percent of the adult U.S. population, or roughly 16 million people over the age of 18. Purchasing power is estimated at between $750 and $900 billion.[69] Not surprisingly, many companies have concluded that the gay market is a highly attractive segment to pursue. Examples include:[70]

- American Airlines created a page on its website specifically for gay, lesbian, bisexual, and transgender (GLBT) consumers. Wyndham Hotels partnered with the airline by giving a 20 percent discount on all reservations made through the page.
- IBM has a "sales team dedicated to bringing GLBT decision-makers in contact with IBM."
- Ikea generated considerable public outcry in 1994 for its gay-themed ad. It reentered the gay market in 2006 with a spot that "shows a black and Asian male couple with their daughter and Golden Retriever and ends with the voiceover: 'Why shouldn't sofas come in flavors, just like families?' " Unlike the reaction in 1994, no public debate was created by this ad.

Any firm that desires to capture the loyalty of the gay community must have internal policies that do not discriminate against gay employees. A recent survey found that 82 percent of gay consumers are more likely to buy from companies they know are gay friendly.[71] The Human Rights Campaign Foundation (www.hrc.org) helps provide such information through its corporate equality index (CEI), which measures how equitably a company treats its GLBT employees, customers, and investors.

Product Issues In many cases the lifestyles of gay consumers do not differ sufficiently from those of other consumers to require product modifications. For example, three of the top four reasons for choosing a hotel were the same for GLBT customers as for heterosexuals. In order of importance, they were convenience, customer service, and recommendations from friends or family.[72] However, product modification opportunities are sometimes possible and beneficial. For example, in the realm of television, content that targets news, concerns, programs, and movies of specific interest to GLBT audiences is increasingly popular. The Logo and here! networks have been launched recently in response to this growing demand. In addition, with the increased focus on same-sex marriage, companies such as Pottery Barn and Tiffany's are modifying their bridal registries to be gender neutral, and websites such as Gayweddings (www.gayweddings.com) are emerging to serve this market.

Another area in which product modifications are often necessary is financial services. As the director of segment marketing for American Express explains:

> Often, gay couples are very concerned about issues like Social Security benefits and estate planning, since same-sex marriages often are not recognized under the law.[73]

Ameriprise has a GLBT web page devoted to this market and scores 100 percent on the CEI index. As their website states:

> Ameriprise Financial was one of the first financial services firms to offer dual client analysis for domestic partners and single people in relationships. Dual client analysis allows financial advisors to help domestic partners create a shared plan for the future. Our financial advisors use a comprehensive approach to financial planning that includes tax, protection, estate, retirement and investment planning strategies.

Communication Issues There are a large number of gay-oriented print media in the United States and Canada. Given the size and spending power of the gay market, it is not surprising that spending in gay-oriented print media has more than tripled since 1997 to its current level of over $350 million. And a large and increasing number of Fortune 500 companies now advertise in gay media.[74]

Compared with the general population, gay consumers tend to be more tech savvy and more likely to search online for information.[75] Marketers are taking this into account in developing their websites.[76] For example, iTunes offers GLBT podcasts, Orbitz has a gay and lesbian page on its travel site, and, as we have seen, Ameriprise has a dedicated web page for the GLBT community. In addition, marketers such as Virgin Mobile are using targeted banner ad campaigns to promote their products through websites that target the GLBT community such as OutTraveler.com, SheWired.com, and gay.com.

Since most products don't require alteration for the gay market, firms may decide to approach the market by placing one of their standard ads in gay-oriented media. Anheuser-Busch, Miller Brewing, Baileys Original Irish Cream, and American Express are among the firms that first approached this market with standard ads. However, a majority of ads (62 percent) in gay print media are now created specifically for gay consumers.[77] The ads may portray a gay couple instead of a heterosexual couple in a standard ad. Or the entire ad may contain a gay theme, such as the Tylenol ad shown in Illustration 3–7.

It has been estimated that roughly half of the gay community rarely or never read gay-oriented publications and spend considerable time using standard media.[78] As one gay man stated, "We are not only reading *Out* and *The Advocate* all the time. If you go into any gay man's apartment you're very likely to see *Vanity Fair* and *People* as well."[79] This is also true online, where eight of the ten top websites visited by gay consumers are general sites, such as Yahoo!, Google, Amazon, CNN, and eBay, which are not specifically devoted to gay issues.[80]

Using ads with gay themes in standard mass media can generate concerns regarding backlash from the portion of the market that does not accept the gay community, as well as the desire to have ads that directly appeal to the largest number of viewers.[81] A recent study compared mainstream ads (heterosexual couples in the ad) with explicitly gay and lesbian ads (male or female couples) or implicit gay and lesbian ads (ads that had gay symbolic icons, such as the rainbow flag, pink triangle, and freedom rings). The study found that gays and heterosexuals equally liked the mainstream ads. In addition, although heterosexuals disliked explicit gay and lesbian ads, their attitudes were not negatively influenced by the implicit gay and lesbian ads. Finally, both explicit and implicit gay and lesbian ads were liked more than mainstream ads by those who identified themselves as gay or lesbian.[82] For marketers wanting to move into the mainstream market with appeals that are as broad as possible and still target gay consumers, this research suggests that using symbolic gay icons (which the mainstream market tends to be relatively unknowledgeable of) appears to be an effective tactic. This is important because research shows that gay consumers reward companies that advertise in gay media outlets and/or use gay themes in their advertising.

Finally, in addition to advertising in gay media, support of gay community events such as Gay Pride week is another important avenue firms use in approaching this market.

ILLUSTRATION 3-7

Ads targeting the gay community can range from standard ads run in gay-oriented media to ads such as as this Tylenol ad with clear gay themes.

Gender-Based Marketing

LO6

As we saw in the chapter's opening vignette, gender roles in the United States are shifting. The shift is going both ways, with more women taking on traditionally male-oriented tasks and more men taking on traditionally female-oriented tasks. It's hard to imagine that just a few generations ago, the prevailing stereotype of an automobile purchase involved a male making the purchase alone. Today, women influence 80 percent of all vehicles sold, make over half of all new vehicle purchases (up from 20 percent in 1984), and purchase 40 percent of all SUVs.[83]

Changes in gender roles for women have been dramatic, with increased participation in the workforce, increased wealth and purchase power, and increased participation in active lifestyles, to name just a few. Marketers of products and services ranging from automobiles, to sportswear, to financial services clearly understand the importance of women as a market segment. Consider the following examples:

- Cadillac targets professional women with campaigns for models such as their CTS featuring Kate Walsh and the tagline "The real question is, when you turn your car on, does it return the favor."
- Harley Davidson has a page on their website called *Women Riders* and sponsors Garage Party events for women, who are an increasing proportion of Harley's customer base.[84]
- Nike has an entire golf and apparel line targeted to women, along with an entire section on its website featuring these products as well as the Nike Training Club app available through iTunes.

The terms *sex* and **gender** are used interchangeably to refer to *whether a person is biologically a male or a female.* **Gender identity** refers to *the traits of femininity* (expressive traits such as tenderness and compassion) *and masculinity* (instrumental traits such as aggressiveness and dominance). These traits represent the ends of a continuum, and individuals have varying levels of each trait, with biological males tending to be toward the masculine end of the continuum and biological females toward the feminine end.[85]

Gender roles are *the behaviors considered appropriate for males and females in a given society.* As the previous discussion of automobile purchasing indicates, gender roles in America have undergone massive changes over the past 30 years. Much of this shift has been for behaviors previously considered appropriate primarily for men to be acceptable for women too. But also, as we saw in the opener, there is a shift for behaviors previously considered appropriate primarily for women to be acceptable for men too.

Gender roles are ascribed roles. An **ascribed role** is based on *an attribute over which the individual has little or no control.* This can be contrasted with an **achievement role,** which is based on *performance criteria over which the individual has some degree of control.* Individuals can, within limits, select their occupational role (achievement role), but they cannot generally determine their gender (ascribed role).

It can be useful to distinguish **traditional** or **modern gender orientations** on the basis of preference for one or the other of two contrasting married lifestyles:

- *Traditional.* A marriage in which the husband assumes the responsibility for providing for the family and the wife runs the house and takes care of the children.
- *Modern.* A marriage in which husband and wife share responsibilities. Both work, and they share homemaking and child care responsibilities.

Americans have certainly moved toward a *preference* for a modern lifestyle, from only 35 percent in 1977 to 71 percent in the most recent polls.[86] In addition, only 25 percent agree that women should return to their traditional roles and 87 percent agree that fathers are just as capable as mothers of caring for their children.[87] However, while males and females both express strong preferences for the modern lifestyle as a general concept, most recognize that it comes with a cost. For example, 80 percent of mothers with children age five or under would prefer to stay home with their children if it were totally up to them,[88] and nearly half of both men and women believe that it was easier when "women stayed at home and men went to work."[89]

As the opener indicated, men's participation in household duties is on the rise. It is important to realize, however, that the focus there was on all men, whether married or single. However, for married men, while participation in household tasks has increased, the general pattern still follows more traditional gender roles. The following Gallup Poll results show the breakout of household chores in terms of who is most likely to do them. The figures for each activity represent the percent response to the question, "Who is most likely to do each of the following in your household?"

Activity	Husband (%)	Wife (%)
Keep the car in good condition	69	13
Do yard work	57	12
Handle investments	35	18
Do grocery shopping	16	53
Do laundry	10	68
Clean house	9	54

Source: F. Newport, "Wives Still Do Laundry, Men Do Yard Work," *Gallup,* 2008 www.gallup.com, accessed May 26, 2008.

ILLUSTRATION 3-8

Women fulfill a multitude of roles today and have a wide range of attitudes about their roles in society. These two ads take radically different approaches to the portrayal of women and women's attitudes.

These numbers have not changed much since the mid-1990s. And the fact that only 2 of the 11 activities are ones for which the male took majority responsibility means wives are left to do most of the work at home even though they also work outside the home. Given that 62 percent believe that "sharing household chores" is very important to a successful marriage,[90] this can lead to strong resentments, as the following quote demonstrates:

> "It's a blowout fight every month," Hope (32 and a book editor) confesses. "It's the only thing we fight about." Hope says getting Cohen (34 and a medical resident) to do his agreed-upon tasks requires constant reminders. "He'll tell me he'll wash the dishes before we go to bed, and maybe he will," she says. "But by around 9:30, with dirty dishes still in the sink, I'm broiling."[91]

With high levels of role overload and stress associated with dual-income families, many Americans are realizing that they can't have it all, and where there is a choice, some are opting for change. Sometimes the change is toward the nontraditional, as in the increasing numbers of "stay-at-home" dads.[92] Sometimes the change is toward the traditional, as in the recent increase in "stay-at-home" moms.[93]

As we have seen, women have a variety of role options and a range of attitudes concerning their gender roles. The ads in Illustration 3–8 reflect two sharply contrasting views of the female role. Next, we examine some of the marketing implications of the changing roles of women in American society.

Market Segmentation Neither the women's nor the men's market is as homogeneous as it once was. At least four significant female market segments exist:[94]

1. *Traditional housewife.* Generally married. Prefers to stay at home. Very home and family centered. Desires to please husband and children. Seeks satisfaction and meaning from household and family maintenance as well as volunteer activities. Experiences strong pressure to work outside the home and is well aware of forgone income opportunity. Feels supported by family and is generally content with role.

2. *Trapped housewife.* Generally married. Would prefer to work but stays at home because of young children, lack of outside opportunities, or family pressure. Seeks satisfaction and meaning outside the home. Does not enjoy most household chores. Has mixed feelings about current status and is concerned about lost opportunities.
3. *Trapped working woman.* Married or single. Would prefer to stay at home but works because of economic necessity or social or family pressure. Does not derive satisfaction or meaning from employment. Enjoys most household activities but is frustrated by lack of time. Feels conflict about her role, particularly if younger children are home. Resents missed opportunities for family, volunteer, and social activities. Is proud of financial contribution to family.
4. *Career working woman.* Married or single. Prefers to work. Derives satisfaction and meaning from employment rather than, or in addition to, home and family. Experiences some conflict over her role if younger children are at home but is generally content. Views home maintenance as a necessary evil. Feels pressed for time.

Although the above descriptions are oversimplified, they indicate the diverse nature of the adult female population. Notice that women may move in and out of these categories over their lifetimes. For example, an otherwise career working woman may feel more like a trapped working woman if she finds it necessary to work while her children are young. And while the career working woman category has grown significantly over the past three decades, the other segments are still sizable, unique, and important.

The male market is likewise diverse in both its attitudes and behaviors toward gender roles, work, and household chores. One classification distinguishes between modern and traditional men, whereby modern men are more focused on such factors as (a) fashion, (b) shopping, and (c) cooking.[95]

Product Strategy Many products are losing their traditional gender typing. Guns, cars, motorcycles, computer games and equipment, golf equipment, financial services, and many other once masculine products are now designed specifically with women in mind. The expanding wealth, independence, and purchasing power of women, and the time pressure on them make them an important target market. Consider the following:

- Women-headed households represent roughly 28 percent of all households. The Barbara K tool line (now Barbara's Way) targeted at women was launched in 2003 and has been highly successful. According to CEO Barbara Kavovit, "Women have made so many strides but can't fix things in their homes." The tools are designed to be stylish and functional, and have special features targeting women, such as cushioned handles.[96]
- Assaults against women are a major social problem. Smith & Wesson launched LadySmith, a line of guns designed specifically for women. They found that "if a woman is going to pull out a gun for personal protection, she doesn't want a cute gun." So rather than "feminize" men's guns with colored handles, Smith & Wesson targeted a key success criterion by redesigning its guns to fit women's hands.
- The high percentage of women working outside the home, particularly when coupled with children, can lead to high levels of time pressure and a resulting need for convenience products and services.[97] A wealth of such products and services have emerged to meet this need, as shown in Illustration 3–9.

As women's roles have expanded, the consumption of potentially harmful products has become socially acceptable for women. This, of course, raises the ethical issue of targeting groups that have not historically been heavy users of products such as alcohol or tobacco.

Marketing Communications A considerable amount of research suggests that males and females process and respond differently to various communications elements, including sexual appeals, music, verbal style, and so forth.[98] As just one example, females respond more favorably to a "help-others" type of appeal for a charity, whereas males respond best to a "self-help" appeal.[99] This is caused by differing worldviews that affect a range of communications responses as well as consumption behaviors.

ILLUSTRATION 3-9

Firms have responded to increased time pressure with new products and positioning strategies.

Men and women also consume different media and use the same media differently. For example in social media, information is a more prominent goal for men (36 percent) than women (28 percent), while finding coupons and promotions is a more prominent goal for women (47 percent) than men (33 percent).[100] Also, types of social network sites women frequent are different from those frequented by men. The top five sites for women and men based on Google Ad Planner data are as follows:

Women	Men
Bebo	Slashdot
MySpace	Reddit
Classmates.com	Digg
Xanga	Last.fm
Ning	Delicious

Source: Statistics from "Study: Males vs. Females in Social Network Sites," at http://royal.pingdom.com, accessed March 1, 2011.

Since women are quite diverse as a group, marketers must also consider such factors as ethnicity, age, life stage, and employment status differences when designing marketing communications. Ads portraying women must be careful about offending any of the various segments.[101] For example, an ad that implied that housework was unimportant or that women who work outside the home are somehow superior to those who do not could insult traditional housewives. Ads that show women primarily as decoration or as clearly inferior to males tend to produce negative responses across all female segments.[102] Despite such negative reactions, many ads still use these tactics.[103] However, some companies are hitting this issue straight on. Dove launched its "Real Beauty" campaign, which features realistic depictions of women, in response to idealized and unrealistic portrayals of women in advertising that have been shown to reduce self-esteem.

Finally, in terms of gender role portrayal, there are still relatively few ads showing men using products traditionally designed for women or performing tasks traditionally performed by women. And according to one study, only one in four men feels that consumer product ads are designed to speak to them.[104] However, this is changing. JIF has moved away from the "Choosy mothers choose JIF," to "Choosy moms and dads choose JIF," along with positive depictions of father and child interactions in their ads. The Dixie Ultra ad in Illustration 3–10 also demonstrates these changing roles. Increases in such portrayals are likely over time.

ILLUSTRATION 3-10

The Dixie Ultra ad is still somewhat unusual in that it portrays a male involved in a traditional female task. Although gender roles are changing, it is much more common to portray women performing traditional male tasks than the reverse.

Retail Strategy As we saw in the chapter opener, men and women shop differently even for the same products. Differences in loyalty, brand switching, coupon usage, and shopping styles within the store all need to be accounted for by retailers as more men take on the grocery shopping task.

In addition, men and women react differently to various aspects of retail and service environments. For example, when there is a service failure, men appear to focus mostly on problem resolution, whereas women also focus on the process by which the problem is resolved. Being able to have a voice in the resolution process is much more important for women than men. Such differences need to be built into employee training programs.[105]

SUMMARY

LO1: Understand core American cultural values

Cultural values are widely held beliefs that affirm what is desirable. Three categories of values that affect behaviors are those related to the self, others, and the environment. Sometimes numerous values are at work in affecting a given trend, as is the case with organic consumption, which is affected by values relating to family and nature.

LO2: Summarize changes in self, environment, and other-oriented values

In terms of *self-oriented* values, we place somewhat less emphasis on hard work as an end in itself, although we continue to work some of the longest hours among industrialized nations. We are trending toward greater emphasis on sensual gratification. And, while the recent recession may have tempered spending, there appears to be a move back toward greater emphasis on immediate gratification. Finally, while religion is important, America remains a relatively secular culture.

Values that affect our relationship to our *environment* have become somewhat more performance oriented and slightly less oriented toward change. There is a strong and growing value placed on protecting the natural environment, and we increasingly value risk taking.

In terms of those values that influence an individual's relationship with *others,* Americans remain individualistic. We have substantially less of a masculine orientation now than in the past. We also place a greater value on older persons and diversity.

LO3: Discuss values as they relate to green marketing

Americans have shifted their view from one of overcoming nature to more of admiring nature. This translates into greater concerns regarding the protection of our environment and the emergence of green marketing. *Green marketing* involves (1) developing products whose production, use, or disposition is less harmful to the environment than the traditional versions of the product; (2) developing products that have a positive impact on the environment; or (3) tying the purchase of a product to an environmental organization or event.

LO4: Discuss values as they relate to cause-related marketing

Americans are high on the value of problem solving. This makes us prone to want to put efforts toward causes that are important to us in an attempt to fix or improve the situation. *Cause-related marketing* is marketing that ties a company and its products to an issue or cause with the goal of improving sales and corporate image while providing benefits to the cause. Companies associate with causes to create long-term relationships with their customers, building corporate and brand equity that should eventually lead to increased sales.

LO5: Discuss values as they relate to marketing to gay and lesbian consumers

The value placed on diversity continues to increase, including openness to alternative lifestyles and family structures including same-sex couples. The *gay market* is estimated at roughly 16 million people over the age of 18 with purchasing power between $750 and $900 billion. Many companies view the gay market as highly attractive and have committed considerable resources to targeting this market with specific products and promotional efforts. Supportive internal policies toward gay employees as well as support for important gay causes are among the critical factors in approaching this market.

LO6: Discuss values as they relate to gender-based marketing

The ongoing shift from a traditionally masculine view toward a balanced masculine-feminine view has resulted in changing gender roles. *Gender roles* have undergone radical changes in the past 30 years. A fundamental shift has been for the female role to become more like the traditional male role. Male roles are also evolving, with men beginning to take on what have traditionally been considered female tasks. Virtually all aspects of our society, including marketing activities, have been affected by these shifts.

KEY TERMS

Achievement role 96
Ascribed role 96
Cause-related marketing (CRM) 90
Cultural values 78
Enviropreneurial marketing 85
Gender 96
Gender identity 96
Gender role 96
Green marketing 88
Greenwashing 89
Modern gender orientation 96
Traditional gender orientation 96
Voluntary simplicity 81

REVIEW QUESTIONS

1. What is a *cultural value?* Do all members of a culture share cultural values?
2. Describe the current American culture in terms of each of the 18 values discussed in this chapter.
3. How is *voluntary simplicity* related to the materialism value? What are the marketing implications of voluntary simplicity? Do these implications vary by product class?
4. What is *green marketing?*
5. What values underlie green marketing?
6. How is *enviropreneurial marketing* related to new product success and market share? Link this to the value of green marketing in creating a competitive advantage.
7. Describe the basic conflict between the environmental movement and many businesses.
8. What is *cause-related marketing?* Why is it often successful?
9. What are the major decisions a firm faces with respect to the gay market?
10. What is meant by *gender?*
11. What is *gender identity?*
12. What is a *gender role?*
13. How does an *ascribed role* differ from an *achievement role?*
14. What is happening to male and female gender roles in America?
15. What are the differences between a traditional and a modern gender role orientation?
16. Describe a segmentation system for the female market based on employment status and gender role orientation.
17. What are some of the major marketing implications of the changing role of women?

DISCUSSION QUESTIONS

18. Describe additional values you feel could, or should, be added to Figure 3–1. Describe the marketing implications of each.
19. Pick the three values you feel the authors of this book were most *in*accurate about in the chapter in describing the *current* American values. Justify your answers.
20. Pick the three values you feel the authors were most *in*accurate about in describing the *emerging* American values. Justify your answers.
21. Respond to the questions in Consumer Insight 3–1.
22. Which values are most relevant to the purchase or use of the following? Are they currently favorable or unfavorable for ownership/use? Are they shifting at all? If so, is the shift in a favorable or unfavorable direction?
    a. Dietary supplements
    b. The Salvation Army
    c. Financial investments (stocks, mutual funds, etc.)
    d. Home theater systems
    e. Tanning salon
    f. Expensive Jewelry
23. Do you believe Americans' concern for the environment is a stronger value than their materialism?

24. What ethical issues do you see relating to green marketing?

25. Explain greenwashing and its possible role in the FTC's revision of the Green Guides.
26. Cause-related marketing is done to enhance a firm's sales or image. Some critics consider such marketing to be unethical. What is your position?

27. In which of the four categories of responders to cause-related marketing are you? Why?
28. Suppose AT&T showed a gay couple using its long-distance service or P&G showed a gay couple using one of its laundry products in ads on network television. Is a backlash by those who do not accept the gay community a likely response? How are such consumers likely to respond? Why?
29. Do you think housewives may be defensive or sensitive about not having employment outside of

the home? If so, what implications will this have for marketing practice?

30. Develop an advertisement for the following for each of the four female market segments described in the chapter.
    a. Bicycles
    b. iPad
    c. Exercise equipment
    d. Breakfast cereal
    e. Vacation cruises
    f. Cosmetics

APPLICATION ACTIVITIES

31. Find and copy or describe an advertisement for an item that reflects Americans' position on the following values:
    a. Active/Passive
    b. Material/Nonmaterial
    c. Hard work/Leisure
    d. Postponed/Immediate gratification
    e. Sensual gratification/Abstinence
    f. Religious/Secular
    g. Cleanliness
    h. Performance/Status
    i. Tradition/Change
    j. Risk taking/Security
    k. Problem solving/Fatalistic
    l. Admire/Overcome nature
    m. Individual/Collective
    n. Limited/Extended family
    o. Diversity/Uniformity
    p. Competition/Cooperation
    q. Youth/Age
    r. Masculine/Feminine
32. Interview a person who consumes one or more organic food items. What values influence this consumption pattern?
33. Interview a salesperson who has been selling the following for at least 10 years. See if this individual has noticed a change in the purchasing roles of women over time.
    a. Electric guitars
    b. Cell phones
    c. Computers
    d. Homes
    e. Financial services
34. Interview a career-oriented working wife and a traditional housewife of a similar age. Report on differences in attitudes toward shopping, products, and so forth.
35. Form a team of five. Have each team member interview five married adult males. Based on these interviews, develop a typology that classifies them by their attitude toward and participation in household or child-rearing activities.
36. Pick two different environmental segments from Table 3–1. Find one advertisement you think is particularly appropriate or effective for each. Copy or describe each ad and justify its selection.
37. Interview a salesperson for each of the following. Ascertain the interest shown in the item by males and females. Determine if males and females are concerned with different characteristics of the item and if they have different purchase motivations.
    a. Art
    b. Automobiles
    c. Golf clubs
    d. Personal care items
    e. Clothing
    f. Gardening tools
38. Interview 10 male and 10 female students. Ask each to describe the typical owner or consumer of the following. If they do not specify, ask for the gender of the typical owner. Then probe to find out why they think the typical owner is of the gender they indicated. Also determine the perceived marital and occupational status of the typical owner and the reasons for these beliefs.
    a. Pet snake
    b. Pasta maker
    c. Large life insurance policy
    d. Power tools
    e. Habitat for Humanity contributor
    f. Personal fitness trainer

REFERENCES

1. Opener based on M. De Mooij and G. Hofstede, "The Hofstede Model," *International Journal of Advertising*, 29 (2010), pp. 85–110; B. Fuller, "Understanding the Male Grocery Shopper," *Promo*, September 15, 2010; and J. Neff, "Time to Rethink Your Message," *Advertising Age*, January 17, 2011.
2. E. Gurel-Atay et al., "Changes in Social Values in the United States," *Journal of Advertising Research*, March 2010, pp. 57–67.
3. Numbers are for 2010 based on a Gallup poll reported at www.gallup.com/poll/1690/religion.aspx, accessed February 20, 2011.
4. W. H. Henley et al., "The Effects of Symbol Product Relevance and Religiosity on Consumer Perceptions of Religious Symbols in Advertising," *Journal of Current Issues and Research in Advertising*, Spring 2009, pp. 89–103.
5. Public Agenda, "New Survey Shows Religious Americans Less Likely to Support Compromise," press release, January 23, 2005, www.publicagenda.org.
6. R. Gardyn, "Breaking the Rules of Engagement," *American Demographics*, July–August 2002, p. 35.
7. B. A. Robinson, "How Many People Go Regularly to Weekly Religious Services?," Ontario Consultants on Religious Tolerance, November 26, 2001, www.religioustolerance.org.
8. Henley et al., "The Effects of Symbol Product Relevance and Religiosity on Consumer Perceptions of Religious Symbols in Advertising."
9. J. Flint, "Angry NFL Slams ABC's 'Desperate Housewives' Promo," *The Wall Street Journal Online*, November 17, 2004, www.wsj.com.
10. L. Petrecca, "Axe Ads Turn up the Promise of Sex Appeal," *USAToday*, April 18, 2007, at www.usatoday.com, accessed February 20, 2011; H-J. Paek et al., "A Cross-Cultural and Cross-Media Comparison of Female Nudity in Advertising," *Journal of Promotion Management*, 13, no. 1/2 (2007), pp. 145–67; and J. Sengupta and D. W. Dahl, "Gender-Related Reactions to Gratuitous Sex Appeals in Advertising," *Journal of Consumer Psychology*, 18 (2008), pp. 62–78.
11. Gurel-Atay et al., "Changes in Social Values in the United States."
12. S. Thompson, "Minor Indulgence Keeps Cookies from Tanking," *Advertising Age*, June 28, 2004, p. S-18.
13. S. Theil, "The Urge to Splurge Is Creeping Back," *Newsweek*, November 29, 2010, www.newsweek.com/urge-splurge-creeping-back-70101.
14. L. J. Shrum, J. E. Burroughs, and A. Rindfleisch, "Television's Cultivation of Material Values," *Journal of Consumer Research*, December 2005, pp. 473–79.
15. Theil, "The Urge to Splurge Is Creeping Back."
16. S. Zavestoski, "The Social-Psychological Bases of Anticonsumption Attitudes," *Psychology & Marketing*, February 2002, p. 155.
17. A. Etzioni, "Voluntary Simplicity," *Journal of Economic Psychology* 19 (1998), pp. 619–43; Zavestoski, "The Social-Psychological Bases of Anticonsumption Attitudes"; M. Craig-Lees and C. Hill, "Understanding Voluntary Simplifiers," *Psychology & Marketing*, February 2002, pp. 197–210; and S. McDonald et al., "Toward Sustainable Consumption," *Psychology & Marketing*, June 2006, pp. 515–34.
18. These statistics drawn from *Statistical Abstract of the United States* (Washington, DC: U.S. Census Bureau, 2011), Labor Force, Employment, and Earnings, tables 644, 602, and 597 respectively.
19. A. C. Brooks, "I Love My Work," *The American*, September/October 2007, accessed February 21, 2011.
20. "Fewer Mothers Prefer Full-Time Work," *PewResearchCenter Publications*, July 12, 2007.
21. "New Survey from Xobni on Email Overload Shows There Is No Such Thing as a Day Off for Americans and Brits," *PR Newswire*, September 2, 2010.
22. See P. Paul, "Targeting Boomers," *American Demographics*, March 2003, pp. 24–26; and J. Consoli, "Where Have All the Young Men Gone?," *Mediaweek*, October 20, 2003, pp. 4–5.
23. M. Slatalla, "Overscheduled?," *Time*, July 24, 2000, p. 79.
24. T. Cahill, "Exotic Places Made Me Do It," *Outside*, March 2002, p. 60.
25. See J. P. Robinson and M. Milke, "Dances with Dust Bunnies," *American Demographics*, January 1997, pp. 37–40; and A. Miller, "The Millennial Mind-Set," *American Demographics*, January 1999, pp. 62–63.
26. P. Tyre, "Clean Freaks," *Newsweek*, June 7, 2004, p. 42.
27. "Cash and Carry," *American Demographics*, May 2000, p. 45.
28. "Creativity at Work," *American Demographics*, December 2002–January 2003, pp. 22–23; D. Kiley, "It's Back . . . Fiat Launches 500, Slights Mass for Creative Class," *Advertising Age*, January 31, 2011, pp. 1 and 8.
29. Gurel-Atay et al., "Changes in Social Values in the United States."
30. "Public Worried but Not Panicked about Economy," *PewResearchCenter Publications*, October 15, 2008.
31. R. E. Dunlap, "The State of Environmentalism in the U.S.," *Gallup*, 2007, www.gallup.com, accessed May 25, 2008; J. M. Jones, "In the U.S., 28% Report Major Changes to Live 'Green,'" *Gallup*, 2008, www.gallup.com, accessed May 25, 2008; *Public Agenda Online*, www.publicagenda.org, accessed May 25, 2008; and J. Loechner, "Consumers Want Proof It's Green," *MediaPost*, April 9, 2009, www.mediapost.com, accessed February 19, 2011.
32. TNS News Center, "TNS Global Study 'The Green Life' Reveals Spectrum of Environmental Attitudes across United States and the World," press release, April 30, 2008, accessed at www.tnsglobal.com on February 20, 2011; J. Gartner, "Consumer Shades of Green Identified," *MatterNetwork.com*, June 9, 2008, accessed February 21, 2011; "Do 'Green' Conscious Consumers Practice What They Preach?," *BusinessWire*, September 29, 2008; and "IRI/TNS Shades of Green Segmentation™," *Data Sheet*, accessed from www.infores.com on February 21, 2011.

33. W. E. Baker and J. M. Sinkula, "Environmental Marketing Strategy and Firm Performance," *Journal of the Academy of Marketing Science,* 33, no. 4 (2005), pp. 461–75; and F. Ross, T. Martinez, and M. Molina, "How Green Should You Be?," *Journal of Advertising Research,* December 2008, pp. 547–63.
34. A. C. Cuneo, "What's in Store," *Advertising Age,* February 25, 2002, p. 1.
35. M. J. Dutta-Bergman and W. D. Wells, "The Values and Lifestyles of Idiocentrics and Allocentrics in an Individualistic Culture," *Journal of Consumer Psychology,* 12, no. 3 (2002), pp. 231–42.
36. B. S. C. Liu, O. Furrer, and D. Sudharshan, "The Relationship between Culture and Behavioral Intentions toward Services," *Journal of Service Research,* November 2001, pp. 118–29.
37. J. Halliday, "Tuners Fit In with Customizer Fare," *Advertising Age,* May 31, 2004, p. S-8.
38. S. A. Grier, A. M. Brumbaugh, and C. G. Thornton, "Crossover Dreams," *Journal of Marketing,* April 2006, pp. 35–51.
39. Ibid.
40. "Millennials' Judgments about Recent Trends Not So Different," *PewResearchCenter Publications,* January 7, 2010.
41. R. Suro, "Movement at Warp Speed," *American Demographics,* August 2000, pp. 61–64.
42. See, e.g., C. A. Lin, "Cultural Values Reflected in Chinese and American Television Advertising," *Journal of Advertising,* Winter 2001, pp. 83–94.
43. C. R. Wiles, J. A. Wiles, and A. Tjernlund, "The Ideology of Advertising," *Journal of Advertising Research,* May–June 1996, pp. 57–66. See also P. Simcock and L. Sudbury, "The Invisible Majority?," *International Journal of Advertising,* 25, no. 1 (2006), pp. 87–106.
44. F. Newport, "Americans Continue to Express Slight Preference for Boys," *Gallup,* July 5, 2007, www.gallup.com, accessed May 26, 2008.
45. *Women's Sports and Physical Activity Facts and Statistics* (EastMeadow: Women's Sports Foundation, May 17, 2008).
46. D. W. Moore, "Americans More Accepting of Female Bosses Than Ever," *Gallup,* May 10, 2002, www.gallup.com, accessed May 26, 2008.
47. J. Ottman, "Innovative Marketers Give New Products the Green Light," *Marketing News,* March 1998, p. 10; and "Investors, Big Businesses See Green in Being Green," *CNN.com,* August 20, 2007, www.cnn.com, accessed December 1, 2008.
48. M. Gunther, "The Green Machine," *Fortune,* August 7, 2006, pp. 42–57; B. Steinberg, "Buy a Spot, Save the Planet," *Advertising Age,* January 11, 2011, pp. 1 and 18; and information available through corporate websites.
49. J. Neff, "Has Green Stopped Giving?," *Advertising Age,* November 8, 2010, pp. 1 and 19; and J. Loechner, "Consumers Want Proof It's Green," *MediaPost,* April 9, 2009.
50. M. Glover, "Why Honda Accord Hybrid Ran Out of Gas," *Knight Ridder Tribune Business News,* June 13, 2007, p. 1.
51. J. Neff, "FTC Goes After Broad Environmental Clams in Long-Awaited Guideline Revision," *Advertising Age,* October 6, 2010; and "Green Means Go on the Enforcement Highway," *Consumer Advertising Law Blog,* at www.consumeradvertisinglawblog.com, accessed February 19, 2011.
52. "Green Guides: Summary of Proposal," at www.ftc.gov, accessed February 18, 2011.
53. See, e.g., P. S. Bronn and A. B. Vrioni, "Corporate Social Responsibility and Cause-Related Marketing," *International Journal of Advertising,* 2 (2001), pp. 207–21.
54. M. J. Barone, A. D. Miyazaki, and K. A. Taylor, "The Influence of Cause-Related Marketing on Consumer Choice," *Journal of the Academy of Marketing Science,* Spring 2000, pp. 248–62; and S. Sen and C. B. Bhattacharya, "Does Doing Good Always Lead to Doing Better?," *Journal of Marketing Research,* May 2001, pp. 225–43.
55. Cone Incorporated, "Multi-Year Study Finds 21% Increase in Americans Who Say Corporate Support for Social Issues is Important in Building Trust," press release, December 8, 2004, www.coneinc.com; and "The Do Well Do Good Public Opinion Survey on Cause-Marketing," Summary Report accessed at www.dowelldogood.net on February 24, 2011.
56. "The Growth of Cause Marketing," *Cause Marketing Forum,* www.causemarketingforum.com, accessed May 26, 2008.
57. P. A. Vlachos et al., "Corporate Social Responsibility," *Journal of the Academy of Marketing Science,* 37 (2009), pp. 170–80.
58. D. J. Webb and L. A. Mohr, "A Typology of Consumer Responses to Cause-Related Marketing," *Journal of Public Policy & Marketing,* Fall 1998, pp. 226–38.
59. J. W. Pracejus and G. D. Olsen, "The Role of Brand/Cause Fit in the Effectiveness of Cause-Related Marketing Campaigns," *Journal of Business Research,* 57 (2004), pp. 635–40; N. J. Rifon et al., "Congruence Effects in Sponsorship," *Journal of Advertising,* Spring 2004, pp. 29–42; and X. Nan and K. Heo, "Consumer Responses to Corporate Social Responsibility (CSR) Initiatives," *Journal of Advertising,* Summer 2007, pp. 63–74.
60. Additional information about these programs can be found on each company's website. See also the Cause Marketing Forum at www.causemarketingforum.com.
61. C. Hays, "Stores That Pop UP and Go Away, on Purpose," *The New York Times,* December 7, 2004, www.nytimes.com/2004/12/07/business/businessspecial/07HAYS.html?_r=0, accessed August 25, 2014. See also S. Hallock, "Taking Aim at Breast Cancer," *Time Magazine,* October 4, 2004, http://content.time.com/time/magazine/article/0,9171,995259,00.html#ixzz2nffbml4b, accessed August 25, 2014.
62. Habitat for Humanity, "Whirlpool Brand and Habitat for Humanity Announce House Build Locations for 2013," press release, February 27, 2013, www.habitat.org/newsroom/2013archive/02_27_2013_Whirlpool_Habitat.aspx, accessed August 25, 2014.
63. P&G, "Bringing Loads of Hope to Colorado," press release, September 20, 2013, http://news.pg.com/blog/sustainability/bringing-loads-hope-colorado, accessed August 25, 2014.
64. S. Rozensher, "The Growth of Cause Marketing: Past, Current, and Future Trends," *Journal of Business & Economics Research (online),* 11, no. 4 (2013), p. 181. For the possible downside effects, see A. Eikenberry, "The Hidden Costs of Cause Marketing," *Stanford Social Innovation Review*, 7, no. 3 (2009), pp. 51–56.

65. J. Chu, "Toms Sets Out to Sell a Lifestyle, Not Just Shoes," *FastCompany.com,* June 17, 2013, www.fastcompany.com/3012568/blake-mycoskie-toms, accessed August 25, 2014; and T. Montague, "The Rise of Storydoing," *FastCompany.com,* August 5, 2013, www.fastcompany.com/3015209/leadership-now/the-rise-of-storydoing-inside-the-staggering-success-of-toms-shoes, accessed August 25, 2014.

66. L. Saad, "Americans' Acceptance of Gay Relations Crosses 50% Threshold," *Gallup Annual Values and Beliefs Survey,* at www.gallup.com, accessed February 24, 2011.

67. "Gay Rights: Seven in 10 Americans Say They Would Favor Hate Crime Laws to Protect Gays and Lesbians," *Public Agenda Online,* www.publicagenda.org, accessed April 18, 2005; and "Most Continue to Favor Gays Serving Openly in Military," *PewResearchCenter Publications,* November 29, 2010, at www.pewresearch.org, accessed February 20, 2011.

68. "The Gay and Lesbian Market in the U.S.," *Packaged Facts,* July 2010.

69. Ibid.

70. Ibid., pp. 181–82; and M. Gunther, "Wal-Mart Becomes Gay-Friendly," *CNNMoney.com,* November 30, 2006, www.cnnmoney.com, accessed May 27, 2008.

71. D. L. Vence, "Pride Power," *Marketing News,* September 1, 2004, pp. 1, 13.

72. "The Gay and Lesbian Market in the U.S.," *Packaged Facts,* February 2007.

73. L. Koss-Feder, "Out and About," *Marketing News,* May 25, 1998, pp. 1, 20.

74. *2009 Gay Press Report* (Mountainside, NJ: 11th Annual Report by Prime Access Inc. and Rivendell Media Company Inc., 2004), available at www.gaymarket.com/agency_reports.html. See also M. Gunther, "Courting the Gay Consumer," *CNNMoney.com,* December 7, 2006.

75. "The Gay and Lesbian Market in the U.S." (2010).

76. R. Greenspan, "Advertisers May Find Gay Dollars Online," July 30, 2003, www.clickz.com.

77. *2009 Gay Press Report.*

78. "The Gay and Lesbian Market in the U.S." (2007).

79. R. Gardyn, "A Market Kept in the Closet," *American Demographics,* November 2001, pp. 37–42; see also J. J. Burnett, "Gays," *Journal of Advertising Research,* January 2000, pp. 75–83.

80. R. Greenspan, "Gays Access News, Influenced by Ads," May 17, 2004, www.clickz.com.

81. J. L. Aaker, A. M. Brumbaugh, and S. A. Grier, "Nontarget Market and Viewer Distinctiveness," *Journal of Consumer Psychology,* 3 (2000), pp. 127–40; and G. Oakenfull and T. Greenlee, "The Three Rules of Crossing Over from Gay Media to Mainstream Media Advertising," *Journal of Business Research,* 57 (2004), pp. 1276–85.

82. G. K. Oakenfull and T. B. Greenlee, "Queer Eye for a Gay Guy," *Psychology & Marketing,* May 2005, pp. 421–39. See also G. K. Oakenfull, M. S. McCarthy, and T. G. Greenlee, "Targeting a Minority without Alienating the Majority," *Journal of Advertising Research,* June 2008, pp. 191–98.

83. For these and other statistics, go to the *About 4-Wheel Drive/Offroading* website at http://4wheeldrive.about.com.

84. C. Krauss, "Harley Woos Female Bikers," *The New York Times,* July 25, 2007.

85. E. Fischer and S. J. Arnold, "Sex, Gender Identity, Gender Role Attitudes, and Consumer Behavior," *Psychology & Marketing,* March 1994, pp. 163–82; see also K. M. Palan, C. S. Areni, and P. Kiecker, "Gender Role Incongruity and Memorable Gift Exchange Experiences," in *Advances in Consumer Research,* ed. M. Gilly and J. Meyers-Levy (Provo, UT: Association for Consumer Research, 2001), pp. 51–57.

86. J. S. Grigsby, "Women Change Places," *American Demographics,* November 1992, p. 48; and "Gender Equality Universally Embraced, but Inequalities Acknowledged," *Pew Global Attitudes Project,* July 1, 2010, at www.pewglobal.org, accessed March 1, 2011.

87. "Child Care: Most People Say Fathers Can Be Just as Caring as Mothers and That Women Should Not Return to Their Traditional Roles," *Public Agenda Online,* www.publicagenda.org, accessed April 24, 2005.

88. "Child Care: Most Women Say That Mothers Who Work Outside the Home Are under More Stress Than Mothers Who Stay Home and Most Mothers Say They Would Prefer to Stay at Home," *Public Agenda Online,* www.publicagenda.org, accessed April 24, 2005.

89. "The Reality of the Working Woman," *Ad Age Insights White Paper,* June 7, 2010, p. 6.

90. "As Marriage and Parenthood Drift Apart Public Is Concerned About Social Impact, *PewResearchCenter Publications,* July 1, 2007.

91. P. Paul, "Whose Job Is This Anyway?," *Time,* October 4, 2004, p. 83.

92. A. Taylor, "Many Fathers Begin to Stay at Home with Children," *Knight Ridder Tribune Business News,* June 20, 2004, p. 1.

93. A. Rock, "From Two Incomes to One," *Money,* January 2005, p. 34.

94. These segments are similar to the four categories popularized by Bartos. See C. M. Schaninger, M. C. Nelson, and W. D. Danko, "An Empirical Evaluation of the Bartos Model," *Journal of Advertising Research,* May 1993, pp. 49–63; and R. Bartos, "Bartos Responds to 'The Bartos Model,'" *Journal of Advertising Research,* January 1994, pp. 54–56.

95. "The U.S. Men's Market," *Packaged Facts,* November 2007.

96. A. Tsao, "Retooling Home Improvement," *BusinessWeek Online,* February 15, 2005, www.businessweek.com.

97. See, e.g., M. Posig and J. Kickul, "Work-Role Expectations and Work Family Conflict," *Women in Management Review* 19, no. 7/8 (2004), pp. 373–86; J. Warner, "Mommy Madness," *Newsweek,* February 21, 2005, p. 42; and "The Female Midlife Crisis," *The Wall Street Journal,* April 7, 2005, p. D1.

98. See, e.g., L. D. Wolin, "Gender Issues in Advertising," *Journal of Advertising Research,* March 2003, pp. 111–29; and S. Putrevu, "Communicating with the Sexes," *Journal of Advertising,* Fall 2004, pp. 51–62.

99. F. F. Brunel and M. R. Nelson, "Explaining Gender Responses to 'Help-Self' and 'Help-Others' Charity Ad Appeals," *Journal of Advertising,* Fall 2000, pp. 15–28.

100. R. H. Levey, "Survey Shows Gender Differences in Retail Social Media Use," *Chief Marketer,* January 4, 2011.

101. See R. Widgery, M. G. Angur, and R. Nataraajan, "The Impact of Employment Status on Married Women's Perceptions of Advertising Message Appeals," *Journal of Advertising Research,* January 1997, pp. 54–62; and S. Feiereisen, A. J. Broderick, and S. P. Douglas, "The Effect and Moderation of Gender Identity Congruity," *Psychology and Marketing* 26, no. 9 (2009), pp. 813–43.

102. M. S. LaTour, T. L. Henthorne, and A. J. Williams, "Is Industrial Advertising Still Sexist?," *Industrial Marketing Management,* 1998, pp. 247–55; and M. Y. Jones, A. J. S. Stanaland, and B. D. Gelb, "Beefcake and Cheesecake," *Journal of Advertising,* Summer 1998, pp. 33–51.

103. For a cross-cultural meta-analysis of this topic, see M. Eisend, "A Meta-Analysis of Gender Roles in Advertising," *Journal of the Academy of Marketing Science* 38 (2010), pp. 418–40.

104. Neff, "Time to Rethink Your Message."

105. J. R. McColl-Kennedy, C. S. Daus, and B. A. Sparks, "The Role of Gender in Reactions to Service Failure and Recovery," *Journal of Service Research,* August 2003, pp. 66–82; see also A. S. Mattila, A. A. Grandey, and G. M. Fisk, "The Interplay of Gender and Affective Tone in Service Encounter Satisfaction," *Journal of Service Research,* November 2003, pp. 136–43.

chapter

4 The Changing American Society: Demographics and Social Stratification

LEARNING OBJECTIVES

LO1 **Understand the critical role that demographics play in influencing consumer behavior.**

LO2 **Define the concept of generations and discuss the generations that exist in America.**

LO3 **Explain the concept of social stratification and the role that socioeconomic factors play.**

LO4 **Identify and discuss the major social classes in America.**

LO5 **Understand how social class is measured.**

LO6 **Discuss the role of social class in developing marketing strategies.**

Technology is hot. And marketers want to know who the heavy users are and what traits characterize them so they can better understand this market and meet their needs. Scarborough Research recently conducted a national survey of adults 18 and older to find what they call the **Digital Savvy** consumer.[1] Digital Savvy consumers *are leading-edge digital users who are early adopters and diffusers of information related to technology in terms of (1) technology ownership, (2) Internet usage, and (3) cell phone feature usage.* Scarborough identified 18 different behaviors relating to these three dimensions that differentiated the Digital Savvy from the general population. Digital Savvy consumers are those who meet 8 or more of the 18 total technology behaviors. They represent 6 percent of the U.S. population, or roughly 14 million adults! Having identified this group, Scarborough went about characterizing it in terms of tech behaviors, demographics, lifestyle, and media usage. Some of the key results include

- *Technology Behaviors:* The Digital Savvy outstrip the general population in every category of technology, including MP3 and DVR ownership, online banking, online streaming video, text messaging, and e-mail use via cell phone.
- *Demographics:* The Digital Savvy have a very distinct demographic profile. They trended younger, white collar, male, higher education, higher income. And while it is commonly believed that technology is mostly a youth market, Digital Savvy consumers are found across all age categories, and the youngest age category is not even the most Digital Savvy. The table below shows the age distribution of Digital Savvy consumers compared with the general population.

Age	General Population (%)	Digital Savvy (%)
18–24	13	22
25–34	18	31
35–44	19	24
45–54	19	16
55–64	14	7
65+	17	1

Source: Adapted from "Understanding the Digital Savvy Consumer," *Scarborough Research,* 2008, www.scarborough.com.

- *Lifestyle:* The Digital Savvy's lifestyles are characterized by luxury purchases (upscale restaurants and luxury cars) and travel to exotic destinations, such as East Asia, the Middle East, and Hawaii. They are heavy online spenders who are also active and athletic (yoga, golf, bowling, adult education) and are sports fans.
- *Media:* The Digital Savvy are heavy users of digital media. In terms of traditional

media, they tend to be slightly higher in radio, about average in newspapers, and somewhat lower in TV except for high-end TV such as pay-per-view and premium channels. They watch news, sports, and family programs (many are married with kids). They also tend to watch ethnically oriented programming because this group trends higher Asian and Hispanic.

Marketers must segment and understand their markets. Demographics are an important aspect in this process, as the opening example suggests. In this chapter, we will discuss the closely related concepts of demographics and social status. As we will see, several demographic variables—income, education, and occupation—serve as dimensions of social status, and they combine with others to determine social class. We will first take a broad look at the demographics of the American society, with particular attention to age and its related concept, generations. Then we will consider social status and the role that demographics play in social status.

DEMOGRAPHICS

Demographics *describe a population in terms of its size, distribution, and structure* (see also Chapter 2). Demographics influence consumption behaviors both directly and by affecting other attributes of individuals, such as their personal values and decision styles.[2] Consider the demographics of the devoted high-end coffee shop crowd:

> Today's most devoted coffee shop patrons are 18- to 34-year-olds and those with annual incomes over $75,000. Forty-two percent of the 18- to 34-year-olds and 46 percent of those who earn more than $75,000 say that when they drink coffee away from home, they head straight for Starbucks-like shops, compared with just 32 percent of all away-from-home coffee drinkers. The younger folks are attracted to the coffee-bar atmosphere, music selections, and what tends to be a younger customer base, while the wealthy simply want the best.[3]

Not surprisingly, marketers frequently segment and describe their markets on the basis of demographics and use that information to select appropriate media and develop effective promotional themes. As the opening example suggests, demographics are often related to values, lifestyles, and media patterns in important ways.

Population Size and Distribution

The population of the United States is approximately 320 million and is expected to surpass 340 million by 2020. The population has grown steadily since 1960 despite birthrates that were on a strong decline through the mid-1970s and birthrates that have held relatively steady since. This steady overall growth can be attributed to longer life expectancies, the large baby boom generation moving through the child-bearing years, and significant immigration. Population growth is expected to remain relatively steady over the next several decades, but the increasing number of deaths due to the aging of the population is expected to result in reduced population growth of about 20 percent over the next five decades. That is, the overall U.S. population will continue to grow, just at a slower rate over time.[4]

Population growth has not been even throughout the United States, nor is it expected to be so in the future. For example, from 2010 to 2020, states like Arizona, Nevada, Texas, and Florida are predicted to grow by at least 15 percent. Growth in these states is being fueled in part by the retirement and migration of older consumers and in part by immigration. In contrast, states like New York, Ohio, Iowa, and North Dakota are expected to grow by less than 2 percent.[5] As we discuss in the next chapter, regions of the country serve as important subcultures whose members have unique tastes and preferences. Several examples of these differences are shown in Figure 4–1.

A Tale of Three Cities **FIGURE 4-1**

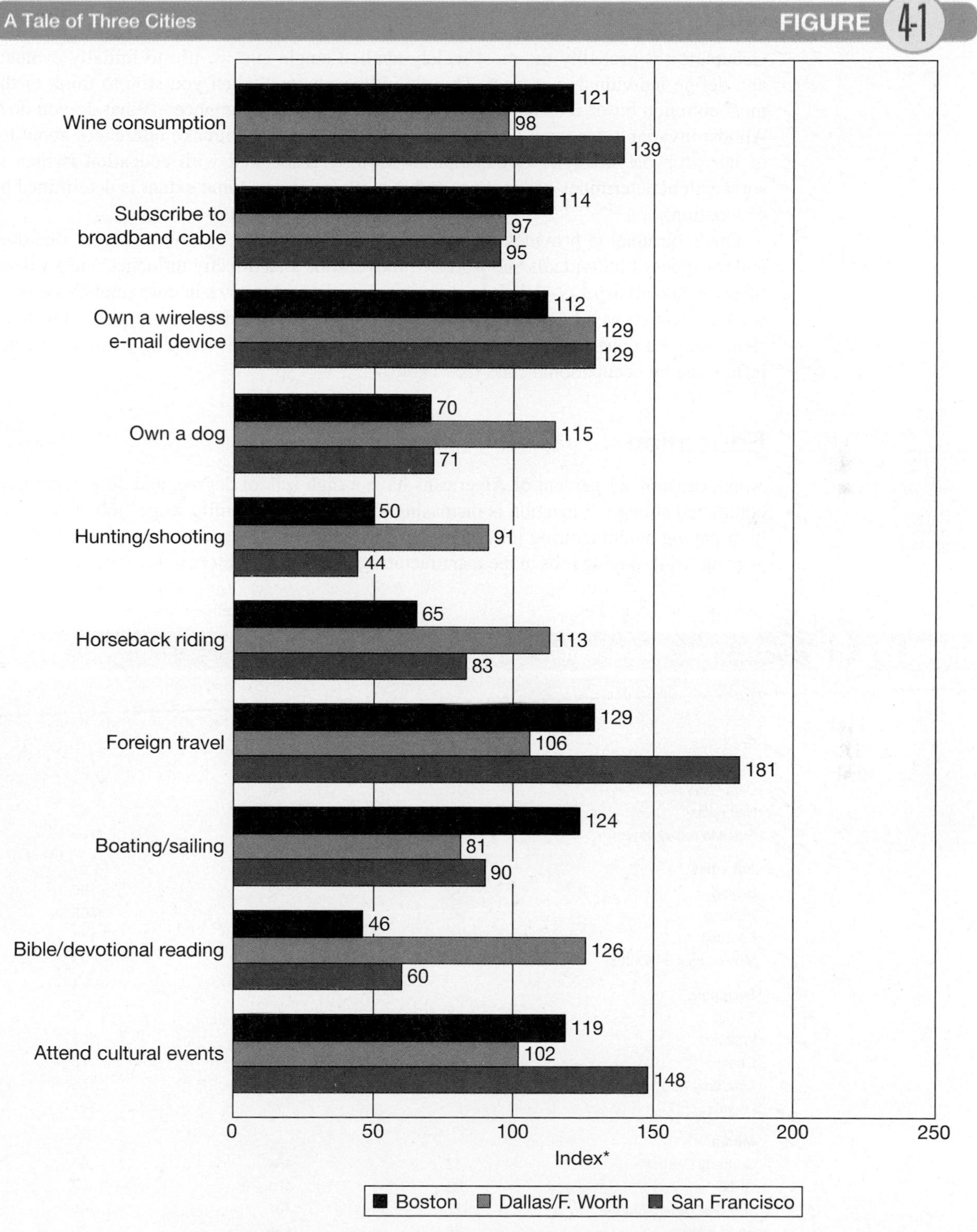

*An Index of 100 represents the average for the entire United States

Source: Data from "The Lifestyle Analyst, 2008 Edition," published by SRDS with data supplied by Equifax Marketing Services. Used by permission.

Occupation

Occupation is probably the most widely applied single cue we use to initially evaluate and define individuals we meet. This should be obvious when you stop to think of the most common bit of information we seek from a new acquaintance: "What do you do?" Almost invariably we want to know someone's occupation to make inferences about his or her probable lifestyle. Occupation is strongly associated with education (which to some extent determines occupation) and income (which to some extent is determined by occupation).

One's occupation provides status and income. In addition, the type of work one does and the types of individuals one works with over time also directly influence one's values, lifestyle, and all aspects of the consumption process. Differences in consumption between occupational classes have been found for products such as beer, detergents, dog food, shampoo, and paper towels. Media preferences, hobbies, and shopping patterns are also influenced by occupational class (see Table 4–1).

Education

Approximately 87 percent of Americans have a high school degree, and 30 percent have completed college. Education is increasingly critical for a "family wage" job. Traditional high-paying manufacturing jobs that required relatively little education are rapidly disappearing. High-paying jobs in the manufacturing and service sectors today require technical

TABLE 4-1 Occupational Influences on Consumption

	Wholesale and Retail Trade	Professional, Scientific, and Technical	Mining and Construction
Products			
Domestic beer	115	122	142
Cigarettes	113	69	140
Diet colas	96	127	66
Satellite radio system	87	143	139
Activities			
Sailing	116	132	195
Hunting	97	60	265
Football	112	115	172
Movies (last 6 months)	109	121	93
Shopping			
Target	101	123	85
Walmart	99	82	102
Costco	98	159	78
Academy Sports	92	89	156
Lowe's	97	118	147
Media			
Comedy Central	132	184	86
CNN	83	101	93
The Wall Street Journal	77	187	148
Food & Wine	86	139	70

Note: 100 = Average level of use, purchase, or consumption.

Source: *Simmons National Consumer Study 2010,* Experian Information Solutions (Costa Mesa, CA 2014).

skills, abstract reasoning, and the ability to read and learn new skills rapidly. Individuals without these skills are generally forced into minimum-wage and often part-time jobs, which will rarely keep a family above the poverty level.[6] As the following data show, education clearly drives income in today's economy.

Since individuals tend to have spouses with similar education levels, these differences are magnified when spousal income is considered.

Income: Workers 18 and Older[7]

Education Level	Males	Females
No high school degree	$24,831	$14,521
High school degree	36,753	24,329
Associate's degree	48,237	32,253
Bachelor's degree	72,868	44,078
Master's degree	88,450	54,517
Professional degree	147,518	87,723

Education influences what one can purchase by partially determining one's income and occupation. It also influences how one thinks, makes decisions, and relates to others.[8] Those with a limited education are generally at a disadvantage.

Not surprisingly, education has a strong influence on one's tastes and preferences, as shown in Table 4–2. However, education seldom provides a complete explanation for consumption patterns. For example, a lawyer earning $30,000 per year as a public defender

Education Level Influences on Consumption **TABLE 4-2**

	Graduated College	Attended College	Graduated High School	Did Not Graduate High School
Products				
Cocktails	103	92	96	113
Beer	70	90	106	168
Motorcycles	87	113	122	70
iPod (Apple)	164	115	65	38
Activities				
Waterskiing	103	114	105	80
Visiting museums	175	103	64	40
Foreign travel (last 3 years)	135	100	84	73
Registered to vote	116	106	96	69
Shopping				
Kmart	75	97	119	107
Neiman Marcus	139	86	88	86
Kentucky Fried Chicken	68	112	110	126
California Pizza Kitchen	198	113	46	42
Media				
Forbes	154	124	69	45
People	129	113	85	52
Nick at Nite	51	90	118	163
Fox News channel	97	101	109	85

Note: 100 = Average level of use, purchase, or consumption.

Source: *Simmons National Consumer Study 2010,* Experian Information Solutions (Costa Mesa, CA 2014).

will have a different lifestyle from a lawyer earning $250,000 per year in private practice, despite similar educational backgrounds.

Income

A household's income level combined with its accumulated wealth determines its purchasing power. While many purchases are made on credit, one's ability to buy on credit is ultimately determined by one's current and past income (wealth).

Most of American history has been characterized by consistently increasing real per capita income. For most middle- and lower-income Americans, this increasing trend stopped in the 1980s, and household incomes were stagnant or declining until they increased again in the mid-1990s.[9] Several notable economic expansions have taken place from the mid-1990s through 2006. The first was from 1993 through 2000 and the second from 2002 through 2006. Economic expansion results in higher incomes and spending power. A major concern, however, is the growing income divide. One study shows that during the 1993–2000 expansion, real incomes of the top 1 percent grew by 10.1 percent while the remaining 99 percent grew by only 2.4 percent. Even more striking, during the 2002–2006 expansion, the top 1 percent of incomes grew by 11 percent compared with just 0.9 percent for the remaining 99 percent. Such increases in wealth concentration mean that not all Americans are benefiting equally from economic expansion in the United States.[10]

Just as Americans have not shared equally in prosperous times, neither have they shared equally in the most recent recession. For example, while the United States lost 1.2 million people previously earning over $100,000, roughly twice that (2.1 million) dropped below $35,000. And while the economy has shown positive signs, consumers are still being affected by the housing market, the high price of gas, and continued economic and global uncertainty. In response, many consumers are buying smaller cars and homes, building fewer new homes, and remodeling less.[11] Target has actually gained business in this environment by repositioning itself more toward value, in part by creating their 5% Rewards program.[12]

How long these trends hold remains to be seen. Consumers with modest incomes often want to "trade up" to luxury brands. Companies, in a strategy termed **class to mass,** have responded by expanding opportunities for less affluent consumers to afford luxury. However, today more than ever, this may require trade-offs. As one retail expert notes:

> Consumers are still willing to trade up. But if someone wants the designer jeans, they'll cut back on something else.[13]

Income *enables* purchases but *does not generally cause or explain them.* For example, a college professor or lawyer may have the same income as a truck driver or plumber. Nonetheless, it is likely that their consumption processes for a variety of products will differ. Occupation and education directly influence preferences for products, media, and activities; income provides the means to acquire them.[14] Thus, income is generally more effective as a segmentation variable when used in conjunction with other demographic variables.

How wealthy one feels may be as important as actual income for some purchases.[15] **Subjective discretionary income (SDI)** is *an estimate by the consumer of how much money he or she has available to spend on nonessentials.* Several studies show that SDI adds considerable predictive power to actual total family income (TFI) measures.[16]

Age

Proper age positioning is critical for many products. Age carries with it culturally defined behavioral and attitudinal norms.[17] It affects our self-concept and lifestyles.[18] Not surprisingly, age influences the consumption of products ranging from beer to toilet paper to vacations. Our age shapes which media we use, where we shop, how we use products, and how we think and feel about marketing activities.[19] Table 4–3 illustrates some consumption behaviors that vary with age. Illustration 4–1 shows an ad with the type of humor appreciated by many young adults.

The estimated age distributions (millions in each age category) of the U.S. population for 2010 and 2020 are shown in the following table.[20]

Age Category	2010	2020	Percentage Change
Under 10	42,132	45,496	+8.0%
10–19	41,103	43,392	+5.6
20–29	43,051	43,112	+0.1
30–39	40,408	44,847	+11.0
40–49	43,638	40,892	−6.3
50–59	41,680	42,578	+2.2
60–69	28,851	38,474	+33.4
Over 69	28,071	37,013	+31.9

Age Influences on Consumption TABLE 4-3

	18–24	25–34	35–44	45–54	55–64	65+
Products						
Tequila	102	140	111	114	90	45
Scotch whiskey	62	105	85	84	127	128
Botox	33	145	199	52	65	83
Blu-ray	138	113	114	110	86	51
Activities						
Skateboarding	297	145	108	49	62	15
Backpacking/hiking	125	129	146	99	80	30
Participating in civil protest	105	116	97	93	106	88
Visiting museums	92	118	107	99	100	82
Shopping						
Belk	88	71	89	95	114	137
Victoria's Secret	200	145	115	81	57	40
Chuck E. Cheese's	128	214	130	75	46	23
The Cheesecake Factory	140	138	97	106	75	58
Media						
Reader's Digest	39	50	75	88	123	203
GQ	237	125	126	83	39	38
AARP, The Magazine	14	9	17	73	192	269
Businessweek	60	74	70	126	112	140

Note: 100 = Average level of use, purchase, or consumption.
Source: *Simmons National Consumer Study 2010,* Experian Information Solutions (Costa Mesa, CA 2014).

ILLUSTRATION 4-1

Age affects how individuals think, feel, and behave. The humor in this ad would be appreciated more by younger consumers than by older consumers.

Even a quick look at these age distributions indicates important changes. Some of the marketing implications include:

- Demand for children's products, such as toys, diapers, and clothes, will grow moderately, as the population under 10 years of age will grow 8 percent over this period.
- The teen market is growing again at a modest rate after a decade in which growth had been minimal or negative. This signals a growth in demand for fashion, music, and technology targeting the teen market.
- Given that marriage and childbirth often occur in the twenties but are increasingly delayed until the thirties, growth in the 30–39 market should provide growth in homes, child care products and services, family cars, and insurance to offset the lack of growth in the 20–29 age group.
- Products consumed by those aged 40 to 49 will decline as this population group grows smaller. This will have significant implications for such industries as financial services, for which this is a key age group.
- The largest growth area is in the 60 and over groups, which will grow at greater than 30 percent. The 60–69 age group will be primarily one- or two-person households, with many retired or near retirement. Vacations, restaurants, second homes, and financial services aimed at this market should flourish. Growth in the 69 and over group will create many opportunities for marketers ranging from beauty aids and travel and leisure to retirement homes and health care.

Age groups, as defined by the census and as presented above, can be useful as a means of understanding and segmenting a market. For example, P&G launched the Oil of Olay ProVital line, targeting women over 50 years old. One of the first spokeswomen for the product was 51-year-old actress Anne Roberts. However, the product line has not been positioned as just an antiwrinkle solution:

> Age is just a number. Many women 50 and over have told us that as they age, they feel more confident, wiser, and freer than ever before. These women are redefining beauty. Our research shows that when it comes to skin, dryness and vitality are their key concerns, not just a few wrinkles.[21]

These comments suggest an important distinction between chronological age (how old you are) and cognitive age (how old you feel). **Cognitive age** is defined as *one's perceived age, a part of one's self-concept.*[22] It is measured by asking people what age they would associate with how they look, feel, and behave. For older consumers, cognitive age is often 10 to 15 years less than chronological age. Similar results have been found for cognitive age in Japan.[23] Better health and higher education, income, and social support lead to reductions in cognitive age. And for many behaviors, cognitive age is more important than chronological age, making age perception a critical marketing consideration. Generational influences, which provide additional richness and insight beyond standard age categories, are discussed next.

UNDERSTANDING AMERICAN GENERATIONS

LO2

A **generation,** or **age cohort,** is *a group of persons who have experienced a common social, political, historical, and economic environment.* Age cohorts, because their shared histories produce unique shared values and behaviors, often function as unique market segments.[24]

Cohort analysis is the process of describing and explaining the attitudes, values, and behaviors of an age group as well as predicting its future attitudes, values, and behaviors.[25] A critical fact uncovered by cohort analysis is that each generation behaves differently from other generations as it passes through various age categories. For example, in 2011 the leading edge of the baby boom generation was eligible to retire at the traditional age of 65. Some opted for earlier retirement, some retired when eligible, and some continue to work, though eligible to retire. However, it would be a mistake to assume that retiring baby boomers will behave like the pre-Depression generation does today. The forces that shaped the lives of these generations were different, and their behaviors will differ throughout their life cycles. As just one example, the computer and Internet skills that baby boomers have acquired will make them much heavier Internet users in their retirement years than is currently true of their parents, who in many cases were bypassed by the most recent technology revolution.

In the following sections, we will examine the six generations that compose the primary American market.[26] The generations, along with their birth years, age range, and approximate size as of 2015, are shown in the table below and described in detail in the sections that follow.

Generation	Birth Years	Age Range	Approximate Size
Pre-Depression	Prior to 1930	86+	6 M
Depression	1930 to 1945	70–85	25 M
Baby Boom	1946 to 1964	51–69	80 M
Generation X	1965 to 1976	39–50	45 M
Generation Y	1977 to 1994	21–38	79 M
Generation Z	1995 to 2009	5–20	69 M

It is important to emphasize that generation is only one factor influencing behavior and the differences within generations are often larger than the differences across generations. In addition, generations do not have sharp boundaries. Those near the age breaks between generations often do not belong clearly to either generation.

Pre-Depression Generation

Born before 1930, this generation represents roughly 6 million Americans as of 2015. High mortality accounts for the rapid reduction in the size of this group (from 12 million in 2010). These individuals grew up in traumatic times. Most were children during the Depression and entered young adulthood during World War II. They have witnessed radical social, economic, and technological change. As a group, they are conservative and concerned with financial and personal security.

As with all generations, the pre-Depression generation is composed of distinct segments, and marketing to it requires a strategy that incorporates such factors as gender, ethnicity, and social class.[27] This generation is part of the broader **mature market,** generally defined as consumers 55 years of age and over. **Gerontographics** is *one segmentation approach to the mature market that incorporates aging processes and life events related to the physical health and mental outlook of older consumers.* Four segments have been identified. *Healthy Indulgers* are physically and mentally healthy and are thus active, independent, and out to enjoy life. *Ailing Outgoers* have health problems that limit their physical abilities, but their positive outlook means they remain active within financial constraints. *Healthy Hermits* are physically healthy, but life events, often the death of a spouse, have reduced their self-concept and they have become withdrawn. *Frail Recluses* have accepted their old-age status and have adjusted their lifestyles to reflect reduced physical capabilities and social roles. *Can you see the marketing implications of these market segments for targeting the mature market?*

The pre-Depression generation faces numerous consumption-related decisions. One is the disposition of valued belongings that they no longer use or that are not appropriate in nursing or retirement homes. These can be emotional decisions for both the elderly person and his or her family members.

> The pin means a great deal to me. I would love for my granddaughter to have it. It will be strange not seeing it in my jewelry box anymore.[28]

Communications strategies need to consider media selection, message content, and message structure. For example, some aspects of information processing, memory, and cognitive performance decline with age. The rapid, brief presentation of information that younger consumers respond to is generally not appropriate for older consumers.[29]

Products related to the unique needs of this segment range from health services to single-serving sizes of prepared foods. As this generation continues to age, assisted-living services are growing rapidly. As more members of this generation experience reduced mobility, shopping will become an increasing problem. Although Internet shopping would seem a good solution, relatively few members of this generation use the Internet.

Depression Generation

Born between 1930 and 1945, this generation represents roughly 25 million Americans as of 2015. These people were small children during the Depression or World War II. They matured during the prosperous years of the 1950s and early 60s. They discovered both

Sinatra and Presley. They "invented" rock and roll and grew up with music and television as important parts of their lives.

Most in this generation have retired or will soon do so. Many have accumulated substantial wealth in the form of home equity and savings, although the most recent economic downturn has eroded the wealth of many in terms of decreased home equity and retirement portfolio values. Those who still work often dominate the top positions in both business and government. Members of this generation are also grandparents with sufficient incomes to indulge their grandchildren, making them a major market for upscale children's furniture, toys, strollers, car seats, and clothing.

ILLUSTRATION 4-2

The mature market is composed of many distinct segments. The Campbell's Healthy Request ad would appeal to the "healthy indulger" segment, which is healthy, content, and out to enjoy life.

Many, particularly those in the younger part of this generation, are still in good health and are quite active. Active lifestyles translate into demand for recreational vehicles, second homes, new cars, travel services, and recreational adult education.[30] Perhaps a bit surprising to younger generations, over half of this generation are online and over half of those online have used the Internet to make travel reservations, and a full three-quarters have used the Internet to look up health information.[31] So-called active adult communities such as Sun City in Phoenix, Arizona, are a major growth arena and will continue to be so as the baby boomers enter their retirement years. These age-restricted communities offer an amazing array of activities and attract relatively wealthy households, many of whom can pay cash for their homes.[32]

Marketers targeting this segment are increasingly using themes that stress an active lifestyle and breaking with stereotypical portrayals of older consumers. A good example of this is Campbell's Healthy Request ads (as shown in Illustration 4–2). Campbell's is appealing to the "healthy indulger" segment described earlier.

Nonetheless, this generation is dealing with the physical effects of aging. In terms of clothing, comfort is important, as attested to by the success of Levi's Action Slacks and Easy Spirit shoes in targeting this segment. However, style simply cannot be overlooked as it plays an important role in maintaining a positive self-concept. Consider the thoughts of Susan, a 71-year-old who shops in department stores:

> Lately, I have found a hard time finding the right clothes. Clothes that I used to wear, that younger people wear, don't look like they used to on me. My body is naturally changing so things don't look good. Please listen to this one. The stuff they have for people over sixty is really horrible . . . and I refuse to wear it. It's old lady looking, very old, and dated. I like stylish slacks and pretty sweaters and nice blouses.[33]

Clearly, nursing home stays and in-home care are more likely for those with serious health issues and those in the older part of this generation[34] and health care is a major concern and a major expenditure. In addition, as this group ages, declines in information processing, memory, and cognitive performance must be considered in creating communications strategies, much like for the pre-Depression generation.[35]

Asset management is important to this group, and firms such as MetLife have developed products and services to meet these needs.[36] Lawyers, accountants, and financial planners also have been attracted to the "wealth transfer" that is expected to occur as the baby boomers inherit the wealth accumulated by their parents. Numbers vary dramatically due to stock market fluctuations and rising health care costs. However, current estimates put the number between $6 and $8 trillion in the coming decades.[37]

In addition, this group of consumers is downsizing homes and possessions just like the pre-Depression generation. And increasing numbers are becoming more tech savvy, even to the point of using eBay to help them downsize! As one such eBay user jokes:

> The end of the bidding cycle is quite exciting, especially for older people whose lives like mine are not that exciting anymore.

SeniorNet is a nonprofit group that helps older consumers learn about computers by offering classes in nursing homes and recreation centers, and eBay has been a strong supporter of their efforts.[38]

Baby Boom Generation

Born during the dramatic increase of births between the end of World War II and 1964, this generation represents nearly 80 million Americans as of 2015. The large size of this generation makes them very important to marketers. Most of this group grew up during the prosperous 1950s and 1960s. They were heavily influenced by the Kennedy assassination, the Vietnam War, recreational drugs, the sexual revolution, the energy crisis, the rapid growth of divorce, and the cold war, as well as rock and roll and the Beatles. Although there are significant differences between the boomers born early in this generation and those born later, boomers are considered to be more self-centered, individualistic, economically optimistic, skeptical, suspicious of authority, and focused on the present than are other generations.[39]

Baby boomers are characterized by high education levels, high incomes, and dual-career households. They are also often characterized by time poverty (particularly young boomers) as they try to manage two careers and family responsibilities. TV is still a major route through which to target this generation. However, baby boomers are more tech savvy than previous generations. The Internet offers the convenience and customization that this generation demands, with roughly two-thirds of boomers using the Internet to make product purchases. Internet usage among boomers is roughly 80 percent, and their use of social networking sites is substantially higher than that of previous generations.[40]

The "empty nest" is increasingly common for this generation, a circumstance that is providing them with both increased discretionary income and time. In fact, baby boomers are 48 percent more likely than the average adult to earn $100,000 or more.[41] As a result, sales of adventure vacations, expensive restaurant meals, second homes, recreational vehicles, maintenance-free homes, personal chefs, and personal trainers should continue to grow.[42] However, boomers are also facing the major challenge of being the caretaker of their parents. One result of this is the rapid growth of assisted-living centers as boomers often don't want their parents living with them and their parents don't want to be a burden.[43]

Retirement is no longer something in the distant future, and many have already made that step. However, surveys indicate that boomers plan to continue and expand the concept of "active retirement" begun by the Depression generation. In one study, two-thirds of 50- to 75-year-olds selected as a definition of retirement: To begin a new, active, and involved chapter in life, starting new activities and setting new goals.[44] Sony has targeted the active boomer as follows:

> Sony spent $25 million to target what it calls the "zoomers," a name that reflects the active lifestyle of this generation. One of their ads featured a "grey-haired astronaut filming Earth with his own camcorder." The tagline: "When your kids ask where the money went, show them the tape." Sony credits a surge in camcorder sales to its renewed focus on this increasingly important segment.[45]

Being a grandparent has or will become a major part of this active retirement period for many boomers. The substantial wealth and spending power of this generation make them prime targets for a whole host of categories including toys, vacations, gift cards, and school supplies.[46]

Clearly, however, as boomers age, their physical needs are changing. Particularly among older boomers, major health problems are increasingly likely and will hamper their active lifestyles. Even for healthy boomers, however, issues of appearance are critical and demand for plastic surgery, baldness treatments, health clubs, cosmetics for both men and women, hair coloring, health foods, and related products continue to expand as this group ages. How well do you feel the baby boom generation is targeted in the Oil of Olay Regenerist ad in Illustration 4–3?

As with the Depression generation, it is important for advertisers to avoid overreliance on themes and models that are too young and not representative of boomers and their life stage. As one boomer indicates:

> I've quit buying clothes from stores who only use young gals in their catalogs. To me it says that they aren't interested in my money.[47]

While it is convenient to provide a general summary of boomer characteristics, it is also important to avoid stereotypes and move toward an understanding of how to segment this large market. Consumer Insight 4–1 discusses some of the stereotypes and also approaches to segmenting the boomer market.

Generation X

Born between 1965 and 1976, this generation represents roughly 45 million Americans as of 2015. It is a smaller generation than the generations before and after it. Generation X reached adulthood during difficult economic times. It is the first generation to be raised mainly in dual-career households, and 40 percent spent at least some time in a single-parent household before the age of 16. The divorce of their parents is often a cause of stress and other problems for the children involved. However, these changes have also caused many members of Generation X to have a very broad view of family, which may include parents, siblings, stepparents, half-siblings, close friends, live-in lovers, and others.

ILLUSTRATION 4-3

The baby boom generation is entering its 50s and 60s. As it matures, it is creating demand for weight-control products, hair dyes, lotions, and other "anti-aging" devices such as the Oil of Olay Regenerist microsculpting serum.

CONSUMER INSIGHT 4-1

Beyond Stereotypes: Segmenting the Boomer Market

The baby boom market is the largest generational segment in America but also one of the most diverse. Such diversity requires that marketers move beyond stereotypes and understand segmentation opportunities that exist. Below we deal with common stereotypes of the boomer market and provide insight as to segmentation opportunities.[48]

- *Boomers all have the same values and outlook*—This is far from true. Boomers are quite different in values and outlook in part due to differences in life experiences relating to health and finances. One study by *Focalyst* finds three boomer segments based on outlook:

  Yesterday (25 percent)—This group believes that life was better in the '50s and is not optimistic about the future. Health and financial issues are major factors for this group. Marketing messages that reassure, comfort, and acknowledge the efforts of this group may be particularly effective.

  Today (30 percent)—This group believes that they live in exciting times and is happy with their lives today. Strong physical and financial health contribute to this positive outlook. Marketing messages that focus on the now, indulgence, and the good life may be particularly effective.

  Tomorrow (45 percent)—This group believes that the future will be better than today and remains positive about the future despite negative financial or health events. This group is highly connected with friends and community, which may explain their positive outlook. Marketing messages that emphasize stability, optimism, and spirituality may be particularly effective.
- *Boomers are self-centered*—The phrase "Me Generation" was created for baby boomers. However, many boomers are much more socially and environmentally conscious than that label suggests. One study estimates that roughly half of all boomers are "Green Boomers," meaning they buy environmentally friendly products.
- *Boomers are not tech savvy*—The Internet and mobile technology are an important part of many boomers' lives. Roughly 80 percent of boomers are online, and roughly half of all boomers engage in wireless Internet use, which includes wireless Internet connection via laptop, checking e-mail via cell phone, using the Internet on a cell phone, and using IM on a cell phone.
- *Boomers are married empty nesters who are downsizing*—Only 25 percent of boomers are married empty nesters. Nearly 40 percent of boomers have children under the age of 18 living at home and many also have boomerang children, and live-in parents. Others are singles who are actively dating. In terms of housing, less than 10 percent of boomers plan to downsize in the next five years.
- *Boomers are all retiring early and wealthy*—Over half of all boomers plan to work and/or volunteer beyond their retirement age. One in six is on their "second career" and about the same percentage are engaged in furthering their education. Although many will continue to work out of enjoyment, many also work due to financial need, increases in retirement age, and so on. Only 10 percent of boomers make $150,000 or more a year, and the net worth of the bottom 20 percent of boomers is a mere $2,480.

Clearly the baby boom generation is large and diverse and marketers must understand the boomer market and its segments in designing appropriate marketing strategies.

Critical Thinking Questions

1. Explain the key factors driving the outlook differences among boomers?
2. What factors explain why only 10 percent of boomers plan to downsize in the next five years?
3. What ethical and social responsibilities do marketers have when marketing to older consumers?

This is the first American generation to seriously confront the issue of reduced expectations. These reduced expectations are based on reality for many in this generation as wages and job opportunities for young workers were limited until the economic boom that started in the mid-1990s. This relative lack of opportunity was in part responsible for this generation's tendency to leave home later and also to return home to live with their parents as younger adults. Not only has the path to success been less certain for this generation, but many Generation Xers do not believe in sacrificing time, energy, and relations to the extent the boomers did for the sake of career or economic advancement.[49]

ILLUSTRATION 4-4

Many Generation X consumers are now parents and companies are targeting their needs in this area.

This generation faces a world racked by regional conflicts and terrorism, an environment that continues to deteriorate, and an AIDS epidemic that threatens their lives. Members of this group tend to blame the Me Generation and the materialism associated with the baby boom generation for the difficult future they see for themselves. Given their early economic challenges, it is perhaps not surprising that this generation appears to be more entrepreneurial in its approach to jobs and less prone to devote their lives to large public corporations. For example, half of all Xers aspire to own their own business, which is 13 percent higher than the average adult.[50]

Generation X is highly educated, with more college attendance and graduates than previous generations. And Xer women are more highly educated than men, giving them increased leverage in the workforce. This is having interesting repercussions in terms of family dynamics. More than 20 percent of Xer women now earn more than their husbands. Given the underlying masculine value predominant for much of America's history, this can be uncomfortable for some couples, although most are finding ways to navigate this change. As one analyst observes:

> At one point, the stereotype was a man might feel inferior to a woman who is at a higher point in her career than he is. I think that's dissipated a bit, where there aren't these built-in expectations of who should be above.[51]

The empowerment of Xer women extends beyond their careers. One study shows that across all generations, Xer women are the highest viewers of home improvement media and the most likely to engage in home improvement projects, including adding a room onto the house.[52]

This generation is moving into its 40s, and although they tended to delay marriage and children, nearly half of Xer households are now married with children under 18.[53] This helped keep the housing market strong during the economic downturn in the early 2000s. It is also the reason that this generation increasingly feels the time crunch typical of child-rearing years. This generation is a major force in the market for cars, appliances, children's products, and travel. The ad in Illustration 4–4 targets Xer parents.

While an important market, Generation X is not always easy to reach. It is both cynical and sophisticated about products, ads, and shopping. It is materialistic and impatient. In many aspects, its tastes are "not baby boom." Thus, it created the grunge look and snowboarding. Magazines such as *Spin, Details,* and *Maxim* were created for this generation, as were the X Games. It responds to irreverence in advertising but not always as well to traditional approaches. Generation Xers want products and messages designed uniquely for their tastes and lifestyles.

Xers are more diverse and open to diversity than previous generations. For example, Xers are 45 percent more likely to be Hispanic. Xers are also more likely to accept alternative lifestyle choices such as gay couples raising children, mothers working outside the home, living together without getting married, and people of different races getting married than are those of previous generations.[54] This generation is also more tech savvy than prior generations, with 86 percent using the Internet and between a half and two-thirds watching videos online, using social networking sites, and sending IMs.

Examples of companies that have targeted the Generation X segment include:

- Volvo redesigned its marketing mix for the S40 sedan to go after the Generation X market and some older Generation Yers. The automaker did tie-ins with Microsoft's Xbox and Virgin Group and created commercials with a hip-hop feel.[55]
- Learn & Master Guitar has a target demographic that is predominantly Generation X men who are increasingly users of Facebook. Learn & Master utilized an ad on Facebook with a visual of a 40-something male and it has done well.[56]

These ads show that successful marketers are adapting to this audience in ways that play not only to their heritage but also to their current life stage and technology use.

Generation Y

Born between 1977 and 1994, this generation represents roughly 79 million Americans as of 2015, thus rivaling the baby boom generation. This segment has grown over the past decade in part due to immigration, as evidenced by the fact that at 22 percent, the Hispanic segment of this market is larger than in any previous generation.[57] These children of the original baby boomers are sometimes referred to as the "echo boom." Overall, it is the first generation to grow up with virtually full-employment opportunities for women, with dual-income households as the standard, with a wide array of family types seen as normal, with significant respect for ethnic and cultural diversity, with computers in the home and schools, and with the Internet. It has also grown up with divorce as the norm,[58] AIDS, visible homelessness (including many teenagers), drug abuse, gang violence, and economic uncertainty. The Columbine shootings, the Oklahoma City bombing, the Clinton–Lewinsky scandal, the collapse of the Soviet Union, and Kosovo were key events for this generation.[59]

Generation Y is characterized by a strong sense of independence and autonomy. They are assertive, self-reliant, emotionally and intellectually expressive, innovative, and curious. They understand that advertisements exist to sell products and are unlikely to respond to marketing hype. They prefer ads that use humor or irony and have an element of truth about them. They like the ability to customize products to their unique needs. Brand names are important to them.[60] Factors they believe make their generation unique include (a) technology use, (b) music and pop culture, (c) tolerance, (d) intelligence, and (e) clothes. Gen Yers are diverse and embrace that diversity with the highest tolerance of any previous generation for alternative lifestyles.[61]

Younger Gen Yers are finishing college and starting careers. Older Gen Yers are starting to get married and have children, with a third falling into that category. Still this generation has the lowest marriage rates of any prior generation as it passed through this age range, while alternative arrangements such as living together increase.[62] Younger Gen Yers have been hit harder by the most recent economic downturn, requiring some to get assistance from family or move back in with parents. This could create longer-term differences between older and younger Gen Yers because coming of age in a down economy can lead to suppressed earnings for a decade or more and also to reduced expectations.[63]

Despite the economic downturn, the size and market potential of Generation Y continue to attract the attention of marketers. Apparel is a major focus since young adults (younger Gen Yers) spend more on apparel than does any other age group.[64] The key is adapting to the tastes of young adults as they move out of their teen years. As one expert puts it, "Where are all these folks going to go when they get tired of shopping in teenage land?"[65] Retailers such as Metropark are blending music and fashion in interesting ways to attract this segment.

> All their stores have "a DJ booth in front and a lounge area in back with sofas, a magazine rack and an array of energy drinks. The boutique sells more than 100 brands, including $219 Paige Premium Denim jeans and $149 hooded sweatshirts from Obey Clothing label."[66]

Other fashion merchandisers are attempting to ease this generation into the workplace with affordable, work-appropriate, yet stylish clothes.

While complete statistics are not yet available, this generation is expected to be at least as highly educated as Generation X, if not more so. In addition, data for older Gen Yers show that the trend of women being more educated than men continues, reflecting ongoing changes in values and gender roles.[67]

Gen Y is more technologically immersed than any previous generation, with 95 percent being online, 66 percent sending IMs, and 83 percent using social network sites.[68] This group is also accustomed to media and TV programs designed for them, such as MTV, Facebook, *Maxim, American Idol,* and *CSI.* Ads targeting this generation must be placed in appropriate magazines and on appropriate Internet sites, television and radio programs, and video games—a strategy called "advergaming."[69]

The portrayal of multiple racial and ethnic groups in ads aimed at this generation is common and important given their multiethnic nature. Similarly, the portrayal of modern female gender roles and alternative lifestyles is more common and important to this group given their diversity and acceptance of that diversity. Traditional mass-marketing approaches that were so successful with older generations often don't work well with Generation Y. Companies must continually push the creative envelope with respect to media and promotional themes to capture this audience. Tapping into consumer-generated buzz is particularly appropriate for this group given their high levels of participation in social media. As seen earlier, music and fashion are often key touch points as well. Illustration 4–5 shows a Van Heusen ad that is designed to tap into the unique aspects of Generation Y, with its creative "institute of style" campaign and use of social media elements.

Generation Z

Born between 1995 and 2009, this generation represents roughly 69 million Americans as of 2015. This generation has also been labeled the Digital Natives, Generation @, and the Net Generation due to the fact that none of the members of this cohort can recall

ILLUSTRATION 4-5

This Van Heusen ad is designed to attract Generation Y through its unique and creative marketing approach.

a time before computers, the Internet, and cell phones. This generation is dealing with global unrest, economic uncertainty, terrorism, the Virginia Tech massacre, cyber-bullying, and global warming.[70] Ethnic diversity is high among this group and comparable to that of Generations X and Y, except that this group currently trends higher in African Americans than do the previous two generations.[71] In addition, due to declining divorce rates, this generation, although certainly accustomed to divorce, often lives in two-parent households.

Many in this group are moving into their tweens (8 to 14) and teens. According to one study, Generation Z values personal responsibility, civic engagement, and diversity. The older members of this generation tend to be driven by their own conscience and by civic responsibility. Compared to Generations X and Y when they were teens and tweens, this group as a whole tends to avoid risky behaviors, acts in a responsible manner, and accepts diversity, including having a gay friend.[72]

Expectations placed on this generation are high and that has produced anxiety to excel at a younger and younger age. One expert indicates of this generation:

> We are seeing an erosion of childhood. Kids aren't allowed to be kids for very long and they're made into little consumers at a very young age. They've grown up in a world which is focused on achievement and outcomes, and some are suffering anxiety about what they do when they finish school already.[73]

Personal ramifications aside, these pressures are expected to result in even higher levels of education for this group compared to previous generations and the gender divide shows no sign of weakening, although it is much too early to make firm predictions. What is known is that teens and tweens, which make up much of this generation, account for an estimated $200 billion in purchasing power.[74] Some of their purchasing power is direct and based on their own earnings, gift money, and allowances. Some of their purchasing power is indirect and based on spending by their parents on items for them. And while the economic downturn has hurt, a recent survey finds that for the teen market:[75]

- While 40 percent have not been affected, the remainder have been negatively affected.
- Teens are shopping smarter (sales and comparison shopping) to weather the economic storm.
- Teens who work do so to buy clothes, save for college, and buy a car.

Beyond spending power, the teenage market is attractive to marketers because preferences and tastes formed during the teenage years can influence purchases throughout life. As the Ford Focus brand manager states, "Although very few of [teenagers] are car buyers now, it is vital to create a relationship with them so they'll think of Ford when it is time to buy a car."[76]

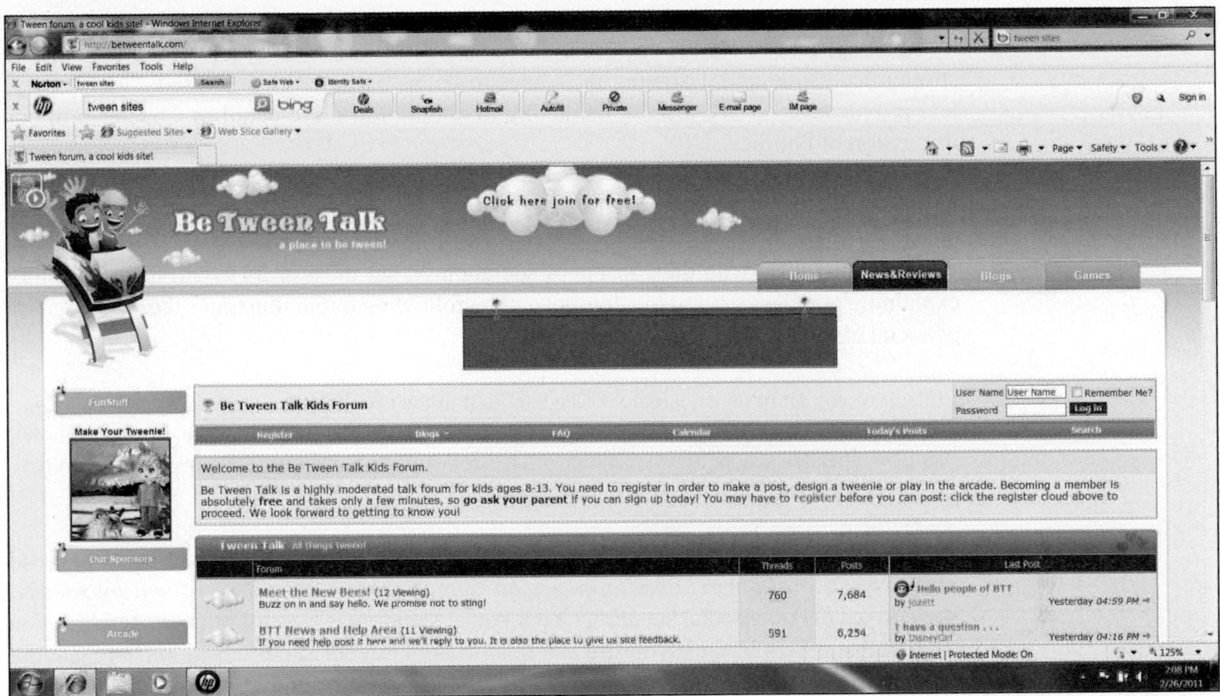

ILLUSTRATION 4-6

The Be Tween Talk social networking site targets the highly attractive Generation Z market.

Marketers targeting teens need to use appropriate language, music, and images. Retailers are realizing that they need to constantly adjust and update their offerings to drive traffic among this active shopper segment that is also easily bored. Consider the following statement by a retail consultant:

> This is the challenge for any store catering to mall rats—the kids come back so often that you're forced to constantly change the displays. Otherwise they get bored and stop coming at all. It's one reason stores need to know how often the regulars return—to see whether the windows and front tables should be changed every week or every seventeen days.[77]

Honesty, humor, diversity, and information appear to be important to teens. And alternative media approaches involving social media are critical. Teens have been found to be high or even the highest in terms of the use of social network sites, sending IMs, reading or posting to blogs, and visiting a virtual world. Illustration 4–6 shows the Be Tween Talk site, which is an example of a social networking site targeting to the teen part of Generation Z. This site provides a forum where teens can focus on their concerns and issues.

Examples of companies that are taking advantage of the tech-savvy nature of Generation Z include:

- Tumblr is a micro-blogging site that allows easy access to blogging from any device, anywhere. It allows posting of photos, video, self-recording audio statements, and IMs and allows posts from Tumblr to be fed to Facebook and Twitter.[78]
- Gatorade knew the teen market was key to its current and future success. So they redesigned their marketing approach toward teens and teen athletes to include a Mobile Locker Room tour, Facebook, and Twitter.[79]

Tweens are late adolescents and early teens. Opportunities exist in music, fashion, cosmetics, video games, and so on. Parents still play an important role in terms of choices for tweens. Aeropostle is one store that is focused on "target the mom." They and others are trying to appeal to both the child and the parent. Some are widening aisles to make them stroller accessible and designing their lines to be, as one mother described, "less snooty, less provocative."[80] We discuss marketing to children in more detail in Chapter 6 in our discussion of families.

SOCIAL STRATIFICATION

LO3 We are all familiar with the concept of social class, but most of us would have difficulty explaining our class system to a foreigner. The following quote illustrates the vague nature of social class:

> Like it or not, all of us are largely defined, at least in the eyes of others, according to a complex set of criteria—how much we earn, what we do for a living, who our parents are, where and how long we attended school, how we speak, what we wear, where we live, and how we react to the issues of the day. It all adds up to our socioeconomic status, our ranking in U.S. society.[81]

The words *social class* and *social standing* are used interchangeably to mean **societal rank**—*one's position relative to others on one or more dimensions valued by society.* How do we obtain a social standing? Your social standing is a result of characteristics you possess that others in society desire and hold in high esteem. Your education, occupation, ownership of property, income level, and heritage (racial or ethnic background, parents' status) influence your social standing, as shown in Figure 4–2. Social standing ranges from the lower class, those with few or none of the socioeconomic factors desired by society, to the upper class, who possess many of the socioeconomic characteristics considered by society as desirable. Individuals with different social standings tend to have different needs and consumption patterns. Thus, a **social class system** can be defined as *a hierarchical division of a society into relatively distinct and homogeneous groups with respect to attitudes, values, and lifestyles.*

"Pure" social classes do not exist in the United States or most other industrialized societies. However, it is apparent that these same societies do have hierarchical groups of individuals and that individuals in those groups do exhibit unique behavior patterns that are different from behaviors in other groups.

What exists is *not a set of social classes* but a *series of status continua.*[82] These status continua reflect various dimensions or factors that the overall society values. In an achievement-oriented society such as the United States, *achievement-related factors* constitute the primary status dimensions. Thus, education, occupation, income, and, to a

FIGURE 4-2 Social Standing Is Derived and Influences Behavior

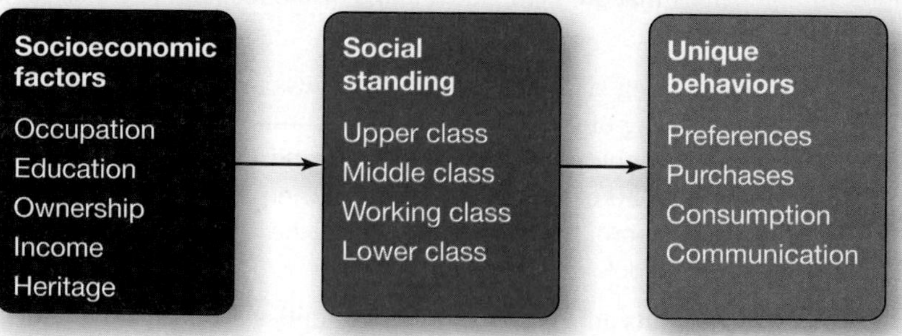

lesser extent, quality of residence and place of residence are important status dimensions in the United States. Race and gender are *ascribed* dimensions of social status that are not related to achievement but still influence status in the United States. Likewise, the status of a person's parents is an ascribed status dimension that also exists in the United States. However, heritage is a more important factor in a more traditional society such as England.[83]

The various status dimensions are clearly related to each other. In a functional sense, the status of one's parents influences one's education, which in turn influences occupation that generates income, which sets limits on one's lifestyle, including one's residence. Does this mean that an individual with high status based on one dimension will have high status based on the other dimensions? This is a question of **status crystallization.** The more consistent an individual is on all status dimensions, the greater the degree of status crystallization for the individual. Status crystallization is moderate in the United States. For example, many blue-collar workers (such as plumbers and electricians) earn higher incomes than many professionals (such as public school teachers).

SOCIAL STRUCTURE IN THE UNITED STATES

LO4

The moderate level of status crystallization in the United States supports the contention that a social class system is not a perfect categorization of social position. However, this does not mean that the population cannot be subdivided into status groups whose members share similar lifestyles, at least with respect to particular product categories or activities. Furthermore, there are many people with high levels of status crystallization who exhibit many of the behaviors associated with a class system. It is useful for the marketing manager to know the characteristics of these relatively pure class types, even though the descriptions represent a simplified abstraction from reality.

A number of different sets of social classes have been proposed to describe the United States. We will use the one developed by Coleman and Rainwater.[84] In their system, shown in Table 4–4, the *upper class* (14 percent) is divided into three groups primarily by differences in occupation and social affiliations. The *middle class* (70 percent) is divided into a middle class (32 percent) of average-income white- and blue-collar workers living in better neighborhoods and a working class (38 percent) of average-income blue-collar workers who lead a "working-class lifestyle." The *lower class* (16 percent) is divided into two groups, one living just above the poverty level and the other visibly poverty-stricken.

The percentage of the American population assigned to each class in the Coleman–Rainwater system closely parallels the way Americans classify themselves.[85] The Coleman–Rainwater groups are described in more detail in the following sections.

Upper Americans

The Upper-Upper Class Members of the upper-upper social class are aristocratic families who make up the social elite. Members with this level of social status generally are the nucleus of the best country clubs and sponsors of major charitable events. They provide leadership and funds for community and civic activities and often serve as trustees for hospitals, colleges, and civic organizations.

The Kennedy family is a national example of the upper-upper class. Most communities in America have one or more families with significant "old money." These individuals

TABLE 4-4 The Coleman-Rainwater Social Class Hierarchy

Upper Americans

- Upper-Upper (0.3%). The "capital S society" world of inherited wealth, aristocratic names.
- Lower-Upper (1.2%). The newer social elite, drawn from current professional, corporate leadership.
- Upper-Middle Class (12.5%). The rest of college graduate managers and professionals; lifestyle centers on careers, private clubs, causes, and the arts.

Middle Americans

- Middle Class (32%). Average pay white-collar workers and their blue-collar friends; live on "the better side of town," try to "do the proper things."
- Working Class (38%). Average pay blue-collar workers; lead "working-class lifestyle" whatever the income, school background, and job.

Lower Americans

- Upper-Lower (9%). "A lower group of people but not the lowest"; working, not on welfare; living standard is just above poverty.
- Lower-Lower (7%). On welfare, visibly poverty-stricken, usually out of work (or have "the dirtiest jobs").

Typical Profile				
Social Class	Percent	Income*	Education	Occupation
Upper Americans				
Upper-upper	0.3%	$1,300,000	Master's degree	Board chairman
Lower-upper	1.2	990,000	Master's degree	Corporate president
Upper-middle	12.5	330,000	Medical degree	Physician
Middle Americans				
Middle class	32.0	61,000	College degree	High school teacher
Working class	38.0	33,000	High school	Assembly worker
Lower Americans				
Upper-lower	9.0	19,700	Some high school	Janitor
Lower-lower	7.0	10,900	Grade school	Unemployed

* Income is 2010 inflation-adjusted dollars using U.S. Consumer Price Index (CPI) data.

Source: R. P. Coleman, "The Continuing Significance of Social Class in Marketing," *Journal of Consumer Research,* December 1983, p. 267. Copyright 1983 by The University of Chicago. Used by permission.

live in excellent homes, drive luxury automobiles, own original art, and travel extensively. They generally stay out of the public spotlight unless it is to enter politics or support a charity or community event.

The Lower-Upper Class The lower-upper class is often referred to as "new rich—the current generation's new successful elite." These families are relatively new in terms of upper-class social status and have not yet been accepted by the upper crust of the community. In some cases, their incomes are greater than those of families in the upper-upper social strata. Bill Gates, founder of Microsoft, and Ted Turner, founder of CNN, are national examples of the lower-upper class. Most communities have one or more families who have acquired great wealth during one generation, many from the high-tech and dot-com boom of the 1990s.

Many members of this group continue to live lifestyles similar to those of the upper-middle class. Other members of the lower-upper class strive to emulate the established

ILLUSTRATION 4-7

The upper classes are willing and able to pay for products and services that not only enhance the quality of their lives but are symbolic of their status.

upper-upper class. Entrepreneurs, sports stars, and entertainers who suddenly acquire substantial wealth often engage in this type of behavior. However, they are frequently unable to join the same exclusive clubs or command the social respect accorded the true "blue bloods." Many respond by aggressively engaging in **conspicuous consumption;** that is, they purchase and use automobiles, homes, yachts, clothes, and so forth primarily to demonstrate their great wealth.[86] Thus, it is not unusual to read about a star professional athlete who owns five or ten luxury cars, multiple homes, and so forth. These individuals are referred as the **nouveaux riches.** Doing the "in thing" on a grand scale is important to this group. High-status brands and activities are actively sought out by the nouveaux riches.

Although small, these groups serve as important market segments for some products and as a symbol of "the good life" to the upper-middle class. Illustration 4–7 shows a product that would appeal to the upper classes.

The Upper-Middle Class The upper-middle class consists of families who possess neither family status derived from heritage nor unusual wealth. Occupation and education are key aspects of this social stratum, as it consists of successful professionals, independent businesspeople, and corporate managers. As shown in Table 4–4, members of this social class are typically college graduates, many with professional or graduate degrees.

Upper-middle-class individuals tend to be confident and forward-looking. They worry about the ability of their children to have the same lifestyle they enjoy. They realize that their success depends on their careers, which in turn depend on education. As a result, having their children get a sound education from the right schools is very important to them.

This group is highly involved in the arts and charities of their local communities. They belong to private clubs where they tend to be quite active. They are a prime market for financial services that focus on retirement planning, estate planning, and college funding issues. They consume fine homes, expensive automobiles, quality furniture, good wines, and nice resorts. Illustration 4–8 contains an advertisement aimed at this group.

This segment of the U.S. population is highly visible, and many Americans would like to belong to it. Because it is aspired to by many, it is an important positioning variable for some products. Figure 4–3 describes the upward-pull strategy often associated with the

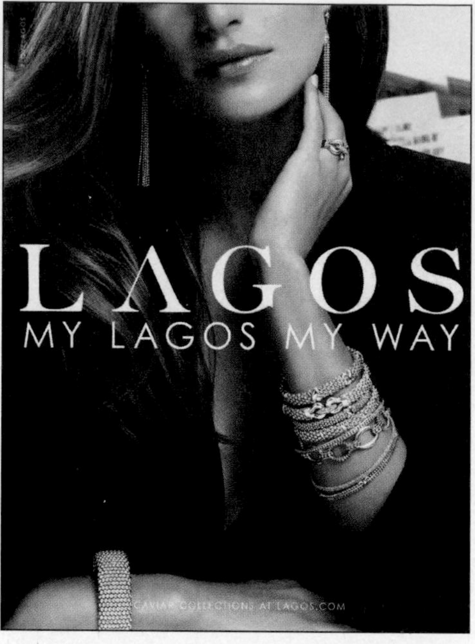

ILLUSTRATION 4-8

An ad such as this would appeal to the upper-middle class. It emphasizes elegance and sophistication.

class to mass approach discussed earlier in the chapter. Illustration 4–9 is an example of the upward-pull strategy as it provides "affordable luxury."

Middle Americans

The Middle Class The middle class is composed of white-collar workers (office workers, school teachers, lower-level managers) and high-paid blue-collar workers (plumbers, factory supervisors). Thus, the middle class represents the majority of the white-collar group and the top of the blue-collar group. The middle-class core typically has some college education though not a degree, a white-collar or a factory supervisor position, and an average income. Many members of this class feel very insecure because of downsizing, outsourcing, and fluctuations in the economy.[87]

The middle class is concerned about respectability. They care what the neighbors think. They generally live in modest suburban homes. They are deeply concerned about the quality of public schools, crime, drugs, the weakening of "traditional family values," and their family's financial security. Retirement is an increasing concern as firms reduce pension plans and health care costs escalate.

Members of the middle class are likely to get involved in do-it-yourself projects. They represent the primary target market for the goods and services of home improvement centers, garden shops, automotive parts houses, as well as mouthwashes and deodorants. With limited incomes, they must balance their desire for current consumption with aspirations for future security. Illustration 4–10 shows an ad for Home Depot which would appeal to this segment with its "Let's Do This" campaign.

The Working Class The working class consists of skilled and semiskilled factory, service, and sales workers. Though some households in this social stratum seek advancement, members are more likely to seek security for and protection of what they already have. This segment suffered seriously during the first half of the 1990s as their average real

FIGURE 4-3 Upward-Pull Strategy Targeted at Middle Class

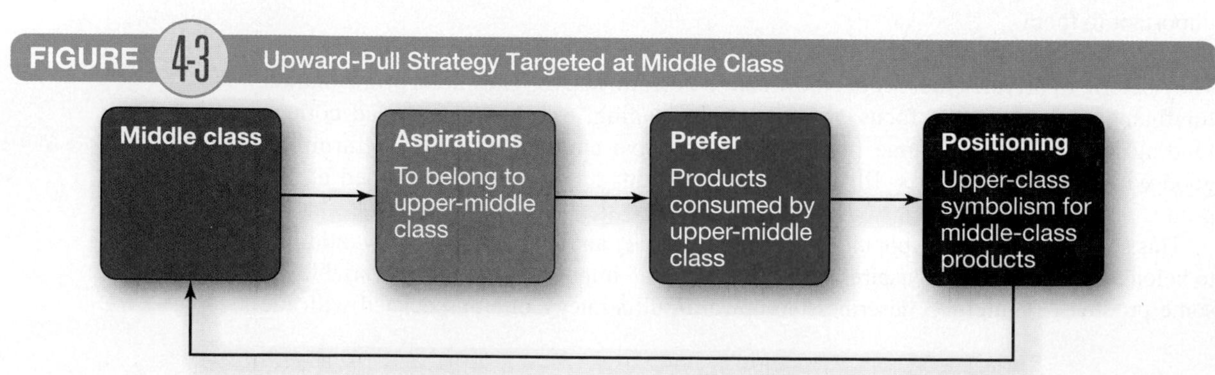

ILLUSTRATION 4-9

This is an example of an upward-pull strategy—positioning a moderately priced product as one that will allow its users to experience some elements of the upper-middle-class lifestyle.

earnings declined. Automation and the movement of manufacturing activities to developing countries also led to economic insecurity. Few of these individuals benefited from the stock market boom of the late 1990s, and many appear to have suffered the consequences of the most recent economic downturn.

Working-class families live in modest homes or apartments that are often located in marginal urban neighborhoods, decaying suburbs, or rural areas. They are greatly concerned about crime, gangs, drugs, and neighborhood deterioration. They generally cannot afford to move to a different area should their current neighborhood or school

ILLUSTRATION 4-10

This Home Depot ad will appeal to the middle class's focus on their homes as well as their desire for value.

ILLUSTRATION 4-11

This Husky Tools product and ad would appeal to the working class, particularly the working-class aristocrats.

become unsafe or otherwise undesirable. With modest education and skill levels, the more marginal members of this class are in danger of falling into one of the lower classes.

Many **working-class aristocrats** dislike the upper-middle class and prefer products and stores positioned at their social-class level.[88] These individuals are proud of their ability to do "real work" and see themselves as the often-unappreciated backbone of America. They are heavy consumers of pickups and campers, hunting equipment, power boats, and beer. Miller Brewing Company gave up attempts to attract a broad audience for its Miller High Life beer. Instead, it is targeting working-class aristocrats with ads that feature bowling alleys, diners, and country music. Homor TLC Inc.'s Huskey Tools are clearly targeted to this segment as shown in Illustration 4–11.

Lower Americans

The Upper-Lower Class The upper-lower class consists of individuals who are poorly educated, have very low incomes, and work as unskilled laborers.[89] Most have minimum-wage jobs. The Fair Minimum Wage Act of 2007 took an important step in helping this group by moving the minimum wage to $7.25 per hour by 2009. This is a substantial improvement but still means that a full-time, 50-week-a-year minimum-wage job is not enough to keep a family of three above the poverty line. This is a major change from the late 1960s, when the minimum wage would support a family of three.

Compounding the problem is that many of these jobs are part-time and few provide benefits such as health insurance or a retirement plan. Consider John Gibson, a 50-year-old part-time janitor in Nashville who makes somewhat more than minimum wage:

> "I'd like to work more," John says. However, he is not qualified for many jobs. "I have to make sacrifices but I get by. When I get my check, the first thing I do is pay my rent." John lives alone in a small efficiency apartment. One of the things John sacrifices in order to get by is eating at fast-food restaurants. Although he likes the food and the convenience, a co-worker convinced him that it was much cheaper to prepare food at home. He minimizes his expenses on clothing by shopping at thrift stores such as the one operated by the Salvation Army.
>
> As a part-time employee, he has no company health insurance, but he is now eligible for some coverage from the state of Tennessee. A few years before he had this coverage he was hospitalized. Afterward, his wages were garnished to cover his bills, and he was forced to rely on social service agencies. Today he spends a great deal of his spare time volunteering at these same agencies. He would enjoy golf but is seldom able to play. He has no pension plan or personal insurance and wonders what his retirement years will be like.[90]

Lack of education tends to be a defining characteristic of this group.[91] Members of the upper-lower class live in marginal housing that is often located in depressed and decayed neighborhoods. Crime, drugs, and gangs are often close at hand and represent very real threats. They are concerned about the safety of their families and their children's future. The lack of education, role models, and opportunities often produces despair that can result in harmful consumption, such as cigarettes and alcohol. It may also produce inefficient purchasing and a short-term time focus.[92]

The marketing system has not served this group effectively. They have a particularly difficult time securing financial services, and many do not have bank accounts. This means that they generally must pay a fee for cashing paychecks and other checks. However, research indicates substantial marketing opportunities in this group. They tend to be value-oriented rather than just cost-focused. They tend to be very brand loyal. Firms such as Walmart and Dollar General have done a good and profitable job serving these consumers.[93]

The Lower-Lower Class Members of the lower-lower social stratum have very low incomes and minimal education. This segment of society is often unemployed for long periods of time and is the major recipient of government support and services provided by nonprofit organizations. Andre Hank, as described in Chapter 1, is an example of an individual who was in the upper-lower class and then wound up in the lower-lower class when he lost his job.

Marketing to the lower classes is frequently controversial. The rent-to-own business flourishes by renting durable goods, such as televisions and refrigerators, to lower-class households who frequently cannot afford to acquire them for cash and lack the credit rating to charge the purchases at regular outlets. While this service appears to meet a real need, the industry is frequently criticized for charging exorbitant interest rates on the purchases.[94]

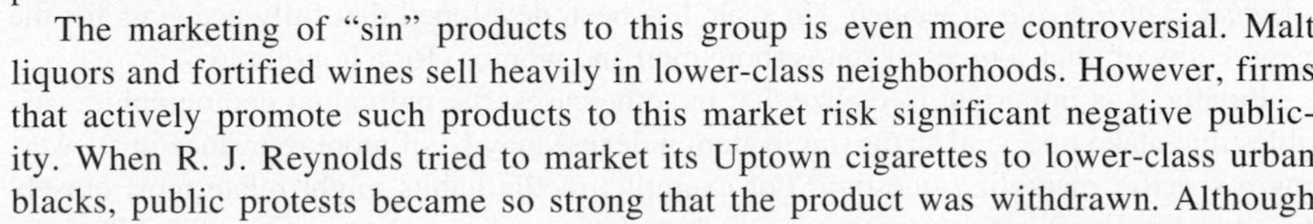

The marketing of "sin" products to this group is even more controversial. Malt liquors and fortified wines sell heavily in lower-class neighborhoods. However, firms that actively promote such products to this market risk significant negative publicity. When R. J. Reynolds tried to market its Uptown cigarettes to lower-class urban blacks, public protests became so strong that the product was withdrawn. Although some might applaud this outcome, the unstated assumption of the protest is that these individuals lack the ability to make sound consumption decisions and thus require protections that other social classes do not require—an assumption that is certainly controversial.

Other firms are criticized for not marketing to the lower classes. Major retail chains, particularly food chains, and financial firms seldom provide services in lower-class neighborhoods. Critics argue that such businesses have a social responsibility to locate in these areas. The businesses thus criticized respond that this is a problem for all of society and the solution should not be forced on a few firms. However, a few sophisticated chain retailers such as Dollar General Corporation have begun to meet the unique needs of this segment. As one specialist in this area said:

> People with lower household incomes are still consumers. They still have to buy food. They still wear clothing. They still have to take care of their kids.[95]

The challenge for business is to develop marketing strategies that will meet the needs of these consumers efficiently and at a reasonable profit to the firm.

THE MEASUREMENT OF SOCIAL CLASS

LO5 There are two basic approaches to measuring social status: a single-item index and a multi-item index. **Single-item indexes** estimate social status on the basis of a single dimension such as education, income, or occupation. Since an individual's overall status is influenced by several dimensions, single-item indexes are generally less accurate. **Multi-item indexes** take into account numerous variables simultaneously and weight these according to a scheme that reflects societal views. We focus here on the classic multi-item approach of Hollingshead.[96]

The Hollingshead **Index of Social Position (ISP)** is a two-item index that is well developed and widely used. The item scales, weights, formulas, and social-class scores are shown in Table 4–5. Notice how, in the United States, occupation is given a higher weight than education. *Why is this?*

It is important to note that multi-item indexes were designed to measure or reflect *an individual's or family's overall social position within a community.* Because of this, it is possible for a high score on one variable to offset a low score on another. Thus, the following three individuals would all be classified as middle class on the ISP scale: (1) someone with an eighth-grade education who is a successful owner of a medium-sized firm; (2) a four-year-college graduate working as a salesperson; and (3) a graduate of a junior college working in an administrative position in the civil service. All of these individuals may well have similar standing in the community. However, it seems likely that their consumption processes for at least some products will differ, pointing out the fact that overall status may mask potentially useful associations between individual status dimensions and the consumption process for particular products.

Another important aspect of these measures is that *they were developed before the rapid expansion of the role of women.* No scale has been developed that fully accounts for the new reality of dual sources of status (both men and women) for a household.

Finally, it is important to realize that in some cases, the individual demographic variables that make up social status (multi-item indexes) may be of more relevance in answering a specific marketing question. For example, media habits might relate most closely to education while leisure activities might relate most closely to occupation. In these

Hollingshead Index of Social Position (ISP)

Occupation Scale (Weight of 7)	
Description	**Score**
Higher executives of large concerns, proprietors, and major professionals	1
Business managers, proprietors of medium-sized businesses, and lesser professionals	2
Administrative personnel, owners of small businesses, and minor professionals	3
Clerical and sales workers, technicians, and owners of little businesses	4
Skilled manual employees	5
Machine operators and semiskilled employees	6
Unskilled employees	7
Education Scale (Weight of 4)	
Description	**Score**
Professional (MA, MS, ME, MD, PhD, LLD, and the like)	1
Four-year college graduate (BA, BS, BM)	2
One to three years of college (also business schools)	3
High school graduate	4
Ten to 11 years of school (part high school)	5
Seven to nine years of school	6
Less than seven years of school	7
ISP score = (Occupation score × 7) + (Education score × 4)	
Classification System	
Social Strata	**Range of Scores**
Upper	11–17
Upper-middle	18–31
Middle	32–47
Lower-middle	48–63
Lower	64–77

Source: Adapted from A. B. Hollingshead and F. C. Redlich, *Social Class and Mental Illness* (New York: John Wiley & Sons, 1958).

instances, marketers are better off using these direct measures of demographics than the more global measures of status. Only when an overall indication of an individual's or family's status is of particular relevance should measures such as the ISP be used. Recent research does suggest that social class is still an important determinant of various consumer behaviors in the United States.[97]

SOCIAL STRATIFICATION AND MARKETING STRATEGY

LO6

While social stratification does not explain all consumption behaviors, it is certainly relevant for some product categories. For clear evidence of this, visit a furniture store in a working-class neighborhood and then an upper-class store such as Ethan Allen Galleries. Another example is the jeans market and in particular Levi Strauss. Figure 4–4 illustrates how Levi Strauss attempts to cover a large portion of the U.S. population by positioning

FIGURE 4-4 Levi Strauss Positioning to Social Class Segments

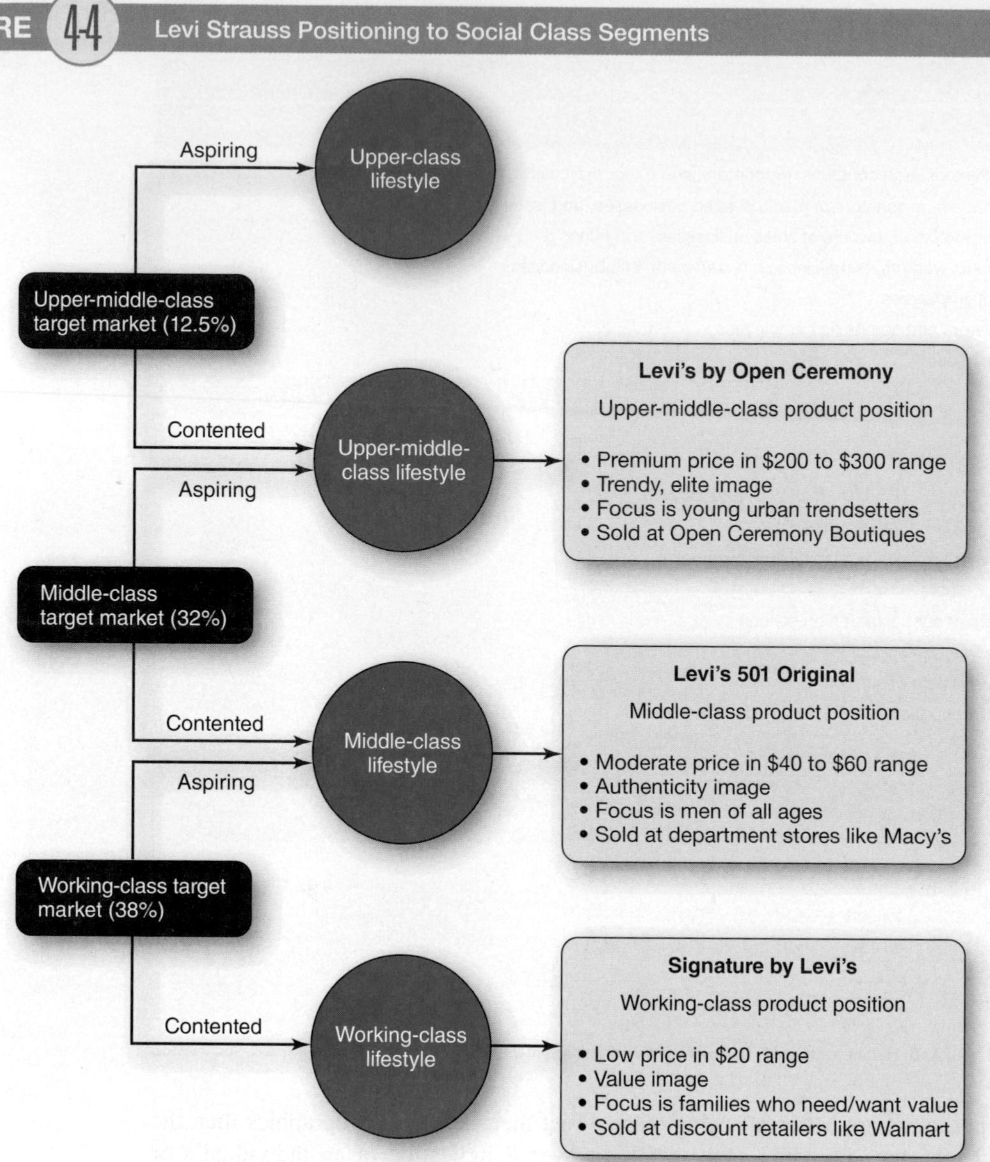

various brands in such a way as to target different social class categories. *How effective do you feel Levi's has been in differentiating and positioning its brands for various social class segments?*

While social class is clearly useful, sometimes looking at overall social class can mask underlying mechanisms and resulting behavioral barriers. The challenge for marketers and consumer advocates is often to dig deeper for the more fundamental aspects *associated with* social class, as discussed in Consumer Insight 4–2.

Finally, moving beyond brands per se to cities and communities can bring up social class issues. For example, many cities are trying to reverse so-called urban blight by working to attract higher-end developers and retailers to revitalize their neighborhoods. One example is Harlem, which has attracted an increasing number of upscale boutique shops, many owned by the "new black middle class," which has enhanced the appeal of Harlem.

CONSUMER INSIGHT 4-2

Social Class, Diet Quality, and the 99 Cent Store

Questions about the link between social class and dietary quality have been examined in a number of ways, including in the medical community.[98] A recent article indicates:

> A large body of epidemiological data shows that diet quality follows a socioeconomic gradient. Whereas hither-quality diets are associated with greater affluence, energy-dense diets that are nutrient-poor are preferentially consumed by persons of lower socioeconomic status (SES) and of more limited economic means.

The article goes on to point out that it is critical to "dig deeper" into the underlying causes associated with social class. In the case of diet, these include the fact that nutritional foods often cost more, and physical access to affordable nutritional foods for disadvantaged groups is often limited. The reason a search for underlying causes is so important is that it has consequences for how groups market high-quality diets to lower-SES/lower-income groups. That is, simply recommending high-cost (but nutritional) foods to low income consumers is likely to be ineffective because the desire to consume a better diet among lower-SES/lower-income consumers would be hindered by inability to pay and limited access (no or few stores nearby that carry such foods).

The following relates the story of a lower-income consumer who was overweight. His access to lower-priced but nutritious foods through the 99 Cent Store became the answer to both of the barriers listed above, as you will see.

> Papa Joe Aviance, a Los Angeles clothing designer and musician who weighed 450 pounds, decided he had to lose weight when he saw a video of himself. "I was 450 pounds—I was two cheeseburgers away from diabetes or high cholesterol, I have been big for pretty much all my life, and I was sick of hating myself. It was now or never." Not able to afford the prices of the vegetables and fruits from high-end food stores like Trader Joe's or Whole Foods, he took up the suggestion of his friend to shop at the 99 Cent Store. His weekly $50 purchase at the 99 Cent Store, which included oatmeal, tuna fish, eggs, salad dressing, vegetables, and fruits, coupled with exercise of daily walks led to a weight loss of 250 pounds over 18 months.

The story confirms the medical article in showing that it is not social class per se that causes poor diet, but other key underlying mechanisms. Faced with inflexible food budgets, persons of lower SES find the relative high price of fruits and vegetables to be a barrier to their diet and choose the lower-priced, energy-dense foods that are high in fats and sugars. These dietary factors contribute to the observed health inequities. Individuals from lower-SES/lower-income groups have higher rates of obesity, diabetes, cardiovascular disease, and dental issues than individuals from higher-SES/higher-income groups.

The Papa Joe Aviance story highlights the key issues that (a) it is not enough to look only at social class in the abstract; (b) marketers and policymakers must look for deeper underlying factors, and address those; and (c) companies such as the 99 Cent Store can play a key role in helping lower-SES groups deal with serious health-related issues by dealing with the underlying factors rather than simply telling everyone that they should eat a healthy diet.

Awareness may be the first key. Generally speaking, American's tend to (incorrectly) believe that wealth is distributed more equally than it is. Moreover, a general awareness of the lack of physical availability of healthy food alternatives is likely lacking as well. A broader understanding of these challenges may be necessary for there to be more companies like the 99 Cent Store that tackle the hurdles facing those on the lower social strata.

Critical Thinking Questions

1. Why is it important for marketers to focus less on social class and more on the underlying mechanisms related to social class that might affect consumers and their behaviors?
2. What challenges are faced by corporations in reducing the barriers to a healthy diet faced by those consumers of lower SES?
3. How might general misperceptions of wealth distribution help to produce well-meaning but misguided approaches to encouraging healthier diets among lower-SES consumers?

At the same time these boutiques have displaced local stores that have traditionally catered to the "long-term, lower class residents."[99] *What are the societal implications of such urban revitalization efforts?*

SUMMARY

LO1: Understand the critical role that demographics play in influencing consumer behavior

American society is described in part by its *demographics,* which include a population's size, distribution, and structure. The structure of a population refers to its age, income, education, and occupation makeup. Demographics are not static. At present, the rate of population growth is moderate, average age is increasing, and the southern and western regions are growing. In addition to actual measures of age and income, subjective measures can provide additional understanding of consumption in the form of *cognitive age* and *subjective discretionary income.*

LO2: Define the concept of generations and discuss the generations that exist in America

An *age cohort* or *generation* is a group of persons who have experienced a common social, political, historical, and economic environment. *Cohort analysis* is the process of describing and explaining the attitudes, values, and behaviors of an age group as well as predicting its future attitudes, values, and behaviors. There are six major generations functioning in America today: pre-Depression, Depression, baby boom, Generation X, Generation Y, and Generation Z.

LO3: Explain the concept of social stratification and the role that socioeconomic factors play

A *social class system* is defined as the hierarchical division of a society into relatively permanent and homogeneous groups with respect to attitudes, values, and lifestyles. A tightly defined social class system does not exist in the United States. What does seem to exist is a series of status continua that reflect various dimensions or factors that the overall society values. Education, occupation, income, and, to a lesser extent, type of residence are important status dimensions in this country. *Status crystallization* refers to the consistency of individuals and families on all relevant status dimensions (e.g., high income and high educational level).

LO4: Identify and discuss the major social classes in America

Although pure social classes do not exist in the United States, it is useful for marketing managers to know and understand the general characteristics of major social classes. Using Coleman and Rainwater's system, we described American society in terms of seven major categories: *upper-upper, lower-upper, upper-middle, middle, working class, upper-lower,* and *lower-lower.*

LO5: Understand how social class is measured

There are two basic approaches to the measurement of social classes: (1) use a combination of several dimensions, a *multi-item index,* or (2) use a single dimension, a *single-item index.* Multi-item indexes are designed to measure an individual's overall rank or social position within the community.

LO6: Discuss the role of social class in developing marketing strategies

Although social class may not play a role in all products or brands, it is obviously relevant in many situations. Brands such as Levi's appear to use social class as a segmenting tool. Targeting those in lower social classes can have ethical implications and choices regarding what products to offer, and what actions to take in this regard must be considered carefully.

KEY TERMS

Age cohort 117
Class to mass 114
Cognitive age 117
Cohort analysis 117
Conspicuous consumption 131
Demographics 110
Digital Savvy 109
Generation 117
Gerontographics 118
Index of Social Position (ISP) 136
Mature market 118
Multi-item indexes 136
Nouveaux riches 131
Single-item indexes 136
Social class system 128
Societal rank 128
Status crystallization 129
Subjective discretionary income (SDI) 114
Working-class aristocrats 134

REVIEW QUESTIONS

1. What are demographics?
2. Why is population growth an important concept for marketers?
3. What trend(s) characterizes the occupational structure of the United States?
4. What trend(s) characterizes the level of education in the United States?
5. What trend(s) characterizes the level of income in the United States?
6. What is meant by *subjective discretionary income?* How does it affect purchases?
7. What trend(s) characterizes the age distribution of the American population?
8. What is cognitive age? How is it measured?
9. What is an age cohort? A cohort analysis?
10. Describe each of the major generations in America.
11. What is a social class system?
12. What is meant by the statement, "What exists is not a set of social classes but a series of status continua"?
13. What underlying cultural value determines most of the status dimensions in the United States?
14. What is meant by *status crystallization?* Is the degree of status crystallization relatively high or low in the United States? Explain.
15. Briefly describe the primary characteristics of each of the classes described in the text (assume a high level of status crystallization).
16. What is meant by the phrase *class to mass* and how does it relate to *upward-pull?*
17. What ethical issues arise in marketing to the lower social classes?
18. What are the two basic approaches used by marketers to measure social class?
19. What are the advantages of multi-item indexes? The disadvantages?
20. Describe the Hollingshead Index of Social Position. Why is occupation weighted more heavily? Would this weighting hold in other cultures?

DISCUSSION QUESTIONS

21. Which demographic shifts, if any, do you feel will have a noticeable impact on the market for the following in the next 10 years? Justify your answer.
    a. Upscale restaurants
    b. Botox treatments
    c. Prescription drugs
    d. Internet shopping
    e. Green products
    f. Newspapers
    g. Charitable contributions
22. Given the projected changes in America's demographics, name five products that will face increasing demand and five that will face declining demand.
23. Why do the regional differences shown in Figure 4–1 exist? What are the implications of such differences for marketers of products such as soft drinks?
24. Will the increasing median age of our population affect the general tone of our society? In what ways?
25. Respond to the questions in Consumer Insight 4–1.
26. Which demographic variable, if any, is most related to the following?
    a. Watching extreme sports on TV
    b. Scuba diving
    c. International travel
    d. In-home chef
    e. Spa treatments
    f. Going to a NASCAR event
27. Describe how each of the following firm's product managers should approach the (*i*) pre-Depression generation, (*ii*) Depression generation, (*iii*) baby boom generation, (*iv*) Generation X, (*v*) Generation Y, and (*vi*) Generation Z.
    a. Pepsi
    b. Panera Bread
    c. The Golf Channel
    d. About.com
    e. The Humane Society
    f. iPod
    g. Facebook
    h. Crest Whitener System

28. Respond to the questions in Consumer Insight 4–2.
29. How will your lifestyle differ from your parents' when you are your parents' age?
30. How could a knowledge of social stratification be used in the development of a marketing strategy for the following?
    a. Jeans
    b. Expensive jewelry
    c. Fishing
    d. Organic milk
    e. Museum attendance
    f. Habitat for Humanity
31. Do you think the United States is becoming more or less stratified over time?
32. Do your parents have a high or low level of status crystallization? Explain.
33. Based on the Hollingshead two-item index, what social class would your father be in? Your mother? What class will you be in at their age?
34. Name two products for which each of the three following demographic variables would be most influential in determining consumption. If you could combine two of the three, which would be the second demographic you would add to each? Justify your answer.
    a. Income
    b. Education
    c. Occupation
35. Name three products for which subjective discretionary income might be a better predictor of consumption than actual income. Justify your answer.
36. How do you feel about each of the ethical issues or controversies the text describes with respect to marketing to the lower classes? What other ethical issues do you see in this area?

37. Is it ethical for marketers to use the mass media to promote products that most members of the lower classes and working class cannot afford?

38. Would your answer to Question 37 change if the products were limited to children's toys?

39. Name five products for which the upward-pull strategy shown in Figure 4–3 would be appropriate. Name five for which it would be inappropriate. Justify your answers.
40. What ethical implications arise from urban renewal efforts such as those in Harlem?

APPLICATION ACTIVITIES

41. On the basis of the demographics of devoted coffee shop patrons, select two magazines in which the industry should advertise (use Standard Rate and Data [SRDS], Mediamark, or Simmons Research Bureau data). Justify your answer.
42. Interview a salesperson at the following locations and obtain a description of the average purchaser in demographic terms. Are the demographic shifts predicted in the text going to increase or decrease the size of this average-purchaser segment?
    a. Mercedes dealership
    b. Electronics store
    c. Vacation cruise
    d. Children's apparel
    e. Harley-Davidson dealership
    f. Pet store
43. Using Standard Rate and Data, Mediamark, or Simmons Research Bureau studies, pick three magazines that are oriented toward the different groups listed below. Analyze the differences in the products advertised and in the types of ads.
    a. Income groups
    b. Age groups
    c. Occupation groups
    d. Education levels
44. Interview three people over 50. Measure their cognitive age and the variables that presumably influence it. Do the variables appear to "cause" cognitive age? Try to ascertain if cognitive age or their chronological age is most influential on their consumption behavior.
45. Interview two members of the following generations. Determine the extent to which they feel the text description of their generation is accurate and how they think their generation differs from the larger society. Also determine what they think about

how they are portrayed in the mass media and how well they are served by business today.
a. Pre-Depression
b. Depression
c. Baby boom
d. Generation X
e. Generation Y
f. Generation Z

46. Interview a salesperson from an expensive, a moderate, and an inexpensive outlet for the following. Ascertain their perceptions of the social classes or status of their customers. Determine if their sales approach differs with differing classes.
a. Men's clothing
b. Women's clothing
c. Furniture
d. Wine

47. Examine a variety of magazines/newspapers and clip or copy an advertisement that positions a product as appropriate for each of the seven social classes described in the text (one ad per class). Explain how each ad appeals to that class.

48. Interview an unskilled worker, a schoolteacher, a retail clerk, and a successful businessperson all in their 30s or 40s. Measure their social status using one of the multi-item measurement devices. Evaluate their status crystallization.

49. Visit a bowling alley and a golf course parking lot. Analyze the differences in the types of cars, dress, and behaviors of those patronizing these two sports.

50. Volunteer to work two days or evenings at a homeless shelter, soup kitchen, or other program aimed at very-low-income families. Write a brief report on your experiences and reactions.

REFERENCES

1. This opener is based on "Understanding the Digital Savvy Consumer," *Scarborough Research,* 2008, www.scarborough.com.
2. See, e.g., M. I. M. Rosa-Diaz, "Price Knowledge," *Journal of Product and Brand Management,* 13, no. 6 (2004), pp. 406–28; and L. Eagle, "Commercial Media Literacy," *Journal of Advertising,* Summer 2007, pp. 101–10.
3. K. Dawidowska, "Caffeine Overload," *American Demographics,* April 2002, p. 16.
4. D. Cohn and G. Livingston, "U.S. Birth Rate Decline Linked to Recession," *Pew Social & Demographic Trends,* April 6, 2010, at http://pewsocialtrends.org, accessed March 10, 2011; and U.S. Census figures.
5. Population Division, U.S. Census Bureau, Interim State Population Projections, April 21, 2005.
6. "Poverty Thresholds by Size of Family Units: 1980–2008," *Income, Expenditures, Poverty, and Wealth* (Washington, DC: U.S. Census Bureau, 2011), table 709.
7. "Mean Earnings by Highest Degree Earned: 2008," *Education* (Washington, DC: U.S. Census Bureau, 2011), table 228.
8. See, e.g., M. Mittila, H. Karjaluoto, and T. Pento, "Internet Banking Adoption among Mature Consumers," *Journal of Services Marketing* 17, no. 5 (2003), pp. 514–28; and V. Mittal, W. A. Kamakura, and R. Govind, "Geographic Patterns in Customer Service and Satisfaction," *Journal of Marketing,* July 2004, pp. 48–62.
9. S. Fulwood III, "Americans Draw Fatter Paychecks," *(Eugene, OR) Register-Guard,* September 27, 1996, p. 1; and E. Kacapyr, "Are You Middle Class?," *American Demographics,* October 1996, pp. 31–35.
10. E. Saez, "Striking It Richer: The Evolution of Top Incomes in the United States," *Pathways Magazine,* Stanford Center for the Study of Poverty and Inequality, Winter 2008, pp. 6–7; updates and data tables available at http://elsa.berkeley.edu/~saez.
11. D. Gross, "The Latte Era Grinds Down," *Newsweek,* October 22, 2007, pp. 46–47.
12. N. Zmuda, "Why the Bad Economy Has Been Good for Target," *Advertising Age,* October 4, 2010.
13. Gross, "The Latte Era Grinds Down."
14. For an example, see F. J. Mulhern, J. D. Williams, and R. P. Leone, "Variability of Brand Price Elasticities across Retail Stores," *Journal of Retailing,* 3 (1998), pp. 427–45.
15. Consumer confidence indexes also consider the subjective nature of spending and represent "leading indicators" of consumer spending. For a discussion, see M. J. Weiss, "Inside Consumer Confidence Surveys," *American Demographics,* February 2003, pp. 22–29.
16. T. C. O'Guinn and W. D. Wells, "Subjective Discretionary Income," *Marketing Research,* March 1989, pp. 32–41; see also P. L. Wachtel and S. J. Blatt, "Perceptions of Economic Needs and of Anticipated Future Income," *Journal of Economic Psychology,* September 1990, pp. 403–15; and J. R. Rossiter, "'Spending Power' and the Subjective Discretionary Income (SDI) Scale," in *Advances in Consumer Research,* vol. 22, ed. F. R. Kardes and M. Sujan (Provo, UT: Association for Consumer Research, 1995), pp. 236–40.
17. P. L. Alreck, "Consumer Age Role Norms," *Psychology & Marketing,* October 2000, pp. 891–909.
18. P. Henry, "Modes of Thought That Vary Systematically with Both Social Class and Age," *Psychology & Marketing,* May 2000, pp. 421–40.
19. For example, see R. Gardyn, "Shopping Attitudes by Life Stage," *American Demographics,* November 2002, p. 33; and D. M. Phillips and J. L. Stanton, "Age-Related Differences in Advertising," *Journal of Targeting, Measurement and Analysis for Marketing,* 13, no. 1 (2004), pp. 7–20.

20. "Resident Population Projections by Sex and Age: 2010 to 2050," *Statistical Abstract of the United States 2008* (Washington, DC: U.S. Bureau of the Census, 2008), table 10.

21. P. Sloan and J. Neff, "With Aging Boomers in Mind, P&G, Den-Mat Plan Launches," *Advertising Age,* April 13, 1998, p. 3.

22. See K. P. Gwinner and N. Stephens, "Testing the Implied Mediational Role of Cognitive Age," *Psychology & Marketing,* October 2001, pp. 1031–48; and A. Mathur and G. P. Moschis, "Antecedents of Cognitive Age," *Psychology & Marketing,* December 2005, pp. 969–94.

23. S. Van Auken, T. E. Barry, and R. P. Bagozzi, "A Cross-Country Construct Validation of Cognitive Age," *Journal of the Academy of Marketing Science,* Summer 2006, pp. 439–55.

24. See A. S. Wellner, "Generational Divide," *American Demographics,* October 2000, pp. 53–58.

25. A. Rindfleisch, "Cohort Generational Influences on Consumer Socialization," in *Advances in Consumer Research,* vol. 21, ed. C. T. Allen and D. R. John (Provo, UT: Association for Consumer Research, 1994), pp. 470–76; and R. T. Rust and K. W. Y. Yeung, "Tracking the Age Wave," in *Advances in Consumer Research,* vol. 22, ed. Kardes and Sujan, pp. 680–85.

26. For a detailed treatment, see J. W. Smith and A. Clurman, *Rocking the Ages* (New York: Harper Business, 1997). See also *Generations 2010* (Washington, D.C.: Pew Research Center, December 2010).

27. See N. Long, "Broken Down by Age and Sex," *Journal of the Market Research Society,* April 1998, pp. 73–91; and G. P. Moschis, "Life Stages of the Mature Market," *American Demographics,* September 1996, pp. 44–51.

28. L. L. Price, E. J. Arnould, and C. F. Curasi, "Older Consumers' Disposition of Special Possessions," *Journal of Consumer Research,* September 2000, p. 192.

29. See C. Yoon, "Age Differences in Consumers' Processing Strategies," *Journal of Consumer Research,* December 1997, pp. 329–40; S. Law, S. A. Hawkins, and F. I. M. Craik, "Repetition-Induced Belief in the Elderly," *Journal of Consumer Research,* September 1998, pp. 91–107; G. P. Moschis, "Consumer Behavior in Later Life," *Research in Consumer Behavior* 9 (2000), pp. 103–28; and G. P. Moschis, "Marketing to Older Adults," *Journal of Consumer Marketing,* 20, no. 6 (2003), pp. 516–25.

30. P. Francese, "The Exotic Travel Boom," *American Demographics,* June 2002, pp. 48–49; and *Growing Old in America* (Bethesda, MD: National Institute on Aging, 2007).

31. *Generations 2010.*

32. J. Schleimer, "Active Adults Uncovered," *Builder,* February 2001, pp. 336–40.

33. J. B. Thomas and C. Peters, "Exploring the Self-Concept, Lifestyles, and Apparel Consumption of Women over Age 65," *International Journal of Retailing & Distribution Management,* 37, no. 12 (2009), pp. 1018–40.

34. M. J. Weiss, "Great Expectations," *American Demographics,* May 2003, pp. 26–35.

35. *Growing Old in America.* See also C. Yoon, C. Cole, and M. P. Lee, "Consumer Decision Making and Aging," *Journal of Consumer Psychology,* 19 (2009), pp. 17–22.

36. See, e.g., R. G. Javalgi, E. G. Thomas, and S. R. Rao, "Meeting the Needs of the Elderly in the Financial Services Market," *Journal of Professional Services Marketing,* 2, no. 2 (2000), pp. 87–105.

37. *Inheritance and Wealth Transfer to Baby Boomers* (Westport, CT: MetLife Mature Market Institute, 2010).

38. J. Saranow, "Online Deaccessioning," *The Wall Street Journal,* June 28, 2004, pp. B1–B2.

39. See, e.g., T. Reisenwitz and R. Iyer, "A Comparison of Younger and Older Baby Boomers," *Journal of Consumer Marketing,* 24, no. 4 (2007), pp. 202–13.

40. *Generations 2010.*

41. *U.S. Baby Boomer Attitudes and Opportunities* (Rockville, MD: Packaged Facts, June 2008).

42. J. Raymond, "The Joy of Empty Nesting," *American Demographics,* May 2000, pp. 49–54; P. Francese, "Big Spenders," *American Demographics,* September 2001, pp. 30–31; P. Francese, "The Coming Boom in Second-Home Ownership," *American Demographics,* October 2001, pp. 26–27; S. Yin, "More at Home on the Road," *American Demographics,* June 2003, pp. 26–27; and S. Yin, "Full Speed Ahead," *American Demographics,* September 2003, pp. 20–21.

43. J. Raymond, "Senior Living," *American Demographics,* November 2000, pp. 58–63.

44. See R. Gardyn, "Retirement Redefined," *American Demographics,* November 2000, pp. 52–57; and H. Schau, M. C. Gilly, and M. Wolfinbarger, "Consumer Identity Renaissance," *Journal of Consumer Research,* August 2009, pp. 255–76.

45. K. Greene, "Marketing Surprise," *The Wall Street Journal,* April 6, 2004, pp. A1, 12.

46. H. Tootelian and S. B. Varshney, "The Grandparent Consumer," *Journal of Consumer Marketing,* 27, no. 1 (2010), pp. 57–63.

47. J. M. Kozar and M. L. Damhorst, "Older Women's Responses to Current Fashion Models," *Journal of Fashion Marketing and Management,* 21, no. 3 (2008), pp. 338–50.

48. This insight is based on "It's Good to Be Green," *Focalyst Insight Report,* December 2007, at www.focalyst.com, accessed March 10, 2011; "How Well Do You Know Boomers?," *Focalyst Insight Report,* April 2008, at www.focalyst.com, accessed March 10, 2011; *Generational Market Research Bundle* (Rockville, MD: Packaged Facts, December 2008); "Yesterday, Today and Tomorrow," *Focalyst Insight Report,* February 2009, at www.focalyst.com, accessed March 10, 2011; "Mobile Access 2010," *Pew Internet & American Life Project,* July 7, 2010, at http://pewinternet.org, accessed March 10, 2011; and "Demographics of Internet Users," *Pew Internet & American Life Project,* 2010, at http://pewinternet.org, accessed March 10, 2011.

49. *Generational Market Research Bundle* (Rockville, MD: Packaged Facts, 2008).

50. *Study of Media and Markets* (Deerfield Beach, FL: Simmons Market Research Bureau, Fall 2005).

51. S. Chen, "Women Marrying Men with Less Education, Income," *CNN.com,* accessed May 17, 2010.

52. "Farther ALONG the X Axis," *American Demographics,* May 2004, pp. 20–24.

53. *Family Households with Own Children under 18 by Type of Family, 2000 and 2009, and by Age of Householder, 2009* (Washington, D.C.: U.S. Census Bureau, Statistical Abstract of the United States, 2011), table 65.

54. "Millenials," *PewResearchCenter Social and Demographic Trends,* February 24, 2010.

55. J. Halliday, "Volvo Goes After Younger Buyers," *Advertising Age,* January 19, 2004, p. 12.
56. "Facebook Targeting," *Affiliate Marketing Blog,* August 4, 2010, at www.legacyaffiliateblog.com, accessed March 13, 2011.
57. *Study of Media and Markets* (Deerfield Beach, FL: Simmons Market Research Bureau, Fall 2007).
58. For a discussion of the consequences of this, see A. Rindfleisch, J. E. Burroughs, and F. Denton, "Family Structure, Materialism, and Compulsive Consumption," *Journal of Consumer Research,* March 1997, pp. 312–25.
59. P. Paul, "Getting inside Gen Y," *American Demographics,* September 2001, pp. 43–49.
60. J. Napoli and M. T. Ewing, "The Net Generation," *Journal of International Consumer Marketing,* 13, no. 1 (2001), pp. 21–34.
61. "Millenials."
62. C. Dougherty, "For Many Adults, Marriage Can Wait, Census Shows," *The Wall Street Journal,* September 28, 2010.
63. R. J. Samuelson, "The Real Generation Gap," *Newsweek,* March 15, 2010; and S. De Hauw and A. De Vos, "Millennials' Career Perspective and Psychological Contract Expectations," *Journal of Business and Psychology,* June 2010, pp. 293–303.
64. P. Paul, "Echo Boomerang," *American Demographics,* June 2001, pp. 45–49; and A. Merrick, "Gap's Greatest Generation?," *The Wall Street Journal Online,* September 15, 2004, www.wsj.com.
65. S. Kang, "Chasing Generation Y," *The Wall Street Journal,* September 1, 2006, p. A11.
66. Ibid.
67. Computed from U.S. Census data.
68. *Generations 2010.*
69. C. La Ferle, S. M. Edwards, and W. Lee, "Teens' Use of Traditional Media and the Internet," *Journal of Advertising Research,* May 2000, pp. 55–65; and H. Fattah and P. Paul, "Gaming Gets Serious," *American Demographics,* May 2002, pp. 38–43.
70. A. Walliker, "Generation Z Comes of Age," *Herald Sun,* February 25, 2008; L. Schmidt and P. Hawkins, "Children of the Tech Revolution," *The Sydney (Australia) Morning Herald,* July 15, 2008; and *Sparxoo 2010 Report: Generation Analysis* (Rochester, NY: Sparxoo, 2010).
71. Based on computations of data from the U.S. Census Bureau.
72. *Good Intentions* (New York, NY: Girl Scout Research Institute, 2009).
73. "Generation Z Comes of Age."
74. "Marketing to Tweens and Teens," *ResearchandMarkets,* product brochure, at www.researchandmarkets.com, accessed March 10, 2011.
75. "Teen Spending," money-management-works.com, accessed March 10, 2011.
76. N. Shepherdson, "New Kids on the Lot," *American Demographics,* January 2000, p. 47.
77. P. Underhill, *Call of the Mall* (New York: Simon and Schuster, 2004), p. 160; see also D. L. Haytko and J. Baker, "It's All at the Mall," *Journal of Retailing,* 80 (2004), pp. 67–83.
78. *Generations 2010;* and *Sparxoo 2010 Report.*
79. J. Zegler, "Gatorade Repositions from Sports Drink to Sports Performance," *Brand Packaging,* September 2010.
80. E. Holmes, "Teen Stores Cater to the Ones with Money," *The Wall Street Journal,* September 23, 2009.
81. K. Labich, "Class in America," *Fortune,* February 7, 1994, p. 114.
82. J. E. Fisher, "Social Class and Consumer Behavior," in *Advances in Consumer Research,* vol. 14, ed. M. Wallendorf and P. Anderson (Provo, UT: Association for Consumer Research, 1987), pp. 492–96.
83. See R. P. Heath, "The New Working Class," *American Demographics,* January 1998, pp. 51–55.
84. R. Coleman, "The Continuing Significance of Social Class in Marketing," *Journal of Consumer Research,* December 1983, p. 265. For a recent discussion of social class in America, see J. Scott and D. Leonhardt, "Shadowy Lines That Still Divide," *New York Times,* May 15, 2005, www.nytimes.com, accessed May 28, 2008.
85. See Heath, "The New Working Class." See also E. Sivadas, G. Mathew, and D. J. Curry, "A Preliminary Examination of the Continuing Significance of Social Class to Marketing," *Journal of Consumer Marketing,* 14, no. 6 (1997), pp. 463–79.
86. See A. M. Kerwin, "Brands Pursue Old, New Money," *Advertising Age,* June 11, 2001, p. S1.
87. See, e.g., R. J. Samuelson, "The End of Entitlement," *Newsweek,* May 26, 2008, p. 39.
88. See J. P. Dickson and D. L. MacLachlan, "Social Distance and Shopping Behavior," *Journal of the Academy of Marketing Science,* Spring 1990, pp. 153–62.
89. See also D. Watson, "In Search of the Poor," *Journal of Economic Psychology,* 21 (2000), pp. 495–515.
90. P. Mergenhagen, "What Can Minimum Wage Buy?," *American Demographics,* January 1996, pp. 32–36.
91. H. Fattah, "The Rising Tide," *American Demographics,* April 2001, pp. 48–53.
92. For a theoretical examination, see P. Henry, "Hope, Hopelessness, and Coping," *Psychology & Marketing,* May 2004, pp. 375–403.
93. Fattah, "The Rising Tide."
94. R. H. Hill, D. L. Ramp, and L. Silver, "The Rent-to-Own Industry and Pricing Disclosure Tactics," *Journal of Public Policy & Marketing,* Spring 1998, pp. 1–10.
95. C. Miller, "The Have-Nots," *Marketing News,* August 1, 1994, p. 2.
96. See A. B. Hollingshead, *Elmstown's Youth* (New York: Wiley, 1949); and W. L. Warner, M. Meeker, and K. Eels, *Social Class in America: A Manual of Procedure for the Measurement of Social Status* (Chicago: Science Research Associates, 1949).
97. Sivadas, Mathew, and Curry, "A Preliminary Examination of the Continuing Significance of Social Class to Marketing"; and T. G. Williams, "Social Class Influences on Purchase Evaluation Criteria," *Journal of Consumer Marketing,* 19, no. 3 (2002), pp. 249–76.
98. Sources for this insight include N. Darmon and A. Drewnowski, "Does Social Class Predict Diet Quality?," *American Journal of Clinical Nutrition,* 87 (2008), pp. 1107–17; D. Ariely, "Americans Want to Live in a Much More Equal Country," *The Atlantic.com,* August 2, 2012, www.theatlantic.com/business/archive/2012/08/americans-want-to-live-in-a-much-more-equal-country-they-just-dont-realize-it/260639/, accessed August 27, 2014; and R. Dillon, "99 Cent Diet Helps Man Lose 250 Pounds with Foods from 99 Cent Store," *Examiner.com*, June 4, 2013, www.examiner.com/article/99-cent-diet-helps-man-lose-250-pounds-with-foods-from-99-cent-store, accessed August 27, 2014.
99. S. Zukin, "New Retail Capital and Neighborhood Change," *City & Community,* March 2009, pp. 47–64.

chapter

5 The Changing American Society: Subcultures

LEARNING OBJECTIVES

LO1 **Understand subcultures and their influence on unique market behaviors.**

LO2 **Analyze the African-American subculture and the unique marketing aspects it entails.**

LO3 **Analyze the Hispanic subculture and the unique marketing aspects it entails.**

LO4 **Analyze the Asian-American subculture and the unique marketing aspects it entails.**

LO5 **Analyze the Native-American, Asian-Indian-American, and Arab-American subcultures and the unique marketing aspects they entail.**

LO6 **Describe the various religious subcultures and their implications for marketing.**

LO7 **Explain the role of geographic regions as subcultures.**

American ethnic subcultures continue to lead the way today in fashion, music, and culture.[1] While we are all Americans, those from specific ethnic subcultures bring with them values, heritage, and culture that influence their choices in ways that are different from so-called mainstream America. African Americans, for example, feel a strong need to embrace their specific ethnic subculture as it relates to activities and family traditions. They also are very likely to support retailers who affirm and respect their cultural heritage by carrying ethnic items and employing people who "look like me."

Sponsorship of ethnic events offers marketers the opportunity to support and nourish the ethnic community in authentic ways. An example of one such effort is the Essence Music Festival. Originally launched in 1995 as a one-time event to celebrate the 25th anniversary of *ESSENCE,* a magazine targeted toward African-American women, the event has thrived to become an annual, massive, multiday festival. Held in the New Orleans Mercedes-Benz Superdome since 1995, the Essence Music Festival is the biggest event of African-American culture and music in the United States, drawing hundreds of thousands of people.

Although the superstar music headliners are a draw, the Essence Music Festival is more than a music fest. Themed from its inception as "the party with a purpose," the Essence Music Festival is designed to give back to the community. It may be the only music-themed event where not only musicians but motivational speakers are featured. A lineup of empowerment seminars and panels on education, careers, beauty, and family are held at a nearby convention center. Included in the program is #YesWeCode "hackathon," which "will bring together nearly 200 of the tech industry's brightest developers, designers, and influential business professionals working alongside 50 high potential youth to solve problems with the goal of transforming their neighborhoods into thriving communities where everyone experiences success regardless of race, gender, abilities or other factors."

Sponsors include Coca Cola, Ford, McDonald's, My Black is Beautiful P&G, State Farm, Walmart, Verizon, AARP, American Cancer Society, Chevron, Colgate, and We tv. According to a company spokesperson for Essence:

> The solution the festival provides is allowing our brand marketers to engage our audience with their brand in relevant ways. For them, the magazine delivers one solution and the website delivers another. The festival really rounds that out with an experiential marketing solution. Whenever we go in to speak with our clients, it's not just with a magazine solution. It's with a full 360, yearlong plan.

Some companies have stumbled in their efforts to market to, and engage, ethnic subcultures. Fully understanding an ethnic group and presenting authentic, respectful, and appropriate messages is critical to success, as demonstrated so well by Essence.

In the previous chapter, we described how changes in American demographics are creating challenges and opportunities for marketers. Another extremely important aspect of the American society is its numerous subcultures, such as the African-American subculture described above. Although American society has always contained numerous subcultures, until recently, many marketers treated it as a homogeneous culture based primarily on Western European values. This view of America was never very accurate, and it is even less so today as non-European immigration, differential birthrates, and increased ethnic identification accentuate the heterogeneous nature of our society.

An array of racial, ethnic, nationality, religious, and regional groups or subcultures characterize American society today. These subcultures are growing at different rates and are themselves undergoing change. In this chapter, we describe the more important subcultures in America. We also highlight the marketing strategy implications of a heterogeneous rather than a homogeneous society.

THE NATURE OF SUBCULTURES

LO1

A **subculture** is *a segment of a larger culture whose members share distinguishing values and patterns of behavior.* The unique values and patterns of behavior shared by subculture group members are based on the social history of the group as well as its current situation. Subculture members are also part of the larger culture in which they exist, and they generally share most behaviors and beliefs with the core culture. As Figure 5–1 indicates, the degree to which an individual behaves in a manner unique to a subculture depends on the extent to which the individual identifies with that subculture.

FIGURE 5-1 Identification with a Subculture Produces Unique Market Behaviors

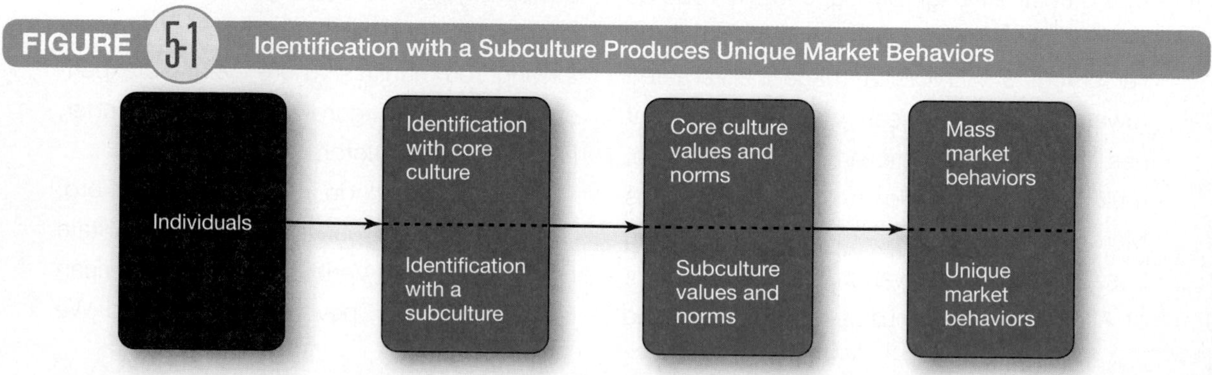

ILLUSTRATION 5-1

It is sometimes important to customize ads to meet the requirements of different ethnic markets.

America has traditionally been viewed as a melting pot or a soup bowl. Immigrants from various countries came to America and quickly (at least by the second generation) surrendered their old languages, values, behaviors, and even religions. In their place, they acquired American characteristics that were largely a slight adaptation of Western European, particularly British, features. The base American culture was vast enough that new immigrants did not change the flavor of the mixture to any noticeable extent. Although this is a reasonable approximation of the experience of most Western European immigrants, it isn't very accurate for African, Hispanic, Asian, or Arabic immigrants. Nor does it accurately describe the experience of Native Americans.

Today, America is perhaps better described as a salad rather than a melting pot or a soup bowl. When a small amount of a new ingredient is added to a soup, it generally loses its identity completely and blends into the overall flavor of the soup. In a salad, each ingredient retains its own unique identity while adding to the color and flavor of the overall salad. However, even in the salad bowl analogy, we should add a large serving of salad dressing, which represents the core American culture and blends the diverse groups into a cohesive society.

Ethnic groups are the most commonly described subcultures, but religions and geographic regions are also the bases for strong subcultures in the United States. Generations, as described in the previous chapter, also function like subcultures. Thus, *we are all members of several subcultures.* Each subculture may influence different aspects of our lifestyle. Our attitudes toward new products or imported products may be strongly influenced by our regional subculture, our taste in music by our generation subculture, our food preferences by our ethnic subculture, and our alcohol consumption by our religious subculture. These subculture influences often result in the need for marketers to adapt one or more aspects of their marketing mix, as seen in Illustration 5–1.

Identifying which subculture, if any, is an important determinant of behavior for a specific product is a key task for marketing managers. In the sections that follow, we describe the major ethnic, religious, and regional subcultures in America. While we will describe the general nature of these subcultures, it must be emphasized that *large variations exist within each subculture.* Our focus in this chapter is on America, but all countries have a variety of subcultures that marketers must consider.

ETHNIC SUBCULTURES

We define **ethnic subcultures** broadly as *those whose members' unique shared behaviors are based on a common racial, language, or national background.* In this chapter, we describe the major ethnic subcultures separately. However, there are many Americans who identify with more than one ethnic group. Romona Douglas, of white, black, and American Indian descent, described her feelings as follows:

> The assumption is that black people are a certain way, and white people are a particular way, and Asians are a certain way. Well, what about multi-racial families? I don't appreciate a McDonald's commercial with a street-wise black person. That is not me, that is not my upbringing. A lot of marketing campaigns are based on stereotypes of mono-racial communities.[2]

We describe the general characteristics of the major ethnic subcultures as a starting point, recognizing that further understanding can be gained by examining multiethnic groups as well. Figure 5–2 provides the current and projected sizes of the major ethnic groups in America.[3] As this figure makes clear, non-European ethnic groups constitute a significant and growing part of our population, from 38 percent in 2010 to 47 percent by 2030. The percentages shown in the figure understate the importance of these ethnic groups to specific geographic regions.[4] Thus, Hispanics are the largest population group in parts of Arizona, California, Florida, New Mexico, and Texas; Asian Americans are the largest group in Honolulu; and African Americans are a majority in parts of the South and urban areas in the Northeast and Midwest. In contrast, states such as Maine, Vermont, and West Virginia are more than 90 percent white.

The relatively faster growth rate of non-European groups is due to a higher birthrate among some of these groups and to greater immigration. Immigration has accounted for over a third of the U.S. population growth over the past several decades. Roughly one million legal immigrants enter the U.S. population each year. In 2009, the sources of these immigrants were as follows:[5]

Latin America	40.8%
Asia	36.5
Europe	9.3
Africa	11.2

FIGURE 5-2 Major Ethnic Subcultures in the United States: 2010–2030

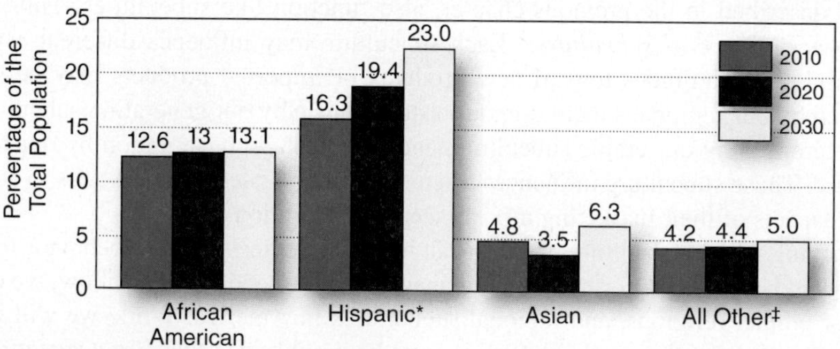

*May be of any race.

‡Includes American Indian, Alaskan Native, Native Hawaiian, Pacific Islander, and two or more races.

Source: "Table 1a. Projected Population of the United States, by Race and Hispanic Origin: 2000 to 2050," *U.S. Interim Projections by Age, Sex, Race, and Hispanic Origin* (Washington, DC: U.S. Bureau of the Census, 2004).

The influx of ethnic immigrants not only increases the size of ethnic subcultures, but also reinforces the unique behaviors and attitudes derived from the group's home culture. In the following sections, we describe the major ethnic subcultures. It is critical to remember that *all subcultures are very diverse, and general descriptions do not apply to all of the members.*

Although one's ethnic heritage is a permanent characteristic, its influence is situational. That is, the degree to which a person's consumption is influenced by his or her ethnicity depends on such factors as who he or she is with, where he or she is, and other physical and social cues.[6] Thus, one's ethnicity might play no role in a decision to grab a quick bite for lunch during a business meeting and a large role in deciding what to prepare for a family dinner.

In addition, ethnicity is only one factor that influences an individual's behavior. As we saw in the previous chapter, demographic factors also play a role. For example, a 45-year-old black doctor earning $90,000 per year and a 45-year-old white doctor with the same income would probably have more consumption behaviors in common than they would with members of their own race who were low-income service workers. As shown below, the various ethnic groups have distinct demographic profiles.[7] Thus, one must use caution in assuming that observed consumption differences between ethnic groups are caused by their ethnicity. These differences often disappear when demographic variables such as income are held constant.

	Whites	Blacks	Hispanics	Asians
Median age (in 2015)	39	33	28	38
High school or more (25 or older)	87%	84%	62%	88%
Bachelor's or more (25 or older)	30%	19%	13%	52%
Families with children under 18	47%	61%	71%	51%
Growth rate (2010–2030)	16%	22%	73%	64%
Median household income	$52,312	$34,218	$37,913	$65,637

Examine Table 5–1. Which of these differences are caused mainly by ethnicity or race, and which are caused by other factors?

Astute marketers are aggressively pursuing opportunities created by increased ethnic diversity. However, successful marketing campaigns targeted at different ethnic groups must be based on a thorough understanding of the attitudes and values of each group, which are discussed next.

AFRICAN AMERICANS

African Americans, or blacks (surveys do not indicate a clear preference for either term among African Americans),[8] constitute roughly 13 percent of the American population. Concentrated in the South and the major metropolitan areas outside the South, African Americans are, on average, younger than the white population and tend to have less education and lower household income levels. However, given the diversity of this segment, opportunities exist for marketers to target diverse members of this group in terms of education and income. For example, one-third of black households earn $50,000 or more and 10 percent earn $100,000 or more.[9] In addition, African Americans represent $1.1 trillion in buying power, which is expected to grow by some 25 percent through 2018, which is higher than the growth for whites.[10] Thus, it is not surprising that marketers are very interested in this group. BMW has recently joined with an "urban-format channel" on Sirius and XM radio and comedian Jamie Foxx to become the automotive partner of the FoxxHole Satellite Radio Channel. The campaign will get "non-scripted on-air mentions LO2

TABLE 5-1 Ethnic Subcultures and Consumption

	White	Black	Hispanic
Products			
Diet colas	109	48	79
Iced tea	93	136	109
Charcoal	96	129	88
Electric espresso/cappuccino maker	103	67	119
Activities			
Dining out (not fast food)	108	67	70
Mountain/rock climbing	91	59	116
Soccer	92	75	240
Record/CD club membership	74	272	129
Shopping			
Dollar General	97	139	81
Talbots	92	125	101
Starbucks	104	45	104
TGI Friday's	84	226	84
Media			
Cosmopolitan	96	88	138
GQ	72	185	133
Better Homes and Gardens	106	84	66
VH1	75	241	117

Note: 100 = Average level of use, purchase, or consumption.
Source: *Simmons National Consumer Study 2010,* Experian Information Solutions (Costa Mesa, CA 2014).

by Foxx and other DJs" and is designed to target the African-American segment through music and comedy. The partnership should help BMW more directly target African Americans, who are currently 4.5 percent of BMW's customers. According to BMW's Vice President of Marketing:

> This partnership allows BMW to promote its brand on satellite radio with a comedian who appreciates the company's cars. . . . What I love about Jamie is he is a BMW enthusiast. He's owned BMWs.

Consumer Segments and Characteristics

It would be a mistake to treat African Americans as a single segment. A recent study of 3,400 African Americans between 13 and 74 years of age identified 11 distinct segments. These segments, described in Table 5–2, show the diversity of this group in terms of numerous factors including demographics, lifestyle, and technology use.[11]

Given the diversity suggested in Table 5–2, marketing strategies that target African Americans as a single market are likely to fail.

Media Usage

African Americans make greater use of mass media than do whites, have different preferences, and report more influence by mass media ads than do whites.[12] While they consume

African-American Segments Identified by Yankelovich TABLE 5-2

New Middle Class (5 percent)—Younger (25–44), highest education and income (1 in 4 earns $100k or more), most suburban, high tech users (55 hours a week on Internet), positive about future, self-describe as Black, feel "Black slang" should be avoided.
Broadcast Blacks (17 percent)—Middle age (2 in 3 over 44), female, lowest income (71 percent earn under $25k), urban, single parent, lowest tech (4 percent online), confident, independent, value education, self-describe as African American, feel "Black slang" should be avoided, strongly support "Buying Black."
Black Is Better (11 percent)—Middle age (35–54); upper-middle income; urban; trend single parent; confident and positive; self-identify as African American; strong emphasis on faith, career, and family; prefer being around people of their own ethnicity; highest spenders on clothing.
Black Onliners (7 percent)—Younger (18–34); male; middle/upper income; brand conscious; place strongest importance on being around people of own ethnicity; most stressed about work, family, academics, and straddling black and white worlds; heaviest users of such technology as blogs and IM.
Digital Networkers (7 percent)—Younger (teens and early twenties), school or early career phase, unmarried, male, suburban, middle/upper income, heavy tech including social networking and IM, less in touch with black solidarity, less-confident attitudes, less religious, prefer to shop online.
Connected Black Teens (12 percent)—Teens living at home, over half raised by single parent, embrace black media, tech savvy, brand conscious and want brands popular with their culture, music focused, positive life attitude, respect elders, not as focused on only interacting with those of same ethnicity.
Boomer Blacks (6 percent)—Oldest segment (average age is 52), upper middle class, heavily (90 percent) online, prefer black advertising, religious, high mistrust in institutions and high awareness of prejudice, prefer being around people of their own ethnicity, strongly support "Buying Black."
Faith Fulfills (10 percent)—Trend older (35+) and female, parents, married, highly religious, spend most time volunteering for religious and nonprofit groups, upper middle class, have positive attitude about future, don't feel they have to hide their blackness, use Internet but not tech forward.
Sick and Stressed (8 percent)—Trend older (45–65), male, suburban, parents, lower-middle income (40 percent earn less than $25k), less optimistic, stressed about health and finances, least likely to lead healthy lifestyle and have health insurance.
Family Struggles (10 percent)—Broad age group, mostly female, parents, lower income status (half earn under $25k), heaviest TV, are mostly online but lighter users, associate heavily with those of same ethnicity, lower use of social network sites, price but not brand conscious.
Stretched Black Straddlers (7 percent)—Young (18–34); female; middle income; trend unmarried; exposed to the greatest racial discrimination; self-identify as Black; report acting differently when around blacks than around other ethnicities; high stress over work, family, and money; newer to technology.

Source: *Black America Today Study* (Radio One and Yankelovich, 2008).

general media, they also desire media specifically targeted at African-American culture, as shown below in terms of top magazines.

Black Men's Top 5 Magazines	Black Women's Top 5 Magazines
1. *Jet*	1. *Ebony*
2. *Ebony*	2. *Jet*
3. *Sports Illustrated*	3. *Essence*
4. *Vibe*	4. *O, The Oprah Magazine*
5. *Time*	5. *People Magazine*

Source: Simmons Market Research Bureau, *Spring 2007 National Consumer Survey.*

The type of TV programming viewed by blacks and whites has evidenced some convergence in the past several decades. However, as with magazines, differences in TV viewing exist that relate to shows dealing with African-American themes, concerns, and issues.

Consider comments from an advertiser in the automobile industry who has worked with Black Entertainment Television (BET):

> We've been working with BET for 15 years. There are precious few TV outlets that specifically target the African American audience. BET is far and away the flagship operation for that. What we like about BET is that it has continued to evolve and diversify its programming. The African American market isn't really one big monolithic market, even though that's what people think. There's a lot of diversity in the market. BET's current programming speaks to the old, the young, and everyone in between.[13]

Although African Americans have historically lagged behind the population as a whole in terms of computer ownership and Internet usage, this is no longer the case. One recent estimate is that 81 percent of African American adults are online, which is only slightly lower than the overall rate of 87 percent. Factors like education play a major role (indeed education is a much stronger determinant of Internet use than is ethnicity), with black college graduates having some of the highest Internet usage.[14] In addition, African-American web users[15]

- Spend more time per day surfing (4.4 hours) compared with the general population (2.3 hours).
- Are more likely than the general population to access the web for news and information across a number of categories, including general news, health, finances, and sports.
- Prefer a black perspective on news and information.

Not surprisingly, black-focused sites such as NetNoir (www.netnoir.net) and AOL's BlackVoices (www.blackvoices.com) are attracting advertisers such as IBM, Hewlett-Packard, Wells Fargo, Walt Disney, and McDonald's. BlackPlanet.com is currently the largest online community for African Americans. It features news, entertainment, and career information from a black perspective.

Finally, African Americans are more likely than whites to use their mobile devices for a variety of activities including text messaging, social networking sites such as Twitter, e-mail, IM, and so on.[16] Clearly, companies such as P&G that utilize social networking approaches in their marketing efforts toward African Americans are tapping into these trends.

Marketing to African Americans

Marketing to African Americans should be based on the same principles as marketing to any other group. Adaptation to fit the requirements of the unique segments identified in Table 5–2 may often be needed, although sometimes a general market approach will be appropriate. Overall, careful use of generalizations (often seen as stereotypes) is important. Consider the following quote by Pepper Miller, president of Hunter-Miller Group, an African-American consulting firm:

> Black Generation Xers spawned one of the greatest marketing and lifestyle phenomena: the Hip Hop Culture. However, not all African American Generation Xers are Hip Hoppers. Yet marketing communications targeting the African American Generation X segment continue to reflect typical and often stereotypical images of Hip Hop's rap culture.[17]

Products African Americans have different skin tones and hair from white Americans. Cosmetics and similar products developed for white consumers are often inappropriate for black consumers. Recognition of this fact by major firms has created aggressive competition for the billions that African Americans spend each year on personal care products and services, including cosmetics, hair care, and skin care. L'Oréal created its SoftSheen-Carson division specifically to serve women in this market. Iman's line of cosmetics, which is sold through such retailers as Walgreens and Target, is similarly targeted to this market (www.i-iman.com). Illustration 5–2 shows a print advertisement for a product designed specifically for the unique needs of the African-American market and another for a product designed to meet the needs of all ethnic groups but that is being promoted to African Americans.

Numerous companies have found it worthwhile to alter their products and target them specifically to African Americans. Beyond hair and skincare, examples include:[18]

- Hallmark has a Mahogany line of greeting cards that feature black characters and sayings.
- Barbie offers African-American dolls.
- GM has designed the Escalade and other models specifically with African Americans in mind.

Communications A common mistake when communicating with any ethnic group is to assume that its members are the same as the larger culture except for superficial differences. Failure to recognize this often results in commercials targeted at African Americans that simply place the firm's standard ad in black media or that replace white actors with black actors, without changing the script, language, setting, or culturally relevant symbols.[19] Jaguar provides a positive example in this regard in that their direct-mail campaign to affluent African Americans (a) modified the race of the actors (black husband and wife), (b) projected positive career images (wife was a surgeon, husband was a sculptor), (c) drew on historically important cultural symbols (they lived in Harlem, historically a mecca of black culture and music), and (d) projected a positive work-related theme in its tagline: "It's not luck that got you where you are." Notice how some aspects of the campaign (black actors and Harlem) are specific to the African-American community, while other aspects (professional careers and the "hard-work" theme) would be effective to the broader American consumer.

The extent to which messages targeted to African Americans need to differ from those targeting other groups varies by situation. For example, sometimes advertisers can simply change the race of the models in the ads and perhaps the consumption setting to help indicate that the product is appropriate for the needs of African Americans. This works when the product, the appeal, and the appropriate language are the same for the black target market and the other groups being targeted. The ad on the left side in Illustration 5–2 is a good example of this approach. In other cases, more specific changes need to be made to communicate how the product is designed to meet the specific needs of African Americans, as in the case of the ad on the right side in Illustration 5–2. In general, the use of black actors and spokespersons is important.[20] This is particularly the case for ethnically relevant products such as cosmetics and for those with strong ethnic identities.[21] Ads such as those in Illustration 5–2 can be run effectively in both black media and general media with a substantial black audience.

Another means of communicating with the African-American and other ethnic communities is **event marketing,** which involves *creating or sponsoring an event that has a particular appeal to a market segment.* For example, church is a major force in the lives of many African Americans. In order to tap into black churchgoers, Chrysler was a sponsor of Patti LaBelle's "The Gospel According to Patti" concert tour in 2006. As part of the sponsorship, Chrysler offered test drives before each concert and donated $5 for

ILLUSTRATION 5-2

African-American consumers have both unique and shared needs relative to other ethnic groups.

each test drive to LaBelle's chosen charity, the University of Pennsylvania's Abramson Cancer Center.[22]

Retailing Retailers often adjust the merchandising mix to meet the needs of African-American shoppers. For example, Albertson's, a national grocery retailer, adapts its merchandising mix in African-American neighborhoods.[23] Surveys reveal that three major store-selection factors for blacks are that the store carries ethnic products (51 percent say that is important), employs people who "look like me" (40 percent), and treats customers of all races and ethnicities with respect (84 percent).[24] This focus on respect is caused by the sad fact that many black shoppers still encounter obviously disrespectful acts such as being closely watched while shopping as well as more subtle discrimination such as slower service.[25] The need for cultural sensitivity training for retail and service employees is clear.[26]

African Americans also use shopping as a form of recreation more than whites.[27] This suggests that stores with black customers should pay particular attention to providing a pleasant and fun shopping environment. Blacks also respond to sales differently than do whites and have differing desires with respect to credit card, cash, and check payments.[28] In addition, research suggests that African Americans are more prone to buy national brands than store brands as a way to signal status, although results in Table 5–2 show that differences in brand consciousness exist across different segments of black consumers.[29] Thus, all aspects of the shopping experience need to be carefully aligned to the needs of the target shoppers.

HISPANICS

LO3

The Bureau of the Census defines **Hispanic** as *a person of Cuban, Mexican, Puerto Rican, South or Central American, or other Spanish culture or origin regardless of race.* Hispanics are, on average, younger than the white non-Hispanic population and tend to have less education and lower household income levels. However, given the diversity of this segment, opportunities exist for marketers to target diverse members of this group in terms of education and income. For example, nearly 40 percent of Hispanic households earn $50,000 or more and 12 percent earn $100,000 or more.[30] In addition, Hispanics represent $1.2 trillion in buying power, which is expected to grow by some 33 percent through 2018, which is higher than the growth for whites.[31]

The Hispanic market is now the largest and fastest-growing ethnic subculture in the United States. By 2030 Hispanics are expected to represent 23 percent of the U.S. population. Marketers are definitely taking notice. Like the other ethnic groups in America, Hispanics are diverse. Many marketers feel that the Hispanic subculture is not a single ethnic subculture but instead is three main and several minor nationality subcultures: Mexican Americans (66 percent), Puerto Ricans (9 percent), Cubans (4 percent), and other Latinos, mainly from Central and South America (14 percent).[32] Each group speaks a slightly different version of Spanish and has somewhat distinct values and lifestyles. Further, each group tends to live in distinct regions of the country: Mexican Americans in the Southwest and California; Puerto Ricans in New York, New Jersey, and Florida; Cubans in Florida; and other Latinos in California, New York, and Florida. Income levels also vary across the groups, with those of Cuban and Puerto Rican descent having somewhat higher incomes than those of Mexican descent.

Others argue that while one must be sensitive to nationality-based differences, the common language, the common religion (Roman Catholic for most Hispanics), and the emergence of national Spanish-language media and entertainment figures create sufficient cultural homogeneity for most products and advertising campaigns. However, at a minimum, the decision to treat Hispanics as a single ethnic subculture needs to take into consideration factors relating to acculturation, language, and generational influences, which we discuss next.

Acculturation, Language, and Generational Influences

Given that roughly 40 percent of growth in the Hispanic population is attributable to immigration, the level of acculturation plays a major role in the attitudes and behaviors of Hispanic consumers. **Acculturation** is *the degree to which an immigrant has adapted to his or her new culture.*[33] Acculturation is highly related to language use and both are strongly influenced by generational factors. A recent study by the Pew Hispanic Center identifies three generations of Hispanic adults:

First-generation adults (63 percent) are those born outside the United States. This generation has the lowest income and education, is most likely to identify themselves as Hispanic (including country of origin), is most likely to have Spanish as their primary language (72 percent), and is most likely to possess traditional values including a masculine view of the family decision hierarchy.

Second-generation adults (19 percent) are those born in the United States to immigrant parents. Compared to the first generation, this generation has higher income and education, is more likely to identify themselves as Americans (though 62 percent still identify as Hispanic), is equally split between being bilingual and having English as the primary language, and is somewhat less likely to ascribe to traditional values.

Third-generation (and beyond) adults (17 percent) are those born in the United States to U.S.-born parents. This group has the highest education and income, is most likely to identify as Americans (57 percent, versus 41 percent who identify themselves as Hispanic), is most likely to have English as the primary language (only 22 percent are bilingual; none are Spanish only), and is also somewhat less likely to ascribe to traditional values.[34]

As this discussion indicates, income, education, language, and identification with Hispanic culture change across generations. However, it is also important to note that most Hispanic adults identify more or less strongly with a Hispanic culture.[35] This strong cultural identity is also true of Hispanic teens, many of whom were born in the United States and would thus be classified as second- and third-generation teens. As discussed

CONSUMER INSIGHT 5-1

Hispanic Teens: The New Bicultural Youth

Hispanic teens constitute about 20 percent of all teenagers but are far more important to marketers than that percentage suggests.[36] First, they currently represent $20 billion in spending power. This is likely to grow dramatically since this segment is projected to grow by 62 percent through 2020, which is six times faster than the overall teen market. More important, these teens are joining black teenagers as fashion and style leaders for the overall teenage market.

Hispanic teens often differ from their parents, who in many cases felt strong pressures to blend in and "be American" (i.e., act and speak like white Americans). These teens don't. Rather, the trend for Hispanic teens is to be bicultural, that is, *acculturating by adding a second culture, not replacing their first culture.* To do so requires a balancing act, particularly in how the divide between inside and outside the home is accomplished. This is particularly challenging given the importance of family, both nuclear and extended, in the Hispanic culture. How this balancing act is enacted is shown in the table on the next page.

And the balancing process leading to biculturalism seems to be working. As three experts describe:

> I'm always amazed by the "Hispanicness" of Hispanic teens. They're speaking Spanish at home, both with friends, English for college and the Internet, but they're very much into the Hispanic culture. Even when they're born here. It's downright breathtaking.
>
> It's not about being bilingual. It's about being bicultural. They are engrossed in the American culture, but they take an incredible amount of pride in being Latino.
>
> It's very cool to be Hispanic at this age. It almost makes them more attractive, exotic. Hispanic teens are brushing up on their Spanish and celebrating their culture.

These bicultural teens read the same English-language magazines and watch the same television programs as their non-Hispanic counterparts. In fact, they are much more likely to read such teen magazines as *Seventeen* and *YM.* One of the magazines targeting the female Hispanic teenager, *Latina,* is mostly English, though most of the ads are in Spanish. However, they also utilize Spanish-language magazines, television, and radio. They grew up listening not only to hip-hop and other popular music but to Hispanic-based rhythms as well—mariachi, banda, and norteño in California; tejano in Texas; salsa in Florida; and meringue in New York.

in Consumer Insight 5–1, Hispanic teens are blending language and culture, setting cultural trends in the general U.S. population, and living truly bicultural and bilingual experiences.

The Hispanic culture is heavily influenced by the Roman Catholic religion. It is family oriented, with the extended family playing an important role across generations (unlike the general U.S. population in which extended family has lost its importance). It is also a masculine culture, and sports are very important to Hispanics, particularly boxing, baseball, and soccer. This masculine orientation manifests itself in many ways, including husband-dominant household decision making.[37]

The Hispanic culture generally has a fairly traditional view of the appropriate role of women. For example, the wife is expected to prepare the food for the family. As a result, food marketers such as Sara Lee and General Mills are engaging in a number of efforts to target Hispanic women. For example, General Mills' website *Que Rica Vida (What a Rich Life)* targets their various brands to Hispanic women and deals with issues of

Identity (Their Base): In-Home and Family	Belong/Blend: Out-of-Home and Friends	Differentiate: U.S. Mainstream
Family	Hispanic friends, but also friends of other nationalities	Use their culture and heritage to show they are different
Experience Latino food and drinks	Latin food and drinks blended with mainstream products—Tacos and Lays Potato Chips	*
Speak Spanish	Speak English	Speak English, Spanish, and Spanglish
Presence of Latin American icons	Mainstream products/brands are more effective in helping them "belong" and be cool and accepted	Successful brands that compete against mainstream brands with Urban or Spanglish twist provides pride in that they are the drivers of those brands
Listen to and watch Spanish music and TV	*	Listen to and watch Spanish and English radio and TV
Family helps maintain cultural identity	Friends provide reassurance it's okay to be who you are and they hang out with other cultures	Are starting to set the trends as African-American (Hip-Hop) culture becomes mainstream

*Data on specific behaviors and attitudes not available.
Source: Adapted from *Nuestro Futuro* (Redwood Shores, CA: Cheskin, 2006), p. 24.

Now they are helping popularize these sounds and variations of them throughout the larger teen population.

Critical Thinking Questions

1. To what extent are Hispanic teenagers leading the teenage market? Justify your response.
2. Many Hispanic teenagers are truly bicultural. What challenges does this present marketers?
3. Explain the role of family in Hispanic teenagers' tendency toward biculturalism.

food, family, and Hispanic-oriented recipes. However, because acculturation can affect gender-role views, it is critical that companies understand their target market on this dimension.[38]

Language is clearly important to the Hispanic market and often strongly intertwined with cultural identity. Generational and immigrant status influence the primary language spoken in a substantial way. Consider the fact that while 38 percent of Hispanics born in the United States speak only English at home, this number is only 4 percent for Hispanics born outside of the United States.[39] Perhaps even more important is that Spanish-language ads are often more effective.[40] Consider the following (and the Windex ad in Illustration 5–3):

> When asked about advertising effectiveness, 38% of Hispanics surveyed found English language ads less effective than Spanish ads in terms of recall and 70% less effective than Spanish ads in terms of persuasion. Many younger and acculturated Latinos mix languages in the form of "Spanglish," in which they speak English peppered with Spanish words. But, when it comes to selling, 56% of Latino adults respond best to advertising when it is presented in Spanish.[41]

ILLUSTRATION 5-3

Spanish language ads such as this Windex ad, are often more effective when marketing to Hispanics. This effect may depend on acculturation level, however.

Given these numbers, it should not be surprising that Univision, a Spanish-language network, is the fifth-largest network in the United States and the top three most watched networks by Hispanics are Spanish-language networks.[42] In addition, recent research shows that the top 53 TV shows watched by Hispanics in the 18-to-49 demographic were in Spanish.[43]

Marketing to Hispanics

Hispanic consumers tend to be highly brand loyal, particularly to marketers who they feel are working to adapt their products and services to meet their distinctive needs. Price is important, but so too is the availability of high-quality national brands. Hispanics tend to be less receptive than the general market to store brands.[44] Marketers are responding with adaptations to various aspects of their marketing mix.

Communications As we saw earlier, Hispanics often speak Spanish and often prefer Spanish-language media. Therefore, although it is possible to reach part of this market using mass media, serious attempts to target Hispanics will often involve Spanish-language media as well. Univision, Telefutura, and Telemundo are the top three Spanish-language TV networks in the United States. Spanish-language radio is widespread, with both local and network stations. And there are numerous Spanish-language magazines, including Spanish versions of such magazines as *Cosmopolitan, Sports Illustrated,* and *Maxim.* There are also many Spanish-language newspapers.

With respect to communication and media, it is important to note that a youth trend is emerging, which will likely shape the future of Hispanic media strategy. Specifically, the 14-to-24-year-old demographic (which will grow rapidly over the next decade)[45] spends more time viewing English-language TV, radio, and print media than Spanish. This group tends to be U.S.-born and more English-dominant in terms of language. In addition, the 18-to-34 demographic views Spanish- and English-language media about equally. In response, Telemundo is offering both bilingual and Spanish-language programming and is developing shows more in touch with the Hispanic youth market, such as the reality show *Protagonistas de Novela.* SiTV is a relatively new cable network that creates and delivers English-language programming with a Latino theme targeted toward younger bicultural Hispanics.[46]

Internet use among Hispanics depends greatly on language and acculturation. For more acculturated, English-speaking Hispanics, Internet use is at 82 percent. For those born outside the United States and thus typically less acculturated, Internet use is at about 50 percent.[47] These general numbers don't tell the entire story because Hispanics (both English and Spanish-dominant) are more likely than non-Hispanic whites to have their own blog or website.[48] And Facebook has 80 percent reach among Hispanics.[49] Online and social network sites are clearly important to companies seeking to target Hispanics. Online sports are available through such sites as ESPN Deportes.com, and Spanish-language

ILLUSTRATION 5-4

Use of the Internet by Hispanics is exploding. Sites such as ESPN Deportes.com are being developed to appeal to the unique needs of this market.

versions of Yahoo! and AOL have been developed. Online Spanish-language communities such as CiudadFutura are also emerging. Hispanic Internet users tend to be relatively young, frequent both English- and Spanish-language sites, and in many cases prefer English-language media. As with traditional media providers, online Hispanic providers will be challenged to deliver content that is relevant to acculturated Hispanics, regardless of language (see Illustration 5–4).[50]

Language translation is a challenge. Examples of translation difficulties include the following:

- Tang introduced itself in its Spanish ads as *jugo de chino,* which worked well with Puerto Ricans, who knew it meant orange juice, but the phrase had no meaning to most other Hispanics.
- A Coors campaign used the word "guey," which in modern slang terms can mean the equivalent of "dude." However, the word can also be used as slang for "idiot" or "stupid." According to one expert, whether or not consumers get the humor is generational.[51]

Successful marketing to Hispanics moves beyond accurate translations into unique appeals and symbols. It requires marketers to be "in-culture," that is, to understand the value system and the overall cultural context of the various Hispanic groups. In fact, value congruence has been found to overcome persuasion shortfalls for second-language ads (e.g., English-language ads to bilingual Hispanics).[52]

- Levi Strauss developed a series for Discovery en Espanol that detailed the journey of a group of young Latinos who traveled along the Pan-American highway to learn more about their cultural heritage. This effort included heavy integration of Levi products and included an interactive site and social media to connect with Hispanic youth.[53]
- Best Buy created a TV spot designed to bridge the gap between younger, tech-savvy Hispanic teens and their older, less-acculturated fathers who often are uncomfortable with technology but, given the patriarchal hierarchy, must "sign off " on the purchase. The slogan reads, "If you're far away, get closer with Best Buy." Best Buy says they designed the spot to get kids and their fathers talking.[54]

Products Historically, other than specialty food products, few marketers developed unique products or services for the Hispanic market. However, given the size and growth of this market, that is changing. For example:

- Home Depot launched a paint line called *Colores Origenes* in some 400 stores that have a heavily Hispanic customer base. Based on research, the names of the colors are designed to specifically communicate to Hispanic customers in terms that evoke Latin tastes, scents, and images.[55]
- In Colorado, Walmart created Denver Bronco T-shirts specifically targeting Hispanic consumers. One version had the phrase "de todo corazón," meaning "with all my heart" in Spanish. Walmart's goal was to combine American sports tradition with symbols of Hispanic culture. The T-shirts became the most popular Denver Bronco's merchandise of the season.[56]
- In addition, marketers are capturing the loyalty developed with their products in Central and South America by distributing them in areas of the United States with large Hispanic populations. For example, Colgate-Palmolive distributes its Mexican household cleaner Fabuloso in Los Angeles and Miami.

Some attempts at adapting products to the Hispanic market have failed because of a failure to truly understand the needs of this market. For example, many Hispanics find the current trend in houses of having the kitchen open onto the family room to be repugnant (Hispanics tend to be uncomfortable having strangers in their kitchens) and find the homes built for Hispanic buyers to be too stereotypical.[57]

Retailing The primary retailing responses to this market have been an increase in the number of bilingual salespeople; the use of Spanish-language signs, directions, and point-of-purchase displays; and merchandise assortments that reflect the needs of the local Hispanic community. The following provide specific examples:

- Walmart has identified Hispanics as one of its six key segments. Not only have they adjusted their traditional stores to include products and destinations such as tortilleria bakeries that appeal to the Hispanic consumer, they also are opening Hispanic Walmart stores called Supermercado de Walmart in metro areas with large Hispanic populations such as Houston, Texas. The stores feature signage, layout, and product assortments designed to appeal very specifically to the Hispanic market. Aspects include cafes serving Latino pastries and coffee as well as full-service meat and fish counters.[58]
- In San Antonio, Texas, a shopping centere called Tianguis Mall has been opened. According to the developers, "Tianguis markets are popular in Latin America, providing shoppers with an open-air retail marketplace. San Antonio's Tianguis Mall will offer the convenience of having the retail stores usually found in neighborhood shopping centers along with restaurants, entertainment and community events in one venue resembling a charming Mexican village."[59]

ASIAN AMERICANS

L04

Asian Americans represent an important subculture. Although relatively small in size, this group will continue to grow. Of particular importance to marketers is that Asian Americans are the highest-educated and highest-income group, with substantial purchasing power. Asian-American purchasing power is estimated at $713 billion and is expected to grow by 37 percent through 2018, which is higher than the growth for whites.[60] However, Asian Americans are also the most diverse group, with numerous nationalities, languages, and

ILLUSTRATION 5-5

Ads on the Zaoboa.sg site would appeal to many Chinese consumers but would not reach most other Asian Americans.

religions. The U.S. Census includes Asian Indians in its summary figures for this group. However, we will discuss them separately in a later section.

Asian Americans are not a single subculture. Consider the Zaoboa.sg website in Illustration 5–5. Ads on this site are probably quite effective with many of the Chinese members of this subculture. However, as Figure 5–3 shows, Chinese represent only a little over a fourth of all Asian Americans, and they share neither a common language nor culture with most of the other groups.

As with Hispanics, language is a major factor. One estimate is that 80 percent of Asian Americans can be reached with "in-language" promotions. Two-thirds of Asian Americans are immigrants, and the percentage of each nationality group that uses primarily its native language is generally high.[61] While language use and proficiency are clearly a function of

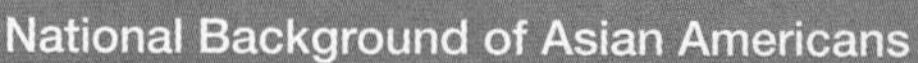

National Background of Asian Americans

FIGURE 5-3

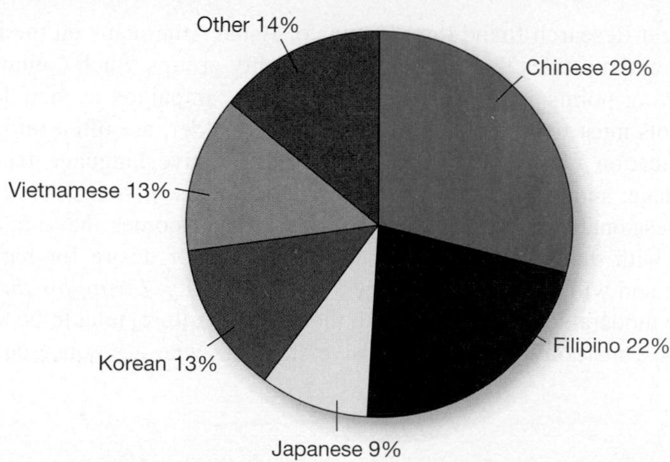

acculturation and age, the following shows a wide variation in English use and proficiency across national background as well:

Country	English Only at Home	Non-English at Home but English Spoken "Very Well"	Non-English at Home but English Spoken Less Than "Very Well"
Vietnam	12	33	55
China	17	36	48
Korea	20	31	49
Philippines	34	44	22
Japan	53	20	27

Source: *The American Community—Asians* (Washington, DC: The Census Bureau, February 2007).

Clearly, this information suggests the need for "in-language" communications, particularly for those from national backgrounds where English proficiency is lower. In addition to proficiency, there is research suggesting that overall, a majority of Asian Americans prefer either in-language or bilingual communication, with only 17 percent preferring English only.[62]

More than languages differ among the groups. In fact, the concept and term *Asian American* was developed and used by marketers and others who study these groups rather than the members themselves. Members of the various nationalities involved generally refer to themselves by their nationality without the term *American,* that is, Vietnamese, not Vietnamese American. An exception is Japanese Americans.[63]

While each nationality group is a distinct culture with its own language and traditions, there are some commonalities across most of these groups. All have experienced the need to adjust to the American culture while being physically distinct from the larger population. Most come from home cultures influenced by Confucianism. Confucianism emphasizes subordination of the son to the father, the younger to the elder, and the wife to the husband. It values conservatism and prescribes strict manners. Their base cultures have also typically placed a very strong value on traditional, extended families. Education, collective effort, and advancement are also highly valued.[64]

Consumer Segments and Characteristics

Market Segment Research found three groups of Asian Americans on the basis of their demographics and attitudes that cut across nationality groups. Such commonalities can be useful starting points when designing marketing campaigns even if language and cultural symbols must be adapted. *Traditionalists* are older, are often retired, and have strong identification with their original culture; the native language tends to be the primary language; and they are not concerned about status. *Established* are older, conservative professionals; are well educated, with strong incomes; have relatively weak identification with their native culture; have less need or desire for native-language programming; and will pay premium prices for high quality. *Living for the Moment* are younger, have moderate identification with their native culture, tend to be bilingual, and are spontaneous, materialistic, and impulsive shoppers who are concerned with status and quality.[65]

Several aspects of the Asian American population may make it easier to target. The first is geographic concentration: 65 percent of both the Asian-American population and their spending power reside in just six states (California, New York, New Jersey, Hawaii, Texas, and Illinois).[66] The second aspect is a trend toward an increase in skilled workers from Mandarin-speaking regions of mainland China. This trend appears to be causing a "gradual shift to Mandarin from Cantonese in Chinese communications."[67]

A final aspect of the Asian-American community that may make it easier to target is one that is common to all subcultures, and that is the youth trend. Roughly a third of Asian Americans are under the age of 25, which is comparable to whites.[68] In addition, this second generation (sometimes referred to as Generation 2.0), which was born in the United States, is, like the African-American and Hispanic youth, still tied to its roots but blending languages and cultures, influencing general U.S. culture, and fueling trends in fashion and music. As in the Hispanic market, English-language media options with Asian-American content targeted at this second generation are increasing. Pepsi aired ads in English on one such venue called *Stir* TV.[69] Also consider the Honda initiative:

> Honda Motor Co. chose to piggyback on Boba, a beverage developed in Taiwan that is all the rage in Asian youth circles. The beverage, also known as bubble tea, consists of "pearls" of black, gummy, tapioca balls that float in the mixture of sweetened iced tea. It has quickly caught on as the soft drink of Asian youth. Honda's idea was to develop drink sleeves that surround hot beverages in the U.S. to promote its youth-oriented cars, like the Civic and Acura RSX. Ponce (manager of emerging markets) got the idea from one of her young Asian co-workers who frequents Boba stores and noticed the number of young Asians who pulled up in Hondas.[70]

Marketing to Asian Americans

As we've seen, there are several Asian-American markets, based primarily on nationality and language. Each of these in turn can be further segmented on degree of acculturation,[71] social class, generation, lifestyle, and other variables. And while this creates challenges for marketers, the purchase power of this group and its various segments is increasingly attractive to marketers and causing them to address these niche markets with creative product, merchandising, and media approaches.

Geographic concentration increases marketing efficiency because targeted nationalities can be reached through specialized media channels. For example, in San Francisco, KTSF offers in-language news and entertainment programming for Chinese and Japanese viewers. Many KTSF advertisers, such as McDonald's, dub their existing ads in Cantonese. Others, such as Colgate-Palmolive, run the ads they are using for the same products in Asia. Major U.S. brands such as State Farm, Wells Fargo, and McDonald's sponsored KTSF's coverage of the 2008 Olympic Games held in Beijing, China.

Direct broadcast satellite (DBS) is also an important TV option. DBS provides a means of reaching virtually all the native-language speakers of any nationality nationwide. For example, EchoStar's Dish network offers a "Chinese Package" called the "Great Wall TV Package," with over 20 channels. DirecTV offers the gamut of language options to the Asian-American audience, including offerings in Vietnamese, Cantonese, and Mandarin, which allow customers to enjoy their favorite programs "from back home."[72]

ILLUSTRATION 5-6

The Walmart ad shown here demonstrates how marketing to Asian Americans involves more than translating ads into the appropriate languages. Acknowledgment of special celebrations and symbols are also important.

Asian Americans are highly tech savvy and heavy users of the Internet. Internet penetration of Asian Americans is estimated at 90 percent.[73] They are also heavy users of social media.[74] Internet-based marketing to the Asian community is growing rapidly. Firms can reach Chinese consumers in their native language on sites such as that shown in Illustration 5–5. Similar sites are gaining popularity among other Asian nationality groups, and firms such as Charles Schwab are using them as communications channels.

Marketing to the various Asian nationality groups should follow the same basic guidelines discussed earlier for Hispanics. Thus, effective communication is more than simply translating ad copy. It also requires adopting and infusing ads with cultural symbols and meanings relevant to each nationality segment. Examine the Walmart ad in Illustration 5–6. This ad is targeted toward a particular Asian nationality group. Notice the various elements that have been incorporated in order to focus attention on and communicate with this segment.

Other examples of successful marketing to Asian Americans include:

- A Los Angeles chain selected four outlets with large numbers of Chinese and Vietnamese customers. At the time of the Moon Festival (an important holiday in many Asian cultures), the store ran ads and distributed coupons for free moon cakes and lanterns. Sales increased by 30 percent in these stores during the promotion. Likewise, Sears advertises the Moon Festival in Mandarin, Cantonese, Vietnamese, or Korean, depending on the population near each outlet. It provides nationality-relevant gifts and entertainment such as traditional dances.
- Western Union sponsors numerous Asian cultural events, such as the Asian-American Expo for the Chinese New Year in Los Angeles. A majority of Asian Americans attend cultural events relevant to their national heritage, so this is an effective strategy.[75] It also partnered with *World Journal* to publish the *Chinese Immigrant Handbook* to offer practical guidance to new immigrants. These represent grassroot, community-based efforts to target the very specific needs of various nationality groups. These efforts supplement their more traditional mass-media approaches using TV, radio, and magazines.[76]

NATIVE AMERICANS

LO5

The number of Native Americans (American Indians and Alaska Natives, in U.S. Census terms) depends on the measurement used. The Census Bureau reports three numbers for Native Americans: (1) one tribe only, (2) one tribe only or in combination with another tribe, and (3) number 2 plus in combination with any other race. The first definition produces an estimate of 2.8 million Native Americans; the total jumps to 4.1 million when the third definition is used. Nearly half live in the West, and 30 percent reside in the South. While many Native Americans live on or near reservations, others are dispersed throughout the country.

There are approximately 550 Native American tribes, each with its own language and traditions. Many of the tribes have reservations and quasi-independent political status. In general, Native Americans have limited incomes,[77] but this varies widely by tribe. The overall buying power of this group is estimated at $96 billion and is expected to grow by 28 percent through 2018, which is higher than the rate for whites.[78] The larger tribes are as follows:

Tribes	One Tribe Only	Multiracial
Cherokee	281,000	730,000
Navajo	269,000	298,000
Sioux	109,000	153,000
Chippewa	106,000	150,000
Choctaw	87,000	159,000
Pueblo	60,000	74,000
Apache	57,000	97,000
Eskimo	46,000	55,000

In recent years, Native Americans have taken increasing pride in their heritage and are less tolerant of inaccurate stereotypes of either their history or their current status. Thus, marketers using Native American names or portrayals must ensure accurate and appropriate use. Native American cuisine is making its way into the American mainstream with efforts from Native American chefs like Arnold Olson. Olson blends European and Native American styles to create interesting dishes such as bison carpaccio and caribou bruschetta. As American interest in and acceptance of diversity continue to grow, unique Native American offerings such as this will become increasingly relevant and popular.[79]

The larger tribes have their own newspapers and radio stations. In addition, there are national Native American–oriented newspapers, radio shows, and magazines.[80] Although each tribe is small relative to the total population, the geographic concentration of each tribe provides easy access for marketers. Sponsorship of tribal events and support for tribal colleges, training centers, and community centers can produce good results for firms that do so over time. For example:

- Indian Summer Inc. is an organization that holds a festival each year to "educate, preserve and promote American Indian cultures, showcase the diversity that exists within tribal cultures, provide economic opportunities to our people and strengthen communication and understanding." Harley Davidson is among the corporate sponsors working to support this event and build a relationship with this market.[81]
- Nike has teamed up with the Indian Health Service to set up educational programs to teach and promote health and fitness on reservations.[82]

ASIAN INDIAN AMERICANS

There are approximately 2.5 million Americans of Indian heritage (from India). This segment of the population is growing rapidly as a result of immigration. Asian Indian Americans are concentrated in New York and California, with significant numbers in New Jersey, Illinois, and Texas as well. As a group, they are well educated, affluent, and fluent in English; yet most retain cultural ties to their Indian background.

Those unfamiliar with India often assume that it is a homogeneous country. However, in some ways it is more like Europe than America. It has 28 states, six union territories, 15 official languages, and dozens of other languages and dialects. Thus, while those who immigrate to America have much in common, they also have many differences based on their background in India.

Although diverse in many ways, most share a number of important cultural traits:

- They place great value on education, particularly their children's education.
- They are concerned with financial security and save at a rate much higher than the average American.
- They do not have a "throw-away" mentality. They shop for value and look for quality and durability.
- Husbands tend to have a dominant role in family decisions.

Asian Indian Americans attend to the general mass media. They can also be targeted via specialty magazines such as *Silicon India* and *Indian Life & Style,* online sites such as IndiaAbroad.com, as well as cable TV, radio stations, and newspapers in regions with significant populations. For example, Western Union advertises to this segment on Eye on Asia, a cable channel focused on this group. National reach is now possible through Echo-Star's Dish Network's South Asia Package with various channels from India. Long-term involvement in the Indian community is an effective way to gain support from this segment:

> Metropolitan Life was a major sponsor of a Navaratri, a religious festival that attracted 100,000 participants from around New York and New Jersey. As one participant said, "One of the chief executives of the company attended the festival, and the company took out a series of ads in the souvenir program. Now we feel we should reward the company for taking an interest in us."[83]

The Internet is also an effective way to market to these consumers. However, such an effort requires a sound knowledge of the community:

> It's December but Namaste.com's holiday rush has been over for two months. Christmas is not the big season for its customers. "To suggest gifting to Indians around Christmas time doesn't make sense. It's the wrong marketing message. Diwali [a festival of lights that happens in late October] is the Indian 'Christmas.'"[84]

ARAB AMERICANS

The 2000 Census identified 1.25 million self-identified Arab Americans in the United States. However the Arab American Institute (the Census Bureau's official designee for analyzing data related to Arab Americans) estimates underreporting by a factor of three and, based on additional research, has estimated the Arab-American population at about 3.5 million. Perhaps no group in America has a more inaccurate stereotype. For example: What is the most common religion of Arab Americans? Sixty-six percent identify themselves as Christians (up from about 50 percent in the early 1990s), and 24 percent are Muslim (down from about 50 percent in the early 1990s).

Arab Americans come from a variety of countries, including Morocco, Algeria, Egypt, Lebanon, Jordan, Saudi Arabia, and Kuwait. They share a common Arabic heritage and the Arabic language. Since World War II, many Arab immigrants have been business proprietors, landowners, or influential families fleeing political turmoil in their home countries. Many of these individuals attended Western or Westernized schools and were fluent in English before arriving.

More than 80 percent of Arab Americans are U.S. citizens, with a majority having been born in the United States. They are somewhat younger than the general population, are better educated, and have a higher-than-average income. They are also much more likely to be entrepreneurs. A third of all Arab Americans live in California, New York, and Michigan.

Most Arab Americans are tired of negative stereotyping and misrepresentations about their culture. Even the film *Aladdin* contained insults and mistakes. Aladdin sings about the "barbaric" country from which he came. A guard threatened to cut off a young girl's hand for stealing food for a hungry child. Such an action would be contrary to Islamic law. The storefront signs in the mythical Arabic land had symbols that made no sense in Arabic or any other language. The aftermath of the September 11, 2001, attacks on the World Trade Center and the Pentagon has aroused some prejudice against these citizens—as well as some enhanced knowledge of their backgrounds and beliefs.

The first rule in reaching this market is to treat its members with respect and accuracy. There are specialized newspapers, magazines, and radio and television stations focused on this market. EchoStar's Dish Network offers an Arabic-language package. And Walmart has begun to adjust its product selection in areas with strong Arab-American populations, such as Dearborn, Michigan, with offerings such as falafel, olives, and Islamic greeting cards. Attention to the unique traditions of this community can pay large dividends.[85]

RELIGIOUS SUBCULTURES

LO6

As discussed in Chapter 3, America is basically a **secular society.** That is, the educational system, government, and political process are not controlled by a religious group, and most people's daily behaviors are not guided by strict religious guidelines. Nonetheless, roughly 82 percent of American adults claim a religious affiliation, 30 percent claim to attend a religious service at least once a week, and 54 percent state that religion is very important in their lives.[86] Interestingly, while some are leaving religion altogether, which accounts for the ongoing decrease in those identifying with a religious affiliation over time, others are switching. A recent study indicates that 44 percent of adults have moved to another religion, moved within the Protestant denomination, or moved out of religion altogether.[87]

The fact that the American culture is largely secular is not viewed as optimal by all of society. Many conservative Christians would prefer a society and legal system more in line with their faith. The intense debates over abortion, prayer in schools, the teaching of evolution versus creationism, homosexual rights, and a host of other issues are evidence of this division in American society.

Religion is important to, and directly influences the behaviors of, many Americans. This includes consuming religiously themed products[88] and avoiding the consumption of other products such as alcohol. The different religions in America prescribe differing values and behaviors. Thus, a number of **religious subcultures** exist in America.

Christian Subcultures

Much of the American value system and the resultant political and social institutions are derived from the Christian, and largely Protestant, beliefs of the early settlers. Although American culture is basically secular, many of its traditions and values are derived from the

REGIONAL SUBCULTURES

LO7

Distinct **regional subcultures** arise as a result of climatic conditions, the natural environment and resources, the characteristics of the various immigrant groups that have settled in each region, and significant social and political events. These distinct subcultures present numerous opportunities and challenges for marketers. Examples include:

- TGI Friday's has a customizable menu that includes a set of 70 standard items plus 30 regional items, including chicken-fried steak, which is a hit in the Southeast but not in some other regions, and a baked brie cheese appetizer that is offered only in Michigan.
- Many national magazines run regional editions. *TV Guide,* for example, had 25 different regional covers for their NFL preview issue. And *Sports Illustrated* often offers special issues devoted to sports in a specific city such as the *Sports Illustrated Boston Collection.*[102]
- Wahoo's, a restaurant in Southern California, Colorado, Texas, and Hawaii (and also now online at www.wahoos.com), offers fish tacos, a menu item that may sound a bit odd to some but is popular among Hispanic consumers.

Although the most effective regional marketing strategies are often based on small geographic areas, we can observe significant consumption differences across much larger regions. Table 5–3 illustrates some of the consumption differences across the four U.S. census regions. Given such clear differences in consumption patterns, marketers realize

TABLE 5-3 Regional Consumption Differences

	Northeast	Midwest	South	West
Products				
Imported beer	124	89	85	115
Tooth whiteners	107	100	94	104
Breakfast pastries	88	108	108	89
Bagels	123	103	83	105
Activities				
Going to concerts	112	96	94	105
Fly fishing	93	106	76	137
Skateboarding	83	85	81	158
College football fan	64	112	131	68
Shopping				
Staples	176	68	78	104
H&M	189	87	48	124
Domino's Pizza	74	85	123	98
Chili's	65	87	128	96
Media				
The New Yorker	141	77	83	117
American Rifleman	66	93	120	102
The Amazing Race (CBS)	105	117	83	106
The Simpsons (FOX)	98	108	88	113

Note: 100 = Average level of use, purchase, or consumption.

Source: *Simmons National Consumer Study 2010,* Experian Information Solutions (Costa Mesa, CA 2014).

that, for at least some product categories, the United States is no more a single market than is the European Union. Since specialized (regional) marketing programs generally cost more than standardized (national) programs, marketers must balance potential sales increases against increased costs. This decision process is exactly the same as described in the section on multinational marketing decisions in Chapter 2.

SUMMARY

LO1: Understand subcultures and their influence on unique market behaviors

The United States is becoming increasingly diverse. Much of this diversity is fueled by immigration and an increase in ethnic pride and by identification with non-European heritages among numerous Americans. Most members of a culture share most of the core values, beliefs, and behaviors of that culture. However, most individuals also belong to several subcultures. A *subculture* is a segment of a larger culture whose members share distinguishing patterns of behavior. An array of ethnic, nationality, religious, and regional subcultures characterizes American society. The existence of these subcultures provides marketers with the opportunity to develop unique marketing programs to match the unique needs of each.

Ethnic subcultures are defined broadly as those whose members' unique shared behaviors are based on a common racial, language, or nationality background. Non-European ethnic groups constitute a significant and growing part of the U.S. population, from 38 percent in 2010 to 47 percent by 2030.

LO2: Analyze the African-American subculture and the unique marketing aspects it entails

African Americans represent a substantial non-European ethnic group at roughly 13 percent of the U.S. population. Although African Americans are younger and tend to have lower incomes than the general population, their rapidly growing education, income, purchasing power, and cultural influence continue to attract marketers to this large and diverse subculture.

LO3: Analyze the Hispanic subculture and the unique marketing aspects it entails

Hispanics represent the largest and fastest-growing ethnic subculture in the United States. Even though Hispanics have a variety of national backgrounds (Mexico, Puerto Rico, Cuba, and so on), the Spanish language, a common religion (Roman Catholicism), and national Spanish-language media and entertainment figures have created a somewhat homogeneous Hispanic subculture.

LO4: Analyze the Asian-American subculture and the unique marketing aspects it entails

Asian Americans are the most diverse of the major ethnic subcultures. They are characterized by a variety of nationalities, languages, and religions. From a marketing perspective, it is not appropriate to consider Asian Americans as a single group. Instead, Asian Americans are best approached as a number of nationality subcultures.

LO5: Analyze the Native-American, Asian-Indian-American, and Arab-American subcultures and the unique marketing aspects they entail

Native Americans, Asian Indian Americans, and *Arab Americans* are smaller but important subcultures. Each is diverse yet shares enough common values and behaviors to be approached as a single segment for at least some products. Geographic concentration and specialized media allow targeted marketing campaigns.

LO6: Describe the various religious subcultures and their implications for marketing

Although the United States is a relatively secular society, roughly 82 percent of American adults claim a religious affiliation and a majority state that religion is important in their lives. A majority of American adults identify themselves as Christian, although the percentage has declined over time. And a variety of *religious subcultures* exist both within and across the Christian faiths and the Jewish, Muslim, and Buddhist faiths. Within each faith, the largest contrast is the degree of conservatism of the members.

LO7: Explain the role of geographic regions as subcultures

Regional subcultures arise as a result of climatic conditions, the natural environment and resources, the characteristics of the various immigrant groups that have settled in each region, and significant social and political events. Regional subcultures affect all aspects of consumption behavior, and sophisticated marketers recognize that the United States is composed of numerous regional markets.

KEY TERMS

Acculturation 157
Born-again Christians 171
Ethnic subcultures 150
Event marketing 155
Hispanic 156
Regional subcultures 174
Religious subcultures 169
Secular society 169
Subculture 148

REVIEW QUESTIONS

1. What is a *subculture?*
2. What determines the degree to which a subculture will influence an individual's behavior?
3. Is the American culture more like a soup or a salad?
4. What is an *ethnic subculture?*
5. How large are the major ethnic subcultures in America? Which are growing most rapidly?
6. What regions are the major sources of America's immigrants?
7. Are the various ethnic subcultures homogeneous or heterogeneous?
8. Describe the influence of education on the Internet use of African Americans. What are the marketing implications?
9. Describe the African-American consumer groups found by the Yankelovich group.
10. What are the basic principles that should be followed in marketing to an African-American market segment?
11. To what extent is the Spanish language used by American Hispanics? How do language and acculturation affect Internet use among Hispanics?
12. Can Hispanics be treated as a single market?
13. Describe the three Hispanic generational groups identified by the Pew Hispanic Center.
14. How homogeneous are Asian Americans?
15. To what extent do Asian Americans use their native language?
16. Describe three emerging aspects that may make the Asian-American population somewhat easier to target.
17. Why is the United States considered to be a *secular society?*
18. Describe the *Roman Catholic subculture.*
19. Describe the *born-again Christian subculture.*
20. Describe the *Jewish subculture.*
21. Describe the *Muslim subculture.*
22. Describe the *Buddhist subculture.*
23. What is a regional subculture? Give some examples.

DISCUSSION QUESTIONS

24. Examine Table 5–1. Which of these differences are mainly caused by ethnicity or race, and which are caused by other factors?
25. Do you agree that America is becoming more like a salad than a soup in terms of the integration of ethnic groups? Is this good or bad?
26. Do you agree with the following statement regarding ethnicity made at one point in time by a Miller Brewing representative? For what types of products is this view most correct? Least correct?

    We used to have an ethnic marketing department up until several years ago. . . . [But now we believe] the things that young Hispanic or young African American or young white people have in common are much stronger and more important than any ethnic difference.

27. Most new immigrants to America are non-European and have limited English-language skills. What opportunities does this present to marketers? Does this raise any ethical issues for marketers?
28. Does a firm's social responsibility play a role in marketing to consumers from various ethnic subcultures whose incomes fall below the poverty line? If so, what?
29. Respond to the questions in Consumer Insight 5–1.
30. Although some of the following have very limited incomes, others are quite prosperous. Does marketing to prosperous members of these groups require a marketing mix different from the one used to reach other prosperous consumers?
    a. African Americans
    b. Hispanics
    c. Asian Americans
31. Describe how each of the following firms' product managers should approach (*i*) the African-American, (*ii*) the Hispanic, (*iii*) the Asian-American, (*iv*) the Asian-Indian-American, (*v*) the Arab-American, or (*vi*) the Native-American markets.
    a. Pepsi
    b. Target
    c. NBA
    d. *Sports Illustrated* magazine
    e. The United Way
    f. Dell laptops
    g. Google.com
    h. Coach handbags
32. What, if any, unique ethical responsibilities exist when marketing to ethnic subcultures?

33. Do you agree that the United States is a secular society? Why or why not?
34. Describe how each of the following firms' product managers should approach the (*i*) Catholic, (*ii*) Protestant, (*iii*) born-again Christian, (*iv*) Jewish, (*v*) Muslim, and (*vi*) Buddhist subcultures.
    a. Red Bull
    b. Wendy's
    c. The NBA
    d. *Maxim* magazine
    e. The United Way
    f. Dell laptops
    g. Facebook
    h. Estée Lauder makeup
35. Will regional subcultures become more or less distinct over the next 20 years? Why?
36. Select one product, service, or activity from each category in Table 5–3 and explain the differences in consumption for the item across the regions shown.

APPLICATION ACTIVITIES

37. Watch two hours of prime-time major network (ABC, CBS, FOX, or NBC) television. What subculture groups are portrayed in the programs? Describe how they are portrayed. Do these portrayals match the descriptions in this text? How would you explain the differences? Repeat these tasks for the ads shown during the programs.
38. Pick a product of interest and examine the Simmons Market Research Bureau or MediaMark studies on the product in your library (these are often in the journalism library on CD-ROM). Determine the extent to which its consumption varies by ethnic group and region. Does consumption also vary by age, income, or other variables? Are the differences in ethnic and regional consumption due primarily to ethnicity and region or to the fact that the ethnic group or region is older, richer, or otherwise different from the larger culture?
39. Examine several magazines or newspapers aimed at a non-European ethnic or nationality group. What types of products are advertised? Why?
40. Interview three members of the following subcultures and ascertain their opinions of how their ethnic or nationality group is portrayed on network television shows and in national ads.
    a. African Americans
    b. Asian Americans
    c. Hispanics
    d. Arab Americans
    e. Asian Indian Americans
    f. Native Americans

41. Interview three members of the following subcultures and ascertain the extent to which they identify with the core American culture, their ethnic subculture within America, or their nationality subculture. Also determine the extent to which they feel others of their ethnic/race group feel as they do and the reasons for any differences.
    a. African Americans
    b. Asian Americans
    c. Hispanics
    d. Arab Americans
    e. Asian Indian Americans
    f. Native Americans
42. Interview three members of the following religious subcultures and determine the extent to which their consumption patterns are influenced by their religion.
    a. Catholics
    b. Protestants
    c. Born-again Christians
    d. Jews
    e. Muslims
    f. Buddhists
43. Interview two students from other regions of the United States and determine the behavior and attitudinal differences they have noticed between their home and your present location. Try to determine the causes of these differences.

REFERENCES

1. Chapter opener is based on L. M. Keefe, "P&G's Multicultural Marketing DNA," *Marketing News,* March 1, 2004, pp. 13–14; T. Nudd, "Nivea Apologizes for Wanting to 'Re-Civilize' Black Man," *Adweek.com,* August 18, 2011, www.adweek.com/adfreak/nivea-apologizes-wanting-re-civilize-black-man-134226, accessed August 29, 2014; F. Kelley, "Essence in New Orleans," *NPR The Record,* July 9, 2012, www.npr.org/blogs/therecord/2012/07/09/156494248/essence-in-new-orleans-a-festival-that-knows-its-audience, accessed August 29, 2014; D. Ramsey, "Essence Music Festival," *theGrio.com,* July 4, 2013, http://thegrio.com/2013/07/04/essence-music-festival-the-magic-and-the-business-behind-this-summers-hottest-ticket/2/, accessed August 29, 2014; and information from Essence website at www.essence.com.
2. C. Fisher, "It's All in the Details," *American Demographics,* April 1998, p. 45.
3. The 2010 percentages are from the 2010 Census and are found at *Overview of Race and Hispanic Origin: 2010* (Washington, DC: U.S. Census Bureau, March 2011). All other data are from *Table 4. Projections of the Population by Sex, Race, and Hispanic Origin for the United States: 2010 to 2050* (Washington, DC: U.S. Census Bureau, August 2008).
4. W. H. Frey, "Micro Melting Pots," *American Demographics,* June 2001, pp. 20–23.
5. R. Monger, *U.S. Legal Permanent Residents: 2009* (Washington, DC: U.S. Department of Homeland Security, 2010), p. 4.
6. M. R. Forehand and R. Deshpande, "What We See Makes Us Who We Are," *Journal of Marketing Research,* August 2001, pp. 336–48.
7. *Statistical Abstract of the United States: 2011* (Washington, DC: U.S. Census Bureau, 2011); and *2008 ASEC Supplement* (Washington, DC: U.S. Census Bureau, 2009).
8. E. Morris, "The Difference in Black and White," *American Demographics,* January 1993, p. 46.
9. "Households by Total Money Income in 2008," *2009 Annual Social and Economic Supplement* (Washington, DC: U.S. Bureau of the Census, 2009).
10. J. M. Humphreys, "The Multicultural Economy 2013," *Selig Center for Economic Growth* (University of Georgia, 2013).
11. Table 5–2 was derived from results presented in *Black America Today* (Radio One and Yankelovich, June 2008); and information found on BlackAmericaStudy.com, accessed April 23, 2011.
12. Y. K. Kim and J. Kang, "The Effects of Ethnicity and Product on Purchase Decision Making," *Journal of Advertising Research,* March 2001, pp. 39–48.
13. J. Adler, "Marketers, Agencies Praise BET's Savvy," *Advertising Age,* April 11, 2005, p. B16.
14. *Demographics of Internet Users* (Washington, DC: Pew Internet & American Life Project, May 2010).
15. E. Burns, "African American Online Population Is Growing," *The ClickZ Network,* October 10, 2005, www.clickz.com, accessed June 7, 2008; "AOL: Some 80 Percent of African-Americans Online," *MarketingVOX,* October 17, 2005, www.marketingvox.com, accessed June 7, 2008; *Black America Today,* 2008; and "Top U.S. Web Brands and Parent Companies for September 2009," Nielsenwire.com, at http://blog.nielsen.com/nielsenwire/online, accessed April 24, 2011.
16. A. Smith, *Technology Trends among People of Color* (Washington, DC: Pew Internet & American Life Project, September 17, 2010).
17. P. Miller, *African Americans Are a Heterogeneous, Not a Homogeneous, Market,* Cablevision Advertising Bureau, 2005, www.onetvworld.org.
18. See, e.g., L. Sanders, "How to Target Blacks?," *Advertising Age,* July 3, 2006, p. 19.

19. See, e.g., B. DeBerry-Spence, "Consumer Creations of Product Meaning in the Context of African-Style Clothing," *Journal of the Academy of Marketing Science,* 36 (2008), pp. 395–408.

20. E. M. Simpson et al., "Race, Homophily, and Purchase Intentions and the Black Consumer," *Psychology & Marketing,* October 2000, pp. 877–99. See also L. A. Perkins, K. M. Thomas, and G. A. Taylor, "Advertising and Recruitment," *Psychology & Marketing,* March 2000, pp. 235–55.

21. C. L. Green, "Ethnic Evaluations of Advertising," *Journal of Advertising,* Spring 1999, pp. 49–63; O. Appiah, "Ethnic Identification on Adolescents' Evaluations of Advertisements," *Journal of Advertising Research,* September 2001, pp. 7–21; and T. E. Whittler and J. S. Spira, "Model's Race," *Journal of Consumer Psychology,* 12, no. 4 (2002), pp. 291–301.

22. *The African-American Market in the U.S.* (New York: Packaged Facts, 2008).

23. D. Howell, "Albertson's Caters to Different Ethnic Markets," *DSN Retailing Today,* October 1, 2001, p. 18.

24. Keefe, "P&G's Multicultural Marketing DNA."

25. T. L. Ainscough and C. M. Motley, "Will You Help Me Please?," *Marketing Letters,* May 2000, pp. 129–36; and T. L. Baker, T. Meyer, and J. D. Johnson, "Individual Differences in Perceptions of Service Failure and Recovery," *Journal of the Academy of Marketing Science,* 36 (2008), pp. 552–64.

26. See V. D. Bush et al., "Managing Culturally Diverse Buyer–Seller Relationships," *Journal of the Academy of Marketing Science,* Fall 2001, pp. 391–404.

27. See, e.g., *The African-American Market in the U.S.*

28. See, e.g., ibid.

29. R. J. Wyatt, B. D. Gelb, and S. Geirger-Oneto, "How Social Insecurity and the Social Meaning of Advertising Reinforce Minority Consumers' Preference for National Brands," *Journal of Contemporary Issues and Research in Advertising,* 30 (Spring 2008), pp. 61–70.

30. "Households by Total Money Income in 2008."

31. Humphreys, "The Multicultural Economy 2013."

32. *The American Community Survey* (Washington, DC: U.S. Census Bureau, 2009).

33. See *Assimilation and Language* (Washington, DC: Pew Hispanic Center, 2004) and *Latino Shoppers* (Rockville, MD: Packaged Facts, 2011).

34. *Generational Differences* (Washington, DC: Pew Hispanic Center, March 2004) and *Statistical Portrait of Hispanics in the United States, 2009* (Washington, DC: Pew Hispanic Center, February 2011). See also R. Villarreal and R. A. Peterson, "Hispanic Identity and Media Behavior," *Journal of Advertising Research,* June 2008, pp. 179–90.

35. G. Berman, *Portrait of the New America* (Coral Gables, FL: Market Segment Group, 2002), p. 21.

36. Based on R. X. Weissman, "Los Niños Go Shopping," *American Demographics,* May 1999, pp. 37–39; H. Stapinski, "Generación Latino," *American Demographics,* July 1999, pp. 63–68; R. Gardyn, "Habla English," *American Demographics,* April 2001, pp. 54–57; J. D. Zbar, "Hispanic Teens Set Urban Beat," *Advertising Age,* June 2001, p. S6; H. Chura, "Sweet Spot," *Advertising Age,* November 12, 2001, p. 1; *Nuestro Futuro* (Redwood Shores, CA: Cheskin, 2006); *Hispanic/Latino Market Profile* (New York: Mediamark Research, 2007); and *Resident Population by Race, Hispanic Origin, and Age* (Washington, DC: U.S. Census Bureau, 2010).

37. C. Webster, "The Effects of Hispanic Identification on Marital Roles in the Purchase Decision Process," *Journal of Consumer Research,* September 1994, pp. 319–31.

38. See, e.g., *Gender Norms and the Role of Extended Family* (Washington, DC: Hispanic Healthy Marriage Initiative, 2006), at www.acf.hhs.gov/healthymarriage/pdf/Gender_Norms.pdf, accessed May 6, 2011; and *Latino Shoppers.*

39. *The American Community Survey* (Washington, DC: U.S. Census Bureau, 2009).

40. *The U.S. Hispanic Market* (New York: Packaged Facts, October 2003); and J. Noriega and E. Blair, "Advertising to Bilinguals," *Journal of Marketing,* September 2008, pp. 69–83.

41. L. Sonderup, "Hispanic Marketing," *Advertising & Marketing Review,* April 2004, www.ad-mkt-review.com.

42. *Hispanic Fact Pack 2010* (New York, NY: Advertising Age, 2010), p. 31.

43. W. R. Ortiz, CableTelevision Advertising Bureau, "Answering the Language Question," press release, www.onetvworld.org, accessed May 9, 2005.

44. *The U.S. Hispanic Market.*

45. L. Wentz, "Rapid Change Sweeps Hispanic Advertising Industry," *AdAge.com,* May 3, 2005, www.adage.com.

46. Information from SiTV website at www.sitv.com, accessed May 6, 2011.

47. *Demographics of Internet Users.*

48. F. Korzenny, "Multicultural Marketing and the Reasons Why," *Journal of Advertising Research,* June 2008, pp. 173–76.

49. *Hispanic Fact Pack 2010.*

50. *Hispanics Online* (New York, NY: eMarketer, May 2010).

51. For these and other examples, see "Marketing to Hispanics," *Advertising Age,* February 8, 1987, p. S23; M. Westerman, "Death of the Frito Bandito," March 1989, pp. 28–32; and L. Wentz, "Debate Swirls over Slang in Coors Spot," *Advertising Age,* May 17, 2004, p. 6.

52. See D. Luna, L. A. Peracchio, and M. D. de Juan, "The Impact of Language and Congruity on Persuasion in Multicultural E-Marketing," *Journal of Consumer Psychology,* 13, no. 1/2 (2003), pp. 41–50; see also Gardyn, "Habla English."

53. *Latino Shoppers.*

54. L. Wentz, "Best Buy Targets Hispanic Patriarchs," *Advertising Age,* August 2, 2004, p. 20.

55. L. Wentz, "Home Depot Paint Line Connects with Hispanics," *Advertising Age,* July 3, 2006, p. 19.

56. J. Garcia and R. Gerdes, "To Win Latino Market, Know Pitfalls, Learn Rewards," *Marketing News,* March 1, 2004, pp. 14, 19.

57. A. S. Wellner, "Gen X Homes In," *American Demographics,* August 1999, p. 61.

58. J. Birchall, "Walmart Targets Latino Mercados with Supermercado do Walmart," *Financial Times,* March 12, 2009;

and "Latino-Focused Wal-Mart, Sam's Club Stores to Open," *Adweek,* March 17, 2009.

59. Information from website at http://tianguismall.com, accessed May 6, 2011.
60. Humphreys, "The Multicultural Economy 2013."
61. See B. Edmundson, "Asian Americans in 2001," *American Demographics,* February 1997, pp. 16–17; "90 Percent of Asian Americans Go Online," *BizReport,* May 10, 2007; and *The Asian-American Market in the U.S.* (Rockville, MD: Packaged Facts, October 2008).
62. "90 Percent of Asian Americans Go Online."
63. M. C. Tharp, *Marketing and Consumer Identity in Multicultural America* (Thousand Oaks, CA: Sage, 2001), p. 259.
64. Ibid., pp. 253–57.
65. *The 1993 Minority Market Report* (Coral Gables, FL: Market Segment Research, 1993).
66. *The American Community—Asians* (Washington, DC: U.S. Census Bureau, February 2007); and Humphreys, "The Multicultural Economy 2013."
67. "Asia Rising." *American Demographics,* July–August 2002, pp. 38–43.
68. Annual Estimates of the Resident Population by Race, Age and Sex for the United States: April 1, 2000 to July 1, 2006 (Washington, DC: U.S. Census Bureau, 2007).
69. D. L. Vence, "Growth in Asian-Am. Spending Fuels Targeted Marketing," *Marketing News,* June 1, 2004, pp. 11–13.
70. "Reaching Generation 2.0," *Advertising Age,* July–August 2002, p. 42.
71. See, e.g., Y.-K. Kim and J. Kang, "Effects of Asian-Americans' Ethnicity and Acculturation on Personal Influences," *Journal of Current Issues and Research in Advertising,* Spring 2001, pp. 43–53.
72. Information accessed from corporate websites.
73. "Annual Asian American Consumer Behavior Study Reveals Key Findings in Retail, Automobile, Insurance, and Telecom Industries," *DiversityBusiness.com,* March 7, 2007, www.diversitybusiness.com, accessed June 8, 2008.
74. Korzenny, "Multicultural Marketing and the Reasons Why."
75. *New Study Reveals Lifestyle Habits and Industry Specific Consumption Behavior among Asian Americans* (Long Beach, CA: interTrend Communications, November 2005).
76. Vence, "Growth in Asian-Am. Spending Fuels Targeted Marketing."
77. "Diversity in America," *American Demographics,* November 2002, p. S17.
78. Humphreys, "The Multicultural Economy 2013."
79. "Native American Food Goes Haute Cuisine," *CNN.com,* September 30, 2004, www.cnn.com.
80. See A. S. Wellner, "Discovering Native America," *American Demographics,* August 2001, p. 21.
81. Information from website at www.indiansummer.org/, accessed May 7, 2011.
82. A. M. Peterson, "Nike Boosts Indians' Health, Its Reputation," *Marketing News,* June 1, 2004, p. 10.
83. This section is based on M. Mogelonsky, "Asian Indian Americans," *American Demographics,* August 1995, pp. 32–39. See also M. M. Cardona, "Segment Marketing Grows as Tool for Financial Services Leaders," *Advertising Age,* November 20, 2000, p. S1.
84. A. S. Wellner, "Every Day's a Holiday," *American Demographics,* December 2000, p. 63.
85. "Arab Americans" section is based on S. El-Badry, "The Arab-American Market," *American Demographics,* January 1994, pp. 22–30; L. P. Morton, "Segmenting to Target Arab Americans," *Public Relations Quarterly,* Winter 2001, pp. 47–48; Arab American Institute, "Survey Reveals Arab American Experiences and Reactions Following 9/11," press release, August 19, 2002; Arab American Institute, "Arab American Demographics," www.aaiusa.org/demographics.htm, accessed May 14, 2005; K. Naughton, "Arab-America's Store," *Newsweek,* March 10, 2008, p. 42; and the Arab American Institute website, http://aaiusa.org, accessed May 7, 2011.
86. Numbers are for 2010 based on a Gallup poll reported at www.gallup.com/poll/1690/religion.aspx, accessed February 20, 2011.
87. "Survey: Americans Switching Faiths, Dropping Out," *CNN.com,* February 25, 2008, www.cnn.com, accessed February 25, 2008.
88. See R. Cimino and D. Lattin, "Choosing My Religion," *American Demographics,* April 1999, pp. 60–65.
89. Gallup poll reported at www.gallup.com/poll/1690/religion.aspx, accessed February 20, 2011. Additional information on religion in the United States can be found at Adherents.com (www.adherents.com), which collects and disseminates statistics from various sources, including two of the most comprehensive surveys of religion in the United States, namely, the National Survey of Religious Identification (NSRI: 1990) and the American Religious Identity Survey (ARIS: 2001) conducted by B. A. Kosmin, S. P. Lachman, and associates.
90. B. Ebenkamp, "The Young and Righteous," *Brandweek,* April 5, 2004, p. 18; and S. Kang, "Pop Culture Gets Religion," *The Wall Street Journal,* May 5, 2004, pp. B1, B2.
91. K. Wheaton, "Chik-fil-A for Sunday Lunch?," *Advertising Age,* July 12, 2010, p. 3.
92. Information on ethnic diversity from ARIS research briefs, www.gc.cuny.edu.
93. Information from website of The Archdiocese of Baltimore at www.archbalt.org/news, accessed May 7, 2011.
94. Information on *Encuentro 2000* from press releases by the U.S. Conference of Catholic Bishops (Washington, DC), including "Growing Asian Impact on Church to Be Felt at *Encuentro 2000,*" May 22, 2000; "Latin Music, Movie on Cuba, Hispanic Cultural Expressions Part of *Encuento 2000* Celebration of Multi-ethnic Church," May 30, 2000; and "Bishops' Agenda Includes Pastoral Framework for Hispanic Ministry," October 11, 2002, www.usccb.org.
95. B. A. Kosmin and P. Lachman, *One Nation under God* (New York: Harmony Books, 1993), p. 245.

96. "Breaking the Rules of Engagement," *American Demographics,* July–August 2002, p. 35.
97. R. Thau, "The New Jewish Exodus," *American Demographics,* June 1994, p. 11.
98. Kosmin and Lachman, *One Nation under God,* p. 12.
99. Estimates here have been hotly debated. For an excellent discussion, see "The Largest Religious Groups in the United States of America," Adherents.com, www.adherents.com.
100. M. Chapman and A. Jamal, "The Floodgates Open," *Enhancing Knowledge Development in Marketing* (Chicago: American Marketing Association, 1996), p. 198.
101. See S. El-Badry, "Understanding Islam in America," *American Demographics,* January 1994, p. 10.
102. B. Horovitz, "Down-Home Marketing," *USA Today,* October 3, 1997, p. 1B.

chapter

6 The American Society: Families and Households

LEARNING OBJECTIVES

LO1 **Explain the concept of household types and their influence on consumption.**

LO2 **Summarize the household life cycle's various stages and marketing implications.**

LO3 **Understand the family decision process.**

LO4 **Describe the role that households play in child socialization.**

LO5 **Explain the sources of ethical concern associated with marketing to children.**

Solo living is on the rise. According to the latest census figures, 27 percent of all households now consist of one person (a 10 percent increase from 1970). Approximately 32 million people live alone. At no other time in history have so many people opted to live alone. According to one expert, the extraordinary upsurge in solo living is the "greatest social change since the baby boom."[1]

Although delaying marriage, divorcing in greater numbers, and living longer as solitary widows or widowers are certainly part of the picture, there is an attitudinal component to it that cuts across age, social, and ethnic distinctions. Specifically, there is a growth in the number of people who *want* to live alone and can afford to do so. Single-person households are more common in metropolitan areas. Over 40 percent of households in San Francisco; Seattle; Minneapolis; Washington, D.C.; Atlanta; and Denver have one occupant. The rise of single-person households is also a global phenomenon, including counties such as France, Japan, Brazil, and China.

The market and marketing implications of single-person households is powerful. Single-person households (average expenditures of $34,471) have a total buying power of $1.9 trillion. They spend 49 percent more than the most affluent "families with children" households ($23,179) and 23 percent more than "married with no children" households ($28,017). From micro-apartments, to single-serving meals, to communal dining, to "solo travel packages" by cruise lines, marketers are adjusting. Indeed, real estate shortages in the metro areas where the "living single" phenomenon has taken hold are pushing the trend toward and development of small living spaces such as micro-apartments. New York City plans to build eighty 300-square-foot micro-apartments, renting at $2000 a month. To do this, it must first change its current zoning law requiring apartments to be at least 400 square feet. Micro-apartments that are 220 square feet are already available in San Jose, California, a city in the heart of technology-heavy, hard-to-find-an-affordable-place-to-rent Silicon Valley. Nearby San Francisco will follow suit, having successfully enacted legislation to change its building code. Small space dwellings have, in turn, sparked a need for space-saving, multipurpose furniture that retailers such as IKEA and Itzy Bitzy are filling.

The rise of single-person households is perhaps the most significant lifestyle trend in the last 50 years and will profoundly influence marketing and the design and delivery of products and service.

Single households, though important and growing, represent just one type of household. This chapter examines the nature and influence of households in American society, the household life cycle, the family decision process, consumer socialization, and marketing to children.

THE NATURE AND INFLUENCE OF AMERICAN HOUSEHOLDS

The Influence of Households

LO1 The household is the basic consumption unit for most consumer goods. Major items such as housing, automobiles, and appliances are consumed more by household units than by individuals. Furthermore, the consumption patterns of individual household members seldom are independent from those of other household members. For example, deciding to grant a child's request for a bicycle may mean spending discretionary funds that could have been used to purchase a weekend away for the parents, new clothing for a sister or brother, or otherwise used by another member of the household. Therefore, it is essential that marketers understand the household as a consumption unit, as shown in Figure 6–1.

Households are important not only for their direct role in the consumption process but also for the critical role they perform in socializing children. The family household is

FIGURE 6-1 The Household Influences Most Consumption Decisions

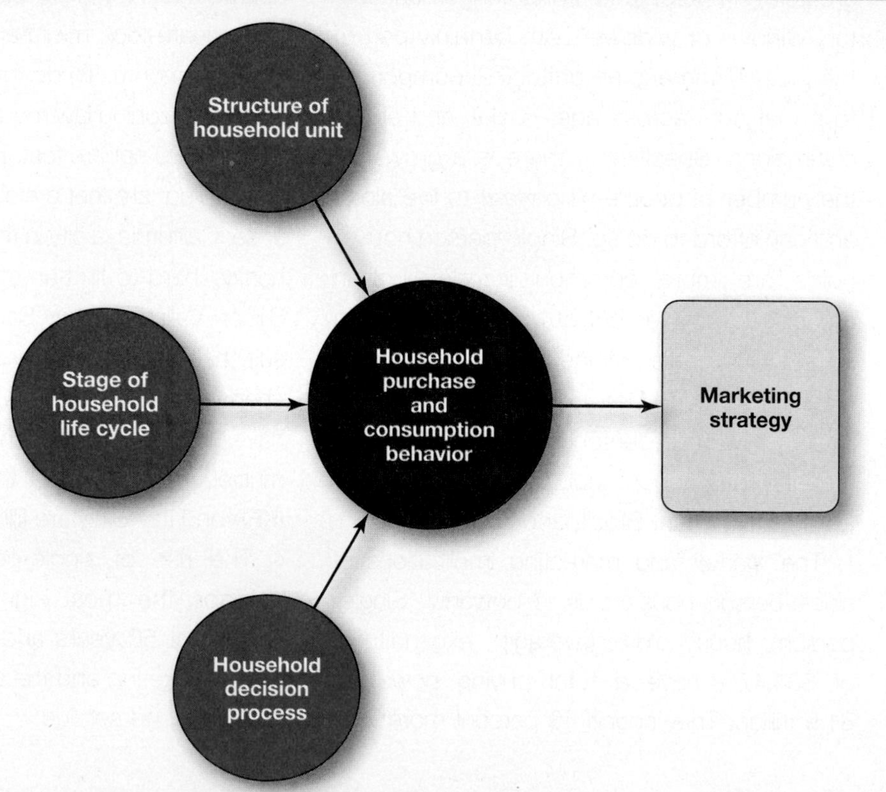

Family and Nonfamily Households

TABLE 6-1

Type of Household	Number (000)	Percentage
All households	**117,181**	**100.0%**
Family households	**78,850**	**67.3**
Married couples	59,118	50.5
Children under 18 at home	*25,129*	*21.4*
No children under 18 at home	*33,989*	*29.0*
Male householder (children under 18 at home)	2,111	1.8
Female householder (children under 18 at home)	8,394	7.2
Other families	9,227	7.9
Nonfamily households	**38,331**	**32.7**
Male householder	17,694	15.1
Living alone	*13,758*	*11.7*
Female householder	20,637	17.6
Living alone	*17,899*	*15.3*

Source: *Households, Families, Subfamilies, and Married Couples: 1980–2009* (Washington, DC: U.S. Census Bureau, 2011), table 5.

the primary mechanism whereby cultural and subcultural values and behavior patterns are passed on to the next generation. Purchasing and consumption patterns are among those attitudes and skills strongly influenced by the family household unit.

Types of Households

There are a variety of types of households. The Census Bureau defines a **household** as *all the people who occupy a housing unit* (a house, apartment, group of rooms, or single room designed to be occupied as separate living quarters). It defines a **family household** as one having *at least two members related by birth, marriage, or adoption, one of whom is the householder* (a householder owns or rents the residence). A **nonfamily household** is a *householder living alone or exclusively with others to whom he or she is not related.* Table 6–1 indicates the current distribution of household types in the United States.[2]

Historically, the family household—and, in particular, the traditional family household—has been an important focus for marketers. The term **traditional family** is typically used to refer to *a married opposite-sex couple and their own or adopted children living at home.* However, this type of family has clearly declined over time, particularly if one considers a traditional family to be one headed by a never-divorced couple. Today, about 20 percent of all households are married couples with children living at home, down from 40 percent in 1970.[3] Some of this decline is due to the increase in *single-parent households.* Much of the decline is due to an increase in the number of *single-person households,* which is a function of (a) young people pushing back marriage until their late 20s (rather than getting married in their early 20s as they did in 1970) and (b) the increase in sole survivors as our population ages.

Step families are also important and growing. The U.S. Census defines a **step family** as *a married-couple family household with at least one child under the age of 18 who is a step-child (i.e., a son or daughter through marriage).* High divorce and remarriage rates mean that a substantial number of American children grow up with stepparents and stepsiblings and often have two such families, one formed by their mother and the other by their father. One study finds that half of all young adults have at least one step relative.[4] Creating and revising relationship identities is critical and difficult and can revolve around consumption activities. Consider the following quote about the challenges of step relationships:

> When mom and dad got divorced and mom remarried, everything changed. We, my father and I, had to find a way to create a sense of who we are without mom. We found that a passion for adventure is something we share, that mom and my sister don't, and we took up scuba diving. Although my stepdad is certainly a part of our family, my mom, sister, and I are a different "we" with many different stories to tell and a distinct history of sharing experiences.[5]

Recognizing the difficult dynamics of step family relationships, Café Press offers cards, t-shirts, mugs, and other products that celebrate step families. One card reads, "It's Love Not Blood that Makes a Forever Family."

Consumer Insight 6–1 discusses another growing family trend, namely, multigenerational families.

In addition, while the Census defines a family in terms of marriage, birth, or adoption, many unmarried couples clearly view themselves as families. There are roughly 6.2 million *unmarried-partner* (opposite and same sex) households in the United States. In many ways, their needs are the same as married couples with similar demographics. However, there are exceptions, such as finding knowledgeable assistance with legal and financial issues concerning joint home ownership, estate planning, and so forth. While same-sex couples can be targeted via specialized media (see Chapter 3), opposite-sex couples can be more difficult to reach since targeted media are lacking.

Clearly, as American households and families evolve away from the traditional family model, marketers must adapt. Kraft recognizes the diversity and importance of families, with ads that portray various family types in scenarios revolving around food. A recent spot features a father and his daughter enjoying a quiet conversation.

Recognizing and adapting to the differing needs of various types of families or the different needs of members within the same family can be a critical success factor. *How well does Campbell's "One Soup Fits All" campaign (see Illustration 6–1) meet the differing needs of today's diverse household?*

LO2

ILLUSTRATION 6-1

This Campbell's Soup ad is attempting to appeal to the needs of different family members and the different household types in which they reside.

THE HOUSEHOLD LIFE CYCLE

The traditional view of the American household life cycle was quite simple. People married by their early 20s; they had several children; these children grew up and started their own families; the original couple retired; and the male would eventually die, followed after a few years by the female. This was known as the *family life cycle,* and it was a useful tool for segmenting markets and developing marketing strategy. The basic assumption underlying the family life cycle approach is that most families pass through an orderly progression of stages, each with its own characteristics, financial situations, and purchasing patterns.

However, as described earlier, American households follow much more complex

CONSUMER INSIGHT 6-1

The Rise of Multigenerational Families

A **multigenerational family** is *a family household containing (a) at least two adult generations or (b) a grandparent and at least one other generation.* Nearly 50 million Americans live in multigenerational households, which is a 33 percent increase since 1980. A number of factors account for this trend, including:[6]

- The increasing immigrant population—this population is more likely to live in multigenerational families. Indeed, nearly a quarter of all Hispanics and Asian Americans live in such households.
- The delay in marriage of younger individuals and the economic recession—because young people have pushed marriage into their late 20s, those in their early 20s are often the most likely to move back in with their parents, and tough economic times have accelerated this trend.
- Medicare cuts and cultural beliefs about caring for an elder parent—there has been an increase in the percentage of those 65 and older moving in with their children. Economic issues may be one factor. However, over half of American adults also believe it is their responsibility to take an elder parent into their home if the parent wants to live with them.

There are different forms of multigenerational family. The first (47 percent) involves two adult generations where the youngest adult is 25 or older. The second (47 percent) involves three or more generations. The third involves a grandparent and grandchild with no parent present. This last category, called the skipped generation, represents 6 percent of all multigenerational families and shows the power of America's aging population in directly parenting and influencing multiple generations of children. It diverges considerably from our traditional notion of aging baby boomers as empty nesters focused on travel and other leisure activities.

Marketers are finding opportunities and challenges in this family type. For example:

- Ameriprise advisors are trained to help women deal with the fact that if they are a caregiver to a family member or friend (and 60 percent are), that it has work and financial consequences that must be planned for.
- Caldwell Banker's real estate agents are trained to position houses for multigenerational families. So, for example, a fifth bedroom could be touted as "in-law quarters."
- Presto created a printer device to which e-mails and pictures can be sent and then directly printed with the push of a button to allow electronic communication with older family members even if they are less technologically proficient.
- For the grandparents raising their grandchildren, opportunities abound that go beyond the typical gift scenario such as diapers, baby food, and other basic need products.

Critical Thinking Questions

1. Do you think the increase in multigenerational families will continue to grow after the economic recession is over?
2. What additional marketing opportunities may exist for multigenerational families?
3. What challenges might marketers face in targeting multigenerational families?

and varied cycles today. Therefore, researchers have developed several models of the **household life cycle (HLC).**[7] All are based on the age and marital status of the adult members of the household and the presence and age of children. A useful version is shown in Figure 6–2.

The HLC assumes that households move into a variety of relatively distinct and well-defined categories over time. There are a variety of routes into most of the categories shown in Figure 6–2, and movement from one category into another frequently occurs. For example, it is common for singles to marry and then divorce within a few years without

FIGURE 6-2 Stages of the Household Life Cycle

Stage	Marital Status		Children at Home		
	Single	Married	None	<6 years	>6 years
Younger (<35)					
Single I	×		×		
Young married		×	×		
Full nest I		×		×	
Single parent I	×			×	
Middle-aged (35–64)					
Single II	×		×		
Delayed full nest I		×		×	
Full nest II		×			×
Single parent II	×				×
Empty nest I		×	×		
Older (>64)					
Empty nest II		×	×		
Single III	×		×		

having children (moving from single to young married back to young single). Or one can become a single parent through divorce or through birth or adoption without a cohabiting partner.

Each category in the household life cycle poses a set of problems that household decision makers must solve. The solution to these problems is bound intimately to the selection and maintenance of a lifestyle and, thus, to consumption. For example, all young couples with no children face a need for relaxation or recreation. Solutions to this common problem differ, with some opting for an outdoors-oriented lifestyle and others choosing a sophisticated urban lifestyle. As these families move into another stage in the HLC, such as the "full nest I" stage, the problems they face change. The amount of time and resources available for recreation usually diminishes. New problems related to raising a child become more urgent.

Each stage presents unique needs and wants as well as financial conditions and experiences. Thus, the HLC provides marketers with relatively homogeneous household segments that share similar needs with respect to household-related problems and purchases, as discussed in Consumer Insight 6–2.

While Figure 6–2 categorizes households into married and unmarried, it is "coupleness" rather than the legal status of the relationship that drives most of the behavior of the household. Committed couples, of the same sex or of opposite sexes, tend to exhibit most of the category-specific behaviors described below whether or not they are married.

Single I This group consists of young (ages 18 to 34), unmarried individuals. There are roughly 69 million people in this age group, with 68 percent of men and 60 percent of women being single. Single I is basically the unmarried members of the Generation Yers, as described in Chapter 4. The aging of the larger Generation Y cohort along with

CONSUMER INSIGHT 6-2

Consumer Life Cycles and Homeowner Remodeling Decisions

Consumers and households move through somewhat predictable phases.[8] As they do so, changes occur in consumption based on these shifts in household characteristics and needs and wants. Housing, of course, is needed at all the household life stages, and a relationship between the type of housing and the consumers' household life stage exists. Consumers who are single and entering the workforce are more likely to rent than own. And while home ownership is an aspiration and reality for many Americans, the challenges associated with changes in the household life cycle can generate the need to either move or remodel. Renovations are costly and can lead to unexpected and hidden costs. Two factors play into renovation decisions:

- Family (and friends) are the single most influential factors in renovation decisions.
- Household life-cycle stage changes can trigger the need for home renovations.

A recent article shows that movements across stages (e.g., from no children to children, from children to no children) can generate the need to renovate and remodel. Some of the mechanisms are as follows:

Prioritizing—Do households balance competing and at times conflicting commitments in how they manage and use space at home?

Embodying—Do household members have particular physical needs, either currently or in the anticipated future, that might affect how the home is arranged?

Adapting—Are households aware of a need to adapt the physical arrangement or material surroundings of their homes?

Clearly these mechanisms can be triggered by a number of factors, but household life-cycle stage and stage changes will have a major (if not *the* major) influence.

An interesting corollary effect involved in remodeling is called the Diderot effect which, in effect, means that one change leads to a cascade of other needed or desired changes. The following quote illustrates this effect:

> I think of my parents, who a year ago remodeled a powder room and redecorated the living room. That work served to highlight the age of the rest of the home, and they have since replaced the garage door and redecorated the guest room, and are now in the process of planning to remodel the kitchen and master bath, finish the basement and redecorate another bedroom. They are neither materialistic nor extravagant, but they want the house to look nice—to be updated and well maintained.

The Diderot effect is a warning to consumers of the hidden costs subsequent to the remodeling, upgrading, and replacement of goods. To the remodeler, the Diderot effect is a promise of possible repeat business from current customers who find, to their surprise, the need for additional remodeling and serves as a reminder to provide quality work.

Critical Thinking Questions

1. Why might the Diderot effect be of interest to marketers?
2. Choose two phases of the household life cycle and describe how one of the mechanisms might be involved in triggering a need for home remodeling.
3. What decision barriers must marketers overcome if consumers are aware of the Diderot effect?

continued delay of marriage has fueled growth in this market.[9] During this time, individuals generally leave home and establish their own distinct identities. It is a time of growth and change, both exciting and positive, and frightening and painful.

This group can be subdivided into those who live with one or both parents and those who live alone or with other individuals. The roughly 44 million single individuals in this age range live as follows:

	Males (%)	Females (%)	Total (%)
Live alone	14	12	13
Live with parent(s)	46	40	43
Live with others	39	48	43

Those who live with parents tend to be younger, with 75 percent being under 25. A significant number are in school or have recently graduated from high school or college and are beginning their working careers. Though people in this group have lower relative incomes, they also have few fixed expenses. They lead active, social lives. They go to bars, movies, and concerts, and purchase sports equipment, clothes, and personal care items.

Although some of those who live with others are involved with a partner, many share quarters with one or more housemates. These individuals have more fixed living expenses than do those who live with their parents, but they generally have ample disposable income as they share rent and other fixed housing costs.

These singles are a good market for the same types of products as those who live at home as well as for convenience-oriented household products. They are also a prime market for nice apartments, sports cars, clothing Club Med vacations, and similar activities. They are beginning to develop financial portfolios such as life insurance, savings, and stocks or mutual funds. The Calvin Klein Jeans ad shown in Illustration 6–2 would appeal to both groups.

ILLUSTRATION 6-2

Young singles are active and often have significant discretionary income. They are an excellent market for a wide array of recreational and leisure items. This Calvin Klein Jeans ad would appeal to their desire for action and romance.

ILLUSTRATION 6-3

This resort is positioned as ideal for couples to escape the pressure of a hectic work schedule for relaxation and romance.

Singles who live alone are older, with 70 percent being over 25. In general, they have higher incomes than the others but also higher expenses because they have no one with whom to share the fixed cost of a house or apartment. They are a good market for most of the same products and services as the other singles.

Young Couples: No Children The decision to marry, or to live together, brings about a new stage in the household life cycle. Marriage is much more likely for the 25- to 34-year-olds (50 percent) than it is for the under-25 crowd (14 percent). The lifestyles of two young singles are greatly altered as they develop a shared lifestyle. Joint decisions and shared roles in household responsibilities are in many instances new experiences.[10] Savings, household furnishings, major appliances, and more comprehensive insurance coverage are among the new areas of problem recognition and decision making to which a young married couple must give serious consideration.

Like the young single stage, the time spent by a young couple in this stage of the HLC has grown as couples either delay their start in having children or choose to remain childless.

Most households in this group have dual incomes and thus are relatively affluent. Compared with full nest I families, this group spends heavily on theater tickets, expensive clothes, luxury vacations, restaurant meals, and alcoholic beverages. They can afford nice cars, stylish apartments, and high-quality home appliances.

Illustration 6–3 contains an ad that would appeal to this group as well as to some members of the single I and full nest I segments. Note that romance plays a major role in the ad. It also plays on the desire to escape worries and everyday responsibilities.

Full Nest I: Young Married with Children Roughly 6 percent of households are young married couples with children. The addition of the first child to a family creates many changes in lifestyle and consumption. Naturally, new purchases in the areas of baby clothes, furniture, food, and health care products occur in this stage. Lifestyles are also greatly altered. The wife may withdraw fully or partly from the labor force (in roughly 62 percent of married couples with a child under six, the wife works outside the home)[11] for several months to several years, with a resulting decline in household income. The couple may have to move to another place of residence because their current apartment may not be appropriate for children. Likewise, choices of vacations, restaurants, and automobiles must be changed to accommodate young children.

Some of the changes in income and annual expenditures that occur as a household moves from childless to the young child stage in their late 20s and early 30s include the following:[12]

Expenditure	Percentage Change
Income	−9.4%
Food at home	24.3
Meals out	−9.6
Alcoholic beverages	−25.0
Adult apparel	−8.3
Children's apparel	215.7
Health care	16.1
Education	−28.8
Personal care products	−2.6

As shown above, discretionary and adult expenditures are reduced by the need to spend on child-related products such as food, health care, and children's apparel as well as to offset the decline in income.

Obtaining competent child care becomes an issue at this stage and remains a major concern of parents at all HLC stages. Households with a stay-at-home spouse confront this issue mainly for evenings out or weekends away. Single-parent and dual-earner households generally require daily child care, which is expensive and often requires parents to make trade-offs from their ideal situation.

Moms across the HLC possess $1.7 trillion in spending power. Examples of companies going after moms in full nest I are given below.

- Kraft, which launched an iPad app called Big Fork Little Fork that provides parents with information on healthy food options for kids and families.[13]
- Club Mom, an online loyalty program that provides advice, resources, and discounts to moms who shop with sponsors such as Chrysler.[14]
- McDonald's, which attempts to attract this segment by providing recreational equipment for the young children in these households.

Illustration 6–4 contains an ad aimed at this market segment. It shows how the choice of recreational activities may change with the addition of young children.

Single Parent I: Young Single Parents Birth or adoption by singles is increasingly common. Roughly 40 percent of children are born to unmarried mothers, a number that has risen by 13 percentage points since 1990. However, as many as 40 percent of these children may actually be born to cohabiting unmarried parents.[15] Divorce, while on the decline since 1980, continues to be a significant part of American society, with 40 percent of first marriages ending in divorce.[16] Although most divorced individuals remarry and most women who bear children out of wedlock eventually get married, 9 percent of American households are single-parent families, and 80 percent of these are headed by women.

The younger members of this group, particularly those who have never been married, tend to have a limited education and a very low income. These individuals are often members of one of the lower social classes, as described in Chapter 4. The older members of this segment and the divorced members receiving support from their ex-spouses are somewhat better off financially, but most are still under significant stress as they raise their young children without the support of a partner who is physically present.

This type of family situation creates many unique needs in the areas of child care, easy-to-prepare foods, and recreation. The need to work and raise younger children creates

ILLUSTRATION 6-4

Parenthood brings both great pleasures and great responsibilities. This ad emphasizes the pleasures of family activities.

enormous time pressures and places tremendous demands on the energy of these parents. Most are renters and so are not a major market for home appliances and improvements. Their purchases focus on getting by and on time- and energy-saving products and services that are not overly expensive.

Middle-Aged Single The middle-aged single category is made up of people who have never married and those who are divorced and have no child-rearing responsibilities. These individuals are in the 35-to-64 age category, which is primarily the Generation X and baby boomers (Chapter 4), although older Generation Y consumers are moving into this category as well.

Middle-aged singles often live alone. In fact, living alone is increasingly viewed as a lifestyle choice that many are willing and able to make, given higher incomes. Middle-aged singles who live alone represented roughly 15 million households, which is about 47 percent of all single-person households. Middle-aged singles have higher incomes than young singles. However, all live-alone singles suffer from a lack of scale economies. That is, a couple or family needs only one dishwasher, clothes dryer, and so forth for everyone in the household; but the single-person household needs the same basic household infrastructure even though only one person uses it. Likewise, many foods and other items come in sizes inappropriate for singles, or the small sizes are disproportionately expensive. Thus, opportunities appear to exist to fill unmet needs among this important and growing market.[17]

The needs of middle-aged singles in many ways reflect those of young singles. But middle-aged singles are likely to have more money to spend on their lifestyles and they are willing to indulge themselves. Thus, they may live in nice condominiums, frequent expensive restaurants, own a luxury automobile, and travel often. They are a major market for gifts, and the males buy significant amounts of jewelry as gifts.

Empty Nest I: Middle-Aged Married with No Children Lifestyle changes in the 1980s and 1990s influenced many young couples to not have children.[18] In other cases, these households represent second marriages in which children from a first marriage are

ILLUSTRATION 6-5

This service and ad would appeal to empty nest I consumers. They have the resources to afford such travel and would welcome the relaxation and escape it promises.

not living with the parent. This group also includes married couples whose children have left home. These three forces have produced a huge market consisting of middle-aged couples without children at home. Roughly 55 percent of married couples in this age group (35 to 64) don't have children under the age of 18. This segment has grown as baby boomers have moved through the latter stages of middle age and into retirement.

Both adults typically will have jobs, so they are very busy. However, the absence of responsibilities for children creates more free time than they have enjoyed since their youth. They also have money to spend on dining out, expensive vacations, second homes, luxury cars, and time-saving services such as housecleaning, laundry, and shopping. They are a prime market for financial services. Less obvious, they are also heavy purchasers of upscale children's products, as gifts for nieces, nephews, grandchildren, and friends' children.

The ad and product in Illustration 6–5 would appeal to this group.

Delayed Full Nest I: Older Married with Young Children Many members of the baby boom generation and Generation X delayed having their first child until they were in their mid-30s. This produced the new phenomenon of a large number of middle-aged, established families entering into parenthood for the first time. Recall from Table 6–1 that married couples with children under 18 make up 21.4 percent of all households. And young married couples make up only 6 percent of all households. However, middle-aged (35 to 64) married couples with children (both delayed full nest I and full nest II) make up roughly 15 percent of all households and represent 71 percent of all married couples with children under 18.[19]

A major difference between delayed full nest I and younger new parents is income. Older new parents' incomes are significantly larger than those of younger new parents. They have had this income flow longer and so have acquired more capital and possessions. They spend heavily on child care, mortgage payments, home maintenance, lawn care, and household furnishings. In addition, they want only the best for their children and are willing and able to spend on them. For example, the specialty diaper and toiletries market is expected to have double-digit growth. And traditional mass marketers such as Kimberly-Clark are pushing high-end products like "pull-up" diapers with glow-in-the-dark animated characters.[20] In addition, delayed full nest I can also spend more on nonchild expenditures such as food, alcohol, and entertainment, and can make more savings and retirement contributions than can younger new parents.

Full Nest II: Middle-Aged Married with Children at Home A major difference between this group and delayed full nest I is age of the children. The children of full nest II are generally over age six and are becoming more independent. The presence of older children creates unique consumption needs, however. Families with children six and older are the primary consumers of lessons of all types (piano, dance, gymnastics, and so on), dental care, soft drinks, presweetened cereals, and a wide variety of snack foods.

Greater demands for space create a need for larger homes and cars. Transporting children to multiple events places time demands on the parents and increases transportation-related expenditures. These factors, coupled with heavy demand for clothing and an increased need to save for college, create a considerable financial burden on households in this stage of the HLC. This is offset somewhat by the tendency of the wife to return to work as the children enter school. This return to work usually entails greater time pressures. ConAgra Foods has found great success tapping parents' desire to simplify mealtime with their easy-to-prepare Banquet Crock-Pot Classics, which have all needed ingredients and can cook all day and be ready to eat in the evening with minimal hassle.[21]

As we saw in Chapter 4, the teenage members (the older part of Generation Z) in these households, as well as teens in the single parent II segment, are important consumers in their own right as well as important influencers on household consumption decisions.

Single Parent II: Middle-Aged Single with Children at Home Single individuals in the 35-to-64 age group who have children are often faced with serious financial pressures. The same demands that are placed on the middle-aged married couple with children are present in the life of a middle-aged single with children. However, the single parent often lacks some or all of the financial, emotional, and time support that the presence of a spouse generally provides. Many individuals in this position are thus inclined to use time-saving alternatives such as ready-to-eat food, and they are likely to eat at fast-food restaurants. The children of this segment are given extensive household responsibilities.

It is important to note that becoming a single parent (through adoption or conception) is increasingly viewed as a lifestyle choice for older, more financially secure women who may or may not plan to marry in the future. Single Mothers by Choice is an organization that recognizes this and offers support and assistance. According to the organization, single women by choice are well-educated, career-oriented women in their 30s and 40s. As a consequence, they often have higher income and financial security than many single parents.[22]

Empty Nest II: Older Married Couples There are about 11 million households in this segment, and it is expected to grow rapidly over the next 10 years as baby boomers age. Many couples in the over-64 age group are either fully or partially retired. However, as we discussed in Chapter 4, improvements in health care and longevity, desire to stay active, and changes in Social Security will likely push retirement age upward over the decades to come. The younger members of this group are healthy, active, and often financially well-off. They have ample time. They are a big market for RVs, cruises, and second homes. They also spend considerable time and money on grandchildren. Increasingly, they take their grandchildren and occasionally their children on vacations. As described in Chapter 4, as they advance in age, health care and assisted living become more important. At this stage and the next, distribution of valued family assets such as family heirlooms, property, and money also becomes important.[23] Illustration 6–6 shows an ad for a product designed to meet one of this segment's needs.

Older Single There are around 17 million older singles in the United States, and this group will continue to grow as baby boomers age. Approximately 70 percent of

ILLUSTRATION 6-6

As consumers mature, their financial situation, free time, and physical and social needs change. This ad would appeal to active members of the empty nest II segment.

all older singles are female, and roughly two-thirds of all older singles live alone. The conditions of being older, single, and generally retired create many unique needs for housing, socialization, travel, and recreation. Many financial firms have set up special programs to work with these individuals. They often have experienced a spouse's death and now are taking on many of the financial responsibilities once handled by the other person. A recent study labeled consumers who were single as the result of the death of a spouse as "single by circumstance" rather than single by choice. Many older singles would fall into the single by circumstance category. Results of the research suggest that older singles who are single by circumstance will be less innovative, more risk averse, more price sensitive, and more likely to engage in coping behaviors, such as spending more time watching television, than their single by choice counterparts.[24] *What are the social and ethical issues involved in marketing to older consumers who are single by circumstance?*

MARKETING STRATEGY BASED ON THE HOUSEHOLD LIFE CYCLE

The HLC is an important segmentation tool given its relation to differences in the needs, wants, constraints, and consumption patterns that are unique to each stage. However, because individuals within each stage may vary on a host of other important factors such as education or income, the HLC becomes more powerful in terms of market segmentation and strategy formulation when it is combined with these factors.

For example, think of how the need for vacations differs as one moves across the stages of the household life cycle. Young singles often desire vacations focused on activities, adventure, and the chance for romance. Young married couples without children would have similar needs but without the desire to meet potential romantic partners. Full nest I and single parent I families need vacations that allow both parents and young children to enjoy themselves. The manner in which these needs will be met will vary sharply across occupational, income, and educational categories. For example, a young professional couple may vacation in Paris or at a resort in the tropics. A white-collar couple may visit a

HLC/Occupational Category Matrix TABLE 6-2

HLC Stage	Occupational Category				
	Executive/Elite Professional	Administrative/ Professional	Technical/Sales/ Clerical	Crafts	Unskilled/ Manual
Single I					
Young married					
Full nest I					
Single parent I					
Single II					
Delayed full nest I					
Full nest II					
Single parent II					
Empty nest I					
Empty nest II					
Single III					

domestic ski resort or visit Hawaii on a package deal. A young blue-collar couple may visit family or go camping.

Table 6–2 presents the **HLC/occupational category matrix.** The vertical axis is the particular stage in the HLC, which determines the problems the household will likely encounter; the horizontal axis is a set of occupational categories, which provide a range of acceptable solutions. This version has been found to be useful across a range of products in segmenting the market and developing appropriate marketing strategies for targeted segments (variables other than or in addition to occupation should be used when appropriate).

An effective use of the matrix is to isolate an activity or problem of interest to the firm, such as preparing the evening meal or providing nutritious snacks, scheduling weekend recreation, or planning a summer vacation. Research, often in the form of focus group interviews, is used to determine the following information for each relevant cell in the matrix:

1. What products or services are now being used to meet the need or perform the activity?
2. What, if any, symbolic or social meaning is associated with meeting the need or using the current products?
3. Exactly how are the current products or services being used?
4. How satisfied are the segment members with the current solutions, and what improvements are desired?

Attractive segments are those that are large enough to meet the firm's objectives and that have needs that current products are not fully satisfying. This approach has been used successfully for movies, regional bakeries, and financial services.[25] *What type of automobile would be best suited for each cell, and what type of ad should promote it?*

FAMILY DECISION MAKING

LO3 **Family decision making** is *the process by which decisions that directly or indirectly involve two or more family members are made.* Decision making by a group such as a family differs in many ways from decisions made by an individual. Consider the purchase of a breakfast cereal that children, and perhaps the adults, will consume. Who recognizes the need for the product? How are the type and brand selected? Does everyone consider the same attributes? A parent typically makes the actual *purchase;* does that mean that the parent also makes the *choice?* Or is the choice made by the children, the other parent, or some combination? Which parents are involved, and how does this change across products and over time? How does it differ by stage in the HLC?

Family purchases are often compared with organizational buying decisions. Although this comparison can produce useful insights, it fails to capture the essence of family decision making. Organizations have relatively objective criteria, such as profit maximization, that guide purchases. Families generally lack such explicit, overarching goals. Most industrial purchases are made by strangers or have little impact on those not involved in the purchase. Most family purchases directly affect the other members of the family.

Most important, *many family purchases are inherently emotional and affect the relationships between the family members.*[26] The decision to buy a child a requested toy or new school clothes is more than simply an acquisition. It is a symbol of love and commitment to the child. The decision to take the family to a restaurant for a meal or to purchase a new television has emotional meaning to the other family members. Disagreements about how to spend money are a major cause of marital discord. The processes families use to make purchase decisions and the outcomes of those processes have important effects on the well-being of the individual family members and the family itself. Thus, while family decision making has some things in common with organizational decision making, it is not the same.

The Nature of Family Purchase Roles

Figure 6–3 illustrates the six roles that frequently occur in family decision making, using a cereal purchase as an example.[27] It is important to note that individuals will play various roles for different decisions.

- *Initiator(s).* The family member who first recognizes a need or starts the purchase process.
- *Information gatherer(s).* The individual who has expertise and interest in a particular purchase. Different individuals may seek information at different times or on different aspects of the purchase.
- *Influencer(s).* The person who influences the alternatives evaluated, the criteria considered, and the final choice.
- *Decisionmaker(s).* The individual who makes the final decision. Of course, joint decisions also are likely to occur.
- *Purchaser(s).* The family member who actually purchases the product. This is typically an adult or a teenager.
- *User(s).* The user of the product. For many products there are multiple users.

Marketers must determine who in the family plays which role. Crayola shifted its advertising budget from children's television to women's magazines because its research

ILLUSTRATION 6-7

Children often determine the products and brands they use. At other times, they influence these choices, but parents play the dominant role. In such cases, the marketer must meet the needs of both the child and the parents.

revealed that mothers rather than children were more likely to recognize the problem, evaluate alternatives, and make the purchase. Illustration 6–7 shows a product designed for use by children that is selected by both the children and the parents and purchased by the parents.

Family decision making has been categorized as *husband-dominant, wife-dominant, joint,* or *individualized.* A moment's reflection will reveal that the above four categories omit critical participants in many family decisions. Until recently, most studies have ignored the influence of children.[28] Yet children, particularly teenagers, often exert a substantial influence on family purchase decisions.[29] Thus, we need to recognize that *child-dominant* and various combinations of *husband, wife,* and *child joint decisions* are also common.

Husband-dominant decisions have traditionally occurred with the purchase of such products as automobiles, liquor, and life insurance. Wife-dominant decisions were more common in the purchase of household maintenance items, food, and kitchen appliances. Joint decisions were most likely when buying a house, living room furniture, and vacations.

The Household Decision-Making Process for Children's Products **FIGURE 6-3**

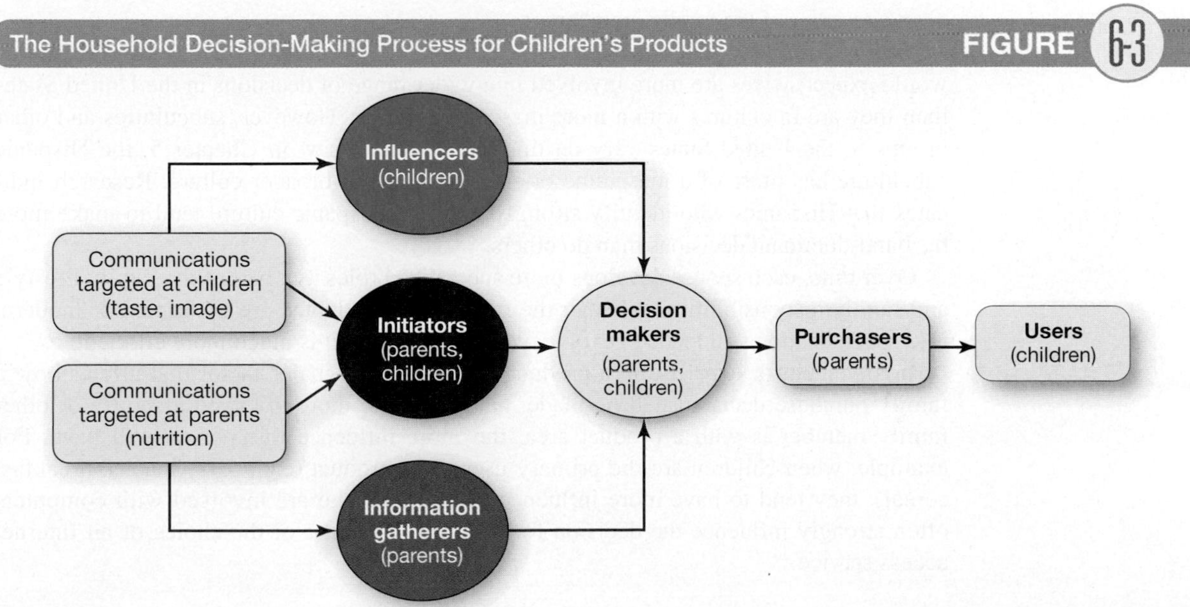

These patterns are much less pronounced today. As women's occupational roles have expanded, so has the range of family decisions in which they participate or dominate.[30] In fact, recent research suggests that the balance has tipped away from husband-dominant decisions even for traditionally male-dominated categories. Across a set of four categories, results are shown in the following table:[31]

	Family Weekend Activities	Large Household Purchases	Household Finances	TV Remote Control
Wife	28%	30%	38%	27%
Husband	16	19	30	26
Share	48	46	28	25

*Numbers don't add to 100 because couples could opt for "don't know" or "it depends" responses.

It is also important to recognize both direct and indirect influences. Parents might choose a Disney vacation without directly consulting their young children, but clearly would be influenced by their perceptions of the children's desires. Different family members often become involved at different stages of the decision process. For example, a child might be the primary initiator of a decision to go to McDonald's, while the parents might be more involved in the timing of that trip and most likely make the purchase itself. Finally, different family members often focus on different attributes. For example, a child may evaluate the color and style of a bicycle while one or both parents evaluate price, warranty, and safety features.

Determinants of Family Purchase Roles

How family members interact in a purchase decision is largely dependent on the *culture and subculture* in which the family exists, the *role specialization* of different family members, the degree of *involvement* each has in the product area of concern, and the *personal characteristics* of the family members.[32]

Today, America has less of a masculine orientation than many other cultures. As one would expect, wives are more involved in a wider range of decisions in the United States than they are in cultures with a more masculine focus.[33] However, subcultures and other groups in the United States vary on this value. As we saw in Chapter 5, the Hispanic subculture has more of a masculine orientation than the broader culture. Research indicates that Hispanics who identify strongly with the Hispanic culture tend to make more husband-dominant decisions than do others.

Over time, each spouse develops more specialized roles as a part of the family lifestyle and family responsibilities. Whether the roles that are adopted are traditional or modern, role specialization still tends to evolve over time because it is much more efficient.

Involvement or expertise in a product area is another major factor that affects how a family purchase decision will be made. Naturally, the more involved a spouse or other family member is with a product area, the more influence this person will have. For example, when children are the primary users of a product (e.g., toys, snacks, breakfast cereal), they tend to have more influence. Teenagers who are involved with computers often strongly influence the decision for a family computer or the choice of an Internet access service.[34]

Decision-Making Influence and Relative Income **FIGURE 6-4**

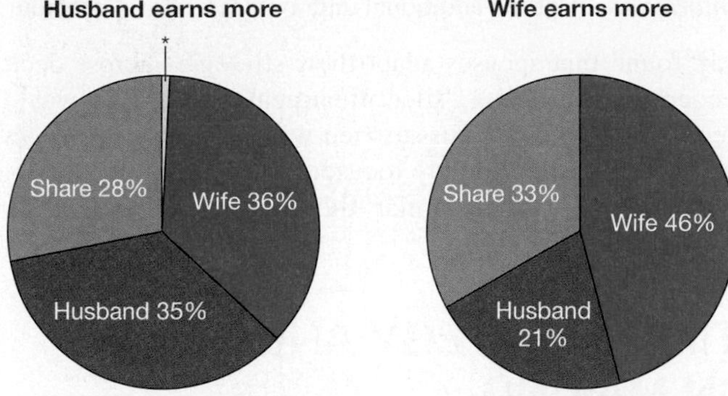

*1 Percent indicated "don't know."

Source: *Women, Men, and the New Economics of Marriage* (Washington, DC: Pew Research Center, January 2010).

Several personal characteristics have an effect on the influence individuals will have on purchase decisions.[35] Education and income are two such personal characteristics. The higher a wife's education and income, the more she will participate in or dominate major decisions.[36] Figure 6–4 shows that when a husband earns more than his wife, major household financial decisions are balanced across wife-dominant, husband-dominant, and shared. However, when a wife earns more than her husband, which is an increasingly common situation, wife-dominant decisions are far more likely.

Personality is also an important determinant of family decision roles. Traits such as aggressiveness, locus of control (belief in controlling one's own situation), detachment, and compliance influence family decision power.[37] For children, age matters. Older children and teens are playing an increasingly stronger role and marketers are communicating directly to them, as with Pottery Barn and *PBteen.* Finally, the stage of the decision process influences decision roles. Purchase decisions evolve from the early stages of problem recognition and information search through choice and purchase. Children and teens tend to have more influence on earlier stages of the family decision process than on later stages.[38]

Conflict Resolution

Given the number of decisions families make daily, disagreements are inevitable. How they are resolved is important to marketers as well as to the health of the family unit. One study revealed six basic approaches that individuals use to resolve purchase conflicts after they have arisen (most couples generally seek to avoid open conflicts):[39]

- *Bargaining.* Trying to reach a compromise.
- *Impression management.* Misrepresenting the facts in order to win.
- *Use of authority.* Claiming superior expertise or role appropriateness (the husband/wife should make such decisions).

- *Reasoning.* Using logical argument to win.
- *Playing on emotion.* Using the silent treatment or withdrawing from the discussion.
- *Additional information.* Getting additional data or a third-party opinion.

Another study found that spouses adapt their strategies across decisions and that when they use coercive means (e.g., silent treatment) to get their way, they are satisfied with the decision *outcome* but dissatisfied with the decision *process*.[40] Although neither study included children, a study focused on how children and parents attempt to influence each other found a similar though more complex set of influence strategies.[41]

MARKETING STRATEGY AND FAMILY DECISION MAKING

Formulating an effective marketing strategy for most consumer products requires a thorough understanding of the family decision-making process in the selected target markets with respect to that product. Table 6–3 provides a framework for such an analysis.

The family decision-making process often varies across market segments such as stages in the family life cycle or subculture. Therefore, a marketer must analyze family decision making *within* each of the firm's defined target markets. Within each target market, the marketer must:

- Discover which family members are involved at each stage of the decision process.
- Determine what their motivations and interests are.
- Develop a marketing strategy that will meet the needs of each participant.

For example, younger children are often involved in the problem recognition stage related to breakfast. They may note a new cartoon character–based cereal or discover that their friends are eating a new cereal. They are interested in identifying with the cartoon character or being like their friends. When they request the new cereal, the parents, generally the mother, may become interested. However, she is more likely to focus on nutrition and price. Thus, a marketer needs to communicate fun, taste, and excitement to

TABLE 6-3 Marketing Strategy Based on the Family Decision-Making Process

Segment: ____________________

Stage in the Decision Process	Family Members Involved	Family Members' Motivation and Interests	Marketing Strategy and Tactics
Problem recognition			
Information search			
Alternative evaluation			
Purchase			
User/consumption			
Disposition			
Evaluation			

children—and nutrition, value, and taste to parents. The children can be reached on Saturday cartoons, appropriate Internet sites, and similar media, while the mother may be more effectively communicated with through magazine ads, package information, and the Internet.

Examine the ad in Illustration 6–8. Use Table 6–3 to analyze this ad in terms of the family decision-making process and marketing strategy.

ILLUSTRATION 6-8

Segmentation analysis regarding family decision making is critical. Who is the target family member for this ad and do the tactics in the ad match their motives?

CONSUMER SOCIALIZATION

LO4

The family provides the basic framework in which consumer socialization occurs. **Consumer socialization** is *the process by which young people acquire skills, knowledge, and attitudes relevant to their functioning as consumers in the marketplace.*[42] We are concerned with understanding both the content of consumer socialization and the process of consumer socialization. The content of consumer socialization refers to what children learn with respect to consumption; the process refers to how they learn it. Before we address these two issues, we need to consider the ability of children of various ages to learn consumption-related skills.

The Ability of Children to Learn

Younger children have limited abilities to process certain types of information. **Piaget's stages of cognitive development** are a widely accepted set of stages of cognitive development:

Stage 1: The period of sensorimotor intelligence (0 to 2 years). During this period, behavior is primarily motor. The child does not yet "think" conceptually, though cognitive development is seen.

Stage 2: The period of preoperational thoughts (3 to 7 years). This period is characterized by the development of language and rapid conceptual development.

Stage 3: The period of concrete operations (8 to 11 years). During these years, the child develops the ability to apply logical thought to concrete problems.

Stage 4: The period of formal operations (12 to 15 years). During this period, the child's cognitive structures reach their greatest level of development, and the child becomes able to apply logic to all classes of problems.

While other approaches exist, the general pattern of less ability to deal with abstract, generalized, unfamiliar, or large amounts of information by younger children is common to all approaches.[43]

A recent study utilized Piaget's stages to help understand different interventions designed to improve dietary intake by children. The two stages examined were younger children (specifically the preoperational stage) and older children (specifically the concrete operational stage). The interventions were incentives (prizes), competition (against a rival school), and a personal pledge that involved signing their name to an in-class poster. Since pledges are more abstract and difficult to understand, they were less effective for the younger children.[44]

The changing capabilities of children to process information as they age present challenges to parents who are attempting to teach their children appropriate consumption behaviors.[45] As we will discuss shortly, this also poses ethical and practical issues for marketers. Children's limited learning capacity is the basis for substantial regulation of advertising to children, which we discuss in depth in Chapter 20.

The Content of Consumer Socialization

The content of consumer learning can be broken down into three categories: consumer skills, consumption-related preferences, and consumption-related attitudes.[46] **Consumer skills** are *those capabilities necessary for purchases to occur such as understanding money, budgeting, product evaluation, and so forth.* A child has to learn how to shop, how to compare similar brands, how to budget available income, and the like. The following example shows an attempt by a parent to teach her adolescent appropriate, from the parent's perspective, shopping rules:

> Son, look at this. This is just going to wash nicer, it will come through the laundry nicer, and you do a lot of the laundry yourself, and I just would rather that it's something that would wash easy, that doesn't have to be ironed, that isn't 100 percent cotton. (Mother with son, age 13)[47]

Consumption-related preferences are *the knowledge, attitudes, and values that cause people to attach differential evaluations to products, brands, and retail outlets.* For example, some parents through their comments and purchases may "teach" their children that Calvin Klein is a prestigious brand name and that prestigious brands are desirable. This information about Calvin Klein's prestige is not necessary to carry out the actual purchase (consumer skills), but it is extremely important in deciding to make a purchase and in deciding what to purchase (consumption-related preferences).[48]

Consumption-related attitudes are *cognitive and affective orientations toward marketplace stimuli such as advertisements, salespeople, warranties, and so forth.*[49] For example, children may learn from their parents or other family members that "you get what you pay for." This would lead them to assume a strong price–quality relationship. Or they may be taught that salespeople are not trustworthy. These attitudes will influence how they react to the various activities undertaken by marketers. What type of attitude is being formed in the following interaction?

> I'm always trying to get her to learn the relative value of things and particularly the impact of advertising and its effect on driving purchases and desires. So we try to talk about that. I point out manipulative or deceptive advertising, and give her a sense of being a critical consumer. (Father with daughter, age 13)[50]

The Process of Consumer Socialization

Consumer socialization occurs through a number of avenues, including advertising and friends. However, family is a primary source of consumer socialization. For example, a recent study of eating patterns found that children cite parents as the most important influence regarding the kinds of foods they eat. This was even true of teenagers, where parental influence was highest, and friends and advertising played a much lesser role.[51] Parents teach their children consumer skills, consumption-related preferences, and consumption-related attitudes. They do so both deliberately and casually through instrumental training, modeling, and mediation.

Instrumental training *occurs when a parent or sibling specifically and directly attempts to bring about certain responses through reasoning or reinforcement.* In other words, a parent may try directly to teach a child which snack foods should be consumed by explicitly discussing nutrition.[52] Or a parent may establish rules that limit the consumption of some snack foods and encourage the consumption of others. The following example shows an approach used with older children:

> One thing that we always talk about when we're looking at something is the price of it. "For what you're buying, is the price worth the quality of what you're buying?" (Mother with son, age 13)[53]

Parents often worry that marketing messages will simply drown out any instrumental training they try to provide. In Illustration 6–9 there is an attempt on the part of the firm to be a partner in the socialization process.

Modeling *occurs when a child learns appropriate, or inappropriate, consumption behaviors by observing others.* Modeling generally, though not always, occurs without direct instruction from the role model and frequently without conscious thought or effort on the part of the child. Modeling is an extremely important way for children to learn relevant skills, knowledge, and attitudes. Children learn both positive and negative consumption patterns through modeling. For example, children whose parents smoke are more likely to start smoking than are children whose parents do not smoke.

ILLUSTRATION 6-9

This company clearly recognizes that it can be a partner with parents in the socialization process.

Mediation *occurs when a parent alters a child's initial interpretation of, or response to, a marketing or other stimulus.* This can easily be seen in the following example:

CHILD: Can I have one of those? See, it can walk!

PARENT: No. That's just an advertisement. It won't really walk. They just make it look like it will so kids will buy them.

The advertisement illustrated a product attribute and triggered a desire, but the parent altered the belief in the attribute and in the believability of advertising in general. This is not to suggest that family members mediate all commercials. However, children often learn about the purchase and use of products during interactions with other family members. Thus, a firm wishing to influence children must do so in a manner consistent with the values of the rest of the family.

The Supermarket as a Classroom

Professor James McNeal developed a five-stage model of how children learn to shop by visiting supermarkets and other retail outlets with a parent.[54]

Stage I: Observing Parents begin taking children to the store with them at a median age of two months. During this stage, children make sensory contact with the marketplace and begin forming mental images of marketplace objects and symbols. In the early months, only sights and sounds are being processed. However, by 12 to 15 months, most children can begin to recall some of these items. This stage ends when children understand that a visit to the market may produce rewards beyond the stimulation caused by the environment.

Stage II: Making Requests At this stage (median age is two years), children begin requesting items in the store from their parents. They use pointing and gesturing as well as statements to indicate that they want an item. Throughout most of this stage, children make requests only when the item is physically present, as they do not yet carry mental images of the products in their minds. In the latter months of stage II, they begin to make requests for items at home, particularly when they are seen on television.

Stage III: Making Selections Actually getting an item off the shelf without assistance is the first act of an independent consumer (median age is three-and-a-half years). At its simplest level, a child's desire is triggered by an item in his or her immediate presence and this item is selected. Soon, however, children begin to remember the store location of desirable items, and they are allowed to go to those areas independently or to lead the parent there.

Stage IV: Making Assisted Purchases Most children learn by observing (modeling) that money needs to be given in order to get things from a store. They learn to value money given to them by their parents and others as a means to acquire things. Soon they are allowed to select and pay for items with their own money. They are now primary consumers (median age is five-and-a-half years).

Stage V: Making Independent Purchases Making a purchase without a parent to oversee it requires a fairly sophisticated understanding of value as well as the ability to visit a store, or a section of a store, safely without a parent. Most children remain in stage IV a long time before their parents allow them to move into stage V (median age is eight years).

McNeal's research indicates that children learn to shop, at least in part, by going shopping. Retailers are developing programs based on these learning patterns. Examples include child-sized shopping carts and kids' clubs.

MARKETING TO CHILDREN

As seen in the opening example, children are a large and growing market. Brand loyalties developed at this age may produce returns for many years. Thus, it is no surprise that marketers are aggressively pursuing these young consumers.

However, marketing to children is fraught with ethical concerns. The major source of these concerns is the limited ability of younger children to process information and to make informed purchase decisions. There are also concerns that marketing activities, particularly advertising, produce undesirable values in children, result in inappropriate diets, and cause unhealthy levels of family conflict. We will examine questionable marketing practices focused on children and the regulations designed to control them in detail in Chapter 20.

Although marketers need to be very sensitive to the limited information-processing skills of younger consumers, ethical and effective marketing campaigns can be designed to meet the needs of children and their parents. All aspects of the marketing mix must consider the capabilities of the child. Consider the following ad and the responses to the ad from children of different ages:

> The ad reads, "Inhale a lethal dose of carbon monoxide and it's called suicide. Inhale a smaller amount and it's called smoking. Believe it or not, cigarette smoke contains the same poisonous gas as automobile exhaust. So if you wouldn't consider sucking on a tailpipe, why would you want to smoke?" A picture of a smoking exhaust pipe was below the copy.
>
> **Seven- and eight-year-olds' responses:**
> "Never stand behind a bus because you could get poisonous in your face." "People sometimes get sick from exhaust."
>
> **Nine- and ten-year-olds' responses:**
> "The person who is driving is smoking." "No matter what kind of smoking it is, it can always make you sick."
>
> **Eleven-year-olds' responses:**
> "You could hurt yourself with that stuff. The same stuff in car exhaust is in cigarettes." "The tailpipe of a car is like the same as smoking and smoking could kill you . . . both of them could kill you."

Only the older children could fully engage in the analogical reasoning required to completely understand the ad. In contrast, a simpler ad that showed a dirty, grimy sock next to an ashtray full of cigarette butts with the word *gross* under the sock and *really gross* under the ashtray was understood by children of all ages (7 through 11).[55]

Reaching children used to mean advertising on Saturday morning cartoons. Now there are many more options, even for the very young. *National Geographic Kids* and *Discovery Girls* are just a few of the many magazines with strong readership among children. Children as young as three are active Internet users. Sites such as 4kidstv.com, Cartoonnetwork.com, and Nick.com are visited by millions of children aged 2 to 11. Direct mail can be an effective means to reach even very young children. Many firms target children or families with young children by forming "kids' clubs." Unfortunately, these clubs sometimes engage in sales techniques that are controversial if not clearly unethical. If done properly, however, they can be fun and educational for the children while delivering responsible commercial messages.

SUMMARY

LO1: Explain the concept of household types and their influence on consumption

The household is the basic purchasing and consuming unit and is, therefore, of great importance to marketing managers of most products. The *family household* consists of two or more related persons living together in a dwelling unit. *Nonfamily households* are dwelling units occupied by one or more unrelated individuals. Family households are a primary mechanism whereby cultural and social-class values and behavior patterns are passed on to the next generation.

LO2: Summarize the household life cycle's various stages and marketing implications

The *household life cycle* is the classification of the household into stages through which it passes over time based on the age and marital status of the adults and the presence and age of children. The household life cycle is a valuable marketing tool because members within each stage or category face similar consumption problems. Thus, they represent potential market segments.

The *HLC/occupational category matrix* is one useful way to use the HLC to develop marketing strategy. One axis is the stages in the HLC, which determine the problems the household will likely encounter; the other is a set of occupational categories, which provide a range of acceptable solutions. Each cell represents a market segment.

LO3: Understand the family decision process

Family decision making involves consideration of questions such as who buys, who decides, and who uses. Family decision making is complex and involves emotion and interpersonal relations as well as product evaluation and acquisition. Household member participation in the decision process varies by *involvement with the specific product, role specialization, personal characteristics,* and one's *culture and subculture.* Participation also varies by stage in the decision process. Most decisions are reached by consensus. If not, a variety of conflict resolution strategies may be employed. Marketing managers must analyze the household decision process separately for each product category within each target market.

LO4: Describe the role that households play in child socialization

Consumer socialization deals with the processes by which young people (from birth until 18 years of age) learn how to become consumers. Children's learning abilities are limited at birth, then slowly evolve with experience over time. Consumer socialization deals with the learning of consumer skills, consumption-related preferences, and consumption-related attitudes. Families influence consumer socialization through direct *instrumental training, modeling,* and *mediation.* Young consumers appear to go through five stages of learning how to shop. This learning takes place primarily in retail outlets in interaction with the parents.

LO5: Explain the sources of ethical concern associated with marketing to children

Marketing to children is fraught with ethical issues. The main source of ethical concern is the limited ability of children to process information and make sound purchase decisions or requests. There are also concerns about the role of advertising in forming children's values, influencing their diets, and causing family conflict. However, ethical and effective marketing programs can be developed for children.

SMARTBOOK™

KEY TERMS

Consumer skills 204
Consumer socialization 203
Consumption-related attitudes 204
Consumption-related preferences 204
Family decision making 198
Family household 185
HLC/occupational category matrix 197

Household 185
Household life cycle (HLC) 187
Instrumental training 205
Mediation 206
Modeling 205
Multigenerational family 187
Nonfamily household 185
Piaget's stages of cognitive development 203
Step family 185
Traditional family 185

REVIEW QUESTIONS

1. The household is described as "the basic consumption unit for consumer goods." Why?
2. What is a *traditional family?* Can a single-parent family be a nuclear family?
3. How does a *nonfamily household* differ from a *family household?*
4. Describe the *multigenerational family.*
5. How has the distribution of household types in the United States been changing? What are the implications of these shifts?
6. What is meant by the *household life cycle?*
7. What is meant by the following statement? "Each stage in the household life cycle poses a series of problems that household decision makers must solve."
8. Describe the general characteristics of each of the stages in the household life cycle.
9. Describe the *HLC/occupational category matrix.* What is the logic for this matrix?
10. What is meant by *family decision making?* How can different members of the household be involved with different stages of the decision process?
11. How does family decision making differ from most organizational decision making?
12. The text states that the marketing manager must analyze the family decision-making process separately within each target market and for each product. Why?
13. What factors influence involvement of a household member in a purchase decision?
14. How do family members attempt to resolve conflict over purchase decisions?
15. What is *consumer socialization?* How is knowledge of it useful to marketing managers?
16. What are Piaget's stages of cognitive development?
17. What do we mean when we say that children learn consumer skills, consumption-related attitudes, and consumption-related preferences?
18. What processes do parents use to teach children to be consumers?
19. Describe each of the five stages children go through as they learn to shop at stores.
20. What ethical issues arise in marketing to children?

DISCUSSION QUESTIONS

21. Respond to the questions in Consumer Insight 6–1.
22. Canada has legislation giving cohabiting couples who have been living together for one year or more the same federal rights and responsibilities as married couples. Should the United States have similar legislation?
23. Rate the stages of the household life cycle in terms of their probable purchase of the following. Justify your answers.
    a. Designer jeans
    b. Trip to Cancun
    c. Diapers
    d. Breakfast bars
    e. Contribution to SPCA
    f. Golf clubs
24. Pick two stages in the household life cycle. Describe how your marketing strategy for the following would differ depending on which group was your primary target market.
    a. Minivan
    b. Razors
    c. Broadway show
    d. Casino
25. Do you think the trend toward nonfamily households will continue? Justify your response.

26. What are the primary marketing implications of Table 6–1?
27. How would the marketing strategies for the following differ by stage of the HLC? (Assume each stage is the target market.)
    a. Cell phone
    b. Scuba gear
    c. Power tools
    d. Children's toys
    e. Detergent
    f. Colleges
28. What are the marketing implications of Figure 6–4?
29. What type of the following would be best suited for each cell in Table 6–2?
    a. Hotel
    b. Television program
    c. Restaurant for the entire household
    d. Lawn mower
30. Name two products for which the horizontal axis in Table 6–2 should be the following. Justify your response.
    a. Occupational category
    b. Income
    c. Education
    d. Social class
31. How can a marketer use knowledge of how family members seek to resolve conflicts?
32. Describe a recent family purchase in which you were involved. Use this as a basis for completing Table 6–3 for a marketer attempting to influence that decision.
33. Describe four types of activities or situations in which direct *instrumental training* is likely to occur.
34. Describe four types of activities or situations in which *modeling* is likely to occur.
35. Describe four types of activities or situations in which *mediation* is likely to occur.
36. Respond to the questions in Consumer Insight 6–2.
37. Are Piaget's stages of cognitive development consistent with the five stages of learning to shop that McNeal identified?

APPLICATION ACTIVITIES

38. Interview a middle school student and determine and describe the household decision process involved in the purchase of his or her
    a. Backpack
    b. Snack foods
    c. Bedroom furniture
    d. Cell phone
    e. Clothing
39. Interview two sporting goods salespersons from different price-level outlets. Try to ascertain which stages in the household life cycle constitute their primary markets and why this is so.
40. Interview one individual from each stage in the household life cycle. Determine and report the extent to which these individuals conform to the descriptions provided in the text.
41. Interview a family with a child under 13 at home. Interview both the parents and the child, but interview the child separately. Try to determine the influence of each family member on the following products *for the child's use.* In addition, ascertain what method(s) of conflict resolution is (are) used.
    a. Toothbrush
    b. Clothes
    c. Cereal
    d. Major toys, such as the Xbox
    e. Television viewing
    f. Fast-food restaurant
42. Interview a couple who have been married for the following periods. Ascertain and report the degree and nature of role specialization that has developed with respect to their purchase decisions. Also determine how conflicts are resolved.
    a. Less than 1 year
    b. 1–5 years
    c. 6–10 years
    d. More than 10 years
43. Pick a product and market segment of interest, and interview three households. Collect sufficient data to complete Table 6–3.

44. Pick a product of interest and, with several fellow students, complete enough interviews to fill the relevant cells in Table 6–2 using the four questions in the text. Develop an appropriate marketing strategy based on this information.

45. Interview several parents of preschool children. Determine the extent to which they agree with Piaget's four stages and McNeal's five stages.

46. Watch several hours of Saturday morning cartoons. What ethical concerns, if any, do they cause?

REFERENCES

1. This opener based on E. Klinenberg, "Solo Nation," *CNN Money,* January 25, 2012, http://finance.fortune.cnn.com/2012/01/25/eric-klinenberg-going-solo/, accessed August 31, 2014; E. Klinenberg, "One's a Crowd," *New York Times Sunday Review,* February 4, 2012, www.nytimes.com/2012/02/05/opinion/sunday/living-alone-means-being-social.html?_r=0, accessed August 31, 2014; G. Ifill and R. Suarez, "Why More Americans Are Living Alone," *pbs.com,* March 27, 2012, www.pbs.org/newshour/bb/social_issues/jan-june12/goingsolo_03-27.html, accessed August 31, 2014; M. Galante, "Why Micro Apartments Are the Next Big Trend in City Living," *BusinessInsider.com,* November 6, 2012, www.businessinsider.com/micro-apartment-trend-2012-10#ixzz2qP0bYtPC, accessed August 31, 2014; E. Klinenberg, *Going Solo* (New York: Penguin Books, 2013); J. Stanton, "A Closer Look at the Single Household," *foodprocessing.com,* August 2013, www.foodprocessing.com/articles/2013/market-view-single-household/, accessed August 31, 2014; and J. Vespa, J. Lewis, and R. Kreider, "America's Families and Living Arrangements," *2012 Population Characteristics* (Washington, DC: U.S. Census Bureau, 2013).
2. For more detailed information, see *America's Families and Living Arrangements: 2007* (Washington, DC: U.S. Census Bureau, 2009).
3. Statistics in this section are drawn primarily from relevant U.S. Census Bureau reports and updates.
4. For more information, see *A Portrait of Stepfamilies* (Washington, DC: Pew Research Center, January 2011).
5. A. M. Epp and L. L. Price, "Family Identity," *Journal of Consumer Research,* June 2008, pp. 50–70.
6. This insight is based on *The Return of the Multi-Generational Family* (Washington, DC: Pew Research Center, March 2010); B. S. Bulik, "We Are Family," *Advertising Age,* August 23, 2010, pp. 1 and 20; and H. El Nasser and P. Overberg, "Census: Households Get Fuller," *USA Today,* September 30, 2010, p. 3A.
7. See C. M. Schaninger and W. D. Danko, "A Conceptual and Empirical Comparison of Alternative Household Life Cycle Models," *Journal of Consumer Research,* March 1993, pp. 580–94; R. E. Wilkes, "Household Life-Cycle Stages, Transitions, and Product Expenditures," *Journal of Consumer Research,* June 1995, pp. 27–42; and C. M. Schaninger and D. H. Lee, "A New Full-Nest Classification Approach," *Psychology & Marketing,* January 2002, pp. 25–58.
8. Insight based on K. Sweet, "250 Years of Consumer Habits," *Professional Remodeler,* November 1, 2004, www.proremodeler.com/250-years-consumer-habits-0, accessed August 31, 2014; *Understanding Homeowners' Renovation Decisions* (London: UK Energy Research Centre, 2013); and *Homeowner Remodeling Survey* (Malvern, PA: Principia Consulting, 2013).
9. See, e.g., N. Donthu and D. I. Gilliland, "The Single Consumer," *Journal of Advertising Research,* November–December 2002, pp. 77–84.
10. See J. Raymond, "For Richer or Poorer," *American Demographics,* July 2000, pp. 59–64.
11. "Employment Status of Women by Marital Status and Presence and Age of Children: 1970 to 2009," *Statistical Abstract of the United States 2011* (Washington, DC: U.S. Bureau of the Census, 2011).
12. Estimates based on *Consumer Expenditure Survey* (Washington, DC: U.S. Bureau of Labor Statistics, 2005–2006).
13. K. Pantel, "Kraft Unveils App for Apple's iPad," *Advertising Age,* July 12, 2010.
14. S. Thompson, "ClubMom Prepares National Rollout," *Advertising Age,* May 3, 2004, p. 24.
15. R. Gardyn, "Unmarried Bliss," *American Demographics,* December 2000, pp. 56–61.
16. For a discussion, including differences across groups, see www.divorcereform.org; and D. Hurley, "Divorce Rate," *New York Times,* April 19, 2005, p. F7.
17. See, e.g., J. Morrow, "A Place for One," *American Demographics,* November 2003, pp. 25–29; and P. Francese, "Well Enough Alone," *American Demographics,* November 2003, pp. 32–33.
18. P. Paul, "Childless by Choice," *American Demographics,* November 2001, pp. 45–50.
19. For additional information, see *The New Demography of American Motherhood* (Washington, DC: Pew Research Center, August 2010).
20. J. Fetto, "The Baby Business," *American Demographics,* May 2003, p. 40; and J. Neff, "P&G Challenges Rival K-C in Trainers Battle," *Advertising Age,* May 17, 2004, p. 10.
21. ConAgra, "New Survey Finds Parents and Children Alike Crave More Time to Talk and Relax Together," press release, January 17, 2005.

22. Information from organization's website at www.singlemothersbychoice.org.

23. T. W. Bradford, "Intergenerational Gifted Asset Dispositions," *Journal of Consumer Research,* June 2009, pp. 93–111.

24. Donthu and Gilliland, "The Single Consumer."

25. For a different approach, see L. G. Pol and S. Pak, "Consumer Unit Types and Expenditures on Food Away from Home," *Journal of Consumer Affairs,* Winter 1995, pp. 403–28.

26. See J. Park, P. Tansuhaj, and E. R. Spangenberg, "An Emotion-Based Perspective of Family Purchase Decisions," *Advances in Consumer Research,* vol. 22, ed. F. R. Kardes and M. Sujan (Provo, UT: Association for Consumer Research, 1995), pp. 723–28.

27. C. Lackman and J. M. Lanasa, "Family Decision-Making Theory," *Psychology & Marketing,* March–April 1993, pp. 81–113.

28. An exception is S. E. Beatty and S. Talpade, "Adolescent Influence in Family Decision Making," *Journal of Consumer Research,* September 1994, pp. 332–41.

29. See J. Cotte and S. L. Wood, "Families and Innovative Consumer Behavior," *Journal of Consumer Research,* June 2004, pp. 78–86; A. Shoham and V. Dalakas, "He Said, She Said . . . They Said," *Journal of Consumer Marketing* 22, no. 3 (2005), pp. 152–60; and E. Bridges and R. A. Briesch, "The 'Nag Factor' and Children's Product Categories," *International Journal of Advertising,* 25, no. 2 (2006), pp. 157–87.

30. See, e.g., M. A. Belch and L. A. Willis, "Family Decision at the Turn of the Century," *Journal of Consumer Behaviour,* 2, no. 2 (2002), pp. 111–24; and N. Razzouk, V. Seitz, and K. P. Capo, "A Comparison of Consumer Decision-Making Behavior of Married and Cohabiting Couples," *Journal of Consumer Marketing,* 24, no. 5 (2007), pp. 264–74.

31. *Women Call the Shots at Home* (Washington, DC: Pew Research Center, September 2008).

32. See C.-N. Chen, M. Lai, and D. D. C. Tarn, "Feminism Orientation, Product Attributes and Husband–Wife Decision Dominance," *Journal of Global Marketing,* 12, no. 3 (1999), pp. 23–39; and C. Webster and M. C. Reiss, "Do Established Antecedents of Purchase Decision-Making Power Apply to Contemporary Couples?," *Psychology & Marketing,* September 2001, pp. 951–72.

33. J. B. Ford, L. E. Pelton, and J. R. Lumpkin, "Perception of Marital Roles in Purchase Decision Processes," *Journal of the Academy of Marketing Science,* Spring 1995, pp. 120–31.

34. See C. K. C. Lee and S. E. Beatty, "Family Structure and Influence in Family Decision Making," *Journal of Consumer Marketing,* 19, no. 1 (2002), pp. 24–41; and G. Slattery and J. Butler, "Teens Are Primary Influencer on Holiday Technology Purchases," *Business Wire,* November 23, 2004, p. 1.

35. See M. C. Reiss and C. Webster, "Relative Influence in Purchase Decision Making," *Advances in Consumer Research,* vol. 24, ed. M. Bruck and D. J. MacInnis (Provo, UT: Association for Consumer Research, 1997), pp. 42–47; and C. Webster, "The Meaning and Measurement of Marital Power," *Advances in Consumer Research,* vol. 25, ed. J. W. Alba and J. W. Hutchinson (Provo, UT: Association for Consumer Research, 1998), pp. 395–99.

36. *Women, Men, and the New Economics of Marriage* (Washington, DC: Pew Research Center, January 2010).

37. C. Webster, "Is Spousal Decision Making a Culturally Situated Phenomenon?," *Psychology & Marketing,* December 2000, pp. 1035–58.

38. See, e.g., M. A. Belch, K. A. Krentler, and L. A. Willis-Flurry, "Teen Internet Mavens," *Journal of Business Research,* 58 (2005), pp. 569–75.

39. C. Kim and H. Lee, "A Taxonomy of Couples Based on Influence Strategies," *Journal of Business Research,* June 1996, pp. 157–68.

40. C. Su, E. F. Fern, and K. Ye, "A Temporal Dynamic Model of Spousal Family Purchase-Decision Behavior," *Journal of Marketing Research,* August 2003, pp. 268–81. See also C. Su et al., "Harmonizing Conflict in Husband-Wife Purchase Decision Making," *Journal of the Academy of Marketing Science,* 36 (2008), pp. 378–94.

41. K. M. Palan and R. E. Wilkes, "Adolescent–Parent Interaction in Family Decision Making," *Journal of Consumer Research,* September 1997, pp. 159–69; see also A. Aribarg, N. Arora, and H. O. Bodur, "Understanding the Role of Preference Revision and Concession in Group Decisions," *Journal of Marketing Research,* August 2002, pp. 336–49.

42. For a thorough review, see D. R. John, "Consumer Socialization of Children," *Journal of Consumer Research,* December 1999, pp. 183–209. See also M. J. Dotson and E. M. Hyatt, "Major Influence Factors in Children's Consumer Socialization," *Journal of Consumer Marketing,* 22, no. 1 (2005), pp. 35–42.

43. See J. Gregan-Paxton and D. R. John, "The Emergence of Adaptive Decision Making in Children," *Journal of Consumer Research,* June 1997, pp. 43–56; T. Davis, "What Children Understand about Consumption Constellations," *Advances in Consumer Research,* vol. 27, ed. S. J. Hoch and R. J. Meyer (Provo, UT: Association for Consumer Research, 2000), pp. 72–78; and E. S. Moore and R. J. Lutz, "Children, Advertising, and Product Experiences," *Journal of Consumer Research,* June 2000, pp. 31–47.

44. S. Raju, P. Rajagopal, and T. J. Gilbride, "Marketing Healthful Eating to Children," *Journal of Marketing,* May 2010, pp. 93–106.

45. Parental responses differ across cultures; see G. M. Rose, "Consumer Socialization, Parental Style, and Developmental Timetables in the United States and Japan," *Journal of Marketing,* July 1999, pp. 105–19.

46. M. Viswanathan, T. L. Childers, and E. S. Moore, "The Measurement of Intergenerational Communication and Influence on Consumption," *Journal of the Academy of Marketing Science,* Summer 2000, pp. 406–24.

47. Palan and Wilkes, "Adolescent–Parent Interaction in Family Decision Making."

48. M. F. Ji, "Children's Relationships with Brands," *Psychology & Marketing,* April 2002, pp. 369–87; and E. S. Moore, W. L. Wilkie, and R. J. Lutz, "Passing the Torch," *Journal of Marketing,* April 2002, pp. 17–37.

49. See T. F. Mangleburg and T. Bristol, "Socialization and Adolescents' Skepticism toward Advertising," *Journal of Advertising,* Fall 1998, pp. 11–20; L. Carlson, R. N. Laczniak,

and J. E. Keith, "Socializing Children about Television," *Journal of the Academy of Marketing Science,* Summer 2001, pp. 276–88; and P. Wright, M. Friestad, and D. M. Boush, "The Development of Marketplace Persuasion Knowledge in Children, Adolescents, and Young Adults," *Journal of Public Policy and Marketing,* Fall 2005, pp. 222–33.

50. Palan and Wilkes, "Adolescent–Parent Interaction in Family Decision Making."
51. P. Dando, "Healthier Fast-Food a Reality," *Advertising Age,* March 29, 2004, p. S-7.
52. See, e.g., C. Kim, H. Lee, and M. A. Tomiuk, "Adolescents' Perceptions of Family Communication Patterns and Some Aspects of Their Consumer Socialization," *Psychology & Marketing,* October 2009, pp. 888–907.
53. Palan and Wilkes, "Adolescent–Parent Interaction in Family Decision Making."
54. J. U. McNeal, *Kids as Consumers* (New York: Lexington Books, 1992); and J. U. McNeal and C. Yeh, "Born to Shop," *American Demographics,* June 1993, pp. 34–39. See also J. B. Schor, *Born to Buy* (New York: Scribner, 2004).
55. L. A. Peracchio and D. Luna, "The Development of an Advertising Campaign to Discourage Smoking Initiation among Children and Youth," *Journal of Advertising,* Fall 1998, pp. 49–56.

chapter

7 Group Influences on Consumer Behavior

LEARNING OBJECTIVES

- **LO1** **Explain reference groups and the criteria used to classify them.**
- **LO2** **Discuss consumption subcultures, including brand and online communities and their importance for marketing.**
- **LO3** **Summarize the types and degree of reference group influence.**
- **LO4** **Discuss within-group communications and the importance of word-of-mouth communications to marketers.**
- **LO5** **Understand opinion leaders (both online and offline) and their importance to marketers.**
- **LO6** **Discuss innovation diffusion and use an innovation analysis to develop marketing strategy.**

For most products and brands, the basic purchase motivation relates to the ability of the product or service itself to meet a need of the consumer. Other purchases are fundamentally different in that consumers buy membership into a group as well. A prime example is the Jeep brand.[1] Many Jeep owners elect to become members of a "Jeep community." These owners attend "brandfests" such as Jeep Jamborees, Jeep 101, and Camp Jeep. At these events, they meet and form relationships with other owners, deepen their involvement with their Jeep vehicles, and become acculturated into the rituals and traditions of the community. The following quote illustrates how Susan, a first-time Jeep owner, began to become a member of this community:

> I've been very happy. I get a lot of communications from Jeep, which I've been so impressed with. Usually you buy a car and you're a forgotten soul. It's kinda like they want you to be part of the family. As soon as I got the invitation for Jeep 101, I registered. I was very excited. But I was also nervous. I didn't think I would end up driving. I was very relieved to see someone in the car with you, 'cause it gave you the confidence to do what you're supposed to. Otherwise, I had visions of abandoning the truck on the hill and saying, "I can't do it!" I thought I might wimp out, but I didn't (smiles).

The Jeep brand has a long tradition of fostering a community spirit. It strives for a balance between grassroots organizing and corporate efforts. Jeep creates events for enthusiasts and venues where members contribute, thereby fostering a sense of community. In addition, Jeep owners organize their own events and clubs that have nothing to do with the company. The Jeep community started offline. Events, organizations, and activities include the following:

- Camp Jeep—This event, hosted each year by Jeep, is a family event with activities including camping, crafts, concerts by such acts as Tim McGraw, and, of course, off-road driving on a specially designed course where owners can test their skills and their Jeep vehicles.
- Jeep Jamboree—These are Jeep-sponsored off-road treks that are fully focused on the off-road driving experience and are held all over the country in such 4 × 4 destinations as Moab, Utah.
- Local Jeep clubs—These are member-created clubs with their own rules, regulations, culture, and leadership. One is the Sacramento Jeepers club, established in 1957. Membership requires owning a

four-wheel-drive Jeep, attending three meetings a year, and driving in three club trips a year.

While the community started offline, it has moved online as well in a number of ways, including

- Jeep's Facebook fan page—Jeep has a fan page on Facebook with over 1 million fans who "like" Jeep. Fans can post questions, videos, and pictures related to their Jeep and Jeep experiences. Jeep can target Facebook users in general by finding those with interests that match the Jeep lifestyle. Jeep can target its fans even more specifically with more refined marketing messages, announcements, and offers.
- Jeep's YouTube channel—The Jeep brand also has a YouTube channel, which is a sponsored YouTube area where Jeep and community members can post videos. Some of the videos are Jeep commercials posted by Jeep and some are videos from members taken at Jeep Jamborees and other off-road events.
- Local club websites—Local clubs also have their own websites that provide information, news, classified ads, discussion forums, and so on. These sites range from simple to elaborate depending on the group's culture, values, and goals.

The Jeep brand has been fostering this community for decades—sometimes leading, sometimes following, and sometimes helping. Though some Jeep owners do not join this community, members tend to be intense, active, and devoted. They are connected to the Jeep brand, the Jeep community, and the lifestyle it represents in a very deep way that permeates their lives and helps define who they are.

As demonstrated in the opening example, even in an individualistic society like America, group memberships and identity are very important to all of us. And while we don't like to think of ourselves as conformists, most of us conform to group expectations most of the time. For example, when you decided what to wear to the last party you attended, you probably based your decision in part on the anticipated responses of the other individuals at the party. This represents a response to group influence and expectations.

TYPES OF GROUPS

LO1

The terms *group* and *reference group* need to be distinguished. A **group** is defined as *two or more individuals who share a set of norms, values, or beliefs and have certain implicitly or explicitly defined relationships to one another such that their behaviors are interdependent.* A **reference group** is *a group whose presumed perspectives or values are being used by an individual as the basis for his or her current behavior.* Thus, a reference group is simply a group that an individual uses as a guide for behavior in a specific situation.

Most of us belong to a number of different groups and perhaps would like to belong to several others. When we are actively involved with a particular group, it generally functions as a reference group. As the situation changes, we may base our behavior on an entirely different group, which then becomes our reference group. We may belong to many groups simultaneously, but we generally use only one group as our primary point of reference in any given situation. This tendency is illustrated in Figure 7–1.

Groups may be classified according to a number of variables. Four criteria are particularly useful: (1) membership, (2) strength of social tie, (3) type of contact, and (4) attraction.

The *membership* criterion is dichotomous: either one is a member of a particular group or one is not a member of that group. Of course, some members are more secure in their membership than others are; that is, some members feel they really belong to a group, while others lack this confidence.

Reference Groups Change as the Situation Changes

FIGURE 7-1

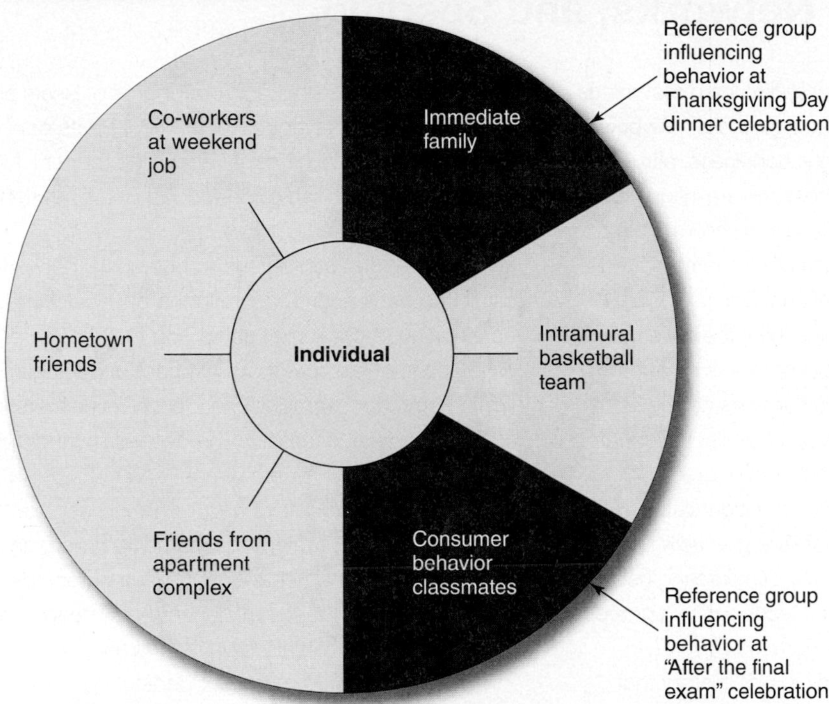

Strength of social tie refers to the closeness and intimacy of the group linkages. **Primary groups,** such as family and friends, involve strong ties and frequent interaction. Primary groups often wield considerable influence. **Secondary groups,** such as professional and neighborhood associations, involve weaker ties and less-frequent interaction.

Type of contact refers to whether the interaction is direct or indirect. Direct contact involves face-to-face interaction; indirect contact does not. The Internet, in particular, has increased the importance of indirect reference groups in the form of *online communities,* which are discussed in more detail later in the chapter.

Attraction refers to the desirability that membership in a given group has for the individual. This can range from negative to positive. Groups with negative desirability—**dissociative reference groups**—can influence behavior just as those with positive desirability do.[2] For example, teenagers tend to avoid clothing styles associated with older consumers. Nonmembership groups with a positive attraction—**aspiration reference groups**—also exert a strong influence. Individuals frequently purchase products thought to be used by a desired group in order to achieve actual or symbolic membership in the group.

Consumer Insight 7–1 shows the power of groups and social networks to influence attitudes and behaviors.

Consumption Subcultures

A **consumption subculture** is a distinctive subgroup of society that self-selects on the basis of a shared commitment to a particular product class, brand, or consumption activity. These groups have (1) an identifiable, hierarchical social structure; (2) a set of shared beliefs or values; and (3) unique jargon, rituals, and modes of symbolic expression.[3] Thus, they are reference groups for their members as well as those who aspire to join or avoid them. LO2

CONSUMER INSIGHT 7-1

Groups, Social Networks, and Seeding

You would probably not be surprised to learn that things like fashion and music spread through social networks.[4] But what about things like obesity, happiness, altruism, or smoking? Research suggests these too are influenced via social networks. Take weight. Research shows that people with similar body mass indices are friends. There are a number of reasonable explanations. One is similarity—people choose others who are like them (be it weight, height, etc.). Another is that social networks establish norms of behavior. The evidence supports norms as a primary explanation for why people of similar weight are friends (part of the same social network or group). Slowly over time, what is considered normal weight within a group or network increases, establishing a "new normal."

Seeding can be an effective way of marketing using the influence of group and opinion leaders within groups. For example, Rick Warren's *The Purpose Driven Life* is the best-selling hardcover book in U.S. history that has been translated into 85 languages. It is a book with Christian topics, relevant to individuals of that faith, but not so much for others who don't share that faith. It is a niche book that spread rapidly and in record numbers to evangelicals for whom the book was relevant, but remained relatively unknown to people outside of this social network. *The Purpose Driven Life* was launched using "seeding," whereby free samples are given away to influential members of existing social networks. Rick Warren nurtured a group of some 1,200 pastors, provided them a free copy of the book, and encouraged them to lead their congregations through the 40-day program.

The phenomenal ability of Beats headphones to grow fivefold and reach $1 billion between 2010 to 2012, despite negative press reviews that suggested Beats headphones were overpriced and underperforming, can in part be explained by seeding Beats headphones to celebrity influential—locker room photos of Beats around the neck of NBA player LeBron James, Beats popping up in Lady Gaga's video "Poker Face," and rapper Lil Wayne wearing $1 million diamond-studded Beats headphones at an NBA game.

The spread of contagion through social networks is difficult to track and measure in the physical world, but data mining of consumer activity on the Internet provides estimations of the spread and impact of contagion. The firm Lotame, for example, can identify influencers in social networks possessing the desired demographics (e.g., women 25–30 years of age) and behavior (e.g., uploaded a video of their child(ren) in the last four hours), send them the contagion (e.g., a movie trailer), and count and track the behaviors and demographics of the people connected to the influencer (e.g., people who viewed the trailer partially or in its entirety).

The downside to contagion, particularly in today's open social media environment, is that it can be difficult to control what is "put out there" and linked to a specific brand and company. Employees who engage in such negative behaviors (e.g., prank and negatively toned videos involving a restaurant's products and/or facilities) can be dismissed, but correcting the damage done can be much more difficult and time-consuming.

Critical Thinking Questions

1. What is seeding and how is it an effective tool for marketers?
2. Use group structure to explain why *The Purpose Driven Life* had little awareness outside a specific social network.
3. In what ways has the Internet enhanced marketers' ability to draw on social networks for marketing purposes?

A number of such subcultures, ranging from hip-hop to gardening to skydiving, have been examined. Each has a set of self-selecting members. They have hierarchies at the local and national levels. And they also have shared beliefs and unique jargon and rituals. Most hobbies and participation sports have consumption-based group subcultures built around them. Consumption need not be shared physically to be a shared ritual that creates and sustains a group.[5]

Note that not all, or even most, product owners or participants in an activity become members of the consumption subculture associated with it. For example, one can enjoy the *Star Trek* TV shows without becoming a member of the associated subculture. Self-selecting into a consumption subculture requires commitment, acquisition of the group's beliefs and values, participation in its activities, and use of its jargon and rituals. Consider the following excerpt regarding the consumption subculture revolving around high-end, limited-edition sneakers, where the most devoted members are called "sneakerheads":

> By 9:35 on a recent Friday night, Dominique Thomas had been camped outside the Niketown store in South Miami for two full days. Thomas, who goes by the street name DK the Line Pimp, had flown in from Denver and was the first in line to buy the $100 Cowboy Air Max 180s, which were scheduled to go on sale at 10 that night. Just 140 pairs of these limited-edition sneakers . . . were manufactured and they would be sold only at the Miami store and only that night. . . . Thomas, 21, reflected on how much getting the shoes meant to him. "Shoes run my life," he said. "Without shoes, I don't exist."[6]

As with other types of groups, members of consumption subcultures vary in their commitment to and interpretation of the group's values and norms. Consider the following quotes from sneakerheads regarding whether or not the sneakers should actually be worn:

> It's just like owning a Porsche. Every time you ride by, everyone looks at you. Well, if you have a rare, sought-after sneaker and you wear it down the street, everyone looks at you . . . .
>
> Most collectors, you can't tell they're sneakerheads. They usually wear really run-of-the-mill sneakers. Real collectors don't want to get their shoes dirty or dusty or worn . . . .[7]

Marketing and Consumption Subcultures Consumption subcultures based on activities obviously are markets for the requirements of the activity itself, such as golf clubs for golfers. However, these groups develop rituals and modes of symbolic communication that often involve other products or services. Golf is renowned for the "uniform" that many of its adherents wear. Clothes, hats, and other items designed for golfers are based as much on providing symbolic meaning as they are for functional benefits.

While these subcultures adopt consumption patterns in large part to affirm their unique identity, the larger market often appropriates all or parts of their symbols, at least for a time. Thus, clothing initially worn by a consumption subculture, such as snowboarders or surfers, for functional or symbolic reasons may emerge as a style for a much larger group. The sneaker culture discussed earlier has given rise to a global market that puts a premium on new and cool styles. The ad in Illustration 7–1 is attempting to appeal to this broader sneaker culture, if not directly at sneakerheads themselves. The name Boxfresh is a reference to hip-hop slang meaning sneakers fresh from the box.

Marketers can and should attempt to use the most respected members of a consumption subculture as a means for identifying trends and influencing consumers in the mass market. Again, the sneaker culture is instructive, as indicated by the director of Adidas's Sports Style Division:

> We have seen the sneaker culture increase over the past several years to the point where, today, bloggers [typically sneakerheads] are integral partners in helping spread the word about coming products. We're putting a lot of effort into this type of consumer, and we're spending a lot of time on them.[8]

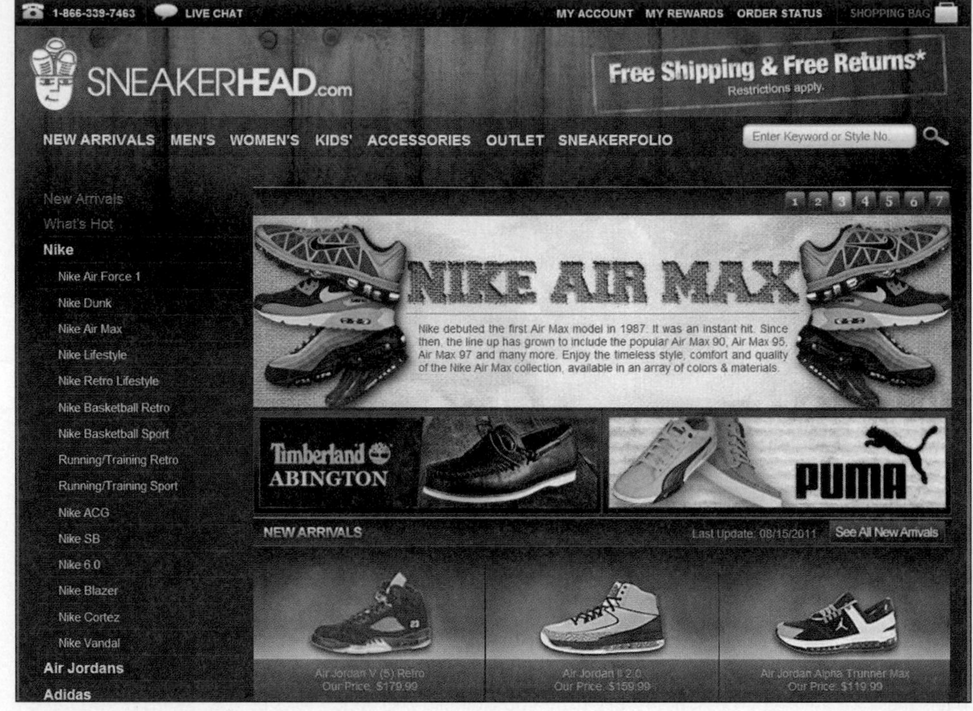

ILLUSTRATION 7-1

Brands may appropriate the slang and symbols of a consumption subculture to appeal to a broader audience.

Brand Communities

Consumption subcultures focus on the interactions of individuals around an activity, product category, or occasionally a brand. A **brand community** is *a nongeographically bound community, based on a structured set of social relationships among owners of a brand and the psychological relationship they have with the brand itself, the product in use, and the firm.*[9] A **community** is *characterized by consciousness of kind, shared rituals and traditions, and a sense of moral responsibility.*[10]

Jeep, along with its owner-enthusiasts, has created a brand community, as described at the beginning of this chapter, as have Harley-Davidson, Saab, Ford Bronco, and MG (a British sports car). The following examples illustrate the nature of brand communities.[11]

Consciousness of Kind
There are several new classes of riders fouling the wind with the misapprehension that merely owning a Harley [Davidson] will transform them into a biker. This is the same type of dangerous ignorance that suggests that giving a dog an artichoke turns him into a gourmet.

Rituals and Traditions
"For the past 7 years, we have sponsored a fall trip. [W]e always go the first weekend in October. [W]e . . . get on the Blue Ridge Parkway [which was] made for MGs, you know—high mountain roads, curves, and hills. We spend Friday and Saturday night in the mountains and then come back. The 1st year we had seven or eight people, last year we had 23 cars."

Moral Responsibility
An MG owner and enthusiast indicates a sense of dedication to help other MG owners even to the point of letting a stranger (who eventually became a friend) stay at his home for free for several nights while waiting on repair parts. "I love it because anyone who has an MG is immediately accepted. . . . I'd help anyone who has an interest in British cars."

Marketing and Brand Communities Brand communities can add value to the ownership of the product and build intense loyalty. A "mere" Jeep owner derives the functional and symbolic benefits associated with owning a Jeep. A member of the Jeep community derives these benefits plus increases in self-esteem from gaining skill in the off-road operation of a Jeep, the ability and confidence to use the Jeep in a wider range of situations, new friendships and social interactions, a feeling of belongingness, a positive association with Chrysler LLC, and a deeper relationship with his or her Jeep.

As the Jeep example suggests, brand communities create value through sets of activities or "practices" that create brand engagement. Four categories of activities and an example of each relating to the Mini Cooper brand are shown in Table 7–1.

From the firm's perspective, building a brand community involves establishing relationships with the owner and helping owners establish relationships with each other. In addition, Table 7–1 suggests a host of activities that can be encouraged and facilitated by both the brand and brand owners to enhance brand value and loyalty. For example, Mini allows individuals to customize their cars during ordering (brand use enhancement via customization) and then track the production and delivery of their vehicle as part of the "birthing" ritual (community engagement via milestoning). The Mini website also features a Mini Owners' Lounge, which is an owners-only area where members share information about upcoming events and so on (social networking via welcoming). One such event is the Mini Getaway Tour. Brand-related events are often termed "brand fests," which are

TABLE 7-1 Value Creation Activities in the Mini Brand Community

Social Networking—Creating, enhancing, and sustaining ties among members by welcoming, empathizing, and governing.

- **Empathizing**—Lending emotional or other support to members
- **Example** (relating to members' "birthing" rituals for their Mini's): Good job Birdman! I'm like you. I watched cameras, checked tracking. . . . You'll treasure having these for your "scrap book" or should I say Minibirds's "baby book"? Jack [the car] was not on a WW ship so there were a lot less options for catching glimpses of the journey. Hang in there. Minibird is almost home!

Community Engagement—Reinforce members' escalating engagement with community by documenting, badging, milestoning, and staking.

- **Milestoning**—Noting significant events in brand ownership and consumption
- **Example** (relating to length of relationship with Mini): The odometer hit 100k miles and I loved my Mini more than ever.

Brand Use—Improving or enhancing the use of the focal brand by customizing, grooming, and commoditizing.

- **Grooming**—Caring for the brand
- **Example** (relating to washing the Mini appropriately): I try to wash at least once a week with a quick detail spray during the middle of the week to keep my Zaino shining. Newt [thread initiator] prepare yourself for an onslaught of posts suggesting that you should keep your car away from those car washes.

Impression Management—Creating positive view of brand community to nonmembers by evangelizing and justifying.

- **Evangelizing**—Sharing about the brand and inspiring others to use the brand
- **Example** (relating to the safety of the Mini): In another MINI forum that I used to visit a lot, there were a few people who had major accidents in their MINIs and I was shocked at just how tough and safe these little cars are. [T]hey weigh more than most small cars and are amazingly rigid and protective from what I've seen.

Source: Adapted from H. J. Schau, A. Muniz Jr., and E. J. Arnould, "How Brand Community Practices Create Value," *Journal of Consumer Research,* September 2009, pp. 30–51.

gatherings of owners and others for the purposes of interacting with one another in the context of learning about and using the brand.

Online Communities and Social Networks

An **online community** is *a community that interacts over time around a topic of interest on the Internet.*[12] These interactions can take place in various forms, including online message boards and discussion groups, blogs, as well as corporate and nonprofit websites. Research indicates that online communities exist for many participants and that there is often a sense of community online, which moves beyond mere interactions to include an affective or emotional attachment to the online group. Studies have found ongoing communications among subsets of these interest groups. In addition, the patterns of communication indicate a group structure, with the more experienced members serving as experts and leaders and the newer members seeking advice and information. These groups develop unique vocabularies, netiquette, and means for dealing with behaviors deemed inappropriate.

Extent of connection can vary dramatically across members. Many members observe the group discussions without participating. Others participate but only at a limited level. Others manage and create content for the group.[13]

The most recent and ongoing evolution relating to online communities involves online social network sites. An **online social network site** is *a web-based service that allows individuals to (1) construct a public or semipublic profile within a bounded system, (2) articulate a list of other users with whom they share a connection, and (3) view and traverse their list of connections and those made by others within the system.*[14] Online social network sites take many forms, including friendship (Facebook and MySpace), media sharing (Flickr and YouTube), events (NASCAR Hookup), corporate or brand (Toyota Friend), and microblogging (Twitter).

Illustration 7–2 shows how Care2, "the world's largest community for good" uses various avenues including a website and Facebook to foster an online community and further solidify brand loyalty.

Marketing and Online Communities and Social Networks

Online communities and social networks are attractive to marketers, who are spending over $4 billion on advertising on social network sites alone, which is nearly 10 percent of all online advertising.[15]

ILLUSTRATION 7-2

Online social network sites such as Care2 shown here, are increasingly popular for both consumers and brands as a way to foster and be connected to a community with similar lifestyles, values, and interests.

Options range from relative standard banner and pop-up ads to more tailored approaches that maximize the specific characteristics of the venue such as sponsored Tweets, branded YouTube channels, or branded fan pages on Facebook.

Online communities and social networks are attractive for a number of reasons, including

- Consumer use is high and rising, with about half of online adults and three-quarters of online teens saying they use social networking sites.[16]
- A majority of consumers who use social network sites use them to share information, including information about brands and products.[17]
- Customer acquisition potential seems high, with 51 percent of firms on Twitter and 68 percent of firms on Facebook indicating they have acquired a customer through these channels.[18]
- Roughly two-thirds of consumers who interact with a brand via social media are more likely to recall the brand, share information about the brand with others, feel connected to the brand, and purchase the brand.[19]

However, consumers don't just want entertainment or marketing; they want content that is relevant and useful to them. A recent study found the following preferences with regard to social media interactions with a firm:

Type of Social Media Interaction	Preference (%)
Providing incentives such as free products and coupons	77
Providing information or solutions to my problems	46
Asking for my feedback on products and services	39
Entertaining me	28
Finding new ways to interact with me	26
Marketing to me	21

Source: Adapted from *2010 Cone Consumer New Media Study Fact Sheet* (Boston, MA: Cone LLC, 2010).

While marketers are still learning about how to most effectively utilize social media, a few general guiding principles have emerged.[20] The first guiding principle is to be *transparent.* In online communities it is critical that companies identify themselves and any posted content as such. Marketers who fail to do so risk being found out and subject to massive criticism from the community. Consider the case of Sony's PSP "Flog," or fake blog, as reported on *The Consumerist* blog:

> [T]he forces of the internet outed a marketing company working for Sony for creating fake PSP blog. The ps3do site says it's written by "Charlie" who wants to get the parents of his friend, "Jeremy," to buy "Jeremy" a PSP for Christmas. The domain name is registered to the *Zipatoni* marketing company.[21]

Indeed, not only are consumers concerned about transparency, so is the FTC, the government body tasked with regulating false and misleading advertising. When Ann Taylor offered a special gift to bloggers who posted coverage about their upcoming line, the FTC investigated. The FTC has issued new guidelines for bloggers requiring them to "clearly disclose any 'material connection' to an advertiser including payments for an endorsement or free product."[22] Since blogs can be and often are a part of social network sites, such issues are directly relevant. More generally it shows how important transparency is when companies interact with online groups.

The second principle is to *be a part of the community.* Online communities often expect that the company will be part of the community and not just market to it. Consider the following excerpt:

> [M]anagers tend to view social media first as a marketing tool, and indeed it is. But consumers are looking for more help, not [marketing] pitches. About two-thirds of U.S. consumers believe that companies should ramp up social media usage to "identify service/support issues and contact consumers to resolve [them].[23]

Search Twitter for a company of interest and gauge the ratio of promotion to customer service. You are likely to find it skewed to promotion, although the better companies will also engage in product and service-failure recovery efforts. Companies such as Target are reacting to customer complaints and issues delivered via Twitter and are reacting to them in real time.

The third principle is to *take advantage of the unique capabilities of each venue.* Many of the social network sites have special areas for corporate advertising and activities that extend beyond traditional banner and pop-up ads. For example, companies can have their own channel on YouTube, which they manage, monitor, and facilitate, as Jeep does. An additional example is the "like" component of Facebook:

> Some companies think that getting someone to click the like button is the end of the game, but in reality it is only the opening kickoff. Consider the case of Adobe Photoshop. With little corporate involvement, it was able to accumulate 240,000 Facebook fans. Many companies would have called that a success. But Adobe wanted to do more. So it enlisted its product management team to run its Facebook page, asking fans what they wanted and learning what topics and ideas resonated with them. Now the page has more than 2 million likes, and fans show their engagement by adding as many as 3000 comments when Adobe posts to the page.[24]

Not only did Adobe utilize a special feature of Facebook (the like function), it managed it in such a way that it was meaningful and engaging to customers and thus created real value, in the form of new product ideas, for the firm.

REFERENCE GROUP INFLUENCES ON THE CONSUMPTION PROCESS

LO3

We all conform in a variety of ways to numerous groups. Sometimes we are aware of this influence, but many times we are not. Before examining the marketing implications of reference groups, we need to examine the nature of reference group influence more closely.

The Nature of Reference Group Influence

Reference group influence can take three forms: *informational, normative,* and *identification.* It is important to distinguish these types since marketing strategies depend on the type of influence involved.

Informational influence *occurs when an individual uses the behaviors and opinions of reference group members as potentially useful bits of information.* This influence is based on either the similarity of the group's members to the individual or the expertise

ILLUSTRATION 7-3

Consumers often use nonmember expert referent groups as a source of information for their purchase decisions.

of the influencing group member.[25] Thus, a person may notice that runners on the track team use a specific brand of nutrition bar. He or she may then decide to try that brand because these healthy and active runners use it. Use by the track team members thus provides information about the brand. Illustration 7–3 shows another form of informational influence whereby a positive nonmember expert referent group endorses or recommends the brand.

Normative influence, sometimes referred to as *utilitarian* influence, *occurs when an individual fulfills group expectations to gain a direct reward or to avoid a sanction.*[26] You may purchase a particular brand of wine to win approval from a colleague. Or you may refrain from wearing the latest fashion for fear of being teased by friends or to fit in with or be accepted by them. As you might expect, normative influence is strongest when individuals have strong ties to the group and the product involved is socially conspicuous.[27] Ads that promise social acceptance or approval if a product is used are relying on normative influence. Likewise, ads that suggest group disapproval if a product is not used, such as a mouthwash or deodorant, are based on normative influence.

Identification influence, also called *value-expressive* influence, *occurs when individuals have internalized the group's values and norms.* These then guide the individuals' behaviors without any thought of reference group sanctions or rewards. The individual has accepted the group's values as his or her own. The individual behaves in a manner consistent with the group's values because his or her values and the group's values are the same.

Figure 7–2 illustrates a series of consumption situations and the type of reference group influence that is operating in each case.

FIGURE 7-2 Consumption Situations and Reference Group Influence

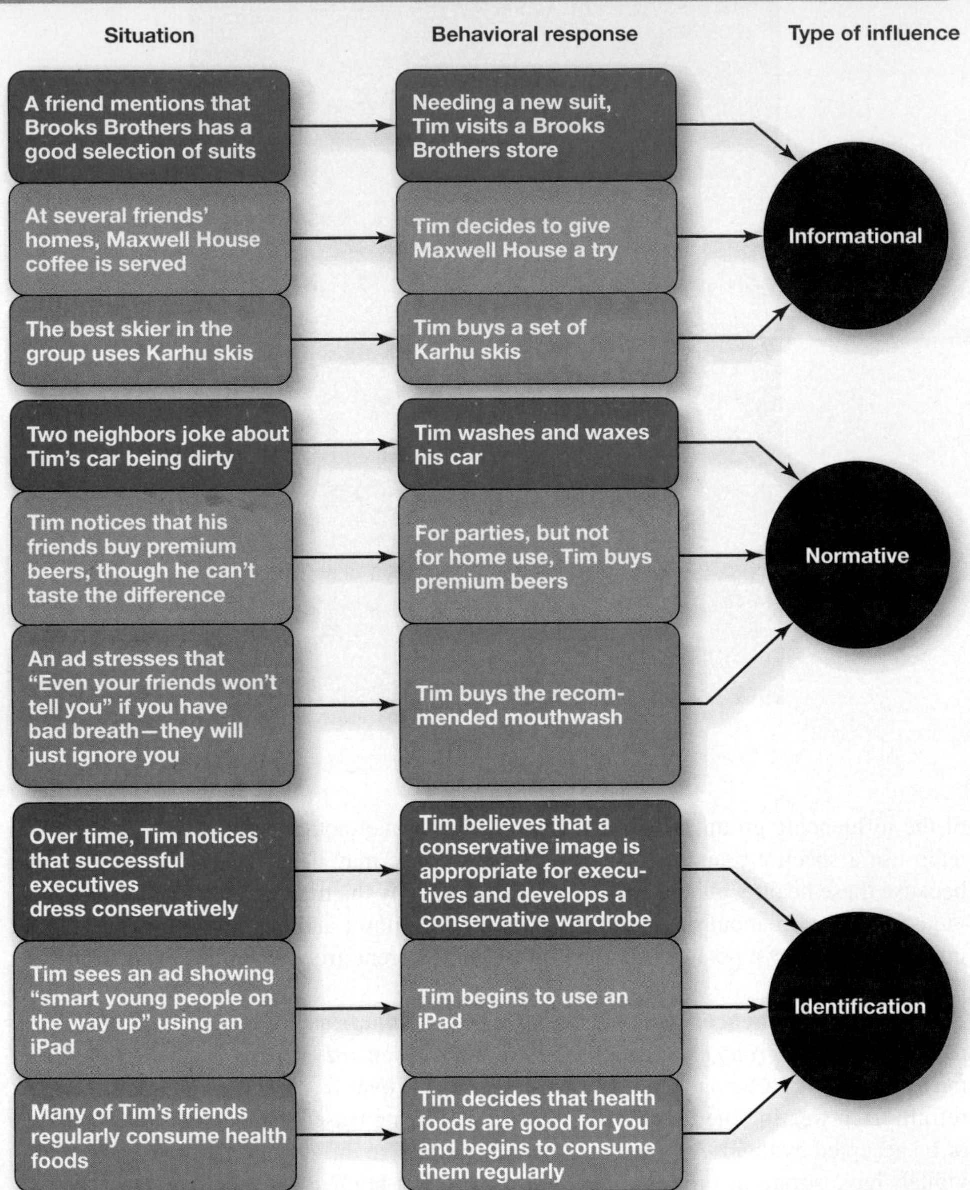

Degree of Reference Group Influence

Reference groups may have no influence in a given situation, or they may influence usage of the product category, the type of product used, or the brand used. Table 7–2 shows how two consumption situation characteristics—necessity/nonnecessity and visible/private consumption—combine to affect the degree of reference group influence likely to operate in a specific situation.

Two Consumption Situation Characteristics and Product/Brand Choice **TABLE** 

	Degree Needed	
	Necessity	**Nonnecessity**
Consumption	Weak reference group influence on product	Strong reference group influence on product
Visible Strong reference group influence on brand	*Public Necessities* Influence: Weak product and strong brand Examples: Shoes Automobiles	*Public Luxuries* Influence: Strong product and brand Examples: Snow board Health club
Private Weak reference group influence on brand	*Private Necessities* Influence: Weak product and brand Examples: Clothes washer Insurance	*Private Luxuries* Influence: Strong product and weak brand Examples: Hot tub Home theater system

Based on Table 7–2, the following two determinants of reference group influence emerge:

- Group influence is strongest *when the use of product or brand is visible to the group.* Products such as running shoes are highly visible. Products such as vitamins are generally not. Reference group influence typically affects only those aspects (e.g., category or brand) that are visible to the group.[28]
- Reference group influence is higher *the less of a necessity an item is.* Thus, reference groups have strong influence on the ownership of products such as snowboards and designer clothes but much less influence on necessities such as refrigerators.

Three additional determinants of reference group influence include:

- In general, *the more commitment an individual feels to a group, the more the individual will conform to the group norms.*
- *The more relevant a particular activity is to the group's functioning, the stronger the pressure to conform to the group norms concerning that activity.* Thus, style of dress may be important to a social group that frequently eats dinner together at nice restaurants and unimportant to a group that meets for basketball on Thursday nights.
- The final factor that affects the degree of reference group influence is *the individual's confidence in the purchase situation.* This can happen even if the product is not visible or important to group functioning as a result of the importance of the decision and a lack of personal decision confidence. Individual personality traits can influence confidence and thus be susceptible to reference group influence.[29]

Figure 7–3 summarizes these determinants, which marketers can use to assess the degree of group influence on their product category and brand.

MARKETING STRATEGIES BASED ON REFERENCE GROUP INFLUENCES

Marketers must first determine the degree and nature of the reference group influence that exists, *or can be created,* for the product in question. Figure 7–3 provides the starting point for this analysis.

FIGURE 7-3 Consumption Situation Determinants of Reference Group Influence

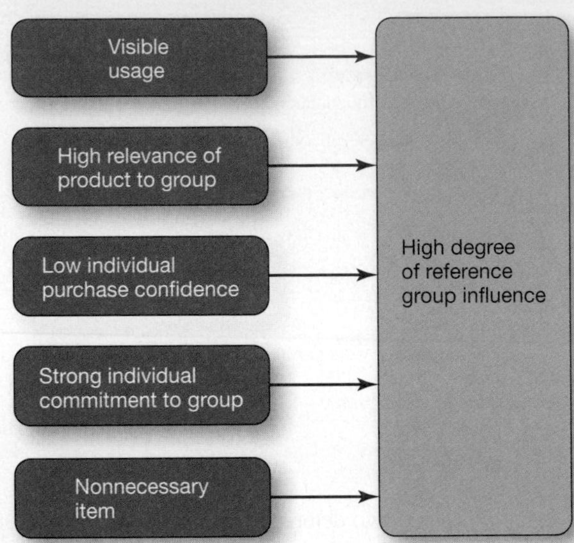

Personal Sales Strategies

The power of groups was initially demonstrated in a classic series of studies. Eight subjects are shown four straight lines on a board—three unequal lines are grouped close together, and another appears some distance from them. The subjects are asked to determine which one of the three unequal lines is closest to the length of the fourth line shown some distance away. The subjects are to announce their judgments publicly. Seven of the subjects are working for the experimenter, and they announce incorrect matches. The order of announcement is arranged so that the naive subject responds last. The naive subject almost always agrees with the incorrect judgment of the others. This is known as the **Asch phenomenon.** Imagine how much stronger the pressures to conform are among friends or when the task is less well defined, such as preferring one brand or style to another.

Consider this direct application of the Asch phenomenon in personal selling. A group of potential customers is brought together for a sales presentation. As each design is presented, the salesperson scans the expressions of the people in the group, looking for the one who shows approval (e.g., head nodding) of the design. The salesperson then asks that person for an opinion because the opinion is certain to be favorable. The person is asked to elaborate. Meanwhile, the salesperson scans the faces of the other people, looking for more support, and then asks for an opinion of the person now showing the most approval. The salesperson continues until the person who initially showed the most disapproval is reached. In this way, by using the first person as a model, and by social group pressure on the last person, the salesperson gets all or most of the people in the group to make a positive public statement about the design. *Do you see any ethical issues in using group influences in this way?*

Advertising Strategies

Marketers often position products as appropriate for group activities. French wines gained an image of being somewhat expensive and snobbish. Many consumers viewed them as appropriate only for very special occasions. Illustration 7–4 shows an ad that positions itself toward a specific group activity.

Marketers use all three types of reference group influence when developing advertisements. Informational influence in advertising was shown earlier in Illustration 7–3. This type of ad uses an expert reference group (e.g., dentists, doctors, and teachers) as the information agent. Another approach is showing members of a group using a product. The message, generally unstated, is that "these types of people find this brand to be the best; if you are like them, you will too."

ILLUSTRATION 7-4

Marketers often position products as appropriate for group activities, as shown in this ad.

Normative group influence is not portrayed in ads as much as it once was. It involves the explicit or implicit suggestion that using, or not using, the brand will result in having members of a group you belong to or wish to join rewarding or punishing you. One reason for the reduced use of this technique is the ethical questions raised by implying that a person's friends would base their reactions to the individual according to his or her purchases. Ads showing a person's friends saying negative things about the person behind his or her back because that person's coffee was not great (yes, there was such an ad campaign) were criticized for playing on people's insecurities and fears.

Identification influence is based on the fact that the individual has internalized the group's values and attitudes. The advertising task is to demonstrate that the product is consistent with the group's—and therefore the individual's—beliefs. This often involves showing the brand being used by a particular type of group, such as socially active young singles or parents of young children.

COMMUNICATIONS WITHIN GROUPS AND OPINION LEADERSHIP

LO4

We learn about new products, services, and brands, as well as retail and information outlets, from our friends and other reference groups in two basic ways. First is by observing or participating with them as they use products and services. Second is by seeking or receiving advice and information from them in the form of **word-of-mouth (WOM) communications.** WOM involves *individuals sharing information with other individuals in a verbal form, including face-to-face, on the phone, and over the Internet.* As indicated in Consumer Insight 7–2, online social media and the Internet continue to transform interpersonal communications and WOM.

Consumers generally trust the opinions of people (family, friends, acquaintances) more than marketing communications because, unlike marketing communications, these personal sources have no reason not to express their true opinions and feelings. As a consequence, WOM can have a critical influence on consumer decisions and business success. It is estimated that two-thirds of all consumer product decisions are influenced by WOM.[30] Recent research shows just how much faith consumers put in WOM versus advertising across a number of products and services. The information

CONSUMER INSIGHT 7-2

Online Social Media, Consumer-Generated Content, and WOM

Social media are part of an ongoing *revolution* online, sometimes referred to as Web 2.0, which involves technologies that allow users to leverage the unique interactive and collaborative capabilities of the Internet. These technologies and formats include online communities, social network sites, consumer review sites, and blogs. Online social media allow users not only to form, join, and communicate with groups and individuals online, but also to create and distribute original content in ways not possible in the past. Such *consumer-generated content* is changing the marketing landscape. Marketers no longer completely control the communications process but now are both observers and participants in an ongoing dialogue that often is driven by consumers themselves.[31]

An example of consumer-generated content in online social network sites is a video titled "Fully Submerged Jeep." It shows an amateur video posted on Metacafe of a Jeep event in which someone takes his Jeep into a pit of water that covers the vehicle completely and comes out the other side unscathed. The video has had over 350,000 views! Jeep is not in control of this content. On the other hand, one Jeep enthusiast provided not only vicarious learning about Jeep but implicit positive WOM about the qualities of Jeep. Others then joined in and posted comments about the video and about Jeep, which kept the "conversation" going. This is the positive side, and for Jeep derives from the devoted members of its brand community.

On the negative side was the Chevy Apprentice Challenge, in which Chevy invited consumers to create their own Tahoe ads with online components and tools provided by the company. The problem was that one in five ads was negative, focusing on the gas guzzler aspect and coming from environmentalists. As one expert noted, the mistake was not in the use of new media but in the mass approach that the company took:

> A much better approach would have been for GM to approach all owners of Tahoes—from soccer moms to hip-hop artists. They could have asked those loyal fans to create commercials using the same material Chevy provided. Or better yet—GM could have allowed them to use their own videos, images, and music to create truly personalized commercials.[32]

below shows the percentage of adults who put people (WOM from friends, family, or other people), as compared with advertising, at the top of their list of best sources for information.

	People	Advertising
Restaurants	83%	35%
Places	71	33
Prescription drugs	71	21
Hotels	63	27
Health tips	61	19
Movies	61	67
Best brands	60	33
Retirement planning	58	9
Automobiles	58	36
Clothes	50	59
Computer equipment	40	18
Websites to visit	37	12

Source: Adapted with the permission of The Free Press, a Division of Simon & Schuster, Inc., from *The Influentials: One American in Ten Tells the Other Nine How to Vote, Where to Eat, and What to Buy,* by Edward Keller and Jonathan Berry. Copyright © 2003 by Roper ASW, LLC. All rights reserved.

When consumer input is requested by firms online, it is called *crowdsourcing.*[33] However, crowdsourcing goes well beyond consumer-generated advertising, which was the focus of the Chevy Apprentice Challenge. Crowdsourcing can involve setting up a forum in which customers can help other customers with their problems, something both Dell and Microsoft have done. It can also involve specific requests by firms for consumer input into product and service design decisions. Illustration 7–5 shows an example.

The statistics presented earlier suggest that nearly 40 percent of social media users would like companies to ask for their input on such decisions. It is important to note, however, that not everyone is highly engaged in generated content online. Different types of consumers generate different types of content at different levels as follows:[34]

- *Creators.* These folks create content of their own—web pages, blogs, video, and video uploads to places like YouTube. Creators tend to be in the teens and early 20s.
- *Critics.* These folks are bloggers and post ratings and reviews. Critics tend to be a bit older than creators—more in the late teens and mid-20s.
- *Joiners.* These folks utilize social networking sites. Joiners range mostly from teens to late 20s. Joiners are a much larger proportion of the population than creators and critics.
- *Spectators.* These folks consume other people's content by reading blogs, watching videos, and so on. Spectators trend young as well, but also garner more members of the older generations.
- *Inactives.* These folks are online but don't participate in social media. Inactives trend older.

Creators and critics are the true leaders of conversation and opinion in Web 2.0. They are, in essence, the opinion leaders and e-fluentials, which we discuss shortly, whose influence cannot be underestimated. Marketers are finding that in this new world of social media, they must think more in terms of joining and participating in the conversation rather than controlling it.

Critical Thinking Questions

1. How do online social media change marketers from controlling communications to participating in and observing it?
2. Beyond age, what do you think are typical characteristics of creators and critics?
3. What strategies might marketers use to work in partnership with creators and critics? What pitfalls do you see?

As this information suggests, the importance of WOM is generally high, and its importance relative to advertising varies somewhat across product types. In addition, traditional mass-media advertising still plays a role, particularly at the earlier stages of the decision process, including building brand awareness.

Negative experiences are powerful motivators of WOM, a factor that must be considered by marketers because negative WOM can strongly influence recipients' attitudes and behaviors.[35] Negative experiences, which are highly emotional and memorable, motivate consumers to talk. While the number varies by situation and product, it is not at all uncommon to find that dissatisfied consumers tell twice as many people about their experience than do satisfied consumers.[36] While merely satisfying consumers (delivering what they expected) may not always motivate WOM, going beyond satisfaction to deliver more than was expected also appears to have the potential to generate substantial WOM. Thus, companies may consider strategies for "delighting" consumers or otherwise creating positive emotional experiences that consumers are motivated to pass along in the form of positive WOM (see Chapter 18).[37] Obviously, it is imperative for companies to provide both consistent product and service quality and quick, positive responses to consumer complaints.

ILLUSTRATION 7-5

Firms are increasingly using social media to request consumer input into product, service design, and marketing decisions.

Moreover, it is important to note that not all personal sources are equal in value. Some folks are known in their circles as the "go-to person" for specific types of information. These individuals actively filter, interpret, or provide product- and brand-relevant information to their family, friends, and colleagues. An individual who does this is known as an **opinion leader.** The process of one person's receiving information from the mass media or other sources and passing it on to others is known as the **two-step flow of communication.** The two-step flow explains some aspects of communication within groups, but it is too simplistic to account for most communication flows. What usually happens is a multistep flow of communication. Figure 7–4 contrasts the direct flow of information from a firm to customers with the more realistic multistep flow of mass communications.

The **multistep flow of communication** involves opinion leaders for a particular product area who actively seek relevant information from the mass media as well as other sources. These opinion leaders process this information and transmit their interpretations of it to some members of their groups. These group members also receive information from the mass media as well as from group members who are not opinion leaders. Figure 7–4 also indicates that these non–opinion leaders often initiate requests for information and supply feedback to the opinion leaders. Likewise, opinion leaders receive information from their followers as well as from other opinion leaders. Note how social media facilitate this multistep flow process online.

FIGURE  Mass Communication Information Flows

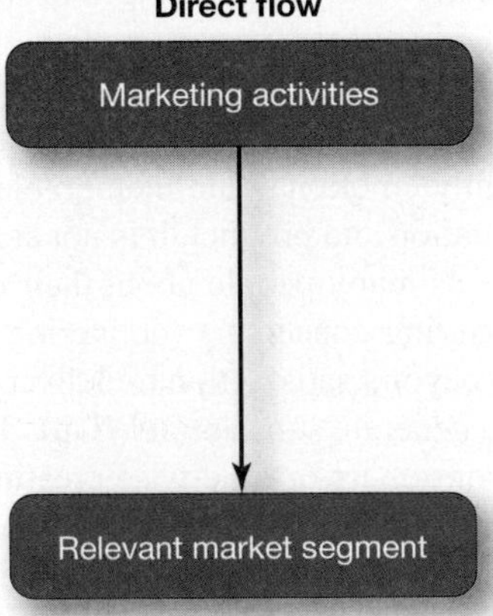

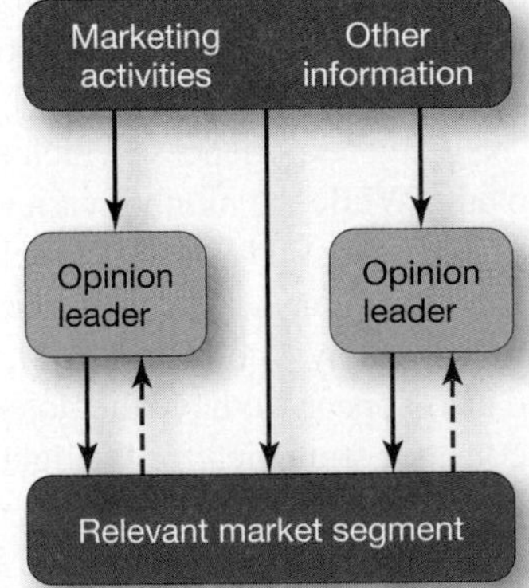

Situations in Which WOM and Opinion Leadership Occur

LO5

The exchange of advice and information between group members can occur *directly* in the form of WOM when (1) one individual seeks information from another or (2) when one individual volunteers information. It can also occur *indirectly* through observation as a byproduct of normal group interaction.

Imagine that you are about to make a purchase in a product category with which you are not very familiar. Further imagine that the purchase is important to you—perhaps a new sound system, skis, or a bicycle. How would you go about deciding what type and brand to buy? Chances are you would, among other things, ask someone you know who you believe is knowledgeable about the product category. This person would be an opinion leader for you. Notice that we have described a *high-involvement* purchase situation in which the purchaser has limited product knowledge about an important decision. Figure 7–5 illustrates how these factors lead to varying levels of opinion leadership.[38]

In addition to *explicitly* seeking or volunteering information, group members provide information to each other through observable behaviors. Consider Hard Candy nail polish:

> Dinah Mohajer, a student at the University of Southern California, made some funky-colored nail polish to match a pair of sandals. Other students saw her and wanted similar polishes. Soon she and her boyfriend were making nail polish in her bathtub. Next she obtained distribution for the polish, now named Hard Candy, in trendy local salons. News photos showing Quentin Tarantino and Drew Barrymore wearing it generated more interest. The actress Alicia Silverstone wore and praised the product on *David Letterman.* In three years sales grew to $30 million.[39]

Hard Candy succeeded mainly through observation. Stylish individuals were seen wearing it on campus (Dinah and her friends). Then other individual style leaders used it (by being distributed through trendy salons, it was seen and purchased by style-conscious individuals). Finally, celebrities were seen in mass media wearing Hard Candy.

FIGURE 7-5 Likelihood of Seeking an Opinion Leader

Product/purchase involvement	Product knowledge: High	Product knowledge: Low
High	Moderate Likelihood	High Likelihood
Low	Low Likelihood	Moderate Likelihood

Obviously, observation and direct WOM often operate together. For example, you might be in the market for a digital camera and notice that a friend uses an Olympus. This might jump-start a conversation about digital cameras, the Olympus brand, and where to find the best deals. And while Hard Candy's success depended heavily on observation, WOM was also involved as friends told other friends.

Characteristics of Opinion Leaders

The most salient characteristic of opinion leaders is greater long-term involvement with the product category than the non–opinion leaders in the group. This is referred to as **enduring involvement,** and it leads to enhanced knowledge about and experience with the product category or activity.[40] This knowledge and experience make opinion leadership possible.[41] Thus, an individual tends to be an opinion leader only for a specific product or activity clusters.

Opinion leadership functions primarily through interpersonal communications and observation. These activities occur most frequently among individuals with similar demographic characteristics. Thus, it is not surprising that opinion leaders are found within all demographic segments of the population and seldom differ significantly on demographic variables from the people they influence. Opinion leaders tend to be more gregarious than others are, which may explain their tendency to provide information to others. They also have higher levels of exposure to relevant media than do non–opinion leaders. And opinion leaders around the world appear to possess similar traits.[42]

Identifying and targeting opinion leaders is important. Offline, opinion leaders can be targeted through specialized media sources. For example, Nike could assume that many subscribers to *Runner's World* serve as opinion leaders for jogging and running shoes.[43] Online, opinion leaders can often be identified in terms of their activity and influence in a given arena.[44] Matt Halfill, a sneakerhead-turned blogger (his blog is NiceKicks), is seen as an opinion leader in the sneaker culture and companies like Nike advertise on his blog.

Market Mavens, Influentials, and e-Fluentials Opinion leaders are specialists. Their knowledge and involvement tend to be product or activity specific. Therefore, while a person might be an opinion leader for motorcycles, she or he is likely to be an opinion seeker for other products, such as cell phones. However, some individuals have information about many different kinds of products, places to shop, and other aspects of markets. They both initiate discussions with others about products and shopping, and respond to requests for market information. These generalized market influencers are **market mavens.** In essence, then, market mavens are a special type of opinion leader.

Market mavens provide significant amounts of information to others across a wide array of products, including durables and nondurables, services, and store types. They provide information on product quality, sales, usual prices, product availability, store personnel characteristics, and other features of relevance to consumers. Market mavens are extensive users of media.[45] They are also more extroverted and conscientious, which drives their tendency to share information with others.[46] Demographically, market mavens tend to be similar to those they influence.

Roper Starch (a market research company) has been tracking a group of generalized market influencers, which are very similar in nature to market mavens, for over 30 years. These consumers, called *Influentials,* represent about 10 percent of the population and have broad social networks that allow them to influence the attitudes and behaviors of the other 90 percent of the population. Influentials are heavy users of print media, such as newspapers and magazines, as well as the Internet and are more likely than the general population to engage in WOM recommendations about products, services, brands, and even what new websites to visit.[47]

Internet mavens also exist. As we saw in Chapter 6, teen Internet mavens are able to influence family decisions that their parents make by operating as important gatekeepers to information on the web.[48] Roper Starch and Burston-Marsteller have identified a related group of consumers they call *e-fluentials*. E-fluentials represent about 10 percent of the adult online community, but their influence is extensive as they communicate news, information, and experiences to a vast array of people both online and offline. E-fluentials actively use the Internet to gather and disseminate information through numerous online avenues including social media. Their number one factor in opening unsolicited e-mails is brand familiarity. Clearly a trusted brand and solid online presence are critical to targeting e-fluentials.[49]

Marketing Strategy, WOM, and Opinion Leadership

Marketers are increasingly relying on WOM and influential consumers as part of their marketing strategies. Driving factors include fragmented markets that are more difficult to reach through traditional mass media, greater consumer skepticism toward advertising, and a realization that opinion leaders and online creators and critics can provide invaluable insights in the research and development process.

This is not to say that marketers have given up on traditional advertising and mass media approaches. Instead, they realize that in many cases they could make their traditional media spending go a lot further if they could tap into these influential consumers who will spread the word either indirectly through observation or directly through WOM. We examine some marketing strategies designed to generate WOM and encourage opinion leadership next.

Advertising Advertising can stimulate and simulate WOM and opinion leadership. *Stimulation* can involve themes designed to encourage current owners to talk about (tell a friend about) the brand or prospective owners to ask current owners (ask someone who owns one) for their impressions.[50] Ads can attempt to stimulate WOM by generating interest and excitement. Dove generated interest using a combination of advertising and so-called pass-it-on tools to stimulate WOM. They ran an ad offering two free bars of Dove to anyone who would recommend three friends, who also got a free bar of soap that was gift-wrapped with the name of the initiating friend on the outside. So instead of a sample from a giant company, it felt like a gift from a friend.[51]

Simulating opinion leadership involves having an acknowledged opinion leader—such as Phil Mickelson for golf equipment—endorse a brand. Illustration 7–6 is an example of this approach. Or it can involve having an apparent opinion leader recommend the product in a "slice of life" commercial. These commercials involve an "overheard" conversation between two individuals in which one person provides brand advice to the other. Finally, advertising can present the results of surveys showing that a high percentage of either knowledgeable individuals ("9 out of 10 dentists surveyed recommend . . .") or typical users recommend the brand.[52]

Product Sampling *Sampling,* sometimes called "seeding," involves getting a sample of a product into the hands of a group of potential consumers. Sampling can be a particularly potent WOM tool when it involves individuals likely to be opinion leaders.

In an attempt to increase the preference for Dockers among the key 24- to 35-year-old urban market, Levi Strauss created the position of "urban networker" in key cities. The networkers identified emerging trendsetters in their cities and tied them to Dockers. This could involve noticing a new band that was beginning to catch on and providing Dockers to the members. The objective was to be associated with emerging urban "happenings" and young influentials as they evolved.[53]

ILLUSTRATION 7-6

Consumers often use personal sources as primary opinion leaders. However, experts whom they don't know personally can also fill this role as can survey results indicating that the brand is recommended by experts or typical users.

BzzAgent (www.BzzAgent.com) recruits everyday people to actively spread WOM about products they like. BzzAgent is adamant that its "agents" acknowledge their association with BzzAgent and provide honest opinions. Most of the WOM occurs offline in normal conversations. Agents receive a free product sample to use and are coached on various WOM approaches. Agents report back to BzzAgent about each WOM episode and redeemable points are rewarded. Importantly, the motive of most is not the points because many don't redeem them. BzzAgent's client list is long and growing and includes Kraft Foods, Goodyear, and Wharton School Publishing. Companies hire BzzAgent to create and field a WOM campaign. Costs vary, but a 12-week campaign involving 1,000 agents can cost $100,000 or more.[54]

Retailing/Personal Selling Numerous opportunities exist for retailers and sales personnel to use opinion leadership. Clothing stores can create "fashion advisory boards" composed of likely style leaders from their target market. An example would be cheerleaders and class officers for a store like Abercrombie & Fitch, which caters to older teens and college students.

Retailers and sales personnel can encourage their current customers to pass along information to potential new customers. When those consumers are given rewards such as discounts, it is called a referral reward program. For example, an automobile salesperson, or the dealership, might provide a free car wash or oil change to current customers who send friends in to look at a new car. Such programs are growing in popularity and companies such as United Airlines, Cingular, and RE/MAX are using them. Research demonstrates that the programs are effective, particularly for encouraging positive WOM to those with whom consumers have weak rather than strong ties.[55]

Creating Buzz **Buzz** can be defined as *the exponential expansion of WOM.* It happens when "word spreads like wildfire" with no or limited mass media advertising supporting it. Buzz drove demand for Hard Candy nail polish, as described earlier. It also made massive successes of Pokémon, Beanie Babies, the original *Blair Witch Project,* the Harry Potter books, and *Toy Story 3.*[56] Marketers create buzz by providing opinion leaders advance information and product samples, having celebrities use the product, placing the product in movies, sponsoring "in" events tied to the product, restricting supply, courting publicity, and otherwise generating excitement and mystique about the brand.

Buzz is generally not supported by large advertising budgets, but it is often created by marketing activities. In fact, creating buzz is a key aspect of *guerrilla marketing*—marketing with a limited budget using nonconventional communications strategies. Guerrilla marketing is about making an "intense connection with individuals and speed[ing] up the natural word-of-mouth process."[57] Examples of guerrilla techniques include:

- Sony Ericsson hired attractive actors to pose as tourists in various metro areas. They would then hand their cell phone/digital camera to locals and ask them to take a picture in an attempt to get the camera in their hands and get them talking about it.
- Blue Cross Blue Shield (BC/BS) hired people to be painted blue and then asked them to roam around Pittsburgh. Nobody knew what the "Blue Crew" campaign was about and it generated enormous buzz. When BC/BS revealed its linkage to the campaign, website traffic increased.[58]

Buzz is not just guerrilla marketing, and guerrilla tactics must be used with care. Consumer advocates are increasingly concerned about certain guerrilla tactics. There are (a) consumer, (b) ethical, and (c) legal issues with stealth or covert marketing efforts. Consider the following example:

> Gillette sponsored an unbranded web site called NoScruf.org. NoScruf stands for the National Organization of Social Crusaders Repulsed by Unshaven Faces. The site was created by Porter Novelli for PR reasons on Gillette's behalf and the .org designation was to further obfuscate Gillette's role.

From a consumer standpoint, research shows that when consumers become aware of such covert marketing efforts, consumer trust, commitment, and purchase intentions are damaged. From an ethical standpoint, hiding a brand's participation in a marketing effort puts consumers at a disadvantage because, when they know, they tend to be more wary of the influence attempt. From a legal standpoint, there is movement in the direction of more stringent guidelines against such covert marketing, with one example being the FTC's new guidelines regarding bloggers and their link to marketers.[59] *Can you see additional ethical concerns surrounding "covert" or "guerrilla" marketing? How is BzzAgent's approach different from Sony Ericsson's?*

Creating buzz is often part of a larger strategy that includes significant mass media advertising. Clairol attempted to create WOM for its True Intense Color line via an online sampling program. It also launched a sweepstakes, "Be the Attraction," with a grand prize of an all-expenses-paid trip for four to the premiere of *Legally Blonde* to fuel the buzz. However, these efforts were soon supplemented with a major mass media advertising campaign.[60]

CONSUMER INSIGHT 7-3

Online Buzz, WOM, and Astrosurfing

As we've seen, the Internet continues to change the nature of interpersonal communications. New avenues are rapidly evolving, and the rewards can be huge for companies that can harness the speed and ease of interconnectivity that the Internet allows. Here are a few examples:

- **Viral marketing** is an online "pass-it-along" strategy. It "uses electronic communications to trigger brand messages throughout a widespread network of buyers." Viral marketing comes in many forms but often involves e-mail. Honda U.K. developed a successful viral marketing campaign that started with "cutting-edge" creativity in the form of a two-minute advertisement called "The Cog." The ad aired in the United Kingdom during the Brazilian Formula 1 Grand Prix to hit likely opinion leaders and was available on Honda's website. That's when the viral aspect kicked in, as people "wowed" by the ad e-mailed it to friends and acquaintances around the world. Honda, Volvo, and Gillette are among a growing list of companies using viral techniques.[61]
- **Blogs** are personalized journals where people and organizations can keep a running dialogue. Blogs can be used in several ways by marketers. First, they can place banner ads in blogs and package ads with blog feeds. Second, they can use product sampling by getting their products in the hands of well-known bloggers in the category with the idea that they will create buzz about them on their blogs. Third, marketers can use blogs by observing important blog sites for marketing intelligence. Fourth, a company can create its own blog and put a company representative in charge of blogging, as Dell has done with Direct2Dell and its chief blogger.[62]
- **Twitter** is a micro-blogging tool. It limits posts to 140 characters. It has evolved quickly into one of the largest and fastest-growing social media outlets. For marketers there are a number of uses for Twitter. First, as we saw earlier, consumers can post complaints or information requests to a brand's Twitter account, to which companies can respond. Second, companies can utilize a Twitter feature called Promoted Tweets. The promotion indicator (like an advertisement) shows up on the Tweet and then the Tweet itself comes up on the search results,

Buzz and WOM are not confined to traditional offline strategies. As discussed in Consumer Insight 7–3, marketers are leveraging increasing numbers of online strategies as well.

DIFFUSION OF INNOVATIONS

LO6

An **innovation** is *an idea, practice, or product perceived to be new by the relevant individual or group.* Whether or not a given product *is* an innovation is determined by the perceptions of the potential market, not by an objective measure of technological change. The manner by which a new product is accepted or spreads through a market is basically a group phenomenon. In this section, we will examine this process in some detail.[63]

even of those who aren't the brand's followers on Twitter. Finally, companies like Sponsored Tweets and Ad.ly are connecting brands with influential tweeters. These tweeters, often celebrities like Charlie Sheen and Kim Kardashian who have millions of followers, get paid for tweeting about specific brands, often at the rate of $1000 or more per tweet. As with regular blogs, full disclosure is an important facet of this model.[64]

- **Customer reviews** and review functionality on a website can be a critical marketing tool. Amazon and others allow consumers to easily post reviews of products on their site. Given the power of WOM, this online version of WOM is a powerful decision influencer. For example, restaurant revenues have been found to increase between 5 and 9 percent if they increase their ranking on Yelp by one star. However, there are at least two factors that marketers must be concerned with regarding online reviews. First, since existing reviews are "public information," they tend to "sway" future reviews in that direction. So, if reviews trend down, that likely feeds more downward bias than if reviews were done independent of knowledge of prior reviews. This is a challenge for both marketers and consumers. Marketers can find themselves in a battle against a misguided trend, and consumers likely are not getting the best, most accurate advice. A second concern is fake reviews, where it is estimated that one in seven reviews is fake. Astrosurfing is the practice whereby companies buy positive reviews of themselves and negative reviews for their competitors. Companies can use algorithms to distinguish genuine and fake reviews and then take legal action. The "buying" of fake reviews by one company for another is akin to false advertising. Samsung was recently fined for hiring people to criticize HTC (a competitor) products.[65]

Clearly marketers are learning how to leverage the WOM potential of the Internet. It will be interesting to see what the future brings!

Critical Thinking Questions

1. What other Internet alternatives exist for interpersonal communication?
2. Do you trust online sources to provide accurate information? What can marketers do to increase consumer trust in online sources?
3. What do you think are typical characteristics of those who are heavy bloggers?

Categories of Innovations

Try to recall new products that you have encountered in the past two or three years. As you reflect on these, it may occur to you that there are degrees of innovation. For example, computer tablets such as Apple's iPad are more of an innovation than is a new fat-free snack. The changes required in one's behavior, including attitudes and beliefs, or lifestyle if a person adopts the new product or service determine the degree of innovation, not the technical or functional changes in the product.

We can place any new product somewhere on a continuum ranging from no change to radical change, depending on the target market's perception of the item. This continuum is often divided into three categories or types of innovations.

Continuous Innovation Adoption of this type of innovation requires relatively minor changes in behavior or changes in behaviors that are unimportant to the consumer.

ILLUSTRATION 7-7

Crest Vivid White Night toothpaste would be considered a continuous innovation by most.

Examples include Crest Vivid White Night toothpaste, Wheaties Energy Crunch cereal, and Purex 3-in-1 laundry sheets. Note that some continuous innovations require complex technological breakthroughs. However, their use requires little change in the owner's behavior or attitude. Crest Vivid White Night Striped toothpaste shown in Illustration 7–7 is another example of a continuous innovation.

Dynamically Continuous Innovation Adoption of this type of innovation requires a moderate change in an important behavior or a major change in a behavior of low or moderate importance to the individual. Examples include digital cameras, personal navigators, mobile apps, and Bella and Birch textured paints that are applied like wallpaper but without glue, using a special applicator. The Shout Color Catcher ad in Illustration 7–8 is a good example of a product that is a dynamically continuous innovation for most consumer groups.

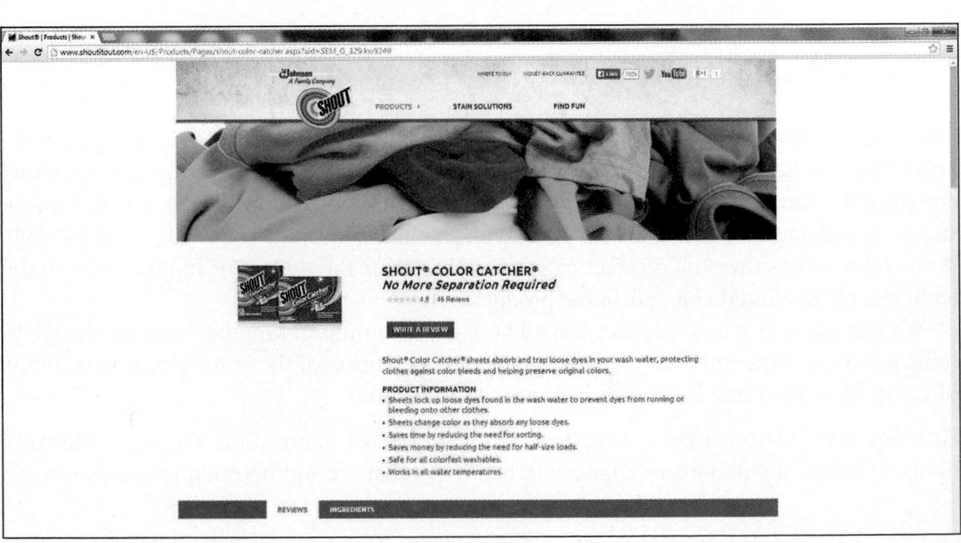

ILLUSTRATION 7-8

Using Shout Color Catcher would require a major change in an area of moderate importance for most individuals. For these individuals, it would be a dynamically continuous innovation.

ILLUSTRATION 7-9

Most consumers will react to this as a discontinuous innovation.

Discontinuous Innovation Adoption of this type of innovation requires major changes in behavior of significant importance to the individual or group. Examples would include the Norplant contraceptive, becoming a vegetarian, and the Toyota FCV hydrogen fuel cell car (see Illustration 7–9).

Most of the new products or alterations introduced each year tend toward the no-change end of the continuum. Much of the theoretical and empirical research, however, has been based on discontinuous innovations. For example, individual consumers presumably go through a series of distinct steps or stages known as the **adoption process** when purchasing an innovation. These stages are shown in Figure 7–6.

Adoption Process and Extended Decision Making

FIGURE  7-6

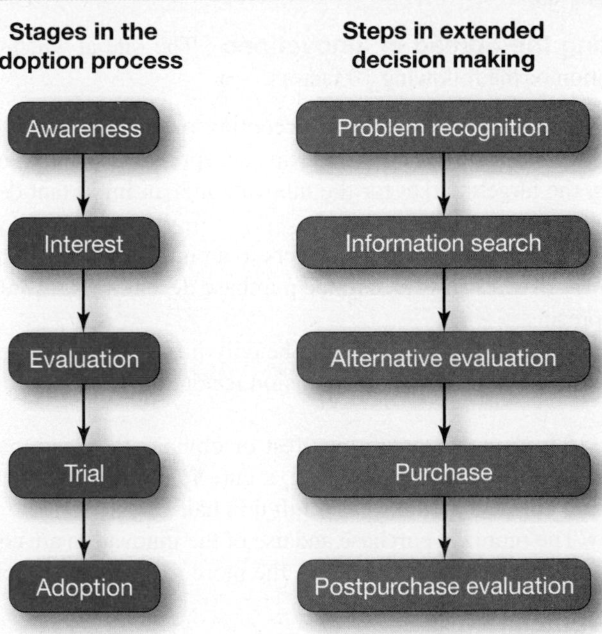

Figure 7–6 also shows the steps in extended decision making, described in Chapter 1. As can be seen, the *adoption process* is basically a term used to describe extended decision making when a new product is involved. As we will discuss in detail in Chapter 14, extended decision making occurs when the consumer is *highly involved* in the purchase. High purchase involvement is likely for discontinuous innovations such as the decision to purchase a hybrid car, and most studies of innovations of this nature have found that consumers use extended decision making.

However, it would be a mistake to assume that all innovations are evaluated using extended decision making (the adoption process). In fact, most continuous innovations probably trigger limited decision making. As consumers, we generally don't put a great deal of effort into deciding to purchase innovations such as Jolt's Wild Grape flavored drink or Glad microwave steaming bags.

Diffusion Process

The **diffusion process** is *the manner in which innovations spread throughout a market.* The term *spread* refers to purchase behavior in which the product is purchased with some degree of regularity.[66] The market can range from virtually the entire society (for a new soft drink, perhaps) to the students at a particular high school (for an automated fast-food and snack outlet).

For most innovations, the diffusion process appears to follow a similar pattern over time: a period of relatively slow growth, followed by a period of rapid growth, followed by a final period of slower growth. This pattern is shown in Figure 7–7. However, there are exceptions to this pattern. In particular, it appears that for continuous innovations such as new ready-to-eat cereals, the initial slow-growth stage may be skipped.

An overview of innovation studies reveals that the time involved from introduction until a given market segment is saturated (i.e., sales growth has slowed or stopped) varies from a few days or weeks to years. This leads to two interesting questions: (1) What determines how rapidly a particular innovation will spread through a given market segment? and (2) In what ways do those who purchase innovations relatively early differ from those who purchase them later?

Factors Affecting the Spread of Innovations The rate at which an innovation is diffused is a function of the following 10 factors.

1. *Type of group.* Some groups are more accepting of change than others. In general, young, affluent, and highly educated groups accept change, including new products, readily. Thus, the target market for the innovation is an important determinant of the rate of diffusion.[67]
2. *Type of decision.* The type of decision refers to an individual versus a group decision. The fewer the individuals involved in the purchase decision, the more rapidly an innovation will spread.
3. *Marketing effort.* The rate of diffusion is heavily influenced by the extent of marketing effort involved. Thus, the rate of diffusion is not completely beyond the control of the firm.[68]
4. *Fulfillment of felt need.* The more manifest or obvious the need that the innovation satisfies, the faster the diffusion. Rogaine, a cure for some types of hair loss, gained rapid trial among those uncomfortable with thin hair or baldness.
5. *Compatibility.* The more the purchase and use of the innovation are consistent with the individual's and group's values or beliefs, the more rapid the diffusion.[69]

Diffusion Rate of an Innovation over Time FIGURE  7-7

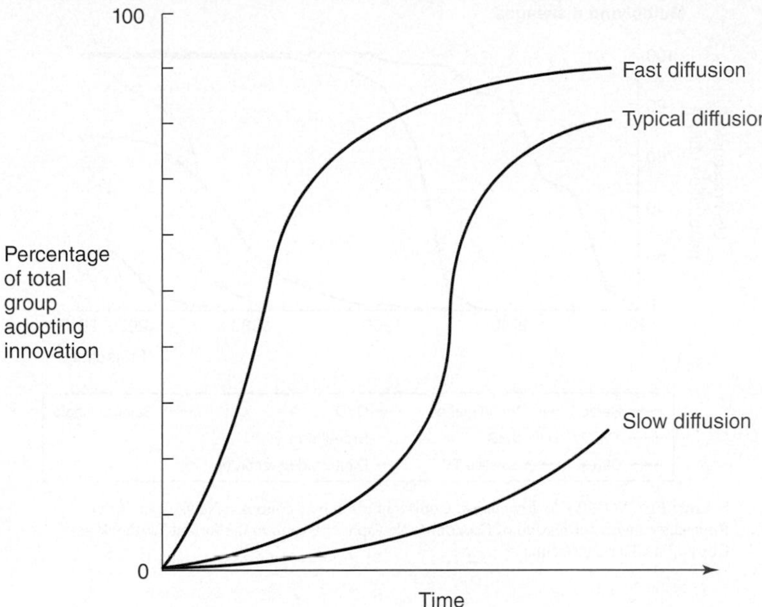

6. *Relative advantage.* The better the innovation is perceived to meet the relevant need compared with existing methods, the more rapid the diffusion. Both the performance and the cost of the product are included in relative advantage. The digital audio tape (DAT) had neither advantage compared with CDs and DVDs and thus never took off.
7. *Complexity.* The more difficult the innovation is to understand and use, the slower the diffusion. The key to this dimension is ease of use, *not* complexity of product. Specialized blogging software is making an otherwise complex task easy and fun.[70]
8. *Observability.* The more easily consumers can observe the positive effects of adopting an innovation, the more rapid its diffusion will be. Cell phones are relatively visible. Laser eye surgery, while less visible, may be a frequent topic of conversation. On the other hand, new headache remedies are less obvious and generally less likely to be discussed.
9. *Trialability.* The easier it is to have a low-cost or low-risk trial of the innovation, the more rapid is its diffusion. The diffusion of products like laser eye surgery has been hampered by the difficulty of trying out the product in a realistic manner. This is much less of a problem with low-cost items such as headache remedies, or such items as camera phones, which can be borrowed or tried at a retail outlet.
10. *Perceived risk.* The more risk associated with trying an innovation, the slower the diffusion. Risk can be financial, physical, or social. Perceived risk is a function of three dimensions: (1) *the probability that the innovation will not perform as desired;* (2) *the consequences of its not performing as desired;* and (3) *the ability (and cost) to reverse any negative consequences.*[71] Thus, many consumers may feel a need for the benefits offered by laser eye surgery and view the probability of its working successfully as being quite high. However, they perceive the consequences of failure as being extreme and irreversible and therefore do not adopt this innovation.

FIGURE 7-8 Diffusion Rates for Consumer Electronics

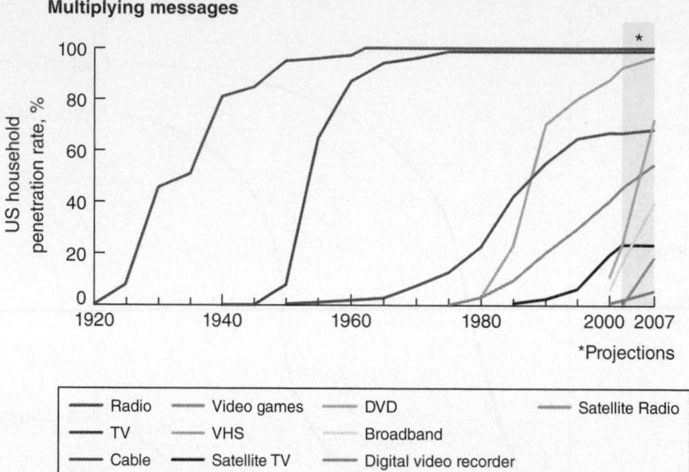

Figure 7–8 shows the diffusion curves for various consumer electronic products. How would you explain the differences in diffusion rates across these products in U.S. households?

Characteristics of Individuals Who Adopt an Innovation at Varying Points in Time The curves shown in Figures 7–7 and 7–8 are cumulative curves that illustrate the increase in the percentage of adopters over time. If we change those curves from a cumulative format to one that shows the percentage of a market that adopts the innovation at any given point in time, we will have the familiar bell-shaped curves shown in Figure 7–9.

Figure 7–9 reemphasizes the fact that a few individuals adopt an innovation very quickly, another limited group is reluctant to adopt the innovation, and the majority of the group adopts at some time in between the two extremes. Researchers have found it useful to divide the adopters of any given innovation into five groups based on the relative time at which they adopt. These groups, called **adopter categories,** are shown in Figure 7–9 and defined below:

Innovators: The first 2.5 percent to adopt an innovation.

Early adopters: The next 13.5 percent to adopt.

Early majority: The next 34 percent to adopt.

Late majority: The next 34 percent to adopt.

Laggards: The final 16 percent to adopt.

How do these groups differ? The following descriptions, though general, provide a good starting point. Clearly, however, research by product category would be necessary in fully understanding specific marketing situations.

Innovators are venturesome risk takers. They are capable of absorbing the financial and social costs of adopting an unsuccessful product. They are cosmopolitan in outlook

Adoptions of an Innovation over Time

FIGURE 7-9

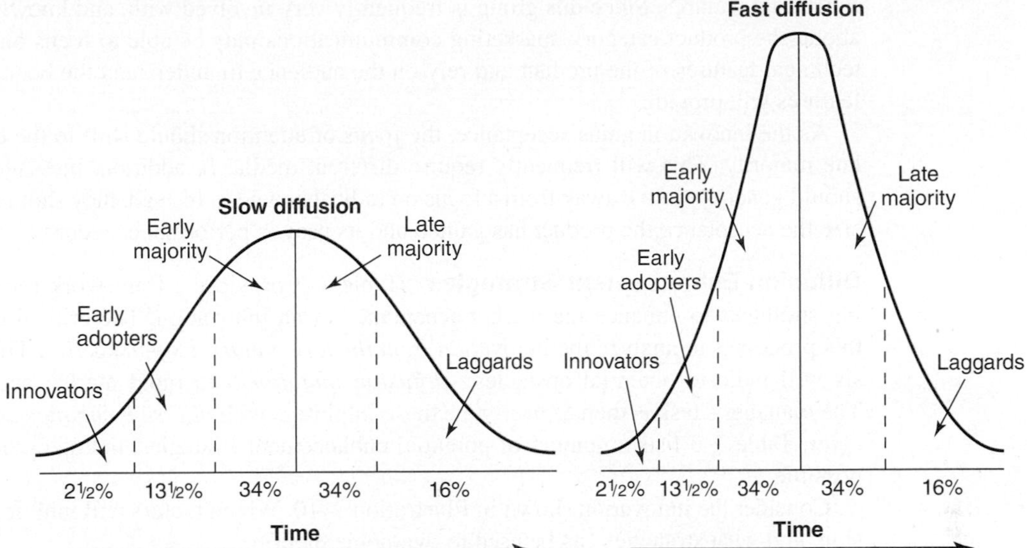

and use other innovators rather than local peers as a reference group. They tend to be younger, better educated, and more socially mobile than their peers. Innovators make extensive use of commercial media, sales personnel, and professional sources in learning of new products.

Early adopters tend to be opinion leaders in local reference groups. They are successful, well educated, and somewhat younger than their peers. They are willing to take a calculated risk on an innovation but are concerned with failure. Early adopters also use commercial, professional, and interpersonal information sources, and they provide information to others.

Early majority consumers tend to be cautious about innovations. They adopt sooner than most of their social group but also after the innovation has proved successful with others. They are socially active but seldom leaders. They tend to be somewhat older, less well educated, and less socially mobile than the early adopters. The early majority relies heavily on interpersonal sources of information.

Late majority members are skeptical about innovations. They often adopt more in response to social pressures or a decreased availability of the previous product than because of a positive evaluation of the innovation. They tend to be older and have less social status and mobility than those who adopt earlier.

Laggards are locally oriented and engage in limited social interaction. They tend to be relatively dogmatic and oriented toward the past. Laggards adopt innovations only with reluctance.

Marketing Strategies and the Diffusion Process

Market Segmentation Since earlier purchasers of an innovation differ from later purchasers, firms should consider a "moving target market" approach. That is, after selecting a general target market, the firm should initially focus on those individuals within the target market most likely to be innovators and early adopters.[72] Messages to this group can often emphasize the newness and innovative characteristics of the product as well as its functional features. Since this group is frequently very involved with, and knowledgeable about, the product category, marketing communications may be able to focus on the new technical features of the product and rely on the audience to understand the benefits these features will provide.[73]

As the innovation gains acceptance, the focus of attention should shift to the early and late majority. This will frequently require different media. In addition, message themes should generally move away from a focus on radical newness. Instead, they should emphasize the acceptance the product has gained and its proven performance record.

Diffusion Enhancement Strategies Table 7–3 provides a framework for developing strategies to enhance the market acceptance of an innovation. The critical aspect of this process is to analyze the innovation *from the target market's perspective.* This analysis will indicate potential obstacles—*diffusion inhibitors*—to rapid market acceptance. The manager's task is then to overcome these inhibitors with *diffusion enhancement strategies.* Table 7–3 lists a number of potential enhancement strategies, but many others are possible.

Consider the innovation shown in Illustration 7–10. Which factors will inhibit its diffusion, and what strategies can be used to overcome them?

TABLE 7-3 Innovation Analysis and Diffusion Enhancement Strategies

Diffusion Determinant	Diffusion Inhibitor	Diffusion Enhancement Strategies
1. Nature of group	Conservative	Search for other markets Target innovators within group
2. Type of decision	Group	Choose media to reach all deciders Provide conflict reduction themes
3. Marketing effort	Limited	Target innovators within group Use regional rollout Leverage buzz
4. Felt need	Weak	Use extensive advertising showing importance of benefits
5. Compatibility	Conflict	Stress attributes consistent with normative values
6. Relative advantage	Low	Lower price Redesign product
7. Complexity	High	Distribute through high-service outlets Use skilled sales force Use product demonstrations Use extensive marketing efforts
8. Observability	Low	Use extensive advertising Target visible events when appropriate
9. Trialability	Difficult	Use free samples to early adopter types Provide special prices to rental agencies Use high-service outlets
10. Perceived risk	High	Use success documentation Obtain endorsement by credible sources Provide guarantees

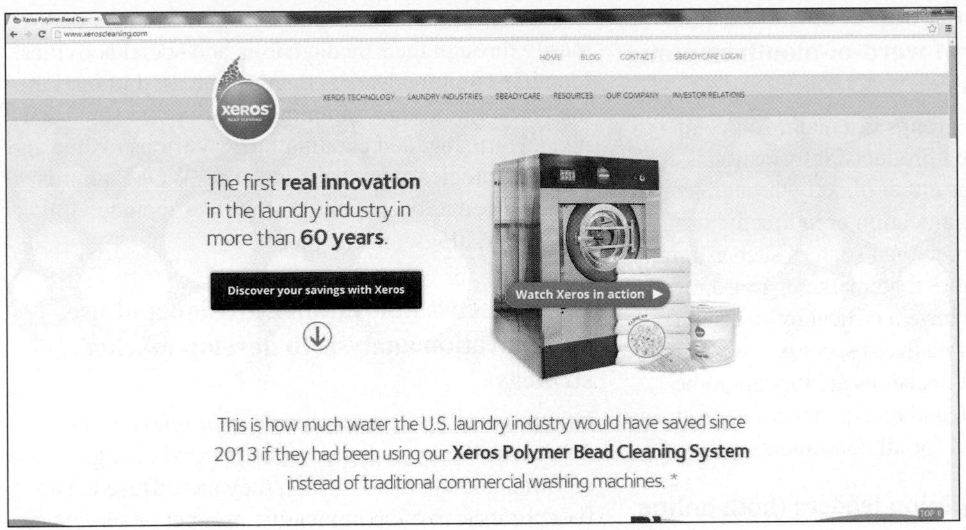

ILLUSTRATION 7-10

Ten factors determine the success of innovations. How do you think this innovation will fare based on these 10 factors?

SUMMARY

SMARTBOOK™

LO1: Explain reference groups and the criteria used to classify them

A *reference group* is a group whose presumed perspectives or values are being used by an individual as the basis for his or her current behavior. Thus, a reference group is simply a group that an individual uses as a guide for behavior in a specific situation. Reference groups, as with groups in general, may be classified according to a number of variables including membership, strength of social tie, type of contact, and attraction.

LO2: Discuss consumption subcultures, including brand and online communities and their importance for marketing

A *consumption subculture* is a group that self-selects on the basis of a shared commitment to a particular product or consumption activity. These subcultures also have (1) an identifiable, hierarchical social structure; (2) a set of shared beliefs or values; and (3) unique jargon, rituals, and modes of symbolic expression. A *brand community* is a nongeographically bound community, based on a structured set of social relationships among owners of a brand and the psychological relationship they have with the brand itself, the product in use, and the firm. Brand communities can add value to the ownership of the product and build intense loyalty. An *online community* is a community that interacts over time around a topic of interest on the Internet. Online communities have evolved over time to include *online social network sites,* which are web-based services that allow individuals to (1) construct a public or semipublic profile within a bounded system, (2) articulate a list of other users with whom they share a connection, and (3) view and traverse their list of connections and those made by others within the system.

LO3: Summarize the types and degree of reference group influence

Informational influence occurs when an individual uses the behaviors and opinions of reference group members as potentially useful bits of information. *Normative influence,* sometimes referred to as utilitarian influence, occurs when an individual fulfills group expectations to gain a direct reward or to avoid a sanction. *Identification influence,* also called value-expressive influence, occurs when individuals have internalized the group's values and norms.

The degree of *conformity* to a group is a function of (1) the visibility of the usage situation, (2) the level of commitment the individual feels to the group, (3) the relevance of the behavior to the functioning of the group, (4) the individual's confidence in his or her own judgment in the area, and (5) the level of necessity reflected by the nature of the product.

LO4: Discuss within-group communications and the importance of word-of-mouth communications to marketers

Communication within groups is a major source of information about certain products. Information is communicated within groups either directly through *word-of-mouth (WOM)* communication or indirectly through observation. WOM via personal sources such as family and friends is trusted more than marketer-based messages and can therefore have a critical influence on consumer decisions and business success. Two-thirds of all consumer product decisions are thought to be influenced by WOM. Negative experiences are a strong driver of negative WOM for all consumers.

LO5: Understand opinion leaders (both online and offline) and their importance to marketers

Opinion leaders are highly knowledgeable about specific products or activities and are seen as the "go-to person" for specific types of information. These individuals actively filter, interpret, or provide product- and brand-relevant information to their family, friends, and colleagues. A defining characteristic of opinion leaders is their enduring involvement with the product category, which leads to their expertise and the trust people have in their opinions.

A special type of opinion leader is *market mavens.* These are individuals who are general market influencers. They have information about many different kinds of products, places to shop, and other aspects of markets. *Internet mavens* describe their online counterparts.

Marketers attempt to identify opinion leaders primarily through their media habits and social activities. Identified opinion leaders then can be used in marketing research, product sampling, retailing/personal selling, advertising, and creating buzz. Various offline and online strategies exist for stimulating WOM, opinion leadership, and buzz. Online strategies include viral marketing, blogs, and Twitter.

LO6: Discuss innovation diffusion and use an innovation analysis to develop marketing strategy

Groups greatly affect the diffusion of innovations. *Innovations* vary in degree of behavioral change required and the rate at which they are diffused. The first purchasers of an innovative product or service are termed *innovators;* those who follow over time are known as *early adopters, early majority, late majority,* and *laggards.* Each of these groups differs in personality, age, education, and reference group membership. These characteristics help marketers identify and appeal to different classes of adopters at different stages of an innovation's diffusion.

The time it takes for an innovation to spread from innovators to laggards is affected by several factors: (1) nature of the group involved, (2) type of innovation decision required, (3) extent of marketing effort, (4) strength of felt need, (5) compatibility of the innovation with existing values, (6) relative advantage, (7) complexity of the innovation, (8) ease in observing usage of the innovation, (9) ease in trying the innovation, and (10) perceived risk in trying the innovation.

KEY TERMS

Adopter categories 244
Adoption process 241
Asch phenomenon 228
Aspiration reference groups 217
Blogs 238
Brand community 220
Buzz 237
Community 220
Consumption subculture 217
Customer reviews 239
Diffusion process 242
Dissociative reference groups 217
Early adopters 245
Early majority 245
Enduring involvement 234
Group 216
Identification influence 225
Informational influence 224
Innovation 238
Innovators 244
Laggards 245
Late majority 245
Market mavens 234
Multistep flow of communication 232
Normative influence 225
Online community 222

REVIEW QUESTIONS

1. How does a *group* differ from a *reference group?*
2. What criteria are used by marketers to classify groups?
3. What is a *dissociative reference group?* In what way can dissociative reference groups influence consumer behavior?
4. What is an *aspiration reference group?* How can an aspiration reference group influence behavior?
5. What is a *consumption-based group* or a *consumption subculture?* How can marketers develop strategy based on consumption subcultures?
6. What is a *brand community?* What are the characteristics of such a group?
7. How can a marketer foster a brand community?
8. What is an *online social network site?* What are the guidelines for marketers operating in online communities and social networking sites?
9. What types of group influence exist? Why must a marketing manager be aware of these separate types of group influence?
10. What five factors determine the strength of reference group influence in a situation?
11. What is the *Asch phenomenon* and how do marketers utilize it?
12. How can a marketer use knowledge of reference group influences to develop advertising strategies?
13. What is an *opinion leader?* How does an opinion leader relate to the *multistep flow of communication?*
14. What characterizes an opinion leader?
15. What determines the likelihood that a consumer will seek information from an opinion leader?
16. How does a *market maven* differ from an *opinion leader?*
17. Explain the role of *enduring involvement* in driving opinion leadership.
18. How can marketing managers identify opinion leaders?
19. How can marketers utilize opinion leaders?
20. What is *buzz?* How can marketers create it?
21. What is a *blog?*
22. What is an *innovation?* Who determines whether a given product is an innovation?
23. What are the various categories of innovations? How do they differ?
24. What is the *diffusion process?* What pattern does the diffusion process appear to follow over time?
25. Describe the factors that affect the diffusion rate for an innovation. How can these factors be utilized in developing marketing strategy?
26. What are *adopter* categories? Describe each of the adopter categories.
27. How can a marketer use knowledge of adopter categories to develop marketing strategy?

DISCUSSION QUESTIONS

28. Respond to the questions in Consumer Insight 7–1.
29. Using college students as the market segment, describe the most relevant reference group(s) and indicate the probable degree of influence on decisions for each of the following:
    a. Brand of toothpaste
    b. Purchase of a hybrid car
    c. Purchase of breakfast cereal
    d. Becoming a vegetarian
    e. Choice of a computer tablet such as the iPad.

Answer Questions 30 to 33 using (a) shoes, (b) barbeque grill, (c) car, (d) toaster, (e) iPad, and (f) adopting a pet from a shelter.

30. How important are reference groups to the purchase of the above-mentioned products or activities? Would their influence also affect the brand or model? Would their influence be informational, normative, or identification? Justify your answers.
31. What reference groups would be relevant to the decision to purchase the product or activity (based on students on your campus)?
32. What are the norms of the social groups of which you are a member concerning the product or activity?
33. Respond to the questions in Consumer Insight 7–2.
34. Describe two groups that serve as aspiration reference groups for you. In what ways, if any, have they influenced your consumption patterns?
35. Describe two groups to which you belong. For each, give two examples of instances when the group has exerted (*a*) informational, (*b*) normative, and (*c*) identification influence on you.
36. Develop two approaches using reference group theory to reduce drug, alcohol, or cigarette consumption among teenagers.
37. What ethical concerns arise in using reference group theory to sell products?
38. Describe a consumption subculture to which you belong. How does it affect your consumption behavior? How do marketers attempt to influence your behavior with respect to this subculture?
39. Do you belong to a brand community? If so, describe the benefits you derive from this group and how it affects your consumption.
40. Do you belong to an online community or social network site? If so, describe the benefits you derive from this group and how it affects your consumption.
41. Answer the following questions for (*i*) Dyson bladeless fan, (*ii*) space flight, (*iii*) cell phone–based GPS.
    a. Is the product an innovation? Justify your answer.
    b. Using the student body on your campus as a market segment, evaluate the perceived attributes of the product.
    c. Who on your campus would serve as opinion leaders for the product?
    d. Will the early adopters of the product use the adoption process (extended decision making), or is a simpler decision process likely?
42. Describe two situations in which you have served as or sought information from an opinion leader. Are these situations consistent with the discussion in the text?
43. Are you aware of market mavens on your campus? Describe their characteristics, behaviors, and motivation.
44. Have you used Twitter recently? Why? How did it work? What marketing implications does this suggest?
45. Identify a recent (*a*) continuous innovation, (*b*) dynamically continuous innovation, and (*c*) discontinuous innovation. Justify your selections.
46. Analyze the Roomba (robotic vacuum cleaner) in terms of the determinants in Table 7–3 and suggest appropriate marketing strategies.
47. Conduct a diffusion analysis and recommend appropriate strategies for the innovation shown in Illustration 7–10.
48. Assume that you are a consultant to firms with new products. You have members of the appropriate market segments rate innovations on the 10 characteristics described in Table 7–3. Based on these ratings, you develop marketing strategies. Assume that a rating of 9 is extremely favorable (e.g., strong relative advantage or a lack of complexity) and 1 is extremely unfavorable. Suggest appropriate strategies for each of the following consumer electronic products (see table).

	Product								
Attribute	**A**	**B**	**C**	**D**	**E**	**F**	**G**	**H**	**I**
Fulfillment of felt need	9	7	3	8	8	5	7	8	9
Compatibility	8	8	8	8	9	2	8	9	8
Relative advantage	9	2	8	9	7	8	9	8	8
Complexity	9	9	9	9	9	3	8	8	7
Observability	8	8	9	1	9	4	8	8	8
Trialability	8	9	8	9	9	2	9	2	9
Nature of group	3	8	7	8	9	9	7	7	3
Type of decision	3	7	8	8	6	7	7	3	7
Marketing effort	6	7	8	7	8	6	3	8	7
Perceived risk	3	8	7	7	3	7	8	8	5

APPLICATION ACTIVITIES

49. Find two advertisements that use reference groups in an attempt to gain patronage. Describe the advertisement, the type of reference group being used, and the type of influence being used.
50. Develop an advertisement for (*i*) breath strips, (*ii*) an energy drink, (*iii*) an upscale club, (*iv*) Red Cross, (*v*) scooters, or (*vi*) vitamins using the following.
    a. An informational reference group influence
    b. A normative reference group influence
    c. An identification reference group influence
51. Interview two individuals who are strongly involved in a consumption subculture. Determine how it affects their consumption patterns and what actions marketers take toward them.
52. Interview an individual who is involved in a brand community. Describe the role the firm plays in maintaining the community, the benefits the person gets from the community, and how it affects his or her consumption behavior.
53. Identify and interview several opinion leaders on your campus for the following. To what extent do they match the profile of an opinion leader as described in the text?
    a. Local restaurants
    b. Sports equipment
    c. Music
    d. Computer equipment
54. Interview two salespersons for the following products. Determine the role that opinion leaders play in the purchase of their product and how they adjust their sales process in light of these influences.
    a. Cell phones
    b. Golf equipment
    c. Computers
    d. Art
    e. Jewelry
    f. Sunglasses
55. Follow a brand on Twitter for a week. What types of marketing strategies are they engaged in and how are they utilizing Twitter to facilitate brand awareness and solve customer problems.

REFERENCES

1. The Chapter 7 opener is based on J. H. McAlexander, J. W. Schouten, and H. F. Koenig, "Building Brand Community," *Journal of Marketing,* January 2002, pp. 38–54, as well as information from various websites, including www.jeep.com, www.youtube.com/user/thejeepchannel, and www.facebook.com/jeep.
2. K. White and D. W. Dahl, "To Be or *Not* Be?," *Journal of Consumer Psychology,* 16, no. 4 (2006), pp. 404–14.
3. J. W. Schouten and J. H. McAlexander, "Subcultures of Consumption," *Journal of Consumer Research,* June 1995, p. 43.
4. N. Christakis and J. Fowler, *CONNECTED* (New York: Little, Brown & Company, 2009); S. Clifford, "Video Prank at Domino's Taints Brand," *nytimes.com,* April 15, 2009, www.nytimes.com/2009/04/16/business/media/16dominos.html?_r=0, accessed September 1, 2014; E. Rosen, The Anatomy of Buzz Revisited: Real-Life Lessons in Word-of-Mouth Marketing (New York: Random House, 2009); J. Sanburn, "How Dr. Dre Made $300 Headphones a Must-Have Accessory," *Time,* January 16, 2013, business.time.com/2013/01/16/how-dr-dre-made-300-headphones-a-must-have-accessory/, accessed September 1, 2014; and D. Gilgoff, "Short Takes: Gauging the impact of 'Purpose Driven Life,' 10 Years on," Belief blog, November 29, 2012, http://religion.blogs.cnn.com/2012/11/29/short-takes-gauging-the-impact-of-purpose-driven-life-10-years-on/, accessed September 1, 2014.
5. B. Gainer, "Ritual and Relationships," *Journal of Business Research,* March 1995, pp. 253–60. See also E. J. Arnould and P. L. Price, "River Magic," *Journal of Consumer Research,* June 1993, pp. 24–45.
6. A. Hamilton and J. DeQuine, "Freaking for Sneakers," *Time,* March 13, 2006.
7. Excerpts from L. Beward, "Sneakerheads Share a Passion for Rare Soles," *McClatchy-Tribune Business News,* July 10, 2009.
8. T. Wasserman, "Sneakerheads Rule," *Adweek,* October 19, 2009, pp. 10–14.
9. Based on McAlexander, Schouten, and Koenig, "Building Brand Community."
10. A. M. Muniz Jr. and T. C. O'Guinn, "Brand Community," *Journal of Consumer Research,* March 2001, p. 413. See also R. P. Bagozzi, "On the Concept of Intentional Social Action in Consumer Behavior," *Journal of Consumer Research,* December 2000, pp. 388–96; and A. M. Muniz Jr. and H. J. Schau, "Religiosity in the Abandoned Apple Newton Brand Community," *Journal of Consumer Research,* March 2005, pp. 737–47.
11. Harley-Davidson example from Schouten and McAlexander, "Subcultures of Consumption." MG examples from T. W. Leigh, C. Peters, and J. Shelton, "The Consumer Quest for Authenticity: The Multiplicity of Meanings within the MG Subculture of Consumption," *Journal of the Academy of Marketing Science,* 34, no. 4 (2006), pp. 481–93.
12. Q. Jones, "Virtual Communities, Virtual Settlements, and CyberArchaeology," *Journal of Computer-Mediated*

Communication, 3, no. 3 (1997), www.ascusc.org/jcmc/vol3/issue3/jones.html; C. Okleshen and S. Grossbart, "Usenet Groups, Virtual Community and Consumer Behaviors," and S. Dann and S. Dann, "Cybercommuning," both in *Advances in Consumer Research,* vol. 25, ed. J. W. Alba and J. W. Hutchinson (Provo, UT: Association for Consumer Research, 1998), pp. 276–82 and 379–85, respectively; C. L. Beau, "Cracking the Niche," *American Demographics,* June 2000, pp. 38–40; and P. Maclaran and M. Catterall, "Researching the Social Web," *Marketing Intelligence and Planning,* 20, no. 6 (2002), pp. 319–26.

13. A. L. Blanchard and M. L. Markus, "The Experienced 'Sense' of a Virtual Community," *Database for Advances in Information Systems,* Winter 2004, pp. 65–79.
14. D. M. Boyd and N. B. Ellison, "Social Network Sites," *Journal of Computer-Mediated Communication,* 13, no. 1 (2007), http://jcmc.indiana.edu, accessed June 17, 2008.
15. Statistics are estimates for 2012 from eMarketer.com.
16. A. Lenhart et al., *Social Media & Mobile Internet Use among Teens and Young Adults* (Washington, DC: Pew Research Center, February 3, 2010).
17. B. Thompson, *How to Use Social Media to Improve Customer Service and Cut Costs* (Birlingame, CA: Customer Think, March 2010).
18. *State of Inbound Marketing Report* (Cambridge, MA: HubSpot, 2010).
19. *2010 Cone Consumer New Media Study Fact Sheet* (Boston, MA: Cone LLC, 2010).
20. For additional information and expertise, visit *Site Logic Marketing* at www.sitelogicmarketing.com and the online marketing blog "Marketing Logic," written by Matt Bailey, Site Logic's president.
21. Excerpt from http://consumerist.com/consumer/blogs/sonys-pspblog-flog-revealed-221384.php.
22. N. Zmuda, "Ann Taylor Investigation Shows FTC Keeping Close Eye on Blogging," *Advertising Age,* April 28, 2010.
23. B. Thompson, *Voice of Customer 2.0* (Birlingame, CA: Customer Think, March 2010).
24. D. A. Williamson, "So You Like My Brand on Facebook. Now What?," *Advertising Age,* May 18, 2011.
25. See T. F. Mangleburg and T. Bristol, "Socialization and Adolescents' Skepticism toward Advertising," *Journal of Advertising,* Fall 1998, pp. 11–20. See also T. F. Mangleburg, P. M. Doney, and T. Bristol, "Shopping with Friends and Teens' Susceptibility to Peer Influence," *Journal of Retailing* 80 (2004), pp. 101–16.
26. See R. J. Fisher and D. Ackerman, "The Effects of Recognition and Group Need on Volunteerism," *Journal of Consumer Research,* December 1998, pp. 262–77.
27. See K. R. Lord, M.-S. Lee, and P. Choong, "Differences in Normative and Informational Social Influence," *Advances in Consumer Research,* vol. 28, ed. M. C. Gilly and J. Meyers-Levy (Provo, UT: Association for Consumer Research, 2001), pp. 280–85.
28. See W. Amaldoss and S. Jain, "Pricing and Conspicuous Goods," *Journal of Marketing Research,* February 2005, pp. 30–42.
29. See, e.g., M. Mourali, M. Laroche, and F. Pons, "Individualistic Orientation and Consumer Susceptibility to Interpersonal Influence," *Journal of Services Marketing,* 19, no. 3 (2005), pp. 164–73.
30. M. Gladwell, "Alternative Marketing Vehicles," *Consumer Insight Magazine* (an ACNielsen publication), Spring 2003, pp. 6–11, www2.acnielsen.com.
31. M. Creamer, "How to Win Web 2.0," *Advertising Age,* November 13, 2006, pp. 3, 57; and "How Businesses Are Using Web 2.0," *McKinsey Quarterly,* March 2007, www.mckinseyquarterly.com, accessed January 18, 2008.
32. "New Media Marketing Plays," *AdvancedBusinessBlogging.com,* May 15, 2006.
33. T. Bunzel, *The Best of Both Worlds,* ebook, available at www.professorppt.com.
34. J. Hempel, "Web Strategies That Cater to Customers," *Inside Innovation* (a *BusinessWeek* publication), June 2007, p. 6.
35. See, e.g., R. N. Laczniak, T. E. DeCarlo, and S. N. Ramaswami, "Consumers' Responses to Negative Word-of-Mouth Communication," *Journal of Consumer Psychology,* 11, no. 1 (2001), pp. 57–73.
36. E. Rosen, *The Anatomy of Buzz* (New York: Doubleday, 2000); see also D. S. Sundaram, K. Mitra, and C. Webster, "Word-of-Mouth Communications," *Advances in Consumer Research,* vol. 25, ed. Alba and Hutchinson, pp. 527–31; and A. A. Bailey, "The Interplay of Social Influence and Nature of Fulfillment," *Psychology & Marketing,* April 2004, pp. 263–78.
37. M. Johnson, G. M. Zinkhan, and G. S. Ayala, "The Impact of Outcome, Competency, and Affect on Service Referral," *Journal of Services Marketing,* 5 (1998), pp. 397–415.
38. For a thorough discussion, see D. F. Duhan, S. D. Johnson, J. B. Wilcox, and G. D. Harrell, "Influences on Consumer Use of Word-of-Mouth Recommendation Sources," *Journal of the Academy of Marketing Science,* Fall 1997, pp. 283–95; and C. Pornpitakpan, "Factors Associated with Opinion Seeking," *Journal of Global Marketing,* 17, no. 2/3 (2004), pp. 91–113.
39. R. Dye, "The Buzz on Buzz," *Harvard Business Review,* November 2000, p. 145.
40. G. M. Rose, L. R. Kahle, and A. Shoham, "The Influence of Employment-Status and Personal Values on Time-Related Food Consumption Behavior and Opinion Leadership," in *Advances in Consumer Research,* vol. 22, ed. F. R. Kardes and M. Sujan (Provo, UT: Association for Consumer Research, 1995), pp. 367–72; and U. M. Dholakia, "Involvement-Response Models of Joint Effects," in *Advances in Consumer Research,* vol. 25, ed. Alba and Hutchinson, pp. 499–506.
41. See M. C. Gilly, J. L. Graham, M. F. Wolfinbarger, and L. J. Yale, "A Dyadic Study of Interpersonal Information Search," *Journal of the Academy of Marketing Science,* Spring 1998, pp. 83–100.
42. R. Marshall and I. Gitosudarmo, "Variation in the Characteristics of Opinion Leaders across Borders," *Journal of International Consumer Marketing,* 8, no. 1 (1995), pp. 5–22.
43. See I. M. Chaney, "Opinion Leaders as a Segment for Marketing Communications," *Marketing Intelligence and Planning,* 19, no. 5 (2001), pp. 302–308.
44. Methods for understanding network influences online are still being developed. For one approach, see M. Trusov, A. V. Bodapati, and R. E. Bucklin, "Determining Influential Users in Internet Social Networks," *Journal of Marketing Research,* August 2010, pp. 643–58.
45. L. F. Feick and L. L. Price, "The Market Maven," *Journal of Marketing,* January 1987, pp. 83–97. See also R. A. Higie, L. F. Feick, and L. L. Price, "Types and Amount of Word-of-Mouth

Communications about Retailers," *Journal of Retailing,* Fall 1987, pp. 260–78; K. C. Schneider and W. C. Rodgers, "Generalized Marketplace Influencers' Attitudes toward Direct Mail as a Source of Information," *Journal of Direct Marketing,* Autumn 1993, pp. 20–28; and J. E. Urbany, P. R. Dickson, and R. Kalapurakal, "Price Search in the Retail Grocery Market," *Journal of Marketing,* April 1996, pp. 91–104.

46. T. A. Mooradian, "The Five Factor Model and Market Mavenism," *Advances in Consumer Research,* vol. 23, ed. K. P. Corfman and J. G. Lynch (Provo, UT: Association for Consumer Research, 1996), pp. 260–63. For additional motivations driving mavens, see G. Walsh, K. P. Gwinner, and S. R. Swanson, "What Makes Mavens Tick?," *Journal of Consumer Marketing,* 21, no. 2 (2004), pp. 109–22.
47. E. Keller and J. Berry, *The Influentials* (New York: Free Press, 2003). See also D. Godes and D. Mayzlin, "Firm-Created Word-of-Mouth Communication," *Harvard Business School Marketing Research Papers,* no. 04-03 (July 2004).
48. M. A. Belch, K. A. Krentler, and L. A. Willis-Flurry, "Teen Internet Mavens," *Journal of Business Research,* 58 (2005), pp. 569–75.
49. I. Cakim, "E-Fluentials Expand Viral Marketing," *iMedia Connection,* October 28, 2002, www.imediaconnection.com; see also information on Burson-Marsteller's website at www.efluentials.com.
50. See also E. Keller and B. Fay, "The Role of Advertising in Word of Mouth," *Journal of Advertising Research,* June 2009, pp. 154–58.
51. Rosen, *The Anatomy of Buzz.*
52. See C. S. Areni, M. E. Ferrell, and J. B. Wilcox, "The Persuasive Impact of Reported Group Opinions on Individuals Low vs. High in Need for Cognition," *Psychology & Marketing,* October 2000, pp. 855–75.
53. A. Z. Cuneo, "Dockers Strives for Urban Credibility," *Advertising Age,* May 25, 1998, p. 6.
54. See R. Walker, "The Hidden (in Plain Sight) Persuaders," *New York Times Magazine,* December 5, 2004; and materials on BzzAgent's website at www.BzzAgent.com.
55. See E. Biyalogorsky, E. Gerstner, and B. Libai, "Customer Referral Management," *Marketing Science,* Winter 2001, pp. 82–95; and G. Ryu and L. Feick, "A Penny for Your Thoughts," *Journal of Marketing,* January 2007, pp. 84–94.
56. Dye, "The Buzz on Buzz," p. 140; and J. Lehrer, "Head Case: The Buzz on Buzz," *The Wall Street Journal,* October 16, 2010, p. C12.
57. T. F. Lindeman, "More Firms Use Unique 'Guerrilla Marketing' Techniques to Garner Attention," *Knight Ridder Tribune Business News,* January 18, 2004, p. 1.
58. Ibid.
59. C. Ashley and H. A. Leonard, "Betrayed by the Buzz?," *Journal of Public Policy and Marketing,* Fall 2009, pp. 212–20.
60. K. Fitzgerald, "Bristol-Meyers Builds Buzz," *Advertising Age,* April 23, 2001, p. 18.
61. A. Dobele, D. Toleman, and M. Beverland, "Controlled Infection!," *Business Horizons* 48 (2005), pp. 143–49.
62. "Two Years after Launching Brand Blogs, Vespa Forgets Them," http://blog.clickz.com, January 2, 2007; R. Ford, "No Wrench Required," *Knight Ridder Tribune Business News,* January 8, 2007, p. 1; J. Jarvis, "Dell Learns to Listen," *BusinessWeek,* October 29, 2007, pp. 118, 120; and presentation by Matt Bailey, president of Site Logic Marketing, November 27, 2007.
63. See also V. Mahajan, E. Muller, and F. M. Bass, "New Product Diffusion Models in Marketing," *Journal of Marketing,* January 1990, pp. 1–26; E. M. Rogers, *Diffusion of Innovations,* 4th ed. (New York: Free Press, 1995). For an alternative to the traditional adoption diffusion model, see C.-F. Shih and A. Venkatesh, "Beyond Adoption," *Journal of Marketing,* January 2004, pp. 59–72.
64. *Who Tweets?* (Washington, DC: Pew Internet, 2009); J. Van Grove, "Sponsored Tweets Launches," *mashable.com,* August 3, 2009, accessed May 23, 2011; "Americans Spend 2 Hours, 12 Minutes per Month on Twitter," *Blog.searchenginewatch.com,* January 26, 2011, accessed March 17, 2011; "How Charlie Sheen and Other Stars Get Paid to Tweet," *blogs.wsj.com,* March 6, 2011, accessed May 25, 2011; and "How Does Twitter Make Money?," *Buzzle.com,* accessed May 23, 2011.
65. D. Pogue, "Critical Mass," *Scientific American,* May 17, 2011, www.scientificamerican.com/article/critical-mass/, accessed September 1, 2014; D. Streitfeld, "In a Race to Out-Rave, 5-Star Web Reviews Go for $5," *nytimes.com,* August 19, 2011, www.nytimes.com/2011/08/20/technology/finding-fake-reviews-online.html, accessed September 1, 2014; D. Streitfeld, "Give Yourself 5 Stars? Online, It Might Cost You," *nytimes.com,* September 22, 2013, www.nytimes.com/2013/09/23/technology/give-yourself-4-stars-online-it-might-cost-you.html?_r=0, accessed September 1, 2014; C. Conner, "Online Reputation," *Forbes.com,* October 30, 2013, www.forbes.com/sites/cherylsnappconner/2013/10/30/online-reputation-new-methods-emerge-for-quashing-fake-defamatory-reviews/, accessed September 1, 2014.
66. See M. I. Nabith, S. G. Bloem, and T. B. C. Poiesz, "Conceptual Issues in the Study of Innovation Adoption Behavior," *Advances in Consumer Research,* vol. 24, ed. M. Bruck and D. J. MacInnis (Provo, UT: Association for Consumer Research, 1997), pp. 190–96.
67. See, e.g., S. L. Wood and J. Swait, "Psychological Indicators of Innovation Adoption," *Journal of Consumer Psychology,* 12, no. 1 (2002), pp. 1–13.
68. See, e.g., E.-J. Lee, J. Lee, and D. W. Schumann, "The Influence of Communication Source and Mode on Consumer Adoption of Technological Innovations," *Journal of Consumer Affairs,* Summer 2002, pp. 1–27.
69. See N. Y.-M. Siu and M. M.-S. Cheng, "A Study of the Expected Adoption of Online Shopping," *Journal of International Consumer Marketing,* 13, no. 3 (2001), pp. 87–106.
70. For a discussion of how type of innovation and consumer expertise interact, see C. P. Moreau, D. R. Lehmann, and A. B. Markman, "Entrenched Knowledge Structures and Consumer Response to New Products," *Journal of Marketing Research,* February 2001, pp. 14–29.
71. For a more complete analysis, see U. M. Dholakia, "An Investigation of the Relationship between Perceived Risk and Product Involvement," *Advances in Consumer Research,* vol. 24, ed. Bruck and MacInnis, pp. 159–67; and M. Herzenstein, S. S. Posavac, and J. J. Brakus, "Adoption of New and Really New Products," *Journal of Marketing Research,* May 2007, pp. 251–60.
72. For a discussion of when this is not appropriate, see V. Mahajan and E. Muller, "When Is It Worthwhile Targeting the Majority Instead of the Innovators in a New Product Launch?," *Journal of Marketing Research,* November 1998, pp. 488–95.
73. See, e.g., Chaney, "Opinion Leaders as a Segment for Marketing Communications."

Part Two CASES*

2-1 BMW TAPS THE EMERGING CHINESE LUXURY MARKET

Companies around the world are focused on the huge potential of the Chinese consumer market. Perhaps nowhere is this more evident than in the automobile market. BMW is one of several Western automotive companies currently doing business in China. They have invested heavily in developing appropriate relationships and distribution outlets since their entry into the market in 2003. China is now BMW's second largest market (ahead of the United States) and ongoing growth is expected. Growth expectations seem reasonable since currently only 50 of every 1,000 Chinese citizens own a car and yet the Chinese auto market is still the largest in the world, outstripping the United States by roughly 40 percent. By 2030, estimates suggest that there will be 400 to 500 vehicles per 1,000 Chinese citizens!

As China's prevalence in the global economy grows, the average earnings of Chinese workers are also increasing. Chinese workers have seen double-digit growth in their earnings in recent years. Along with this greater purchasing power has come a desire for more consumer goods and services. Beyond a growing economy and incomes, several other factors are contributing to greater automobile ownership in China, including

- Increasing availability of credit.
- Expanding automobile dealer networks.
- Widespread road construction in rural areas.
- Greater purchase ability due to higher savings (saving is a Chinese cultural norm).

As China's consumer culture becomes more prolific, the newly rich Chinese place more emphasis on status and especially favor European luxury brands. Many Chinese consumers also spend disproportionate amounts of their income on cars. For example, those who make more than 50,000 yuan per year buy vehicles for prices that are roughly equivalent to their annual income. According to BMW Brilliance's senior vice president, 2010 yielded a 70 percent increase in luxury car sales and he expects further growth in the Chinese luxury vehicles market over the next five years.

Tapping this highly desirable market is not without its challenges. Business is done differently in China. China maintains legal restrictions on foreign ownership that essentially requires joint ventures within which technology and trade secrets are shared. In addition, foreign automakers entering China must spend time developing *guanxi,* a form of relationship based on trust and interpersonal relationships. Consider the following comment by one Chinese expert:

> You really have to do your homework and research the kind of connections you want to create and drive them by yourself. Otherwise, you won't end up with the right relationships or will find them too hard to sustain. [Some multinational companies] don't have the patience or willingness to give equal respect to local partners and understand what they can do and offer. Their local knowledge and expertise is undermined and overlooked. That's bad for business and doesn't sustain Guanxi between partners.

Chinese consumers also have their own unique tastes and preferences. In response, BMW has modified their product offerings to better suit these unique wants and desires. Among the customized automobiles that BMW has developed are:

- ***Special edition China-only models***—These have lengthened wheelbases and more limo-like features. Unlike the U.S. market, the expanding Chinese middle class does not favor SUVs, but prefers the luxurious features of European sedans.
- ***Adaptations to regional preferences***—Northern Chinese prefer larger vehicles than those in the South because they associate size with prestige or social status, so regional adaption is desirable.
- ***Electric and hybrid vehicles***—Electric and hybrid vehicles are becoming more popular than traditional gas-only engines due, in part, to China's worsening traffic jams. In response, BMW recently unveiled a new plug-in hybrid that will be built in Shenyang, China, and will only be available in China.

Discussion Questions

1. There is often a natural tendency to assume that in collectivist cultures such as that in China, luxury products would not be popular.

*Part Two Cases are contributed by Carolyn Findley Musgrove, Assistant Professor of Marketing, Indiana University Southeast.

a. Explain how luxury products such as the BMW automobile might fulfill needs even within the traditional collectivist value-set of China.

b. Explain other factors that might be driving the desire for luxury in China.

2. Develop a sample advertisement for BMW in China. Include the major theme, the key copy points, and the visual that you would utilize. Explain and defend your choices based on the case and materials in Chapter 2.

3. Growth in car ownership in China is expected to explode in the next 20 years. This will, for many Chinese, involve buying and owning a car for the very first time. In terms of adoption of innovation (see Chapter 7) for these first-time buyers:

   a. What type of innovation is the car for Chinese consumers who have never owned one? Explain.

   b. The current car owners in China, comprising 5 percent of the population, would fall into which adoption categories?

   c. Analyze the likelihood that such growth can be achieved, using Table 7–2 as a structure.

   d. Do you think the values and desires of later adopters in China will be different from the 5 percent who currently own cars? Explain.

4. The automobile is an innovation that is not as widespread in China as in other countries. Chapter 7 discusses the innovation process and factors affecting the spread of innovations. Figures 7–7 through 7–9 give examples of various diffusion curves based on different diffusion rates. Draw two separate adoption curves, one for rural consumers and one for urban consumers in China. Defend your answer based on demographics, values, and lifestyle factors.

5. BMW and other foreign auto makers are adapting their products to better suit the Chinese market. To what extent should BMW customize their offerings to local tastes and preferences? What are the risks of extreme customization?

6. Developing *guanxi* is a vital part of business in China. Using the text and case, explain how a Western company could build *guanxi* with their Chinese business partner.

7. China is not the only Asian country with a large population that represents opportunity for new customers who have their own unique tastes. Similar to BMW Brilliance, BMW India serves the Indian market and launches certain models especially for India. Discuss factors that make India attractive to BMW. Compare and contrast India and China in terms of the key elements that BMW must address.

Source: "BMW Group," *China CSR Map.org*, www.chinacsrmap.org; D. Lienert, "The Rising Chinese Car Market," *Forbes.com*, December 15, 2003, www.forbes.com; S. Chen, "How China Buys Cars," *Forbes*, July 31, 2007, www.forbes.com; N. Madden, "Winning Consumers in China," *Advertising Age White Paper*, May 1, 2009, http://adage.com; E. Gilligan, "How to Make Business Connections in China," *Harvard Business Review*, January 20, 2009, http://blogs.hbr.org; "Chinese Workers Earning More Pay and Power," *Association for Operations Management*, August 6, 2010, www.apics.org; "China Is Now BMW's Second Largest Market, Topping the U.S.," *www.BMWcoop.com*, August 8, 2010, www.bmwcoop.com; "Luxury Car Sales in China May Reach 1.1 Million Units by 2015," *InAutoNews.com*, September 10, 2010, www.inautonews.com; C. Lee, "BMW Brilliance's Senior Vice President Is Optimistic about Chinese Luxury Car Market," *Gasgoo.com*, January 13, 2011, http://autonews.gasgoo.com; "Earthquake Dents Japan's Chances in China's Luxury Car Market," *Reuters*, March 15, 2011, www.reuters.com; "BMW to Unveil a 5-Series Plug-in Hybrid Prototype for China," *AutoObserver.com*, April 7, 2011, www.autoobserver.com; L. Dian-Wei, "International Auto Brands Thrive by Catering to Chinese Consumers," *WantChinaTimes.com*, May 1, 2011, www.wantchinatimes.com; K. Chan, "China Market a Big Draw for International Car Companies: But Automakers Find That Deals Come with a Big Price Tag," *Pittsburgh Post Gazette*, May 3, 2011, www.post-gazette.com; and J. Kell, "China's Auto Market to Overcome Oil's Rise—JD Power," *The Wall Street Journal*, June 14, 2011, http://online.wsj.com.

2–2 CVS CAREMARK DISCONTINUES THE SALE OF TOBACCO PRODUCTS

According to the American Cancer Society, smoking has resulted in $96 million in health care costs from 2000 to 2014. A well-established link exists between tobacco use and cancer. Public awareness of the dangers of smoking has led to shifting cultural norms, such that smoking is increasingly viewed as negative. Cigarette smoking in the United States has been on the decline since the 1950s. However, about one out of five Americans continues to smoke cigarettes. Cigarette smoking and cancer have been strongly linked particularly for lung, oral, and throat cancer where, for both men and women, smoking has been found to account for half or more of the cancer cases in these regions of the body.

Overall cancer rates (not specific to smoking) across gender and ethnicity in the United States are also shown in the following table.

Lung and Bronchus Cancer Incidence by Sex and Ethnicity, United States, 2006–2010

	Non-Hispanic White	African American	Asian American or Pacific Islander	American Indian or Alaska Native	Hispanic/ Latino
Male	82.9	94.7	48.8	70.2	45.9
Female	59.9	50.4	28.0	52.1	26.6
Total	138.6	220.0	75.0	104.1	124.2

*Rates are per 100,000 population.
Source: American Cancer Society, Surveillance Research, 2014.

One pharmacy company is taking a stand against smoking and its negative health effects. In 2007, CVS merged with Caremark to become CVS Caremark and undertook a repositioning campaign. Beyond being a chain of drug stores, CVS Caremark is a pharmacy benefit manager that works with insurance companies and employers to control drug costs. The CVS Caremark website refers to the company as "a pharmacy innovation company helping people on their pathway to better health." In mid-September, ahead of its October 1, 2014, deadline, CVS Caremark discontinued the sale of tobacco products in an effort to better serve their customers and society. According to the CVS Caremark CEO and president, Larry Merlo:

> Ending the sale of cigarettes and tobacco products at CVS/pharmacy is simply the right thing to do for the good of our customers and our company. The sale of tobacco products is inconsistent with our purpose—helping people on their path to better health. As the delivery of health care evolves with an emphasis on better health outcomes, reducing chronic disease and controlling costs, CVS Caremark is playing an expanded role through our 26,000 pharmacists and nurse practitioners. By removing tobacco products from our retail shelves, we will better serve our patients, clients and health care providers while positioning CVS Caremark for future growth as a health care company. Cigarettes and tobacco products have no place in a setting where health care is delivered. This is the right thing to do.

An essential part of this repositioning is the introduction of a variety of basic health care services within the retail locations, from flu shots to strep throat tests. The shortage of primary care doctors and provisions in the Affordable Care Act has created an opportunity for pharmacies to play a larger role in the nation's health care. The stage is set for retail clinics to grow at a rate of 25 to 30 percent over the next few years, reaching to 2,800 in 2015, up from 1,400 in 2012. CVS Caremark already has 800 "MinuteClinics" and plans to grow that number to 1,500 by 2017. According to Larry Merlo:

> We have about 26,000 pharmacists and nurse practitioners helping patients manage chronic problems like high cholesterol, high blood pressure and heart disease, all of which are linked to smoking. We came to the decision that cigarettes and providing health care just don't go together in the same setting.

There is much speculation over how this change will affect CVS Caremark, both financially and in the public perception. In order to make this change, CVS Caremark will lose $2 billion in annual revenue from tobacco products. This amount translates into 17 cents less earnings annually per share of stock. The company is planning ways to offset the impact on profits such as a smoking cessation program with the goal of helping half of a million Americans quit smoking.

Aside from the financial impact, CVS Caremark is reaping benefits. In the public eye, this move is largely seen favorably. Results of a Gallup Poll of 5,550 Americans over the age of 18 show that the discontinuance of tobacco sales has enhanced the image of CVS Caremark in the perceptions of many consumers. The following tables provide a sample of the Gallup Poll results. The first displays general reactions to CVS Caremark's decision, while the second breaks the respondents into groups based on their level of engagement with CVS Caremark. According to Larry Merlo, "The feedback has been overwhelmingly positive."

Reaction to CVS's Decision to Stop Selling Tobacco Products in Its Stores

	Strongly Disagree (1)	(2)	(3)	(4)	Strongly Agree (5)	Don't Know/ Refused
This decision helps me better understand CVS's mission and purpose.	7%	8%	19%	31%	27%	8%
This decision helps me better understand what makes CVS different from its competitors.	8%	8%	23%	29%	24%	9%

Note: Percentages may not add to 100 percent due to rounding.
Source: Gallup Poll 2014.

Perceptions of Consumers by Level of Engagement with CVS

	Fully Engaged	Indifferent	Actively Disengaged
Are you aware of CVS's recent decision to discontinue the sale of tobacco products (for example, cigarettes)? (% Yes)	96%	82%	80%
The decision helps me better understand CVS's mission and purpose. (% Strongly Agree)	64%	24%	16%
This decision helps me better understand what makes CVS different from its competitors. (% Strongly Agree)	61%	26%	15%
Based on CVS's decision to discontinue the sale of tobacco products, are you more or less likely to shop at CVS? (% More Likely to Shop at CVS)	47%	27%	23%

Note: Percentages may not add to 100 percent due to rounding.
Source: Gallup Poll 2014.

Discussion Questions

1. What type of marketing strategy is CVS using?
2. Chapter 2 deals with global nonverbal communication, which can find application in specific regions and countries as well. Which nonverbal category does cigarette smoking fall under?
3. Chapter 3 discusses several American cultural values. Smoking can relate to individual values from each of the three categories. Decide which of the values in each of the following categories best relates to smoking and describe that relationship.
   a. Other-oriented values
   b. Environment-oriented values
   c. Self-oriented values
4. What impact do you think CVS's decision to stop selling tobacco products will have on (a) its long-term sales and (b) smoking trends in America?
5. The case mentions that since the 1950s there has been a cultural trend away from smoking. Young people today may have different perceptions and levels of exposure to the shifts in cultural norms dealing with smoking than those in other generations. Perform a brief interview with members of different generational groups to find out how perceptions may differ for different age cohorts. Compare and contrast their perceptions and stories of how smoking was normally treated in different periods of American history. Interviewees should be drawn from at least three of the following generations:
   a. Pre-Depression generation
   b. Depression generation
   c. Baby boom generation
   d. Generation X
   e. Generation Y
   f. Generation Z
6. What type of reference group would best describe smokers today? How would your answer differ if you were referring to smokers in the early to mid-1900s?

The following questions are based on the tables provided in the case.

7. Which groups have the highest incidence of lung/bronchus cancer (in terms of ethnicity and sex)? Would this group be a good target market for CVS Caremark?
8. What effect has CVS Caremark's decision had on public perceptions of the retailer?
9. Do you feel that the consumers who are fully engaged, indifferent, or actively disengaged represent the best target market for CVS Caremark? Why?
10. Based on your answers for Questions 6 and 8, devise a marketing strategy for CVS Caremark to market their smoking cessation program to an ideal target market (as described by demographics, ethnicity, and level of engagement). Make sure to consider the sections of Chapter 5 that discuss nuances of ethnic subcultures.

Source: L. Saad, "One in Five U.S. Adults Smoke, Tied for All-Time Low," *Gallup.com,* August 22, 2012, www.gallup.com; Cancer Facts and Figures 2014 (Atlanta, GA: American Cancer Society, 2014), www.cancer.org/acs/groups/content/@research/documents/webcontent/acspc-042151.pdf, accessed September 21, 2014; *Tobacco: The True Cost of Smoking* (Atlanta, GA: American Cancer Society, July 7, 2014), www.cancer.org; M. Herper, "Kicking the Habit: CVS to Stop Selling Tobacco, Sacrificing $2 Billion in Sales for Public Health and Future Growth," *Forbes.com,* February 5, 2014, www.forbes.com; E. Landaum, "CVS Stores to Stop Selling Tobacco," *CNN.com,* February 5, 2014, www.cnn.com; T. Martin and M. Esterl, "CVS to Stop Selling Cigarettes," *The Wall Street Journal,* February 5, 2014, http://online.wsj.com; S. Strom, "CVS Vows to Quit Selling Tobacco Products," *New York Times,* February 5, 2014, www.nytimes.com; CVS Caremark, "About Us," July 20, 2014, http://info.cvscaremark.com; P. Corbett, "CVS Caremark Not Quite Quitting Tobacco," *USA Today,* February 12, 2014, www.usatoday.com; and N. Devorak and D. Yu, "Why CVS May Not Get Burned by Its Tobacco Decision," *GALLUP Business Journal,* March 18, 2014, http://businessjournal.gallup.com.

2-3 BEATS BY DRE RISE TO THE TOP

In 2006, rapper Dr. Dre and music industry mogul James Iovine began an endeavor that would change the face of the premium headphones market. They saw an opportunity to increase the numbers of consumers who listened to music primarily on mobile devices. While listening to music on cell phones and tablets has convenient mobility, most consumers were using cheap plastic earbuds that came with their devices. In addition, digital music download piracy was increasing. Together, Dr. Dre and Mr. Iovine launched a company called Beats by Dre with the purpose of dramatically enhancing the listening experience for consumers using mobile devices for music delivery. Ultimately, the goal is for the listener to have an experience likened to the sound in the record studio. According to Mr. Iovine:

> You've got to be lucky enough to identify a problem where you think you can help. . . . Apple was selling $400 iPods with $1 earbuds. Dre told me, "Man, it's one thing that people steal my music. It's another thing to destroy the feeling of what I've worked on."

After two years in development with consumer electronics manufacturer Monster, Beats by Dre introduced Beats headphones. The headphones are priced from $99 to $450, well above many of its competitors. However, Beats headphones have a unique appeal. They carry the "cool factor" of Dr. Dre and a heavy emphasis on bass. Beats headphones have been wildly popular with consumers, carrying a 70 percent market share in the premium headphones category in 2014. It is also the highest-selling brand of headphones for consumers between 17 and 35 years of age.

Consistent with the "cool factor," marketing Beats headphones has taken a grass-roots approach. According to Mr. Iovine:

> We aren't buying a lot of ads. We market it our way. We're from the music business where you never get a lot of money to market. . . . They're making a beautiful white object with all the music in the world in it. I'm going to make a beautiful black object that will play it back. Dre and I decided to market this product just like it was Tupac or U2 or Guns N' Roses. . . . We sold half a billion worth of product before we paid for one ad.

While in development, Mr. Iovine would keep various designs in his office and would ask celebrities, such as musicians Will.i.am, Gwen Stephani, and Pharrell Williams, to try them and give feedback, which spread early awareness. Co-marketing has been a favorite strategy of Beats, having partnered many other brands, such as HP laptops, Chrysler 300s, and Radio Shack. Beats is also expanding into related product areas, including portable wireless speakers and automobile speaker systems.

Beats also sent complementary headphones to many influential celebrities in the music and sports industries, such as Lady Gaga, P. Diddy, Michael Phelps, Justin Beiber, and Ellen DeGeneres. When the public saw their favorite celebrities sporting Beats headphones, the popularity skyrocketed. *Ad Age* reports that celebrity endorsements have been shown to improve sales by as much as 20 percent. As part of an ambush marketing campaign, just before the 2008 Olympics, Beats sent customized headphones in the national colors to Lebron James. James immediately asked for 15 more and the entire U.S. Olympic basketball team arrived in Shanghai wearing Beats headphones. All this was despite the fact that Beats was not an official Olympic sponsor. As a result of these efforts, Beats headphones have become a fashion accessory in pop culture.

In early 2014, Beats began its own music streaming service called Beats Music. A streaming service helps to counteract the digital piracy issue. Not only do the musicians receive higher royalties from streaming, but they can also connect directly with the fans by controlling their profile, selling merchandise, and updating fans on upcoming events and releases. The music streaming industry is growing fast. In 2014, there were roughly 29 million subscribers of music streaming services, and many more using free streaming services like Pandora. By 2018, predictions suggest there will be around 191 million subscribers. Beats Music provides a free trial and is converting 70 percent of those consumers into subscribers. Roughly 1,000 consumers subscribed to Beats Music daily in 2014.

In the summer of 2014, Dr. Dre and Mr. Iovine sold both the electronics and music streaming businesses to Apple for $3 billion. Further, the paid agreed to work for Apple in an advisory role, while maintaining some equity. Analysts suggest that perhaps Dr. Dre will be able to bring the "cool" back to Apple. According to Apple CEO Tim Cook:

> Music is such an important part of all of our lives and holds a special place within our hearts at Apple. That's why we have kept investing in music and are bringing together these extraordinary teams so we can continue to create the most innovative music products and services in the world.

Mr. Iovine mirrored that sentiment:

> I've always known in my heart that Beats belonged with Apple. The idea when we started the company was inspired by Apple's unmatched ability to marry culture and technology. Apple's deep commitment to music fans, artists, songwriters and the music industry is something special.

This match has much promise; however, it remains to be seen how the corporate cultures of the two companies will align. Dr. Dre reportedly is a workaholic who disregards artificial deadlines, which might cause some friction with Apple. However, like Apple, Dr. Dre prides himself on a lack of marketing research. Apple has also historically had a market orientation, believing that consumers do not know what they want until someone shows it to them. Only time will tell how fruitful Beats and Apple will be together. But the projections show that they are poised for success.

Discussion Questions

1. Please reference the other-oriented, environment-oriented, and self-oriented values in the text. Choose a few of these values and explain how they are relevant to Beats by Dre and Beats Music?
2. Refer to the generation groups and social classes in Chapter 4 and the ethnic subcultures in Chapter 5. With all of these concepts in mind, describe an ideal target market segment for Beats Music?
3. Refer to Table 5–2 in Chapter 5, entitled, "African-American Segments Identified by Yankelovich." Imagine that Beats has decided to target African Americans. Which of these segments would be the best target market for Beats? Explain your answer.
4. Refer to the three categories of innovation in Chapter 7. Which category of innovation do the following products belong? Justify your answer.
   a. Beats headphones
   b. Beats Music
5. Think in terms of family decision making from Chapter 6. What members of the household are likely to play each of the following roles in the purchase decision for Beats Music or Beats headphones?
   a. Initiators
   b. Information gatherers
   c. Influencers
   d. Decision makers
   e. Purchasers
   f. Users
6. Reference the section of Chapter 7 on reference group influence.
   a. Are Beats headphones a necessity or non-necessity?
   b. Are Beats headphones visible or private?
   c. Given your answers for (a) and (b), how has Beats by Dre capitalized on this in the past?
   d. Do you feel reference group influence will play an important role in the success of Beats? Explain your answer.
7. Review the section of Chapter 7 on marketing strategy, WOM, and opinion leadership. Which strategy or strategies of those listed has Beats by Dre used to become so popular in its market?

Source: M. Bush, "Beats by Dr. Dre," *Advertising Age,* November 15, 2010, www.adage.com; T. Fishburne, "The Power of Ambush Marketing," *Tom Fishburne: Marketoonist,* August 12, 2012, www.tomfishburne.com; J. Sanburn, "How Dr. Dre Made $300 Headphones a Must-Have Accessory," *Time Magazine,* January 16, 2013, www.business.time.com; J. Dorris, "Beats with a Billion Eyes," *Slate,* September 11, 2013, www.slate.com; "Beliebing in Streaming," *The Economist,* March 22, 2014, www.economist.com; A. Diallo, "Beats Music to take Streaming Mass Market," *Forbes,* January 12, 2014, www.forbes.com; B. Helm, "How Dr. Dre's Headphone Company Became a Billion-Dollar Business," *Inc.,* May 1, 2014, www.inc.com; L. Johnston, "Apple Buys Beats for $3B," *Twice,* May 28, 2014, www.twice.com; H. Karp, "Apple's New Beat: What Steve Jobs and Dr. Dre have in Common," *The Wall Street Journal,* June 6, 2014, www.wsj.com; and J. Solsman, "Beat Music Turns 7 out of 10 Free Trial Users to Paying Ones," *CNet.com,* March 20, 2014, www.cnet.com.

2–4 HOW SOCIAL MEDIA NEARLY BROUGHT DOWN UNITED AIRLINES

Online social media and social networking are growing at an exponential rate and provide a means for consumers to voice their opinions about products and services. As of 2011, the number of social media users was as follows:

- Twitter—175 million
- Facebook—500 million
- Facebook Mobile—200 million
- YouTube—100 million views per day and 700 billion playbacks annually

It is increasingly common for consumers to vent their dissatisfaction via one or more of these social media outlets, sometimes in the form of videos. Often these videos go viral, meaning that millions of consumers become aware of the product or service failure in a very short period of time. One iconic example is Dave Carroll, a traveling musician, whose guitar was ruined by United Airlines' baggage handlers. United refused to take responsibility and Dave Carroll retaliated via social media. It all began when Carroll noticed his guitar being mishandled:

> On that first leg of the flight we were seated at the rear of the aircraft and upon landing and waiting to deplane in order to make our connection a woman sitting behind me, not aware that we were musicians cried out: "My god they're throwing guitars out there." Our bass player Mike looked out the window in time to see his bass being heaved without regard by the United baggage handlers. My $3500 710 Taylor had been thrown before his.

When Carroll got his guitar back, the neck was broken (despite having been in a protective case). He immediately notified United Airlines. He found it very difficult to find anyone who was sympathetic or would take responsibility for his damaged guitar. He was passed from employee to employee, in person and via phone and e-mail, at several airports and call centers in various U.S. states, Canada, and India. After nine months of pursuing the issue, a United Airlines customer service representative sent him an e-mail that said the airline would not be taking responsibility for the guitar (other than a rejected offer of $1200 in flight vouchers) and would no longer communicate with him about the matter. As noted by Carroll:

> The system is designed to frustrate affected customers into giving up their claims. . . . I told [the service representative] that I would be writing three songs about United Airlines and my experience in the whole matter. I would then make videos for these songs and offer them for free download on YouTube and my own website, inviting viewers to vote on their favorite United song. My goal: to get one million hits in one year.

Carroll's first video has had over 10 million views. Within four days of Carroll's first video going online, United Airlines' stock price fell 10 percent, equaling a loss of $180 million (the cost of approximately 51,000 replacement guitars). After his videos went viral, United Airlines attempted to smooth things over with a $3,000 donation to the Thelonious Monk Institute of Jazz. However, it was too late to stop Carroll from proceeding with his video series. Since then, Carroll has been featured on *Today,* CNN, and *Jimmy Kimmel* and his "United Breaks Guitars" song has been number one on the Country Western download charts in iTunes in the United Kingdom.

Clearly social media can be a means for consumers to vent negative word-of-mouth (WOM). However, it may also be a very useful and positive way for companies to communicate with and learn from their consumers. Researchers at Forrester believe that social influence can be viewed as a pyramid containing three groups. As in any target marketing scenario, companies must manage their relationships with each of these three types of influencers in unique ways to encourage them to spread positive WOM through their social networks.

- *Social broadcasters,* the group at the top of the pyramid, are the few, most well-connected individuals who have many other users who look to them for advice. However, the other users in their network may not know these individuals personally, so they may not have a high level of trust. Other users may consider the advice of social broadcasters about products and services as one part of a larger information search. Social broadcasters dislike traditional PR and want to be respected by marketers because of their broad audience. The best way to reach social broadcasters is through offers uniquely customized for them that reflect an appreciation for their opinions.
- *Mass influencers,* the group in the middle of the pyramid, produce 80 percent of the influence impressions about products and services, while making up only 16 percent of the influencers. This group is less tech savvy and motivated than the social broadcasters, but they influence people they know in real life as well as others. The best way to reach mass influencers is to give them gossip fodder. Giving them content that they cannot resist sharing with others encourages them to spread the marketer's message to a larger audience.
- *Potential influencers,* the group at the base of the pyramid, makes up the largest group, with some 80 percent of the influencers. These individuals have smaller networks that consist primarily of people they know and trust in offline. The potential influencers group is not very tech savvy or as motivated as the other two groups. The best way to reach this group is to give them helpful content that is simple for them to spread to others.

Table A provides demographic information on the users of three popular social network sites.

Demographics of Online Social Network Users TABLE A

	YouTube	Twitter	Facebook
Gender			
Male	101	92	91
Female	98	106	108
Age			
3–12	79	62	67
13–17	173	112	186
18–34	123	153	144
35–49	79	87	71
50+	67	58	49
Race/Ethnic Group			
Caucasian	83	88	96
African American	152	184	145
Asian	156	77	117
Hispanic	168	129	73
Other	98	91	98
Kids in Household			
No kids 0–17	93	90	87
Has kids 0–17	108	113	117
Household Income			
$0–$30K	102	95	75
$30–$60K	95	96	89
$60–$100K	96	98	108
$100K+	105	107	116
Education			
No college	112	108	105
College	90	94	98
Graduate school	88	89	88

Index = 100, Population = Total Internet population.
Source: Quantcast, June 2010.

Discussion Questions

1. When Dave Carroll posted his video on YouTube, it went viral. What American value do you feel motivated consumers to pass along this "video complaint" to others?
2. Of the three groups of influencers identified by Forrester, which group or groups do you think were most likely responsible for Dave Carroll's video going viral? Explain.
3. Based on your answers to 1 and 2, develop a marketing strategy for United to "recover" from their service failure. Specifically, address the following:
   a. What "message" should United be sending to the general public?
   b. What "media" outlets (traditional, online, or social) should they be using?
   c. Develop a video or ad concept that United could place on social media that could help offset consumer anger over their service failure.
   d. Identify which of the three Forrester groups United should focus on with their recovery campaign and defend your answer.
4. Chapter 7 defines and discusses opinion leaders. Are the individuals who create viral complaint videos opinion leaders? Why or why not?
5. Chapter 7 also discusses guiding principles that marketers should use when engaging in social media. How should have United Airlines or other companies who have had similar issues operate based on these principles?
6. Several companies are using crowdsourcing as a way for customers to help solve each other's problems. How might companies harness the power of crowdsourcing to combat instances of viral negative WOM?
7. Besides being a method of communication, online social networks are also innovations that are being diffused. Are online social networks continuous, dynamically continuous, or discontinuous innovations?
8. Describe the typical user of each of the three social networks described in Table A.

Source: D. Carroll, "United Breaks Guitars," 2009, www.DaveCarrollMusic.com; C. Ayres, "Revenge Is Best Served Cold—on YouTube," *The Times,* July 22, 2009, www.timesonline.co.uk; R. Sawhney, "Broken Guitar Has United Playing the Blues to the Tune of $180 Million," *Fast Company,* July 28, 2009, www.fastcompany.com; D. Dybwad, "The State of Online Word-of-Mouth Marketing," *Mashable.com*, April 24, 2010, http://mashable.com; "Facebook.com," *Quantcast.com*, June 10, 2011, www.quantcast.com; "Twitter.com," *Quantcast.com*, June 10, 2011, www.quantcast.com; "Youtube.com," *Quantcast.com*, June 10, 2011, www.quantcast.com; J. Hird, "20+ Mindblowing Social Media Statistics," *E-consultancy: Digital Marketers United,* March 25, 2011, http://econsultancy.com; and P. Laya, "Statistics," *YouTube Pressroom,* June 18, 2011, www.youtube.com.

2-5 RICH, ANGRY BIRDS

Angry Birds is a simple and extremely popular video game that has taken the world by storm. Angry Birds is a mobile app whose franchise is also expanding to video game consoles, board games, cookbooks, and toys. In the game, the goal is to retrieve the stolen bird eggs from the enemy pigs and kill the pigs. Players use a slingshot to launch wingless birds through the air to destroy pigs and various structures that are housing the pigs. If the players complete their mission of killing all the pigs within the allotted time and number of birds, they pass to the next level, where different pigs and structures await to be killed and destroyed. As players progress through the stages of the game, new types of birds and features, such as explosives, become available. Numerous free updates, additional content, and holiday promotions help keep consumers hooked on this game.

The global market for applications, or "apps," is already huge and continues to grow at an exponential rate. In 2010 alone, the global app market accounted for $6.8 billion in sales. Analysts project that this market will see double-digit growth and be worth $25 billion by 2015. Currently over 2 million apps are available and North America produces the most revenue in the app market. However, Asia has the highest number of total app downloads. Of all the apps out there, Angry Birds may be one of the most popular of all time. Angry Birds is downloaded more than 1 million times a day and played for more than 200 million minutes a day.

An executive for the company is exuberant about the app, stating, "Angry Birds is going to be bigger than Mickey Mouse and Mario." A combination of factors has helped lead to Angry Birds' success.

- Angry Birds also received a boost from celebrities giving their endorsement by telling fans that they are hooked on the game (e.g., Anja Pärson, a Swedish skier).
- The company made Angry Birds very simple to use, increasing its "addictive power."
- The unpredictability of the game also lures in consumers.
- The company engages in customer relationship management and maintains communication with its customers through social media.

However, above all, one company executive attributes Angry Birds' initial success to the Apple platform, which is where Angry Birds started.

> It [Apple] has opened up for innovation and given us a huge market. The game itself is made possible by the touch technology, which hit the market at the right time with the growth of smart phones and the launch of the App Store. The key is to offer it for free and reach volume. You need to get the game out to the masses. . . . It is important to continue being number one in the app store. When you manage to do this, the challenge is to build an even greater audience.

The Angry Birds franchise continues to grow and engage consumers by partnering with other organizations and developing new innovations. Soon, they hope to allow users to get special game features as a function of their location. And the company is offering Angry Birds merchandise like speakers in the shape of the Angry Birds characters for assorted electronic devices.

In regard to cause-related marketing, the company behind Angry Birds (Rovio) has joined BirdLife International in the fight to save threatened birds from extinction. Rovio is helping to raise awareness of bird extinction issues through the in-game that directs players to visit BirdLife International's web page to learn more about their programs. Likewise, BirdLife's web page hosts a trivia question about bird extinction that produces a secret level of Angry Birds for those players who visit its site.

Discussion Questions

1. The Angry Birds game is a type of innovation.
   a. Identify whether it is a continuous, dynamically continuous, or discontinuous innovation.
   b. Conduct an innovation analysis of Angry Birds using Table 7–2 as the basis (for the purposes of analysis, focus on consumers who already use mobile apps).
2. Rovio is engaging in cause-related marketing by teaming up with BirdLife International, a nonprofit organization. How well does this cause "fit" Angry Birds? Discuss the impact that this cause-related marketing partnership could have for Angry Birds.
3. Examine the four cause-related marketing (CRM) consumer segments in Chapter 3. Detail each segment's likely response to the CRM partnership that Angry Birds has with BirdLife International.
4. Angry Birds and many other apps are available in numerous countries. What are some factors that app designers should consider when entering into a foreign market?
5. Angry Birds is appealing to young children because of its simplicity and cartoonish quality. Clearly, children are one of the market segments that Angry Birds is targeting. It is involved in, or is planning, such initiatives as clothing, toys, and Angry Birds Happy Meals. Chapter 6 discusses marketing to children and the consumer socialization process. What ethical concerns should Rovio consider when marketing to children?

6. Angry Birds has been widely popular among Americans. What American values discussed in Chapter 3 help explain why Angry Birds is appealing to such a large audience. Defend your answer.

Source: World Mobile Applications Market—Advanced Technologies, Global Forecast (2010–2015), *MarketsandMarkets.com*, August 2010, www.marketsandmarkets.com; E. Ericksen and A. Abdymomunov, "Angry Birds Will Be Bigger Than Mickey Mouse and Mario," *MIT Entrepreneurship Review*, February 18, 2011, http://miter.mit.edu; "Help for the World's Angriest Birds," *BirdLife.org*, April 21, 2011, www.birdlife.org; C. Holt, "Angry Birds Review," Macworld, 2011, www.macworld.com; G. Sin, "Angry Birds Speakers + Stand from Gear4 to Land in Stores in September," *ZDNet.com*, June 13, 2011, www.zdnet.com; R. Kim and K. Tofel, "Angry Birds Seeks NFC in Location," *Bloomberg Businessweek*, June 14, 2011, www.businessweek.com; and M. Silverman, "Angry Birds Hits 1 Million Downloads a Day," *Mashable.com*, June 17, 2011, http://mashable.com.

2-6 AMERICAN BEAGLE OUTFITTERS: APRIL FOOL'S JOKE TURNED REALITY

American Eagle Outfitters is a well-established retailer that is often found in mainstream shopping malls. It targets teens and young adults of both sexes with trendy clothing and accessories. American Eagle is actually one of the most popular clothing retailers in its market. A survey of teenagers revealed that American Eagle has higher "brand relevance" than its competitors, Aeropostale and Abercrombie & Fitch.

On March 24, 2014, American Eagle announced that it would be offering a new line, dog apparel to match the human clothing sold in its stores, called American Beagle Outfitters. The American Beagle website featured pictures of pooches modeling fashions for small, medium, and large dogs. It even launched a "dogumentary" on social media explaining the new line and the idea behind its creation. The dogumentary features two American Eagle employees. One cannot stand the thought of her dog wearing Halloween costumes all year long and another who believes "he's a pioneer as well as a prisoner of his own ambition." According to American Eagle's press release:

> Designed to perfectly match their owner's on-trend American Eagle wardrobe, the canine collection features must-haves such as slimming doggy jeggings, fur-friendly bikinis and statement accessories, creating head-to-tail looks that complement the unique style and personality of every pooch, big and small.

Following the announcement, consumers were urged to sign up on the waiting list for access to the dog apparel and receive a 20 percent discount. Further, for a certain period, American Eagle offered a $1 donation to the ASPCA with each order. American Eagle ultimately donated $100,000.

However, with April Fool's Day just around the corner, many people speculated that the new dog apparel line was merely an April Fool's joke. This idea was supported by the fact that the company would not say when the products would be available or how they would be priced. Further, the American Eagle spokesperson refused to answer when directly asked whether this promotion was an April Fool's joke, citing a nondisclosure agreement.

When April Fool's Day arrived, American Eagle admitted that American Beagle was an April Fool's joke. But, since it was so popular among consumers, American Eagle decided to go ahead and produce the doggie fashion line. According to Michael Leedy, the chief marketing officer:

> We originally felt that April Fool's Day was the perfect opportunity for us to engage with our consumers in a fun, lighthearted way, all while supporting the ASPCA. Due to the tremendous positive response and excitement from our customers for the American Beagle Outfitters line, we decided to make a limited-edition collection for Holiday 2014.

This campaign created a fair amount of publicity in many news outlets, in no small part due to the April Fool's aspect. The company also encouraged consumers to submit photos of their own dogs' style with the hashtag #AEOStyle for a chance to be featured on the American Beagle website. This helped to build engagement with both the American Eagle and American Beagle brands.

Pet ownership has been increasing over the last two decades. According to the National Pet Owners Survey, from the American Pet Products Association (APPA), a record 82.5 million American households owned at least one pet in 2012, which amounts to 68 percent of the households. The IBISWorld report estimates the pet ownership rate to increase by 2.2 percent each year through at least 2018.

This increase in pet ownership is due to a number of factors. While there was still growth in the pet products industry during the recession, now that there is a

Pet Owners' Behavior during Recession (2008) TABLE 

Holiday Gifts

- 81% of respondents purchase gifts for their pups during the holidays
- 69% spend up to \$50; 24% spend \$50–\$100; only 3% spend more than \$150
- 59% expect to spend the same amount on gifts for their dog as they did last year

Trading Personal Services for Dog Services

- 67% would cancel their travel plans if they could not afford to pay to board their dog
- 65% would regularly eat Ramen noodles before they would skimp on their dogs' high quality food
- 59% would color their own hair in the kitchen sink in order to keep groomer appointments

Cutbacks Owners Are Willing to Make for Their Dog

- Eat more meals at home (97%)
- Cancel gym membership (72%)
- Cancel cable or satellite service (50%)
- Curb spending on new clothes (94%)
- Push back plans for home remodeling (89%)
- Forgo buying new car or buy a less expensive model (88%)

Money-Saving Techniques

- 52% look for sales and/or clip coupons before shopping for pet products
- 48% are purchasing fewer toys/treats and other nonessential dog supplies
- 34% have begun buying dog food in bulk

Source: American Kennel Club, 2008.

slow recovery taking place, consumers have more disposable income to care for pets. Refer to Table A for examples of modification of consumption habits that dog owners made during a time of recession (2008) in order to provide the best care for their pets. More importantly, there is a cultural shift taking place such that consumers increasingly view dogs as members of the family, rather than companion animals or outdoor protectors. Many consumers now view themselves as "pet parents" and their dogs as "fur babies." In a survey of women, 90 percent of respondents indicated that they think of their pets as family members. According to a Consumer Products and Trends Survey, pet ownership is highest among empty-nesters, single professionals, and couples without children. These groups have more disposable income due to not having (human) children, and many are looking to their dogs to fill the role of someone to care for and nurture. See Table B for information on activities that pet owners engage in

Survey of *Consumer Reports* Readers TABLE B

	Dog Owners	Cat Owners
Fed the pet human food	63%	41%
Taught it tricks	57	14
Let it sleep with you	55	75
Gave it holiday gifts	55	43
Took it on vacation	45	7
Signed a card with its name or photo	40	29
Put photos of it on social media sites	32	23
Dressed it in outfits	18	5

Source: *Consumer Reports,* 2012.

with dogs and cats. According to Bob Vetere, president of the APPA:

> Pets are acquiring a more significant role in the family, and with that, they are tending to be treated more in human terms. . . . People are pampering their pets more than ever . . . from interactive and innovative toys to dog walking, doggy day-care and pet-friendly hotels, restaurants and airlines.

American Eagle is not the first human apparel retailer to get into pet apparel. Americans are spending more than \$1 billion on dog apparel and many retailers want a piece of the pie. High-end fashion retailers such as Ralph Lauren, Burberry, Juicy Couture, and Kiehl's also offer dog apparel. There is even a Pet Fashion Week in New York City. According to Angie McKaig, CEO of PamperedPuppy.com:

> As more designers come into the marketplace with really unique designs, they catch the eye of someone who might not have bought dog clothes before, people who say to me, "I think this stuff is dumb normally."

A survey of visitors to the dog apparel and accessories site PamperedPuppy.com revealed that more than 60 percent of the visitors owned at least four pieces of clothing, four collars, and ten toys per dog. The APPA has been tracking spending on pets for two decades. In 2013 alone, Americans spent \$55.7 billion on their pets. The APPA 2013/2014 National Pet Owners Survey projects spending on pets to increase in the coming years. The booming pet industry is presenting a growing area of opportunity for American (B)Eagle Outfitters, as well as many other retailers. According to Mr. Vetere:

> The pet industry continues to see unprecedented growth. The survey reveals pet owners are willing to spend money on their pets despite a downturn in the economy.

Discussion Questions

1. Given the unusual circumstances of American Eagle's launch of its American Beagle line, do you feel that this April Fool's prank was genuinely a prank-turned reality or do you think that it was actually a planned launch and American Eagle was testing the waters in a way that created consumer engagement and buzz in the marketplace? Or perhaps you have another opinion? Explain your answer.
2. As part of the launch, American Beagle allowed consumers to sign up for early sales before the dog apparel were released.
   a. What category of adopters discussed in the section of Chapter 7 on diffusion of innovations would the consumers that signed up early fall into?
   b. What are some possible reasons behind American Beagle offering early sign-ups?
3. Chapter 3 describes four consumer types with respect to their responses to cause-related marketing. Describe how each of the following groups would have a different perspective on cause-related marketing and how they would react to the American Beagle campaign partnering with ASPCA.
   a. Skeptics
   b. Balancers
   c. Attribution-oriented consumers
   d. Socially concerned consumers
4. Referring to Question 3, to which of those groups of perspectives on cause-related marketing do you personally belong? Why? Explain your answer thoroughly.
5. Chapter 4 discusses several generational groups. Which generational group do you think would serve as the best target market for American Beagle dog apparel? Would more than one be viable? Explain your answer.
6. Chapter 6 describes various stages in the household life cycle. Which of these stages would serve as the best target market for American Beagle dog apparel? Would more than one be viable? Explain your answer.
7. Refer to Table A, which shows results of a survey in the midst of the recession in 2008. Now that there has been some economic recovery, the results may differ.
   a. Perform a survey of modern-day pet owners asking the same questions. Compare and contrast your results with those from 2008.
   b. Record the generation for your respondents and perform a cross-tab analysis based on those data.
   c. Record household life cycle stage and perform a cross-tab analysis based on those data.

Source: S. Thompson, "What's Next? Pup Tents in Bryant Park?," *Advertising Age,* January 29, 2007, www.adage.com; P. Kennedy and M. McGarvey, "Animal-Companion Depictions in Women's Magazine Advertising," *Journal of Business Research,* 61, no. 5 (May 2008), pp. 424–30; "Current Economic Woes No Competition for Americans' Dedication to Their Dogs," *American Kennel Club,* December 8, 2008, www.akc.org; "American Eagle Outfitters' Canine Collection, American Beagle Outfitters, Goes from April Fool's Joke to Real-Life Dog Fashion Line," *PR Newswire,* April 1, 2014, www.prnewswire.com; C. Brough, "Pet Businesses Will Prosper: Industry Trends for 2014 and Beyond," *Multi Briefs,* 2014, www.multibriefs.com; D. Hirschhorn, "Holy Shih Tzu! Americans Spend $56 Billion on Pets Last Year," *Time Magazine,* March 13, 2014, www.time.com; "How We Dote on Dogs and Cats," *Consumer Reports,* October 2012, www.consumerreports.com; L. Lowe, "See American Eagles' New Line for Dogs: 'American Beagle Outfitters'," *Parade,* March 26, 2014, www.parade.condenast.com; S. Maheshwari, "American Eagle Says It's Starting a Dog Brand Called American Beagle Outfitters," *Buzzfeed,* March 24, 2014, www.buzzfeed.com; S. Maheshwari, "American Eagle May Shine Brightest in the 'Post-Apocalyptic Future of Teen Retail,' Analysts Say," *Buzzfeed,* February 21, 2014, www.buzzfeed.com; N. Ogunnaike, "This is Not a Joke: American Beagle, a Dog Clothing Line for American Eagle, to Launch in Fall," *Glamour Magazine,* April 1, 2014, www.glamour.com; and "The Pet Services Industry Today," *Zoom Room,* 2014, www.zoomroomonline.com.

2-7 TIDE GOES AFTER GREEN WITH NEW PODS

Green household cleaners are gaining popularity, despite an ongoing recession and decline in the overall laundry category. In particular, the green laundry category has seen 50 percent annual growth, which, if sustained, would put sales in this category at $700 million by 2014. Despite a growing interest in the environment, consumers often use too much detergent, which has numerous negative effects on the environment, including faster equipment failure and the need to dispose of it, wasted detergent, and potential contamination of the water supply.

P&G (Procter and Gamble) has responded to the problem of excess detergent usage per load with new Tide Pods liquid detergent tabs for the U.S. market. Premeasured tablets and sachets are popular in Europe but have not yet gained popularity in the United States.

Consumers usually learn their laundry habits from their parents during their adolescence, and such habits are often difficult to change. However, P&G is spending $150 million in marketing for new Tide Pods with the goal of this innovation bringing sales growth back to a declining laundry category. Bob McDonald, P&G chairman-CEO, said, "I think you're going to see [Tide Pods] will return market growth to the laundry category. P&G projects that liquid-filled tabs could ultimately take 30% share of the U.S. laundry market."

However, Tide Pods are quite different from what American consumers have become accustomed to in their appearance, patented design, and usage. They have a swirl pattern of orange and blue in two chambers on top of a larger white chamber within a fishbowl-style container with a flip top lid. The film that packages the detergent is water soluble. Tide Pods are twice as concentrated as Liquid Tide, but consumers do not have to worry about using too much detergent. Tide Pods use a reduced amount of water and packaging, as well as help prevent the problems associated with detergent overdosing.

In consumer tests, Tide Pods perform very well, with up to 40 percentage-point increases from pre- to post-use satisfaction. Consumers feel that Tide Pods simplify laundry by allowing consumers to spend as little time and effort as possible, while providing excellent cleansing and stain-fighting qualities. However, some consumers dislike Tide Pods, especially those who prefer to mix their own solutions of detergent, fabric softener, and/or oxy-cleaners. According to Alex Keith, VP of North American Laundry at P&G:

> There are always going to be doers of laundry who want to be that master chemist. But we know over 70% of women out there are asking for a solution that provides excellent results with minimal time and effort. So some of them are chemists because they want to be, and some of them are chemists because they think they have to be.

In addition to quantitative tests, qualitative tests of Tide Pods are also showing promise. In product tests, women who use Tide Pods show very positive reactions, and some even ask for free samples. Tide Pods will likely attract green consumers as well as consumers who were previously using Tide liquid and powder detergents. This is because Tide Pods possess environmentally friendly qualities while carrying the Tide brand name, which is known for strength and quality.

Understanding the traits of green laundry users is important in developing marketing strategies for Tide Pods. One study found the following demographic traits of mass-market green household cleaner brands:

- Families with children.
- Those who work full time.
- Hispanics and African Americans.

Discussion Questions

1. Table 3–1 describes a green segmentation scheme of consumers that includes psychographic and demographic information. Choose four of the eight segments and describe the likely reaction that each segment will have to the introduction of Tide Pods.
2. Chapter 7 discusses diffusion of innovations.
   a. Identify whether Tide Pods is a continuous, dynamically continuous, or discontinuous innovation.
   b. Then, evaluate Tide Pods as an innovation based on Table 7–2 (use college students as the group of consumers for this example).
3. Consumer tests show that some people are reluctant to use premeasured laundry tablets because they learned from their parents to do laundry differently.
   a. How does this apprehensive attitude toward Tide Pods relate to the consumer socialization process discussed in Chapter 6?
   b. Recall and discuss examples of how your family has influenced your own consumer behaviors.
4. Chapter 7 discusses influencers.
   a. Who are likely to be the influencers for Tide Pods?
   b. How can P&G best target and utilize them?
5. How could P&G build buzz or WOM for Tide Pods?
6. Using the demographic characteristics of green cleaners listed in the case, develop a marketing campaign including (a) a core theme, (b) body copy, (c) key visual aspects, and (d) media considerations for one or more target groups.

Source: "The Proctor & Gamble Company," *International Directory of Company Histories,* vol. 67 (New York, NY: Saint James Press, 2005); *Green Household Cleaning Products in the U.S.* (Rockville, MD: Packaged Facts, June 2010); E. Byron, "The Great American Soap Overdose," *The Wall Street Journal,* January 25, 2010, http://online.wsj.com; J. Neff, "P&G Reinvents Laundry with $150 Million Tide Pods Launch," *Advertising Age,* April 26, 2011, http://adage.com; "Tide Is Betting $150 Million That You'll Like Laundry Pods," *GoGreenZine.com,* April 27, 2011, http://gogreenezine.com; J. Neff, "Can P&G Laundry Pod Breathe Life into the Category?," *Advertising Age,* May 2, 2011, p. 5; M. Murphy, "Church & Dwight CEO Praises, Then Zings, Competitor P&G," *FoxBusiness.com,* May 12, 2011, www.foxbusiness.com; and "P&G Delays Tide Pods to '12, Too Much Demand," *Business Courier,* May 27, 2011, http://assets.bizjournals.com.

2–8 HISPANIC MARKETING IN ONLINE AND MOBILE FORMATS

The Hispanic market is the fastest-growing ethnic segment and bears considerable economic importance. It is being heralded as the last true growth opportunity. From 2010 to 2050, the Hispanic population in the United States is expected to grow by 167 percent, compared to 42 percent for the total population. For many consumer packaged goods, Hispanics are expected to be the sole driver of sales growth. According to the vice president of advertising and sales of Univision, all of the growth in beverage sales will come from Hispanics and the growth in automotive sales for Hispanics is expected to be double that of non-Hispanics. According to Monica Gill, senior vice president of public affairs and government relations at Nielson:

> Latinos are emerging as a powerhouse of economic influence, presenting marketers an increasingly influential consumer group that can translate into business impact. The key is to recognize that today's modern Latino is "ambicultural" with the ability to seamlessly pivot between English and Spanish languages and to embrace two distinct cultures. Understanding how to connect with this unique consumer profile will be key to successful engagement.

Each year, *Advertising Age* publishes its Hispanic Fact Pack, which provides valuable information about the sought-after demographic to marketers in many industries. The following five tables provide insights from the report as they relate to Hispanic use of social media, mobile marketing, and online purchasing.

HISPANICS AND SOCIAL NETWORKING

Tables A and B provide information about Hispanics' use of various social networking websites and how those websites affect the segment's attitudes. Table B details additional information about Hispanic attitudes relative to those of non-Hispanics.

HISPANICS AND MOBILE MARKETING

Tables C and D display information about the mobile platform preferences of Hispanics and the activities in which this segment engages. The activities in Table D are further broken down into generational groups.

Social Networking: Largest Multiplatform Web Properties among U.S. Hispanics by Unique Visitors TABLE 

				Hispanic Composition	
Rank	Properties	Unique Visitors in Thousands	Percent Reach (%)	Percent (%)	Index
1	Facebook	31,463	82.1	15.9	104
2	Twitter	18,892	49.3	16.3	106
3	LinkedIn	8,577	22.4	12.5	81
4	Pinterest	7,394	19.3	12.6	82
5	Tumblr	6,480	16.9	16.5	108
6	AddThis	3,476	9.1	14.4	94
7	Yahoo Profile	2,475	6.5	14.7	96
8	Goodreads	2,149	5.6	13.7	89
9	Quizlet	1,813	4.7	17.6	115
10	Ask.fm	1,504	3.9	27.9	182
	Total Internet: Hispanic all	38,332	100	15.3	100
	Social media/social networking	34,429	89.8	15.5	101

Note: Percent reach here is the percent of all Hispanic Internet users (38.3 million). Multiplatform data include both desktop and mobile platforms and are inclusive of website, video, and app content.

Source: *ComScore,* May 2014, http://comscore.com.

Attitudes Toward Social Media TABLE 

People Who Agree	Percent Hispanic (%)	Percent Non-Hispanic (%)	Percent of All (%)
I am more likely to purchase products I see advertised on a social sharing/networking website.	10.9	8.3	8.6
I am more likely to purchase products I see used or recommended by friends on social sharing/networking websites.	18.3	17.8	17.8
I like to follow my favorite brand or companies on social sharing/networking websites.	23.5	20.2	20.6
Social sharing/networking websites are a way for me to tell people about companies and products that I like.	23.9	20.2	20.8
I sometimes post ratings or reviews online for other consumers to read.	18.2	17.8	17.9
I pay attention to ratings and reviews posted online by other consumers.	27.1	29.3	28.9
I often click on links or items posted by other people on social sharing/networking websites.	29.0	33.8	33.1
I often access social sharing/networking websites from different devices.	29.8	33.1	32.6

Mobile Platform Share among Hispanics TABLE 

Smartphones			
Rank	Platform	Share (%)	Audience
1	Google (Android)	55.9	16,995
2	Apple (iOS)	38.1	11,582
3	Microsoft (Windows)	3.2	986
4	Blackberry	2.5	773
5	Symbian	0.1	38
6	Other	0.1	20
	Total	100.0	30,405
Tablets			
Rank	Platform	Share (%)	Audience
1	Google (Android)	56.4	8,414
2	Apple (iOS)	47.0	7,011
3	Microsoft (Windows)	2.8	423
4	Blackberry	0.7	101
5	HP	0.6	87
	Total	100.0	14,925

Note: Share based on three-month averages ended May 2014. Audience is in thousands.

Source: *ComScore,* 2014, http://comscore.com.

Smartphone User Activities in the Last Seven Days TABLE 

	Percent Who Used This Function in the Last Week (%)						
Category	Hispanic	Non-Hispanic	Hispanic Millennials	Non-Hispanic Millennials	Hispanic 35+	Non-Hispanic 35+	All Users
Camera	51.5	51.6	54.2	53.4	48.4	50.5	51.5
Download app	66.4	61.3	66.8	62.1	65.9	60.8	62.1
E-mail	79.4	82.2	78.7	83.3	80.1	81.6	81.8
GPS	41.3	38.8	42.5	43.2	40.0	36.2	39.2
IM/chat	38.1	23.1	39.4	24.3	36.6	22.4	25.4
Listen to music	37.9	30.2	41.4	33.9	34.0	28.0	31.4
Play games	52.0	50.1	54.5	50.8	49.1	49.8	50.4
Read newspapers/periodicals	17.3	16.6	19.0	17.5	15.3	16.0	16.7
Social network/blog	74.1	69.3	77.1	73.2	70.8	67.0	70.0
Talk	91.6	92.0	91.4	92.0	91.8	92.0	91.9
Messaging	93.4	91.5	93.8	90.6	93.0	92.1	91.8
Visit websites	91.6	88.0	91.0	89.0	92.2	87.5	88.6
Watch/download/stream video	52.2	37.2	58.0	42.6	45.7	34.1	39.5

Source: *Experian Marketing Services,* 2014, http://experian.com/marketing-services. Data based on Experian Marketing Services' Simmons Connect Study, Fall 2013, for the dates of October 2013 through January 2014.

HISPANICS AND ONLINE PURCHASES

Finally, Table E illustrates the purchase behavior of Hispanic consumers relative to that of all American adults. This purchase behavior is further subdivided into the particular type of device.

Discussion Questions

1. What are the opportunities and challenges facing marketers that are targeting the lucrative Hispanic market through online and mobile marketing?
2. Based on the information in Tables A, B, C, D, and E, develop an overall marketing strategy for targeting the Hispanic market.
3. Based on the information in Tables A, B, C, D, and E, develop an advertising campaign including (*i*) overall positioning strategy and core theme, (*ii*) key advertising copy points, (*iii*) visual elements, and (*iv*) key media outlets.
4. Based on the information in Tables A, B, C, D, and E, develop training materials for entry-level marketing professionals (specifically those working for a company whose target segment is or includes Hispanic consumers) to enhance their interactions with consumers and to enhance their selection of media outlets when communicating with consumers.

Source: G. Llopis, "5 Steps to Capturing the Hispanic Market—The Last True Growth Opportunity," *Forbes,* September 3, 2013, www.forbes.com; and Crain Communications, Inc., "Advertising Age, 11th Annual Hispanic Fact Pack," *Advertising Age,* July 28, 2014.

Purchases via Device by Category: TABLE 

	Percent Who Have Purchased Using a . . . (%)					
	Personal Computer		Tablet		Cell Phone	
Category	Hispanic	All Adults	Hispanic	All Adults	Hispanic	All Adults
Apparel/accessories	54.0	59.4	52.3	47.4	36.8	29.4
Electronics	50.9	51.6	51.8	41.5	31.5	20.8
Food	22.3	22.7	32.7	23.1	15.1	11.8
Stocks/bonds/mutual funds	12.9	14.0	19.7	15.1	6.5	6.2
Tickets to movies/events	45.5	45.1	40.8	34.1	19.4	15.4
Toys/games	38.1	33.4	43.7	34.9	17.6	11.7
Travel services/reservations	52.4	58.5	40.2	32.6	17.2	10.7
Auction items	24.0	24.5	26.9	25.6	21.2	13.9
Charitable donations	17.4	16.7	18.5	16.3	16.8	11.0
Books	41.9	43.0	43.7	45.8	14.6	13.9
Music	36.3	37.5	48.0	41.6	23.8	17.0

Source: *Experian Marketing Services,* 2014, http://experian.com/marketing-services. Data based on Experian Marketing Services' Simmons New Media Study, for the dates of January 26, 2014, through February 2, 2014. Base of device owners for each device (e.g., 54 percent of Hispanics who own a computer have purchased apparel/accessories using their computer vs. 59 percent of all computer owners).

part III INTERNAL INFLUENCES

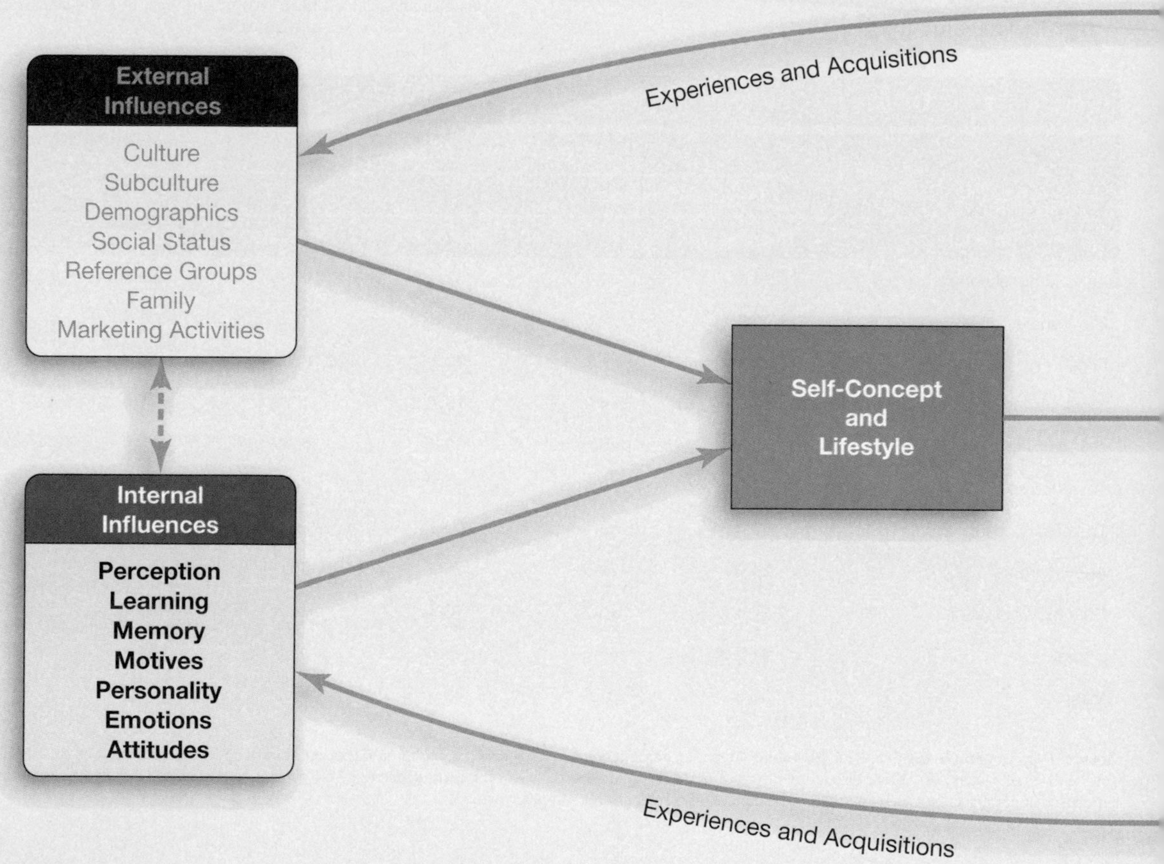

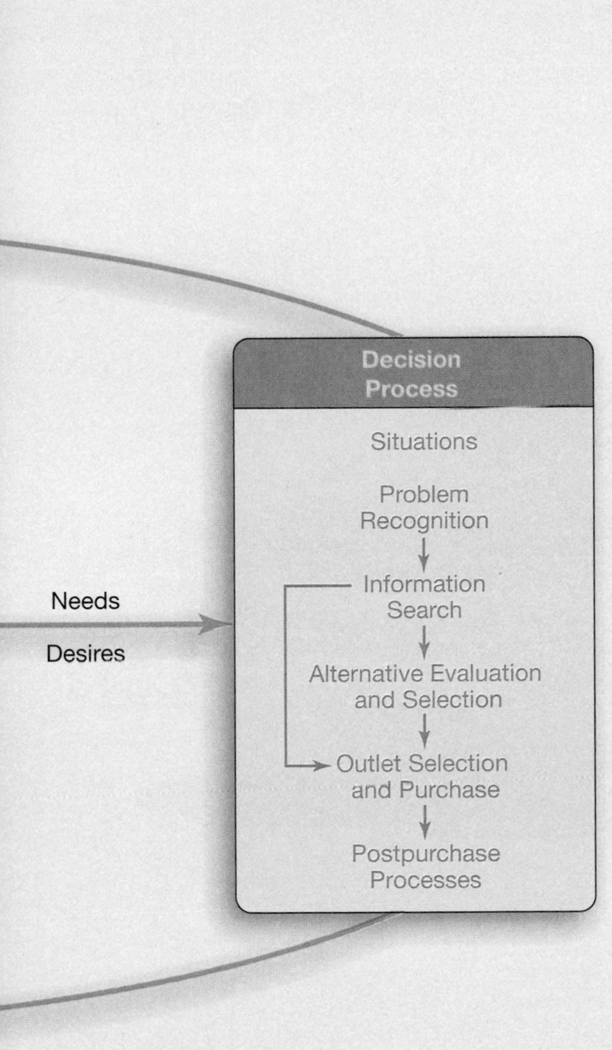

The highlighted areas of our model, internal influences and self-concept and lifestyle, are the focal points of this part of the text. Our attention shifts from forces that are basically outside the individual to processes that occur primarily within the individual.

Part III begins in Chapter 8 with a discussion of perception, the process by which individuals access and assign meaning to environmental stimuli. In Chapter 9, we consider learning and memory. Chapter 10 covers motivation, personality, and emotion. Chapter 11 focuses on the critical concept of attitudes and the various ways attitudes are formed and changed.

As a result of the interaction of the external influences described in the previous part of the text and the internal processes examined in this part, individuals form self-concepts and desired lifestyles, as discussed in Chapter 12. These are the hub of our model of consumer behavior. Self-concept refers to the way individuals think and feel about themselves as well as how they would like to think and feel about themselves. Their actual and desired lifestyles are the way they translate their self-concepts into daily behaviors, including consumption behaviors.

chapter 8 Perception

LEARNING OBJECTIVES

L01 **Describe the nature of perception and its relationship to consumer memory and decisions.**

L02 **Explain exposure, the types of exposure, and the resulting marketing implications.**

L03 **Explain attention, the factors that affect it, and the resulting marketing implications.**

L04 **Explain interpretation, the factors that affect it, and the resulting marketing implications.**

L05 **Discuss how perception can enhance strategies for retailing, branding, advertising, and packaging.**

You may have noticed that brands are showing up more and more in your favorite TV shows, movies, music videos, and video games. This is not by accident. The technique is called *product placement,* and spending on product placements in the United States is $4 billion and growing at an annualized rate of over 30 percent. There is now a whole area of the media and PR business devoted to matching brands and shows to hit the right demographics with the right branded message. One company that has devoted substantial resources to product placement is General Motors through its Chevy brand. Examples include:[1]

- *Glee.* This break-out hit TV show has an audience that trends younger female. Chevy aired one episode where Mr. Schuester, a teacher on the show, is shown driving a yellow convertible Corvette. Such placements will continue according to Chevy, who is also a sponsor and advertiser for the show.
- *Men of a Certain Age.* This show targets older men and centers heavily around Chevy since one of the main characters helps run a Chevrolet dealership and another main character also works there. This goes well beyond typical product placement because so much of the show happens at the dealership. This may account for the fact that their placements here generate 75 percent more recall and 65 percent higher purchase consideration than other placement venues. However, GM also notes that it is much more work intensive than other placements, with folks from GM, the show, and the ad agency all playing a role.
- *Hawaii Five-O.* This TV show hits a broad demographic and Chevy brands are well integrated into the show. The main character, Steve McGarrett, drives a Chevy Silverado and his partner, Danny "Danno" Williams, drives a Camaro. The automobiles are featured extensively in the episodes, as the detectives move around the Island fighting crime.

There are a number of reasons for the increase in product placements. A major factor is the rise of the digital video recorder (DVR), which allows consumers to avoid advertising by fast-forwarding through it. At their best, product placements put brands into the natural flow of the storyline and thus create positive branded messages that are virtually impossible for consumers to avoid. According to Nielson, product placements work best when there is a good "fit" between the brand and the show (think sports cars and crime fighting on *Hawaii Five-O*), when the characters praise the features of the brand (dialogue of this sort happens often on *Men of a Certain Age,* but notice that a character's use of the brand is an implied endorsement), and when an ad for the product appears during the commercial break (Chevy does this as well).

Perception is a process that begins with consumer exposure and attention to marketing stimuli and ends with consumer interpretation. As the opening examples suggest, exposure and attention are highly selective—meaning that consumers process only a small fraction of the available information. And as we will see, interpretation can be a highly subjective process. Thus reality and consumer perceptions of that reality are often quite different. Marketers wishing to communicate their brand message effectively to consumers must understand the nature of perception and the many factors influencing it.

THE NATURE OF PERCEPTION

LO1

Information processing is *a series of activities by which stimuli are perceived, transformed into information, and stored.* Figure 8–1 illustrates a useful information-processing model having four major steps or stages: exposure, attention, interpretation, and memory. The first three of these constitute **perception.**

FIGURE 8-1 Information Processing for Consumer Decision Making

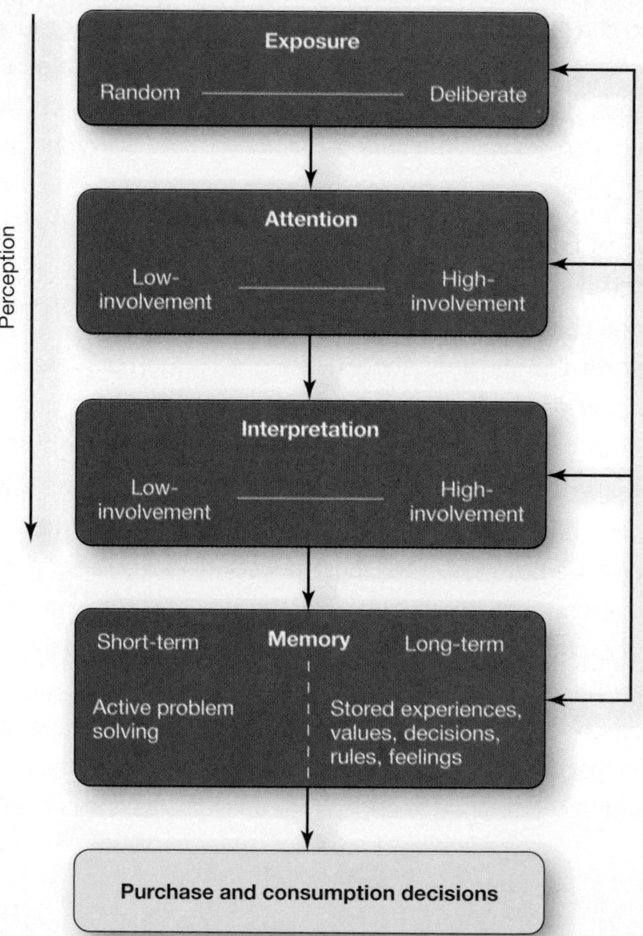

Exposure occurs when a stimulus such as a banner ad comes within range of a person's sensory receptor nerves—vision, in this example. *Attention* occurs when the stimulus (banner ad) is "seen" (the receptor nerves pass the sensations on to the brain for processing). *Interpretation* is the assignment of meaning to the received sensations. *Memory* is the short-term use of the meaning for immediate decision making or the longer-term retention of the meaning.

Figure 8–1 and the above discussion suggest a linear flow from exposure to memory. However, *these processes occur virtually simultaneously and are clearly interactive.* For example, a person's memory influences the information he or she is exposed to and attends to and the interpretations the person assigns to that information. At the same time, memory itself is being shaped by the information it is receiving.

Both perception and memory are extremely selective. Of the massive amount of information available, individuals can be exposed and attend to only a limited amount. The meaning assigned to a stimulus is as much or more a function of the individual as it is the stimulus itself. Further, much of the interpreted information will not be available to active memory when the individual makes a purchase decision.

This selectivity, sometimes referred to as **perceptual defenses,** means that *individuals are not passive recipients of marketing messages.* Rather, consumers largely determine the messages they will encounter and notice as well as the meaning they will assign them. Clearly, the marketing manager faces a challenging task when communicating with consumers.

EXPOSURE

LO2

Exposure *occurs when a stimulus is placed within a person's relevant environment and comes within range of his or her sensory receptor nerves.* Exposure provides consumers with the *opportunity* to pay attention to available information but in no way guarantees it. For example, have you ever been watching television and realized that you were not paying attention to the commercials being aired? In this case, exposure occurred, but the commercials will probably have little influence due to your lack of attention.

An individual can be exposed to only a minuscule fraction of the available stimuli. There are now hundreds of television channels, thousands of radio stations, and innumerable magazines and websites. In-store environments are also cluttered with tens of thousands of individual items and in-store advertising. Even in today's multitasking society there are limits.[2]

So what determines exposure? Is it a random process, or is it purposeful? Most of the stimuli to which individuals are exposed are "self-selected." That is, people deliberately seek out exposure to certain stimuli and avoid others. Generally, people seek *information that they think will help them achieve their goals.* An individual's goals and the types of information needed to achieve those goals are a function of that person's existing and desired lifestyle and such short-term motives as hunger or curiosity.

Of course, people are also exposed to a large number of stimuli on a more or less random basis during their daily activities. While driving, they may hear commercials, see billboards and display ads, and so on that they did not purposefully seek out.

Selective Exposure

The highly selective nature of consumer exposure is a major concern for marketers because failure to gain exposure results in lost communication and sales opportunities. For example, consumers are highly selective in the way they shop once they enter a store. One study found that only 21 percent of U.S. shoppers visited each aisle in the store. The remainder avoided exposure to products in aisles they didn't shop. Consumers in France, Belgium, and Holland are also highly selective shoppers, while consumers in Brazil and the United Kingdom are more likely to shop all the aisles.[3]

Media exposure is also of great concern to marketers. Media are where marketers put their commercial messages and include television, radio, magazines, direct mail, billboards, and the Internet. The impact of the active, self-selecting nature of media exposure can be seen in the zipping, zapping, and muting of television commercials. **Zipping** occurs when one fast-forwards through a commercial on a prerecorded program. **Zapping** involves switching channels when a commercial appears. **Muting** is turning the sound off during commercial breaks. Zipping, zapping, and muting are simply mechanical ways for consumers to selectively avoid exposure to advertising messages, often referred to as **ad avoidance.**

The nearly universal presence of remote controls makes zipping, zapping, and muting very simple. Indeed, existing and emerging technologies give consumers more and more control over exposure to television commercials. One such technology is the digital video recorder (DVR) offered by companies such as TiVo. Consumer Insight 8–1 explores how the DVR is reshaping the media landscape and how marketers are responding.

Avoidance of commercials is a global phenomenon that extends beyond TV to include radio, the Internet, magazines, and newspapers. Ad avoidance depends on numerous psychological and demographic factors. A study by Initiative examined ad avoidance globally and across various media. The study found that ad avoidance is increased by lifestyle (busy and hectic lifestyle), social class (higher social class), and demographics (men and younger consumers).[4]

In addition, ad avoidance appears to increase as advertising clutter increases and as consumer attitudes toward advertising become more negative. Consumers tend to dislike (and actively avoid) advertising when it is perceived to be boring, uninformative, and intrusive.[5] In China, for example, where the novelty of advertising and product variety is wearing off, ad avoidance is on the rise and feelings about advertising are becoming more negative.[6] In online settings, marketers have devised "pop-up" ads that are difficult or impossible for viewers to eliminate. At the extreme, movie theaters now air ads *prior* to the movie because the theater provides a captive audience and enhances ad recall beyond that of TV.[7] Such techniques should be used with care, however, because consumers may react very negatively to such forced exposure.[8] In fact, one study found that many online users are so turned off by pop-up ads that they use software or settings to avoid them completely![9]

As seen in the opening example, in response to ad avoidance, marketers increasingly seek to gain exposure by placing their brands within entertainment media, such as in movies and television programs, in exchange for payment or promotional or other consideration. Such **product placement** provides exposure that consumers don't try to avoid—it shows how and when to use the product and enhances the product's image. Product placement agents read scripts and meet with set designers to identify optimal placement opportunities.[10] While product placement is commonplace in the United States, it is not universally accepted. In the United Kingdom, for example, product placement was illegal until just recently. Moreover, while product placements are now allowed, they must be accompanied by a "P" logo at the beginning, end, and after ad breaks, when there are "paid-for-references." The logic behind the disclosure is that it will alert consumers that the placements are essentially advertisements.[11] *What effect do you think such disclosure will have on product placement effectiveness? Do you believe that such a requirement should be enforced in the United States? What are the ethical issues involved?*

CONSUMER INSIGHT 8-1

Living in a DVR World

DVRs allow for digital recording of programs and "time-shifted" viewing. Currently some 40 percent of U.S. households have a DVR and that number is expected to grow.[12] A major concern for marketers is increased ad avoidance. DVR viewers of prerecorded content skip ads at more than twice the rate of those who view the same content live. And 50 to 90 percent of DVR users fast-forward through at least some commercials.[13]

Other research is more optimistic. Several studies point out that most viewers who zip through DVR commercials still "notice" the ads and, in fact, will stop and view commercials they are interested in.[14] And Innerscope Research recently found that DVR users who fast-forwarded through TV ads were more "engaged" with the ads than those who did not.[15]

Clearly, marketers need to think beyond traditional models as DVR technology transforms how consumers watch TV. One strategy being tested is compressing ads so consumers see a shortened version of the ad, which plays in real time during fast-forwarding.[16] With such a strategy, research suggests that the key is simplicity and having key brand information in the center of the screen, where it is most likely to be noticed.[17] Other strategies now in use include the following:[18]

- *Still-frame ads.* This strategy keeps the visual relatively static for 30 seconds, giving marketers a chance to present their package, brand, and logo and have it visible even during fast-forwarding. *Brotherhood,* a show set in Providence, Rhode Island, used the cityscape focal visual. When fast-forwarded, the clouds move and the audio is made to be quite dramatic.
- *Hybrid ads.* Hybrid ads mimic the show the audience is watching. These tie-ins to shows seem to be particularly effective at staving off ad skipping. Guinness used a hybrid to mimic *Mythbusters,* the show in which the ad aired. This ad yielded 41 percent higher recall than a regular Guinness ad!
- *Interactive ads.* TiVo recently added an interactive "tag" icon that appears while the ad is playing, which takes consumers to more detailed brand information and additional ads. Sony has created ads with multiple endings that viewers select with their remote. Interactivity provides marketers with *more* freedom in a DVR context to deliver relevant brand information and content to consumers who want it.
- *Dynamic ad placement.* DirecTV is now using technology that allows "seamless insertion of household addressable ads into both live and recorded video content from the DVR hard drive." Such micro-targeting can offer consumers ads that are much more relevant to their needs and goals, a critical factor in attitudes toward advertising in general and attention to specific ads in particular.[19]

Beyond such adaptations, networks are also eyeing alternative delivery platforms that would not involve the DVR. The goal would be to have such platforms replace the DVR. CBS did research that showed that many consumers would be willing to accept commercials in return for not having to pay $10 per month for their DVR. This would appear to be dependent on the availability of "anytime" viewing of popular shows and that is just the type of strategy being examined. According to a CBS representative:

> I call DVRs a transitional technology. The DVR will be supplanted by streaming and VOD [video on demand] that will give the consumer the ability to watch the shows any way they want to and to do so in a way that is much more advertiser-friendly.

Critical Thinking Questions

1. Do you think that later adopters of DVRs will be less interested in "ad avoidance" capabilities? Will this change as they "learn" to use their DVR?
2. Can you think of other strategies beyond those discussed that could be used to reduce consumers' tendency to skip ads even with a DVR?
3. Do you agree with CBS that the DVR is a transitional technology?

ILLUSTRATION 8-1

Marketers increasingly use non-traditional media approaches to gain exposure for their messages.

Movies and television are just some of the avenues being used. Marketers increasingly seek exposure by placing their messages in ever more unique media, such as on the side of trucks and taxis, in airplanes, at events, and in video games. Outdoor and video games are major growth areas for advertisers in this regard. Outdoor is branching out in many new ways beyond traditional billboards. Adidas created an outdoor display to launch a new store in Amsterdam that mimicked a shoe box, except that it was 6 feet tall, 6 feet deep, and 24 feet wide! And for the World Cup in Germany, Adidas used a 215-foot-long cutout image of Oliver Kahn (a goalkeeper for one of the German teams) diving for a soccer ball that spanned across the autobahn (see Illustration 8–1).[20] Such outdoor efforts provide eye-catching visuals that are virtually impossible to ignore.

Video game advertising is perhaps the fastest-growing alternative media. It allows for exposure to younger males, who tend to be the gamers and avoid traditional media. As one expert notes:

> Advertisers have seen that young males, specifically 18- to 24-year-olds, are increasingly turning their backs on TV and multiplexes in favor of video games and the Internet. Making the area [ads in video games] even more attractive [is] a recent study from Nielson and game publisher Activision [which] shows that gamers not only accept brands embedded into games but can be persuaded to buy the products if the integration is relevant and authentic.[21]

As a result, the Yankee Group estimates that while ad spending in some media is growing in the 4 to 5 percent range (TV and magazines) and some is even shrinking (newspapers), ad spending in video games is growing by over 30 percent per year and is nearing the $1 billion mark.[22]

Voluntary Exposure

Although consumers often avoid commercials and other marketing stimuli, sometimes they actively seek them out for various reasons, including purchase goals, entertainment, and information. As we saw earlier, consumers actively seek out aisles containing items they want to buy.[23] And many viewers look forward to the commercials developed for the Super Bowl. Perhaps more impressive is the positive response consumers have to **infomercials**—*program-length television commercials with a toll-free number and/or web address through which to order or request additional information.* These positively affect brand attitudes and purchase intentions.[24] And they are more likely to be viewed by early adopters and opinion leaders.[25] This latter effect implicates a critical indirect influence of infomercials through word-of-mouth communications. It also highlights the role that information and relevance play in driving voluntary exposure to marketing messages.

Exposure to online messages and advertising can also be voluntary or involuntary. As we saw earlier, exposure to banner ads and pop-ups is generally *involuntary,* as consumers encounter them while seeking other information or entertainment. However, a consumer who clicks on the banner or pop-up (*click through*) is now *voluntarily* being exposed to the target site and its marketing message.

Consumers also voluntarily expose themselves to marketing messages by deliberately visiting firms' homepages and other marketer sites. For example, if you are buying a new car, you might visit manufacturer sites such as www.toyota.com and independent sites such as www.edmunds.com. You might also register online to receive coupons or regular updates or newsletters about a company's products and services. The voluntary and self-selected nature of such online offerings, where consumers "opt in" to receive e-mail-based promotions, is often referred to as **permission-based marketing.**[26] Consumers control the messages they are exposed to and, consequently, are more receptive and responsive to those messages. Permission-based marketing concepts are also being used to enhance the effectiveness of *mobile marketing* on cell phones.[27] Finally, note that online viral and buzz marketing (Chapter 7) rely heavily on consumer voluntary exposure and distribution of marketing messages.

ATTENTION

LO3

Attention *occurs when the stimulus activates one or more sensory receptor nerves, and the resulting sensations go to the brain for processing.* Attention requires consumers to allocate limited mental resources toward the processing of incoming stimuli, such as packages seen on store shelves or banner ads on the web. As we discussed earlier, the marketing environment is highly cluttered and consumers are constantly bombarded by thousands of times more stimuli than they can process. Therefore, consumer attention is selective. As one advertising agency director stated,

> Every year it gets more and more important to stand out and be noticed, to be loud but simple, and to say something relevant and compelling because there is less and less opportunity to talk to consumers and you can't waste any chances.[28]

The ad in Illustration 8–2 is very likely to attract attention. What factors determine and influence attention? Perhaps you are in the market for a DVD player. Once in the DVD

ILLUSTRATION 8-2

This ad uses stimulus factors including color and interestingness to capture attention.

aisle, you focus your attention on the various brands to make a purchase. However, a loud announcement briefly pulls your attention away from the display. Later, you lose concentration and begin focusing on nearby products you hadn't noticed before. These products were available all the time but were not processed until a deliberate effort was made to do so. As this example demonstrates, attention always occurs within the context of a situation. The *same individual* may devote different levels of attention to the *same stimulus* in *different situations.* Attention is determined by these three factors: the *stimulus,* the *individual,* and the *situation.*

Stimulus Factors

Stimulus factors are physical characteristics of the stimulus itself. Stimulus characteristics such as ad size and color are under the marketer's control and can attract attention independent of individual or situational characteristics. The attention garnered by stimulus factors tends to be relatively automatic. So even if you *think* you are not interested in a car (individual characteristic), a large and colorful car ad (stimulus characteristics) may be hard to ignore.

Size Larger stimuli are more likely to be noticed than smaller ones. This is certainly the case on store shelves where shelf space is at a premium and more shelf space can translate into greater attention and sales.[29] As a consequence, consumer-products companies often pay what are called *slotting allowances* to retailers to secure shelf space. The Federal Trade Commission estimates that companies spend $9 billion annually on such slotting fees.[30]

The Impact of Size on Advertising Readership FIGURE 8-2

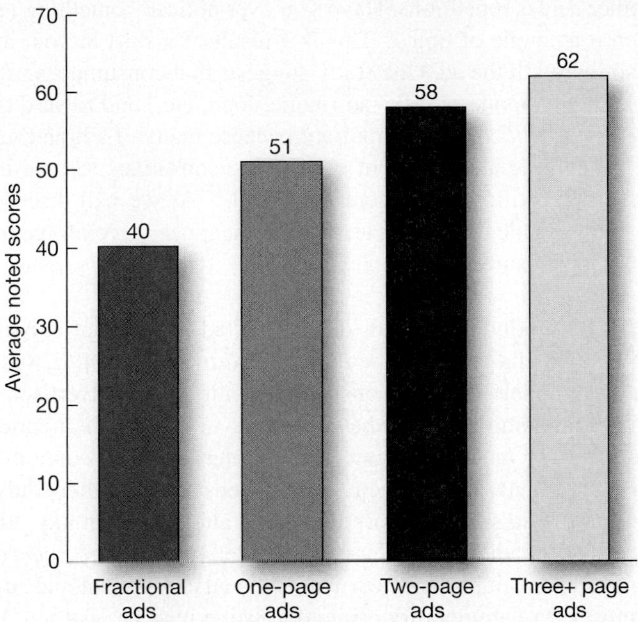

Source: © D. L. Mothersbaugh, G. R. Franke, and B. A. Huhmann 2015.

Size also affects attention to advertising. Figure 8–2 indicates the relative attention-attracting ability of various sizes of magazine ads, with larger ads garnering more attention than smaller ads. Larger banner ads also attract more attention, which might help explain why banner and online ads continue to increase in size.[31] And larger Yellow Pages ads get more attention and have higher call rates. In one study, consumers seeking a business from the Yellow Pages attended to more than 90 percent of the quarter-page ads but only a quarter of the small listings.[32]

Intensity The *intensity* (e.g., loudness, brightness, length) of a stimulus can increase attention. For instance, the longer a scene in an advertisement is held on-screen, the more likely it is to be noticed and recalled.[33] In online contexts, one aspect of intensity is *intrusiveness,* or the degree to which one is forced to see or interact with a banner ad or pop-up in order to see the desired content. A study in which the banner ad was the only thing on the screen for a brief period before the consumer was connected to the sought-after site produced over three times the level of noticing the ad compared with a standard banner format, and almost 25 times the click-through rate.[34] As we saw earlier, however, caution is advised in using intrusiveness because of negative attitudes and ad avoidance.

Repetition is related to intensity. It is the number of times an individual is exposed to a given stimulus, such as an ad or brand logo, over time. Attention generally decreases across repeated exposures, particularly when those exposures occur in a short period of time (intensity is high). For example, attention to multiple inserts of the same print ad within the same magazine issue has been found to drop by 50 percent from the first to the third exposure.[35]

However, the decrease in overall attention caused by repetition needs to be interpreted in view of two factors. First, consumers may shift the *focus* of their attention from one part of the ad to another across repetitions. Have you ever noticed something new about an ad after you've seen it a couple of times? This is a result of a shift in your attention as you become more familiar with the ad. One study suggests that consumers shift their attention away from the brand component of the ad (name, logo, etc.) and toward the text component.[36] This *attention reallocation* is important because many of a brand's features can be communicated through the ad's text, but convincing consumers to read is difficult. The second factor is that repetition often increases recall.[37] As we will discuss in Chapter 9, subsequent exposures, while generating less attention, appear to reinforce the learning that occurred on the first exposure.

Attractive Visuals Individuals tend to be attracted to pleasant stimuli and repelled by unpleasant stimuli. This explains the ability of *attractive visuals,* such as mountain scenes and attractive models, to draw consumer attention to an advertisement. In fact, an ad's visual or pictorial component can have a strong influence on attention independent of other characteristics. One study found that greater graphics content increased how much time consumers spent at an online retailer's website.[38] Another study of over 1,300 print ads found that the ad's picture garnered more attention than any other ad element (e.g., brand and text elements) regardless of its size. This *picture superiority* effect on attention demonstrates the importance of an ad's visual component and suggests why the heavy use of pictures in contemporary print advertising may be justified. However, since attention is limited, drawing attention to one element of an ad can detract from others. For example, increasing picture size in a print ad reduces the amount of attention consumers pay to the brand.[39]

Any factor that draws attention to itself and away from the brand and its selling points has to be used with caution. An ad's visual component represents one such factor. Attractive models represent another. One company found that putting a provocatively dressed model in its print ad drew attention away from their product and toward the model. As a consequence, consumer recall of their brand name 72 hours after exposure to the ad was reduced by 27 percent![40]

Color and Movement Both *color* and *movement* serve to attract attention, with brightly colored and moving items being more noticeable. Certain colors and color characteristics create feelings of excitement and arousal, which are related to attention. Brighter colors are more arousing than dull. And *warm* colors, such as reds and yellows, are more arousing than *cool* colors, such as blues and grays.[41]

In-store, a brightly colored package or display is more apt to receive attention. Retailers interested in encouraging impulse purchases may utilize red in their displays given its ability to attract attention and generate feelings of excitement.[42] Also, point-of-purchase displays with moving parts and signage are more likely to draw attention and increase sales. Thus, companies like Eddie Bauer are choosing dynamic digital signage over static displays.[43]

Color and movement are also important in advertising. Thus, banner ads with dynamic animation attract more attention than similar ads without dynamic animation.[44] In a study of Yellow Pages advertising, color ads were attended to sooner, more frequently, and longer than noncolor ads.[45] Figure 8–3 shows the relative attention-attracting ability of black-and-white and of four-color magazine ads of different sizes.

Illustration 8–3 shows two Konica Copier ads that are identical except for the use of color. The ad with the color was noticed by significantly more readers than was the black-and-white ad.

Color and Size Impact on Attention*

FIGURE 8-3

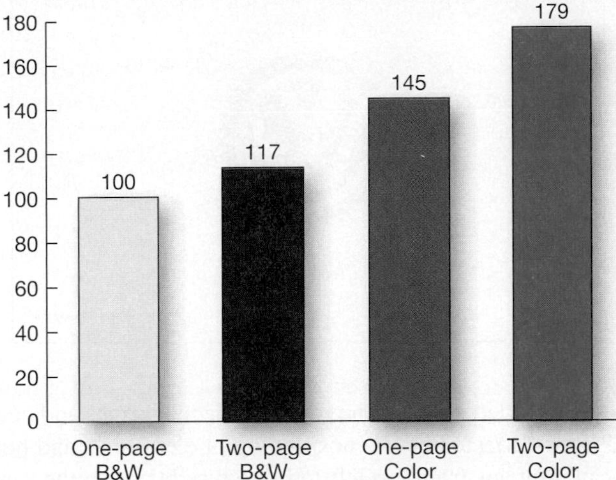

*Readership of a one-page black-and-white ad was set at 100.

Source: "How Important Is Color to an Ad?," *Starch Tested Copy,* February 1989, p. 1, Roper Starch Worldwide, Inc.

Position *Position* refers to the placement of an object in physical space or time. In retail stores, items that are easy to find or that stand out are more likely to attract attention. End caps and kiosks are used for this reason. In addition, because items near the center of a consumer's visual field are more likely to be noticed than those on the periphery, consumer goods manufacturers compete fiercely for eye-level space in grocery stores.[46]

Position effects in advertising often depend on the medium and how consumers normally interact with that medium. In print contexts, ads on the right-hand page receive more

ILLUSTRATION 8-3

Color can attract attention to an ad. In this case, the color Konica ad had a noted score of 62 percent, compared with 44 percent for the identical Konica black-and-white ad.

ILLUSTRATION 8-4

This Volkswagen print ad makes effective use of isolation to capture and hold attention.

attention than those on the left based on how we peruse magazines and newspapers. Attention within an ad is also affected by the positioning of elements[47] and how we read. U.S. readers tend to scan print ads from top left to bottom right, much the same way we read. As a consequence, so-called *high-impact* zones in print ads and other print documents tend to be more toward the top and left of the ad. In online contexts, vertical banners attract more attention than horizontal banners, perhaps because they stand out from the typically horizontal orientation of most print communications.[48] In television, the probability of a commercial being viewed and remembered drops sharply as it moves from being the first to air during a break to the last to air because consumers often engage in other activities during commercial breaks.[49]

Isolation *Isolation* is separating a stimulus object from other objects. In-store, the use of stand-alone kiosks is based on this principle. In advertising, the use of "white space" (placing a brief message in the center of an otherwise blank or white advertisement) is based on this principle, as is surrounding a key part of a radio commercial with a brief moment of silence.[50] Teh Volkswagen ad in Illustration 8–4 shows an effective print ad that uses isolation.

Format Catalog merchants wishing to display multiple items per page often create an environment in which the competition for attention across items reduces attention to all the items. However, with proper arrangement and formatting, this competition for attention can be reduced and sales improved.[51] *Format* refers to the manner in which the message is presented. In general, simple, straightforward presentations receive more attention than complex presentations. Elements in the message that increase the effort required to process the message tend to decrease attention. Advertisements that lack a clear visual point of reference or have inappropriate movement (too fast, slow, or "jumpy") increase the processing effort and decrease attention. Likewise, audio messages that are difficult to understand because of foreign accents, inadequate volume, or a speech rate that is too fast[52] also reduce attention.

Contrast and Expectations Consumers pay more attention to stimuli that *contrast* with their background than to stimuli that blend with it. Nissan's use of color ads in newspapers demonstrates an effective use of contrast.[53]

Contrast is related to the idea of expectations. Expectations drive our perceptions of contrast. Packaging, in-store displays, and ads that differ from our expectations tend to get noticed. For example, ads that differ from the type of ad consumers *expect* for a product category often motivate more attention than ads that are more typical for the product category.[54]

ILLUSTRATION 8-5

This print ad will likely generate considerable attention because of its original approach.

One concern of marketers is that once a promotion becomes familiar to consumers, it will lose its ability to attract attention. **Adaptation level theory** suggests that if a stimulus doesn't change, over time we adapt or habituate to it and begin to notice it less. Thus, an ad that we initially notice when it's new may lose its ability to capture our attention as we become familiar with it. This familiarity effect is not uncommon. However, one study finds that by being original (that is, unexpected, surprising, unique), an advertisement can continue to attract attention even after consumers are familiar with it.[55] Illustration 8–5 shows a print ad that is unique and original, when compared with the typical ad for this product.

Interestingness What one is interested in is generally an individual characteristic. Snowboarders would be likely to attend to ads or shop in stores related to that activity, whereas nonboarders would not. However, there are characteristics of the message, store, and in-store display themselves that cause them to be of interest to a large percentage of the population. For example, in-store displays that use "tie-ins" to sporting events and movies appear to generate considerably more interest, attention, and sales than simple brand signs.[56]

In advertising, factors that increase curiosity, such as a plot, the possibility of a surprise ending, and uncertainty as to the point of the message until the end, can increase interest and the attention paid to the ad. In fact, while many DVR users skip commercials, one study found that more than 90 percent watched *certain* ads because they found them interesting.[57] Another study found that consumers were more likely to continue watching TV ads that were highly entertaining.[58]

Information Quantity Finally, *information quantity* represents the number of cues in the stimulus field. Cues can relate to the features of the brand itself, typical users of the brand, typical usage situations, and so on. This information can be provided on packaging, in displays, on websites, and in ads.

Information helps consumers make decisions. But is more information better? In advertising, the answer is that it depends on a number of factors, including the media used. In print advertising, information appears to attract attention, while in TV advertising, information appears to reduce attention. One explanation is that increases in information quantity in TV ads quickly lead to **information overload** because (unlike the situation with print ads) consumers have no control over the pace of exposure.[59] Information overload occurs when consumers are confronted with so much information that they cannot or will not attend to all of it. The result can be suboptimal decisions.[60]

Individual Factors

Individual factors are characteristics that distinguish one individual from another. Generally speaking, consumer motivation and ability are the major individual factors affecting attention.

Motivation *Motivation* is a drive state created by consumer *interests* and *needs.* Interests are a reflection of overall lifestyle as well as a result of goals (e.g., becoming an accomplished guitar player) and needs (e.g., hunger). *Product involvement* indicates motivation or interest in a specific product category. Product involvement can be temporary or enduring. You might be temporarily involved with dishwashers if yours stops working, but involved with guitars and music your entire life. Either way, product involvement motivates attention. For example, several studies show that product involvement increases the amount of attention paid to print ads and, in particular, to the ad's body copy rather than picture.[61] So the picture superiority effect we discussed earlier may play less of a role when consumers are highly involved with the product being advertised. Another study found that consumers were more likely to click on banners for products they were involved with. *External* stimulus characteristics like animation had less influence on these consumers because they were already *internally* motivated.[62]

One way marketers have responded to consumer interests and involvement is by developing smart banners for the Internet. **Smart banners** are *banner ads that are activated based on terms used in search engines.*[63] Such *behavioral targeting* strategies are available for general websites as well, and they appear to be quite effective. For example, during one ad campaign, surfers on www.wsj.com who visited travel-related columns were targeted as potential travelers and "were 'followed' around the site and served American Airlines ads, no matter what section of wsj.com they were reading."[64] Attention was higher for these targeted ads, as was brand and message recall.

Ability *Ability* refers to the capacity of individuals to attend to and process information. Ability is related to knowledge and familiarity with the product, brand, or promotion. An audiophile, for example, is more capable of attending to highly detailed product information about stereo equipment than a novice. As a consequence, experts can attend to more information, more quickly and more effectively, than novices can and tend to be less plagued by information overload. One study found that consumers with higher education and greater health-related experience were more likely to pay attention to the highly detailed technical information in "direct-to-consumer" pharmaceutical ads.[65]

Brand familiarity is an ability factor related to attention. Those with high brand familiarity may require less attention to the brand's ads because of their high existing knowledge. For example, one exposure appears to be all that is needed to capture attention and generate click-through with banner ads when brand familiarity is high. In contrast, the click-through rate is very low on the first exposure when brand familiarity is low, but increases dramatically on the fifth exposure.[66] Consumers with low brand familiarity appear to require more banner attention to yield the knowledge and trust needed to drive further attention via click-through to the site.

Situational Factors

Situational factors include stimuli in the environment other than the focal stimulus (i.e., the ad or package) and temporary characteristics of the individual that are induced by the environment, such as time pressures or a crowded store. Clutter and program involvement are two major situational factors affecting attention.

Clutter *Clutter* represents the density of stimuli in the environment. In-store research suggests that cluttering the environment with too many point-of-purchase displays decreases the attention consumers pay to a given display. This explains why companies such as Walmart have made a concerted effort to reduce the number of displays in their stores.[67] In advertising, consumers pay less attention to a commercial in a large cluster of commercials than they do to one in a smaller set.[68] You may have noticed cable channels moving more to a single-sponsor format and actually promoting the fact that their programs will have fewer commercials!

Program Involvement *Program involvement* refers to how interested viewers are in the program or editorial content surrounding the ads (as opposed to involvement with the ad or brand). In general, the audience is attending to the medium because of the program or editorial content, not the advertisement. So the question remains: Does involvement with the program or editorial content influence attention to the ad? The answer is clearly yes, in a positive direction, as demonstrated by Figure 8–4.

However, research shows that even when program involvement is low, marketers can increase attention by enhancing the quality of the ad itself. *Ad quality* represents how well a message is constructed in terms of being believable and appealing, and in communicating the core message effectively.[69]

Nonfocused Attention

Thus far we have been discussing a fairly high-involvement attention process in which the consumer focuses attention on some aspect of the environment as a result of stimulus, individual, or situational factors. However, stimuli may be attended to without deliberate or conscious focusing of attention. A classic example is the *cocktail party effect,* whereby an individual engaged in a conversation with a friend isn't consciously aware of other conversations at a crowded party until someone in another group says something relevant such as mentioning her name. This example suggests we are processing a host of stimuli at a subconscious level, and mechanisms in our brain evaluate this information to decide what warrants deliberate and conscious attention.[70] In fact, the idea behind *hemispheric lateralization* is that different parts of our brain are better suited for focused versus nonfocused attention.

Hemispheric Lateralization **Hemispheric lateralization** is a term applied to activities that take place on each side of the brain. The left side of the brain is primarily responsible for verbal information, symbolic representation, sequential analysis, and the ability

Involvement with a Magazine and Advertising Effectiveness

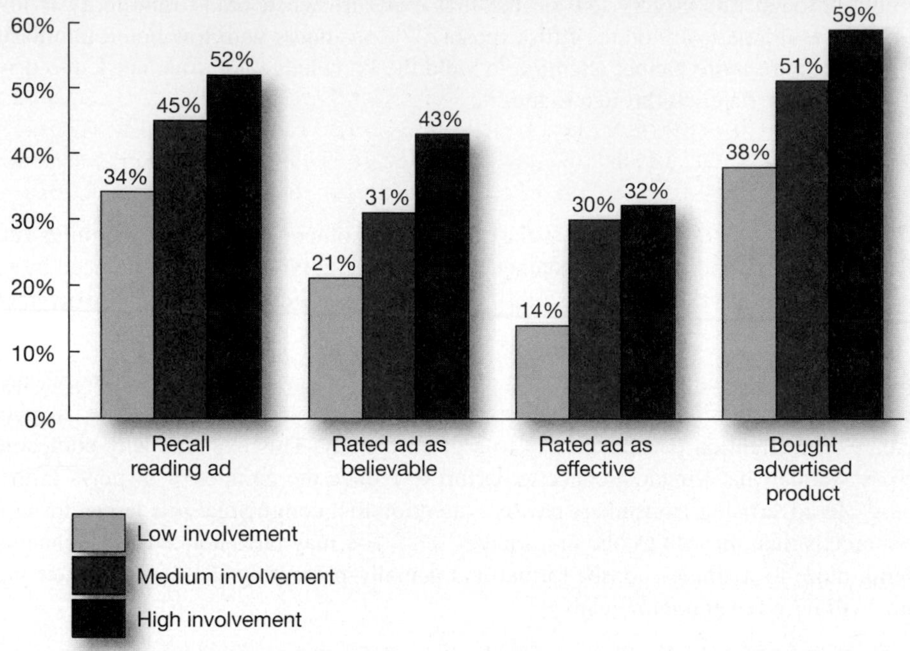

Source: *Cahners Advertising Research Report 120.1 and 120.12* (Boston: Cahners Publishing, undated).

to be conscious and report what is happening. It controls those activities we typically call *rational thought.* The right side of the brain deals with pictorial, geometric, timeless, and nonverbal information without the individual being able to verbally report it. It works with images and impressions.

The left brain needs fairly frequent rest. However, the right brain can easily scan large amounts of information over an extended time period. This led Krugman to suggest that "it is the right brain's picture-taking ability that permits the rapid screening of the environment—to select what it is the left brain should focus on."[71] One study of banner ads found evidence of preconscious screening. Web surfers seem able to spot a banner ad without actually looking directly at it. As a consequence, direct attention to banner ads occurred only 49 percent of the time. It seems that experience with the web allows consumers to build up knowledge about banner characteristics (typical size and location) that is used to avoid direct attention.[72]

However, just because consumers don't pay direct attention to an advertisement doesn't mean it can't influence them. For example, brands contained in ads to which subjects are exposed but pay little or no attention (incidental exposure) nonetheless are more likely to be considered for purchase.[73]

Subliminal Stimuli A message presented so fast or so softly or so masked by other messages that one is not aware of seeing or hearing it is called a **subliminal stimulus.** A subliminal ad is different from a "normal" ad in that it "hides" key persuasive information within the ad by making it so weak that it is difficult or impossible for an individual to physically detect. Normal ads present key persuasive information to consumers so that it is easily perceived.

Subliminal advertising has been the focus of intense study and public concern. It's one thing for consumers to decide not to pay attention to an ad. It's quite another for advertisers to try to bypass consumers' perceptual defenses by using subliminal stimuli.

Two books triggered public interest in masked subliminal advertising.[74] The author "documents" numerous advertisements that, once you are told where to look and what to look for, appear to contain the word *sex* in ice cubes, phalli in mixed drinks, and nude bodies in the shadows. Such masked symbols, deliberate or accidental, do not appear to affect standard measures of advertising effectiveness or influence consumption behavior. Likewise, research on messages presented too rapidly to elicit awareness indicates that such messages have little or no effect.[75] In addition, there is no evidence marketers are using subliminal messages.[76]

INTERPRETATION

LO4

Interpretation is *the assignment of meaning to sensations.* Interpretation is related to how we comprehend and make sense of incoming information based on characteristics of the stimulus, the individual, and the situation.

Several aspects of interpretation are important to consider. First, it is generally a relative process rather than absolute, often referred to as **perceptual relativity.** It is often difficult for people to make interpretations in the absence of some reference point. Consider the following actual scenario:

> An episode of QVC Network's *Extreme Shopping* program offers Muhammad Ali's boxing robe (priced at over $12,000), followed by Jane Mansfield's former mansion (almost $3.5 million), and a Volkswagen Beetle painted by Peter Max ($100,000). Then, signed and personalized Peter Max prints were offered for about $200.

In line with the notion of relativity, consumers interpreted the print price as lower when it followed the higher-priced items.[77]

A second aspect of interpretation is that it tends to be subjective and open to a host of psychological biases. The subjective nature of interpretation can be seen in the distinction between *semantic meaning,* the conventional meaning assigned to a word such as found in the dictionary, and *psychological meaning,* the specific meaning assigned a word by a given individual or group of individuals based on their experiences, their expectations, and the context in which the term is used.

Marketers must be concerned with psychological meaning as it is the subjective experience, not objective reality, that drives consumer behavior. A firm may introduce a high-quality new brand at a lower price than competitors because the firm is more efficient. However, if consumers interpret the lower price to mean lower quality (and they often do), the new brand will not be successful regardless of the objective reality.[78]

A final aspect of interpretation is that it can be a cognitive "thinking" process or an affective "emotional" process. **Cognitive interpretation** is *a process whereby stimuli are placed into existing categories of meaning.*[79] As we saw earlier, ads are categorized as expected or unexpected, a process that can vary by culture and individual.[80] In countries like France where ads are more sexually explicit, nudity may be seen as more appropriate than in the United States. Products are also categorized. When DVD players were first introduced, most consumers probably grouped them in the same category as VCRs, but with further experience put them in separate categories. Radically "new" products (discontinuous innovation) are the most difficult to categorize, and marketers need to provide consumers with assistance to gain understanding and acceptance.[81]

ILLUSTRATION 8-6

Consumers have emotional responses to or interpretations of ads as well as cognitive ones. This ad is likely to produce an emotional or feeling response in many members of its target audience.

Affective interpretation is *the emotional or feeling response triggered by a stimulus such as an ad.* Emotional responses can range from positive (upbeat, exciting, warm) to neutral (disinterested) to negative (anger, fear, frustration). Like cognitive interpretation, there are "normal" (within-culture) emotional responses to many stimuli (e.g., most Americans experience a feeling of warmth when seeing pictures of young children with kittens). Likewise, there are also individual variations to this response (a person allergic to cats might have a negative emotional response to such a picture). Consumers confronting new products or brands often assign them to emotional as well as cognitive categories.[82] The ad shown in Illustration 8–6 is likely to trigger an emotional interpretation as well as a cognitive one.

Consumer Insight 8–2 deals with the issue of how consumers deal with multiple cues simultaneously in interpreting a brand, service, or experience, and how marketers are tapping into the skills of specialists called *synners* to help them design appropriate multifaceted "cue sets."

Individual Characteristics

Marketing stimuli have meaning *only* as individuals interpret them.[83] Individuals are not passive interpreters of marketing and other messages but actively assign meaning based on their needs, desires, experiences, and expectations.

Traits Inherent physiological and psychological traits, which drive our needs and desires, influence how a stimulus is interpreted. From a *physiological* standpoint, consumers differ in their sensitivity to stimuli. Some children are more sensitive to the bitter taste of certain chemicals found in green, leafy vegetables such as spinach.[84] Tab (a diet cola containing

CONSUMER INSIGHT 8-2

I Smell Orange, I Taste Blue, I Feel Silver, I Hear Squiggles

The critical importance of cues—brand name, logo, sound, packaging, color, font, smell, feel, taste—to product perception, and particularly interpretation, is widely accepted by marketers. Companies spend heavily to develop the right brand names and design the right logos to communicate who they are, what they stand for, what they promise—in some cases, cleverly so, with special messages—the arrow in FedEx, the kiss in Hershey's kisses, the 31 in Baskin Robbins 31 flavors.[85]

Microsoft's understanding of the importance of sound to its brand led it to use many musicians from around the world to compose the "inspiring, universal, optimistic, futuristic, sentimental, sexy, emotional . . ." musical notes for a new system launch. Intel's use of the four note "Intel bong" is so well known that consumers can sing it on request. Harley-Davidson deemed the sound of its HOG engine to be so important to its identity that it sought, although unsuccessfully, to trademark it.

Each cue is a part that together creates the perception of the whole product. Marketers know that the whole is more than the sum of its parts, but understanding how all the parts fit together is challenging. This is where synners, as people with synesthesia call themselves, come in. Synners have a neurological condition that crosses two or more senses—letters have colors, sounds have tastes—and puts them in a particularly good position to evaluate how the parts interact and contribute to the whole. An estimated one out of 27 people is a synner, including musician John Mayer, Nobel laureate physicist Richard Feynman, and rapper Kanye West. As a group, synners appear to have better memories and score higher on tests of creativity.

Marketers have come to appreciate synners' unique potential and have begun to incorporate their input into product planning and design. Ford Motor Co., for example, recently created the custom position *specialist in cross-sensory harmonization* for one of its engineers who is a synner. As his job title implies, he is responsible for working with the designers and engineers to coordinate the parts of the car—sound, look, feel, smell—into a harmonizing whole that Ford wants consumers to have of its cars.

Marketing attention afforded to synners reflects the increased usage of multisensory marketing to carve out brand image in a world of ever greater competition for consumer attention. This is one reason, for example, that organizations such as Zappos (e-tailer of clothing and shoes renowned for its customer care) are conducting workshops to expose their employees to an appreciation of consumer experiences with a multisensory consideration. Of course, there have been previous instances of multisensory marketing—Skittles' tagline "Taste the Rainbow"—but these were scattered. What we are witnessing now is a more focused, defined, and formal strategy that recognizes the potential of synners. Some synners are not waiting for incumbent firms to recognize their potential and have formed their own businesses such as 12.29, an olfactory branding firm founded by two synners that helps hotels, banks, and fashion runways choose the right scent.

Critical Thinking Questions

1. Did you know about the insider messages in the FedEx, Hershey's and Baskin-Robbins logos? Do you know of any others?
2. What sensory cues do you strongly associate with brands? Stores?
3. When the cues are at odds with one another, consumers get mixed messages that can lead to confusion and declines in sales (e.g., Pepsi Crystal's taste was cola, but its color was like water). What are other products that flopped because of the mismatch of cues?

ILLUSTRATION 8-7

Colors often have learned associations that are used in ads to convey product characteristics and meanings.

saccharine) maintains a small but fiercely loyal customer base, most likely among those who (unlike most of us) don't physiologically perceive saccharine as bitter.

From a *psychological* standpoint, consumers have natural cognitive, emotional, and behavioral predispositions. As just one example, some people experience emotions more strongly than others, a trait known as *affect intensity.* A number of studies have found that consumers who are higher in affect intensity experience stronger emotional reactions to any given advertisement.[86] We discuss other personality differences in Chapter 10.

Learning and Knowledge The meanings attached to such "natural" things as time, space, relationships, and colors are learned and vary widely across cultures, as we saw in Chapter 2. Consumers also learn about marketer-created stimuli like brands and promotions through their experiences with them. This experience and knowledge affect interpretations. One general finding is that consumers tend to interpret information in ways that favor their preferred brands. In one study, those higher in loyalty to a firm tended to discredit negative publicity about the firm and thus were less affected by it.[87] Similarly, another study found that consumers infer more positive motives from a company's price increase if the company has a strong reputation.[88]

The ad in Illustration 8–7 uses color to reinforce an interpretation that consumers have learned. *What meanings are associated with the colors in Illustration 8–7?*

Expectations Individuals' interpretations of stimuli tend to be consistent with their *expectations,* an effect referred to as the *expectation bias.* Most consumers expect dark brown pudding to taste like chocolate, not vanilla, because dark pudding is generally chocolate flavored and vanilla pudding is generally cream colored. In a taste test, 100 percent of a sample of college students accepted dark brown *vanilla* pudding as chocolate.[89] Thus, their expectations, cued by color, led to an interpretation that was inconsistent with objective reality.

Consumers' expectations are the result of learning and can be formed very quickly, as the old saying "first impressions matter" suggests. Once established, these expectations can wield enormous influence[90] and can be hard to change. Many consumers expect, for example, that well-known brands are higher quality. As a consequence, consumers frequently evaluate the performance of a well-known brand as higher than that of an *identical* product with an unknown brand name. Many consumers have also come to expect that brands with some sort of in-store signage are on sale. As a consequence, one study found that brands with promotional signs on them in retail stores are interpreted as having reduced prices even though the signs don't indicate a price reduction and the prices aren't actually reduced.[91]

Situational Characteristics

A variety of situational characteristics have an impact on interpretation, including temporary characteristics of the individual, such as time pressure and mood,[92] and physical characteristics of the situation, such as the number and characteristics of other individuals present and the nature of the material surrounding the message in question.

Basically, the situation provides a context within which the focal stimulus is interpreted. The **contextual cues** present in the situation play a role in consumer interpretation *independent* of the actual stimulus. There are innumerable contextual cues in any given marketing context—here we examine just a few examples. *Color* can be a contextual cue. A recent study of online advertising examined various aspects of background color present during web page loads. Certain color characteristics were found to elicit feelings of relaxation (blue was more relaxing than red) and these feelings increased perceptions of faster web page loading even when actual speeds were identical.[93]

The *nature of the programming* surrounding a brand's advertisements can also be a contextual cue. Both Coca-Cola and General Foods have refused to advertise some products during news broadcasts because they believe that "bad" news might affect the interpretation of their products. According to a Coca-Cola spokesperson:

> It's a Coca-Cola corporate policy not to advertise on TV news because there's going to be some bad news in there, and Coke is an upbeat, fun product.[94]

The previous example expresses a concern about the impact that the content of the material surrounding an ad will have on the interpretation of the ad. As Coca-Cola suspects, it appears that ads are evaluated in a more positive light when surrounded with positive programming.[95] In addition, effects can be even more specific and have implications for marketing globally. Research finds that death-related content, which is prevalent in news programming, cues consumer thoughts of patriotism and thus increases consumer preferences for domestic versus foreign brands. Foreign brands can overcome this, however, with pro-domestic claims.[96]

Stimulus Characteristics

The stimulus is the basic entity to which an individual responds and includes the product, package, advertisement, in-store display, and so on. Consumers react to and interpret basic traits of the stimulus (size, shape, color), the way the stimulus is organized, and changes in the stimulus. As we have seen, all these processes are likely to be heavily influenced by the individual and the situation.

Traits Specific traits of the stimulus, such as size, shape, and color, affect interpretation. The meaning of many stimulus traits is learned. Color is one trait in which learning

ILLUSTRATION 8-8

Consumers are exposed to many more ads than they can read or even notice. Marketers often use rhetorical figures to capture the audience's attention.

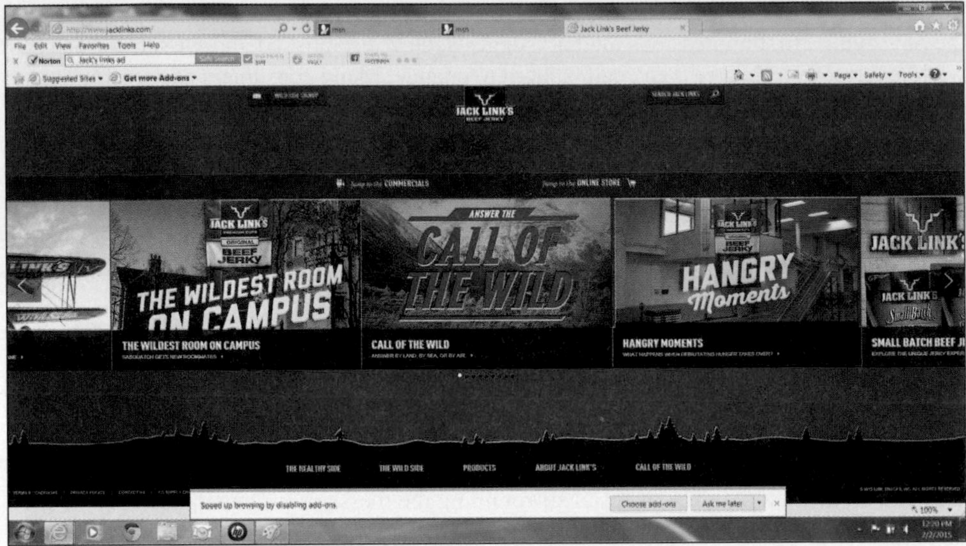

affects meaning. Canada Dry's sugar-free ginger ale sales increased dramatically when the can was changed to green and white from red. Red is interpreted as a "cola" color and thus conflicted with the taste of ginger ale.[97] White space in ads is another trait involving learned meaning. That is, over time consumers have come to believe that white space in an ad means prestige, high price, and quality. As a consequence, marketers can positively influence product perceptions by what they *don't* say in an ad![98]

Another general trait is the extent to which the stimulus is unexpected, a trait sometimes referred to as *incongruity*. Incongruity increases attention, as we saw earlier. However, it also increases liking, in part because of the pleasure consumers derive from "solving the puzzle" presented by the incongruity. As a consequence, products and ads that deviate somewhat from established norms (without going too far) are often better liked. Incongruity often requires that consumers go beyond what is directly stated or presented in order to make sense of the stimulus. These inferences, which we discuss later in the chapter, are an important part of interpretation. Rhetorical figures such as rhymes, puns, and metaphors have been shown to increase consumer attention and influence their feelings and perceptions of the brand. **Rhetorical figures** *involve the use of an unexpected twist or artful deviation in how a message is communicated either visually in the ad's picture or verbally in the ad's text or headline.*[99] Illustration 8–8 provides an example of how Jack Link's® uses Rhetorical Figures in their promotions to grab attention.

Organization **Stimulus organization** refers to *the physical arrangement of the stimulus objects.* Organization affects consumer interpretation and categorization. For example, you likely perceive the letters that make up the words you are reading as words rather than as individual letters. This effect is enhanced by the fact that each word has letters that are close together and is separated by larger spaces, a principle called *proximity.* We discuss this and other principles next.

Proximity refers to the fact that *stimuli positioned close together are perceived as belonging to the same category.* Sometimes proximity comes from the stimulus itself. For example, when consumers read the headline "Have a safe winter. Drive Bridgestone Tires," they tend to infer from the proximity of the two statements that the ad means Bridgestone Tires will help them have a safe winter. However, the headline does not explicitly make that claim. *What ethical implications exist?*

Sometimes proximity results from the relationship of the stimulus to its context, as in ambush marketing. **Ambush marketing** involves *any communication or activity that implies, or from which one could reasonably infer, that an organization is associated with an event, when in fact it is not.* A common form of ambush marketing is to advertise heavily during the event. Proximity would lead many to believe that the company was a sponsor of the event even if it was not.[100]

ILLUSTRATION 8-9

This Puma Body Train ad draws on figure–ground to make the focal image stand out from the background.

Closure involves *presenting an incomplete stimulus with the goal of getting consumers to complete it and thus become more engaged and involved.* Advertisers will often use incomplete stimuli in this manner because closure is often an automatic response engaged in by consumers in order to interpret message meaning. Not surprisingly, increasing consumer ad involvement also increases recall, as we will discuss more in Chapter 9.[101]

Figure–ground involves *presenting the stimulus in such a way that it is perceived as the focal object to be attended to and all other stimuli are perceived as the background.* This strategy is often used in advertising, where the goal is to make the brand stand out as the prominent focal object to which consumers will attend. Absolut, a Swedish vodka, uses figure–ground very effectively. Each ad uses the natural elements in the ad to "form" the figure of a bottle, as with Absolut Mandarin where the bottle is formed by pieces of orange peel. The Puma ad in Illustration 8–9 provides another example.

Changes In order to interpret stimulus change, consumers must be able to categorize and interpret the new stimulus relative to the old. Interpreting change requires the ability to both detect change and then assign meaning to that change. Sometimes consumers won't be able to detect a change. Sometimes they can detect a change but interpret it as unimportant.

The physiological ability of an individual to distinguish between similar stimuli is called **sensory discrimination.** This involves such variables as the sound of stereo systems, the taste of food products, or the clarity of display screens. The minimum amount that one brand can differ from another (or from its previous version) with the difference still being noticed is referred to as the **just noticeable difference (j.n.d.).** The higher the initial level of an attribute, the greater that attribute must be changed before the change will be noticed. Thus, a small addition of salt to a pretzel would not likely be noticed unless that pretzel contained only a small amount of salt to begin with.

As a general rule, *individuals typically do not notice relatively small differences between brands or changes in brand attributes.* Makers of candy bars have used this principle for years. Since the price of cocoa fluctuates widely, they simply make small adjustments in the size of the candy bar rather than altering price. Since marketers want some product changes, such as reductions in the size, to go unnoticed, they may attempt to make changes that fall below the j.n.d. This strategy, sometimes referred to as *weighting out,* appears to be on the increase. However, if and when consumers do notice, the potential backlash may be quite severe.[102] *What is your evaluation of the ethics of this practice?*

After *noticing* a change or difference, consumers must *interpret* it. Some changes are meaningful and some are not. The relationship between change and consumers' valuation of that change tends to follow the pattern discussed for j.n.d. The higher the initial level of an attribute, the greater the attribute must change before it is seen as meaningful. For example, consumers underestimate the calories in a meal more as the portion size of the meal increases. This *mis*interpretation has important individual and societal consequences for obesity and portion control.[103]

Change is often interpreted with respect to some *referent state.* The referent state might be a brand's prior model or a competitor's model. *Reference price* is also a referent state. Consumers can bring *internal* reference prices with them based on prior experience. Also, marketers can provide a reference in the form of *manufacturer's suggested retail price (MSRP).* Consumers then are more likely to interpret the sale price with respect to the MSRP, which, if favorable, should increase perceived value of the offer and likelihood of purchase.[104]

Consumer Inferences

When it comes to marketing, "what you see is not what you get." That's because interpretation often requires consumers to make inferences. An **inference** *goes beyond what is directly stated or presented.* Consumers use available data *and* their own ideas to draw conclusions about information that is not provided.

Quality Signals Inferences are as numerous and divergent as consumers themselves. However, some inferences related to product quality are relatively consistent across consumers. Here consumers use their own experiences and knowledge to draw inferences about product quality based on a nonquality cue.

Price-perceived quality is an inference based on the popular adage "you get what you pay for." Consumers often infer that higher-priced brands possess higher quality than do lower-priced brands.[105] Consumers sometimes take price discounts as a signal of lower quality, which is a major concern for companies such as General Motors that rely heavily on such tactics.[106]

Advertising intensity is also a quality signal. Consumers tend to infer that more heavily advertised brands are of higher quality.[107] One reason is that effort is believed to predict success, and ad spending is seen as an indicator of effort. Any factor related to advertising expense such as medium, use of color, and repetition can increase quality perceptions and choice.[108]

Warranties are another quality signal, with longer warranties generally signaling higher quality. Consumers infer that a firm wouldn't offer a longer warranty if it weren't confident in the quality of its products because honoring the warranty would be expensive.[109]

Price, advertising, and warranties are just a few quality cues. Others include *country of origin (COO),* in which consumers interpret products more positively when they are manufactured in a country they perceive positively,[110] as well as *brand* effects, where well-known brands are perceived as higher quality than are unknown brands.

In general, quality signals operate more strongly when consumers lack the expertise to make informed judgments on their own, when consumer motivation or interest in the decision is low, and when other quality-related information is lacking.

Interpreting Images Consumer inferences from visual images are becoming increasingly important as advertisers increase their use of visual imagery.[111] Note how visuals dominate many print ads. For example, Clinique ran an ad that pictured a tall, clear glass of mineral water and ice cubes. A large slice of lime was positioned on the lip of the glass. In the glass with the ice cubes and mineral water were a tube of Clinique lipstick and a container of cheek base. Nothing else appeared in the ad. *What does this mean?*

ILLUSTRATION 8-10

Pictures and imagery do more than merely represent reality. They convey feelings and meanings that often cannot be expressed in words.

Obviously, in order to interpret the Clinique ad, consumers must infer meaning. Until recently, pictures in ads were thought to convey reality. If so, the Clinique ad is nonsensical. Is Clinique guilty of ineffective advertising? No. All of us intuitively recognize that pictures do more than represent reality; they supply meaning. Thus, one interpretation of the Clinique ad is "Clinique's new summer line of makeup is as refreshing as a tall glass of soda with a twist."

The verbal translation of the meaning conveyed by images is generally incomplete and inadequate. A picture is worth a thousand words not just because it may convey reality more efficiently than words but because it may convey meanings that words cannot adequately express.

Marketers must understand the meanings their audiences assign to various images and words, and use them in combination to construct messages that will convey the desired meaning. They must be sensitive to cultural differences since interpretation is highly contingent on shared cultural experience. For example, consumers in some cultures (termed high-context cultures) tend to "read between the lines." These consumers are very sensitive to cues in the communications setting such as tone of voice. On the other hand, consumers in low-context cultures tend to ignore such cues and focus more on the message's literal or explicit meaning. One study has found that consumers in high-context cultures such as the Philippines are more likely to infer implicit meanings from ad visuals than are those in low-context cultures such as the United States.[112] Illustration 8–10 is an example of an ad based heavily on imagery. *What does this ad mean to you? Would it mean the same to older consumers? Consumers from other cultures?*

Missing Information and Ethical Concerns When data about an attribute are missing, consumers may assign it a value based on a presumed relationship between that attribute and one for which data are available; they may assign it the average of their assessments of the available attributes; they may assume it to be weaker than the attributes for which data are supplied; or any of a large number of other strategies may be used.[113]

Consider the following hypothetical ad copy:

- The Subaru Outback gets better gas mileage than the Toyota Camry.
- It has more cargo space than the Chevy Volt.
- It has more power than the Toyota RAV4.

Some consumers would infer from this that the Subaru gets better gas mileage than the Volt and the RAV4; has more cargo space than the Camry and the RAV4; and has more power than the Volt and the Camry.[114] These claims are not stated in the ad, making it clear that certain types of information portrayal may lead to incorrect inferences and suboptimal consumer decisions. Thus, a factually correct ad could still mislead some consumers. *Are such ads ethical?*

Consumers can be misled in a number of different ways. One way is that companies can make *direct claims* that are false. Claiming that a food or food ingredient is "mushroom in origin" when it is really a fungus or mold appears to fall into this category. This is the easiest form of deception to detect and prosecute under the law. However, other types of deception are more subtle. These fall under the broad category of *claim-belief discrepancies,* whereby a communication leads consumers to believe something about the product that is not true even though it doesn't present a direct false claim. For example, the Federal Trade Commission (FTC) felt that Kraft Foods' early ads for Kraft Cheese Singles might be misleading based on claim-belief discrepancy. That's because their ads focused on the importance of calcium and the fact that each slice was made from five ounces of milk. The FTC's concern was that reasonable consumers would infer that Kraft Cheese Singles contained the same amount of calcium as five ounces of milk even though this was not directly stated in their ads. This inference is wrong because processing milk into cheese reduces calcium content. Since parents might use Kraft Cheese Singles as a calcium source for their kids, this was of particular concern. Although more difficult from a legal standpoint, the FTC can and does hold companies responsible for claim-belief discrepancies as we see with Kraft.[115] Our understanding and regulation of deception continue to evolve as we gain a better understanding of consumer information processing. This is discussed in more detail in Chapter 20.

PERCEPTION AND MARKETING STRATEGY

LO5

Perception holds critical implications for marketing strategy in a number of areas. We turn to these next.

Retail Strategy

Retailers often use exposure very effectively. Store interiors are designed with frequently purchased items (canned goods, fresh fruits and vegetables, meats) separated so that the average consumer will travel through more of the store. This increases total exposure. High-margin items are often placed in high-traffic areas to capitalize on increased exposure.

Shelf position and amount of shelf space influence which items and brands are allocated attention. Point-of-purchase displays also attract attention and boost sales.[116] And **cross-promotions,** whereby signage in one area of the store promotes complementary products in another (milk signage in the cookie aisle), can also be effective. Recently, retailers have begun to reduce clutter by cutting out marginal, unimportant, and redundant SKUs (stock-keeping units—individual items such as brands, sizes, and versions) within a category. Consumer perceptions and sales tend to go up when the reduction in clutter does not reduce variety and choice.[117]

Another important aspect of the retail environment is *ambient scent.* Pleasant smells in a retail store can increase product evaluations by boosting emotions. In some cases this occurs even when the scent is inconsistent with the product being evaluated (e.g., pine scent and orange juice).

Brand Name and Logo Development

Shakespeare notwithstanding, marketers do not believe that "a rose by any other name would smell as sweet." Mountain Dew's marketing director ascribes part of the success of Code Red to its name: "Had it been called 'Mountain Dew Cherry' it would've done very differently."[118] Brand names can influence anything from color preference to food taste. One study found that people preferred avocado to light green even though the actual color was exactly the same. Another found that young kids liked the taste of foods such as carrots, milk, and apple juice more when they came in a McDonald's package![119] Effects such as this can be related back to expectation biases. That is, the name sets up an expectation that, in turn, biases people's perceptions of the actual experience. Given the tendency toward global brands, it is easy to imagine how complex creating an appropriate name can be.[120]

Linguistic Considerations Sometimes brand names start out having no inherent meaning but gain associations over time as consumers gain experience with them. Ford and Toyota are examples. However, marketers increasingly tap into linguistic characteristics of words to create brand names with inherent meaning right from the start. One aspect is inherent *semantic meaning* or *morpheme.* NutraSweet took advantage of morphemes to imply nutritious and sweet. And Dodge has brought back its "Hemi" engine, a name associated with high performance.[121] A second aspect is sound or *phonemes.* Sounds of letters and words can symbolize product attributes. For example, heavier sounding vowels (Frosh) might be better used to suggest richer, creamier ice cream than lighter sounding vowels (Frish).[122]

Lexicon and other naming companies such as NameLab use these concepts to create names that convey appropriate meanings. Lexicon selected the Blackberry name for Research in Motion's handheld device because *berry* suggests small, the "b" sound is associated strongly with relaxation, and the two "b" sounds at the beginning of *black* and *berry* are light and crisp, suggesting speed. Thus, a name that suggests a handheld that is small, easy to use, and fast—every consumer's dream![123]

Branding Strategies Marketers engage in numerous strategies to leverage strong existing brand names. One is **brand extension,** where an existing brand extends to a new category with the same name such as Levi Strauss putting its Levi name on a line of upscale men's suits. Another is **co-branding,** an alliance in which two brands are put together on a single product. An example is "Intel Inside" Compaq computers. Brand extensions and co-branding can be positive or negative, as we'll discuss in Chapter 9. A key issue is *perceived fit* between the core brand and the extension or the two co-brands. Really poor fit (too much incongruity) is bad, as people find it hard to categorize and make sense of the new brand. For example, the Levi men's suit was a flop because the core Levi image of relaxed and casual did not fit a formal, upscale suit.[124]

Logo Design and Typographics How a product or service name is presented—its *logo*—is also important.[125] Figure 8–5 shows a number of brands that have changed their logos over time. *Do you think the new logos are better or worse? In what ways are they better or worse?*

FIGURE 8-5 Recent Logo Redesigns

Brand	Original	Update
Pepsi		
Reebok	Reebok	Reebok
BP	BP	bp
Belk	Belk	belk MODERN. SOUTHERN. STYLE.

Perhaps in trying to answer these questions, you realized that you don't have any criteria for making suggestions. Such criteria are hard to come by and we are just now beginning to understand why some logos work better than others. One study provides guidance, finding that logo symbols (such as Prudential's Rock) that are natural, moderately elaborate, and symmetrically balanced lead to higher levels of logo liking. *Natural* logos depict commonly experienced objects; *elaborate* logos entail complexity; *symmetrical* logos are visually balanced.

Beyond the logo symbol is also the shape and form of the letters in their name, which relates to typeface and type font. Intuitively, for example, you might think that a fancy *scripted* font signals elegance and is better suited for a fountain pen than for a mountain bike. Turns out you would be right! Different fonts do evoke different meanings and an appropriate fit between the font and product can increase choice of the brand, independent of the name.[126] *Given these various criteria, can you now assess the logo redesigns?*[127]

Selective Exposure to Magazines Based on Demographic Characteristics

TABLE 

Demographic Characteristics	Better Homes & Gardens	Cosmopolitan	Maxim	National Geographic	Family Circle
Gender					
Male	26	29	151	120	17
Female	169	166	52	85	177
Age					
18–24	33	263	169	64	17
25–34	50	143	195	56	39
35–44	78	112	132	86	93
45–54	108	76	76	89	87
55–64	131	41	43	132	126
65+	174	23	14	161	207
Education					
College graduate	107	109	123	126	99
High school graduate	108	90	105	75	118
Household income					
Less than $25,000	95	74	60	106	119
$25,000–49,999	105	98	84	91	123
$50,000–59,999	104	120	113	107	93
$60,000–74,999	99	113	105	103	89
$75,000 or more	99	106	126	100	80

Note: 100 = Average level of use, purchase, or consumption.

Source: *Simmons National Consumer Study 2010,* Experian Information Solutions (Costa Mesa, CA 2014).

Media Strategy

The explosion of media alternatives makes it difficult and expensive to gain exposure to key target audiences.[128] However, the fact that the exposure process is often selective rather than random is the underlying basis for effective media strategies. Specifically, firms must determine to which media the consumers in the target market are most frequently exposed and place ad messages in those media. As one executive stated:

> We must look increasingly for matching media that will enable us best to reach carefully targeted, emerging markets. The rifle approach rather than the old shotgun.[129]

Consumer involvement can drive media exposure and strategy. For high-involvement products, ads should be placed in media outlets with content relevant to the product. Specialized media such as *Runner's World* or *Vogue* tend to attract readers who are interested in and receptive to ads for related products. In contrast, ads for low-involvement products should be placed in reputable media independent of content, as long as they are frequented by the target market.[130] In a situation such as this, the marketer must find media that the target market is interested in and place the advertising message in those media. Target markets as defined by age, ethnic group, social class, or stage in the family life cycle have differing media preferences, which can then be used to select media outlets. Table 8–1 illustrates selective exposure to several magazines based on demographic characteristics.

As we saw earlier, video game player demographics skew toward young males (for console games, average age is 26 and 68 percent are male). Companies like Burger King, who are desperate to obtain media exposure among this demographic, are moving ad dollars to in-game video ads and product placements.[131]

Technology continues to radically alter media targeting choices. Consider the impact of GPS technology on outdoor mobile ads:

> While a cab travels from one end of a city to the other, an electronic billboard on top changes according to location and time of day. Thanks to a satellite feed and global positioning system, the bright, attention-getting ads on the taxi roof keep changing. As the cab passes by a college, an ad for a bookstore appears. While the cab moves through the business district at noon, an ad for a local deli fills the screen. As the cab travels through a Hispanic neighborhood, a Spanish-language ad for a snack food is shown.[132]

Advertisements

Advertisements must perform two critical tasks: capture attention and convey meaning. Unfortunately, the techniques appropriate for accomplishing one task are often counterproductive for the other.

What if you had to design a campaign to increase users for your firm's toilet bowl freshener, but research shows your target market has little inherent interest in the product. What do you do? Two strategies seem reasonable. One is to *utilize stimulus characteristics* such as bright colors or surrealism to attract attention. The second is to *tie the message to a topic in which the target market is interested.*

However, using factors unrelated to the product category to attract attention must be done with caution. First, it may detract attention away from the core brand message because stimuli compete for limited attention. That's why companies often try to use humor, sex appeal, and celebrities in ways that are relevant to the product or message. Second, it may negatively affect *interpretation.* For example, humor in an insurance ad may result in the brand's being interpreted as unreliable.

Package Design and Labeling

Packages must attract attention and convey information, and various aspects from color to shape to typography can interact in complex ways in affecting consumer perceptions.[133] Packaging has functional and perceptual components. Consider the candy coating of M&M's. It is functional because it keeps the chocolate from melting in your hands. But it is also perceptual. The bright colors are interesting and unique even though they don't taste different. One study varied the color variety (7 versus 10 colors) in a bowl of M&M's and found that as variety went up, consumers ate more![134] M&M's has refocused on color by introducing bolder colors and emphasizing color in its ads. As one executive states, "We've always had color as a unique point of difference, but we wanted to reinforce that message in a fresh, contemporary way."[135]

Bright colors, tall packages, and unusual shapes can be used to attract attention, convey meaning, and influence consumption.[136] For example, consumers tend to believe that taller, more elongated packages contain more than shorter packages of the same volume (e.g., a can of soda). As a consequence, a recent study shows that consumers of beverages buy fewer bottles than cans but perceive that the volume they buy is the same. Notice how package options such as an elongated bottle can influence perceived consumption in ways that reduce product sales and revenues.[137] Look at Illustration 8–11. Which appears to contain more? If you said Acqua Panna, you were influenced by the elongation bias (they all contain exactly the same amount of liquid: one liter).

ILLUSTRATION 8-11

Package design can strongly influence perceived volume and consumption levels. Which package do you think contains more beverage?

Packages also contain product information and warnings. Ethical and legal considerations require marketers to place warning labels on a wide array of products such as cigarettes, alcoholic beverages, and many over-the-counter drugs. On the one hand, there is the desire to effectively alert users to potential risks. On the other hand, there is a desire to avoid detracting unduly from product image. The key from an ethical and legal standpoint is to not err on the side of image at the expense of the consumer. Well-designed warnings appear to be at least somewhat effective. Factors reducing their effectiveness include overly technical or complex language and a failure to indicate the positive consequences of compliance.[138]

SUMMARY

LO1: Describe the nature of perception and its relationship to consumer memory and decisions

Perception consists of those activities by which an individual acquires and assigns meaning to stimuli. Perception occurs in three stages, namely, exposure, attention, and interpretation. If and when perception occurs, the meaning derived from a stimulus is typically transferred to memory, where it is stored and can be later retrieved when consumers are making purchase decisions.

LO2: Explain exposure, the types of exposure, and the resulting marketing implications

Exposure occurs when a stimulus comes within range of one of an individual's primary sensory receptors. People are exposed to only a small fraction of the available stimuli. And when consumers actively avoid certain marketing stimuli, this is referred to as *selective exposure.* Selective exposure in the advertising area is termed *ad avoidance.* Marketers try to overcome avoidance by using tactics such as *product placement* and *hybrid ads.* It should be noted, however, that consumers seek out some marketing stimuli voluntarily. Examples include Super Bowl ads, ads that go viral online, and company-based e-mails that consumers choose to receive through *permission-based marketing.*

LO3: Explain attention, the factors that affect it, and the resulting marketing implications

Attention occurs when the stimulus activates one or more of the sensory receptors and the resulting sensations go into the brain for processing. People *selectively attend* to stimuli as a function of stimulus, individual, and situational factors. *Stimulus factors* are physical characteristics of the stimulus itself, such as contrast, size, intensity, attractiveness, color, movement, position, isolation, format, and information quantity. *Individual factors* are characteristics of the individual, such as motivation and ability. *Situational factors* include stimuli in the environment other than the focal stimulus and temporary characteristics of the individual that are induced by the environment. Clutter and program involvement are situational factors of particular interest to marketers. Marketers can utilize all these factors to better develop stimuli that attract consumer attention in today's cluttered environment.

Nonfocused attention occurs when a person takes in information without deliberate effort. *Hemispheric lateralization* is a term applied to activities that take place on each side of the brain. The left side of the brain is concerned primarily with those activities typically called rational thought and the ability to be conscious and report what is happening. The right side of the brain deals with pictorial, geometric, timeless, and nonverbal information without the individual's being able to verbally report it.

A message presented so fast or so softly or so masked by other messages that one is not aware of seeing or hearing it is called a *subliminal message.* Subliminal messages have generated a great deal of interest but are not generally thought to affect brand choice or other aspects of consumer behavior in a meaningful way.

LO4: Explain interpretation, the factors that affect it, and the resulting marketing implications

Interpretation is the assignment of meaning to stimuli that have been attended to. Interpretation tends to be relative rather than absolute (perceptual relativity) and subjective rather than objective. Two general forms of interpretation are cognitive and affective. *Cognitive interpretation* appears to involve a process whereby new stimuli are placed into existing categories of meaning. *Affective interpretation* is the emotional or feeling response triggered by the stimulus.

Interpretation is largely a function of individual traits, learning, and expectations that are triggered by the stimulus and moderated by the situation. Stimulus characteristics are critical. *Stimulus organization* is the physical arrangement of the stimulus objects and relates to the perceptual principles of *proximity, closure,* and *figure–ground.* Marketers can use these principles to design effective communication strategies. *Stimulus change* and consumer reactions to it are also of concern and have consequences in relation to such strategies as "weighting out," whereby marketers attempt to reduce the quantity offered in increments that consumers won't detect.

Interpretation often involves consumer inferences. *Inferences* go beyond what is directly stated or presented and help explain consumer use of *quality signals* (e.g., higher price means higher quality), their *interpretation of images,* and how they deal with *missing information.* Inferences also help explain how consumers can be misled by marketing messages even when those messages are *literally* true.

LO5: Discuss how perception can enhance strategies for retailing, branding, advertising, and packaging

Marketers use their knowledge of perception to enhance strategies in a number of areas including retailing, branding, advertising, and packaging. For retailing, issues surrounding store and shelf location are important determinants of perception. For branding, issues surrounding the selection of brand names, extensions, and appropriate logos have important implications for perception. Advertising strategies and media selection are heavily influenced by considering factors that enhance exposure and attention. Packaging is a functional aspect of products, but also perceptual in that it can capture consumer attention and influence their brand interpretations.

KEY TERMS

Ad avoidance 276
Adaptation level theory 285
Affective interpretation 290
Ambush marketing 295
Attention 279
Brand extension 299
Brand familiarity 286
Closure 295
Co-branding 299
Cognitive interpretation 289
Contextual cues 293
Cross-promotions 298
Exposure 275
Figure–ground 295
Hemispheric lateralization 287
Inference 296
Infomercials 279
Information overload 286
Information processing 274
Interpretation 289
Just noticeable difference (j.n.d.) 295
Muting 276
Perception 274
Perceptual defenses 275
Perceptual relativity 289
Permission-based marketing 279
Product placement 276
Proximity 294
Rhetorical figures 294
Sensory discrimination 295
Smart banners 286
Stimulus organization 294
Subliminal stimulus 288
Zapping 276
Zipping 276

REVIEW QUESTIONS

1. What is *information processing?* How does it differ from *perception?*
2. What is meant by *exposure?* What determines which stimuli an individual will be exposed to? How do marketers utilize this knowledge?
3. What are *zipping, zapping,* and *muting?* Why are they a concern to marketers?
4. What are *infomercials?* How effective are they?
5. What is *ad avoidance?* How is *DVR technology* affecting it? How are marketers dealing with this phenomenon?
6. What is meant by *attention?* What determines which stimuli an individual will attend to? How do marketers utilize this?
7. What stimulus factors can be used to attract attention? What problems can arise when stimulus factors are used to attract attention?
8. What is *adaptation level theory?*
9. What is *information overload?* How should marketers deal with information overload?
10. What impact does *program involvement* have on the attention paid to commercials embedded in the program?
11. What is a *contextual cue?* Why is it of interest to marketers?
12. What is meant by *nonfocused attention?*
13. What is meant by *hemispheric lateralization?*
14. What is meant by *subliminal perception?* Is it a real phenomenon? Is it effective?
15. What is meant by *interpretation?*
16. What determines how an individual will interpret a given stimulus?
17. What is the difference between *cognitive* and *affective* interpretation?
18. What is the difference between *semantic* and *psychological* meaning?
19. What is *sensory discrimination?* What is a *just noticeable difference (j.n.d.)?*
20. What is a *consumer inference?* Why is this of interest to marketers?
21. How does a knowledge of information processing assist the manager in the following?
    a. Formulating retail strategy
    b. Developing brand names and logos
    c. Formulating media strategy
    d. Designing advertisements
    e. Designing packages and labels
22. What is *co-branding?* Is it effective?
23. What is a *cross-promotion* retail strategy? Provide two examples.
24. How can *rhetorical figures* enhance attention?
25. What is a *smart banner?* How does this relate to selective attention?
26. What is *figure–ground?*
27. What ethical concerns arise in applying knowledge of the perceptual process?

28. What is *ambush marketing?*

DISCUSSION QUESTIONS

29. Given that smoking scenes in movies increase the positive image and intention to smoke among youth, what regulations, if any, should apply to this?
30. How could a marketing manager for the following use the material in this chapter to guide the development of a national advertising campaign (choose one)? To assist local retailers or organizations in developing their promotional activities? Would the usefulness of this material be limited to advertising decisions?
    a. The Salvation Army
    b. Smartphones
    c. Qdoba Mexican Grill
    d. Lucky Jeans
    e. Belkin WiFi equipment
31. Respond to the questions in Consumer Insight 8–1.
32. Hershey recently created a line of upscale chocolates called "Cacao Reserve *by Hershey's*." The company created fancy packaging, priced the product at the high end, and did little mass marketing for its new product. Initial sales were disappointingly slow even though the premium chocolate market is growing nicely, with brands like Ghirardelli faring well. As a consequence, Hershey almost immediately (within six months) dropped its prices and started mass advertising. Using concepts in this chapter, why do you think Hershey failed in its move into the premium chocolate market? Do you think the adjustments were the most appropriate, or could Hershey have taken other steps?
33. Pick three brand names that utilize a *morphemic* approach and three that utilize a *phonemic* approach. Are the morphemes and phonemes consistent with the overall positioning of these brands?
34. Develop a brand name for (*a*) an MP3 player, (*b*) an R&B music store, (*c*) an Internet grocery shopping service, (*d*) a mobile app, or (*e*) a pet-walking service. Justify your name.
35. Develop a logo for (*a*) an MP3 player, (*b*) an R&B music store, (*c*) an Internet grocery shopping service, (*d*) a mobile app, or (*e*) a pet-walking service. Justify your design.
36. Evaluate the in-text ads in Illustrations 8–1 through 8–10. Analyze the attention-attracting characteristics and the meaning they convey. Are they good ads? What risks are associated with each?
37. Develop three co-branded products: one that would be beneficial to both individual brands, one that would benefit one brand but not the other, and one that would benefit neither brand. Explain your logic.
38. Find an ad that you feel might mislead consumers through a *claim-belief discrepancy*. What inference processes are you assuming?

APPLICATION ACTIVITIES

39. Find and copy or describe examples of advertisements that specifically use stimulus factors to attract attention. Look for examples of each of the various factors discussed earlier in the chapter and try to find their use in a variety of promotions. For each example, evaluate the effectiveness of the stimulus factors used.
40. Repeat Question 40, but this time look for advertisements using individual factors.
41. Complete Question 34 and test your names on a sample of students. Justify your testing procedure and report your results.
42. Complete Question 35 and test your logos on a sample of students. Justify your testing procedure and report your results.
43. Find two brand names that you feel are particularly appropriate and two that you feel are not very appropriate. Explain your reasoning for each name.
44. Find and describe a logo that you feel is particularly appropriate and one that you feel is not very appropriate. Explain your reasoning.
45. Interview three students with a DVR about their behavior during television breaks when watching prerecorded programming. Do they watch any ads? Why? What do you conclude?
46. Interview three students about how they respond to banner ads and the extent to which they attend to various commercial messages on the Internet.
47. Go to a health food or alternative medicines store or section of a store. Find three products that make health claims. Evaluate the likely effectiveness of any disclaimers that they contain.

48. Find and copy or describe an ad or other marketing message that you think makes unethical use of the perceptual process. Justify your selection.
49. Develop an ad but omit information about some key product attributes. Show the ad to five students. After they have looked at the ad, give them a questionnaire that asks about the attributes featured in the ad and about the missing attributes. If they provide answers concerning the missing attributes, ask them how they arrived at these answers. What do you conclude?

REFERENCES

1. This insight is based on E. Nussbaum, "Product Integration, *30 Rock,* and the Trouble with Using Brands to Write TV," *New York,* October 13, 2008, pp. 32–37 and 90; J. Plambeck, "Product Placement Grows in Music Videos," *New York Times,* July 5, 2010; "Corvette Placement on 'Glee' Hits Right Note for Chevy," *Los Angeles Times,* September 30, 2010; B. Steinberg, "Chevy Takes on Ambitious Role in TNT's 'Men' Program," *Advertising Age,* January 17, 2011, p. 3.
2. For an interesting discussion, see J. J. Pilotta and D. Schultz, "Simultaneous Media Experience and Synesthesia," *Journal of Advertising Research,* March 2005, pp. 19–26.
3. R. Liljenwall, "Global Trends in Point-of-Purchase Advertising," in *The Power of Point-of-Purchase Advertising,* ed. R. Liljenwall (Washington, DC: Point-of-Purchase Advertising International, 2004), ch. 10.
4. "Ad Avoidance Highest among Key Target Groups, Says Study," *Businessline,* October 21, 2004, p. 1. See also J. Rojas-Mendez, G. Davies, and C. Madran, "Universal Differences in Advertising Avoidance Behavior," *Journal of Business Research,* 62 (2009), pp. 947 54.
5. S. M. Edwards, H. Li, and J.-H. Lee, "Forced Exposure and Psychological Reactance," *Journal of Advertising,* Fall 2002, pp. 83–95; H. Li, S. M. Edwards, and J.-H. Lee, "Measuring the Intrusiveness of Advertisements," *Journal of Advertising,* Summer 2002, pp. 37–47; S. Shavitt, P. Vargas, and P. Lowrey, "Exploring the Pole of Memory for Self-Selected Ad Experiences," *Psychology & Marketing,* December 2004, pp. 1011–32; and C. H. Cho and H. J. Cheon, "Why Do People Avoid Advertising on the Internet?," *Journal of Advertising,* Winter 2004, pp. 89–97.
6. A. C. B. Tse and R. P. W. Lee, "Zapping Behavior during Commercial Breaks," *Journal of Advertising Research,* May 2001, pp. 25–28; and M. Savage, "China Turning On, but Tuning Out," *Media,* May 7, 2004, p. 19.
7. P. Paul, "Coming Soon: More Ads Tailored to Your Tastes," *American Demographics,* August 2001, pp. 28–31.
8. Edwards, Li, and Lee, "Forced Exposure and Psychological Reactance."
9. "Pop-Ups—End of an Era?," *NOP World United Business Media,* September 29, 2003, www.unitedbusinessmedia.com.
10. C. A. Russell, "Investigating the Effectiveness of Product Placements in Television Shows," *Journal of Consumer Research,* December 2002, pp. 306–18; S. A. McKechnie and J. Zhou, "Product Placement in Movies," *International Journal of Advertising,* 22, no. 3 (2003), pp. 349–74; M. Wiles and A. Danielova, "The Worth of Product Placement in Successful Films," *Journal of Marketing,* July 2009, pp. 44–63; and P. M. Homer, "Product Placements," *Journal of Advertising,* Fall 2009, pp. 21–31. For examples when negative effects can occur, see E. Cowley and C. Barron, "When Product Placement Goes Wrong," *Journal of Advertising,* Spring 2008, pp. 89–98.
11. E. Hall, "Nestle Breaks First Product-Placement TV Buy in U.K.," *Advertising Age,* March 3, 2011.
12. "No More Skipping Ads?," *Los Angeles Times,* October 11, 2010.
13. R. Greenspan, "DVRs Not Necessarily Ad-Killers," *ClickZ.com,* May 24, 2004; "Jupiter: DVR Ad Skipping Threatens $8B in Advertising," *MarketingVOX.com,* May 4, 2006; "Ad Spots in the DVD Era," *Broadcast Engineering,* August 2007, p. 106; and R. Dana and S. Kang, "Answer to Vexing Question: Who's Not Watching Ads," *The Wall Street Journal,* October 17, 2007, p. B2.
14. J. Mandese, "Study: DVRs 'Recapture' 96% of TV Ad Zapping," *MediaPost's Media Daily News,* May 25, 2004, www.mediapost.com; "New Age for Ads," *Cablefax Daily,* December 6, 2007, www.cablefax.com; and H. Dawley, "As to Worries Over Ad-Skipping, Skip It," *Media Life Research,* www.medialifemagazine.com, May 18, 2006.
15. A. Ambruster, "Don't Give Up on TV Ads Just Yet," *Television-Week,* July 23–30, 2007, p. 16.
16. B. A. S. Martin, V. T. L. Nguyen, and J.-Y. Wi, "Remote Control Marketing," *Marketing Intelligence and Planning,* 20, no. 1 (2002), pp. 44–48.
17. S. A. Brasel and J. Gips, "Breaking Through Fast-Forwarding," *Journal of Marketing,* November 2008, pp. 31–48.
18. See D. Kiley, "Learning to Love the Dreaded TiVo," *BusinessWeek,* April 17, 2006, p. 88; C. Limbardi, "TV Advertising's DVR Challenge," *News.com,* May 23, 2006; K Ritchi, "Fast-Forwarding Is So Passe Advertisers Want in on DVR and Providers Are Finally Listening," *Boards,* January 2007, p. 13; B. Steinberg, "In the End, It's the Last Ad in a Pod They Recall," *Television Week,* June 11, 2007, p. 13; and S. Vranica, "New Ads Take on TiVo," *The Wall Street Journal,* October 5, 2007, p. B4.
19. NDS Ltd., "DirecTV Chooses NDS Dynamic to Support Addressable Advertising," press release, March 22, 2011, www.nds.com, accessed May 27, 2011.
20. The Adidas outdoor efforts found in the following: "Adidas and Guerrilla Marketing," *Outdoor Advertising Blog,* 1outdooradvertising.blogspot.com, August 13, 2007; and "Giant Adidas Ad," *Advertising Age,* June 5, 2006, p. 15.
21. T. L. Stanley, "Advergames, Content Role Juice up Marketer's Game," *Advertising Age,* February 6, 2006, p. S-3; see also L. Schneider and T. B. Cornwell, "Cashing in on Crashes via Brand Placement in Computer Games," *International Journal of Advertising,* 24, no. 3 (2005), pp. 321–43.

22. P. Lehman, "Mad Ave Clicks with the Gamers," *IN,* November 2007, p. 28; and "Interactive Marketing and Media Fact Pack," *Advertising Age,* 2006, p. 46.
23. Liljenwall, "Global Trends in Point-of-Purchase Advertising."
24. M. Singh, S. K. Balasubramanian, and G. Chakraborty, "A Comparative Analysis of Three Communication Formats," *Journal of Advertising,* Winter 2000, pp. 59–75.
25. M. T. Elliot and P. S. Speck, "Antecedents and Consequences of Infomercials," *Journal of Direct Marketing,* Spring 1995, pp. 39–51.
26. "DoubleClick's 2004 Consumer Email Study," October 2004, www.doubleckick.com.
27. A. Z. Cuneo, "Wireless Giants Leap into Third-Screen Marketing," *Advertising Age,* September 11, 2006, p. 39.
28. S. Thompson, "Media Recipe," *Advertising Age,* October 23, 2000, p. 42.
29. K. Bouffard, "Analyst Says Grocers' Cut in Shelf Space for Orange Juice Hurts Citrus Sales," *Knight Ridder Tribune Business News,* July 22, 2004, p. 1.
30. M. Rappaport, "Food Product Makers Secure Supermarket Shelf Space by Paying Slotting Fees," *Knight Ridder Tribune Business News,* January 14, 2004, p. 1.
31. X. Drèze and F. Xavier Hussherr, "Internet Advertising," *Journal of Interactive Marketing,* Autumn 2003, pp. 8–23; "A NotSo-Banner Year," *Marketing News,* April 29, 2002, p. 3; and H. Robinson, A. Wysocka, and C. Hand, "Internet Advertising Effectiveness," *International Journal of Advertising,* 26, no. 4 (2007), pp. 527–41.
32. G. L. Lohse, "Consumer Eye Movement Patterns on Yellow Pages Advertising," *Journal of Advertising,* Spring 1997, pp. 61–73; A. M. Abernethy and D. N. Laband, "The Customer Pulling Power of Different-Sized Yellow Pages Advertisements," *Journal of Advertising Research,* May–June 2002, pp. 66–72; and A. M. Abernethy and D. N. Laband, "The Impact of Trademarks and Advertising Size on Yellow Page Call Rates," *Journal of Advertising Research,* March 2004, pp. 119–25.
33. J. R. Rossiter and R. B. Silberstein, "Brain-Imaging Detection of Visual Scene Encoding in Long-Term Memory for TV Commercials," *Journal of Advertising Research,* March 2001, pp. 13–21. See also S. L. Crites Jr., and S. N. Aikman-Eckenrode, "Making Inferences Concerning Physiological Responses," *Journal of Advertising Research,* March 2001, p. 25; and J. R. Rossiter et al., "So What?," *Journal of Advertising Research,* May 2001, pp. 59–61.
34. C.-H. Cho, J.-G. Lee, and M. Tharp, "Different Forced-Exposure Levels to Banner Ads," *Journal of Advertising Research,* July 2001, pp. 45–54; and W. W. Moe, "A Field Experiment to Assess the Interruption Effect of Pop-Up Promotions," *Journal of Interactive Marketing,* Winter 2006, pp. 34–44.
35. R. Pieters, E. Rosbergen, and M. Wedel, "Visual Attention to Repeated Print Advertising," *Journal of Marketing Research,* November 1999, pp. 424–38.
36. R. Pieters and M. Wedel, "Attention Capture and Transfer in Advertising," *Journal of Marketing,* April 2004, pp. 36–50.
37. S. N. Singh et al., "Does Your Ad Have Too Many Pictures?," *Journal of Advertising Research,* January 2000, pp. 11–27.
38. P. J. Danaher, G. W. Mullarkey, and S. Essegaier, "Factors Affecting Web Site Visit Duration," *Journal of Marketing Research,* May 2006, pp. 182–94.
39. Pieters and Wedel, "Attention Capture and Transfer in Advertising."
40. Telecom Research, Inc., *What the Eye Does Not See, the Mind Does Not Remember,* undated.
41. G. J. Gorn, A. Chattopadhyay, T. Yi, and D. W. Dahl, "Effects of Color as an Executional Cue in Advertising," *Management Science,* October 1997, pp. 1387–99.
42. L. Haugen and C. Weems, "P-O-P Advertising Design and Creativity," in *The Power of Point-of-Purchase Advertising,* ch. 6.
43. L. Rostoks, "Sales from POP Advertising Are Measureable," *Canadian Grocer,* July–August 2001, p. 19; and J. McCarthy, "Point of Purchase Last Chance to Dance," *Marketing Magazine,* March 2004, p. 33.
44. C.-H. Cho, "How Advertising Works on the WWW," *Journal of Current Issues and Research in Advertising,* Spring 1999, pp. 33–49; see also S. S. Sunder and S. Kalyanaraman, "Arousal, Memory, and Impression-Formation Effects of Animation Speed in Web Advertising," *Journal of Advertising,* Spring 2004, pp. 7–17.
45. Lohse, "Consumer Eye Movement Patterns on Yellow Pages Advertising." See also K. V. Fernandez and D. L. Rosen, "The Effectiveness of Information and Color in Yellow Pages Advertising," *Journal of Advertising,* Summer 2000, pp. 62–73.
46. D. Alexander, "Food Industry Giants Spend Big Money for Prime Supermarket Shelf Space," *Knight Ridder Tribune Business News,* December 14, 2003, p. 1.
47. C. Garcia, V. Ponsoda, and H. Estebaranz, "Scanning Ads," *Advances in Consumer Research,* vol. 27, ed. S. J. Hoch and R. J. Meyer (Provo, UT: Association for Consumer Research, 2000), pp. 104–109.
48. Drèze and Hussherr, "Internet Advertising."
49. D. D. McAdams, "Is Anybody Paying Attention?," *Broadcasting and Cable,* August 7, 2000, p. 38.
50. See G. D. Olsen, "Creating the Contrast," *Journal of Advertising,* Winter 1995, pp. 29–44.
51. C. Janiszewski, "The Influence of Display Characteristics on Visual Exploratory Search Behavior," *Journal of Consumer Research,* December 1998, pp. 290–301.
52. A. Chattopadhyay, D. W. Dahl, R. J. B. Ritchie, and K. N. Shahin, "Hearing Voices," *Journal of Consumer Psychology,* 13, no. 3 (2003), pp. 198–204.
53. J. Roumelis, "How to Get Noticed . . . Fast," *Marketing Magazine,* May 6, 2002, p. 26.
54. R. C. Goodstein, "Category-Based Applications and Extensions in Advertising," *Journal of Consumer Research,* June 1993, pp. 87–99; see also Y. H. Lee, "Manipulating Ad Message," *Journal of Advertising,* Summer 2000, pp. 29–43.
55. R. Pieters, L. Warlop, and M. Wedel, "Breaking through the Clutter," *Management Science,* June 2002, pp. 765–81.
56. "Signposts," *Advertising Age,* May 21, 2001, p. 3.
57. T. Elkin, "PVR Not Yet a Big Threat," *Advertising Age,* May 6, 2002, p. 55. See also L. F. Allwitt, "Effects of Interestingness on Evaluations of TV Commercials," *Journal of Current Issues and Research in Advertising,* Spring 2000, pp. 41–53; and W. Friedman, "72.3% of PVR Viewers Skip Commercials," *AdAge.com,* July 2, 2002, www.adage.com.

58. J. W. Elpers, M. Wedel, and R. Pieters, "Why Do Consumers Stop Viewing Television Commercials?," *Journal of Marketing Research,* November 2003, pp. 437–53.

59. Pieters, Warlop, and Wedel, "Breaking through the Clutter"; and Elpers, Wedel, and Pieters, "Why Do Consumers Stop Viewing Television Commercials?"

60. B. Lee and W. Lee, "The Effect of Information Overload on Consumer Choice Quality in an On-Line Environment," *Psychology & Marketing,* March 2004, pp. 159–83.

61. Pieters and Wedel, "Attention Capture and Transfer in Advertising"; and R. Pieters and M. Wedel, "Goal Control of Attention to Advertising," *Journal of Consumer Research,* August 2007, pp. 224–33.

62. C.-H. Cho, "The Effectiveness of Banner Advertisements," *Journalism and Mass Communication Quarterly,* Autumn 2003, pp. 623–45.

63. See W. Dou, R. Linn, and S. Yang, "How Smart Are 'Smart Banners'?," *Journal of Advertising Research,* July 2001, pp. 31–43.

64. K. Oser, "Targeting Web Behavior Pays, American Airlines Study Says," *Advertising Age,* May 17, 2004, p. 8; see also L. Sherman and J. Deighton, "Banner Advertising," *Journal of Interactive Marketing,* Spring 2001, pp. 60–64.

65. A. M. Menon, A. D. Deshpande, M. Perri III, and G. M. Zinkhan, "Consumers' Attention to the Brief Summary in Print Direct-to-Consumer Advertisements," *Journal of Public Policy and Marketing,* Fall 2003, pp. 181–91.

66. M. Dahlen, "Banner Advertisements through a New Lens," *Journal of Advertising Research,* July 2001, pp. 23–30.

67. J. Spaeth, "Post-Promotion Evaluation," in *The Power of Point-of-Purchase Advertising,* ch. 6; and Liljenwall, "Global Trends in Point-of-Purchase Advertising."

68. R. G. M. Pieters and T. H. A. Bijmolt, "Consumer Memory for Television Advertising," *Journal of Consumer Research,* March 1997, pp. 362–72; see also E. Riebe and J. Dawes, "Recall of Radio Advertising in Low and High Advertising Clutter Formats," *International Journal of Advertising,* 25, no. 1 (2006), pp. 71–86.

69. "The Involvement Index," *Magazine Involvement Alliance,* 2004.

70. For more detail, see T. L. Chartrand, "The Role of Conscious Awareness in Consumer Behavior," *Journal of Consumer Psychology,* 15, no. 3 (2005), pp. 203–10; A. Dijksterhuis and P. K. Smith, "What Do We Do Unconsciously?," *Journal of Consumer Psychology,* 15, no. 3 (2005), pp. 225–29; L. A. Peracchio and D. Luna, "The Role of Thin-Slice Judgments in Consumer Psychology," *Journal of Consumer Psychology,* 16, no. 1 (2006), pp. 25–32; and T. L. Chartrand et al., "Nonconscious Goals and Consumer Choice," *Journal of Consumer Research,* August 2008, pp. 189–201.

71. H. E. Krugman, "Sustained Viewing of Television," *Journal of Advertising Research,* June 1980, p. 65; and H. E. Krugman, "Low Recall and High Recognition of Advertising," *Journal of Advertising Research,* February–March 1986, pp. 79–86.

72. Drèze and Hussherr, "Internet Advertising."

73. S. Shapiro, D. J. MacInnis, and S. E. Heckler, "The Effects of Incidental Ad Exposure on the Formation of Consideration Sets," *Journal of Consumer Research,* June 1997, pp. 94–104; and S. Shapiro, "When an Ad's Influence Is beyond Our Conscious Control," *Journal of Consumer Research,* June 1999, pp. 16–36.

74. W. B. Key, *Subliminal Seduction* (Englewood Cliffs, NJ: Prentice Hall, 1973); and W. B. Key, *Media Sexploitation* (Englewood Cliffs, NJ: Prentice Hall, 1976).

75. C. Trappey, "A Meta-Analysis of Consumer Choice and Subliminal Advertising," *Psychology & Marketing,* August 1996, pp. 517–30; S. J. Broyles, "Subliminal Advertising and the Perpetual Popularity of Playing to People's Paranoia," *Journal of Consumer Affairs,* 40, no. 2 (2006), pp. 392–406. In contrast, see A. B. Aylesworth, R. C. Goodstein, and A. Kalra, "Effect of Archetypical Embeds on Feelings," *Journal of Advertising,* Fall 1999, pp. 73–81.

76. M. Rogers and C. A. Seiler, "The Answer Is No," *Journal of Advertising Research,* March 1994, pp. 36–45.

77. T. F. Stafford, "Alert or Oblivious?," *Psychology & Marketing,* September 2000, pp. 745–60.

78. See D. Grewal, K. B. Monroe, and R. Krishnan, "The Effects of Price-Comparison Advertising," *Journal of Marketing,* April 1998, pp. 46–59; and D. Grewal, R. Krishnan, J. Baker, and N. Borin, "The Effects of Store Name, Brand Name, and Price Discounts," *Journal of Retailing,* 3 (1998), pp. 331–52.

79. M. Viswanathan and T. L. Childers, "Understanding How Product Attributes Influence Product Categorization," *Journal of Marketing Research,* February 1999, pp. 75–94; and J. Gregan-Paxton, S. Hoeffler, and M. Zhao, "When Categorization Is Ambiguous," *Journal of Consumer Psychology,* 15, no. 2 (2005), pp. 127–40.

80. Goodstein, "Category-Based Applications and Extensions in Advertising."

81. G. P. Moreau, D. R. Lehmann, and A. B. Markman, "Entrenched Knowledge Structures and Consumer Responses to New Products," *Journal of Marketing Research,* February 2001, pp. 14–29; and G. Page Moreau, A. B. Markham, and D. R. Lehmann, "'What Is It?' Categorization Flexibility and Consumers' Responses to Really New Products," *Journal of Consumer Research,* March 2001, pp. 489–98.

82. J. Z. Sojka and J. L. Giese, "Thinking and/or Feeling," *Advances in Consumer Research,* vol. 24, ed. M. Bruck and D. J. MacInnis (Provo, UT: Association for Consumer Research, 1997), pp. 438–42; and J. A. Ruth, "Promoting a Brand's Emotional Benefits," *Journal of Consumer Psychology,* 11, no. 2 (2001), pp. 99–113.

83. See S. Ratneshwar, "Goal-Derived Categories," *Journal of Consumer Psychology,* 10, no. 3 (2001), pp. 147–57.

84. B. Turnbull and E. Matisoo-Smith, "Taste Sensitivity to 6-*n*-propylthiouracil Predicts Acceptance of Bitter-Tasting Spinach in 3–6-y-Old Children," *American Journal of Clinical Nutrition,* 76 (2002), pp. 1101–105.

85. J. O'Dell, "Harley-Davidson Quits Trying to Hog Sound," *LA Times,* June 21, 2000, http://articles.latimes.com/2000/jun/21/business/fi-43145, accessed September 1, 2014; J. Rohrlich, "Who Created the Windows Start-Up Sound?," *minyanville.com,* May 25, 2010, http://www.minyanville.com/businessmarkets/articles/intel-microsoft-research-in-motion-apple/5/25/2010/id/28465, accessed September 1, 2014; J. Pritchard, N. Coolbear, and J. Ward, "Enhanced Associative Memory for Colour (but Not Shape or Location) in Synaesthesia," *Cognition,* May 2013. pp. 230–34; C. Winter, "The Mind's Eye," *Bloomberg Businessweek,* January 9, 2014; W. Leung, "Synesthesia Can Be a blessing. Just Ask Kanye West," *The Globe and Mail,* February 10 2013, www.theglobeandmail.com/life/

health-and-fitness/health/synesthesia-can-be-a-blessing-just-ask-kanye-west/article8414660/, accessed September 1, 2014; and L. Spinney, "Synesthesia Sells," *NewScientist,* www.slate.com/articles/health_and_science/new_scientist/2013/09/cultural_synesthesia_in_marketing_tiffany_cadbury_and_corona_use_multiple.html, accessed September 1, 2014.

86. For a discussion, see J. E. Escalas, M. C. Moore, and J. E. Britton, "Fishing for Feelings?," *Journal of Consumer Psychology,* 14, nos. 1 & 2 (2004), pp. 105–14.

87. R. Ahluwalia, R. E. Burnkrant, and H. R. Unnava, "Consumer Response to Negative Publicity," *Journal of Marketing Research,* May 2000, pp. 203–14.

88. M. C. Campbell, "Perceptions of Price Unfairness," *Journal of Marketing Research,* May 1999, pp. 187–99; see also L. Xia, K. B. Monroe, and J. L. Cox, "The Price Is Unfair!," *Journal of Marketing,* October 2004, pp. 1–15.

89. G. Tom et al., "Cueing the Consumer," *Journal of Consumer Marketing,* Spring 1987, pp. 23–27. See also D. S. Kempf and R. N. Laczniak, "Advertising's Influence on Subsequent Product Trial Processing," *Journal of Advertising,* Fall 2001, pp. 27–40.

90. See K. R. Evans et al., "How First Impressions of a Customer Impact Effectiveness in an Initial Sales Encounter," *Journal of the Academy of Marketing Science,* Fall 2000, pp. 512–26.

91. J. J. Inman, L. McAlister, and W. D. Hoyer, "Promotion Signal," *Journal of Consumer Research,* June 1990, pp. 74–81.

92. See M. G. Meloy, "Mood-Driven Distortion of Product Information," *Journal of Consumer Research,* December 2000, pp. 345–58.

93. G. J. Gorn, A. Chattopadhyay, J. Sengupta, and S. Tripathi, "Waiting for the Web," *Journal of Marketing Research,* May 2004, pp. 215–25.

94. "GF, Coke Tell Why They Shun TV News," *Advertising Age,* January 28, 1980, p. 39.

95. A. B. Aylesworth and S. B. MacKenzie, "Context Is Key," *Journal of Advertising,* Summer 1998, pp. 17–31; Q. Chen and W. D. Wells, "Attitude toward the Site," *Journal of Advertising Research,* September 1999, pp. 27–37; and B. M. Tennis and A. B. Bakker, "Stay Tuned," *Journal of Advertising,* Fall 2001, pp. 15–25. See also S. Shapiro, D. J. MacInnis, and C.W. Park, "Understanding Program-Induced Mood Effects," *Journal of Advertising,* Winter 2002, pp. 15–26.

96. J. Liu and D. Smeesters, "Have You Seen the News Today?," *Journal of Marketing Research,* April 2010, pp. 251–62.

97. R. Alsop, "Color Grows More Important in Catching Consumers' Eyes," *The Wall Street Journal,* November 29, 1989, p. B1.

98. J. W. Pracejus, G. D. Olsen, and T. C. O'Guinn, "How Nothing Became Something," *Journal of Consumer Research,* June 2006, pp. 82–90.

99. D. L. Mothersbaugh, B. A. Huhmann, and G. R. Franke, "Combinatory and Separative Effects of Rhetorical Figures on Consumers' Effort and Focus in Ad Processing," *Journal of Consumer Research,* March 2002, pp. 589–602; E. F. McQuarrie and D. Glenn Mick, "Visual and Verbal Rhetorical Figures under Directed Processing versus Incidental Exposure to Advertising," *Journal of Consumer Research,* March 2003, pp. 579–87; S. Bulmer and M. Buchanan-Oliver, "Advertising across Cultures," *Journal of Current Issues and Research in Advertising,* Spring 2006, pp. 57–71; and J. Argo, M. Popa, and M. C. Smith, "The Sound of Brands," *Journal of Marketing,* July 2010, pp. 97–109.

100. T. Meenaghan, ed., "Ambush Marketing," special issue, *Psychology & Marketing,* July 1998.

101. J. Sengupta and G. J. Gorn, "Absence Makes the Mind Grow Sharper," *Journal of Marketing Research,* May 2002, pp. 186–201.

102. T. Howard, "Pay the Same, Get Less as Package Volume Falls," *USA Today,* March 17, 2003, p. 3b.

103. R. Bryant and L. Dundes, "Portion Distortion," *Journal of Consumer Affairs,* Winter 2005, pp. 399–408; and P. Chandon and B. Wansink, "Is Obesity Caused by Calorie Underestimation?," *Journal of Marketing Research,* February 2007, pp. 84–99.

104. A. Krishna, R. Briesch, D. R. Lehmann, and H. Yuan, "A Meta-Analysis of the Impact of Price Presentation on Perceived Savings," *Journal of Retailing,* 78 (2002), pp. 101–18; L. D. Compeau, J. Lindsey-Mullikin, D. Grewal, and R. D. Petty, "Consumers' Interpretations of the Semantic Phrases Found in Reference Price Advertisements," *Journal of Consumer Affairs,* Summer 2004, pp. 178–87; and T. Mazumdar, S. P. Raj, and I. Sinha, "Reference Price Research," *Journal of Marketing,* October 2005, pp. 84–102.

105. P. Raghubir, "Free Gift with Purchase," *Journal of Consumer Psychology,* 14, nos. 1 & 2 (2004), pp. 181–86.

106. S. Chatterjee, T. B. Heath, and S. Basuroy, "Failing to Suspect Collusion in Price-Matching Guarantees," *Journal of Consumer Psychology,* 13, no. 3 (2003), pp. 255–67; and J. Halliday, "GM Incentive Plans Could Damage Brand," *Advertising Age,* September 27, 2004, p. 1.

107. A. Kirmani, "Advertising Repetition as a Signal of Quality," *Journal of Advertising,* Fall 1997, pp. 77–86.

108. G. L. Lohse and D. L. Rosen, "Signaling Quality and Credibility in Yellow Pages Advertising," *Journal of Advertising,* Summer 2001, pp. 73–85.

109. A. Kirmani and A. R. Rao, "No Pain, No Gain," *Journal of Marketing,* April 2000, pp. 66–79; and D. Soberman, "Simultaneous Signaling and Screening with Warranties," *Journal of Marketing Research,* May 2003, pp. 176–92.

110. Z. Gurhan-Canli and D. Maheswaran, "Cultural Variations in Country of Origin Effects," *Journal of Marketing Research,* August 2000, pp. 309–17; Z. Gurhan-Canli and D. Maheswaran, "Determinants of Country-of-Origin Effects," *Journal of Consumer Research,* June 2000, pp. 96–108; and P. Chao, G. Wuhrer, and T. Werani, "Celebrity and Foreign Brand Name as Moderators of Country-of-Origin Effects," *International Journal of Advertising,* 24, no. 2 (2005), pp. 173–92.

111. B. J. Phillips and E. F. McQuarrie, "The Development, Change, and Transformation of Rhetorical Style in Magazine Advertisements 1954–1999," *Journal of Advertising,* 31, no. 4 (2003), pp. 1–13; L. A. Peracchio and J. Meyers-Levy, "Using Stylistic Properties of Ad Pictures to Communicate with Consumers," *Journal of Consumer Research,* June 2005, pp. 29–40; and J. Z. Sojka and J. L. Giese, "Communicating through Pictures and Words," *Psychology & Marketing,* December 2006, pp. 995–1014.

112. B. J. Phillips, "The Impact of Verbal Anchoring on Consumer Response to Image Ads," *Journal of Advertising,* Spring 2000, pp. 15–24; E. F. McQuarrie and D. G. Mick, "Visual Rhetoric in Advertising," *Journal of Consumer Research,* June 1999, pp. 37–54; and M. Callow and L. Schiffman, "Implicit Meaning in Visual Print Advertisements," *International Journal of Advertising,* 21 (2002), pp. 259–77.

113. See R. Kivetz and I. Simonson, "The Effects of Incomplete Information on Consumer Choice," *Journal of Marketing Research,* November 2000, pp. 427–48.

114. M. J. Barone and P. J. Miniard, "How and When Factual Ad Claims Mislead Consumers," *Journal of Marketing Research,* February 1999, pp. 58–74; M. J. Barone, K. M. Palan, and P. W. Miniard, "Brand Usage and Gender as Moderators of the Potential Deception Associated with Partial Comparative Advertising," *Journal of Advertising,* Spring 2004, pp. 19–28; and M. J. Barone, K. C. Manning, and P. W. Miniard, "Consumer Response to Retailers' Use of Partially Comparative Pricing," *Journal of Marketing,* July 2004, pp. 37–47.

115. For an excellent discussion, see I. L. Preston, *The Tangled Web They Weave* (Madison, WI: University of Madison Press, 1994).

116. L. Petrak, "Capturing Consumer Attention," *National Provisioner,* October 2003, pp. 52–53.

117. P. Boatwright and J. C. Nunes, "Reducing Assortment," *Journal of Marketing,* July 2001, pp. 50–63. See also E. van Herpen and R. Pieters, "The Variety of an Assortment," *Marketing Science,* Summer 2002, pp. 331–41; S. J. Hoch, E. T. Bradlow, and B. Wansink, "Rejoinder to 'The Variety of an Assortment,'" *Marketing Science,* Summer 2002, pp. 342–46; A. Chernev, "When More Is Less and Less Is More," *Journal of Consumer Research,* September 2003, pp. 170–83; and S. Thompson, "Kraft Vows to Kick Addiction to Extensions," *Advertising Age,* August 23, 2004, p. 1.

118. H. Chura, "Pepsi-Cola's Code Red Is White Hot," *Advertising Age,* August 27, 2001, p. 24.

119. "What's in a Name?," *Global Cosmetics Industry,* August 2002, p. 42. See also E. G. Miller and B. E. Kahn, "Shades of Meaning," *Journal of Consumer Research,* June 2005, pp. 86–92; J. L. Skorinko et al., "A Rose by Any Other Name . . . ," *Psychology and Marketing,* December 2006, pp. 975–93; and "Study: Food in McDonald's Wrapper Tastes Better to Kids," *CNN.com,* accessed August 7, 2007. See also R. Raghunathan, R. W. Naylor, and W. D. Hoyer, "The Unhealthy = Tasty Intuition," *Journal of Marketing,* October 2006, pp. 170–84.

120. S. Zhang and B. H. Schmitt, "Creating Local Brands in Multilingual International Markets," *Journal of Marketing Research,* August 2001, pp. 313–25.

121. S. Freeman, "Revived 'Hemi' Engine Helps Chrysler Juice Up Its Sales," *The Wall Street Journal,* April 30, 2004, p. B1.

122. R. R. Klink, "Creating Brand Names with Meaning," *Marketing Letters* 11, no. 1 (2000), pp. 5–20; and E. Yorkston and G. Menon, "A Sound Idea," *Journal of Consumer Research,* June 2004, pp. 43–51.

123. S. Begley, "New ABCs of Branding," *The Wall Street Journal,* August 26, 2002, p. B1.

124. I. P. Levin and A. M. Levin, "Modeling the Role of Brand Alliances in the Assimilation of Product Evaluations," *Journal of Consumer Psychology* 9, no. 1 (2000), pp. 43–52; and K. K. Desai and K. I. Keller, "The Effects of Ingredient Branding Strategies on Host Brand Extendibility," *Journal of Marketing,* January 2002, pp. 73–93.

125. See J. Tantillo, J. D. Lorenzo-Aiss, and R. E. Mathisen, "Quantifying Perceived Differences in Type Styles," *Psychology & Marketing,* August 1995, pp. 447–57; and C. Janiszewski and T. Meyvis, "Effects of Brand Logo Complexity, Repetition, and Spacing on Processing Fluency and Judgment," *Journal of Marketing Research,* June 2001, pp. 18–32.

126. T. L. Childers and J. Jass, "All Dressed Up with Something to Say," *Journal of Consumer Psychology* 12, no. 2 (2002), pp. 93–106; J. R. Doyle and P. A. Bottomley, "Font Appropriateness and Brand Choice," *Journal of Business Research,* 57 (2004), pp. 873–80; and J. R. Doyle and P. A. Bottomley, "Dressed for the Occasion," *Journal of Consumer Psychology,* 16, no. 2 (2006), pp. 112–23. See also P. W. Henderson, J. L. Giese, and J. A. Cote, "Impression Management Using Typeface Design," *Journal of Marketing,* October 2004, pp. 60–72.

127. P. W. Henderson and J. A. Cote, "Guidelines for Selecting or Modifying Logos," *Journal of Marketing,* April 1998, pp. 14–30; and J. T. Landry, "Making Logos Matter," *Harvard Business Review,* March–April 1998, pp. 16–17.

128. M. Peers, "Buddy, Can You Spare Some Time?," *The Wall Street Journal,* January 26, 2004, p. B1; and B. Frank, "'Missing' Men Prove Prescient," *Advertising Age,* August 23, 2004, p. 16.

129. "Ford Boss Outlines Shift to 'Rifle' Media," *Advertising Age,* October 26, 1981, p. 89. See also P. J. Danaher, "Wearout Effects in Target Marketing," *Marketing Letters,* 3 (1996), pp. 275–87.

130. P. N. Shamdasani, A. J. S. Stanaland, and J. Tan, "Location, Location, Location," *Journal of Advertising Research,* July 2001, pp. 7–20.

131. Lehman, "Mad Ave Clicks with the Gamers."

132. J. Guterman, "Outdoor Interactive," *American Demographics,* August 2001, p. 32.

133. O. Ampuero and N. Vila, "Consumer Perceptions of Product Packaging," *Journal of Consumer Marketing,* 23, no. 2 (2006), pp. 100–112.

134. B. E. Kahn and B. Wansink, "The Influence of Assortment Structure on Perceived Variety and Consumption Quantities," *Journal of Consumer Research,* March 2004, pp. 519–33.

135. S. Thompson, "M&M's Wraps Up Promo with Color," *Advertising Age,* March 8, 2004, p. 4.

136. B. Wansink and K. Van Ittersum, "Bottoms Up!," *Journal of Consumer Research,* December 2003, pp. 455–63; V. Folkes and S. Matta, "The Effect of Package Shape on Consumers' Judgments of Product Volume," *Journal of Consumer Research,* September 2004, pp. 390–401; and J. Hoegg and J. W. Alba, "Taste Perception," *Journal of Consumer Research,* March 2007, pp. 490–498.

137. S. Yang and P. Raghubir, "Can Bottles Speak Volumes?," *Journal of Retailing,* 81, no. 4 (2005), pp. 269–81.

138. E. Lepkowska-White and A. L. Parsons, *Journal of Consumer Affairs,* Winter 2001, pp. 278–94; and V. A. Taylor and A. B. Bower, "Improving Product Instruction Compliance," *Psychology & Marketing,* March 2004, pp. 229–45; see also J. J. Argo and K. J. Main, "Meta-Analyses of the Effectiveness of Warning Labels," *Journal of Public Policy and Marketing,* Fall 2004, pp. 193–208.

chapter 9

Learning, Memory, and Product Positioning

LEARNING OBJECTIVES

LO1 **Describe the nature of learning and memory.**

LO2 **Explain the types of memory and memory's role in learning.**

LO3 **Distinguish the different processes underlying high- and low-involvement learning.**

LO4 **Summarize the factors affecting information retrieval from memory.**

LO5 **Understand the application of learning to brand positioning, equity, and leverage.**

Learning and memory can be tricky things for consumers and marketers. How we learn or "come to know" something is complex and multifaceted. Once we have learned something, it is hard to "unlearn" it even when we are told or suspect that it is false. Marketers must deal with the challenge of understanding learning and memory and the implications this has for marketing messages and product design.

Some bizarre, funny, and not-so-funny examples of learning and the difficulty of unlearning include:[1]

- The flies etched in urinals in men's restrooms apparently act as "targets," resulting in 80 percent less "spilling." How men "learn" to aim for the target is not well understood.
- People given large-size buckets of five-day-old stale popcorn mindlessly eat 57 percent more popcorn than people given medium-size buckets of the same popcorn. One source of such "mindless" eating could be the "clean your plate" mantra "learned" at an early age by many children in the United States.
- We "learn" from an early age that buttons get responses via video games, door bells, and so on. Interestingly, research suggests that most "cross walk" buttons are not hooked up to anything and yet people push them endlessly in expectation of an effect.
- We have "learned" that certain noises signal successful action. Thus, while smartphones don't need a "click" for button action success (keyboard or camera), consumers often want the noise because they find it hard to "unlearn" the "noise = successful action" link.
- We have "learned" how cars should sound with combustion engines both as an operator and as pedestrians trying to stay safe. The Nissan Leaf hybrid car runs so quietly that drivers could not tell that their car was running. A synthesizer in the dashboard hooked up to speakers in the hood plays an engine sound to provide drivers with the needed feedback. To warn other people of its approach, an artificial roaring noise was added to the silent ENV hydrogen cell motorcycle.

In this chapter, we discuss the nature of learning and memory, conditioning and cognitive theories of learning, and factors affecting retrieval. Implications for marketing managers are discussed throughout, culminating with an examination of product positioning and brand equity in the final sections.

NATURE OF LEARNING AND MEMORY

LO1 Learning is essential to the consumption process. In fact, consumer behavior is largely *learned* behavior. People acquire most of their attitudes, values, tastes, behaviors, preferences, symbolic meanings, and feelings through learning. Culture, family, friends, mass media, and advertising provide learning experiences that affect the type of lifestyle people seek and the products they consume. Consider, for example, how often your movie choices are influenced by what you read online and discussions you have with friends.

Learning is *any change in the content or organization of long-term memory or behavior*[2] and is the result of information processing. In the previous chapter, we described information processing as *a series of activities by which stimuli are perceived, transformed into information, and stored.* The four activities in the series are exposure, attention, interpretation, and memory.

As Figure 9–1 indicates, different information processing systems handle different aspects of learning. The perceptual system deals with information intake through exposure and attention and, as we discussed in Chapter 8, may be conscious or unconscious. Short-term memory deals with holding information temporarily while it is interpreted and transferred into long-term memory. Long-term memory deals with storing and retrieving information to be used in decisions.

These processes are highly interrelated. For example, a consumer may notice his or her favorite brand of soda on the store shelf because of a purchase goal stored in long-term

FIGURE 9-1 Information Processing, Learning, and Memory

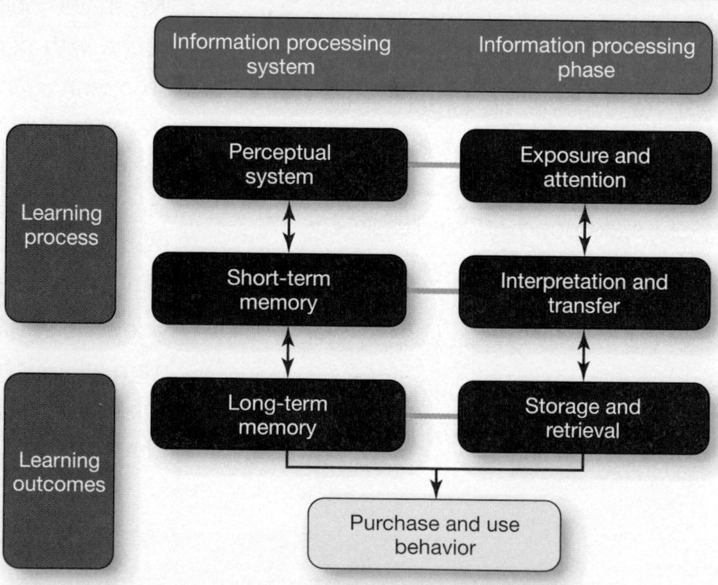

memory. The soda's current price is brought into short-term memory through the perceptual system for processing. But a reference price may also be retrieved from long-term memory as a comparison point. Finally, price perceptions associated with the consumer's favorite brand may be updated and stored in long-term memory as a consequence of the comparison process.

MEMORY'S ROLE IN LEARNING

L02

Memory is the total accumulation of prior learning experiences. As Figure 9–1 suggests, memory is critical to learning. It consists of two interrelated components: short-term and long-term memory.[3] These are *not* distinct physiological entities. Instead, **short-term memory (STM),** or *working memory,* is that portion of total memory that is currently activated or in use. **Long-term memory (LTM)** is that portion of total memory devoted to permanent information storage.

Short-Term Memory

STM has a limited capacity to store information and sensations. In fact, it is not used for storage in the usual sense of that term. It is more like a computer file that is currently in use. Active files hold information while it is being processed. After processing is complete, the reconfigured information is printed or returned to more permanent storage such as the hard drive. A similar process occurs with STM. Individuals use STM to hold information while they analyze and interpret it. They may then transfer it to another system (write or type it), place it in LTM, or both. Thus, STM is closely analogous to what we normally call thinking. *It is an active, dynamic process, not a static structure.*

STM Is Short Lived Information in working memory decays quickly. The memory span for prices, for example, is about 3.7 seconds.[4] The short-lived nature of STM means that consumers must constantly refresh information through **maintenance rehearsal** or it will be lost. Maintenance rehearsal is *the continual repetition of a piece of information in order to hold it in current memory for use in problem solving or transferal to LTM.* Repeating the same formula or definition several times before taking an exam is an example. Marketers frequently simulate this by repeating the brand name or a key benefit in a prominent manner several times in an ad.

STM Has Limited Capacity The limited capacity of STM means that consumers can hold only so much information in current memory. The capacity of STM is thought to be in the range of five to nine bits of information. A bit can be an individual item or a related set of items. Organizing individual items into groups of related items that can be processed as a single unit is called *chunking.* Chunking can greatly aid in the transfer (and recall) of information from memory. A recent study of toll-free *vanity numbers* shows the power of chunking. Memory for completely numeric numbers was 8 percent, memory for combinations of numbers and words (800-555-HOME) was 44 percent, and memory for all words (800-NEW-HOME) was 58 percent! The number of bits goes down as the words become meaningful chunks replacing meaningless numbers.[5]

Marketers can help consumers chunk product information by organizing detailed attribute information in messages around the more general benefits that they create. Interestingly, consumers who are product experts are better able to chunk due to highly organized memory structures. As a consequence, experts are better able to learn information and avoid information overload.[6]

ILLUSTRATION 9-1

Successful brands must enter into memory in a favorable manner, and they must be recalled when required. The brand name, visual, and ad text will enhance elaborative activities appropriate for the product.

Elaborative Activities Occur in STM STM is often termed working memory because that's where information is analyzed, categorized, and interpreted—that is, STM is where **elaborative activities** take place. Elaborative activities are *the use of previously stored experiences, values, attitudes, beliefs, and feelings to interpret and evaluate information in working memory as well as to add relevant previously stored information.* Elaborative activities serve to redefine or add new elements to memory.

Suppose your firm has developed a new product for consumers who want to use their electronic devices safely while driving. The product is a voice-activated program that allows you to give commands to your MP3 player and to your cell phone, hands free. How will this product be categorized? The answer depends in large part on *how* it is presented. How it is presented will influence the nature of the elaborative activities that will occur, which in turn will determine how the product is remembered. Illustration 9–1 shows how the elements of an advertisement can work together to enhance elaborative activities.

Elaborative activities can involve both concepts and imagery. **Concepts** are abstractions of reality that capture the meaning of an item in terms of other concepts. They are similar to a dictionary definition of a word. **Imagery** involves concrete sensory representations of ideas, feelings, and objects. It permits a direct recovery of aspects of past experiences.

Thus, imagery processing involves the recall and mental manipulation of sensory images, including sight, smell, taste, and tactile (touch) sensations.

Pictures can increase imagery, particularly when they are *vivid,* meaning they are relatively concrete representations of reality rather than an abstraction. Pictures are not the only factor to increase imagery, however. Words and phrases in an ad can also encourage consumers to conjure up their own images (e.g., "picture it . . .," "feel it . . .," "imagine . . .").

Marketers need to make sure that the words and pictures work together. For example, if the ad text invites consumers to engage in imagery processing but provides them with a boring picture, then consumers will be turned off to the message and less likely to buy the brand.[7]

Whether consumers are processing concepts or images, a key issue in learning and memory is the *extent of elaboration.* A major determinant of elaboration is consumer motivation or involvement. Elaboration is enhanced when consumers are more involved or interested in the brand, product, or message at hand (as we saw earlier, it also is facilitated by consumer expertise). Elaboration increases the chances that information will be transferred to LTM and be retrieved at a later time by increasing the processing attention directed at that information and by establishing meaningful linkages between the new information and existing information. These linkages or associations are an important part of LTM, as discussed next.

Long-Term Memory

LTM is viewed as *an unlimited, permanent storage.* It can store numerous types of information, such as concepts, decision rules, processes, and affective (emotional) states. Marketers are particularly interested in **semantic memory,** which is *the basic knowledge and feelings an individual has about a concept.* It represents the person's understanding of an object or event at its simplest level. At this level, a brand such as Acura might be categorized as "a luxury car."

Another type of memory of interest to marketers is **episodic memory.** This is *the memory of a sequence of events in which a person participated.* These personal memories of events such as a first date, graduation, or learning to drive can be quite strong. They often elicit imagery and feelings. Marketers frequently attempt to evoke episodic memories either because their brand was involved in them or to associate the positive feelings they generate with the brand. Flashbulb memories are a special type of episodic memory. **Flashbulb memory** is *acute memory for the circumstances surrounding a surprising and novel event.*[8]

Key aspects of flashbulb memories include the following:

- They are vividly detailed and therefore highly enduring over time.
- They contain specific situational detail about location, people, activities, and felt emotions.
- They are held with a high degree of confidence.
- They are perceived as special and different from memories of ordinary or mundane experiences.

Marketers worry not only about *what* information is stored in LTM but also *how* this information is organized. Two important memory structures are schemas and scripts.

Schemas Both concepts and episodes acquire depth of meaning by becoming associated with other concepts and episodes. A pattern of such associations around a particular concept is termed a **schema** or *schematic memory,* sometimes called a *knowledge structure.* Schematic memory is a complex web of associations. Figure 9–2 provides a simplified example of a schema by showing how one might associate various concepts with Mountain Dew to form a network of meaning for that brand. Notice that our hypothetical

FIGURE 9-2 A Partial Schematic Memory for Mountain Dew

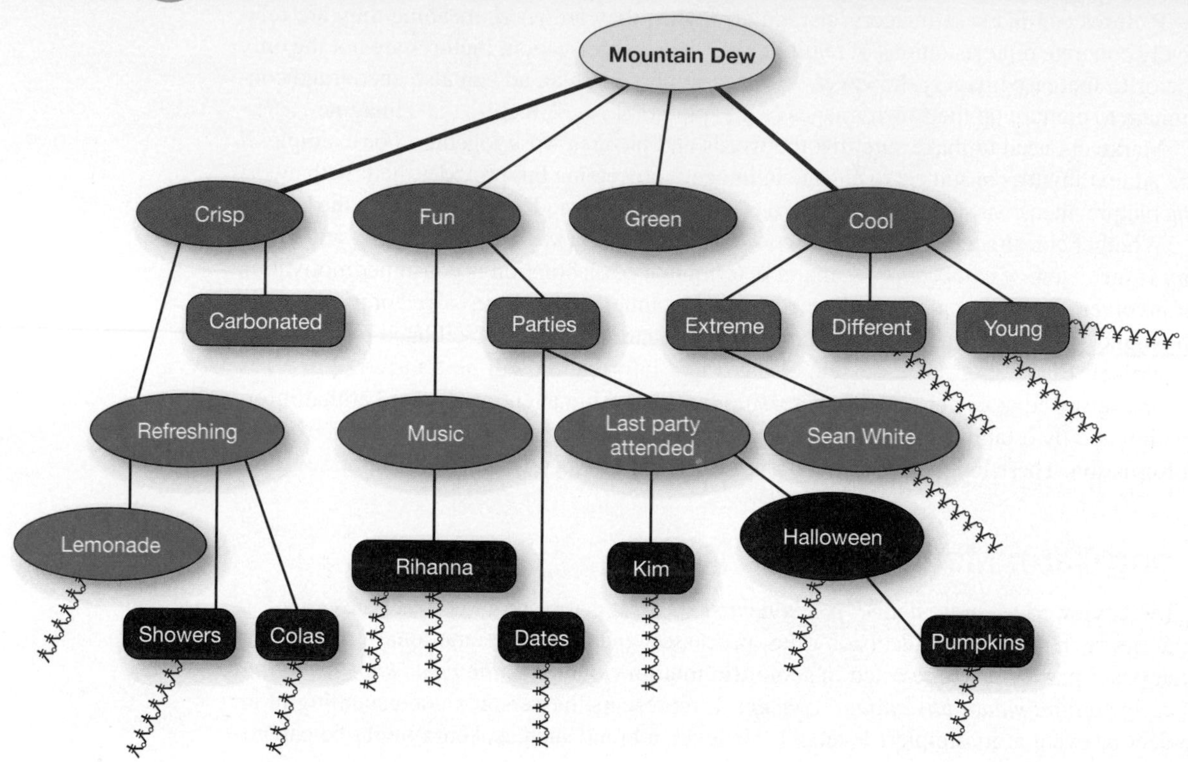

schema contains *product characteristics, usage situations, episodes,* and *affective reactions.* The source of some of the schema is personal experience, but other aspects may be completely or partially based on marketing activities.[9] The schematic memory of a brand is the same as the brand image, which we discuss later in the chapter. It is what the consumer thinks of and feels when the brand name is mentioned.

In the partial schema shown in Figure 9–2, concepts, events, and feelings are stored in *nodes* within memory. Thus, the concept "cool" is stored in a node, as are "music," "fun," and "Halloween." Each of these is associated either directly or indirectly with Mountain Dew. *Associative links* connect various concepts to form the complete meaning assigned to an item.

Associative links vary in terms of how strongly and how directly they are associated with a node. In our example, crisp, fun, green, and cool are directly associated with Mountain Dew. However, one or two of these may be strongly associated with the brand, as crisp and cool are shown to be by the bold lines in our example. Other nodes, such as fun and green, may have weaker links. Without reinforcement, the weaker links may disappear or fade over time (e.g., the Halloween party linkage). Over the longer run, so will the stronger ones (e.g., the cool linkage). Marketers spend enormous effort attempting to develop strong, easily activated links between their brands and desirable product benefits.[10] The various ways in which these linkages are established and strengthened (reinforced) are discussed in the next section, on learning.

The memory activation shown in Figure 9–2 originated with the name of a particular brand. If the activation had begun with the concept "cool," would Mountain Dew arise as a node directly linked to cool? It would depend on the total context in which the memory was being activated. In general, multiple memory nodes are activated simultaneously. Thus, a question like "What is a cool soft drink?" might quickly activate a memory schema that links Mountain Dew directly to cool. However, a more abstract question like "What is cool?" might not because of its relatively weak and indirect connection to beverages and sodas.[11] Marketers expend substantial effort to influence the schema consumers have for their brands. We will discuss this process in detail later in the chapter.

Marketers also strive to influence the schema consumers have for consumption situations. For example, consumers likely have very different beverage schemas for situations such as jogging, where thirst is a key component, than for a party, where socializing and relaxing are key components. The beverage schema for jogging might include products such as water and soda and brands such as Dasani and Pepsi. The beverage schema for a party might include products such as wine and beer and brands such as Yellow Tail and Budweiser. Brands in the schematic memory that come to mind (are recalled) for a specific problem or situation such as thirst are known as the *evoked set.*

The usage situation schema to which a brand attaches itself can have major ramifications. For example, if Canada Dry Ginger Ale associated itself strongly with a "party" situation as a mixer for cocktails, then it is much less likely to be retrieved as part of the evoked set when consumers are thinking of other usage situations, such as those involving thirst.[12] We will discuss how the evoked set influences consumer decision making in Chapter 15.

Scripts *Memory of how an action sequence should occur,* such as purchasing and drinking a soft drink to relieve thirst, is a special type of schema known as a **script.** Scripts are necessary for consumers to shop effectively. One of the difficulties new forms of retailing have is teaching consumers the appropriate script for acquiring items in a new manner. This is the problem facing firms wanting to sell products via the Internet. Before these firms can succeed, their target markets must learn appropriate scripts for Internet shopping. Green marketing efforts relate in part to teaching consumers appropriate scripts for disposal that include recycling.

Retrieval from LTM The likelihood and ease with which information can be recalled from LTM is termed **accessibility.** Every time an informational node or a link between nodes is activated (accessed) in memory, it is strengthened. Thus, accessibility can be enhanced by rehearsal, repetition, and elaboration. For example, Coca-Cola might be one of the brands that always comes to mind (is retrieved) when you think of sodas because you have seen so many ads for that brand. This accessibility effect for brands is called *top-of-mind awareness.* In addition, accessibility is related to the strength and number of incoming linkages. In essence, when a concept is linked to other concepts in memory, its accessibility increases as a result of the multiple retrieval pathways. Thus, elaboration enhances retrieval by creating a rich associative network. Finally, accessibility is related to the strength and directness of links to nodes, with stronger and more direct linkages being more accessible. Thus, *cool* and *crisp* are highly accessible associations related to Mountain Dew, while *parties* and *refreshing* are less accessible. Clearly, marketers want strong and direct linkages between their brand and critical product features.

Retrieving information from LTM is not a completely objective or mechanical task. If asked to recall the sponsor of the last summer Olympics, some consumers will not remember instantly and certainly. These individuals may *construct* a memory based on limited recall and a series of judgments or inferences. For example, many might "recall" Nike because it is a dominant firm in sports equipment and apparel. Thus, it would "make sense" for Nike to be the sponsor, which could lead some consumers to believe that Nike was indeed a sponsor of the event even if it was not.[13] Therefore, memory is sometimes shaped and changed as it is accessed.

Finally, retrieval may involve *explicit* or *implicit* memories. Traditionally, we have thought of remembering, and thus memory, as the ability to recall specific items or events. If you read this chapter and then try to answer the review questions at the end without referring back to the chapter, you are engaging in traditional memory recall. This is referred to as **explicit memory,** which is characterized by *the conscious recollection of an exposure event.* In contrast, **implicit memory** involves *the nonconscious retrieval of previously encountered stimuli.* It is a sense of familiarity, a feeling, or a set of beliefs about an item without conscious awareness of when and how they were acquired. An example of implicit memory relates to brand placements. One study found that over time, a brand's image becomes increasingly similar to the TV show in which it appears, even when consumers don't remember seeing the brand placements![14]

LEARNING UNDER HIGH AND LOW INVOLVEMENT

LO3 We have described learning as any change in the content or organization of long-term memory or behavior. In addition, we have described LTM in terms of schemas or associational networks. So how do people *learn* these associations? For example, how do consumers *learn* that Mountain Dew is cool or that Walmart has low prices?

A moment's reflection will reveal that people learn things in different ways. For example, buying a car or stereo generally involves intense, focused attention and processing. The outcome of these efforts is rewarded by better choices. However, most learning is of a much different nature. Even if they don't care for baseball, most people know who is playing in the World Series each year because they hear about it frequently. And people can identify clothes that are stylish even though they never really think much about clothing styles.

As just described, learning may occur in either a high-involvement or a low-involvement situation. Recall from Chapter 8 that information processing (and therefore learning) may be conscious and deliberate in high-involvement situations. Or it may be nonfocused and even nonconscious in low-involvement situations. A **high-involvement learning** situation is one in which *the consumer is motivated to process or learn the material.* For example, an individual reading *PC Magazine* prior to purchasing a computer is probably highly motivated to learn relevant material dealing with the various computer brands. A **low-involvement learning** situation is one in which *the consumer has little or no motivation to process or learn the material.* A consumer whose television program is interrupted by a commercial for a product he or she doesn't currently use or feel a desire for generally has little motivation to learn the material presented in the commercial. Much, if not most, consumer learning occurs in relatively low-involvement contexts.[15]

As we will see in the following sections, the way a communication should be structured differs depending on the level of involvement the audience is expected to have. Illustration 9–2 shows the FEL-PRO ad that assumes high-involvement learning and the Campbell's Select ad based on low-involvement learning. *Why does one ad assume a highly involved audience and the other a low-involvement audience? What differences do you notice between these two ads? Do those differences make sense?*

Figure 9–3 shows the two general situations and the five specific learning theories that we are going to consider. *Level of involvement is the primary determinant of how material is learned.* The solid lines in the figure indicate that operant conditioning and analytical reasoning are common learning processes in high-involvement situations. Classical conditioning and iconic rote learning tend to occur in low-involvement situations. And vicarious learning/modeling is common in both low- and high-involvement situations. We will discuss each of these theories in the following pages.

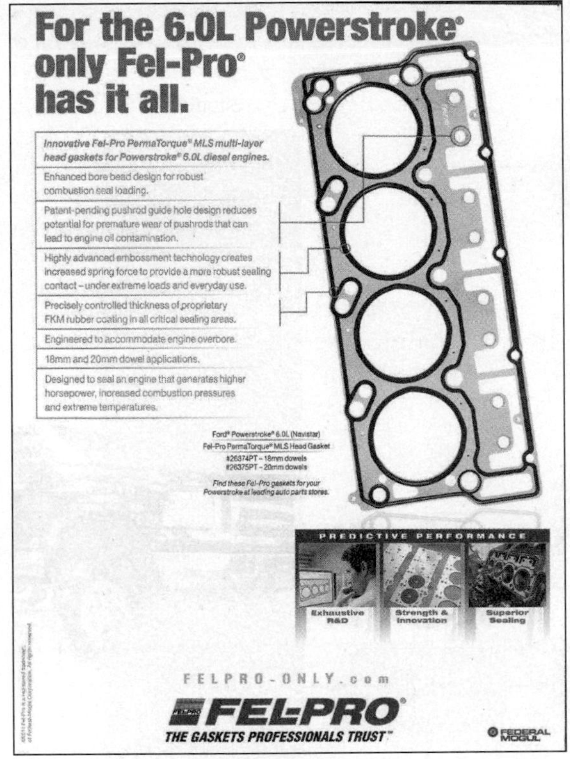

ILLUSTRATION 9-2

An important judgment in designing an ad is the level of involvement the audience will have as shown by the FEL-PRO and Campbell's Select ads.

Conditioning

Conditioning is probably most appropriately described as a set of procedures that marketers can use to increase the chances that an association between two stimuli is formed or learned. The word *conditioning* has a negative connotation to many people and brings forth images of robot-like humans. However, the general procedure simply involves presenting two stimuli in close proximity so that eventually the two are perceived (consciously or unconsciously) to be related or associated. That is, consumers learn that the stimuli go (or do not go) together.

There are two basic forms of conditioned learning: classical and operant. *Classical conditioning* attempts to create an association between a stimulus (e.g., brand name) and some response (e.g., behavior or feeling). *Operant conditioning* attempts to create an association between a response (e.g., buying a brand) and some outcome (e.g., satisfaction) that serves to reinforce the response.

Classical Conditioning Imagine that you are marketing a new brand of pen and want consumers to feel positively about that pen. How might classical conditioning help you to associate positive feelings with your unfamiliar brand? The classical conditioning procedure would have you pair the unknown brand repeatedly together with some other stimulus that you know already *automatically* elicits positive feelings or emotions, such as popular music in an ad. The goal would be that, eventually, after repeatedly pairing the brand name and the music, the brand name alone will elicit the same positive feelings produced by the music.

The process of using an established relationship between one stimulus (music) and response (pleasant feelings) to bring about the learning of the same response (pleasant feelings) to a different stimulus (the brand) is called **classical conditioning.** Figure 9–4 illustrates this type of learning. Hearing popular music (unconditioned stimulus) automatically elicits a positive emotion (unconditioned response) in many individuals. If

FIGURE 9-3 Learning Theories in High- and Low-Involvement Situations

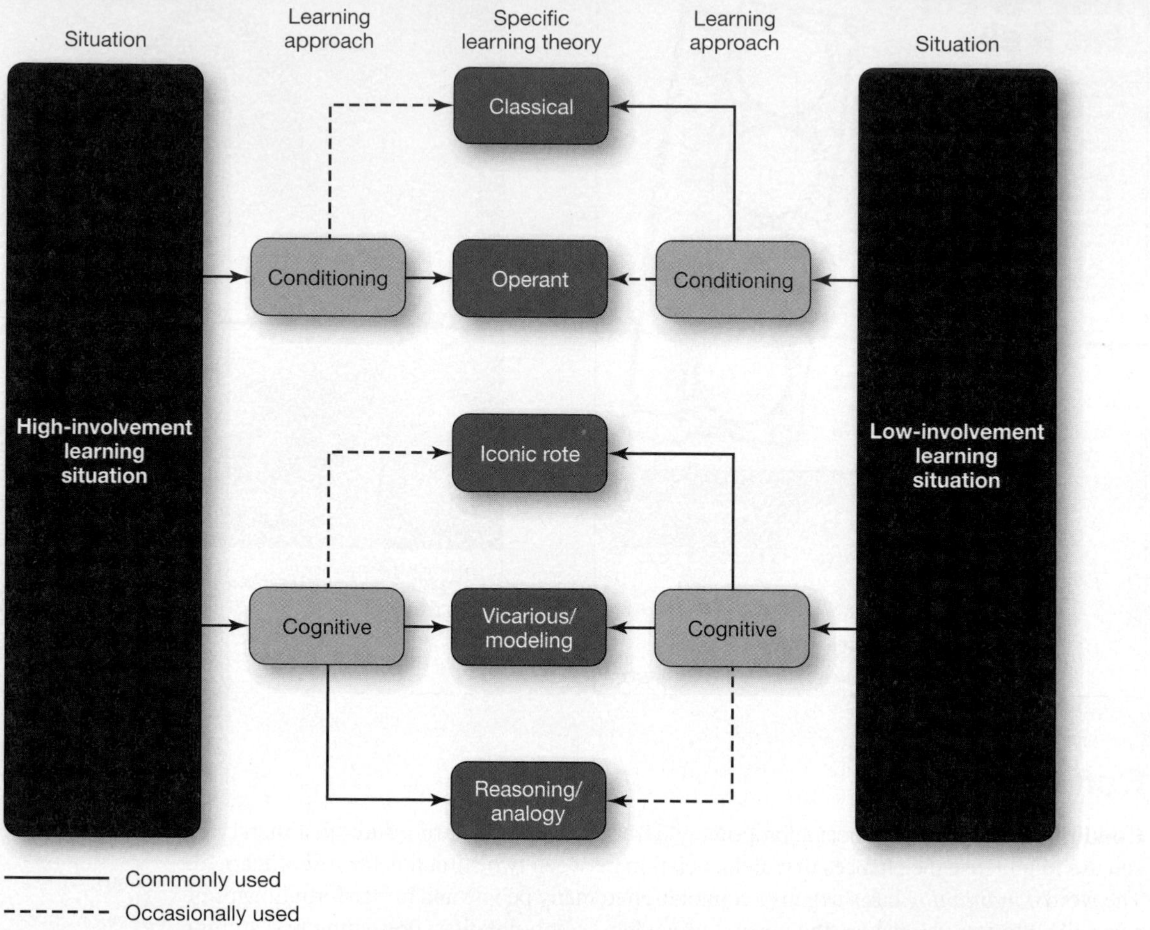

Situation | Learning approach | Specific learning theory | Learning approach | Situation

High-involvement learning situation

Conditioning

Cognitive

Classical

Operant

Iconic rote

Vicarious/ modeling

Reasoning/ analogy

Conditioning

Cognitive

Low-involvement learning situation

——— Commonly used

- - - - - Occasionally used

FIGURE 9-4 Consumer Learning through Classical Conditioning

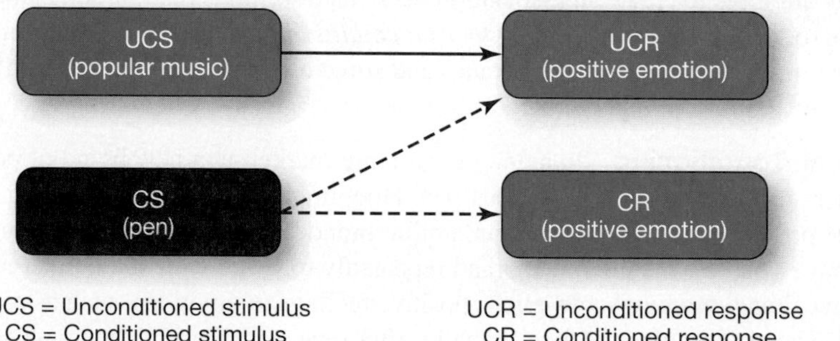

this music is consistently paired with a particular brand of pen or other product (conditioned stimulus), the brand itself may come to elicit the same positive emotion (conditioned response).[16] In addition, some features, such as the masculine/feminine qualities of the unconditioned stimulus, may also become associated with the conditioned stimulus.

That is, using a scene showing males or females in an activity that elicits positive emotions may not only cause a positive emotional response to a brand consistently paired with it, but also cause the brand to have a masculine or a feminine image.[17] Thus, classical conditioning can lead to positive attitudes by influencing brand feelings and beliefs. This is important because, as we will see in later chapters, attitudes influence information search, trial, and brand choice.

Other marketing applications of classical conditioning include:

- Consistently advertising a product on exciting sports programs may result in the product itself generating an excitement response.
- An unknown political candidate may elicit patriotic feelings by consistently playing patriotic background music in his or her commercials and appearances.
- Christmas music played in stores may elicit emotional responses associated with giving and sharing, which in turn may increase the propensity to purchase.

Learning via classical conditioning is most common in low-involvement situations, where relatively low levels of processing effort and awareness are involved.[18] However, after a sufficient number of low-involvement "scannings" or "glances at" the advertisement, the association may be formed or learned.

Operant Conditioning **Operant conditioning** (or instrumental learning) involves rewarding desirable behaviors such as brand purchases with a positive outcome that serves to reinforce the behavior.[19] The more often a response is reinforced, the more likely it will be repeated in the future as consumers *learn* that the response is associated with a positive outcome.

Imagine that you are marketing a snack called Pacific Snax's Rice Popcorn. You believe your product has a light, crisp taste that consumers will like. But how can you influence them to learn to consume your brand? One option, based on the operant conditioning procedure, would be to distribute a large number of free samples through the mail, at shopping malls, or in stores. Many consumers would try the free sample (desired response). To the extent that the taste of Rice Popcorn is indeed pleasant (a positive outcome that serves as a reinforcement), the probability of continued consumption is increased. This is shown graphically in Figure 9–5.

Unlike the relatively automatic associations created by classical conditioning, operant conditioning requires that consumers first engage in a deliberate behavior and come to understand its power in predicting positive outcomes that serve as reinforcement. As suggested in Figure 9–3, such learning is common under conditions of higher involvement.

Operant conditioning often involves influencing consumers to purchase a specific brand or product (desired response). Thus, a great deal of marketing strategy is aimed at securing an initial trial. Free samples (at home or in the store), special price discounts on

Consumer Learning by Operant Conditioning FIGURE 9-5

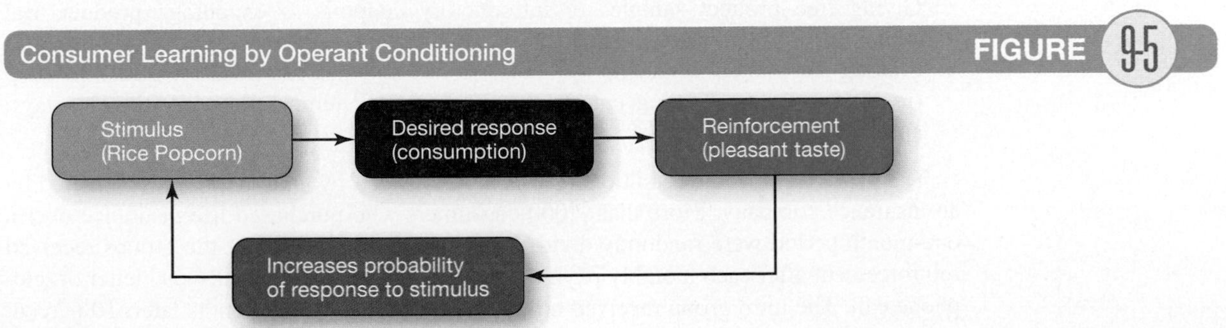

FIGURE 9-6 The Process of Shaping in Purchase Behavior

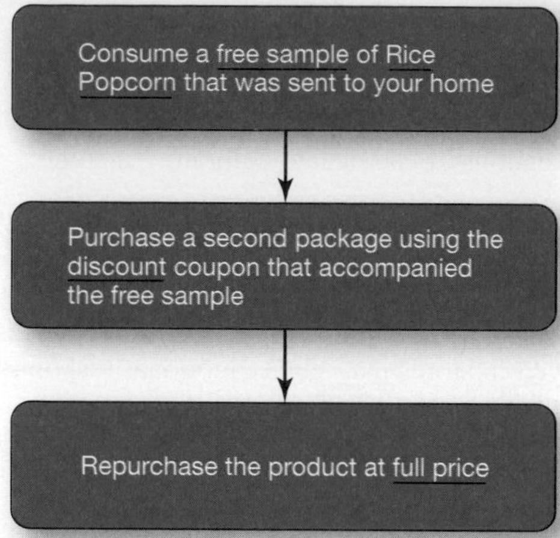

new products, and contests all represent rewards offered to consumers to try a particular product or brand. If they try the brand under these conditions and like it (reinforcement), they are likely to take the next step and purchase it in the future. This process of encouraging partial responses leading to the final desired response (consume a free sample, buy at a discount, buy at full price) is known as **shaping** and is illustrated in Figure 9–6.

In one study, 84 percent of those given a free sample of a chocolate while in a candy store made a purchase, whereas only 59 percent of those not provided a sample made a purchase. Thus, shaping can be very effective. Illustration 9–3 shows an ad for Ciba Vision Dailies lenses. This ad is designed to induce trial, the first step in shaping.

While reinforcement increases the likelihood of behavior such as a purchase being repeated, a negative consequence (punishment) has exactly the opposite effect. Thus, the purchase of a brand that does not function properly greatly reduces the chances of future purchases of that brand. This underscores the critical importance of consistent product quality.

Operant conditioning is used widely by marketers. The most common application is to offer consistent-quality products so that the use of the product to meet a consumer need is reinforcing. Other applications include:

- Direct mail or personal contact after a sale that congratulates the purchaser for making a wise purchase.
- Giving extra reinforcement for purchasing a particular brand, such as rebates, toys in cereal boxes, or discount coupons.
- Giving free product samples or introductory coupons to encourage product trial (shaping).
- Making store interiors, shopping malls, or downtown areas pleasant places to shop (reinforcing) by providing entertainment, controlled temperature, exciting displays, and so forth.

The power of operant conditioning was demonstrated by an experiment conducted by an insurance company. More than 2,000 consumers who purchased life insurance over a one-month period were randomly divided into three groups. Two of the groups received reinforcement after each monthly payment in the form of a nice "thank-you" letter or telephone call. The third group received no such reinforcement. Six months later, 10 percent of the members of the two groups that received reinforcement had terminated their policies, while 23 percent of those who had not received reinforcement had done so! Reinforcement (being thanked) led to continued behavior (sending in the monthly premium).[20]

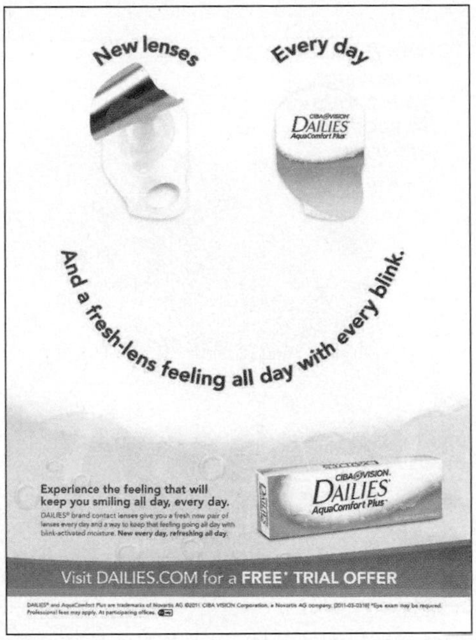

ILLUSTRATION 9-3

Marketers design products that they hope will meet consumer needs. When a need is met by a product, the probability of its being purchased in the future increases. A critical step in the process is the initial purchase or trial of the product. This ad encourages such a trial as shown by the Ciba Vision Dailies ad.

Cognitive Learning

Cognitive learning encompasses all the mental activities of humans as they work to solve problems or cope with situations. It involves learning ideas, concepts, attitudes, and facts that contribute to our ability to reason, solve problems, and learn relationships without direct experience or reinforcement. Cognitive learning can range from very simple information acquisition (as in iconic rote learning) to complex, creative problem solving (as in analytical reasoning). Three types of cognitive learning are important to marketers.

Iconic Rote Learning Learning *a concept or the association between two or more concepts in the absence of conditioning* is known as **iconic rote learning.** For example, one may see an ad that states "Ketoprofin is a headache remedy" and associate the new concept "ketoprofin" with the existing concept "headache remedy." Notice the distinction from conditioning in that there is neither an unconditioned stimulus (classical) nor a direct reward or reinforcement (operant) involved.

Also, it is important to point out that unlike more complex forms of cognitive learning, iconic rote learning generally involves considerably less cognitive effort and elaboration.[21] A substantial amount of low-involvement learning involves iconic rote learning. Numerous repetitions of a simple message that occur as the consumer scans the environment may result in the essence of the message being learned. Through iconic rote learning, consumers may form beliefs about the characteristics or attributes of products without being aware of the source of the information. When the need arises, a purchase may be made based on those beliefs.[22]

Vicarious Learning or Modeling It is not necessary for consumers to directly experience a reward or punishment to learn. Instead, they can observe the outcomes of others' behaviors and adjust their own accordingly.[23] Similarly, they can use imagery to anticipate the outcome of various courses of action. This is known as **vicarious learning** or **modeling.**

This type of learning is common in both low- and high-involvement situations. In a high-involvement situation, such as purchasing a new suit shortly after taking a job, a consumer may deliberately observe the styles worn by others at work or by role models from other environments, including advertisements. Many ads encourage consumers to imagine the feelings and experience of using a product.[24] Such images not only enhance learning about the product, but may even influence how the product is evaluated after an actual trial.

A substantial amount of modeling also occurs in low-involvement situations. Throughout the course of their lives, people observe others using products and behaving in a great variety of situations. Most of the time they pay little attention to these behaviors. However,

ILLUSTRATION 9-4

Ads not only convey information and elicit feelings; they can challenge existing assumptions, even implicit assumptions, and cause readers to think and reexamine their beliefs.

over time they learn that certain behaviors, and products, are appropriate in some situations and others are not.

Analytical Reasoning The most complex form of cognitive learning is **analytical reasoning.** In reasoning, individuals engage in creative thinking to restructure and recombine existing information as well as new information to form new associations and concepts. Information from a credible source that contradicts or challenges one's existing beliefs will often trigger reasoning.[25] The ad in Illustration 9–4 challenges implicit consumer beliefs.

One form of analytical reasoning is the use of analogy. **Analogical reasoning** is *an inference process that allows consumers to use an existing knowledge base to understand a new situation or object.* That is, it allows consumers to use knowledge about something they are familiar with to help them understand something they are not familiar with. For example, if you have not tried or adopted a digital reader such as the Kindle or nook, you may learn about it by relating it to your laptop computer and Word documents. Your computer allows for digital storage and downloading of documents which you "open" and "read" on a screen. You might reason that this is much like downloading, opening, and reading any digital content on any digital device. Given the similarities, you might correctly infer that digital readers allow for convenient and mobile access to your online books and magazines. You may also incorrectly infer that flipping through pages and finding your place will be difficult and that reading in such a format will be "hard on your eyes." Thus, from the analogical comparison you could come away with a relatively complete (though in some areas perhaps inaccurate) set of beliefs about the digital reader based on its similarity to your laptop computer and the Word documents you already use.[26]

Learning to Generalize and Differentiate

Regardless of which approach to learning is applicable in a given situation, consumers' ability to differentiate and generalize from one stimulus to another (for example, one brand to another) is critical to marketers.

Stimulus discrimination or differentiation refers to the *process of learning to respond differently to similar but distinct stimuli.* This process is critical for marketers who want consumers to perceive their brands as possessing unique and important features compared with other brands. For example, the management of Bayer aspirin feels that consumers should not see its aspirin as being the same as other brands. In order to obtain a premium price or a large market share, Bayer must teach consumers that its aspirin is distinct from other brands. Stimulus discrimination is an important consideration in brand image and product positioning, discussed later in the chapter.[27]

Stimulus discrimination is critical when brand scandals erupt. Scandals don't always hurt just the scandalized brand but can damage competitors in that industry, an effect termed *spillover.* One of the best ways for competitors to protect against spillover from scandals is to be highly differentiated from the scandalized brand.[28]

TABLE 9-1 Summary of Learning Theories with Examples of Involvement Level

Theory	Description	High-Involvement Example	Low-Involvement Example
Classical conditioning	A response elicited by one object is elicited by a second object if both objects frequently occur together.	The favorable emotional response elicited by the word *America* comes to be elicited by a car brand after repeated exposure to its *Made in America* campaign. This response is in addition to any cognitive learning that may have occurred.	The favorable emotional response elicited by a song in an ad for a new breath mint comes to be elicited by that brand after repeated pairing with the song even though the consumer pays little attention to the ad.
Operant conditioning	A response that is reinforced is more likely to be repeated when the same (or similar) situation arises in the future.	A suit is purchased after extensive thought and the consumer finds that it is comfortable and doesn't wrinkle. A sport coat made by the same firm is later purchased because of the positive experience with their suits.	A familiar brand of peas is purchased without much thought due to the low importance of the decision. The peas taste "fresh," so the consumer continues to purchase this brand.
Iconic rote learning	A concept or the association between two concepts is learned without conditioning.	A consumer with little expertise about Blu-ray players tries hard to learn brand information by examining it carefully several times. Learning is limited, however, because his or her lack of expertise inhibits elaboration.	A consumer learns a company's most recent jingle because it is catchy and can't stop replaying it in his or her head.
Vicarious learning or modeling	Behaviors are learned by watching the outcomes of others' behaviors or by imagining the outcome of a potential behavior.	A consumer carefully watches the reactions that other co-workers have to her friend's new briefcase before deciding to buy one.	A child learns that people dress up for special occasions without really ever thinking about it.
Analytical reasoning	Individuals use thinking to restructure and recombine existing and new information to form new associations and concepts.	A consumer buying a car carefully processes information about a new gas/electric hybrid car by using the analogy of homes powered by solar energy.	When a store is out of black pepper, a consumer buys white pepper instead based on the quick reasoning that "pepper is pepper."

Stimulus generalization, often referred to as the *rub-off effect, occurs when a response to one stimulus is elicited by a similar but distinct stimulus.*[29] Thus, a consumer who learns that Nabisco's Oreo cookies taste good and therefore assumes that the company's new Oreo Chocolate Cones will also taste good has engaged in stimulus generalization. Stimulus generalization is common and provides a major source of brand equity and opportunities for brand extensions, which are discussed later in the chapter.

Summary of Learning Theories

Theories of learning help us understand how consumers learn across a variety of situations. We have examined five specific learning theories: classical conditioning, operant conditioning, iconic rote learning, vicarious learning/modeling, and analytical reasoning. Each of these learning theories can operate in a high- or a low-involvement situation, although some are more common in one type of situation than another. Table 9–1 summarizes these theories and provides examples from both high- and low-involvement contexts.

LEARNING, MEMORY, AND RETRIEVAL

Chrysler's growth slowed considerably in the late 2000s,[30] as did Gillette's in the early 2000s,[31] Saturn's in the early 1990s,[32] and L&M cigarettes' in the 1980s.[33] In each case, at least some of the decline in growth was attributed to sharply reduced advertising. As one executive stated, LO4

> Some time after the company moved away from advertising and marketing, it became clear that people would quickly forget about our products if we didn't support them in the marketplace.[34]

These examples emphasize that marketers want consumers to learn *and* remember positive features, feelings, and behaviors associated with their brands. However, consumers forget. In conditioned learning, forgetting is often referred to as **extinction** because the desired response (e.g., pleasant feelings or brand purchase) decays or dies out if learning is not repeated and reinforced. In cognitive learning, forgetting is often referred to as a **retrieval failure** because information that is available in LTM cannot be accessed, that is, retrieved from LTM into STM.

Two aspects of forgetting that are of concern to marketers are the *likelihood of forgetting* in any given situation and the *rate of forgetting*. Figure 9–7 illustrates a commonly found rate of forgetting for advertising. In this study, aided and unaided recall of four advertisements from *American Machinist* magazine were measured. As can be seen, the probability of ad recall (likelihood) dropped rapidly over the first five days and then stabilized (rate).

At times, marketers or regulatory groups desire to accelerate forgetting or extinction. For example, the American Cancer Society and other organizations offer programs designed to help individuals "unlearn" smoking behavior. Manufacturers want consumers to forget unfavorable publicity or outdated product images. *Corrective advertising,* a

FIGURE 9-7 Forgetting over Time: Magazine Advertisement

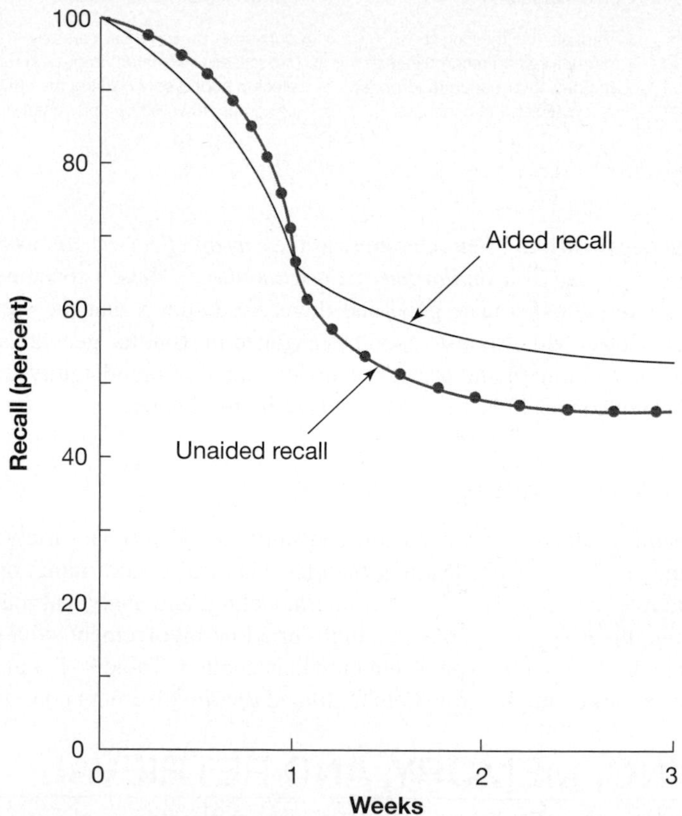

Source: LAP Report #5260.1 (New York: Weeks McGraw-Hill, undated). Reprinted with permission from McGraw-Hill Companies, Inc.

government requirement that firms remove inaccurate learning caused by past advertising, is described in Chapter 20.

Consumers forget brands, brand associations, and other information for a variety of reasons. First, learning may be weak to begin with. Second, information from competing brands and ads may cause memory interference. Third, the response environment (e.g., the retail store) may not be set up to encourage retrieval of previously learned information (e.g., from advertising). We turn to these issues next.

Strength of Learning

How can the HIV Alliance teach you to minimize your AIDS risk so that you will not forget? Or how can Neutrogena teach you about its line of sunless tanning products so you remember key features when shopping at CVS? That is, what is required to bring about a long-lasting learned response?

One factor is strength of learning. The stronger the original learning (e.g., of nodes and links between nodes), the more likely relevant information will be retrieved when required. *Strength of learning* is enhanced by six factors: *importance, message involvement, mood, reinforcement, repetition,* and *dual coding.*

Importance Importance refers to the value that consumers place on the information to be learned. Importance might be driven by inherent interest in the product or brand, or by the need to make a decision in the near future. The more important it is for the individual to learn a particular behavior or piece of information, the more effective and efficient he or she becomes in the learning process. This is largely due to the greater elaborative activities involved in fully processing and categorizing the material.

One emerging area of interest to marketers is how bilingual consumers process and recall second-language ads. For example, if Hispanic consumers process an ad in English, will it still be as effective as when they process the same ad in Spanish? Generally speaking, processing an ad in a second language is more difficult. This tends to reduce learning and recall for ads in a consumer's second language. Does this mean that second-language ads can never be effective? The answer appears to depend on importance. When importance is high, bilingual consumers expend more processing effort to understand the second-language ad, leading to greater learning and recall.[35]

Importance is one dimension that separates high-involvement learning situations from low-involvement situations. Therefore, high-involvement learning tends to be more complete than low-involvement learning.[36] Unfortunately, marketers are most often confronted with consumers in low-involvement learning situations.

Message Involvement When a consumer is not motivated to learn the material, processing can be increased by causing the person to become involved *with the message itself.* For example, playing an instrumental version of a popular song with lyrics related to product attributes ("Like a rock" in Chevrolet pickup ads) may cause people to "sing along," either out loud or mentally. This deepened involvement with the message, relative to merely listening to the lyrics being sung, increases the extent of processing of the message and memory of the associated features or theme.[37]

In Chapter 8 we discussed various strategies for increasing consumer attention including incongruity, rhetoric, incomplete messages, and interesting ads with plots and surprise endings. These strategies also tend to enhance message involvement and thus lead to stronger learning and memory.[38]

Several issues regarding message involvement are important to consider. First, there is evidence that scent may be important to memory. One study found that positive scents present during exposure to an ad increased attention to the ad and resulted in higher brand recall. Not surprisingly, marketers are currently developing technologies that will allow for "scent-emitting" technologies for Internet applications and in-store kiosks![39]

A second issue is the role of suspense. Sometimes marketers wait until the very end of a message to reveal the brand name in an attempt to attract interest and attention. However, this strategy must be used with caution because waiting until the end of an ad to reveal the brand gives consumers little opportunity to integrate new information into their existing brand schemas. As a result, the associative linkages are weaker and memory is reduced. These results suggest that marketers should strongly consider mentioning the brand relatively early in any marketing message.[40]

A final issue regards message strategies that highlight a brand's personal relevance to the consumer. One such strategy is self-referencing. **Self-referencing** indicates that consumers are relating brand information to themselves. The "self" is a powerful memory schema, and integrating brand information into this schema enhances learning and memory. Self-referencing can be encouraged in ads by using nostalgia appeals, which encourage consumers to remember past personal experiences.[41] It can also be encouraged by using language such as "you" and "your" (second-person pronoun).

Mood Get happy, learn more? Research indicates that this is indeed true. A positive mood during the presentation of information such as brand names enhances learning. A positive mood during the reception of information appears to enhance its relational elaboration—it is compared with and evaluated against more categories. This produces a more complete and stronger set of linkages among a variety of other brands and concepts, which in turn enhances retrieval (access to the information).[42]

Learning enhancement caused by a positive mood suggests the types of programs that marketers attempting to encourage consumer learning should advertise on. Likewise, it suggests that those commercials that enhance one's mood would also increase learning.[43]

Reinforcement Anything that increases the likelihood that a given response will be repeated in the future is considered **reinforcement.** While learning frequently occurs in the absence of reinforcement, reinforcement has a significant impact on the speed at which learning occurs and the duration of its effect.

A *positive reinforcement* is a pleasant or desired consequence. A couple who likes Mexican food sees an ad for a new Chipotle Mexican Grill in their area and decides to try it. They enjoy the food, service, and atmosphere. They are now more likely to select the Chipotle Mexican Grill the next time they dine out.

A *negative reinforcement* involves the removal or the avoidance of an unpleasant consequence. Vicks ads promise to relieve sinus pain and pressure. If they convince a consumer to try the sinus formula and it performs well, this consumer is likely to purchase and use it again in the future and, based on stimulus generalization, perhaps try other Vicks products as well.

Illustration 9–5 is an ad for KitchenAid which provides an additional example of reinforcement in that it suggests the positive outcomes of using their brand.

ILLUSTRATION 9-5

Reinforcement is anything that increases the probability that a response will be repeated in the future. This KitchenAid ad utilizes positive reinforcement.

CONSUMER INSIGHT 9-1

Earworms—Music That Gets Stuck in Our Heads

Through repetitive exposure, consumers unintentionally, inattentively, unknowingly learn the jingles, and songs, which lie dormant for days, months, years, even decades in the consumers' memory that on occasion can be triggered and brought to awareness by a fragrance, a few musical notes, a flash of a picture. Such recall may be accompanied by the feeling of surprise—the unearthing of buried information—and nostalgia—memories tied to the music. Soon, however, the tune returns to its state of dormancy.[44]

However, some jingles and songs in memory refuse to be "turned off" and play in an endless, repetitive loop in our heads for hours, days, and, for a small minority, even weeks or months. They pop up and demand to be sung or hummed repeatedly. They are called *earworms.* Some 98 percent of people have experienced this annoying condition. In a recent study, the top four earworms were

- Chili's "Baby Back Ribs" jingle.
- "Who Let the Dogs Out" by Baha Men.
- "We Will Rock You" by Queen.
- Kit-Kat candy-bar jingle ("Gimme a Break . . .").

Music most likely to cause an earworm is simple, upbeat, and repetitive and has an element of the unexpected—like a rhythmic variation, a shifting time signature, or an extra beat.

Music is a ubiquitous component of commercials. Sometimes the music is created specifically for the product—Chili's "Baby Back Ribs," Dr. Pepper's "I'm a Pepper." Sometimes the music is a piece of popular music specially culled to appeal to the target market (e.g., Apple's use of U-2's "Vertigo") and sometimes music is selected for its ability to enhance the features of the product—Rolling Stone's "Start Me Up" for a new Windows release.

As annoying as earworms can be, they do prove that music serves as a hook of sorts for brands. A better understanding of earworms may be key to a better understanding of the automaticity of music and memory.

Critical Thinking Questions

1. Have you experienced earworms? What song got stuck in your head? How long did it last?
2. What is your opinion of musicians licensing their music to advertisements? Is this "selling out" or is it a smart way for a win-win for marketers and musicians?
3. What are the (dis)advantages of using popular music in advertisements? Original music?

Punishment is the opposite of reinforcement. It is any consequence that decreases the likelihood that a given response will be repeated in the future. If the couple who tried the Chipotle Mexican Grill described earlier thought that the service was bad or that the food was poorly prepared, they would be unlikely to patronize it in the future.

Obviously, it is critical for marketers to determine precisely what reinforces consumer purchases so they can design promotional messages and products that encourage initial and repeat purchases.

Repetition Repetition enhances learning and memory by increasing the accessibility of information in memory or by strengthening the associative linkages between concepts.[45] Quite simply, the more times people are exposed to information or engage in a behavior, the more likely they are to learn and remember it. For example, compared with one showing of a Miller Lite beer commercial, three showings during a championship baseball game produced two-and-one-third times the recall.[46] For reasons that are not completely clear, certain music "motivates" automatic self-repetition on the part of the consumer, which creates stronger learning and brand associations, as discussed in Consumer Insight 9–1.

The effects of repetition depend, of course, on importance and reinforcement. Less repetition of an advertising message is necessary for someone to learn the message if the subject matter is important or if there is a great deal of relevant reinforcement. Since many advertisements do not contain information of current importance to consumers or direct rewards for learning, repetition plays a critical role in the promotion process for many products.[47] As we saw earlier, classical conditioning and iconic rote learning (low-involvement learning) rely heavily on repetition.

Figure 9–8, shows how ad repetition affects recall for low and high awareness brands. High repetition works better than low and the gains in recall are more pronounce the longer the campaign runs and for low awareness brands.[48]

Both the number of times a message is repeated and the timing of those repetitions affect the extent and duration of learning and memory.[49] Figure 9–9 illustrates the relationship between repetition timing and product recall for a food product. One group of homemakers, represented by the curved line in the figure, was exposed to a food product advertisement

FIGURE 9-8 Impact of Repetition on Brand Awareness for High- and Low-Awareness Brands

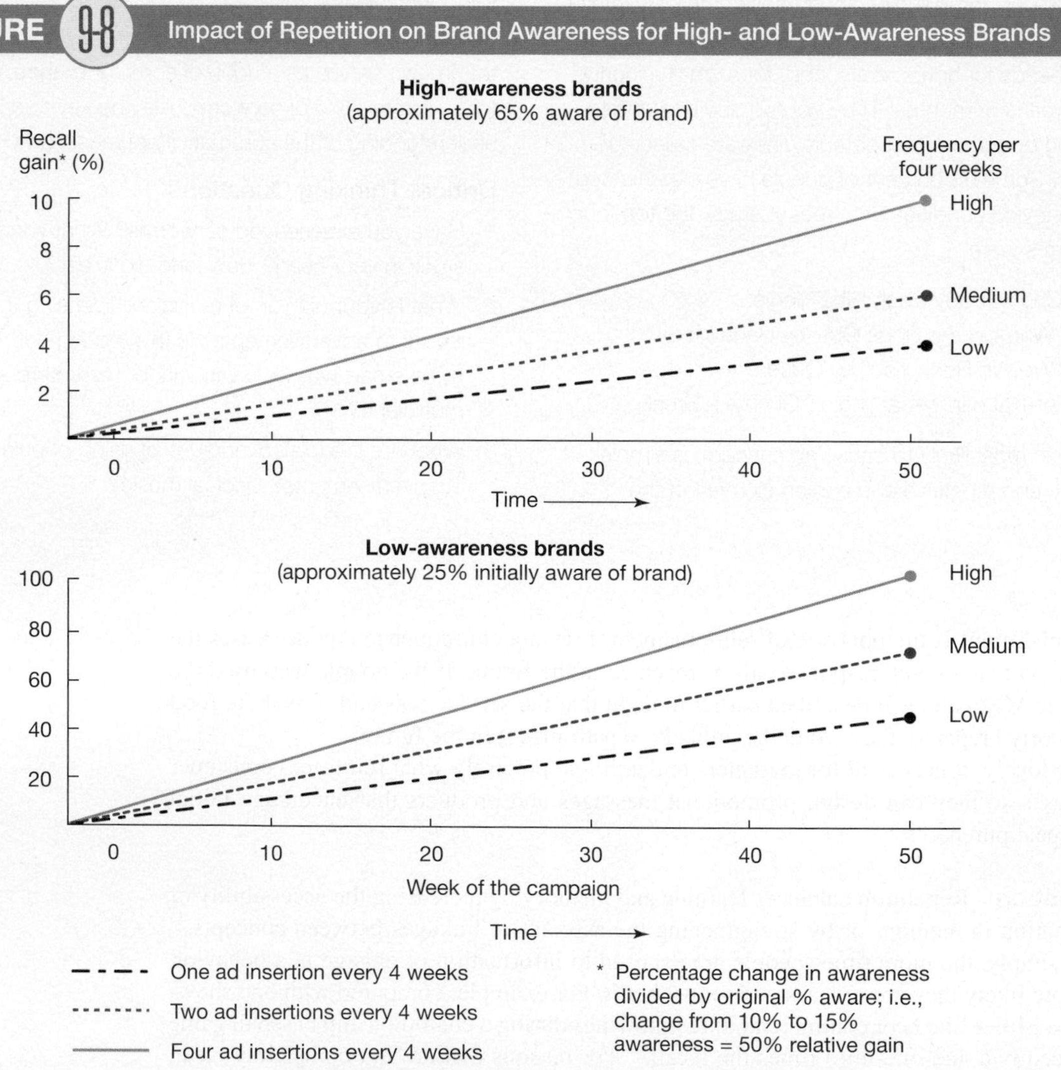

Source: *A Study of the Effectiveness of Advertising Frequency in Magazines.* © 1993 Time Inc. Reprinted by permission.

once a week for 13 consecutive weeks. For this group, product recall increased rapidly and reached its highest level during the 13th week. Forgetting occurred rapidly when advertising stopped, and recall was virtually zero by the end of the year.

A second group of homemakers was exposed to the same 13 direct-mail advertisements. However, they received one ad every four weeks. The zigzag line in the figure shows the recall pattern for this group. In this case, learning increased throughout the year, but substantial forgetting occurred between message exposures.

Given a finite budget, how should a firm allocate its advertising across a budget cycle—should it concentrate it all at once or spread it out over time? The answer depends on the task. Any time it is important to produce widespread knowledge of the product rapidly, such as during a new-product introduction, frequent (close together) repetitions should be used. This is referred to as **pulsing.** Thus, political candidates frequently hold back a significant proportion of their media budgets until shortly before the election and then use a media blitz to ensure widespread knowledge of their desirable attributes. More long-range programs, such as store or brand image development, should use more widely spaced repetitions.[50]

Repetition Timing and Advertising Recall

FIGURE 

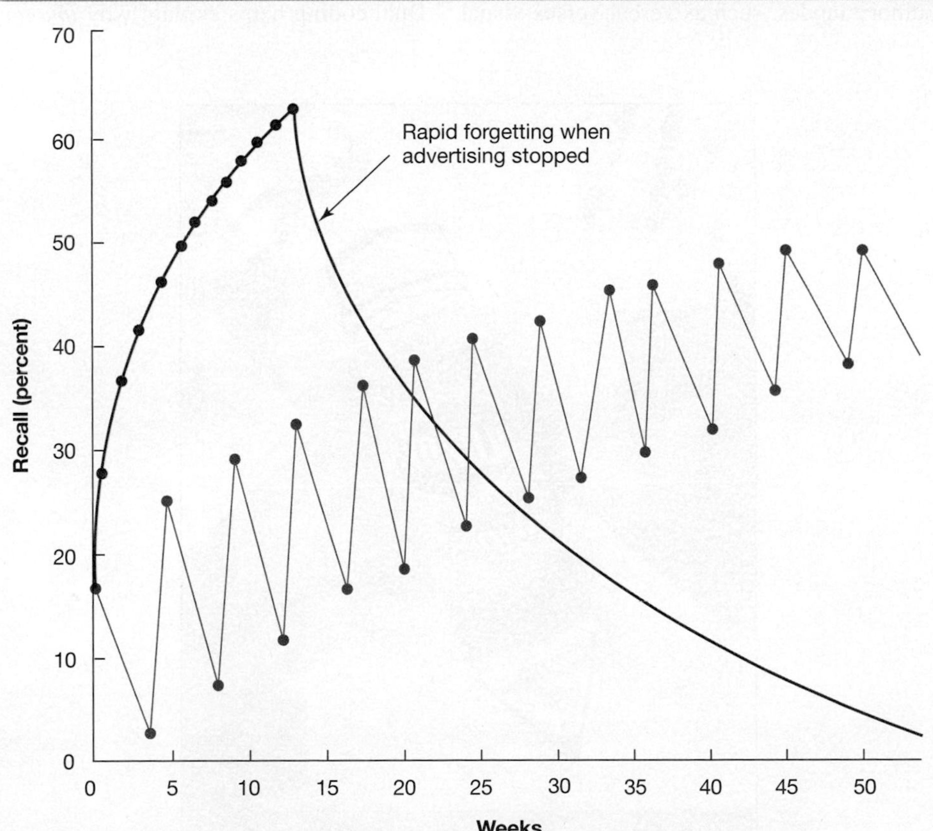

Source: Reprinted from H. J. Zielski, "The Remembering and Forgetting of Advertising," *Journal of Marketing,* January 1959, p. 240, with permission from The American Marketing Association. The actual data and a refined analysis were presented in J. L. Simon, "What Do Zielski's Data Really Show about Pulsing?," *Journal of Marketing Research,* August 1979, pp. 415–20.

Marketers must walk a fine line in terms of repetition. Too much repetition can cause consumers to actively shut out the message, evaluate it negatively, or disregard it, an effect called **advertising wearout.**[51] One strategy for avoiding wearout is to utilize variations on a common theme.[52] For example, ads for Target continually emphasize core brand themes and the "red dot" symbol. However, they have done so over time in different and interesting ways, including roaming animated spokes characters, a white dog with a red dot around one eye, and so on. Cross-cultural research suggests that a consistent theme with a varied execution is an effective strategy for avoiding advertising wearout in Southeast Asia as well.[53]

Dual Coding Consumers can store (code) information in different ways. Storing the same information in different ways (dual coding) results in more internal pathways (associative links) for retrieving information. This in turn can increase learning and memory.

One example of dual coding is when consumers learn information in two different contexts—for example, a consumer sees two ads for the same brand of dandruff shampoo, one with an office theme and one with a social theme. The varied theme (context) provides multiple paths to the brand and therefore enhances recall later on. Illustration 9–6 shows one theme that Clorox uses for its disinfectant products. It has other themes as well. By using multiple themes for its disinfectant products, Clorox can enhance consumer memory beyond its traditional bleach products.

Another example of dual coding relates to information being stored in different memory modes, such as verbal versus visual.[54] Dual coding helps explain why *imagery*

ILLUSTRATION 9-6

Using varied themes across ads can aid dual coding and enhance memory. Note the differences between this Clorox ad and others you may have seen.

enhances memory. High-imagery stimuli leave a dual code because they are stored in memory on both verbal and pictorial dimensions, whereas low-imagery stimuli are coded only verbally. As a consequence, high-imagery brand names such as Jolt and Mustang are substantially easier to learn and remember than low-imagery names.

Echoic memory—memory of sounds, including words—is another memory mode that appears to have characteristics distinct from visual and verbal memory.[55] This provides the opportunity for dual coding when the sound component of a message (e.g., background music) conveys similar meanings to that being conveyed by the verbal message.[56]

Learning and memory appear to be enhanced when the key ideas communicated through one mode are consistent with those communicated through other modes.[57] For example, one study finds that having the picture (visual) and text (verbal) convey consistent ideas makes it easier for bilingual consumers to process an ad in their second language. The result is greater learning and memory of the second-language ad.[58]

Memory Interference

Sometimes consumers have difficulty retrieving a specific piece of information because other related information in memory gets in the way. This effect is referred to as **memory interference.** A common form of interference in marketing is due to competitive advertising. For example, seeing an ad for Canada Dry Ginger Ale might interfere with your memory of Mountain Dew. Competitive advertising makes it harder for consumers to recall any given advertisement and its contents. And even if they can recall the contents of a specific ad, they will often have a hard time associating that ad with a specific brand. As a consequence, competitive advertising can either reduce memory for the brand claims made in a specific advertisement or lead to brand-claim confusion across advertisements for competing brands.[59]

Competitive advertising interference increases as the number of competing ads within the same product category increases and as the similarity of those ads to each other increases. Given the high levels of advertising clutter, it should not be surprising that this is an area of concern for marketers and advertisers. The major question is, *What can marketers do to decrease competitive interference?* A number of strategies exist, many related to the learning and memory concepts we discussed earlier.

Avoid Competing Advertising One strategy is to avoid having your ad appear in the same set of ads (same pod in a TV format) as your competitors'. Some companies actually pay a premium to ensure this exclusivity. Another strategy, called *recency planning,* involves trying to plan advertising exposures so that they occur as close in time to a consumer purchase occasion as possible. The idea behind this concept is that reducing the time to purchase reduces the chances that an ad for a competing brand will be seen prior to purchase.[60]

Strengthen Initial Learning Another strategy is to increase the strength of the initial learning because stronger learning is less subject to memory interference. Evidence for the value of this strategy comes from the fact that memory interference is less pronounced in high-involvement contexts and for highly familiar brands. This is not surprising when you consider that high-involvement learning should result in stronger brand schemas and that brand schemas for familiar brands are stronger than those for unfamiliar brands.[61]

Additional evidence for the role of learning comes from advertising strategies that encourage dual coding. Specifically, brands can reduce competitive interference by showing different ad versions for the same brand (shampoo ad in office context and social context) or by varying the modality across exposures (radio ad followed by a print ad).[62]

Interestingly, while strong initial learning of a brand's key attributes can yield positive memory effects, it can also make it harder for the brand to add or change attributes. That is, the strong initial learning interferes with consumer learning and memory for new brand information.[63] This can make brand *repositioning* a challenging task. Repositioning is discussed later in the chapter.

Reduce Similarity to Competing Ads Ads within the same product class (e.g., ads for different brands of cell phone) have been shown to increase interference, as have ads that are similar to competing ads. Similarity can be in terms of ad claims, emotional valence, and ad execution elements such as background music or pictures. Interestingly, similarity between ad execution elements can lead to memory interference even when the ads are for brands in different product categories (print ads for bleach and soda each picturing mountain scenes). Just as unique ads can break through advertising clutter to garner greater attention, unique ads are also more resistant to competitive memory interference.[64]

Provide External Retrieval Cues Retrieval cues provide an external pathway to information that is stored in memory. The reason that brand names are so important is because they can serve as a retrieval cue. Seeing a brand name can trigger recall of brand information stored in memory, as well as retrieval of images and emotions associated with prior advertisements for the brand.

However, brand name is not always enough to trigger recall of prior advertising for the brand. For example, seeing the brand on a store shelf may not be sufficient to cue consumers' memory for prior advertising. This is of major consequence for marketers because failure to recall prior advertising information and emotion during purchase reduces advertising effectiveness. In this case, marketers can use point-of-purchase displays or package cues that link directly back to the advertisements for that brand.[65] For example, during the "Got Milk?" campaign, in-store signage with the "Got Milk?" slogan was used to remind consumers about the TV ads that emphasized how awful it feels to run out of milk. Quaker Oats applied this concept as well by placing a photo of a scene from its Life cereal commercial on the cereal box. This enhanced the ability of consumers to recall both affect and information from the commercial and was very successful.

Response Environment

Retrieval is also affected by the similarity of the retrieval (response) environment to the original learning environment and type of learning.[66] Thus, the more the retrieval situation offers cues similar to the cues present during learning, the more likely effective retrieval is to occur. One strategy is to configure the retrieval environment to resemble the original learning environment. The "Got Milk?" and Life cereal examples discussed earlier represent attempts by marketers to match the in-store retrieval environment to the learning environment by providing retrieval cues.

Another strategy is to configure the learning environment to resemble the most likely retrieval environment. Suppose a chewing gum brand knows that its retrieval environment will be in retail stores. In this case, conditioning a positive feeling to the *brand and package* by consistently pairing a visual image of the package with pleasant music would likely be most appropriate. This is because the response environment (the store shelf) visually presents consumers with brand packages. And, because learning was conditioned to a visual of the brand's package (learning environment configured to match the retrieval environment), seeing the package on the shelf will likely elicit the learned response.

BRAND IMAGE AND PRODUCT POSITIONING

Brand Image

LO5

Brand image refers to *the schematic memory of a brand.* It contains the target market's interpretation of the product's attributes, benefits, usage situations, users, and manufacturer/marketer characteristics. It is what people think of and feel when they hear or see a brand name. It is, in essence, the set of associations consumers have *learned* about the brand.[67] *Company image* and *store image* are similar except that they apply to companies and stores rather than brands.

The importance of branding and brand image can be seen in the fact that products that have traditionally been unbranded such as water, apples, and meat are increasingly being branded. Consider the meat industry. It must deal with a number of issues, not the least of which is that many consumers see meat as difficult and time-consuming to prepare. As one industry expert said:

> A lot of consumers don't have the time and expertise to take a raw roast and cook it for six to eight hours, so what we have to do in this industry is understand that and do something about it.[68]

Tyson has responded by offering a line of fully cooked chicken, pork, and beef meals that are fast, easy, and safe to prepare. This move builds nicely on Tyson's strong reputation for quality fresh meat products and its prepackaged lunch meats. Given today's consumers' dual concerns over convenience and food safety, Tyson is well positioned with a strong and consistent image that consumers trust and can relate to. The ability to benefit from a brand image is called *brand equity,* which we discuss in the next section.

Brand image is a major concern of both industrial and consumer goods marketers. Consider the following headlines from recent marketing publications:

Buick Leads GM's Efforts at Reinvention

How Microsoft got Hip

Moto's Regaining Its Mojo by Putting Consumer First

Pepsi Max Drops the Diet, Aims to Rekindle Cola War

How powerful are brand images? Think of Nike, McDonald's, Kate Spade, Hershey's, Coke, Discovery Channel, Amazon.com, and Midas. For many consumers, each of these names conjures up a rich pattern of meanings and feelings. These meanings and imagery are powerful drivers of consumer decision making, which explains why strong brands also tend to be market leaders in terms of sales and profits. Examine Illustration 9–7. *What meanings and imagery are elicited by the Lee Jeans brand? Does this brand have a strong image?*

Brand images can hinder as well as help products.[69] Hershey's recently tried to enter

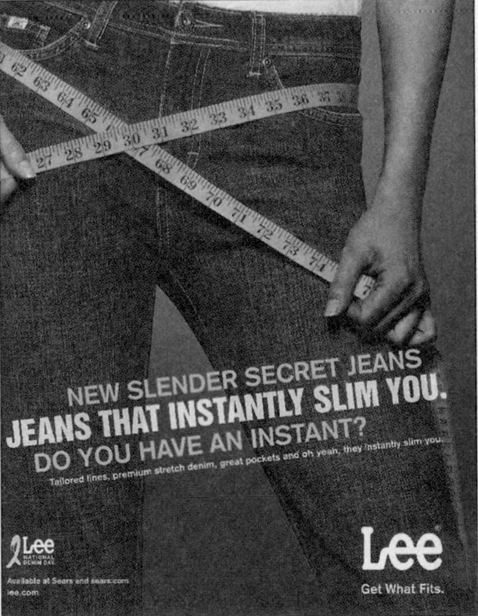

ILLUSTRATION 9-7

Brand names such as Lee Jeans provide an anchor to which consumers can attach meaning. This allows marketers to invest in product improvements and communications with a reasonable possibility of benefiting from those investments.

the upscale chocolate market with the name Cacao Reserve *by Hershey's.* The product has not performed well, most likely because consumers don't equate Hershey's with premium. Hershey's has a strong image. However, its image as an everyday chocolate hinders its move into the premium market. In this case, Hershey's may have been better off using a *new brand strategy* with no ties to the Hershey's name. We discuss this strategy later in the chapter.

Product Positioning

Product positioning is a *decision by a marketer to try to achieve a defined brand image relative to competition within a market segment.* That is, marketers decide that they want the members of a market segment to think and feel in a certain way about a brand relative to competing brands. The term *product positioning* is most commonly applied to decisions concerning brands, but it is also used to describe the same decisions for stores, companies, and product categories.

Product positioning has a major impact on the long-term success of the brand, presuming the firm can create the desired position in the minds of consumers. A key issue in positioning relates to the need for brands to create product positions that differentiate them from competitors in ways that are meaningful to consumers.[70] A brand that fails to differentiate itself from competitors (stimulus discrimination) will generally find it difficult to generate consumer interest and sales.

Consider Saturn. Its original positioning emphasized customer service and the retail experience. This differentiated Saturn from the competition and resulted in strong sales. However, its ads stopped focusing on customer service in 2002 and after that sales slumped. As a result, it switched advertising agencies with the hopes of *repositioning* its brand in the minds of customers by focusing back on customer service.[71] These efforts ultimately failed and the Saturn line was discontinued.

An important component of brand image is the appropriate usage situations for the product or brand. Often marketers have the opportunity to influence the usage situations for which a product or brand is seen as appropriate. What do you think of when you think of cranberry sauce? Odds are that Thanksgiving and perhaps Christmas are part of your image of cranberry sauce. In fact, these are probably the only usage situations that came to mind. However, in one study, sales for cranberry sauce increased almost 150 percent over a three-month period after consumers saw advertisements promoting nontraditional uses. Thus, expanding the usage situation component of cranberry sauce's product position could dramatically increase its sales.[72]

The terms *product position* and *brand image* are often used interchangeably. In general, however, product position involves an explicit reference to a brand's image relative to another brand or the overall industry. It is characterized by statements such as "HP printers are the most reliable printers available." Brand image generally considers the firm's image without a direct comparison to a competitor. It is characterized by statements such as "HP printers are extremely reliable."

Once a marketer decides on an appropriate product position, the marketing mix is manipulated in a manner designed to achieve that position in the target market.[73] For example, Sunkist Growers offers a fruit jelly candy called Sunkist Fruit Gems that comes in various fruit flavors. It is positioned as a "healthful, natural" snack for adults and children. From a product standpoint, the candy is made from pectin (a natural ingredient from citrus peels) and contains no preservatives and less sugar than most fruit jelly candies. Thus, the product itself communicates the desired position.

However, other aspects of the marketing mix can also contribute. For example, Sunkist could distribute the candy through the produce departments of supermarkets. Notice how distribution then supports the desired product position or image. A consumer receiving a message that this is a healthful, natural product should be more receptive when the product is found near other healthful, natural products such as apples and oranges.

Marketing managers frequently fail to achieve the type of product image or position they desire because they fail to anticipate or test for consumer reactions. Toro's initial lightweight snowthrower was not successful. Why? It was named the Snowpup, and consumers interpreted this to mean that it was a toy or lacked sufficient power. Sales success came only after a more macho, power-based name was utilized—first Snowmaster and later Toro.

Perceptual mapping offers marketing managers a useful technique for measuring and developing a product's position. Perceptual mapping takes consumers' perceptions of how similar various brands or products are to each other and relates these perceptions to product attributes. Figure 9–10 is a perceptual map for various chocolate candy brands. This perceptual map also provides the ideal points for five market segments—I_1, I_2, I_3, I_4, I_5. The size of the circle around the ideal point represents the relative size of the segment, with segment 4 (I_4) being the largest and segment 5 (I_5) being the smallest. These ideal points represent the image or characteristics each segment desires in a chocolate candy. If the chocolate candies in this map were all that existed, it would indicate that segment 2 consumers are not being offered many of the products they want. Target has recently positioned a brand to target this segment with Choxie (the tagline is "Choxie is chocolate with moxie."). Still, opportunities remain to target segment 2. Is Dove well positioned? It appears not; that is, Dove would benefit from *repositioning* toward segment 2. We discuss repositioning in the next section. Notice that even though segment 3 is relatively large, there is also a considerable amount of competition, something of importance when deciding which segments to target with new brands. *What segment and competitor factors would make it more difficult to enter segment 5 than segment 2?*

Perceptual Map for Chocolate Candy FIGURE 9-10

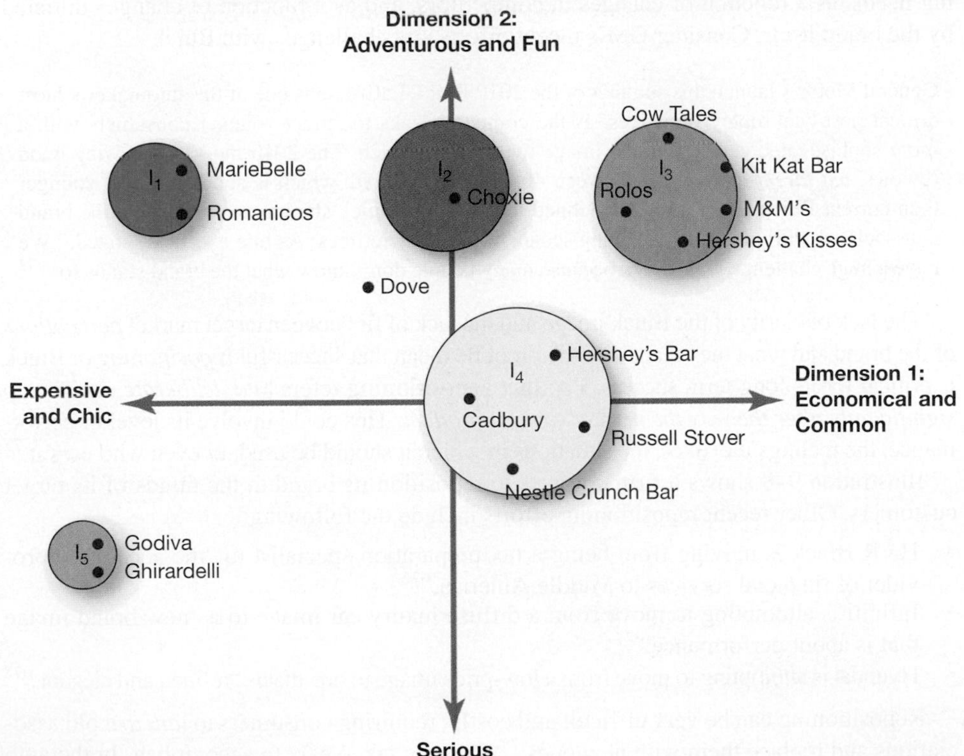

ILLUSTRATION 9-8

Repositioning a product involves making all aspects of the product consistent with the new position. This includes product features, price, communications, and distribution channels.

Product Repositioning

The images consumers have of brands change over time as a function of their own changing needs, as a function of changes in competitors, and as a function of changes initiated by the brand itself. Consider GM's recent efforts and challenges with Buick:

> General Motor's launch this summer of the 2010 Buick LaCrosse is one of the automaker's most critical post-bankruptcy initiatives, as the company seeks to attract younger consumers with a more sophisticated car design and image overhaul to match. The 2010 model is drawing good reviews, *but target consumers* [between 46 and 55 years old, which is about 10 years younger than current Buick buyers] are disinclined to even visit Buick showrooms given that the brand is associated with plush, easy-driving sedans favored by retirees. As one executive stated, "We have a huge challenge with Buick because many people don't know what the brand stands for."[74]

The lack of clarity of the Buick image and the lack of fit between target market *perceptions* of the brand and what they want in an automobile mean that successful *repositioning* of Buick is critical for its long-term success. **Product repositioning** refers to *a deliberate decision to significantly alter the way the market views a product.* This could involve its level of performance, the feelings it evokes, the situations in which it should be used, or even who uses it.[75]

Illustration 9–8 shows a firm's efforts to reposition its brand in the minds of its target customers. Other recent repositioning efforts include the following:

- H&R Block is moving from being a tax preparation specialist to "the accessible provider of financial services to Middle America."[76]
- Infiniti is attempting to move from a diffuse luxury car image to a "new brand image that is about performance."[77]
- Hyundai is attempting to move from a low-price image to one that is "refined and elegant."[78]

Repositioning can be very difficult and costly, requiring consumers to *unlearn* old associations and replace them with new ones.[79] This can take years to accomplish. In the auto industry, it is estimated that repositioning can take up to 10 years. According to one industry expert, "People's perceptions change very slowly."[80]

Repositioning may also require drastic action. For example, Hardee's was able to reverse plummeting sales only after completely walking away from the thin patties common in fast-food hamburgers and focusing exclusively on its now signature Thickburger made from Black Angus beef.[81] Sometimes companies will even change their brand name to allow a fresh start. For example, when Bell Atlantic and GTE Wireless merged, they changed their name to Verizon.

BRAND EQUITY AND BRAND LEVERAGE

Brand equity is *the value consumers assign to a brand above and beyond the functional characteristics of the product.*[82] For example, many people pay a significant premium for Bayer aspirin relative to store brands of aspirin although they are chemically identical.

Brand equity is nearly synonymous with the reputation of the brand. However, the term *equity* implies economic value.[83] Thus, brands with "good" reputations have the potential for high levels of brand equity, whereas unknown brands or brands with weak or negative reputations do not. The outcomes of brand equity include increased market share, decreased consumer price sensitivity, and enhanced marketing efficiency.[84]

Brand equity is based on the product position of the brand. A consumer who believes that a brand delivers superior performance, is exciting to use, and is produced by a company with appropriate social values is likely to be willing to pay a premium for the brand, to go to extra trouble to locate and buy it, to recommend it to others, to forgive a mistake or product flaw, or to otherwise engage in behaviors that benefit the firm that markets the brand. Thus, one source of economic value from a positive brand image results from consumers' behaviors toward existing items with that brand name.[85]

Another source of value for a brand image is that consumers may assume that the favorable aspects of the image associated with an existing product will apply to a new product with the same brand name. This is based on the principle of stimulus generalization described earlier in this chapter. **Brand leverage,** often termed *family branding, brand extensions,* or *umbrella branding,* refers to *marketers capitalizing on brand equity by using an existing brand name for new products.*[86] If done correctly, consumers will assign some of the characteristics of the existing brand to the new product carrying that name. Relatively recent brand extensions include Starbucks ice cream, Listerine breath strips, and Campbell's tomato juice.

However, stimulus generalization does not occur just because two products have the same brand name. There must be a connection between the products. Pace is finally leveraging its brand equity beyond salsas by extending its name into related products such as refried beans, taco sauces, and bean dip. According to Pace's brand manager:

> We feel we have the ability to expand into Mexican meals, it's just now about choosing the right products and aligning with what consumers are making.[87]

In contrast, Campbell's was not able to introduce a spaghetti sauce under the Campbell's name (it used Prego instead). Consumer research found that

> Campbell's, to consumers, says it isn't authentic Italian. Consumers figured it would be orangy and runny like our tomato soup.[88]

Successful brand leverage generally requires that the original brand have a strong positive image and that the new product fit with the original product on at least one of four dimensions:[89]

1. *Complement.* The two products are used together.
2. *Substitute.* The new product can be used instead of the original.

CONSUMER INSIGHT 9-2

Art Infusion: A Path to Greater Brand Extendibility

Marketers would like their brands to be more extendable in many cases because it increases their options to leverage existing brand equity. Research has found that one path to increased brand extendibility is by using visual art in a brand's advertising. For example, Vincent Van Gogh's painting "Starry Night" was used as the "art" visual in an ad for a brand of MP3 player called Consul (this was the core product and brand). The "non-art" visual was a picture of a night sky. These two ads were used to advertise the Consul MP3 player and then consumers were asked about both the Consul MP3 player and about their perceptions of two possible extensions, namely, Consul clothing (a lower-fitting extension with MP3 players) and Consul digital radios (a higher-fitting extension with MP3 players). The following effects were found when comparing the effects of the art visual advertisement to the non-art visual advertisement:[90]

- The art visual in the ad increased brand image for the Consul MP3 player.
- The art visual in the ad increased the perceived fit of the extensions and therefore . . .
- The art visual increased the perceived extendibility of the Consul brand from MP3 players to both clothing and digital radios.

These effects are worth a bit more explanation. First, visual art has been shown to elicit perceptions of luxury and exclusiveness that spill over (that is, generalize) to the brand in a relatively automatic way. This explains why the art visual enhanced the image of the Consul MP3 brand. Second, visual art in an ad increases consumers' cognitive flexibility, allowing them to see connections between objects that are more different than they would otherwise be able to do. This increases perceived fit even for extensions that are lower in fit, such as when Consul moved from an MP3 player to clothing. Both of these effects operate in such a way that having an art visual in an advertisement increases the extendibility of the brand in the minds of consumers from MP3 players to digital radios and clothing.

The positive effects of visual art occur even when consumers are not familiar with the visual art in question (in this case Van Gogh's "Starry Night"), which means that the use of visual art in advertising does not require that the target audience be art connoisseurs.

Critical Thinking Questions

1. Why does visual art increase brand image?
2. Why does visual art enhance cognitive flexibility?
3. Are there some product categories for which art infusion would not work? Explain.

3. *Transfer.* Consumers see the new product as requiring the same manufacturing skills as the original.
4. *Image.* The new product shares a key image component with the original.

It is important for marketers to understand what the key "fit" criteria are for consumers. For example, one study found that consumers would prefer Fruit Loops lollipops over Fruit Loops hot cereal. Apparently, the key fit criterion of concern was not the *transfer* of manufacturing capability, but rather the *image* component of taste.[91]

It is also important for marketers to realize that the more the new product category is a "stretch" for the brand, the more their advertising messages must help to explain how the products fit together.[92] For example, Revlon tried to launch its own vitamins with the expression "Now, Revlon beauty begins from the inside-out." Notice how the slogan associates cosmetics and vitamins in terms of beauty.

Finally, it is important for marketers to realize that the way in which they advertise a brand can enhance perceptions of fit and make a brand more extendable into a broader set of product categories. One such approach, the use of visual art, is discussed in Consumer Insight 9–2.

ILLUSTRATION 9-9

Brand extensions are most likely to succeed when the new product is closer to existing products as with Fabreze. However, the greatest rewards are sometimes associated with extensions into more distinct product categories as with Special K.

Examples of successful and unsuccessful brand extensions include the following:

- Harley-Davidson has applied its name successfully to a wide variety of products, but its Harley-Davidson wine coolers were not successful.
- Levi Strauss failed in its attempt to market Levi's tailored suits for men.
- Country Time could not expand from lemonade to apple cider.
- LifeSavers gum did not succeed.
- Coleman successfully expanded from camping stoves and lanterns into a complete line of camping equipment.
- Oil of Olay bar soap is successful in large part because of the equity of the Oil of Olay lotion.

Illustration 9–9 shows ads for two different product offerings that demonstrate the concept of brand extension. Which of the two, Fabreze or Special K, is closest to its existing products?

Sometimes brand extensions are not feasible. When marketers want to target distinct market segments with an image distinct from the original brand, they generally need to create a new brand rather than extend the existing one. Toyota did this when moving into the luxury automobile market with the new brand Lexus, as did Honda with the new brand Acura. These new brands have images that are distinct from the original brand. Using unique brand names for this purpose avoids diluting or confusing the original brand image.

Brand extensions can also involve risks, one being that a failure of any product with a brand name can hurt all the products with the same brand name (consumers generalize both good and bad outcomes).[93] Another risk is diluting the original brand image.[94]

A strong image is generally focused on a fairly narrow set of characteristics. Each additional product added to that product name alters the image somewhat. If too many or too dissimilar products are added to the brand name, the brand image may become diffuse or confused.[95] For instance, were Porsche to offer a ski boat that competed on price rather than performance, it could damage its core image, particularly among existing owners.[96] Some observers feel that Nike is in danger of such a brand dilution as it attaches its name to an ever-wider array of products.

SUMMARY

LO1: Describe the nature of learning and memory

Learning is any change in the content or organization of long-term memory or behavior and is the result of information processing. Information processing is a series of activities by which stimuli are perceived, transformed into information, and stored. The four activities in the series are exposure, attention, interpretation, and memory. Thus memory is both an outcome of learning and a part of the process of learning. For example, when interpreting the price of a brand, consumers may retrieve information about competitor prices (prior learning) and once the comparison is made, store their price perception about the new brand in memory (new learning).

LO2: Explain the types of memory and memory's role in learning

Memory is the result of learning, which involves information processing. Most commonly, information goes directly into *short-term memory* (STM) for processing, where two basic activities occur: maintenance rehearsal and elaborative activities. *Maintenance rehearsal* is the continual repetition of a piece of information in order to hold it in current memory. *Elaborative activities* are the use of stored experiences, values, attitudes, and feelings to interpret and evaluate information in current memory.

Long-term memory (LTM) is information from previous information processing that has been stored for future use. LTM undergoes continual restructuring as new information is acquired. Information is stored in LTM in associative networks, or schemas. Consumers often organize information in LTM around brands in the form of *brand schemas.* These schemas represent the brand's image in terms of key attributes, feelings, experiences, and so on.

LO3: Distinguish the different processes underlying high- and low-involvement learning

Consumers learn in various ways, which can be broadly classified into high- versus low-involvement learning. *High-involvement learning* occurs when an individual is motivated to acquire the information. *Low-involvement learning* occurs when an individual is paying only limited or indirect attention to an advertisement or other message. Low-involvement learning tends to be limited as a result of a lack of elaborative activities.

Learning can also be classified as either conditioned or cognitive. There are two forms of conditioned learning: classical and operant. *Classical conditioning* attempts to create an association between a stimulus (e.g., brand name) and some response (e.g., behavior or feeling) and is generally low involvement in nature. *Operant conditioning* attempts to create an association between a response (e.g., buying a brand) and some outcome (e.g., satisfaction) that serves to reinforce the response and is generally high involvement in nature.

The *cognitive* approach to learning encompasses the mental activities of humans as they work to solve problems, cope with complex situations, or function effectively in their environment. Cognitive learning includes *iconic rote learning* (generally low involvement), *vicarious learning/modeling* (low or high involvement), and *analytical reasoning* (generally high involvement).

Stimulus generalization is one way of transferring learning by generalizing from one stimulus situation to other, similar ones. *Stimulus discrimination* refers to the opposite process of learning—responding differently to somewhat similar stimuli. The ability of consumers to differentiate and generalize is critical for successful brand positioning and leverage.

LO4: Summarize the factors affecting information retrieval from memory

Once learned, information is *retrieved* from LTM for use in evaluations and decisions. *Retrieval failures* or *extinction* of a learned response represents a reduction in marketing effectiveness. Retrieval depends on strength of initial learning, memory interference, and the response environment. *Strength of learning* depends on six basic factors: importance, message involvement, reinforcement, mood, repetition, and dual coding. *Importance* refers to the value that the consumer places on the information to be learned—greater importance increases learning and retrieval. *Message involvement* is the degree to which the consumer is interested in the message itself—the greater the message involvement, the greater the learning and retrieval. *Reinforcement* is anything that increases the likelihood that a response will be repeated in the future—the greater the reinforcement, the greater the learning and retrieval. *Mood* is the temporary mental state or feeling of the consumer. Learning and memory appear to be greater in positive mood conditions. *Repetition* refers to the number of times that we are exposed to the information or that we engage in a behavior. Repetition increases learning and memory but can also lead to *wearout. Dual coding* involves creating multiple complementary pathways to a concept in LTM. Dual coding increases learning and retrieval.

Memory interference occurs when consumers have difficulty retrieving a specific piece of information because other related information in memory gets in the way. A common form of memory interference is due to competitive advertising. Competitive interference increases with increased advertising clutter. But it can be reduced by avoiding competitive clutter, strengthening learning, reducing similarity to competitor ads, and providing retrieval cues.

The *response environment* can also be critical to retrieval. Matching the response environment to the learning environment, or matching the learning environment to the response environment, can enhance the ease and likelihood of retrieval.

LO5: Understand the application of learning to brand positioning, equity, and leverage

Brand image, a market segment or individual consumer's schematic memory of a brand, is a major focus of marketing activity. *Product positioning* is a decision by a marketer to attempt to attain a defined and differentiated brand image, generally in relation to specific competitors. A brand image that matches a target market's needs and desires will be valued by that market segment. Such a brand is said to have *brand equity* because consumers respond favorably toward it in the market. In addition, these consumers may be willing to assume that other products with the same brand name will have some of the same features, which relates to how consumers learn to generalize from one stimulus to another. Introducing new products under the same name as an existing product is referred to as *brand leverage* or *brand extension.*

KEY TERMS

REVIEW QUESTIONS

1. What is *learning?*
2. What is *memory?*
3. Define *short-term memory* and *long-term memory.*
4. Discuss the nature of *short-term memory* in terms of its endurance and capacity.
5. What is *maintenance rehearsal?*
6. What is meant by *elaborative activities?*
7. What is meant by *imagery* in working memory?
8. What is *semantic memory?*
9. How does a *schema* differ from a *script?*
10. What is *episodic memory* and how does it relate to *flashbulb memory?*
11. Describe *low-involvement learning.* How does it differ from *high-involvement learning?*
12. What do we mean by *cognitive learning* and how does it differ from the *conditioning theory* approach to learning?
13. Distinguish between learning via *classical conditioning* and learning that occurs via *operant conditioning.*
14. What is *iconic rote learning?* How does it differ from classical conditioning? Operant conditioning?
15. Define *modeling.*
16. What is meant by learning by *analytical reasoning?*
17. Describe *analogical reasoning.*
18. What is meant by *stimulus generalization?* When do marketers use it?
19. Define *stimulus discrimination.* Why is it important?
20. Explain *extinction* and *retrieval failure* and why marketing managers are interested in them.
21. What factors affect the *strength of learning?*
22. How does *self-referencing* relate to *strength of learning* and retrieval?
23. What is *memory interference* and what strategies can marketers use to deal with it?
24. Why is it useful to match the retrieval and learning environments?
25. What is a *brand image?* Why is it important?
26. What is *product positioning? Repositioning?*
27. What is *perceptual mapping?*
28. What is *brand equity?*
29. What does *leveraging brand equity* mean?

DISCUSSION QUESTIONS

30. How would you determine the best product position for the following?
    a. A brand of tablet computer
    b. A cell phone targeting children
    c. A local animal shelter
    d. A line of power tools targeting women
    e. A brand of toothpaste
31. Is low-involvement learning really widespread? Which products are most affected by low-involvement learning?
32. Almex and Company introduced a new coffee-flavored liqueur in direct competition with Hiram Walker's tremendously successful Kahlua brand. Almex named its new entry Kamora and packaged it in a bottle similar to that of Kahlua, using a pre-Columbian label design. The ad copy for Kamora reads, "If you like coffee—you'll love Kamora." Explain Almex's marketing strategy in terms of learning theory.
33. Describe the brand images the following brands have among students on your campus.
    a. BlackBerry smartphone
    b. Your student government
    c. Pepsi Max
    d. Toyota Prius Hybrid
    e. The United Way
    f. Chevy Volt
34. In what ways, if any, would the brand images you described in response to the previous question differ with different groups, such as (*a*) middle-aged professionals, (*b*) young blue-collar workers, (*c*) high school students, and (*d*) retired couples?
35. What role does *dual coding* play in the learning process?
36. Respond to the questions in Consumer Insight 9–1.
37. Evaluate Illustrations 9–1 through 9–5 in light of their apparent objectives and target market.
38. Respond to the questions in Consumer Insight 9–2.

APPLICATION ACTIVITIES

39. Fulfill the requirements of Question 33 by interviewing three male and three female students.
40. Answer Question 34 based on interviews with five individuals from each group.
41. Pick a consumer convenience product, perhaps a personal care product such as suntan lotion or toothpaste, and create advertising copy stressing (*a*) a positive reinforcement, (*b*) a negative reinforcement, and (*c*) a punishment.
42. Find and describe three advertisements, one based on cognitive learning, another based on operant conditioning, and the third based on classical conditioning. Discuss the nature of each advertisement and how it utilizes that type of learning.
43. Find and describe three advertisements that you believe are based on low-involvement learning and three that are based on high-involvement learning. Justify your selection.
44. Select a product and develop an advertisement based on low-involvement learning and one on high-involvement learning. When should each be used (be specific)?
45. Find two advertisements for competing brands that you feel do a good job of avoiding competitive advertising interference and two that you think do not. Justify your selection.
46. Visit a grocery store and examine product packages or point-of-purchase information that could serve as retrieval cues for a brand's ongoing advertising campaign. Write a brief report of your findings and describe the nature and effectiveness of the retrieval cues utilized. Could they have been better? Explain.
47. Select a product that you feel has a good product position and one that has a weak position. Justify your selection. Describe an ad or package for each product and indicate how it affects the product's position.
48. Select a product, store, or service of relevance to students on your campus. Using a sample of students, measure its brand image. Develop a marketing strategy to improve its image.
49. Develop a campaign to reduce the risk of AIDS for students on your campus by teaching them the value of
    a. Abstinence from sex outside of marriage
    b. Safe sex
50. Find a recent brand extension that you feel will be successful and one that you feel will fail. Explain each of your choices.

REFERENCES

1. This opener is based on R. Krulwich, "There's a Fly in My Urinal," *npr.com*, December 18, 2009, www.npr.org/templates/story/story.php?storyId=121310977, accessed September 1, 2014; B. Wansink, *Mindless Eating* (New York: Bantam, 2010); "Placebo Buttons," *abcnews.go.com* video, May 23, 2010, http://abcnews.go.com/GMA/video/placebo-buttons-pushing-10722406, accessed September 1, 2014; M. Wright, "5 Fake Sounds Designed to Help Humans," *Sharp Company Blog*, June 20, 2011, www.humansinvent.com/#!/889/5-fake-sounds-designed-to-help-humans/, accessed September 1, 2014.
2. A. A. Mitchell, "Cognitive Processes Initiated by Exposure to Advertising," in *Information Processing Research in Advertising*, ed. R. Harris (New York: Erlbaum, 1983), pp. 13–42.
3. For differing views, see A. J. Malter, "An Introduction to Embodied Cognition," *Advances in Consumer Research*, vol. 23, ed. K. P. Corfman and J. G. Lynch (Provo, UT: Association for Consumer Research, 1996), pp. 272–76; and M. E. Hill, R. Radtke, and M. King, "A Transfer Appropriate Processing View of Consumer Memory," *Journal of Current Issues and Research in Advertising*, Spring 1997, pp. 1–21.
4. M. Vanhuele, G. Laurent, and X. Drèze, "Consumers' Immediate Memory for Prices," *Journal of Consumer Research*, September 2006, pp. 163–72.
5. J. Fetto, "Call Me Vain," *American Demographics*, November 2002, p. 15.
6. See K. Mason, T. Jensen, S. Burton, and D. Roach, "The Accuracy of Brand and Attribute Judgments," *Journal of the Academy of Marketing Science*, Summer 2001, pp. 307–17; and S. Putrevu, J. Tan, and K. R. Lord, "Consumer Responses to Complex Advertisements," *Journal of Current Issues and Research in Advertising*, Spring 2004, pp. 9–24.
7. P. K. Petrova and R. B. Cialdini, "Fluency of Consumption Imagery and the Backfire Effects of Imagery Appeals," *Journal of Consumer Research*, December 2005, pp. 442–52.
8. G. Wolters and J. J. Goodsmit, "Flashbulb and Event Memory of September 11, 2001, *Psychological Reports*, June 2005, pp. 605–19; H. A. Roehm Jr. and M. L. Roehm, "Can Brand Encounters Inspire Flashbulb Memories?," *Psychology & Marketing*, January 2007, pp. 25–40; and A. Bohn and D. Bernsten, "Pleasantness Bias in Flashbulb Memories," *Memory*

and Cognition, April 2007, pp. 565–77. See also H. Ahn, M. W. Liu, and D. Soman, "Memory Markers," *Journal of Consumer Psychology,* 19 (2009), pp. 508–16.

9. K. A. Braun, "Postexperience Advertising Effects on Consumer Memory," *Journal of Consumer Research,* March 1999, pp. 319–34; and M. Supphellen, O. Eismann, and L. E. Hem, "Can Advertisements for Brand Extensions Revitalize Flagship Products?," *International Journal of Advertising,* 23 (2004), pp. 173–96.
10. M. Morrin, J. Lee, and G. M. Allenby, "Determinants of Trademark Dilution," *Journal of Consumer Research,* September 2006, pp. 248–57.
11. See E. J. Cowley, "Recovering Forgotten Information," in *Advances in Consumer Research,* vol. 21, ed. C. T. Allen and D. R. John (Provo, UT: Association for Consumer Research, 1994), pp. 58–63.
12. K. K. Desai and W. Hoyer, "Descriptive Characteristics of Memory-Based Consideration Sets," *Journal of Consumer Research,* December 2000, pp. 309–23. See also P. Nedungadi, A. Chattopadyay, and A.V. Muthukrishnan, "Category Structure, Brand Recall, and Choice," *International Journal of Research in Marketing,* 18 (2001), pp. 191–202; and E. Cowley and A. A. Mitchell, "The Moderating Effect of Product Knowledge on the Learning and Organization of Product Information," *Journal of Consumer Research,* December 2003, pp. 443–54.
13. G. Venkataramani and M. T. Pham, "Relatedness, Prominence, and Constructive Sponsor Identification," *Journal of Marketing Research,* August 1999, pp. 299–312.
14. K. B. Monroe and A. Y. Lee, "Remembering versus Knowing," *Journal of the Academy of Marketing Science,* Spring 1999, pp. 207–25; and E. A. van Reijmersdal, P. C. Neijens, and E. G. Smit, "Effects of Television Brand Placement on Brand Image," *Psychology & Marketing,* May 2007, pp. 403–20.
15. S. A. Hawkins, S. J. Hoch, and J. Meyers-Levy, "Low-Involvement Learning," *Journal of Consumer Psychology,* 11, no. 1 (2001), pp. 1–11.
16. See R. P. Grossman and B. D. Till, "The Persistence of Classically Conditioned Brand Attitudes," *Journal of Advertising,* Spring 1998, pp. 23–31; J. Kim, J.-S. Lim, and M. Bhargava, "The Role of Affect in Attitude Formation," *Journal of the Academy of Marketing Science,* Spring 1998, pp. 143–52; W. E. Baker, "When Can Affective Conditioning and Mere Exposure Directly Influence Brand Choice?," *Journal of Advertising,* Winter 1999, pp. 31–46; B. D. Till and R. L. Priluck, "Stimulus Generalization in Classical Conditioning," *Psychology & Marketing,* January 2000, pp. 55–72; and B. D. Till, S. M. Stanley, and R. Priluck, "Classical Conditioning and Celebrity Endorsers," *Psychology and Marketing,* February 2008, pp. 179–96.
17. B. D. Till and R. L. Priluck, "Conditioning of Meaning in Advertising," *Journal of Current Issues and Research in Advertising,* Fall 2001, pp. 1–8
18. For discussions of the role of awareness in classical conditioning, see C. Janiszewski and L. Warlop, "The Influence of Classical Conditioning Procedures on Subsequent Attention to the Conditioned Brand," *Journal of Consumer Research,* September 1993, pp. 171–89; R. Priluck and B. D. Till, "The Role of Contingency Awareness, Involvement, and Need for Cognition in Attitude Formation," *Journal of the Academy of Marketing Science,* 32, no. 3 (2004), pp. 329–44; and I. Kirsch et al., "The Role of Cognition in Classical and Operant Conditioning," *Journal of Clinical Psychology,* April 2004, pp. 369–92.
19. See, e.g., W. H. Motes and A. G. Woodside, "Purchase Experiments of Extra-ordinary and Regular Influence Strategies Using Artificial and Real Brands," *Journal of Business Research,* 53 (2001), pp. 15–35; and Kirsch et al, "The Role of Cognition in Classical and Operant Conditioning."
20. B. J. Bergiel and C. Trosclair, "Instrumental Learning," *Journal of Consumer Marketing,* Fall 1985, pp. 23–28. See also W. Gaidis and J. Cross, "Behavior Modification as a Framework for Sales Promotion Management," *Journal of Consumer Marketing,* Spring 1987, pp. 65–74.
21. E. Heit, J. Briggs, and L. Bott, "Modeling the Effects of Prior Knowledge on Learning Incongruent Features of Category Members," *Journal of Experimental Psychology: Learning, Memory, and Cognition,* September 2004, pp. 1065–81.
22. See J. W. Pracejus, "Is More Always Better?," in *Advances in Consumer Research,* vol. 22, ed. F. R. Kardes and M. Sujan (Provo, UT: Association for Consumer Research, 1995), pp. 319–22; and K. P. Gwinner and J. Eaton, "Building Brand Image through Event Sponsorship," *Journal of Advertising,* Winter 1999, pp. 47–57.
23. T. P. Ballinger, M. G. Palumbo, and N. T. Wilcox, "Precautionary Saving and Social Learning across Generations," *The Economic Journal,* October 2003, pp. 920–47.
24. For a way to measure such images, see L. A. Babin and A. C. Burns, *Psychology & Marketing,* May 1998, pp. 261–78.
25. S. P. Jain and D. Maheswaran, "Motivated Reasoning," *Journal of Consumer Research,* March 2000, pp. 358–71.
26. J. Gregan-Paxton, J. D. Hibbard, F. F. Brunel, and P. Azar, "So That's What That Is," *Psychology & Marketing,* June 2002, pp. 533–50; and J. Gregan-Paxton and P. Moreau, "How Do Consumers Transfer Existing Knowledge?," *Journal of Consumer Psychology,* 13, no. 4 (2003), pp. 422–30. See also M. R. Goode, D. W. Dahl, and C. P. Moreau, "The Effect of Experiential Analogies on Consumer Perceptions and Attitudes," *Journal of Marketing Research,* April 2010, pp. 274–86.
27. For an application to trademark infringement, see C. Pullig, C. J. Simmons, and R. G. Netemeyer, "Brand Dilution," *Journal of Marketing,* April 2006, pp. 52–66.
28. M. L. Roehm and A. M. Tybout, "When Will a Brand Scandal Spill Over, and How Should Competitors Respond?," *Journal of Marketing Research,* August 2006, pp. 366–373.
29. See Till and Priluck, "Stimulus Generalization in Classical Conditioning."
30. J. Halliday, "Chrysler Hikes Spending to 'Re-establish' Three Brands," *Advertising Age,* November 9, 2009, p. 4.
31. M. Maremont, "Gillette Chief Says Cost-Cutting Plan Will Take Time," *The Wall Street Journal,* June 7, 2001, p. B2.
32. "Behind Saturn's Stumble," *Advertising Age,* January 24, 1994, p. 22.
33. "L&M Lights Up Again," *Marketing & Media Decisions,* February 1984, p. 69.
34. Ibid.
35. D. Luna and L. A. Peracchio, "Where There Is a Will . . .," *Psychology & Marketing,* July–August 2002, pp. 573–93; see

also R. S. Wyer Jr., "Language and Advertising Effectiveness," *Psychology & Marketing,* July–August 2002, pp. 693–712.

36. See R. G. M. Pieters, E. Rosbergen, and M. Hartog, "Visual Attention to Advertising," *Advances in Consumer Research,* vol. 23, ed. Corfman and Lynch, pp. 242–48; and S. M. Leong, S. H. Ang, and L. L. Tham, "Increasing Brand Name Recall in Print Advertising among Asian Consumers," *Journal of Advertising,* Summer 1996, pp. 65–81.
37. M. L. Roehm, "Instrumental vs. Vocal Versions of Popular Music in Advertising," *Journal of Advertising Research,* May 2001, pp. 49–58. See also W. E. Baker and R. J. Lutz, "An Empirical Test of an Updated Relevance–Accessibility Model," *Journal of Advertising,* Spring 2000, pp. 1–13.
38. See, e.g., M. Wedel and R. Pieters, "Eye Fixations on Advertisements and Memory for Brands," *Marketing Science,* Fall 2000, pp. 297–312.
39. M. Morrin and S. Ratneshwar, "Does It Make Sense to Use Scents to Enhance Brand Memory?," *Journal of Marketing Research,* February 2003, pp. 10–25.
40. W. E. Baker, H. Honea, and C. A. Russell, "Do Not Wait to Reveal the Brand Name," *Journal of Advertising,* Fall 2004, pp. 77–85; see also W. E. Baker, "Does Brand Name Imprinting in Memory Increase Brand Information Retention?," *Psychology & Marketing,* December 2003, pp. 1119–35.
41. See R. E. Burnkrant and H. R. Unnava, "Effects of Self-Referencing on Persuasion," *Journal of Consumer Research,* June 1995, pp. 17–26; and P. Krishnamurthy and M. Sujan, "Retrospection versus Anticipation," *Journal of Consumer Research,* June 1999, pp. 55–69.
42. K. R. Lord, R. E. Burnkrant, and H. R. Unnava, "The Effects of Program-Induced Mood States on Memory for Commercial Information," *Journal of Current Issues and Research in Advertising,* Spring 2001, pp. 1–14; and S. J. Newell, K. V. Henderson, and B. T. Wu, "The Effects of Pleasure and Arousal on Recall of Advertisements during the Super Bowl," *Psychology & Marketing,* November 2001, pp. 1135–53.
43. T. Ambler and T. Burne, "The Impact of Affect on Memory of Advertising," *Journal of Advertising Research,* March 1999, pp. 25–39; and S. Youn et al., "Commercial Liking and Memory," *Journal of Advertising Research,* May 2001, pp. 7–13.
44. Consumer Insight 9–1 is based on J. Kellaris, "Dissecting Earworms," in *Proceedings of the Society for Consumer Psychology Winter 2003 Conference,* ed. C. Page and S. Posavac (New Orleans, LA: American Psychological Society, 2003), pp. 220–22; K. Bruno, "Best-Ever Advertising Jingles," *forbes.com,* June 30, 2010, www.forbes.com/2010/06/30/advertising-jingles-coca-cola-cmo-network-jingles_slide_7.html, accessed September 1, 2014; A. Scott, "Start Me Up," *bizjournals.com,* June 28, 2011, www.bizjournals.com/seattle/blog/techflash/2011/06/bill-gates-mick-jagger-deal.html?ana=from_rss&utm_source=feedburner&utm_medium=feed&utm_campaign=Feed%253A+TechFlash+%2528TechFlash+-+Seattle%2527s+Technology+News+Source%2529, accessed September 1, 2014; T. Faulkner, "How Commercial Jingles Work," *howstuffworks.com,* http://money.howstuffworks.com/commercial-jingle2.htm, accessed September 1, 2014; and S. Watson, "Why Do Songs Get Stuck in My Head?," *howstuffworks.com,* http://science.howstuffworks.com/life/songs-stuck-in-head1.htm, accessed September 1, 2014.
45. See P. Malaviya, J. Meyers-Levy, and B. Sternthal, "Ad Repetition in a Cluttered Environment," *Psychology & Marketing,* March 1999, pp. 99–118.
46. J. O. Eastlack Jr., "How to Get More Bang from Your Television Bucks," *Journal of Consumer Marketing,* Third Quarter 1984, pp. 25–34. See also L. W. Turley and J. R. Shannon, "The Impact and Effectiveness of Advertisements in a Sports Arena," *Journal of Services Marketing,* 14, no. 4 (2000), pp. 323–36.
47. See Hawkins, Hoch, and Meyers-Levy, "Low-Involvement Learning."
48. See also J. P. Jones, "Single-Source Research Begins to Fulfill Its Promise," *Journal of Advertising Research,* May 1995, pp. 9–16.
49. See S. N. Singh, S. Mishra, N. Bendapudi, and D. Linville, "Enhancing Memory of Television Commercials through Message Spacing," *Journal of Marketing Research,* August 1994, pp. 384–92; E. Ephron, "More Weeks, Less Weight," *Journal of Advertising Research,* May 1995, pp. 18–23; and H. Noel, "The Spacing Effect," *Journal of Consumer Psychology,* 16, no. 3 (2006), pp. 306–20.
50. For more on spacing effects, see C. Janiszewski, H. Noel, and A. G. Sawyer, "A Meta-Analysis of the Spacing Effect in Verbal Learning," *Journal of Consumer Research,* June 2003, pp. 138–49; S. L. Appleton-Knapp, R. A. Bjork, and T. D. Wickens, "Examining the Spacing Effect in Advertising," *Journal of Consumer Research,* September 2005, pp. 266–76; and A. G. Sawyer, H. Noel, and C. Janiszewski, "The Spacing Effects of Multiple Exposures on Memory," *Journal of Advertising Research,* June 2009, pp. 193–97.
51. See M. H. Blair and M. J. Rabuck, "Advertising Wearin and Wearout," *Journal of Advertising Research,* September 1998, pp. 7–25; D. W. Stewart, "Advertising Wearout," *Journal of Advertising Research,* September 1999, pp. 39–42; and M. C. Campbell and K. L. Keller, "Brand Familiarity and Advertising Repetition Effects," *Journal of Consumer Research,* September 2003, pp. 292–304.
52. D. Schumann, R. E. Petty, and D. S. Clemons, "Predicting the Effectiveness of Different Strategies of Advertising Variation," *Journal of Consumer Research,* September 1990, pp. 192–202.
53. C. Yoo, H. Bang, and Y. Kim, "The Effects of a Consistent Ad Series on Consumer Evaluations," *International Journal of Advertising,* 28, no. 1 (2008), pp. 105–23.
54. W. J. Bryce and R. F. Yalch, "Hearing versus Seeing," *Journal of Current Issues and Research in Advertising,* Spring 1993, pp. 1–20; and A. C. Burns, A. Biswas, and L. A. Babin, "The Operation of Visual Imagery as a Mediator of Advertising Effects," *Journal of Advertising,* June 1993, pp. 71–85.
55. T. Clark, "Echoic Memory Explored and Applied," *Journal of Consumer Marketing,* Winter 1987, pp. 39–46. See also C. E. Young and M. Robinson, "Video Rhythms and Recall," *Journal of Advertising Research,* July 1989, pp. 22–25.
56. J. J. Kellaris, A. D. Cox, and D. Cox, "The Effect of Background Music on Ad Processing," *Journal of Marketing,* October 1993, pp. 114–25. See also M. Hahn and I. Hwang, "Effects of Tempo and Familiarity of Background Music on Message Processing in TV Advertising," *Psychology & Marketing,* December 1999, pp. 659–75.

57. K. R. Lord and S. Putrevu, "Communicating in Print," *Journal of Current Issues and Research in Advertising,* Fall 1998, pp. 1–18.

58. D. Luna and L. A. Peracchio, "Moderators of Language Effects in Advertising to Bilinguals," *Journal of Consumer Research,* September 2001, pp. 284–95.

59. See R. D. Jewell and H. R. Unnava, "When Competitive Interference Can Be Beneficial," *Journal of Consumer Research,* September 2003, pp. 283–91; and A. Kumar and S. Krishnan, "Memory Interference in Advertising," *Journal of Consumer Research,* March 2004, pp. 602–11.

60. See M. Dahlen and J. Nordfalt, "Interference Effects of a Purchase on Subsequent Advertising within the Category," *Journal of Current Issues and Research in Advertising,* Spring 2004, pp. 1–8.

61. R. J. Kent and C. T. Allen, "Competitive Interference Effects in Consumer Memory for Advertising," *Journal of Marketing,* July 1994, pp. 97–105; A. Kumar, "Interference Effects of Contextual Cues in Advertisements on Memory for Ad Content," *Journal of Consumer Psychology,* 9, no. 3 (2000), pp. 155–66; S. Law, "Can Repeating a Brand Claim Lead to Memory Confusion?," *Journal of Marketing Research,* August 2002, pp. 366–78; K. A. Braun-LaTour and M. S. LaTour, "Assessing the Long-Term Impact of a Consistent Advertising Campaign on Consumer Memory," *Journal of Advertising,* Summer 2004, pp. 49–61; and M. Laroche, M. Cleveland, and I. Maravelakis, "Competitive Advertising Interference and Ad Repetition Effects," *International Journal of Advertising,* 25, no. 3 (2006), pp. 271–307.

62. H. R. Unnava and D. Sirdeshmukh, "Reducing Competitive Ad Interference," *Journal of Marketing Research,* August 1994, pp. 403–11.

63. Jewell and Unnava, "When Competitive Interference Can Be Beneficial"; and K. L. Keller, S. E. Heckler, and M. J. Houston, "The Effects of Brand Name Suggestiveness on Advertising Recall," *Journal of Marketing,* January 1998, pp. 48–57.

64. Kumar, "Interference Effects of Contextual Cues in Advertisements on Memory for Ad Content."

65. M. C. Macklin, "The Effects of an Advertising Retrieval Cue on Young Children's Memory and Brand Evaluations," *Psychology & Marketing,* May 1994, pp. 291–311; Keller, Heckler, and Houston, "The Effects of Brand Name Suggestiveness on Advertising Recall"; and N. T. Tavassoli and Y. H. Lee, "The Differential Interaction of Auditory and Visual Advertising Elements with Chinese and English," *Journal of Marketing Research,* November 2003, pp. 468–80.

66. See J. W. Park, "Memory-Based Product Judgments," and E. J. Cowley, "Altering Retrieval Sets," both in *Advances in Consumer Research,* vol. 22, ed. Kardes and Sujan, pp. 159–64 and 323–27, respectively; and M. E. Hill and M. King, "Comparative vs. Noncomparative Advertising," *Journal of Current Issues and Research in Advertising,* Fall 2001, pp. 33–52.

67. S. M. J. Van Osselaer and J. W. Alba, "Consumer Learning and Brand Equity," *Journal of Consumer Research,* June 2000, pp. 1–16; W. R. Dillon et al., "Understanding What's in a Brand Rating," *Journal of Marketing Research,* November 2001, pp. 415–29; and K. L. Keller, "Brand Synthesis," *Journal of Consumer Research,* March 2003, pp. 595–600.

68. S. Thompson, "Meat Gets Branded," *Advertising Age,* September 24, 2001, p. 6.

69. S. M. J. Van Osselear and J. W. Alba, "Locus of Equity and Brand Extension," *Journal of Consumer Research,* March 2003, pp. 539–50.

70. For a discussion of perceived differences generated by trivial attributes, see S. M. Broniarczyk and A. D. Gershoff, "The Reciprocal Effects of Brand Equity and Trivial Attributes," *Journal of Marketing Research,* May 2003, pp. 161–75.

71. J. Halliday, "Losing Its Brand Soul," *Advertising Age,* February 5, 2007, pp. 4, 35.

72. B. Wansink, "Making Old Brands New," *American Demographics,* December 1998, pp. 53–58.

73. See, e.g., C. Young, "Brain Waves, Picture Sorts®, and Branding Moments," *Journal of Advertising Research,* August 2002, pp. 42–53; E. Maoz and A. M. Tybout, "The Moderating Role of Involvement and Differentiation in the Evaluation of Brand Extensions, *Journal of Consumer Psychology,* 12, no. 2 (2002), pp. 119–31; F. Völckner and H. Sattler, "Drivers of Brand Extension Success," *Journal of Marketing,* April 2006, pp. 18–34; and H. Mao and H. S. Krishnan, "Effects of Prototype and Exemplar Fit on Brand Extension Evaluations," *Journal of Consumer Research,* June 2006, pp. 41–49.

74. N. O'Leary, "Buick Leads GM's Efforts at Reinvention," *Adweek,* July 20, 2009, p. 4.

75. See V. Gerson, "Showing Customers Your Best Face," *Bank Marketing,* January 1999, pp. 26–30; and D. James, "Image Makeovers Require Gentle Touch," *Marketing News,* July 2, 2001, p. 4.

76. M. Cardona, "Block's Less Taxing Future," *Advertising Age,* January 15, 2001, p. 6.

77. J. Halliday, "New Q45 Effort," *Advertising Age,* March 2001, p. 8.

78. J. Halliday, "Hyundai and Kia Head Upscale via Different Routes," *Advertising Age,* November 1, 2004, p. 12.

79. Jewell and Unnava, "When Competitive Interference Can Be Beneficial"; and K. K. Desai and S. Ratneshwar, "Consumer Perceptions of Product Variants Positioned on Atypical Attributes," *Journal of the Academy of Marketing Science,* Winter 2003, pp. 22–35.

80. J. Halliday, "Little Else Matters," *Advertising Age,* August 16, 2004, p. 6.

81. K. Macarthur, "Hardee's," *Advertising Age,* November 1, 2004, p. S-18.

82. M. Supphellen, "Understanding Core Brand Equity," *International Journal of Marketing Research,* 42, no. 3 (2000), pp. 319–38; M. M. Mackay, "Application of Brand Equity Service Measures in Service Markets," *Journal of Services Marketing,* 15, no. 3 (2001), pp. 21–29; D. A. Aaker and R. Jacobson, "The Value of Brand Attitude in High-Technology Markets," *Journal of Marketing Research,* November 2001, pp. 485–93; and S. Brown, R. V. Kozinets, and J. F. Sherry Jr., "Teaching Old Brands New Tricks," *Journal of Marketing,* July 2003, pp. 19–33.

83. A. Chaudhuri, "How Brand Reputation Affects the Advertising–Brand Equity Link," *Journal of Advertising Research,* June 2002, pp. 33–43.

84. P. Chandon, B. Wansink, and G. Laurent, "A Benefit Congruency Framework of Sales Promotion Effectiveness," *Journal of Marketing,* October 2000, pp. 65–81.

85. N. Dawar and M. M. Pillutla, "Impact of Product-Harm Crises on Brand Equity," *Journal of Marketing Research,* May 2000, pp. 215–26; H. Kim, W. G. Kim, and J. A. An, "The Effect of Consumer-Based Brand Equity on Firms' Financial Performance," *Journal of Consumer Marketing,* 20, no. 4 (2003), pp. 335–51; and D. DelVecchio and D. C. Smith, "Brand-Extension Price Premiums," *Journal of the Academy of Marketing Science,* Spring 2005, pp. 184–96.

86. See T. Erdem and B. Sun, "An Empirical Investigation of the Spillover Effects of Advertising and Sales Promotions in Umbrella Branding," *Journal of Marketing Research,* November 2002, pp. 408–20; and J. H. Washburn, B. D. Till, and R. Priluck, "Brand Alliance and Customer-Based Brand-Equity Effects," *Psychology & Marketing,* July 2004, pp. 487–508.

87. S. Thompson, "Campbell Extends Pace beyond Salsa," *Advertising Age,* August 30, 2004, p. 10.

88. H. Schlossberg, "Slashing through Market Clutter," *Marketing News,* March 5, 1990, p. 6.

89. Maoz and Tybout, "The Moderating Role of Involvement and Differentiation in the Evaluation of Brand Extensions."

90. This insight is based on H. Hagtvedt and V. M. Patrick, "Art and the Brand," *Journal of Consumer Psychology,* 18 (2008), pp. 212–22; H. Hagtvedt and V. M. Patrick, "Art Infusion," *Journal of Marketing Research,* June 2008, pp. 379–89; and H. Hagtvedt and V. M. Patrick, "The Broad Embrace of Luxury," *Journal of Consumer Psychology,* 19 (2009), pp. 608–18.

91. S. M. Broniarczyk and J. W. Alba, "The Importance of the Brand in Brand Extension," *Journal of Marketing Research,* May 1994, pp. 214–28; see also T. Meyvis and C. Janiszewski, "When Are Broader Brands Stronger Brands?," *Journal of Consumer Research,* September 2004, pp. 346–57.

92. S. Bridges, K. L. Keller, and S. Sood, "Communication Strategies for Brand Extensions," *Journal of Advertising,* Winter 2000, pp. 1–12; and R. Klink and D. C. Smith, "Threats to the External Validity of Brand Extension Research," *Journal of Marketing Research,* August 2001, pp. 326–35; see also Völckner and Sattler, "Drivers of Brand Extension Success"; and C. Blankson and S. P. Kalafatis, "Congruence between Positioning and Brand Advertising," *Journal of Advertising Research,* March 2007, pp. 79–94.

93. V. Swaminathan, R. J. Fox, and S. K. Reddy, "The Impact of Brand Extension Introduction on Choice," *Journal of Marketing,* October 2001, pp. 1–15.

94. Effects can be negative or positive. See, e.g., D. R. John, B. Loken, and C. Joiner, "The Negative Impact of Extensions," *Journal of Marketing,* January 1998, pp. 19–32; Z. Gurhan-Canli and D. Maheswaran, "The Effects of Extensions on Brand Name Dilution and Enhancement," *Journal of Marketing Research,* November 1998, pp. 464–73; and S. Balachander and S. Ghose, "Reciprocal Spillover Effects," *Journal of Marketing,* January 2003, pp. 4–13.

95. For exceptions, see Meyvis and Janiszewski, "When Are Broader Brands Stronger Brands?"

96. A. Kirmani, S. Sood, and S. Bridges, "The Ownership Effect in Consumer Response to Brand Line Stretches," *Journal of Marketing,* January 1999, pp. 88–101.

chapter

10 Motivation, Personality, and Emotion

LEARNING OBJECTIVES

LO1 **Define motivation and summarize the motivation sets put forth by Maslow and McGuire.**

LO2 **Articulate motivation's role in consumer behavior and marketing strategy.**

LO3 **Define personality and the various theories of personality.**

LO4 **Discuss how brand personality can be used in developing marketing strategies.**

LO5 **Define emotions and list the major emotional dimensions.**

LO6 **Discuss how emotions can be used in developing marketing strategies.**

Brands, like people, have personalities. Brand personality, as we will see later in the chapter, is a set of human characteristics that become associated with a brand. These characteristics contribute to a brand's image. Personality traits and other brand associations can be affected in positive and negative ways by numerous factors including advertising, word-of-mouth, direct product experience, and so on. Toyota, which has enjoyed amazing success in the United States, has found itself struggling with brand image since safety issues relating to its accelerator pedal and system resulted in a recall of nearly 6 million vehicles. The overall result was a major reduction in Toyota perceptions, as shown below.[1]

For both owners and non-owners, perceptions of reliability and quality went down after the recall and these effects were stronger for non-owners. Owners appear to be giving Toyota a bit more of the benefit of the doubt, although even there the declines are substantial. Specifically, among Toyota owners, there was a 23-point drop in reliability and a 44-point drop in those who perceived Toyota to be of higher quality than domestics. Reliability is a brand personality trait associated with competence. Clearly Toyota's image has suffered and that has translated into reduced quality perceptions and purchase intentions, as the percentage of Toyota owners who would consider buying a Toyota in the future dropped 16 points after the recall.

Toyota is working hard to fix its image problem. Among other things, it has a "recall information" page on its website and has launched its "Safety First" advertising campaign, which states, in part:

> At Toyota, we're committed to providing our customers with safe, reliable cars. That's why we're

	Toyota Owners		Toyota Non-Owners	
	Before Recall	After Recall	Before Recall	After Recall
Reliable brand	95%	72%	89%	61%
Unreliable brand	5	28	6	39
Quality lower than domestics	4	18	5	34
Quality equal to domestics	25	49	43	53
Quality higher than domestics	70	33	47	13

Source: Adapted from B. Steinberg, "Lightspeed Survey: Toyota's Loss of Consumer Trust Is Domestic Rivals' Gain," *Advertising Age*, February 8, 2010, p. 2.

currently spending $1 million per hour to enhance the technology and safety of our vehicles. And we've also made our comprehensive star safety system standard on every vehicle we make.

There is evidence that Toyota is coming back. Although they dropped as far as fourth place in U.S. sales after the recall, more recent sales numbers put them in third place behind Ford and GM.

As the opening example suggests, brand personality is critical to brand image and consumer behavior. It is also part of three interrelated aspects of consumer behavior, namely, motivation, personality, and emotions. *Motivation* is the energizing force that activates behavior and provides purpose and direction to that behavior. It helps answer the question of "why" consumers engage in specific behaviors. *Personality* reflects the relatively stable behavioral tendencies that individuals display across a variety of situations. It helps answer the question of "what" behaviors consumers choose to engage in to achieve their goals. *Emotions* are strong, relatively uncontrollable feelings that affect our behavior. Emotions are triggered by a complex interplay between motives, personality, and external factors. Indeed, the three concepts are closely interrelated and are frequently difficult to separate.

THE NATURE OF MOTIVATION

LO1

Motivation is the reason for behavior. A **motive** is a construct representing an unobservable inner force that stimulates and compels a behavioral response and provides specific direction to that response. A motive is why an individual does something. The terms *need* and *motivation* are often used interchangeably. This is because when a consumer feels a gap between a desired state and his or her actual current state, a need is recognized and experienced as a drive state referred to as motivation. Needs and motives influence what consumers perceive as relevant and also influence their feelings and emotions. For example, a consumer who feels hungry is motivated to satisfy that need, will view food and ads for food as personally relevant, and will experience negative emotions prior to eating and positive emotions after eating.

There are numerous theories of motivation. This section describes two particularly useful approaches. The first approach, *Maslow's need hierarchy,* is a macro theory designed to account for most human behavior in general terms. The second approach, based on McGuire's work, uses a fairly detailed set of motives to account for specific aspects of consumer behavior.

Maslow's Hierarchy of Needs

Maslow's hierarchy of needs is based on four premises:[2]

1. All humans acquire a similar set of motives through genetic endowment and social interaction.
2. Some motives are more basic or critical than others.
3. The more basic motives must be satisfied to a minimum level before other motives are activated.
4. As the basic motives become satisfied, more advanced motives come into play.

Thus, Maslow proposed a need hierarchy shared by all. Table 10–1 illustrates this hierarchy, briefly describes each level, and provides marketing examples.

Marketing Strategies and Maslow's Need Hierarchy

I. Physiological: Food, water, sleep, and, to an extent, sex are physiological motives.

Products Health foods, medicines, sports drinks, low-cholesterol foods, and exercise equipment.

Themes BAND-AID: "Blister-proof your feet."

Quaker Oats: "Eating oatmeal is good for your heart."

NordicTrack: "Only NordicTrack gives you a total-body workout."

II. Safety: Seeking physical safety and security, stability, familiar surroundings, and so forth are manifestations of safety needs.

Products Smoke detectors, preventive medicines, insurance, retirement investments, seat belts, burglar alarms, and sunscreen.

Themes Sleep Safe: "We've designed a travel alarm that just might wake you in the middle of the night—because a fire is sending smoke into your room. You see, ours is a smoke alarm as well as an alarm clock."

Partnership for a Drug-Free America: "Heroin: Dying's the Easy Part."

State Street Investing: "Precise in a world that isn't."

III. Belongingness: Belongingness motives are reflected in a desire for love, friendship, affiliation, and group acceptance.

Products Personal grooming, foods, entertainment, clothing, and many others.

Themes Olive Garden Restaurants: "When You're Here, You're Family."

Tums: "You are important. You are loved. You should take your calcium."

Grand Marnier: "Add flavor to good company."

IV. Esteem: Desires for status, superiority, self-respect, and prestige are examples of esteem needs. These needs relate to the individual's feelings of usefulness and accomplishment.

Products Clothing, furniture, liquors, hobbies, stores, cars, and many others.

Themes Sheaffer: "Your hand should look as contemporary as the rest of you."

New Balance: "One more woman chasing a sunset. One more woman going a little farther. One more woman simply feeling alive. One less woman relying on someone else."

BMW: "The Ultimate Driving Machine."

V. Self-Actualization: This involves the desire for self-fulfillment, to become all that one is capable of becoming.

Products Education, hobbies, sports, some vacations, gourmet foods, museums.

Themes U.S. Navy: "Accelerate Your Life."

Gatorade: "Is it in you?"

Outward Bound School: "Minds in Motion."

Maslow's theory is a good guide to general behavior. It is not an ironclad rule, however. Numerous examples exist of individuals who sacrificed their lives for friends or ideas, or who gave up food and shelter to seek self-actualization. However, we do tend to regard such behavior as exceptional, which indicates the general validity of Maslow's overall approach.[3] It is important to remember that any given consumption behavior can satisfy more than one need. Likewise, the same consumption behavior can satisfy different needs at different times. For example, a number of motives could cause one to join one of the branches of the U.S. Military. The Marines' "The Few, The Brave" ad in Illustration 10–1 appeals to self-actualization.

McGuire's Psychological Motives

Maslow presented a hierarchical set of five basic motives, and other researchers have proposed hundreds of additional, very specific motives. McGuire developed a classification system that organizes these various theories into 16 categories.[4] This system helps

ILLUSTRATION 10-1

Appeals to self-actualization focus on individuals challenging themselves and reaching their full potential as shown in this Marines ad.

marketers isolate motives likely to be involved in various consumption situations. McGuire first divides motivation into four main categories using two criteria:

1. Is the mode of motivation cognitive or affective?
2. Is the motive focused on preservation of the status quo or on growth?

Cognitive motives focus on the person's need for being adaptively oriented toward the environment and achieving a sense of meaning. *Affective* motives deal with the need to reach satisfying feeling states and to obtain personal goals. *Preservation-oriented* motives emphasize the individual as striving to maintain equilibrium, while *growth* motives emphasize development. These four main categories are then further subdivided on the bases of source and objective of the motive:

3. Is this behavior actively initiated or in response to the environment?
4. Does this behavior help the individual achieve a new internal or a new external relationship to the environment?

The third criterion distinguishes between motives that are actively or internally aroused versus those that are a more passive response to circumstances. The final criterion is used to categorize outcomes that are internal to the individual and those focused on a relationship with the environment.

McGuire's 16 motives and their implications for marketing are briefly described in the following sections.

Cognitive Preservation Motives ***Need for Consistency (active, internal)*** A basic desire is to have all facets of oneself consistent with each other.[5] These facets include attitudes, behaviors, opinions, self-images, views of others, and so forth. *Cognitive dissonance* is a common motive of this type. For example, making a major purchase is not consistent with the need to save money. This inconsistency motivates the individual to reduce it (see Chapter 18).

Understanding the need for consistency is also important for structuring advertising messages relating to attitude change. A need for internal consistency means consumers are reluctant to accept information that disagrees with existing beliefs. Thus, marketers wishing to change attitudes must use highly credible sources or other techniques to overcome this (see Chapter 11).

Need for Attribution (active, external) This set of motives deals with our need to determine who or what causes the things that happen to us and relates to an area of research called **attribution theory.**[6] Do we attribute the cause of a favorable or unfavorable outcome to ourselves or to some outside force?

Need for attribution is extremely relevant to consumer reactions to promotional messages (in terms of credibility). Because consumers do not passively receive messages but rather attribute "selling" motives and tactics to ads and the advice of sales personnel, they

ILLUSTRATION 10-2

Consumers generally attribute selling motives to ads and disbelieve or discount the message. One approach to gain message acceptance is to use a credible source.

do not believe or they discount many sales messages.[7] Marketers use a variety of means to overcome this. One approach is to use a credible spokesperson, as seen in Illustration 10–2. This technique is discussed in depth in Chapter 11.

Need to Categorize (passive, internal) People have a need to categorize and organize the vast array of information and experiences they encounter in a meaningful yet manageable way,[8] so they establish categories or mental partitions to help them do so. Prices are often categorized such that different prices connote different categories of goods. Automobiles over $20,000 and automobiles under $20,000 may elicit two different meanings because of information categorized on the basis of price level. Many firms price items at $9.95, $19.95, $49.95, and so forth. One reason is to avoid being categorized in the over $10, $20, or $50 group.

Need for Objectification (passive, external) These motives reflect needs for observable cues or symbols that enable people to infer what they feel and know. Impressions, feelings, and attitudes are subtly established by viewing one's own behavior and that of others and drawing inferences as to what one feels and thinks. In many instances, clothing plays an important role in presenting the subtle meaning of a desired image and consumer lifestyle. Brands play a role in this, as shown in Figure 10–1.

Cognitive Growth Motives ***Need for Autonomy (active, internal)*** The need for independence and individuality is a characteristic of the American culture, as described in Chapter 2. All individuals in all cultures have this need at some level. Americans are taught that it is proper and even essential to express and fulfill this need (in contrast to Eastern countries such as Japan, which value affiliation).

ILLUSTRATION 10-3

Americans respond positively to ads and products that encourage uniqueness and individuality.

Owning or using products and services that are unique is one way consumers express their autonomy.[9] Marketers have responded to this motive by developing limited editions of products and providing wide variety and customization options. In addition, many products are advertised and positioned with independence, uniqueness, or individuality themes, as shown in Illustration 10–3.

Need for Stimulation (active, external) People often seek variety and difference out of a need for stimulation.[10] Such variety-seeking behavior may be a prime reason for brand switching and some so-called impulse purchasing.[11] The need for stimulation is curvilinear and changes over time.[12] That is, individuals experiencing rapid change generally become satiated and desire stability, whereas individuals in stable environments become bored and desire change.

Teleological Need (passive, internal) Consumers are pattern matchers who have images of desired outcomes or end states with which they compare their current situation. Behaviors are changed and the results are monitored in terms of movement toward the desired end state. This motive propels people to prefer mass media such as movies, television programs, and books with outcomes that match their view of how the world should work (e.g., the good guys win). This has obvious implications for advertising messages.

Utilitarian Need (passive, external) These theories view the consumer as a problem solver who approaches situations as opportunities to acquire useful information or new skills. Thus, a consumer watching a situation comedy on television not only is being entertained but is learning clothing styles, lifestyle options, and so forth. Likewise, consumers may approach ads and salespeople as a source of learning for future decisions as well as for the current one.

Affective Preservation Motives ***Need for Tension Reduction (active, internal)*** People encounter situations in their daily lives that create uncomfortable levels of stress. In order to effectively manage tension and stress, people are motivated to seek ways to reduce arousal. Recreational products and activities are often promoted in terms of tension relief. Illustration 10–4 contains a product and appeal focused on this need.

Need for Expression (active, external) This motive deals with the need to express one's identity to others. People feel the need to let others know who and what they are by their actions, which include the purchase and use of goods. The purchase of many products, such as clothing and automobiles, allows consumers to express an identity to others because the products have symbolic meanings. For example, fashion-oriented watches such as Swatch satisfy more than the functional need to tell time—they allow consumers to express who they are.

Need for Ego Defense (passive, internal) The need to defend one's identity or ego is another important motive. When one's identity is threatened, the person is motivated to protect his or her self-concept and utilize defensive behaviors and attitudes. Many products can provide ego defense. A consumer who feels insecure may rely on well-known brands for socially visible products to avoid any chance of making a socially incorrect purchase.

ILLUSTRATION 10-4

Today's hurried lifestyles often produce uncomfortable levels of tension. Products that relieve this stress fulfill a fundamental need.

Need for Reinforcement (passive, external) People are often motivated to act in certain ways because they were rewarded for behaving that way in similar situations in the past. This is the basis for operant learning. Products designed to be used in public situations (clothing, furniture, and artwork) are frequently sold on the basis of the amount and type of reinforcement that will be received. Keepsake Diamonds has exploited this motive with an ad that states, "Enter a room and you are immediately surrounded by friends sharing your excitement."

Affective Growth Motives ***Need for Assertion (active, internal)*** Many people are competitive achievers who seek success, admiration, and dominance. Important to them are power, accomplishment, and esteem. As Illustration 10–5 shows, the need for assertion underlies numerous ads.

Need for Affiliation (active, external) Affiliation refers to the need to develop mutually helpful and satisfying relationships with others. It relates to altruism and seeking acceptance and affection in interpersonal relations. As we saw in Chapter 7, group membership is a critical part of most consumers' lives, and many consumer decisions are based on the need to maintain satisfying relationships with others. Marketers frequently use such affiliation-based themes as "Your kids will love you for it" in advertisements.[13]

Need for Identification (passive, internal) The need for identification results in the consumer's playing various roles. A person may play the role of college student, sorority member, bookstore employee, fiancée, and many others. One gains pleasure from adding new, satisfying roles and by increasing the significance of roles already adopted. Marketers encourage consumers to assume new roles (become a skateboarder) and position products as critical for certain roles ("No working mother should be without one").

ILLUSTRATION 10-5

Consumer need for assertion underlies the strategy for this ad.

Need for Modeling (passive, external) The need for modeling reflects a tendency to base behavior on that of others. Modeling is a major means by which children learn to become consumers. The tendency to model explains some of the conformity that occurs within reference groups. Marketers use this motive by showing desirable types of individuals using their brands. American Express, for example, used Kate Winslet and Beyonce in its "My life. My card" campaign.

MOTIVATION THEORY AND MARKETING STRATEGY

LO2

Consumers do not buy products; instead, they buy motive satisfaction or problem solutions. For example, a study of Porsche buyers in the United States found that some were motivated by power and status (need for assertion), others by excitement and adventure (need for stimulation), and others by escapism (need for tension reduction). Such motives are not constrained to the United States. A study of car buyers in India found fairly similar motives. For example, they found a "Potency" buyer group interested in power (need for assertion), a "Utility" buyer group interested in basic transportation (utilitarian need), an "Adventure" buyer group interested in fun (need for stimulation), and a "Liberation" buyer group interested in freedom (need for autonomy).[14] Thus, firms must discover the motives that their products and brands can satisfy and develop marketing mixes around these motives.

An important question that often arises is, "Do marketers create needs?" The answer depends in part on what is meant by the term *need.* If it is used to refer to the basic motives described in this chapter, it is clear that marketers seldom if ever *create* a need. Human genetics and experience basically determine motives. Long before marketing or advertising appeared, individuals used perfumes, clothing, and other items to gain acceptance, display status, and so forth. However, marketers do create demand. **Demand** is *the willingness to buy a particular product or service.* It is caused by a need or motive, but it is not the motive. For example, a mouthwash ad might use a theme suggesting that without mouthwash people will not like you because you have bad breath. This message ties mouthwash to an existing need for affiliation in hopes of creating demand for the brand.

The following sections examine how motives relate to various aspects of marketing strategy.

Discovering Purchase Motives

Suppose a marketing researcher asked a consumer why he or she wears J. Crew clothes (or owns a mountain bike, or uses cologne, or whatever). Odds are the consumer would offer several reasons, such as "They're in style," "My friends wear them," "I like the way they fit," or "They look good on me." However, there may be other reasons that the consumer is reluctant to admit or perhaps is not even aware of: "They show that I have money," "They make me sexually desirable," or "They show I'm trendy and urbane." All or any combination of the above motives could influence the purchase of clothes or many other items.

The first group of motives mentioned above were known to the consumer and admitted to the researcher. Motives that are known and freely admitted are called **manifest motives.** Any of the motives we have discussed can be manifest; however, motives that conform to a society's prevailing value system are more likely to be manifest than are those in conflict with such values.

The second group of motives described above either were unknown to the consumer or were such that he or she was reluctant to admit them. Such motives are **latent motives.** Figure 10–1 illustrates how the two types of motives might influence a purchase.

The first task of the marketing manager is to determine the combination of motives influencing the target market. Manifest motives are relatively easy to determine. Direct questions (Why do you purchase J. Crew clothing?) will generally produce reasonably accurate assessments of manifest motives.

Latent and Manifest Motives in a Purchase Situation FIGURE 10-1

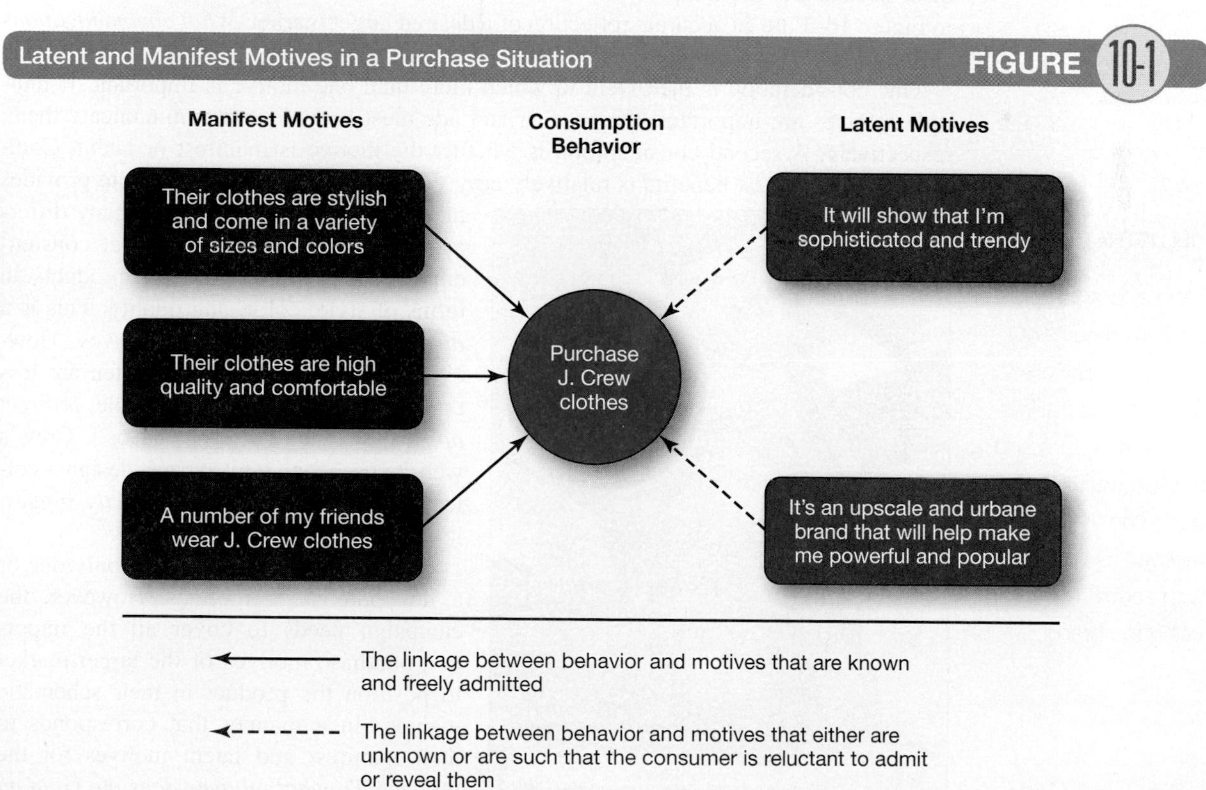

Determining latent motives is substantially more complex. Motivation research or **projective techniques** are designed to provide information on latent motives. One example is the third-person technique whereby consumers provide reasons why "other people" might buy a certain brand. Oreo used projective techniques and was surprised to find that "many regarded Oreo as almost 'magical.'" As a result, "Unlocking the Magic of Oreo" became a campaign theme.[15] For more details on projective techniques, see Appendix A and Table A–1.

Beyond projective techniques, a popular tool for identifying motives is **laddering,** or constructing a **means–end** or **benefit chain.**[16] A product or brand is shown to a consumer, who names all the benefits that product might provide. For each of these benefits, the respondent is then asked to identify further benefits. This is repeated until no additional benefits are identified.

For example, a respondent might mention "fewer colds" as a benefit of taking a daily vitamin. When asked the benefit of fewer colds, one respondent might identify "more efficient at work" and "more energy." Another might name "more skiing" and "looking better." Both use the vitamin to reduce colds but as a means to different ultimate benefits. *How should vitamin ads aimed at each of these two consumers differ?*

Marketing Strategies Based on Multiple Motives

Once a manager has isolated the combination of motives influencing the target market, the next task is to design the marketing strategy around the appropriate set of motives. This involves everything from product design to marketing communications. The nature of these decisions is most apparent in the communications area. Suppose the motives shown in Figure 10–1 are an accurate reflection of a desired target market. *What communications strategy should the manager use?*

One consideration is the extent to which more than one motive is important. If multiple motives are important, the product and ads must provide and communicate them, respectively. A second consideration is whether the motive is manifest or latent. Communicating manifest benefits is relatively easy. For example, J. Crew's website provides hundreds of thumbnails of its many different products by category so that consumers can visually evaluate its products in terms of style, color, and quality. This is a *direct appeal* to manifest motives. However, because latent motives often are less than completely socially desirable, *indirect appeals* frequently are used. So, J. Crew's website uses font, white space, designer collections, and so forth, to *indirectly suggest* its upscale and trendy nature.

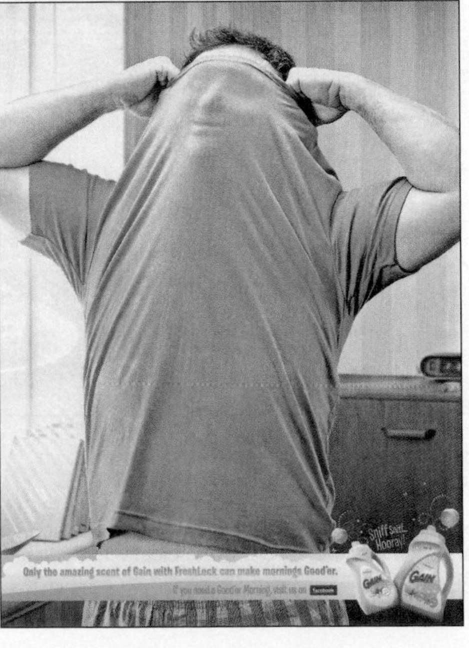

ILLUSTRATION 10-6

Most ads like this ad for Gain detergent appeal to multiple motives and desires. Both the picture and the text should be based on the set of motives associated with acquiring and using the brand.

Any given ad may focus on only one or a few purchasing motives. However, the campaign needs to cover all the important purchase motives of the target market to position the product in their schematic memory in a manner that corresponds to their manifest and latent motives for the product. *To what motives does the Gain ad shown in Illustration 10–6 appeal?*

Motivation and Consumer Involvement

As we have seen in previous chapters, involvement is an important determinant of how consumers process information and learn. We will also see in future chapters that involvement is an important determinant of how consumers form attitudes and make purchase decisions. **Involvement** is a motivational state caused by consumer perceptions that a product, brand, or advertisement is relevant or interesting.[17] Needs play a strong role in determining what is relevant or interesting to consumers. For example, watches may be involving because they tell time (utilitarian need), because they allow for self-expression (expressive need), or because they provide a way to fit in (affiliation need).[18] In addition, the situation itself may influence involvement. For example, some consumers may be involved with computers on an ongoing basis (enduring involvement), while others may only be involved in specific situations such as an upcoming purchase (situational involvement).

Involvement is important to marketers because it affects numerous consumer behaviors. For example, consumer involvement increases attention, analytical processing, information search, and word-of-mouth.[19] Involvement is also important to marketers because it affects marketing strategies. For example, high-involvement consumers tend to be product experts and are more persuaded by ads that include detailed product information. On the other hand, low-involvement consumers lack product expertise and are more persuaded by images, emotion, and message source. As a consequence, you will often find highly informational ads for automobiles in magazines such as *Car and Driver* that are targeted at high-involvement consumers. Alternatively, image and emotional approaches are often the norm in general-interest magazines, where involvement is likely moderate to low.

Marketing Strategies Based on Motivation Conflict

With the many motives consumers have, there are frequent conflicts between motives. Resolution of a motivational conflict often affects consumption patterns. In many instances, the marketer can analyze situations that are likely to result in a motivational conflict, provide a solution to the conflict, and thus encourage purchase of their brand. We address the three key types of motivation conflict next.

Approach–Approach Motivational Conflict A consumer who must choose between two attractive alternatives faces **approach–approach conflict.** The more equal the attractions, the greater the conflict. A consumer who recently received a large cash gift for graduation (situational variable) might be torn between a trip to Hawaii (perhaps powered by a need for stimulation) and a new mountain bike (perhaps driven by the need for assertion). This conflict could be resolved by a timely ad designed to encourage one or the other action. Or a price modification, such as "buy now, pay later," could result in a resolution whereby both alternatives are selected.

Approach–Avoidance Motivational Conflict A consumer facing a purchase choice with both positive and negative consequences confronts **approach–avoidance conflict.** Consumers who want a tan but don't want to risk the skin damage and health risks associated with extended sun exposure face this situation. Neutrogena's Instant Bronze sunless tanner resolves this problem by allowing consumers the aesthetic and social benefits of having a tan (approach) without the risk of skin cancer (avoidance).

Avoidance–Avoidance Motivational Conflict A choice involving only undesirable outcomes produces **avoidance–avoidance conflict.** When a consumer's old washing machine fails, this conflict may occur. The person may not want to spend money on a new washing machine, or pay to have the old one repaired, or go without one. The availability of credit is one way of reducing this motivational conflict. Advertisements emphasizing the importance of regular maintenance for cars, such as oil filter changes, also use this type of motive conflict: "Pay me now, or pay me (more) later."

Marketing Strategies Based on Regulatory Focus

Consumers are often strategic in terms of the behaviors they choose to attain a desired outcome. Some of this, we will see later, is a function of personality. Some of this relates to the particular set of motives that happen to be salient or important when consumers are reacting to stimuli and making decisions. The salience of particular sets of motives triggers consumers to regulate their behavior in different ways in order to achieve desired outcomes. Two prominent sets of motives are termed promotion and prevention. **Promotion-focused motives** revolve around a desire for growth and development and are related to consumers' hopes and aspirations. **Prevention-focused motives** revolve around a desire for safety and security and are related to consumers' sense of duties and obligations.[20]

Regulatory focus theory suggests that consumers will react differently depending on which broad set of motives is most salient. When promotion-focused motives are more salient, consumers seek to gain positive outcomes, think in more abstract terms, make decisions based more on affect and emotion, and prefer speed versus accuracy in their decision making. When prevention-focused motives are more salient, consumers seek to avoid negative outcomes, think in more concrete terms, make decisions based more on factual substantive information, and prefer accuracy over speed in their decision making. In essence, when promotion-focused motives are most salient, consumers are "eager," more risk-seeking decision makers looking for ways to maximize the possibility that they will attain the most positive possible outcomes. When prevention-focused motives are most salient, consumers are "vigilant," more risk-averse decision makers looking for ways to minimize the chances that they will experience negative outcomes and attempt to avoid making mistakes.

Considerable insight has been gained into the motives, characteristics, and decision-making styles that distinguish a promotion focus from a prevention focus. These differences have important marketing consequences, some of which we have already addressed, and some of which will be addressed in later chapters. Table 10–2 describes differences and the marketing-related dimensions to which they relate.

Whether promotion or prevention motives are most salient depends both on the individual and on the situation. Both prevention and promotion motives reside in each person simultaneously. However, as a result of early childhood experiences, one or the other tends to dominate in each person. This aspect is called *chronic accessibility*. That is, these aspects have been a key focus for so long for these consumers that they tend to be brought to mind when stimuli and decisions are encountered. One aspect of this that has important implications for marketers and market segmentation is the fact that promotion-focused individuals tend to possess more independent self-concepts while prevention-focused individuals tend to possess more interdependent self-concepts. As we saw in Chapter 2, such differences relate to global differences across Western (individualistic) and Eastern (interdependent) cultures. Thus, marketers in Asia should expect that, on average, consumers will be more naturally prevention focused than those in the United States and Western Europe and would benefit from adapting their strategies accordingly. For example, it appears that ads that "frame" the message in terms of acquiring positive outcomes work better in the United States than in China, whereas ads that frame the message in terms of avoiding losses work better in China than in the United States.

Situational factors, such as characteristics of the decision, the environment, and so on, can also *temporarily* make one orientation more prominent. Examples that marketers can use include:

- *Ad theme:* achievement (promotion) versus avoidance (prevention).
- *Message frame:* benefits to be gained (promotion) versus losses to be avoided (prevention).

Differences in Regulatory Focus

TABLE 

Dimension	Promotion-Focused	Prevention-Focused
Motives	Hopes, wishes, aspirations Regulate nurturance needs Growth and development	Obligations, responsibilities Regulate security needs Status quo
Characteristics		
• Time	Long-term focus	Short-term focus
• Mental imagery	Abstract	Concrete
• Desired steady state	Change	Stability
• Desired feelings	Fun and enjoyment	Safety and security
• Failure emotions	Dejection	Agitation
• Desired self-trait	Creativity	Self-control
• Self-concept	Independent	Interdependent
Decision Making		
• Style	Eager style to maximize gains	Vigilant style to minimize losses
• Meta-goals	Speed over accuracy	Accuracy over speed
• Ad cue effects	Affect and emotion	Product facts
• Choice of compromise brand	Lower probability	Higher as compromise brand is less extreme and thus less risky
• Importance of "fit" in brand extensions	Less important	More important as fit reduces risk

- *Advertising context:* ad placement in shows, magazines, or websites that are likely to elicit a promotion focus (e.g., *O Magazine,* which focuses on ideals and aspirations) versus those likely to elicit a prevention focus (e.g., *The Evening News,* which tends to focus on negative events).

Consumer Insight 10–1 examines one situational component related to regulatory focus.

PERSONALITY

LO3

While motivations are the energizing and directing force that makes consumer behavior purposeful and goal directed, the personality of the consumer helps guide and further direct the behaviors chosen to accomplish goals in different situations. **Personality** is *an individual's characteristic response tendencies across similar situations.* Thus, two consumers might have equal needs for tension reduction but differ in their level of extroversion, and, as a consequence, engage in very different behaviors designed to satisfy that need.

While there are many theories of personality, those found to be most useful in a marketing context are called *trait theories.* Trait theories examine personality as an individual difference and thus allow marketers to segment consumers as a function of their personality differences. Trait theories assume that (1) all individuals have internal characteristics or traits related to action tendencies and (2) there are consistent and measurable differences between individuals on those characteristics. To demonstrate, imagine how you might respond if you were asked to describe the personality of a friend. You might say that one of your friends is aggressive, competitive, and outgoing. What you have described are the behavioral tendencies or *traits* your friend has exhibited over time across a variety of situations. Most trait theories state that traits are inherited or formed at an early age and are relatively unchanging over the years. Differences between personality theories center on which traits or characteristics are the most important.

CONSUMER INSIGHT 10-1

When Consumers Wait Until the Last Minute to Buy

Sometimes consumers put off purchase decisions until the last minute. Have you ever still been shopping on Christmas Eve? Have you ever waited until right before a vacation to book a flight and hotel? Well, you are not alone and the consequences are significant. A recent study examined how people react to different advertising themes when they were either booking a last-minute summer vacation or planning for a winter-break vacation many months away. Two ad themes for an online travel service were created, with differing taglines, as follows:[21]

- Prevention-focused ad: *Don't get stuck at home! Don't get ripped off!*
- Promotion-focused ad: *Give yourself a memorable vacation! Get the best deals!*

After viewing the ads, consumers were asked how much they would pay for a ticket from the service. The results may surprise you because scaring people sometimes led to a willingness to pay more, but not always. *Can you predict when the prevention-focused ad worked better and when the promotion-focused ad worked better?* Here are the results:

- Last-minute summer vacation (how much would you pay for a ticket?):
  - Prevention-focused ad: $672
  - Promotion-focused ad: $494
- Future winter-break vacation (how much would you pay for a ticket?):
  - Prevention-focused ad: $415
  - Promotion-focused ad: $581

This may seem odd until you consider the fact that when consumers are shopping at the last minute (last-minute summer vacation in the example above), their goals are prevention-focused such as minimizing losses and mistakes. The prevention-focused ad worked best in this situation because it played into consumer fears about those losses. Alternatively, when consumers are shopping well in advance (future winter-break vacation in the example above), their goals are promotion-focused such as personal growth and aspirations. The promotion-focused ad worked best in this situation because it played into those consumer desires and aspirations.

> According to Jennifer Aaker, an expert in this area: [It's] about how people are motivated by hope and optimism on one hand and by fear on the other.

For holiday marketers, the results seem clear—utilize positive (promotion-focused) messages early on and negative (prevention-focused) messages close to the holiday. Last-minute shoppers beware!

Critical Thinking Questions

1. Why is it that fear-based appeals are not always the most effective?
2. How might airlines and hotels be able to determine and utilize decision timing in their online marketing efforts?
3. Do you see any ethical issues associated with applying knowledge of decision timing to decisions about promotional themes? Explain.

Multitrait Approach

Some trait research attempts to examine a consumer's entire personality profile across a set of relatively exhaustive dimensions. Specifically, *multitrait personality theory* identifies several traits that in combination capture a substantial portion of the personality of the individual. The multitrait theory used most commonly by marketers is the **Five-Factor Model.**[22] This theory identifies five basic traits formed by genetics and early learning. These core traits interact and manifest themselves in behaviors triggered by situations. Table 10–3 lists the five traits and some of their manifestations.

TABLE 10-3 The Five-Factor Model of Personality

Core Trait	Manifestation
Extroversion	Prefer to be in a large group rather than alone Talkative when with others Bold
Instability	Moody Temperamental Touchy
Agreeableness	Sympathetic Kind to others Polite with others
Openness to experience	Imaginative Appreciative of art Find novel solutions
Conscientiousness	Careful Precise Efficient

The Five-Factor Model has proven useful in such areas as understanding bargaining and complaining behavior[23] and compulsive shopping.[24] There is evidence that it may have validity across cultures.[25] The advantage of a multitrait approach such as this is the broad picture it allows of the determinants of behavior. For example, suppose research focused on the single dimension of extroversion and found that those who complained about a dissatisfactory purchase tended to be extroverts. *What insights does this provide for training those who deal with consumer complaints? What training insights are added if we also learn such people are conscientious?* Clearly, the more we know, the better we can satisfy these customers.

Single-Trait Approach

Single-trait theories emphasize one personality trait as being particularly relevant to understanding a particular set of behaviors. They do not suggest that other traits are nonexistent or unimportant. Rather, they study a single trait for its relevance to a set of behaviors, in our case, consumption-related behaviors. Three such consumer traits are described next. We emphasize that given the strong interrelationship between motivation and personality, it is not uncommon for personality traits to evidence motivational aspects.[26] Traits labeled as "needs" often reflect these motivational bases.

Consumer Ethnocentrism **Consumer ethnocentrism** *reflects an individual difference in consumers' propensity to be biased against the purchase of foreign products.*[27] Consumers low in ethnocentrism tend to be more open to other cultures, less conservative, and more open to purchasing foreign-made products. Consumers high in ethnocentrism tend to be less open to other cultures, more conservative, and more likely to reject foreign-made products in favor of domestics. As a consequence, Lexington furniture is tapping into pro-American sentiments by actively promoting the "Made in America" status of its Bob Timberlake line to retailers and consumers.[28] Consumer ethnocentrism is a global phenomenon, thus also affecting perceptions of American brands doing business in other countries.[29]

Need for Cognition *Need for cognition (NFC)* reflects an individual difference in consumers' propensity to engage in and enjoy thinking.[30] Compared with low-NFC individuals, those high in NFC engage in more effortful processing of persuasive communications, prefer verbal to visual information, and are less swayed by the opinions of others. NFC has obvious implications for marketing communications. In addition, research linking NFC to demographic characteristics such as gender (e.g., women are generally higher in NFC) helps to make this personality factor more actionable in terms of media targeting.[31]

Consumers' Need for Uniqueness *Consumers' need for uniqueness* reflects an individual difference in consumers' propensity to pursue differentness relative to others through the acquisition, utilization, and disposition of consumer goods.[32] It affects what consumers own and value, why they own it, and how they use it. The concept fits with the increasingly common marketing practice of deliberate scarcity—producing less of an item than the predicted demand. Such a strategy helps preserve the uniqueness of the product and enhances the distinctiveness and status of those who own it.

THE USE OF PERSONALITY IN MARKETING PRACTICE

LO4

Sometimes consumers choose products that fit their personality. For example, a timid person might forgo a flashy car because "it's just not me." Other times, consumers use products to bolster an area of their personality where they feel weak. Thus, a timid person who wants to feel more assertive might drive a powerful, flashy sports car. Clearly, products and brands help consumers express their personality.

Brand image is what people think of and feel when they hear or see a brand name (Chapter 9). A particular type of image that some brands acquire is a **brand personality.** Brand personality is *a set of human characteristics that become associated with a brand.* Consumers perceive brand personalities in terms of five basic dimensions, each with several facets, as shown in Figure 10–2. A scale has been developed to measure brand personality in the United States and, with adaptations, in countries such as Russia and Chile.[33]

Researchers have drawn the following conclusions about brand personality:[34]

- Consumers readily assign human characteristics to brands.
- Brand personalities create expectations about key brand characteristics.
- Brand personalities are often the basis for a long-term relationship with the brand.

Not surprisingly, marketers are paying increasing attention to brand personality. Jaguar, Reebok, and Sprite are just a few of the many companies that are currently attempting to enhance their brand personalities to better target key customer groups. Jaguar is trying to be less "aloof," Reebok wants to be "hip and aggressive," and Sprite wants more "street cred."[35]

The ability of a brand's personality to affect customer relationships is critical, and one study provides key insights. Specifically, consumer relationships with "sincere" brands were found to deepen over time along the lines of a "friendship." Alternatively, consumer relationships with "exciting" brands were found to weaken over time along the lines of a "short-lived fling." This advantage for sincere brands required, however, that the brand consistently deliver high quality.[36]

Nonprofits can also benefit from understanding and managing brand personality. One study shows that nonprofits (compared to for-profits) are generally seen as warmer but less competent. Warmth is related to the sincerity dimension of Figure 10–2. Competence is related to reliability and effectiveness, as shown in Figure 10–2. The perceived lack of competence hinders consumer willingness to buy from (or donate to) a nonprofit despite perceptions of the organization's good intentions. However, cues that enhance credibility, such as an endorsement from a credible source, can bridge this gap and therefore increase purchase/donation intentions for the nonprofit firm.[37]

Dimensions of Brand Personality

FIGURE 10-2

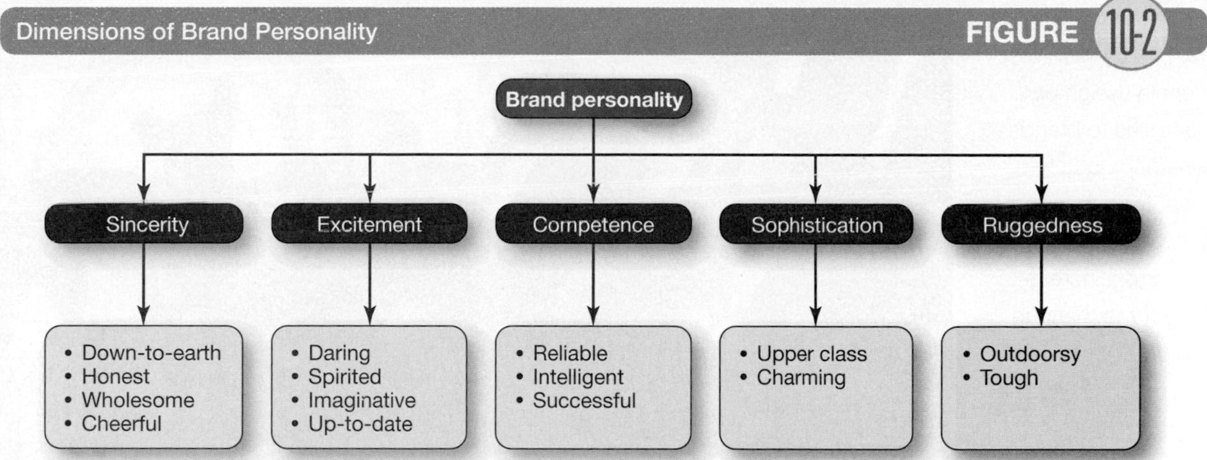

Communicating Brand Personality

Since brand personality can serve as a way to target specific market segments, marketers need to manage and communicate brand personality. Bourjois, a French cosmetics company, created unique makeup sets that communicate distinctive personalities. They used "various cocktails, holiday destinations, [and] fashion statements that have different personality attributes" on their packaging. One set, for example, used the martini and the name *Fabulous Flirtini.* According to their branding company Dragon Rouge, the strategy was to

> [offer] several different color stories with the same theme to capture as many consumers as possible and to promote a range of personalities to connect with a range of consumers. At the same time the sets reflected the core attributes of Bourjois: profusion of color, joie de vivre, whimsy, sassy and fun.[38]

As you can see, numerous elements can be used to communicate brand personality. Three important advertising tactics are celebrity endorsers, user imagery, and executional factors.[39]

Celebrity Endorsers Celebrity endorsers are often a useful way to personify a brand since the characteristics and meanings of the celebrity can be transferred to the brand. Examples include:[40]

- Nike and Serena Williams—edgy, individualistic brand.
- Revlon and Halle Berry—sexy, confident brand.

User Imagery User imagery involves showing a typical user along with images of the types of activities they engage in while using the brand. User imagery helps define who the typical user is in terms of his or her traits, activities, and emotions. The emotion and tone of the activities can also transfer to the brand. Examples include:[41]

- Mountain Dew—features young, active users engaged in fun and exciting activities.
- Hush Puppies—features "hip young people in a wooded setting."

Executional Factors Executional factors go beyond the core message to include "how" it is communicated. The "tone" of the ad (serious vs. quirky), the appeal used (fear vs. humor), the logo and typeface characteristics (*scripted font* may signal sophistication), the pace of the ad, and even the media outlet chosen can all communicate a brand's personality. Examples include:[42]

- *Tone.* Listerine in Canada wanted a way to be both lighthearted and powerful, so it leveraged an action-hero theme from a popular movie. Listerine went from "old-fashioned and serious" to "powerful and larger than life."

ILLUSTRATION 10-7

People assign personalities to brands whether marketers want them to or not. Therefore, marketing managers increasingly try to manage the brand personalities of their products.

- *Media.* Hush Puppies placed ads in fashion magazines such as *W* and *InStyle* to establish a more hip, fashionable personality.
- *Pace.* Molson in Canada wanted a "spirited, adventurous and slightly naughty" personality, so it created TV ads in which "a festive Latin beat is punctuated with fast-moving, sexually charged party scenes."
- *Logo.* Reebok wanted to invigorate its brand toward a younger, hipper image, so it created the new "Rbk" logo. According to one executive, "Creating a short code gave permission to the youth culture to look at the brand again without the old baggage."

What type of brand personality is created by the ad in Illustration 10–7? What advertising elements are being used?

EMOTION

LO5

Emotions are strong, relatively uncontrolled feelings that affect behavior.[43] Emotions are strongly linked to needs, motivation, and personality. Unmet needs create motivation that is related to the arousal component of emotion. Unmet needs generally yield negative emotions, while met needs generally yield positive emotions. As a result, products and brands that generate positive consumption emotions increase consumer satisfaction and loyalty.[44] Personality also plays a role. For example, some people are more emotional than others, a consumer trait termed *affect intensity.* Consumers higher in affect intensity experience stronger emotions and are more influenced by emotional appeals.[45]

All emotional experiences tend to have several common elements. First, emotions are often triggered by environmental events (e.g., viewing an ad, consuming a product that meets a need). However, they can also be initiated by internal processes such as imagery. As we have seen, advertisers frequently use imagery to evoke specific emotional responses.

Nature of Emotions FIGURE 10-3

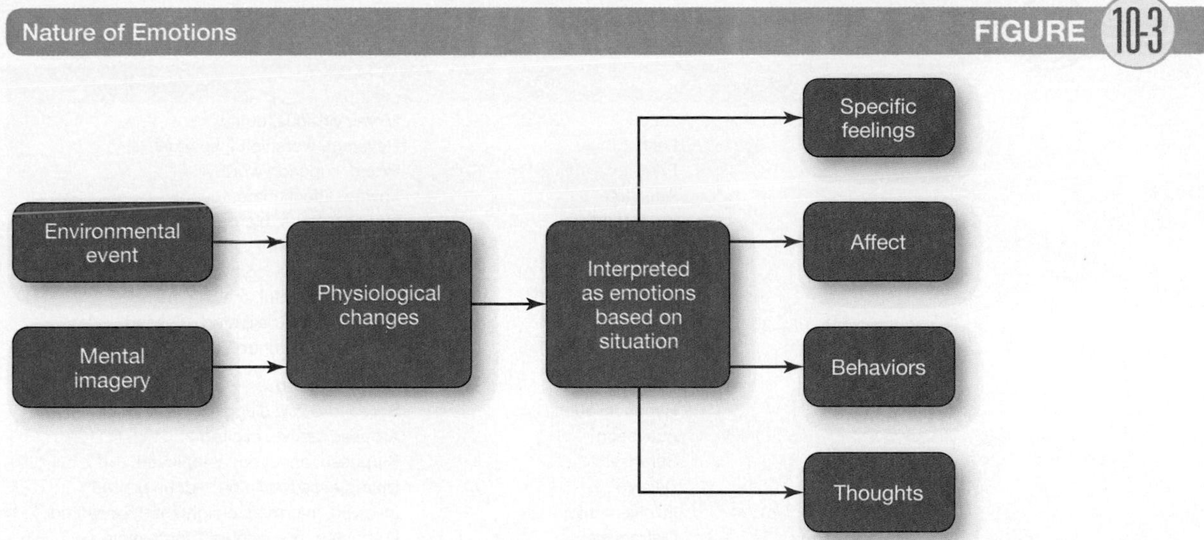

Second, emotions are accompanied by *physiological changes* such as (1) eye pupil dilation, (2) increased perspiration, (3) more rapid breathing, (4) increased heart rate and blood pressure, and (5) enhanced blood sugar level. Third, emotions generally, though not necessarily, are accompanied by *cognitive thought.*[46] The types of thoughts and our ability to think rationally vary with the type and degree of emotion.[47]

A fourth characteristic is that emotions have associated *behaviors.* While the behaviors vary across individuals and within individuals across time and situations, there are unique behaviors characteristically associated with different emotions: fear triggers fleeing (avoidance) responses, anger triggers striking out (approach), grief triggers crying, and so forth.[48]

Finally, emotions involve *subjective feelings.* In fact, it is the feeling component we generally refer to when we think of emotions. Grief, joy, anger, and fear feel very different. These subjectively determined feelings are the essence of emotion. These feelings have a specific component we label as the emotion, such as sad or happy. In addition, emotions carry an evaluative, or a like–dislike, component.

We use **emotion** to refer to the identifiable, specific feeling, and *affect* to refer to the liking–disliking aspect of the specific feeling. Emotions are generally evaluated (liked and disliked) in a consistent manner across individuals and within individuals over time, but there are cultural, individual, and situational variations.[49] For example, few of us generally want to be sad or afraid, yet we occasionally enjoy a movie or book that scares or saddens us.

Figure 10–3 reflects current thinking on the nature of emotions.

Types of Emotions

If asked, you could doubtless name numerous emotions. Thus, it is not surprising that researchers have attempted to categorize emotions into manageable clusters. Some researchers have suggested that three basic dimensions—pleasure, arousal, and dominance (PAD)—underlie all emotions. Specific emotions reflect various combinations and levels of these three dimensions. Table 10–4 lists the three primary PAD dimensions, a variety of emotions or emotional categories associated with each dimension, and indicators or items that can be used to measure each emotion.

Emotional Dimensions, Emotions, and Emotional Indicators

Dimension	Emotion	Indicator/Feeling
Pleasure	Duty	Moral, virtuous, dutiful
	Faith	Reverent, worshipful, spiritual
	Pride	Proud, superior, worthy
	Affection	Loving, affectionate, friendly
	Innocence	Innocent, pure, blameless
	Gratitude	Grateful, thankful, appreciative
	Serenity	Restful, serene, comfortable, soothed
	Desire	Desirous, wishful, craving, hopeful
	Joy	Joyful, happy, delighted, pleased
	Competence	Confident, in control, competent
Arousal	Interest	Attentive, curious
	Hypoactivation	Bored, drowsy, sluggish
	Activation	Aroused, active, excited
	Surprise	Surprised, annoyed, astonished
	Déjà vu	Unimpressed, uninformed, unexcited
	Involvement	Involved, informed, enlightened, benefited
	Distraction	Distracted, preoccupied, inattentive
	Surgency	Playful, entertained, lighthearted
	Contempt	Scornful, contemptuous, disdainful
Dominance	Conflict	Tense, frustrated, conflictful
	Guilt	Guilty, remorseful, regretful
	Helplessness	Powerless, helpless, dominated
	Sadness	Sad, distressed, sorrowful, dejected
	Fear	Fearful, afraid, anxious
	Shame	Ashamed, embarrassed, humiliated
	Anger	Angry, agitated, enraged, mad
	Hyperactivation	Panicked, confused, overstimulated
	Disgust	Disgusted, revolted, annoyed, full of loathing
	Skepticism	Skeptical, suspicious, distrustful

Source: Adapted from M. B. Holbrook and R. Batra, "Assessing the Role of Emotions on Consumer Responses to Advertising," *Journal of Consumer Research,* December 1987, pp. 404–20. Copyright © 1987 by the University of the Chicago. Used by permission.

EMOTIONS AND MARKETING STRATEGY

Emotions play a role in a wide range of marketing situations relating to products, retailing, consumer coping, and advertising. We examine each of these in the following sections.

Emotion Arousal as a Product and Retail Benefit

Emotions are characterized by positive or negative evaluations. Consumers actively seek products whose primary or secondary benefit is emotion arousal.[50] Movies, books, and music are obvious examples,[51] as are resort destinations such as Las Vegas and adventure travel programs. Recent advertisements designed to fuel consumer emotion and excitement about brands include Bacardi rum's "Shake up your night," Pontiac G6's "Move like a shaker," and Chevrolet's "An American Revolution." Beyond products and brands, retailers also feature events and environments that arouse emotions such as excitement. For example, websites using avatars are perceived as more social, which enhances pleasure, arousal, perceived hedonic value, and purchase intentions.[52]

One specific emotion that is getting increased attention in terms of relationship marketing is **gratitude.** Gratitude in a consumer context is *the emotional appreciation for benefits received.* Firms can invest in relationship improvements in many ways including time, effort, investments in equipment specific to the customer, and so on. Research shows that these relationship marketing efforts on the part of the firm lead to the following outcomes:

- Increased consumer gratitude.
- Increased consumer trust in the firm.
- Increased customer purchases.
- Increased "gratitude-based reciprocity" behaviors.

Gratitude-based reciprocity behaviors include (a) buying products based on gratitude for the relationship marketing efforts, (b) giving more business to the firm due to feelings of "owing" them, and (c) buying a broader set of products from the firm as a "payback" for their prior relationship marketing efforts and positive word-of-mouth. Gratitude, it turns out, is a powerful emotion. It causes consumers to want to reward firms for their relationship marketing efforts in ways that lead to greater sales and positive word-of-mouth.[53]

Although consumers seek positive emotions the majority of the time, this is not always the case, as when we enjoy a sad movie. Additionally, products can arouse negative emotions such as the frustration and anger we feel when high-tech gadgets are difficult to use.[54]

Emotion Reduction as a Product and Retail Benefit

Few people like to feel sad, powerless, humiliated, or disgusted. Responding to this, marketers design or position many products to prevent or reduce the arousal of unpleasant emotions. The most obvious of these products are the various over-the-counter medications designed to deal with anxiety or depression. Food and alcohol are consumed, often harmfully, to reduce stress. Flowers are heavily promoted as an antidote to sadness. Weight-loss products and other self-improvement products are frequently positioned primarily in terms of guilt-, helplessness-, shame-, or disgust-reduction benefits. Personal grooming products often emphasize anxiety reduction as a major benefit. Charities frequently stress guilt reduction or avoidance as a reason for contributing.[55]

Consumer Coping in Product and Service Encounters

Consumers must cope with the negative emotions they experience in various marketing situations. **Coping** *involves consumer thoughts and behaviors in reaction to a stress-inducing situation designed to reduce stress and achieve more desired positive emotions.*[56] Avoidance is a common mechanism. For example, when a decision involves a trade-off that evokes strong negative emotions (e.g., price versus safety), consumers will often delay the purchase to avoid making a decision.[57] In retail settings, consumers in a bad mood attempt to cope by avoiding salespeople they perceive as happy. However, if they are forced to deal with a happy salesperson, it makes them feel worse, which reduces salesperson effectiveness.[58] *What marketing and training aspects relating to service personnel does this suggest?*

One typology of coping strategies categorizes three broad types in response to negative emotions emanating from stressful events such as bad customer service or product failure. The three types are:[59]

- *Active coping.* Thinking of ways to solve the problem, engaging in restraint to avoid rash behavior, and making the best of the situation.
- *Expressive support seeking.* Venting emotions and seeking emotional and problem-focused assistance from others.
- *Avoidance.* Avoiding the retailer mentally or physically or engaging in complete self-denial of the event.

Each strategy can have positive and negative marketing consequences. Active coping may involve working with the company to resolve the situation or switching from the firm altogether. Likewise, consumers may vent to the company (expressive support seeking), which is desirable, or they may vent to friends (negative WOM), which is damaging. Finally, denial (avoidance) may result in customer retention, but physical avoidance of the retailer will result in lost sales. As you can see, proper training of service personnel to handle product and service failures as well as the careful design of retail and service facilities to reduce stressors is critical.

Consumer ability to *effectively* cope with stressful situations relates to the concept of **consumer emotional intelligence,** which is defined as *a person's ability to skillfully use emotional information to achieve a desirable consumer outcome.* It is an ability variable rather than a personality trait. Consumers higher in emotional intelligence are better at perceiving, facilitating, understanding, and managing emotional information. For example, a consumer with higher emotional intelligence may understand better how to channel his or her feelings of anger over a service failure to obtain a solution that is desirable to the consumer.[60] A failure to appropriately channel such feelings can result in "rage episodes," which appear to be on the increase in the United States. In response, firms need to better understand what triggers rage episodes and train their employees so they can (a) engage in behaviors to minimize their likelihood and (b) train their employees to effectively and safely handle such rage episodes when they do occur.[61]

Emotion in Advertising

Emotion arousal is often used in advertising regardless of whether it is specifically relevant to the brand's performance. Consider the following recent headlines:

- Under Armour taps raw emotion.
- Kleenex for Men to play on emotion in TV return.
- Emotional appeal of laundry to replace performance claims in ads.

Illustration 10–8 provides an example of the effective use of emotion to attract attention to an ad and to position a brand.

Emotions can play a variety of roles in advertising. Emotional content in ads *enhances their attention, attraction, and maintenance capabilities.* Advertising messages that trigger the emotional reactions of joy, warmth, and suspense[62] are more likely to be attended to than are more neutral ads. As we saw in Chapter 8, attention is a critical early step in the perception process.

Emotions are characterized by a state of heightened physiological arousal. Individuals become more alert and active when aroused. Given this enhanced level of arousal,

ILLUSTRATION 10-8

Emotional appeals can play a powerful role in developing a brand image.

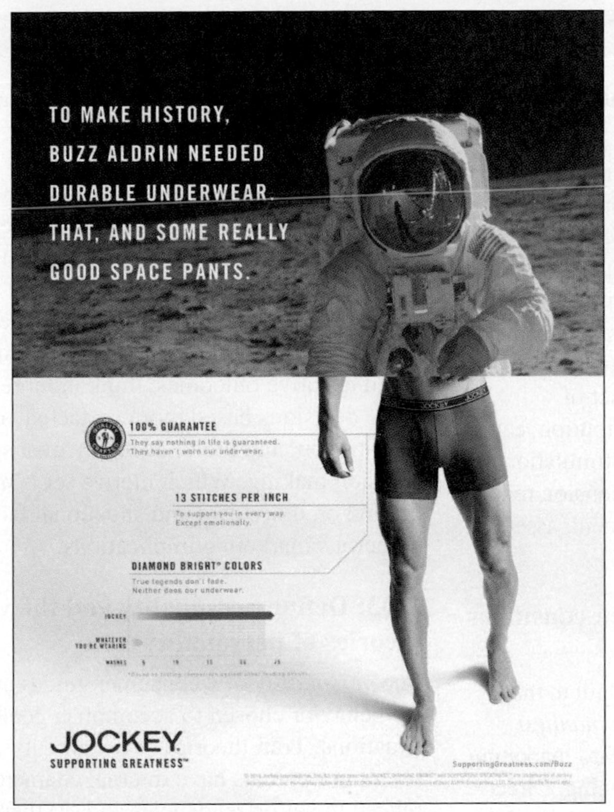

ILLUSTRATION 10-9

Emotional appeals can capture attention and enhance the retention of advertising messages. They can also help humanize the brand and associate feelings with it.

emotional messages may be processed more thoroughly than neutral messages. More effort and increased elaboration activities may occur in response to the emotional state.[63] As a consequence of this greater attention and processing, emotional ads *may be remembered better than neutral ads.*[64]

Emotional advertisements that *trigger a positively evaluated emotion will enhance liking of the ad itself.*[65] For example, warmth is a positively valued emotion that is triggered by experiencing directly or vicariously a love, family, or friendship relationship. Ads high in warmth are liked more than neutral ads. Liking an ad has a positive impact on liking the product and purchase intentions.[66] As you might suspect, ads that irritate or disgust consumers can create negative reactions to the advertised brand.[67]

Repeated exposure to positive-emotion-eliciting ads *may increase brand preference through classical conditioning.*[68] Repeated pairings of positive emotion (unconditioned response) with the brand name (conditioned stimulus) may result in the positive affect occurring when the brand name is presented. *Brand preference may also occur in a direct, high-involvement way.* A person having a single or few exposures to an emotional ad may simply decide he or she likes the product. This is a much more conscious process than implied by classical conditioning. Such a process seems more likely for hedonic products involving high levels of emotional value rather than utilitarian products. For hedonic products, ad-evoked emotion is a relevant cue on which to base a product evaluation.[69]

Advertising using emotional appeals continues to be popular. For example, Zippo launched an emotion-based campaign for its lighters. It used eight print ads, each with a picture of an engraved lighter and a simple headline, "True Love Is not Disposable." A spokesperson said of the campaign, "We wanted to make a human, emotional attachment."[70] Illustration 10–9 shows how Jockey taps into emotions through the use of humor.

SUMMARY

LO1: Define motivation and summarize the motivation sets put forth by Maslow and McGuire

Consumer motivations are energizing forces that activate behavior and provide purpose and direction to that behavior. There are numerous motivation theories. Maslow's need hierarchy states that basic motives must be minimally satisfied before more advanced motives are activated. It proposes five levels of motivation: physiological, safety, belongingness, esteem, and self-actualization.

McGuire developed a more detailed set of motives—the needs for consistency, attribution, categorization, objectification, autonomy, stimulation, desired outcomes (teleological), utility, tension reduction, expression, ego defense, reinforcement, assertion, affiliation, identification, and modeling.

LO2: Articulate motivation's role in consumer behavior and marketing strategy

Consumers are often aware of and will admit to the motives causing their behavior. These are *manifest motives.* They can be discovered by standard marketing research techniques such as direct questioning. Direct advertising appeals can be made to these motives. At other times, consumers are unable or unwilling to admit to the motives that are influencing them. These are *latent motives.* They can be determined by motivation research techniques such as word association, sentence completion, and picture response (see Appendix Table A–1). Although direct advertising appeals can be used, indirect appeals are often necessary. Both manifest and latent motives are operative in many purchase situations.

Involvement is a motivational state caused by consumer perceptions that a product, brand, or advertisement is relevant or interesting. Consumer needs play a strong role in shaping involvement, and marketers must adapt their strategies depending on the level (high versus low) and type (enduring versus situational) of involvement exhibited by their target audience.

Because of the large number of motives and the many different situations that consumers face, motivational conflict can occur. In an *approach–approach conflict,* the consumer faces a choice between two attractive alternatives. In an *approach–avoidance conflict,* the consumer faces both positive and negative consequences in the purchase of a particular product. And finally, in an *avoidance–avoidance conflict,* the consumer faces two undesirable alternatives.

Regulatory focus theory suggests that consumers react differently depending on whether promotion-focused or prevention-focused motives are most salient. When promotion-focused motives are more salient, consumers seek to gain positive outcomes, think in more abstract terms, make decisions based more on affect and emotion, and prefer speed versus accuracy in their decision making. When prevention-focused motives are more salient, consumers seek to avoid negative outcomes, think in more concrete terms, make decisions based more on factual substantive information, and prefer accuracy over speed in their decision making. Which motive set is more salient can depend on individual and situational factors and has numerous marketing implications.

LO3: Define personality and the various theories of personality

The *personality* of a consumer guides and directs the behavior chosen to accomplish goals in different situations. Trait theories of personality assume that (1) all individuals have internal characteristics or traits related to action tendencies and (2) there are consistent and measurable differences between individuals on those characteristics. Most of these theories assume that traits are formed at an early age and are relatively unchanging over the years.

Multitrait theories attempt to capture a significant portion of a consumer's total personality using a set of personality attributes. The Five-Factor Model of personality is the most widely used multitrait approach. Single-trait theories focus on one aspect of personality in an attempt to understand a limited part of consumer behavior. Various traits related specifically to consumer behavior include consumer ethnocentricity, need for cognition, and consumers' need for uniqueness.

LO4: Discuss how brand personality can be used in developing marketing strategies

Brands, like individuals, have personalities, and consumers tend to prefer products with brand personalities that are pleasing to them. Consumers also prefer advertising messages that portray their own or a desired personality. Brand personality can be communicated in a number of ways, including celebrity endorsers, user imagery, and executional ad elements such as tone and pace.

LO5: Define emotions and list the major emotional dimensions

Emotions are strong, relatively uncontrollable feelings that affect our behavior. Emotions occur when environmental events or our mental processes trigger physiological changes such as increased heart rate. These changes are interpreted as specific emotions resulting from the situation. They affect consumers' thoughts and behaviors. The major dimensions of emotion are pleasure, arousal, and dominance. Each of these major dimensions has specific emotions and feelings associated with it.

LO6: Discuss how emotions can be used in developing marketing strategies

Marketers design and position products to both arouse and reduce emotions. In addition, consumers must cope with stressful marketing situations such as service and product failures. The various coping mechanisms can be beneficial or detrimental to the firm depending on various factors and require that marketers consider not only their responses to failure but also service-setting design to reduce consumer stressors. Advertisements include emotion-arousing material to increase attention, degree of processing, remembering, and brand preference through classical conditioning or direct evaluation.

KEY TERMS

Approach–approach conflict 363
Approach–avoidance conflict 363
Attribution theory 356
Avoidance–avoidance conflict 363
Benefit chain 362
Brand personality 368
Consumer emotional intelligence 374
Consumer ethnocentrism 367
Coping 373
Demand 360
Emotion 371
Five-Factor Model 366
Gratitude 372
Involvement 363
Laddering 362
Latent motives 361
Manifest motives 361
Maslow's hierarchy of needs 354
Means–end chain 362
Motivation 354
Motive 354
Personality 365
Prevention-focused motives 364
Projective techniques 362
Promotion-focused motives 364
Regulatory focus theory 364

REVIEW QUESTIONS

1. What is a *motive?*
2. What is meant by a *motive hierarchy?* How does Maslow's hierarchy of needs function?
3. Describe each level of Maslow's hierarchy of needs.
4. Describe each of McGuire's motives.
5. Describe *attribution theory.*
6. What is meant by *motivational conflict* and what relevance does it have for marketing managers?
7. What is a *manifest motive?* A *latent motive?* How is each measured?
8. How do you appeal to manifest motives? Latent motives?
9. Describe the following motivation research techniques (see Appendix A and Appendix Table A–1 for details):
   a. Association
   b. Completion
   c. Construction
10. What is the relationship between *involvement* and *motivation?*
11. Describe *regulatory focus theory.*
12. What is *personality?*
13. What is *consumer ethnocentrism* and why is it important to global marketers?
14. How can knowledge of personality be used to develop marketing strategy?
15. What is an *emotion?* What are the basic dimensions of emotion?
16. What physiological changes accompany emotional arousal?
17. What factors characterize emotions?
18. What is consumer *gratitude* and what outcomes are associated with this emotion?
19. How do marketers use emotions in product design and advertising?
20. What is *coping* and what are the general types of coping mechanisms used by consumers?

DISCUSSION QUESTIONS

21. How could Maslow's motive hierarchy be used to develop marketing strategy for the following?
    a. American Bird Conservancy
    b. Redkin shampoo
    c. Purell hand sanitizer
    d. Chipotle Mexican Grill
    e. BlackBerry
    f. Crest Whitestrips
22. Which of McGuire's motives would be useful in developing a promotional campaign for the following? Why?
    a. Cadillac CTS
    b. Precision Cuts (hair salon chain)
    c. Nokia cell phones
    d. Just for Men hair coloring
    e. Twitter
    f. Habitat for Humanity
23. Describe how motivational conflict might arise in purchasing, patronizing, or giving to the following:
    a. Greenpeace
    b. Chevy Volt
    c. Walmart
    d. Red Bull energy drink
    e. Taco Bell restaurant
    f. Home security system
24. Describe the manifest and latent motives that might arise in purchasing, shopping at, or giving to the following:
    a. Yukon hybrid
    b. Saks Fifth Avenue
    c. Bose sound system
    d. Kitten
    e. Mercedes Benz convertible
    f. iPhone
25. Do marketers create needs? Do they create demand? What ethical issues are relevant?

26. Respond to the questions in Consumer Insight 10–1.
27. How might knowledge of personality be used to develop an advertising campaign for the following?
    a. Rainforest Action Network (an environmental group)
    b. Smartphones
    c. American Express financial services
    d. Ready-to-drink iced tea
    e. J. Crew women's shoes
    f. Clinique cosmetics
28. Using Table 10–3, discuss how you would use one of the core personality source traits in developing a package design for an organic, shade-grown coffee.
29. How would the media preferences of those on each end of the consumer need for uniqueness continuum differ?
30. How would the shopping behaviors of those on each end of the ethnocentrism continuum differ?
31. How would you use emotion to develop a marketing strategy for each of the following?
    a. Visa card use
    b. Sky diving
    c. Orthodontist
    d. Silk (soy milk)
    e. Honda Civic Hybrid
    f. Iceland
32. List all the emotions you can think of. Which ones are not explicitly mentioned in Table 10–4? Where would you place them in this table?

APPLICATION ACTIVITIES

33. Develop an advertisement for one of the items in Question 21 based on relevant motives from McGuire's set.
34. Repeat Question 33 using Maslow's need hierarchy.
35. Repeat Question 33 using emotions.
36. Find and copy or describe two advertisements that appeal to each level of Maslow's hierarchy. Explain why the ads appeal to the particular levels and speculate on why the firm decided to appeal to these levels.
37. Find and copy or describe an ad that contains direct appeals to manifest motives and indirect appeals to latent motives. Explain how and why the ad is using each approach.
38. Select a product of interest and use motivation research techniques to determine the latent purchase motives for five consumers (see Appendix A and Appendix Table A–1 for details).

39. Have five students describe the personality of the following. To what extent are their descriptions similar? Why are there differences?
    a. Swatch watches
    b. Prada sunglasses
    c. Toyota
    d. Dell computer
    e. Cheesecake Factory restaurant
    f. The university bookstore
40. Find and copy an ad that you feel communicates a strong brand personality. Describe that personality in terms of the dimensions in Figure 10–2. Describe the various techniques used in the ad (e.g., celebrity endorser, user imagery, and executional factors) and how that links to the personality they are communicating.
41. Find and copy an ad with strong emotional appeals and another ad from the same product category with limited emotional appeals. Why do the companies use different appeals?
    a. Have 10 students rank or rate the ads in terms of their preferences and then explain their rankings or ratings.
    b. Have 10 different students talk about their reactions to each ad as they view it. What do you conclude?
42. Ask two students to describe the coping mechanisms they use when dealing with product or service failures. Identify factors that cause their coping to be beneficial (e.g., complaining to the company) rather than detrimental (e.g., negative WOM) to the firm.

REFERENCES

1. This chapter opening is based on B. Ellis and P. Valdes-Dapena, "Toyota's Big Recall Halts Sales, Production of 8 Models," *CNNMoney.com*, February 10, 2010; "Toyota Announces January 2010 Recall for 2.3 Million Vehicles to Fix Sticky Accelerator Pedal," www.autos.aol.com, January 21, 2010, accessed June 6, 2011; B. Steinberg, "Lightspeed Survey," *Advertising Age,* February 2010, pp. 2 and 18; "U.S. Auto Sales by Brand—February 2011," www.goodcarbadcar.net, accessed June 6, 2011; and information from Toyota's website at www.toyota.com.
2. A. H. Maslow, *Motivation and Personality,* 2nd ed. (New York: Harper & Row, 1970).
3. See R. Yalch and F. Brunel, "Need Hierarchies in Consumer Judgments of Product Designs," *Advances in Consumer Research,* vol. 23, ed. K. P. Corfman and J. G. Lynch (Provo, UT: Association for Consumer Research, 1996), pp. 405–10.
4. W. J. McGuire, "Psychological Motives and Communication Gratification," in *The Uses of Mass Communications,* ed. J. G. Blumler and C. Katz (Newbury Park, CA: Sage, 1974), pp. 167–96; and W. J. McGuire, "Some Internal Psychological Factors Influencing Consumer Choice," *Journal of Consumer Research,* March 1976, pp. 302–19.
5. See A. G. Woodside and J.-C. Chebat, "Updating Heider's Balance Theory in Consumer Behavior," *Psychology & Marketing,* May 2001, pp. 475–95.
6. M. C. Campbell and A. Kirmani, "Consumers' Use of Persuasion Knowledge," *Journal of Consumer Research,* June 2000, pp. 69–83; and R. N. Laczniak, T. E. DeCarlo, and S. N. Ramaswami, "Consumers' Responses to Negative Word-of-Mouth Communication," *Journal of Consumer Psychology,* 11, no. 31 (2001), pp. 57–73.
7. See M. Friestad and P. Wright, "Persuasion Knowledge," *Journal of Consumer Research,* June 1995, pp. 62–74.
8. See B. H. Schmit and S. Zhang, "Language Structure and Categorization," *Journal of Consumer Research,* September 1998, pp. 108–22; and J. A. Rosa and J. F. Porac, "Categorization Bases and Their Influence on Product Category Knowledge Structures," *Psychology & Marketing,* June 2002, pp. 503–32.
9. M. Lynn and J. Harris, "The Desire for Unique Consumer Products," *Psychology & Marketing,* September 1997, pp. 601–16.
10. R. K. Ratner, B. E. Kahn, and D. Kahneman, "Choosing Less-Preferred Experiences for the Sake of Variety," *Journal of Consumer Research,* June 1999, pp. 1–15; and R. K. Ratner and B. E. Kahn, "The Impact of Private versus Public Consumption on Variety-Seeking Behavior," *Journal of Consumer Research,* September 2002, pp. 246–57.
11. M. Trivedi, "Using Variety-Seeking-Based Segmentation to Study Promotional Response," *Journal of the Academy of Marketing Science,* Winter 1999, pp. 37–49; M. Trivedi and M. S. Morgan, "Promotional Evaluation and Response among Variety Seeking Segments," *Journal of Product and Brand Management,* 12, no. 6 (2003), pp. 408–25; and J. Chen and S. Paliwoda, "The Influence of Company Name in Consumer Variety Seeking," *Brand Management,* February 2004, pp. 219–31.
12. See D. Goldman, "Pain? It's a Pleasure," *American Demographics,* January 2000, pp. 60–61; and J. J. Inman, "The Role of Sensory-Specific Satiety in Attribute-Level Variety Seeking," *Journal of Consumer Research,* June 2001, pp. 105–19.
13. See G. M. Zinkhan, J. W. Hong, and R. Lawson, "Achievement and Affiliation Motivation," *Journal of Business Research,* March 1990, pp. 135–43.
14. Porsche example from A. Taylor III, "Porsche Slices Up Its Buyers," *Fortune,* January 6, 1995, p. 24. Indian car example from "New Car Buyers in India Seek Emotive Needs," *indiatelevision.com,* December 21, 2004, at www.indiatelevision.com, accessed June 7, 2011.
15. C. Rubel, "Three Firms Show That Good Research Makes Good Ads," *Marketing News,* March 13, 1995, p. 18.
16. T. J. Reynolds and J. C. Olson, *Understanding Consumer Decision Making* (Mahwah, NJ: Erlbaum, 2001); G. S. Mort and T. Rose, "The Effect of Product Type on Value Linkages

in the Means-End Chain," *Journal of Consumer Behaviour,* March 2004, pp. 221–34; and F. Huber, S. C. Beckmann, and A. Herrmann, "Means-End Analysis," *Psychology & Marketing,* September 2004, pp. 715–37.

17. See J. L. Zaichkowsky, "The Personal Involvement Inventory," *Journal of Advertising,* December 1994, pp. 59–70.

18. See P. Quester and A. L. Lim, "Product Involvement/Brand Loyalty," *Journal of Product and Brand Management,* 12, no. 1 (2003), pp. 22–38.

19. See U. M. Dholakia, "A Motivational Process Model of Product Involvement and Consumer Risk Perception," *European Journal of Marketing,* 35, no. 11/12 (2001), pp. 1340–60; and C.-W. Park and B.-J. Moon, "The Relationship between Product Involvement and Product Knowledge," *Psychology & Marketing,* November 2003, pp. 977–97.

20. This section on regulatory focus, including Table 10–2, is based on the following: E. T. Higgins, "Beyond Pleasure and Pain," *American Psychologist,* December 1997, pp. 1280–300; J. L. Aaker and A. Y. Lee, "'I' Seek Pleasures and 'We' Avoid Pains," *Journal of Consumer Research,* June 2001, pp. 33–49; A. Chernev, "Goal-Attribute Compatibility in Consumer Choice," *Journal of Consumer Psychology,* 14, nos. 1 & 2 (2004), pp. 141–50; M. T. Pham and T. Avnet, "Ideals and Oughts and the Reliance on Affect versus Substance in Persuasion," *Journal of Consumer Research,* March 2004, pp. 503–18; A. Bosmans and H. Baumgartner, "Goal-Relevant Emotional Information," *Journal of Consumer Research,* December 2005, pp. 424–34; J. L. Aaker and A. Y. Lee, "Understanding Regulatory Fit," *Journal of Marketing Research,* February 2006, pp. 15–19; T. Avnet and E. T. Higgins, "How Regulatory Fit Affects Value in Consumer Choices and Opinions," *Journal of Marketing Research,* February 2006, pp. 1–10; Y.-J. Kim, "The Role of Regulatory Focus in Message Framing in Antismoking Advertisements for Adolescents," *Journal of Advertising,* Spring 2006, pp. 143–51; J. Yeo and J. Park, "Effects of Parent-Extension Similarity and Self Regulatory Focus on Evaluations of Brand Extensions," *Journal of Consumer Psychology,* 16, no. 3 (2006), pp. 272–82; M. Mourali, U. Bockenholt, and M. Laroche, "Compromise and Attraction Effects under Prevention and Promotion Motivations," *Journal of Consumer Research,* August 2007, pp. 234–47; and A. Y. Lee, P. A. Keller, and B. Sternthal, "Value from Regulatory Construal Fit," *Journal of Consumer Research,* February 2010, pp. 735–47.

21. This insight is based on "No Time before Valentine's Day?," *Science Daily,* January 27, 2008; C. Mogilner, J. L. Aaker, and G. L. Pennington, "Time Will Tell," *Journal of Consumer Research,* February 2008, pp. 670–81; and S. Vedantam, "Care to Know the Motivation Behind That Gift, Love?," *Washington Post,* February 11, 2008, p. A3.

22. See J. S. Wiggins, *The Five-Factor Model of Personality* (New York: Guilford Press, 1996).

23. E. G. Harris and J. C. Mowen, "The Influence of Cardinal-, Central-, and Surface-Level Personality Traits on Consumers' Bargaining and Complaint Behaviors," *Psychology & Marketing,* November 2001, pp. 1155–85.

24. J. C. Mowen and N. Spears, "Understanding Compulsive Buying among College Students," *Journal of Consumer Psychology,* 8, no. 4 (1999), pp. 407–30.

25. W. Na and R. Marshall, "Validation of the 'Big Five' Personality Traits in Korea," *Journal of International Consumer Marketing,* 12, no. 1 (1999), pp. 5–19.

26. See N. Brody and H. Ehrlichman, *Personality Psychology* (Englewood Cliffs, NJ: Prentice Hall, 1998); and A. Deponte, "Linking Motivation to Personality," *European Journal of Personality,* 18 (2004), pp. 31–44.

27. See S. Sharma, T. A. Shimp, and J. Shin, "Consumer Ethnocentrism," *Journal of the Academy of Marketing Science,* Winter 1995, pp. 26–37; and G. Balabanis and A. Diamantopoulos, "Domestic Country Bias, Country-of-Origin Effects, and Consumer Ethnocentrism," *Journal of the Academy of Marketing Science,* Winter 2004, pp. 80–95.

28. J. Linville, "Lexington Touts Timberlake as 'Made in America' Line," *Furniture Today,* October 13, 2003, p. 98.

29. M. Supphellen and K. Gronhaug, "Building Foreign Brand Personalities in Russia," *International Journal of Advertising,* 22, no. 2 (2003), pp. 203–26; and H. Kwak, A. Jaju, and T. Larsen, "Consumer Ethnocentrism Offline and Online," *Journal of the Academy of Marketing Science,* Summer 2006, pp. 367–85.

30. C. S. Areni, M. E. Ferrell, and J. B. Wilcox, "The Persuasive Impact of Reported Group Opinions on Individuals Low vs. High in Need for Cognition," *Psychology & Marketing,* October 2000, pp. 855–75; and J. Z. Sojka and J. L. Giese, "The Influence of Personality Traits on the Processing of Visual and Verbal Information," *Marketing Letters,* February 2001, pp. 91–106.

31. See, e.g., L. K. Waters and T. D. Zakrajsek, "Correlates of Need for Cognition Total and Subscale Scores," *Educational and Psychological Measurement,* Spring 1990, pp. 213–17.

32. K. T. Tian, W. O. Bearden, and G. L. Hunter, "Consumers' Need for Uniqueness," *Journal of Consumer Research,* June 2001, pp. 50–66. See also K. T. Tian and K. McKenzie, "The Long-Term Predictive Validity of the Consumers' Need for Uniqueness Scale," *Journal of Consumer Psychology,* 10, no. 3 (2001), pp. 171–93.

33. J. L. Aaker, "Dimensions of Brand Personality," *Journal of Marketing Research,* August 1997, pp. 347–56. For international adaptations, see Supphellen and Gronhaug, "Building Foreign Brand Personalities in Russia"; J. I. Rojas-Mendez, I. Erenchun-Podlech, and E. Silva-Olave, "The Ford Brand Personality in Chile," *Corporate Reputation Review,* Fall 2004, pp. 232–51; and Y. Sung and S. F. Tinkham, "Brand Personality Structures in the United States and Korea," *Journal of Consumer Psychology,* 15, no. 4 (2005), pp. 334–50.

34. Aaker, "Dimensions of Brand Personality." Also see T. Triplett, "Brand Personality Must Be Managed or It Will Assume a Life of Its Own," *Marketing News,* May 9, 1994, p. 9.

35. K. Greenberg, "Levinson: Jaguar Ads to Stress Quality, Youth, a Bit of Humor," *Brandweek,* April 26, 2004, p. 32; B. Russak, "Calling the Shots," *Footwear News,* October 25, 2004, p. 42; and K. MacArthur and J. Neff, "Sprite Shifts Gears in Quest for Street Cred," *Advertising Age,* January 26, 2004, p. 1.

36. J. Aaker, S. Fournier, and S. A. Brasel, "When Good Brands Do Bad," *Journal of Consumer Research,* June 2004, pp. 1–16.

37. J. Aaker, K. D. Vohs, and C. Mogilner, "Nonprofits Are Seen as Warm and For-Profits as Competent," *Journal of Consumer Research,* August 2010, pp. 224–37.

38. From http://dragonrouge-usa.com/, accessed February 24, 2008.

39. For a detailed discussion, see D. A. Aaker, R. Batra, and J. G. Meyers, *Advertising Management,* 4th ed. (Englewood Cliffs, NJ: Prentice Hall, 1992), ch. 8. See also T. T. T. Wee,

"Extending Human Personality to Brands," *Brand Management,* April 2004, pp. 317–30.

40. A. Nagel and M. Prior, "Revlon Gets Ready for 2005," *WWD,* August 13, 2004, p. 8; and S. Kang, "Nike, Serena Williams Partner Up," *The Wall Street Journal,* December 12, 2003, p. B2.
41. S. O'Loughlin, "Hush Puppies Steps into a New Image," *Brandweek,* June 23, 2003, p. 14.
42. Russak, "Calling the Shots"; O'Loughlin, "Hush Puppies Steps into a New Image"; "Listerine Mouthwash and PocketPaks," *Marketing Magazine,* November 18, 2002, p. C9; and M. Warren, "Molson Debuts a Saucy Brazilian," *Marketing Magazine,* March 24, 2003, p. 2.
43. For a thorough discussion, see R. P. Bagozzi, M. Gopinath, and P. U. Nyer, "The Role of Emotions in Marketing," *Journal of the Academy of Marketing Science,* Spring 1999, pp. 184–207. See also M. E. Hill et al., "The Conjoining Influences of Affect and Arousal on Attitude Formation," *Research in Consumer Behavior,* 9 (2000), pp. 129–46.
44. See, e.g., D. M. Phillips and H. Baumgartner, "The Role of Consumption Emotions in the Satisfaction Response," *Journal of Consumer Psychology,* 12, no. 3 (2002), pp. 243–52; and D. Martin et al., "The Role of Emotion in Explaining Consumer Satisfaction and Future Behavioural Intention," *Journal of Services Marketing,* 22, no. 3 (2008), pp. 224–36.
45. See, e.g., D. J. Moore and P. M. Homer, "Dimensions of Temperament," *Journal of Consumer Psychology,* 9, no. 4 (2000), pp. 231–42.
46. J. A. Ruth, F. F. Brunel, and C. C. Otnes, "Linking Thoughts to Feelings," *Journal of the Academy of Marketing Science,* Winter 2002, pp. 44–58.
47. See B. J. Babin, J. S. Boles, and W. R. Darden, "Salesperson Stereotypes, Consumer Emotions, and Their Impact on Information Processing," *Journal of the Academy of Marketing Science,* Spring 1995, pp. 94–105.
48. For a discussion of coping strategies, see S. Yi and H. Baumgartner, "Coping with Negative Emotions in Purchase-Related Situations," *Journal of Consumer Psychology,* 14, no. 3 (2004), pp. 303–17.
49. See L. Dube and M. S. Morgan, "Trend Effects and Gender Differences in Retrospective Judgments of Consumption Emotions," *Journal of Consumer Research,* September 1996, pp. 156–62; J. L. Aaker and P. Williams, "Empathy versus Pride," *Journal of Consumer Research,* December 1998, pp. 241–61; and M. Geuens and P. D. Pelsmacker, "Affect Intensity Revisited," *Psychology & Marketing,* May 1999, pp. 195–209.
50. J. A. Ruth, "Promoting a Brand's Emotion Benefits," *Journal of Consumer Psychology,* 11, no. 2 (2001), pp. 99–113.
51. See K. T. Lacher and R. Mizerski, "An Exploratory Study of the Responses and Relationships Involved in the Evaluation of, and in the Intention to Purchase, New Rock Music," *Journal of Consumer Research,* September 1994, pp. 366–80.
52. L. C. Wang et al., "Can a Retail Web Site Be Social?," *Journal of Marketing,* July 2007, pp. 143–57.
53. I. Soscia, "Gratitude, Delight, or Guilt," *Psychology and Marketing,* October 2007, pp. 871–94; and R. W. Palmatier et al., "The Role of Customer Gratitude in Relationship Marketing," *Journal of Marketing,* September 2009, pp. 1–18.
54. S. L. Wood and C. Page Moreau, "From Fear to Loathing?," *Journal of Marketing,* July 2006, pp. 44–57.
55. B. A. Huhmann and T. P. Brotherton, "A Content Analysis of Guilt Appeals in Popular Magazine Advertisements," *Journal of Advertising,* Summer 1997, pp. 35–45.
56. Based on A. Duhachek, "Coping," *Journal of Consumer Research,* June 2005, pp. 41–53.
57. M. F. Luce, "Choosing to Avoid," *Journal of Consumer Research,* March 1998, pp. 409–33.
58. N. M. Puccinelli, "Putting Your Best Face Forward," *Journal of Consumer Psychology,* 16, no. 2 (2006), pp. 156–62.
59. Duhachek, "Coping."
60. B. Kidwell, D. M. Hardesty, and T. L. Childers, "Consumer Emotional Intelligence," *Journal of Consumer Research,* June 2008, pp. 154–66.
61. J. R. McColl-Kennedy et al., "Consumer Rage Episodes," *Journal of Retailing,* 85, no. 2 (2009), pp. 222–37.
62. See L. F. Alwitt, "Suspense and Advertising Responses," *Journal of Consumer Psychology,* 12, no. 1 (2002), pp. 35–49.
63. H. Mano, "Affect and Persuasion," *Psychology & Marketing,* July 1997, pp. 315–35; and A. M. Isen, "An Influence of Positive Affect on Decision Making in Complex Situations," *Journal of Consumer Psychology,* 11, no. 2 (2001), pp. 75–85.
64. A. Y. Lee and B. Sternthal, "The Effects of Positive Mood on Memory," *Journal of Consumer Research,* September 1999, pp. 115–27; K. R. Lord, R. E. Burnkrant, and H. R. Unnava, "The Effects of Program-Induced Mood States on Memory for Commercial Information," *Journal of Current Issues and Research in Advertising,* Spring 2001, pp. 1–14; and S. J. Newell, K. V. Henderson, and B. T. Wu, "The Effects of Pleasure and Arousal on Recall of Advertisements during the Super Bowl," *Psychology & Marketing,* November 2001, pp. 1135–53.
65. M. Royo-Vela, "Emotional and Informational Content in Commercials," *Journal of Current Issues and Research in Advertising,* Fall 2005, pp. 13–38; and C. Chang, "Context-Induced and Ad-Induced Affect," *Psychology & Marketing,* September 2006, pp. 757–82.
66. W. Janssens and P. De Pelsmacker, "Emotional or Informative?," *International Journal of Advertising,* 24, no. 3 (2005), pp. 373–94; and J. Kim and J. D. Morris, "The Power of Affective Response and Cognitive Structure in Product-Trial Attitude Formation," *Journal of Advertising,* Spring 2007, pp. 95–106.
67. B. M. Fennis and A. B. Bakker, "Stay Tuned—We Will Be Right Back after These Messages," *Journal of Advertising,* Fall 2001, pp. 15–25; J. D. Morris et al., "The Power of Affect," *Journal of Advertising Research,* May–June 2002, pp. 7–17; and T. A. Shimp and E. W. Stuart, "The Role of Disgust as an Emotional Mediator of Advertising Effects," *Journal of Advertising,* Spring 2004, pp. 43–53.
68. E. Walther and S. Grigoriadis, "Why Sad People Like Shoes Better," *Psychology & Marketing,* October 2004, pp. 755–73; and P. R. Darke, A. Chattapadhyay, and L. Ashworth, "The Importance and Functional Significance of Affective Cues in Consumer Choice," *Journal of Consumer Research,* December 2006, pp. 322–28.
69. See R. Adaval, "Sometimes It Just Feels Right," *Journal of Consumer Research,* June 2001, pp. 1–17.
70. C. Beardi, "Zippo's Eternal Flame," *Advertising Age,* August 13, 2001, p. 4.

chapter

11 Attitudes and Influencing Attitudes

LEARNING OBJECTIVES

- **LO1** **Define attitude and its role in consumer behavior.**
- **LO2** **Summarize the three components of attitudes.**
- **LO3** **Discuss attitude change strategies associated with each attitude component.**
- **LO4** **Describe the elaboration likelihood model of persuasion.**
- **LO5** **Describe the role of message source, appeal, and structure on attitudes.**
- **LO6** **Discuss segmentation and product development applications of attitudes.**

Companies like Nike, Gatorade, and American Express spend billions on celebrity endorsements each year. In fact, it is estimated that 25 percent or more of ads in the United States contain a celebrity and that spending on celebrity endorsers is roughly $30 billion annually. In many ways, the use of celebrities as product endorsers makes sense. As we will discuss later in the chapter, celebrities can break through the clutter and grab consumer attention as well as enhance consumer perceptions and attitudes toward the brands they endorse. The downside is when endorsers engage in questionable personal behaviors. What is particularly interesting, however, is which companies decide to stick with their endorsers through scandals while others fire them. Let's look at three examples.[1]

Michael Phelps. This Olympic swimmer, who has broken most if not all of the swimming records, has had problems in his personal life. The most recent was a picture that surfaced after the Beijing Olympics showing Phelps smoking a marijuana pipe. Kellogg dropped Phelps, while Speedo did not. Here are statements from each company:

> KELLOGG: Michael's most recent behavior is not consistent with the image of Kellogg.
>
> SPEEDO: In light of Michael Phelps' statement yesterday, Speedo would like to make it clear that it does not condone such behavior and we know that Michael truly regrets his actions. Michael Phelps is a valued member of the Speedo team and a great champion. We will do all that we can to support him and his family.

Tiger Woods. Perhaps the most gifted golfer of his generation, if not of all time, Tiger Woods has performed miracles on the golf course. Unfortunately, personal scandals involving infidelity came crashing down. Tag Heuer dropped Tiger; Nike did not. Here are statements from each company:

> TAG HEUER: We recognize Tiger Woods as a great champion, but we have to take account of the sensitivity of some consumers in relation to recent events.
>
> NIKE: Tiger has been a part of Nike for more than a decade. He is the best golfer in the world and one of the greatest athletes of his era. We look forward to his return to golf. He and his family have Nike's full support.

Why such different reactions by each company? No one knows for sure, but in looking at these examples, it appears that it may be a function of what the company gains or loses from the endorser and the scandal. Speedo and Nike arguably gain the most from Phelps and

Woods because of the product performance credibility they bring to their sports brands. Personal scandals may do little to damage this dimension. Alternatively, Kellogg and Tag Heuer appear to have used Phelps and Woods for general credibility and image and these clearly took a hit when the scandals broke.

Outside of sports, Subway has been dealing with the undesirable behavior of its main endorser, Jared Fogle. Jared lost 245 pounds eating low-fat Subway sandwiches but had recently gained back 40 pounds. Rather than walking away from Jared, they took it as an opportunity to highlight the humanness of Jared in having weight struggles. They entered and trained him for the New York City Marathon. According to Subway:

> Jared is kind of like the everyman. He has his ups and downs, and though he hasn't had crazy ups, this one got a lot of attention.

Researchers in sports have reached similar conclusions. Namely, sports fans love the human side of athletes and love a great "comeback" story.

LO1 As the chapter's opening example indicates, brands and organizations attempt to influence consumer attitudes and their resulting consumption behaviors.

An **attitude** is *an enduring organization of motivational, emotional, perceptual, and cognitive processes with respect to some aspect of our environment.* It is a learned predisposition to respond in a consistently favorable or unfavorable manner with respect to a given object. Thus, an attitude is the way one thinks, feels, and acts toward some aspect of his or her environment, such as a retail store, television program, or product.[2] Attitudes are formed as the result of all the factors we have discussed in previous chapters, and they represent an important influence on an individual's lifestyle. In this chapter, we examine attitude components, general attitude change strategies, and the effect of marketing communications on attitudes.

ATTITUDE COMPONENTS

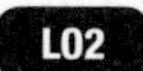

As Figure 11–1 illustrates, it is useful to consider attitudes as having three components: cognitive (beliefs), affective (feelings), and behavioral (response tendencies). Each of these attitude components is discussed in more detail below.

Cognitive Component

The **cognitive component** consists of *a consumer's beliefs about an object.* For most attitude objects, people have a number of beliefs. For example, an individual may believe that AMP beverages

- Are popular with younger consumers.
- Provide consumers with lots of energy.
- Contain a lot of vitamins.
- Are priced competitively with other energy drinks.
- Are made by a sports-oriented company.

The total configuration of beliefs about this beverage brand represents the cognitive component of an attitude toward AMP. Beliefs can be about the emotional benefits of owning or using a product (one can believe it would be exciting to own or drive a convertible) as well as about objective features.[3] Many beliefs about attributes are evaluative

Attitude Components and Manifestations FIGURE 11-1

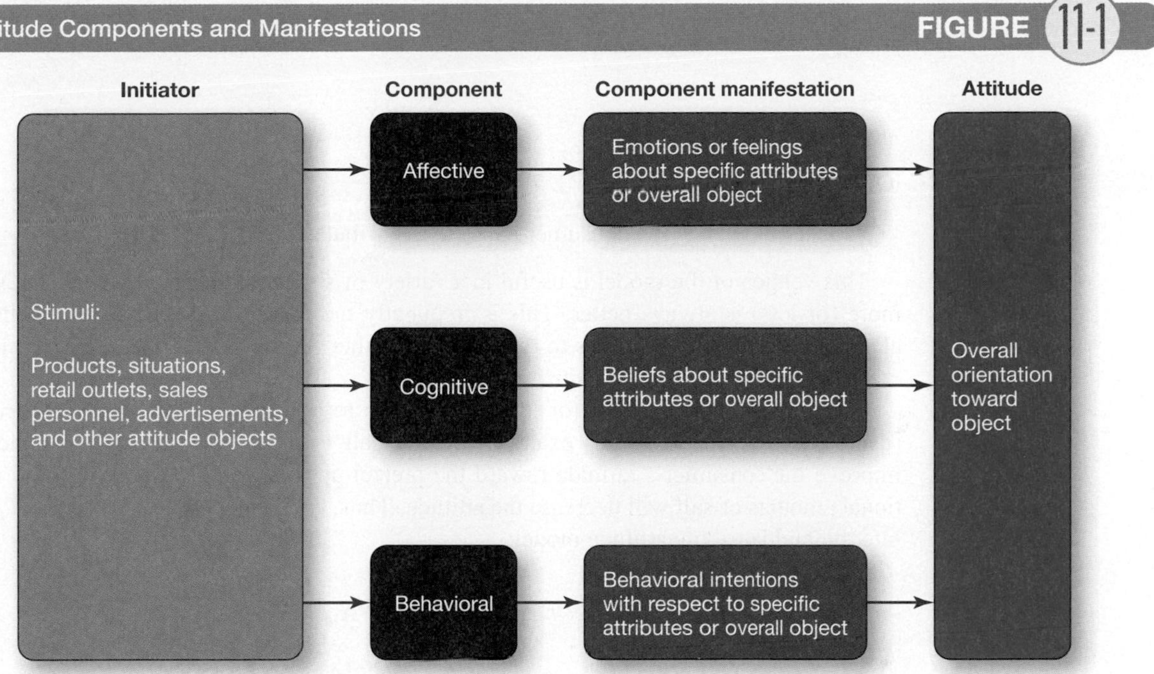

in nature; for example, high gas mileage, attractive styling, and reliable performance are generally viewed as positive beliefs. This brings up the distinction between a *feature* and a *benefit,* both of which are beliefs. A product may have five milligrams of sodium per serving (a nonevaluative *feature* belief), which means that it is low in sodium and better for your health (both evaluative *benefit* beliefs). Marketers must promote benefits rather than features, especially for less knowledgeable consumers and for complex products. Otherwise consumers will not know how to evaluate and respond to the claims.[4] For example, Quaker Oats helps consumers interpret the nutritional information on its package with statements such as "the soluble fiber in oatmeal helps reduce cholesterol."

The more positive beliefs associated with a brand, the more positive each belief is, and the easier it is for the individual to recall the beliefs, the more favorable the overall cognitive component is presumed to be.[5] And because all the components of an attitude are generally consistent, the overall attitude is more favorable. This logic underlies what is known as the **multiattribute attitude model.**

Multiattribute Attitude Model There are several versions of this model. The simplest is

$$A_b = \sum_{i=1}^{n} X_{ib}$$

where

A_b = Consumer's attitude toward a particular brand b

X_{ib} = Consumer's belief about brand b's performance on attribute i

n = Number of attributes considered

This version assumes that all attributes are equally important in determining our overall evaluation. However, a moment's reflection suggests that frequently a few attributes, such as price, quality, or style, are more important than others. Thus, it is often necessary to add an importance weight for each attribute:

$$A_b = \sum_{i=1}^{n} W_i X_{ib}$$

where

W_i = The importance the consumer attaches to attribute i

This version of the model is useful in a variety of situations. However, it assumes that more (or less) is always better. This is frequently the case. More miles to the gallon is always better than fewer miles to the gallon, all other things being equal. This version is completely adequate for such situations.

For some attributes, more (or less) is good up to a point, but then further increases (decreases) become bad. For example, adding salt to a saltless pretzel will generally improve the consumer's attitude toward the pretzel up to a point. After that point, additional amounts of salt will decrease the attitude. Thus, we need to introduce an *ideal point* into the multiattribute attitude model:

$$A_b = \sum_{i=1}^{n} W_i |I_i - X_{ib}|$$

where

I_i = Consumer's ideal level of performance on attribute i

Because multiattribute attitude models are widely used by marketing researchers and managers, we will work through an example using the weighted, ideal point model. The simpler models would work in a similar manner.

Imagine that Coca-Cola gathers data on a set of beliefs about Diet Coke from a segment of consumers (more details on measuring the various attitude components can be found in Appendix A and Appendix Table A–3). These consumers perceive Diet Coke to have the following levels of performance (the *X*s) and desired performance (the *I*s) on four attributes:

	(1)	(2)	(3)	(4)	(5)	(6)	(7)	
Low price			I	X				High price
Sweet taste		I				X		Bitter taste
High status			I		X			Low status
Low calories	IX							High calories

This segment of consumers believes (the *X*s) that Diet Coke is average priced, very bitter in taste, somewhat low in status, and extremely low in calories. Their ideal soda (the *I*s) would be slightly low priced, very sweet in taste, somewhat high in status, and extremely low in calories. Because these attributes are not equally important to consumers, they are assigned weights based on the relative importance a segment of consumers attaches to each.

A popular way of measuring importance weights is with a 100-point *constant-sum scale.* For example, the importance weights shown below express the relative importance of the four soft-drink attributes such that the total adds up to 100 points.

Attribute	Importance
Price	10
Taste	30
Status	20
Calories	40
	100 points

In this case, calories are considered the most important attribute, with taste slightly less important. Price is given little importance.

From this information, we can index this segment's attitude toward Diet Coke as follows:

$$
\begin{aligned}
A_{\text{Diet Coke}} &= (10)(|3 - 4|) + (30)(|2 - 6|) + (20)(|3 - 5|) + (40)(|1 - 1|) \\
&= (10)(1) + (30)(4) + (20)(2) + (40)(0) \\
&= 170
\end{aligned}
$$

This involves taking the absolute difference between the consumer's ideal soft-drink attributes and beliefs about Diet Coke's attributes and multiplying these differences by the importance attached to each attribute. In this case, the attitude index is computed as 170. Is this good or bad? Because an attitude index is relative, to fully evaluate it, we must compare it with the segment's attitudes toward competing brands. However, if Diet Coke were perceived as the ideal soft drink, an attitude index of zero would result. Thus, the closer to zero an attitude index calculated in this manner is, the better. It is important to note that, in general, the multiattribute attitude model merely *represents* a process that is much less precise and structured than implied by the model.

Affective Component

Feelings or *emotional reactions to an object* represent the **affective component** of an attitude. A consumer who states "I like Diet Coke" or "Diet Coke is a terrible soda" is expressing the results of an emotional or affective evaluation of the product. This overall evaluation may be simply a vague, general feeling developed without cognitive information or beliefs about the product. Or it may be the result of several evaluations of the product's performance on each of several attributes. Thus, the statements "Diet Coke tastes bad" and "Diet Coke is not good for your health" imply a negative affective reaction to specific aspects of the product that, in combination with feelings about other attributes, will determine the overall reaction to the brand.

Marketers are increasingly turning their attention to the affective or "feeling" component of attitudes to provide a richer understanding of attitudes than that based solely on the cognitive or "thinking" component. As a consequence, marketers now commonly distinguish *utilitarian* or functional benefits and attitudes from *hedonic* or emotional benefits and attitudes.[6] For example, one study found that consumer acceptance of handheld Internet devices was influenced by both utilitarian benefits such as usefulness and hedonic aspects such as fun to use.[7] Another study found that in some cases hedonic aspects of giving blood such as fear and joy were stronger determinants of overall attitude toward blood donation than utilitarian beliefs.[8]

In addition, marketers are beginning to consider both form *and* function in product designs and focus considerable attention on the aesthetic aspects of design (appearance,

ILLUSTRATION 11-1

Aesthetically pleasing or interesting product designs can evoke powerful emotional responses that are such a critical aspect of the affective component of attitudes.

sensory experience). The iPod and iPad are examples of products with high **aesthetic appeal** that tap consumers' affective reactions by going beyond the cognitive associations of functionality.[9] Illustration 11–1 shows an ad for a product high in aesthetic appeal.

Affective reactions to a specific product or benefit can vary by situation and individual. For example, a consumer's belief that Diet Coke has caffeine may result in positive feelings if he or she needs to stay awake to work late but negative feelings if he or she wants to get to sleep quickly. The Swanson ad in Illustration 11–2 is an example of an affective ad which will likely bring about emotional reactions to a number of the captions, such as "feeling like an artist."

Marketers sometimes measure the affective component on verbal scales much like those used to measure the cognitive component (for more detail, see Appendix A and Appendix Table A–3). So, consumers might be asked to rate Diet Coke overall (or specific attributes such as taste) on the following dimensions by placing an *X* in the appropriate space:

	(1)	(2)	(3)	(4)	(5)	(6)	(7)	
Good	_____	_____	_____	_____	_____	_____	_____	Bad
Like	_____	_____	_____	_____	_____	_____	_____	Dislike
Happy	_____	_____	_____	_____	_____	_____	_____	Sad
Pleasant	_____	_____	_____	_____	_____	_____	_____	Unpleasant

SAM and AdSAM® However, sometimes marketers want to tap feelings and emotions more directly and bypass the cognitive processing that often goes along with verbal scales. One such measure is based on the pleasure-arousal-dominance (PAD) approach to emotions discussed in Chapter 10. This measure, termed SAM (Self-Assessment Manikin), provides visual representations of 232 "emotional adjectives" underlying PAD. SAM (and AdSAM®, which applies SAM to ad planning) is a graphical character that is manipulated to portray emotions and more directly tap emotional responses. From a global standpoint, SAM is effective across different cultures and languages because the pictorial representations don't require translation or alteration.[10] Examples of AdSAM® for each dimension of PAD are shown below (top panel—pleasure; middle—arousal; bottom—dominance):

Behavioral Component

The **behavioral component** of an attitude is *one's tendency to respond in a certain manner toward an object or activity.* A series of decisions to purchase or not purchase Diet Coke or to recommend it or other brands to friends would reflect the behavioral component. Brand interest, as represented by tendencies to seek out the brand on store shelves or search for brand information, also reflects the behavioral component. The behavioral

ILLUSTRATION 11-2

Individuals differ in their affective reactions to product characteristics. Likewise, the same individual will react differently to the same attribute in different situations. Would you enjoy an experience that induced the following, as shown within this Swanson ad?

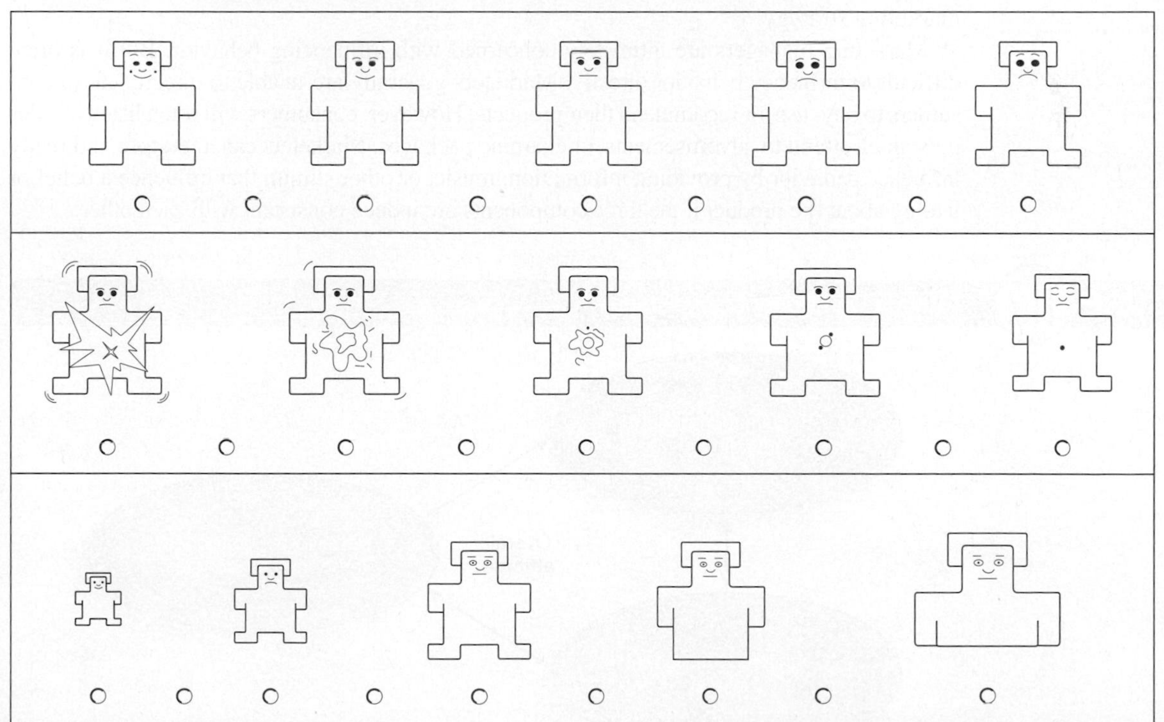

Source: Copyright 2000 AdSam Marketing LLC.

component provides response tendencies or behavioral intentions. *Actual behaviors reflect these intentions as they are modified by the situation in which the behavior will occur.*

Direct versus Indirect Approach Actual behaviors and response tendencies are most often measured by fairly direct questioning (for more detail, see Appendix A and Appendix Table A–3). For example, consumers might be asked about their intentions to buy Diet Coke, as follows:

How likely is it that you will buy Diet Coke the next time you purchase a soft drink (put an X *in the appropriate space)?*

Definitely Will	Probably Will	Might	Probably Will Not	Definitely Will Not
____	____	____	____	____

Such direct questioning may work well for most consumption, but not so well for sensitive topics such as alcohol, pornography, and eating patterns where consumers may understate negative behaviors or intentions. In these cases, asking *indirect* questions such as estimating the behaviors of other people similar to themselves (neighbors, those with similar jobs, etc.) may help reduce the bias.

Component Consistency

Figure 11–2 illustrates a critical aspect of attitudes: *All three attitude components tend to be consistent.*[11] This means that a change in one attitude component tends to produce related changes in the other components. This tendency is the basis for a substantial amount of marketing strategy.

Marketing managers are ultimately concerned with influencing behavior. But it is often difficult to influence behavior directly. Marketers generally are unable to directly cause consumers to buy, use, or recommend their products. However, consumers will often listen to sales personnel, attend to advertisements, or examine packages. Marketers can, therefore, indirectly influence behavior by providing information, music, or other stimuli that influence a belief or feeling about the product if the three components are indeed consistent with each other.

FIGURE 11-2 Attitude Component Consistency

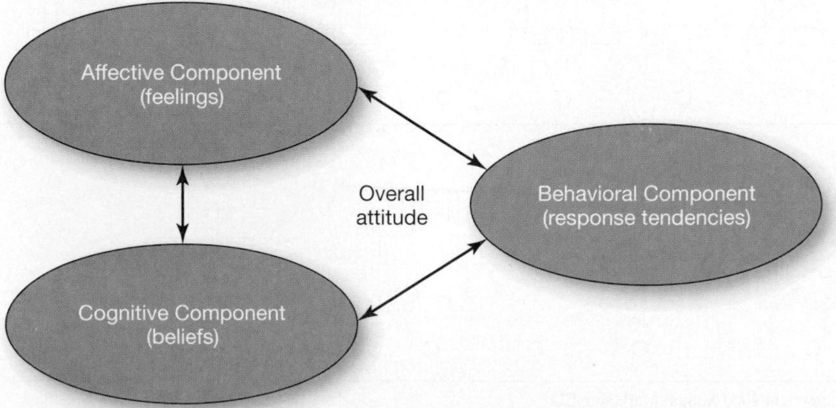

Some research has found only a limited relationship among the three components.[12] Let's examine the sources of this inconsistency by considering an example. Suppose an individual reports positive beliefs and affect toward the iPod but does not own an iPod or purchases another brand. At least six factors may account for inconsistencies between *measures* of beliefs and feelings and *observations* of behavior.

1. *Lack of need.* A favorable attitude requires a need or motive before it can be translated into action. Thus, the consumer may not feel a need for a portable player or might already own an acceptable, though less preferred, brand.
2. *Lack of ability.* Translating favorable beliefs and feelings into ownership requires ability. The consumer might not have sufficient funds to purchase an iPod; thus, she might purchase a less-expensive brand.
3. *Relative attitudes.* In the prior example, only attitudes toward the iPod were considered. However, purchases often involve trade-offs across competing brands. Thus, a consumer may have a relatively high attitude toward iPod but a slightly higher attitude toward a competing brand. In a choice situation, relative attitudes are a stronger predictor of behavior.
4. *Attitude ambivalence.* While consumers often strive to hold consistent beliefs, feelings, and intentions toward a specific attitude object, this is not always the case. Sometimes a consumer has an **ambivalent attitude,** which involves *holding mixed beliefs and/or feelings about an attitude object.* Think of seafood. A consumer with an ambivalent attitude toward seafood would agree that "Sometimes I feel seafood tastes good, but other times I feel it tastes bad." Ambivalent attitudes are less stable over time and less predictive of behavior. Firms should avoid ambivalent attitudes by creating consistent messages and experiences over time. Firms may also attempt to gain market share by creating ambivalence among customers of competing brands.[13]
5. *Weak beliefs and affect.* If the cognitive and affective components are weakly held, and if the consumer obtains additional information while shopping, then the initial attitudes may give way to new ones. Specifically, stronger attitudes or those attitudes held with more confidence tend to be stronger predictors of behavior. Attitudes can be weak because of ambivalence. However they can also be weak because of a general lack of experience with the brand. Thus, direct (and consistently positive) experience tends to yield attitudes that are more strongly and confidently held.[14] As a consequence, companies often spend enormous amounts of money on coupons and free samples to generate direct product experience.

   In addition to direct experience, factors related to strength of learning such as importance, message involvement, reinforcement, and repetition (see Chapter 9) are also related to attitude strength because attitudes are generally learned.
6. *Interpersonal and situational influences.* An individual's attitudes were measured above. However, many purchase decisions involve others directly or indirectly. Thus, a shopper may purchase something other than an iPod to better meet the needs of the entire family. Situation and other consumers' expectations in those situations can also play a role. For example, it may be seen by some as more desirable to purchase and use an iPod in front of friends (even though they themselves like another brand better) because their friends think the iPod is the coolest brand.

In summary, attitude components—cognitive, affective, and behavioral—tend to be consistent. However, as we see, the degree of apparent consistency can be reduced by a variety of factors. Marketers must incorporate these factors when developing persuasive messages and strategies.

ATTITUDE CHANGE STRATEGIES

Marketers often attempt to influence consumer behavior by changing one or more of the underlying attitude components. Such influence can be positive, as we saw in the chapter's opening vignette. However, social, ethical, and regulatory concerns arise when companies attempt to promote potentially harmful consumption behaviors or when persuasion attempts are deemed deceptive.

Change the Cognitive Component

A common and effective approach to changing attitudes is to focus on the cognitive component.[15] Four basic marketing strategies—change beliefs, shift importance, add beliefs, and change ideal—are used for altering the cognitive structure of a consumer's attitude.

Change Beliefs This strategy involves shifting beliefs about the performance of the brand on one or more attributes.[16] Illustration 11–3 shows one example. Another example is Radio Shack, which is repositioning itself as a more modern and contemporary retailer. They have nicknamed the store "The Shack" and are trying to change existing merchandise beliefs as follows:

> Consumers thought this was a place that had private labels and off brands, when in fact we've got leading national brands across every one of our categories. So the goal from the outset was to close those gaps in brand perception [beliefs] and business reality.[17]

Attempts to change beliefs generally involve providing facts or statements about performance. It is important to realize that some beliefs are strongly held and thus hard to change. As a consequence, marketers may have more success changing overall brand attitudes by targeting weaker brand beliefs that are more vulnerable to persuasion attempts.[18]

Shift Importance Most consumers consider some product attributes to be more important than others. Marketers often try to convince consumers that those attributes on which their brands are relatively strong are the most important. For example, General Motors uses detailed narratives of drivers in distress to emphasize the importance of instant communications and emergency assistance, which its proprietary OnStar system provides.

Sometimes evaluative factors that would otherwise not be prominent to consumers can be enhanced by cues in the ad. One study created ads with references to Asian culture (e.g., picture of the Great Wall of China) to enhance "ethnic self-awareness." When ethnic self-awareness was enhanced, Asian consumers reacted more positively to ads containing an Asian spokesperson.[19]

Add Beliefs Another approach to changing the cognitive component of an attitude is to add new beliefs to the consumer's belief structure. For example, the California Pomegranate Council wants consumers to know that beyond possessing vitamins and minerals (already known), new research shows that pomegranates contain "powerful antioxidants [that] help retard aging and can neutralize almost twice as many free radicals as red wine and seven times as many as green tea."[20]

Change Ideal The final strategy for changing the cognitive component is to change the perceptions of the ideal brand or situation. Thus, many conservation organizations strive to

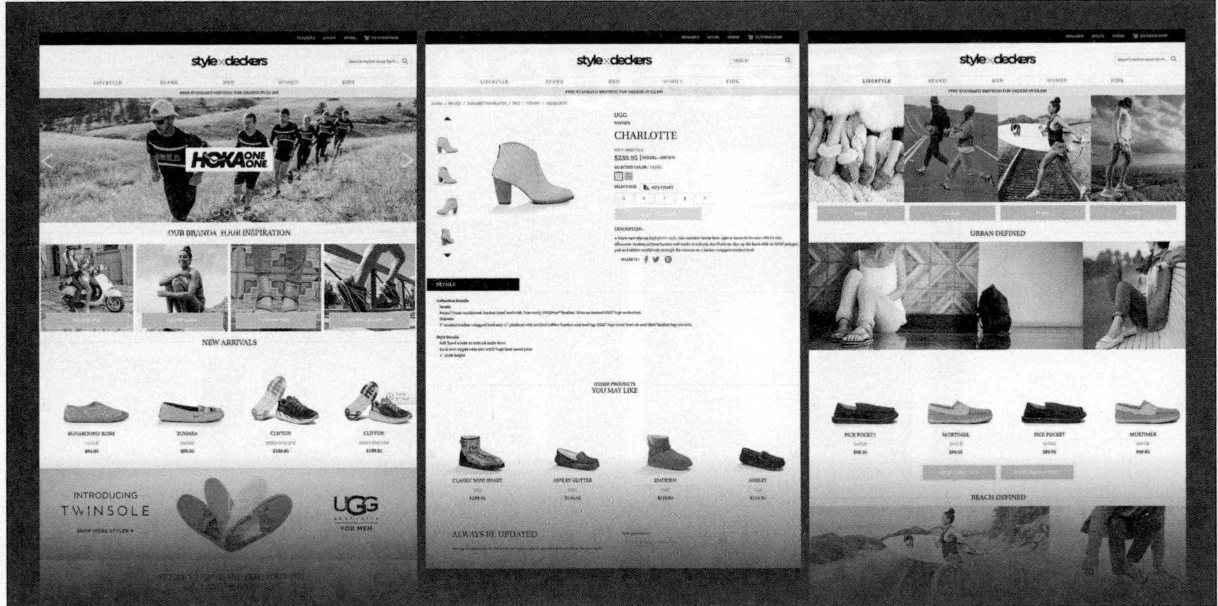

ILLUSTRATION 11-3

The cognitive component of an attitude can be altered by changing current beliefs, adding new beliefs, shifting the importance of beliefs, or changing the beliefs about the ideal product.

influence our beliefs about the ideal product in terms of minimal packaging, nonpolluting manufacturing, extensive use of recycled materials, and nonpolluting disposition after its useful life.

Change the Affective Component

Firms increasingly attempt to influence consumers' liking of their brands without directly influencing either beliefs or behavior. If the firm is successful, increased liking will tend to lead to increased positive beliefs,[21] which could lead to purchase behavior should a need for the product arise. Or, perhaps more common, increased liking will lead to a tendency to purchase the brand should a need arise,[22] with purchase and use leading to increased positive beliefs. Marketers use three basic approaches to directly increase affect: classical conditioning, affect toward the ad itself, and mere exposure.

Classical Conditioning One way of directly influencing the affective component is through classical conditioning (see Chapter 9). In this approach, a stimulus the audience likes, such as music, is consistently paired with the brand name. Over time, some of the positive affect associated with the music will transfer to the brand.[23] Other liked stimuli, such as pictures, are frequently used for this reason.

Affect toward the Ad or Website As we saw in Chapter 10, liking the advertisement (attitude toward the ad, or Aad) generally increases the tendency to like the brand (attitude toward the brand, or Abr).[24] Somewhat similar results are associated with liking the website on which an ad appears (Aweb).[25] Using humor, celebrities, or emotional appeals increases Aad and Aweb. For example, vivid websites with rich sensory content that appeal to multiple senses produce more positive Aweb than do less vivid sites.[26] Illustration 11–4 contains an ad that relies on positive affect.

Ads that arouse negative affect or emotions such as fear, guilt, or sorrow can also enhance attitude change. For example, an ad for a charity assisting refugees could show pictures that would elicit a variety of unpleasant emotions such as disgust or anger and still be effective.[27]

ILLUSTRATION 11-4

Ads can change the affective component of an attitude toward a brand without altering the belief structure if the ad itself elicits a positive response (is liked). Ads that are primarily pictorial are often used for this purpose, though the pictures themselves convey cognitive as well as emotional meanings.

Mere Exposure While controversial, there is evidence that affect or brand preference may also be increased by **mere exposure.**[28] That is, simply presenting a brand to an individual on a large number of occasions might make the individual's attitude toward the brand more positive. A common explanation of the mere exposure effect is that "familiarity breeds liking." Thus, the repetition of advertisements for low-involvement products may well increase liking (through enhanced familiarity) and subsequent purchase of the advertised brands without altering the initial belief structure. Mere exposure effects underlie the use of simple reminder ads as well as product placements.[29]

Classical conditioning, Aad, and mere exposure can alter affect directly and, by altering affect, alter purchase behavior without first changing beliefs. This has a number of important implications:

- Ads designed to alter affect need not contain any cognitive (factual or attribute) information.
- Classical conditioning principles should guide such campaigns.
- Aad and ad-evoked affect are critical for this type of campaign unless mere exposure is being used.
- Repetition is critical for affect-based campaigns.
- Cognitively based measures may be inappropriate to assess advertising effectiveness.

As these guidelines suggest, classical conditioning, Aad, and mere exposure tend to occur in low-involvement situations (see Chapter 9). There is at least one major exception, however. When emotions and feelings are important product performance dimensions, then such feelings and emotions are relevant to the evaluation. In these situations, Aad can readily influence Abr under high involvement. As we discussed earlier in the chapter, hedonic (versus utilitarian) products are those for which affect and emotion are relevant performance criteria. Not surprisingly, hedonic products are those for which affect, emotions, and Aad can play a role in more conscious, high-involvement settings.[30]

Change the Behavioral Component

Behavior, specifically purchase or use behavior, may precede the development of cognition and affect. Or it may occur in contrast to the cognitive and affective components. For example, a consumer may dislike the taste of diet soft drinks and believe that artificial sweeteners are unhealthy. However, rather than appear rude, the same consumer may accept a diet drink when offered one by a friend due to social norms. Drinking the beverage may alter her perceptions of its taste and lead to liking; this in turn may lead to increased learning, which changes the cognitive component.

Behavior can lead directly to affect, to cognitions, or to both simultaneously.[31] Consumers frequently try new brands or types of low-cost items in the absence of prior knowledge or affect. Such purchases are as much for information (Will I like this brand?) as for satisfaction of some underlying need such as hunger.

Internet marketers have been particularly concerned about their ability to simulate direct experiences for products in a virtual context. A recent study finds that for experiential products such as sunglasses, creating a *virtual direct experience* (in this case, a video that simulated viewing the content with and without the sunglasses) led to more positive beliefs, affect, and purchase intentions.[32] The ability to simulate experiences with products in an online context relates to the issue of "touch," which is a major online purchasing factor discussed in Chapter 17.

Changing behavior prior to changing affect or cognition is based primarily on operant conditioning (see Chapter 9). Thus, the key marketing task is to induce people to purchase or consume the product while ensuring that the purchase or consumption will indeed be rewarding.[33] Coupons, free samples, point-of-purchase displays, tie-in purchases, and price reductions are common techniques for inducing trial behavior. Because behavior often leads to strong positive attitudes toward the consumed brand, a sound distribution system (limited stockouts) is important to prevent current customers from trying competing brands.

INDIVIDUAL AND SITUATIONAL CHARACTERISTICS THAT INFLUENCE ATTITUDE CHANGE

LO4

Attitude change is determined by individual and situational factors as well as marketing activities.[34] Individual factors include gender, need for cognition, consumer knowledge, ethnicity, and, as we saw in Chapter 10, regulatory focus. Situational factors include program context, level of viewer distraction, and buying occasion.

Marketers continue to focus considerable attention on consumer involvement, which has both an individual (intrinsic interest) and situational (current need to make a purchase decision) component. Consumer involvement is an important motivational factor that influences elaborative processing, learning, and attitudes. The **elaboration likelihood model (ELM)** is a theory about how attitudes are formed and changed under varying conditions of involvement. Thus, the ELM integrates select individual, situational, and marketing factors to understand attitudes.[35]

The ELM suggests that involvement is a key determinant of how information is processed and attitudes are changed. High involvement results in a *central route* to attitude

FIGURE 11-3 The Elaboration Likelihood Model

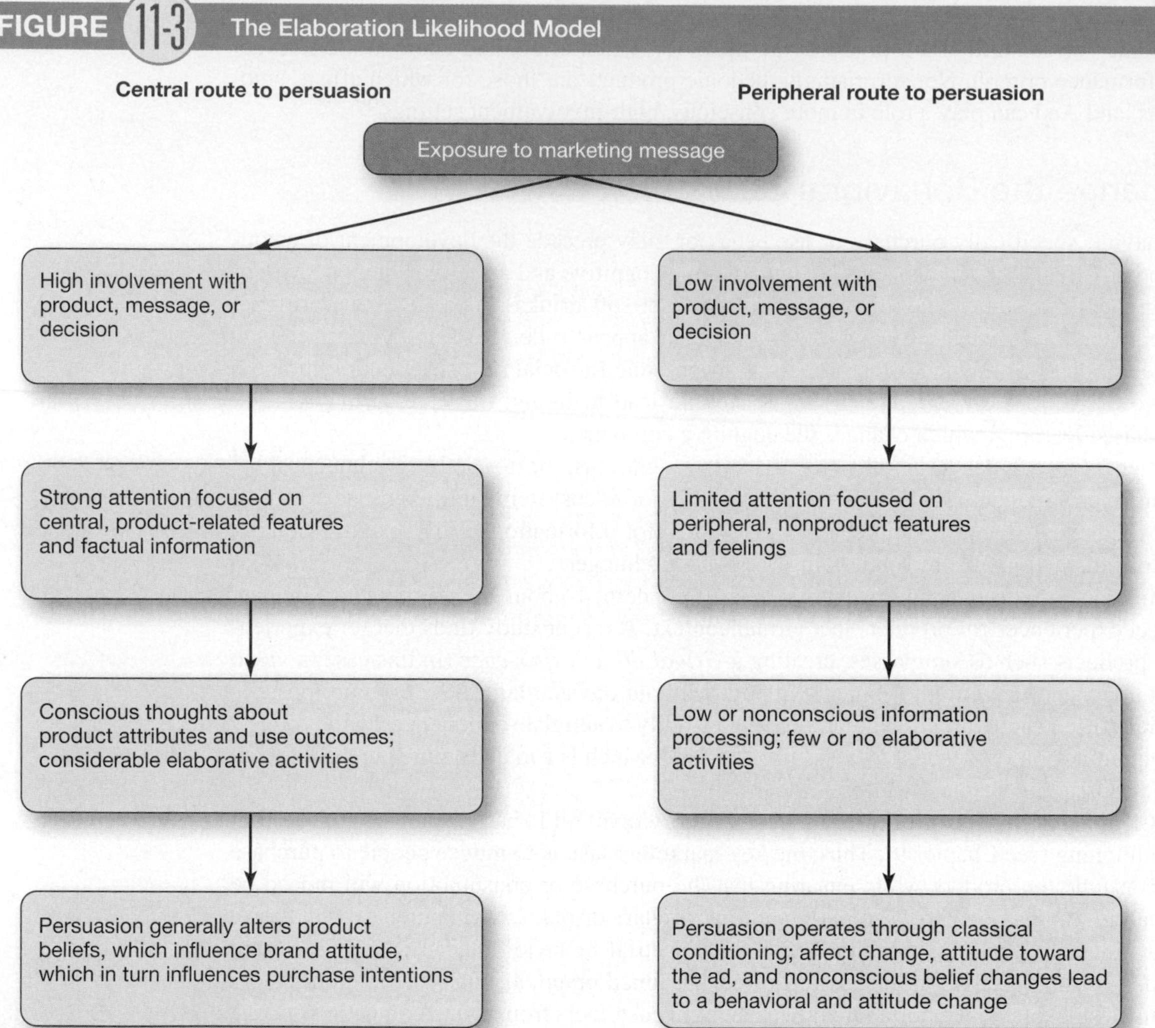

change by which consumers deliberately and consciously process those message elements that they believe are relevant to a meaningful and logical evaluation of the brand (see Figure 11–3). These elements are elaborated on and combined into an overall evaluation. The multiattribute attitude model represents a high-involvement view of attitude change.

In contrast, low involvement results in a *peripheral route* to attitude change in which consumers form impressions of the brand based on exposure to readily available cues in the message regardless of their relevance to the brand or decision. Attitudes formed through the peripheral route are based on little or no elaborative processing. Classical conditioning, Aad, and mere exposure represent low-involvement views of attitude change.

The ELM suggests that vastly different communications strategies are required to communicate effectively with high- versus low-involvement consumers. In general, detailed factual information (central cues) is effective in high-involvement, central-route situations. Low-involvement, peripheral-route situations generally require limited information and instead rely on simple affective and cognitive cues such as pictures, music, and characteristics of people in the ad (peripheral cues). *Which persuasion route is most likely being used in Illustration 11–4?*

Cue Relevance and Competitive Situation

Generally speaking, compared with attitudes formed under the peripheral route, attitudes formed under the central route tend to be stronger, more resistant to counterpersuasion attempts, more accessible from memory, and more predictive of behavior.[36]

However, it is important to realize that central route processing involves extensive processing of *decision-relevant* information or cues. And what consumers find relevant can vary by product and situation. For example, an attractive picture can be peripheral or central. In an ad for orange soda, a picture of cute puppies would be a peripheral cue (and influence attitudes under low involvement), while a picture of fresh, juicy orange slices would be a central cue (and influence attitudes under high involvement).[37] Similarly, emotions likely represent a central cue for hedonic products and thus influence attitudes under high involvement.

In addition, the competitive situation can also work to enhance the role of peripheral cues even under high involvement. For example, if competing brands are comparable in terms of their product features (central cues), highly involved consumers prefer the brand with the strongest peripheral cues in its advertising.[38] The basic idea is that relative attitudes are critical in competitive settings and peripheral cues become the tiebreaker between otherwise equivalent (parity) brands. As you can see, the role of peripheral cues can extend beyond low-involvement settings in certain competitive situations.

Consumer Resistance to Persuasion

Consumers are not passive to persuasion attempts. Instead, consumers are often skeptical (an individual characteristic) and resist persuasion.[39] Also, consumers frequently infer an advertiser's intent and respond in light of that presumed selling intent.[40] For example, a recent ad for California Almonds stated, "It's uncanny how we raise indulgence and lower cholesterol." A consumer could respond to the ad as follows: "Of course they're going to tell me almonds are healthy for me. They're trying to sell more almonds. I'm still not convinced." To help reduce the likelihood of such responses, the ad makes use of the American Heart Association and scientific research to bolster its health claims.

Strongly held attitudes are harder to change than weakly held attitudes. Think of something you feel strongly about—perhaps your school or your favorite sports team. What would be required to change your attitude? Clearly, it would be difficult. Consumers tend to avoid messages that are counter to their attitudes (e.g., committed smokers tend to avoid antismoking ads). And if they do encounter such messages, they tend to (a) discredit the source as unreliable, (b) discount the importance of the issue or attribute at hand, and (c) if all else fails, "contain" the negative information so it doesn't "spill over" to the entire brand.[41] These behaviors are particularly likely for loyal customers of a brand—thus, it is possible to see why loyal customers can be so valuable to firms.

COMMUNICATION CHARACTERISTICS THAT INFLUENCE ATTITUDE FORMATION AND CHANGE

LO5

In this section, we describe communication techniques that can be used to form and change attitudes. Obviously, as with all aspects of consumer behavior, individual and situational characteristics interact with the communication features to determine effectiveness.

Source Characteristics

The source of a communication represents "who" delivers the message. Sources include people (celebrities, typical consumers), animated spokescharacters (Jolly Green Giant, Mr. Peanut), and organizations (the company, a third-party endorser). The source of a message is important because consumers respond differently to the same message delivered by different sources.

Source Credibility Persuasion is easier when the target market views the message source as highly credible. **Source credibility** consists of *trustworthiness* and *expertise.* A source that has no ulterior motive to provide anything other than complete and accurate information would generally be considered trustworthy. However, product knowledge is required for a source to have expertise. Thus, a friend might be trustworthy but lack expertise. Alternatively, salespeople and advertisers may have ample knowledge but be viewed with skepticism by consumers.

Individuals who are recognized experts and who have no apparent motive to mislead can be powerful sources because of their ability to reduce risk.[42] An example is 1-800-PetMeds®, with its TV advertisements in which a veterinarian discusses pain management options for your pet. Relatively unknown individuals similar to those in the target market can be effective spokespersons as well, but for different reasons. In a **testimonial ad,** *a person, generally a typical member of the target market, recounts his or her successful use of the product, service, or idea.*[43] Testimonials are important on the web as well. Amazon and other online marketers offer customer reviews, which appear to be important determinants of attitudes and purchase behavior.[44] Similarity of the source enhances the believability and relevance of these testimonials.

Independent *third-party endorsements* by organizations such as the American Dental Association (ADA) are widely viewed as both trustworthy and expert by consumers and are actively sought by marketers. Such endorsements appear to be used by consumers as brand quality cues.[45] The remarkable success of Crest toothpaste is largely attributable to the ADA endorsement. Other examples include:

- The American Heart Association—Quaker Oats and Subway.
- J.D. Power and Associates—Edward Jones.
- Good Housekeeping Seal of Approval—LiftMaster garage doors.

Of course, the company itself is the most obvious source of most marketing messages. This means developing a corporate reputation or image for trustworthiness can greatly enhance the impact of the firm's marketing messages.[46]

Source credibility can influence persuasion in various situations. First, a credible source can enhance attitudes when consumers lack the ability or motivation to form direct judgments of the product's performance.[47] This is more of a low-involvement process. Second, a credible source can enhance message processing and acceptance. In fact, expert sources can increase attitudes in some high-involvement settings as a result of their perceived decision relevance.[48]

Cultural differences can also play a role. For example, Thai consumers are more influenced by expert sources than are Canadian consumers. Thai consumers are more risk averse and more likely to defer to authority, thus making them more prone to external sources of influence.[49]

One factor that can diminish the credibility of any source is if consumers believe that the firm is paying the source for his or her endorsement.[50] This is especially relevant for celebrities and athletes who are paid large sums for their endorsements.

Celebrity Sources Celebrities are widely used in advertising. Marketers are increasingly using culturally diverse celebrities to reach an ethnically diverse U.S. population. Eva Mendes (Pantene), Kobe Bryant (Nike), Penelope Cruz (Lancome Tresor Fragrance), and Michelle Wie (Omega watches) are just a few such celebrities with endorsement contracts or their own product lines.

A visible use of celebrity endorsers in recent years has been the mustache campaign for milk. Illustration 11–5 clearly targets the growing ethnic market in the United States.

ILLUSTRATION 11-5

Ethnic celebrities are increasingly common in U.S. advertisements as a way to target specific ethnic subcultures.

Celebrity sources are effective for a variety of reasons:[51]

- *Attention.* Celebrities may attract attention to the advertisement. Consumers tend to be curious about celebrities and are drawn to ads in which they appear.
- *Attitude toward the ad.* A celebrity's likeability and popularity often translate into higher Aad, which can enhance brand attitudes.
- *Trustworthiness.* Despite being paid for their endorsements, celebrities often develop strong and credible public personas that consumers trust—and this trust translates into purchases. One study finds that private actions are just as important as professional achievements for many consumers, which explains why personal scandals can lead to a company firing an endorser, as we saw in the opener.[52]

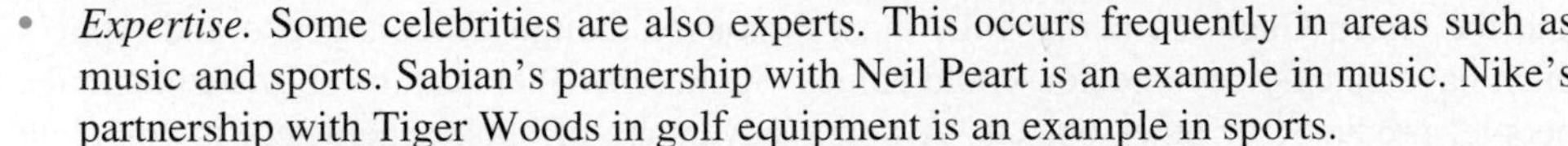

- *Expertise.* Some celebrities are also experts. This occurs frequently in areas such as music and sports. Sabian's partnership with Neil Peart is an example in music. Nike's partnership with Tiger Woods in golf equipment is an example in sports.
- *Aspirational aspects.* Consumers may identify with or desire to emulate the celebrity. As a consequence, they may imitate the behavior and style of a celebrity through purchases of similar brands and styles. For example, popular actresses often lead the way in terms of clothing and hair styles for young women.
- *Meaning transfer.* Consumers may associate known characteristics of the celebrity with attributes of the product that coincide with their own needs or desires. For example, urban youth looking for "street cred" see celebrity athletes like Alan Iverson as powerful icons. As one executive states, "He's from the streets. They admire him."[53]

As the last point suggests, effectiveness of a celebrity endorser can generally be improved by matching the image of the celebrity with the personality of the product and the actual or desired self-concept of the target market.

When the three components shown in Figure 11–4 are well matched, effective attitude formation or change can result.[54] For example, "Avril Lavigne, known for her pairing of frilly dresses and combat boots, will bring her style to the juniors department at Kohl's department stores. The edgy, pop-rock star's clothing line 'Abbey Dawn' was named after her childhood nickname."[55] In this case, there should be a strong match between the celebrity, the clothing line, and the teen and tween female consumers who want to emulate the singer's style and personality. Sometimes images don't mesh and should be avoided. For example, Burger King canceled talks with Paris Hilton when it decided her racy image might be too extreme for the franchise.[56] A recent study also supports the importance of match-up in sports marketing in China.[57]

Using a celebrity as a company spokesperson creates special risks. One risk is overexposure. If a celebrity endorses many products, consumers' reactions may become less positive. Thus, marketers might consider limiting the number of products "their" celebrities endorse.[58] An additional risk, as we saw in the opening example, is that negative behavior involving the spokesperson will affect the individual's credibility and, in turn,

FIGURE 11-4 Matching Endorser with Product and Target Audience

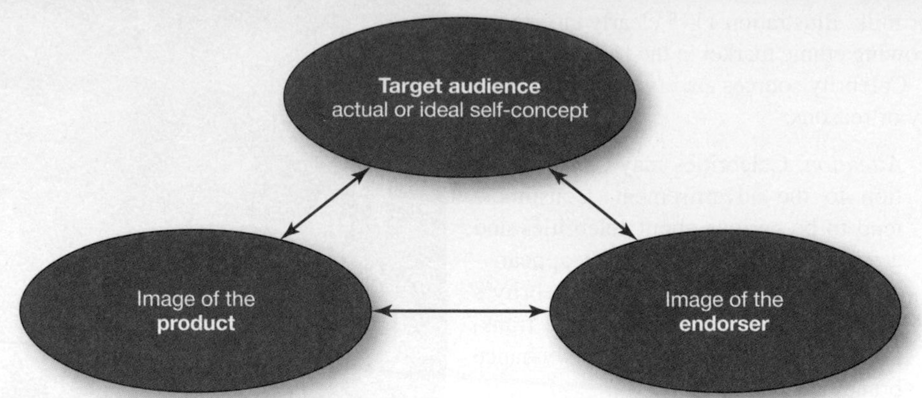

damage the firm's image.[59] Rawlings and Nike terminated their deals with Michael Vick after his indictment for dog fighting. And to protect its family image, NASCAR was quick to penalize Dale Earnhardt Jr. for using profanity in an interview. And PLBS, a Pittsburgh company that made Big Ben Beef Jerky, terminated its contract with Ben Roethlisberger after several off-field scandals, citing their "morals clause."

Rather than use celebrities, many firms are creating **spokescharacters.**[60] Tony the Tiger and the Green Giant are perhaps the most famous, although Geico's gecko and Aflac's duck have quickly become household names. Spokescharacters can be animated animals, people, products, or other objects. A major advantage of spokescharacters is complete image control. This eliminates many of the problems associated with real celebrities. Such characters come to symbolize the brand and give it an identity that competitors cannot easily duplicate. Illustration 11–6 shows how spokescharacters are used as product symbols.

Sponsorship **Sponsorship,** *a company providing financial support for an event* such as the Olympics or a concert, is one of the most rapidly growing marketing activities and a multibillion-dollar industry.[61] Sponsorships in North America continue to grow and total spending exceeds $16 billion per year.[62] One high-profile example is Nextel's replacement of Winston as NASCAR's title sponsor.[63] Another example is Coke's sponsorship of the FIFA World Cup.[64] The potential to generate goodwill in sports sponsorships is particularly high among rabid fans.[65] These fans may react along these lines: "Reebok supports my team, so I'm going to support Reebok."

Sponsorships often work in much the same manner as using a celebrity endorser, and the matchup described in Figure 11–4 is important (where the sponsor replaces the endorser in Figure 11–4). Mismatches can generate consumer backlash such as the negative reactions over an Ohio hospital's plan to name its children's emergency and trauma center after Abercrombie & Fitch, a company that advocacy groups see as engaging in "not-exactly-child-friendly advertising."[66] Sponsor match-up is important in countries such as France and Australia as well.[67]

Finally, it is important to remember that sponsorships should be promoted through offline, online, and social media to maximize awareness and effectiveness.

Appeal Characteristics

As you would expect, the nature of the appeal, or "how" a message is communicated, affects attitude formation and change.

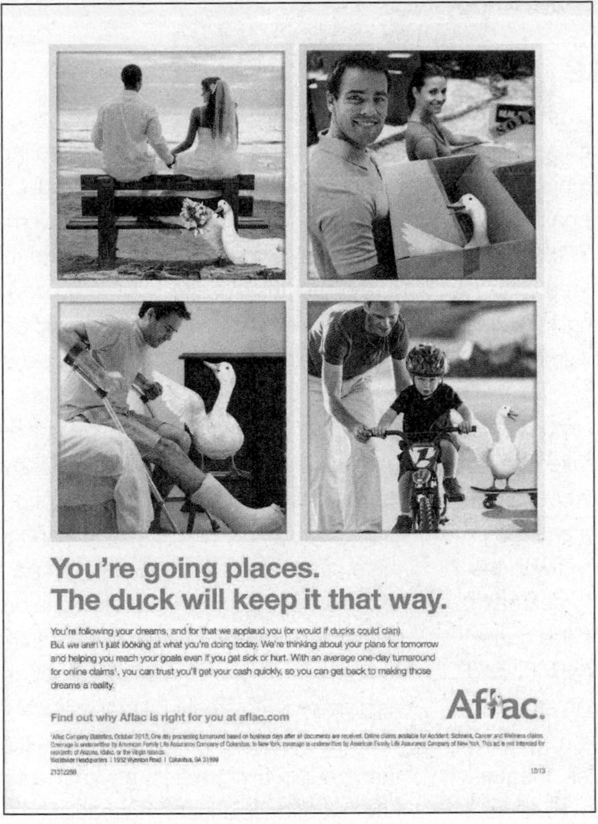

ILLUSTRATION 11-6

Spokescharacters are gaining popularity. They can add credibility to a message as well as attract attention. Some come to serve as a symbol of the product.

Fear Appeals

The picture at the top of an ad is a snapshot of a young couple sitting together on their back deck. The headline reads: "I woke up in the hospital. Patti never woke up." The copy describes how carbon monoxide poisoning caused the tragedy. The ad, one of a series of similar ads, is for First Alert carbon monoxide detector.

Fear appeals use *the threat of negative (unpleasant) consequences if attitudes or behaviors are not altered.* Fear appeals have been studied primarily in terms of physical fear (physical harm from smoking, unsafe driving, and eating genetically modified foods), but social fears (disapproval of one's peers for incorrect clothing, bad breath, or smoking) are also used in advertising.[68]

There is some evidence that individuals avoid or distort extremely threatening messages. At the same time, fear appeals tend to be more effective as higher levels of fear are aroused. Thus, those using fear appeals want to maximize the level of fear aroused while not presenting a threat so intense as to cause the consumer to distort, reject, or avoid the message. This task is difficult because individuals respond differently to threats. Thus, the same "threatening" advertisement may arouse no fear in one individual or group and a high level of fear in another.[69] To further complicate matters, creating fear may not be enough. Recent research suggests that making people feel *accountable* to act by playing on guilt or regret emotions (e.g., ad for heart attack prevention medicine showing what the family goes through if you fail to act and die from a heart attack) may also be necessary to induce desired behaviors.[70] Consumer Insight 11–1 provides an example of both the tripartite attitude approach and fear appeals in the efforts to decrease cigarette consumption in the United States.

CONSUMER INSIGHT 11-1

Scare You Smokeless

Prior to the 1970s, cigarette smoking was a "perceived and promoted" healthy habit recommended by doctors, Santa Claus, and infants.[71] Cigarettes were packed with the c-rations provided to soldiers during WWII.[72] Celebrities, including lovable cartoon characters Fred Flintstone and Barney Rubble of the long-running TV series *The Flintstones,* promoted the enjoyment of smoking cigarettes.[73]

Today smoking cigarettes is understood to be an unhealthy habit. The three-pronged effort—affective, behavioral, cognitive—to decimate cigarette consumption, along with antismoking advertisements and the increase in cigarette prices, has been credited with the decline of smoking in the United States.[74] To decrease consumer top-of-the mind awareness (cognitive component), cigarette advertising was banned from TV and radio (1971).[75] To make it harder to engage in smoking behavior, 38 states have some form of ban on smoking in enclosed public areas—restaurants, offices, theatres (behavioral component).[76] To induce fear as a deterrent (affective component), cigarette packages were required to carry warning labels proclaiming its health hazard (1984).[77]

In recent years, the suggestion for the United States to follow in the footsteps of 40 other countries, including Thailand, England, and Canada, to include graphics—photos of diseased lungs and rotting teeth—to the health warning labels has been championed as a technique to aid efforts to prevent, decrease, and eliminate the consumption of tobacco.[78] It is a more severe form of the fear appeal discussed previously and designed to operate directly via the affective component of attitudes (though it also likely indirectly operates via cascading effects on thoughts and behaviors). Research in other countries where the effort has been ongoing finds that consumers report that the graphic images help them to decrease cigarette consumption and prevent initial use.[79] Whether or not the enactment of such a requirement in the United States would lead to similar results will remain moot. The courts have recently ruled that requiring cigarette manufacturers to include graphics is a violation of the First Amendment right of free speech.[80]

Cigarette manufacturers and governmental regulation bodies will now have to contend with the recent arrival of e-cigarettes. A battery-powered device that looks like a cigarette, e-cigarettes or electronic cigarettes vaporize a liquid solution that can deliver nicotine or non-nicotine flavorings smoke free. Too new to be a real commercial threat, but growing too fast to be ignored, cigarette manufacturers are hedging their bets by buying e-cigarette companies (in 2012, Lorillard bought e-cigarette company Blu for $135 million; in 2014 Altria announced it was buying e-cigarette company Green Smoke for $110 million) and developing their own e-cigarette brands, MarkTen (Altria) and Vuse (Reynolds). With insufficient information to know whether e-cigarettes will act as a deterrent or as a gateway to smoking conventional cigarettes and whether their long-term effect is less threatening to health than traditional cigarettes, governmental regulating bodies have waded tepidly into the regulation waters.[81]

E-cigarettes are an interesting case study in attitude formation for new products. Companies are marketing the products as safe (cognitive component) and the users as sophisticated and individualistic (affective component), which will likely drive adoption in the future by consumers. Government regulating bodies are finding it hard to form "attitudes" towards this new nicotine delivery device due to the lack of information and research with which to form those attitudes. As we can see, attitudes are important for consumers, marketers, and government regulators.

Critical Thinking Questions

1. Describe each attitude component used in deterring cigarette smoking in the United States.
2. Using what you know about fear appeals, do you think the graphic approach will work better than verbal warnings?
3. Find and evaluate an advertisement for e-cigarettes using the information from this chapter.

ILLUSTRATION 11-7

Fear appeals such as this Internet Segura ad, can be effective at forming, reinforcing, and/or changing attitudes. The ethics of such appeals should be examined carefully before they are used.

Examine Illustration 11–7. *Is this Internet Segura ad an effective use of a fear appeal?*

Fear appeals are frequently criticized as unethical. Frequent targets of such criticisms are fear appeals based on social anxieties about bad breath, body odor, dandruff, or soiled clothes. The thrust of these complaints is that these appeals raise anxieties unnecessarily; that is, the injury or harm that they suggest will occur is unlikely to occur or is not really harmful. Fear appeals used to produce socially desirable behaviors such as avoiding drug use or avoiding acknowledged physical risks such as carbon monoxide poisoning are subject to much less criticism.[82]

Humorous Appeals At almost the opposite end of the spectrum from fear appeals are **humorous appeals.**[83] Ads built around humor appear to increase attention to and liking of the ad, particularly for those individuals high in *need for humor.*[84] It also increases attitude toward the brand.[85] The overall effectiveness of humor is generally increased when the humor relates to the product or brand in a meaningful way and is viewed as appropriate for the product by the target audience.[86] Illustration 11–8 shows an ad that makes effective use of humor.

Here is another effective use of humor:

Snickers' "You're just not you when you're hungry" featured Betty White whining during a touch football game, before eating a Snickers bar offered by a friend, and then turning back into himself. This ad aired during the Super Bowl and won *USA Today*'s ad meter award.[87] The humor points to how being hungry makes one grumpy and that Snickers satisfies that hunger.

ILLUSTRATION 11-8

Humor is widely used in advertising to attract attention and alter attitudes.

While it is generally recommended that humor be relevant, companies have been successful using humor that is only loosely tied to the product (e.g., Geico's Gecko ads in which the confusion between the two creates the humor, even though the Gecko has nothing to do with auto insurance). In these cases, humor attracts attention, and the positive emotional response may transfer to the brand via classical conditioning or Aad.[88] Humorous ads also involve risk. What is considered funny varies across individuals, cultures, and situations.[89] Humor viewed as demeaning or insulting can cost a company image and sales.

Comparative Ads **Comparative ads** *directly compare the features or benefits of two or more brands* (see Illustration 11–9). Comparative ads are often more effective than noncomparative ads in generating attention, message and brand awareness, greater message processing, favorable sponsor brand attitudes, and increased purchase intentions and behaviors. However, comparative ads can also have negative consequences for the sponsor brand such as lower believability, lower attitude toward the ad and sponsor brand, and

ILLUSTRATION 11-9

Comparison ads can be very effective at changing attitudes about lesser-known brands.

more positive attitude toward the competitor brand(s).[90] Available evidence suggests that comparative ads should follow these guidelines:[91]

- Comparative advertising may be particularly effective for promoting new or little-known brands with strong product attributes to create their position or to upgrade their image by association. When established brands use comparative ads, they may appear "defensive." This may be particularly true if comparisons are seen as overly derogatory.
- Comparative advertising is likely to be more effective if its claims are substantiated by credible sources. Also, research should be used to determine the optimal number of claims.
- Audience characteristics, especially brand loyalty associated with the sponsoring brand, are important. Users of the named competitor brands appear to resist comparative claims.
- Since comparative ads are more interesting than noncomparatives (and more offensive), they may be effective in stagnant categories where noncomparative ads have ceased to be effective.
- Print media appear to be better vehicles for comparative advertisements because print lends itself to more thorough comparisons.
- Care must be used with *partially* comparative ads because of their misleading potential. A partially comparative ad contains comparative and noncomparative information and may lead consumers to believe the sponsor brand is superior on all attributes, not just the compared attributes.

Emotional Appeals Emotional or feeling ads are being used with increasing frequency. **Emotional ads** are *designed primarily to elicit a positive affective response rather than to provide information or arguments.* Emotional ads such as those that arouse feelings of warmth trigger physiological reactions (see Chapter 10). Emotional advertisements may enhance persuasion by increasing[92]

- Attention and processing of the ad and, therefore, ad recall.
- Liking of the ad.
- Product liking through classical conditioning.
- Product liking through high-involvement processes.

As we discussed previously, whether emotional ads operate through classical conditioning and Aad (low involvement) or through more analytical high-involvement processes depends on the relevance of the emotion to evaluating key aspects of the product.

In addition, emotional ads appear to work better than rational or informational ads for heavy (versus light) users of a brand and more established (versus new) brands in a market. This effect may be due to the fact that heavy users and established brands already have an established knowledge base for attribute information, making emotions a more compelling differentiating feature.[93] The Prize Not Fighter ad by the Humane Society in Illustration 11–10 is designed to elicit emotional responses.

ILLUSTRATION 11-10

Ads such as the Humane Society's Prize Not Fighter ad evoke powerful emotional responses in some individuals. These emotional responses often facilitate attitude change.

Value-Expressive versus Utilitarian Appeals **Value-expressive appeals** attempt to build a personality for the product or create an image of the product user. **Utilitarian appeals** involve informing the consumer of one or more functional benefits that are important to the target market. Which is best under what conditions?

ILLUSTRATION 11-11

Utilitarian appeals such as the Ballistic Wallet ad generally work best with functional products; value-expressive appeals such as the Sally Hansen ad work best with products designed to enhance one's image or provide other intangible benefits.

Both theory and some empirical evidence indicate that *utilitarian* appeals are most effective for functional products and *value-expressive* appeals are most effective for products designed to enhance self-image or provide other intangible benefits.[94] Which to use can be difficult when, as in the case of automobiles, many consider the product primarily utilitarian while many others consider it primarily value-expressive. Some marketers hedge their bets in such situations by appealing to both aspects simultaneously. Illustration 11–11 contains an example of each approach. Which appeal is primarily being used in the Sally Hansen ad versus the Ballistic Wallet ad?

Research also indicates that banner ads on websites should differ for the two types of products. For utilitarian products, banner ads serve primarily to transport consumers to the more detailed target ads or sites. For value-expressive products, banner ads should influence attitudes on the basis of exposure to the banner ad itself, not on clickthrough to the target ad.[95]

Message Structure Characteristics

One-Sided versus Two-Sided Messages In advertisements and sales presentations, marketers generally present only the benefits of their product without mentioning any negative characteristics it might possess or any advantages a competitor might have. These are **one-sided messages** because only one point of view is expressed. The idea of a **two-sided message,** presenting both good and bad points, is counterintuitive, and most marketers are reluctant to try such an approach. However, two-sided messages are generally more effective than one-sided messages in changing a strongly held attitude. One reason is because they are unexpected and increase consumer trust in the advertiser. They are particularly effective with highly educated consumers. One-sided messages are most effective at reinforcing existing attitudes. However, product type, situational variables, and advertisement format influence the relative effectiveness of the two approaches.[96]

Positive versus Negative Framing **Message framing** refers to presenting one of two equivalent value outcomes either in positive or gain terms (positive framing) or in negative or loss terms (negative framing). There are various *types* of message frames and the type of frame influences whether positive or negative framing is better.[97] The simplest form appears to be **attribute framing,** where only a single attribute is the focus of the frame. A classic example is describing ground beef as either 80 percent fat free (positive frame) or 20 percent fat (negative frame). In attribute framing situations, positive framing yields the most positive evaluations because it emphasizes the desirable aspects of the specific attribute.

Goal framing is where "the message stresses either the positive consequences of performing an act or the negative consequences of not performing the act."[98] The act could be purchasing a specific brand, having a yearly mammogram, and so on. In each case the act is beneficial. However, in the positive frame, the benefits of the act are emphasized (e.g., increased chance of finding a tumor), while in the negative frame, the risks of not engaging in the act are emphasized (e.g., decreased chance of finding a tumor). In goal framing situations, the *negative* frame is generally more effective. This is likely due to the risk-averse nature of consumers coupled with the risk-enhancing nature of the negative goal frame.

Framing effects can vary across products, consumers, and situations. Thus, decisions to use positive or negative framing should ultimately be based on research for the specific product and market.[99]

Nonverbal Components In Chapter 9, we discussed how pictures enhance imagery and facilitate learning. Pictures, music, surrealism, and other nonverbal cues are also effective in attitude change. Emotional ads, described earlier, often rely primarily or exclusively on nonverbal content to arouse an emotional response. Nonverbal ad content can also affect cognitions about a product. For example, an ad showing a person drinking a new beverage after exercise provides information about appropriate usage situations without stating "good to use after exercise." Thus, nonverbal components can influence attitudes through affect, cognition, or both.

MARKET SEGMENTATION AND PRODUCT DEVELOPMENT STRATEGIES BASED ON ATTITUDES

LO6

Market Segmentation

Identifying market segments is a key aspect of marketing. Properly designed marketing programs should be built around the unique needs of each market segment. The importance of various attributes is one way of defining customer needs for a given product. *Segmenting consumers on the basis of their most important attribute or attributes* is called **benefit segmentation.**[100]

To define benefit segments, a marketer needs to know the importance that consumers attach to various product or service features. This allows consumers who seek the same benefits to be grouped into segments. Additional information about consumers within each segment can then be obtained to develop a more complete picture of each segment. Based on this information, separate marketing programs can be developed for each of the selected target segments.

Product Development

While the importance consumers attach to key attributes provides a meaningful way to understand needs and form benefit segments, the ideal levels of performance indicate the consumers' desired level of performance in satisfying those needs. These ideal levels of

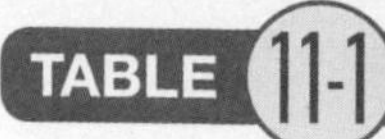

TABLE 11-1 Using the Multiattribute Attitude Model in the Product Development Process

A. Ideal soft drink*

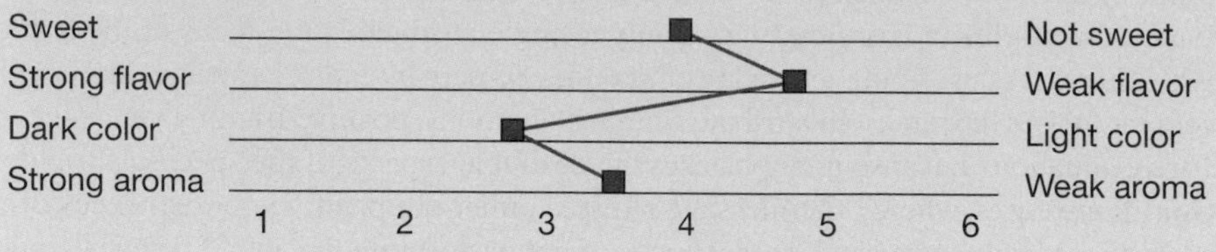
Sweet
Strong flavor
Dark color
Strong aroma
Not sweet
Weak flavor
Light color
Weak aroma
1
2
3
4
5
6

B. Product concept*

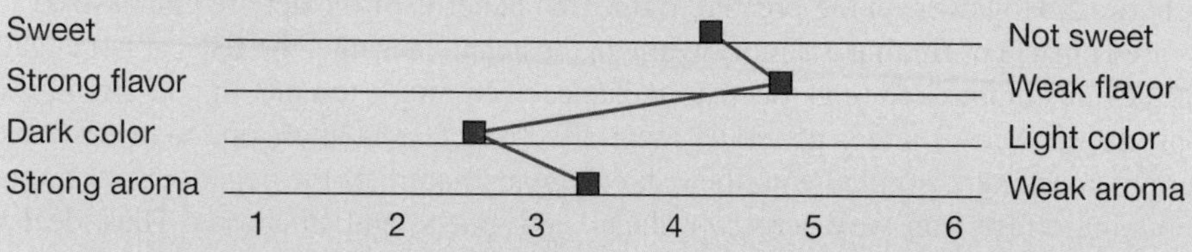
Sweet
Strong flavor
Dark color
Strong aroma
Not sweet
Weak flavor
Light color
Weak aroma
1
2
3
4
5
6

C. Actual product*

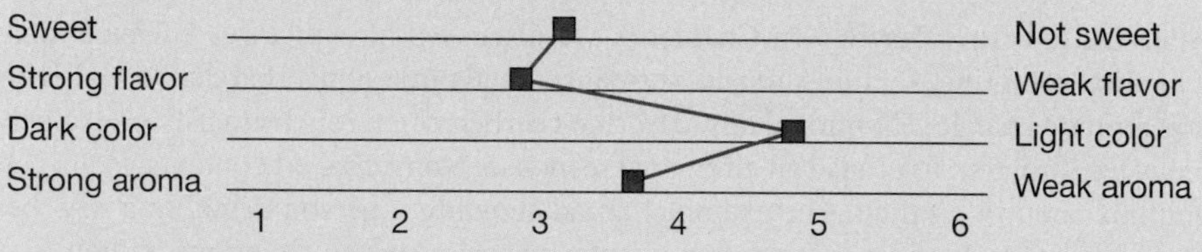
Sweet
Strong flavor
Dark color
Strong aroma
Not sweet
Weak flavor
Light color
Weak aroma
1
2
3
4
5
6

D. Attitude toward concept and product

$$
\begin{aligned}
A_{\text{concept}} &= 25\,|\,4.17 - 4.43\,| + 25\,|\,4.63 - 4.90\,| + 25\,|\,3.16 - 2.60\,| + 25\,|\,3.64 - 3.62\,| \\
&= 25(.15) + 25(.27) + 25(.56) + 25(.02) \\
&= 25
\end{aligned}
$$

$$
\begin{aligned}
A_{\text{product}} &= 25\,|\,4.17 - 3.25\,| + 25\,|\,4.63 - 3.17\,| + 25\,|\,3.16 - 4.64\,| + 25\,|\,3.64 - 3.68\,| \\
&= 25(.92) + 25(1.46) + 25(1.48) + 25(.04) \\
&= 97.5
\end{aligned}
$$

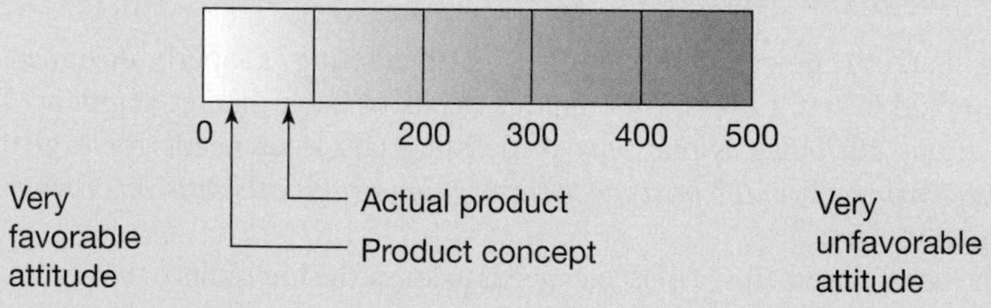
0
200
300
400
500
Very favorable attitude
Actual product
Product concept
Very unfavorable attitude

*Measured on a six-point semantic differential scale.

performance can provide valuable guidelines in developing a new product or reformulating an existing one.

Table 11–1 describes how Coca-Cola used this approach in developing a new soft drink.[101] The first step is constructing a profile of a consumer segment's ideal level of performance on key soft drink attributes. As shown in Table 11–1, four attributes were identified for a particular type of soft drink, and ideal performance was obtained from consumer ratings as shown in section A.

A second step is creating a product concept that closely matches the ideal profile. The concept could be a written description, picture, or actual prototype. As section B in Table 11–1 shows, consumers evaluated the product concept developed by Coca-Cola as being fairly close to their ideal on each of the four attributes. Only color appears to be off target slightly by being a little too dark.

The next step is translating the concept into an actual product. When Coca-Cola did this and presented the product to the consumers, they did not perceive it to be similar to either the product concept or their ideal (see section C in Table 11–1). Although the actual product achieved a reasonable attitude rating, the product concept scored higher (section D, Table 11–1). Thus, the product could benefit from further improvements to better align it with the ideal profile. This same basic procedure can be used to help design ads, packages, or retail outlets.

SUMMARY

LO1: Define attitude and its role in consumer behavior

Attitudes can be defined as the way people think, feel, and act toward some aspect of their environment. A result of all the factors discussed so far in the text, attitudes influence, as well as reflect, the lifestyle individuals pursue.

LO2: Summarize the three components of attitudes

Attitudes have three components: cognitive, affective, and behavioral. The *cognitive component* consists of the individual's beliefs or knowledge about the object. It is generally assessed by using a version of the multiattribute attitude model. Feelings or emotional reactions to an object represent the *affective component* of the attitude and can be assessed in various ways including AdSAM®. The *behavioral component* reflects overt actions and statements of behavioral intentions with respect to specific attributes of the object or the overall object. In general, all three components tend to be consistent with each other. However, a number of factors can create inconsistencies and marketers must understand and incorporate these in their marketing research and communications strategies.

LO3: Discuss attitude change strategies associated with each attitude component

Attitude change strategies can focus on affect, behavior, cognition, or some combination. Attempts to change affect generally rely on classical conditioning. Change strategies focusing on behavior rely more on operant conditioning. Changing cognitions usually involves information processing and cognitive learning. It can involve changing beliefs about such things as a brand's attribute levels, shifting the importance of a given attribute, adding beliefs about new attributes, or changing the perceived ideal point for a specific attribute or for the brand concept overall.

LO4: Describe the elaboration likelihood model of persuasion

The *elaboration likelihood model (ELM)* is a theory about how attitudes are formed and changed under varying conditions of involvement. The ELM suggests different communications strategies depending on involvement. In general, detailed factual information (central cues) is effective in high-involvement, central route situations. Low-involvement, peripheral route situations generally require limited information and instead rely on simple affective and cognitive cues such as pictures, music, and characteristics of people in the ad (peripheral cues). The ELM has found general support. However, what is perceived as relevant can depend on the situation (e.g., attractive model and hair may be "central" in shampoo ad but "peripheral" in car ad), and the nature of competition can bolster the role of peripheral cues even under high involvement.

LO5: Describe the role of message source, appeal, and structure on attitudes

Three communication characteristics are important to attitudes. They are source characteristics, message appeal characteristics, and message structure characteristics.

In terms of source characteristics, *source credibility* is composed of two dimensions: trustworthiness and expertise. Persuasion is much easier when the message source is viewed as highly credible. Celebrities are widely used as product or company spokespersons. They are most effective when their image matches the personality of the product and the actual or desired self-concept of the target market.

In terms of message appeals, the appeals used to change attitudes are important and are varied. *Fear appeals* use threat of negative consequences if attitudes or behaviors are not altered. *Humorous appeals* can also be effective in influencing attitudes. However, the humorous message must remain focused on the brand or main selling point to be maximally effective. *Comparative ads* produce mixed results. They are most effective for unknown brands having a strong functional advantage. The decision to use a *value-expressive* or *utilitarian appeal* depends on whether the brand fills value-expressive or utilitarian needs. However, this is complicated when the brand fills both types of needs. *Emotional appeals* have been found to have a strong effect on attitudes toward both the ad and the product.

Message structure has three facets. *Two-sided* (versus *one-sided*) *messages* can increase trust and message acceptance, but effects depend on characteristics of the individual and situation. *Message framing* effects—presenting equivalent value outcomes either in positive (positive framing) or negative (negative framing) terms—depend on type of frame. Positive *attribute framing* tends to work best whereas negative *goal framing* tends to work best. *Nonverbal* aspects of the ad, such as pictures, surrealism, and music, also affect attitudes.

LO6: Discuss segmentation and product development applications of attitudes

Consumer evaluations, feelings, and beliefs about specific product features form the basis for market segmentation strategies, such as *benefit segmentation,* and for new-product development strategies.

KEY TERMS

Aesthetic appeal 388
Affective component 387
Ambivalent attitude 391
Attitude 384
Attribute framing 407
Behavioral component 388
Benefit segmentation 407
Cognitive component 384
Comparative ads 404
Elaboration likelihood model (ELM) 395
Emotional ads 405
Fear appeals 401
Goal framing 407
Humorous appeals 403
Mere exposure 394
Message framing 407
Multiattribute attitude model 385
One-sided messages 406
Source credibility 398
Spokescharacters 400
Sponsorship 400
Testimonial ad 398
Two-sided message 406
Utilitarian appeals 405
Value-expressive appeals 405

REVIEW QUESTIONS

1. What is an *attitude?*
2. What are the components of an attitude?
3. Are the components of an attitude consistent? What factors reduce the apparent consistency among attitude components?
4. What is the *multiattribute attitude model?*
5. What is *attitude ambivalence?*
6. What strategies can be used to change the following components of an attitude?
   a. Affective
   b. Behavioral
   c. Cognitive
7. What is meant by *mere exposure?*
8. What is the *elaboration likelihood model?*
9. What strategies can consumers use to resist persuasion? Which consumers are most likely to do so?
10. What are the two characteristics of the source of a message that influence its ability to change attitudes? Describe each.
11. What is *source credibility?* What causes it?
12. Why are celebrity sources sometimes effective? What risks are associated with using a celebrity source?

13. Name five possible characteristics of an appeal that would influence or change attitudes. Describe each.
14. Are *fear appeals* always effective in changing attitudes? Why?
15. What characteristics should *humorous ads* have?
16. Are *emotional appeals* effective? Why?
17. Are *comparative appeals* effective? Why?
18. What is a *value-expressive appeal?* A *utilitarian appeal?* When should each be used?
19. What are the three characteristics of the message structure that influence its ability to change attitudes? Describe each.
20. What is meant by *positive message framing* and *negative message framing?* How does the effectiveness of a positive versus negative frame vary depending on whether it's a *goal frame* or *attribute frame?*
21. What are the nonverbal components of an ad? What impact do they have on attitudes?
22. When is a *two-sided message* likely to be more effective than a *one-sided message?*
23. How can attitudes guide new-product development?
24. What is a *benefit segment?*

DISCUSSION QUESTIONS

25. Which version of the multiattribute attitude model and which attributes would you use to assess student attitudes toward the following? Justify your answer.
    a. Student health system
    b. Target store
    c. Hybrid automobiles
    d. Cats as pets
    e. Amp
26. Respond to the questions in Consumer Insight 11–1.
27. Assume you wanted to improve or create favorable attitudes among college students toward the following. Would you focus primarily on the affective, cognitive, or behavioral component? Why?
    a. ASPCA
    b. BMW motorcycles
    c. Organic eggs
    d. Sky diving
    e. Not driving after drinking
    f. Using the bus for most local trips
    g. Oreo cookies
    h. Volunteering for Habitat for Humanity
28. Suppose you used the multiattribute attitude model and developed a fruit-based carbonated drink that was successful in the United States. Could you use the same model in the following countries? If not, how would it have to change?
    a. India
    b. Chile
    c. Qatar
29. Suppose you wanted to form highly negative attitudes toward smoking among college students.
    a. Which attitude component would you focus on? Why?
    b. Which message characteristic would you use? Why?
    c. What type of appeal would you use? Why?
30. What communications characteristics would you use in an attempt to improve college students' attitudes toward the following?
    a. Buick
    b. Levis
    c. Volunteering at a local shelter
    d. Gmail
    e. MADD
    f. White-water rafting
31. Is it ethical to use fear appeals to increase demand for the following?
    a. Complexion medication among teenagers
    b. Dandruff-control shampoos among adults
    c. Emergency response devices among elderly consumers
    d. Weight-loss supplements for young women
32. Name two appropriate and two inappropriate celebrity spokespersons for each of the products or causes in Question 27. Justify your selection.
33. What benefit segments do you think exist for the following?
    a. Crossroads Guitar Festival
    b. NASCAR
    c. Major art museums
    d. Jazz concert

APPLICATION ACTIVITIES

34. Find and copy two magazine or newspaper advertisements, one based on the affective component and the other on the cognitive component. Discuss the approach of each ad in terms of its copy and illustration and what effect it creates in terms of attitude. Also discuss why the marketer might have taken that approach in each advertisement.
35. Repeat Activity 34 for utilitarian and value-expressive appeals.
36. Identify a television commercial that uses a humorous appeal. Then interview five individuals not enrolled in your class and measure their
    a. Awareness of this commercial
    b. Recall of the brand advertised
    c. Recall of relevant information
    d. Liking of the commercial
    e. Preference for the brand advertised

    Evaluate your results and assess the level of communication that has taken place in terms of these five consumers' exposure, attention, interpretation, and preferences for this product and commercial.
37. Describe a magazine, Internet, or television advertisement, or a package that uses the following. Evaluate the effectiveness of the ad or package.
    a. Aesthetic appeal
    b. Source credibility
    c. Celebrity source
    d. Testimonial
    e. Fear appeal
    f. Humorous appeal
    g. Emotional appeal
    h. Comparative approach
    i. Extensive nonverbal elements
    j. A two-sided appeal
    k. Positive message framing
    l. Negative message framing
38. Measure another student's ideal beliefs and belief importance for the following. Examine these ideal beliefs and importance weights and then develop a verbal description (i.e., concept) of a new brand for these items that would satisfy this student's needs. Next, measure that student's attitude toward the concept you have developed in your verbal description.
    a. Sunglasses
    b. Spa
    c. Automobile
    d. Credit card
    e. Dietary supplements
    f. Charity
39. Use the multiattribute attitude model to assess 10 students' attitudes toward several brands in the following product categories. Measure the students' behavior with respect to these brands. Are they consistent? Explain any inconsistencies.
    a. Television news program
    b. Sports drinks
    c. Healthy dinners
    d. Fast-food restaurants
    e. Exercise
    f. Coffee shops
40. Develop two advertisements for the following with college students as the target. One ad should focus on the cognitive component and the other on the affective component.
    a. Timex sport watches
    b. Toyota Prius
    c. Red Bull energy drink
    d. Reducing smoking
    e. Increasing exercise
    f. Reebok athletic shoes
41. Repeat Activity 40 using utilitarian and value-expressive appeals.
42. Develop a positively framed and an equivalent negatively framed message about a product attribute. Have five students react to these messages. What do you conclude?

REFERENCES

1. This opener is based on "Michael Phelps' Sponsors Sticking with Him after Bong Photo," *Associated Press,* February 2, 2009; K. Hein, "Are Celebrity Endorsers Really Worth the Trouble?," *Brandweek,* February 9, 2009; "Nike Won't Drop Tiger Woods," www.x17online.com/celebrities, December 12, 2009, accessed June 6, 2011; Y. Upadhyay and S. K. Singh, "When Sports Celebrity Doesn't Perform," *Vision,* January–June 2010; E. B. York, "Celeb Dieters," *Advertising Age,* February 15, 2010, p. 10; D. Tilkin, "Study on Tiger," www.kval.com/news/business, February 11, 2011, accessed June 6, 2011; and L. I. Alpert, "Tag Heuer Drops Tiger," *New York Post,* June 10, 2011.

2. See R. E. Petty, D. T. Wegener, and L. R. Fabriger, "Attitudes and Attitude Change," *Annual Review of Psychology,* 48 (1997), pp. 609–38.
3. J. A. Ruth, "Promoting a Brand's Emotional Benefits," *Journal of Consumer Psychology,* 11, no. 2 (2001), pp. 99–113.
4. B. Wansink and M. M. Cheney, "Leveraging FDA Health Claims," *Journal of Consumer Affairs,* 39, no. 2 (2005), pp. 386–98.
5. See M. Wanke, G. Bohner, and A. Jurkowitsch, "There Are Many Reasons to Drive a BMW," *Journal of Consumer Research,* September 1997, pp. 170–77.
6. K. E. Voss, E. R. Spangenberg, and B. Grohmann, "Measuring the Hedonic and Utilitarian Dimensions of Consumer Attitude," *Journal of Marketing Research,* August 2003, pp. 310–20; T. Lageat, S. Czellar, and G. Laurent, "Engineering Hedonic Attributes to Generate Perceptions of Luxury," *Marketing Letters,* July 2003, pp. 97–109; and R. Chitturi, R. Raghunathan, and V. Mahajan, "Delight by Design," *Journal of Marketing,* May 2008, pp. 48–63.
7. G. C. Bruner II and A. Kumar, "Explaining Consumer Acceptance of Handheld Internet Devices," *Journal of Business Research,* 58 (2005), pp. 553–58.
8. C. T. Allen et al., "A Place for Emotion in Attitude Models," *Journal of Business Research,* 58 (2005), pp. 494–99.
9. C. Page and P. M. Herr, "An Investigation of the Processes by Which Product Design and Brand Strength Interact to Determine Initial Affect and Quality Judgments," *Journal of Consumer Psychology,* 12, no. 2 (2002), pp. 133–47; and H. Hagtvedt and V. M. Patrick, "Art Infusion," *Journal of Marketing Research,* June 2008, pp. 379–89.
10. J. D. Morris et al., "The Power of Affect," *Journal of Advertising Research,* May–June 2002, pp. 7–17; and J. D. Morris, "Observations: SAM," *Journal of Advertising Research,* November–December 1995, pp. 63–68.
11. For an excellent review, see P. A. Dabholkar, "Incorporating Choice into an Attitudinal Framework," *Journal of Consumer Research,* June 1994, pp. 100–18. See also Morris et al., "The Power of Affect"; P. E. Grimm, "A_b Components' Impact on Brand Preference," *Journal of Business Research,* 58 (2005), pp. 508–17; and P. M. Homer, "Relationships among Ad-Induced Affect, Beliefs, and Attitudes," *Journal of Advertising,* Spring 2006, pp. 35–51.
12. R. E. Petty and J. A. Krosnick, *Attitude Strength* (Mahwah, NJ: Erlbaum, 1995); S. J. Kraus, "Attitudes and the Prediction of Behavior," *Personality and Social Psychology Bulletin,* 21 (1995), pp. 58–75; R. Madrigal, "Social Identity Effects in a Belief-Attitude-Intentions Hierarchy," *Psychology & Marketing,* February 2001, pp. 145–65; and W. E. Baker, "The Diagnosticity of Advertising Generated Brand Attitudes in Brand Choice Contexts," *Journal of Consumer Psychology,* 11, no. 2 (2001), pp. 129–39.
13. S. O. Olsen, J. Wilcox, and U. Olsson, "Consequences of Ambivalence on Satisfaction and Loyalty," *Psychology & Marketing,* March 2005, pp. 247–69; and C. Homburg, N. Koschate, and W. D. Hoyer, "The Role of Cognition and Affect in the Formation of Customer Satisfaction," *Journal of Marketing,* July 2006, pp. 21–31. See also C. A. Roster and M. L. Richins, "Ambivalence and Attitudes in Consumer Replacement Decisions," *Journal of Consumer Psychology,* 19 (2009), pp. 48–61.
14. See, e.g., J. R. Priester et al., "The A^2SC^2 Model: The Influence of Attitudes and Attitude Strength on Consideration and Choice," *Journal of Consumer Research,* March 2004, pp. 574–87; and B. Johnson, "Consumers Cite Past Experience as the No. 1 Influencer When Buying," *Advertising Age,* November 20, 2006, p. 21.
15. See S. A. Hawkins, S. J. Hoch, and J. Meyers-Levy, "Low-Involvement Learning," *Journal of Consumer Psychology,* 11, no. 31 (2001), pp. 1–11.
16. For guidelines on structuring message arguments to enhance beliefs, see C. S. Areni, "The Proposition–Probability Model of Argument Structure and Message Acceptance," *Journal of Consumer Research,* September 2002, pp. 168–87.
17. N. Zmuda, "Rebranding Resuscitates 90-Year-Old Radio Shack," *Advertising Age,* April 12, 2010, p. 16.
18. See A. Drolet and J. Aaker, "Off-Target?," *Journal of Consumer Psychology,* 12, no. 1 (2002), pp. 59–68; and A. H. Tangari et al. "How Do Antitobacco Campaign Advertising and Smoking Status Affect Beliefs and Intentions?," *Journal of Public Policy and Marketing,* Spring 2007, pp. 60–74.
19. M. R. Forehand and R. Deshpande, "What We See Makes Us Who We Are," *Journal of Marketing Research,* August 2001, pp. 336–48. See also J. K. Maher and M. Hu, "The Priming of Material Values on Consumer Information Processing of Print Advertisements," *Journal of Current Issues and Research in Advertising,* Fall 2003, pp. 21–30.
20. From website at www.pomegranates.org/techinfo.html, accessed June 10, 2011.
21. For a discussion of program-induced affect and extremity of beliefs, see R. Adaval, "How Good Gets Better and Bad Gets Worse," *Journal of Consumer Research,* December 2003, pp. 352–67.
22. See M. J. J. M. Candel and J. M. E. Pennings, "Attitude-Based Models for Binary Choices," *Journal of Economic Psychology* 20 (1999), pp. 547–69; and H.-P. Erb, A. Bioy, and D. J. Hilton, "Choice Preferences without Inferences," *Journal of Behavioral Decision Making,* July 2002, pp. 251–62.
23. See, e.g., W. E. Baker, "When Can Affective Conditioning and Mere Exposure Directly Influence Brand Choice?," *Journal of Advertising,* Winter 1999, pp. 31–46; and B. D. Till and R. L. Priluck, "Stimulus Generalization in Classical Conditioning," *Psychology & Marketing,* January 2000, pp. 55–72.
24. See, e.g., R. E. Goldsmith, B. A. Lafferty, and S. J. Newell, "The Impact of Corporate Credibility and Celebrity Credibility on Consumer Reaction to Advertisements and Brands," *Journal of Advertising,* Fall 2000, pp. 43–54; and K. S. Coulter, "An Examination of Qualitative vs. Quantitative Elaboration Likelihood Effects," *Psychology & Marketing,* January 2005, pp. 31–49.
25. J. S. Stevenson, G. C. Bruner II, and A. Kumard, "Webpage Background and Viewer Attitudes," *Journal of Advertising Research,* January 2000, pp. 29–34; and G. C. Bruner II and A. Kumard, "Web Commercials and Advertising Hierarchy-of-Effects," *Journal of Advertising Research,* January 2000, pp. 35–43. See also L. Dailey, "Navigational Web Atmospherics," *Journal of Business Research,* 57 (2004), pp. 795–803.

26. J. R. Coyle and E. Thorson, "The Effects of Progressive Levels of Interactivity and Vividness in Web Marketing Sites," *Journal of Advertising,* Fall 2001, pp. 65–77.

27. See M.-H. Huang, "Is Negative Affect in Advertising General or Specific?," *Psychology Marketing,* May 1997, pp. 223–40. See also P. S. Ellen and P. F. Bone, "Does It Matter if It Smells?," *Journal of Advertising,* Winter 1998, pp. 29–39.

28. A. Rindfleisch and J. J. Inman, "Explaining the Familiarity-Liking Relationship," *Marketing Letters,* 1 (1998), pp. 5–19; E. L. Olson and H. M. Thjomoe, "The Effects of Peripheral Exposure to Information on Brand Preference," *European Journal of Marketing,* 37, no. 1/2 (2003), pp. 243–55; and G. Menon and P. Raghubir, "Ease-of-Retrieval as an Automatic Input in Judgments," *Journal of Consumer Research,* September 2003, pp. 230–43.

29. S. Auty and C. Lewis, "Exploring Children's Choice," *Psychology & Marketing,* September 2004, pp. 697–713.

30. See Ruth, "Promoting a Brand's Emotional Benefits"; R. Adaval, "Sometimes It Just Feels Right," *Journal of Consumer Research,* June 2001, pp. 1–17; M. T. Pham et al., "Affect Monitoring and the Primacy of Feelings in Judgment," *Journal of Consumer Research,* September 2001, pp. 167–88; and C. W. M. Yeung and R. S. Wyer Jr., "Affect, Appraisal, and Consumer Judgment," *Journal of Consumer Research,* September 2004, pp. 412–24.

31. See D. S. Kempf, "Attitude Formation from Product Trial," *Psychology & Marketing,* January 1999, pp. 35–50.

32. D. A. Griffith and Q. Chen, "The Influence of Virtual Direct Experience (VDE) on On-line Ad Message Effectiveness," *Journal of Advertising,* Spring 2004, pp. 55–68.

33. See G. J. Gaeth et al., "Consumers' Attitude Change across Sequences of Successful and Unsuccessful Product Usage," *Marketing Letters,* 1 (1997), pp. 41–53; and L. A. Brannon and T. C. Brock, "Limiting Time for Response Enhances Behavior Corresponding to the Merits of Compliance Appeals," *Journal of Consumer Psychology,* 10, no. 3 (2001), pp. 135–46.

34. See, e.g., M. L. Roehm and B. Sternthal, "The Moderating Effect of Knowledge and Resources on the Persuasive Impact of Analogies," *Journal of Consumer Research,* September 2001, pp. 257–72; M. Moorman, P. C. Neijens, and E. G. Smit, "The Effects of Magazine-Induced Psychological Responses and Thematic Congruence on Memory and Attitude toward the Ad in a Real-Life Setting," *Journal of Advertising,* Winter 2002, pp. 27–40; and S. Putrevu, J. Tan, and K. R. Lord, "Consumer Responses to Complex Advertisements," *Journal of Current Issues and Research in Advertising,* Spring 2004, pp. 9–24.

35. See R. E. Petty, J. T. Cacioppo, and D. Schumann, "Central and Peripheral Routes to Advertising Effectiveness," *Journal of Consumer Research,* September 1993, pp. 135–46; J. Meyers-Levy and P. Malaviya, "Consumers' Processing of Persuasive Advertisements," *Journal of Marketing,* 63 (1999), pp. 45–60; C. S. Areni, "The Effects of Structural and Grammatical Variables on Persuasion," *Psychology & Marketing,* April 2003, pp. 349–75; and D. D. Rucker and R. E. Petty, "Increasing the Effectiveness of Communications to Consumers," *Journal of Public Policy and Marketing,* Spring 2006, pp. 39–52. For additional perspectives, see T. P. Novak and D. L. Hoffman, "The Fit of Thinking Style and Situation," *Journal of Consumer Research,* June 2009, pp. 56–72; and M. L. Cronley, S. P. Mantel, and F. R. Kardes, "Effects of Accuracy Motivation and Need to Evaluate on Mode of Attitude Formation and Attitude-Behavior Consistency," *Journal of Consumer Psychology,* 20 (2010), pp. 274–81.

36. See, e.g., Petty and Krosnick, *Attitude Strength.* For a discussion of attitude persistence under low involvement, see J. Sengupta, R. C. Goodstein, and D. S. Boninger, "All Cues Are Not Created Equal," *Journal of Consumer Research,* March 1997, pp. 351–61.

37. P. W. Miniard et al., "Picture-Based Persuasion Processes and the Moderating Role of Involvement," *Journal of Consumer Research,* June 1991, pp. 92–107.

38. P. W. Miniard, D. Sirdeshmukh, and D. E. Innis, "Peripheral Persuasion and Brand Choice," *Journal of Consumer Research,* September 1992, pp. 226–39; and T. B. Heath, M. S. McCarthy, and D. L. Mothersbaugh, "Spokesperson Fame and Vividness Effects in the Context of Issue-Relevant Thinking," *Journal of Consumer Research,* March 1994, pp. 520–34. See also B. Yoo and R. Mandhachitara, "Estimating Advertising Effects on Sales in a Competitive Setting," *Journal of Advertising Research,* September 2003, pp. 310–21; and S. S. Posavac et al., "The Brand Positivity Effect," *Journal of Consumer Research,* December 2004, pp. 643–51.

39. T. F. Mangleburg and T. Bristol, "Socialization and Adolescents' Skepticism toward Advertising," *Journal of Advertising,* Fall 1998, pp. 11–21; C. Obermiller and E. R. Spangenberg, "On the Origin and Distinctiveness of Skepticism toward Advertising," *Marketing Letters,* November 2000, pp. 311–22; and D. M. Hardesty, J. P. Carlson, and W. O. Bearden, "Brand Familiarity and Invoice Price Effects on Consumer Evaluations," *Journal of Advertising,* Summer 2002, pp. 1–15.

40. M. C. Campbell and A. Kirmani, "Consumers' Use of Persuasion Knowledge," *Journal of Consumer Research,* June 2000, pp. 69–83; R. Ahluwalia and R. E. Burnkrant, "Answering Questions about Questions," *Journal of Consumer Research,* June 2004, pp. 26–42; and D. M. Hardesty, W. O. Bearden, and J. P. Carlson, "Persuasion Knowledge and Consumer Reactions to Pricing Tactics," *Journal of Retailing,* 83, no. 2 (2007), pp. 199–210.

41. R. Ahlusalia, "Examination of Psychological Processes Underlying Resistance to Persuasion," *Journal of Consumer Research,* September 2000, pp. 217–32.

42. A. Wang, "The Effects of Expert and Consumer Endorsements on Audience Response," *Journal of Advertising Research,* December 2005, pp. 402–12; R. Arora, C. Stoner, and A. Arora, "Using Framing and Credibility to Incorporate Exercise and Fitness in Individual's Lifestyle," *Journal of Consumer Marketing,* 23, no. 4 (2006), pp. 199–207; and D. Biswas, A. Biswas, and N. Das, "The Differential Effects of Celebrity and Expert Endorsements on Consumer Risk Perceptions," *Journal of Advertising,* Summer 2006, pp. 17–31.

43. R. D. Reinartz, "Testimonial Ads," *Bank Marketing,* March 1996, pp. 25–30; J. Nicholson, "Testimonial Ads Defend Client Turf," *Editor & Publisher,* October 23, 1999, p. 33; and O. Appiah, "The Effectiveness of 'Typical-User' Testimonial Advertisements on Black and White Browsers' Evaluations of Products on Commercial Websites," *Journal of Advertising Research,* March 2007, pp. 14–27.

44. Wang, "The Effects of Expert and Consumer Endorsements on Audience Response."

45. D. H. Dean, "Brand Endorsement, Popularity, and Event Sponsorship as Advertising Cues Affecting Pre-Purchase Attitudes," *Journal of Advertising,* Fall 1999, pp. 1–11; and D. H. Dean and A. Biswas, "Third-Party Organization Endorsement of Products," *Journal of Advertising,* Winter 2001, pp. 41–57.

46. Goldsmith, Lafferty, and Newell, "The Impact of Corporate Credibility and Celebrity Credibility on Consumer Reaction to Advertisements and Brands"; B. A. Lafferty, R. E. Goldsmith, and S. J. Newell, "The Dual Credibility Model," *Journal of Marketing Theory and Practice,* Summer 2002, pp. 1–12; and Z. Gurhan-Canli and R. Batra, "When Corporate Image Affects Product Evaluations," *Journal of Marketing Research,* May 2004, pp. 197–205.

47. S. P. Jain and S. S. Posavac, "Prepurchase Attribute Verifiability, Source Credibility, and Persuasion," *Journal of Consumer Psychology,* 11, no. 3 (2001), pp. 169–80.

48. See P. M. Homer and L. R. Kahle, "Source Expertise, Time of Source Identification, and Involvement in Persuasion," *Journal of Advertising,* 19, no. 1 (1990), pp. 30–39.

49. C. Pornpitakpan and J. N. P. Francis, "The Effect of Cultural Differences, Source Expertise, and Argument Strength on Persuasion," *Journal of International Consumer Marketing,* 13, no. 1 (2001), pp. 77–101.

50. D. J. Moore, J. C. Mowen, and R. Reardon, "Multiple Sources in Advertising Appeals," *Journal of the Academy of Marketing Science,* Summer 1994, pp. 234–43. See also N. Artz and A. M. Tybout, "The Moderating Impact of Quantitative Information on the Relationship between Source Credibility and Persuasion," *Marketing Letters* 10, no. 1 (1999), pp. 51–62.

51. Sengupta, Goodstein, and Boninger, "All Cues Are Not Created Equal"; B. Z. Erdogan, M. J. Baker, and S. Tagg, "Selecting Celebrity Endorsers," *Journal of Advertising Research,* May–June 2001, pp. 39–48; M. R. Stafford, N. E. Spears, and C.-K. Hsu, "Celebrity Images in Magazine Advertisements," *Journal of Current Issues and Research in Advertising,* Fall 2003, pp. 13–20; and A. J. Bush, C. A. Martin, and V. D. Bush, "Sports Celebrity Influence on the Behavioral Intentions of Generation Y," *Journal of Advertising Research,* March 2004, pp. 108–18.

52. Knowledge Networks, "Michael Jordan Trumps Tiger, Lance in Influence on Purchase Consideration," press release, October 27, 2003, www.knowledgenetworks.com.

53. M. Tenser, "Endorser Qualities Count More Than Ever," *Advertising Age,* November 8, 2004, p. S2.

54. B. D. Till and M. Busler, "The Match-Up Hypothesis," *Journal of Advertising,* Fall 2000, pp. 1–13; Erdogan, Baker, and Tagg, "Selecting Celebrity Endorsers"; A. B. Bower and S. Landreth, "Is Beauty Best?," *Journal of Advertising,* Spring 2001, pp. 1–12; and R. Batra and P. M. Homer, "The Situational Impact of Brand Image Beliefs," *Journal of Consumer Psychology,* 14, no. 3 (2004), pp. 318–30.

55. "Avril Lavigne's Style Comes to Kohl's," *StarNewsOnline.com,* March 12, 2008. See also J. Chebatoris, "Avril Lavigne Is Sew Cool," *Newsweek,* March 17, 2008, p. 69.

56. K. Macarthur, "BK and Paris," *Advertising Age,* August 30, 2004, p. 6.

57. M. T. Liu, Y. Huang, and J. Minghua, "Relations among Attractiveness of Endorsers, Match-up, and Purchase Intention in Sport Marketing in China," *Journal of Consumer Marketing,* 24, no. 6 (2007), pp. 358–65.

58. C. Tripp, T. D. Jensen, and L. Carlson, "The Effects of Multiple Product Endorsements by Celebrities on Consumers' Attitudes and Intentions," *Journal of Consumer Research,* March 1994, pp. 535–47; and J. R. Priester and R. E. Petty, "The Influence of Spokesperson Trustworthiness on Message Elaboration, Attitude Strength, and Advertising Effectiveness," *Journal of Consumer Psychology,* 13, no. 4 (2003), pp. 408–21.

59. B. D. Till and T. A. Shimp, "Endorsers in Advertising," *Journal of Advertising,* Spring 1998, pp. 67–82; and T. A. Louie, R. L. Kulik, and R. Jacobson, "When Bad Things Happen to the Endorsers of Good Products," *Marketing Letters,* February 2001, pp. 13–23.

60. J. A. Garretson and R. W. Niedrich, "Spokes-Characters," *Journal of Advertising,* Summer 2004, pp. 25–36; and J. A. Garretson and S. Burton, "The Role of Spokescharacters as Advertisement and Package Cues in Integrated Marketing Communications," *Journal of Marketing,* October 2005, pp. 118–32.

61. For an excellent overview, see T. Meenaghan, "Understanding Sponsorship Effects," *Psychology & Marketing,* February 2001, pp. 95–122; see also B. Walliser, "An International Review of Sponsorship Research," *International Journal of Advertising,* 22 (2003), pp. 5–40.

62. "North American Sponsorship Spending Seen Up in '08," *Reuters.com,* January 22, 2008, www.reuters.com.

63. R. Thomaselli, "Nextel Sees Payoff as NASCAR Sponsor," *Advertising Age,* May 31, 2004, p. 3.

64. R. Thomaselli, "Offical Sponsors Score with World Cup," *Advertising Age,* July 26, 2010, p. C-3.

65. R. Madrigal, "The Influence of Social Alliances with Sports Teams on Intentions to Purchase Corporate Sponsors' Products," *Journal of Advertising,* Winter 2000, pp. 13–24.

66. N. Zmuda, "Children's Hospital in Hot Water over Corporate Sponsorships," *AdAge.com,* March 12, 2008, http://adage.com.

67. S. R. McDaniel, "An Investigation of Match-Up Effects in Sport Sponsorship Advertising," *Psychology & Marketing,* March 1999, pp. 163–84; N. J. Rifon et al., "Congruence Effects in Sponsorships," *Journal of Advertising,* Spring 2004, pp. 29–42; T. B. Cornwell, S. W. Pruitt, and J. M. Clark, "The Relationship between Major-League Sports' Official Sponsorship Announcements and the Stock Prices of Sponsoring Firms," *Journal of the Academy of Marketing Science,* 33, no. 4 (2005), pp. 401–12; and N. D. Fleck and P. Quester, "Birds of a Feather Flock Together," *Psychology & Marketing,* November 2007, pp. 975–1000.

68. C. Pechmann et al., "What to Convey in Antismoking Advertisements for Adolescents," *Journal of Marketing,* April 2003, pp. 1–18; M. S. LaTour and J. F. Tanner Jr., "Randon," *Psychology & Marketing,* May 2003, pp. 377–94; and J. P. Dillard and J. W. Anderson, "The Role of Fear in Persuasion," *Psychology & Marketing,* November 2004, pp. 909–26.

69. P. A. Keller and L. G. Block, "Increasing the Persuasiveness of Fear Appeals," *Journal of Consumer Research,* March 1996,

pp. 448–60; M. S. LaTour and H. J. Rotfeld, "There Are Threats and (Maybe) Fear-Caused Arousal," *Journal of Advertising,* Fall 1997, pp. 45–59; and M. Laroche et al., "A Cross-Cultural Study of the Persuasive Effect of Fear Appeal Messages in Cigarette Advertising," *International Journal of Advertising,* 3 (2001), pp. 297–317.

70. K. Passyn and M. Sujan, "Self-Accountability Emotions in Fear Appeals," *Journal of Consumer Research,* March 2006, pp. 583–89.

71. M. N. Gardner and A. M. Brandt, "The Physician in US Cigarette Advertisements, 1930–1953," *American Journal of Public Health,* February 2006, pp. 222–32.

72. R. R. Vernellia, *The History of Tobacco* (Boston University Medical Center, Community Outreach Health Information System, 1999), http://academic.udayton.edu/health/syllabi/tobacco/history.htm, accessed August 27, 2014.

73. "Hanna-Barbera Production *Flintstones*—Winston Compilation (1960)," UCSF Tobacco Industry Videos, https://archive.org/details/tobacco_djq03d00, accessed August 27, 2014.

74. S. Egan, "Why *Smoking* Rates Are at New Lows," *The New York Times,* June 25, 2013, http://well.blogs.nytimes.com/2013/06/25/why-smoking-rates-are-at-new-lows/, accessed August 27, 2014.

75. 15 U.S.C. § 1335, "Unlawful Advertisements on Medium of Electronic Communication" (Cornell University Law School: Legal Information Institute), www.law.cornell.edu/uscode/text/15/1335, accessed August 27, 2014.

76. "U.S. Smoking Bans, State By State," *Huffington Post,* May 25, 2011, www.huffingtonpost.com/2011/02/23/smoking-bans-state-by-sta_n_826672.html#s244139title=Alabama_, accessed August 27, 2014.

77. "Highlights: Warning Labels," *Center for Disease Control and Prevention,* www.cdc.gov/tobacco/data_statistics/sgr/2000/highlights/labels/, accessed August 27, 2014.

78. G. T. Fong, D. Hammond, and S. C. Hitchman, "The Impact of Pictures on the Effectiveness of Tobacco Warnings," *Bulletin of the World Health Organization,* August 2009, pp. 640–43.

79. A. C. Villanti, J. Cantrell, J. L. Pearson, D. M. Vallone, and J. M. Rath, "Perceptions and Perceived Impact of Graphic Cigarette Health Warning Labels on Smoking Behavior among U.S. Young Adults," *Nicotine & Tobacco Research,* March 14, 2014, pp. 469–77.

80. S. Almasy, "FDA Changes Course on Graphic Warning Labels for Cigarettes," *CNN,* March 20, 2013, www.cnn.com/2013/03/19/health/fda-graphic-tobacco-warnings/, accessed August 27, 2014.

81. M. McArdle, "E-Cigarettes: A $1.5 Billion Industry Braces for FDA Regulation," *Bloomberg Businessweek,* February 6, 2014, www.businessweek.com/articles/2014-02-06/e-cigarettes-fda-regulation-looms-for-1-dot-5-billion-industry#p1, accessed August 27, 2014.

82. See M. S. LaTour, R. L. Snipes, and S. J. Bliss, "Don't Be Afraid to Use Fear Appeals," *Journal of Advertising Research,* March 1996, pp. 59–66.

83. D. L. Alden, A. Mukherjee, and W. D. Hoyer, "The Effects of Incongruity, Surprise and Positive Moderators and Perceived Humor in Television Advertising," *Journal of Advertising,* Summer 2000, pp. 1–14; K. Flaherty, M. G. Weinberger, and C. S. Gulas, "The Impact of Perceived Humor, Product Type, and Humor Style in Radio Advertising," *Journal of Current Issues and Research in Advertising,* Spring 2004, pp. 25–36; and J. Elpers, A. Mukherjee, and W. D. Hoyer, "Humor in Television Advertising," *Journal of Consumer Research,* December 2004, pp. 592–98.

84. T. W. Cline, M. B. Altsech, and J. J. Kellaris, "When Does Humor Enhance or Inhibit Ad Responses?," *Journal of Advertising,* Fall 2003, pp. 31–45.

85. M. Eisend, "A Meta-Analysis of Humor in Advertising," *Journal of the Academy of Marketing Science,* 37 (2009), pp. 191–203.

86. See, e.g., H. S. Krishnan and D. Chakravarti, "A Process Analysis of the Effects of Humorous Advertising Executions on Brand Claims Memory," *Journal of Consumer Psychology,* 13, no. 3 (2003), pp. 230–45.

87. E. B. York, "Snickers Uses Humor to Satisfy Generations of Hunger," *Advertising Age,* March 29, 2010, p. 22.

88. H. Chung and X. Zhao, "Humour Effect on Memory and Attitude," *International Journal of Advertising,* 22 (2003), pp. 117–44; and Y. Zhang and G. M. Zinkhan, "Responses to Humorous Ads," *Journal of Advertising,* Winter 2006, pp. 113–27.

89. D. L. Fugate, J. B. Gotlieb, and D. Bolton, "Humorous Services Advertising," *Journal of Professional Services Marketing,* 21, no. 1 (2000), pp. 9–22; M. F. Toncar, "The Use of Humour in Television Advertising," *International Journal of Advertising,* 20 (2001), pp. 521–39; and K. Macarthur, "Subway Cans Schtick to Focus on Food in Its Creative," *Advertising Age,* March 1, 2004, p. 4.

90. D. Grewal et al., "Comparative versus Noncomparative Advertising," *Journal of Marketing,* October 1998, pp. 1–15; M. E. Hill and M. King, "Comparative vs. Noncomparative Advertising," *Journal of Current Issues and Research in Advertising,* Fall 2001, pp. 33–52; K. C. Manning et al., "Understanding the Mental Representations Created by Comparative Advertising," *Journal of Advertising,* Summer 2001, pp. 27–39; L. D. Compeau, D. Grewal, and R. Chandrashekaran, "Bits, Briefs, and Applications," *Journal of Consumer Affairs,* Winter 2002, pp. 284–94; and J. R. Priester et al., "Brand Congruity and Comparative Advertising," *Journal of Consumer Psychology,* 14, no. 1/2 (2004), pp. 115–23.

91. A. Chattopadhyay, "When Does Comparative Advertising Influence Brand Attitude?," *Psychology & Marketing,* August 1998, pp. 461–75; M. J. Barone and P. W. Miniard, "How and When Factual Ad Claims Mislead Consumers," *Journal of Marketing Research,* February 1999, pp. 58–74; S. V. Auken and A. J. Adams, "Across- versus Within-Class Comparative Advertising," *Psychology & Marketing,* August 1999, pp. 429–50; A. B. Sorescu and B. D. Gelb, "Negative Comparative Advertising," *Journal of Advertising,* Winter 2000, pp. 25–40; S. P. Jain, B. Buchanan, and D. Maheswaran, "Comparative versus Non-comparative Advertising," *Journal of Consumer Psychology*, 9, no. 4 (2000), pp. 201–11; A. V. Muthukrishnan, L. Warlop, and J. W. Alba, "The Piecemeal Approach to Comparative Advertising," *Marketing Letters,* 12, no. 1 (2001), pp. 63–73; S. P. Jain and S. S. Posavac, "Valenced

Comparisons," *Journal of Marketing Research,* February 2004, pp. 46–58; and M. J. Barone, K. M. Palan, and P. W. Miniard, "Brand Usage and Gender as Moderators of the Potential Deception Associated with Partial Comparative Advertising," *Journal of Advertising,* Spring 2004, pp. 19–28.

92. See, e.g., M. E. Hill et al., "The Conjoining Influences of Affect and Arousal on Attitude Formation," *Research in Consumer Behavior,* 9 (2000), pp. 129–46; J. D. Morris et al., "The Power of Affect," *Journal of Advertising Research,* May–June 2002, pp. 7–17; M.-H. Huang, "Romantic Love and Sex," *Psychology & Marketing,* January 2004, pp. 53–73; and D. J. MacInnis and G. E. de Mello, "The Concept of Hope and Its Relevance to Product Evaluation and Choice," *Journal of Marketing,* January 2005, pp. 1–14.

93. R. K. Chandy et al., "What to Say When," *Journal of Marketing Research,* November 2001, pp. 399–414; and R. D. Jewell and H. R. Unnava, "Exploring Differences in Attitudes between Light and Heavy Brand Users," *Journal of Consumer Psychology,* 14, no. 1/2 (2004), pp. 75–80.

94. J. S. Johar and M. J. Sirgy, "Value-Expressive versus Utilitarian Advertising Appeals," *Journal of Advertising,* September 1991, pp. 23–33; S. Shavitt, "Evidence for Predicting the Effectiveness of Value-Expressive versus Utilitarian Appeals," *Journal of Advertising,* June 1992, pp. 47–51; M. E. Slama and R. B. Singley, "Self-Monitoring and Value-Expressive vs. Utilitarian Ad Effectiveness," *Journal of Current Issues and Research in Advertising,* Fall 1996, pp. 39–49; L. Dube, A. Chattopadhyay, and A. Letarte, "Should Advertising Appeals Match the Basis of Consumers' Attitudes?," *Journal of Advertising Research,* November 1996, pp. 82–89; and J.-S. Chiou, "The Effectiveness of Different Advertising Message Appeals in the Eastern Emerging Society," *International Journal of Advertising,* 21 (2002), pp. 217–36.

95. M. Dahlen and J. Bergendahl, "Informing and Transforming on the Web," *International Journal of Advertising,* 20, no. 2 (2001), pp. 189–205.

96. A. E. Crowley and W. D. Hoyer, "An Integrative Framework for Understanding Two-Sided Persuasion," *Journal of Consumer Research,* March 1994, pp. 561–74; G. Bohner et al., "When Small Means Comfortable," *Journal of Consumer Psychology,* 13, no. 4 (2003), pp. 454–63; and M. Eisend, "Understanding Two-Sided Persuasion," *Psychology & Marketing,* July 2007, pp. 615–40.

97. I. P. Levin, S. L. Schneider, and G. J. Gaeth, "All Frames Are Not Created Equal," *Organizational Behavior and Human Decision Processes,* November 1998, pp. 149–88.

98. Ibid.

99. P. A. Keller, I. M. Lipkus, and B. K. Rimer, "Affect, Framing, and Persuasion," *Journal of Marketing Research,* February 2003, pp. 54–64; J. Meyers-Levy and D. Maheswaran, "Exploring Message Framing Outcomes When Systematic, Heuristic, or Both Types of Processing Occur," *Journal of Consumer Psychology,* 14, no. 1/2 (2004), pp. 159–67; and B. Shiv, J. A. E. Britton, and J. W. Payne, "Does Elaboration Increase or Decrease the Effectiveness of Negatively versus Positively Framed Messages?," *Journal of Consumer Research,* June 2004, pp. 199–208.

100. See, e.g., J. W. Peltier and J. A. Schribrowsky, "The Use of Need-Based Segmentation for Developing Segment-Specific Direct Marketing Strategies," *Journal of Direct Marketing,* Fall 1997, pp. 53–62; and R. Ahmad, "Benefit Segmentation," *International Journal of Marketing Research,* 45 (2003), pp. 373–88.

101. H. E. Bloom, "Match the Concept and the Product," *Journal of Advertising Research,* October 1977, pp. 25–27.

chapter

12 Self-Concept and Lifestyle

LEARNING OBJECTIVES

LO1 **Describe self-concept, how it is measured, and how it is used to position products.**

LO2 **Define lifestyle and its relationship to the self-concept and to psychographics.**

LO3 **Explain specific lifestyle typologies and summarize those for luxury sports cars and technology.**

LO4 **Explain general lifestyle typologies and summarize those for VALS™ and PRIZM®.**

LO5 **Discuss international lifestyles and one existing segmentation scheme.**

In Chapter 2 we identified a cross-cultural group we called the global youth, with similar values and consumption patterns across culture. A new study suggests another such group based on luxury consumption that can be termed the global elite. The global market for luxury is estimated at $2 trillion and growing. Brands such as Gucci, Armani, and Louis Vuitton are vying for their share of this global market in the fashion arena. Four fashion lifestyle segments emerged in a study that examined female consumers in the United States, Korea, and Europe. The segments and their characteristics are:[1]

- *Conspicuous consumers* (19 percent)—love prestige brands; they value the status that luxury brands give them. They are concerned with others' opinions. They are less price conscious, willing to sacrifice to have lux brands, and believe lux brands offer higher quality. They won't search brands they don't know. Marketing emphasis should be prestige and status.
- *Information seekers* (27 percent)—want luxury brands as well but spend considerable time searching out information about lux brands, including brands they don't know very well. They do so to keep up with fashion and trends, which are things they are very interested in. Marketing emphasis should be quality and trends.
- *Sensation seekers* (30 percent)—value the aesthetics in fashion. Color is particularly important, as is their belief that they "have an eye for fashion." They are less influenced by fashion information than are information seekers because they believe they know fashion. Marketing emphasis should be eye-catching, coordinated fashion.
- *Utilitarian consumers* (25 percent)—want comfort and functionality in their clothing. They feel that clothes' shopping is a chore, which is very different from the other segments that enjoy shopping and searching for fashion and luxury in different ways. They are price conscious. Marketing emphasis should be function and value.

An additional aspect of the study was that how consumers reacted to fashion advertising was more influenced by their shopper lifestyle typology than by their country of origin. So, for example, whether from the United States, Korea, or Europe, women in the conspicuous consumer segment were more similar to each other in their reactions to luxury ads and brands than they were to those from their own country but in a different segment. Such similarities across countries offer strong support for the notion of a global elite consumer who can be marketed to in a similar manner regardless of the country in which she resides as shown in the Delta "Keep Climbing" ad.

In this chapter, we will discuss the meaning of lifestyle and the role it plays in developing marketing strategies. Lifestyle is, in many ways, an outward expression of one's self-concept. That is, the way an individual chooses to live, given the constraints of income and ability, is heavily influenced by that person's current and desired self-concept. Therefore, we begin the chapter with an analysis of the self-concept. We then describe lifestyles, the ways lifestyle is measured, and examples of how lifestyle is being used to develop marketing programs.

SELF-CONCEPT

LO1

Self-concept is defined as *the totality of the individual's thoughts and feelings having reference to himself or herself as an object.* It is an individual's perception of and feelings toward him- or herself. In other words, your self-concept is composed of the attitudes you hold toward yourself.

The self-concept can be divided into four basic parts, as shown in Table 12–1: actual versus ideal, and private versus social. The actual–ideal distinction refers to the individual's perception of *who I am now* (**actual self-concept**) and *who I would like to be* (**ideal self-concept**). The private self refers to *how I am or would like to be to myself* (**private self-concept**), and the social self is *how I am seen by others or how I would like to be seen by others* (**social self-concept**).

Interdependent/Independent Self-Concepts

The self-concept is important in all cultures. However, those aspects of the self that are most valued and most influence consumption and other behaviors vary across cultures. Researchers have found it useful to categorize self-concepts into two types: independent and interdependent, also referred to as one's separateness and connectedness.[2]

An independent construal of the self is based on the predominant Western cultural belief that individuals are inherently separate. The **independent self-concept** *emphasizes personal goals, characteristics, achievements, and desires.* Individuals with an independent self-concept tend to be individualistic, egocentric, autonomous, self-reliant, and self-contained. They define themselves in terms of what they have done, what they have, and their personal characteristics.[3]

An interdependent construal of the self is based more on the common Asian cultural belief in the fundamental connectedness of human beings. The **interdependent self-concept** *emphasizes family, cultural, professional, and social relationships.* Individuals with an interdependent self-concept tend to be obedient, sociocentric, holistic, connected, and relation oriented. They define themselves in terms of social roles, family relationships, and commonalities with other members of their groups.

Independent and interdependent self-concepts are not discrete categories; rather, they are constructs used to describe the opposite ends of a continuum along which most cultures lie.

TABLE 12-1 Dimensions of a Consumer's Self-Concept

Dimensions of Self-Concept	Actual Self-Concept	Ideal Self-Concept
Private self	How I actually see myself	How I would like to see myself
Social self	How others actually see me	How I would like others to see me

However, as we emphasized in Chapter 2, most cultures are heterogeneous. Therefore, within a given culture, subcultures and other groups will vary on this dimension, as will individuals.[4] For example, women across cultures tend to have more of an *interdependent* self-concept than do men.[5]

Variation in the degree to which an individual or culture is characterized by an independent versus an interdependent self-concept has been found to influence message preferences, consumption of luxury goods, and the types of products preferred. For example, ads emphasizing acting alone and autonomy tend to be effective with consumers with independent self-concepts, whereas ads emphasizing group membership work better with consumers with interdependent self-concepts.[6] The ad in Illustration 12–1 should be effective with individuals whose independent self-concept is dominant.

ILLUSTRATION 12-1

Ads work best when their appeal matches the dominant type of self-concept held by the target market. This ad will be effective with the independent self-concept common in Western cultures.

However it is also important to note that ads themselves can cue self-concepts and make them more salient at least for some consumers. In a study of Gen X Chinese consumers, individualistic ads made the independent self-concept more salient, while collectivist ads made the interdependent self-concept more salient. This makes sense if you view these consumers as younger and bicultural in that they are navigating between traditional and emerging value sets. Ads, therefore, can influence the weight placed on a given value set.[7]

Possessions and the Extended Self

Some products acquire substantial meaning to an individual or are used to signal particularly important aspects of that person's self to others. Belk developed a theory called the *extended self* to explain this.[8] The **extended self** consists of *the self plus possessions;* that is, people tend to define themselves in part by their possessions. Thus, some possessions are not just a manifestation of a person's self-concept; they are an integral part of that person's self-identity. People are, to some extent, what they possess. If one were to lose key possessions, he or she would be a somewhat different individual.[9]

While these key possessions might be major items, such as one's home or automobile, they are equally likely to be smaller items with unique meanings, such as a souvenir, a photograph, a pet, or a favorite cooking pan. Such objects have meaning to the individual beyond their market value. Consider these statements from consumers who lost their possessions in natural disasters and who had ample insurance to replace them:

> Yea, we got better stuff, but it doesn't mean anything to us. It's just stuff.
>
> You can't put back or replace what you had. It was too personal—it was customized.[10]

Products become part of one's extended self for a variety of reasons. Souvenirs often become part of the extended self as representations of memories and feelings:

> You can't really tell what Paris is like . . . you know, a lot of it is just feelings; feelings you can't put into words, or [that] pictures cannot capture. . . . They [a hat and blouse] are just reminders.
>
> I had a really wonderful trip and really sort of discovered myself; you know, I learned to be independent on my own. I really didn't have the money to buy this [necklace and boomerang charm], but I decided I wanted something really permanent. . . . The boomerang is a symbol of going back there sometime.[11]

Gifts often take on important meanings as representations of relationships:

> That gift was my grandfather's ring. . . . Even now when I look at it, I think about its past with him and the journeys it took around the world in the Navy back in World War II.
>
> The key chain is special because every so often, when I think about who gave it to me, it brings back old thoughts and feelings. It is a symbol of friendship between us, and it keeps us in touch.[12]

Some products become embedded with meaning, memories, and value as they are used over time, as with an old baseball glove. At other times, a single peak experience with a product such as a mountain bike can propel the product into the extended self. A **peak experience** is *an experience that surpasses the usual level of intensity, meaningfulness, and richness and produces feelings of joy and self-fulfillment.*[13] Finally, products that are acquired or used to help consumers with major life transitions (e.g., leaving home, first job, marriage) are also likely to be or become part of the extended self.[14]

Extended self can also relate to nonproduct entities such as activities (golfing), other people (my best friend), TV shows (*Star Trek*), and sports teams (Green Bay Packers).

A scale has been developed to measure the extent to which an item has been incorporated into the extended self.[15] It is a Likert scale (see Appendix A) in which consumers express levels of agreement (from strongly agree to strongly disagree on a seven-point scale) to the following statements:

- My _____ helps me achieve the identity I want to have.
- My _____ helps me narrow the gap between what I am and what I try to be.
- My _____ is central to my identity.
- My _____ is part of who I am.
- If my _____ is stolen from me I will feel as if my identity has been snatched from me.
- I derive some of my identity from my _____.

Owning a product affects a person even if it does not become an important part of the person's extended self. The **mere ownership effect,** or the *endowment effect,* is *the tendency of an owner to evaluate an object more favorably than a nonowner.* This occurs almost immediately upon acquiring an object and increases with time of ownership. Thus, people tend to value an object more after acquiring it than before. People also tend to value objects they own more highly than they value similar objects owned by others.[16]

The extent to which brands become part of the extended self appears to be affected by individual differences in **brand engagement.** Brand engagement *refers to the extent to which an individual includes important brands as part of his or her self-concept.*

Sample items used to measure brand engagement include "I have a special bond with the brands that I like," "I often feel a personal connection between my brands and me," and "Part of me is defined by important brands in my life."[17] Research shows that the strongest predictor of brand engagement is materialism. It also shows that consumers with higher brand engagement like products better when the brand logo is prominently displayed on the product. *Which segment from the opener do you feel is highest in brand engagement and materialism? What design aspects relating to logo would be important to this group? Explain.*

The concept of the extended self and the mere ownership effect have numerous implications for marketing strategy. One is that communications that cause potential consumers to *visualize product ownership* may result in enhanced product evaluations. Product sampling or other trial programs may have similar results.

Measuring Self-Concept

Using the self-concept in marketing requires that it be measurable. The most common measurement approach is the semantic differential (see Appendix A). Malhotra has developed a set of 15 pairs of adjectives, shown in Table 12–2. These have proven effective in describing the ideal, actual, and social self-concepts of individuals as well as the images of automobiles and celebrities. *Using this scale, determine your actual and desired private and social self-concepts.*

This instrument can be used to ensure a match between the self-concept (actual or ideal) of a target market, the image of a brand, and the characteristics of an advertising spokesperson. For example, in its decision to sign Serena Williams to a multiyear endorsement contract, Nike undoubtedly saw a match between the desired self-concept of young women, the desired image for Nike's women's athletic apparel line, and the image of Serena Williams.[18]

Measurement Scales for Self-Concepts, Person Concepts, and Product Concepts TABLE 12-2

1. Rugged	___	___	___	___	___	___	___	Delicate
2. Excitable	___	___	___	___	___	___	___	Calm
3. Uncomfortable	___	___	___	___	___	___	___	Comfortable
4. Dominating	___	___	___	___	___	___	___	Submissive
5. Thrifty	___	___	___	___	___	___	___	Indulgent
6. Pleasant	___	___	___	___	___	___	___	Unpleasant
7. Contemporary	___	___	___	___	___	___	___	Noncontemporary
8. Organized	___	___	___	___	___	___	___	Unorganized
9. Rational	___	___	___	___	___	___	___	Emotional
10. Youthful	___	___	___	___	___	___	___	Mature
11. Formal	___	___	___	___	___	___	___	Informal
12. Orthodox	___	___	___	___	___	___	___	Liberal
13. Complex	___	___	___	___	___	___	___	Simple
14. Colorless	___	___	___	___	___	___	___	Colorful
15. Modest	___	___	___	___	___	___	___	Vain

Source: N. K. Malhotra, "A Scale to Measure Self-Concepts, Person Concepts, and Product Concepts," *Journal of Marketing Research*, published by the American Marketing Association; reprinted with permission. November 1981, p. 462.

Using Self-Concept to Position Products

People's attempts to obtain their ideal self-concept, or maintain their actual self-concept, often involve the purchase and consumption of products, services, and media.[19] This process is described in Figure 12–1. While this figure implies a rather conscious and deliberate process, many times that is not the case. For example, a person may drink diet colas because his desired self-concept includes a trim figure, but he is unlikely to think about the purchase in these terms. However, as the following statement illustrates, sometimes people do think in these terms:

> And I feel if you present yourself in the right way, people will start to notice. But this leads back to image and self-worth, which can be achieved through having the right clothes and a good haircut. . . . [H]aving a good portrait of yourself on the outside can eventually lead to an emotionally stable inside.[20]

All this suggests that marketers should strive to develop product images that are consistent with the self-concepts of their target markets.[21] While everyone's self-concept is unique, there is also significant overlap across individuals and groups, which is one basis for market segmentation. For example, many consumers see themselves as environmentalists. Companies and products that create an image of being concerned about or good for the environment are likely to be supported by these consumers.

Consumers maintain and enhance their self-concepts not only by what they consume, but by what they avoid.[22] Some consumers make a point of avoiding certain product categories, such as red meat, or certain brands, such as Nike, as part of maintaining "who they are."

In general, consumers prefer brands that match their self-concepts. However, it is important to realize that the degree to which such "self-image congruity" influences brand preference and choice depends on a number of product, situational, and individual factors. First, self-image congruity is likely to matter more for products such as perfume where value-expressive *symbolism* is critical than for more utilitarian products such as a garage door opener. Second, self-image congruity (especially ideal social self) is likely to matter more when the situation involves *public* or *conspicuous consumption* (e.g., having a beer with friends at a bar) than when consumption is private (e.g., having a beer at home).[23]

FIGURE 12-1 The Relationship between Self-Concept and Brand Image Influence

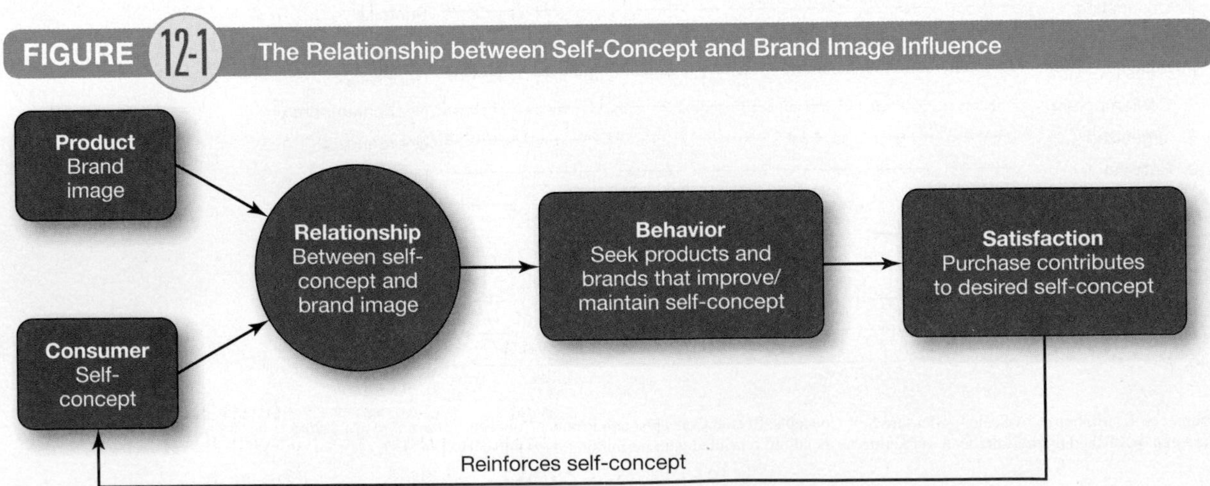

Finally, self-image congruity is likely to matter more for consumers who place heavy weight on the opinions and feelings of others (called *high self-monitors*) than for consumers who do not (called *low self-monitors*), particularly in public situations where consumption behaviors can be observed by others.[24]

Look at Illustration 12–2 and the various aspects of self-concept listed in Table 12–2. *Which aspect(s) of self-concept does this ad appeal to?*

ILLUSTRATION 12-2

Ads that position products to match the self-concept of the target market are generally successful. Such ads can appeal to the consumer's actual or ideal, private or social self.

Marketing Ethics and the Self-Concept

The self-concept has many dimensions. Marketers have been criticized for focusing too much attention on the importance of being beautiful, with *beautiful* being defined as young and slim with a fairly narrow range of facial features. Virtually all societies appear to define and desire beauty, but the intense exposure to products and advertisements focused on beauty in America today is unique. Critics argue that this concern leads individuals to develop self-concepts that are heavily dependent on their physical appearance rather than other equally or more important attributes.

Consider the following statements from two young women:

> I never felt that I looked right. Like I can see outfits that I'd love to wear, but I know that I could never wear them. I probably could wear them and get away with it, but I'd be so self-conscious walking around that I'd be like, "oh, my God." Like I always try to look thinner and I guess everybody does.
>
> I am pretty content with my hair because I have good hair. I have good eyesight (laughs) so I don't have to wear glasses or anything that would make my face look different from what it is. In terms of bad points, well there is a lot. I got a lot of my father's features. I wish I had more of my mother's. My hands are pretty square. I have a kind of a big butt. Then, I don't have that great of a stomach.[25]

These young women have self-concepts that are partly negative as a result of their perceptions of their beauty relative to the standard portrayed in the media. Critics of advertising claim that most individuals, but particularly young women, acquire negative components to their self-concepts because very few can achieve the standards of beauty presented in advertising. Recent research indicates that similar negative self-evaluations occur in males as a result of idealized images of both physical attractiveness and financial success.[26]

The ethical question is complex. No one ad or company has this type of impact. It is the cumulative effect of many ads across many companies reinforced by the content of the mass media that presumably causes some to be overly focused on their physical beauty. And, as stated earlier, concern with beauty existed long before advertising.

Consumer Insight 12–1 delves deeper into the Dove campaigns and the complex issues involved.

CONSUMER INSIGHT 12-1

Mind the Gap—The Real You and the Ideal You

The consumers' actual self is how they see themselves. The consumers' ideal self is how they would like to see themselves. A gap, sometimes small, sometimes big, may exist between the ideal self and the actual self, as discussed earlier in this chapter.

In 2004 Unilever, the parent company of Dove, conducted a survey of 3,200 women in 10 countries (the United States, Japan, Canada, Argentina, the Netherlands, Great Britain, France, Portugal, Italy, and Brazil) to understand what beauty means to women. The study revealed that only 2 percent of women saw themselves as beautiful. Ninety-eight percent of women's perception of their actual beauty fell short of their ideal. The study had identified a gap between women's ideal self-concept and actual self-concept.[27]

Following on the heels of the study, Dove launched the Dove Campaign for Real Beauty to zero in on the gap. The campaign sought to broaden the definition of beauty beyond the stereotypic narrow confines. The campaign included billboard, print, TV, video, and digital advertisements. The billboards featured a woman and two tick box options such as "Fat or Fit?" or "Withered or Wonderful?" and invited passersby to visit a website to cast their votes. The print ads, "featuring six real women with real bodies and real curves," were "created to debunk the stereotype that only thin is beautiful."[28] The enormously successful campaign was showered with media attention and recognized with awards.[29] It also received criticism: the models "are still head-turners, with straight white teeth, no visible pores, and not a cell of cellulite. . . . [T]hey represent a beauty standard still idealized and, for the overwhelming majority of consumers, still pretty damn unattainable."[30]

The next phase of the Dove Real Beauty campaign, Dove Real Beauty Sketch, was launched in 2013 as three- and seven-minute, web-only commercials. A forensic artist sketched two portraits of the person, one as she described herself concealed behind a screen out of the artist's sight—the real self—and another sketch as a stranger described her. The two sketches revealed that strangers saw these women as more attractive than women saw themselves. The video, capturing the heartfelt emotional response by the women—tears, surprise—when they saw the two portraits of themselves went viral and generated substantial buzz.[31] This campaign, like the previous ones, received both support—"a real expression of the insecurity of so many women who tend to sell themselves short"—and criticism—"pandering, soft-focus fake empowerment ads."

Dove is in the beauty business. Its Dove Campaign for Real Beauty focused on acceptance of real beauty beyond the stereotypical beauty ideal. Its Dove Sketch campaign showed women that they are more beautiful than they see themselves. Both campaigns have received accolades for bringing to light the overemphasis of the importance of physical beauty to women's self-concept. Both campaigns have been criticized for its focus on women's beauty and their underlying message of the importance of physical beauty. Hate it or love it, authentic or fake, the campaigns have sold a lot of Dove products.

Critical Thinking Questions

1. Are you aware of the Dove Campaign for Real Beauty? Dove Sketch campaign? What was your initial reaction? Has your reaction changed over time?
2. Dove's parent company Unilever owns Slimfast and Axe. Does this make the Dove Real Beauty and Dove Sketch campaigns a sham? Or can the campaigns still be authentic?
3. The 2004 TV, print, and billboard Dove campaign and the 2013 web-only Dove campaign illustrate the increasing power of social media and viral marketing. What are other social media–driven successful advertising campaigns?

THE NATURE OF LIFESTYLE

LO2

As Figure 12–2 indicates, **lifestyle** is basically *how a person lives.* It is how a person enacts her or his self-concept and is determined by past experiences, innate characteristics, and current situation. One's lifestyle influences all aspects of consumption behavior and is a function of inherent individual characteristics that have been shaped and formed through social interaction as the person has evolved through the life cycle.

The relationship between *lifestyle* and *self-concept* was demonstrated in a recent study comparing various lifestyle-related activities, interests, and behaviors across those with independent versus interdependent self-concepts. *Independents* were more likely to seek adventure and excitement through travel, sports, and entertainment; to be opinion leaders; and to prefer magazines over TV. *Interdependents* were more likely to engage in home and domestic-related activities and entertainment, including cooking at home and from scratch. Interdependents were also more likely to engage in social activities revolving around family and the community.[32]

Individuals and households both have lifestyles. Although household lifestyles are in part determined by the individual lifestyles of the household members, the reverse is also true.

Individuals' *desired* lifestyles influence their needs and desires and thus their purchase and use behavior. Desired lifestyle determines many of a person's consumption decisions, which in turn reinforce or alter that person's lifestyle.

Marketers can use lifestyle to segment and target specific markets. As the chapter's opening vignette illustrates, luxury brands need to adjust their approach to the fashion lifestyle segments. Similarly, those who live the extreme sports lifestyle have a specific pattern of attitudes, behaviors, and purchase patterns that marketers must be aware of and adapt to. Illustration 12–3 shows an ad targeted at the extreme sports enthusiast.

Consumers are seldom explicitly aware of the role lifestyle plays in their purchase decisions. For example, few consumers would think, "I'll have a Starbucks coffee at a Starbucks outlet to maintain my lifestyle." However, individuals pursuing an active, social lifestyle might purchase Starbucks in part because of its convenience, its "in" status, and the presence

Lifestyle and the Consumption Process FIGURE 12-2

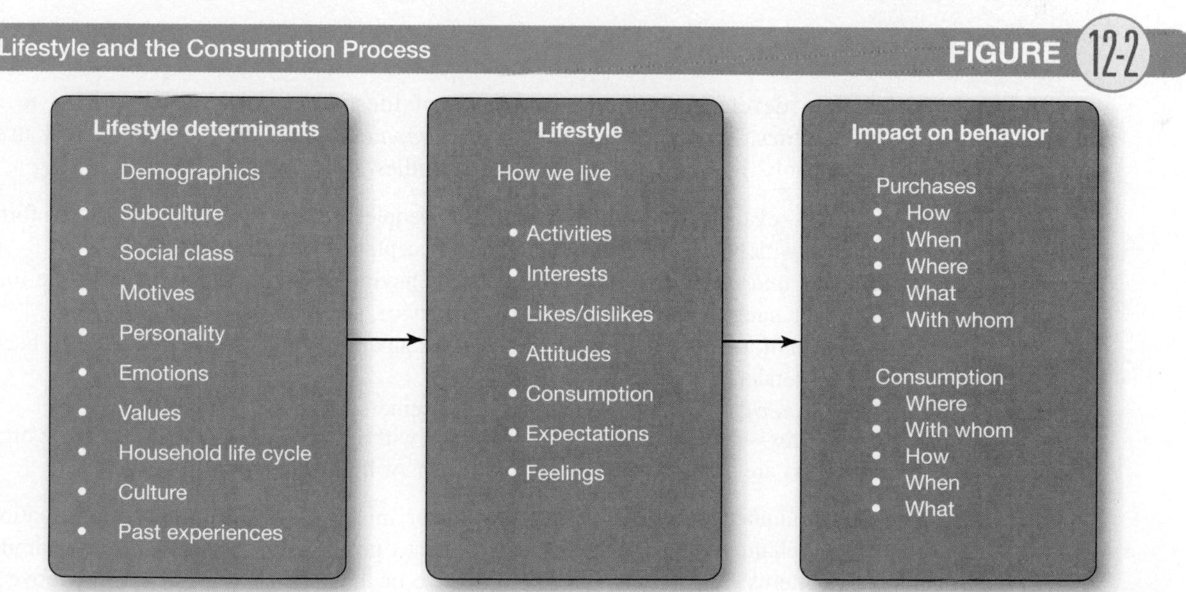

ILLUSTRATION 12-3

This ad targets the lifestyle of extreme sports enthusiasts.

of others at Starbucks outlets. Thus, lifestyle frequently provides the basic motivation and guidelines for purchases, although it generally does so in an indirect, subtle manner.

Measurement of Lifestyle

Attempts to develop quantitative measures of lifestyle were initially referred to as **psychographics.**[33] In fact, the terms *psychographics* and *lifestyle* are frequently used interchangeably. Psychographics or lifestyle studies typically include the following:

- *Attitudes*—evaluative statements about other people, places, ideas, products, and so forth.
- *Values*—widely held beliefs about what is acceptable or desirable.
- *Activities and interests*—nonoccupational behaviors to which consumers devote time and effort, such as hobbies, sports, public service, and church.
- *Demographics*—age, education, income, occupation, family structure, ethnic background, gender, and geographic location.
- *Media patterns*—the specific media the consumers utilize.
- *Usage rates*—measurements of consumption within a specified product category; often consumers are categorized as heavy, medium, or light users or as nonusers.

A large number of individuals, often 500 or more, provide the above information. Statistical techniques are used to place them into groups whose members have similar response patterns. Most studies use the first two or three dimensions described above to group individuals. The other dimensions are used to provide fuller descriptions of each group. Other studies include demographics as part of the grouping process.[34]

General versus Specific Lifestyle Schemes

LO3

Lifestyle measurements can be constructed with varying degrees of specificity. At one extreme, marketers can study the general lifestyle patterns of a population. These general lifestyle approaches are not specific to any one product or activity, so they have broad applicability in developing marketing strategies for a wide range of products and brands. General approaches include VALS™ and PRIZM®, which are discussed in later sections of this chapter.

At the other extreme, firms can conduct very specific lifestyle studies focused on those aspects of individual or household lifestyles most relevant to their product or service. For these studies, lifestyle measurement is product or activity specific. Let's take an in-depth look at two specific lifestyle schemes.

Luxury Sports Cars Porsche examined the lifestyles of its buyers. What they found surprised them a bit because although key demographics (e.g., high education and income) were similar across their buyers, their lifestyles and motivations were quite different. The segments and their descriptions are listed below:[35]

- *Top Guns* (27 percent). Ambitious and driven, this group values power and control and expects to be noticed.
- *Elitists* (24 percent). These old-family-money "blue-bloods" don't see a car as an extension of their personality. Cars are cars no matter what the price tag.
- *Proud Patrons* (23 percent). This group purchases a car to satisfy themselves, not to impress others. A car is a reward for their hard work.
- *Bon Vivants* (17 percent). These thrill seekers and "jet-setters" see cars as enhancing their already exciting lives.
- *Fantasists* (9 percent). This group uses their car as an escape, not as a means to impress others. In fact, they feel a bit of guilt for owning a Porsche.

How would Porsche's marketing approach need to be changed across these different lifestyle segments?

Technology How technology is used by consumers is of critical importance to marketers. Numerous technology and Internet lifestyle profiles exist such as the Technographics segmentation scheme by Forrester Research.[36] Experian Information Systems provides another typology, based on an extensive analysis of attitudes, lifestyle, and adoption and usage patterns related to technology. The segments and their descriptions are listed below:[37]

- *Wizards* (31 percent). Characterized by the statement "Technology is life." Enthusiastic and adventurous users of new technology. Driven by desire for new technology as means for improving all aspects of life. Demographics: Young adults and students (youngest group with mean age of 42); household income, at $79k, is slightly below average; 31 percent nonwhite; trend single and male. Tech lifestyle: First to buy new electronic equipment, likely to purchase products advertised on cell phone, high use for gaming and social aspects. Latest technology includes iPhone, Blu-ray, and Internet TV.
- *Journeymen* (13 percent). Characterized by the statement "Technology is an important part of my life." A notch down from wizards on enthusiasm, this group nonetheless is knowledgeable and confident in their use of new technology. Demographics: Young and established adults (average age is 43); household income, at $104k, is above average; 27 percent nonwhite; trend married with kids. Tech lifestyle: Shop online, e-mail a key influence on shopping, technology a big changer of how they work and spend leisure time. Latest technology includes Blackberry and DVR.
- *Apprentices* (31 percent). Characterized by the statement "Technology is changing my life." Take advantage of new technology, but there is room to grow, and they are willing to grow and learn. Affordability is the key barrier, not attitudes.

ILLUSTRATION 12-4

Experian Information Systems has identified four lifestyle segments related to technology. To which segment(s) will this ad most appeal?

Demographics: Established and middle-aged (average age is 48); household income, at $95k, is slightly above average; 17 percent nonwhite; trend married and female. Tech lifestyle: Technology is used to search and has changed how they gather information. Technology is a major source of information and shopping. Latest technology includes DVD drive on computer, LCD TV, and satellite radio.

- *Novices* (25 percent). Characterized by the statement "Technology has a limited impact on my life." This group is disconnected from emerging technology and resistant to change. Want simple and easy-to-use devices. Attitudinally not engaged. Demographics: Mature adults and retirees (average age is 55); household income, at $61k, is below average; 18 percent nonwhite; trend grandparents. Tech lifestyle: Confused by technology, use cell phone only for calling. E-mail is one of the few online activities. Latest technology includes portable DVD player and DVR in satellite box.

To which of these groups will the ad in Illustration 12–4 appeal?

While specific lifestyle studies are useful, many firms have found general lifestyle studies to be of great value also. Two popular general systems are described next.[38]

THE VALS™ SYSTEM

LO4

By far the most popular application of psychographic research by marketing managers is Strategic Business Insights' (SBI) VALS™ program. **VALS** provides a systematic classification of American adults into eight distinct consumer segments.[39]

VALS is based on enduring psychological characteristics that correlate with purchase patterns. Respondents are classified according to their *primary motivation,* which serves as one of VALS's two dimensions. As we saw in Chapter 10, motives are critical determinants of behavior. Motives have strong linkages to personality and self-concept. Indeed, a core premise behind VALS is that "People buy products and services and seek experiences that fulfill characteristic motives and give shape, substance, and satisfaction to their lives." Three primary motivations underlie VALS:

- *Ideals motivation.* These consumers are guided in their choices by their beliefs and principles rather than by feelings or desire for social approval. They purchase functionality and reliability.
- *Achievement motivation.* These consumers strive for a clear social position and are strongly influenced by the actions, approval, and opinions of others. They purchase status symbols.
- *Self-expression motivation.* These action-oriented consumers strive to express their individuality through their choices. They purchase experiences.

These three orientations determine the types of goals and behaviors that individuals will pursue. Table 12–3 provides more detailed descriptions of the goals, motivations, and behavioral tendencies of each motivational group.

The second dimension, termed *resources,* reflects the ability of individuals to pursue their dominant self-orientation. It refers to the full range of psychological, physical, demographic, and material means on which consumers can draw. Resources generally increase from adolescence through middle age and then remain relatively stable until they begin to decline with older age. Resources are an important part of VALS because they can aid or inhibit a consumer's ability to act on his or her primary motivation.

On the basis of these two concepts, SBI has identified eight general psychographic segments, as shown in Figure 12–3. Table 12–4 provides selected characteristics for each segment. Each of these segments is described briefly next.

The VALS™ Segments

Innovators are successful, sophisticated, take-charge people with high self-esteem. They are change leaders and are the most receptive to new ideas and technologies. Their purchases reflect cultivated tastes for upscale, niche products and services as demonstrated by the Jaguar ad in Illustration 12–5.

Underlying Differences across VALS™ Motivational Types

TABLE 

	Primary Motivation		
	Ideals	**Achievement**	**Self-Expression**
They are	Information seeking	Goal oriented	Spontaneous
They make	Choices based on principles	Choices to enhance position	Choices to have emotional impact
They buy	Functionality and reliability	Success symbols	Experiences
They seek	Understanding	Social approval	Adventure, excitement, novelty
They pursue	Self-development	Self-improvement	Self-reliance
They resist	Impulse	Risk	Authority
They ask	What "should" I do?	What are others like me doing?	What do I feel like doing?

Source: Strategic Business Insights (SBI), www.strategicbusinessinsights.com/vals.

FIGURE 12-3 VALS™ Framework

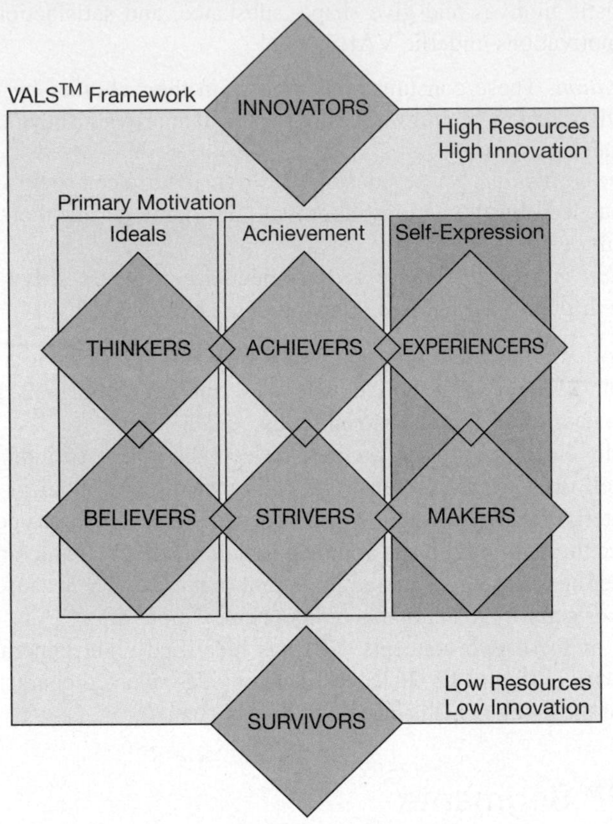

Source: Strategic Business Insights (SBI), www.strategicbusinessinsights.com/vals.

TABLE 12-4 VALS Segments: Selected Characteristics

	Innovators	Thinkers	Believers	Achievers	Strivers	Experiencers	Makers	Survivors
Percent of United States	10	11	16.5	14	11.5	13	12	12
Median age	45	56	52	41	28	24	46	70
Married	65	75	63	72	34	25	68	45
Work full time	72	55	47	70	52	55	59	13
Used Internet last 30 days	98	88	61	93	70	85	68	29
Bought last vehicle used	39	37	50	45	59	53	59	44
Buy organic	26	13	6	9	5	9	6	4
Walk for exercise	52	46	29	37	20	18	26	22
Played golf in past year	18	16	6	15	7	10	7	3
Contributed to NPR/PBS	23	13	3	3	0	0	0	3
Top media	Internet	Newspaper	TV	Internet	Radio	Magazine	Radio	TV
Preferences	Print	Internet	Radio	Magazine	TV	Internet	TV	Newspaper

Note: Except for age and media, numbers represent percent of each group that possesses the characteristic.
Source: Strategic Business Insights (SBI), www.strategicbusinessinsights.com/vals.

ILLUSTRATION 12-5

This Jaguar ad is targeted toward the Innovators' desire for growth and their taste for the finer things in life.

Thinkers are mature, satisfied, comfortable, and reflective. They tend to be well educated and actively seek out information in the decision-making process. They favor durability, functionality, and value in products.

Believers are strongly traditional and respect rules and authority. Because they are fundamentally conservative, they are slow to change and technology averse. They choose familiar products and established brands.

ILLUSTRATION 12-6

This ad for TomTom Runner GPS Watch would appeal to the Achievers' desire to demonstrate success and for products that help them be in control of their lives.

Achievers have goal-oriented lifestyles that center on family and career. They avoid situations that encourage a high degree of stimulation or change. They prefer premium products that demonstrate success to their peers. The TomTom ad in Illustration 12–6 would appeal to the Achievers' desire to demonstrate success and for products that help them be in control of their lives—as emphasized in its "See more. Achieve more" campaign.

Strivers are trendy and fun loving. They have little discretionary income and tend to have narrow interests. They favor stylish products that emulate the purchases of people with greater material wealth. Many Strivers believe that life isn't fair.

Experiencers appreciate the unconventional. They are active and impulsive,

ILLUSTRATION 12-7

Experiencers are impulsive and social. They like new and offbeat things, as shown in this NewMexicoEarth.org ad.

seeking stimulation from the new, offbeat, and risky. They spend a comparatively high proportion of their income on fashion, socializing, and entertainment. The NewMexicoEarth.org ad in Illustration 12–7 would be particularly appealing to this segment.

Makers value practicality and self-sufficiency. They choose hands-on constructive activities and spend leisure time with family and close friends. Because they prefer value to luxury, they buy basic products. Makers prefer to "buy American." The product shown in Illustration 12–8 would appeal to this group.

Survivors lead narrowly focused lives. Because they have the fewest resources, they do not exhibit a primary motivation and often feel powerless. They are primarily concerned about safety and security, so they tend to be brand loyal and buy discounted merchandise. As described in Chapter 4, meeting the needs of these consumers is a challenge for both marketers and public policymakers.

GEO-LIFESTYLE ANALYSIS (NIELSEN PRIZM®)

PRIZM® is a state-of-the-art geo-demographic classification system from The Nielsen Company that merges U.S. Census data with extensive data on product consumption and media usage patterns. The output is a set of 66 lifestyle segments. Each household in the United States can be profiled in terms of these lifestyle groups. The logic of **geo-demographic analysis** is as follows:

> People with similar cultural backgrounds, means and perspectives naturally gravitate toward one another. They choose to live amongst their peers in neighborhoods offering affordable advantages and compatible lifestyles. Once settled in, people naturally emulate their neighbors. They adopt similar social values, tastes and expectations. They exhibit shared patterns of consumer behavior toward products, services, media and promotions.[40]

PRIZM Social and Life Stage Groups

PRIZM organizes its 66 individual segments into broader social and life stage groups.[41] The broadest social groupings are based on "urbanicity." Urbanicity is determined by population density, relates to where people live, and is strongly related to the lifestyles people lead. The four major social groups are:

- *Urban*—major cities with high population density.
- *Suburban*—moderately dense "suburban" areas surrounding metropolitan areas.
- *Second city*—smaller, less densely populated cities or satellites to major cities.
- *Town & Rural*—low-density towns and rural communities.

The broadest life stage groups are based on age and the presence of children. As we saw in Chapter 6, these factors strongly influence consumption patterns and lifestyle. The three major life stage groups are:

- *Younger years*—singles and couples; under 35 years of age without kids, or middle aged without kids *at home.*

ILLUSTRATION 12-8

Makers focus on their families and homes. They are practical and value functional products. This product taps into their self-sufficiency motives.

- *Family life*—households with children *living at home.*
- *Mature years*—singles and couples; age 55 and over, or age 45–64 without children *at home.*

PRIZM gets even finer-grained detail by further dividing each social and life stage group by level of affluence (e.g., income and wealth) because affluence is a strong demographic determinant of activities, consumption patterns, and lifestyle. When possible, Nielsen also merges its general PRIZM information with clients' customer databases as a way to further enhance precision.

Sample PRIZM Segments

We briefly describe six specific segments and use them in demonstrating how PRIZM can be used in developing a successful marketing strategy (for all segments, visit www.MyBestSegments.com).

- *Young Digerati* (Urban/Younger Years—PRIZM segment 04). The Young Digerati are tech-savvy and live in fashionable neighborhoods on the urban fringe. Affluent, highly educated, and ethnically mixed, Young Digerati communities are typically filled with trendy apartments and condos, fitness clubs and clothing boutiques, casual restaurants, and all types of bars—from juice to coffee to microbrew. They watch the Independent Film Channel and drive cars like the Audi A3.
- *Blue Blood Estates* (Suburban/Family—PRIZM segment 02). This is a family portrait of suburban wealth: a place of million-dollar homes and manicured lawns, high-end cars, and exclusive private clubs. The nation's second-wealthiest lifestyle is characterized by married couples with children, graduate degrees, a significant percentage of

Asian Americans, and six-figure incomes earned by business executives, managers, and professionals. They watch video-on-demand and drive cars like the Audi A8.

- *Big Fish, Small Pond* (Town/Mature—PRIZM segment 09). Older, upper-class, college-educated professionals, the members of Big Fish, Small Pond are often among the leading citizens of their small-town communities. These upscale, empty-nesting couples enjoy the trappings of success, including belonging to country clubs, maintaining large investment portfolios, and spending freely on computer technology. They watch events on TV like *The Triple Crown* and drive cars like the Cadillac DTS.
- *Pools & Patios* (Suburban/Mature—PRIZM segment 15). Formed during the postwar baby boom, Pools & Patios has evolved from a segment of young suburban families to one for older, empty-nesting couples. In these stable neighborhoods graced with backyard pools and patios—a large proportion of homes were built in the 1950s and 1960s—residents work as white-collar managers and professionals, and are now at the top of their careers. They watch shows like *24* and drive cars like a Subaru Forester.
- *Young & Rustic* (Town/Younger Years—PRIZM segment 48). Young & Rustic is composed of middle-age, restless singles. These folks tend to be lower-middle-income and high-school-educated, and live in tiny apartments in the nation's exurban towns. With their service industry jobs and modest incomes, these folks still try to fashion fast-paced lifestyles centered on sports, cars, and dating. They watch shows like *WWE Wrestling* and drive cars like the Dodge Ram Diesel.
- *Golden Ponds* (Town/Mature—PRIZM segment 55). Golden Ponds is mostly a retirement lifestyle, dominated by downscale singles and couples over 65 years old. Found in small bucolic towns around the country, these high-school-educated seniors live in small apartments on less than $35,000 a year; one in five resides in a nursing home. For these elderly residents, daily life is often a succession of sedentary activities such as reading, watching TV, playing bingo, and doing craft projects. They watch shows like *The Price is Right* and drive cars like the Mercury Sable.

An Application of PRIZM

Marketing a Las Vegas Casino One Las Vegas casino used PRIZM to identify its core consumers and markets and identify opportunities for future growth. It merged its own customer database with the PRIZM system in order to categorize each customer in its database into one of the 66 segments. With these data, it was able to find out which segments represented its core customers. These segments included *Young Digerati; Big Fish, Small Pond;* and *Pools & Patios.* While consumers in these segments differ in various ways, they are all highly educated, affluent professionals who like to travel.

The casino also looked at which segments were least attractive for its business. These included the *Young and Rustics* and *Golden Ponds.* Given the casino's core customer, these results make sense because both of these segments are less-educated, lower-income consumers who tend to engage in sedentary activities or activities close to home.

Finally, the casino searched for attractive segments that held opportunity but were currently being underleveraged. One such segment was the *Blue Blood Estates,* which holds key similarities to the casino's core customers in terms of education, income, and travel.

Having identified high-opportunity segments, the casino realigned and refocused its marketing efforts to specifically target those groups while also staying true to its core. By understanding its core customers, and where households that looked like its core customers existed in target markets, it was successful in attracting new and profitable customers in a cost-effective manner.

INTERNATIONAL LIFESTYLES

LO5

The VALS and PRIZM systems presented in this chapter are oriented to the United States. In addition, VALS has systems for Japan and the United Kingdom. As we saw in Chapter 2, marketing is increasingly a global activity. If there are discernible lifestyle segments that cut across cultures, marketers can develop cross-cultural strategies around these segments. Although language and other differences would exist, individuals pursuing similar lifestyles in different cultures should be responsive to similar product features and communication themes.

Not surprisingly, a number of attempts have been made to develop such systems.[42] Large international advertising agencies and marketing research firms are leading the way. Roper Starch Worldwide, a global marketing research and consulting company, surveyed roughly 35,000 consumers across 35 countries in Asia, North and South America, and Europe.[43] Their goal was a global segmentation scheme based on core underlying values. According to one executive,

> We're looking for the bedrock values, the fundamental stable things in people's lives that determine who they are, to understand the underlying motivations that drive their attitudes as well as their behavior.[44]

Their survey uncovered six global lifestyle segments, as described in Table 12–5. While these segments exist in all the countries studied, the percentage of the population in each group varied by country. For example, Asia has a high proportion of Strivers. Aside from language, the MEI.com ad in Illustration 12–9 has a global appeal to the Strivers segment. This type of ad is often used by marketers to target similar lifestyle groups across different cultures, allowing for a relatively standardized ad theme.

Global Lifestyle Segments Identified by Roper Starch Worldwide TABLE 

Strivers (23 percent)—value material and professional goals and are driven by wealth, status, and power. They like computers and cell phones but have little time for media beyond newspapers. Middle aged, and skewing male, Strivers are found disproportionately (33 percent) in Asia.
Devouts (22 percent)—value duty, tradition, faith, obedience, and respect for elders. They are the least media involved and least interested in Western brands. Skewing female, Devouts are most common in developing Asia (e.g., Philippines), Africa, and the Middle East and least common in developed Asia (e.g., Japan) and Western Europe.
Altruists (18 percent)—are interested in social issues and the welfare of society. They are well educated and older, with a median age of 44. Skewing female, Altruists are most common in Latin America and Russia.
Intimates (15 percent)—value close personal relationships and family. They are heavy users of broadcast media, enjoy cooking and gardening, and are good targets for familiar consumer brands. Gender balanced, Intimates are more common in Europe and the United States (25 percent) and less common in developing Asia (7 percent).
Fun Seekers (12 percent)—value adventure, pleasure, and excitement. They are heavy users of electronic media, are fashion conscious, and like going to restaurants, bars, and clubs. Fun Seekers are the youngest, the most global in their lifestyles, roughly gender balanced, and more common in developed Asia.
Creatives (10 percent)—are interested in knowledge, education, and technology. They are the heaviest users of media, particularly books, magazines, and newspapers. They also lead the way in technology, including owning a computer and surfing the net. Gender balanced, Creatives are more common in Latin America and Western Europe.

Source: Global Lifestyle Segments, Roper Starch Worldwide.

ILLUSTRATION 12-9

This MEI.com ad would have strong appeal to Strivers.

SUMMARY

LO1: Describe self-concept, how it is measured, and how it is used to position products

The *self-concept* is one's beliefs and feelings about oneself. There are four types of self-concept: *actual self-concept, social self-concept, private self-concept,* and *ideal self-concept.* The self-concept is important to marketers because consumers purchase and use products to express, maintain, and enhance their self-concepts. Marketers, particularly those in international marketing, have found it useful to characterize individuals and cultures by whether they have a predominantly *independent self-concept* (the individual is the critical component) or an *interdependent self-concept* (relationships are of primary importance).

An individual's self-concept, the way one defines oneself, typically includes some of the person's possessions. The self-concept including the possessions one uses to define oneself is termed the *extended self.* Marketers can position products and brands as a means to enhance an individual's self-concept in terms of the extended self. Sometimes products and brands can be positioned to help maintain the self-concept, as when the ideal and actual self-concepts are consistent. At other times, products and brands can be positioned to enhance the self-concept, as when the actual self-concept is lower than the ideal.

LO2: Define lifestyle and its relationship to the self-concept and to psychographics

Lifestyle can be defined simply as how one lives. It is a function of a person's inherent individual characteristics that have been shaped through social interaction as the person moves through his or her life cycle. It is how an individual expresses his or her self-concept through actions.

Psychographics is the primary way that lifestyle is made operationally useful to marketing managers. This is a way of describing the psychological makeup or lifestyle of consumers by assessing such lifestyle dimensions as activities, interests, opinions, values, and demographics. Lifestyle measures can be macro and reflect how individuals live in general, or micro and describe their attitudes and behaviors with respect to a specific product category or activity.

LO3: Explain specific lifestyle typologies and summarize those for luxury sports cars and technology

Lifestyle measurements can be constructed with varying degrees of specificity. At one extreme, firms can conduct very specific lifestyle studies focused on those aspects of individual or household lifestyles most

SMARTBOOK™

relevant to their product or service. For these studies, lifestyle measurement is product or activity specific. Porsche conducted a lifestyle segmentation study for its brand and found various segments with very different purchase motives. Experian examined technology users and found very different groups in terms of their attitudes, usage, and adoption of emerging technologies.

LO4: Explain general lifestyle typologies and summarize those for VALS™ and PRIZM®

At the other extreme, marketers can study the general lifestyle patterns of a population. These general lifestyle approaches are not specific to any one product or activity, so they have broad applicability in developing marketing strategies for a wide range of products and brands. General approaches include VALS and PRIZM.

The *VALS* system divides the United States into eight groups: Innovators, Thinkers, Believers, Achievers, Strivers, Experiencers, Makers, and Survivors. These groups were derived on the basis of two dimensions. The first, *primary motivation,* has three categories: *ideals* (those guided by their basic beliefs and values), *achievement* (those striving for a clear social position and influenced by others), and *self-expression* (those who seek self-expression, physical activity, variety, and excitement). The second dimension is the physical, mental, and material *resources* to pursue one's dominant motivation.

Geo-demographic analysis is based on the premise that individuals with similar lifestyles tend to live near each other. PRIZM is a system that examines demographic and consumption data down to the individual household with 66 lifestyle segments organized around social groupings and life stage.

LO5: Discuss international lifestyles and one existing segmentation scheme

In response to the rapid expansion of international marketing, a number of attempts have been made to develop lifestyle measures applicable across cultures. Roper Starch Worldwide conducted a large multinational survey and found six global lifestyle segments based on core values.

KEY TERMS

Actual self-concept 420
Brand engagement 422
Extended self 421
Geo-demographic analysis 434
Ideal self-concept 420
Independent self-concept 420
Interdependent self-concept 420
Lifestyle 427
Mere ownership effect 422
Peak experience 422
Private self-concept 420
PRIZM 434
Psychographics 428
Self-concept 420
Social self-concept 420
VALS 430

REVIEW QUESTIONS

1. What is a *self-concept?* What are the four types of self-concept?
2. How do marketers use insights about the self-concept?
3. How can one measure the self-concept?
4. How does an *interdependent self-concept* differ from an *independent self-concept?*
5. What is the *extended self?*
6. What is a *brand engagement?*
7. What ethical issues arise in using the self-concept in marketing?
8. What do we mean by *lifestyle?* What factors determine and influence lifestyle?
9. What is *psychographics?*
10. When is a product- or activity-specific psychographic instrument superior to a general one?
11. What are the dimensions on which VALS is based? Describe each.
12. Describe the VALS system and each segment in it.
13. What is *geo-demographic analysis?*
14. Describe the PRIZM system.
15. Describe the global lifestyle segments identified by Roper Starch Worldwide.

DISCUSSION QUESTIONS

16. Use Table 12–2 to measure your four self-concepts. To what extent are they similar? What causes the differences? To what extent do you think they influence your purchase behavior?
17. Use Table 12–2 to measure your self-concept (you choose which self-concept and justify your choice). Also measure the images of three celebrities you admire. What do you conclude?
18. Respond to the questions in Consumer Insight 12–1.
19. What possessions are part of your extended self? Why?
20. Is your self-concept predominantly independent or interdependent? Why?
21. What ethical concerns are associated with ads that portray a standardized ideal image of beauty?

22. For each of the following products, develop one ad that would appeal to a target market characterized by predominantly independent self-concepts and another ad for a target market characterized by predominantly interdependent self-concepts.
    a. Amazon.com
    b. Mini Cooper automobile
    c. Timex watch
    d. Polo Ralph Lauren clothing
23. Use the self-concept theory to develop marketing strategies for the following products:
    a. The National Alzheimer Association contributions
    b. BMW
    c. Army ROTC recruitment
    d. A&W root beer
    e. Purell
    f. Carnival Cruiseline
24. Does VALS make sense to you? What do you like or dislike about it?
25. How would one use VALS to develop a marketing strategy?
26. Develop a marketing strategy based on VALS for
    a. Starbucks
    b. Grand Canyon kayak vacation
    c. Sirius satellite radio
    d. Kawasaki jet ski
    e. Triumph motorcycles
    f. NBA
27. Develop a marketing strategy for each of the eight VALS segments for
    a. Verizon wireless
    b. Vacation package
    c. DeVinci Gourmet coffee syrups
    d. CNN
    e. Facial cleansers
    f. Walmart
28. Does PRIZM make sense to you? What do you like or dislike about it? Is it really a measure of lifestyle?
29. How would one use PRIZM to develop a marketing strategy?
30. Develop a marketing strategy for each of the Roper Starch global lifestyle segments for the products in Question 26. What challenges do you face in trying to market these products to global market segments?
31. The following quote is from Paul Casi, president of Glenmore distilleries: "Selling cordials is a lot different from selling liquor. Cordials are like the perfume of our industry. You're really talking high fashion and you're talking generally to a different audience—I don't mean male versus female—I'm talking about lifestyle."
    a. In what ways do you think the lifestyle of cordial drinkers would differ from that of those who drink liquor but not cordials?
    b. How would you determine the nature of any such differences?
    c. Of what use would knowledge of such lifestyle differences be to a marketing manager introducing a new cordial?
32. How is one likely to change one's lifestyle at different stages of the household life cycle? Over one's life, is one likely to assume more than one of the VALS lifestyle profiles described?
33. To which VALS category do you belong? To which do your parents belong? Which will you belong to when you are your parents' age?
34. Generalizing from the global fashion lifestyles in the opener, develop a marketing strategy for
    a. A spa
    b. Makeup
    c. Jewelry
    d. Shoes
    e. Clothes

APPLICATION ACTIVITIES

35. Develop an instrument to measure the interdependent versus independent self-concept.
36. Use the instrument you developed in Activity 35 to measure the self-concepts of 10 male and 10 female students, all of the same nationality. What do you conclude?
37. Develop your own psychographic instrument (set of relevant questions) that measures the lifestyles of college students.
38. Using the psychographic instrument developed in Activity 37, interview 10 students (using the questionnaire instrument). On the basis of their responses, categorize them into lifestyle segments.
39. Find and copy or describe ads that would appeal to each of the eight VALS segments.
40. Find and copy or describe ads that would appeal to each of the PRIZM segments discussed in the text.
41. Repeat Activity 40 for the Roper Starch Worldwide global lifestyle segments.
42. Repeat Activity 40 for the Experian Technology segments.

REFERENCES

1. Opening example is based on E. Ko et al., "Cross-National Market Segmentation in the Fashion Industry," *International Marketing Review* 24, no. 5 (2007), pp. 629–51; C. R. Taylor, "Lifestyle Matters Everywhere," *Advertising Age,* May 19, 2008, p. 24; and "Global Luxury Market Foresees Recovery," www.fibre2fashion.com, October 30, 2009, accessed June 11, 2011.
2. N. Y. Wong and A. C. Ahuvia, "Personal Taste and Family Face," *Psychology & Marketing,* August 1998, pp. 423–41; and T. Sun, M. Horn, and D. Merrit, "Values and Lifestyles of Individualists and Collectivists," *Journal of Consumer Marketing,* 21, no. 5 (2004), pp. 318–31.
3. See, e.g., E. C. Hirschman, "Men, Dogs, Guns, and Cars: The Semiotics of Rugged Individualism," *Journal of Advertising,* Spring 2003, pp. 9–22.
4. C. L. Wang and J. C. Mowen, "The Separateness–Connectedness Self-Schema," *Psychology & Marketing,* March 1997, pp. 185–207.
5. C. L. Wang et al., "Alternative Modes of Self-Construal," *Journal of Consumer Psychology,* 9, no. 2 (2000), pp. 107–15.
6. See A. Reed II, "Activating the Self-Importance of Consumer Selves," *Journal of Consumer Research,* September 2004, pp. 286–95; Sun, Horn, and Merrit, "Values and Lifestyles of Individualists and Collectivists"; N. Agrawal and D. Maheswaran, "The Effects of Self-Construal and Commitment on Persuasion," *Journal of Consumer Research,* March 2005, pp. 841–49; C. J. Torelli, "Individuality or Conformity?," *Journal of Consumer Psychology,* 16, no. 3 (2006), pp. 240–48; J. H. Leigh and Y. Choi, "The Impact of Attributions about Life Events on Perceptions of Foreign Products," *Psychology & Marketing,* January 2007, pp. 41–68; and A. B. Monga and L. Lau-Gesk, "Blending Cobrand Personalities," *Journal of Marketing Research,* August 2007, pp. 389–400.
7. M. Zhang, "The Effect of Advertising Appeals in Activating Self-Construals," *Journal of Advertising,* Spring 2009, pp. 63–81.
8. R. W. Belk, "Possessions and the Extended Self," *Journal of Consumer Research,* September 1988, pp. 139–68; and R. Belk, "Extended Self and Extending Paradigmatic Perspective," *Journal of Consumer Research,* June 1989, pp. 129–32. See also M. L. Richins, "Valuing Things," *Journal of Consumer Research,* December 1994, pp. 504–21; M. L. Richins, "Special Possessions and the Expression of Material Values," *Journal of Consumer Research,* December 1994, pp. 522–31; and A. C. Ahuvia, "Beyond the Extended Self," *Journal of Consumer Research,* June 2005, pp. 171–84.
9. See S. S. Kleine, R. E. Kleine III, and C. T. Allen, "How Is a Possession 'Me' or 'Not Me'?," *Journal of Consumer Research,* December 1995, pp. 327–43.
10. S. Sayre and D. Horne, "I Shop, Therefore I Am," *Advances in Consumer Research,* vol. 23, ed. K. P. Corfman and J. G. Lynch (Provo, UT: Association for Consumer Research, 1996), pp. 323–28.
11. See L. L. Love and P. S. Sheldon, "Souvenirs," *Advances in Consumer Research,* vol. 25, ed. J. W. Alba and J. W. Hutchinson (Provo, UT: Association for Consumer Research, 1998), pp. 170–74.
12. C. S. Areni, P. Kiecker, and K. M. Palan, "Is It Better to Give Than to Receive?," *Psychology & Marketing,* January 1998, pp. 81–109. See also C. F. Curasi, L. L. Price, and E. J. Arnould, "How Individuals' Cherished Possessions Become Families' Inalienable Wealth," *Journal of Consumer Research,* December 2004, pp. 609–22.
13. K. J. Dodson, "Peak Experiences and Mountain Biking," *Advances in Consumer Research,* vol. 23, ed. Corfman and Lynch, pp. 317–22.
14. C. H. Noble and B. A. Walker, "Exploring the Relationships among Liminal Transitions, Symbolic Consumption, and the Extended Self," *Psychology & Marketing,* January 1997, pp. 29–47.
15. E. Sivadas and K. A. Machleit, "A Scale to Determine the Extent of Object Incorporation in the Extended Self," in *Marketing*

Theory and Applications, vol. 5, ed. C. W. Park and D. C. Smith (Chicago: American Marketing Association, 1994).

16. S. Sen and E. J. Johnson, "Mere-Possession Effects without Possession in Consumer Choice," *Journal of Consumer Research,* June 1997, pp. 105–17; M. A. Strahilevitz and G. Loewenstein, "The Effect of Ownership History of the Valuation of Objects," *Journal of Consumer Research,* December 1998, pp. 276–89; and K. P. Nesselroade Jr., J. K. Beggan, and S. T. Allison, "Possession Enhancement in an Interpersonal Context," *Psychology & Marketing,* January 1999, pp. 21–34.
17. D. Sprott, S. Czellar, and E. Spangenberg, "The Importance of a General Measure of Brand Engagement," *Journal of Marketing Research,* February 2009, pp. 92–104. The full set of eight measurement items can be found on page 93 of their article.
18. S. Kang, "Nike, Serena Williams Partner Up," *The Wall Street Journal,* December 12, 2003, p. B2.
19. J. G. Helgeson and M. Supphellen, "A Conceptual and Measurement Comparison of Self-Congruity and Brand Personality," *International Journal of Market Research,* 46, no. 2 (2004), pp. 205–33; L. N. Chaplin and D. R. John, "The Development of Self-Brand Connections in Children and Adolescents," *Journal of Consumer Research,* June 2005, pp. 119–29; J. E. Escalas and J. R. Bettman, "Self-Construal, Reference Groups, and Brand Meaning," *Journal of Consumer Research,* December 2005, pp. 378–89; C. Yim, K. Chan, and K. Hung, "Multiple Reference Effects in Service Evaluations," *Journal of Retailing* 83, no. 1 (2007), pp. 147–57; and V. Swaminathan, K. L. Page, and Z. Gurhan-Canli, "'My' Brand or 'Our' Brand," *Journal of Consumer Research,* October 2007, pp. 248–59.
20. S. J. Gould, "An Interpretive Study of Purposeful, Mood Self-Regulating Consumption," *Psychology & Marketing,* July 1997, pp. 395–426.
21. See J. W. Hong and G. M. Zinkhan, "Self-Concept and Advertising Effectiveness," *Psychology & Marketing,* January 1995, pp. 53–77; A. Mehta, "Using Self-Concept to Assess Advertising Effectiveness, *Journal of Advertising Research,* January 1999, pp. 81–89; and M. J. Barone, T. A. Shimp, and D. E. Sprott, "Product Ownership as a Moderator of Self-Congruity Effects," *Marketing Letters,* February 1999, pp. 75–85.
22. E. N. Banister and M. K. Hogg, "Mapping the Negative Self," and A. M. Muniz and L. O. Hamer, "Us versus Them," both in *Advances in Consumer Research,* vol. 28, ed. M. C. Gilly and J. Meyers-Levy (Provo, UT: Association for Consumer Research, 2001), pp. 242–48 and 355–61, respectively.
23. For a broader discussion of situational factors, see T. R. Graeff, "Consumption Situations and the Effects of Brand Image on Consumers' Brand Evaluations," *Psychology & Marketing,* January 1997, pp. 49–70.
24. M. K. Hogg, A. J. Cox, and K. Keeling, "The Impact of Self-Monitoring on Image Congruence and Product/Brand Evaluation," *European Journal of Marketing,* 34, no. 5/6 (2000), pp. 641–66.
25. J. Meyers-Levy and L. A. Peracchio, "Understanding the Socialized Body," *Journal of Consumer Research,* September 1995, p. 147.
26. C. S. Gulas and K. McKeage, "Extending Social Comparison," *Journal of Advertising,* Summer 2000, pp. 17–28; and D. Smeesters and N. Mandel, "Positive and Negative Media Image Effects on the Self," *Journal of Consumer Research,* March 2006, pp. 576–82.
27. N. Etcoff, S. Orbach, J.Scott, and H. D'Agostino, "Findings of the Global Study on Women, Beauty and Well-Being," *Unilever White Paper,* September 2004, www.clubofamsterdam.com/contentarticles/52%20Beauty/dove_white_paper_final.pdf.
28. "The Dove® Campaign for Real Beauty," Dove company website, www.dove.us/social-mission/campaign-for-real-beauty.aspx, accessed August 28, 2014.
29. J. Neff, "Ten Years In, Dove's 'Real Beauty' Seems to Be Aging Well," *Advertising Age,* January 22, 2014, http://adage.com/article/news/ten-years-dove-s-real-beauty-aging/291216/, accessed August 28, 2014; and N. Bahadur, "Dove 'Real Beauty' Campaign Turns 10: How a Brand Tried to Change the Conversation about Female Beauty," *Huffington Post,* February 6, 2014, www.huffingtonpost.com/2014/01/21/dove-real-beauty-campaign-turns-10_n_4575940.html, accessed August 28, 2014.
30. B. Garfield, "Women May Be 'Real' but Product Is Baloney," *Advertising Age,* July 25, 2005. http://search.proquest.com.proxy.lib.csus.edu/abicomplete/docview/208354959/D01FA10D961D49AAPQ/1?accountid=10358, accessed August 28, 2014.
31. E. Spitznagel, "How Those Dove 'Real Beauty Sketch' Ads Went Viral," *Bloomberg Businessweek,* April 26, 2013, www.businessweek.com/articles/2013-04-26/how-those-dove-real-beauty-sketch-ads-went-viral#p1, accessed August 28, 2014; and J. Grose, "The Story Behind Dove's Mega Viral 'Real Beauty Sketches' Campaign," *Fast Company,* www.fastcocreate.com/1682823/the-story-behind-doves-mega-viral-real-beauty-sketches-campaign, accessed August 28, 2014.
32. M. J. Dutta-Bergman and W. D. Wells, "The Values and Lifestyles of Idiocentrics and Allocentrics in an Individualistic Culture," *Journal of Consumer Psychology,* 12, no. 3 (2002), pp. 231–42.
33. See E. H. Demby, "Psychographics Revisited," *Marketing Research,* Spring 1994, pp. 26–30.
34. See F. W. Gilbert and W. E. Warren, "Psychographic Constructs and Demographic Segments," *Psychology & Marketing,* May 1995, pp. 223–37.
35. Based on A. Taylor III, "Porsche Slices Up Its Buyers," *Fortune,* January 16, 1995, p. 24.
36. Based on a Forrester Research report by J. Kolko, "Why Techno-Graphics *Still* Works," December 14, 2004. Used by permission of Forrester Research.
37. Segment descriptions from *2010 Technology Adoption Consumer Report* (Costa Mesa, CA: Experian, Spring 2010).
38. For a critical review and alternative approach, see D. B. Holt, "Poststructuralist Lifestyle Analysis," *Journal of Consumer Research,* March 1997, pp. 326–50. Alternative lifestyle systems are also described in C. Walker and E. Moses, "The Age of Self-Navigation," *American Demographics,* September 1996,

pp. 36–42; and P. H. Ray, "The Emerging Culture," *American Demographics,* February 1997, pp. 29–56.

39. Based on material provided by Strategic Business Insights.
40. *How to Use PRIZM* (Claritas Inc., 1986), p. 1.
41. Information regarding PRIZM is based on *Prizm*$_{NE}$*: The New Evolution Segment Snapshots* (Claritas Inc., 2003); other information from Claritas Inc., 2005; information from www.claritas.com/MyBestSegments/tutorials/Nielsen_PRIZM/engage.html, accessed June 11, 2011; and information from www.claritas.com/MyBestSegments, accessed June 11, 2011.
42. For example, see M. T. Ewing, "Affluent Asia," *Journal of International Consumer Marketing,* 12, no. 2 (1999), pp. 25–37.
43. This material, including information in Table 12–6, is based on S. Elliott, "Research Finds Consumers Worldwide Belong to Six Basic Groups That Cross National Lines," *New York Times,* June 25, 1998, p. D8; and T. Miller, "Global Segments from 'Strivers' to 'Creatives,'" *Marketing News,* July 20, 1998, p. 11.
44. Elliott, "Research Finds Consumers Worldwide Belong to Six Basic Groups That Cross National Lines."

Part Three CASES*

3–1 PATAGONIA'S ECO-FASHION PUSH

Concerns about the environment continue to grow. Consumers are becoming more educated about environmental friendliness with over one-third of consumers believing that it is important for companies to be environmentally conscious. Not surprisingly, green-household products had the highest adoption rate of all consumer goods categories in six out of the eight countries that were included in a recent survey.

While automobiles often garner the lion's share of media attention regarding the environment, consumers also voice concerns about the impact of the products that they eat and wear. According to one expert:

> Early in the study, we asked consumers what green products they were looking for, and they were looking for products that were closer to them—that they put in their body or on their body.

In terms of what consumers are putting on their bodies, environmentally friendly apparel, also called *eco-fashion,* is becoming increasingly popular. Consumers favor natural fibers in their clothing over synthetic materials. A survey from Cotton Incorporated found that 83 percent of consumers believe that clothing made from 100 percent natural fibers is better for the environment than other clothing materials. However, consumers also consider their awareness of a brand's corporate actions, values, recycling and packaging efforts, sustainability, and supply chain decisions when making decisions about environmentally friendly apparel.

Patagonia is an apparel company that shares the environmentally conscious values of many consumers. Since 1985, Patagonia has donated at least one percent of annual sales to environmental charities. Patagonia's One Percent for the Planet program has influenced other companies to follow its lead. Patagonia is continuously looking for new ways to be more environmentally friendly. According to Patagonia's founder, Yvon Chouinard:

> We're switching all our nylon to something called Nylon 6, which can be recycled infinitely. We're recycling cotton; we're recycling wool. We send polyester back to Japan, where it gets melted down into its original polymer. Of course, the best thing to do is make clothing so it never wears out, right?

Patagonia's 2011 fall collection continued the theme of environmental responsibility. The fabrics used were environmentally friendly. Thirty-six percent of their fabrics were Bluesign approved. Bluesign is an independent auditor that requires members to establish management systems to improve environmental performance as follows:

> Bluesign® members agree at the outset to establish management systems for improving environmental performance in five key areas of the production process—resource productivity, consumer safety, water emissions, air emissions, and occupational health and safety. Members regularly report their progress and must meet improvement goals to maintain their status; bluesign® technologies performs regular audits.

In addition, all styles currently being released are eligible for the Common Threads Recycling Initiative. In this program, consumers are encouraged to reduce clothing consumption, repair worn clothing when possible, reuse clothing by donating it to others, and recycle worn clothing when beyond repair.

Patagonia's designs are popular among everyday consumers and celebrities. Brad Pitt has been seen sporting Patagonia clothing, which may have had something to do with him being named one of Hollywood's "Greenest Stars."

In 2010, Cotton Incorporated conducted a Consumer Environment Survey to study consumers' attitudes about environmental friendliness in the apparel industry. They segmented consumers into five groups based on their attitudes and behaviors regarding environmentally friendly apparel, as shown in Table A.

*Part Three cases are contributed by Carolyn Findley Musgrove, Assistant Professor of Marketing, Indiana University Southeast.

TABLE A Attitudes and Behaviors of Green Apparel Consumers

Consumer segment	%	Attitudes and Behaviors
Dark green	7	Very likely to seek out environmentally friendly apparel; would be extremely bothered and complain if company engaged in practices that were not environmentally friendly.
Green	9	Very likely to seek out environmentally friendly apparel.
Light green	54	Somewhat or moderately likely to seek out environmentally friendly apparel.
Pale green	14	Do not seek out environmentally friendly apparel.
Non-green	16	Do not seek out environmentally friendly apparel; would not be bothered if firm engaged in practices that were not environmentally friendly.

Source: Cotton Incorporated's 2010 *Consumer Environment Survey.*

Further, the researchers at Cotton Incorporated profiled each of these five green consumer segments based on the characteristics of apparel that play the most important role in their apparel purchases. A summary of each segment's profile is available in Table B.

Finally, Cotton Incorporated's researchers profiled each of the green consumer segments, with demographic information shown in Table C.

Discussion Questions

1. Using the information provided in the tables, which of the five green segments identified by Cotton International would you target if you were marketing a clothing line in each of the following situations. Explain your choices.
   a. Well-known brand name that is moderately environmentally friendly but has the potential for mass appeal.
   b. Well-known brand name with a track record of environmental friendliness and a high natural-fiber content.
   c. Moderately well-known brand name, with low prices, that has been cited in the past for behaving in ways that are not environmentally friendly.
2. The green segmentation scheme presented in this case is particular to green apparel. Compare and contrast the green apparel segments with the green segments described in Table 3–1 of the text.
3. The case mentions that Brad Pitt has been spotted in the media wearing Patagonia clothing. In what ways is this potentially positive for the brand?
4. Consider that Patagonia was going to sign a celebrity endorser to their brand.
   a. What factors should Patagonia consider when choosing a celebrity endorser?
   b. What celebrity would be a good endorser for Patagonia? Justify your answer.

TABLE  Purchase Drivers for the Green Apparel Segments

% of Consumers Citing the Factor as Important in Apparel Purchases	Dark Green (%)	Green (%)	Light Green (%)	Pale Green (%)	Non-green (%)
Fit	99	99	97	99	96
Color	96	92	86	86	85
Style	96	93	90	88	84
Price	96	94	94	93	93
Environmental friendliness	93	84	55	27	12
Fiber content	91	82	67	51	44
Laundering instructions	87	79	66	57	47
Brand name	76	74	51	39	34

Source: Cotton Incorporated's 2010 *Consumer Environment Survey.*

5. Chapter 12 outlines the VALS lifestyle segments. Which of these lifestyle segments is the most likely target market for Patagonia products? Could more than one group be a good target market? Justify your answer.

6. In terms of Cotton Incorporated's five green consumer segments for apparel, their purchase motivations, and their demographics, describe a target market for Patagonia.

Source: J. Pearson, "Hollywood Goes Green!," *Star Magazine,* 2007, www.starmagazine.com; S. Casey, "Patagonia: Blueprint for Green Business," *Fortune,* May 29, 2007, money.cnn.com; T. Foster, "Patagonia's Founder on Why There's 'No Such Thing as Sustainability,'" *Fast Company,* July 1, 2009, www.fastcompany.com; "Shades of the Green Consumer," *Cotton Incorporated Supply Chain Insights,* 2010; E. Grady, "Patagonia Launches Common Threads Initiative to Curb Clothing Consumption," *Treehugger.com,* November 15, 2010, www.treehugger.com; "Introducing the Common Threads Initiative," *Patagonia.com,* 2011, www.patagonia.com; "Seventh Gen and Whole Foods Top Green Brands Ranking," *Environmental Leader,* June 10, 2011, www.environmentalleader.com; E. Grady, "Patagonia Steps Up Sustainability in New Fall 2011 Styles," *Treehugger.com,* June 12, 2011, www.treehugger.com; and "Survey: People Getting Smarter about Going Green," *Ad Age Blogs,* June 13, 2011, http://adage.com.

TABLE C Demographics of Green Consumers

	Dark Green (%)	Green (%)	Light Green (%)	Pale Green (%)	Non-green (%)
Gender					
Male	51	46	39	31	45
Female	49	54	62	69	55
Age					
Average age (years)	39	36	38	38	38
14 to 24	12	20	20	20	21
25 to 34	23	23	17	13	15
35 to 44	30	27	25	26	26
45 to 54	36	30	39	41	39
Income					
Average annual (000)	70	64	61	58	63
Ethnicity					
Caucasian	57	63	64	67	67
African American	16	10	12	13	15
Hispanic	14	16	17	14	12
Asian	8	8	5	1	3
Other	6	3	3	4	2
Education Level					
Less than high school diploma	6	15	10	15	13
High school graduate	27	34	34	36	33
Some college	21	18	26	30	26
College degree or higher	46	34	30	19	29
Children in the Household					
Yes	59	60	51	47	50
No	41	40	49	53	50
Region					
South	35	45	35	33	40
West	26	19	25	26	18
Midwest	20	21	20	25	26
Northeast	19	15	20	18	15

Source: Cotton Incorporated's 2010 *Consumer Environment Survey.*

3–2 DOMINO'S REFORMULATION

Domino's Pizza long held a reputation for quick delivery service and terrible pizza. Consumer focus groups described Domino's pizza crust as being similar to cardboard, the pizza as mass produced, the sauces as ketchup, and the cheese as bland. For years, executives at Domino's were aware of many people's feelings about its pizza but chose to focus on its core competency of delivery service instead of product quality. However, delivery speed was not enough and Domino's recognized that it needed better-quality pizza as well.

Domino's recently introduced a reformulated version of its pizza with higher quality and more flavorful ingredients. It launched an extensive advertising and promotional campaign that poked fun at its own brand by announcing that the old pizza recipe was awful, but its new recipe was wonderful. Commercials featured focus groups giving negative evaluations of the old pizza recipe and Domino's employees talking about complaints received about the pizza, with the promise of the new pizza being much better. According to Domino's CEO:

> It wasn't a hard choice to change the pizza. But it was absolutely a calculated risk to advertise it this way. There was no Plan B. If it didn't work, there was no going back. You can't say your old pizza was bad and this new pizza is great and expect to go back to the old formula if people don't like it. This new pizza was dramatically different. It tasted better—there was no question. We knew all we had to do was get people to try it. We were doing it through the absolute teeth of the recession, and we knew it would result in a higher-cost pizza.

Consumers' reactions to the new pizza recipe were mixed, but generally positive. Some critics claimed that adding spices does not constitute a reinvention of the recipe. However, two months into the campaign, Domino's new pizza recipe beat Pizza Hut and Papa John's by a wide margin in taste tests. One customer wrote on Domino's Facebook page:

> I seriously hated Domino's in the past. Only had it a couple times and it made my stomach upset and it was average at best. I recently moved and tried Domino's again since there's not much for delivery where I moved to. We are totally turned around by the taste! We have ordered again since 2 more times and plan to order a lot more in the future. Way to turn things around Domino's, keep up the fantastic work!!!

Table A provides demographic data for low- and high-frequency Domino's customers.

The reaction to the advertising campaign itself was very good. Late-night talk show hosts such as Conan O'Brien and Stephen Colbert picked up on Domino's ads and featured them in exaggerated comedy pieces that helped to put Domino's new pizza recipe in the

Demographics for Low- and High-Frequency Domino's Customers — TABLE A

	1–5 Visits per Month	6+ Visits per Month
Age		
18–24	179	214
25–34	139	114
35–44	127	113
45–54	100	100
55–64	80	44
65+	39	90
Gender		
Male	93	97
Female	105	102
Ethnicity		
White	79	30
Hispanic	154	297
Black	179	353
Asian	73	44
Household Income		
<$25K	115	180
$25K–$49K	92	92
$50K–$74K	90	60
$75K–$99K	103	119
$100K–$149K	108	34
$150K+	87	51
Children at Home		
No	77	81
Yes	144	137

Note: Numbers are indexed to 100, where 100 is the average; for example, 115 would represent 15 percent above average.

Source: Experian Simmons' Fall 2009 *National Consumer Study*.

national spotlight. Because of its campaign, Domino's was named runner-up for Advertising Age's Marketer of the Year Award. Domino's was also named the Pizza Chain of the Year by *Pizza Today,* the industry's leading trade publication.

Part of the success of Domino's new campaign is that it actively engages customers in a number of ways. For example, Domino's actively seeks feedback from social media as well as providing various contests and activities for its customers. For example:

- In the "Taste Bud Bounty Hunter" program, customers nominate others who have not tried the new pizza. Those customers who "convert the most taste buds" win a year of free pizza. The potential customers who have not tried the new pizza have the potential to end up on a Domino's commercial.
- In the "Show Us Your Pizza" program, customers send in photos of the pizza that they ordered from Domino's to be used in a national advertising campaign for cash prizes.

In a commitment to transparency, Domino's solicits customers' positive and negative comments through social media. It also promised to never edit photographs of its pizza in advertisements.

The combination of a higher-quality product and a successful marketing campaign resulted in a positive financial impact. Domino's posted a 14.3 percent increase in same-store sales in the first quarter of 2010, beating McDonald's highest-ever gain of 14.2 percent. The following quarter saw a 14.5 percent increase in sales. The true test will be whether Domino's increase in popularity has longevity. Domino's intends to continue the wave of revamping its menu by moving on to chicken. Again, it is soliciting customer ideas and opinions.

Discussion Questions

1. Domino's is repositioning its brand with new recipes and extensive advertising and promotional campaigns.
   a. Why can repositioning the brand be very difficult?
   b. What characteristics of Domino's rebranding effort may help it ultimately succeed in the long term?
2. What message structure characteristic discussed in Chapter 11 does Domino's use in its campaign? What consumer emotions are stimulated by this type of message structure?
3. Chapter 9 discusses several learning theories. What learning theory is Domino's using to teach consumers that its product is improved?
4. Using the demographic information given in Table A and your own experience and knowledge, characterize the segment of "high-frequency" user that Domino's would want to target.
5. Develop a brand "schema" for the old version and the new version of Domino's brand image. Discuss the marketing implications of the differences.
6. Is Domino's new pizza recipe an innovation? If so, what type of innovation is it? Explain your answer.

Source: A. Sauer, "Is the Domino's Rebrand Too Honest?," *BrandChannel,* January 5, 2010, www.brandchannel.com; B. Garfield, "Domino's Does Itself a Disservice by Coming Clean About Its Pizza," *Advertising Age,* January 11, 2010, p. 22; "U.S. Foodservice Landscape 2010: Restaurant Industry and Consumer Trends, Momentum and Migration," *Packaged Facts,* May 2010; D. Brady, "J. Patrick Doyle," *Bloomberg Businessweek,* May 3, 2010, p. 1; E. York, "Domino's Claims Victory with New Strategy: Pizza Wasn't Good, We Fixed It," *Advertising Age,* May 10, 2010, p. 4; R. Parekh, "Runner-Up: Domino's," *Advertising Age,* October 18, 2010, p. 19; M. Brandau, "Pizza Revamp Drives Domino's Results," *Nation's Restaurant News,* March 1, 2011, www.nrn.com; and S. Gregory, "Domino's New Recipe: (Brutal) Truth in Advertising," *Time Magazine,* May 5, 2011, http://www.time.com/time.

3-3 LET'S MOVE! CAMPAIGN CELEBRITIES ENDORSING SODA?!

In February 2010, First Lady Michelle Obama launched her Let's Move! Campaign. Let's Move! is an effort to improve the lives of young Americans through healthier diets and more active lifestyles. This effort is especially needed at a time when childhood obesity has become a problem of epic proportions in the United States. The key to making progress within Let's Move! is through developing collaborative partnerships with various stakeholders, including families, schools, food companies, legislators, and even celebrities. According to the Let's Move! website:

> We've seen substantial commitments from parents, business leaders, educators, elected officials, military leaders, chefs, physicians, athletes, childcare providers, community and faith leaders, and kids themselves to improve the health of our nation's children. Thanks to these efforts, families now have access to more of the information they need to make healthier decisions for their children. Young people now have more opportunities for physical activity in their communities. Food in schools has been dramatically improved. And more Americans now have access to healthy, affordable food right in their communities.

In the few years since the launch of the campaign, child obesity remains a problem in the United States, but some headway has been made in several states, such as New York, Mississippi, and Philadelphia. In March 2014, Partnership for a Healthier America published a report that extolled its members for putting more grocers in poor areas and healthier foods in restaurants. Sixteen member food manufacturers have pledged to cut 1.5 trillion calories from their products by 2015. Also, the American Beverage Association participated by placing calorie labels on the front of beverages. While the progress is yet modest, a fundamental shift in the lifestyles of America's youth is something that takes time to evolve.

One major method that Mrs. Obama has utilized to popularize the Let's Move! Campaign among young people is partnering with celebrities. Celebrity endorsements are a well-established strategy in marketing that can lend credibility to brands. Several celebrities and athletes have participated in and endorsed the Let's Move! Campaign in various ways. Even Mrs. Obama herself has used her own celebrity to endorse companies that partner with the Let's Move! Campaign. Recently, Subway restaurants joined the initiative by pledging to offer nutritious foods on its kid's menu and to meet the same federal restrictions that are placed on school lunches. In a show of appreciation, Mrs. Obama held a news conference at a Washington, D.C., Subway restaurant, where she ate lunch with athletes who endorse Subway and a group of school children and parents. According to Sam Kass, the executive director of Let's Move!:

> We hope that both companies and athletes and celebrities will put their marketing resources and voices behind the healthier products. . . . Having celebrities and athletes of great presence really helps us get the message out. They're cultural icons who have real powerful voices in our communities and particularly for young people—they really respond to messages and their leadership. We certainly want to harness the power of these voices to help create a healthier country. That is really an important component of what we are doing.

Unfortunately, not all of the celebrities who have partnered with Let's Move! have delivered consistent messages to the young people whom they influence. While the campaign does not have official spokespeople, the celebrities have an informal obligation to serve as role models of the message they are promoting. An organization called Center for Science in the Public Interest (CSPI) has been monitoring the behavior of the Let's Move! celebrity partners. According to executive director Michael Jacobson:

> It's unfortunate, the high number of high-profile entertainers that have supported the campaign do commercials promoting fast food. The message is completely inconsistent with Let's Move!. Presumably, some percentage of the population notices that inconsistency and thinks less of the Let's Move! Campaign and the celebrity. Kids are especially influenced by celebrities. They think if they consume their product, a little of that glamour or athletic prowess will rub off on them. . . . Ideally the First Lady and Let's Move! would adopt a policy of using celebrities to get out the message, but ensuring they don't have the Achilles heel of junk food promotion.

Three celebrities, in particular, that partnered with the Let's Move! Campaign have drawn the ire of critics for their endorsement of sodas: Michelle Kwan, Beyoncé, and Shaquille O'Neal. Each of these celebrities went on to endorse sugar-laden, unhealthful drinks after lending their celebrity to the Let's Move! Campaign. The Let's Move! Campaign specifically speaks out against sodas and encourages young Americans to consume water or unsweetened beverages instead, so these moves in favor of sodas are very contradictory and erode the credibility of both the celebrities themselves and the campaign. According to Mr. Jacobson:

> You can't do a photo-op with the first lady promoting exercise one day and sell disease-promoting sodas the rest of the year.

Michelle Kwan is a U.S. Olympic figure skater who hosted the kick-off event for the 2014 Let's Read! Let's Move! summer program, which encouraged children to be active, eat healthful food, and read during the summer. Ms. Kwan is also a member of the President's Council on Fitness, Sports, and Nutrition. The conflict arose when Ms. Kwan also became one of Coca-Cola's "Four Pack" of athletes promoting its soda during the Sochi winter games. The fact that both campaigns would want Ms. Kwan as an endorser is logical considering their similar target markets. However, their messages on soda are very different. The President's Council on Fitness suggests:

> Drink water instead of sugary drinks: Cut calories by drinking water or unsweetened beverages. Soda, energy drinks and sports drinks are a major source of added sugar and calories in American diets. Try adding a slice of lemon, lime or watermelon or a splash of 100-percent juice to your glass of water if you want some flavor.

Meanwhile, Coca-Cola prefers a message that is more focused on "balance":

> Physical activity is vital to the health and well-being of consumers. It is essential in helping to maintain energy balance—the balance between "calories in" and "calories out"—for overall fitness and health.

Beyoncé Knowles (known as simply "Beyoncé") is a singer who is popular among young people. She participated in the Let's Move! Campaign by creating a music video called "Move Your Body" that featured her dancing in a school cafeteria with children and eating an apple. Only two years later, critics noticed that she partnered with Pepsi in a $50 million promotion deal. The CSPI issued an open letter to Beyoncé criticizing this move. Neither Beyoncé nor her representatives answered CSPI.

> Your image is one of success, health, talent, fitness, and glamour. But by lending your name and image to PepsiCo, you are associating those positive attributes with a product that is quite literally sickening Americans.

Another celebrity who is drawing fire for soda associations is retired NBA star Shaquille O'Neal. He joined Mrs. Obama at an elementary school to lead children in aerobic exercises. He was officially there in the capacity of a Reebok representative, but was still involved with the Let's Move! Campaign. Not long after, Mr. O'Neal launched his own line of sodas, Soda Shaq Cream Soda drinks with AriZona Beverages. The sodas, which contain 270 empty calories each, even feature Mr. O'Neal's face prominently on the packaging. According to Mr. Jacobson at CSPI:

> Clearly, Shaq knows better. He has said he avoids soda himself, and worries about obesity and diabetes. But he's now using his name, face and reputation to make those health problems even bigger. It's shameful hypocrisy, presumably motivated by money.

Other athletes who have participated in the Let's Move! Campaign have also endorsed other nonsoda, unhealthful food choices. For example, Eli Manning promoted Double Stuff Oreos and Dunkin' Donuts and David Beckham promoted Burger King.

Experts warn that in order to avoid criticisms of hypocrisy, celebrities should endorse products and ideas that they actually believe in and use in reality. In fact, China has proposed regulations to encourage truth in advertising that would prohibit celebrities from endorsing products that they do not use themselves. According to Denise Lamberston, the founder/partner of the LMS agency, which specializes in celebrity partnerships:

> Marketing is much more transparent now due to the internet and social media. This couldn't be more eloquently illustrated than with celebrity endorsements. As a celebrity, if you sign on to endorse a beverage, you better drink that beverage and none of its competitors. Because access to images of you carrying that drink, consuming that drink and buying that drink is photographed and available immediately on the internet, the consumer will call you out in a split second for not being authentic. Blogs & editorial follow suit, and quickly the story changes.

Before partnering with a celebrity to endorse a product, there are several legal measures that organizations can have in place to reduce the risk. First, the arrangement should not legally violate any previous agreements with third parties and the celebrity should agree that he or she will not enter into any subsequent agreements with other competing organizations for a period of time. Second, there should be a morals clause that would allow the agreement to be terminated for criminal or morally reprehensible behavior. The wording of this clause should be very specific in order to avoid any ambiguity or post facto disagreement between celebrities and organizations about what behaviors qualify. Finally, the agreement should ensure that celebrity endorsements on social media are compliant with federal regulations. For example, endorsement tweets should use hashtags that clearly identify them as sponsored content, such as #ad or #sponsored.

Ultimately, an ongoing debate exists as to whether celebrity endorsements are even effective. A study by Experian Marketing Services showed that 43 percent of viewers are less likely to buy products that have celebrity endorsements, unless the celebrity is an expert in the area. Ace Metrix, an advertising analytics agency, reported that television ads that contain celebrities have poorer performance than those without celebrities. The worst-performing advertisements were those in which a celebrity endorsed a product that was perceived as unlikely for the celebrity to actually use. Finally, a 2014 article in the journal *Social Influence* reported that celebrity endorsements are a risk that often does not pay off. Margaret Campbell, of Colorado University Boulder's Leeds School of Business, said:

> The overall message to marketers is be careful, because all of us, celebrities or not, have positives and negatives to our personalities, and those negatives can easily transfer to a brand.

A 2012 article in the *Journal of Advertising Research* reported that athlete celebrity endorsements are effective for increasing sales both in an absolute sense and relative to competitors. Further, each time the athlete has an achievement, the sales and stock returns jump. A Nielsen study found that consumers are five times more likely to purchase products that are endorsed by credible, third-party sources, which indicates that celebrity endorsements are effective provided that the celebrity is a credible expert in the product category. This is where it is important for the celebrity's actual use of the product be believable. Please see Table A for a listing of several celebrity endorsements that may have varying levels of believability in terms of the celebrity's use of the product. Conversely, a Harris Interactive study showed that 53 percent of adults believe that celebrity endorsements of political and social causes are very effective. There is also some evidence that celebrity endorsements are more effective on children than adults. According to Andrew Cheyne, a researcher of advertising that targets children at Berkeley Media Studies Group:

> One reason any campaign wants a popular celebrity spokesperson is because kids are attracted to them no matter what they are doing. Kids look up to them, and they want to be like them. We can't expect kids to turn off that admiration when the same person is selling sugar. At best, kids might be confused. At worst, they'll think the messages about soda are the same as the messages about water, and those two beverages aren't the same.

Celebrity Endorsers and Sponsors TABLE 

Celebrity	Sponsor
Melissa Joan Hart	Disney Paint
Justin Bieber	OPI
David Hasselhoff	Lean Pockets
Lisa Rinna	Depends
Bill Wyman	Signature Metal Detector
Mr. T	FlavorWave Oven Turbo
Eva Longoria	Lay's Potato Chips
Shannen Doherty	EducationConnection
Snoop Dogg	Norton Anti-Virus Software
Kiss	Kiss Kasket
Brooke Shields	La-Z-Boy
Bruce Willis	"Die Hard" Cologne
John Cena	Fruity Pebbles
Sylvester Stallone	Protein Pudding
Nelly	"Pimp Juice"
Lil' Romeo	"Rap Snacks"
Jeff Foxworthy	Beef Jerky
Hulk Hogan	"Hulkster" Cheeseburger
Danny DeVito	Limoncello

Discussion Questions

1. Chapter 11 discusses source characteristics and celebrity endorsements. Three constructs that influence the effectiveness of a celebrity endorser are expertise, aspirational aspects, and meaning transfer. Think in the context of the Let's Move! Campaign.
   a. Evaluate Michelle Kwan on these three aspects relative to the Let's Move! Campaign.
   b. Evaluate Beyoncé on these three aspects relative to the Let's Move! Campaign.
   c. Evaluate Shaquille O'Neal on these three aspects relative to the Let's Move! Campaign.
2. Chapter 11 also discusses fit between a celebrity endorser and the product that he or she endorses. Do you feel that there is a better fit between the Let's Move! Campaign and each of the following celebrities or between their endorsed soda brand and each of the following celebrities. Justify your answer.
   a. Michelle Kwan
   b. Beyoncé
   c. Shaquille O'Neal
3. Review the celebrity endorsements listed in the table.
   a. Choose three celebrity/product pairs that you feel are the best in terms of fit. Justify your selection.
   b. Choose three celebrity/product pairs that you feel are the worst in terms of fit. Justify your selection.
   c. Compare and contrast your choices from part a and part b.

4. Chapter 8 discusses consumer inferences. Reflect on what you read about the Let's Move! promotions and the celebrity endorsers' subsequent behavior.
   a. What aspect of consumer inferences in Chapter 8 is related to this situation?
   b. How might that aspect affect the inferences that consumers draw about the Let's Move! Campaign? How about for the celebrities discussed in the case?
5. Chapter 9 discusses schemas, which are also known as schematic memories and knowledge structures. Construct a schema diagram for each of the following celebrities as brands.
   a. Michelle Kwan
   b. Beyoncé
   c. Shaquille O'Neal
6. Chapter 10 discusses Maslow's hierarchy of needs. Which of the needs in Maslow's hierarchy of needs does the Let's Move! Campaign hope to activate in young consumers by encouraging them to make healthful food and exercise choices? (Hint: Multiple needs could be correct.)
7. Chapter 4 discusses several generational groups.
   a. Which of the generational groups is the target market for the Let's Move! Campaign?
   b. Based on what you know about the generations listed in Chapter 4, make suggestions about how the Let's Move! Campaign might better communicate with the generation you selected in part a.

Source: A. Elberse and J. Verluen, "The Economic Value of Celebrity Endorsements," *Journal of Advertising Research,* June 2012, pp. 149–65; M. Bittman, "Why Do Stars Think It is OK to Sell Sodas?," *New York Times,* January 5, 2013, http://opinionator.blogs.nytimes.com; P. Kaur, "Does Celebrity Endorsement Actually Work?," *Marketing Interactive,* February 24, 2013, www.marketing-interactive.com; "Let's Move Slowly!," *The Economist,* March 9, 2013, www.economist.com; A. Sifferlin, "Let's Move: But Not with Shaq and Beyonce," *Time,* September 16, 2013, http://healthland.time.com; S. Brewster, "'Let's Read! Let's Move!': Michelle Kwan Kicks Off Education Department Program," *Huffington Post,* July 10, 2013, www.huffingtonpost.com; K. Harrington, "Save Your Money: Celebrity Endorsements Not Worth the Cost," *Forbes,* January 31, 2014, www.forbes.com; "Health Group Questions Michelle Kwan's Dual Roles as Both Member of the President's Council on Fitness and Coke Ambassador," *Center for Science in the Public Interest,* February 18, 2014, www.cspinet.org; M. Jacobson, "Kwan Should Stop Spinning for Coke," *Huffington Post,* March 25, 2014, www.huffingtonpost.com/; L. Kornowski, "No One Cares about Celebrity Endorsements, Says Study Likely to Freak Kim Kardashian Out," *Huffington Post,* April 25, 2014, www.huffingtonpost.com; Let's Move!, "Accomplishments," September 2014, www.letsmove.gov/; R. Lynch, "13 Celebrity Endorsement Deals That Backfired," *Los Angeles Times,* February 26, 2014, www.latimes.com; R. Mann, "China Cracks Down on Laughable Celebrity Endorsements: New Law Requires Celebs to Actually Use the Products They Pitch," *Ad Week,* September 2, 2014, www.adweek.com; C. May, "Health Group Upset Shaq Promoting 'Let's Move!' with First Lady While Selling Soda," *Daily Caller,* September 5, 2013, http://dailycaller.com; K. McQuade, "Strangest Celebrity Partnerships Like David Hasselhoff and Frozen Food," *Huffington Post,* July 18, 2013, www.huffingtonpost.com; M. Salup, "The Evolution of Celebrity Endorsements," *Huffington Post,* February 24, 2014, www.huffingtonpost.com; K. Thompson, "Michelle Obama Touts Subway's Kids Menu," *Washington Post,* January 23, 2014, www.washingtonpost.com; and J. Thomas, "Want a Celebrity Endorsement on Twitter? 3 Legal Precautions to Know," *Entrepreneur.com,* March 25, 2014, www.entrepreneur.com.

3–4 ATTENTION MILLENNIALS! AUTOMOBILE MANUFACTURERS ADAPT FOR YOU

Millennials (Generation Y in the text) are the largest generation since their parents constituted the previous largest generation: the baby boomers. The Millennial generation encompasses a fairly wide range of ages, but the oldest of the group are now in their early 30s and are living very grown-up lives, complete with major consumer purchases. This generation is very attractive to marketers because of its sheer size and purchasing power. Yet, the Millennials think about brands and make purchases differently and are much more in tune with digital communication than any other generation.

Not long ago, parents struggled to keep their children from watching too much television. Now, as those children are coming of age, television advertisers have the opposite problem as they compete for the attention of Millennials. Young people are still consuming media at very high rates, but now they are in many new places other than television, like social media and mobile devices. To illustrate, in 1983, 100 million Americans watched the finale of *Mash* on television, compared to a mere 10 million that watched the finale of *Breaking Bad* on live television. Meanwhile, advertising on small mobile screens does not carry the same effect as advertising in traditional media once did.

Consumers are increasingly ignoring and disregarding advertising. This lack of attention to advertising is compounded by Americans engaging in other activities while viewing traditional media. (See Tables A and B for statistics regarding these factors for various demographic groups, including Millennials.)

According to the CEO of Starcom MediaVest, one of the largest advertising buying agencies:

> I am nervous about us all being out of a job a year from now if Reed Hastings [chief executive of Netflix] takes over the world.

Millennials in particular are the subject of many marketing research companies. Various recent surveys show that this generation spends more time on social media, particularly on mobile devices, than any other group.

TABLE A Types of Advertisements Most Ignored and Disregarded

	Total	Gender		Age				Education		
		Male	Female	18–34	35–44	45–54	55+	H.S. or Less	Some College	College Grad+
	%	%	%	%	%	%	%	%	%	%
Any (NET)	91	90	92	90	92	88	93	89	92	94
Internet banner ads	43	42	45	42	47	43	43	40	46	46
Internet search engine ads	20	20	21	21	21	19	20	17	22	23
Television ads	14	15	13	9	13	14	20	17	12	12
Radio ads	7	7	8	11	7	5	6	8	7	7
Newspaper ads	6	6	5	7	4	7	5	6	5	6
None of these	9	10	8	10	8	12	7	11	8	6

Source: Harris Interactive Poll of American Adults.

TABLE B Activities Done While Watching Television

	Total	Gender		Age				Education		
		Male	Female	18–34	35–44	45–54	55+	H.S. or Less	Some College	College Grad+
	%	%	%	%	%	%	%	%	%	%
Surf the Internet using a computer	56	53	59	68	59	55	45	52	57	62
Read a book, magazine, or newspaper	44	37	51	42	41	44	47	35	50	51
Go on a social networking site (e.g., Facebook, Twitter)	40	34	45	57	47	36	21	33	44	46
Text on my mobile phone	37	35	39	57	46	38	14	28	41	47
Shop online	29	27	31	40	33	27	19	22	31	39
Surf the Internet using my mobile phone	18	20	16	30	23	15	6	10	19	29
Read a book on an eReader device (e.g., Kindle, Nook)	7	6	9	6	8	9	7	5	10	9
Surf the Internet on a tablet computer (e.g., iPad, Xoom)	7	8	6	7	13	4	5	6	5	11
Something else	30	26	33	32	26	28	30	26	33	32
None	14	18	11	8	12	16	20	19	12	10
Not applicable	3	4	2	5	3	2	2	3	2	4

Source: Harris Interactive Poll of American Adults.

Millennials spend 14.5 hours per week on average on mobile devices. However, while it is less than that of Generation X and baby boomers, they still spend 25 hours per week on average watching television. In response, advertisers are expected to spend $17.7 billion on mobile advertising in 2014, which is double the amount spent in 2013. Thirty-six percent of Millennials say that digital advertising is the most influential media for brand decisions, while 19 percent of Millennials say the same for television advertising. Meanwhile, 44 percent of Millennials want to have an open dialogue with brands using social channels. A full 55 percent of Millennials feel that a recommendation from a friend is the strongest influence of brand choice. Often, these recommendations are created sharing branded content on social media.

Automobile manufacturers are particularly attracted to Millennials and many of them are having to learn new ways to appeal as they focus their efforts on this group. They are trying new approaches to the product offerings, like flashy colors. Also, many automobile manufacturers are attempting to garner the attention of Millennials through nontraditional tactics involving consumer engagement and entertaining, quirky content on social media. Volkswagen, Ford, Toyota, and Mini Cooper have had some success through advertising on Buzzfeed, an entertaining website known for viral content that targets Millennials. Jonathan Perelman, vice president of agency strategy and industry development at Buzzfeed, states:

> The power for auto brands, really any brand, but really for automotive brands is you can tell a really compelling, sometimes funny story that's adding value to the consumer so that they're not only going to want to engage with that ad, but also share it with their friends. There's an implied endorsement that you as my friend understand what I like. You're going to have a significant lift in your feelings toward the brand. That's the power today in social content marketing. Being able to be in the conversation, adding value to the consumer and tapping into the networks where people are already communicating.

According to Chris Travell, vice president of strategic consulting for Maritz Research:

> Millennials are an important group of buyers in the industry today, and not just in terms of sheer size. They are also helping to refine the vehicle shopping and ownership experience. These younger buyers are much more connected than previous car buyers. The manufacturer that develops a strategy that resonates with millennial buyers will increase the likelihood of consideration the next time that customer is in the market. In turn, this will increase the likelihood of selling a car to that customer.

However, there is a wide disparity among Millennials' responses to automobile manufacturers' efforts. Fiat failed miserably with its "Endless Fun" campaign, which featured seven-year-old memes and .gifs featuring bizarre images of things like people dancing around a Fiat in horse masks. Honda chose an unconventional method by mocking how other advertisers focus on Millennial stereotypes in its #UnBuenFit campaign.

Ford is one automobile manufacturer that seems to have tapped into ways of communicating with Millennials that has been very effective. Ford has been the number one brand in purchase consideration for Millennials for the past several years. According to Sheryl Connelly, global consumer trends and futuring manager at Ford:

> This group of consumers is an incredible market opportunity, but the way that millennials interact with brands is totally different from earlier generations. Understanding their priorities helps us market to them, so that we're giving a message that is relevant to them.

Ford has discovered a formula that turns Millennial consumers into brand ambassadors and it appears to be working. Amy Marentic, Ford's global car and crossover marketing manager, explains Ford's approach to Millennials:

> We're turning a 108-year old brand over to consumers. I'm very serious about that. Our market share with Millennials has increased significantly. . . . We're now the top selling brand to all Millennials . . . don't be afraid to turn your brand over to others.

Ford points to several techniques that have led to its success. The first is to get Millennials talking to each other about the brand. When Ford was preparing to launch its Fiesta model in the United States, it gave 100 of the vehicles to influential, web-savvy Millennials, who were dubbed as "Fiesta Agents." Ms. Marentic said:

> We gave them a Fiesta for six months, and gave them gas and insurance, and they had to do monthly missions for us and then put the results online. If I tell them how great the new Ford Fiesta is, they won't notice, but when their friends and family tell them, they'll pay attention.

Second, Ford appeals to Millennials' love of technology through new technology called MyFord Touch. MyFord Touch performs many tasks while consumers are driving, including syncing their phones, reading their texts, adjusting the temperature, and making dinner suggestions.

> [Millennials] are always on and they want their experience in the car to be always on. It understands 10,000 voice commands.

Finally, Ms. Marentic suggests that Ford's success with Millennials comes from being edgy and entertaining.

For example, in order to improve the formerly stuffy image of the Ford Focus, Ford created a spokescharacter named Doug that is only present on social media such as Twitter and YouTube. Doug is a rude-mannered and irreverent orange sock puppet. For example, when Doug is informed by a Ford marketing executive that the Focus has double French stitching on the seats. Doug replies:

> How many times have I sat in single-French-stitched seats and said, "I might as well be at the town dump sitting on garbage cans"?

This is precisely the untraditional type of content that Ford has used to successfully capture the attention of Millennials that remains so elusive for other automobile manufacturers and brands.

Discussion Questions

1. Chapter 8 discusses factors that affect consumer attention. How do the following situational factors play a role in Millennials' attention to Ford's promotions?
   a. Clutter
   b. Program involvement
2. Chapter 11 discusses appeal characteristics in advertising. Use Google Videos or Google Images to find examples of the advertisements for the Ford Fiesta advertising campaigns. Evaluate those advertisements based on
   a. Appeal characteristics
   b. Message structure characteristics
3. Chapter 8 discusses stimulus factors in advertising. Use Google Videos or Google Images to find examples of the advertisements for the Ford Fiesta's advertising campaigns. Evaluate those advertisements based on the following stimulus factors:
   a. Size
   b. Intensity
   c. Attractive visuals
   d. Color and movement
   e. Position
   f. Isolation
   g. Format
   h. Contrast and expectations
   i. Interestingness
   j. Information quantity
4. Evaluate the information displayed in Tables A and B. Imagine you are a marketing manager for an automobile manufacturer that is targeting Millennials. Your goal is to gain the attention of your target market. Use that information to answer the following questions.
   a. According to Table A, which types of media are least likely to be ignored by Millennials?
   b. How do the media that are least likely to be ignored compare with what media other surveys show Millennials prefer?
   c. Assume that television advertising is a part of your promotional mix. How would you handle the fact that a large part of your target market is multitasking while watching television?
   d. Imagine that your target market is a different demographic. How would your answers to the previous parts of this question change?
5. Chapter 9 discusses strength of learning. Ford is hoping that Millennials learn that Ford is focused on their needs and wants. So far, it appears to be working. Strength of learning is enhanced by the following six factors. Evaluate Ford's marketing to Millennials on these factors.
   a. Importance
   b. Message involvement
   c. Mood
   d. Reinforcement
   e. Repetition
   f. Dual coding
6. Chapter 9 also discusses brand image and product positioning. Think about Ford and other automobile manufacturer's brand images. Then, construct a perceptual map that includes several automobile manufacturers that are targeting Millennials.
7. Chapter 12 discusses VALS. To which category (ideals, achievement, self-expression) does Ford's approach appear to be targeted in attracting Millennials? Explain.

Sources: "Are Advertisers Wasting Their Money?," *Harris Interactive: A Nielsen Company,* December 3, 2010, www.harrisinteractive.com; C. Arreola, "Honda Targets Latino Millennials in Unconventional Way," *Latina,* July 18, 2014, www.latina.com; V. Bond, "How Car Marketers Harness the Viral Power of Buzzfeed to Reach Millennials," *Automotive News,* December 1, 2013, www.autonews.com; "Distracted TV Viewers," *Harris Interactive: A Nielsen Company,* June 15, 2011, www.harrisinteractive.com; D. Fenn, "4 Tips from Ford on Marketing to Millennials," *CBS Money Watch,* June 22, 2011, www.cbsnews.com; I. Slutsky, "Ford and Twitter Talk Keys to Marketing to Millennials," *Advertising Age,* August 19, 2011, http://adage.com; "Traditional or Digital Ads? Millennials Show Mixed Feelings," *EMarketer,* April 15, 2014, www.emarketer.com; B. Tuttle, "Selling Cars to Millennials: Quirky Models, Flashy Colors Aim to Get Gen Y Out of Neutral," *Time,* November 20, 2012, http://business.time.com; S. Vranica, "Millennials Spend 14.5 Hours per Week on Smartphones," *The Wall Street Journal,* July 2, 2014, http://blogs.wsj.com; "Ford Now Leads Sales Consideration with Millennials," *Ford Motor Company,* August 19, 2014, http://corporate.ford.com; J. Fromm, "Ford Recognizes Millennial Consumer Marketing Trends," *Future Cast Millennial Marketing Insights,* 2014, http://millennialmarketing.com; J. Gapper, "Advertisers Have Lost the Attention of a Generation," *Financial Times,* June 18, 2014, www.ft.com; "Millennials: The New Age of Brand Loyalty," *Adroit Digital,* 2014, www.adroit.digital.com; J. Perez, "Fiat Tries to Target Millennials with New Ads, Fails Miserably," *Yahoo! Auto,* June 18, 2014, https://autos.yahoo.com.

3–5 IS YOUR DOG A CHEESEHEAD? TARGETING THE PREMIUM PET MARKET

The market for pet products and services is large and growing, with a current estimated size of $47 billion. It's not just dry dog food anymore. Pet owners refer to themselves as "pet parents," put their animals in "pet motels," and pamper them with spa-like treatments. Pet owners, it seems, are a very interesting and committed group of folks. Increasingly, pet owners are "humanizing" their pets, with 92 percent considering their pets to be another member of the family. According to survey results from the American Animal Hospital Association, of pet owners surveyed, 63 percent tell their pets they love them at least once a day, 59 percent celebrate their pet's birthday, and 66 percent prepare special foods for their pet!

These purchases, attitudes, and behaviors belong to the premium pet market, which consists of some 17 million people across a number of subsegments, including (1) affluents ($150,000+ annual income), (2) specialty shoppers (shop only in specialty stores and online), (3) married with children, (4) empty nesters, (5) dual-income households with no kids, and (6) singles with no children. No longer does the presence of children drive pet ownership and spending. Today, pet ownership and pampering is a lifestyle, with pets being part of the family. Table A contains demographic data pertaining to the premium pet market compared with the baseline of all households who own a dog or cat (for example, 18- to 24-year-olds index 91, which means they are 9 percent less likely to have premium pet owners in that age group than the average pet household).

TABLE A Premium Pet Demographics versus Average Pet Owners

	Premium Pet Owners
Percent of households	**32.9%**
Age	
18–24 years	91
25–34	71
35–44	121
45–54	128
55–64	115
65–74	47
75+	41
Education	
Graduate degree	201
College graduate	154
High school graduate or less	55
Occupation	
Management	181
Professional/technical	149
Sales	120
Administrative support	110
Labor	90
Race/Ethnic Group	
White	103
Hispanic	76
Black	74
Asian	188
Gender	
Male	112
Female	92
Region	
Northeast	125
Southeast	100
Southwest	85
Pacific	98
Household Income	
$50,000–74,999	30
$75,000–99,999	164
$100,000–149,999	304
$150,000+	304
Marital Status	
Single	88
Married	124
Divorced	64
Widowed	42
Number of Children	
None	104
One	92
Two	104
Three+	75

Note: 100 = Average household that owns a dog or cat.

Source: Simmons Market Research Bureau, *Study of Media and Markets,* Fall 2006.

(Continued)

While brands such as Purina and Hartz are major players in the mass market for pet supplies and products, numerous smaller brands exist that fill various niches in the market. One such company that is riding this premium pet wave is Complete Natural Nutrition, which sells all natural products for discerning pet parents. A core aspect of their approach is that their products are human food "disguised" as pet treats. According to their website:

> Complete Natural Nutrition is a health "solutions" company for discriminating pets whose parents accept nothing less than the very best. In 2005, Complete Natural Nutrition set out to develop products that would make a significant difference in the daily lives of dogs and cats. We understood that pet parents did not need another treat, cookie, raw hide or body part to feed their companion pet. Rather, we set out to provide frustrated pet parents with treat solutions for pets with specific health issues like diabetes, overweight, finicky, allergies or on restricted diets. We set out to provide discriminating pet parents, who read labels and who want US made and US sourced ingredients, with the world's healthiest pet treats.

They offer Cheese Please, made from 100 percent pure Wisconsin cheese, which they describe as "a human snack disguised as a training treat." A 7 oz. bag sells for $15.99. They also offer different Real Food Toppers such as beef, chicken, and salmon, which are 100 percent meat. Each 4 oz. bag sells for $15.99. Complete Natural Nutrition products can be bought (a) online at their website, (b) through specialty online stores, and (c) through specialty retail pet stores.

Discussion Questions

1. Visit Complete Natural Nutrition's website (www.completenaturalnutrition.com). What types of attitude change strategies are they utilizing? Do you think they are effective?
2. What learning approach and principles would you use to teach consumers about Complete Natural Nutrition's products such as Cheese Please and Real Food Toppers? Is this reflected in the company's website?
3. Develop a psychographic profile relating to the type of person who would be most likely to purchase pet food products from Complete Natural Nutrition. That is, generate a list of attitudes, values, activities, and interests that are specifically related to having a dog that Cheese Please and Real Food Toppers buyers would likely possess.
4. Based on the demographic data in Table A, what would be the best target(s) market for Cheese Please and Real Food Toppers, assuming they are targeting the premium market?
5. Develop an ad or marketing approach to create a positive attitude toward Cheese Please or Real Food Toppers, focusing on the following components:
   a. Cognitive
   b. Affective
   c. Behavioral
6. Develop an ad or marketing approach to create a positive attitude toward Cheese Please or Real Food Toppers, using the following:
   a. Humor
   b. Emotion
   c. Utilitarian appeal
   d. Value-expressive appeal
   e. Celebrity endorser
   f. Self-concept
   g. Fear

Source: J. Fetto, "'Woof, Woof' Means, 'I Love You,'" *American Demographics,* February 2002, p. 11; R. Gardyn, "Animal Magnetism," *American Demographics,* May 2002, pp. 30–37; *Market Trends: Premium Pet Demographics and Product Purchasing Preferences* (Rockville, MD: Packaged Facts, August 2007); and information from Complete Natural Nutrition's website, accessed July 13, 2011.

3–6 HELLO KITTY MANIA

Hello Kitty is a Japanese cartoon character that has maintained global popularity since 1974. Hello Kitty is a very cute cat with rounded features and no mouth. Sanrio, the makers of Hello Kitty, have produced and disseminated a huge assortment of Hello Kitty–themed merchandise. In doing so, some have even claimed that Hello Kitty "conquered the world." Hello Kitty has become a national icon of sorts for Japan, as she has served as an ambassador for UNICEF for both Japan and the United States and has even played a role as a Japanese diplomatic envoy to China.

Hello Kitty has become a brand phenomenon throughout the globe for generations of consumers. Hello Kitty originally targeted young girls and preteens in the 1970s. After its popularity began to wane in the 1980s, Sanrio repositioned Hello Kitty as retro in the 1990s to appeal to a much wider range of female consumers. Hello Kitty products were marketed to the adult women who were familiar with Hello Kitty from their childhoods. In the early 2000s, popularity waned again but was revived by partnerships with luxury products and jewelry. Hello Kitty's image graces over 50,000 products, which are sold in over 70 countries. Over the last 40 years, Hello Kitty has grown into a brand worth $7 billion and generates over $789 million in revenue annually.

The Hello Kitty brand is heavily licensed and has been used in co-branding campaigns with a wide variety of retail brands. In 2012, *Forbes* named it one of the best-selling license entertainment products. Numerous brands have collaborated with Hello Kitty, including Target, Sephora, McDonald's, Walmart, Forever 21, Tervis, Fender, Uglydoll, Kidrobot, the NFL, the MLB, Minnetonka, Vans, Swarovski, and many more. Hello Kitty has gotten into the transportation business as well. Eva Air is flying Hello Kitty airplanes out of Taiwan. Star Cruises is sailing Hello Kitty cruises in Singapore and Malaysia. In 2014, Hello Kitty reached a 40-year milestone, without any shortage of limited-edition products to commemorate the date. The Japanese American National Museum in Los Angeles also honored Hello Kitty's 40th anniversary.

Hello Kitty's popularity among so many consumers of various ages in countries all over the world is a much-discussed topic among many Hello Kitty enthusiasts to the executives at Sanrio. In part, the answer lies in Japanese popular culture and the Japanese love for *kawaii. Kawaii* means cuteness and it pervades Japanese society. The use of cute cartoon characters with rounded features and pastel colors is extremely prevalent in Japanese culture and branding. *Kawaii* is much more than a style or trend. It is embedded in social and gender roles of young Japanese women and even dictates their behavior. For example, *kawaii* young women often act silly and speak in squeaky voices.

Japanese companies like Sanrio have successfully exported *kawaii* culture to the rest of world. The cuteness serves as a comfort of sorts for people living in congested urban lifestyles. Japanese companies take care to cultivate and protect their *kawaii* image. According to Yauko Nakamura, the president of a Tokyo-based marketing company:

> Japanese products are made to be *kawaii* so that they are liked by women. In Japan, women hold the spending power. Even for things that women don't purchase themselves, such as a car, they have a strong say in the final decision.

Several experts in Japanese culture give similar responses. Hello Kitty can be anything for anyone. The appeal of Hello Kitty comes from her reflections of each consumer's unique projections. According to the author of *Japanamerica: How Japanese Pop Culture Has Invaded the U.S.*:

> Kitty's appeal is that she's an emotional blank slate. As one of her designers told me: "Kitty feels like you do. We project upon that mouth-less, expressionless kitten, making her the perfectly interactive toy or doll or marketing tool in an age where interactivity is not only desired, it's expected."

Sanrio's public relations manager Kazuo Tohmatsu said:

> Hello Kitty represents the deep desire among all people, regardless of nationality or race, to feel joy and happiness, without having to qualify it at any deep intellectual level. Hello Kitty doesn't judge. She lets you feel how you feel without forcing you to question why.

David Marchi, senior manager of brand management and marketing at Sanrio, views Hello Kitty in a similar way:

> She is not graphically portrayed with a visual mouth, and it lends to her appeal. When you look at her she can be everything and anything. She can appeal to a little girl, an alternative teen, an executive. She can be for anyone.

Still, others focus on Hello Kitty's symbolization of desirable virtues. For example, Helen McCarthy, an author and expert on Japanese animation and comics, said:

> Hello Kitty stands for the innocence and sincerity of childhood and the simplicity of the world. Women and girls all over the world are happy to buy in to the image of the trusting, loving childhood in a safe neighborhood that Hello Kitty represents. They don't want to let go of that image, so as they grow up, they hang onto Hello Kitty out of nostalgic longing—as if by keeping a symbolic object, they can somehow keep hold of a fragment of their childhood self.

Finally, according to Nick Currie, an Osaka-based musician and cultural commentator:

> Hello Kitty symbolizes some essential Japanese virtues: agreeableness, harmony, commerce, cuteness, nature, fertility, affluence and the avoidance of aggression. She [also] represents the irresistible idiocy of consumer culture, hardwired to our neurological system. We shop with almost the same reflexes that make us stretch out to stroke a big-eyed, fluffy kitten. That may be a universal impulse.

Consumers of a wide range of ages adore the brand and often begin to incorporate Hello Kitty in to their self-concepts. Many customers have adopted the habit of collecting Hello Kitty items. This practice is especially encouraged by many releases of special limited-edition collector items. However, some fans' passion for collecting Hello Kitty merchandise develops into an obsession as they go to what many people would call extremes.

Meet Natasha Goldsworth, one of the world's most avid collectors of Hello Kitty memorabilia. For her, Hello Kitty is more than a hobby; it is a lifestyle and a huge part of her identity. At 29 years of age, she has been collecting for over 15 years and has filled every room of her apartment with Hello Kitty with all manner of items including jewelry, handbags, furniture, clothing, appliances, décor, doll houses, and over 4,000 plush Hello Kitty toys. She also edits and maintains a website devoted to Hello Kitty called hellokitty4u.com. According to Ms. Goldsworth:

> I live in my little pink lagoon with all my kitties, they cheer me up and I like having them around me. Before people come over I do have to warn them about my kitty kingdom because some people just can't handle it. . . . I'm actually thinking about moving into a bigger place. There just isn't enough room for all of my kitties.

Ms. Goldsworth is currently seeking a romantic partner and would like to be married, but her obsessive collecting of Hello Kitty paraphernalia has become an obstacle to her previous romantic pursuits. When it comes to a decision between a potential romantic partner and her Hello Kitty collection, Hello Kitty is victorious. Ms. Goldsworth says:

> Boyfriends in the past have tried to make me give her up, so I got rid of them. It's part of who I am and I'm not changing for anybody. . . . Others have asked me to sell my collection and I've had to tell them no. If a man doesn't like my kitty kingdom and can't accept me for who I am then I'm not interested in them.

Ms. Goldsworth estimates she has spent nearly $80,000 on her Hello Kitty collection. However, she makes other financial sacrifices to support her habit, such as sacrificing vacations and eating out for years. Her most valuable Hello Kitty possession is a limited-edition cuddly Hello Kitty wearing a handmade Hanita wedding dress. Once she finds her future husband who is supportive of her Hello Kitty–centric lifestyle, she plans to wear a human-sized replica of that same dress.

> When I get married I want to wear the same Hanita dress. My dad's already agreed to wear a pink tie and I want to have Hello Kitty on top of the wedding cake.

To Ms. Goldsworth and other extreme Hello Kitty enthusiasts, collecting Hello Kitty merchandise is a way of life. This lifestyle is known as collection obsession and the object of collection (Hello Kitty in this case) becomes engrained in the collector's identity. It is important to note that obsessive collecting is distinct from hoarding. Hoarders keep almost everything. They have a very anxious time organizing and throwing anything away because of a belief that they will use the items again. Several television programs have featured examples of extreme hoarders. Obsessive collectors, on the other hand, accumulate only particular objects, are meticulously organized, know exactly how many items are in the collection and where they are located, and enjoy proudly displaying their collections. According to Julie Pike, a clinical psychologist from the Anxiety Disorder Treatment Center in Durham, NC:

> With hoarding, we look at three main behaviors: one acquiring too many possessions; second, having great difficulty discarding something; and three difficulty organizing. . . .
>
> Unlike hoarders, collectors are proud, not ashamed, of their possessions. More likely, collectors have an obsession or preoccupation. Most of us have a degree of that rather than the ends of a continuum. But if collectors get in a place where they are spending so much money that they can't pay their mortgage, that's a problem. Or if they are spending so much time at it that they can't go to their job or leave their house.

Discussion Questions

1. Chapter 8 discusses branding strategies. One of the ways that the Hello Kitty brand became disseminated so widely is by using a co-branding strategy with many other brands.
   a. What are some of the brands mentioned in the case that partnered with Hello Kitty?
   b. Discuss the perceived fit between each of those brands and Hello Kitty.
   c. Discuss the target market for each of those co-branded offerings. Are the target markets the same? If not, how do they differ?
   d. Perform an Internet search to discover more brands with which Hello Kitty is currently partnering.
   e. Repeat the analysis in parts b and c for the new brands that you uncovered in your Internet search.
   f. What characteristics of Hello Kitty make it able to be a successful co-branding partner with so many other types of brands?
2. Chapter 9 discusses brand image and product positioning. Reflect on Hello Kitty as a brand and then answer the following:
   a. Describe Hello Kitty's brand image.
   b. Based on your answers from the question about co-branding, select a product category from the co-branded Hello Kitty products and brainstorm a short list of competitors in the market for that product category.
   c. Construct a perceptual map that includes a Hello Kitty co-branded product and your list of brainstormed products in that category.
   d. Write a short narrative describing the process you used to develop the perceptual map and your interpretation of the content of the perceptual map.
3. Chapter 10 covers McGuire's psychological motives. Review the cognitive preservation motives, cognitive growth motives, affective preservation motives, and affective growth motives. Which of these motives could describe why Hello Kitty enthusiasts, such as Ms. Goldsworth, accumulate such large Hello Kitty collections?
4. Chapter 11 discusses spokescharacters, a communication characteristic that influences attitudes. The case describes how Hello Kitty served as a spokescharacter for UNICEF for many years, as well as a diplomatic tool for Japanese-Chinese diplomacy. Some characteristics that influence the success of celebrity sources include their expertise, aspirational aspects, and meaning transfer. How do these characteristics apply to Hello Kitty as a spokescharacter?
5. Chapter 12 discusses self-concept and lifestyle. Think about Ms. Goldsworth as an example of an obsessive Hello Kitty collector.
   a. Do you feel that her Hello Kitty possessions have become part of Ms. Goldsworth's extended self? Explain your rationale.
   b. Think about the concepts of actual self-concept, ideal self-concept, private self-concept, and social self-concept. Using her quotes in the case, interpret how these self-concepts may differ for Ms. Goldsworth.
6. Review the VALS segments discussed in Chapter 12. In which of these segments do you think obsessive collectors (who are able to fund the purchases required for large collections) would best fit?

Source: B. Bremner, "In Japan, Cute Conquers All," *Bloomberg Businessweek,* June 24, 2002, www.businessweek.com; E. Walker, "Top Cat: How 'Hello Kitty' Conquered the World," *The Independent,* May 21, 2008, www.independent.co.uk; K. Webley, "Hoarding: How Collecting Stuff Can Destroy Your Life," *Time,* April 26, 2010, http://content.time.com; D. Dana, "Japan Grows Its Soft Power through the Export of Kawaii," *Investoralist,* January 19, 2010, www.investoralist.com; J. Sholl, "What Is the Difference between Compulsive Hoarding and Collecting?," *Psychology Today,* December 17, 2010, www.psychologytoday.com; R. Lamb, "Swarovski Flaunts Hello Kitty Collection with Facebook-First Approach," *Luxury Daily,* July 7, 2011, www.luxurydaily.com; S. James, "'My Collection Obsession': One Man's Collector Is Another's Hoarder," *ABC News,* August 17, 2011, http://abcnews.go.com; S. Harwin, "Forever 21 and Sanrio Team Up for Hello Kitty Forever Collection," *Catster,* November 21, 2012, www.catster.com; "Tervis Introduces New Hello Kitty Collection," *Gift Shop,* August 13, 2012, www.giftshopmag.com; M. Keane, "The Cutesy Hello Kitty Character Came to Be Popular with Everyone from Small Children to Motorcycle Gangs," *The Wall Street Journal,* April 12, 2013, http://online.wsj.com; Z. Bissonnette, "Hobbies: When Collection Becomes Compulsion, Think 'Sell,'" *CNBC,* July 15, 2013, www.cnbc.com; S. Parsons, "'Kawaii' Culture," *Japan in Perspective,* May 16, 2013, www.japaninperspective.com; T. Borchard, "10 Things You Should Know about Compulsive Hoarding," *Psych Central,* http://psychcentral.com; M. Fitzpatrick, "Hello Kitty at 40: The Cat That Conquered the World," *BBC,* August 18, 2014, www.bbc.com; J. Howenstine, "Hello Kitty × Vans 2014 Collection," *Nice Kicks,* June 16, 2014, www.nicekicks.com; B. London, "'If a Man Doesn't Like My Kitty Kingdom, Then I'm Not Interested': 29-Yr-Old Woman Has Spent over £50,000 on Her Hello Kitty Obsession . . . and Yes, She Is Still Single," *Mail Online,* June 11, 2014, www.dailymail.co.uk; "Minnetonka for Hello Kitty Collaboration Debuts for Fall 2014," *Hello Kitty Junkie,* July 30, 2014, www.hellokittyjunkie.com; J. Osterheldt, "At 40, Hello Kitty Is Timeless," *Kansas City Star,* June 25, 2014, www.kansascity.com; and P. St. Michel, "The Rise of Japan's Creepy-Cute Craze," *The Atlantic,* April 14, 2014, www.theatlantic.com.

3-7 XEROX'S ONGOING BATTLE TO REPOSITION

Xerox is a fantastic example of brand positioning. So fantastic, in fact, that its name has become synonymous with the photocopier industry and is often used as a verb. Xerox has very strong global brand recognition and has historically been a leader in its industry. However, this well-known brand position may actually be a hindrance to the company as Xerox attempts to reposition itself in consumers' minds in an evolving competitive landscape. In an age of digital media and cloud computing, businesses have much less need for copier and fax machines. Xerox has moved into several other areas of business but continues to struggle to shift consumer perceptions along with it.

Xerox has experienced multiple failed brand reposition attempts. In the early 1970s Xerox wanted consumers to think of the brand as a leader in the information systems and data processing business, but Xerox Data Systems was abandoned after spending millions of dollars. Likewise, Xerox later failed with its Telecopier, XTEN network, and Team Xerox attempts to reposition the company. These previous repositioning failures have not deterred Xerox from trying to reposition again.

After decades, Xerox's most recent attempts to reposition the brand began in 2008 when the company introduced a new corporate logo. This change extended to product design, product naming, and building signage. According to Richard Wergan, the Xerox director of worldwide branding:

> We are a very different company today than we were when our current brand architecture was developed. The new logo is meant to disrupt the mental model of Xerox as just a copier company.

Research at the time showed that the old corporate logo (called a wordmark) had become too familiar and consumers did not pay it much attention. The new logo included a red sphere that is representative of a globe and worldwide connections, was encircled by intersecting graphic ribbons, and used FS Albert font with curved edges. Internal documents at Xerox described the logo as

> I am FS Albert. I am a modern and approachable font. My rounded corners make me more human and less technical.

In 2010, Xerox acquired a company called Affiliated Computer Services, or ACS, a well-established business processing company that aids its clients with digital documents like credit card applications, medical billing, mass-transit ticketing systems, and municipal paperwork. With this acquisition, just over half of Xerox's revenue came from business solution services, rather than sales of copier and fax equipment. Xerox launched its most expensive advertising campaign to date in an effort to shift the company's image to that of a business solutions services provider. Ursula Burns, Xerox CEO, said that

> [this campaign] aimed at disrupting old perceptions of the Xerox brand and positioning the new Xerox as the world's leading enterprise for business process and document management.

The advertisements in this campaign focused on Xerox's business solutions relationships with several well-known clients, such as Procter & Gamble, Target, Ducati, the New York Mets, the University of Notre Dame, and Marriot International. These organizations happily allowed their brand names to be used in the campaign. In each advertisement, employees or spokescharacters were shown dealing with back-office functions that were interfering with their core purpose. For example, one including P&G portrayed Mr. Clean attempting to scan documents with one hand while cleaning a table with another hand. The advertisements targeted businesspeople with decision-making power. In order to reach this target, ads were placed in airports, in business publications like *The Wall Street Journal,* and on business news channels like CNBC.

Unfortunately, the 2010 advertising campaign did not have the intended effect. Rather, Xerox's client companies garnered more benefits from the ads, while Xerox continued to be viewed as a copier company. However, CEO Ursula Burns still had heart and knew that repositioning the Xerox brand and a business services brand would not happen overnight. She said:

> We need to expand even further into business process outsourcing and IT outsourcing. It's a $500 billion industry and so we have a long way to go before we tap that market. We're showing proof points as we go along. But you can't be confused about the reality. It's all about managing this transition, so that you don't fall in love too much with the future to the point where you hate the past.

Determined to reposition the brand to thrive in the digital services marketplace and compete with the likes of IBM and Accenture, Xerox pushed on. Another approach that Xerox used was to change perceptions through content in social media marketing. Xerox partnered with *Forbes* and *The Week* to create Xerox-branded pages that post content on topics like analyzing big data and managing the millennial generation. According to Jay Bartlett, Xerox vice president of global social marketing:

> Everything across our social media channels and content we're developing is very much about driving thought leadership in these spaces you'd never expect to see our name. This is really the notion that content and social go hand in glove. We married the two, and we think that's a recipe to help us utilize word-of-mouth marketing to help with our repositioning.

In 2013, Xerox launched a new advertising campaign that recognized that the enduring perception among consumers was that Xerox was in the business of copy machines and leveraged that fact to highlight its business services in a humorous way. Chista Carone, Xerox's chief marketing officer at the time, describes the rationale and a spot from that campaign:

> It became clear that we needed to draw the connection between who we were and who we are. We needed to get back to the basics of explaining our purpose and giving people a reason to believe that the copier company could stand for so much more than copies. That's why our latest campaign, which broke in February, acknowledges our past, even embraces it, while helping people connect the dots to today's Xerox. It's a no-nonsense, straight-talk effort. One 30-second spot from Young & Rubicam opens with a woman standing in front of—yes!—a copying machine. "When I say Xerox, I know what you're thinking," she says, then prints an image of a transit map. "Transit fares, as in the 37 billion transit fares we help collect each year." Another commercial features the same woman proclaiming that revolutionizing an industry is a hard act to follow, and then explaining some of the breadth and scale of services offered by Xerox.

That year marked the 75th anniversary of the first xerographic image. Xerox did not let this occasion pass unnoticed or uncelebrated. According to CEO Ursula Burns:

> Now is the time when many companies would look back, and we certainly will, but only for a moment. The real focus of our celebration will be the future and how Xerox will continue to simplify how work gets done.

"Simplifying how work gets done" is a message and position that Xerox hopes will resonate with businesspeople. This theme is present in its press releases and throughout the content in its own website and sponsored pages. For example, each of Xerox's seven outsourcing services incorporates the message on the webpage. Please see the table for examples of this.

Outsourcing Service	Simplifying Message
Human Resources	Did you know Xerox is the second largest benefits and pensions administrator globally? It's just one of the ***surprising ways Xerox is helping companies simplify how work gets done.*** . . .
Customer Care	Did you know Xerox has 175 customer care centers globally, staffed with over 46,000 agents? It's just one of the ***surprising ways Xerox is helping companies simplify how work gets done.*** . . .
Finance & Accounting	Did you know Xerox has over 24,000 professionals operating in over 90 global service centers? It's just one of the ***surprising ways Xerox is helping companies simplify how work gets done.*** . . .
Document Management	Did you know Gartner positions Xerox as a leader in the 2013 Gartner Magic Quadrant for managed print services? It's because Xerox finds ***surprising ways to help simplify how work gets done.*** . . .
Healthcare	Did you know Xerox offers services that touch two out of every three insured lives in the U.S.? It's because Xerox has surprising ways to help every area of the health care industry ***simplify how work gets done.*** . . .
Transportation	Did you know Xerox ranks #1 as a provider of worldwide transportation services to governments? It's because Xerox has proven solutions to help ***simplify the way the world moves.*** . . .

Will Xerox's latest efforts successfully reposition the brand to consumers as a business services company? Or will Xerox forever be relegated to the position as a photocopier giant? Xerox appears to be making the right moves, but only time will tell.

Discussion Questions

1. Chapter 9 discusses schemas, which are also known as schematic memories and knowledge structures. Construct a schema diagram for Xerox.
2. Chapter 9 also discusses product positioning, repositioning, and perceptual mapping.
   a. Construct a perceptual map that includes the Xerox brand before 2008 (before recent repositioning efforts).

b. Construct a perceptual map that includes the Xerox brand in current times.
c. Discuss how Xerox's position differs (or does not differ) between the two perceptual maps from part a and part b.

3. Chapter 9 further discusses brand equity and brand leverage. Xerox has strong brand equity because it has been a well-known and established brand for many years.
   a. According to the chapter, successful brand leverage requires that the original brand have a strong positive image and that the new product fit with the original product on at least one of what four dimensions?
   b. In which of these four dimensions does the business services solutions "product" fit with the original Xerox brand?
4. Chapter 11 discusses appeal characteristics in advertising. Use Google Videos or Google Images to find examples of the advertisements for either Xerox's 2010 or 2013 advertising campaigns. Evaluate those advertisements based on
   a. Appeal characteristics
   b. Message structure characteristics
5. Chapter 8 discusses stimulus factors in advertising. Use Google Videos or Google Images to find examples of the advertisements for either Xerox's 2010 or 2013 advertising campaigns. Evaluate those advertisements based on the following stimulus factors:
   a. Size
   b. Intensity
   c. Attractive visuals
   d. Color and movement
   e. Position
   f. Isolation
   g. Format
   h. Contrast and expectations
   i. Interestingness
   j. Information quantity
6. Discuss aspects of learning (Chapter 9) that have made it difficult for Xerox to change the brand perceptions held by consumers.

Source: D. Kiley, "Xerox Gets a Brand Makeover," *BusinessWeek,* January 7, 2008, www.businessweek.com; D. Maggiore, "Xerox Stretches Its Brand Positioning," *Innis Maggiore Ad Agency,* September 17, 2010, www.innismaggiore.com; D. Mattoli, "Xerox Touts Its Business-Services Side," *The Wall Street Journal,* September 2, 2010, http://online.wsj.com; Fast Company Staff, "Fresh Copy: How Ursula Burns Reinvented Xerox," November 19, 2011, www.fastcompany.com; E. Schwartz, "CEO Strategy: Charting 'Dual Transformation' at Xerox and Barnes & Noble," *Innosight,* December 2012, www.innosight.com; C. Carone, "Xerox's Brand Repositioning Challenge," *Advertising Age,* March 12, 2013, http://adage.com; J. Sternberg, "How Content Drives Xerox's Transformation," *Digiday,* June 21, 2013, http://digiday.com; Street Authority, "Climb Aboard the Xerox Transformation," *MSN Money,* June 27, 2013, http://money.msn.com; "Xerox Celebrates 75th Anniversary of the Creation of Xerography," *PIWorld,* October 17, 2013, www.piworld.com; and L. Abinanti, "Xerox Gets Positioning Right," *Messages That Matter,* April 15, 2014, www.messagesthatmatter.com.

3-8 DELL TAKES AN EMOTIONAL APPROACH

Dell Computers is taking a new approach in promoting its products: emotional branding. Dell recently launched its "More You" advertising campaign. The "More You" campaign emphasizes its users' self-identification in an effort to turn Dell into a lifestyle brand. According to Dell:

> We realized it was important to connect more emotionally with customers. Most competitors are neglecting the fact that technology is empowering people's lives. It will help people think, "It's about me."

This is not Dell's first venture into the realm of emotional branding. According to BrandIndex, Dell's 2010 "You Can Touch Dell" and "The Power to Do More" campaigns have helped boost sales, but Dell still lags behind HP and Apple in reputation and overall customer satisfaction.

The "More You" advertisements, which target Generation Y consumers, highlight Dell's new personalization features. The ads focus on customers and how they use Dell laptops, desktops, tablets, and smartphones in their daily routines as an avenue to express themselves. The customers' names are written in the Dell corporate font. The ads feature a variety of consumers from a variety of backgrounds who use Dell technology to satisfy a wide range of needs. Examples include a young lady who identifies herself as a Justin Beiber fan and uses Dell products to make a Justin Beiber shrine; a lady who uses Dell to "keep an eye on her boyfriend even if he doesn't know he's [her] boyfriend"; a gardening enthusiast who uses Dell to "plant ideas in [her] head";

and a grandmother who uses Dell products to maintain contact with her grandchildren. According to Dell:

> The humanity comes across well. That is what we are trying to do. It gives you insight into the lives of these people. . . . We have found our value proposition. A year ago, consumers didn't know what we stood for in consumer computing. Now our emphasis is on giving you seamless access to your digital life, service that is second to none, and value.

There has been debate over the superiority of emotional versus rational appeals in advertising for decades. Advocates of rational appeals, or hard sell, argue that facts and rational arguments sell products most effectively. Advocates of emotional appeals, or soft sell, argue that brands that inspire emotional responses from consumers are much more powerful and create more engagement. According to Les Binet, European director of DDB Matrix:

> A lot of clients, especially in the U.S., are schooled in the rational [approach]—finding a product difference and then using advertising to convey a message rather than build a relationship. They don't understand the power of emotions.

This could be a problem because recent research in the United Kingdom suggests that emotional campaigns are nearly twice as likely to produce large profit gains as rational campaigns. Of particular interest to marketers is that emotional campaigns reduce price sensitivity, which is especially vital in times of economic downturn. The reason emotional campaigns reduce price sensitivity is that they create a sense of differentiation between the brand and its competitors. The negative side to emotional campaigns is that short-term results are difficult to measure because their effects on awareness and brand image tend to take longer to unfold. Conversely, rational (informational) campaigns provide measureable short-term results but do not perform as well in the long term.

Emotional branding may be of greatest importance when there is a high degree of competitive parity between brands. Competitors can quickly imitate any functional, tangible changes to the product, leaving marketers with little unique rational claims. However, competitors cannot imitate the feelings that consumers experience when they see an emotional advertisement for a brand or consume the product. Dell is taking a lesson from Apple's computer advertising: not talking about computers themselves, in their advertisements. Instead, they are focusing on the personality, lifestyle, and feelings that the brand produces for consumers.

Discussion Questions

1. Dell is using emotional appeals in the "More You" advertising campaign. Chapter 10 identifies three basic emotions.
   a. Which of these three primary emotions is Dell trying to elicit with this campaign (you can select more than one)? Justify your answer.
   b. Table 10–4 gives examples of various emotions that are covered within the three primary dimensions. Using this list, as well as other descriptors, describe the specific emotions that the "More You" campaign could elicit.
2. Chapter 11 discusses source characteristics.
   a. Other than Dell, who serves as the source in the "More You" advertisements?
   b. What is the technical term for the types of sources that are present in the "More You" advertisements?
   c. How does this type of source impact source credibility?
3. Dell's "More You" advertisements feature customers talking about how they use Dell products to satisfy a need. Chapter 10 discusses Maslow's hierarchy of needs. Which of these needs could Dell products help satisfy for consumers? Justify your answer.
4. Dell is targeting members of Generation Y with their "More You" campaign. Using what you know from Chapter 4:
   a. How well does Dell's approach align with the characteristics of Gen Y?
   b. What else could Dell do to better reach this demographic?
5. Chapter 11 discusses the appropriateness of value-expressive versus utilitarian appeals in various contexts.
   a. Are Dell's products functional products or are they designed to enhance self-image or provide other benefits?
   b. Based on your answer to part a, what does the text suggest is the most appropriate appeal?

6. At the time of the writing of this case, Dell had just launched the "More You" campaign. Go online and research the consumer reactions and impact for the brand that the campaign produced. Summarize your findings and comment on how they relate to this case.

Source: E. Hall, "IPA: Effective Ads Work on the Heart, Not the Head," *Advertising Age,* July 16, 2007; D. Hill, "CMOS Win Big by Letting Emotions Drive Advertising," *Advertising Age,* August 27, 2007; S. McKee, "Brands: The Power of Emotion," *BusinessWeek,* November 8, 2007, www.businessweek.com; H. Pringle, "Why Emotional Messages Beat Rational Ones," *Advertising Age,* March 2, 2009; M. Hachman, "Dell's 'More You' Ads Mean a Renewed Consumer Push," *PC Magazine,* July 5, 2011, www.pcmag.com; S. Shayon, "Dell's 'More You': Dude, You're Getting a Lifestyle Brand," *Brand Channel,* July 5, 2011, www.brandchannel.com; I. Sherr, "Dell Ads to Focus on Human Side of Technology," *The Wall Street Journal,* July 5, 2011, http://online.wsj.com; and K. Daniels, "Dell(NASDAQ:DELL) to Launch New Campaign," *eMoney Daily,* July 6, 2011, www.emoneydaily.com.

3-9 CAMPBELL'S TARGETS GROWING MALE GROCERY SHOPPERS

Traditional gender roles are shifting in the United States. While women are still primarily responsible for household duties, an increasing number of men are taking on this task. This shift has been caused by a variety of factors, including

- Dual-income households with high time pressure.
- Women with more education and higher incomes than their husbands.
- Necessity borne from higher unemployment among men with the recent economic recession.
- Generational shifts in attitudes such that younger men are increasingly willing to take an active role in parenting and household duties.
- Changing media portrayal of men such that men are now more often shown engaging in traditionally "female" roles or activities such as grocery shopping.

A recent television commercial featured a father shopping at a Walmart store and purchasing P&G products. According to one expert:

> [It] is no longer seen as an emasculating thing to be in the kitchen. Obviously, Emeril Lagasse is a big, burly masculine guy and there's nothing effeminate about his approach to the kitchen, and I think that's an empowering thing for men to see.

Grocery shopping, in particular, is a household responsibility that is increasingly performed by men. In 2010, more than half of men aged 18–63 identified themselves as the primary grocery shoppers in their households. Among fathers, the percentage increases to 60 percent. However, less than 25 percent of men felt that marketers are targeting them with advertisements for packaged goods. The overwhelming majority of advertisements and promotional campaigns for grocery items are targeted toward women.

One brand that is targeting men is Campbell's Soup with their Chunky Soup line, which includes 23 varieties. According to Campbell's:

> Extensive research revealed men today are facing what we call a "male meal dilemma"—they're having trouble finding convenient, satisfying foods that taste good and that they feel good about eating. We saw an opportunity for Chunky to help solve that dilemma. We took what people love about Chunky and made it even better, with more high-quality, nutritious ingredients that taste great and fill you up.

Campbell's Chunky Soup has used print, radio, and television advertisements featuring male actors to reach their target demographic: males in their 30s. For several years Campbell's has partnered with the NFL in promotional campaigns. One popular campaign included advertisements of the mothers of NFL players encouraging their sons to eat Chunky Soup. Chunky Soup and the NFL have formed the Campbell's Chunky/NFL Tackling Hunger program, which hosts an annual contest, named Click-for-Cans. In order to participate, consumers must go to a website each day and click on their favorite team. Every team receives a donation of canned goods to its local food bank. However, at the end of the contest the teams from the NFC and AFC with the most clicks get a larger donation of canned goods as well as bragging rights.

In light of this shift in grocery-shopping responsibility, Campbell's and other brands found in grocery stores should be aware of differences in the way that men and women shop for groceries. Men are not only buying products that are traditionally viewed as masculine, like meat and beer, but they are buying many of the same products as their female counterparts. For example, popular products among male grocery shoppers are canned seafood, herbal packaged tea, prepared ready-to-serve lasagna, health bars, refrigerated yogurt,

The Grocery Shopping Habits of Men and Women

TABLE 

	Men (%)	Women (%)
Money-Saving Strategies		
Shop at multiple stores to find the lowest prices	35	43
Buy more "all-purpose" cleaning supplies to reduce number of items needed	31	43
Buy less variety to reduce the number of items needed	24	25
Shopping Behaviors		
Look at a store circular either before or at the store	49	59
Make additional unplanned purchases after seeing products/deals in store	44	54
Stock up on certain items because they were on sale	44	54
Seek out and buy store brands to save money	33	36
Choose products because of loyalty card discounts	19	22
List-Making Behaviors		
List categories to buy (e.g., coffee, frozen pizza, toothpaste, vitamins)	56	51
Use a store circular to make the list	37	46
Make a list based on ingredients needed for recipes	33	46
List specific brands to buy	16	14
List specific private label/store brand items to buy	12	8
Brand-Selection Process Based on		
Previous usage and trust of the brands	73	78
Coupons from home	40	52
Newspaper circulars from home	38	45
Requested by a household member	30	44
Signs or displays in the store	23	27
Product label/packaging	16	19

Source: SymphonyIRI, *MarketPulse,* January 2011.

and dishwasher rinsing aids. Please see Table A for the results of a survey of U.S. adult respondents who had shopped for groceries within the past 24 hours that shows differences in grocery shopping behavior.

Discussion Questions

1. Images of men shown performing duties that were traditionally considered to be feminine, such as the Walmart example, encourage an attitude shift about what roles are acceptable for men and women. How does this relate to the attitude change strategies discussed in Chapter 11?
2. Interpret the information contained in Table A.
   a. Describe the similarities and differences between how men and women grocery shop.
   b. Using this knowledge, how could a marketer of a packaged good grocery item effectively target men?
3. Campbell's and the NFL have joined forces in advertising and promotional campaigns by forming the Campbell's Chunky/NFL Tackling Hunger program that provides canned goods to food banks.
   a. What branding strategy are Campbell's and the NFL using?

b. Chapters 8 and 9 discuss fit among branding partners. How well does the NFL fit with Campbell's Chunky Soup?

4. Chapter 9 discusses product positioning.
   a. What is Campbell's Chunky Soup's product positioning?
   b. Create a perceptual map that includes Campbell's Chunky Soup and other soup brands. Use masculine/feminine as one axis and be creative with the other axis.
5. Chapter 6 discusses the nature of family purchase roles. In a grocery shopping context, how might each of the roles differ in a family consisting of a husband, wife, and child, based on traditional gender roles versus evolving gender roles?
   a. Initiator
   b. Information gatherer
   c. Influencer
   d. Decision maker
   e. Purchaser
   f. User

Source: A. Newman, "The Man of the House: More Men Than Ever Are Cooking, Cleaning and Caring for Kids—So Why Aren't Household Brands Targeting Them?," *Adweek,* August 11, 2008, www.adweek.com; R. Adams, "Campbell's Soup Sacks NFL Mothers," *The Wall Street Journal,* August 27, 2008, http://online.wsj.com; "Campbell's Revamps Chunky Soup Line," *Adweek,* September 2, 2009, www.adweek.com; "Mr. Grocery Buyer," *GourmetAds Food and Wine Advertising,* 2011, www.gourmetads.com; J. Neff, "Time to Rethink Your Message: Now the Cart Belongs to Daddy," *Advertising Age,* January 17, 2011, http://adage.com; R. Neill, "Grocery Shopping Man Style," *Life Inc. on Today,* May 24, 2011, http://lifeinc.today.com; A. Gurbels, "Soup's on at Local Food Bank, Thanks to Jaguar Fans," *Jacksonville Business Journal,* June 14, 2011, www.bizjournals.com; and "Food Shopper Insights: Grocery Shopping Trends in the U.S.," *Packaged Facts,* July 2011.

part

IV CONSUMER DECISION PROCESS

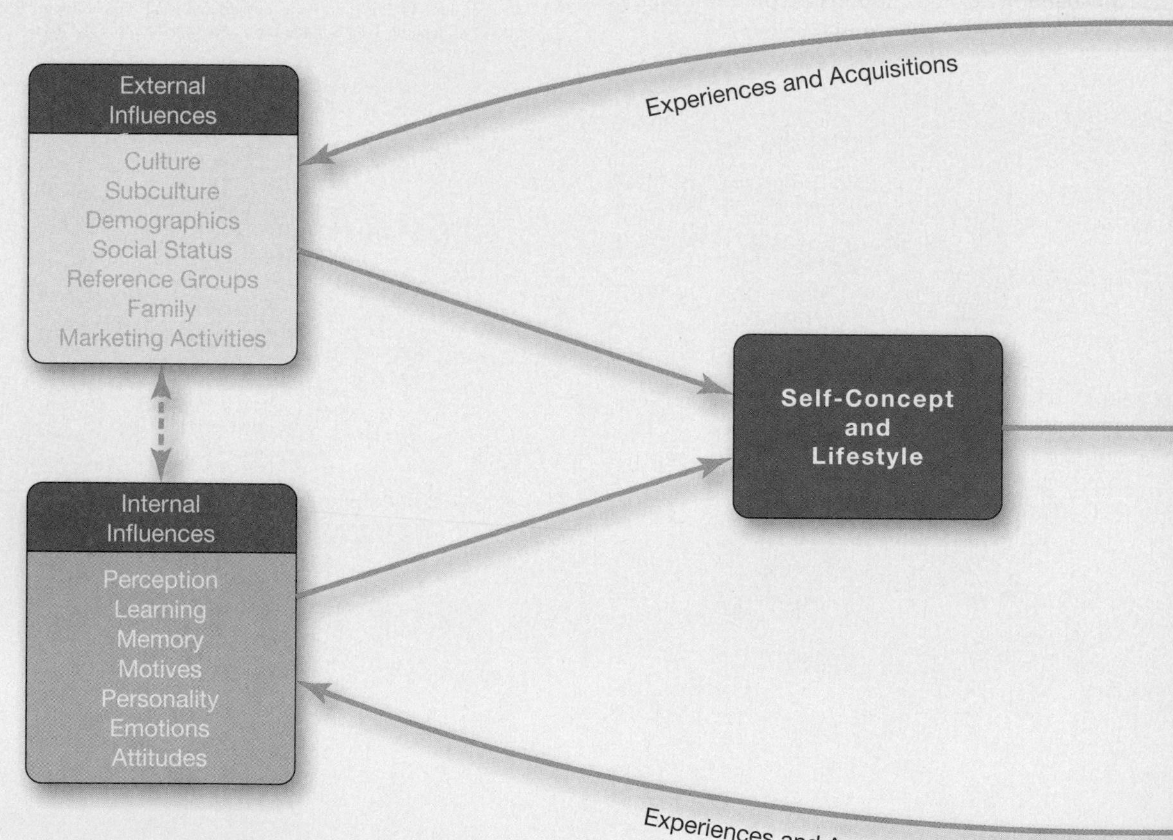

Up to now, we have focused on various sociological and psychological factors that contribute to different patterns of consumer behavior. Though these various influences play a significant role in behavior, all behavior takes place within the context of a situation. Chapter 13 provides a discussion of the impact situational variables have on consumer behavior.

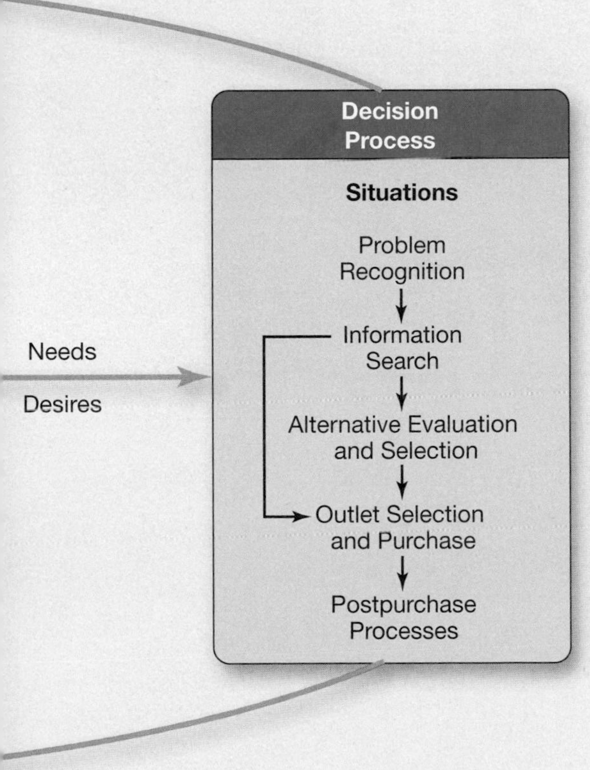

Of particular importance to marketers is how situations and internal and external sources of influence affect the purchase decision process. The extended consumer decision process, shown on this page, is composed of a sequence of activities: problem recognition, information search, brand evaluation and selection, outlet choice and purchase, and postpurchase processes. However, extended decision making occurs only in those relatively rare situations when the consumer is highly involved in the purchase. Lower levels of purchase involvement produce limited or nominal decision making. Chapter 14 describes those various types of decisions and their relationship to involvement. It also analyzes the first stage of the process—problem recognition.

Information search, in various forms including onlinc, mobile, and offline, constitutes the second stage of the consumer decision process and is discussed in Chapter 15. Chapter 16 examines the alternative evaluation and selection process. Chapter 17 deals with outlet selection and the in-store and online influences that often determine final brand choice. The final stage of the consumer decision process, presented in Chapter 18, involves behaviors after the purchase. These include postpurchase dissonance, product use and disposition, and satisfaction and loyalty. Both cognitive (thinking) and emotional (feeling) processes are important at each stage of the decision process.

chapter

13 Situational Influences

LEARNING OBJECTIVES

LO1 **Define *situational influence*.**

LO2 **Explain the four types of situations and their relevance to marketing strategy.**

LO3 **Summarize the five characteristics of situations and their influence on consumption.**

LO4 **Discuss ritual situations and their importance to consumers and marketers.**

LO5 **Describe the use of situational influence in developing marketing strategy.**

Did you realize that companies change their marketing tactics geographically depending on the weather and how it is changing? How weather is *changing* is the critical part here because it creates "situations" into which marketers can offer their products as solutions. For example, when temperatures are temporarily *colder than usual,* consumers will deviate from their normal purchase pattern. Sometimes this means buying more of a certain item such as Campbell's Slow Kettle Style Soup to provide a nice hot meal on a cold winter's day. Sometimes this means buying different products such as a heavier jacket.[1] Planalytics is a major global player in helping marketers track and react to changing weather situations. It is a geographically based system that looks at what we will later term "momentary conditions." Planalytics offers a Weather-Driven Demand (WDD) approach, which they describe, in part, as "a numerical representation of the consumer need for a product or service caused by perceived changes in the weather at a time/location intersection." This perception change by time/location intersection creates a situation of which marketers attempt to take advantage. As Planalytics' COO states:

> That's where the marketing gold that needs to be mined is. Marketing into a situation that's favorable to your product [causes] the numbers to go off the chart.

Examples of clients who use Planalytics to adjust their marketing efforts include

- *Campbell Soup.* Campbell Soup has created a "misery index" that is based on weather changes, such as within day, within week, year over year, and so on, with bonus points for snow or rain. When the misery index hits a certain mark, Campbell will deliver chicken soup ads to that market. It has over 30 such geographic markets that it tracks and targets in this way and is also in the process of creating a flu index.
- *Lands' End.* This global retailer uses weather information to plan and forecast inventories, tweak merchandising and promotional offerings, and so on. It also examines historical demand as a function of "unusual" weather patterns and discounts future estimates accordingly. So, for example, if there was an unusually hot spring season in the United Kingdom one year, with sales of certain items (e.g., light apparel such as shorts) being high, they will discount next year's estimates accordingly to avoid having overstocks.

New media options are available as well. Google can track "trending" weather-related phrases such as "hot chocolate" and launch appropriate "new search campaigns within hours." So, what's your weather situation?

As the model we have used to organize this text indicates, the purchase decision and consumption process always occur in the context of a specific situation. Therefore, before examining the decision process, we must first develop an understanding of situations. In this chapter, we will examine the situations in which consumption occurs, the way situations influence consumption behaviors, key characteristics of situations, the nature of ritual situations, and situation-based marketing strategies.

THE NATURE OF SITUATIONAL INFLUENCE

LO1 Consumers do not respond to stimuli such as advertisements and products presented by marketers in isolation; instead, they respond to marketing influences and the situation simultaneously. To understand a consumer's behavior, we must know about the *consumer;* about the primary *stimulus* object, such as a product or advertisement to which the consumer is responding; and about the *situation* in which the response is occurring.[2]

We define **situational influence** as *all those factors particular to a time and place that do not follow from a knowledge of the stable attributes of the consumer and the stimulus and that have an effect on current behavior.*[3] Thus, with one exception, the situation stands apart from the consumer and the stimulus. The exception is in the case of *temporary* (as opposed to stable) characteristics of a consumer or stimulus that are specific to the situation and sometimes even caused by it. For example, a consumer may generally be upbeat (stable trait), but just prior to viewing a firm's ad sees a disturbing news flash that puts her in a bad mood. This bad mood is a transient state (situational factor) caused by the surrounding media context in which the focal ad appears. Other such temporary conditions include illness and time pressure. Consumer involvement also includes a situation-specific component. That is, some consumers are involved only when they have to make a purchase.

A key marketing finding is that consumers often react and behave very differently depending on the situation. We discussed some of these effects in earlier chapters. For example, an ad or in-store display that might otherwise attract consumer attention may not do so in a cluttered environment (Chapter 8). Or an ad that might be persuasive in a non-purchase situation may be much less persuasive in a purchase situation where consumers are on the market to buy (Chapter 11). The interplay between situation, marketing, and the individual is shown in Figure 13–1.

Consumer behavior occurs within four broad categories or types of situations: the communications situation, the purchase situation, the usage situation, and the disposition situation.

The Communications Situation

LO2 The situation in which consumers receive information has an impact on their behavior. Whether one is alone or in a group, in a good mood or bad, in a hurry or not influences the degree to which one sees and listens to marketing communications. Is it better to advertise on a happy or sad television program? A calm or exciting program? These are some of the questions managers must answer with respect to the **communications situation.**[4] Marketers often attempt to place their ads in appropriate media contexts to enhance their effectiveness. Some even go so far as to mandate that their ads be "pulled" when programming content negative to their company or industry will appear. Recent examples include Morgan Stanley and BP. *What are the ethical implications of such policies?*[5]

A marketer is able to deliver an effective message to consumers who are interested in the product and are in a receptive communications situation. However, finding high-interest potential buyers in receptive communications situations is a difficult challenge.

The Situation Interacts with the Marketing Activity and the Individual to Determine Behavior **FIGURE 13-1**

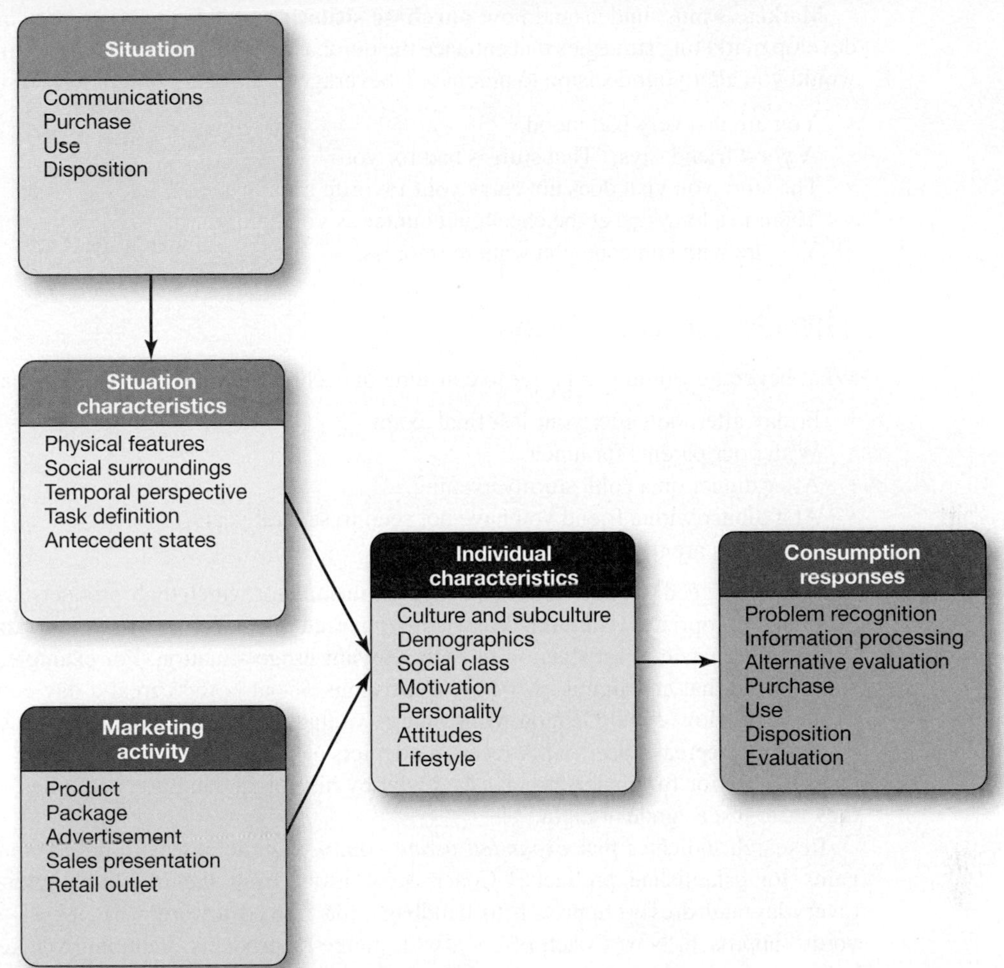

For example, consider the difficulty a marketer would have in communicating to you in the following communications situations:

- Your favorite team just lost the most important game of the year.
- Final exams begin tomorrow.
- Your roommates watch only comedy programs.
- You have the flu.
- You are driving home on a cold night, and your car heater doesn't work.

The Purchase Situation

The situation in which a purchase is made can influence consumer behavior. Mothers shopping with children are more apt to be influenced by the product preferences of their children than when shopping without them. A shortage of time, such as trying to make a purchase between classes, can affect the store-choice decision, the number of brands considered, and the price the shopper is willing to pay. At an even more basic level, whether or not a consumer is in a "purchase mode" influences a whole host of behaviors from advertising responses to shopping. Consider, for example, how differently you might behave at Best Buy if you were there only to browse versus being there to replace a broken Blu-ray player.

Marketers must understand how **purchase situations** influence consumers in order to develop marketing strategies that enhance the purchase of their products. For example, how would you alter your decision to purchase a beverage in the following purchase situations?

- You are in a very bad mood.
- A good friend says, "That stuff is bad for you!"
- The store you visit does not carry your favorite brand.
- There is a long line at the checkout counter as you enter the store.
- You are with someone you want to impress.

The Usage Situation

What beverage would you prefer to consume in each of the following usage situations?

- Friday afternoon after your last final exam.
- With your parents for lunch.
- After dinner on a cold, stormy evening.
- At a dinner with a friend you have not seen in several years.
- When you are feeling sad or homesick.

Marketers need to understand the **usage situations** for which their products are, or may become, appropriate. Using this knowledge, marketers can communicate how their products create consumer satisfaction in each relevant usage situation. For example, a recent study found that consuming two 1.5-cup servings of oat-based cereal a day could lower cholesterol. How could General Mills take advantage of this finding to increase sales of its oat-based cereal Cheerios? A recent ad depicts a dad coming home late from work and having Cheerios for dinner. When asked why by his young daughter, he replies, "Because they taste just as good at night."

Research indicates that *expanded usage situation* strategies can produce major sales gains for established products.[6] Coach went away from the traditional two-occasion (everyday and dressy) approach to handbags and moved toward what it calls a "usage voids" approach. Now Coach offers a wide range of products, including weekend bags, coin purses, clutches, and wristlets in a variety of colors and fabrics. The goal is to get consumers more attuned to the various usage situations available in which to accessorize and then create bags to fit the situations.[7] Dunkin' Donuts found that over half of donut consumption was for breakfast, but roughly 34 percent was for nonbreakfast snacks. In response, the company has

> created simple yet imaginative make-at-home snack and dessert recipes, such as Cocoa Donut and Strawberry Grilled Cheese, to encourage consumers to think of and use the company's products in new ways. [They are also tapping the specialty occasions market with] limited-time offers, such as the heart-shaped Valentine's "Cupid's Choice."[8]

The GoGo Squeez ad in Illustration 13–1 provides another example of a company trying to expand the usage situations for its brand.

The Disposition Situation

Consumers must frequently dispose of products or product packages after or before product use. As we will examine in detail in Chapter 18, decisions made by consumers regarding the **disposition situation** can create significant social problems as well as opportunities for marketers.

Some consumers consider ease of disposition an important product attribute. These people may purchase only items that can be easily recycled. Often disposition of an existing product must occur before or simultaneously with the acquisition of the new product. For example, most consumers must remove their existing bed before using a new one. Marketers need to understand how situational influences affect disposition decisions in order to develop more effective and ethical products and marketing programs. Government and environmental organizations need the same knowledge in order to encourage socially responsible disposition decisions.

ILLUSTRATION 13-1

Many products become defined for particular usage situations. Firms that are able to expand the range of usage situations deemed appropriate for their brands can capture significant sales gains. This GoGo Squeez ad is attempting to show how its applesauce can be consumed in various situations.

How would your disposition decision differ in these situations?

- You have finished a soft drink in a can at a mall. There is a trashcan nearby, but there is no sign of a recycling container.
- You have finished reading the newspaper after class, and you note that you are running late for a basketball game.
- You and two friends have finished soft drinks. Both your friends toss the recyclable cans into a nearby garbage container.
- A local charity will accept old refrigerators if they are delivered to the charity. Your garbage service will haul one to the dump for $15. You just bought a new refrigerator. You don't know anyone (or you do know someone) with a pickup or van.

SITUATIONAL CHARACTERISTICS AND CONSUMPTION BEHAVIOR

LO3

The situations discussed above can be described on a number of dimensions that determine their influence on consumer behavior. The five key dimensions or characteristics are physical surroundings, social surroundings, temporal perspectives, task definition, and antecedent states.[9] These characteristics have been studied primarily in the United States. While the same characteristics of the situation exist across cultures, a marketer should not assume that the response to these characteristics would be the same. For example, a crowded store might cause a different emotional reaction among American consumers than among consumers in India.[10]

Physical Surroundings

Physical surroundings include decor, sounds, aromas, lighting, weather, and configurations of merchandise or other materials surrounding the stimulus object. Physical surroundings are a widely used type of situational influence, particularly for retail applications. Consumer Insight 13–1 sheds further light onto one aspect of the physical retail environment, namely mannequins.

CONSUMER INSIGHT 13-1

Mannequins, More Than Just Store Dummies

Perhaps equally as true as the statement "the clothes make the man"[11] is the statement "the mannequin makes the clothes." Forty-two percent of consumers polled in a recent study stated that what they saw displayed on a mannequin influenced their purchase decision.[12]

With the forecast that "All department stores will become museums, and all museums will become department stores," threatening to become ever more real with online retail encroachment into their sales, brick-and-mortar stores are fighting back with an army of mannequins. The plain white faceless, sometimes headless, torso mannequin that quietly blended unnoticed into the background has been replaced with a new breed of mannequins that scream with attention-arresting poses, and astoundingly realistic physical features.

To be more than the colorless, uniform clothes-hanger mannequins of yesteryear, mannequins today are being created to personalize the brand. For example, Nike mannequins come alive in action poses to communicate the energy and dynamism of athleticism, and the runway model poses of Guess mannequins exemplify fashion sophistication and confidence.

Mannequins have long been the silent salespersons, ranking third, after friends and family, in influencing purchasing behavior. It turns out that realistic, larger-sized mannequins are better sales people. Recent research shows that women are three times more likely to buy clothes when they see them on a mannequin related to their size. Macy's, Nordstrom, and the British Debenhams department stores are using or report plans to use more realistic, full-bodied mannequins. Developed after an extensive study that involved scanning thousands of women's bodies to arrive at a better understanding of women's proportions, the mannequins in David's Bridal, the largest chain of bridal stores in the United States, have thicker waists and realistic imperfections.

Another trend in mannequin realism centers not so much on creating more realistic body types, but on providing mannequins with realistic details including pierced ears, tattoos, movable limbs to better display clothes, and articulated fingers to better show off rings. Mannequins have progressed beyond being a silent salesperson. Some mannequins are also data collectors. EyeSee Mannequins are traditional-looking mannequins, except they have eyes fitted with a camera lens that captures data on passersby. The data are fed to facial recognition software; mined for shoppers' age, gender, and ethnicity; and used in forecasting models to develop marketing campaigns and store displays. Mindful of consumer privacy, EyeSee mannequins do not record or send data of a sensitive nature such as biometric data.

Much more than just store dummies, mannequins contribute to the brick-and-mortar shopping experience, exuding appeal to entice consumers to visit stores, poising provocatively to capture consumer attention, and sized and detailed to motivate consumers to make purchases. Mannequins serve as a store ambassador, evangelizing brand image and selling clothes.

Critical Thinking Questions

1. Have you noticed the new mannequins in stores where you shop for clothes? What is your reaction?
2. The new types of mannequins have centered more on women than men. Would men be more likely to buy clothes displayed on mannequins related to their size?
3. Digital mannequins collect data from passersby who are unaware that they are being recorded. Is this ethical?

External retail factors such as the architecture, arrangement, and assortment of retailers are an important influence on consumer shopping experiences. In addition, store interiors are often designed to create specific feelings in shoppers that can have an important cueing or reinforcing effect on purchase. All physical aspects of the store, including lighting,

ILLUSTRATION 13-2

Retail store interiors should provide a physical environment consistent with the nature of the target market, the product line, and the desired image of the outlet.

layout, presentation of merchandise, fixtures, floor coverings, colors, sounds, odors, and dress and behavior of sales personnel, combine to produce these feelings, which in turn influence purchase tendencies.[13] A retail clothing store specializing in extremely stylish, modern clothing would want its fixtures, furnishings, and colors to reflect an overall mood of style, flair, and newness (see Illustration 13–2). In addition, the store personnel should carry this theme in terms of their own appearance and apparel. Compare this with the interior of a so-called discount retailer, also shown in the illustration. It is important to note that one is not superior to the other. Each attempts to create an appropriate atmosphere for its target audience.

The sum of all the physical features of a retail environment is referred to as the **store atmosphere** or environment (see Chapter 17). Store atmosphere influences consumer judgments of store quality and image. It also has been shown to influence shoppers' moods and their willingness to visit and linger. **Atmospherics** is *the process managers use to manipulate the physical retail environment to create specific mood responses in shoppers.*[14] Atmospherics is also important online and is receiving increasing attention from marketers.[15]

Atmosphere is referred to as **servicescape** when describing a service business such as a hospital, bank, or restaurant.[16] Figure 13–2 classifies services according to the reason the customer is using the service and the length of time the service will be used. The consumption purpose is categorized along a continuum from strictly utilitarian, such as dry cleaning, to completely hedonic, such as a massage. The time can range from a few minutes to days or weeks. Physical characteristics and the feelings and image they create become increasingly important as hedonic motives and the time involved with the service increase. Thus, the physical characteristics of a vacation resort may be as important as or more important than the intangible services provided.

It is important that Figure 13–2 be interpreted correctly. It indicates that the physical environment at Starbucks is more important to the service experience than the physical features of dry cleaners are. *This does not mean that the physical aspects of dry cleaners are not important.* Indeed, an organized, professional-appearing dry cleaning establishment is likely to produce more satisfied customers than one with the opposite characteristics. What the figure does indicate is that the relative importance of

FIGURE 13-2 Typology of Service Environments

Time Spent in Facility	Consumption Purpose: Utilitarian	----------	Hedonic
Short [minutes]	Dry cleaner Bank	Fast food Hair salon	Facial Coffee at Starbucks
Moderate [hour(s)]	Medical appointment Legal consultation	Business dinner Exercise class	Theater Sporting event
Extended [day(s)]	Hospital Trade show	Conference hotel Training center	Cruise Resort

tangible physical features increases as one moves to extended, hedonic consumption experiences.

Having established the importance of the physical environment, we will now examine some of its components.

Colors As we saw in Chapter 8, certain colors and color characteristics create feelings of excitement and arousal that are related to attention. Bright colors are more arousing than dull colors. And *warm* colors, such as reds and yellows, are more arousing than *cool* colors, such as blues and greys.[17] Which color would be best for store interiors? The answer is, it depends. For the dominant interior color, cool colors (e.g., blue) should probably be used because they increase sales and customer satisfaction.[18] However, the attention-getting nature of warm colors should not be overlooked and can be used effectively as an accent color in areas where the retailer wants to attract attention and drive impulse purchases.[19] Cool colors also appear to be capable of reducing wait time perceptions by inducing feelings of relaxation.[20]

As we saw in Chapter 2, the meaning of colors varies across cultures. Therefore, this and all other aspects of the physical environment should be designed specifically for the cultures involved.

Aromas There is increasing evidence that odors can affect consumer shopping.[21] One study found that a scented environment produced a greater intent to revisit the store, higher purchase intention for some items, and a reduced sense of time spent shopping.[22] Another study found that one aroma, but not another, increased slot machine usage in a Las Vegas casino.[23] A third study found that the presence of a certain aroma in a retail setting increased pleasure, arousal, time spent, and money spent at the retailer.[24] A fourth study found that a pleasantly scented environment enhanced brand recall and evaluations, particularly for unfamiliar brands. The pleasant scent increased the time spent evaluating the brands (attention), which, in turn, increased memory.[25]

Given these results, it is not surprising that a billion-dollar *environmental fragrancing* industry has developed around the use of ambient scents.[26] However, marketers still have a lot to learn about if, when, and how scents can be used effectively in a retail environment.[27] In addition, scent preferences are highly individualized; a pleasant scent to one

TABLE 13-1

The Impact of Background Music on Restaurant Patrons

Variables	Slow Music	Fast Music
Service time	29 min	27 min
Customer time at table	56 min	45 min
Customer groups leaving before seated	10.5%	12.0%
Amount of food purchased	$55.81	$55.12
Amount of bar purchases	$30.47	$21.62
Estimated gross margin	$55.82	$48.62

Source: R. E. Milliman, "The Influence of Background Music on the Behavior of Restaurant Patrons," in the *Journal of Consumer Research*, September 1986, p. 289. Copyright © 1986 by the University of Chicago. Used by permission.

individual may be repulsive to another. Moreover, some shoppers object to anything being deliberately added to the air they breathe, and others worry about allergic reactions.[28]

Music Music influences consumers' moods, which influence a variety of consumption behaviors both in traditional retailer settings and in online settings.[29] Is slow-tempo or fast-tempo background music better for a restaurant? Table 13–1 indicates that slow music increased gross margin for one restaurant by almost 15 percent per customer group compared with fast music. However, before concluding that all restaurants should play slow music, examine the table carefully. Slow music appears to have relaxed and slowed down the customers, resulting in more time in the restaurant and substantially more purchases from the bar. Restaurants that rely on rapid customer turnover might be better off with fast-tempo music.

Other aspects of music besides tempo are also important. For example, research suggests that matching music to the musical preferences of the target audience is critical to positive retail outcomes such as satisfaction and enjoyment, browsing time, spending, perceived service quality, and positive word-of-mouth. In addition, research suggests that music that creates moderate levels of arousal (versus extremely low or high) yields the most positive retail outcomes.[30]

Because of the impact that music can have on shopping behavior, firms exist to develop music programs to meet the unique needs of specific retailers. An emerging trend is having music more in the foreground so it becomes part of the shopping experience and drives store image. AEI, a major supplier of foreground music, does intense research on the demographics and psychographics of each client store's customers. The age mix, buying patterns, and traffic flows of each part of the day are analyzed. AEI characterizes its approach as

> [creating] environments where sounds, video, lighting and architecture blend together to give a brand a voice, creating emotional attachments that encourage consumers to shop longer, increase spending and return often.[31]

Firms such as Abercrombie & Fitch, Banana Republic, Bath & Body Works, and Eddie Bauer use companies like AEI to create appropriate and consistent shopping environments throughout their chains.

Crowding Crowding generally produces negative outcomes for both the retail outlet and the consumer.[32] As more people enter a store or as more of the space of the store is filled with merchandise, an increasing percentage of the shoppers will experience a feeling of being crowded, confined, or claustrophobic. Most consumers find these feelings to be unpleasant and will take steps to change them. The primary means of doing so is to spend less time in the store by buying less, making faster decisions, and using less of the available information. This in turn tends to produce less satisfactory purchases, an unpleasant shopping trip, and a reduced likelihood of returning to the store.

Marketers should design their outlets in ways that will help reduce consumers' perceptions of crowding. This is difficult because retail shopping tends to occur at specific times, such as holiday weekends. Retailers must balance the expense of having a larger store than required most of the time against the cost of having dissatisfied customers during key shopping periods. Using extra personnel, opening additional checkout lines, and implementing similar measures can enhance the flow of consumers through a store during peak periods and reduce the crowding sensation. In addition, recent research shows that music tempo can be important. Specifically, music with a slow tempo offsets the negative emotions experienced as a result of crowding. Because music tempo adjustments are less expensive than store expansion or new personnel, this is an important finding for retail strategy.[33]

Marketers need to be sensitive to cross-cultural differences because personal space and resulting crowding perceptions can vary from culture to culture. For example, one study found that when the activity is for fun, such as an amusement park or concert, Middle East consumers perceive less crowding and appreciate crowding more than North American consumers.[34]

Social Surroundings

Social surroundings are *the other individuals present in the particular situation.* People's actions are frequently influenced by those around them. What would you wear in each of the following situations?

- Studying alone for a final.
- Meeting at the library with a date to study for a final.
- Going to a nice restaurant with a date.
- Meeting a prospective employer for lunch.

Illustration 13–3 shows a company that is positioning its brand for casual rather than formal social settings.

Social influence is a significant force acting on our behavior because individuals tend to comply with group expectations, particularly when the behavior is visible (see Chapter 7). Thus, shopping, a highly visible activity, and the use of many publicly consumed brands are subject to social influences.[35] This is particularly true of those who are highly susceptible to interpersonal influence, a stable personality trait. As just one example, a recent study finds that consumers are more likely to engage in variety-seeking behavior in public (versus private) consumption situations even if it means consuming products they like less. The reason is that consumers feel that others view them more positively (more fun, interesting, exciting) if their purchases show more variety. This tendency is stronger for those more susceptible to interpersonal influence.[36]

Marketers have recently begun to examine the role of social influence on embarrassment. **Embarrassment** is *a negative emotion influenced by both the product and the situation.* Certain products are more embarrassing than others (condoms, hearing aids, etc.) and embarrassment is driven by the presence of others in the purchase or usage situation. Because embarrassment can deter purchases, this is an important area for marketers. One

ILLUSTRATION 13-3

Styles vary depending on the social situation in which they will be worn.

finding is that familiarity with purchasing the product reduces embarrassment, so marketers might try advertisements that show the purchase of a potentially embarrassing product in which no awkwardness or embarrassment occurs. For extremely sensitive products (e.g., adult diapers), strategies might include home delivery options with discreet labeling to completely avoid the social component.[37]

Shopping can provide a social experience outside the home for making new acquaintances, meeting existing friends, or just being near other people. Some people seek status and authority in shopping because the salesperson's job is to wait on the customer. This allows these individuals a measure of respect or prestige that may otherwise be lacking in their lives. Thus, consumers, on occasion, shop *for* social situations rather than, or in addition to, products. The presence of others *during* the shopping trip can also influence impulse buying. Results show that compared with shopping alone, shopping with close friends increased impulse buying, while shopping with close family members decreased impulse buying. It seems that consumers believe that norms differ such that their friends view impulse buying as more acceptable than family.[38]

Frequently, marketing managers will not have any control over social characteristics of a situation. For example, when a television advertisement is sent into the home, the advertising manager cannot control whom the viewer is with at the time of reception. However, the manager can use the knowledge that some programs are generally viewed alone (weekday, daytime programs), some are viewed by the entire family (prime-time family comedies), and others are viewed by groups of friends (Super Bowl). The message presented can be structured to these viewing situations. Marketers can also use social consumption

ILLUSTRATION 13-4

In the United States and other countries, dual-career and single-parent families have caused consumers to feel time starved. Internet shopping provides many such consumers both time savings and control over when they shop. This Zappos ad would appeal to this consumer.

themes in their ads to enhance the likelihood that consumers will consider the social component in their decisions. For example, a recent study found that brand personality (fun and sophistication) conveyed by a celebrity endorser in an ad only enhanced purchase intentions when a social context was evoked.[39]

Temporal Perspectives

Temporal perspectives are *situational characteristics that deal with the effect of time on consumer behavior.* Time as a situational factor can manifest itself in a number of ways.[40] The amount of time available for the purchase has a substantial impact on the consumer decision process. In general, the less time there is available (i.e., increased time pressure), the shorter will be the information search, the less available information will be used, and the more suboptimal purchases will be made.[41] In addition, research suggests that time pressure decreases perceptions of retailer service quality.[42]

Limited purchase time can also result in a smaller number of product alternatives being considered. The increased time pressure experienced by many dual-career couples and single parents tends to increase the incidence of brand loyalty, particularly for nationally branded products. The obvious implication is that these consumers feel safer with nationally branded or "known" products, particularly when they do not have the time to engage in extensive comparison shopping.

Time as a situational influence affects consumers' choice of stores and behaviors in those stores.[43] A number of retail firms have taken advantage of the temporal perspective factor. Perhaps the most successful of these is the 7-Eleven chain, which caters almost exclusively to individuals who either are in a hurry or want to make a purchase after regular shopping hours.

Internet shopping is growing rapidly in part as a result of the time pressures felt by many dual-career and single-parent households. Shopping on the Internet has two important time-related dimensions. First, it has the potential to reduce the amount of time required to make a specific purchase. Second, it provides the consumer with almost total control over *when* the purchase is made (see Chapter 17). These features are among the major reasons for the rapid growth in Internet outlets and sales (see the Zappos ad in Illustration 13–4).

Task Definition

Task definition is *the reason the consumption activity is occurring.* The major task dichotomy used by marketers is between purchases for self-use versus gift giving.

Gift Giving Consumers use different shopping strategies and purchase criteria when shopping for gifts versus shopping for the same item for self-use.[44] Consumers give gifts for many reasons. Social expectations and ritualized consumption situations such as birthdays often require gift giving independent of the giver's actual desires.[45] Gifts are also given to elicit return favors in the form of either gifts or actions. And, of course, gifts are given as an expression of love and caring.[46]

The type of gift given and desired varies by occasion and gender.[47] One study found that wedding gifts tend to be *utilitarian,* while birthday gifts tend to be *fun.* Thus, both the general task definition (gift giving) and the specific task definition (gift-giving occasion) influence purchase behavior, as does the relationship between the giver and the recipient.

Gift giving produces anxieties on the part of both givers and receivers.[48] Gifts communicate symbolic meaning on several levels. The gift item itself generally has a known, or knowable, price that can be interpreted as a measure of the esteem the giver has for the receiver. The image and functionality of the gift implies the giver's impression of the image and personality of the receiver. It also reflects on the image and thoughtfulness of the giver.

The nature of a gift can signify the type of relationship the giver has or desires with the receiver.[49] A gift of stationery implies a very different desired relationship between two individuals than does a gift of cologne. Consider the following:

> The biggest moment of revelation, the moment I knew he was "serious" about me, was when he showed up with a gift for my daughter. Other men had shown the typical false affection for her in order to get on my good side, but he was only civil and polite to her, never gushy. One day, however, he showed up with a very nice skateboard for my daughter. . . . The gift marked a turning point in our relationship. I think for him it marked the time that he decided it would be OK to get serious about a woman with a child.[50]

As the example above indicates, the act of giving/receiving a gift can alter the relationship between the giver and the receiver. In addition, items received as gifts often take on meaning associated with the relationship or the giver. For example, a gift may be cherished and protected because it symbolizes an important friendship.[51]

Of course, gift giving is culture specific (see Chapter 2).[52] For example, in characterizing gift giving in Korea (collectivist) compared with the United States (individualistic), one expert summarized:

> Koreans reported more gift giving occasions, a wider exchange network, more frequent giving of practical gift items, especially cash gifts, strong face-saving and group conformity motivations, more social pressure to reciprocate, higher gift budget, and frequent workplace giving.[53]

Antecedent States

Features of the individual person that are not lasting characteristics, such as momentary moods or conditions, are called **antecedent states.** For example, most people experience states of depression or excitement from time to time that are not normally part of their individual makeup.

Moods **Moods** are *transient feeling states that are generally not tied to a specific event or object.*[54] They tend to be less intense than emotions and may operate without the individual's awareness. Although moods may affect all aspects of a person's behavior, they generally do not completely interrupt ongoing behavior as an emotion might. Individuals use such terms as *happy, cheerful, peaceful, sad, blue,* and *depressed* to describe their moods.

Moods both affect and are affected by the consumption process.[55] Moods influence decision processes, the purchase and consumption of various products, and perceptions of service.[56] Positive moods appear to be associated with increased browsing and impulse purchasing. Negative moods also increase impulse and compulsive purchasing in some consumers. One explanation is that some shopping behaviors play both a mood

ILLUSTRATION 13-5

Consumers' moods vary over the course of time. Astute firms develop products and services relevant to the various moods consumers experience or want to experience.

maintenance (positive moods) and mood enhancement (negative moods) role.[57]

Mood can also play an important role in the communications situation. Such effects are often called *program context effects* and relate to the nature of the programming surrounding the focal ad (see Chapter 8). The television, radio, and magazine content viewed just prior to the focal ad can influence consumers' moods and arousal levels, which, in turn, influence their information-processing activities.[58] A basic finding is that ad and brand attitudes are often influenced in a mood-congruent manner. Thus, a TV show that puts a consumer in a positive mood (elicits positive affective reactions) should improve ad and brand attitudes compared with one that puts the consumer in a negative mood. However, in cases where so-called negative programming is also liked by the viewer (a sad movie that a viewer loves), then program liking can still provide a positive boost in ad and brand attitudes.[59] Given such complexities, marketers must pretest their ads in contexts as close to their expected programming environment as possible.

Consumers actively manage their mood states (see Illustration 13–5).[60] That is, consumers often seek situations, activities, or objects that will alleviate negative moods or enhance positive ones. Products and services are one means consumers use to manage their mood states. Thus, a person feeling bored, sad, or down might view a situation comedy on television, go to a cheerful movie, visit a fun store, eat at an upbeat restaurant, or purchase a new Blu-ray disc, shirt, or other fun product.[61] Consumers may engage in such mood-regulating behavior both at a nonconscious level and also at a deliberate, conscious level:

> [T]here are certain products that I purchase specifically to make me feel better. For instance, occasionally, I enjoy smoking a cigar. Certainly the cigar serves no other purpose than to make me feel good.
>
> While other cosmetics, perfumes and nice clothes can make me feel good, they seldom have the same power to transform my temperament like a manicure and pedicure can.[62]

Marketers attempt to influence moods and to time marketing activities with positive mood-inducing events.[63] Many companies prefer to advertise during light television programs because viewers tend to be in a good mood while watching these shows. Restaurants, bars, shopping malls, and many other retail outlets are designed to induce positive moods in patrons. As discussed earlier, music is often played for this reason. Finally, marketers can position their products and services in terms of mood enhancement.

Momentary Conditions Whereas moods reflect states of mind, *momentary conditions reflect temporary states of being,* such as being tired, being ill, having extra money, being broke, and so forth. However, for conditions, as for moods, to fit under the definition of antecedent states, they must be momentary and not constantly with the individual. Hence, an individual who is short of cash only momentarily will act differently from someone who is always short of cash.[64]

As with moods, individuals attempt to manage their momentary conditions, often through the purchase or consumption of products and services. For example, individuals feeling tired or sleepy during the day may drink a cup of coffee or a soft drink or eat a candy bar. Massages are consumed to relieve sore muscles. A variety of medications are sold to relieve

ILLUSTRATION 13-6

This product is designed to help consumers cope with an uncomfortable momentary condition.

physical discomfort associated with overexertion, colds, allergies, and so forth. Pawnshops provide cash for individuals temporarily needing funds, as do banks and other financial institutions. Thus, a great deal of marketing activity is directed toward momentary conditions. Illustration 13–6 is an ad for a product designed to relieve a momentary condition.

RITUAL SITUATIONS

L04

Rituals are receiving increasing attention by marketing scholars and practitioners. A **ritual situation** can be described as *a socially defined occasion that triggers a set of interrelated behaviors that occur in a structured format and that have symbolic meaning.*[65] Ritual situations can range from completely private to completely public. A completely private ritual situation would be an individual's decision to drink a private toast or say a private prayer on the anniversary of an event with special meaning to the individual. A couple who celebrates their first date by returning to the same restaurant every year is involved in a more public ritual. Weddings tend to be even more public. Finally, national and global holidays present very public ritual situations.

Ritual situations are of major importance to marketers because they often involve prescribed consumption behaviors. Every major American holiday (ritual situation) has consumption rituals associated with it. For example, more than 60 percent of the toy industry's sales occur at Christmas.

ILLUSTRATION 13-7

Ritual situations generally have consumption patterns associated with them. This brand is tapping into ritual situations.

While there is significant variation across individuals and households, there is enough shared behavior that marketers can develop products and promotions around the common ritual situations that arise each year. For example, candy marketers produce and promote a wide array of candies for Valentine's Day and Halloween. Illustration 13–7 shows how one marketer is capitalizing on consumption rituals.

Marketers also attempt to change or create consumption patterns associated with ritual situations.[66] Mother's Day is a $10 billion occasion in which card giving is largely a ritual behavior created by marketers.[67] Halloween cards are now being promoted as part of the Halloween ritual.[68] And many firms seek to make their products and services part of the consumption pattern associated with "coming of age." These occasions are often marked with religious ceremonies and after-ceremony parties. Traditionally, these events have tended to focus on religious aspects and responsibility to family and community. For example:

> In Latin America, the quinceañera, a celebration dating back to the Aztecs that commemorates the spiritual and physical coming of age of a 15-year-old girl, is typically observed with a ceremony in the Catholic church and a backyard party for family members.[69]

The "after-ceremony" celebrations range from simple and inexpensive to elaborate and costly. However, the trend is definitely toward more elaborate and costly parties with modern themes, expensive catering and entertainment, and interactive activities to entertain hundreds of guests. For example:

> One Hispanic family spent $30,000 to celebrate their daughter's quinceañera with "a horsedrawn, pumpkin-shaped crystal carriage with liveried servants in powdered wigs, a silver tulle gown and a gala at which 260 guests danced until dawn in the shadow of Sleeping Beauty's castle at Disneyland."[70]

Ritual situations can also result in injurious consumption. Binge or excessive drinking is a serious health and social problem on many college campuses, though its incidence appears to be on the decline. Recent research suggests that this can be understood as a ritual behavior in that it is triggered by social occasions (e.g., birthdays), involves a set of interrelated behaviors and routines (e.g., start drinking on game days at a specific time), and results in special meaning and rewards for participants (e.g., fun, acceptance by group). When approached from this perspective, more effective strategies for minimizing such behaviors may result.

SITUATIONAL INFLUENCES AND MARKETING STRATEGY

LO5

In the previous sections, we described a variety of marketing strategies based on situational influences. Here we will focus more specifically on the process by which such strategies can be developed.

It is important to note that individuals do not encounter situations randomly. Instead, most people "create" many of the situations they face. Thus, individuals who choose to engage in physically demanding sports such as jogging, tennis, or racquetball are indirectly choosing to expose themselves to the situation of "being tired" or "being thirsty." This allows marketers to develop products, advertising, and segmentation strategies based on the situations that individuals selecting various lifestyles are likely to encounter.

After identifying the different situations that might involve the consumption of a product, marketers must determine which products or brands are most likely to be purchased or consumed across those situations. One method of approaching this is to jointly scale situations and products. An example is shown in Figure 13–3. Here, *use situations* that ranged from "private consumption at home" to "consumption away from home where there is a concern for other people's reaction to you" were scaled in terms of their similarity and relationship to products appropriate for that situation.

For use situation I, "to clean my mouth upon rising in the morning," toothpaste and mouthwash are viewed as most appropriate (see Figure 13–3). However, use situation II, "before an important business meeting late in the afternoon," involves both consumption away from home and a concern for the response from others. As a result, mint-flavored gums or candies are preferred. *Where do you think a product like Listerine Breath Strips would be located on this map?*

Use Situations and Product Positioning FIGURE 13-3

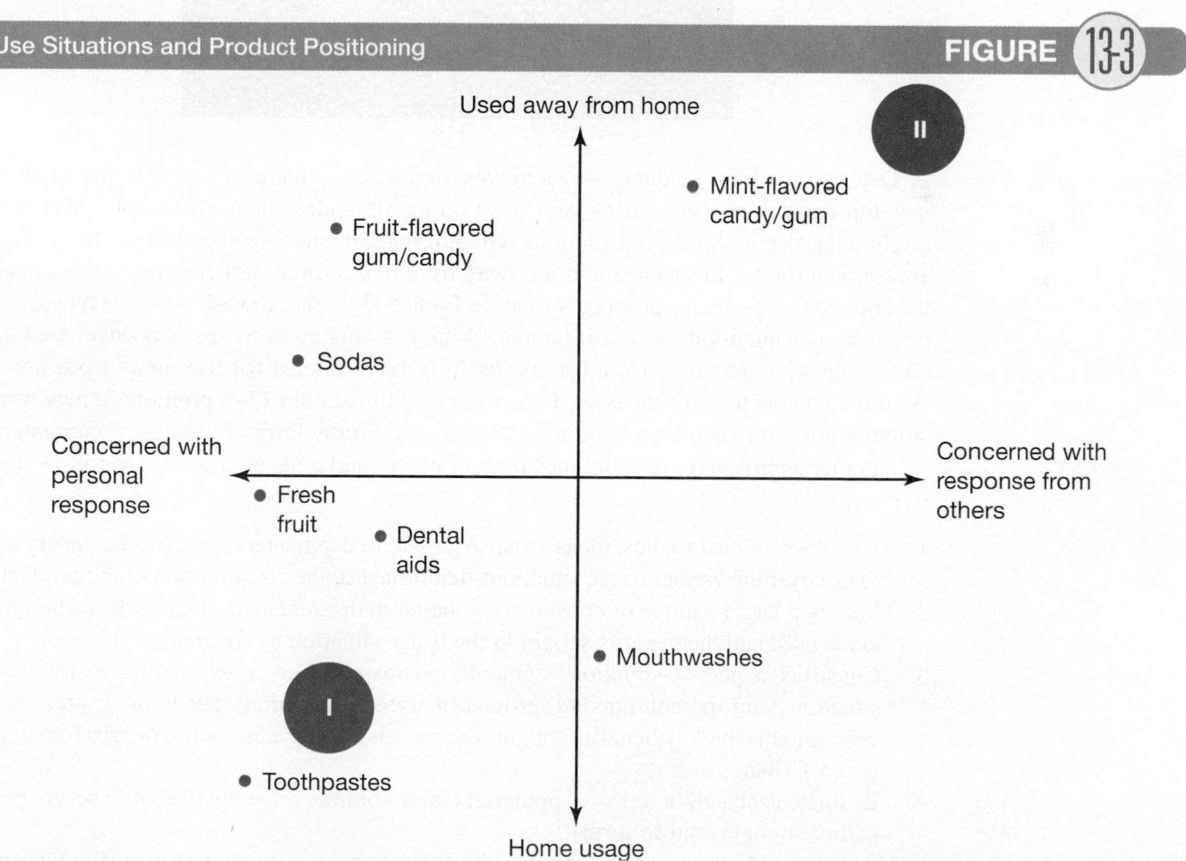

I = Use situation: "To clean my mouth upon rising in the morning."
II = Use situation: "Before an important business meeting late in the afternoon."

ILLUSTRATION 13-8

This ad shows new use situations for Arla LactoFree milk.

Determining how products are *currently used* across situations can help the marketer develop appropriate advertising and positioning strategies. In our example, Wrigley's might advertise its Spearmint Gum as having breath-freshening capabilities that make it appropriate for use in social situations away from home. Or a marketer may try to change the situations for which a product is used. In Figure 13–3, mouthwash is not seen as appropriate for consumption away from home. What if a version of Scope was developed that one swallowed after use? Could it successfully be promoted for use away from home? Would it be able to compete against breath strips? Illustration 13–8 promotes a new usage situation for Arla LactoFree milk in its "Say Yes to Frothy Fruity Smoothies" campaign.

Another approach for developing situation-based marketing strategies is to follow these five steps:[71]

1. Use observational studies, focus group discussions, depth interviews, and secondary data to discover the various usage situations that influence the consumption of the product.
2. Survey a larger sample of consumers to better understand and quantify how the product is used and the benefits sought in the usage situation by the market segment.
3. Construct a person–situation segmentation matrix. The rows are the major usage situations and the columns are groups of users with unique needs or desires. Each cell contains the key benefits sought. (Table 13–2 illustrates such a matrix for suntan lotion.) Then:
4. Evaluate each cell in terms of potential (sales volume, price level, cost to serve, competitor strength, and so forth).
5. Develop and implement a marketing strategy for those cells that offer sufficient profit potential given your capabilities.

Person–Situation Segments for Suntan Lotions TABLE 

Suntan Lotion Use Situation	Potential Users of Suntan Lotion				General Situation Benefits
	Young Children	Teenagers	Adult Women	Adult Men	
Beach/boat activities	Prevent sunburn/skin damage	Prevent sunburn while tanning	Prevent sunburn/ skin change/ dry skin	Prevent sunburn	Container floats
Home/pools sunbathing	Prevent sunburn/skin damage	Tanning without sunburn	Tanning without skin damage or dry skin	Tanning without sunburn/skin damage	Lotion won't stain clothes or furniture
Tanning booth		Tanning	Tanning with moisturizer	Tanning	Designed for sunlamps
Snow skiing		Prevent sunburn	Prevent sunburn/ skin damage/ dry skin	Prevent sunburn	Antifreeze formula
Person benefits	Protection	Tanning	Protection and tanning with soft skin	Protection and tanning	

Source: Adapted from P. Dickson, "Person–Situation: Segmentation's Missing Link," *Journal of Marketing,* Fall 1982, pp. 56–64. Published by the American Marketing Association. Reprinted with permission.

SUMMARY

LO1: Define *situational influence*

Situational influence is all those factors particular to a time and place that do not follow from a knowledge of the stable attributes of the consumer and the stimulus and that have an effect on current behavior.

LO2: Explain the four types of situations and their relevance to marketing strategy

Four categories of situations are communications, purchase, usage, and disposition situations. The situation in which consumers receive information is the communications situation. The situation in which a purchase is made is the purchase situation. The situation in which the product or service is used is the usage situation. The situation in which a product or product package is disposed of either after or before product use is the disposition situation. Each type of situation has marketing implications such as within what programming to advertise (communications situation), the effect of other people on an individual's shopping behavior in-store (buying situation), the ability to expand beyond traditional uses for a given product (usage situation), and the factors contributing to recycling behavior (disposition situation).

LO3: Summarize the five characteristics of situations and their influence on consumption

Five characteristics of situations have been identified. *Physical surroundings* include geographical and institutional location, decor, sound, aromas, lighting, weather, and displays of merchandise or other material surrounding the product. Retailers are particularly concerned with the effects of physical surroundings. The sum of all the physical features of a retail environment is referred to as the *store atmosphere* or environment. *Atmospherics* is the process managers use to manipulate the physical retail environment to create specific mood responses in shoppers. Atmosphere is referred to as *servicescape* when describing a service business such as a hospital, bank, or restaurant.

Social surroundings deal with other persons present who could have an impact on the individual consumer's behavior. The characteristics of the other persons present, their roles, and their interpersonal interactions are potentially important social situational influences.

Temporal perspectives relate to the effect of time on consumer behavior, such as effects of time of day, time since last purchase, time since or until meals or payday, and time constraints imposed by commitments. Convenience stores have evolved and been successful by taking advantage of the temporal perspective factor.

Task definition reflects the purpose or reason for engaging in the consumption behavior. The task may reflect different buyer and user roles anticipated by the individual. For example, a person shopping for dishes to be given as a wedding present is in a different situation from a person buying dishes for personal use.

Antecedent states are features of the individual person that are not lasting or relatively enduring characteristics. *Moods* are temporary states of depression or high excitement, and so on, which all people experience. *Momentary conditions* are such things as being tired, being ill, having a great deal of money (or none at all), and so forth.

LO4: Discuss ritual situations and their importance to consumers and marketers

A *ritual situation* can be described as a set of interrelated behaviors that occur in a structured format, that have symbolic meaning to consumers, and that occur in response to socially defined occasions. Ritual situations can range from completely private to completely public. They are of major importance to marketers because they often involve prescribed consumption behaviors.

LO5: Describe the use of situational influence in developing marketing strategy

Situational influences may have direct influences, but they also interact with product and individual characteristics to influence behavior. In some cases, the situation will have no influence whatsoever because the individual's characteristics or choices are so intense that they override everything else. But the situation is always potentially important and therefore of concern to marketing managers.

KEY TERMS

Antecedent states 483
Atmospherics 477
Communications situation 472
Disposition situation 475
Embarrassment 480
Moods 483
Physical surroundings 475
Purchase situations 474
Ritual situation 485
Servicescape 477
Situational influence 472
Social surroundings 480
Store atmosphere 477
Task definition 482
Temporal perspectives 482
Usage situations 474

REVIEW QUESTIONS

1. What is meant by the term *situation?* Why is it important for a marketing manager to understand situational influences on purchasing behavior?
2. What are *physical surroundings* (as a situational variable)? Give an example of how they can influence the consumption process.
3. How does crowding affect shopping behavior?
4. What is *store atmosphere?*
5. What is *atmospherics?*
6. What is a *servicescape?*
7. What are *social surroundings* (as a situational variable)? Give an example of how they can influence the consumption process.
8. What is *temporal perspective* (as a situational variable)? Give an example of how it can influence the consumption process.
9. What is *task definition* (as a situational variable)? Give an example of how it can influence the consumption process.
10. Why do people give gifts?

11. How might the receipt of a gift affect the relationship between the giver and the receiver?
12. What are *antecedent conditions* (as a situational variable)? Give an example of how they can influence the consumption process.
13. What is a *mood?* How does it differ from an *emotion?* How do moods influence consumption behavior?
14. How do people manage their moods?
15. How do moods differ from *momentary conditions?*
16. What is meant by the statement, "Situational variables may interact with product or personal characteristics"?
17. Are individuals randomly exposed to situational influences? Why or why not?
18. What are *ritual situations?* Why are they important?
19. Describe a process for developing a situation-based marketing strategy.

DISCUSSION QUESTIONS

20. Discuss the potential importance of each type of situational influence in developing a marketing strategy to promote the purchase of (gifts to/shopping at):
    a. Audubon Society
    b. Subway
    c. iPhone
    d. Coca-Cola Zero
    e. 7-Eleven
    f. Eyewear
21. What product categories seem most susceptible to situational influences? Why?
22. Flowers are appropriate gifts for women for many situations but seem to be appropriate for men only when they are ill. Why is this so? How might 1-800-FLOWERS change this?
23. How could the store atmosphere at the following be improved?
    a. The main library on campus
    b. The bank lobby near campus
    c. A diner near campus
    d. A convenience store near campus
    e. The student advising office
24. Speculate on what a matrix like the one shown in Table 13–2 would look like for the following:
    a. Tablet computer
    b. Eyewear
    c. Ice cream
    d. Shoes
    e. Motor scooter
    f. Coffee
25. Does Table 13–1 have implications for outlets other than restaurants? If yes, which ones and why?
26. Do your shopping behavior and purchase criteria differ between purchases made for yourself and purchases made as gifts? How?
27. Describe a situation in which a mood (good or bad) caused you to make an unusual purchase.
28. Describe a relatively private ritual that you or someone you know has. What, if any, consumption pattern is associated with it?
29. Describe the consumption rituals your family has associated with the following ritual situations:
    a. Family birthdays
    b. Summer vacations
    c. Winter holiday
    d. Halloween
    e. Mother's Day
    f. Father's Day
    g. New Year's Eve
30. Respond to the questions in Consumer Insight 13–1.

APPLICATION ACTIVITIES

31. Interview five people who have recently purchased the following. Determine the role, if any, played by situational factors.
    a. Cell phone
    b. Jewelry
    c. Motorcycle
    d. A fast-food restaurant meal
    e. A cup of coffee
    f. Health insurance
32. Interview a salesperson for the following. Determine the role, if any, this individual feels situational variables play in his or her sales.
    a. Renter's insurance
    b. BMX bikes
    c. Fine chocolates
    d. Flowers
33. Conduct a study using a small (five or so) sample of your friends in which you attempt to isolate the situational factors that influence the type, brand, or amount of the following purchased or used.
    a. Health club
    b. Clothing
    c. Movie attendance
    d. Volunteer work
    e. TV dinners
    f. Car tires
34. Create a list of 10 to 20 use situations relevant to campus area restaurants. Then interview 10 students and have them indicate which of these situations they have encountered, and ask them to rank these situations in terms of how likely they are to occur. Discuss how a restaurant could use this information in trying to appeal to the student market.
35. Visit three stores selling the same product line. Describe how the atmosphere differs across the stores. Why do you think these differences exist?
36. Visit three local coffee shops. Describe how the servicescapes differ across the shops. Why do you think these differences exist?
37. What kind of online atmosphere does each of the following have? How would you improve it?
    a. Toyota.com
    b. Harley-Davidson.com
    c. Nike.com
    d. Charities.org
    e. Cabelas.com
    f. Cheerios.com
38. Copy or describe an advertisement that is clearly based on a situational appeal. Indicate
    a. Which situational variable is involved.
    b. Why the company would use this variable.
    c. Your evaluation of the effectiveness of this approach.
39. Create graduation gift, anniversary gift, and self-use ads for the following. Explain the differences across the ads:
    a. Trip abroad
    b. Gourmet coffee maker
    c. Magazine subscription
    d. Set of dishes
    e. Blender
    f. Watch
40. Interview five students and determine instances where their mood affected their purchases. What do you conclude?
41. Interview five students and determine the consumption rituals they have with respect to the following. What do you conclude?
    a. New Year's Day
    b. Spring break
    c. Memorial Day
    d. Valentine's Day
    e. Mother's Day
    f. Father's Day

REFERENCES

1. This opener is based on H. Kimball, "Cold Weather Means Hot Demand for Soup, Boots," *newser,* January 11, 2010, www.newser.com, accessed June 15, 2011; N. Zmuda and E. B. York, "Marketers Make Most of Falling Mercury," *Advertising Age,* January 11, 2010, pp. 1 & 20; and information from Planalytics' website at www.planalytics.com, accessed June 15, 2011.
2. See K. S. Lim and M. A. Razzaque, "Brand Loyalty and Situational Effects," *Journal of International Consumer Marketing* 4 (1997), pp. 95–115.
3. R. W. Belk, "Situational Variables and Consumer Behavior," *Journal of Consumer Research,* December 1975, p. 158.

4. See K. R. Lord, R. E. Burnkrant, and H. R. Unnava, "The Effects of Program-Induced Mood States on Memory for Commercial Information," *Journal of Current Issues and Research in Advertising,* Spring 2001, pp. 1–14; S. Shapiro, D. J. MacInnis, and C. W. Park, "Understanding Program-Induced Mood Effects," *Journal of Advertising,* Winter 2002, pp. 15–26; P. De Pelsmacker, M. Geuens, and P. Anckaert, "Media Context and Advertising Effectiveness," *Journal of Advertising,* Summer 2002, pp. 49–61; S. Jun et al., "The Influence of Editorial Context on Consumer Response to Advertisements in a Specialty Magazine," *Journal of Current Issues and Research in Advertising,* Fall 2003, pp. 1–11; and C. Yoon, M. P. Lee, and S. Danziger, "The Effects of Optimal Time of Day on Persuasion Processes in Older Adults," *Psychology and Marketing,* May 2007, pp. 475–95.

5. L. Sanders and J. Halliday, "BP Institutes 'Ad-Pull' Policy for Print Publications," *AdAge.com,* May 24, 2005.

6. B. Wansink, "Making Old Brands New," *American Demographics,* December 1997, pp. 53–58.

7. E. Byron, "Case by Case," *The Wall Street Journal,* November 17, 2004, p. A1.

8. "Glazed Still Tops among Donuts," *Baking Management,* May 23, 2011.

9. I. Sinha, "A Conceptual Model of Situation Type on Consumer Choice Behavior and Consideration Sets," in *Advances in Consumer Research,* vol. 21, ed. C. T. Allen and D. R. John (Provo, UT: Association for Consumer Research, 1994), pp. 477–82. See also Byron, "Case by Case."

10. See J. A. F. Nicholls et al., "Situational Influences on Shoppers," *Journal of International Consumer Marketing* 9, no. 2 (1996), pp. 21–39; and J. A. F. Nicholls, T. Li, and S. Roslow, "Oceans Apart," *Journal of International Consumer Marketing* 12, no. 1 (1999), pp. 57–72.

11. Mark Twain, in *Brainy Quotes,* www.brainyquote.com/quotes/quotes/m/marktwain104599.html, accessed August 28, 2014.

12. Consumer Insight 13–1 is based on A. D'Innocenzio, "Mannequin Makeovers Include Back Fat, Tattoos, Pubic Hair and Bigger Waists," *National Post,* January 28, 2014, http://life.nationalpost.com/2014/01/28/mannequin-makeovers-include-back-fat-tattoos-pubic-hair-and-bigger-waists/, accessed August 28, 2014; R. Walker, "Museum Quality," *New York Times Magazine,* January 9, 2005, www.nytimes.com/2005/01/09/magazine/09CONSUMED.html, accessed August 28, 2014; S. Clifford, "Stores Demand Mannequins with Personality (Heads Optional)," *New York Times,* June 15, 2011, www.nytimes.com/2011/06/16/business/16mannequin.html, accessed August 28, 2014; K. Bishop, "Store Uses Plus-Size Mannequins to Reflect True Shape of Shoppers," *NBC News,* November 6, 2013, www.nbcnews.com/business/consumer/store-uses-plus-size-mannequins-reflect-true-shape-shoppers-f8C11542388, accessed August 28, 2014; J. Stern, "Department Store Mannequins Are Watching You. No, Really," *ABC News,* November 26, 2012, http://abcnews.go.com/Technology/department-store-mannequins-watch-eyesee-analyzes-shoppers-webcams/story?id=17813441, accessed August 28, 2014; and N. Anitha and C. Selvaraj, "The Effects of Mannequins on Consumers' Perception and Shopping Attitude," *Information Processing and Management,* 2010, pp. 641–47.

13. See E. Sherman, A. Mathur, and R. B. Smith, "Store Environment and Consumer Purchase Behavior," *Psychology & Marketing,* July 1997, pp. 361–78; and J. Baker et al., "The Influence of Multiple Design Cues on Perceived Merchandise Value and Patronage Intentions," *Journal of Marketing,* April 2002, pp. 120–41.

14. For an extensive review, see L. W. Turley and R. E. Milliman, "Atmospheric Effects on Shopping Behavior," *Journal of Business Research* 49 (2000), pp. 193–211. See also A. d'Astous, "Irritating Aspects of the Shopping Environment," *Journal of Business Research* 49 (2000), pp. 149–56; and A. Sharma and T. F. Stafford, "The Effect of Retail Atmospherics on Customers' Perceptions of Salespeople and Customer Persuasion," *Journal of Business Research* 49 (2000), pp. 183–91.

15. P. Sautter, M. R. Hyman, and V. Lukosius, "E-Tail Atmospherics," *Journal of Electronic Commerce Research* 5, no. 1 (2004), pp. 14–24; and E. E. Manganari, G. J. Siomkos, and A. P. Vrechopoulos, "Store Atmosphere in Web Retailing," *European Journal of Marketing* 43, no. 9/10 (2009), pp. 1140–53.

16. M. J. Bitner, "Servicescapes," *Journal of Marketing,* April 1992, pp. 57–71. See also K. D. Hoffman, S. W. Kelley, and B. C. Chung, "A CIT Investigation of Servicescape Failures and Associated Recovery Strategies," *Journal of Services Marketing* 17, no. 4/5 (2003), pp. 322–40.

17. G. J. Gorn, A. Chattopadhyay, T. Yi, and D. W. Dahl, "Effects of Color as an Executional Cue in Advertising," *Management Science,* October 1997, pp. 1387–99.

18. See J. A. Bellizzi and R. E. Hite, "Environmental Color, Consumer Feelings, and Purchase Likelihood," *Psychology & Marketing,* September 1992, pp. 347–63.

19. B. E. Kahn and L. McAlister, *Grocery Revolution* (Reading, MA: Addison-Wesley, 1997).

20. G. J. Gorn, A. Chattopadhyay, J. Sengupta, and S. Tripathi, "Waiting for the Web," *Journal of Marketing Research,* May 2004, pp. 215–25.

21. D. J. Mitchell, B. E. Kahn, and S. C. Knasko, "There's Something in the Air," *Journal of Consumer Research,* September 1995, pp. 229–38.

22. E. R. Spangenberg, A. E. Crowley, and P. W. Henderson, "Improving the Store Environment," *Journal of Marketing,* April 1996, pp. 67–80.

23. A. R. Hirsch, "Effects of Ambient Odors on Slot-Machine Usage in a Las Vegas Casino," *Psychology & Marketing,* October 1995, pp. 585–94.

24. M. Morrison et al., "In-Store Music and Aroma Influences on Shopper Behavior and Satisfaction," *Journal of Business Research* 64 (2011), pp. 558–64.

25. M. Morrin and S. Ratneshwar, "The Impact of Ambient Scent on Evaluation, Attention, and Memory for Familiar and Unfamiliar Brands," *Journal of Business Research* 49 (2000), pp. 157–65.

26. See, e.g., "Environmental Fragrancing," *Labnews.co.uk,* May 26, 2011, accessed June 15, 2011.

27. P. F. Bone and P. S. Ellen, "Scents in the Marketplace," *Journal of Retailing* 75, no. 2 (1999), pp. 243–62.

28. P. Sloan, "Smelling Trouble," *Advertising Age,* September 11, 1995, p. 1.

29. See S. Oakes, "The Influence of the Musicscape within Service Environments," *Journal of Services Marketing* 4, no. 7 (2000), pp. 539–56; Morrison et al., "In-Store Music and Aroma Influences on Shopper Behavior and Satisfaction"; and S. Morin, L. Dube, and J. C. Chebat, "The Role of Pleasant Music in Servicescapes," *Journal of Business Research* 83, no. 1 (2007), 115–30.

30. J. C. Sweeney and F. Wyber, "The Role of Cognitions and Emotions in the Music-Approach-Avoidance Behavior Relationship," *Journal of Services Marketing* 16, no. 1 (2002), pp. 51–69; and C. Caldwell and S. A. Hibbert, "The Influence of Music Tempo and Musical Preference on Restaurant Patrons' Behavior," *Psychology & Marketing,* November 2002, pp. 895–917.

31. B. Zimmers, "Business Deals Put AEI Music CEO in Good Mood," *Puget Sound Business Journal,* June 23, 2000, p. 44; see also C. A. Olson, "Shopping to the Music Made Easy," *Billboard,* July 31, 1999, pp. 73–74.

32. See K. A. Machleit, S. A. Eroglu, and S. P. Mantel, "Perceived Retail Crowding and Shopping Satisfaction," *Journal of Consumer Psychology* 9, no. 1 (2000), pp. 29–42. For an exception, see F. Pons, M. Laroche, and M. Mourali, "Consumer Reactions to Crowded Retail Settings," *Psychology & Marketing,* July 2006, pp. 555–72.

33. S. A. Eroglu, K. A. Machleit, and J. C. Chebat, "The Interaction of Retail Density and Music Tempo," *Psychology & Marketing,* July 2005, pp. 577–89.

34. Pons, Laroche, and Mourali, "Consumer Reactions to Crowded Retail Settings."

35. T. R. Graeth, "Consumption Situations and the Effects of Brand Image on Consumers' Brand Evaluations," *Psychology & Marketing,* January 1997, pp. 49–70. See also S. Ramanathan and A. L. McGill, "Consuming with Others," *Journal of Consumer Research,* December 2007, pp. 506–24.

36. R. K. Ratner and B. E. Kahn, "The Impact of Private versus Public Consumption on Variety-Seeking Behavior," *Journal of Consumer Research,* September 2002, pp. 246–57.

37. See, e.g., D. W. Dahl, R. V. Manchanda, and J. J. Argo, "Embarrassment in Consumer Purchase," *Journal of Consumer Research,* December 2001, pp. 473–81. See also D. Grace, "How Embarrassing!," *Journal of Service Research,* February 2007, pp. 271–84.

38. X. Luo, "How Does Shopping with Others Influence Impulsive Purchasing?," *Journal of Consumer Psychology* 15, no. 4 (2005), pp. 288–94.

39. R. Batra and P. M. Homer, "The Situational Impact of Brand Image Beliefs," *Journal of Consumer Psychology* 14, no. 3 (2004), pp. 318–30.

40. L. A. Brannon and T. C. Brock, "Limiting Time for Responding Enhances Behavior Corresponding to the Merits of Compliance Appeals," *Journal of Consumer Psychology* 10, no. 3 (2001), pp. 135–46; and R. Suri and K. B. Monroe, "The Effects of Time Constraints on Consumers' Judgments of Prices and Products," *Journal of Consumer Research,* June 2003, pp. 92–104.

41. S. M. Nowlis, "The Effect of Time Pressure on the Choice of Brands That Differ in Quality, Price, and Product Features," *Marketing Letters,* October 1995, pp. 287–96; R. Dhar and S. M. Nowlis, "The Effect of Time Pressure on Consumer Choice Deferral," *Journal of Consumer Research,* March 1999, pp. 369–84; and R. Pieters and L. Warlop, "Visual Attention during Brand Choice," *International Journal of Research in Marketing,* February 1999, pp. 1–16.

42. S. D. Strombeck and K. L. Wakefield, "Situational Influences on Service Quality Evaluations," *Journal of Services Marketing* 22, no. 5 (2008), pp. 409–19.

43. P. Van Kenhove, K. De Wulf, and W. Van Waterschoot, "The Impact of Task Definition on Store-Attribute Saliences and Store Choice," *Journal of Retailing* 75, no. 1 (1999), pp. 125–37; and P. Van Kenhove and K. De Wulf, "Income and Time Pressure," *International Review of Retail, Distribution and Consumer Research,* April 2000, pp. 149–66.

44. See B. H. Schmitt and C. J. Shultz II, "Situational Effects on Brand Preferences for Image Products," *Psychology & Marketing,* August 1995, pp. 433–46.

45. T. M. Lowrey, C. C. Otnes, and J. A. Ruth, "Social Influences on Dyadic Giving over Time," *Journal of Consumer Research,* March 2004, pp. 547–58.

46. For a review and framework, see D. Larsen and J. J. Watson, "A Guide Map to the Terrain of Gift Value," *Psychology & Marketing,* August 2001, pp. 889–906; see also G. Saad and T. Gill, "An Evolutionary Psychology Perspective on Gift Giving among Young Adults," *Psychology & Marketing,* September 2003, pp. 765–84.

47. M. A. McGrath, "Gender Differences in Gift Exchanges," *Psychology & Marketing,* August 1995, pp. 371–93; and K. M. Palan, C. S. Areni, and P. Kiecker, "Gender Role Incongruency and Memorable Gift Exchange Experiences," and J. F. Durgee and T. Sego, "Gift-Giving as a Metaphor for Understanding New Products That Delight," both in *Advances in Consumer Research,* vol. 28, ed. M. C. Gilly and J. Meyers-Levy (Provo, UT: Association for Consumer Research, 2001), pp. 51–57 and 64–69, respectively.

48. D. B. Wooten, "Qualitative Steps toward an Expanded Model of Anxiety in Gift-Giving," *Journal of Consumer Research,* June 2000, pp. 84–95.

49. See, e.g., J. A. Ruth, C. C. Otnes, and F. F. Brunel, "Gift Receipt and the Reformulation of Interpersonal Relationships," *Journal of Consumer Research,* March 1999, pp. 385–402.

50. R. W. Belk and G. S. Coon, "Gift Giving as Agapic Love," *Journal of Consumer Research,* December 1993, pp. 404–405. See also J. A. Ruth, F. F. Brunel, and C. C. Otnes, "An Investigation of the Power of Emotions in Relationship Realignment," *Psychology & Marketing,* January 2004, pp. 29–52.

51. C. S. Areni, P. Kiecker, and K. M. Palan, "Is It Better to Give Than to Receive?," *Psychology & Marketing,* January 1998, pp. 81–109.

52. A. Joy, "Gift Giving in Hong Kong and the Continuum of Social Ties," *Journal of Consumer Research,* September 2001, pp. 239–55; and S. L. Lotz, S. Shim, and K. C. Gehrt, "A Study of Japanese Consumers' Cognitive Hierarchies in Formal and Informal Gift-Giving Situations," *Psychology & Marketing,* January 2003, pp. 59–85.

53. S.-Y. Park, "A Comparison of Korean and American Gift-Giving Behaviors," *Psychology & Marketing,* September 1998, pp. 577–93.

54. See R. P. Bagozzi, M. Gopinath, and P. U. Nyer, "The Role of Emotion in Marketing," *Journal of the Academy of Marketing Science,* Spring 1999, pp. 184–206; and H. T. Luomala and M. Laaksonen, "Contributions from Mood Research," *Psychology & Marketing,* March 2000, pp. 195–233.
55. M. B. Holbrook and M. P. Gardner, "Illustrating a Dynamic Model of the Mood-Updating Process in Consumer Behavior," *Psychology & Marketing,* March 2000, pp. 165–94.
56. J. P. Forgas and J. Ciarrochi, "On Being Happy and Possessive," *Psychology & Marketing,* March 2001, pp. 239–60; and R. Adaval, "Sometimes It Just Feels Right," *Journal of Consumer Research,* June 2001, pp. 1–17.
57. D. W. Rook and M. P. Gardner, "In the Mood," *Research in Consumer Behavior* 6 (1993), pp. 1–28; W. R. Swinyard, "The Effects of Mood, Involvement, and Quality of Store Experience on Shopping Intentions," *Journal of Consumer Research,* September 1993, pp. 271–80; and R. J. Faber and G.A. Christenson, "In the Mood to Buy," *Psychology & Marketing,* December 1996, pp. 803–19. See also N. Garg, B. Wansink, and J. J. Inman, "The Influence of Incidental Affect on Consumers' Food Intake," *Journal of Marketing,* January 2007, pp. 194–206, for an application of mood to food choice.
58. See Reference 4.
59. See, e.g., K. S. Coulter, "The Effects of Affective Responses to Media Context on Advertising Evaluations," *Journal of Advertising,* Winter 1998, pp. 41–51.
60. H. T. Luomala and M. Laaksonen, "A Qualitative Exploration of Mood-Regulatory Self-Gift Behaviors," *Journal of Economic Psychology* 20 (1999), pp. 147–82.
61. H. Mano, "The Influence of Pre-Existing Negative Affect on Store Purchase Intentions," *Journal of Retailing* 75, no. 2 (1999), pp. 149–73.
62. S. J. Gould, "An Interpretive Study of Purposeful, Mood Self-Regulating Consumption," *Psychology & Marketing,* July 1997, pp. 395–426.
63. See M. G. Meloy, "Mood-Driven Distortion of Product Information," *Journal of Consumer Research,* December 2000, pp. 345–58.
64. See P. A. Walsh and S. Spiggle, "Consumer Spending Patterns," in *Advances in Consumer Research,* vol. 21, ed. Allen and John, pp. 35–40; and N. Karlsson, T. Garling, and M. Selart, "Explanations of Prior Income Changes on Buying Decisions," *Journal of Economic Psychology* 20 (1999), pp. 449–63.
65. See B. Gainer, "Ritual and Relationships," *Journal of Business Research,* March 1995, pp. 253–60.
66. See C. C. Otnes and L. M. Scott, "Something Old, Something New," *Journal of Advertising,* Spring 1996, pp. 33–50.
67. "$10 Billion for Mom," *CNNmoney,* April 21, 2004, http://money.cnn.com/.
68. A. Z. Cuneo, "Using Halloween to Scare Up Sales," *Advertising Age,* October 8, 2001, p. 4.
69. A. Chozick, "Fairy-Tale Fifteenths," *The Wall Street Journal,* October 15, 2004, p. B1.
70. Ibid.
71. For a similar approach, see R. Brodie, "Segmentation and Market Structure When Both Consumer and Situational Characteristics Are Explanatory," *Psychology & Marketing,* September 1992, pp. 395–408.

chapter

14 Consumer Decision Process and Problem Recognition

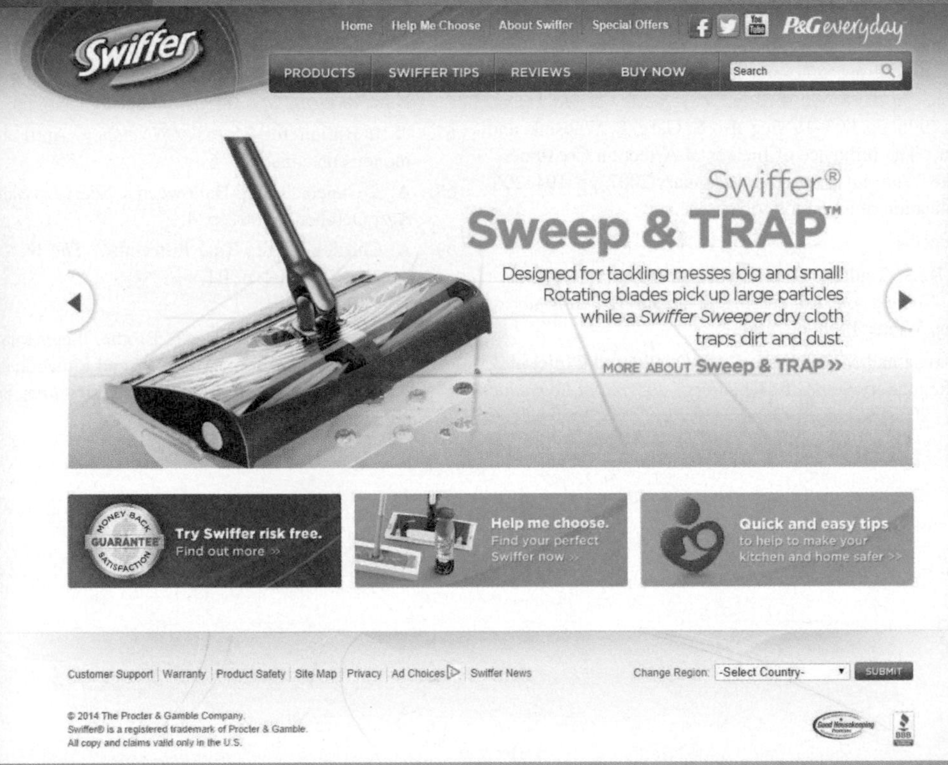

LEARNING OBJECTIVES

LO1 **Describe the impact of purchase involvement on the decision process.**

LO2 **Explain problem recognition and how it fits into the consumer decision process.**

LO3 **Summarize the uncontrollable determinants of problem recognition.**

LO4 **Discuss the role of consumer problems and problem recognition in marketing strategy.**

The plug to the lamp is one of the eight cords in the power strip, but which one? You are going to have to trace the cord from the lamp to the power strip, which is underneath the desk. You rummage through your desk drawer looking for a rubber band. You know you have rubber bands somewhere among the scattering of paper clips, pens, ties, and odds and ends. It's a mess. These are a few examples of common problems we all have. They are a bit irritating and annoying, but not really of any great importance and not likely to occur with frequency. So we just work around them. These *work-around problems* fall in the category of "nominal decision making," a type of decision making that in effect involves no decision per se.

Prior to social media, the doyenne of solutions to work-around problems was Heloise, who offered her Helpful Hints.[1] Now with social media as part of our daily lives, and most notably with the popularity of Pinterest, Heloise-like "life hacks" have sprung up, offering help for problems you never knew you had, like using recycled bread tags to label and identify cords in the power strip and using old tins to organize your messy desk drawers. These enthusiastically, freely offered solutions parallel the product strategy to increase sales by suggesting other ways to use the products besides the obvious. For example, Arm and Hammer Baking Soda offers many other versatile uses of its baking soda besides baking—as a deodorizer for rugs and refrigerators and as an ingredient to build a model of an active volcano.

For consumers engaged in nominal decision making, store signage and display may remind them to make purchases that they might otherwise forget. Some stores print coupons of the consumer's previously purchased products on the back of the customer's receipts to serve as reminders.

It's very likely that most households in the United States have cleaning products—detergents, dishwashing liquids, cleanser, bleach—that clean "well enough." Consumers are likely not actively involved in looking for alternatives. However, if you are Proctor and Gamble, faced with increasingly shorter product life cycles, you are forced to innovate and continuously improve solutions currently on the market. Enter P&G's Swiffer line of cleaning products that promises to make sweeping, dusting, vacuuming better and easier. Vacuum cleaners are a common household appliance that perform well enough and are infrequently replaced. Then Dyson introduced improvements—bagless vacuum cleaners with "cyclone" efficiency, wheels that eliminated annoying run-ins with furniture—solving problems that you didn't know you had.

With the rise of crowd sourcing—Quirky, Kickstarter—the ability to develop and market solutions to "problems you didn't know you had" can now extend beyond the Procter and Gambles of the world to individual consumers. Examples include Quirky Bandits, rubber bands with hooks to "keep pens and drawing supplies together, fasten sunglasses to the rearview mirror," and Cordies, to organize the cords on desks by "reining in all these loose chords to reduce tangling."

The consumer decision process begins with problem recognition. Nominal problems are those that involve little to no thought. For nominal problems, consumers follow habit and buy the same brand. They perform the same behavior to *work around* the problem. But solutions offered may be so clever that they knock consumers into awareness of the existence of problems they didn't know they had.

This chapter examines the nature of the consumer decision process and analyzes the first step in that process: problem recognition. Within problem recognition, we focus on (1) the process of problem recognition, (2) the uncontrollable determinants of problem recognition, and (3) marketing strategies based on the problem recognition process.

TYPES OF CONSUMER DECISIONS

L01

The term *consumer decision* produces an image of an individual carefully evaluating the attributes of a set of products, brands, or services and rationally selecting the one that solves a clearly recognized need for the least cost. It has a rational, functional connotation. Consumers do make many decisions in this manner; however, many other decisions involve little conscious effort. Further, many consumer decisions focus not on brand attributes but rather on the feelings or emotions associated with acquiring or using the brand or with the situation in which the product is purchased or used. Thus, a brand may be selected not because of an attribute (price, style, functional characteristics) but because "it makes me feel good" or "my friends will like it."[2]

Although purchases and related consumption behavior driven by emotional or situational needs have characteristics distinct from the traditional attribute-based model, the decision process model provides useful insights into all types of consumer purchases. As we describe the process of consumer decision making in this and the next four chapters, we will indicate how it helps us understand emotion-, situation-, and attribute-based decisions.

Consumer decisions are frequently the result of a single problem, for example, running low on gasoline. At other times, they result from the convergence of several problems, such as an aging automobile and a growing feeling of inadequacy or low self-esteem. Furthermore, once the decision process begins, it may evolve and become more complex with multiple goals. A consumer noticing a simple need for gas may want to minimize the price paid, avoid one or more brands because of their environmental record, and decide to find a station with food service attached. This consumer may wind up choosing between a station with a lower price and its own food service, or another station with a higher price but with a preferred food outlet such as Taco Bell attached, or perhaps spending the extra time to buy gas at one and food at the other.[3]

As Figure 14–1 indicates, there are various types of consumer decision processes.[4] As the consumer moves from a very low level of involvement *with the purchase* to a high level of involvement, decision making becomes increasingly complex. While purchase involvement is a continuum, it is useful to consider nominal, limited, and extended decision making as general descriptions of the types of processes that occur along various points on the continuum. Keep in mind that the types of decision processes are not distinct but rather blend into each other.

Before describing each type of decision process, we must clarify the concept of purchase involvement. We define **purchase involvement** as *the level of concern for, or*

Involvement and Types of Decision Making

FIGURE 14-1

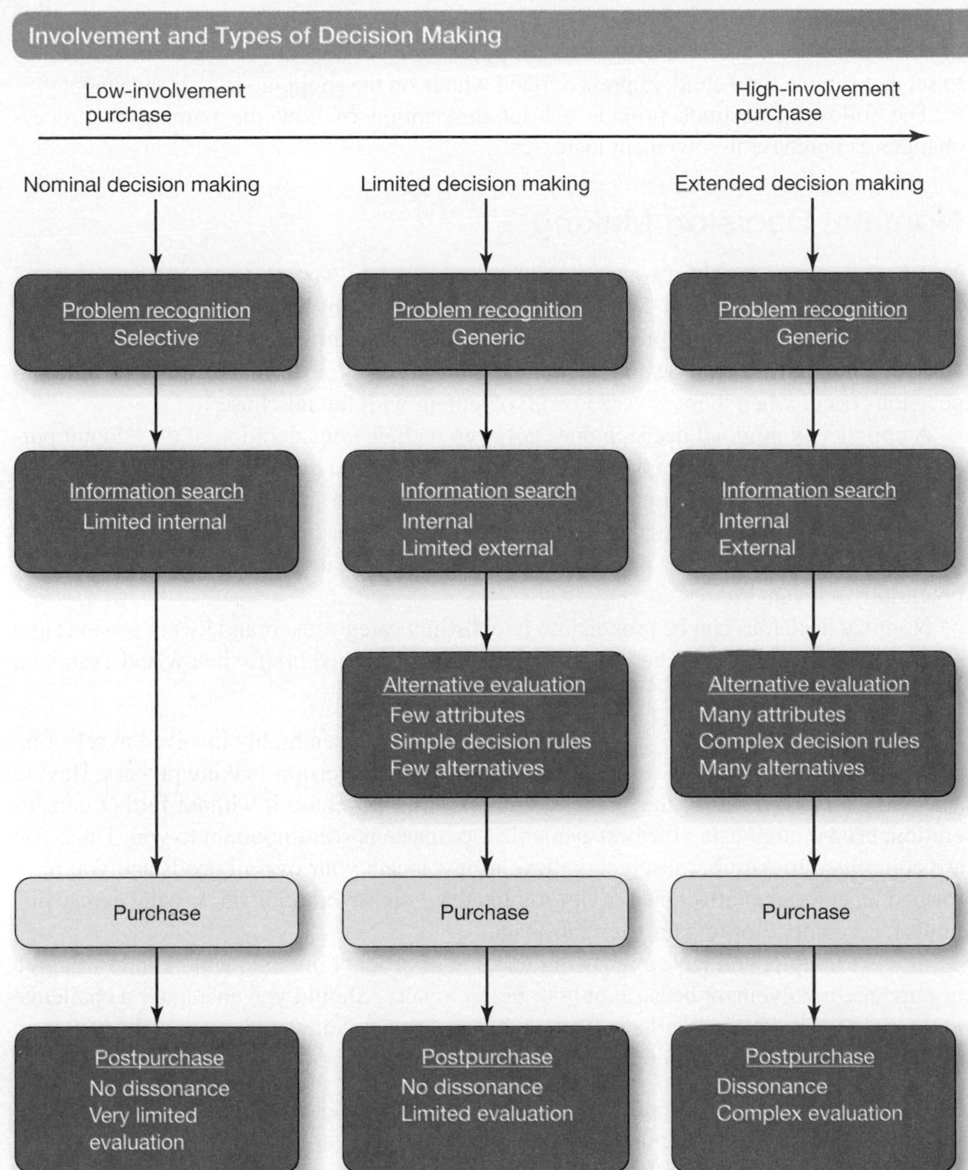

interest in, the purchase process triggered by the need to consider a particular purchase. Thus, purchase involvement is a *temporary state* of an individual or household. It is influenced by the interaction of individual, product, and situational characteristics.

Note that purchase involvement is *not* the same as **product involvement** or enduring involvement. A consumer may be very involved with a brand (Starbucks or Dodge) or a product category (coffee or cars) and yet have a very low level of involvement with a particular purchase of that product because of brand loyalty, time pressures, or other reasons. For example, think of your favorite brand of soft drink or other beverage. You may be quite loyal to that brand, think it is superior to other brands, and have strong, favorable feelings about it. However, when you want a soft drink, you probably just buy your preferred brand without much thought.

Or a consumer may have a rather low level of involvement with a product (school supplies or automobile tires) but have a high level of purchase involvement because he or she desires to set an example for a child, impress a friend who is on the shopping trip, or save money.

The following sections provide a brief description of how the purchasing process changes as purchase involvement increases.

Nominal Decision Making

Nominal decision making, sometimes referred to as *habitual decision making,* in effect *involves no decision per se.* As Figure 14–1 indicates, a problem is recognized, internal search (long-term memory) provides a single preferred solution (brand), that brand is purchased, and an evaluation occurs only if the brand fails to perform as expected. Nominal decisions occur when there is very low involvement with the purchase.

A completely nominal decision does not even include consideration of the "do not purchase" alternative. For example, you might notice that you are nearly out of Aim toothpaste and resolve to purchase some the next time you are at the store. You don't even consider not replacing the toothpaste or purchasing another brand. At the store, you scan the shelf for Aim and pick it up without considering alternative brands, its price, or other potentially relevant factors.

Nominal decisions can be broken into two distinct categories: brand loyal decisions and repeat purchase decisions. These two categories are described briefly below and examined in detail in Chapter 18.

Brand Loyal Purchases At one time, you may have been highly involved in selecting a brand of toothpaste and, in response, used an extensive decision-making process. Having selected Aim as a result of this process, you may now purchase it without further consideration, even though using the best available toothpaste is still important to you. Thus, you are committed to Aim because you believe it best meets your overall needs and you have formed an emotional attachment to it (you like it). You are brand loyal. It will be very difficult for a competitor to gain your patronage.

In this example, you have a fairly high degree of product involvement but a low degree of purchase involvement because of your brand loyalty. Should you encounter a challenge to the superiority of Aim, perhaps through a news article, you would most likely engage in a high-involvement decision process before changing brands.

Repeat Purchases In contrast, you may believe that all ketchup is about the same and you may not attach much importance to the product category or purchase. Having tried Del Monte and found it satisfactory, you now purchase it whenever you need ketchup. Thus, you are a repeat purchaser of Del Monte ketchup, but you are not committed to it.

Should you encounter a challenge to the wisdom of buying Del Monte the next time you need ketchup, perhaps because of a point-of-sale price discount, you would probably engage in only a limited decision process before deciding on which brand to purchase.

Limited Decision Making

Limited decision making involves internal and limited external search, few alternatives, simple decision rules on a few attributes, and little postpurchase evaluation. It covers the middle ground between nominal decision making and extended decision making. In its simplest form (lowest level of purchase involvement), limited decision making is similar to nominal decision making. For example, while in a store you may notice a point-of-purchase display for Jell-O and pick up two boxes without seeking information beyond your memory that "Jell-O tastes good" or "Gee, I haven't had Jell-O in a long time." In addition, you may have considered no other alternative except possibly a very limited examination of a "do not buy" option. Or you may have a decision rule that you buy the cheapest brand of instant coffee available. When you run low on coffee (problem recognition), you simply examine coffee prices the next time you are in the store and select the cheapest brand.

Limited decision making also occurs in response to some emotional or situational needs. For example, you may decide to purchase a new brand or product because you are bored with the current, otherwise satisfactory, brand. This decision might involve evaluating only the newness or novelty of the available alternatives.[5] Or you might evaluate a purchase in terms of the actual or anticipated behavior of others. For example, you might order or refrain from ordering wine with a meal depending on the observed or expected orders of your dinner companions.

In general, limited decision making involves recognizing a problem for which there are several possible solutions. There is internal and a limited amount of external search. A few alternatives are evaluated on a few dimensions using simple selection rules. The purchase and use of the product are given very little evaluation afterward, unless there is a service problem or product failure.

Extended Decision Making

As Figure 14–1 indicates, **extended decision making** involves an extensive internal and external information search followed by a complex evaluation of multiple alternatives and significant postpurchase evaluation. It is the response to a high level of purchase involvement. After the purchase, doubt about its correctness is likely and a thorough evaluation of the purchase takes place. Relatively few consumer decisions reach this level of complexity. However, products such as homes, personal computers, and complex recreational items such as home theatre systems are frequently purchased via extended decision making.

Even decisions that are heavily emotional may involve substantial cognitive effort. For example, a consumer may agonize over a decision to take a ski trip or visit parents even though the needs being met and the criteria being evaluated are largely emotions or feelings rather than attributes per se, and are therefore typically fewer in number with less external information available.

As Figure 14–1 illustrates, problem recognition is the first stage of the decision process. We will describe this stage and discuss the marketing applications associated with it in the remainder of this chapter. We devote the next four chapters to the remaining four stages of the consumer decision process and discuss the relevant marketing applications in those chapters.

Our discussion of the decision process is based primarily on studies conducted in America. Where appropriate throughout this section of the text, we will point out some of the similarities and differences in decision making across cultures. As just one example relating to family decision making (Chapter 6), researchers found that in China, the more patriarchal social structure leads to more husband-dominated decisions and fewer joint husband-wife decisions than in the United States.[6] Given shifting values, particularly among the youth in Southeast Asia as discussed in Chapter 2, this result is likely to also be a function of the age of the couples in question.

THE PROCESS OF PROBLEM RECOGNITION

LO2

A day rarely passes in which a person does not face multiple problems that are resolved by consuming products and services. Routine problems of depletion, such as the need to get gasoline as the gauge approaches empty or the need to replace a frequently used food item, are readily recognized, defined, and resolved. The unexpected breakdown of a major appliance such as a refrigerator creates an unplanned problem that is also easily recognized but is often more difficult to

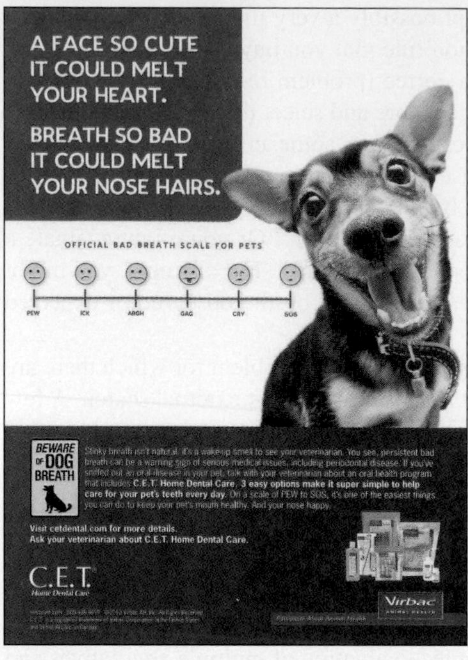

ILLUSTRATION 14-1

Marketers often attempt to cause consumers to recognize potential problems for which the marketer has a solution. As this ad illustrates, this sometimes involves making consumers aware of problems well before they arise.

resolve. Recognition of other problems, such as the need for a camera phone or a GPS system in the car, may take longer, as they may be subtle and evolve slowly over time.

Feelings, such as boredom, anxiety, or the "blues," may arise quickly or slowly over time. Such feelings are often recognized as problems subject to solution by purchasing behavior (I'm sad; I think I'll go to the mall/to a movie/to a restaurant). At other times, such feelings may trigger consumption behaviors without deliberate decision making. A person feeling restless may eat snack food without really thinking about it. In this case, the problem remains unrecognized (at the conscious level) and the solutions tried are often inappropriate (eating may not reduce restlessness).

Marketers develop products to help consumers solve problems. They also attempt to help consumers recognize problems, sometimes well in advance of their occurrence (see Illustration 14–1).

The Nature of Problem Recognition

Problem recognition is the first stage in the consumer decision process. **Problem recognition** is the result of a discrepancy between a desired state and an actual state that is sufficient to arouse and activate the decision process.[7] An **actual state** is *the way an individual perceives his or her feelings and situation to be at the present time.* A **desired state** is *the way an individual* wants *to feel or be at the present time.* For example, you probably don't want to be bored on Friday night. If you find yourself alone and becoming bored, you would treat this as a problem because your actual state (being bored) and your desired state (being pleasantly occupied) are different. You could then choose to watch a television program, rent a video, call a friend, go out, or take a wide array of other actions.

The kind of action taken by consumers in response to a recognized problem relates directly to the problem's importance to the consumer, the situation, and the dissatisfaction or inconvenience created by the problem.

Without recognition of a problem, there is no need for a decision. This condition is shown in Figure 14–2, when there is no discrepancy between the consumer's desired state (what the consumer would like) and the actual state (what the consumer perceives as already existing). Thus, if Friday night arrives and you find yourself engrossed in a novel, your desire to be pleasantly occupied (desired state) and your condition of enjoying a novel would be consistent, and you would have no reason to search for other activities.

On the other hand, when there is a discrepancy between a consumer desire and the perceived actual state, recognition of a problem occurs. Figure 14–2 indicates that any time the desired state is perceived as being greater than or less than the actual state, a problem exists. For example, being pleasantly occupied (desired state) would generally exceed being bored (actual state) and result in problem recognition. However, if your roommate suddenly showed up with a rowdy party, you might find yourself with more stimulation (actual state) than the medium level you actually desire. This too would result in problem recognition.

The Process of Problem Recognition FIGURE 14-2

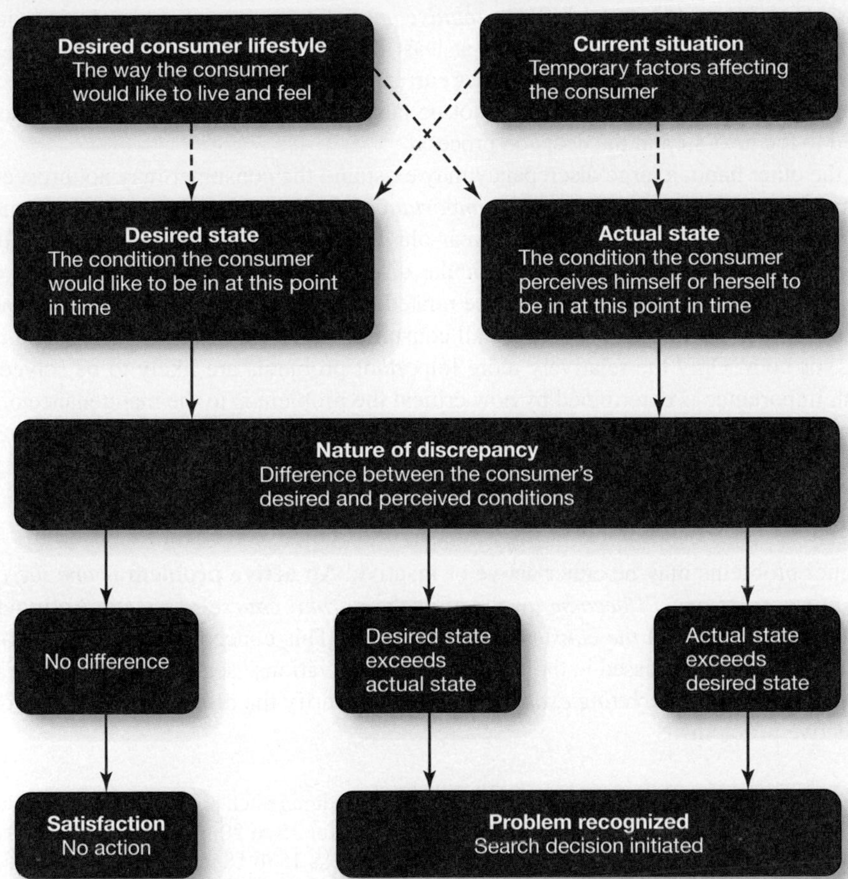

In Figure 14–2, consumer desires are shown to be the result of the desired lifestyle of the consumer (as described in Chapter 12) and the current situation (time pressures, physical surroundings, and so forth, as described in Chapter 13). Thus, a consumer whose self-concept and desired lifestyle focus on outdoor activities will desire frequent participation in such activities. A current situation of new snow in the mountains or warm weather at the beach would tend to increase that person's desire to be engaged in outdoor sports.

Perceptions of the actual state are also determined by a consumer's lifestyle and current situation. Consumers' lifestyles are a major determinant of their actual state because that is how they choose to live given the constraints imposed by their resources. Thus, a consumer who has chosen to raise a family, have significant material possessions, and pursue a demanding career is likely to have little free time for outdoor activities (actual state). The current situation—a day off work, a big project due, or a sick child—also has a major impact on how consumers perceive the actual situation.

It is important to note that it is the consumer's *perception* of the actual state that drives problem recognition, not some objective reality. Consumers who smoke cigars may believe that this activity is not harming their health because they do not inhale. These consumers do not recognize a problem with this behavior despite the reality that it is harmful.

The Desire to Resolve Recognized Problems The level of one's desire to resolve a particular problem depends on two factors: (1) *the magnitude of the discrepancy between the desired and actual states* and (2) *the relative importance of the problem.* An individual could desire to have a car that averages at least 25 miles per gallon while still meeting certain size and power desires. If his or her current car obtains an average of 22 miles per gallon, a discrepancy exists, but it may not be large enough to motivate the consumer to proceed to the next step in the decision process.

On the other hand, a large discrepancy may exist and the consumer may not proceed to information search because the *relative importance* of the problem is small. A consumer may desire a new Honda and own a 15-year-old Toyota. The discrepancy is large. However, the relative importance of this particular discrepancy may be small compared with other consumption problems such as those related to housing, utilities, and food. Relative importance is a critical concept because all consumers have budget constraints, time constraints, or both. Only the relatively more important problems are likely to be solved. In general, importance is determined by how critical the problem is to the maintenance of the consumer's desired lifestyle.

Types of Consumer Problems

Consumer problems may be either active or inactive. An **active problem** is *one the consumer is aware of or will become aware of in the normal course of events.* An **inactive problem** is *one of which the consumer is not aware.* (This concept is very similar to the concept of felt need discussed in the "Diffusion of Innovations" section of Chapter 7.) The following is a *classic marketing example* that should clarify the distinction between active and inactive problems.

Timberlane Lumber Co. acquired a source of supply of Honduran pitch pine. This natural product lights at the touch of a match even when damp and burns for 15 to 20 minutes. It will not flare up and is therefore relatively safe. It can be procured in sticks 15 to 18 inches long and 1 inch in diameter. These sticks can be used to ignite fireplace fires, or they can be shredded and used to ignite charcoal grills.

Prior to marketing the product, Timberlane commissioned a marketing study to estimate demand and guide in developing marketing strategy. Two large samples of potential consumers were interviewed. The first sample was asked how they lit their fireplace fires and what problems they had with this procedure. Almost all the respondents used newspaper, kindling, or both, and very few experienced any problems. The new product was then described, and the respondents were asked to express the likelihood that they would purchase such a product. Only a small percentage expressed any interest. However, a sample of consumers that were paid to use the new product for several weeks felt it was a substantial improvement over existing methods and expressed a strong desire to continue using the product. Thus, the problem was there (because the new product was strongly preferred over the old by those who tried it), but most consumers were not aware of it. This is an *inactive problem.* Before the product can be successfully sold, the firm must activate problem recognition.

In contrast, a substantial percentage of those interviewed about lighting charcoal fires expressed a strong concern about the safety of liquid charcoal lighter. These individuals expressed great interest in purchasing a safer product. This is an *active problem.* Timberlane need not worry about problem recognition in this case. Instead, it can concentrate on illustrating how its product solves the problem that the consumers already know exists.

As this example indicates, active and inactive problems require different marketing strategies. Active problems require the marketer only to convince consumers that its brand is the

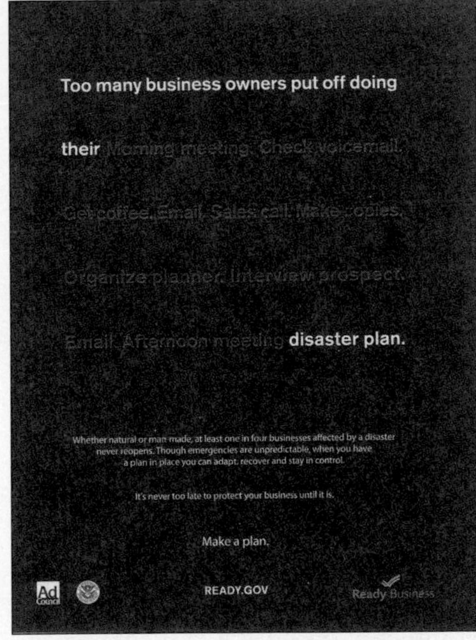

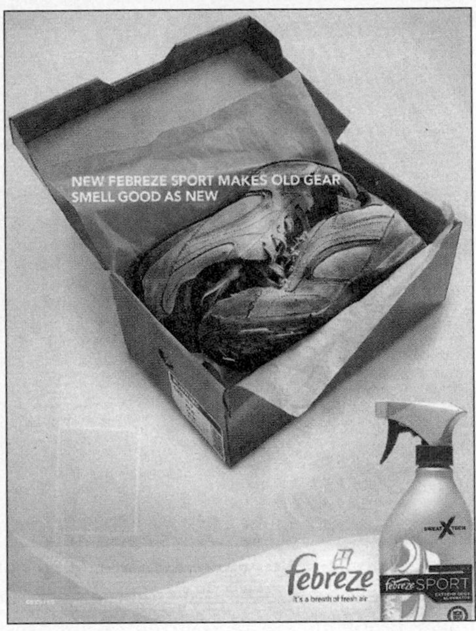

ILLUSTRATION 14-2

Often, marketers need to trigger problem recognition in market segments as with Ready.gov relating to disaster planning. However, at other times, the market is well aware of the problem and the communication can focus on the brand's ability to solve the problem as with Febreze.

superior solution. Consumers are already aware of the problem. In contrast, inactive problems require the marketer to convince consumers that they *have* the problem *and* that the marketer's brand is a superior solution to the problem. This is a much more difficult task.

Illustration 14–2 shows two ads, one for Febreze relating to an active problem and one for Ready.gov pertaining to an inactive problem. The ad on the left first must make consumers aware of a problem (inactive) they likely didn't know of. The ad on the right assumes consumers are aware of the problem (active) and simply focuses on its unique ability to solve it.

UNCONTROLLABLE DETERMINANTS OF PROBLEM RECOGNITION

LO3

A discrepancy between what is desired by a consumer and what the consumer has is the necessary condition for problem recognition. A discrepancy can be the result of a variety of factors that influence consumer desires, perceptions of the existing state, or both. These factors are often beyond the direct influence of the marketing manager, such as a change in family composition. Figure 14–3 summarizes the major nonmarketing factors that influence problem recognition. The marketing factors influencing problem recognition are discussed in the next section of this chapter.

Most of the nonmarketing factors that affect problem recognition are fairly obvious and logical. Most were described in some detail in prior chapters. For example, as we discussed in Chapter 2, a person's culture affects almost all aspects of his or her desired state. Thus, the desire to be recognized as an independent, unique person with distinctive behaviors and possessions differs sharply between American and Japanese consumers because of cultural influences.

Previous decisions and individual development were not discussed in earlier chapters. A previous decision to buy a bike or skis could lead to a current desire to have a car rack

FIGURE 14-3 Nonmarketing Factors Affecting Problem Recognition

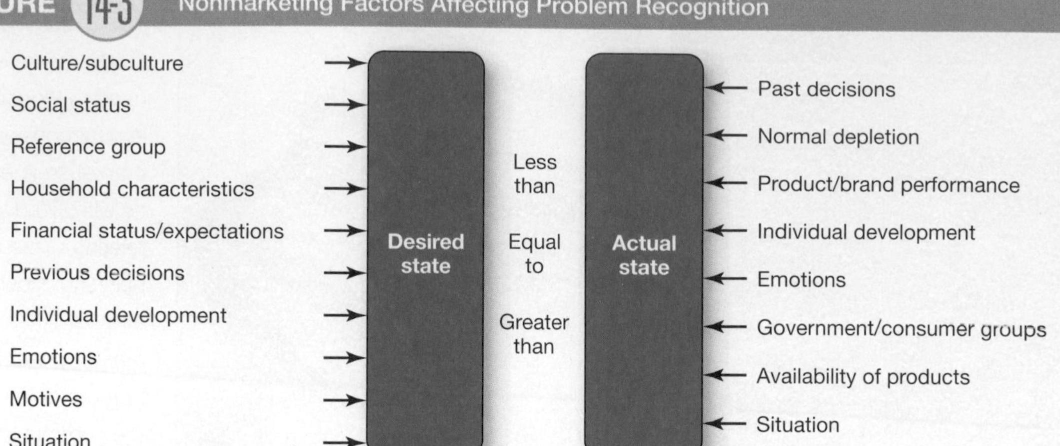

to carry them. A decision to become a homeowner may trigger desires for numerous home and garden items. Past decisions may also deplete purchasing power with the result that fewer problems are recognized or are assigned sufficient importance to trigger action.[8] Prior decisions can influence future decisions even within the same category. One study finds that consumers get tired of food items such as cereal and pretzels, not because they don't like the brand, but because, from a sensory (taste) standpoint, they become bored. Consumers solve this "problem" by variety seeking—that is, they switch to other products. The good news for marketers is that the boredom relates to taste and not the brand itself. So if the brand can offer variety to consumers, they will switch to different *options* but stay loyal to the *brand.* Kellogg's and other food marketers offer huge variety to accommodate this uncontrollable element. Just a few of Kellogg's cereals, for example, are their Corn Flakes, Froot Loops, and Special K.[9]

Individual development causes many changes in desired and actual states. For example, as individuals gain skills, their desires related to those skills change. Beginning skiers, musicians, and gardeners typically desire products and capabilities that will no longer be appropriate as their skills increase. Emotional and psychological development (or lack thereof) can also be related to the need to trigger problem recognition. Recent concerns over cyber bullying have led Facebook to develop a campaign called "mean stinks" in an effort to get young girls to realize the seriousness of hateful words about others on social media.

Government agencies and various consumer groups also actively attempt to trigger problem recognition, often in relation to the consumption of various products. Warning labels on alcohol and cigarettes are two examples of these types of efforts, as are antismoking campaigns and campaigns that stress the dangers of drinking and driving. The NYC.gov ad is geared toward triggering problem recognition, illustrating the negative effects of smoking, as shown in Illustration 14–3.

MARKETING STRATEGY AND PROBLEM RECOGNITION

LO4

Marketing managers have four concerns related to problem recognition. First, they need to know the problems consumers are facing. Second, they must know how to develop the marketing mix to solve consumer problems. Third, managers occasionally want to cause

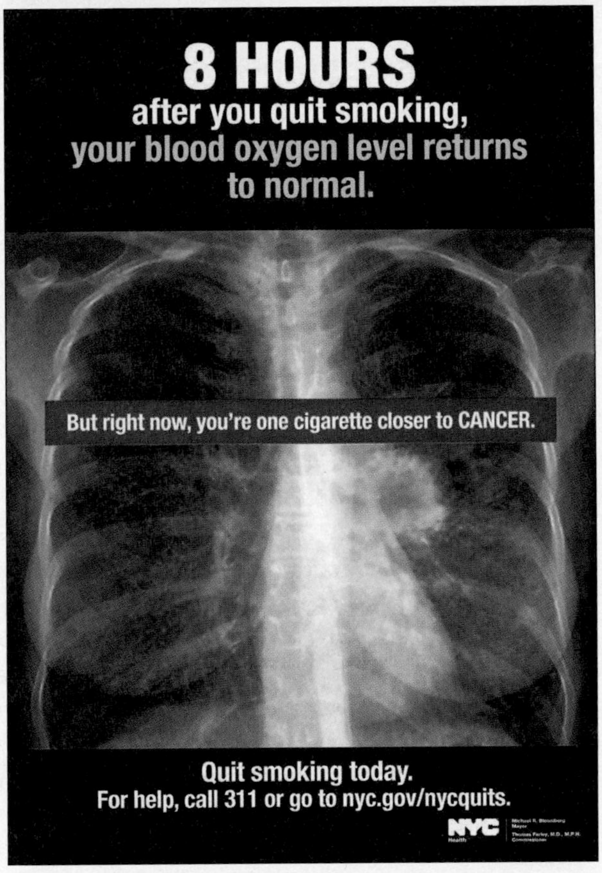

ILLUSTRATION 14-3

Government agencies and socially conscious groups and corporations often attempt to generate problem recognition in consumers. This is often done in an attempt to change behaviors that are harmful to the individual or society. The NYC.gov ad is an example of an attempt to generate problem recognition and the negative effects of smoking.

consumers to recognize problems. Finally, there are times when they desire to suppress problem recognition among consumers. The remainder of this chapter discusses these issues.

Discovering Consumer Problems

Simple *intuition* is perhaps the most common approach to discovering consumer problems. Its benefits are that it is relatively inexpensive, fast, and easy. Its drawbacks are that the intuition, because it tends to be generated by an individual, may be wrong or not apply to a wide range of consumers, thus increasing the likelihood of failure for new product introductions. Thus, marketing research is often conducted as a substitute for, or as a complement to, intuition as a means for increasing the success rate of new products. Numerous research approaches exist for uncovering consumer problems. A number of the relatively well-established approaches are discussed next. In addition, Consumer Insight 14–1 discusses a new online approach based on monitoring consumer online and social media.

Activity and Product Analysis *Activity analysis* focuses on a particular activity, such as preparing dinner, maintaining the lawn, or swimming. Then, surveys or focus groups (see Appendix A) attempt to determine what problems consumers encounter during the performance of the activity. For example, a shampoo company could use

CONSUMER INSIGHT 14-1

Identifying Consumer Problems Using Online and Social Media

Traditional methods of discovering consumer problems have tended toward direct questioning of consumers. Today's online environment, however, can be seen as a potential goldmine for identifying consumer problems at both the category and brand level by monitoring the "conversations" happening online. Sometimes those conversations will be happening on a brand's own online and social media outlets, as when a consumer tweets a company about a recent product failure. Sometimes these conversations will be happening in the broader social media environment, as when bloggers discuss product failures or general needs in a specific product area. Consider the following statements from Radian6, a leader in the field of social media measurement:[10]

> Problems, needs, and wish lists from your potential customers or your competitor's customers are being tossed out to the social web all the time. From product reviews to casual statements about what's not working right, consumers are giving you loads of intelligence about what problems they need you to solve.

Tracking is not enough—responding to problems and concerns is a critical part of the whole package. That is, it is not enough to know, via postings on your brand's Facebook fan page that there are problems with your newest software release. It is critical that those problems be solved in a timely and appropriate manner. Radian6's comments are informative here as well:

> [It's] about understanding how your business solves problems for people, and then connecting with them in a meaningful, helpful way when they need you most. It's not about a sales pitch. It's about creating a solution for someone that they're asking for.

Sounds simple right? Think again. Online and social media outlets (both the company's and general) are extensive. Imagine trying to monitor all of the conversations or "chatter" happening in cyberspace at any given time and filtering that down to usable information. One study by Forrester Research notes numerous such venues including customer forums, blogs, Facebook, and Twitter. And that's before you consider the company's website and e-mail. These options are a growing source of potential consumer feedback and input. The challenge is how to track, consolidate, interpret, and react to all of the online chatter. The interpretation part can be difficult particularly for non-brand-specific problems. It's easy to know when a customer is complaining that your software has a specific flaw; it's much harder to recognize those broader consumer needs that lead to truly breakthrough innovations. Though tracking specific types of key words can help, the interpretation process is still difficult and as yet not well understood. Companies such as Radian6 offer proprietary solutions to help companies through these and the many challenges associated with this form of consumer problem discovery.

Critical Thinking Questions

1. What are some advantages of online and social media tracking compared to traditional methods?
2. In what ways might the viral nature of a given topic be important to marketers in assessing the importance of a given problem?
3. Do you see any ethical concerns related to this approach? Explain.

such an approach to develop products specifically for the hair-related problems associated with swimming in chlorinated pools. *Product analysis* is similar to activity analysis but examines the purchase or use of a particular product or brand. Thus, consumers may be asked about problems associated with using their mountain bikes or laptop computers.

Problem Analysis Problem analysis is different in that it *starts* with a problem and asks respondents to indicate which activities, products, or brands are associated with (or perhaps could eliminate) those problems. For example, a study dealing with packaging problems could include questions such as:

_____ packages are hard to open.

Packages of _____ are hard to reseal.

Packages of _____ don't fit on the shelf.

Packages of _____ waste too many resources.

ILLUSTRATION 14-4

A key task of marketers is to identify consumer problems and position their brands as solutions for them.

Human Factors Research Human factors research attempts to determine human capabilities in areas such as vision, strength, response time, flexibility, and fatigue and the effect on these capabilities of lighting, temperature, and sound. Many methods can be employed in human factors research. However, observational techniques such as slow-motion and time-lapse photography, video recording, and event recorders are particularly useful. This type of research can sometimes identify functional problems that consumers are unaware of. For example, it can be used in the design of such products as lawnmowers, kitchen utensils, smartphone keyboards, and computers to minimize user fatigue.

Emotion Research Marketers are increasingly conducting research on the role of emotions in problem recognition and resolution. Common approaches are surveys, focus group research, and personal interviews that examine the emotions associated with certain problems (see Table 10–4 for specific survey measures for emotions). For example, researchers are beginning to examine how consumers cope with the negative emotions associated with product or service failures. Findings suggest that certain emotions (e.g., anger) are associated with certain coping strategies (e.g., confrontation). This type of research is critical to marketers in helping them anticipate consumer reactions to problems and train their customer service personnel to respond appropriately.[11] For subtle or sensitive problems and emotions, projective techniques (see Appendix A, Table A–1) may be necessary.[12]

Responding to Consumer Problems

Once a consumer problem is identified, the manager may structure the marketing mix to solve the problem. This can involve developing a new product or altering an existing one, modifying channels of distribution, changing pricing policy, or revising advertising strategy. For example, in Illustration 14–4 the product is being positioned as a unique solution to a problem.

As you approach graduation, you will be presented with opportunities to purchase insurance, acquire credit cards, and solve other problems associated with the onset of financial independence and a major change in lifestyle. These opportunities reflect various firms' knowledge that many individuals in your situation face problems that their products will help solve.

Weekend and night store hours and, in part, the rapid growth of Internet stores are a response of retailers to the consumer problem of limited weekday shopping opportunities. Solving this problem has become particularly important to families with both spouses employed.

The examples described above represent only a small sample of the ways marketers react to consumer problem recognition. Each firm must be aware of the consumer problems it can solve, which consumers have these problems, and the situations in which the problems arise.

Helping Consumers Recognize Problems

There are occasions when the manager will want to cause problem recognition rather than react to it. In the earlier example, Timberlane faced having to activate problem recognition in order to sell its product as a fireplace starter. Toy marketers are attempting to reduce their dependence on the Christmas season by activating problem recognition at other times of the year. For example, Fisher-Price has had "rainy day" and "sunny day" promotions in the spring and summer months. Illustrations 14–1 and 14–2, presented earlier, show attempts to activate problem recognition.

Generic versus Selective Problem Recognition Two basic approaches to causing problem recognition are *generic problem recognition* and *selective problem recognition.* These are analogous to the economic concepts of generic and selective demand.

Generic problem recognition involves a *discrepancy that a variety of brands within a product category can reduce.* Generally, a firm will attempt to influence generic problem recognition when the problem is latent or of low importance and one of the following conditions exists:

- It is early in the product life cycle.
- The firm has a high percentage of the market.
- External search after problem recognition is apt to be limited.
- It is an industrywide cooperative effort.

Telephone sales programs often attempt to arouse problem recognition, in part because the salesperson can then limit external search to one brand. Advertising for food-related cooperatives such as milk, beef, and pork frequently focuses on generic problem recognition. Illustration 14–5 is an example of one of the most notable ongoing campaigns of this type. Note that the ad does not promote a specific brand.

Firms with large market shares in a product category often focus on generic problem recognition because any sales increase will probably come to their brands. However, a smaller firm that generates generic problem recognition for its product category may be generating more sales for its competitors than for itself. But even firms with large market share can lose share if generic problem recognition campaigns are not done carefully. In the early 1990s, Borden increased marketing efforts for its popular Creamette pasta brand substantially and promoted recipes using pasta. Its sales increased only 1.6 percent, compared with the industry's growth of 5.5 percent.[13] Its efforts apparently helped the sales of its competitors more than its own sales.

Selective problem recognition involves *a discrepancy that only one brand can solve.* The ad shown in Illustration 14–6 is focused on creating selective problem recognition. Firms attempt to cause selective problem recognition to gain or maintain market share, whereas increasing generic problem recognition generally results in an expansion of the total market.

ILLUSTRATION 14-5

This ad will generate problem recognition that any brand could resolve. This is known as generic problem recognition.

ILLUSTRATION 14-6

This ad will generate problem recognition that is best solved by one brand. This is known as selective problem recognition.

ILLUSTRATION 14-7

This Maui Jim ad attempts to influence the desired state by showing the optimal outcomes that are possible.

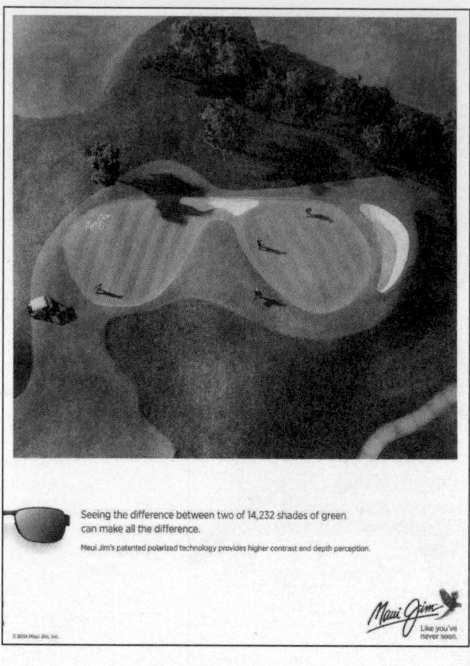

Approaches to Activating Problem Recognition How can a firm influence problem recognition? Recall that problem recognition is a function of the (1) *importance* and (2) *magnitude* of a discrepancy between the desired state and an existing state. Thus, a firm can attempt to influence the size of the discrepancy by altering the desired state or perceptions of the existing state. Or the firm can attempt to influence perceptions of the importance of an existing discrepancy.

Many marketing efforts attempt to *influence the desired state;* that is, marketers often advertise the benefits their products will provide, hoping that these benefits will become desired by consumers. The Maui Jim ad in Illustration 14–7 attempts to influence the desired state by showing just how good the product can make you look. Do you feel Maui Jim is effective in influencing consumers to buy its products?

It is also possible to *influence perceptions of the existing state* through advertisements. Many personal care and social products take this approach. "Even your best friend won't tell you . . ." or "Kim is a great worker but this coffee . . ." are examples of messages designed to generate concern about an existing state. The desired states are assumed to be fresh breath and good coffee. These messages are designed to cause individuals to question if their existing state coincides with this desired state.

Illustration 14–8 is designed to target an undesirable actual state that the product is designed to correct.

Critics frequently question the ethics of activating problem recognition. This is particularly true for problems related to status or social acceptance. This debate is generally discussed in terms of marketers' "creating needs," which we discussed in Chapter 10.

The Timing of Problem Recognition Consumers often recognize problems at times when purchasing a solution is difficult or impossible, as the following examples demonstrate:

- We decide we need snow chains when caught in a blizzard.
- We become aware of a need for insurance *after* an accident.
- We desire a flower bed full of tulips in the spring but forgot to plant bulbs in the fall.
- We want cold medicine when we are sick but don't feel like driving to the store.

In some instances, marketers attempt to help consumers solve such problems after they arise. For example, some pharmacies will make home deliveries. However, the more common strategy is to trigger problem recognition in advance of the actual problem (see Illustration 14–1). That is, it is often to the consumer's and marketer's advantage for the consumer to recognize and solve potential problems *before* they become actual problems.

Some companies, particularly insurance companies, attempt to initiate problem recognition through mass media advertising; others rely more on point-of-purchase displays and other in-store influences (see Chapter 17). Retailers, as well as manufacturers, are

ILLUSTRATION 14-8

Focusing on the actual state is a way to activate problem recognition and ultimately change behaviors.

involved in this activity. For example, prior to snow season, the following sign was placed on a large rack of snow shovels in the main aisle of a large hardware store:

REMEMBER LAST WINTER
WHEN YOU *NEEDED*
A SNOW SHOVEL?
THIS YEAR BE PREPARED!

Suppressing Problem Recognition

As we have seen, competition, consumer organizations, and governmental agencies occasionally introduce information in the marketplace that triggers problem recognition that particular marketers would prefer to avoid. The American tobacco industry has made strenuous attempts to minimize consumer recognition of the health problems associated with cigarette smoking. For example, a Newport cigarette advertisement showed a happy, laughing couple under the headline "Alive with pleasure." This could easily be interpreted as an attempt to minimize any problem recognition caused by the mandatory warning at the bottom of the advertisement: "Warning: The Surgeon General has determined that cigarette smoking is dangerous to your health."

Obviously, marketers do not want their current customers to recognize problems with their brands. Effective quality control and distribution (limited out-of-stock situations) are important in this effort. Packages and package inserts that assure the consumer of the wisdom of his or her purchase are also common.

SUMMARY

LO1: Describe the impact of purchase involvement on the decision process

Consumer decision making becomes more extensive and complex as *purchase involvement* increases. The lowest level of purchase involvement is represented by *nominal decisions:* A problem is recognized, long-term memory provides a single preferred brand, that brand is purchased, and only limited postpurchase evaluation occurs. As one moves from *limited decision making* toward *extended decision making,* information search increases, alternative evaluation becomes more extensive and complex, and postpurchase evaluation becomes more thorough.

LO2: Explain problem recognition and how it fits into the consumer decision process

Problem recognition involves the existence of a discrepancy between the consumer's desired state (what the consumer would like) and the actual state (what the consumer perceives as already existing). Both the desired state and the actual state are influenced by the consumer's lifestyle and current situation. If the discrepancy between these two states is sufficiently large and important, the consumer will begin to search for a solution to the problem.

LO3: Summarize the uncontrollable determinants of problem recognition

A number of factors beyond the control of the marketing manager can affect problem recognition. The desired state is commonly influenced by (1) culture/subculture, (2) social status, (3) reference groups, (4) household characteristics, (5) financial status/expectations, (6) previous decisions, (7) individual development, (8) emotions, (9) motives, and (10) the current situation. The actual state is influenced by (1) past decisions, (2) normal depletion, (3) product/brand performance, (4) individual development, (5) emotions, (6) government/consumer groups, (7) availability of products, and (8) the current situation.

LO4: Discuss the role of consumer problems and problem recognition in marketing strategy

Before marketing managers can respond to problem recognition generated by outside factors, they must be able to *identify* consumer problems. Surveys and focus groups using *activity, product,* or *problem analysis* are commonly used. *Human factors research* approaches the same task from an observational perspective. *Emotion research* focuses on the role of emotions in problem recognition and resolution. And, as Consumer Insight 14–1 points out, tracking of online and social media is proving to be an increasingly powerful tool as well.

Once managers are aware of problem recognition patterns among their target market, they can react by designing the marketing mix to solve the recognized problem. This may involve product development or repositioning, a change in store hours, a different price, or a host of other marketing strategies.

Marketing managers often want to influence problem recognition rather than react to it. They may desire to generate *generic problem recognition,* a discrepancy that a variety of brands within a product category can reduce, or to induce *selective problem recognition,* a discrepancy that only one brand in the product category can solve.

Attempts to *activate problem recognition* generally do so by focusing on the desired state. However, attempts to make consumers aware of negative aspects of the existing state are also common. In addition, marketers attempt to influence the timing of problem recognition by making consumers aware of potential problems before they arise.

Finally, managers may attempt to minimize or suppress problem recognition by current users of their brands.

KEY TERMS

Active problem 504
Actual state 502
Desired state 502
Extended decision making 501
Generic problem recognition 510
Inactive problem 504
Limited decision making 500
Nominal decision making 500
Problem recognition 502
Product involvement 499
Purchase involvement 498
Selective problem recognition 510

REVIEW QUESTIONS

1. What is meant by *purchase involvement?* How does it differ from product involvement?
2. How does consumer decision making change as purchase involvement increases?
3. What is the role of *emotion* in the consumer decision process?
4. How do *nominal, limited,* and *extended decision making* differ? How do the two types of nominal decision making differ?
5. What is *problem recognition?*
6. What influences the motivation to resolve a recognized problem?
7. What is the difference between an *active* and an *inactive problem?* Why is this distinction important?
8. How does lifestyle relate to problem recognition?
9. What are the main uncontrollable factors that influence the *desired* state?
10. What are the main uncontrollable factors that influence the *existing* state?
11. How can you measure problem recognition?
12. In what ways can marketers react to problem recognition? Give several examples.
13. How does *generic problem recognition* differ from *selective problem recognition?* Under what conditions would a firm attempt to influence generic problem recognition? Why?
14. How can a firm cause problem recognition? Give examples.
15. How can a firm suppress problem recognition?

DISCUSSION QUESTIONS

16. What products do you think *generally* are associated with nominal, limited, and extended decision making? Under what conditions, if any, would these products be associated with a different form of decision making?
17. What products do you think *generally* are purchased or used for emotional reasons? How would the decision process differ for an emotion-driven purchase compared to a more functional purchase?
18. What products do you think *generally* are associated with brand-loyal decision making and which with repeat-purchase decision making? Justify your response.
19. Describe a purchase you made using nominal decision making, one using limited decision making, and one using extended decision making. What caused you to use each type of decision process?
20. Describe two recent purchases you have made. What uncontrollable factors, if any, triggered problem recognition? Did they affect the desired state, the actual state, or both?
21. How would you measure consumer problems among the following?
    a. College students
    b. Children aged 2 to 4
    c. Internet shoppers
    d. New residents in a town
    e. Vegans
    f. Newly married couples
22. How would you determine the existence of consumer problems of relevance to a marketer of the following?
    a. Women's spa
    b. Internet retail outlets
    c. Online health food store
    d. Public library
    e. Hawaiian vacation resort
    f. Mountain bikes
23. Discuss the types of products that resolve specific problems that occur for most consumers at different stages of their household life cycle.
24. How would you activate problem recognition among college students for the following?
    a. Volunteering time at the Salvation Army
    b. Student recreation center
    c. A vegan diet
    d. Rooms To Go
    e. Using a designated driver if drinking
    f. Laundry service

25. How would you influence the time of problem recognition for the following?
    a. Fire alarm battery replacement
    b. Gift basket
    c. Car tune-up
    d. Air conditioner filters
    e. Health insurance
    f. Vitamins
26. Respond to the questions in Consumer Insight 14–1.

APPLICATION ACTIVITIES

27. Interview five students and identify three consumer problems they have recognized recently. For each problem, determine
    a. The relative importance of the problem.
    b. How the problem occurred.
    c. What caused the problem (i.e., change in desired or actual states).
    d. What action they have taken.
    e. What action is planned to resolve each problem.
28. Track a brand's Twitter account for a week. Write a report on the role that Twitter and other social media can play in identifying consumer problems. As part of the report, discuss whether or not you believe that some venues are better than others at providing insights for general versus brand-specific problems.
29. Interview three students and identify recent instances when they engaged in nominal, limited, and extended decision making (a total of nine decisions). What specific factors appear to be associated with each type of decision?
30. Interview three students and identify five products that each buys using a nominal decision process. Identify those that are based on brand loyalty and those that are merely repeat purchases. What characteristics, if any, distinguish the brand-loyal products from the repeat products?
31. Find and describe an advertisement that is attempting to activate problem recognition. Analyze the advertisement in terms of the type of problem and the action the ad is suggesting. Also, discuss any changes you would recommend to improve the effectiveness of the ad in terms of activating problem recognition.
32. Using two consumers from a relevant market segment, conduct an activity analysis for an activity that interests you. Prepare a report on the marketing opportunities suggested by your analysis.
33. Using two consumers from a relevant market segment, conduct a product analysis for a product that interests you. Prepare a report on the marketing opportunities suggested by your analysis.
34. Conduct a problem analysis, using a sample of five college freshmen. Prepare a report on the marketing opportunities suggested by your analysis.
35. Interview five smokers and ascertain what problems they see associated with smoking.
36. Interview someone from the local office of the American Cancer Society concerning its attempts to generate problem recognition among smokers.

REFERENCES

1. This opener is based on S. McNamara, "25 Clever Ideas to Make Life Easier," November 1, 2011, *Mum's Grapevine,* http://mumsgrapevine.com.au/2011/11/25-clever-ideas_household-tips_storage-ideas/, accessed August 28, 2014; L. Deal, "Solutions to Problems That I Didn't Know That I Had," *Pinterest,* www.pinterest.com/lindsayfayedeal/solutions-to-problems-that-i-didn-t-know-that-i-ha/, accessed August 28, 2014; information from Arm and Hammer Company website, www.armandhammer.com/solutions.aspx, accessed August 28, 2014; T. Luna, "Long CVS Receipts Spark Social Media Sensation," *Boston Globe,* August 31, 2013, www.bostonglobe.com/business/2013/08/30/long-cvs-receipts-spark-social-media-sensation/VzQeVzNmBB3ECqy6vQtj1N/story.html, accessed August 28, 2014; information from Swiffer company website, www.swiffer.com/, accessed August 28, 2014; information from Dyson company website, www.dyson.com/, accessed August 28, 2014; and information from Quirky company website, www.quirky.com/, accessed August 28, 2014.
2. See B. Shiv and J. Huber, "The Impact of Anticipating Satisfaction on Consumer Choice," *Journal of Consumer Research,* September 2000, pp. 202–16; and M. T. Pham et al., "Affect Monitoring and the Primacy of Feelings in Judgment," *Journal of Consumer Research,* September 2001, pp. 167–88.
3. See J. R. Bettman, M. F. Luce, and J. W. Payne, "Constructive Consumer Choice," *Journal of Consumer Research,* December 1998, pp. 187–217.

4. For more complex but valuable approaches, see ibid.; and R. Lawson, "Consumer Decision Making within a Goal-Driven Framework," *Psychology & Marketing,* August 1997, pp. 427–49.

5. M. Trivedi, F. M. Bass, and R. C. Rao, "A Model of Stochastic Variety-Seeking," *Marketing Science,* Summer 1994, pp. 274–97; S. Menon and B. E. Kahn, "The Impact of Context on Variety Seeking in Product Choice," *Journal of Consumer Research,* December 1995, pp. 285–95; and R. K. Ratner, B. E. Kahn, and D. Kahneman, "Choosing Less-Preferred Experiences for the Sake of Variety," *Journal of Consumer Research,* June 1999, pp. 1–15.

6. J. B. Ford, M.S. LaTour, and T. L. Henthorne, "Perception of Marital Roles in Purchase Decision Processes," *Journal of the Academy of Marketing Science,* 23, no. 2 (1995), pp. 120–31.

7. See C. J. Hill, "The Nature of Problem Recognition and Search in the Extended Health Care Decision," *Journal of Services Marketing,* 15, no. 6 (2001), pp. 454–79.

8. D. Soman, "Effects of Payment Mechanism on Spending Behavior," *Journal of Consumer Research,* March 2001, pp. 460–74.

9. See H. C. M. Van Trijp, W. D. Hoyer, and J. J. Inman, "Why Switch? Product Category-Level Explanations for True Variety-Seeking Behavior," *Journal of Marketing Research,* August 1996, pp. 281–92; and J. J. Inman, "The Role of Sensory-Specific Satiety in Attribute-Level Variety Seeking," *Journal of Consumer Research,* June 2001, pp. 105–20.

10. This insight is based on D. Alston, "Social Media Monitoring—Top 10 Reasons for Monitoring Brands," *TopRank,* May 2008, www.toprankblog.com, accessed June 16, 2011; *CMOs Must Connect the Dots of the Online Brand* (Cambridge, MA: Forrester Research, Inc., June 27, 2010); *Brands Cannot Ignore Offline Conversations* (Cambridge, MA: Forrester Research, Inc., September 3, 2010); and information found at Radian6's website, www.radian6.com, accessed June 16, 2011.

11. S. Yi and H. Baumgartner, "Coping with Negative Emotions in Purchase-Related Situations," *Journal of Consumer Psychology,* 14, no. 3 (2004), pp. 303–17.

12. See, e.g., G. Zaltman, "Metaphorically Speaking," *Marketing Research,* Summer 1996, pp. 13–20; and C. B. Raffel, "Vague Notions," *Marketing Research,* Summer 1996, pp. 21–23.

13. E. Lesly, "Why Things Are So Sour at Borden," *BusinessWeek,* November 22, 1993, p. 84.

chapter

15 Information Search

LEARNING OBJECTIVES

LO1 **Discuss internal and external information search and their role in different decision types.**

LO2 **Summarize the types of information consumers search for.**

LO3 **Describe the categories of decision alternatives relating to the evoked set.**

LO4 **Discuss available information sources and the role of Internet and mobile search.**

LO5 **Discuss the major cost–benefit factors driving the amount of external search.**

LO6 **Summarize the marketing strategies based on information search patterns.**

Consumers still watch TV and lots of it. And TV (in particular TV ads) can be a valuable information source for some products and services. The difference is that now there is a growing trend for consumers to watch TV with a second screen—cell phone or tablet—in hand.[1] The second screen allows marketers to extend the reach of their commercials and to provide consumers with additional routes for information search. Take the eBay iPad app, "Watch with eBay," for example. The app synchronizes a TV show with the consumer's tablet or cell phone to combine TV watching and searching/shopping—or so-called couch commerce. Users enter in their zip code, cable provider, channel, and the show they are watching and the app will display relevant products from eBay's millions of listings. That is, "Watch with eBay" is both a search and shopping tool. SpotSynch is a similar app but provides information and options (and the ability to buy products) from various retailers not just eBay. The time lapse between advertising exposures to search to purchase is very short in many cases due to the nominal or limited decision machining context involved (see Chapter 14) and the ease and convenience of searching and shopping using these apps.

Shazam is an app that enables consumers to identify a song from just a few bars of music and is so well known it has become a verb. Hold up your cell phone or tablet to the TV (or radio or other broadcast device) while a tune is playing and Shazam will identify it. Not only will the name of the song and the artist surface (in a sense, automated information search), but Shazam will even take you to a website to purchase the music. Recently, Shazam has moved beyond music to partner with marketers to integrate TV programs and ads with the consumer's second-screen experience. So, for example, viewers who Shazammed a Toyota ad aired during the 2012 Super Bowl could enter a contest to win a Camry car.

In a new twist to product placement, one episode (March 18, 2014) of the TBS comedy *Cougar Town* was simulcast by Target at ShopCougarTown.com. On the online broadcast of *Cougar Town,* products from the Target line by designer Nate Berkus—baskets, pillows—were flagged by flashing red crosses. Scrolling over a red cross paused the show to display information about the product (consumer-driven interactive search) and provided further links to purchase the product.

Today's TV viewing consumers have more power at their disposal related to information search and purchase through the second screen. The increasing trend for consumers to watch TV with cell phone or tablet in hand provides marketers with opportunities to engage consumers watching TV programs. A major current challenge is that the majority of consumers are not using their second screens to engage in activities related to the TV program (instead surfing unrelated materials while TV commercials are airing) because they find second-screen content lacking. Zeebox's SpotSynch, shown at the beginning of the chapter, is an example of how moving forward, marketers know they must enhance the value of the consumer search experience and interface via the second screen.

This chapter examines the information search stage of the decision process that occurs after problem recognition. Within information search, we focus on (1) the amount and type of search, (2) categories of decision alternatives relating to the evoked set, (3) sources and channels of information including the Internet and mobile, (4) the cost–benefit factors driving external search, and (5) marketing strategies based on information search patterns.

THE NATURE OF INFORMATION SEARCH

LO1

Once a problem is recognized, relevant information from long-term memory is used to determine such things as (1) if a satisfactory solution is known, (2) what the characteristics of potential solutions are, and (3) what appropriate ways exist to compare solutions. This is **internal search.** If a resolution is not reached through internal search, then the search process is focused on external information relevant to solving the problem. This is **external search,** which can involve independent sources, personal sources, marketer-based information, and product experience.[2] It is important to note that even in extended decision making with extensive external search, the initial internal search generally produces a set of guides (e.g., must-have attributes) or decision constraints (e.g., maximum price that can be paid) that limit and guide external search. Search has benefits such as finding a lower price or getting higher quality. However, search has costs that tend to limit the amount of search even for very important decisions. That is, information search involves mental as well as physical activities that consumers must perform that take time, energy, and money.

As discussed in Chapter 14, the amount of search depends on purchase involvement, which is a major determinant of the type of decision process consumers engage in. Purchase involvement, and the amount of external search, increases as consumers move from nominal decision making to extended decision making. Internal information tends to dominate in nominal decision making, where typically a consumer recalls a single satisfactory solution and purchases it without further search or evaluation. External search tends to dominate in extended decision making, where typically a consumer examines and evaluates numerous alternatives across numerous criteria using information from many sources. For limited decision making, external search can play a moderate role in some instances, particularly when the consumer is aware of several possible alternative solutions to his or her problem and therefore must search and evaluate on a limited basis to make a choice.[3]

Search after problem recognition can also be limited by prior search and learning. That is, deliberate external search also occurs in the absence of problem recognition. **Ongoing search** is done both *to acquire information for possible later use and because the process itself is pleasurable.* For example, individuals highly involved with an activity, such as tennis, are apt to seek information about tennis-related products on an ongoing basis without a recognized problem with their existing tennis equipment (recall that enduring involvement is characteristic of opinion leaders). In addition, consumers acquire a substantial amount of relevant information on an ongoing basis without deliberate search—through low-involvement learning (see Chapter 9).

TYPES OF INFORMATION SOUGHT

A consumer decision requires information on the following:[4] LO2

1. The appropriate evaluative criteria for the solution of a problem.
2. The existence of various alternative solutions.
3. The performance level or characteristic of each alternative solution on each evaluative criterion.

Information search, then, seeks each of these three types of information, as shown in Figure 15–1.

Evaluative Criteria

Suppose you are provided with money to purchase a laptop computer, perhaps as a graduation present. Assuming you have not been in the market for a computer recently, your first thought would probably be, "What features do I want in a computer?" You would then engage in internal search to determine the features or characteristics required to meet your needs. These desired characteristics are your *evaluative criteria.* If you have had limited experience with computers, you might also engage in external search to learn which characteristics a good computer should have. You could check with friends, read reviews in *PC Magazine* online, talk with sales personnel, visit computer websites, post questions on an online discussion board, or personally inspect several computers. Illustration 15–1 shows an example of how a company is trying to focus consumers toward an attribute on which it excels but that consumers may not automatically have in mind when selecting a brand.

A detailed discussion of evaluative criteria appears in Chapter 16.

Appropriate Alternatives

After and while searching for appropriate evaluative criteria, you would probably seek *appropriate alternatives*—in this case, brands or, possibly, stores. In general, there are five groupings of alternatives. First is the set of all possible alternatives that could solve a consumer problem. Within this set there are four categories of decision alternatives. The **awareness set** is composed of *those brands consumers are aware of.* The **inert set** is composed of *those brands consumers are aware of and view in a neutral manner.* These LO3

Information Search in Consumer Decisions FIGURE 15-1

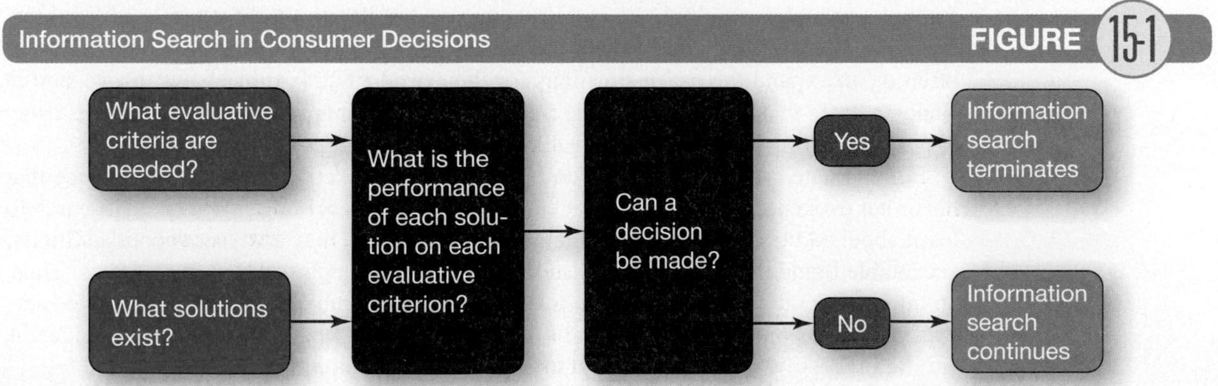

ILLUSTRATION 15-1

Consumers often search for information on appropriate evaluative criteria to use. This ad seeks to influence the criteria used and position the brand accordingly.

are brands that might be seen as acceptable by consumers if their favorite alternative is not available. These are also brands for which consumers will be open to positive information although they will not be actively seeking it out. The **inept set** is composed of *those brands consumers are aware of and view negatively.* These brands are ones for which consumers will generally not process or accept positive information even if readily available.

The **evoked set** (also called the **consideration set**) is composed of *those brands or products one will evaluate for the solution of a particular consumer problem.*[5] Note that while evoked sets are frequently composed of brands from a single product category (brands of cereals or computers), this need not be the case because substitute products can also play a role.[6] For example, one landscaping company found that consumers often view landscaping as a "home improvement decision." As a consequence, their landscaping services often compete with other home improvement products such as interior decorating instead of, or in addition to, other landscaping services.

In addition, the evoked set or consideration set often varies with the usage situation. For example, pancakes may only be in a consumer's consideration set for weekend breakfast situations because they are too inconvenient for busy weekday mornings. Companies will often try to expand the usage situations for their products in various ways, as we saw in Chapter 13. In this example, premade frozen pancakes that are toaster-ready may be a way to get pancakes into the weekday breakfast consideration set.[7]

Finally, note that if a consumer does not have an evoked set or lacks confidence that his or her evoked set is adequate, that consumer will probably engage in external search to learn about additional alternatives. In addition, consumers may also learn about additional acceptable brands as an incidental aspect of moving through the decision process. Thus, an important outcome of information search is the development of a *complete* evoked set.

Figure 15–2 illustrates the general relationships among these classes of alternatives. A similar process operates with respect to retail outlet selection.[8]

Categories of Decision Alternatives FIGURE 15-2

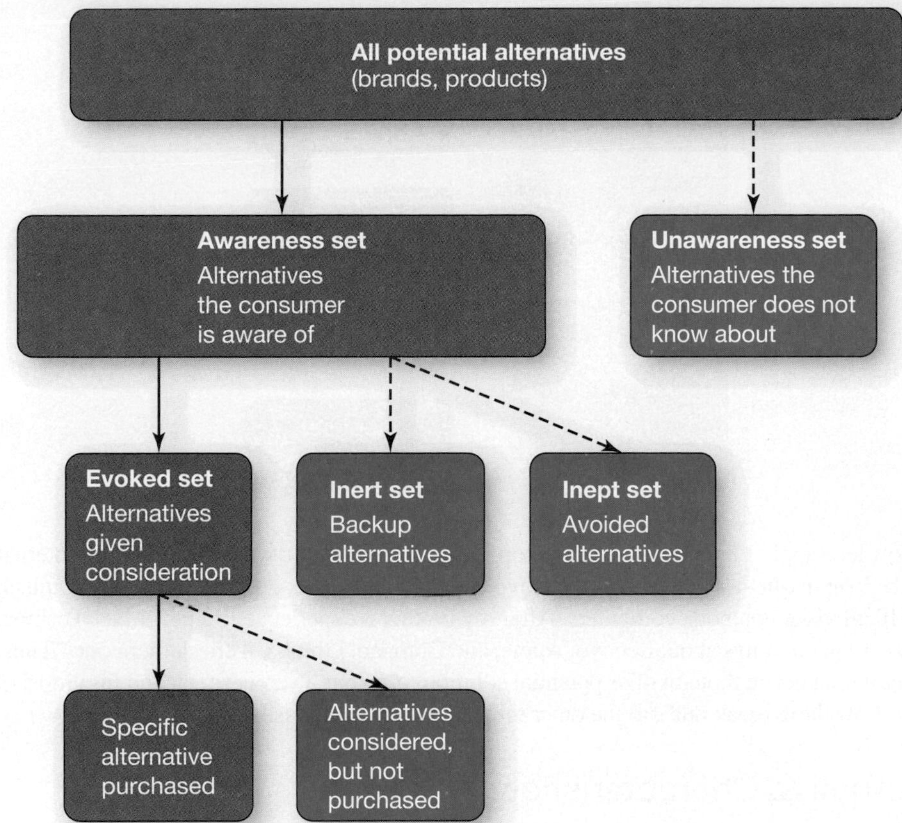

One study examined the awareness and evoked sets across numerous product categories. Several results and strategic implications of this study are worth noting.

- The awareness set was always larger than the evoked set. That is, consumers know about more brands than they will seriously consider. And because awareness does not equal consideration and because consideration is necessary for a chance at being chosen, marketers are very concerned (once they have built sufficient awareness) about moving their brands into consumer evoked sets and must engage in persuasive messaging and other strategies to do so.
- The evoked set for some categories—for example, mouthwash and toothpaste—were basically one brand. This means that for categories, nominal decision making (choosing one brand repeatedly over time) is the norm. Later in the chapter we will discuss the use of disruption strategies for brands in this situation that are not in a consumer's evoked set.
- The evoked sets for some categories were somewhat large, but that may be due to variety seeking. For example, the evoked set for fast food was five brands. However, one can imagine that consumers are loyal to brands of fast-food restaurants *within* type, but they variety seek or otherwise switch across situations. So, McDonald's may be the hamburger alternative, KFC the chicken alternative, Pizza Hut the pizza alternative, Taco Bell the Mexican alternative, and so on.

FIGURE 15-3 Example of Decision Alternatives for Laptop Computers

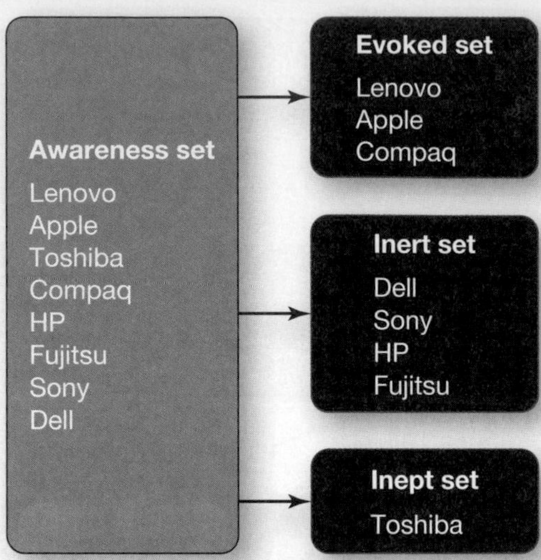

Now let's apply Figure 15–2 to our laptop example. Again, you would start with an internal search. You might say to yourself, "Lenovo, Compaq, Toshiba, Apple, Dell, Sony, Fujitsu, and HP all make notebook computers. After my brother's experience, I'd never buy Toshiba. I've heard good things about Lenovo, Apple, and Compaq. I think I'll check them out." Thus, the eight brands you thought of as potential solutions are your awareness set, and Figure 15–3 shows how these break out into the other three categories of decision alternatives.

Alternative Characteristics

To choose among the brands in the evoked set, the consumer compares them on relevant evaluative criteria. This process requires the consumer *to gather information about each brand on each pertinent evaluative criterion.* In our example of a computer purchase, you might collect information on the price, memory, processor, weight, screen clarity, and software package for each brand you are considering. In addition, emotional considerations relating to comfort, styling, and ease of use may factor in as well.

SOURCES OF INFORMATION

LO4

Refer again to our laptop computer example. We suggested that you might recall what you know about computers, check with friends and an online discussion board, consult *Consumer Reports* and read reviews in *PC Magazine,* talk with sales personnel, or personally inspect several computers to collect relevant information. The following represent the five primary sources of information available to consumers:

- *Memory* of past searches, personal experiences, and low-involvement learning.
- *Personal sources,* such as friends, family, and others.
- *Independent sources,* such as magazines, consumer groups, and government agencies.
- *Marketing sources,* such as sales personnel, websites, and advertising.
- *Experiential sources,* such as inspection or product trial.

These sources are shown in Figure 15–4. Each of these sources has an offline, online, and mobile component.[9] As just one example, offline marketing sources such as TV advertising and brochures correspond to online banner ads and corporate websites, and mobile ads.

Information Sources for a Purchase Decision **FIGURE 15-4**

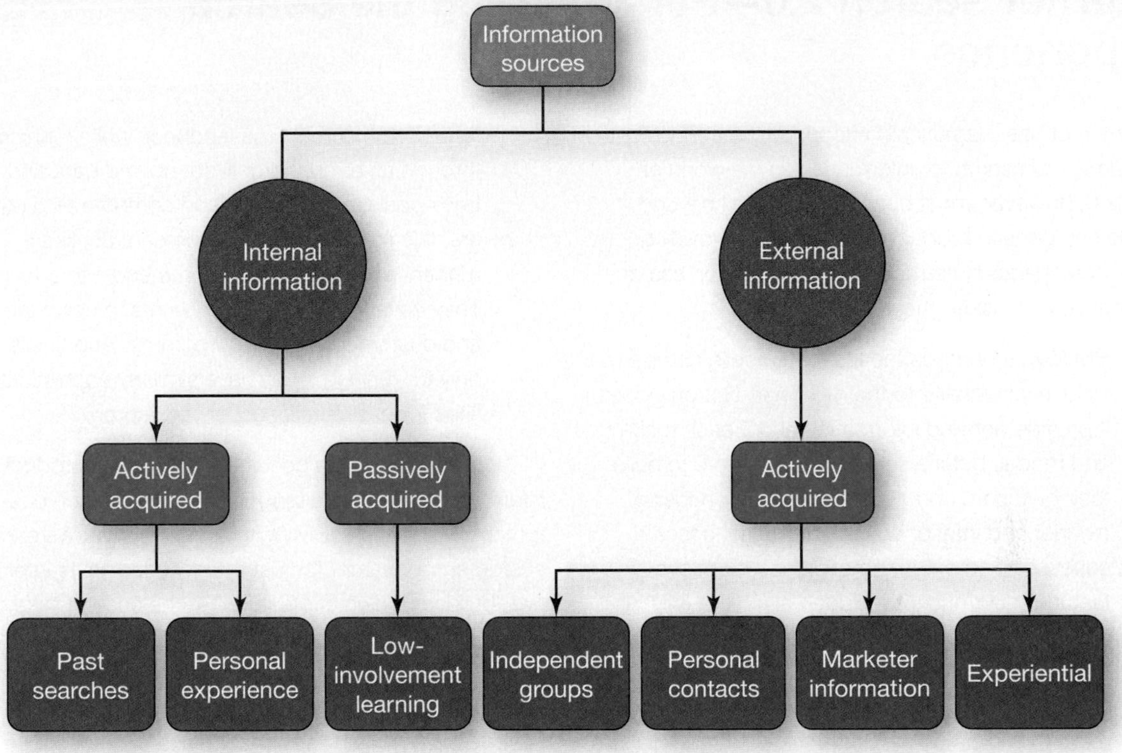

Information sources
Internal information
External information
Actively acquired
Passively acquired
Actively acquired
Past searches
Personal experience
Low-involvement learning
Independent groups
Personal contacts
Marketer information
Experiential

Internal information is the primary source used by most consumers most of the time (nominal and limited decision making). However, note that information in long-term memory was *initially* obtained from external sources. Thus, a consumer may resolve a consumption problem using only or mainly stored information. At some point, however, the individual acquired that information from an external source, such as direct product experience, friends, or low-involvement learning.

Marketing-originated messages are only one of five potential information sources, and they are frequently reported to be of limited *direct* value in consumer decisions.[10] However, marketing activities influence all five sources. Thus, the characteristics of the product, the distribution of the product, and the promotional messages about the product provide the underlying or basic information available in the market. An independent source such as *Consumer Reports* bases its evaluation on the functional characteristics of the product, as do personal sources such as friends. Marketers are continually looking for ways to get their information channeled through non-marketing sources. As we discussed in Chapter 7, product sampling to influential bloggers (with appropriate disclosure) is just one means of getting the word out through non-marketing channels.

In addition, although consumers may not use (or believe they use) advertising or other marketer-provided data as immediate input into many purchase decisions, there is no doubt that continual exposure to advertising frequently influences the perceived need for the product, the composition of the awareness and evoked sets, the evaluative criteria used, and beliefs about the performance levels of each brand.[11] As a consequence, the long-term *total* influence of advertising and other marketer-provided information on consumer decision making and sales can be substantial.

CONSUMER INSIGHT 15-1

Internet Search 2.0—Personalizing the Search Experience

The Internet has dramatically expanded the ability of consumers to search for information. In the world of Web 2.0, however, most companies go well beyond simple and *generic* product information by providing highly personalized information and information search experiences. Consider the following:[12]

- BMW was perhaps the first automobile company to take its website to the next level. Not only does it provide detailed information about each make and model, but it also allows consumers to build their own cars from the "ground up," choosing exterior and interior colors, packages, accessories, and so on. Information about options, features, and price is included along the way, as are realistic 360° visuals. According to one BMW representative, its website changes the way consumers search for and purchase their cars, with many coming into the dealership with their BMW already "picked out." Other features of its site include BMW TV, links to BMW brand communities, and a news feed.
- Nike's website has various pages relating to its shoes and apparel. However, it goes well beyond a place to find out information about shoes. For example, Nike+ is an online interactive tool that interfaces with special Nike equipment to allow runners to get real-time feedback while running through an armband or iPod, upload data and track goals, and connect and compete with others. It is so popular that 90 percent of Nike+ runners say they would recommend it to a friend. They have a runner's blog, forums, a news tab, and customized training programs. And this is only for running. They have similarly sophisticated sites for basketball, soccer, and so on.

Note how each site goes beyond *generic* product information by personalizing information to each customer. In the case of BMW, its search tool allows each customer to "search" for just the right car via its interactive "build your own car feature." In the case of Nike, the interactive tool customizes the information it provides to each user based on personal goals and performance. Personalizing information search is critical to a more positive and engaging information search experience.

Critical Thinking Questions

1. What is the difference between generic information and personalized information?
2. How does personalized information create greater customer engagement?
3. What influence might Internet search have on the role of salespeople?

Internet Search

The Internet gives consumers unprecedented access to information. Global Internet usage continues to grow rapidly, and more than two billion people are online around the world. Asia (922 million), Europe (476 million), and North America (272 million) have the highest number of Internet users. Growth potential is strongest for regions such as Africa, Asia, and Latin America, where Internet usage as a percent of the total population is still relatively low. Asia overshadows other regions of the world in terms of current users and potential growth, in view of its population size (3.9 billion), growing middle class, and increased access to low-cost technology.[13] Consumer Insight 15–1 shows some of the various ways in which companies use the Internet to create an information search "experience" that is more engaging, easier, and faster, and extends the search environment to include virtual trial and interactive tools.

Nearly 90 percent of U.S. adults have used the Internet and growth of new users has slowed considerably. Early on, Internet users were predominantly young, educated, white males. Today, the demographic characteristics of Internet users look much more like those of the population in general. The demographic factors with any real remaining influence are age (Internet usage decreases with age), education, and income (Internet usage increases with both education and income).[14] Perhaps not surprisingly, given this demographic information, six of the top 10 reasons for nonuse of the Internet are related (directly and indirectly) to age, income, and education. These reasons, in order of importance, are (1) no computer, (2) too expensive, (3) too difficult, (4) don't have access, (5) too old to learn, and (6) don't know how.[15]

ILLUSTRATION 15-2

The Internet is an important source of information as well as a place to purchase products and services. Marketers often use traditional mass media ads to encourage consumers to visit their websites.

The Internet is a major and often preferred avenue through which consumers search for information.[16] Consider the following:[17]

- *Online information is expected.* Most Internet users *expect* to find information about a product or brand of interest to them on a company's website.
- *Online information boosts offline sales.* Internet users are more likely to purchase a company's product offline if its website provides product-related information.
- *Online sources are viewed as valuable.* Corporate and third-party websites match or beat traditional TV and print advertising as an information source in many categories.
- *Online sources reduce the salesperson's role.* Internet users tend to require considerably less purchase assistance from a salesperson.

Not surprisingly, the second most important activity online is *using a search engine to find information.* And seven of the top 20 activities on the Internet are tied to information search or purchase, as follows:[18]

Activity	%
Use search engine to find information	87%
Look for health-related information	83
Look for information about a hobby or interest	83
Research a product/service before buying it	78
Buy a product	66
Buy or make a travel reservation	66
Use an online classified ad or site	53

Source: Pew Internet & American Life Project, www.pewinternet.org.

It is important to note, however, that traditional media can be effective at guiding consumers' information search activities to company websites, as shown in Illustration 15–2.

Search engines such as Google, Yahoo, and MSN are important search tools for consumers. Online search prior to purchase is the norm for most Internet users. In fact, search engines are the number one online shopping tool, followed by coupon sites, retailer e-mails, online reviews, and shopping comparison sites. Notice that all the tools listed are sources of some form of information and thus play a role in the information search and acquisition process. The influence of online search cannot be overestimated because[19]

- Ninety-four percent of online purchases are preceded by online search.
- Seventy-four percent of offline purchases are likely to be preceded by online search.
- Consumers who "pre-search" and are exposed to online ads spend 41 percent more in-store.

The nature of search terms used by consumers is critical for marketers to understand so that they can build these into their search marketing strategies. One study categorized search terms into *brand only* (retailer's brand), *generic* (general product-related terms), and *brand-item* (brand plus generic). As shown in Figure 15–5, most of the search leading up to the purchase was generic—that is, general product-related terms that did not include any of the retailers being tracked in the study. As you might expect, generic search dominated early in the search process (3 to 12 weeks out), while branded search dominated just prior to purchase.[20] *What strategic implications do these results hold for online marketers?*

Economic considerations are a major motivator of online search.[21] For example, car buyers who used the Internet were able to make decisions faster and get a better buy—on average by $741.[22] And coupon sites, which are increasingly popular, help consumers get better deals with ease. However, *information overload* (see Chapter 8) is a challenge on the Internet. General search engines are useful. However, more specialized services and tools continue to evolve to aid consumers more specifically in their search and decision making. Comparison shopping sites are a popular version of these services. Comparison

FIGURE 15-5 The Nature of Search Using Online Search Engines

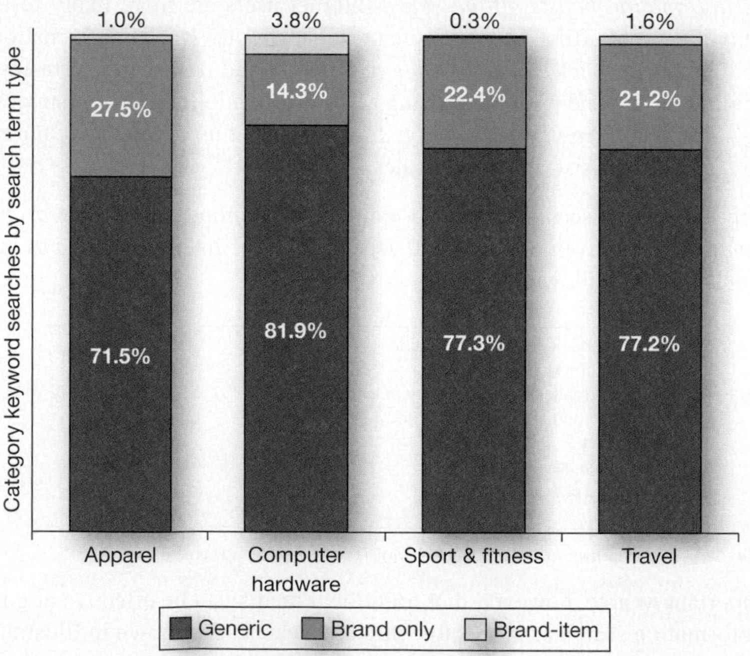

Source: "The Nature of Search Using Online Search Engines," *Search before the Purchase* (New York: DoubleClick, February 2005), p. 2. Copyright: DoubleClick, Inc., 2005.

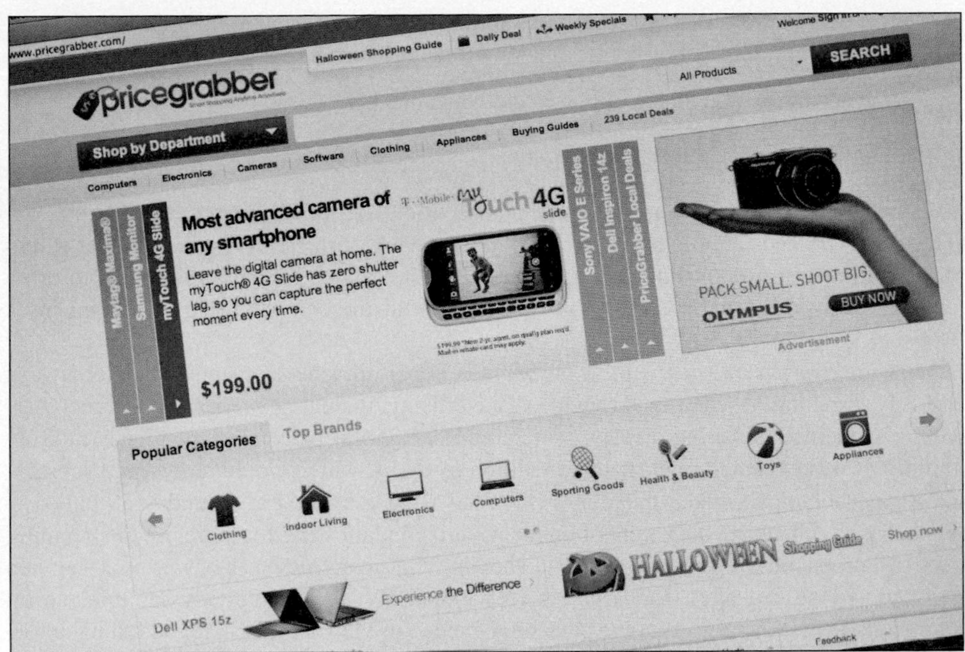

ILLUSTRATION 15-3

Online shopping services are increasingly popular as a way for consumers to deal with the enormous amount of information on the Internet.

sites often focus on price but can be designed to filter brands based on a broader set of evaluative criteria set by the consumer (see Illustration 15–3). These services use **bots,** or software "robots," that do the shopping/searching for users, and are therefore often referred to as *shopping bots.*[23] Examples include BizRate.com, mySimon.com, and NexTag.com.

In addition to marketer-based information, the Internet contains personal sources of information in bulletin boards and chat rooms as well as in the brand review features of many shopping services.[24] One study finds that consumer reviews are utilized heavily (72 percent) by consumers during online search for performance information.[25] As discussed in Chapter 7, WOM and personal sources are influential because of consumer trust in these sources.

Marketing Strategy and Information Search on the Internet As the online population increasingly mirrors the general population, segmentation and target marketing are increasingly critical to online success. Consider the following:

> Where higher education marketing is different is the complexity of the audiences. A college . . . in particular has to please—if you are talking about the institutional Web site—alumni, donors, current students, prospective students, parents (and) the media. It's daunting sometimes.

Furman University decided that its general website was inadequate for admissions. So the university created a separate website to target high school students interested in the institution. The site is designed to target this tech-savvy group specifically, with virtual tours, message boards, and online student journals (with no editing by administration!).[26]

Obviously, universities are not the only ones who must deal with diverse consumer needs and characteristics. For example, consumers of various ethnicities in the United States often prefer and primarily use ethnic (versus mainstream) websites.[27] Global marketers must adapt as well. A recent study finds that Japanese websites use less individualistic approaches than do U.S. websites.[28]

More specifically, with respect to the Internet's role in information search and decision making, marketers have at least three major strategic issues to deal with:

1. How can they drive their information to consumers?
2. How can they drive consumers to their information?
3. How (if at all) can online selling be utilized or integrated with existing channels?

The first two issues are addressed in this section. The third is covered in Chapter 17. The first two issues are highly interrelated in that many of the strategies companies use to drive information to consumers (e.g., banner ads) are also designed, ultimately, to drive consumers to additional sources of information about the company (e.g., the company's website).

Driving a firm's information to consumers is important since consumers are not always actively searching. One way is through web advertising, including *banner ads.* Internet marketing spending (including display, search, and behavioral placement) continues to grow rapidly. It was expected to grow to $55 billion by 2014, which would represent a substantial proportion of all media spending, which has been estimated at around $150 billion.[29] Broadband is changing the nature of online advertising, allowing for more use of streaming media. For example, in response to data showing that many new car buyers visit the web prior to visiting a dealer, Honda placed its national TV ads for the Odyssey minivan on numerous websites. Viewers could click on the video or view it and ask for additional information. This goes beyond the traditional banner ad approach, and yet both drive the brand and information to the consumer.[30]

E-mail is also an important tool for pushing information to consumers. Many consumers see e-mail as a replacement for direct mail. However, spam (unsolicited e-mails) is not well received by consumers. Thus, *permission-based e-mail* (PBE), in which the consumer "opts in" to receive e-mail, is the norm for most reputable marketers. Even with PBE, marketers need to be careful—too many e-mails that lack relevance may still be viewed as spam.[31]

As we saw earlier, social media such as Facebook and Twitter can be used to drive a firm's information to consumers in a number of ways. Facebook allows for the delivery of ads to its members. Twitter has an ad option called promoted tweets, where a promotion code shows up on the tweet and then the tweet comes up in search results (see Chapter 7).[32]

Driving consumers to a firm's information is a daunting and important task given the explosion in the amount and sources of information on the web. Companies have websites to which they want consumers to go and return frequently.[33] Various strategies are possible. Offline media are one avenue for calling attention to a website. In fact, given that many younger consumers watch TV and surf the web simultaneously (see opener), research is demonstrating "upticks" in search volume on search engines such as Google *in real time,* based on traditional TV ads that attract consumer interest. That is, consumers see a TV ad for a product of interest, then use Google to search for more information. This behavioral outcome of traditional advertising online is an important step in driving consumers to a company's information and to the next stage in the decision process.[34]

Banner ads are another way to drive traffic to websites. While *click-through rates* (percentage who click through to the corporate website) are generally low, marketers are looking beyond immediate click-through to measures that include brand awareness, brand attitudes, and purchase intentions. The idea is that boosting awareness and attitudes will drive *long-term* website visits and purchases.

Website visits that occur as a result of *exposure* to an online ad but that do not occur at the time of exposure have been termed *view-throughs.* It is estimated that "half or more of the ad-related visits in a campaign are attributed to the view-through effect as opposed to direct clicks." And, beyond view-through, as online ads become more interactive, other metrics are possible. Mini Cooper used an interactive banner that allowed viewers to see various owner profiles. Useful metrics here would be the interaction rate (percent that interacted in some way with the ad such as paging through the owner profiles) and time spent with the ad.[35]

As you might expect, appropriate or targeted ad placement is helpful in increasing online ad performance across various outcomes including click-through rates. For example, Dolby ran interactive banners relating to thunder and the outdoors. The campaign did well overall but did markedly better (e.g., 60 percent higher click-through rate) when placed on the National Geographic site because of the higher relevance of these themes to the site's viewers.[36]

Social networking sites are also getting into the act. MySpace offers targeted advertising based on member profiles and indicates that ad performance increases by as much as 300 percent by using their targeted approach.[37] Facebook has similar ad-targeting features, and can also target based on the "Fan" status of a member, whereby ads are only delivered to Facebook members who have "liked" a given brand.[38] Given that relevance is a key driver of attention, interest, and engagement as measured by processing and click-throughs (Chapter 8), such personalized targeting can be extremely effective. Levi's is using interactive videos placed in social media in China to tap the self-expression needs of urban youth. The interactive videos allow users to tailor the experience through different destinations and plots, and are designed ultimately to "drive users" to key Levi product information and images.[39]

Behavioral targeting is another form of targeting that is based not on what people say but what they actually do online. Specifically, **behavioral targeting** *involves tracking consumer click patterns on a website and using that information to decide on banner ad placement.*[40] Pepsi used behavioral targeting to promote Aquafina to consumers interested in healthy lifestyles. Online behavioral tracking helped them determine which consumers were the "healthy lifestyles" consumers, and then ads for Aquafina were delivered to those consumers across over 4,000 websites. The result was a 300 percent greater click-through rate for the targeted Aquafina campaign compared to their previous nontargeted campaigns. Again, the perceived relevance of the message to the target audience is a key factor to the success of behavioral targeting.[41] Concerns over privacy and transparency are driving efforts at industry self-regulation, which could or already do include "no-tracking lists" and privacy browsing features.

As we saw earlier, online consumers are heavy users of search engines. Not surprisingly, spending on search-related marketing efforts (including ads and search optimization activities discussed shortly) is the largest single category of Internet marketing, and represents 60 percent of all Internet marketing spending.[42] Because search results are ordered and consumers often don't *drill down* beyond the first page of listings, keyword selection and other techniques relating to search engine optimization are critical for the firm in terms of getting its website the highest priority listing for the most appropriate search terms. **Search engine optimization (SEO)** *involves techniques designed to ensure that a company's web pages "are accessible to search engines and focused in ways that help improve the chances they will be found."*[43]

SEO strategies are critical to Internet search success. One estimate is that the top five spots on a Google search can be worth $50 to $100 million per year depending on the industry and company. A recent report found that searching for the generic keyword "home repair" did not get Home Depot in the top 10 listings. Rather, it came in at number 16 (and on page 2) behind such brands as Lowe's, This Old House, and BobVila.com. The problem, according to one expert, is that Home Depot failed to place key "category-defining keywords [such as 'home repair'] in the URLs."[44] This is in line with our earlier discussion of the critical nature of generic terms in the consumer Internet search process. SEO relates to what is termed "organic" or natural search results. Paid or "sponsored" listings are also available through programs such as Google's Adword program, in which companies pay for "sponsored" listings for specific search terms.

Website design is also critical. While we will discuss this issue more in Chapter 17, it is clear that driving *ongoing and repeat* traffic to a website requires such factors as relevant and frequently updated content. Techniques can include product-related news features, user-related discussion forums, updates on new products and features, and so on. RSS (really simple syndication) feeds that pull information on an ongoing basis from various online sources can be used to keep sites relevant and current. Marketers can also offer opt-in e-mail updates, which can trigger site visits.[45]

Mobile Search

Mobile search and marketing appears to be the next major growth arena for firms. Roughly 84 percent of U.S. adults have a mobile phone (a small but growing segment of mobile phone users also has a tablet device such as the iPad, which is also included as a mobile device).[46] Not surprising, U.S. Mobile advertising spending (including display, search, and messaging-based ads) is estimated between $1.5 and $3 billion.[47] While this is just a fraction of the nearly $150 billion spent overall on measured media, it is expected to continue to grow, particularly as the functionality of smartphones takes off and users become more comfortable operating and using phones as an information, decision, and buying tool. A recent study of mobile phone users by Experian found five segments, as follows:[48]

- *Mobirati* (19 percent)—are younger, grew up with cell phones, phone central to life. Trend high on interest in services to use phone to buy in store, accepting ads if get value in return, using information to decide social activities like where to eat.
- *Mobile Professionals* (17 percent)—are both younger and older, use phone for business and personal life. Phone features are critical and phone is an information tool. Trend high on wanting features beyond just calling, and on using phone in many ways to get information they need.
- *Social Connectors* (22 percent)—are younger, communication is key, mobile device helps them connect socially. Trend high on feeling that text messages are just as meaningful as a "real" conversation, and feeling that their phone connects them to their social world.
- *Pragmatic Adopters* (22 percent)—are older, cell phones came later in their lives. Learning to use beyond just calling. More functional, but still quite important because they are one of the highest income segments.
- *Basic Planners* (20 percent)—are older, not into mobility or technology. Use cell phone for basic calling. Trend high on using cell phone only for emergencies and only for basic calling.

Clearly these segments and their characteristics are important to marketers in relation to information search and product purchasing. In particular, the Mobirati and Mobile Professionals are key users of search and buying features of cell phones and to some degree are open to mobile "push" marketing in the form of advertisements. Pragmatic Adopters seem to be worth pursuing because of their willingness to learn new features and adopt new functionality beyond basic calling, and also because they have high incomes.

One area of particular importance to marketers is local mobile search. **Local mobile search** is defined as *searches for information from a mobile device pertaining to the current (or future planned) geographic location of a consumer.* Google provides a useful illustration of this type of search and marketing efforts related to it. Punch the key words

"Italian restaurant" into Google on your mobile phone and what you will get will be heavily skewed to "local" search results. That is, Google knows your location based on your phone's location and will deliver results that not only list Italian restaurants close to you, but also provide a map of how to get there, the phone number for each restaurant, and so on. You could also select alternate locations as when you are planning to go on a vacation and want to search for restaurants ahead of time. Google can also deliver relevant mobile banner ads to you through its AdWords location-based targeting program.[49]

You may have noticed from the mobile segment descriptions that some consumers are much more likely to use their cell phones for local mobile search. Pew Research finds that two of the top eight local search categories include search for (1) local restaurants and businesses and (2) local coupons and discounts. Clearly, "apps" for local information are a key strategic point that we will also return to later. Roughly 74 percent of U.S. adults access local information via their mobile devices including local mobile apps. As with Internet usage, the major demographic differences in local mobile search and app usage are age, education, and income (with local mobile search/app usage decreasing with age and increasing with education and income.[50]

Marketing Strategy and Mobile Search

Mobile browsers and apps appear to be a critical part of local mobile search strategies. Examine Figure 15–6. Notice how local mobile search is changing how consumers find stores and brands, and also how they search for information. Consumers have historically

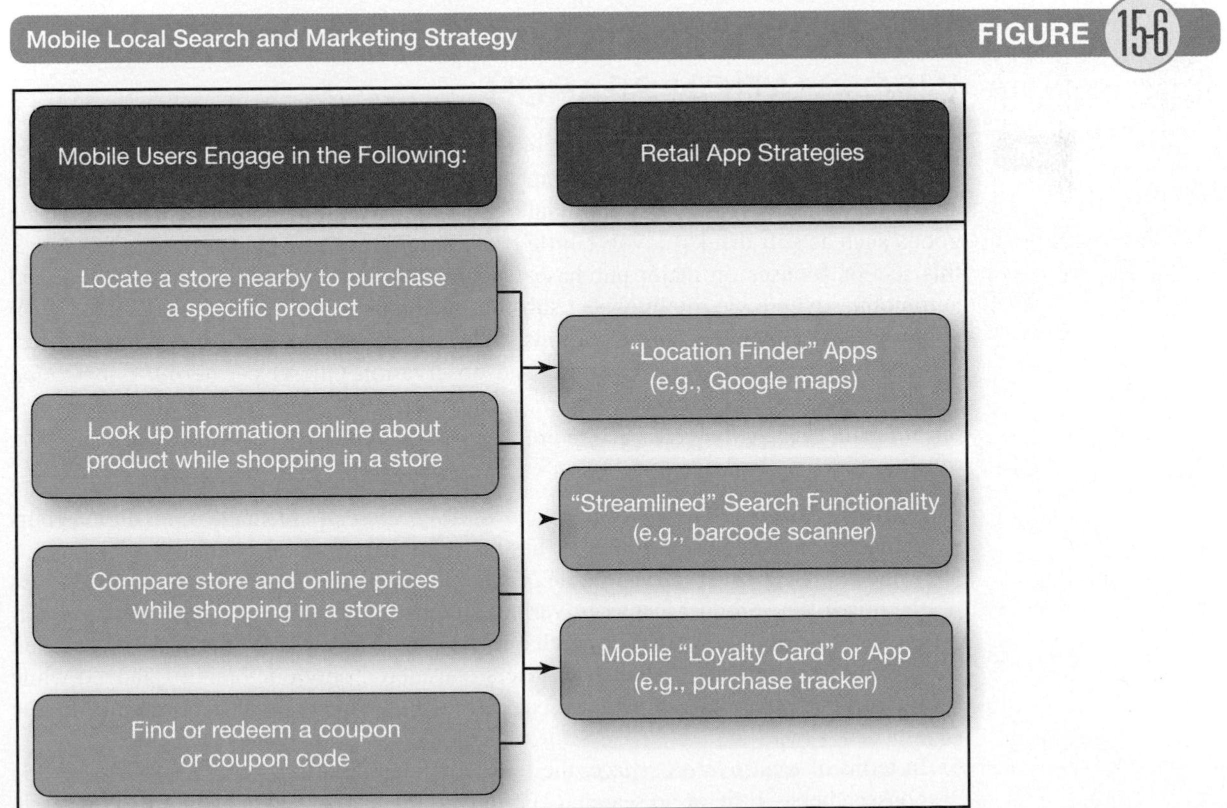

searched for information that was available "within" a store while they were at the store and searched for information "outside" of the store either prior to or after their store search. No longer is that the case, with many mobile users searching for information "outside" the store while shopping in the store. This gives retailers and in-store sales personnel somewhat less control over the shopping experience and puts the consumer more in the driver's seat. Clearly, however, retailers must figure out how to be a part of this emerging new search pattern and design or participate in apps and programs that resonate with consumers. Walmart was reluctant to share prices with price-matching apps at first, but has relented.

Many useful search and shopping apps exist. Consider RetrevoQ, which provides mobile local search via an app or Twitter:

> RetrevoQ uses texts and tweets to dispense [information]. Shoppers can text 41411 or tweet @retrevoq including the make and model of the electronics product they're considering, and RetrevoQ will respond with advice on whether it's a good buy, a fair price, the price range available online for that product and a link to reviews at Retrevo.com, a consumer-electronics shopping and review site.

Such functionality, ease, and possible search benefits make it clear why this and other apps are becoming increasingly popular with shoppers. Why go from store to store to make sure you are getting the lowest price when Shopsavvy will conduct the search for you while you are in the store from your mobile phone.[51] Figure 15–6 provides additional directions for thinking about the kinds of local mobile apps that consumers may want.

Consumer Insight 15–2 examines additional strategic considerations in the mobile marketing arena.

AMOUNT OF EXTERNAL INFORMATION SEARCH

LO5 Marketers are particularly interested in external information search, as this provides them with direct access to the consumer. How much external information search do consumers actually undertake? Nominal and limited decision making (e.g., convenience goods such as soft drinks) involve little or no external search by definition. Therefore, this section focuses on major purchases such as appliances, professional services, and automobiles where we might expect substantial amounts of direct external search prior to purchases. However, across various measures (stores visited, brands considered, sources utilized, total overall search) one observation emerges: *external information search is skewed toward limited search, with the greatest proportion of consumers performing little external search immediately prior to purchase.* Consider the following results:

- Surveys of *shopping behavior* have shown a significant percentage of all durable purchases are made after the consumer has visited only one store.[52]
- Although the *number of alternative brands or models considered* tends to increase as the price of the product increases, various studies show small consideration sets as follows: (1) nearly half of watch purchasers considered only one brand *and* one model; (2) 27 percent of major appliance buyers considered only one brand;[53] and (3) while Internet use increased automobile search, Internet searchers still only examined three models.[54]
- In terms of *total overall search,* the following classification scheme can be used: (1) nonsearchers—little or no search, (2) limited information searchers—low to moderate

CONSUMER INSIGHT 15-2

Push and Pull Strategies in Mobile Marketing

Mobile marketing strategies can be viewed similarly to those on the Internet—that is, driving information to consumers (push strategies) and driving consumers to information (pull strategies).[55]

Mobile Push. Driving information to consumers on mobile devices can involve a variety of strategies. One strategy that will continue to grow as more consumers use mobile Internet is ads placed on mobile web pages. As with computer-based approaches, mobile ads can be targeted to be most relevant to the specific mobile content being viewed. Another strategy is permission-based or opt-in text messaging promotions. According to SmartReply, a media consulting group, the best text message programs involve the following:

- Building an "opt-in" database—this can be done through traditional and e-mail marketing in which consumers are asked to text in or register at a specific website.
- Developing the text-message "ad"—should include (a) a hook relating to why they are being contacted; (b) a call to action, such as entering a code to get a discount; and (c) an "opt-out" option.
- Rolling out the campaign—involves delivering the text promotion to those on the opt-in list.

Adidas used a variation of this approach as sponsor for the NBA All-Star week. It had game information, store events, athlete appearances, and shoe releases as part of its promotions. Consumers opted in and then could access all the promotional materials at any time during the week by texting "originals."

Mobile Pull. Driving consumers to information on mobile devices can also involve a number of strategies. One is to use traditional media to build awareness about a mobile site or promotional event. AT&T held a mobile contest on U.S. college campuses for a free Dave Matthews Band concert to the school that could generate the most "invitations" sent through text messaging for the band to play at their school. To generate awareness and drive students to its mobile space, AT&T blanketed college campuses with posters telling students to "Text DMB to 959" or "visit ATTBLUEROOM.COM to enter." As we have seen, mobile search is another important option. Mobile Internet use is increasing rapidly and the functionality and geo-targeting capabilities of providers such as Google and Yahoo allow marketers to drive traffic to not only traditional websites and mobile content, but also to local restaurants and retailers.

Critical Thinking Questions

1. With cell phones even less easily controlled and monitored than home computers, what ethical and regulatory issues are raised regarding mobile marketing to children?
2. Beyond the approaches discussed above, what other mobile marketing approaches are emerging? Are they effective? Explain.
3. What challenges do marketers face as they have to create campaigns that span mobile, Internet, and traditional media?

search, and (3) extended information searchers—high search. Eight separate studies spanning almost 50 years (1955 to 2003), multiple products and services (appliances, automobiles, and professional services), and two countries (America and Australia) show remarkable consistency in terms of the total external information search undertaken—namely, extended searchers only account for between seven and 20 percent of buyers.[56]

The following section tries to explain why, even for high-involvement products and services, external search immediately prior to purchases is often low.

COSTS VERSUS BENEFITS OF EXTERNAL SEARCH

Buyers appear to weigh the benefits of search against the costs they incur. Search benefits include such aspects as lower price, higher quality, greater comfort with purchase, and so on. Search costs include time; money; hassle; the opportunity costs of other, more enjoyable forgone activities; and so on. All else equal, greater perceived benefits increase search, while greater perceived costs reduce search. When buyers perceive that the next brand (or store, or bit of information) will cost them more than it will benefit them, they stop searching. On the benefits side, given ongoing search and incidental learning, as discussed earlier, the amount of accumulated knowledge can be substantial for many consumers and thus lower the benefits of search *just prior to purchase.* On the costs side, the Internet can greatly lower search costs. When it does, it increases search and leads to better consumer decisions and a more enjoyable shopping experience.[57]

In this section, we examine four basic types of factors that influence the expected benefits and perceived costs of search both online and offline: *market characteristics, product characteristics, consumer characteristics,* and *situation characteristics* (see Table 15–1).[58]

Market Characteristics

Market characteristics (or, more accurately, consumer perceptions of them) include the number of alternatives, price range, store distribution, and information availability.[59] Obviously, the greater the *number of alternatives* (products, stores, brands) available to resolve a particular problem, the more external search there is likely to be. At the extreme, there is no need to search for information in the face of a complete monopoly such as utilities or driver's licenses. However, too many brands or too many noncomparable models across stores can frustrate consumer search efforts and lead to lower search or search within one store. Some marketers strategically develop a large number of models so that key accounts can have exclusive models and avoid direct price competition with other retailers on those exact models.[60] *What ethical concerns are raised by this practice?*

The *perceived range of prices* among equivalent brands in a product class is a major factor in stimulating external search. For example, shopping 36 retail stores in Tucson for five popular-branded toys produced a total low cost of $51.27 and a total high cost of $105.95. Clearly, efficient shopping for those products in that market would provide a significant financial gain. Pricing strategies such as price matching can affect consumer price perceptions. A recent study suggests that consumers interpret such policies as signaling lower prices, which, under high search costs, yields less search.[61] It appears that the percentage savings available from shopping may be as important as the dollar amount. The chance to save $50 when purchasing a $200 item appears to motivate more search than is the case when purchasing a $5,000 item.[62] This relates to the perceptual relativity discussed in Chapter 8.

Store distribution—the number, location, and distances between retail stores in the market—affects the number of store visits a consumer will make before purchase. Because store visits take time, energy, and, in many cases, money, a close proximity of stores will often increase this aspect of external search.[63]

In general, *information availability,* including format, is directly related to information use.[64] However, too much information can cause information overload and the use of less information. In addition, readily available information tends to produce learning over time, which may reduce the need for additional external information immediately prior to a purchase.[65]

TABLE 15-1

Factors Affecting External Search Immediately Prior to Purchase

Influencing Factor	Increasing the Influencing Factor Causes External Search to:
I. Market Characteristics	
A. Number of alternatives	Increase
B. Price range	Increase
C. Store concentration	Increase
D. Information availability	Increase
1. Advertising	
2. Point of purchase	
3. Websites	
4. Sales personnel	
5. Packaging	
6. Experienced customers	
7. Independent sources	
II. Product characteristics	
A. Price	Increase
B. Differentiation	Increase
C. Positive products	Increase
III. Consumer characteristics	
A. Learning and experience	Decrease
B. Shopping orientation	Mixed
C. Social Status	Increase
D. Age and household life cycle	Mixed
E. Product involvement	Mixed
F. Perceived risk	Increase
IV. Situation characteristics	
A. Time availability	Increase
B. Purchase for self	Decrease
C. Pleasant surroundings	Increase
D. Social surroundings	Mixed
E. Physical/mental energy	Increase

Product Characteristics

Perceived product *differentiation*—feature and quality variation across brands—is associated with increased external search.

In addition, consumers appear to enjoy shopping for *positive products*—those whose acquisition results in positive reinforcement (e.g., flowers, sports equipment). In contrast, shopping for *negative products*—those whose primary benefit is negative reinforcement, or the removal of an unpleasant condition (e.g., grocery shopping, auto repairs)—is viewed as less pleasant. All else equal, consumers engage in more external search for positive products.[66]

Consumer Characteristics

A variety of consumer characteristics affect perceptions of expected benefits, search costs, and the need to carry out a particular level of external information search.[67] As described earlier, the first step a consumer normally takes in response to a problem or opportunity is a search of memory for an appropriate solution. If the consumer finds a solution that he or she is confident is satisfactory, external search is unlikely.[68] However, overconfidence can lead to inadequate search and poor choices. It can also make it harder for companies to reposition their brands when consumers wrongly assume they "know" about the brand.[69]

A satisfying *experience* with a particular brand is a positively reinforcing process. It increases the probability of a repeat purchase of that brand and decreases the likelihood of external search.[70] However, at least some familiarity with a product class is necessary for external search to occur. For example, external search prior to purchasing a new automobile is high for consumers who have a high level of *general knowledge about cars* and low for those who have a substantial level of knowledge about existing brands.[71] Thus, consumers facing a completely unfamiliar product category may lack sufficient general knowledge to conduct an external search.

Consumers tend to form general approaches or patterns of external search. These general approaches are termed *shopping orientations.*[72] For example, some individuals engage in extensive ongoing information search because they are market mavens, as described in Chapter 7. This orientation would generally reduce the need to search *just prior to a purchase* as adequate existing knowledge would exist. Other orientations would have different effects.

External search tends to increase with various measures of *social status* (education, occupation, and income), though middle-income individuals search more than those at higher or lower levels. *Age* of the shopper is inversely related to information search. External search appears to decrease as the age of the shopper increases. This may be explained in part by increased learning and product familiarity gained with age. New households and individuals moving into new stages of the *household life cycle* have a greater need for external information than established households.

Consumers who are *highly involved with a product category* generally seek information relevant to the product category on an ongoing basis.[73] This ongoing search and the knowledge base it produces may reduce their need for external search immediately before a purchase, although variety-seeking needs can override this effect.[74]

The *perceived risk* associated with unsatisfactory product performance, either instrumental or symbolic, increases information search prior to purchase.[75] Higher perceived risk is associated with increased search and greater reliance on personal sources of information and personal experiences. Perceived risk can be situational, such as the higher risk felt when buying wine for a dinner party versus for personal consumption at home. Risk can also be perceived as high when a consumer has little prior purchase experience in the product category, in which case information search may help reduce perceived risk.[76] We will discuss perceived risk further in Chapter 17.

Situation Characteristics

As indicated in Chapter 13, situational variables can have a major impact on search behavior. For example, recall that one of the primary reactions of consumers to crowded store conditions is to minimize external information search. *Temporal perspective* is probably the most important situational variable with respect to search behavior. As the time available to solve a particular consumer problem decreases, so does the amount of external information search.[77]

Gift-giving situations (*task definition*) tend to increase perceived risk, which, as we have seen, increases external search. Likewise, multiple-item purchase tasks such as buying a bike and a bike rack or several items for a meal produce increased levels of information search.[78] Shoppers with limited physical or emotional energy (*antecedent state*) will search for less information than others. Pleasant *physical surroundings* increase the tendency to search for information, at least *within* that outlet. *Social surroundings* can increase or decrease search, depending on the nature of the social setting (see Chapter 13 for a more complete discussion).

MARKETING STRATEGIES BASED ON INFORMATION SEARCH PATTERNS

LO6

Sound marketing strategies take into account the nature of information search engaged in by the target market prior to purchase. Two dimensions of search are particularly appropriate: the type of decision influences the level of search and the nature of the evoked set influences the direction of the search. Table 15–2 illustrates a strategy matrix based on these two dimensions. This matrix suggests the six marketing strategies discussed in the following sections. As you will see, although there is considerable overlap between the strategies, each has a unique thrust.

Maintenance Strategy

If the brand is purchased habitually by the target market, the marketer's strategy is to maintain that behavior. This requires consistent attention to product quality, distribution (avoiding out-of-stock situations), and a reinforcement advertising strategy. In addition, the marketer must defend against the disruptive tactics of competitors. Thus, it needs to maintain product development and improvements and to counter short-term competitive strategies, such as coupons, point-of-purchase displays, or rebates.

Morton salt and Del Monte canned vegetables have large repeat purchaser segments that they have successfully maintained. Budweiser, Marlboro, and Crest have large brand-loyal purchaser segments. They have successfully defended their market positions against assaults by major competitors in recent years. In contrast, Liggett & Myers lost 80 percent of its market share when it failed to engage in maintenance advertising.[79] Quality control problems caused Schlitz to lose substantial market share.

The Temptations ad in Illustration 15–4 shows the use of a maintenance strategy against the challenge of competitors. Note that the ad stresses the improvements to the product.

Disrupt Strategy

If the brand is not part of the evoked set and the target market engages in nominal decision making, the marketer's first task is to *disrupt* the existing decision pattern. This is a difficult task since the consumer does not seek external information or even consider alternative brands before a purchase. Low-involvement learning over time could generate a positive product position for the brand, but this alone would be unlikely to shift behavior.

In the long run, a major product improvement accompanied by attention-attracting advertising could shift the target market into a more extensive form of decision making. In the short run, attention-attracting advertising aimed specifically at breaking habitual decision making can be successful. This advertising might be targeted via online and social media

Marketing Strategies Based on Information Search Patterns

TABLE 

Position	Target Market Decision-Making Pattern		
	Nominal Decision Making (no search)	Limited Decision Making (limited search)	Extended Decision Making (extensive search)
Brand in evoked set	Maintenance strategy	Capture strategy	Preference strategy
Brand not in evoked set	Disrupt strategy	Intercept strategy	Acceptance strategy

ILLUSTRATION 15-4

Firms with a significant group of loyal or repeat purchasers such as Temptations Cat Treats, must continually improve their products and communicate their advantages to their consumers.

as well with a strong but simple benefits-based approach. Free samples, coupons, rebates, and tie-in sales are common approaches to disrupting nominal decision making. Thus, participation in local mobile coupon app programs could be helpful. Likewise, striking package designs and point-of-purchase displays may disrupt a habitual purchase sequence.[80] Comparative advertising is also often used for this purpose.

Illustration 15–5 is an example of a disrupt strategy. The ad tries to convince consumers to change to the advertised brand based on several key benefits.

Capture Strategy

Limited decision making generally involves a few brands that are evaluated on only a few criteria, such as price or availability. Much of the information search occurs at the point of purchase or in readily available media prior to purchase. If the brand is one given this type of consideration by the target market, the marketer's objective is to capture as large a share of the purchases as practical.

Because these consumers engage in limited search, the marketer needs to know where they search and what information they are looking for. In general, the marketer will want to supply information, often on price and availability, on its website, on mobile apps, in local media including efforts related to local mobile search, and at the point of purchase through

ILLUSTRATION 15-5

Firms trying to disrupt the habitual purchase or consumption patterns of consumers who do not even consider their brand need attention-attracting ads and a strong benefit or other inducement to try the brand.

displays and adequate shelf space. The marketer will also be concerned with maintaining consistent product quality and adequate distribution.

Intercept Strategy

If the target market engages in limited decision making and the brand is not part of the evoked set, the objective will be to intercept the consumer during the search for information on the brands in the evoked set or during general search for related information. Again, the emphasis will be on local media with cooperative advertising and at the point of purchase with displays, shelf space, package design, and so forth. Coupons can also be effective. The marketer will have to place considerable emphasis on attracting the consumers' attention because they will not be seeking information on the brand. The behavioral targeting strategy used by Snapple on iVillage's website is a great example of an online intercept strategy. As one ad executive stated:

> The big trick with this product was changing [the audience's perception] of Snapple-a-Day from an on-the-go, quirky product to something that has real health benefits for women and that has to be more of a planned purchase.[81]

The promotion shown in Illustration 15–6 would be effective as part of a capture or intercept strategy.

In addition to the strategies mentioned above, low-involvement learning, product improvements, and free samples can be used to move the brand into the target market's evoked set.

Preference Strategy

Extended decision making with the brand in the evoked set requires a preference strategy. Because extended decision making generally involves several brands, many attributes, and a number of information sources, a simple capture strategy may not be adequate. Instead, the marketer needs to structure an information campaign that will result in the brand being preferred by members of the target market.

The first step is a strong position on those attributes important to the target market.[82] This will be discussed in considerable detail in Chapter 16. Next, information must be provided in all the appropriate sources. This may require extensive advertising to groups

ILLUSTRATION 15-6

The ad shown here reflects an intercept strategy in that it gives consumers an immediate incentive to purchase its brand.

ILLUSTRATION 15-7

Honda's website assumes an extended search process. It provides substantial data on numerous product features.

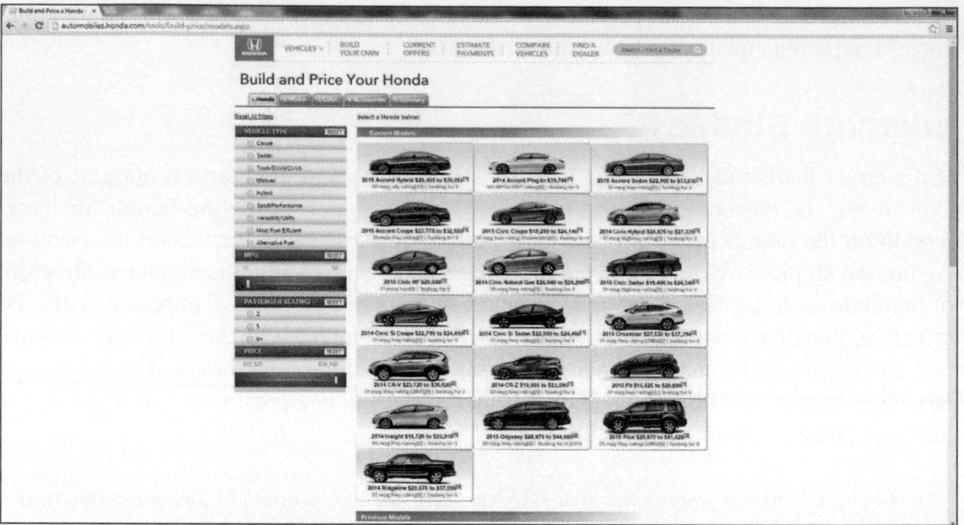

or influential online participants (e.g., bloggers) who will recommend it to others (e.g., druggists for over-the-counter drugs, veterinarians, and county agents for agricultural products). Independent groups should be encouraged to test the brand, and sales personnel should be provided detailed information on the brand's attributes. In addition, it may be wise to provide the sales personnel with extra motivation (e.g., extra commissions paid by the manufacturer) to recommend the product. Point-of-purchase displays and pamphlets should also be available. A well-designed website is essential.

Illustration 15–7 shows Honda's web site is part of an effective preference strategy. It assumes an involved search, provides detailed information relative to multiple product attributes, and so on.

Acceptance Strategy

Acceptance strategy is similar to preference strategy. However, it is complicated by the fact that the target market is not seeking information about the brand. Therefore, in addition to the activities involved in the preference strategy described above, the marketer must attract the consumers' attention or otherwise motivate them to learn about the brand. This can be difficult, but various automakers over the years have gone as far as to pay customers to test drive their cars (Chrysler) or loan their cars to opinion leaders (Ford) in an effort to move their brand into consumer consideration sets by encouraging trial and/or positive WOM.

The Internet can play an important role in an acceptance strategy. Since keyword searches prior to a purchase tend to be generic, this opens up important opportunities for companies that are not in the evoked set to engage in search engine optimization strategies to give their brand exposure to the consumer during the decision process—hopefully, to the point of moving the brand into consumers' evoked sets. Obviously, a well-designed website is a critical part of this strategy.

Long-term advertising designed to enhance low-involvement learning is another useful technique for gaining acceptance. Extensive advertising with strong emphasis on attracting attention can also be effective. The primary objective of these two approaches is not to sell the brand; rather, the objective is to move the brand into the evoked set. Then, when a purchase situation arises, the consumer will seek additional information on this brand.

SUMMARY

LO1: Discuss internal and external information search and their role in different decision types

Following problem recognition, consumers typically engage in some form and amount of search. *Internal search* is accessing relevant information from long-term memory to be used to determine if a satisfactory solution is known, what the characteristics of potential solutions are, what the appropriate ways to compare solutions are, and so forth. If a resolution is not reached through internal search, then the search process is focused on external information relevant to solving the problem. This is *external search,* which can involve independent sources, personal sources, marketer-based information, and product experience. Internal information tends to dominate in nominal decision making, whereas external search tends to dominate in extended decision making. For limited decision making, external search can play a moderate role in some instances.

LO2: Summarize the types of information consumers search for

Information may be sought on (1) the appropriate *evaluative criteria* for the solution of the problem, (2) the existence of various *alternative solutions,* and (3) the *performance* of each alternative solution on each evaluative criterion.

LO3: Describe the categories of decision alternatives relating to the evoked set

From the set of all possible alternatives that could solve a consumer problem, the following are the categories of decision alternatives: alternatives that consumers are aware of (*awareness set*), alternatives that consumers are aware of and view in a neutral manner (*inert set*), alternatives that consumers are aware of and view negatively (*inept set*), and alternatives that consumers are aware of and view positively (*evoked set*). The evoked set (also called the *consideration set*) represents the alternatives that the consumer seeks additional information on during the remaining internal and external search process. Therefore, marketers are first concerned with making sure their brand is in the awareness set. But, because awareness does not equal consideration and because consideration is necessary for a chance at being chosen, marketers are also very concerned about moving their brands into consumer evoked sets and must engage in persuasive messaging and other strategies to do so.

LO4: Discuss available information sources and the role of Internet and mobile search

Consumer internal information (information stored in memory) may have been actively acquired in previous searches and personal experiences, or it may have been passively acquired through low-involvement learning. In addition to their own *memory,* consumers can seek information from the following four major types of external sources: (1) *personal sources,* such as friends and family; (2) *independent sources,* such as consumer groups, paid professionals, and government agencies; (3) *marketing sources,* such as sales personnel and advertising; and (4) *experiential sources,* such as direct product inspection or trial. Each of these sources of information can be accessed through the Internet or mobile devices. Internet and mobile search options are dramatically changing the way in which consumers search for information prior to a purchase and provide marketers with many unique opportunities and challenges.

LO5: Discuss the major cost–benefit factors driving the amount of external search

Explicit external information search *after* problem recognition is often limited. It is often suggested that consumers generally should engage in relatively extensive external search prior to purchasing an item in order to reap higher benefits of the purchase such as higher brand quality or lower price. However, this view ignores the fact that information search is not free. It takes time, energy, and money and can often require giving up more desirable activities. Therefore, consumers should engage in external search only to the extent that the expected benefits, such as a lower price or a more satisfactory purchase, outweigh the expected costs. Numerous aspects affect the perceived costs and/or benefits of search. They can be *market characteristics* (e.g., number of brands), *product characteristics* (e.g., price), *consumer characteristics* (e.g., prior search and learning), and *situational characteristics* (e.g., time availability).

LO6: Summarize the marketing strategies based on information search patterns

Sound marketing strategy takes into account the nature of information search engaged in by the target market. The level of search and the brand's position in or out of the evoked set are two key dimensions. Based on these two dimensions, the following six potential information strategies are suggested: (1) *maintenance,* (2) *disrupt,* (3) *capture,* (4) *intercept,* (5) *preference,* and (6) *acceptance.*

KEY TERMS

Awareness set 521
Behavioral targeting 531
Bots 529
Consideration set 522
Evoked set 522
External search 520
Inept set 522
Inert set 521
Internal search 520
Local mobile search 532
Ongoing search 520
Search engine optimization (SEO) 531

REVIEW QUESTIONS

1. When does *information search* occur? What is the difference between internal and external information search?
2. What kind of information is sought in an external search for information?
3. What are *evaluative criteria* and how do they relate to information search?
4. How does a consumer's *awareness set* influence information search?
5. What roles do the *evoked set, inert set,* and *inept set* play in a consumer's information search?
6. What are the primary sources of information available to consumers?
7. What is *behavioral targeting?*
8. What is *search engine optimization?*
9. What is *local mobile search?*
10. How do nonsearchers, limited information searchers, and extended information searchers differ in their search for information?
11. What factors might influence the search effort of consumers who are essentially one-stop shoppers? How do these factors differ in terms of how they influence limited information searchers and extended information searchers?
12. What factors have to be considered in the total cost of the information search? How might these factors be different for different consumers?
13. Explain how different *market characteristics* affect information search.
14. How do different *consumer characteristics* influence a consumer's information search effort?
15. How do *product characteristics* influence a consumer's information search effort?
16. How do *situational characteristics* influence a consumer's information search effort?
17. Describe the information search characteristics that should lead to each of the following strategies:
    a. Maintenance
    b. Disrupt
    c. Capture
    d. Intercept
    e. Preference
    f. Acceptance
18. Describe each of the strategies listed in Question 17.

DISCUSSION QUESTIONS

19. Pick a product/brand that you believe would require each strategy in Table 15–2 (six products in total). Justify your selection. Develop a specific marketing strategy for each (six strategies in total).
20. Which product classes are most likely to have evoked sets of one? Relate this to the type of decision process.

21. Use a shopping service such as NexTag to help you choose a brand of digital camera. In what way does it help you form your evoked or consideration set? Is information overload a problem? Explain.
22. Do you have a local mobile search app? If so, what is your evaluation of it? If no, why not?
23. What information sources do you think students on your campus use when acquiring the items listed below? Consider the various sources listed in Figure 15–4 in developing your answer. Do you think there will be individual differences? Why?
    a. Movies
    b. Restaurants
    c. Apartment
    d. Computer
    e. Fitness equipment
    f. A charity contribution
    g. Dress clothes
    h. Cell phones
24. What factors contribute to the size of the awareness set, evoked set, inert set, and inept set?
25. Discuss factors that may contribute to external information search and factors that act to reduce external search for information before purchase or adoption of the following:
    a. Car insurance
    b. International travel
    c. Exercise club
    d. Formal wear
    e. Eye wear
    f. Counseling services
26. Is it ever in the best interest of a marketer to encourage potential customers to carry out an extended prepurchase search? Why or why not?
27. What implications for marketing strategy does Figure 15–2 suggest?
28. What implications for online marketing strategy does Figure 15–5 suggest?
29. What role, if any, should the government play in ensuring that consumers have easy access to relevant product information? How should it accomplish this?
30. Respond to the questions in Consumer Insight 15–1.
31. Describe a recent purchase in which you engaged in extensive search and one in which you did little prepurchase search. What factors caused the difference?
32. What is your awareness set, evoked set, inert set, and inept set for the following? In what ways, if any, do you think your sets will differ from the average member of your class? Why?
    a. Automobiles
    b. Energy drinks
    c. Car insurance providers
    d. Jewelry stores
    e. Book stores
    f. Laptop computers
    g. Restaurants

APPLICATION ACTIVITIES

33. Develop an appropriate questionnaire and complete Question 23 using information from five students not in your class. Prepare a report discussing the marketing implications of your findings.
34. For the same products listed in Question 32, ask five students to list all the brands they are aware of in each product category. Then have them indicate which ones they might buy (evoked set), which ones they are indifferent toward (inert set), and which brands they strongly dislike and would not purchase (inept set). What are the marketing implications of your results?
35. Develop a short questionnaire designed to measure the information search consumers engage in prior to purchasing an expensive recreational or entertainment item or service. Your questionnaire should include measures of types of information sought, as well as sources that provide this information. Also include measures of the relevant consumer characteristics that might influence information search, as well as some measure of past experience with the products. Then interview two recent purchasers of each product, using the questionnaire you have developed. Analyze each consumer's response and classify each consumer

in terms of information search. What are the marketing implications of your results?

36. For each strategy in Table 15–2, find one brand that appears to be following that strategy. Describe in detail how it is implementing the strategy.

37. Develop a questionnaire to determine which products college students view as positive and which they view as negative. Measure the shopping effort associated with each type. Explain your overall results and any individual differences you find.

REFERENCES

1. The opener is based on L. Rao, "eBay Debuts Standlone [sic] 'Couch Commerce' iPad App to Purchase Items, Watch with eBay," *TechCrunch,* March 12, 2012, http://techcrunch.com/2012/03/12/ebay-debuts-standlone-couch-commerce-ipad-app-to-purchase-items-seen-on-tv-watch-with-ebay/, accessed August 29, 2014; G. Hayes, "Rebooting 2nd Screen & Social TV: Interactive TV 3.0," *Personalizemedia,* May 29, 2013, www.personalizemedia.com/rebooting-2nd-screen-social-tv-interactive-tv-3-0/, accessed August 29, 2014; A. A. Newman, "Like That Vase on the TV? Click Your Phone to Buy It," *New York Times,* March 17, 2014, www.nytimes.com/2014/03/18/business/media/like-that-vase-on-the-tv-click-your-phone-to-buy-it.html?_r=0, accessed August 29, 2014; A. Satariano, "Shazam's TV Strategy," *Bloomberg Businessweek,* July 5, 2012, www.businessweek.com/articles/2012-07-05/shazams-tv-strategy, accessed August 29, 2014; C. Palist, "Watch with eBay," *Huffington Post,* March 14, 2012, www.huffingtonpost.com/2012/03/14/ebays-watch-with-ebay-app_n_1344304.html, accessed August 29, 2014; N. Summers, "Second-Screen TV App Zeebox Launches SpotSynch, Matching Clickable Ads to TV Shows and Commercials," *TNW,* February 12, 2013, http://thenextweb.com/apps/2013/02/12/second-screen-tv-app-zeebox-launches-spotsynch-showing-users-clickable-ads-alongside-tv-commercials/#!AqG71, accessed August 29, 2014; M. Ballve, "Chart of the Day: The Beginnings of Second Screen Commerce," *Business Insider,* February 11, 2013, www.businessinsider.com/chart-of-the-day-mobile-activity-2013-2, accessed August 29, 2014; and T. Spangler, "TV Viewers Aren't Thrilled with Second-Screen Synchronized Content, Study Finds," *Variety,* January 9, 2014, http://variety.com/2014/digital/news/tv-viewers-arent-thrilled-with-second-screen-synchronized-content-study-finds-1201040757/, accessed August 29, 2014.
2. G. Punji and R. Brookes, "Decision Constraints and Consideration-Set Formation in Consumer Durables," *Psychology & Marketing,* August 2001, pp. 843–63.
3. An outstanding discussion of the trade-off consumers make between memory-based decisions (internal search) and external search is in J. R. Bettman, M. F. Luce, and J. W. Payne, "Constructive Consumer Choice Processes," *Journal of Consumer Research,* December 1998, pp. 187–217.
4. See, e.g., R. Smith and B. Deppa, "Two Dimensions of Attribute Importance," *Journal of Consumer Marketing,* 26, no. 1 (2009), pp. 28–38.
5. S. S. Posavac, D. M. Sanbonmatsu, and E. A. Ho, "The Effects of the Selective Consideration of Alternatives on Consumer Choice and Attitude-Decision Consistency," *Journal of Consumer Psychology,* 12, no. 3 (2002), pp. 203–13; T. Erdem and J. Swait, "Brand Credibility, Brand Consideration, and Choice," *Journal of Consumer Research,* June 2004, pp. 191–98; M. Paulssen and R. P. Bagozzi, "A Self-Regulatory Model of Consideration Set Formation," *Psychology & Marketing,* October 2005, pp. 785–812; and J. R. Hauser et al., "Disjunctions of Conjunctions, Cognitive Simplicity, and Consideration Sets," *Journal of Marketing Research,* June 2010, pp. 485–96.
6. E. M. Felcher, P. Malaviya, and A. L. McGill, "The Role of Taxonomic and Goal-Derived Product Categorization in, within, and across Category Judgments," *Psychology & Marketing,* August 2001, pp. 865–87.
7. P. Aurier, S. Jean, and J. L. Zaichkowsky, "Consideration Set Size and Familiarity with Usage Context," *Advances in Consumer Research,* vol. 27, ed. S. J. Hoch and R. J. Meyer (Provo, UT: Association for Consumer Research, 2000), pp. 307–13; and K. K. Desai and W. D. Hoyer, "Descriptive Characteristics of Memory-Based Consideration Sets," *Journal of Consumer Research,* December 2000, pp. 309–23.
8. R. R. Brand and J. J. Cronin, "Consumer-Specific Determinants of the Size of Retail Choice Sets," *Journal of Services Marketing,* 11, no. 1 (1997), pp. 19–38.
9. L. R. Klein and G. T. Ford, "Consumer Search for Information in the Digital Age," *Journal of Interactive Marketing,* Summer 2003, pp. 29–49; B. T. Ratchford, M.-S. Lee, and D. Talukdar, "The Impact of the Internet on Information Search for Automobiles," *Journal of Marketing Research,* May 2003, pp. 193–209; H. Li, T. Daugherty, and F. Biocca, "The Role of Virtual Experience in Consumer Learning," *Journal of Consumer Psychology,* 13, no. 4 (2003), pp. 395–407; A. E. Schlosser, "Experience Products in the Virtual World," *Journal of Consumer Research,* September 2003, pp. 184–98; and D. A. Griffith and Q. Chen, "The Influence of Virtual Direct Experience (VDE) on On-line Ad Message Effectiveness," *Journal of Advertising,* Spring 2004, pp. 55–68.
10. For a review and conflicting evidence, see A. A. Wright and J. G. Lynch Jr., "Communications Effects of Advertising versus Direct Experience When Both Search and Experience Attributes Are Present," *Journal of Consumer Research,* March 1995, pp. 108–18.
11. See C. F. Mela, S. Gupta, and D. R. Lehmann, "The Long-Term Impact of Promotion and Advertising on Consumer Brand Choice," *Journal of Marketing Research,* May 1997, pp. 248–61; and M. J. Sirgy et al., "Does Television Viewership Play a Role in the Perception of Quality of Life?," *Journal of Advertising,* Spring 1998, pp. 125–42.

12. This Consumer Insight is based on information found on the various corporate websites.
13. *World Internet Usage Statistics News and World Population Stats* (Bogota, Colombia: Miniwatts Marketing Group, March 2011).
14. *The Web at 25 in the U.S.* (Washington, DC: Pew Internet & American Life Project, February 2014).
15. *Generations 2010* (Washington, DC: Pew Internet & American Life Project, December 2010).
16. S. Hays, "Has Online Advertising Finally Grown Up?," *Advertising Age,* April 1, 2002, p. C1.
17. "Counting on the Internet," *Pew Internet & American Life Project,* December 29, 2002, www.pewinternet.org; Klein and Ford, "Consumer Search for Information in the Digital Age"; Ratchford, Lee, and Talukdar, "The Impact of the Internet on Information Search for Automobiles"; *DoubleClick's Touch-points II,* DoubleClick research report, March 2004, www.doubleclick.com; *Double-Click's Touch-points III,* DoubleClick research report, July 2005, www.doubleclick.com; and B. T. Ratchford, D. Talukdar, and M. Lee, "The Impact of the Internet on Consumers' Use of Information Sources for Automobiles," *Journal of Consumer Research,* June 2007, pp. 111–19.
18. "Internet Activities," *Pew Internet & American Life Project,* www.pewinternet.org, accessed June 18, 2011.
19. comScore, "Yahoo! and comScore Study Finds Online Consumers Who Pre-Shop on the Web Spend More In-Store," press release, July 30, 2007, www.comscore.com, accessed June 19, 2011; *State of the U.S. Online Retail Economy through Q1 2009* (Reston, VA: comScore, 2009); D. M. Arbesman, "Online Shopper Intelligence Study Released," *compete pulse,* February 22, 2010, http://blog.complete.com, accessed June 15, 2011; and "Study Shows Online Shoppers Are Doing Their Homework," *e-commerce news,* February 26, 2010, http://ecommercejunkie .com, accessed June 15, 2011.
20. *Search before the Purchase,* DoubleClick research report, February 2005, www.doubleclick.com.
21. J. L. Joines, C. W. Scherer, and D. A. Scheufele, "Exploring Motivations for Consumer Web Use and Their Implications for E-commerce," *Journal of Consumer Marketing,* 20, no. 2 (2003), pp. 90–108.
22. Ratchford, Lee, and Talukdar, "The Impact of the Internet on Information Search for Automobiles."
23. L. Gentry and R. Calantone, "A Comparison of Three Models to Explain Shop-Bot Use on the Web," *Psychology & Marketing,* November 2002, pp. 945–56; and Y. Xu and H. Kim, "Order Effect and Vendor Inspection in Online Comparison Shopping," *Journal of Retailing,* 84, no. 4 (2008), pp. 477–86.
24. B. Bickart and R. M. Schindler, "Internet Forums as Influential Sources of Consumer Information," *Journal of Interactive Marketing,* Summer 2001, pp. 31–40; and P. Chatterjee, "Online Reviews," *Advances in Consumer Research,* vol. 28, ed. M. C. Gilly and J. Meyers-Levy (Provo, UT: Association for Consumer Research, 2001), pp. 129–33.
25. J. Loechner, "Online Research a Significant Part of Consumer Buying," *MediaPost,* February 22, 2011, www.mediapost.com, accessed June 15, 2011.
26. A. Parmar, "Student e-union," *Marketing News,* April 1, 2004, pp. 14–15.
27. "Ethnic Groups Online," *eMarketer,* June 20, 2005.
28. N. Singh and H. Matsuo, "Measuring Cultural Adaptation on the Web," in *Advances in Consumer Research,* vol. 30, ed. P. A. Keller and D. W. Rook (Provo, UT: Association for Consumer Research, 2003), pp. 271–72.
29. "Want Consumer Engagement?," *Launchfire,* October 5, 2009, www.launchfire.com, accessed June 15, 2011.
30. J. Halliday, "Half Hit Web before Showrooms," *Advertising Age,* October 4, 2004, p. 76.
31. E-mail material based on *DoubleClick's 2004 Consumer E-mail Study,* DoubleClick, October 2004, www.doubleclick.com.
32. *Who Tweets?* (Washington, DC: Pew Internet, 2009); J. Van Grove, "Sponsored Tweets Launches," *mashable.com*, August 3, 2009, accessed May 23, 2011; and "How Does Twitter Make Money," *Buzzle.com,* accessed May 23, 2011.
33. J. S. Ilfeld and R. S. Winer, "Generating Web Traffic," *Journal of Advertising Research,* October 2002, pp. 49–61.
34. D. Zigmond and H. Stipp, "Assessing a New Advertising Effect," *Journal of Advertising Research,* June 2010, pp. 162–68.
35. R. E. Bruner and M. Gluck, *Best Practices for Optimizing Web Advertising Effectiveness,* DoubleClick, May 2006, www.doubleclick.com.
36. Ibid.
37. C. McCarthy, "MySpace Gets 'Hyper' with Targeted Ads," *CNET News.com,* November 5, 2007, http://news.cnet.com/; and J. Kirk, "MySpace User Ad Targeting Will Be Optional," *The Industry Standard,* April 29, 2008, www.thestandard.com.
38. J. Smith, "10 Powerful Ways to Target Facebook Ads Every Performance Advertiser Should Know," *Inside Facebook,* July 27, 2009, www.insidefacebook.com, accessed June 19, 2011.
39. N. Madden, "Levi's Partners with Tudou for Interactive Video Campaign," *Advertising Age,* December 22, 2010.
40. W. Dou, R. Linn, and S. Yang, "How Smart Are 'Smart Banners'?," *Journal of Advertising Research,* 41, no. 4 (2001), pp. 31–43.
41. E. Steel, "How Marketers Hone Their Aim Online," *The Wall Street Journal,* June 19, 2007.
42. "Search Marketing Fact Pack 2008," *Advertising Age,* November 8, 2008.
43. D. Sullivan, "Intro to Search Engine Optimization," *SearchEngineWatch.com*, October 14, 2002.
44. B. S. Bulik, "Meet the Brands Hiding on Google," *Advertising Age,* April 27, 2010.
45. See, e.g., T. P. Novak, D. L. Hoffman, and Y.-F. Yung, "Measuring the Customer Experience in Online Environments," *Marketing Science,* Winter 2000, pp. 22–42; and J. R. Coyle and E. Thorson, "The Effects of Progressive Levels of Interactivity and Vividness in Web Marketing Sites," *Journal of Advertising,* Fall 2001, pp. 65–77.
46. *How Mobile Devices Are Changing Community Information Environments* (Washington, DC: Pew Internet & American Life Project, March 14, 2011).
47. Estimates from *eMarketer.* This and related information available at www.emarketer.com/reports.

48. Segment information from *2010 American Mobile Consumer Report* (Costa Mesa, CA: Experian Information Systems, Inc., March 5, 2010); H. Leggatt, "Experian Segments Mobile Users by Behavior/Attitudes," *BizReport,* March 8, 2010, www.bizreport.com, accessed June 18, 2011; and J. Loechner, "Holiday Layaway," *MediaPost,* August 17, 2010, www.mediapost.com, accessed June 15, 2011. See also M. Pihlstrom and G. J. Brush, "Comparing the Perceived Value of Information and Entertainment Mobile Services," *Pscychology & Marketing,* August 2008, pp. 732–55.
49. R. Aronauer, "Going Mobile to Market," *Sales & Marketing Management,* June 2007; and "Search Marketing Fact Pack 2008."
50. *Location-Based Services* (Washington, DC: Pew Internet & American Life Project, September 12, 2014).
51. N. Zmuda, "Yes, There's an App for That Too," *Advertising Age,* March 1, 2010, p. 8.
52. R. A. Westbrook and C. Farnell, "Patterns of Information Source Usage among Durable Goods Buyers," *Journal of Marketing Research,* August 1979, pp. 303–12; and J. E. Urbany, P. R. Dickson, and W. L. Wilkie, "Buyer Uncertainty and Information Search," *Journal of Consumer Research,* September 1989, pp. 208–15.
53. Urbany, Dickson, and Wilkie, "Buyer Uncertainty and Information Search"; and *Warranties Rule Consumer Follow-Up* (Washington, DC: Federal Trade Commission, 1984), p. 26.
54. Ratchford, Lee, and Talukdar, "The Impact of the Internet on Information Search for Automobiles."
55. Consumer Insight 15–2 is based on M. Kamvar and S. Baluja, "A Large Scale Study of Wireless Search Behavior," in *Proceedings of SIGCHI Conference on Human Factors in Computing Systems,* ed. R. Ginter et al. (Montreal: Conference on Human Factors in Computing Systems, 2006), pp. 701–709; "Search Marketing," in *Advertising Age Fact Pack 2007* (New York: Crain Communications, November 5, 2007); *Best Practices: A Blueprint for Building a Retail Mobile Marketing Program* (Irvine, CA: SmartReply, 2007); "Case Studies," *MobileMarketing Magazine,* November 19, 2007, p. 22; and "Special Report: Interactive Marketing," *promomagazine.com,* accessed April 15, 2008.
56. G. Katona and E. Mueller, "A Study of Purchase Decisions," in *Consumer Behavior: The Dynamics of Consumer Reaction,* ed. L. Clark (New York: New York University Press, 1955), pp. 30–87; J. Newman and R. Staelin, "Prepurchase Information Seeking for New Cars and Major Household Appliances," *Journal of Marketing Research,* August 1972, pp. 249–57; J. Claxton, J. Fry, and B. Portis, "A Taxonomy of Prepurchase Information Gathering Patterns," *Journal of Consumer Research,* December 1974, pp. 35–42; G. C. Kiel and R. A. Layton, "Dimensions of Consumer Information Seeking Behavior," *Journal of Marketing Research,* May 1981, pp. 233–39; J. B. Freiden and R. E. Goldsmith, "Prepurchase Information-Seeking for Professional Services," *Journal of Services Marketing,* Winter 1989, pp. 45–55; Urbany, Dickson, and Wilkie, "Buyer Uncertainty and Information Search"; G. N. Souter and M. M. McNeil, *Journal of Professional Services Marketing,* 11, no. 2 (1995), pp. 45–60; and Klein and Ford, "Consumer Search for Information in the Digital Age."
57. J. G. Lynch Jr. and D. Ariely, "Wine Online," *Marketing Science,* Winter 2000, pp. 83–103; D. Ariely, "Controlling the Information Flow," *Journal of Consumer Research,* September 2000, pp. 233–48; and Ratchford, Lee, and Talukdar, "The Impact of the Internet on Information Search for Automobiles."
58. For a similar model of online search, see S. Kulviwat, C. Guo, and N. Engchanil, "Determinants of Online Search," *Internet Research,* 14, no. 3 (2004), pp. 245–53; and A. L. Jepsen, "Factors Affecting Consumer Use of the Internet for Information Search," *Journal of Interactive Marketing,* Summer 2007, pp. 21–34.
59. D. R. Lichtenstein, N. M. Ridgway, and R. G. Netemeyer, "Price Perceptions and Consumer Shopping Behavior," *Journal of Marketing Research,* May 1993, pp. 234–45.
60. M. N. Bergen, S. Dutta, and S. M. Shugan, "Branded Variants," *Journal of Marketing Research,* February 1996, pp. 9–19.
61. J. Srivastava and N. Lurie, "A Consumer Perspective on Price-Matching Refund Policies," *Journal of Consumer Research,* September 2001, pp. 296–307.
62. D. Grewal and H. Marmorstein, "Market Price Variation, Perceived Price Variation, and Consumers' Price Search Decisions for Durable Goods," *Journal of Consumer Research,* December 1994, pp. 453–60.
63. See B. G. C. Dellaert, "Investigating Consumers' Tendency to Combine Multiple Shopping Purposes and Destinations," *Journal of Marketing Research,* May 1998, pp. 177–89.
64. See C. Moorman, "Market-Level Effects of Information," *Journal of Marketing Research,* February 1998, pp. 82–98; and A. D. Miyazaki, D. E. Sprott, and K. C. Manning, "Unit Prices on Retail Shelf Labels," *Journal of Retailing,* 76, no. 1 (2000), pp. 93–112.
65. See C. M. Fisher and C. J. Anderson, "The Relationship between Consumer Attitudes and Frequency of Advertising in Newspapers for Hospitals," *Journal of Hospital Marketing,* 7, no. 2 (1993), pp. 139–56.
66. S. Widrick and E. Fram, "Identifying Negative Products," *Journal of Consumer Marketing,* no. 2 (1983), pp. 59–66.
67. See D. D'Rozario and S. P. Douglas, "Effect of Assimilation on Prepurchase Information-Search Tendencies," *Journal of Consumer Psychology,* 8, no. 2 (1999), pp. 187–209; and C. Merrill, "Where the Cars Are Caliente," *American Demographics,* January 2000, pp. 56–59.
68. J. Lee and J. Cho, "Consumers' Use of Information Intermediaries and the Impact on Their Information Search Behavior in the Financial Market," *Journal of Consumer Affairs,* 39, no. 1 (2005), pp. 95–120.
69. J. W. Alba and J. W. Hutchinson, "Knowledge Calibration," *Journal of Consumer Research,* September 2000, pp. 123–49.
70. C. M. Heilman, D. Bowman, and G. P. Wright, "The Evolution of Brand Preferences and Choice Behaviors of Consumers New to a Market," *Journal of Marketing Research,* May 2000, pp. 139–55. See also D. Mazursky, "The Effects of Invalidating Information on Consumers' Subsequent Search Patterns," *Journal of Economic Psychology,* April 1998, pp. 261–77.
71. See J. A. Barrick and B. C. Spilker, "The Relations between Knowledge, Search Strategy, and Performance in Unaided and Aided Information Search," *Organizational Behavior and Human Decision Processes,* 90 (2003), pp. 1–18.

72. See T. Williams, M. Slama, and J. Rogers, "Behavioral Characteristics of the Recreational Shopper," *Journal of Academy of Marketing Science,* Summer 1985, pp. 307–16; J. R. Lumpkin, J. M. Hawes, and W. R. Darden, "Shopping Patterns of the Rural Consumer," *Journal of Business Research,* February 1986, pp. 63–81; and W. W. Moe, "Buying, Searching, or Browsing," *Journal of Consumer Psychology,* 13, no. 1/2 (2003), pp. 29–39.

73. See U. M. Dholakia, "Involvement-Response Models of Joint Effects," *Advances in Consumer Research,* vol. 25, ed. J. W. Alba and J. W. Hutchinson (Provo, UT: Association for Consumer Research, 1998), pp. 499–506.

74. T. H. Dodd, B. E. Pinkleton, and A. W. Gustafson, *Psychology & Marketing,* May 1996, pp. 291–304. See also J. R. McColl-Kennedy and R. E. Fetter Jr., "An Empirical Examination of the Involvement to External Search Relationship," *Journal of Services Marketing,* 15, no. 2 (2001), pp. 82–98.

75. G. R. Dowling and R. Staelin, "A Model of Perceived Risk and Intended Risk-Handling Activity," *Journal of Consumer Research,* June 1994, pp. 119–34. See also J. B. Smith and J. M. Bristor, "Uncertainty Orientation," *Psychology & Marketing,* November 1994, pp. 587–607.

76. A. Chaudhuri, "Product Class Effects on Perceived Risk," *International Journal of Research in Marketing,* May 1998, pp. 157–68; and K. Mitra, M. C. Reiss, and L. M. Capella, "An Examination of Perceived Risk, Informational Search, and Behavioral Intentions," *Journal of Services Marketing,* 13, no. 3 (1999), pp. 208–28.

77. See, e.g., M. W. H. Weenig and M. Maarleveld, "The Impact of Time Constraint on Information Search Strategies in Complex Choice Tasks," *Journal of Economic Psychology,* 23 (2002), pp. 689–702. For an exception, see C. J. Hill, "The Nature of Problem Recognition and Search in the Extended Health Care Decision," *Journal of Services Marketing,* 15, no. 6 (2001), pp. 454–79.

78. A. G. Abdul-Muhmin, "Contingent Decision Behavior," *Journal of Consumer Psychology,* 8, no. 1 (1999), pp. 91–111.

79. "L&M Lights Up Again," *Marketing and Media Decisions,* February 1984, p. 69.

80. L. L. Garber, "The Package Appearance in Choice," in *Advances in Consumer Research,* vol. 22, ed. F. R. Kardes and M. Sujan (Provo, UT: Association for Consumer Research, 1995), pp. 653–60.

81. K. Oser, "Snapple Effort Finds Women as They Browse," *Advertising Age,* May 3, 2004.

82. See, e.g., Erdem and Swait, "Brand Credibility, Brand Consideration, and Choice."

chapter

16 Alternative Evaluation and Selection

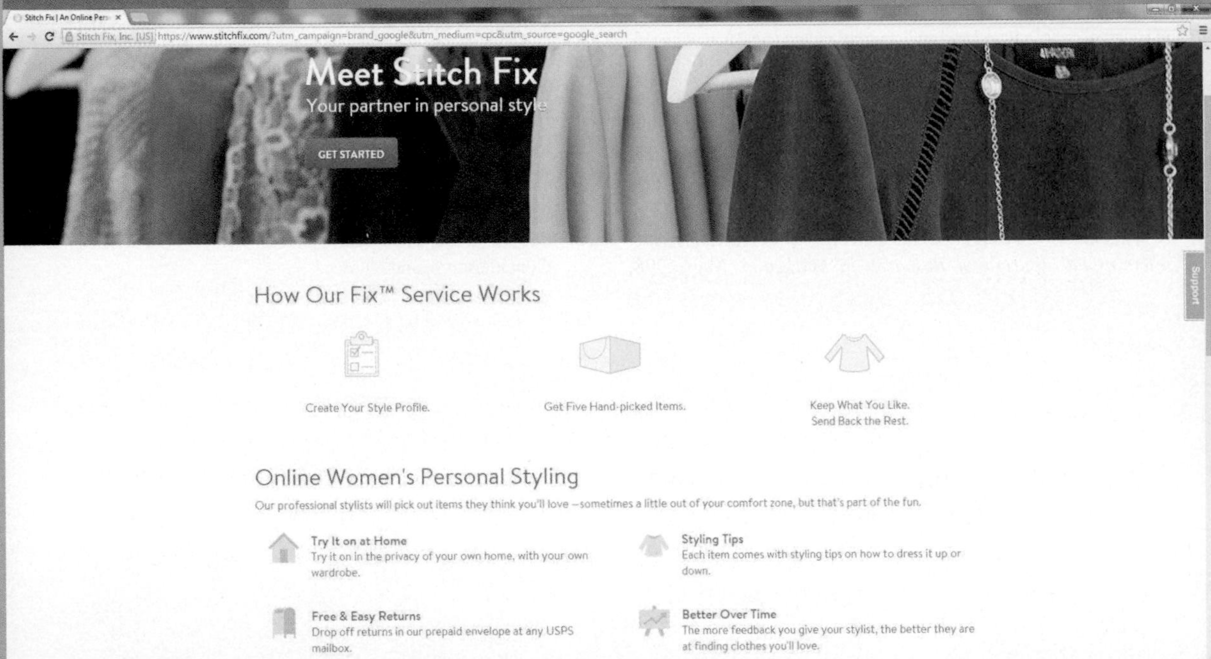

LEARNING OBJECTIVES

LO1 **Discuss how actual consumer choice often differs from rational choice theory.**

LO2 **Summarize the types of choice processes consumers engage in.**

LO3 **Explain evaluative criteria and their measurement.**

LO4 **Describe the role of evaluative criteria in consumer judgment and marketing strategy.**

LO5 **Summarize the five decision rules for attribute-based choice and their strategic relevance.**

One goal of consumer decision making is to make the best decision possible and another goal is to have (the freedom of) many alternatives from which to choose. These two goals clash when the consumer has too many alternatives and feels overwhelmed. This is choice overload. It is more likely to occur when the choice is one with which the consumer lacks expertise and familiarity, one that is important to the consumer, and one that offers numerous alternatives each possessing numerous, varied, non-overlapping features. A consumer faced with the decision of choosing the best health insurance from the list of dozens of alternatives on the government health exchange is more likely to experience choice overload and describe the situation as a nightmare, while the consumer who is choosing an ice cream from 32 flavors is likely to describe the situation as a fun experience. In choice overload situations, consumers are likely to make poorer choices and feel greater dissatisfaction with their choice, for which they blame themselves.[1]

Faced with choice overload, consumers may exhibit choice paralysis, choosing to make no decision, which, of course, can hurt consumers and marketers alike. The "decision" to not choose has been shown to be equally likely in relatively trivial decisions such as choosing not to buy a jar of jam when presented 30 alternatives, as it is with more important decisions such as (not) enrolling in 401(k) retirement plans. Fortunately, consumers can use heuristics to simplify decisions and thus avoid possible negative consequences of not choosing. These are rules of thumb or mental shortcuts, such as "buy the most popular brand" or "buy the lowest price," that consumers use to aid the decision process. Heuristics serve the practical purpose of helping consumers make "satisficing" choices that, while not "maximally best," are still good enough.

The proliferation of brands and line extensions both online and offline increases the likelihood of choice overload. Supermarkets, for example, carry something like 40,000 brands—15 types of Thomas' English Muffins, 27 versions of Crest toothpaste. However, instead of more, Costco, the giant warehouse retailer, has adopted a practice of carrying fewer selections. This practice may be as much a contributor to Costco's success as its discount pricing practice. Research shows that people buy more with limited offerings and are more satisfied with their choices.

Online retailers, facing no space barrier, may offer consumers so many alternatives that consumers suffer choice overload, a situation that may contribute to consumer abandonment of their merchandise-filled shopping carts.

E-tailers like Stitch Fix, Fancy, Quarterly, Birch Box, and Kiwi Crate are attempting to address the problem of choice overload by eliminating consumer choice altogether. Stitch Fix, a "personal stylist for women," begins the shopping process by having customers fill out a survey on their preferences. This helps the consumer think through what he or she wants. The data form the basis of an algorithm that generates recommendations for the customer. The shopper can also provide a link to her Pinterest, which provides more granular information that the shopper's personal stylist can use to hand-pick items. For the $20 styling fee, the shopper receives a five-item box or "fix" of clothing and accessories, each averaging $65. Items the shopper doesn't want can be returned at no cost to the shopper.

Choice overload is a reality and yet most consumers like to feel like they have adequate options to choose from. The task for marketers is to hit the sweet spot and offer enough, but not so much that it triggers choice overload. To that end, marketing strategies include product assortment optimization—determining an appropriate number of alternatives, with meaningful differentiation—and strategies to ease the consumer decision-making process—structuring the decision process and lessening perceived risk.

As the opening examples suggest, consumers make decisions in a variety of ways, with a variety of overarching goals, and the decisions they make range from simple to complex. The decision stage after problem recognition and information search is alternative evaluation and selection. Alternative selection is also referred to as consumer choice and in reality consumers are often evaluating alternatives for choice even during the search process. Consumer evaluation and choice of alternatives is the focus of this chapter.

CONSUMER CHOICE AND TYPES OF CHOICE PROCESS

LO1

Marketers sometimes assume that the process underlying consumer choice follows *rational choice theory.* Rational choice theory implicitly or explicitly assumes a number of things about consumer choice that often are not true. These assumptions are discussed next.

- ***Assumption 1:*** Consumers seek one optimal solution to a problem and choose on that basis.

  However, increasingly, marketers are coming to understand that these conditions don't always describe consumer choice. First, consumers don't always have the goal of finding the "optimal brand" for them. Instead, there are alternative metagoals, where a **metagoal** refers to *the general nature of the outcome being sought.* In addition to selecting the optimal alternative, metagoals include minimizing decision effort or maximizing the extent to which a decision is justifiable to others.[2] Consider nominal decision making from Chapter 14. Consumers who are low in purchase involvement may engage in little or no external search because they can recall from memory a brand that is at least satisfactory. In this case, consumers will usually choose this brand with no further search or decision effort, even though it may not be the optimal brand for them. This is because, given low purchase involvement, other goals come into play such as minimizing search and decision effort.
- ***Assumption 2:*** Consumers have the skill and motivation to find the optimal solution.

  However, marketers are increasingly aware that consumers often don't have the ability or the motivation to engage in the highly demanding task of finding the optimal solution. For example, consumers are subject to **bounded rationality**—*a limited* *capacity for processing information.*[3] Moreover, as suggested in Chapter 14, most decisions do not generate enough purchase involvement to motivate consumers to seek the optimal solution through extended decision making. As the opening example suggests, many websites in the United States are attempting to help consumers deal with the information overload that accompanies too many choices.

In the United Kingdom, choice overload was the motivation behind a site called Just Buy This One, which recommends only one brand within a product category and price range with three reasons why it's the best choice. According to a company executive:

> We knew that 25% of people are overwhelmed by the choice on price comparison sites and we decided to create something utterly simple and extremely useful. Online shopping used to be the simple solution, but it's gotten too crowded.[4]

- ***Assumption 3:*** The optimal solution does not change as a function of situational factors such as time pressure, task definition, or competitive context.

  However, marketers are increasingly aware that preferences can and do shift as a function of the situation (Chapter 13). For example, limited decision making is more likely when we are tired or hurried. In addition, when new brands are added to the competitive set, it can alter consumer choices, as we discuss later in the chapter.

Thus, as you read this chapter, it is important to keep in mind that consumer decisions (a) are often not rational in the sense of finding the optimal solution, (b) are not optimal due to the cognitive and time limits of consumers, and (c) are malleable in that they change based on the situation. In addition, it is important to keep in mind that consumer decisions are much more circular, emotional, and incomplete than our formal examination here might suggest.

Types of Consumer Choice Processes

Let's begin by examining the three general types of decision processes that consumers can engage in. You will notice that some are not even based on a comparison of brands and their features, which is often a major (and sometimes incorrect) assumption made by marketing managers. The three choice processes are affective choice, attitude-based choice, and attribute-based choice. While we describe them separately for simplicity, it is important to keep in mind that these are not mutually exclusive and combinations may be used in a single decision. First, let's look at three decision scenarios involving a digital camera: L02

Scenario 1 (Affective Choice). As a consumer shops at a local store, one camera catches her eye: she examines it, looking at the lines and overall look. She thinks the camera looks sleek, modern, and cool. She examines another camera but thinks it looks too serious and boring. After a few more minutes of contemplation about what a great impression she would make using the first camera to take pictures at parties and weddings, she decides to buy the first camera.

Scenario 2 (Attitude-Based Choice). The consumer remembers that her friend's Olympus Stylus worked well and looked "good"; her parents had a Kodak Easyshare that also worked well but was rather large and bulky; and her old Fujifilm FinePix had not performed as well as she had expected. At her local electronics store she sees that the Olympus and Kodak models are about the same price and decides to buy the Olympus Stylus.

Scenario 3 (Attribute-Based Choice). After consulting the Internet to determine what features she is most interested in, the consumer then goes to her local electronics store and compares the various brands on the features most important to her—namely, camera size, zoom, automatic features, and storage size. She mentally ranks each model on these attributes and her general impression of each model's quality. On the basis of these evaluations, she chooses the Olympus Stylus.

These three scenarios relate to different choice processes. The first scenario represents affective choice.[5] **Affective choice** tends to be more holistic in nature. The brand is not decomposed into distinct components, each of which is evaluated separately from the whole. The evaluation of such products is generally focused on the way they will make the user feel as they are used. The evaluation itself is often based exclusively or primarily on the immediate emotional response to the product or service.[6] Decisions based on affect use the "How do I feel about it" heuristic or decision rule.[7] Consumers imagine or picture using the product or service and evaluate the feeling that this use will produce.[8]

Consumer use of the affective choice process is affected by underlying purchase motives. Affective choice is most likely when the underlying motive is consummatory rather than instrumental. **Consummatory motives** *underlie behaviors that are intrinsically rewarding to the individual involved.* **Instrumental motives** *activate behaviors designed to achieve a second goal.* For example, the consumer in Scenario 1 is clearly motivated primarily by the emotional rewards involved in having and using a camera that makes her look trendy and fashionable (consummatory motive), whereas other consumers may be motivated by having a camera that takes high-quality pictures that can be enjoyed later (instrumental motive).[9] Illustration 16–1 shows ads appealing to each of these motives. How do the Huntsman Springs and Oil of Olay ads differ in motive appeals?

Marketers continue to learn more about affect-based decisions.[10] It is clear that such decisions require different strategies than the more cognitive decisions generally considered in marketing. For those decisions that are likely to be affective in nature (largely triggered by consummatory motives), marketers should design products and services that will provide the appropriate emotional responses.[11] They also should help consumers visualize how they will feel during and after the consumption experience.[12] This is particularly important for new brands or products and services. Consumers who have experience with a product or brand have a basis for imagining the affective response it will produce. Those who do not may incorrectly predict the feelings the experience will produce. For example, individuals imagining a

ILLUSTRATION 16-1

The Huntsman Springs ad on the left appeals to a consummatory motive by showing that the product or consumption is rewarding in and of itself. The Oil of Olay ad on the right appeals to an instrumental motive by showing that the product is a means to an end.

white-water rafting trip may conclude that it would produce feelings of terror rather than exhilaration. Illustration 16–2 shows an ad that helps consumers envision the positive experiences and accompanying feelings they would have if they owned the product.

ILLUSTRATION 16-2

This ad encourages an affect-based choice by encouraging consumers to imagine the pleasure they will derive from owning the product.

The second scenario represents attitude-based choice. **Attitude-based choice** *involves the use of general attitudes, summary impressions, intuitions, or heuristics; no attribute-by-attribute comparisons are made at the time of choice.*[13] It is important to note that many decisions, even for important products, appear to be attitude-based. Recall from Chapters 14 and 15 that most individuals collect very little product information from external sources immediately before a purchase. They are most likely making attitude-based decisions.

Motivation, information availability, and situational factors interact to determine the likelihood that attitude-based choices are made. As one would suspect, the lower the motivation to make an optimal decision, the more likely an attitude-based choice will be made. This relates to purchase involvement and nominal and limited decision making in Chapter 14, which are likely to be heavily skewed toward attitude-based choice. When information is difficult to find or access, or when consumers face time pressures, attitude-based choices are more likely. Notice how time pressures increase the perceived cost of search and make attitude-based choices from memory appear much more attractive.

The third scenario represents attribute-based choice. **Attribute-based choice** *requires the knowledge of specific attributes at the time the choice is made, and it involves attribute-by-attribute comparisons across brands.* This is a much more effortful and time-consuming process than the global comparisons made when affective and attitude-based choices are involved. It also tends to produce a more nearly optimal decision. Again, motivation, information availability, and situational factors interact to determine the likelihood that attitude-based choices are made.

Consumers with high purchase involvement or motivation are more likely to make attribute-based choices, which most resemble the extended decision-making approach we discussed in Chapter 14. More accessible brand and attribute information increases the likelihood that attribute-based choices are made. This can be used by marketers of brands that have important attribute-based advantages but that lack strong reputations or images in the target market. The approach would be to provide attribute-based comparisons in an easy-to-process format, such as a brand-by-attribute matrix. Such a matrix could be presented in ads, on packages, in point-of-purchase displays, on the brand's website, and so on. An appropriate comparison format and structure is critical to making the firm's brand the focal point of comparison.[14] This could be done by listing the brand first, perhaps in bold or colored type.

The ads in Illustration 16–3 show the differences between attribute-based and attitude-based choice strategies. The Viviscal ad on the left focuses on specific features of the brand and would be consistent with an attribute-based choice. The EXY Sharker Skateboard ad on the right focuses on the brand and an overall impression of the product and its users and would be consistent with an attitude-based choice.

ILLUSTRATION 16-3

The Viviscal ad on the left encourages attribute-based choice with primacy given to its key product features. Ads such as this EXY Sharker Skateboard ad on the right assume or encourage attitude-based choice by focusing on brand, overall performance, and image rather than specific product features.

It is important to note that these three processes are not always used in isolation. For example, affective or emotional criteria can be considered along with functional criteria. Sometimes consumers are more driven by emotions and end up choosing functionally inferior brands.[15] Such trade-offs between hedonic and utilitarian attributes are important for marketers to consider in developing products and promotional campaigns. In addition, sometimes affective and attitude-based processes can be used by consumers to establish or narrow their consideration sets. This type of *phased* decision making is common, and understanding the role of affect and attitudes in the formation of the evoked set is critical for marketers.

Given the nature, complexity, and importance of attribute-based choice to both consumers and marketers, the focus of the remainder of the chapter is on issues related to attribute-based choice. Figure 16–1 provides an overview of the stages of the attribute-based choice process.

LO3

EVALUATIVE CRITERIA

Attribute-based choices rely heavily on a comparison of brands on one or more attributes. These attributes are called evaluative criteria because they are the dimensions on which the brands are evaluated. **Evaluative criteria** are *the various dimensions, features, or benefits a consumer looks for in response to a specific problem.* While functional attributes are common, evaluative criteria can also be emotions (the pleasure associated with eating chocolate cake) and the reactions of important reference group members (for socially

Alternative Evaluation and Selection for Attribute-Based Choice FIGURE 16-1

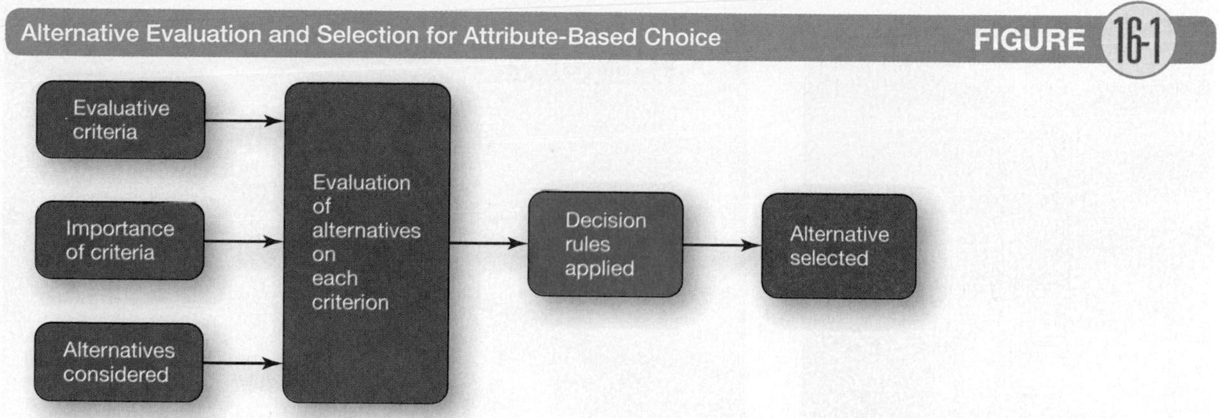

consumed products). Before purchasing a computer, you might be concerned with cost, speed, memory, operating system, display, and warranty. These would be your evaluative criteria. Someone else could approach the same purchase with an entirely different set of evaluative criteria.

Evaluative criteria are perceived and utilized by consumers in a number of ways including extremes (lower price or more miles per gallon is better), limits (it must not cost more than $100; it must get more than 25 miles per gallon), or ranges (any price between $85 and $99 is acceptable).[16] For new product categories, consumers must often first determine which levels of various criteria are desirable. For example, a consumer who buys a barbecue grill for the first time and has limited experience with grills may have to determine if he prefers gas to charcoal, domed or traditional shape, and so forth. After purchase and use, these preference levels become more firmly established and stable.[17]

Nature of Evaluative Criteria

Evaluative criteria are typically associated with desired benefits. Thus, consumers want fluoride (evaluative criteria) in their toothpaste to reduce cavities (benefit). It is often more persuasive for marketers to communicate brand benefits rather than (or in addition to) evaluative criteria because it is the benefits that consumers specifically desire. The ad in Illustration 16–4 focuses primarily on product benefits rather than technical features.

ILLUSTRATION 16-4

Consumers are generally interested in product features only in relation to the benefits those features provide. This ad emphasizes core benefits rather than the technical characteristics that generate those benefits.

Evaluative criteria can differ in type, number, and importance. The *type of evaluative criteria* a consumer uses in a decision varies from *tangible* cost and performance features to *intangible* factors such as style, taste, prestige, feelings generated, and brand image.[18] Illustration 16–5 shows how two similar products stress different types of evaluative criteria. The Blue Wilderness ad on the left

ILLUSTRATION 16-5

The Blue Wilderness and Purina ads are for the same product category but assume differing evaluative processes by consumers.

stresses tangible attributes and technical performance. The Purina ad on the right focuses more on intangible attributes and feelings.

For fairly simple products such as toothpaste, soap, or facial tissue, consumers use relatively few evaluative criteria. On the other hand, the purchase of an automobile, smartphone, or house may involve numerous criteria. Individual characteristics such as product familiarity and age and situational characteristics such as time pressure also affect the number of evaluative criteria considered.[19] For example, time pressure tends to reduce the number of attributes examined.[20]

The *importance* that consumers assign to each evaluative criterion is of great interest to marketers. Three consumers could use the same six evaluative criteria shown in the following table when considering a laptop computer. However, if the importance rank they assigned each criterion varied as shown, they would likely purchase different brands.

	Importance Rank for		
Criterion	**Consumer A**	**Consumer B**	**Consumer C**
Price	**1**	6	3
Processor	5	**1**	4
Display quality	3	3	**1**
Memory	6	**2**	5
Weight	4	4	**2**
After-sale support	**2**	5	6

Consumer A is concerned primarily with cost and support services. Consumer B wants computing speed and power (as represented by processor and memory). Consumer C is concerned primarily with ease of use (as represented by display and weight). If each of these three consumers represented a larger group of consumers, we would have three distinct market segments based on the importance assigned to the same criteria.

Evaluative criteria and their importance affect which brands consumers select. They also influence if and when a problem will be recognized. For example, consumers who attach more importance to automobile styling relative to cost buy new cars *more frequently* than do those with the opposite importance rankings.[21] Thus, marketers want to understand which criteria consumers use to evaluate their brands so they can develop and communicate appropriate brand features to the target market. Also, marketers sometimes want to change the evaluative criteria that consumers utilize in ways that benefit their brands.[22] Thus measuring evaluative criteria is an important marketing activity.

Measurement of Evaluative Criteria

Before a marketing manager or a public policy decision maker can develop a sound strategy to affect consumer decisions, he or she must determine

- Which evaluative criteria are used by the consumer.
- How the consumer perceives the various alternatives on each criterion.
- The relative importance of each criterion.

Therefore, it is often difficult to determine which criteria consumers are using in a particular brand-choice decision, particularly if emotions or feelings are involved. This is even more of a problem when trying to determine the relative importance they attach to each evaluative criterion.

Determination of Which Evaluative Criteria Are Used To determine which criteria are used by consumers in a specific product decision, the marketing researcher can use either direct or indirect methods of measurement.

Direct methods include asking consumers what criteria they use in a particular purchase or, in a focus group setting, noting what consumers say about products and their attributes. However, consumers sometimes will not or cannot verbalize their evaluative criteria for a product, particularly if emotions or feelings are involved. For example, Hanes Corporation suffered substantial losses ($30 million) on its L'erin cosmetics line when, *in response to consumer interviews,* it positioned it as a functional rather than a romantic or emotional product. Eventually, the brand was successfully repositioned as glamorous and exotic, although consumers did not *express* these as desired attributes.[23]

Thus, *indirect* measurement techniques such as **projective techniques** (Appendix A, Table A-1), which allow the respondent to indicate the criteria someone else might use, are often helpful. The "someone else" will likely be a *projection* of the respondent, of course—thus, the marketer can indirectly determine the evaluative criteria that would be used.

Perceptual mapping is another useful indirect technique for determining evaluative criteria. First, consumers judge the similarity of alternative brands. This generally involves having the consumer look at possible pairs of brands and indicate which pair is most similar, which is second most similar, and so forth until all pairs are ranked. These similarity judgments are processed via a computer to derive a perceptual map of the brands. No evaluative criteria are specified by the consumer. The consumer simply ranks the similarity between all pairs of alternatives, and a perceptual configuration is derived in which the consumer's still-unnamed evaluative criteria are the dimensions of the configuration.

For example, consider the perceptual map of beers shown in Figure 16–2. This configuration was derived from a consumer's evaluation of the relative similarity of these brands of beer. The horizontal axis is characterized by physical characteristics such as taste, calories, and fullness. The vertical axis is characterized by price, quality, and status. Naming each axis, and thus each evaluative criterion, is done using judgment. This procedure allows marketers to understand consumers' perceptions and the evaluative criteria they use to differentiate brands.

Perceptual Mapping of Beer Brand Perceptions

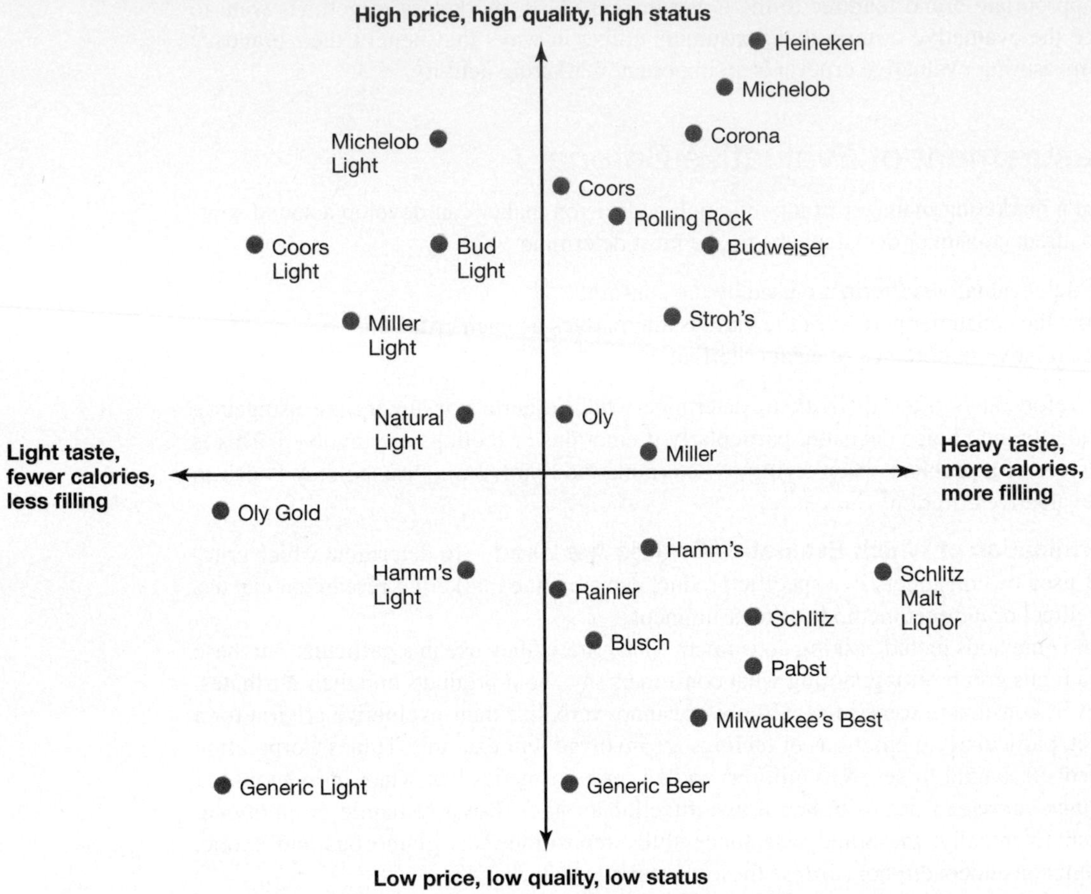

Determination of Consumers' Judgments of Brand Performance on Specific Evaluative Criteria A variety of methods are available for measuring consumers' judgments of brand performance on specific attributes. These include *rank ordering scales, semantic differential scales,* and *Likert scales* (see Appendix A and Appendix Table A-3). The semantic differential scale is probably the most widely used technique.

None of these techniques are very effective at measuring emotional responses to products or brands. Projective techniques can provide some insights. SAM, the graphical approach designed to tap more directly into the pleasure–arousal–dominance dimensions of emotions (see Chapter 11), is also a useful option.

Determination of the Relative Importance of Evaluative Criteria The importance assigned to evaluative criteria can be measured either by direct or by indirect methods. No matter which technique is used, the usage situation should be specified because attribute importance often changes with the situation. The *constant sum scale* is the most common method of direct measurement (see Chapter 11).

The most popular indirect measurement approach is **conjoint analysis.** In conjoint analysis, the consumer is presented with a set of products or product descriptions in which the evaluative criteria vary. For example, the consumer may be presented with the description of 24 different laptop computers that vary on four criteria. Two might be as follows:

Intel Core Duo 2.4 GHz	Intel Core Duo 2.0 GHz
Energy Star compliant (yes)	Energy Star compliant (no)
5.1 pounds	4 pounds
$1,250	$850

The consumer ranks all 24 such descriptions in terms of his or her preference for those combinations of features. Using these preference ranks, sophisticated computer programs derive the relative importance consumers assign to each level of each attribute tested (see Appendix A and Appendix Figure A-1 for details).

Conjoint analysis was used by Sunbeam in reformulating its food processor line for various segments. Sunbeam tested 12 different attributes: price, motor power, number of blades, bowl shape, and so forth. Various segments emerged *based on the relative importance of these attributes.* In order of importance, the key attributes for two segments were as follows. These results helped Sunbeam develop models specifically for each of these segments and that better met their needs on important evaluative criteria.

Cheap/Large Segment	Multispeed/Multiuse Segment
$49.99 price	$99.99 price
4-quart bowl	2-quart bowl
Two speeds	Seven speeds
Seven blades	Functions as blender and mixer
Heavy-duty motor	Cylindrical bowl
Cylindrical bowl	Pouring spout

INDIVIDUAL JUDGMENT AND EVALUATIVE CRITERIA

LO4

If you were buying a laptop computer, you would probably make direct comparisons across brands on features such as price, weight, and display clarity. These comparative judgments might not be completely accurate. For example, the display that is the easiest to read in a five-minute trial might not be the easiest to read over a two-hour work session. For other attributes, such as quality, you might not be able to make direct comparisons. Instead, you might rely on brand name or price to indicate quality. In addition, consumer perceptions of the importance of product features are influenced by various external factors. The accuracy of direct judgments, the use of one attribute to indicate performance on another (surrogate indicator), and variations in attribute importance are critical issues for marketers.

Accuracy of Individual Judgments

The average consumer is not adequately trained to judge the performance of competing brands on complex evaluative criteria such as quality or durability. For more straightforward criteria, however, most consumers can and do make such judgments. Prices generally can be judged and compared directly. However, even this can be complex. Is a six-pack of 12-ounce cans of Coca-Cola selling for $2.49 a better buy than two liters priced at $1.59 each? Consumer groups have pushed for unit pricing (pricing by common measurements such as cost per ounce) to make such comparisons simpler. The federal truth-in-lending law was passed to facilitate direct price comparisons among alternative lenders.

ILLUSTRATION 16-6

Marketers sometimes use price, warranty, brand, or country of origin as surrogate indicators of quality. The ad for Grana Padano Cheese uses country of origin as an indicator of quality.

The ability of an individual to distinguish between similar stimuli is called **sensory discrimination** (see Chapter 8). This could involve such variables as the sound of stereo systems, the taste of food products, or the clarity of display screens. The minimum amount that one brand can differ from another, with the difference still being noticed, is referred to as the *just noticeable difference (j.n.d.)*. As we saw in Chapter 8, this ability is not well developed in most consumers. In general, research indicates that *individuals typically do not notice relatively small differences between brands or changes in brand attributes.* In addition, the complexity of many products and services as well as the fact that some aspects of performance can be judged only after extensive use makes accurate brand comparisons difficult.[24]

The inability of consumers to accurately evaluate many products can result in inappropriate purchases (buying a lower-quality product at a higher price than necessary).[25] This is a major concern of regulatory agencies and consumer groups as well as for marketers of high-value brands.

Use of Surrogate Indicators

Consumers frequently use an observable attribute of a product to indicate the performance of the product on a less observable attribute.[26] For example, a consumer might infer that because a product has a relatively high price, it must also be of high quality. *An attribute used to stand for or indicate another attribute* is known as a **surrogate indicator.** As discussed in Chapter 8, consumers often use such factors as price, advertising intensity, warranties, brand, and country of origin as surrogate indicators of quality—what we termed quality signals. Illustration 16–6 shows an ad for Grana Padano Cheese. This ad is attempting to take advantage of a surrogate indicator of quality.

In general, surrogate indicators operate more strongly when consumers lack the expertise to make informed judgments on their own, when consumer motivation or interest in the decision is low, and when other quality-related information is lacking. Unfortunately, the relationship between surrogate indicators and functional measures of quality is often modest at best.[27] Obviously, when consumers rely on surrogates that have little relationship to actual quality, they are likely to make suboptimal decisions.

Surrogate indicators are based on consumers' beliefs that two features such as price level and quality level generally go together. Consumers also form beliefs that certain variables do not go together—such as *lightweight* and *strong; rich taste* and *low calories;* and *high fiber* and *high protein.*[28] Marketers attempting to promote the presence of two or more variables that many consumers believe to be mutually exclusive have a high risk of failure unless very convincing messages are used. Thus, it is important for marketers to fully understand consumers' beliefs about the feasible relationships of attributes related to their products.

The Relative Importance and Influence of Evaluative Criteria

The importance of evaluative criteria varies among individuals and also within the same individual over time. That is, although consumers often have a general sense of how important various criteria are, this can be influenced by a number of factors. These include the following:

- *Usage situation.* The situation in which a product or service is used (Chapter 13) can have important influences on the criteria used to make a choice. For example, speed of service and convenient location may be very important in selecting a restaurant over a lunch break but relatively unimportant when selecting a restaurant for a special occasion.[29]
- *Competitive context.* Generally speaking, the lower the variance across competing brands on a given evaluative criterion, the less influence it is likely to have in the decision process.[30] For example, you might think that the weight of a notebook computer is important. However, if all the brands you are considering weigh between 4 and 5 pounds, this attribute may suddenly become less of a factor in your decision.
- *Advertising effects.* Advertising can affect the importance of evaluative criteria in a number of ways. For example, an ad that increases attention and elaborative processing of an attribute can increase its perceived importance and/or influence in the decision.[31] As we saw in Chapters 8 and 9, contrast, prominence, and imagery are just a few of the tactics that can be used to enhance attention and elaboration.

Evaluative Criteria, Individual Judgments, and Marketing Strategy

Obviously, marketers must understand the evaluative criteria consumers use relative to their products and develop products that excel on those features. All aspects of the marketing communications mix must then communicate this excellence.

Marketers must also recognize and react to the ability of individuals to judge evaluative criteria, as well as to their tendency to use surrogate indicators. For example, most new consumer products are initially tested against competitors in blind tests. A **blind test** is one in which *the consumer is not aware of the product's brand name.* Such tests enable the marketer to evaluate the functional characteristics of the product and to determine if an advantage over a particular competitor has been obtained without the contaminating, or halo, effects of the brand name or the firm's reputation. *Can you see any drawbacks to only using blind tests in evaluating the market potential of products?*

Marketers also make direct use of surrogate indicators. Hyundai's 10-year, 100,000-mile warranty was a milestone in the industry when introduced over a decade ago. The goal was to overcome low-quality perceptions related to another surrogate—namely country of origin. That is, consumers in the United States were unsure of the quality of Korean-made automobiles at the time, and the warranty was designed to overcome this.

For image products such as fine wines, imported beers, and so forth, higher prices tend to signal higher quality. Therefore, although, for most products, higher prices lead to lower quantity demanded, for such image-based products, higher prices generally drive higher demand due to the quality that is inferred based on the higher price.

Brand names are also a strong surrogate for quality. Elmer's glue emphasized the well-established reputation of its brand in promoting its new super glue: ads for Elmer's

Wonder Bond said, "Stick with a name you can trust." Firms with a limited reputation can sometimes form *brand alliances* with a reputable firm and gain from the quality associated with the known brand. Thus, a new brand of ice cream that used a branded ingredient such as M&Ms would gain from M&Ms' quality image.[32] Country-of-origin themes such as "Made in America," "Italian Styling," or "German Engineering" are also common.

Marketers must also understand the factors that influence consumer perceptions of the importance of evaluative criteria. Understanding that attributes may be important but wield little influence on decisions because of similarity across competitors is a critical insight. It speaks to the need for marketers to examine critical *points of differentiation* on which the brand can be positioned. Advertising themes that emphasize specific usage occasions for which the brand is particularly appropriate can be effective, as can strategies such as imagery that draw attention to attributes on which the firm's brand excels.

DECISION RULES FOR ATTRIBUTE-BASED CHOICES

LO5 As we describe some of the choice rules consumers use to select among alternatives, remember that these rules are representations of imprecise and often nonconscious or low-effort mental processes. The following example is a good representation of a consumer using a complex choice rule (compensatory with one attribute weighted heavily):

> I really liked the Ford [minivan] a lot, but it had the back tailgate that lifted up instead of the doors that opened. I suspect that if that had been available we might have gone with the Ford instead because it was real close between the Ford and the GM. The lift gate in the back was the main difference, and we went with the General Motors because we liked the doors opening the way they did. I loved the way the Ford was designed on the inside. I loved the way it drove. I loved the way it felt and everything, but you are there manipulating all these kids and groceries and things and you have got to lift this thing, and it was very awkward. It was hard to lift, and if you are holding something you have got to steer all the kids back, or whack them in the head. So that was a big thing. You know it was a lot cheaper than the GM. It was between $1,000 and $2,000 less than General Motors, and because money was a factor, we did go ahead and actually at one point talk money with a [Ford] dealer. But we couldn't get the price difference down to where I was willing to deal with that tailgate is what it comes down to.[33]

Despite the fact that the choice rules we describe are not precise representations of consumer decisions, they do enhance our understanding of how consumers make decisions and provide guidance for marketing strategy.

Suppose you have six laptop computers in your evoked set and you have assessed them based on six evaluative criteria: price, weight, processor, battery life, after-sale support, and display quality. Further, suppose that each brand excels on one attribute but falls short on one or more of the remaining attributes, as shown in Table 16–1.

Which brand would you select? The answer would depend on the decision rule you utilize. Consumers commonly use five decision rules: conjunctive, disjunctive, elimination-by-aspects, lexicographic, and compensatory. More than one rule may be used in any given decision. The most common instance of this is using a relatively simple rule to reduce the number of alternatives considered and then to apply a more complex rule to choose among the remaining options.[34] An example would be eliminating from consideration all those apartments that are too far from campus or that rent for more than $700 per month (conjunctive decision rule). The choice from among the remaining apartments might involve carefully trading off among features such as convenience of location, price,

TABLE 16-1 Performance Levels on the Evaluative Criteria for Six Laptop Computers

	Consumer Perceptions*					
Evaluative Criteria	Acer	HP	Compaq	Dell	Lenovo	Toshiba
Price	5	3	3	4	2	1
Weight	3	4	5	4	3	4
Processor	5	5	5	2	5	5
Battery-life	1	3	1	3	1	5
After-sale support	3	3	4	3	5	3
Display quality	3	3	3	5	3	3

*1 = Very poor; 5 = Very good.

presence of a pool, and size of rooms (compensatory rule). Note that some online shopping services such as Price Grabber complete the first phase in this process by filtering out all brands that don't meet the consumer's criteria.

The first four rules we will describe are *noncompensatory* rules. This means that a high level of one attribute cannot offset a low level of another. In the apartment example, the consumer would not consider an apartment that was right next to campus if it costs more than $700 per month. An excellent location could not compensate for an inappropriate price. In contrast, the last rule we will describe is a *compensatory* rule in which consumers average across attribute levels. This allows a high level of one value to offset a low value of another.

Finally, note that the conjunctive and disjunctive decision rules may produce a set of acceptable alternatives, whereas the remaining rules generally produce a single "best" alternative.

Conjunctive Decision Rule

The **conjunctive decision rule** establishes minimum required performance standards for each evaluative criterion and selects the first or all brands that meet or exceed these minimum standards. Thus, in making the decision on the computer, you would say, "I'll consider all (or I'll buy the first) brands that are acceptable on the attributes I think are important." For example, assume that the following represent your minimum standards:

Price	3
Weight	4
Processor	3
Battery life	1
After-sale support	2
Display quality	3

Any brand of computer falling below any of these minimum standards (cutoff points) would be eliminated from further consideration. Referring to Table 16–1, we can see that four computers are eliminated—Lenovo, Acer, Dell, and Toshiba. These are the computers that failed to meet all the minimum standards. Under these circumstances, the two remaining brands may be equally satisfying. Or you might use another decision rule to select a single brand from these two alternatives.

ILLUSTRATION 16-7

This ad tries to assure consumers that its brand has every feature they might need. This is consistent with consumers using a conjunctive decision rule.

Because individuals have limited ability to process information, the conjunctive rule is frequently used to reduce the size of the information processing task to some manageable level. This is often done in the purchase of such products as homes, computers, and bicycles; in the rental of apartments; or in the selection of vacation options. A conjunctive rule is used to eliminate alternatives that are out of a consumer's price range, are outside the location preferred, or do not offer other desired features. After eliminating those alternatives not providing these features, the consumer may use another decision rule to make a brand choice among those remaining alternatives that satisfy these minimum standards.

The conjunctive decision rule is commonly used in many low-involvement purchases as well. In such a purchase, the consumer generally evaluates a set of brands one at a time and selects the first brand that meets all the minimum requirements.

If the conjunctive decision rule is used by a target market, it is critical to meet or surpass the consumers' minimum requirement on each criterion. For low-involvement purchases, consumers often purchase the first brand that does so. For such products, extensive distribution and dominant shelf space are important. It is also necessary to understand how consumers "break ties" if the first satisfactory option is not chosen. The ad in Illustration 16–7 tries to assure consumers that its brand has every feature they might need.

Disjunctive Decision Rule

The **disjunctive decision rule** *establishes a minimum level of performance for each important attribute* (often a fairly high level, which sets the performance standard very high and makes it hard for a brand to attain). All brands that meet or exceed the performance level for *any* key attribute are considered acceptable. Using this rule, you would say, "I'll consider all (or buy the first) brands that perform really well on any attribute I consider important." Assume that you are using a disjunctive decision rule and the attribute cutoff points shown below:

Price	5
Weight	5
Processor	Not critical
Battery life	Not critical
After-sale support	Not critical
Display quality	5

You would find Acer (price), Compaq (weight), and Dell (display quality) to warrant further consideration (see Table 16–1). As with the conjunctive decision rule, you might purchase the first brand you find acceptable, use another decision rule to choose among the three, or add additional criteria to your list.

When the disjunctive decision rule is used by a target market, it is critical to meet or surpass the consumers' requirements on at least one of the key criteria. This should be emphasized in advertising messages and on the product package. Because consumers often purchase the first brand that meets or exceeds one of the requirements, extensive distribution and dominant shelf space are important. Again, it is also necessary to understand how consumers break ties if the first satisfactory option is not chosen. Illustration 16–8 stresses one important attribute and would be appropriate for consumers who placed a high importance on this attribute and used a disjunctive decision rule.

Elimination-by-Aspects Decision Rule

The **elimination-by-aspects decision rule** requires the consumer to rank the evaluative criteria in terms of their importance and to establish a cutoff point for each criterion. All brands are first considered on the most important criterion. Those that do not meet or exceed the cutoff point are dropped (eliminated) from further consideration. If more than one brand remains in the set after this first elimination phase, the process is repeated on those brands for the second most important criterion. This continues until only one brand remains. Thus, the consumer's logic is, "I want to buy the brand that has a high level of an important attribute that other brands do not have."

Consider the rank order and cutoff points shown below. What would you choose using the elimination-by-aspects rule?

	Rank	Cutoff Point
Price	1	3
Weight	2	4
Display quality	3	4
Processor	4	3
After-sale support	5	3
Battery life	6	3

Price would eliminate Lenovo and Toshiba (see Table 16–1). Of those remaining, Compaq, HP, and Dell meet or exceed the weight hurdle (Acer is eliminated). Notice that Toshiba also meets the minimum weight requirement but would not be considered because it had been eliminated in the initial consideration of price. Only Dell meets or exceeds the third requirement, display quality.

ILLUSTRATION 16-8

The disjunctive decision rule selects products that meet or exceed high standards on any important attribute.

Using the elimination-by-aspects rule, you end up with a choice that has all the desired features of all the other alternatives, plus one more.

For a target market using the elimination-by-aspects rule, it is critical to meet or surpass the consumers' requirements on one more (in order) of the criteria used than the competition. This competitive superiority should be emphasized in advertising messages and on the product package. Firms can also attempt to alter the relative importance that consumers assign to the evaluative criteria. The ad in Illustration 16–9 is consistent with this rule. It indicates that the brand has desirable features other competitors do not have.

Lexicographic Decision Rule

The **lexicographic decision rule** *requires the consumer to rank the criteria in order of importance.* The consumer then selects the brand that performs *best* on the most important attribute. If two or more brands tie on this attribute, they are evaluated on the second most important attribute. This continues through the attributes until one brand outperforms the others. The consumer's thinking is something like this: "I want to get the brand that does best on the attribute of most importance to me. If there is a tie, I'll break it by choosing the one that does best on my second most important criterion."

The lexicographic decision rule is similar to the elimination-by-aspects rule. The difference is that the lexicographic rule seeks maximum performance at each stage, whereas the elimination-by-aspects seeks satisfactory performance at each stage. Thus, using the lexicographic rule and the data from the elimination-by-aspects example above would result in the selection of Acer because it has the best performance on the most important attribute.

ILLUSTRATION 16-9

Elimination-by-aspects choices seek a brand that has a high level of an attribute that other brands do not have.

Had Acer been rated a 4 on price, it would be tied with Dell. Then, Dell would be chosen based on its superior weight rating.

When this rule is being used by a target market, the firm should try to be superior to the competition on *the* key attribute. This competitive superiority should be emphasized in advertising. It is essential that the product at least equal the performance of all other competitors on the most important criterion. Outstanding performance on lesser criteria will not matter if a competitor is superior on the most important attribute. If a competitive advantage is not possible on the most important feature, attention should be shifted to the second most important (assuming equal performance on the most important one). If it is not possible to meet or beat the competition on the key attribute, the firm must attempt to make another attribute more important.

The Tostitos ad shown in Illustration 16–10 emphasizes one key feature, presumably the most important to its target market. To the extent that its customers use a lexicographic rule, this ad should be effective in driving choice of this brand.

Compensatory Decision Rule

The four previous rules are *noncompensatory* decision rules because very good performance on one evaluative criterion cannot compensate for poor performance on another evaluative criterion. On occasion, consumers may wish to average out some very good features with some less attractive features of a product in determining overall brand preference. That appears to be the case with the new minipackage craze being used by companies such as Frito-Lay, Nabisco, and Keebler. Some consumers have complained that the prices are high on a per-serving basis. Frito-Lay and others are counting on the fact that the

ILLUSTRATION 16-10

Consumers using a lexicographic decision rule select the brand or service that performs best on their most important attribute. The Tostitos ad emphasizes it is made with real cheese.

convenience and calorie-control elements of their new 100-calorie packets will offset price in the minds of their target consumer. That is, they assume the target market will use a compensatory decision rule for this product. It appears this is the case, as explained by one customer who balked at the notion of buying in bulk and then measuring out 100-calorie servings into baggies:

> If you want to mess with those baggies, that's fine. But for those of us in the real world, we'll take the 100 cal packs. Sure, we might pay a few more pennies per ounce, but we also can't sneak any extra in while refilling.[35]

The **compensatory decision rule** states that *the brand that rates highest on the sum of the consumer's judgments of the relevant evaluative criteria will be chosen.* This can be illustrated as

$$R_b = \sum_{i=1}^{n} W_i B_{ib}$$

where

R_b = overall rating of brand b

W_i = importance or weight attached to evaluative criterion i

B_{ib} = evaluation of brand b on evaluative criterion i

n = number of evaluative criteria considered relevant

This is the same as the multiattribute attitude model described in Chapter 11. If you used the relative importance scores shown below, which brand would you choose using the compensatory rule?

	Importance Score
Price	30
Weight	25
Processor	10
Battery life	05
After-sale support	10
Display quality	20
Total	100

Using this rule, you would choose Dell because it has the highest preference (see Table 16–1). The calculations for Dell are as follows:

$$R_{\text{Dell}} = 30(4) + 25(4) + 10(2) + 5(3) + 10(3) + 20(5)$$
$$= 120 + 100 + 20 + 15 + 30 + 100$$
$$= 385$$

Products and services targeting consumers likely to use a compensatory rule can offset low performance on some features with relatively high performance on others. However, it is important to have a performance level at or near the competition's on the more important features because they receive more weight in the decision than do other attributes. Recall the description of the minivan purchase from the beginning of this section. This customer preferred most of the features of the Ford but bought the GM because Ford was very weak on one key attribute. However, the consumer did express a willingness to change the decision had the price differential been greater. Thus, for compensatory decisions, the total mix of the relevant attributes must be considered to be superior to those of the competition.

The compensatory rule tends to be the most time-consuming and mentally taxing. Also, consumers often find it difficult to consider more than a few attributes at a time in the trade-off process. In addition, as competitors enter the market, they can change the attractiveness of existing alternatives. This situational effect is discussed in Consumer Insight 16–1.

Summary of Decision Rules

As shown below, each decision rule yields a somewhat different choice. Therefore, marketers must understand which decision rules are being used by target consumers in order to position a product within this decision framework.

Decision Rule	Brand Choice
Conjunctive	HP, Compaq
Disjunctive	Dell, Compaq, Acer
Elimination-by-aspects	Dell
Lexicographic	Acer
Compensatory	Dell

CONSUMER INSIGHT 16-1

Situational Influences on Consumer Choice

Rational choice theory suggests that consumer choices and preferences should be independent of the context. As a simple example, it is assumed that consumers will evaluate a $5 discount the same way regardless of context. However, this is not the case. Consumers tend to perceive the value of the $5 discount as higher when it is on a product originally priced at $10 and lower on a product originally priced at $100. The reason goes back to Chapter 8 and relative preferences. Consumers appear to evaluate the $5 savings *in the context of* or *relative to* the original price of the product.

In a similar way, consumers are affected by the competitive context in which they make choices, or what we referred to in Chapter 13 as the purchase situation. There are numerous context effects on consumer choice. Here we discuss the compromise effect.[36] We begin with Choice Set 1 (left graph), in which there are two apartments (A and B) evaluated on two attributes (distance from campus in miles and quality on a 1–100 scale where 100 is the best). As the graph on the left shows, option A is farther from campus (a negative) but of higher quality (a positive), whereas option B is nearer to campus (a positive) but of lower quality (a negative). Choosing between these apartments involves a *compensatory choice process* in which distance and quality must be traded off against each other. As configured here, the apartments split the market equally. That is, 50 percent of the students chose option A (presumably weighting quality more heavily) and 50 percent chose option B (presumably weighting distance more heavily).

Now consider Choice Set 2 (right graph). In this context, there is a third apartment that consumers are aware of but that is not currently available. It is closer than A or B in terms of distance (a positive) but poorer than A or B in terms of quality (a negative). Rational choice theory assumes that if an option such as C is included, consumers should still prefer the brands the same way as they did previously. Particularly because option C is not even available, rational choice theory would suggest that options A and B would hold steady at 50 percent of the market each. However, this is not what happens. Instead, adding option C, even though not available for rent, increases B's share up to 66 percent!

This is called the compromise effect because adding option C made option B the compromise solution. It is a compromise between the two extremes of A (farthest away, best quality) and C (nearest, worst quality). Consumers prefer compromise options and find them easy to justify (a metagoal). The compromise effect seems

Research clearly indicates that people do use these decision rules.[37] Low-involvement purchases generally involve relatively simple decision rules (conjunctive, disjunctive, elimination-by-aspects, or lexicographic) because consumers will attempt to minimize the mental cost of such decisions.[38] High-involvement decisions and purchases involving considerable perceived risk tend to increase evaluation efforts and often may involve not only more complex rules (compensatory) but stages of decision making, with different attributes being evaluated using different rules at each stage.[39] Of course, individual, product, and situational characteristics also influence the type of decision rule used.[40]

A marketing manager must first determine which rule or combination of rules the target consumers will most likely use in a particular purchase situation and then develop the appropriate marketing strategy.

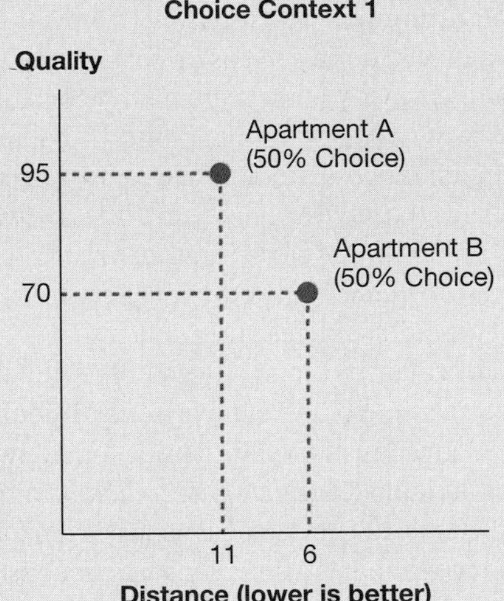

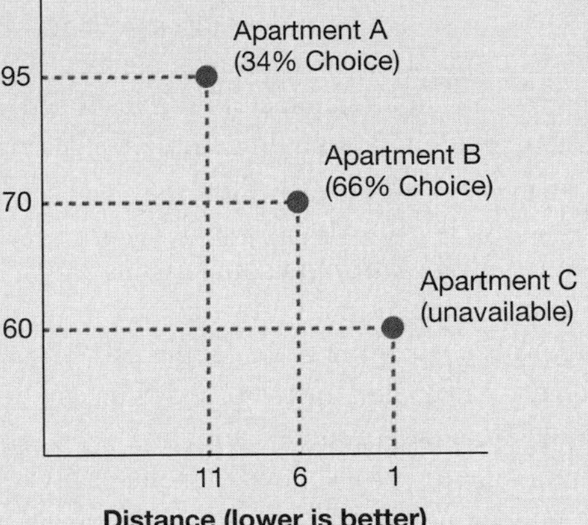

strongest when the compromise brand is the more familiar brand in the set.

The compromise effect has important implications for marketers. Real estate agents who want to sell a particular property might first show their clients an unavailable property that makes their available property seem like the compromise option to increase the chances their client will purchase it. For retailers, because consumers often search and evaluate alternatives online and then go to a physical store to purchase the selected brand, an "online only" option (option C) could be created to make their in-store options seem like compromise options to increase their choice share.

Critical Thinking Questions

1. Why does the compromise effect contradict rational choice theory?
2. Beyond being easy to justify, can you think of other reasons why consumers prefer compromise options?
3. Do you see any ethical issues related to strategies designed to position brands as compromise alternatives? Explain.

SUMMARY

SMARTBOOK™

LO1: Discuss how actual consumer choice often differs from rational choice theory

Rational choice theory assumes that (1) consumers seek one optimal solution to a problem and choose on that basis, (2) consumers have the skill and motivation to find the optimal solution, and (3) the optimal choice does not change as a function of the situation. However, all of these assumptions have been shown to be incorrect for at least some consumer decisions. Reasons include that consumers have alternative *metagoals,* consumers are subject to *bounded rationality,* and situations actually influence consumer perceptions of the optimal choice.

LO2: Summarize the types of choice processes consumers engage in

Affective choice tends to be more holistic in nature. The brand is not decomposed into distinct components, each of which is evaluated separately from the whole. Decisions based on affect use the "How do I feel about it" heuristic or decision rule and tend to occur in reponse to *consummatory motives.*

Attitude-based choice involves the use of general attitudes, summary impressions, intuitions, or heuristics; no attribute-by-attribute comparisons are made at the time of choice. Lower purchase involvement, scarce information, and certain situational factors such as time pressure increase the likelihood of attitude-based choice.

Attribute-based choice requires the knowledge of specific attributes at the time the choice is made, and it involves attribute-by-attribute comparisons across brands. This is a much more effortful and time-consuming process than the global comparisons made when affective and attitude-based choices are involved. It also tends to produce a more nearly optimal decision. Higher purchase involvement, easily accessible brand-attribute information, and situational factors such as lower time pressure increase the likelihood of attribute-based choice.

LO3: Explain evaluative criteria and their measurement

Evaluative criteria are the various features or benefits a consumer looks for in response to a specific problem. They are the performance levels or characteristics consumers use to compare different brands in view of their particular consumption problem.

The measurement of (1) which evaluative criteria are used by the consumer, (2) how the consumer perceives the various alternatives on each criterion, and (3) the relative importance of each criterion is a critical first step in utilizing evaluative criteria to develop marketing strategy. The measurement task is not easy, although a number of techniques are available including *perceptual mapping,* the *constant-sum scale,* and *conjoint analysis.*

LO4: Describe the role of evaluative criteria in consumer judgment and marketing strategy

The ability of an individual to distinguish between similar stimuli is called *sensory discrimination.* Some evaluative criteria such as price, size, and color can be judged easily and accurately by consumers. Other criteria, such as quality, durability, and health benefits, are much more difficult to judge. In general, research indicates that *individuals typically do not notice relatively small differences between brands or changes in brand attributes.* In addition, the complexity of many products and services and the fact that some aspects of performance can be judged only after extensive use make accurate brand comparisons difficult. In such cases, consumers often use price, brand name, or some other variable as a *surrogate indicator* of quality. Marketers can use surrogate cues as a means to affect consumer choice in situations where consumers find it difficult to make accurate assessments of alternatives. Marketers can also attempt to influence the relative importance of attributes in such a way as to favor their brands through advertising as well as position in regards to specific usage occasions.

LO5: Summarize the five decision rules for attribute-based choice and their strategic relevance

When consumers judge alternative brands on several evaluative criteria, they must have some method to select one brand from the various choices. Decision rules serve this function. A decision rule specifies how a consumer compares two or more brands. Five commonly used decision rules are *disjunctive, conjunctive, lexicographic, elimination-by-aspects,* and *compensatory.* The decision rules work best with functional products and cognitive decisions. Marketing managers must be aware of the decision rule(s) used by the target market because different decision rules require different marketing strategies.

KEY TERMS

Affective choice 554
Attitude-based choice 555
Attribute-based choice 555
Blind tests 563
Bounded rationality 552
Compensatory decision rule 570
Conjoint analysis 560
Conjunctive decision rule 565
Consummatory motives 554
Disjunctive decision rule 566
Elimination-by-aspects decision rule 567
Evaluative criteria 556
Instrumental motives 554
Lexicographic decision rule 568
Metagoal 552
Perceptual mapping 559
Projective techniques 559
Sensory discrimination 562
Surrogate indicator 562

REVIEW QUESTIONS

1. What is *rational choice* theory?
2. What is meant by *bounded rationality*?
3. What is a *metagoal*?
4. What are three common metagoals for consumer decisions?
5. What is *affective choice,* and when is it most likely to occur?
6. What is the difference between *consummatory motives* and *instrumental motives*?
7. How does *attribute-based choice* differ from *attitude-based choice*? When is each most likely?
8. What are *evaluative criteria,* and on what characteristics can they vary?
9. How can you determine which evaluative criteria consumers use?
10. What methods are available for measuring consumers' judgments of brand performance on specific attributes?
11. How can the importance assigned to evaluative criteria be assessed?
12. What is *sensory discrimination,* and what role does it play in the evaluation of products? What is meant by a *just noticeable difference*?
13. What are *surrogate indicators*? How are they used in the consumer evaluation process?
14. What factors influence the *importance* of evaluative criteria?
15. What is the *conjunctive decision rule*?
16. What is the *disjunctive decision rule*?
17. What is the *elimination-by-aspects decision rule*?
18. What is the *lexicographic decision rule*?
19. What is the *compensatory decision rule*?
20. How can knowledge of consumers' evaluative criteria and criteria importance be used in developing marketing strategy?
21. How can knowledge of the decision rules consumers might use in a certain purchase assist a firm in developing marketing strategy?

DISCUSSION QUESTIONS

22. Respond to the questions in Consumer Insight 16–1.
23. Would you use an attribute-based or an attitude-based decision approach to purchasing (or renting or giving to) the following? Which, if any, situational factors would change your approach?
    a. Adopting a pet from a shelter
    b. A movie
    c. A digital reader
    d. A BBQ grill
    e. A personal trainer
    f. Athletic shoes
    g. A new shampoo
    h. An apartment
    i. A smartphone
    j. Habitat for Humanity
24. Repeat Question 23 but speculate on how your instructor would answer. In what ways might his or her answer differ from yours? Why?
25. For which, if any, of the options in Question 23 would you make an affective decision? What role would situational factors play?
26. What metagoals might you have, and what would be their relative importance to you, in purchasing (or renting or giving to) the options in Question 23?
27. List the evaluative criteria and the importance of each that you would use in purchasing (or renting or giving to) the options in Question 23. Would situational factors change the criteria? The importance weights? Why?
28. Repeat Question 27 but speculate on how your instructor would answer. In what ways might his or her answer differ from yours? Why?
29. Describe a purchase decision for which you used affective choice, one for which you used attitude-based choice, and one for which you used attribute-based choice. Why did the type of decision process you used vary?
30. Identify five products for which surrogate indicators may be used as evaluative criteria in a brand choice decision. Why are the indictors used, and how might a firm enhance their use (i.e., strengthen their importance)?

31. The table below represents a particular consumer's evaluative criteria, criteria importance, acceptable level of performance, and judgments of performance with respect to several brands of mopeds. Discuss the brand choice this consumer would make when using the lexicographic, compensatory, and conjunctive decision rules.

Evaluative Criteria	Criteria Importance	Minimum Acceptable Performance	Alternative Brands					
			Motron	Vespa	Cimatti	Garelli	Puch	Motobecane
Price	30	4	2	4	2	4	2	4
Horsepower	15	3	4	2	5	5	4	5
Weight	5	2	3	3	3	3	3	3
Gas economy	35	3	4	4	3	2	4	5
Color selection	10	3	4	4	3	2	5	2
Frame	5	2	4	2	3	3	3	3

Note: 1 = Very poor; 2 = Poor; 3 = Fair; 4 = Good; and 5 = Very good.

32. Describe the decision rule(s) you used or would use in buying (or renting or giving to) the options listed in Question 23. Would you use different rules in different situations? Which ones? Why? Would any of these involve an affective choice?
33. Describe your last two major and your last two minor purchases. What role did emotions or feelings play? How did they differ? What evaluative criteria and decision rules did you use for each? Why?
34. Discuss surrogate indicators that could be used to evaluate the perceived quality of the products or activities listed in Question 23.

APPLICATION ACTIVITIES

35. Present 10 students with the choice set from the left panel of Consumer Insight 16–1 and present a different set of 10 students with the choice set from the right panel. Do you observe the compromise effect (choice share of option B goes up with the addition of the nonavailable option C)? Have the students who chose the compromise alternative explain their choice—what reasons do they provide?
36. Conduct an extensive interview with two students who recently made a major purchase. Have them describe the process they went through. Report your results. If each represented a market segment, what are the strategy implications?
37. Develop a list of evaluative criteria that students might use in evaluating alternative apartments they might rent. After listing these criteria, go to the local newspaper or student newspaper, select several apartments, and list them in a table similar to the one in Question 31. Then have five other students evaluate this information and have each indicate the apartment he or she would rent if given only those alternatives. Next, ask them to express the importance they attach to each evaluative criterion, using a 100-point constant sum scale. Finally, provide them with a series of statements that describe different decision rules and ask them to indicate the one that best describes the way they made their choice. Calculate the choice they should have made given their importance ratings and stated decision rules. Have them explain any inconsistent choices. Report your results.
38. Develop a short questionnaire to elicit the evaluative criteria consumers might use in selecting the following. Also, have each respondent indicate the relative importance he or she attaches to each of the evaluative criteria. Then, working with several other students, combine your information and develop a segmentation strategy based on consumer evaluative criteria and criteria importance. Finally, develop an advertisement for each market segment to indicate that their needs would be served by your brand.
    a. Wrist watch
    b. Running shoes

c. Movie
d. Fast-food restaurant
e. Credit card
f. Charity
g. Home theatre system
h. Health club

39. Set up a taste test experiment to determine if volunteer taste testers can perceive a just noticeable difference between three different brands of the following. To set up the experiment, store each test brand in a separate but identical container and label the containers *L, M,* and *N.* Provide volunteer taste testers with an adequate opportunity to evaluate each brand before asking them to state their identification of the actual brands represented as *L, M,* and *N.* Evaluate the results and discuss the marketing implications of these results.
    a. Colas
    b. Diet colas
    c. Lemon-lime drinks
    d. Carbonated waters
    e. Chips
    f. Orange juices

40. For a product considered high in social status, develop a questionnaire that measures the evaluative criteria of that product, using both a *direct* and an *indirect* method of measurement. Compare the results and discuss their similarities and differences and which evaluative criteria are most likely to be used in brand choice.

41. Find and copy or describe an ad that uses a surrogate indicator. Is it effective? Why? Why do you think the firm uses this approach?

42. Find and copy or describe an ad that attempts to change the importance consumers assign to product class evaluative criteria. Is it effective? Why? Why do you think the firm uses this approach?

43. Find and copy or describe two ads that are based on affective choice. Why do you think the firm uses this approach? Are the ads effective? Why?

44. Interview a salesperson for one of the following products. Ascertain the evaluative criteria, importance weights, decision rules, and surrogate indicators that he or she believes consumers use when purchasing this product. What marketing implications are suggested if their beliefs are accurate for large segments?
    a. Luxury cars
    b. Kitchen furniture
    c. Air purification systems
    d. Cosmetics
    e. Ski clothes
    f. Fine art

REFERENCES

1. This chapter opener is based on A. M. Tybout and B. J. Calder, eds., *Kellogg on Marketing,* 2nd ed. (New York: John Wiley & Sons, 2010), pp. 351–52; S. S. Iyengar and M. R. Lepper, "When Choice Is Demotivating: Can One Desire Too Much of a Good Thing?," *Journal of Personality and Social Psychology,* 2000, pp. 995–1006; R. H. Thaler and C. R. Sustein, *Nudge: Improving Decisions about Health, Wealth, and Happiness* (New Haven: Yale University Press, 2008), pp. 109–10; P. M. Todd and G. Gigerenzer, "Simple Heuristics That Make Us Smart," *Behavioral and Brain Sciences,* 2000, pp. 727–41; A. E. Weiss, "Keep It Simple: Avoid Giving Your Customers Decision Overload," *The Guardian,* March 13, 2014, www.theguardian.com/small-business-network/2014/mar/13/avoid-giving-customers-decision-overload, accessed August 29, 2014; "Supermarket Choice Overload: Consumer Reports," *Local SYR,* February 4, 2014, www.localsyr.com/story/d/story/supermarket-choice-overload-consumer-reports/25371/xybHtf6gOEeL5YJD12lpJA, accessed August 29, 2014; M. Little, "Costco's Strategy for Avoiding the Bullwhip," blog post on *Supply Chain Management,* September 10, 2013, http://cmuscm.blogspot.com/2013/09/costcos-strategy-for-avoiding-bullwhip.html, accessed August 29, 2014; P. Boatwright and J. C. Nunes, "Reducing Assortment: An Attribute-Based Approach," *Journal of Marketing,* July 2001, pp. 50–63; N. LaPorte, "The Anti-Zappos Subscription Shopping Finds Its Niche," *Fast Company,* March 2014, pp. 44, 46; and A. Chernev and R. Hamilton, "Assortment Size and Option Attractiveness in Consumer Choice Among Retailers," *Journal of Marketing Research,* June 2009, pp. 410–20.
2. See, for example, J. R. Bettman, M. F. Luce, and J. W. Payne, "Constructive Consumer Choice Processes," *Journal of Consumer Research,* December 1998, pp. 187–217; C. L. Brown and G. S. Carpenter, "Why Is the Trivial Important?," *Journal of Consumer Research,* March 2000, pp. 372–85; J. Swait and W. Adamowicz, "The Influence of Task Complexity on Consumer Choice," *Journal of Consumer Research,* June 2001, pp. 135–48; and M. Heitmann, D. R. Lehmann, and A. Herrmann, "Choice Goal Attainment and Decision and Consumption Satisfaction," *Journal of Marketing Research,* May 2007, pp. 234–50. See also O. Amir and D. Ariely, "Decisions by Rules," *Journal of Marketing Research,* February 2007, pp. 142–52.

3. For a discussion and related research, see G. A. Haynes, "Testing Boundaries of the Choice Overload Phenomenon," *Psychology and Marketing,* March 2009, pp. 204–12.

4. E. Hall, "Overwhelmed U.K. Online Shoppers Can Justbuythisone," *Advertising Age,* December 16, 2010.

5. B. Mittal, "A Study of the Concept of Affective Choice Mode for Consumer Decisions," in *Advances in Consumer Research,* vol. 21, ed. C. T. Allen and D. R. John (Provo, UT: Association for Consumer Research, 1994), p. 256.

6. J. F. Durgee and G. C. O'Connor, "Why Some Products 'Just Feel Right,'" in *Advances in Consumer Research,* vol. 22, ed. F. R. Kardes and M. Sujan (Provo, UT: Association for Consumer Research, 1995), p. 652.

7. See M. T. Pham et al., "Affect Monitoring and the Primacy of Feelings in Judgment," *Journal of Consumer Research,* September 2001, pp. 167–87. See also P. R. Darke, A. Chattopadhyay, and L. Ashworth, "The Importance and Functional Significance of Affective Cues in Consumer Choice," *Journal of Consumer Research,* December 2006, pp. 322–28.

8. M. T. Pham, "Representativeness, Relevance, and the Use of Feelings in Decision Making," *Journal of Consumer Research,* September 1998, pp. 144–59. For a more elaborate model of affective appraisal and its influence on subsequent judgment, see C. W. M. Yeung and R. S. Wyer Jr., "Affect, Appraisal, and Consumer Judgment," *Journal of Consumer Research,* September 2004, pp. 412–24.

9. See also R. Dhar and K. Wertenbroch, "Consumer Choice between Hedonic and Utilitarian Goods," *Journal of Marketing Research,* February 2000, pp. 60–71.

10. See B. Shiv and A. Fedorikhin, "Heart and Mind in Conflict," *Journal of Consumer Research,* December 1999, pp. 278–91.

11. J. A. Ruth, "Promoting a Brand's Emotional Benefits," *Journal of Consumer Psychology,* 11, no. 2 (2001), pp. 99–113; and J. C. Sweeney and G. N. Soutar, "Consumer Perceived Value," *Journal of Retailing,* 77 (2001), pp. 203–20.

12. See P. Krishnamurthy and M. Sujan, "Retrospection versus Anticipation," *Journal of Consumer Research,* June 1999, pp. 55–69. See also B. Shiv and J. Huber, "The Impact of Anticipating Satisfaction on Consumer Choice," *Journal of Consumer Research,* September 2000, pp. 202–16; and C. P. S. Fong and R. S. Wyer Jr., "Cultural, Social, and Emotional Determinants of Decisions under Uncertainty," *Organizational Behavior and Human Decision Processes,* 90 (2003), pp. 304–22.

13. This section is based on S. P. Mantell and F. R. Kardes, "The Role of Direction of Comparison, Attribute-Based Processing, and Attitude-Based Processing in Consumer Preference," *Journal of Consumer Research,* March 1999, pp. 335–52. For a discussion of the specific role of advertising-based attitudes, see W. E. Baker, "The Diagnosticity of Advertising Generated Brand Attitudes in Brand Choice Contexts," *Journal of Consumer Psychology,* 11, no. 2 (2001), pp. 129–39.

14. See R. Dhar, S. M. Nowlis, and S. J. Sherman, "Comparison Effects on Preference Construction," *Journal of Consumer Research,* December 1999, pp. 293–306.

15. C. Qui, Y. H. Lee, and C. W. M. Yeung, "Suppressing Feelings," *Journal of Consumer Psychology,* 19 (2009), pp. 427–39.

16. G. Kalyanaram and J. D. C. Little, "An Empirical Analysis of Latitude of Price Acceptance in Consumer Package Goods," *Journal of Consumer Research,* December 1994, pp. 408–18.

17. See S. Hoeffler and D. Ariely, "Constructing Stable Preferences," *Journal of Consumer Psychology,* 8, no. 2 (1999), pp. 113–39; and A. V. Muthukrishnan and F. R. Kardes, "Persistent Preferences for Product Attributes," *Journal of Consumer Research,* June 2001, pp. 89–102.

18. P. H. Bloch, "Seeking the Ideal Form," *Journal of Marketing,* July 1995, pp. 16–29; and Dhar and Wertenbroch, "Consumer Choice between Hedonic and Utilitarian Goods." See also D. Horsky, P. Nelson, and S. S. Posavac, "Stating Preference for the Ethereal but Choosing the Concrete," *Journal of Consumer Psychology,* 14, no. 1/2 (2004), pp. 132–40.

19. D. J. Mitchell, B. E. Kahn, and S. C. Knasko, "There's Something in the Air," *Journal of Consumer Research,* September 1995, pp. 229–38; D. R. Lichtenstein, R. G. Netemeyer, and S. Burton, "Assessing the Domain Specificity of Deal Proneness," *Journal of Consumer Research,* December 1995, pp. 314–26; D. R. Lichtenstein, S. Burton, and R. G. Netemeyer, "An Examination of Deal Proneness across Sales Promotion Types," *Journal of Retailing,* 2 (1997), pp. 283–97; and V. Ramaswamy and S. S. Srinivasan, "Coupon Characteristics and Redemption Intentions," *Psychology & Marketing,* January 1998, pp. 50–80.

20. See, e.g., R. Pieters and L. Warlop, "Visual Attention during Brand Choice," *International Journal of Research in Marketing,* 16 (1999), pp. 1–16.

21. B. L. Bagus, "The Consumer Durable Replacement Buyer," *Journal of Marketing,* January 1991, pp. 42–51.

22. A. Kirmani and P. Wright, "Procedural Learning, Consumer Decision Making, and Marketing Choice," *Marketing Letters,* 4, no. 1 (1993), pp. 39–48; G. S. Carpenter, R. Glazer, and K. Nakamoto, "Meaningful Brands from Meaningless Differentiation," *Journal of Marketing Research,* August 1994, pp. 339–50; and S. M. Broniarczyk and A. D. Gershoff, "Meaningless Differentiation Revisited," in *Advances in Consumer Research,* vol. 24, ed. M. Bruck and D. J. MacInnis (Provo, UT: Association for Consumer Research, 1997), pp. 223–28.

23. B. Abrams, "Hanes Finds L'eggs Methods Don't Work with Cosmetics," *The Wall Street Journal,* February 3, 1983, p. 33.

24. See S. H. Ang, G. J. Gorn, and C. B. Weinberg, "The Evaluation of Time-Dependent Attributes," *Psychology & Marketing,* January 1996, pp. 19–35.

25. P. M. Parker, "Sweet Lemons," *Journal of Marketing Research,* August 1995, pp. 291–307; S. Shapiro and M. T. Spence, "Factors Affecting Encoding, Retrieval, and Alignment of Sensory Attributes in a Memory-Based Brand Choice Task," *Journal of Consumer Research,* March 2002, pp. 603–17; and B.-K. Lee and W.-N. Lee, "The Effect of Information Overload on Consumer Choice Quality in an On-Line Environment," *Psychology & Marketing,* March 2004, pp. 159–83.

26. See A. Kirmani and A. R. Rao, "No Pain, No Gain," *Journal of Marketing,* April 2000, pp. 66–79.

27. See, e.g., V. P. Norris, "The Economic Effects of Advertising," *Current Issues and Research in Advertising,* 1984, pp. 39–134; S. Burton and D. R. Lichtenstein, "Assessing the Relationship between Perceived and Objective Price-Quality," in *Advances in Consumer Research,* vol. 27, ed. M. E. Goldberg, G. Gorn, and

R. W. Pollay (Provo, UT: Association for Consumer Research, 1990), pp. 715–22; and D. J. Faulds, O. Grunewald, and D. Johnson, "A Cross-National Investigation of the Relationship between the Price and Quality of Consumer Products," *Journal of Global Marketing,* 8, no. 1 (1994), pp. 7–25.

28. K. M. Elliott and D. W. Roach, "Are Consumers Evaluating Your Products the Way You Think and Hope They Are?," *Journal of Consumer Marketing,* Spring 1991, pp. 5–14; and J. Baumgartner, "On the Utility of Consumers' Theories in Judgments of Covariation," *Journal of Consumer Research,* March 1995, pp. 634–43.

29. See S. Ratneshwar et al., "Benefit Salience and Consumers' Selective Attention to Product Features," *International Journal of Research in Marketing,* 14 (1997), pp. 245–59; R. Dhar and I. Simonson, "Making Complementary Choices in Consumption Episodes," *Journal of Marketing Research,* February 1999, pp. 29–44; and J. K. H. Lee and J. H. Steckel, "Consumer Strategies for Purchasing Assortments within a Single Product Class," *Journal of Retailing,* 75, no. 3 (1999), pp. 387–403.

30. See, e.g., P. W. J. Verlegh, H. N. J. Schifferstein, and D. R. Wittink, "Range and Number-of-Levels Effects in Derived and Stated Measures of Attribute Importance," *Marketing Letters,* 13, no. 1 (2002), pp. 41–52.

31. M. P. Gardner, "Advertising Effects on Attributes Recalled and Criteria Used for Brand Evaluations," *Journal of Consumer Research,* December 1983, pp. 310–18; S. B. MacKenzie, "The Role of Attention in Mediating the Effect of Advertising on Attribute Importance," *Journal of Consumer Research,* September 1986, pp. 174–95; and G. D. Olsen, "Creating the Contrast," *Journal of Advertising,* Winter 1995, pp. 29–44.

32. A. R. Rao, L. Qu, and R. W. Ruekert, "Signaling Unobservable Product Quality through a Brand Ally," *Journal of Marketing Research,* May 1999, pp. 258–68; and C. Janiszewski and S. M. J. van Osselaer, "A Connectionist Model of Brand-Quality Associations," *Journal of Marketing Research,* August 2000, pp. 331–50.

33. C. J. Thompson, "Interpreting Consumers," *Journal of Marketing Research,* November 1997, p. 443. Published by the American Marketing Association; reprinted with permission.

34. See G. Haubl and V. Trifts, "Consumer Decision Making in Online Shopping Environments," *Marketing Science,* Winter 2000, pp. 2–21.

35. S. Thompson, "Food Marketers Count on Snacks," *Advertising Age,* April 24, 2006, p. 4.

36. This insight is based on I. Simonson, "Choice Based on Reasons," *Journal of Consumer Research,* September 1989, pp. 158–74; S. Sheng, A. M. Parker, and K. Nakamoto, "Understanding the Mechanism and Determinants of Compromise Effects," *Psychology & Marketing,* July 2005, pp. 591–608; and F. Sinn et al., "Compromising the Compromise Effect," *Marketing Letters,* December 2007, pp. 223–36.

37. M. L. Ursic and J. G. Helgeson, "The Impact of Choice and Task Complexity on Consumer Decision Making," *Journal of Business Research,* August 1990, pp. 69–86; P. L. A. Dabholkar, "Incorporating Choice into an Attitudinal Framework," *Journal of Consumer Research,* June 1994, pp. 100–18; and T. Elrod, R. D. Johnson, and J. White, "A New Integrated Model of Non-compensatory and Compensatory Decision Strategies," *Organizational Behavior and Human Decision Processes,* 95 (2004), pp. 1–19.

38. See E. Coupey, "Restructuring," *Journal of Consumer Research,* June 1994, pp. 83–99.

39. See D. L. Alden, D. M. Stayman, and W. D. Hoyer, "Evaluation Strategies of American and Thai Consumers," *Psychology & Marketing,* March 1994, pp. 145–61; and J. E. Russo and F. Lecleric, "An Eye-Fixation Analysis of Choice Processes for Consumer Nondurables," *Journal of Consumer Research,* September 1994, pp. 274–90.

40. See J. G. Helgeson and M. L. Ursic, "Information Load, Cost/Benefit Assessment and Decision Strategy Variability," *Journal of the Academy of Marketing Science,* Winter 1993, pp. 13–20; W. J. McDonald, "The Roles of Demographics, Purchase Histories, and Shopper Decision-Making Styles in Predicting Consumer Catalog Loyalty," *Journal of Direct Marketing,* Summer 1993, pp. 55–65; M. S. Yadav, "How Buyers Evaluate Product Bundles," *Journal of Consumer Research,* September 1994, pp. 342–53; A. V. Muthukrishnan, "Decision Ambiguity and Incumbent Brand Advantage," *Journal of Consumer Research,* June 1995, pp. 98–109; and D. E. Hansen and J. G. Helgeson, "Consumer Response to Decision Conflict from Negatively Correlated Attributes," *Journal of Consumer Psychology,* 10, no. 3 (2001), pp. 150–69.

chapter

17 Outlet Selection and Purchase

LEARNING OBJECTIVES

LO1 **Describe how retailing is evolving.**

LO2 **Discuss the Internet and mobile as part of multi- and omni-channel shopping.**

LO3 **Explain the retail and consumer attributes that affect outlet selection.**

LO4 **Summarize the in-store and online influences on brand choice.**

LO5 **Understand how purchase plays a role in the shopping process.**

Brick-and-mortar stores are fighting for their survival using technology—the very thing that in many ways threatens its existence—to do so.[1] Here are some examples:

Window Displays. It isn't that consumers are going to the mall any less; it's that they are visiting fewer stores. Having shopped online, they have narrowed their selection of alternatives and have less need to visit as many stores as they had in the past. This creates a greater challenge for window displays purposed to convert passersby to shoppers. With the help of technology, the staid, flat, static window displays can be transformed into visual hooks that hijack consumer attention, encourage consumer interaction, and drive foot traffic into stores. For example, using (Kinect technology) sensors, the Nike Hyperdunk+shoes window display lets you measure how high you can jump (to dunk a basketball) as follows:

> [Y]ou stand on a street-side blue dot and jump as high as you can. Then, the system asks if you'd like to save your score—you respond by touching a "yes" or "no" decal on the window, which makes the entire plate glass window feel like a touch screen (though really, the camera is just tracking the movement of your hand). You can compare yourself, Strava-style, to others on a web ranking site.[2]

For its "Merry Kissmass" holiday window display, retailer Ted Baker created a giant digital Mistletoe atop the entrance of its New York City store. Consumers were invited "to take 'selfies' kissing in front of a digital backdrop and tag them (hashtag) KissTed on Instagram or Twitter. The photos, displayed on another screen, were entered into a contest to win a romantic getaway."

Shoppertainment. Brick-and-mortar stores have the opportunity to create "shoppertainment" experiences for consumers using technology to help design environments that are emotionally engaging, entertaining, and memorable. A showcase example is the 44,000-square-foot Burberry flagship store on Regent Street in London. Housed in the remodeled 1820 Prince Regent building, the Burberry store is theatrical and technologically integrated throughout. Upon entering the store, consumers see the world's tallest indoor retail screen (over 22 feet), self-supporting stone staircases, and well placed scatterings of "bespoke blackened bronze lanterns, furniture, plasterwork, timber paneling and flooring, traditional glass signage," all of which provide the intended effect—giving customers the feeling that they have arrived at Burberry World Live, the Burberry web landing page. Mirrors instantly transform into screens to show "runway footage and exclusive video and satellite technology-enabled live streaming of events." At set times throughout the day, "disruptive digital takeovers" occur and all 500 speakers and 100 screens are synchronized to show the same thing. RFID (radio-frequency identification)-tagged merchandise trigger mirrors in the store and in the fitting rooms to turn into video screens that provide the consumer with product information they would not otherwise have—design, stitching, history—and in the process create touch points for consumers to form deep engagement with the brand. To make purchasing web-easy, iPad-armed Burberry personnel not only can answer questions about inventory and place orders, but also can take payment on the spot, eliminating the need for customers to carry merchandise to cashiers and wait in line to pay for products. The store is designed to provide a website user experience in a brick-and-mortar store.

Inventory. The advantage of web stores for unlimited inventory can be matched by brick-and-mortar stores that extend their physical inventory with virtual inventory displayed on large-screen kiosks, touch-screen order points, and online kiosks. One example is the virtual footwear wall piloted by Adidas, the global athletic retailer. The wall, which includes LCD touch screens that allow consumers to create shoes and see them rendered in 3-D, has led to substantial increase in sales.

Tracking Consumers. Web stores can track consumer wanderings on the Internet by following the trail of cookies (bits of software code). Now a number of firms (RetailNext, Euclid Elements, Nomi, ShopperTrak, Brickstream, WirelessWerx, Shopperception) are using technology—smartphones' unique Wi-Fi address, heat maps, sensors that track radio signals from mobile phones—to allow brick-and-mortar stores to do the same in the physical world. Brick-and-mortar stores can capture data—consumer wanderings in the store, the amount of time they spent at various locations, the items they considered, the number of passersby who entered the store, the length of time of their stay, whether or not they return—that can be analyzed to provide information vital for planning staffing needs, merchandise decisions, store layouts, and window displays to attract customers and influence shoppers. In addition, with knowledge of consumer in-store location, retailers can send information and offers—coupons, discounts—about merchandise to the consumer's smartphone (Shopperception, Shopkick, and Snapett) when consumers are in the vicinity of the merchandise.

Clearly, retailing is an exciting area of marketing. *What's next on the retail horizon?*

Before, during, or after searching for information and selecting a brand, consumers select a retail outlet from which to make a purchase. Brands are critical to retail outlets because brands are a major determinant of which outlets consumers will shop. Retail outlets are critical to brands because retailers provide brands with the access to the consumers they desire. The Husky ad in Illustration 17–1 provides an example of the importance of retail outlets and brands to each other as the brand and several retailers are advertised simultaneously.

Our focus in this chapter is to describe the evolving retail landscape, the factors affecting outlet selection, and the in-store (and online) determinants of brand choice.

THE EVOLVING RETAIL SCENE

As the opening examples illustrate, retailing is changing dramatically, particularly as a function of technology. We use *retail outlet* to refer to any source of products or services for consumers. This has moved well beyond physical stores and catalogs to include the Internet, interactive TV ads, and mobile shopping apps. Roughly 20 years ago, the following description of the future of retailing by Bill Gates, founder of Microsoft, seemed far-fetched. However, much if not all of what he predicted has already happened or is now happening, along with a few things he didn't predict. Consider his statement:

ILLUSTRATION 17-1

This Husky ad shows how marketers often use advertising to create brand demand and to direct consumers to appropriate outlets.

L01

> You're watching "Seinfeld" on TV, and you like the jacket he's wearing. You click on it with your remote control. The show pauses and a Windows-style dropdown menu appears at the top of the screen, asking if you want to buy it. You click "yes." The next menu offers you a choice of colors; you click on black. Another menu lists your credit cards asking which one you'll use for this purchase. Click on MasterCard or whatever. Which address should the jacket go to, your office or your home or your cabin? Click on one address and you're done—the menus disappear and "Seinfeld" picks up where it left off.
>
> Just as you'll already have taught the computer about your credit cards and addresses, you will have had your body measured by a 3-D version of supermarket scanners, so the system will know your exact size. And it will send the data electronically to a factory, where robots will custom tailor the jacket to your measurements. An overnight courier service will deliver it to your door the next morning.[3]

Today, computers can learn and recall consumer information and preferences in a number of ways including behavioral tracking, full-body scanners exist that allow for custom-fitted apparel, and many cable providers are experimenting with interactive TV ads that allow users to get more information about products in the ads and even, as in the case of Reebok, purchase them.[4]

Beyond interactive TV ads is the concept of interactive TV shows in which brands within the shows can be searched and bought using the TV remote. If you think this seems far-fetched, go to www.clikthrough.com, where you can watch music videos by popular artists in which the brands and products in the videos are searchable and buyable.

> In Katy Perry's video *Waking Up in Vegas,* a man is wearing a black shirt. Click on the shirt and a box appears that provides more information about the shirt. Click on the "shop now" button, and it takes you to the Neiman Marcus online store where you can buy the shirt.

Our main focus in the current chapter is on Internet (online) and store (bricks-and-mortar) retailing with additional discussion focused on the increasing role of mobile apps in terms of their influence on how consumers shop both online and in store. Also, other forms of nonstore retailing such as catalogs, telemarketing, direct mail, and TV (referred to as **in-home shopping**) continue to be important and are discussed. The integration of the Internet and mobile has given rise to an additional issue that we discuss, namely, multi- and omni-channel marketing and consumers.

Internet Retailing

As indicated in Chapter 15, the Internet is a major information source. It is also a major retail channel and one aspect of in-home shopping. The following table shows the current size of Internet retailing.[5]

Current Size of Internet Retailing	
U.S. Internet users (millions)	288
Total U.S. (nontravel) retail expenditures online (billions)	$279
Online spending as a percent of all retail spending	11
Total web-influenced in-store sales (billions)	$1,543

Several aspects of this table specifically, and Internet shopping more generally, are worth noting. First, annual growth in the number of Internet users is relatively low, at about 3 percent. This is because most of the U.S. adult population is already online. Second, annual growth in online sales remains steady at 12 percent (this number depends substantially on the product class). Third, estimates indicate that between 66 and 88 percent of Internet users have purchased a product online at some point. Thus, future growth in online sales will continue to come more from increasing the amount of online spending from *existing* buyers than from increasing the number of Internet users. One estimate by Forrester indicates that in 2010, 70 percent of the increase in online sales came from existing online shoppers buying more.[6] And there is still substantial room to grow. Even if you take away grocery sales, which have very low Internet penetration, the online sales are still only about 15 percent of retail sales. Finally, the Internet has a major influence on in-store sales, which further increases its importance as a retail channel. Such "cross-channel" effects are discussed later in the chapter.

The top five categories of online spending continue to include (1) travel, (2) apparel (including accessories and footwear), (3) computers and peripherals, (4) automotive (autos and parts), and (5) consumer electronics. Consumers shop online for various reasons, many of them similar to those for shopping from catalogs:[7]

Reason	Online Shopping	Catalog Shopping
Convenience	67%	62%
Price was right	41	40
Unique merchandise	33	40
Past experience with company	28	39
Wanted product delivered	16	31
No time to go to store	13	17
Recommendation from a friend	7	7
Impulse	4	5

Source: *Catalog Age*. Reprinted with the permission of Primedia Business Magazines & Media Inc.

Until recently, many industry experts predicted the demise of catalogs. However, catalogs and the Internet appear to work in a complementary fashion. For example, one study found that when consumers received a physical catalog, it nearly doubled their chances of buying at the retailer's website and increased their spending by 16 percent.[8]

Characteristics of Online Shoppers Obviously, online shoppers must first be Internet users. As we saw in Chapter 15, Internet users tend to be younger and have higher income and education levels than the general population, although these differences are diminishing. Pew Research estimates that currently 66 percent of all U.S. adult Internet users have made a purchase online at some time. The demographic characteristics of Internet buyers are similar to Internet users. Namely, they are younger (under 65 versus 65+ is the major difference), are non-Hispanic, have higher education levels, earn higher income,

ILLUSTRATION 17-2

Different consumers use the Internet in different ways to browse and shop. Which shopper segment is this website trying to target?

and are broadband users.[9] In addition, online experience appears to increase online buying.[10] And online attitudes, experiences, and behavior influence online buying, as suggested by the following shopping segments found by Experian.[11] Illustration 17–2 shows a screenshot of retailer Jambu footwear. Can you pick which shopping segment it is targeting?

- *Upscale Clicks and Bricks* (17 percent) are 68 percent more likely than average to have bought online in the past 12 months. Higher income and middle age, this segment is most likely to buy online, but also buy in-store on par with average consumer. Heavy online research prior to buying.
- *Virtual Shoppers* (26 percent) are 10 percent more likely than average to have bought online in the past 12 months. Younger and split between higher and lower income, this group tends to use the Internet to find good deals.
- *Status Strivers* (20 percent) are 4 percent more likely than average to have bought online in the past 12 months. Younger and heavily female, this group sees shopping as fun and as a form of recreation. Like to browse and shop to keep up with trends. Highest mall shoppers.
- *Mall Maniacs* (10 percent) are 15 percent less likely than average to have bought online in the past 12 months. Middle income, this group likes trying new things. They enjoy shopping. Second highest mall shoppers.
- *Just the Essentials* (14 percent) are 27 percent less likely than average to have bought online in the past 12 months. Older and middle income, this group is only looking for functional necessity. Score lower than average on all forms of shopping.
- *Original Traditionalists* (13 percent) are 55 percent less likely than average to have bought online in past the 12 months. Older and lower income, this group is brand and store loyal, buy American, buy green. Roughly average on mall shopping. Highest catalog shoppers.

A study of Asian consumers yielded a similar set of segments.[12] Clearly, in order for online buying to continue growing, marketers must overcome barriers that suppress online buying, particularly of the Status Strivers and Mall Maniacs. This is not a simple proposition. These consumers enjoy shopping and the "fun" factor in shopping. Many probably enjoy the social aspect of shopping with others that the Internet generally lacks. Interestingly, the Just the Essentials group may be attracted to the ease of buying online and the ability to get good deals and may not mind if Internet shopping is functional.

Barriers to Internet Shopping For some products, people, and situations, the Internet offers a better combination of selection, convenience, price, and other attributes than do catalogs, traditional stores, or other outlets. However, in many cases, consumers prefer traditional retail stores. Indeed, traditional offline stores are still the top-ranked *purchasing* channel for most consumers in most categories, followed by the Internet and catalogs.[13] An obvious barrier to Internet shopping is online access, although, as we've seen in Chapter 15, this is diminishing rapidly. For those who are online, other barriers exist. Forrester Research found that for those who were online but had never made a purchase, the following reasons were contributing factors.[14] Research suggests similar reasons for Asian consumers as well.[15]

Reason	%
Lack of "touch"	36
Don't want to give personal financial information	32
Delivery costs too high	29
Returns will be a hassle	26
Prefer to research online, buy offline	24
Feel no need to buy online	23
Can't speak to sales assistant online	14

Source: Forrester Research, 2010.

These and other barriers relate to the issue of converting browsers to buyers, a major concern to Internet marketers looking to enhance online sales. Consumer Insight 17–1 discusses online conversion strategies.

Store-Based Retailing

The majority of retail sales take place in physical stores, and this will remain true for the foreseeable future. However, traditional store-based retailing is certainly vulnerable in ways that play into the hands of in-home retailers. Consider the results of a Roper survey asking consumers why they don't like shopping in stores:[16]

Reason	Percent
Salespeople are poorly informed	74
Waiting in long lines	73
Hard time finding things	64
Parking and traffic	64
Dealing with crowds	58
Hard to get someone to wait on you	54
The time it takes to shop	38
Don't like shopping	34

Source: From Roper Reports Telephone Survey, August 2003.

Obviously, for many people, in-store shopping is perceived as neither fun nor an efficient use of time. However, retailers are fighting back with different formats.[17] Lifestyle centers that mimic small-town retailing of the past with sidewalks, restaurants, and parks, in an outdoor setting, are emerging to generate excitement and adapt to the changing shopping habits of consumers. Brand stores are emerging as major sales volume outlets as well as promotional devices for brands, such as Levi's, Nike, and Reebok. Stores within stores are also being tried. Walmart has eyeglasses, banks, and restaurants all under one roof. Giant superstores such as Walmart and Home Depot are experimenting with smaller versions of its larger stores.[18]

ILLUSTRATION 17-3

One way store-based retailers add value for their customers is by providing a fun shopping environment as shown by this Mall of America Visitors Guide.

Apart from different formats, traditional department stores have tried to create "destination areas" within their stores that enhance their overall image and drive ongoing store traffic. For example, Macy's has bridal salons in select locations, and Target and Kmart offer designer collections to draw consumers in.[19] In fact, Target's use of designer fashion collections has created a trendier image than that created by Walmart and others.

More and more, retailers are trying to enhance the experiential component of their stores through layout, music, personal shoppers, and so on. Some stores are targeted at the experiential component. American Girl stores don't just sell dolls; they also offer experiences such as dining and parties! Part of this appears to play off of the socialization of children to the shopping experience as well as mother–daughter and father–daughter shopping experiences (see Chapter 6). Similarly Bass Pro Shops sell products, but also have aquariums to showcase fish, a shooting range, a restaurant, and so on. Dick's Sporting Goods has a golf club test range for trying and fitting golf clubs to the individual, and some locations even have a rock climbing wall!

As you can see, as the functionality of the web has made competing on that dimension more difficult for traditional retailers, they are focusing on becoming giant entertainment centers, an emphasis on the social element. For example, the Mall of America near Minneapolis is built around an amusement park. It also has a miniature golf course, nightclubs, theme restaurants, and an aquarium (see Illustration 17–3). Retailing is clearly an exciting, competitive area. Those retailers who best understand their consumers will be the ones to prosper in the future.

The Internet as Part of a Multi-Channel Strategy

Most retailers are not solely online. Instead, they engage in multi-channel marketing, meaning they utilize multiple retail channels to reach their customers. Various channels include physical stores, the Internet, catalogs, and so on. A multi-channel approach can LO2

CONSUMER INSIGHT 17-1

Converting Website Visitors to Buyers

With about 90 percent of U.S. adults online and roughly two-thirds having made an online purchase, online sales will only grow by increasing how frequently and how much consumers buy online. The following provides a set of guidelines for online retailers to help them convert website visitors to buyers.

- *Appropriate Landing Page.* Bad landing pages can be purchase killers. An example is clicking on an Esurance-sponsored link after searching for homeowner's insurance and having the landing page be about *auto* insurance. Companies are trying to target their landing pages specifically to the type of consumer who is clicking through. For example, Elite Island Resorts set up two landing pages to target different travel buyers.[20]
- *Deal with Privacy and Security Concerns.* Online privacy and security are top online buying deterrents and represent billions in lost sales. **Online privacy concerns** *relate to consumer fears regarding how personal information about them that is gathered online might be used.* Online privacy concerns include targeting children, being inundated with marketing messages, and identity theft.[21]

  Four approaches to reducing online privacy concerns seem possible. First is direct control through "opt-in" features that let consumers choose directly how their information is used.[22] Second is the use of direct trust signals such as privacy statements and the incorporation and communication of security verification systems such as VeriSign.[23] These signals can increase trust, reduce privacy concerns, and enhance purchases, but sometimes they do not. A third approach is to use an indirect signal relating to a firm's investment in its website. An example would be a firm that uses "Shockwave technology to allow a user to experience an online demonstration and roll over the product image to gather additional information," versus one that conveys the same information but does so "through text and static graphics." Research shows that when consumers perceive that firms have invested more in their website, this increases trust and online purchase likelihood.[24] A final approach is to use brand as an indirect signal of trust. Research shows that consumers are more likely to provide transaction-specific information to a trusted retailer than to one with whom they are unfamiliar.[25]

  The approach a firm should use depends on the type of web visitor, with searchers (search-task directed) more responsive to the indirect website investment signal and browsers (pleasure

take many forms and can be successful for a number of reasons. For example, regional in-store retailers such as that shown in Illustration 17–4 can use the Internet to instantly become national and international in scope. On the flip side, the Internet allows traditional retailers such as JCPenney and Saks Fifth Avenue to reach smaller communities where they could not otherwise operate economically.

The increase in multi-channel marketing reflects shifts in consumer shopping. Consumers are increasingly likely to be **multi-channel shoppers**—that is, consumers who browse and/or purchase in more than one channel. Research suggests that[26]

- The most common form is online to store (search online, buy at a physical store). This is the preferred style for over 75 percent of multi-channel shoppers, followed distantly by roughly seven percent of shoppers who prefer to search in the store and buy online.
- Roughly 78 percent of Internet shoppers utilize two or more channels to browse and buy.

directed) more responsive to the direct privacy statement signal.

- *Deal with Lack of Touch.* The lack of touch or ability to physically handle, test, or try products prior to purchase is a top concern and affects product categories such as apparel and home decorating, where it can be difficult to simulate experience attributes (e.g., fit for apparel, color and texture for home decorating).[27] Internet marketers are becoming much more sophisticated in terms of creating *virtual product experiences* using such techniques as 3-D simulations and rich media, made practical by the increased penetration of broadband. In the apparel area, for example, "virtual try-on" functionality allows consumers to see how clothing looks on a model. MVM (My Virtual Model) allows consumers to create their own model and try on various fashion brands and styles.[28]
- *Deal with Lack of Social Element.* In-store retailing allows for the social element, which is a major shopping motive and lacking in many online shopping sites. To deal with this, some online retailers are creating sites that incorporate a social shopping experience. One example is Kaboodle, which combines online shopping with social networking to allow consumers to shop online with their friends. Also, online retailers like Lands' End are increasingly adding video and text chat with a sales associate. An even more social dimension is being created by "humanlike" online assistants such as IKEA's Anna. Such assistants lead to perceptions that the website is more social, which creates positive emotions and increases purchase intentions.[29]
- *Deal with Shopping Cart Abandonment.* Roughly 70 percent of all shopping carts that consumers start get abandoned prior to a purchase. That's a lot of revenue left on the table and marketers are seeing the opportunity. One recent study found that e-mail campaigns that are specifically targeted (e.g., mention the items abandoned, promote core brand values, provide some sort of promotion because price and delivery charges are often major factors) and timed (after 24 hours, 90 percent of abandoned carts will stay that way). Done correctly, one estimate is each e-mail (or series in a campaign) to a consumer who abandoned an online cart yields an average of $17.90, meaning those who abandon carts can be re-engaged and converted to buyers.[30]

Critical Thinking Questions

1. What other strategies can online retailers use to increase the purchase likelihood of website visitors?
2. Do you think the social element even matters online? Explain.
3. Why do you think campaigns targeting shopping cart abandonment are so successful?

ILLUSTRATION 17-4

An Internet sales site instantly converts a local or regional firm into a national and even international one.

- Multi-channel shoppers have higher incomes and spend 15 to 30 percent more with a retailer than single-channel shoppers.
- Similar multi-channel shoppers and shopping patterns exist in Europe.

Multi-Channel Shoppers Browse in One Channel and Purchase in Another

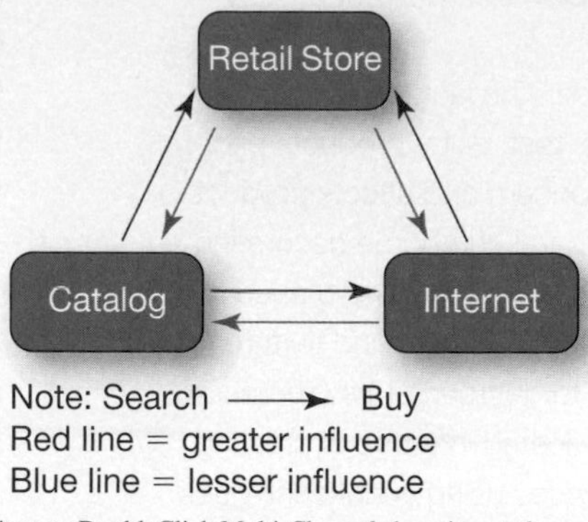

Source: DoubleClick Multi-Channel shopping study—Holiday 2003, www.internetretailer.com, January 2004.

Retail channels tend to be complementary, as shown in Figure 17–1, because no retailing format is optimal on all dimensions. Thus, the Internet can be used to overcome a lack of informed salespeople or the inconvenience of researching products in-store, while in-store can provide "touch" and immediacy of purchasing.[31] Figure 17–1 also emphasizes the ongoing importance of catalogs as drivers of both online and retail store purchases, even though, early on, catalogs were predicted to die at the hand of Internet retailing.

Mobile as Part of an Omni-Channel Strategy

A new form of shopper called the *omni-channel shopper* is emerging due to the emergence of mobile shopping apps. **Omni-channel shoppers** are *consumers who browse and/or purchase in more than one channel simultaneously*. That is, while in a store, they might scan a product's bar code into a mobile shopping app that takes them to the web and compares prices for that branded item across several local stores. Or they might use a mobile app that looks for deals and coupons at that store. Or they might search the Internet using their phone to get more information about the product or find online recommendations. The key is simultaneous channel engagement. In the examples just mentioned, the channels are in-store, mobile, and Internet. Figure 17–2 depicts omni-channel shopping, where three channels are being engaged simultaneously within a physical store as enabled by mobile apps that access the Internet.

Omni-channel shoppers are digital savvy, with heavy reliance on mobile and mobile shopping apps. Omni-channel shoppers are younger Gen Yers as well as upscale and tech-savvy Gen X and older Gen Yers. Omni-channel shoppers spend 15 to 30 percent more with a retailer than multi-channel shoppers and are a critical new target for retailers. Consider the following statement by a Macy's executive:

> We talk a lot at Macy's about "omnichannel" retailing. Our customer is multi-dimensional. She is busy at work and out with friends. She always has her mobile device in her hand. She's active on Facebook and Twitter and YouTube and a dozen other social media sites. We want that customer to be able to interact with Macy's no matter where she is or how she shops. It makes no difference to us whether she buys something in our store or online, or whether she is shopping from her desktop computer or her Droid or her iPad. Macy's best customers are those who shop us in-stores and online. We have a whole series of strategies in place to drive our store customers to the Web, and our online customer to the stores. Today's customer is not monolithic. And that's the way we are approaching our customer.[32]

Omni-Channel Shoppers Browse and Purchase in Multiple Channels Simultaneously **FIGURE 17-2**

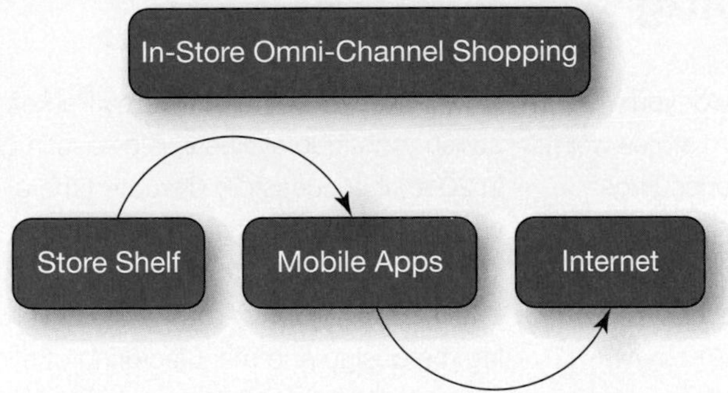

Marketing across channels, though rewarding in terms of consumer spending, is quite challenging. Consider the major task of coordinating a seamless look and feel across channels, while making sure to be plugged into the appropriate mobile apps and optimized for the major search engines. Major tech companies like IBM are now advising companies like Macy's about how to best handle such issues. Consumer Insight 17–2 explores additional examples and approaches to multi- and omni-channel consumers and marketing.

ATTRIBUTES AFFECTING RETAIL OUTLET SELECTION

LO3

The selection of a specific retail outlet involves a comparison of the alternative outlets on the consumer's evaluative criteria. This section considers a number of evaluative criteria commonly used by consumers to select retail outlets. While much of the research on outlet selection relates to choosing among retail stores (e.g., JCPenney versus Sears), when applicable we also draw linkages to choosing among online retailers (e.g., Buybooks.com versus Amazon.com) based on emerging evidence.

Outlet Image

A given consumer's or target market's perception of all the attributes associated with a retail outlet is generally referred to as the **store image.** This is the same as the concept of *brand image* discussed in Chapter 9. One study found the following nine dimensions and 23 components of these nine dimensions of store image.[33] Notice that the store atmosphere component is primarily affective, or feeling in nature.

Store Image

Dimension	Components
Merchandise	Quality, selection, style, and price
Service	Layaway plan, sales personnel, easy return, credit, and delivery
Clientele	Customers
Physical facilities	Cleanliness, store layout, shopping ease, and attractiveness
Convenience	Location and parking
Promotion	Advertising
Store atmosphere	Congeniality, fun, excitement, comfort
Institutional	Store reputation
Posttransaction	Satisfaction

Source: J. D. Lindquist, "Meaning of Image," *Journal of Retailing,* Winter 1974, pp. 29–38.

CONSUMER INSIGHT 17-2

Multi-Channel Shopping

IKEA, the giant Swedish retailer of all things for your home, has giant brick-and-mortar showroom stores well known for their meandering pathways that encourage wanderings throughout the store—the better for consumers to see and buy things. IKEA also has an easy-to-navigate website from which consumers can order goods. Plus it mails a catalog to consumers' homes. Even with this "triple threat" IKEA still has not solved the consumer's problem of determining how things such as sofas, chairs, and tables will look in their homes—that is, until IKEA introduced its augmented reality app. This is how it works. A consumer flipping through the IKEA catalog sees something she likes—say a sofa. She scans the page with her smartphone or tablet. Then she places the catalog where she would likely place the sofa—say against the wall and in front of the window. Using her smart device, she can see how the sofa would look in her home. The virtual reality app, available for 100 of the 300 products in the IKEA catalog, is likely to be helpful to the 14 percent of IKEA customers who buy the wrong size furniture and the 70 percent of IKEA customers who don't know the size of their home.[34]

Retailers who started out as pure play web stores have discovered the value and benefits of adding brick-and-mortar stores. Warby Parker, the purveyor of stylish, boutique eyewear, is a case in point. Introduced in 2010, it successfully disrupted the eyewear industry with the implementation of its e-commerce model, selling eyewear directly to consumers. It was able to offer prices below industry standards by vertically integrating the design and manufacturing of eyewear, thereby eliminating the practice of paying (exorbitant) brand licensing fees. Taking a page out of Apple's retail store, its newly opened Soho New York brick-and-mortar store is designed with the focus on the consumer experience. The 20-foot-wide store has the feel of an old library—terrazzo floor, brass library lamps, rolling ladders, (meticulously selected) musty books (that consumers can buy). Rather than locked behind glass cases, eyewear is out in the open for consumers to try. Consumers can view themselves in one of the mirrors that surround the store or take a photo of themselves in a custom photobooth—an experience more novel than a selfie taken with a cell phone. To complete the offering, an in-house optometrist is available seven days a week to provide $50 eye exams booked online.

E-tailers can use their webstore data—customer characteristics and location, sales volume—to guide

This study focused on stores; the components and, probably, the dimensions will require adjusting for use with other types of retail outlets. For example, a recent study of *online retailer image* found the following seven dimensions and related components that influenced online outlet selection.[35] *Which dimensions and components of store image translate the most to an online context and which the least?*

Online Retailer Image

Dimension	Components
Usefulness	Good product offers and information, value, aligned with interests
Enjoyment	Fun, attractive, pleasant to browse
Ease of use	Easy to use and navigate, flexible site
Trustworthiness	Reputation, information safety and security
Style	Helpful, friendly, knowledgeable, calm
Familiarity	Advertising online and offline, general familiarity
Settlement	Fast and flexible delivery and transactions

Source: Reprinted from H. van der Heijden and T. Verhage, "Online Store Image," *Information and Management* 41 (2004), pp. 609–17.

decisions for their physical store—store location, store size, merchandise. For example, analysis of its web shopper guided webstore Bonobos, the purveyor of upscale men's clothing, to open its physical stores, Guideshop, to solve the problem of customers' desire to try on clothes before they buy them online. Customers make appointments (usually lasting 45 minutes) to visit a Guideshop store for fittings. Guideshops are smaller stores (700 square feet) that carry sufficient inventory—khaki chinos in all 11 waist sizes and 4 inseam lengths—for store personnel to fit and size customers. Customers can then purchase clothing from the Bonobos website during their visit or at a later time of their choosing.

Analysis of webstore data may suggest that rather than a flagship store, the e-tailer is better served with a less expensive pop-up store in a high foot traffic area for a short amount of time (a few days to several months). This is an option that Etsey, seller of handmade products, and even eBay, the online auction house, have used. Like an old-fashioned craft fair, Etsy's pop-up stores provided a physical space for its sellers to showcase their handmade products. Sellers used laptops to show their inventory and used smart devices to transact sales using Paypal and Square. E-bay's first physical store, its Christmas emporium in London, was housed in a container box. Opened for four days of holiday shopping, it attracted 2,500 customers. The store's virtual inventory consisted of 350 top-rated products projected onto walls, each accompanied by social media recommendations and bearing a QR (quick response) code that consumers could scan with mobile devices to pay eBay. By establishing an offline presence, these online retailers are doubling down benefits from the interaction of their physical and web markets. Physical stores showcase selected merchandise that consumers can touch and feel while relying on their e-stores' virtual merchandise for their backroom inventory. The physical store can attract new customers while simultaneously creating buzz for its web market customers.

Critical Thinking Questions

1. What products are currently marketed web-only that in your opinion should remain web-only versus those that should consider establishing a (permanent, pop-up) physical store?
2. Some traditional retailers (Macy's, Nordstrom's, Walmart) have made themselves multi-channel. They have established web stores, allowing customers the convenience to buy online and return in store. Has this convenience encouraged you to buy products that you otherwise wouldn't have?
3. Would you consider yourself an omni-channel shopper? What is the value of this approach to you as a consumer?

As these studies suggest, overall retailer image (both Internet and store-based) relates to both functional and affective dimensions. The importance of the affective component cannot be overstated.

Marketers make extensive use of image data in formulating retail strategies.[36] First, marketers control many of the elements that determine an outlet's image. Second, differing groups of consumers desire different things from various types of retail outlets. Thus, a focused, managed image that matches the target market's desires on both affective and functional elements is essential for most retailers. For example, fashion retailers build affective image by relying on designer collections to enhance their high-end, fashion-forward appeal, as shown in Illustration 17–5.

Other outlets focus on more functional attributes. For example, Amazon.com and Buy.com focus heavily on breadth of merchandise and price. And stores like 7-Eleven focus almost exclusively on convenience (easy access, extended hours, and quick service) for consumers in those situations where convenience is the key attribute.

ILLUSTRATION 17-5

Designer collections are one way retailers can enhance their image and position their stores appropriately for their target customers.

Retailer Brands

Closely related to store image are **store brands.** At the extreme, the store or outlet is the brand. The Gap, Victoria's Secret, and Body Shop International are examples. All the items carried in the store are the store's own brand. Traditionally, retailers carried only manufacturers' brands, and only a few, such as Sears and Montgomery Wards, developed their own house or store brands. In the 1970s, many stores began to develop store brands as low-price alternatives to national brands, and many continue with this approach.[37]

Increasingly, however, retailers such as Walmart and Target are developing and promoting high-quality brands with either the store's name or an independent name. Such brands not only provide attractive margins for these outlets; if they are developed appropriately, they also become an important attribute of the outlet. That is, they are another reason for the consumer to shop that store.[38] And importantly, no other outlet can carry this brand. The key to success of store brands seems clear—high quality at a reasonable price. The traditional pattern of providing reasonable quality at a low price is no longer necessarily optimal.[39] In fact, emphasizing quality over price may be particularly beneficial if the brand carries the store's name or will become associated with the store. In fact, a recent study finds that, at least up to a point, increased consumer use of retailer brands (e.g., Target's Archer Farms) leads to increased loyalty to that retailer (Target).[40]

Expenditures of Individuals Drawn to a Store by an Advertised Item — FIGURE 17-3

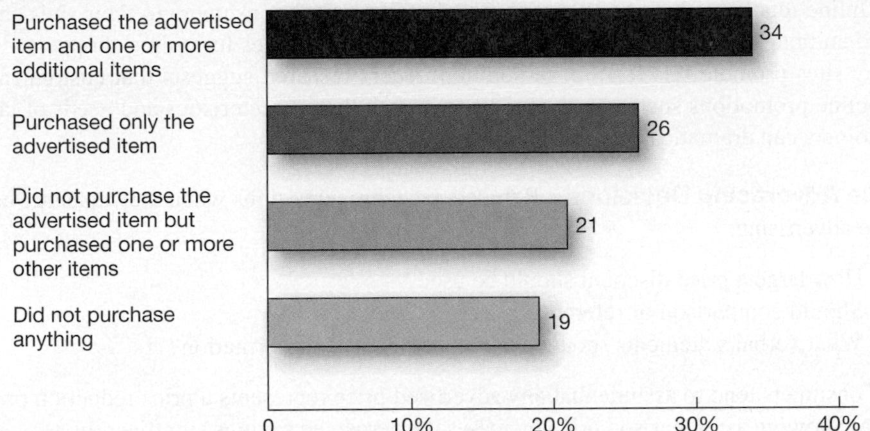

Retail Advertising

Retailers use advertising to communicate their attributes, particularly sale prices, to consumers. It is clear that price advertising (traditional, online, and mobile) can attract people to stores. Revealing results were obtained in a major study involving newspaper ads in seven cities for a range of product categories (motor oil, sheets, digital watches, pants, suits, coffee makers, dresses, and mattresses). The impact of the retail advertisements varied widely by product category. For example, 88 percent of those who came to the store in response to the advertisement for motor oil purchased the advertised item, compared with only 16 percent of those responding to the dress ad. Approximately 50 percent of the shoppers overall purchased the advertised item that attracted them to the store.

As Figure 17–3 illustrates, purchases of the advertised item understate the total impact of the ad. *Sales of additional items to customers who came to purchase an advertised item* are referred to as **spillover sales.** Spillover sales in this study equaled sales of the advertised items; that is, for every $1 spent on the sale item by people who came to the store in response to the advertising, another $1 was spent on some other item(s) in the store.[41]

Another study produced the results shown below:[42]

	Reason for Visiting Store	
Action	**Purchase Promoted Item**	**Other Reason**
Dollars spent on promoted items	$11.30	$ 3.27
Dollars spent on regular items	18.48	21.90
Total	$29.78	$25.17
Store profit	$ 5.64	$ 5.77

Retailers evaluating the benefits of price or other promotions must consider the impact on overall store sales and profits, not just those of the advertised item. And while a large percentage of retail advertising stresses price, particularly sales price, studies continue to show that price is frequently not the prime reason consumers select a retail outlet.[43] Thus, many retailers could benefit by emphasizing service, selection, or the affective benefits of their outlets. Affective benefits may be particularly effective for hedonic rather than utilitarian products.[44]

Online retailers advertise in mass media both to attract consumers to their sites and to build an image. Price and value are clearly important attributes for online shoppers,[45] and many sites promote this feature. In addition, recent research suggests that customization of online promotions such as e-mail to better match the characteristics and needs of target customers can dramatically increase online store traffic.[46]

Price Advertising Decisions Retailers face three decisions when they consider using price advertising:

1. How large a price discount should be used?
2. Should comparison or reference prices be used?
3. What verbal statements should accompany the price information?

Consumers tend to assume that any advertised price represents a price reduction or sale price. Showing a comparison price increases the perceived savings significantly. However, the strength of the perception varies with the manner in which the comparison or reference price is presented. A **reference price** is *a price with which other prices are compared.* In the claim, "Regularly $9.95, now only $6.95," $9.95 is the reference price. An **external reference price** is *a price presented by a marketer for the consumer to use to compare with the current price.* An **internal reference price** is *a price or price range*[47] *that a consumer retrieves from memory to compare with a price in the market.*[48]

Although there are situational influences and individual differences,[49] most consumers understand external reference prices and are influenced by them but do not completely believe them.[50] The reason for the lack of belief is the practice of some retailers of using inflated reference prices. These inflated prices could be "suggested list prices" in markets where virtually all sales are at a lower level. Or they may reflect prices that the store set for the merchandise originally that were too high and produced few sales. The price reduction being shown then merely corrects an earlier pricing error but does not provide meaningful benefit to the consumer. Because price and sale advertising have a strong impact on consumer purchases, the FTC and many states have special guidelines and regulations controlling their use.[51]

The best approach for retailers seems to be to present the sale price and (1) the dollar amount saved if it is large, (2) the percentage saved when it is large, and (3) both if both are large. Thus, $10 savings on a $200 item should show the dollar savings but not the percentage savings. A $10 saving on a $20 item could emphasize both the dollar and the percentage savings. A $1 saving on a $3 item should focus on the percentage savings.[52] The regular price could be shown in any of these conditions.[53] The regular price (the price on which the savings are calculated) should be the price at which the store normally sells a reasonable volume of the brand being discounted.

Such words or phrases as "now only," "compare at," or "special" appear to enhance the perceived value of a sale. However, this varies by situation, initial price level and discount size, consumer group, and retail outlet.[54] Is "50 percent off" or "buy one, get one free" likely to be perceived as a better value? It depends in large part on the nature of the item being promoted. For stock-up items such as detergent, they are viewed as equivalent. However, for perishable items such as bread, the "50 percent off" is seen as a better value.[55]

Retailers need to use caution in how they use price advertising. Such advertising signals not only the price of the advertised items but also the price level of the store.[56] And because price level, quality, service, and other important attributes are often linked in the consumer's mind, inappropriate price advertising can have a negative effect on the store's image.[57]

ILLUSTRATION 17-6

This sale ad focuses primarily on the dollar savings. Should the percentage savings also be stressed?

The ad in Illustration 17–6 places primary emphasis on the dollar savings but not the reference price or the sale price. To the extent that the target audience "knows" that the regular price for this item is high, they will use this internal reference price or range in making a judgment. And because the dollar savings are relatively large, the research we have reviewed suggests that presenting the dollar savings is sound strategy.

Outlet Location and Size

Location plays an important role in consumer store choice. If all other things are approximately equal, the consumer generally will select the closest store.[58] Likewise, the size of an outlet is an important factor. Unless the customer is particularly interested in fast service or convenience, he or she would tend to prefer larger outlets over smaller outlets, all other things being equal.[59] Interestingly, some of the major online players are "superstores" such as Amazon.com. Thus, retailer size appears to play a role online as well.

The **retail attraction model,** also called the **retail gravitation model,** is used to calculate the level of store attraction based on store size and distance from the consumer. In the retail gravitation model, store size is measured in square footage and assumed to be a measure of breadth of merchandise. The distance or travel time to a store is assumed to be a measure of the effort, both physical and psychological, to reach a given retail area.

The effect of distance or travel time varies by product.[60] For a convenience item or minor shopping good, distance is important because shoppers are unwilling to travel very far for such items. However, major high-involvement purchases such as automobiles or specialty items such as wedding dresses generate greater willingness to travel.

Willingness to travel also varies with the size of the shopping list for that trip.[61] Thus, a consumer who would not be willing to travel very far to purchase three or four convenience items may willingly go much farther if 20 or 30 such items are to be purchased on the same trip.

Consumers often combine shopping trips and purposes.[62] Thus, a consumer may visit a health club, have lunch with a friend, pick up the laundry, shop for food for the next few days, and pick up a prescription on one trip. Thus, retail patronage is in part a function of an outlet's location in relation to other outlets and consumers' travel patterns. Combining outlets or adding departments in response to such shopping patterns can produce value for customers and increased revenue for the firm.[63] For example, many supermarkets also have pharmacies.

CONSUMER CHARACTERISTICS AND OUTLET CHOICE

The preceding discussion by and large has focused on store attributes independently of the specific characteristics of the consumers in the target market. However, different consumers have vastly differing desires and reasons for shopping. This section of the chapter examines two consumer characteristics that are particularly relevant to store choice: perceived risk and shopper orientation.

Perceived Risk

The purchase of products involves the risk (see Chapter 15) that they may not perform as expected. Such a failure may result in a high

- *Social cost* (e.g., a hairstyle that is not appreciated by one's peers).
- *Financial cost* (e.g., an expensive pair of shoes that become too uncomfortable to wear).
- *Time cost* (e.g., a television repair that requires the set to be taken to the shop, left, and then picked up later).
- *Effort cost* (e.g., a flash drive that is loaded with several hours of work before it fails).
- *Physical cost* (e.g., a new medicine that produces a harmful side effect).

The first of these is generally termed *social risk*; the next three are often considered to be *economic risk.* Product categories vary in the level and type of risk generally associated with them.[64] Table 17–1 shows that socks and gasoline are low in economic and social risk, while hairstyles and small gifts are low in economic risk but high in social risk. Other products, such as personal computers and auto repairs, are low in social risk but high in economic risk. Finally, automobiles and living room furniture are high in both economic and social risk.[65] Table 17–1 also indicates the role of the situation in perceived risk. Wine is shown as low in both social and economic risk when used for personal consumption but high in social risk when served while entertaining.

The perception of these risks differs among consumers, depending in part on their past experiences and lifestyles. For this reason, **perceived risk** is considered a consumer characteristic as well as a product characteristic.[66] For example, while many individuals would feel no social risk associated with the brand of car owned, others would.

Like product categories, retail outlets are perceived as having varying degrees of risk. Traditional outlets are perceived as low in risk, whereas more innovative outlets such as online are viewed as higher risk.[67]

TABLE 17-1 The Economic and Social Risk of Various Types of Products

Social Risk	Economic Risk: Low	Economic Risk: High
Low	Wine (personal use) Socks Kitchen supplies Pens/pencils Gasoline	Personal computer Auto repairs Clothes washer Insurance Doctor/lawyer
High	Fashion accessories Hairstyles Gifts (inexpensive) Wine (entertaining) Deodorant	Business suits Living room furniture Automobile Snowboard Ski suit

The above findings lead to a number of insights into retailing strategy,[68] including the following:

- Nontraditional outlets need to minimize the perceived risk of shopping, particularly if they sell items with either high economic or social risk. Lands' End attempts to reduce perceived risk by emphasizing toll-free ordering, 24-hour toll-free customer service telephones with trained assistants, and a 100 percent satisfaction guarantee. Word-of-mouth from satisfied customers reinforces these advertised policies.
- Nontraditional outlets need brand-name merchandise in those product categories with high perceived risk. Most Internet retailers feature such items.
- Traditional outlets and websites of well-known retailers have a major advantage with high-perceived-risk product lines. These lines should generally be their primary strategy focus. Low-risk items can be used to round out the overall assortment.
- Economic risks can be reduced through warranties, reasonable return policies, security verification systems, and so forth. As we've seen, such factors are critical to online shopping where financial security concerns are high. Social risk is harder to reduce. A skilled sales force, known brands, and satisfaction guarantees can help reduce this type of risk.

Illustration 17–7 shows how one retailer reduces perceived risk by providing a product-replacement guarantee.

Shopping Orientation

Individuals go shopping for more complex reasons than simply acquiring a product or set of products. Diversion from routine activities, exercise, sensory stimulation, social interactions, learning about new trends, and even acquiring interpersonal power ("bossing" clerks) are nonpurchase reasons for shopping.[69] Of course, the relative importance of these motives varies both across individuals and within individuals over time as the situation changes.[70] See again Illustration 17–3, which shows how malls can provide an inviting environment for activities in addition to shopping.

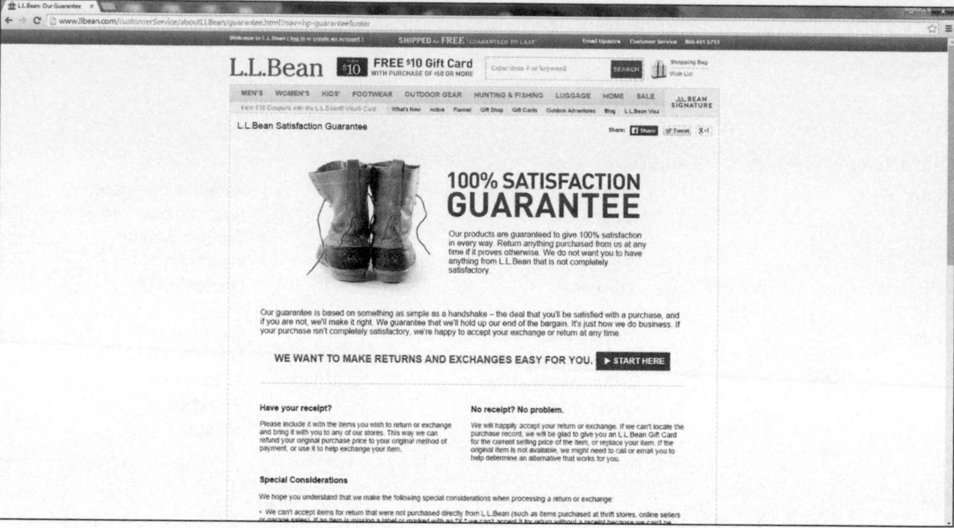

ILLUSTRATION 17-7

Guaranteeing complete satisfaction no matter what can greatly reduce the perceived risk of a purchase, particularly one made via catalog or online.

A shopping style that puts particular emphasis on certain activities or shopping motivations is called a **shopping orientation.** Shopping orientations are closely related to general lifestyle and are subject to similar influences. A recent study examined the shopper motivations of consumers across four different types of retailers (traditional malls, outlet malls, discount stores, and category killers) and found five shopping orientation segments that operated across all four types of retailers.[71]

1. *Apathetic Shoppers* (16 percent of mall shoppers) have no particular shopping motive and are "indifferent toward shopping."
2. *Enthusiast Shoppers* (22 percent of mall shoppers) enjoy shopping and are motivated by many aspects of shopping including recreational and social aspects, and "obtain entertainment value" from shopping.
3. *Destination Shoppers* (21 percent of mall shoppers) are motivated primarily by the anticipated utility of obtaining brand name and image-enhancing products and not by other factors such as socializing.
4. *Basic Shoppers* (22 percent of mall shoppers) are motivated primarily by getting exactly what they want in the least amount of time. Shopping is necessary but not recreational or social.
5. *Bargain Seekers* (20 percent of mall shoppers) are motivated by their perceived role as a shopper who gets good deals and lower prices. Recreational and social aspects of shopping are not of interest.

Clearly *Destination Shoppers* may seek out boutique shops to find their brand name products. However, they also shop at Target and other discounters who have added designer labels to their line-up. And attracting *Enthusiast Shoppers* requires the addition of recreational and social aspects to the retail environment to keep it fun and interesting. Music, layout, store personnel, and displays all work together to create such environments. *Bargain Seekers* may not be the appropriate target for all retail stores, but traditional malls are now adding such retailers as Walmart and Home Depot as anchor stores to cater to the needs of this segment. And *Basic Shoppers* are being offered the convenience of such service-oriented retailers as Lens Crafters and Supercuts.

IN-STORE AND ONLINE INFLUENCES ON BRAND CHOICES

L04

It is not uncommon to enter a retail outlet with the intention of purchasing a particular brand but to leave with a different brand or additional items. Influences operating within the retail outlet induce additional information processing and subsequently affect the final purchase decision. This portion of the chapter examines seven variables that singularly and in combination influence brand decisions inside a retail outlet (either a store or website): *point-of-purchase materials, price reductions, outlet atmosphere, stockout situations, website design, mobile and mobile apps,* and *sales personnel.* We begin by examining the extent and nature of unplanned purchases.

The Nature of Unplanned Purchases

The fact that consumers often purchase brands different from or in addition to those planned has led to an interest in unplanned purchases. **Unplanned purchases** are defined as *purchases made in a retail outlet that are different from those the consumer planned to make prior to entering that retail outlet.* While the term *unplanned purchase* implies a lack of rationality or alternative evaluation, this is not necessarily true. For example, the decision to purchase Del Monte rather than Green Giant peas because Del Monte is on sale is certainly not illogical.

Viewing most in-store and online purchase decisions as the result of additional information processing within the retail outlet leads to more useful marketing strategies than does viewing such purchases as random or illogical.[72] This approach allows the marketer to utilize knowledge of the target market, its motives, and the perception process to increase sales of specific items. Point-of-Purchase Advertising International (POPAI) uses the following definitions regarding in-store purchases:

- *Specifically planned.* A specific brand or item decided on before visiting the store and purchased as planned.
- *Generally planned.* A prestore decision to purchase a product category such as vegetables but not the specific item.
- *Substitute.* A change from a specifically or generally planned item to a functional substitute.
- *Unplanned.* An item bought that the shopper did not have in mind on entering the store.
- *In-store decisions.* The sum of generally planned, substitute, and unplanned purchases.

Unplanned purchases as defined above can be further subdivided into two categories: reminder purchases and impulse purchases. A *reminder purchase* would occur when a consumer notices Band-Aids in a store and remembers that she is almost out at home.[73] An **impulse purchase** would occur when a consumer sees a candy bar in the store and purchases it with little or no deliberation as the result of a sudden, powerful urge to have it.[74]

Figure 17–4 and Table 17–2 illustrate the extent of purchasing (in the United States and Canada) that is not specifically planned. It reveals that consumers make most item or brand decisions *after* entering the store. Interestingly, high levels of in-store decision making have also been found in the United Kingdom (76 percent), France (76 percent), Belgium (69 percent), Holland (80 percent), Australia (70 percent), and Brazil (88 percent).[75] *Can you explain differences in terms of cultural values?*

The research by POPAI regarding in-store decision rates has recently been confirmed by a 2008 OgilvyAction study of "six retail channels in the U.S." based on nearly 7,000 shopper intercept interviews. From this, they concluded that "72.4 percent of shoppers make in-store purchase decisions at the category, brand or quantity level."[76]

FIGURE 17-4 Supermarket Decisions: Two-Thirds Are Made In-Store

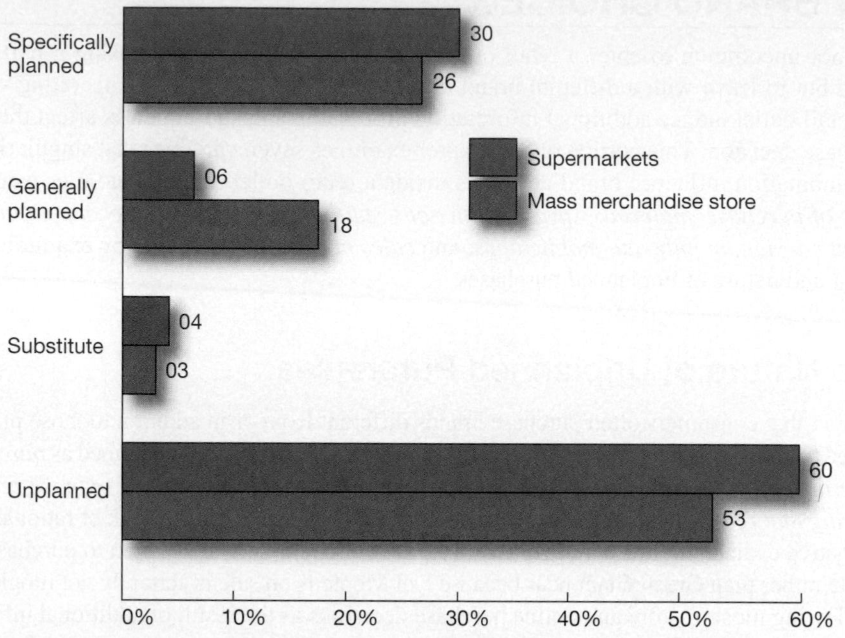

Source: *1995 POPAI Consumer Buying Habits Study* (Washington, DC: Point-of-Purchase Institute, 1995), p. 18, www.popai.com.

TABLE 17-2 In-Store Purchase Behavior

Product	Specifically Planned	Generally Planned	+	Substituted	+	Unplanned	=	In-Store Decisions
Total study average*	30%	6%		4%		60%		70%
Hair care*	23	4		5		68		77
Magazines/newspapers*	11	3		1		84		89
Oral hygiene products*	30	5		5		61		71
Automotive oil*	21	–		–		79		79
Tobacco products*	32	6		–		61		68
Coffee*	42	5		6		47		58
First-aid products*	7	10		–		83		93
Cereal*	33	9		6		52		67
Soft-drinks*	40	3		5		51		60
Mixers	23	6		4		68		77
Fresh fruits, vegetables*	67	7		1		25		33
Cold remedies†	28	35		19		18		72
Toothpaste/toothbrushes†	38	31		16		15		62
Antacids/laxatives†	39	37		12		12		61
Facial cosmetics†	40	34		11		15		60

Sources: **1995 POPAI Consumer Buying Habits Study* (Englewood, NJ: Point-of-Purchase Advertising Institute, 1995);
†*1992 POPAI/Horner Canadian Drug Store Study* (Englewood, NJ: Point-of-Purchase Advertising Institute, 1992).

However, overall statistics can hide the fact that the rate of in-store and unplanned purchasing varies by product, consumer, and situation.

- ***Product.*** You may have noticed in Table 17–2 that some grocery items such as fresh fruits and vegetables, soft drinks, coffee, and antacids have relatively higher specifically planned rates. The rates of planning look even higher if you include generally planned. Interestingly, a recent grocery shopping study found that "94 percent of U.S. households prepare a written shopping list prior to grocery shopping, and 72 percent of shoppers never or only occasionally buy items not on the list."[77] It should be noted that grocery lists often include what POPAI would term "generally planned" and thus would still fall under "in-store" decisions. That's because as long as consumers must make some sort of decision, be it product type, brand, or size, then there is a chance for the retailer to have influence in the store.
- ***Consumer.*** While overall POPAI estimates in-store decisions are made 70 percent of the time, this is higher in China (88 percent) and much lower in Germany (38 percent).[78] Considering the cultural, historical, and value-related factors that drive such differences, it is critical for marketers to understand on a country-by-country basis.
- ***Situation.*** When consumers choose a retailer for its lower prices and are only shopping one store during their outing (e.g., a trip to Walmart to shop for groceries for the week), unplanned purchases are higher.[79]

In conclusion, while the rate and nature of consumer in-store decisions vary as a function of numerous factors, consumers still make a substantial number of decisions "in-store." Thus, marketing efforts to influence in-store decisions are substantial as well. Such efforts are discussed next.

Point-of-Purchase Materials

Point-of-purchase (P-O-P) materials are common in the retailing of many products, and the impact these materials have on brand sales can be substantial. Recent research by POPAI examined the sales increase or "lift" generated by the addition of various types of P-O-P materials in supermarkets.[80] They examined both store-shelf and product-display materials. Shelf-based materials are placed in the main shelf for the product category and include price signage, coupon dispensers, shelf talkers, and dangling signage. Product display materials are those included with product displays located at the ends of aisles (end caps), on the store floor, and so on. Figure 17–5 provides a visual representation of the lift provided by four different shelf-based P-O-P materials.

The Sales Impact of Shelf-Based Point-of-Purchase Materials **FIGURE 17-5**

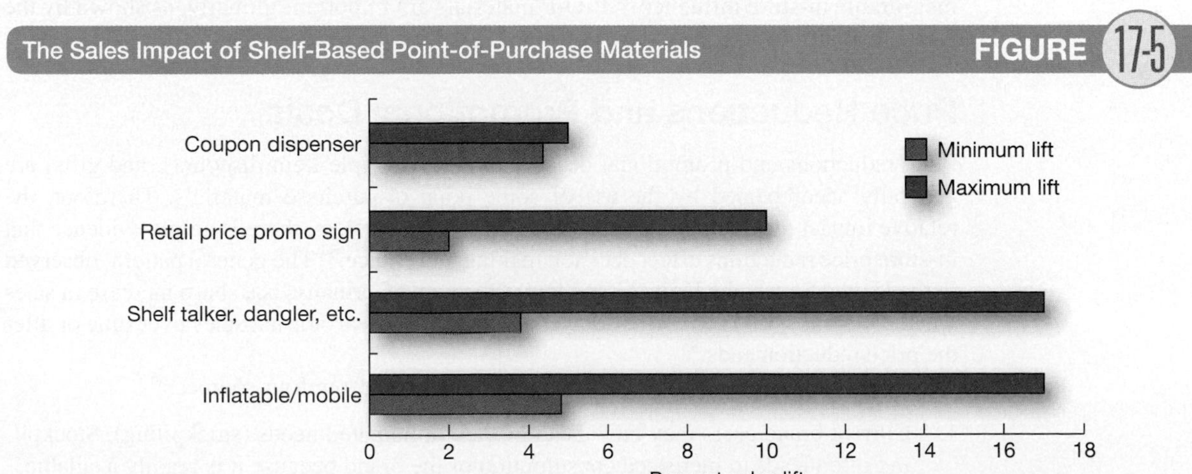

Source: *2001 POPAI P-O-P Measure UP: Learnings from the Supermarket Class of Trade Study* (Washington, DC: POPAI, 2001), www.popai.com.

ILLUSTRATION 17-8

Point-of-purchase displays such as these Nestle displays, are effective across cultures.

This figure demonstrates that the effectiveness of P-O-P materials can vary substantially. Effectiveness can also vary across brands and products. Factors such as frequency of promotion, brand familiarity, prevalence of certain types of P-O-P, and extent of P-O-P change can influence effectiveness. Many of these factors relate to the ability to capture consumer attention (Chapter 8). Consider the following comment from a POPAI report:

> When consumers visit the main shelf and the same types of P-O-P advertisements are presented from week to week and brand-to-brand, they appear to be less receptive to the message.[81]

Thus, the relative prevalence of price promotion signs and coupon dispensers may help to explain why they provide less lift than do other approaches. Despite variability across type, category, and brand, P-O-P materials are an important and increasingly measurable in-store influence.[82] P-O-P materials are important globally, as shown by the Nestle displays in Illustration 17–8.

Price Reductions and Promotional Deals

Price reductions and promotional deals (coupons, multiple-item discounts, and gifts) are generally accompanied by the use of some point-of-purchase materials. Therefore, the relative impact of each is sometimes not clear.[83] Nonetheless, there is ample evidence that in-store price reductions affect decision making and choice.[84] The general pattern, observed in the United States, the United Kingdom, Japan, and Germany, is a sharp increase in sales when the price is first reduced, followed by a return to near-normal sales over time or after the price reduction ends.[85]

Sales increases in response to price reductions come from four sources:[86]

1. Current brand users may buy ahead of their anticipated needs (stockpiling). Stockpiling often leads to increased consumption of the brand because it is readily available.
2. Users of competing brands may switch to the reduced-price brand. These new brand buyers may or may not become repeat buyers of the brand.

3. Nonproduct category buyers may buy the brand because it is now a superior value to the substitute product or to "doing without."
4. Consumers who do not normally shop at the store may come to the store to buy the brand.

ILLUSTRATION 17-9

Retail website designs such as that shown in the Gardner's Supply website should create an appropriate atmosphere or feelings as well as provide content and functionality.

High-quality brands tend to benefit more than brands from lower-quality tiers when prices are reduced, and they suffer less when prices are raised.[87]

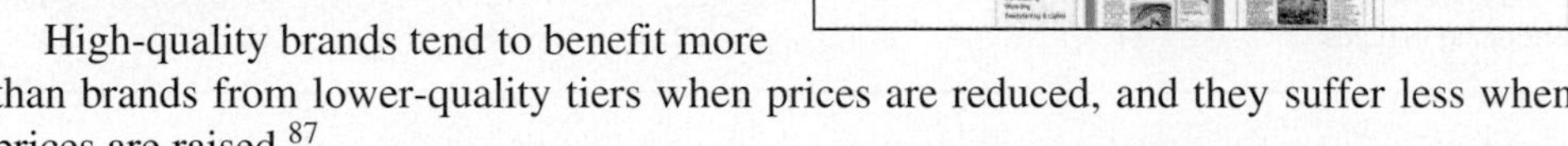

As discussed earlier under price advertising, consumers judge store quality and image in part on the basis of the number and nature of reduced-price items in the store.[88] Therefore, retailers need to carefully consider their sale price policies in view of both the sales of the discounted items and the impact these discounts will have on the store image. In addition, shoppers who purchase a large number of items at one time prefer stores with "everyday low prices"—all items in the store have relatively low prices but few are reduced beyond that level ("on sale")—to stores with somewhat higher standard prices but many sale items.[89] Is a shirt from an Internet retailer priced at $24.95 plus $5.00 shipping and handling a better or worse deal than the same shirt priced at $29.95 with shipping and handling free? Consumers tend to perceive the former to be a better deal than the latter. Research has shown that *partitioned prices* (the first scenario above) produced greater demand and a lower recalled total cost than the combined price (the second scenario).[90]

Outlet Atmosphere

Store atmosphere is influenced by such attributes as lighting, layout, presentation of merchandise, fixtures, floor coverings, colors, sounds, odors, and the dress and behavior of sales and service personnel (see Chapter 13).

Atmosphere is referred to as **servicescape** when describing a service business such as a hospital, bank, or restaurant.[91] **Atmospherics** is the process managers use to manipulate the physical retail or service environment to create specific mood responses in shoppers. Internet retailers also have *online atmospheres* that are determined by graphics, colors, layout, content, entertainment features, interactivity, tone, and so forth.[92] *What type of atmosphere is portrayed in the Gardner's Supply site shown in Illustration 17–9?*

A store's atmosphere affects the shopper's mood/emotions and willingness to visit and linger. It also influences the consumer's judgments of the quality of the store and the store's image.[93] Similarly, recent research shows that online atmospherics influence shopping behavior. For example, one study found that designing a website to elicit affective responses such as pleasure and arousal leads to increased willingness to browse.[94] Another study found that when a website offers restricted navigation, negative emotions (due to consumers' felt loss of control) occur, which lead to website avoidance.[95] Perhaps more important, positive mood/emotion induced while in the store or website increases satisfaction with the store or website, which can produce repeat visits and store loyalty.[96]

A major component of store atmosphere is the *number, characteristics, and behavior of other customers.*[97] Crowding must be considered because it can generate negative emotions and reduce browsing. And training staff how to appropriately deal with unruly customers is critical because the behaviors of other customers can influence the overall atmosphere.[98]

Music can have a major impact on the store environment (see Chapter 13). It can influence the time spent in the store or restaurant, the mood of the consumer, and the overall impression of the outlet.[99] However, it is important to match the music to the target audience. As shown below, baby boomers responded positively to classic rock music in a supermarket setting, but older adults did not:[100]

	Baby Boomers			Older Adults		
	Classic Rock	Big Band	Top 40	Classic Rock	Big Band	Top 40
Items purchased	31	11	15	4	12	14
Dollars spent	34	21	21	16	17	24
Shopping minutes	27	16	29	21	30	28

Marketers are also beginning to investigate the impact of *odors* on shopping behaviors (see Chapter 13).[101] Early studies suggest that odors can have a positive effect on the shopping experience, particularly if they are consistent with other aspects of the atmosphere such as the music being played.[102] However, like music, odor preference varies across customers, so caution must be used to ensure that the aroma is not offensive to target customers.[103]

Figure 17–6 illustrates the way store atmosphere influences shopper behavior. Several aspects in this figure are noteworthy. First, the physical environment interacts with

FIGURE 17-6 Store Atmosphere and Shopper Behavior

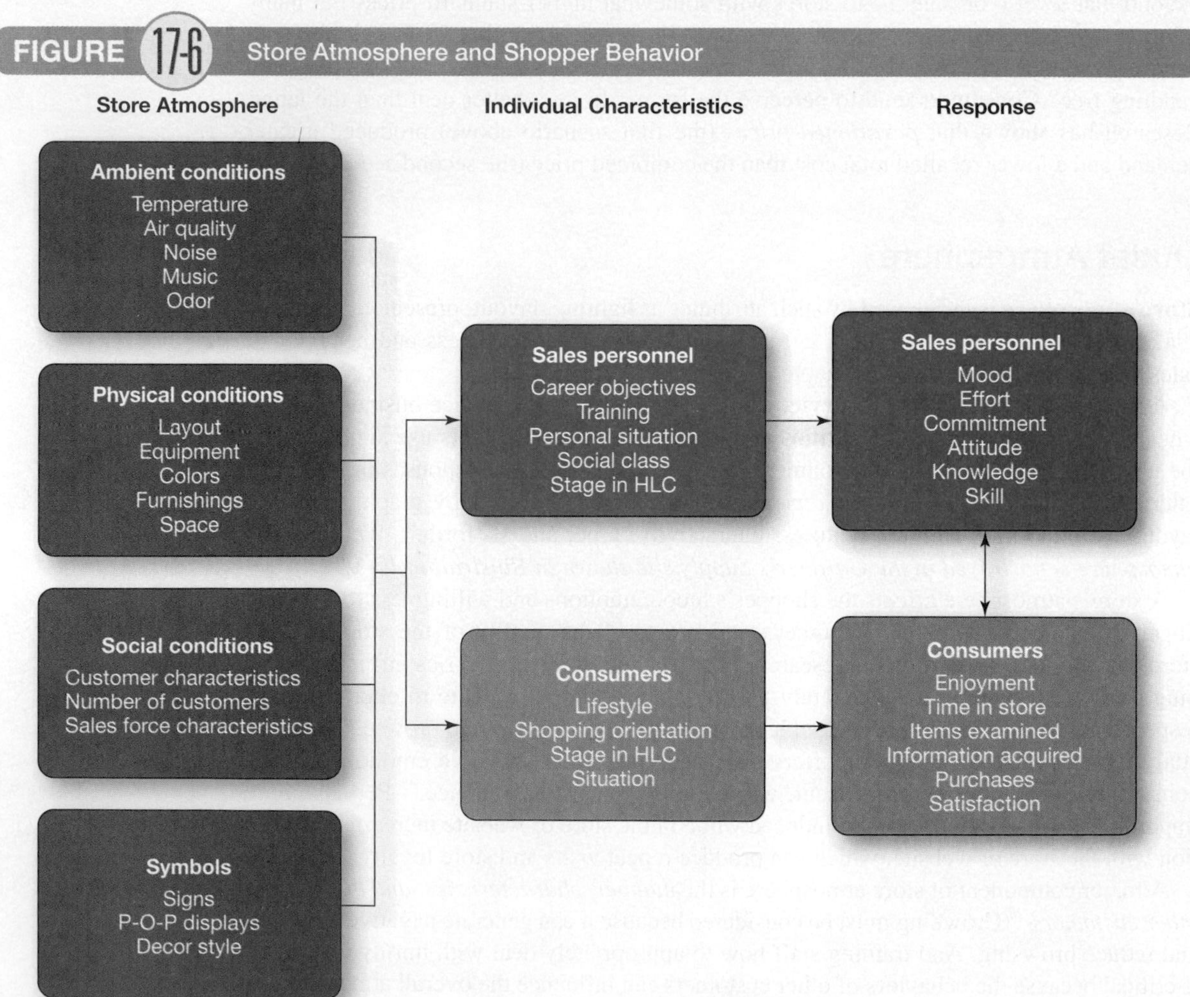

Source: "Framework for Understanding Environment-User Relationships in Service Organizations," Figure 2 in M. J. Bitner, "Servicescapes: The Impact of Physical Surroundings on Customers and Employees," from the April 1992 issue of the *Journal of Marketing.* Used by permission.

individual characteristics. Thus, an atmosphere that would produce a favorable response in teenagers might produce a negative response in older shoppers. Second, store atmosphere influences sales personnel and customers, whose interactions then influence each other. Finally, while this model focuses on store-based retailing, emerging research will continue to advance our understanding of online atmospherics.

Stockouts

Stockouts, *the store being temporarily out of a particular brand,* obviously affect a consumer's purchase decision. The consumer must then decide whether to (a) buy the same brand but at another store, (b) switch brands, (c) delay the purchase and buy the desired brand later at the same store, or (d) forgo the purchase altogether. Stockouts can also produce negative attitudes and/or word-of-mouth concerning the original store or positive attitudes and/or word-of-mouth concerning the substitute store or brand.

Three types of perceived costs affect the likely response of a consumer to a stockout.[104] *Substitution costs* refer to the reduction in satisfaction the consumer believes a replacement size, brand, or product will provide. This is a function of the consumer's commitment or loyalty to the preferred brand and the perceived similarity of potential substitutes.[105] *Transaction costs* refer to the mental, physical, time, and financial costs of purchasing a substitute product or brand. *Opportunity costs* are the reduction in satisfaction associated with forgoing or reducing consumption of the product.[106]

Website Functioning and Requirements

Recent research suggests that roughly 7 in 10 online shopping carts are started but abandoned prior to purchase. This means billions in potential lost sales. The top five reasons for shopping cart abandonment are as follows:[107]

Shipping and handling costs too high	44%
Not ready to make the purchase	41
Wanted to compare prices on other sites	27
Product price higher than willing to pay	25
Wanted to save products in cart for later consideration	24

Clearly, there are many areas in which the design and functioning of retail websites can be improved. Obviously, managing shipping charges is important and companies are responding. Amazon.com offers Amazon Prime, a member-based program where consumers pay a fixed annual fee for free second-day shipping and reduced-rate overnight. Some re-targeting efforts toward abandoned carts utilize e-mail marketing campaigns focused in part on some sort of promotional deal as we saw earlier in this chapter, in part because price and delivery charges are important online components. Complexity of the online buying process is also a problem. As a consequence, online retailers are simplifying and streamlining the online checkout process.[108] Some companies, such as Lands' End, are offering live chat, which connects consumers to a customer service representative at any point in the checkout process to answer questions and offer help. Security is an ongoing concern. Various website strategies are possible, as we discussed earlier. In addition, credit card companies are getting into the game with *single-use numbers.* Consumers who were offered and adopted this controlled payment option increased their online purchases between 50 and 200 percent.[109]

Improving Website Functionality

Website Factor	Percent
More detailed product information	45
Better search capabilities	36
Live help options	29
Better navigation	26
Make it easier to contact store	25
Improve the checkout process	22
More offers tailored to my interests or needs	16
Provide better access via mobile and social media	8

Source: *Consumer Shopping Experiences, Preferences, and Behaviors* (Cambridge, MA: ATG, October 2010).

A recent study by ATG asked consumers how the online shopping experience could be improved.[110] Many of the factors that consumers suggested appear to be capable of increasing online purchase rates. Some of the major factors are shown in Table 17–3.

Clearly consumers who abandoned carts because they were not ready (second highest reason) may have been unprepared due to their perception that they didn't have good enough information to make a choice. Thus, more detailed information and easier-to-access information (via search and navigation) should increase online purchases. Personalized offerings tend to motivate purchases because they are more directly relevant to consumer problems.

Mobile and Mobile Apps

While mobile marketing is still in its relative infancy, it is clearly the next horizon for marketers. As we saw in Chapter 15, local mobile search is changing how consumers find stores and brands within stores. And, as Figure 17–2 and the omni-channel consumer suggest, mobile phones and apps are increasingly playing a role in how consumers shop *in the store.* Price comparison and coupon apps as well as mobile search functionality allow consumers to search for brands, prices, and deals while standing in a physical store. In no small way, mobile and mobile apps have become an in-store influence and can interact with other in-store elements to influence shopping in numerous ways that were historically not possible. And retailers, even powerful ones like Walmart, don't want to get left behind. Walmart has always been reluctant to provide pricing information publicly, but since the advent of price-comparison mobile apps, they have decided to do so in order to avoid being excluded from this important source of shopping influence. *Can you think of interesting ways that marketers could allow for mobile phones to interact with elements of the store and store shelf that would positively influence retail sales?*

Sales Personnel

For most low-involvement purchases in the United States, self-service is predominant. As purchase involvement increases, the likelihood of interaction with a salesperson also increases. Thus, most studies of effectiveness in sales interactions have focused on high-involvement purchases such as insurance, automobiles, or industrial products. There is no simple explanation for effective sales interactions. Instead, the effectiveness of sales efforts is influenced by the interactions of[111]

- The salesperson's knowledge, skill, and authority.
- The nature of the customer's buying task.
- The customer–salesperson relationship.

Thus, specific research is required for each target market and product category to determine the optimal personnel selling strategy.

Consider the following shopping experience:

> I also had lousy service in the store. The sales guy seemed to be trying to sell me the cheaper shoe to get me out the door. . . . The thing that irritated me was that I thought I was a fairly knowledgeable shopper and I thought that they should understand some of these things. . . . They weren't very knowledgeable. . . . I got the impression they didn't like their jobs.[112]

Is this consumer likely to return to this outlet? Will he recommend it to his friends? It is clear that knowledgeable, helpful salespeople enhance the shopping experience, while those who are not have the opposite effect.

In the online context, marketers are testing online sales clerks that interact with customers as they shop on their website. These online sales clerks are called *avatars* and can be defined as "virtual characters that can be used as company representatives." One study found that avatars increased store attitude, product attitude, and purchase likelihood. It also found that for high-involvement products, expert avatars were more influential because of their increased credibility, while for lower-involvement products, attractive-looking avatars were more effective as a result of their likeability.[113]

PURCHASE

LO5

Once the consumer has selected the brand and retail outlet, he or she must complete the transaction. This involves what is normally called *purchasing* or *renting* the product. In traditional retail environments, this was straightforward and did not generally stop or delay purchases, with the possible exception of major and more complex purchases such as a home or car. However, as we saw earlier, many consumers starting to make an online purchase quit without making one for a variety of reasons. Making online purchasing itself easier is clearly an important factor. Mobile and social network purchase options are emerging and will likely increase rapidly. Simplifying these will also be important.

Credit plays a major role in consumer purchases, and new technologies are being tested on an ongoing basis. And research indicates that the ability to pay by credit card rather than cash substantially increases consumers' willingness to pay and the amount they purchase.[114] Thus, it may be to the retailer's advantage to encourage credit card use even though it must pay a percentage of these sales to the credit card companies.

Businesses need to simplify the actual purchase as much as possible. This involves strategies as simple as managing the time spent in line at the checkout register to more complex operations, such as computerized credit checks to minimize credit authorization time. Many businesses appear to overlook the fact that the actual purchase act is generally the last contact the consumer will have with the store on that trip. Although first impressions are important, so are final ones. Store personnel need to be not only efficient at this activity but also helpful and personable. And online retailers need to minimize the complexity, hassle, and stress involved.

SUMMARY

LO1: Describe how retailing is evolving

Retail outlet refers to any source of products or services for consumers. Retailing has moved well beyond traditional physical stores and catalogs to include the Internet, interactive TV ads, and mobile shopping apps. Computers learn and recall consumer information and preferences; full-body scanners allow for custom-fit apparel; and interactive TV ads and shows do or will allow for product information search and purchase from the ad or show. The Internet and mobile phones and apps are changing the way consumers shop both prior to and during a store visit in unprecedented ways that are influencing the stores and brands that consumers choose.

LO2: Discuss the Internet and mobile as part of multi- and omni-channel shopping

Internet retailing and other forms of in-home retailing including catalogs are increasingly important retail outlets. While store-based retailing continues to dominate in terms of overall sales, consumers increasingly use in-home options such as the Internet and catalogs in combination with retail stores in what is known as *multi-channel shopping*. Retailers often operate in various formats (catalog, retail store, and Internet) to leverage the benefits that consumers derive from each.

In addition, mobile phones and apps have led to a form of shopping and shopper termed omni-channel. *Omni-channel shoppers* are consumers who browse and/or purchase in more than one channel *simultaneously*. Mobile phones and apps allow consumers to search for information, prices, coupons, and discounts, while standing in a physical store. Multi- and omni-channel consumers spend more at a given retailer than single-channel consumers, and retailers such as Macy's are courting these customers heavily with online and mobile functionality.

LO3: Explain the retail and consumer attributes that affect outlet selection

The decision process used by consumers to select a retail outlet is the same as the process described for selecting a brand. The only difference is in the nature of the evaluative criteria used. Retail outlet *image* is an important evaluative criterion. Store-based image and online retailer image are both important, although the dimensions consumers use to judge them vary. *Store brands* can both capitalize on a store's image and enhance, or detract from, it. *Outlet location and size* are important, with closer and larger outlets generally being preferred over more distant and smaller ones. Consumer characteristics such as *perceived risk* and *shopping orientation* are also important determinants of outlet choice.

LO4: Summarize the in-store and online influences on brand choice

While in a retail outlet, consumers often purchase a brand or product that differs from their plans before entering. Such purchases are referred to as *unplanned purchases*. Most of these decisions are the result of additional information processing induced by in-store or online stimuli. However, some are impulse purchases made with little or no deliberation in response to a sudden, powerful urge to buy or consume the product. Such variables as *point-of-purchase displays, price reductions, outlet atmosphere, website design, mobile and mobile apps, sales personnel,* and brand or product *stockouts* can have a major impact on sales patterns.

LO5: Understand how purchase plays a role in the shopping process

Once the outlet and brand have been selected, the consumer must acquire the rights to the item. This often involves credit. Whether purchasing is in-store, online, or via mobile or on social networks, the retailer's job is to simplify the process because it will enhance the likelihood of purchase and enhance their image.

SMARTBOOK™

KEY TERMS

Atmospherics 605
External reference price 596
Impulse purchase 601
In-home shopping 583
Internal reference price 596
Multi-channel shoppers 588
Omni-channel shoppers 590
Online privacy concerns 588
Perceived risk 598

Reference price 596
Retail attraction (gravitation) model 597
Servicescape 605
Shopping orientation 600
Spillover sales 595
Stockouts 607
Store atmosphere 605
Store brands 594
Store image 591
Unplanned purchases 601

REVIEW QUESTIONS

1. The consumer faces the problems of both what to buy and where to buy it. How do these two types of decisions differ?
2. How is the retail environment changing?
3. Describe Internet retailing.
4. What is *multi-channel shopping* and what implications does it hold for retailer strategy?
5. What is *omni-channel shopping* and what implications does it hold for retailer strategy?
6. What is meant by *online privacy concern?* Why is it a particularly important issue for online shoppers?
7. Describe the six segments of shoppers in terms of the Internet.
8. What is a *store image* and what are its dimensions and components?
9. Describe *Internet retailer image* and compare/contrast it with *store image.*
10. What is a *store brand?* How do retailers use store brands?
11. What key decisions do retailers make with respect to retail price advertising?
12. What is meant by the term *spillover sales?* Why is it important?
13. How does the size of and distance to a retail outlet affect store selection and purchase behavior?
14. How is store choice affected by the *perceived risk* of a purchase?
15. What is meant by *social risk?* How does it differ from *economic risk?*
16. What is a *shopping orientation?*
17. Describe five motivation-based shopping orientations across retail type.
18. What is meant by an *in-store purchase decision?* Why is it important?
19. What is meant by an *impulse purchase?* Why is it important?
20. Once in a particular retail outlet, what in-store and/or online characteristics can influence brand and product choice? Give an example of each.
21. Describe the impact of point-of-purchase displays on retail sales.
22. Describe the impact of price reductions and deals on retail sales.
23. What is meant by *store atmosphere? Online atmosphere?* How do they affect consumer behavior?
24. What is a *servicescape?*
25. Why do consumers planning to make a purchase at an online outlet often fail to do so?
26. What are frequent problems consumers encounter while shopping online?
27. What can happen in response to a *stockout?*

DISCUSSION QUESTIONS

28. Name two mobile apps that affect the choice of brands in the store?
29. Does the image of a retail outlet affect the image of the brands it carries? Do the brands carried affect the image of the retail outlet?
30. What challenges face multi-channel retailers in managing their image across channels?
31. Respond to the questions in Consumer Insight 17–1.
32. How are social and economic risks associated with the following products likely to affect the outlet choice behavior of consumers? How would the perception of these risks differ by consumer? Situation?
    a. Sports car
    b. Athletic shoes (for running)
    c. Wine (as a gift)
    d. Hairdresser

e. Mountain bike
f. Mouthwash
g. Cell phone
h. Movie for a date

33. Describe an appropriate strategy for an online store such as Target for each of the motivation-based shopping orientations described in the text.
34. Describe an appropriate strategy for an online store such as J. Crew for each of the five shopper segments related to Internet shopping described in the text.
35. Suggest other methods for developing motivation-based shopping orientations.
36. How should retailer strategies to encourage unplanned purchases differ depending on the type of unplanned purchase generally associated with the product category?
37. What in-store characteristics could traditional retailers use to enhance the probability of purchase among individuals who visit a store? Describe each factor in terms of how it should be used, and describe its intended effect on the consumer for the following products:
    a. Perfume
    b. Ice cream
    c. Coffee after a meal
    d. Flowers from a supermarket
    e. B12 drinkable shots
    f. Motor oil
38. What website characteristics could online retailers use to enhance the probability of purchase among individuals who visit their websites? Describe each factor in terms of how it should be used, and describe its intended effect on the consumer for the following products:
    a. Dorm furniture from Target.com
    b. Electronics from Amazon.com
    c. Laptop from HP.com
    d. Backpack from REI.com
    e. Apparel from JCPenney.com
    f. Cosmetics from Macys.com
    g. Tools from Sears.com
39. What type of store atmosphere is most appropriate for each of the following retailer types? Why?
    a. Bookstore serving college students
    b. Cosmetic section of Sears
    c. Auto dealership service department
    d. Consumer electronics
    e. Mercedes automobiles
    f. Inexpensive furniture
    g. Thai food restaurant
40. Repeat Question 39 (except for *c* and *g*) for online retailers.
41. How would you respond to a stockout of your preferred brand (or model) of the following? What factors other than product category would influence your response?
    a. SUV
    b. Cereal
    c. Deodorant
    d. Dress shirt/blouse
    e. Perfume/aftershave lotion
    f. Soft drink

APPLICATION ACTIVITIES

42. Describe the current state of Internet retailing.
43. Pick a residential area in your town and develop a gravitational model for (*a*) nearby supermarkets or (*b*) shopping malls. Conduct telephone surveys to test the accuracy of your model.
44. Develop a questionnaire to measure the image of the following. Have 10 other students complete these questionnaires. Discuss the marketing implications of your results.
    a. Target
    b. Americangirl.com
    c. Subway
    d. Local coffee shop
    e. BMW.com
    f. Walmart
    g. Saks Fifth Avenue
45. Have 10 students on your campus describe their shopping orientations in terms of animals as

follows: "Think about an animal that best describes you as a shopper and explain what it is about your shopping behavior that makes this animal an appropriate metaphor." Combine your descriptions with those of two other students. Do any patterns emerge? What are the retailing implications?

46. For several of the products listed in Table 17–2, interview several students not enrolled in your class and ask them to classify their last purchase as specially planned, generally planned, substitute, or unplanned. Then combine your results with those of your classmates to obtain an estimate of student behavior. Compare student behavior with the behavior shown in Table 17–2 and discuss any similarities or differences.
47. Arrange with a local retailer (convenience store, drugstore, or whatever) to temporarily install a point-of-purchase display. Then set up a procedure to unobtrusively observe the frequency of evaluation and selection of the brand before and while the display is up. Describe your findings.
48. Visit two retail stores selling the same type of merchandise and prepare a report on their use of P-O-P materials. Explain any differences.
49. Interview the manager of a drug, department, or grocery store on their views of P-O-P materials and price advertising.
50. Develop an appropriate questionnaire and construct a new version of Table 17–2, using products relevant to college students. What are the marketing implications of this table?
51. Determine, through interviews, the general shopping orientations of students on your campus. What are the marketing implications of your findings?
52. Interview 10 students on your campus and determine their attitudes toward and use of the Internet and online shopping. Place each into one of the six shopper segments described in the text. Do they fit into these segments? Combine your results with those of four other students. What do you conclude?

REFERENCES

1. This chapter opener is based on J. Reingold, "Is Brick-and-Mortar Retail in a Death Spiral?," *Fortune,* November 26, 2013, http://features.blogs.fortune.cnn.com/2013/11/26/is-brick-and-mortar-retail-in-a-death-spiral/, accessed August 29, 2014; C. Phillips, "Expert Predictions: The Demise of Bricks and Mortar Retail," *Power Retail,* February 6, 2013, www.powerretail.com.au/hot-topics/demise-of-bricks-and-mortar-retail/, accessed August 29, 2014; J. Wang, "Retailers Entice Shoppers with a Visual Hook," *Orange County Register,* January 21, 2014, www.heraldonline.com/2014/01/29/5618838/retailers-entice-shoppers-with.html, accessed August 29, 2014; K. Campbell-Dollaghan, "Nike's Kinect-Powered Window Displays Are Watching You," *Fast Company,* March 26, 2013, www.fastcodesign.com/1672213/nikes-kinect-powered-window-displays-are-watching-you, accessed August 29, 2014; "Ted Baker 'Merry Kissmas' Interactive Christmas Window Display," *BWD,* http://thebwd.com/ted-baker-merry-kissmas-interactive-christmas-window-display/, accessed August 29, 2014; C. W. Smith, "Burberry Regent Street," *Retail Innovation,* http://retail-innovation.com/burberry-regent-street/, accessed August 29, 2014; E. Williams, "Heritage Meets Digital in New Flagship Burberry Store," *Creative Review,* September 14, 2012, www.creativereview.co.uk/cr-blog/2012/september/burberry-mixes-heritage-with-digital-high-tech-in-new-london-store, accessed August 29, 2014; Burberry, "Burberry Regent Street Fact Sheet," press release, September 2012, www.emtecnica.com/burberry-regent-street-fact-sheet.pdf, accessed August 29, 2014; B. Andersen and W. Eckstein, "What's in Store—How Technology Is Transforming the Retail Industry," *KPMG,* June 2013, www.kpmg.com/US/en/services/Advisory/management-consulting/management-consulting-by-function/Documents/kpmg-retail-brick-and-mortar.pdf, accessed August 29, 2014; B. Johns, "Adidas' Digital Signage Boosts Sales By 40%," *Integrated Solutions for Retailers,* February 2013, www.retailsolutionsonline.com/doc/adidas-boosts-sales-with-digital-signage-0001?sectionCode=Spotlight&templateCode=EnhancedStandard&user=1863032&source=nl:36447, accessed August 29, 2014; S. Kessler, "Here's What Brick-and-Mortar Stores See When They Track You," *Fast Company,* August 1, 2013, www.fastcompany.com/3015060/heres-what-brick-and-mortar-stores-see-when-they-track-you, accessed August 29, 2014; O. Kharif, "Retailers Enlist the Smartphone to Encourage Shopping," *Bloomberg Businessweek,* April 4, 2013, www.businessweek.com/articles/2013-04-04/retailers-enlist-the-smartphone-to-encourage-shopping, accessed August 29, 2014; and A. Flaherty, "New Technology Helps Stores Track Your Every Move This Season," *Huffington Post,* November 30, 2013, www.huffingtonpost.com/2013/11/30/stores-track-you_n_4363811.html, accessed August 29, 2014.

2. Campbell-Dollaghan, "Nike's Kinect-Powered Window Displays Are Watching You."

3. S. Sherman, "Will the Information Superhighway Be the Death of Retailing?," *Fortune,* April 18, 1994, p. 17.

4. L. Petrecca, "Interactive TV Ads Are Clicking with Viewers," *USA Today,* July 11, 2008, www.usatoday.com, accessed June 24, 2011.

5. Information in table based on "Internet User Forecast by Country," *eTForecasts,* www.etforecosts.com, accessed June 24, 2011; "Forrester Forecast," *WorldTech24,* March 8, 2010, www.worldtech24.com, accessed June 15, 2011; and S. Mulpuru et al., *US Online Retail Forecast, 2010 to 2015* (Cambridge, MA: Forrester Research, Inc., February 28, 2011).

6. Mulpuru et al., *US Online Retail Forecast, 2010 to 2015.*

7. S. Chiger, "Consumer Shopping Survey: Part III," *Catalog Age,* November 1, 2001, pp. 1–4. Used by permission of Multichannel Merchant Magazine (formerly Catalog Age). Similar reasons for online shopping were found as recently as 2008 by Forrester Research. For details, visit http://blogs.forrester.com.

8. "USPS Study Shows Mailed Catalogs Boost Online Spending," *directmag.com,* September 28, 2004.

9. *Online Shopping* (Washington, DC: Pew Internet & American Life Project, February 13, 2008).

10. S. M. Kerner, "More Broadband Usage Means More Online Spending," *clickz.com,* October 8, 2004.

11. *Retail Shopper Segments* (Costa Mesa, CA: Experian Information Solutions, Inc., July 2009); and J. Loechner, "Holiday Layaway," *MediaPost,* www.mediapost.com, accessed June 15, 2011.

12. See, e.g., A. K. Kau, Y. E. Tang, and S. Ghose, "Typology of Online Shoppers," *Journal of Consumer Marketing,* 20, no. 2 (2003), pp. 139–56.

13. See, e.g., *US eCommerce Forecast: 2008 to 2012* (Cambridge, MA: Forrester Research, Inc., January 18, 2008).

14. *Why Some Consumers Don't Buy Online* (Cambridge, MA: Forrester Research, Inc., Research Report, 2005). *North American Technographics Retail Online Benchmark Recontact Survey* (Cambridge, MA: Forrester Research, Inc., 2010).

15. Kau, Tang, and Ghose, "Typology of Online Shoppers."

16. From Roper Reports Telephone Survey, August 2003.

17. See A. Z. Cuneo, "What's in Store?," *Advertising Age,* February 25, 2002, p. 1; and R. V. Kozinets et al., "Themed Flagship Brand Stores in the New Millennium," *Journal of Retailing,* 78 (2002), pp. 17–29.

18. S. M. Pardy, "For Retailers, Best Things That Come in Small Packages Include Stores," *CoStar,* May 16, 2007, www.costar.com, accessed June 25, 2011.

19. A. Z. Cuneo, "On Target," *Advertising Age,* December 11, 2000, p. 1.

20. A. Klaassen, "Ion Interactive Develops System to Turn Online Visitors into Customers," *Advertising Age,* December 11, 2006, p. 32.

21. See H. Smith, S. J. Milberg, and S. J. Burke, "Information Privacy: Individuals' Concerns about Organizational Practices," *MIS Quarterly,* 20, no. 2 (1996), pp. 167–96; and M. Metzger, "Effects of Site, Vendor, and Consumer Characteristics on Web Site Trust and Disclosure," *Communication Research* 33, no. 3 (2006), pp. 155–79.

22. For a description of the FTC's approach in this area and its fit with consumer concerns, see K. B. Sheehan and M. G. Hoy, "Dimensions of Privacy Concern among Online Consumers," *Journal of Public Policy & Marketing,* Spring 2000, pp. 62–73. See also J. Phelps, G. Nowak, and E. Ferrell, "Privacy Concerns and Consumer Willingness to Provide Personal Information," *Journal of Public Policy & Marketing,* Spring 2000, pp. 27–41; and K. B. Sheehan and T. W. Gleason, "Online Privacy," *Journal of Current Issues and Research in Advertising,* Spring 2001, pp. 31–41.

23. See, e.g., A. D. Miyazaki and A. Fernandez, "Consumer Perceptions of Privacy and Security Risks for Online Shopping," *Journal of Consumer Affairs,* 35, no. 1 (2001), pp. 27–44; E. B. Andrade, V. Kaltcheva, and B. Weitz, "Self-Disclosure on the Web," in *Advances in Consumer Research,* vol. 29, ed. S. M. Broniarczyk and K. Nakamoto (Provo, UT: Association for Consumer Research, 2002), pp. 350–53; A. D. Miyazaki and S. Krishnamurthy, "Internet Seals of Approval," *Journal of Consumer Affairs,* 36, no. 1 (2002), pp. 28–49; G. R. Milne and M. J. Culnan, "Strategies for Reducing Online Privacy Risks," *Journal of Interactive Marketing,* Summer 2004, pp. 15–29; and T. B. White, "Consumer Disclosure and Disclosure Avoidance," *Journal of Consumer Psychology,* 14, no. 1/2 (2004), pp. 41–51.

24. A. E. Schlosser, T. B. White, and S. M. Lloyd, "Converting Web Site Visitors into Buyers," *Journal of Marketing,* April 2006, pp. 133–48.

25. *Personal Information That US Internet Users Are Willing to Share with Internet Retailers, by Trust Level, 2004* (New York: eMarketer, 2005); and E. Xie, H. Teo, and W. Wan, "Volunteering Personal Information on the Internet: Effects of Reputation, Privacy Notices, and Rewards on Online Consumer Behavior," *Marketing Letters,* 17, no. 1 (2006), pp. 61–74.

26. The sections on multi-channel and omni-channel marketing are based on U. Konus, P. C. Verhoef, and S. A. Neslin, "Multichannel Shopper Segments and Covariates," *Journal of Retailing,* 84, no. 4 (2008), pp. 398–413; W. Kwon and S. J. Lennon, "Reciprocal Effects between Multichannel Retailers' Offline and Online Brand Images," *Journal of Retailing,* 82, no. 3 (2009), pp. 376–90; "Have You Met the Omni-Channel Shoppers?," *BizReport,* October 23, 2009, www.bizreport.com, accessed June 25, 2011; *Cross-Channel Shopping Behaviors* (Cambridge, MA: Forrester Research Inc., 2010); *Perfect Storm* (San Mateo, CA: Coremetrics, 2010); *Fuel Your Marketing Efforts* (San Mateo, CA: Coremetrics, 2010); *Cross-Channel Commerce* (Cambridge, MA: ATG, March 2010); and *Understanding Consumer Patterns and Preferences in Multi-Channel Retailing* (Somers, NY: IBM, 2011).

27. See, e.g., K.-P. Chiang and R. R. Dholakia, "Factors Driving Consumer Intention to Shop Online," *Journal of Consumer Psychology,* 13, no. 1/2 (2003), pp. 177–83; and R. W. Hamilton and D. V. Thompson, "Is There a Substitute for Direct Experience?," *Journal of Consumer Research,* December 2007, pp. 546–55.

28. L. R. Klein, "Creating Virtual Product Experiences," *Journal of Interactive Marketing,* Winter 2003, pp. 41–55; J. Nantel, "My Virtual Model," *Journal of Interactive Marketing,* Summer 2004, pp. 73–86; and J. Kim and S. Forsythe, "Adoption of Virtual Try-On Technology for Online Apparel Shopping," *Journal of Interactive Marketing,* Spring 2008, pp. 45–59.

29. L. Wang et al., "Can a Retail Web Site Be Social?," *Journal of Marketing,* July 2007, pp. 143–57.

30. "Shopping Cart Abandonment Emails Generate $17.90 per Email," *See Why,* http://seewhy.com/blog, accessed June 25, 2011; "Analysis: Promotions Make Big Impact on Abandoned Shopping Carts," *See Why,* http://seewhy.com/blog, accessed June 25, 2011; and *Retargeting Browsers and Abandoners* (San Mateo, CA: Coremetrics, 2011).

31. See also K. C. Gehrt and R.-N. Yan, "Situational, Consumer, and Retailer Factors Affecting Internet, Catalog, and Store Shopping," *International Journal of Retail and Distribution Management,* 32, no. 1 (2004), pp. 5–18.

32. B. Kilcourse, "Gaming Google," *Retail Systems Research,* March 1, 2011.

33. J. D. Lindquist, "Meaning of Image," *Journal of Retailing,* Winter 1974, pp. 29–38; see also M. R. Zimmer and L. L. Golden, "Impressions of Retail Stores," *Journal of Retailing,* Fall 1988, pp. 265–93.

34. This Consumer Insight is based on M. Wilson, "Ikea's New Catalog Magically Transforms into Furniture," *Fast Company,* August 2, 2013, www.fastcodesign.com/1673164/ikeas-new-catalog-magically-transforms-into-your-furniture, accessed August 29, 2014; L. Stinson, "So Smart: New Ikea App Places Virtual Furniture in Your Home," *Wired Magazine,* August 20, 2013, www.wired.com/design/2013/08/a-new-ikea-app-lets-you-place-3d-furniture-in-your-home/, accessed August 29, 2014; R. Empson, "Warby Parker Opens Retail Store in NYC, with Boston Up Next, Beats Google & Amazon to the Offline Punch," *Techcrunch,* April 4, 2013, http://techcrunch.com/2013/04/13/warby-parker-opens-retail-store-in-nyc-with-boston-up-next-beats-google-amazon-to-the-offline-punch/, accessed August 29, 2014; C. Chaey, "Take a Look Inside Warby Parker's New NYC Flagship Store," *Fast Company,* April 12, 2013, www.fastcompany.com/3008182/where-are-they-now/take-look-inside-warby-parkers-new-nyc-flagship-store, accessed August 29, 2014; S. Clifford, "Once Proudly Web Only, Shopping Sites Hang Out Real Shingles," *New York Times,* December 18, 2012, www.nytimes.com/2012/12/19/business/shopping-sites-open-brick-and-mortar-stores.html?_r=0, accessed August 29, 2014; O. St. John, "Bonobos Opens Stores That Don't Sell Anything," *USA Today,* March 12, 2013, www.usatoday.com/story/money/business/2013/03/12/savvy-small-business-bonob s-ants/1916885/, accessed August 29, 2014; L. Bustos, "Why Online Pure Plays Are Opening Physical Shops," *Get Elastic ecommerce,* February 4, 2013, www.getelastic.com/why-online-pure-plays-are-opening-physical-shops/, accessed August 29, 2014; and P. Marsden, "e-Bay's London Pop-Up Shop: A Vision of Social Commerce Tomorrow?," *Digital Intelligence Today,* December 4, 2012, http://digitalintelligencetoday.com/EBAYS-LONDON-POP-UP-SHOP-A-VISION-OF-SOCIAL-COMMERCE-TOMORROW/, accessed August 29, 2014.

35. H. van der Heijden and T. Verhagen, "Online Store Image," *Information and Management,* 41 (2004), pp. 609–17. See also J. R. Coyle and E. Thorson, "The Effects of Progressive Levels of Interactivity and Vividness in Web Marketing Sites," *Journal of Advertising,* Fall 2001, pp. 65–77; C. Page and E. Lepkowska-White, "Web Equity," *Journal of Consumer Marketing,* 19, no. 3 (2002), pp. 231–48; E. J. Johnson, S. Bellman, and G. L. Lohse, "Cognitive Lock-In and the Power Law of Practice," *Journal of Marketing,* April 2003, pp. 62–75; and P. Katerattanakul and K. Siau, "Creating a Virtual Store Image," *Communications in ACM,* December 2003, pp. 226–32. See also B. B. Holloway and S. E. Beatty, "Satisfiers and Dissatisfiers in the Online Environment," *Journal of Service Research,* May 2008, pp. 347–64.

36. See N. Sirohi, E. W. McLaughlin, and D. R. Witink, "A Model of Consumer Perceptions and Store Loyalty Intentions for a Supermarket Retailer," *Journal of Retailing,* 2 (1998), pp. 223–45; and K. Macarthur, "What's in a Name?," *Advertising Age,* April 17, 2006, p. 43.

37. See S. Burton, D. R. Lichtenstein, R. G. Netemeyer, and J. A. Garretson, "A Scale for Measuring Attitude toward Private Label Products," *Journal of the Academy of Marketing Science,* Fall 1998, pp. 293–306.

38. See M. Corstjens and R. Lal, "Building Store Loyalty through Store Brands," *Journal of Marketing Research,* August 2000, pp. 281–91.

39. P. S. Richardson, A. K. Jain, and A. Dick, "Household Store Brand Proneness," *Journal of Retailing,* 2 (1996), pp. 159–85; and S. C. Choi and A. T. Coughlan, "Private Label Positioning," *Journal of Retailing,* 82, no. 2 (2006), pp. 79–93. For a conflicting view, see K. L. Ailawadi, S. A. Neslin, and K. Gegdenk, "Pursuing the Value-Conscious Consumer," *Journal of Marketing,* January 2001, pp. 71–89.

40. K. L. Ailawadi, K. Pauwels, and J. E. M. Steenkamp, "Private-Label Use and Store Loyalty," *Journal of Marketing,* November 2008, pp. 19–30.

41. *The Double Dividend* (New York: Newspaper Advertising Bureau Inc., February 1977).

42. F. J. Mulhern and D. T. Padgett, "The Relationship between Retail Price Promotions and Regular Price Purchases," *Journal of Marketing,* October 1995, pp. 83–90. For similar results, see S. Burton, D. R. Lichtenstein, and R. G. Netemeyer, "Exposure to Sales Flyers and Increased Purchases in Retail Supermarkets," *Journal of Advertising Research,* September 1999, pp. 7–14.

43. See, e.g., V. Severin, J. J. Louviere, and A. Finn, "The Stability of Retail Shopping Choices over Time and across Countries," *Journal of Retailing,* 77 (2001), pp. 185–202.

44. See, e.g., P. Chandon, B. Wansink, and G. Laurent, "A Benefit Congruency Framework of Sales Promotion Effectiveness," *Journal of Marketing,* October 2000, pp. 65–81.

45. See, e.g., van der Heijden and Verhagen, "Online Store Image."

46. A. Ansari and C. F. Mela, "E-Customization," *Journal of Marketing Research,* May 2003, pp. 131–45.

47. See C. Janiszewski and D. R. Lichtenstein, "A Range Theory of Price Perception," *Journal of Consumer Research,* March 1999, pp. 353–68.

48. See R. A. Briesch, L. Krishnamurthi, and T. Mazumdar, "A Comparative Analysis of Reference Price Models," *Journal of Consumer Research,* September 1997, pp. 202–14; R. W. Niedrich, S. Sharma, and D. H. Wedell, "Reference Price and Price Perceptions," *Journal of Consumer Research,* December 2001, pp. 339–54; and P. K. Kopalle, and J. Lindsey-Mullikin, "The Impact of External Reference Price on Consumer Price Expectations," *Journal of Retailing,* 79 (2003), pp. 225–36. For a different approach, see K. B. Monroe and A. Y. Lee, "Remembering versus Knowing," *Journal of the Academy of Marketing Science,* Spring 1999, pp. 207–25.

49. See V. Kumar, K. Karande, and W. J. Reinartz, "The Impact of Internal and External Reference Prices on Brand Choice," *Journal of Retailing,* 3 (1998), pp. 401–26.

50. T. A. Suter and S. Burton, "Reliability and Consumer Perceptions of Implausible Reference Prices in Retail Prices," *Psychology & Marketing,* January 1996, pp. 37–54; M. S. Yadav and K. Seiders, "Is the Price Right?," *Journal of Retailing,* 1998, pp. 311–29; and L. D. Compeau and D. Grewal, "Comparative Price Advertising," *Journal of Public Policy & Marketing,* Fall 1998, pp. 257–73. See also M. J. Barone, K. C. Manning, and P. W. Miniard, "Consumer Response to Retailers' Use of Partially Comparative Pricing," *Journal of Marketing,* July 2004, pp. 37–47.

51. See A. Biswas et al., "Consumer Evaluation of Reference Price Advertisements," *Journal of Public Policy & Marketing,* Spring 1999, pp. 52–65.

52. T. B. Heath, S. Chatterjee, and K. R. France, "Mental Accounting and Changes in Price," *Journal of Consumer Research,* June 1995, pp. 90–97.

53. See S.-F. S. Chen, K. B. Monroe, and Y.-C. Lou, "The Effects of Framing Price Promotion Messages on Consumers' Perceptions and Purchase Intentions," *Journal of Retailing,* 3 (1998), pp. 353–72; and M. R. Stafford and T. F. Stafford, "The Effectiveness of Tensile Pricing Tactics in the Advertising of Services," *Journal of Advertising,* Summer 2000, pp. 45–60.

54. See A. Biswas and S. Burton, "Consumer Perceptions of Tensile Price Claims in Advertisements," *Journal of the Academy of Marketing Science,* Summer 1993, pp. 217–30; K. N. Rajendran and G.-J. Tellis, "Contextual and Temporal Components of Reference Price," *Journal of Marketing,* January 1994, pp. 22–39; and D. Grewal, H. Marmorstein, and A. Sharma, "Communicating Price Information through Semantic Cues," *Journal of Consumer Research,* September 1996, pp. 148–55.

55. I. Sinha and M. F. Smith, "Consumers' Perceptions of Promotional Framing of Price," *Psychology & Marketing,* March 2000, pp. 257–75.

56. See D. Simester, "Signaling Price Image Using Advertised Prices," *Marketing Science,* 14, no. 2 (1995), pp. 166–88; and J. Srivastave and N. Lurie, "A Consumer Perspective on Price-Matching Refund Policies," *Journal of Consumer Research,* September 2001, pp. 296–307.

57. G. S. Bobinski Jr., D. Cox, and A. Cox, "Retail 'Sale' Advertising, Perceived Retailer Credibility, and Price Rationale," *Journal of Retailing,* 3 (1996), pp. 291–306.

58. See, e.g., Severin, Louviere, and Finn, "The Stability of Retail Shopping Choices over Time and across Countries."

59. See I. Simonson, "The Effect of Product Assortment on Buyer Preferences," *Journal of Retailing,* 75, no. 3 (1999), pp. 347–70; and R. E. Stassen, J. D. Mittelstaedt, and R. A. Mittelstaedt, "Assortment Overlap," *Journal of Retailing,* 75, no. 3 (1999), pp. 371–86.

60. C. S. Craig, A. Ghosh, and S. McLafferty, "Models of the Retail Location Process: A Review," *Journal of Retailing,* Spring 1984, pp. 5–33.

61. See D. R. Bell, T.-H. Ho, and C. S. Tang, "Determining Where to Shop," *Journal of Marketing Research,* August 1998, pp. 352–69.

62. See B. G. C. Dellaert et al., "Investigating Consumers' Tendency to Combine Multiple Shopping Purposes and Destinations," *Journal of Marketing Research,* May 1998, pp. 177–88.

63. See P. R. Messinger and C. Narasimhan, "A Model of Retail Formats Based on Consumers' Economizing on Shopping Time," *Marketing Science,* 1 (1997), pp. 1–23.

64. A. Chaudhuri, "Product Class Effects on Perceived Risk," *International Journal of Research in Marketing,* May 1998, pp. 157–68; and R. Batra and I. Sinha, "Consumer-Level Factors Moderating the Success of Private Label Brands," *Journal of Retailing,* 76, no. 2 (2000), pp. 175–91.

65. Based on V. Prasad, "Socioeconomic Product Risk and Patronage Preferences of Retail Shoppers," *Journal of Marketing,* July 1975, p. 44.

66. G. R. Dowling and R. Staelin, "A Model of Perceived Risk and Intended Risk-Handling Activity," *Journal of Consumer Research,* June 1994, pp. 119–34; L. W. Turley and R. P. LeBlanc, "An Exploratory Investigation of Consumer Decision Making in the Service Sector," *Journal of Services Marketing,* 7, no. 4 (1993), pp. 11–18; and J. B. Smith and J. M. Bristor, "Uncertainty Orientation," *Psychology & Marketing,* November 1994, pp. 587–607.

67. R. B. Settle, P. L. Alreck, and D. E. McCorkle, "Consumer Perceptions of Mail/Phone Order Shopping Media," *Journal of Direct Marketing,* Summer 1994, pp. 30–45; C. R. Jasper and S. J. Ouellette, "Consumers' Perception of Risk and the Purchase of Apparel from Catalogs," *Journal of Direct Marketing,* Spring 1994, pp. 23–36; and D. Biswas and A. Biswas, "The Diagnostic Role of Signals in the Context of Perceived Risks in Online Shopping," *Journal of Interactive Marketing,* Summer 2004, pp. 30–45.

68. See also J. C. Sweeney, G. N. Soutar, and L. W. Johnson, "The Role of Perceived Risk in the Quality–Value Relationship," *Journal of Retailing,* 75, no. 1 (1999), pp. 75–105.

69. See K. L. Wakefield and J. Baker, "Excitement at the Mall," *Journal of Retailing,* 74, no. 4 (1998), pp. 515–39; H. McDonald, P. Darbyshire, and C. Jevons, "Shop Often, Buy Little," *Journal of Global Marketing,* 13, no. 4 (2000), pp. 53–71; J. A. F. Nicholls et al., "Inter-American Perspectives from Mall Shoppers," *Journal of Global Marketing,* 15, no. 1 (2001), pp. 87–103; B. Jin and J.-O. Kim, "Discount Store Retailing in Korea," *Journal of Global Marketing,* 15, no. 2 (2001),

pp. 81–107; and J. L. Joines, C. W. Scherer, and D. A. Scheufele, "Exploring Motivations for Consumer Web Use and Their Implications for E-commerce," *Journal of Consumer Marketing,* 20, no. 2 (2003), pp. 90–108.

70. See M. A. Eastlick and R. A. Feinberg, "Gender Differences in Mail-Catalog Patronage Motives," *Journal of Direct Marketing,* Spring 1994, pp. 37–44; "The Call of the Mall," *EDK Forecast,* October 1994, pp. 1–3; "Black, Hip, and Primed to Shop," *American Demographics,* September 1996, pp. 52–58; and J. A. F. Nicholls et al., "The Seven Year Itch?," *Journal of Consumer Marketing,* 19, no. 2 (2002), pp. 149–65.

71. These segments and how retailers are targeting them are based on J. Ganesh, K. E. Reynolds, and M. G. Luckett, "Retailer Patronage Behavior and Shopper Typologies," *Journal of the Academy of Marketing Science,* May 2007, pp. 369–81.

72. See J. E. Russo and F. Lecleric, "An Eye Fixation Analysis of Choice Processes for Consumer Nondurables," *Journal of Consumer Research,* September 1994, pp. 274–90.

73. See L. G. Block and V. G. Morwitz, "Shopping Lists as an External Memory Aid for Grocery Shopping," *Journal of Consumer Psychology,* 8, no. 4 (1999), pp. 343–75.

74. See D. W. Rook and R. J. Fisher, "Normative Influences on Impulsive Buying Behaviors," *Journal of Consumer Research,* December 1995, pp. 305–13; R. Puri, "Measuring and Modifying Consumer Impulsive Buying Behavior," *Journal of Consumer Psychology,* 5, no. 2 (1996), pp. 87–113; U. M. Dholakia, "Temptation and Resistance," *Psychology & Marketing,* November 2000, pp. 955–82; and R. F. Baumeister, "Yielding to Temptation," *Journal of Consumer Research,* March 2002, pp. 670–76.

75. R. Liljenwall, "Global Trends in Point-of-Purchase Advertising," in *The Power of Point-of-Purchase Advertising,* ed. R. Liljenwall (Washington, DC: Point-of-Purchase Advertising International, 2004), p. 191.

76. "Shopping Decisions Made In-Store," *Archibald Container Corporation,* October 2, 2008.

77. B. Hurst, "Shopping Impulses Hit 'Before the Store,'" *RetailWire,* January 19, 2011, www.retailwire.com, accessed January 21, 2011.

78. "Shopper Decisions Made In-Store," *WPP,* www.wpp.com, accessed June 13, 2011.

79. D. R. Bell, D. Corsten, and G. Knox, "From Point of Purchase to Path to Purchase," *Journal of Marketing,* January 2011, pp. 31–45.

80. *P-O-P Measures Up* (Washington, DC: Point-of-Purchase Advertising Institute, 2001).

81. Ibid.

82. See *POPAI/Horner Drug Store Study* (Englewood, NJ: Point-of-Purchase Advertising Institute, 1992); A. J. Greco and L. E. Swayne, "Sales Response of Elderly Consumers to P-O-P Advertising," *Journal of Advertising Research,* September 1992, pp. 43–53; *POPAI/Kmart/Procter & Gamble Study of P-O-P Effectiveness* (Englewood, NJ: Point-of-Purchase Advertising Institute, 1993); *P-O-P Measures Up;* and T. Lee, "Experts Say Point-of-Purchase Advertising Can Influence Shoppers' Choices," *Knight Ridder Tribune Business News,* January 19, 2002. For an exception, see C. S. Areni, D. F. Duhan, and P. Kiekeer, "Point-of-Purchase Displays, Product Organization, and Brand Purchase Likelihoods," *Journal of the Academy of Marketing Science,* Fall 1999, pp. 428–41.

83. See E. T. Anderson and D. I. Simester, "The Role of Sale Signs," *Marketing Science,* 2 (1998), pp. 139–55.

84. See, e.g., G. A. Taylor, "Coupon Response in Services," *Journal of Retailing,* 77 (2001), pp. 139–51; C. M. Heilman, K. Nakamoto, and A. G. Rao, "Pleasant Surprises," *Journal of Marketing Research,* May 2002, pp. 242–52; and D. M. Hardesty and W. O. Bearden, "Consumer Evaluations of Different Promotion Types and Price Presentations," *Journal of Retailing,* 79 (2003), pp. 17–25.

85. A. S. C. Ehrenberg, K. Hammond, and G. J. Goodhardt, "The After-Effects of Price-Related Consumer Promotions," *Journal of Advertising Research,* July 1994, pp. 11–21; and P. Papatla and L. Krishnamurthi, "Measuring the Dynamic Effects of Promotions on Brand Choice," *Journal of Marketing Research,* February 1996, pp. 20–36.

86. See C. F. Mela, K. Jedidi, and D. Bowman, "The Long-Term Impact of Promotions on Consumer Stockpiling Behavior," *Journal of Marketing Research,* May 1998, pp. 250–62; and J. E. Urbany, P. R. Dickson, and A. G. Sawyer, "Insights into Cross- and Within-Store Price Search," *Journal of Retailing,* 76, no. 2 (2000), pp. 243–58. See also M. Zeelenberg and M. van Putten, "The Dark Side of Discounts," *Psychology & Marketing,* August 2005, pp. 611–22, for the negative effects of postpromotion when loyal customers miss a discount opportunity.

87. K. Sivakumar and S. P. Raj, "Quality Tier Competition," *Journal of Marketing,* July 1997, pp. 71–84; and S. M. Nowlis and I. Simonson, "Sales Promotions and the Choice Context as Competing Influences on Consumer Decision Making," *Journal of Consumer Psychology,* 9, no. 1 (2000), pp. 1–16.

88. D. Grewal, R. Krishnan, J. Baker, and N. Borin, "The Effect of Store Name, Brand Name, and Price Discounts on Consumers' Evaluations and Purchase Intentions," *Journal of Retailing,* 3 (1998), pp. 331–52.

89. D. R. Bell and J. M. Lattin, "Shopping Behavior and Consumer Preference for Store Price Format," *Marketing Science,* 17, no. 1 (1998), pp. 66–88. See also R. Lal and R. Rao, "Supermarket Competition," *Marketing Science,* 16, no. 1 (1997), pp. 60–80.

90. V. G. Morwitz, E. A. Greenleaf, and E. J. Johnson, "Divide and Prosper," *Journal of Consumer Research,* November 1998, pp. 453–63.

91. K. L. Wakefield and J. G. Blodgett, "The Effect of the Servicescape on Customers' Behavioral Intentions in Leisure Service Settings," *Journal of Services Marketing,* 10, no. 6 (1996), pp. 45–61; K. L. Wakefield and J. G. Blodgett, "Customer Response to Intangible and Tangible Service Factors," *Psychology & Marketing,* January 1999, pp. 51–68; and B. D. Keillor, G. T. M. Hult, and D. Kandemir, "A Study of the Service Encounter in Eight Countries," *Journal of International Marketing,* 12, no. 1 (2004), pp. 9–35.

92. See C. Mathwick, N. Malhotra, and E. Rigdon, "Experiential Value," *Journal of Retailing,* 77 (2001), pp. 39–56; P. D. Lynch, R. J. Kent, and S. S. Srinivasan, "The Global Internet Shopper," *Journal of Advertising Research,* May 2001, pp. 15–23; T. P. Novak, D. L. Hoffman, and A. Duhachek, "The Influence of Goal-Directed and Experiential Activities on Online Flow Experiences," *Journal of Consumer Psychology,* 13, no. 1/2 (2003), pp. 3–16; A. P. Vrechopoulos et al., "Virtual Store Layout," *Journal of Retailing,* 80, no. 1 (2004), pp. 13–22; and J. H. Song and G. M. Zinkhan, "Determinants of Perceived Web Site Interactivity," *Journal of Marketing,* March 2008, pp. 99–113.

93. E. Sherman, A. Mathur, and R. B. Smith, "Store Environment and Consumer Purchase Behavior," *Psychology & Marketing,* July 1997, pp. 361–78; and J. Baker et al., "The Influence of Multiple Store Environment Cues on Perceived Merchandise Value and Patronage Intentions," *Journal of Marketing,* April 2002, pp. 120–41.

94. S. A. Eroglu, K. A. Machleit, and L. M. Davis, "Empirical Testing of a Model of Online Store Atmospherics and Shopper Responses," *Psychology & Marketing,* February 2003, pp. 139–50. See also S. Menon and B. Kahn, "Cross-Category Effects of Induced Arousal and Pleasure on the Internet Shopping Experience," *Journal of Retailing,* 78 (2002), pp. 31–40.

95. L. Dailey, "Navigational Web Atmospherics," *Journal of Business Research,* 57 (2004), pp. 795–803.

96. B. Babin and W. R. Darden, "Good and Bad Shopping Vibes," *Journal of Business Research,* March 1996, pp. 210–60; K. Chang, "The Impact of Perceived Physical Environments on Customers' Satisfaction and Return Intentions," *Journal of Professional Services Marketing,* 21, no. 2 (2000), pp. 75–85; D. Grewal et al., "The Effects of Wait Expectations and Store Atmosphere Evaluations on Patronage Intentions in Service-Intensive Retail Stores," *Journal of Retailing,* 79 (2003), pp. 259–68; Menon and Kahn, "Cross-Category Effects of Induced Arousal and Pleasure on the Internet Shopping Experience"; and Eroglu, Machleit, and Davis, "Empirical Testing of a Model of Online Store Atmospherics and Shopper Responses."

97. See K. A. Machleit, S. A. Eroglu, and S. P. Mantel, "Perceived Retail Crowding and Shopping Satisfaction," *Journal of Consumer Psychology,* 9, no. 1 (2000), pp. 29–42; K. Harris and S. Baron, "Consumer-to-Consumer Conversations in Service Settings," *Journal of Service Research,* February 2004, pp. 287–303; J. J. Argo, D. W. Dahl, and R. V. Manchanda, "The Influence of Mere Social Presence in a Retail Context," *Journal of Consumer Research,* September 2005, pp. 207–12; and K. Zhang, S. E. Beatty, and D. L. Mothersbaugh, "A CIT Investigation of Other Customers' Influence in Services," *Journal of Services Marketing,* 24, no. 5 (2010), pp. 389–99.

98. S. J. Grove and R. P. Fisk, "The Impact of Other Customers' Service Experiences," *Journal of Retailing,* 1 (1997), pp. 63–85.

99. See, e.g., S. Oakes, "The Influence of Musicscape within Service Environments," *Journal of Services Marketing,* 4, no. 7 (2000), pp. 539–56; J. C. Sweeney and F. Wyber, "The Role of Cognitions and Emotions in the Music-Approach-Avoidance Behavior Relationship," *Journal of Services Marketing,* 16, no. 1 (2002), pp. 51–69; C. Caldwell and S. A. Hibbert, "The Influence of Music Tempo and Musical Preference on Restaurant Patrons' Behavior," *Psychology & Marketing,* November 2002, pp. 895–917; and S. Morin, L. Dube, and J. C. Chebat, "The Role of Pleasant Music in Servicescapes," *Journal of Retailing,* 83, no. 1 (2007), pp. 115–30.

100. C. S. Gulas and C. D. Schewe, "Atmospheric Segmentation," in *Enhancing Knowledge Development in Marketing,* ed. R. Achrol and A. Mitchell (Chicago: American Marketing Association, 1994), pp. 325–30. Similar results are in J. D. Herrington and L. M. Capella, "Effects of Music in Service Environments," *Journal of Services Marketing,* 2 (1996), pp. 26–41.

101. D. J. Mitchell, B. E. Kahn, and S. C. Knasko, "There's Something in the Air," *Journal of Consumer Research,* September 1995, pp. 229–38; A. R. Hirsch, "Effects of Ambient Odors on Slot-Machine Usage in a Las Vegas Casino," *Psychology & Marketing,* October 1995, pp. 585–94; M. Wilkie, "Scent of a Market," *American Demographics,* August 1995, pp. 40–49; P. Sloan, "Smelling Trouble," *Advertising Age,* September 11, 1995, p. 1; E. R. Spangenberg, A. E. Crowley, and P. W. Henderson, "Improving the Store Environment," *Journal of Marketing,* April 1996, pp. 67–80; and P. F. Bone and P. S. Ellen, "Scents in the Marketplace," *Journal of Retailing,* 75, no. 2 (1999), pp. 243–62.

102. A. S. Mattila and J. Wirtz, "Congruency of Scent and Music as a Driver of In-Store Evaluations and Behavior," *Journal of Retailing,* 77, no. 2 (2001), pp. 273–89.

103. See A. M. Fiore, X. Yah, and E. Yoh, "Effects of Product Display and Environmental Fragrancing on Approach Responses and Pleasurable Experiences," *Psychology & Marketing,* January 2000, pp. 27–54.

104. K. Campo, E. Gijsbrechts, and P. Nisol, "Towards Understanding Consumer Response to Stock-Outs," *Journal of Retailing,* 76, no. 2 (2000), pp. 219–42.

105. G. J. Fitzsimons, "Consumer Response to Stockouts," *Journal of Consumer Research,* September 2000, pp. 249–67.

106. See, e.g., L. M. Sloot, P. C. Verhoef, P. H. Franses, "The Impact of Brand Equity and the Hedonic Level of Products on Consumer Stock-Out Reactions," *Journal of Retailing,* 81, no. 1 (2005), pp. 15–34.

107. "Reasons Why Website Visitors Abandoned Their Shopping Carts," *See Why,* June 3, 2010, http://seewhy.com/blog, accessed June 13, 2011.

108. M. Prince, "Online Retailers Turn to New Shopping Carts to Drive Sales," *The Wall Street Journal Online,* November 10, 2004.

109. "Single-Use Numbers Increase Confidence, Boost Online Spending, Study Says," *InternetRetailer.com,* February 3, 2005.

110. *Consumer Shopping Experiences, Preferences, and Behaviors* (Cambridge, MA: ATG, October 2010).

111. See, e.g., R. Lacey, J. Suh, and R. M. Morgan, "Differential Effects of Preferential Treatment on Relational Outcomes," *Journal of Service Research,* February 2007, pp. 241–56; and R. Di Mascio, "The Service Models of Frontline Employees," *Journal of Marketing,* July 2010, pp. 63–80.

112. B. B. Stern, G. J. Thompson, and E. J. Arnould, "Narrative Analysis of a Marketing Relationship," *Psychology & Marketing,* 3 (1998), pp. 195–214.

113. M. Holzwarth, C. Janiszewski, and M. M. Neumann, "The Influence of Avatars on Online Consumer Shopping Behavior," *Journal of Marketing,* October 2006, pp. 19–36.

114. D. Prelec and D. Simester, "Always Leave Home without It," *Marketing Letters,* February 2001, pp. 5–12; and D. Soman, "Effects of Payment Mechanism on Spending Behavior," *Journal of Consumer Research,* March 2001, pp. 460–74.

chapter

18 Postpurchase Processes, Customer Satisfaction, and Customer Commitment

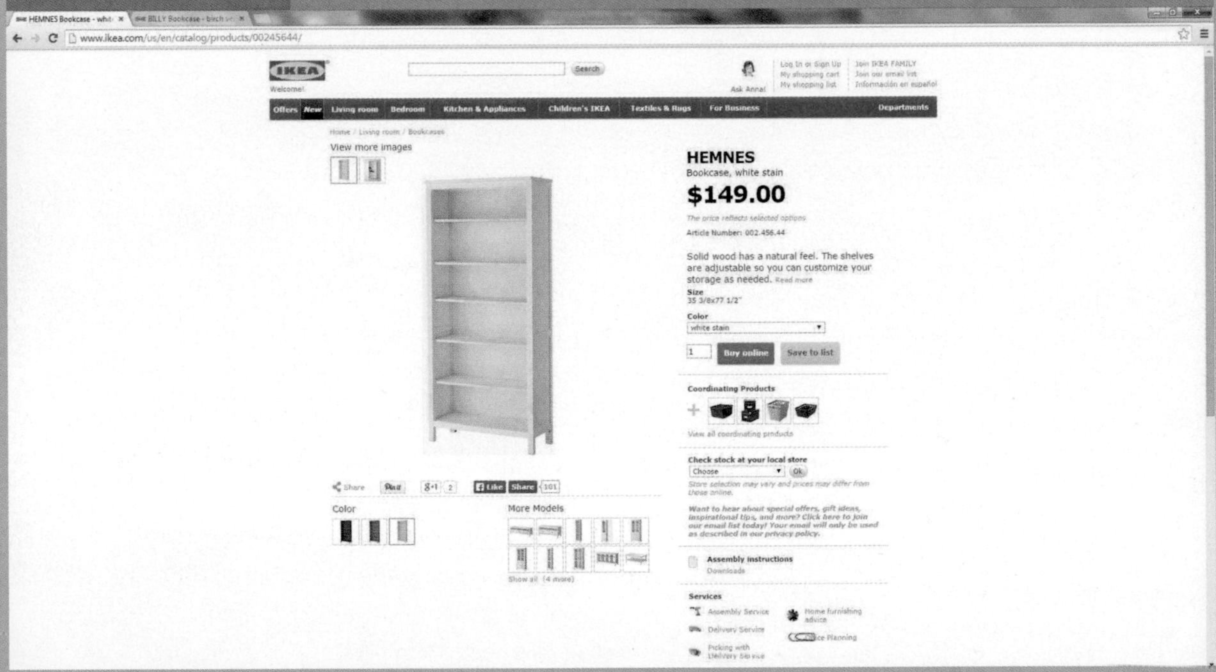

LEARNING OBJECTIVES

LO1 **Describe the various postpurchase processes engaged in by consumers.**

LO2 **Define and discuss postpurchase dissonance.**

LO3 **Discuss the issues surrounding product use and nonuse and their importance to marketers.**

LO4 **Summarize disposition options and their relevance to marketers and public policy.**

LO5 **Explain the determinants and outcomes of satisfaction and dissatisfaction.**

LO6 **Describe the relationship between satisfaction, repeat purchase, and customer commitment.**

Once consumers have purchased a product or service, postpurchase issues of usage, disposition, and postpurchase valuation and satisfaction kick in. Just as we have found biases in perception and decision making "prepurchase," such biases exist "postpurchase" as well. The following are just a few examples:

- *Product use.* Consumers given larger-sized containers of popcorn eat (53 percent) more than consumers given medium-sized containers. Consumers given larger ice cream scoopers served themselves more ice cream than consumers given smaller ice cream scoopers. In "mindless" eating, people are unaware that their eating behavior is influenced by seemingly irrelevant environmental factors—size of container, serving utensil.[1]
- *Product value based on consumer effort.* Consumers who purchase products that must be assembled value them more than those that come assembled (sometimes termed the *IKEA effect*). The IKEA effect is *retroactive,* occurring after *successful* completion of the necessary assembly. The IKEA effect suggests that products sold "with some assembly required" may be adding labor-infused value to the products.[2]
- *Product value based on ownership.* Consumers who own a product will, on average, require a significantly higher price to sell it than the average price consumers shopping for the product are willing to pay. This increased valuation of the product bestowed by "mere" ownership is known as the *endowment effect* and has been repeatedly demonstrated with a wide range of goods—candy bars, pens, mugs, hats, tee shirt—and might explain why consumers keep old products rather than sell or donate them even after a replacement has been found and purchased.[3]

How we use and value products and services is subject to a host of influences, postpurchase. Postpurchase and the various processes and influences involved are the focus of this chapter.

FIGURE 18-1 Postpurchase Consumer Behavior

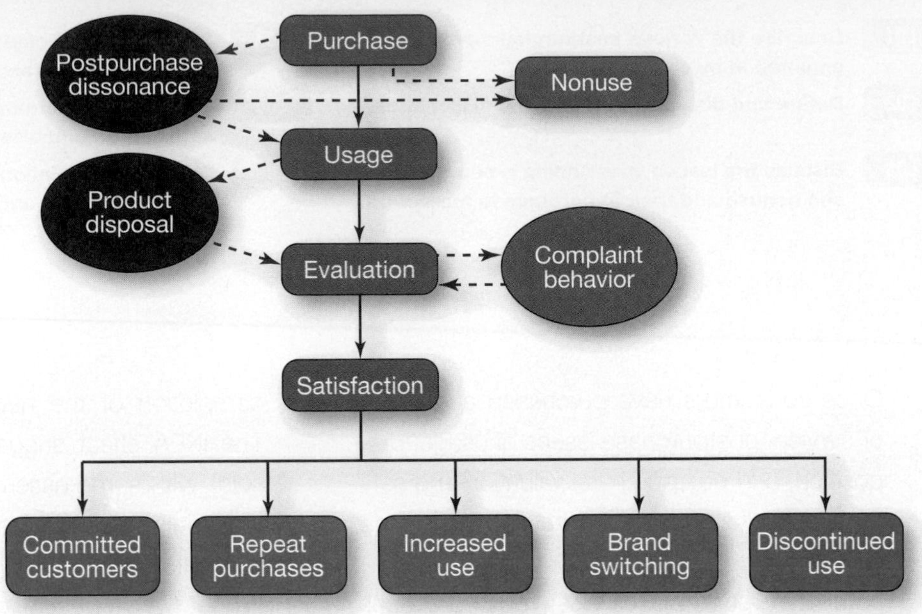

Purchase is followed by a number of processes including use, evaluation, and, in some cases, satisfaction, and consumer responses related to satisfaction include repurchase, positive word-of-mouth, and loyalty. Evaluation can also lead to dissatisfaction, which is sometimes associated with complaining, as well as erosion of loyalty, brand switching, and negative word-of-mouth. Appropriate responses to product and service failure are critical, including putting in processes to track potential problems such as call centers and the social media options discussed in Chapter 7. Once a problem is recognized, appropriate action is important as a way to try to reverse or eliminate the negative outcomes of dissatisfaction. Effective CRM programs and high-quality service, as discussed in the opener, are often important aspects of marketing strategy designed to either deliver high satisfaction or deal effectively with dissatisfaction when it occurs.

L01

Figure 18–1 shows the relationships among these various processes, which are the focus of this chapter. It also indicates that immediately following a purchase, and often prior to usage, consumers may feel doubt or anxiety, known as postpurchase dissonance.

POSTPURCHASE DISSONANCE

L02

> I still like it [a dining room set] a whole lot better than what we used to have. But I think if we had taken longer we would have gotten more precisely what we wanted. I mean we got a great deal. You couldn't get that for that price, so I am happy with the money part of it, but some days I wish we had spent more and gotten something a bit different.[4]

This is a common consumer reaction after making a difficult, relatively permanent decision. Doubt or anxiety of this type is referred to as **postpurchase dissonance.**[5] Some, but not all, consumer purchase decisions are followed by postpurchase dissonance. The probability and magnitude of such dissonance are a function of:

- *The degree of commitment or irrevocability of the decision.* The easier it is to alter the decision, the less likely the consumer is to experience dissonance.
- *The importance of the decision to the consumer.* The more important the decision, the more likely dissonance will result.
- *The difficulty of choosing among the alternatives.* The more difficult it is to select from among the alternatives, the more likely the experience and magnitude of dissonance. Decision difficulty is a function of the number of alternatives considered, the number of relevant attributes associated with each alternative, and the extent to which each alternative offers attributes not available with the other alternatives.
- *The individual's tendency to experience anxiety.* Some individuals have a higher tendency to experience anxiety than do others. The higher the tendency to experience anxiety, the more likely the individual will experience postpurchase dissonance.

Dissonance does not generally occur for low-involvement nominal and limited decision making. These decisions are relatively easy and unimportant. Dissonance is most common in high-involvement extended decision making, where trade-offs among desirable attributes create conflict (as in the price–quality trade-off made in the dining room decision above). Such trade-offs create negative emotions and decision delay.[6] Thus, when such trade-offs exist, salespeople and ads could attempt to refocus consumer attention on the positive aspects of the decision or provide incentives to make a purchase even in the face of the difficult trade-off.

After the purchase, consumers may use one or more of the following approaches to reevaluate or alter the decision to reduce dissonance:

- Increase the desirability of the brand purchased.
- Decrease the desirability of rejected alternatives.
- Decrease the importance of the purchase decision.
- Reverse the purchase decision (return the product before use).

Advertising and follow-up sales efforts can have a huge effect on postpurchase dissonance because consumers, in their reevaluation process, often search for and are receptive to information that confirms the wisdom of their purchase. Direct mailers, follow-up calls, and e-mails can all be effective. Johnston & Murphy sends follow-up e-mails thanking customers for their recent purchase, pointing them to its website, and soliciting feedback. Such communications can go a long way in reducing dissonance and increasing satisfaction. Illustration 18–1 provides an additional example of the reinforcement potential of advertising in the postpurchase process.

A concept very similar to postpurchase dissonance is **consumption guilt.** Consumption guilt occurs when *negative emotions or guilt feelings are aroused by the use of a product or a service.* A person driving a large car may experience some negative feelings due to concern over resource utilization and pollution. The example below illustrates consumption guilt quite clearly:

> I have to count calories much more than I did before. I still buy a sundae once in a while but the joy of eating ice cream will probably forever be connected with guilt over eating something so unhealthy. When I think about it, I realize that most products make me feel good and bad at the same time.[7]

Marketers of products whose target markets might experience consumption guilt need to focus on validating the consumption of the product. They need to find ways to give the consumer permission or a rationale for indulging in that consumption act.[8]

ILLUSTRATION 18-1

Advertisements for high-involvement purchase items can serve to confirm the wisdom of a purchase as well as influence new purchasers.

PRODUCT USE AND NONUSE

Product Use

LO3 Most consumer purchases involve nominal or limited decision making and therefore arouse little or no postpurchase dissonance. Instead, the purchaser or some other member of the household uses the product without first worrying about the wisdom of the purchase. And as Figure 18–1 shows, even when postpurchase dissonance occurs, it is still generally followed by product use.

Marketers need to understand how consumers use their products for a variety of reasons. Understanding both the functional and symbolic ways in which a product is used can lead to more effective product designs and marketing campaigns. For example, the existence of the sneakerhead consumption subculture (Chapter 7) has influenced many aspects of sneaker design and marketing, including the creation of expensive, limited-edition designs that are targeted specifically to the sneakerhead collector.

Use innovativeness refers to *a consumer using a product in a new way.*[9] Marketers who discover new uses for their products can greatly expand sales.

- Arm & Hammer discovered that consumers were using its baking soda for a variety of noncooking uses, such as deodorizing refrigerators. It now advertises such uses and has developed product packaging, such as its Fridge Fresh Air Filters, specific to such uses. It also has a section on its website where consumers can submit their own "solutions" to common household problems using Arm & Hammer baking soda.

- WD-40, a lubricant, is renowned for the wide array of applications that consumers suggest for it, including as an additive to fish bait and for removing gum from a carpet.
- Bounce had a contest where consumers submitted stories that were merged into an online booklet that can be found on its website. Company lawyers cleared the stories and deleted any that could be harmful to consumers or the environment.

ILLUSTRATION 18-2

As shown by this Crest ProHealth ad, marketers can leverage the fact that certain products are used together by developing product mixes consisting of complementary products.

Just as the Internet can be used as a way to observe and track consumer problems, it can also be used as a means for tracking innovative product uses. And web-based submission options on a brand's website make direct collection of such ideas easier than ever.[10]

Marketers can frequently take advantage of the fact that the use of one product may require, be enhanced by, or suggest the use of other products. The Crest ProHealth ad in Illustration 18–2 provides a great example of the concept. Crest is promoting the use of its toothbrushes, toothpaste, and mouthwash together for an "enhanced felling of clean and a healthier mouth." Consider houseplants and fertilizer; bikes and helmets; dresses and shoes. Retailers can promote such items jointly, display them together, or train their sales personnel to make relevant complementary sales.

Stringent product liability laws and aggressive civil suits also are forcing marketing managers to examine how consumers use their products. These laws have made firms responsible for harm caused by products *not only when the product is used as specified by the manufacturer but in any reasonably foreseeable use of the product.* Thus, the manufacturer must design products with both the primary purpose *and* other potential uses in mind. This requires substantial research into how consumers actually use products.

When marketers discover confusion about the proper way to use a product, it is often to their advantage to teach consumers how to use it and engage in marketing communications that increase the chances of proper use. After all, how many consumers blame themselves when a product failure occurs as a result of their own failure to follow usage instructions?[11] At other times, a firm can gain a competitive advantage by redesigning the product so that it is easier to use properly.

Product Nonuse

As Figure 18–1 indicates, not all purchases are followed by use. **Product nonuse** occurs when a consumer actively acquires a product that is not used or used only sparingly relative to potential use.[12]

For many products and most services, the decisions to purchase and to consume are made simultaneously. A person who orders a meal in a restaurant is also deciding to eat the meal at that time. However, a decision to purchase food at a supermarket requires a second decision to prepare and consume the food. The second decision occurs at a different point in time and in a different environment from the first. Thus, nonuse can occur because the situation or the purchaser changes between the purchase and the potential usage occasion. For example, a point-of-purchase display featuring a new food item shown as part of an appealing entrée might cause a consumer to imagine an appropriate usage situation and to

ILLUSTRATION 18-3

Advertisements, such as this Kellogg's Nutri-Grain ad, can encourage purchases, consumption of previously purchased items, or both.

purchase the product. However, without the stimulus of the display, the consumer may not remember the intended use or may just never get around to it. Nonuse situations such as the following are common:[13]

Wok. "I wanted to try and cook stirfry, but I didn't take time out to use it."

Skirt. "My ingenious idea was that I'd lose a few pounds and fit into the size 4 rather than gain a few and fit into the size 6. Obviously, I never lost the weight, so the skirt was snug."

Gym membership. "Couldn't get in the groove to lift."

In such cases, the consumer has wasted money and the marketer is unlikely to get repeat sales or positive referrals. Many such purchases are difficult for the marketer to correct after the purchase. In other cases, consumers would have used the product if reminded or motivated at the proper time. In the last example above, good records would indicate that this member was not using the gym. A personal letter, e-mail, or telephone invitation to come in might be enough to get this person started.

Some products are known to be kept on hand by consumers; that is, they stock up on certain items. In this case, a major goal of advertising should be to encourage people to consume the product at the next appropriate occasion and perhaps even suggest situations that would be appropriate. Since consumers have the product available, the task is not to encourage purchase but to motivate near-term consumption such as including Kellogg's Nutri-Grain bar into consumers' regular breakfast routines, as suggested in Illustration 18–3.

The division between the initial purchase decision and the decision to consume is particularly strong with catalog and online purchases. In effect, two decisions are involved in these purchases: the initial decision to order the product and a second decision to keep or return the item when it is received. Not only is it likely that several days will have passed between the two decisions, but substantially different information is available at the "keep or return" decision point. In particular, consumers can physically touch, try on, or otherwise experience the item.

Obviously, online and catalog retailers want to maximize the percentage of items kept rather than returned. Intuitively, one might think that a strict return policy would accomplish this. However, such a policy might also reduce the number of initial orders. In fact, a liberal return policy appears to maximize initial orders and may also minimize returns. Such a policy reduces perceived risk and signals higher quality (surrogate indicator), which increases initial orders. Consumers also tend to perceive items ordered under liberal return policies as having higher quality after receiving them, which reduces returns.[14] In addition to return policies, online tools that can better represent products so that a maximal fit to consumer needs is attained can help. Scanner-based, full-body measurement technology that also makes recommendations about sizes, styles, and brands (Chapter 17) should dramatically increase how well clothing fits even if it is ordered online without first trying it on. This should reduce returns and company costs and increase customer satisfaction.

DISPOSITION

LO4

Disposition of the product or the product's container may occur before, during, or after product use. Or for products that are completely consumed, such as an ice cream cone, no disposition may be involved.

The United States produces several hundred million tons of refuse a year.[15] Packaging is an important component. Millions of pounds of product packages are disposed of every day. These containers are thrown away as garbage or litter, used in some capacity by the consumer, or recycled. Creating packages that utilize a minimal amount of resources is important for economic reasons as well as being a matter of social responsibility. Many firms are responding to this issue, as the examples below illustrate:

- Crate & Barrel stopped using white bleached board in its famous black and white boxes and switched to more renewable fiber that contains postconsumer recyclable material.
- Casio redesigned its consumer and channel-based packaging so as to reduce the total amount of materials used.

Beyond packaging is the physical product that continues to exist even though it may no longer meet a consumer's needs either in an instrumental (no longer works) or symbolic (no longer the latest trend) way. Either situation requires disposition. For some consumers, recycling is more prominent than others (see Chapter 4 on green marketing), and companies and government organizations are working to encourage recycling and make it more convenient. Still, only about a third of solid waste (trash) is recycled.[16]

Exploding demand and short product life spans for high-tech gadgets such as cell phones, personal computers, and various other personal electronics devices are creating growing concerns over **e-waste.** Both instrumental and symbolic considerations can drive e-waste. Consumer and corporate solutions are necessary and evolving, although one recent estimate is that only one in four computers is recycled![17] Examples of efforts to reduce e-waste include the following:

- TechForward offers a guaranteed buy-back plan for electronics products.[18]
- Sony has developed a recycling plan whereby it will offset pound-for-pound that amount of materials recycled for new products produced. Sony is partnering with a recycling company and banking on the project's paying for itself as a result of the value of such ingredients as copper typically found in e-waste. Big issues are consumer awareness and convenience.[19]

ILLUSTRATION 18-4

Proper product disposition is important to many consumers and therefore to many firms and industries.

- Companies such as HP and Office Depot are engaged in ongoing efforts related to print cartridges. HP provides a self-addressed, postage-paid envelope in which you can return used ink cartridges to its recycling center. Office Depot offers discounts through their customer rewards program for those who return used cartridges.

Figure 18–2 illustrates the various alternatives for disposing of a product or package. Unfortunately, while "throw it away" is only one of many disposition alternatives, it is by far the most widely used by many consumers. Environmental groups work hard to change these behaviors, as do some firms and other organizations (see Illustration 18–4). Other firms, however, continue to use unnecessary or hard-to-recycle packaging and product components.

Product Disposition and Marketing Strategy

Why should a marketing manager be concerned about the disposition of a used product? Perhaps the best reason is the cumulative effect that these decisions have on the quality of the environment and the lives of current and future generations. However, there are also short-term economic reasons for concern. Disposition decisions affect the purchase decisions of both the individual making the disposition and other individuals in the market for that product category.

There are five major ways in which disposition decisions can affect a firm's marketing strategy. First, for most durable goods, consumers are reluctant to purchase a new item until they have "gotten their money's worth" from the old one. These consumers mentally depreciate the value of a durable item over time. If the item is not fully mentally depreciated, they are reluctant to write it off by disposing of it to acquire a new one. Allowing old items to be traded in is one way to overcome this reluctance.[20]

Second, disposition sometimes must occur before acquisition of a replacement because of space or financial limitations. For example, because of a lack of storage space, a family living in an apartment may find it necessary to dispose of an existing bedroom set before acquiring a new one. Or someone may need to sell his current bicycle to raise supplemental funds to pay for a new bicycle. Thus, it is to the manufacturer's and retailer's advantage to assist the consumer in the disposition process.

Third, frequent decisions by consumers to sell, trade, or give away used products may result in a large used-product market that can reduce the market for new products.

Disposition Alternatives

FIGURE 18-2

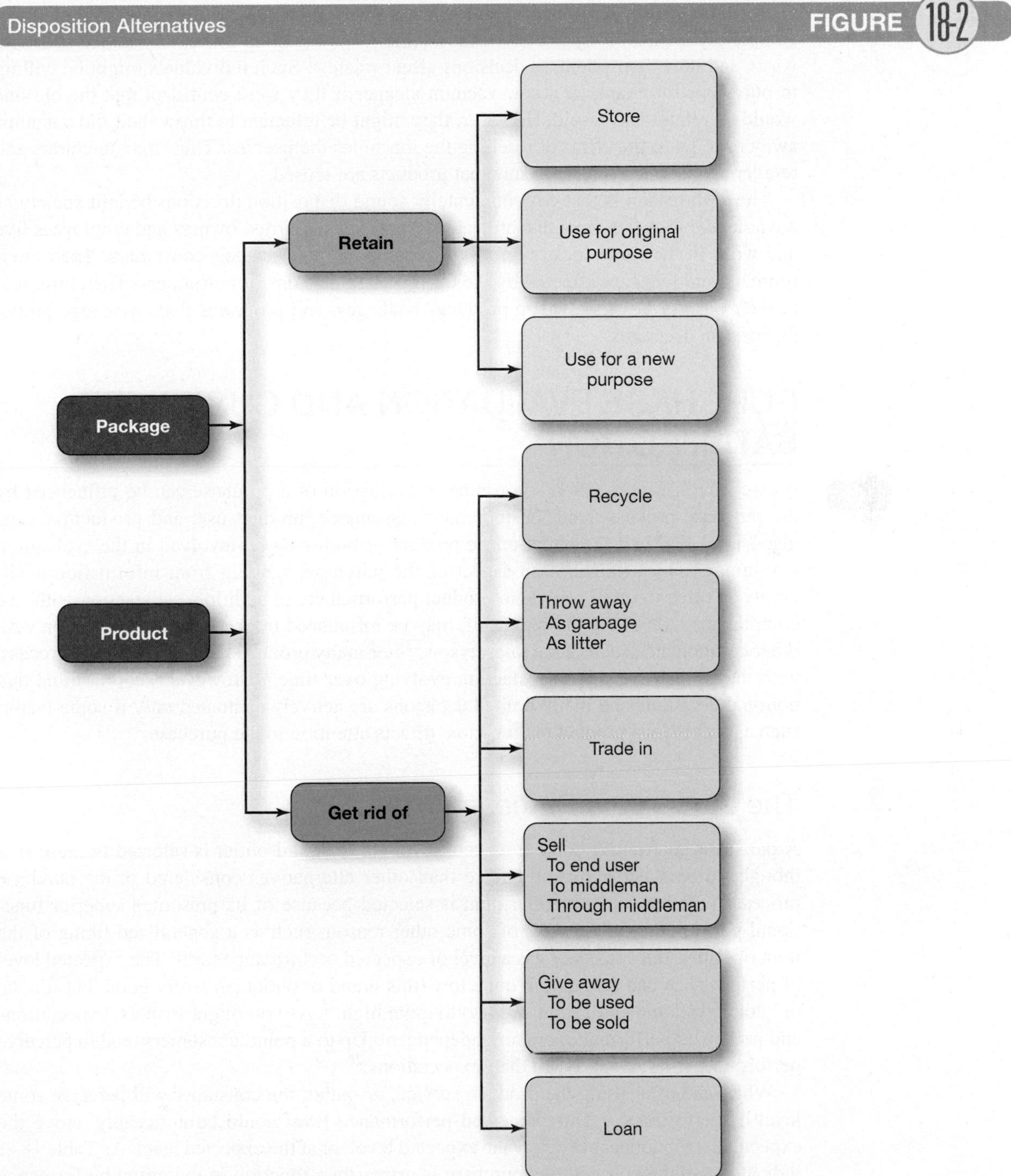

A **consumer-to-consumer sale** occurs when *one consumer sells a product directly to another with or without the assistance of a commercial intermediary.* Garage sales, swap meets, flea markets, classified ads, and online outlets such as eBay exist as a result of consumer demand to buy and sell used items. In addition, consumers may give or sell their used items to resellers. Thrift stores, featuring used clothing, appliances, and furniture, run by both commercial and nonprofit groups, are an important part of the economy.

A fourth reason for concern with product disposition is that the United States is not completely a throwaway society. Many Americans continue to be very concerned with waste and how their purchase decisions affect waste.[21] Such individuals might be willing to purchase, for example, a new vacuum cleaner if they were confident that the old one would be rebuilt and resold. However, they might be reluctant to throw their old vacuums away or to go to the effort of reselling the machines themselves. Thus, manufacturers and retailers could take steps to ensure that products are reused.

The fifth reason is that environmentally sound disposition decisions benefit society as a whole and thus the firms that are part of that society. Firms' owners and employees live and work in the same society and environment as many of their consumers. Their environment and lives are affected by the disposition decisions of consumers. Therefore, it is in their best interest to develop products, packages, and programs that encourage proper disposition decisions.

PURCHASE EVALUATION AND CUSTOMER SATISFACTION

LO5

As we saw in Figure 18–1, a consumer's evaluation of a purchase can be influenced by the purchase process itself, postpurchase dissonance, product use, and product/package disposition. Further, the outlet or the product or both may be involved in the evaluation. Consumers may evaluate each aspect of the purchase, ranging from information availability to price to retail service to product performance. In addition, satisfaction with one component, such as the product itself, may be influenced by the level of satisfaction with other components, such as the salesperson.[22] For many products, this is a dynamic process, with the factors that drive satisfaction evolving over time.[23] However, keep in mind that nominal decisions and many limited decisions are actively evaluated only if some factor, such as an obvious product malfunction, directs attention to the purchase.[24]

The Evaluation Process

A particular alternative such as a product, brand, or retail outlet is selected because it is thought to be a better overall choice than other alternatives considered in the purchase process. Whether that particular item is selected because of its presumed superior functional performance or because of some other reason, such as a generalized liking of the item or outlet, the consumer has a level of expected performance for it. The expected level of performance can range from quite low (this brand or outlet isn't very good, but it's the only one available and I'm in a hurry) to quite high.[25] As you might suspect, expectations and perceived performance are not independent. Up to a point, consumers tend to perceive performance to be in line with their expectations.[26]

While and after using the product, service, or outlet, the consumer will perceive some level of performance. This perceived performance level could be noticeably above the expected level, noticeably below the expected level, or at the expected level. As Table 18–1 indicates, satisfaction with the purchase is primarily a function of the initial performance expectations and perceived performance relative to those expectations.[27]

Two general expectation levels are presented in Table 18–1. The first is when consumers expect the brand to perform below some minimum level and requires a bit of explanation. Choice of such brands and outlets is not typical because they would normally be in a consumer's inept set (see Chapter 15). However, three situations will drive choice in this case: (1) where available alternatives don't exist (the iPhone was only available on AT&T until

Expectations, Performance, and Satisfaction

TABLE 18-1

	Expectation Level	
Perceived Performance Relative to Expectation	Below Minimum Desired Performance	Above Minimum Desired Performance
Better	Satisfaction*	Satisfaction/Commitment
Same	Nonsatisfaction	Satisfaction
Worse	Dissatisfaction	Dissatisfaction

*Assuming the perceived performance surpasses the minimum desired level.

recently), (2) in an emergency situation (your tire goes flat and the repair service only carries a brand you find undesirable), or (3) when family decisions result in a suboptimal choice for some family members (the child is thrilled with Chuck E. Cheese; the parents are not).

Table 18–1 shows that an outlet or brand whose performance confirms a low-performance expectation generally will result in neither satisfaction nor dissatisfaction but rather with what can be termed *nonsatisfaction.* That is, the consumer is not likely to feel disappointment or engage in complaint behavior. However, this purchase will not reduce the likelihood that the consumer will search for a better alternative the next time the problem arises.

A brand whose perceived performance falls below expectations generally produces dissatisfaction. If the discrepancy between performance and expectation is sufficiently large, or if initial expectations were low, the consumer may restart the entire decision process. Most likely, he or she will place an item performing below expectations in the inept set and no longer consider it. In addition, the consumer may complain or initiate negative word-of-mouth communications.

When perceptions of product performance match expectations that are at or above the minimum desired performance level, satisfaction generally results. Likewise, performance above the minimum desired level that exceeds a lower expectation tends to produce satisfaction. Satisfaction reduces the level of decision making the next time the problem is recognized; that is, a satisfactory purchase is rewarding and encourages one to repeat the same behavior in the future (nominal decision making). Satisfied customers are also likely to engage in positive word-of-mouth communications about the brand, which can lead to the acquisition of new customers.

Product performance that exceeds expected performance will generally result in satisfaction and sometimes in commitment. Commitment, discussed in depth in the next section, means that the consumer is enthusiastic about a particular brand and is somewhat immune to actions by competitors.

The need to develop realistic consumer expectations poses a difficult problem for the marketing manager. For a brand or outlet to be selected, the consumer must view it as superior on the relevant combination of attributes. Therefore, the marketing manager naturally wants to emphasize its positive aspects. If such an emphasis creates expectations in the consumer that the item cannot fulfill, a negative evaluation may occur. Negative evaluations can produce brand switching, unfavorable word-of-mouth communications, and complaint behavior. Thus, the marketing manager must balance enthusiasm for the product with a realistic view of the product's attributes.

Determinants of Satisfaction and Dissatisfaction Because performance expectations and actual performance are major factors in the evaluation process, we need to understand the dimensions of product and service performance. A major study of the reasons customers switch service providers found competitor actions to be a relatively minor cause. Most customers did not switch from a satisfactory provider to a better provider. Instead, they switched because of perceived problems with their current service provider. The nature of these problems and the percentage listing each as a reason they changed providers follow (the percentages sum to more than 100 because many customers listed several reasons that caused them to switch):[28]

- *Core service failure* (44 percent). Mistakes (booking an aisle rather than the requested window seat), billing errors, and service catastrophes that harm the customer (the dry cleaners ruined my wedding dress).
- *Service encounter failures* (34 percent). Service employees were uncaring, impolite, unresponsive, or unknowledgeable.
- *Pricing* (30 percent). High prices, price increases, unfair pricing practices, and deceptive pricing.
- *Inconvenience* (21 percent). Inconvenient location, hours of operation, waiting time for service or appointments.
- *Responses to service failures* (17 percent). Reluctant responses, failure to respond, and negative responses (it's your fault).
- *Attraction by competitors* (10 percent). More personable, more reliable, higher quality, and better value.
- *Ethical problems* (7 percent). Dishonest behavior, intimidating behavior, unsafe or unhealthy practices, or conflicts of interest.
- *Involuntary switching* (6 percent). Service provider or customer moves, or a third-party payer such as an insurance company requires a change.

Other studies have found that waiting time has a major impact on evaluations of service. Consumers have particularly negative reactions to delays over which they believe the service provider has control and during which they have little to occupy their time.[29] *What are the marketing strategy implications of these results?*

Failure on a given product or service characteristic often has a stronger effect on consumers than success on that same characteristic, something referred to as the *negativity bias.*[30] Thus, depending on the attributes and decision rule involved (see Chapter 16), this could mean first meeting expectations across all relevant features before maximizing performance on a few.

Firms are using technology as a way to deliver more convenient service both online and in the store. Price check scanners in the store or mobile local price apps can make the in-store experience more satisfying. And website functionality such as avatars and text and video chat with customer representatives can be critical to customer satisfaction online. When technology fails or is complicated to use, consumers typically experience dissatisfaction. In the case of online checkout, such factors can result in lost sales as consumers abandon their shopping carts (see Chapter 17).

For many products, there are two dimensions to performance: instrumental and expressive, or symbolic. **Instrumental performance** relates *to the physical functioning of the product.* **Symbolic performance** relates to *aesthetic or image-enhancement performance.* For example, the durability of a sport coat is an aspect of instrumental performance, whereas styling represents symbolic performance. Complete satisfaction requires adequate performance on both dimensions. However, for at least some product categories such as clothing, "[d]issatisfaction is caused by a failure of instrumental performance, while complete satisfaction also requires the symbolic functions to perform at or above the expected levels."[31]

In addition to symbolic and instrumental performance, products also provide affective performance. **Affective performance** is *the emotional response that owning or using the* *product or outlet provides.*[32] It may arise from the instrumental or symbolic performance or from the product itself; for example, a suit that produces admiring glances or compliments may produce a positive affective response. Or the affective performance may be the primary product benefit, such as for an emotional movie or novel.

Research regarding online satisfiers and dissatisfiers finds the following four dimensions to be important:[33]

- ***Website Design and Interaction:*** Includes factors such as information quality, navigation, price, merchandise availability, purchase process, and order tracking.
- ***Security and Privacy:*** Includes factors related to security such as fraud and identity theft and privacy related to unwanted marketing efforts.
- ***Fulfillment and Reliability:*** Includes factors such as timely delivery, order accuracy, billing accuracy, and the quality of the merchandise.
- ***Customer Service:*** Includes factors relating to service level such as customer support, ability and ease of communication, as well as factors relating to returns such as clear and fair return policies.

A study of German consumers finds similar drivers of satisfaction with online retailers.[34] Finally, research suggests that in multi-channel contexts involving the Internet, the issue of integration is critical in that content, processes, image, and so on should be consistent to the extent possible and appropriate across different channels within a company or brand.[35]

DISSATISFACTION RESPONSES

Figure 18–3 illustrates the major options available to a dissatisfied consumer. The first decision is whether or not to take any external action. By taking no action, the consumer decides to live with the unsatisfactory situation. This decision is a function of the importance of the purchase to the consumer, the ease of taking action, the consumer's existing

Dissatisfaction Responses — FIGURE 18-3

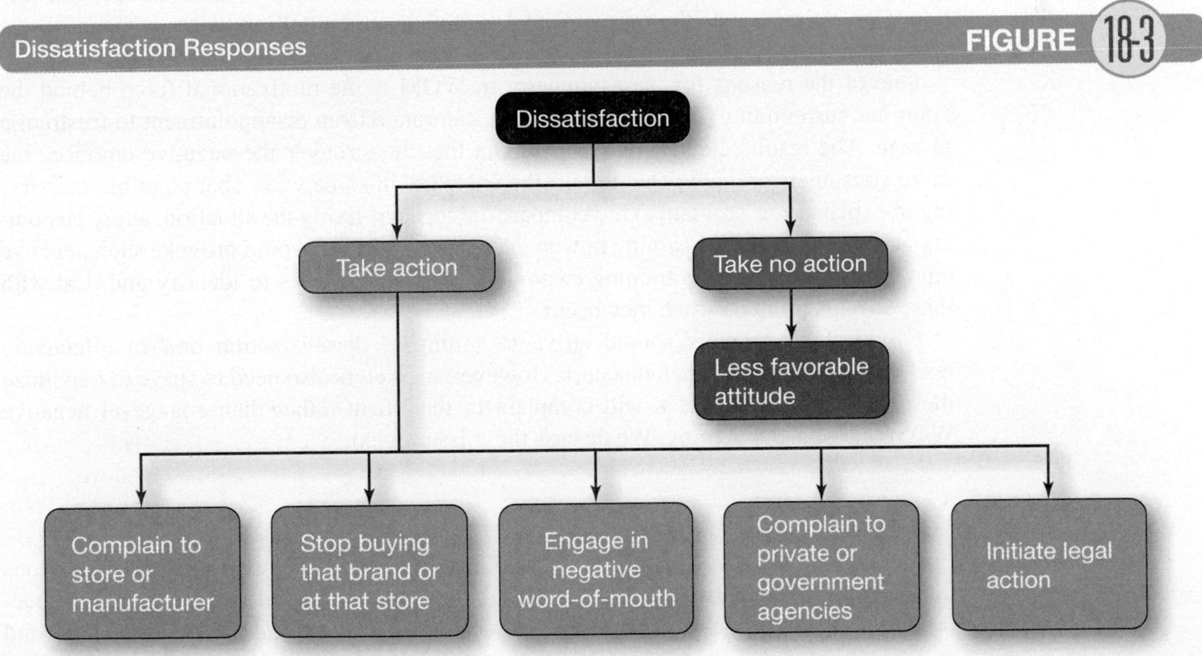

level of overall satisfaction with the brand or outlet, and the characteristics of the consumer involved. It is important to note that even when no external action is taken, the consumer is likely to have a less favorable attitude toward the store or brand.[36]

Consumers who take action in response to dissatisfaction generally pursue one or more of five alternatives. As Figure 18–3 indicates, the most favorable of these alternatives from a company's standpoint is for consumers to complain to it. This at least gives the company a chance to resolve the problem. Many times, however, consumers do not complain to the company, but instead take actions such as switching brands or engaging in negative word-of-mouth (WOM).

Consumers are satisfied with the vast majority of their purchases. Still, because of the large number of purchases they make each year, most individuals experience dissatisfaction with some of their purchases. For example, one study asked 540 consumers if they could recall a case in which one or more of the grocery products they normally purchase were defective. They recalled 1,307 separate unsatisfactory purchases.

These purchases produced the following actions (the study did not measure negative word-of-mouth actions such as warning friends):

- 25 percent of these unsatisfactory purchases resulted in brand switching.
- 19 percent caused the shopper to stop buying the products.
- 13 percent led to an in-store inspection of future purchases.
- 3 percent produced complaints to the manufacturer.
- 5 percent produced complaints to the retailer.
- 35 percent resulted in the items being returned.

In a similar study of durable goods, 54 percent of the dissatisfied customers said they would not purchase the brand again (brand switching) and 45 percent warned their friends (negative WOM) about the product.[37]

As we discussed in Chapter 7, WOM is a critical factor in consumer behavior. Consumers trust WOM more than many other sources and, therefore, tend to rely on it heavily when making decisions. Unfortunately for companies, when it comes to WOM, there appears to be an asymmetry—that is, dissatisfaction yields more WOM than does satisfaction. One estimate puts the ratio at 2 to 1, with consumers telling twice as many people about a negative product or service experience than a positive one.[38]

One of the reasons for the asymmetry in WOM is the motivational force behind the emotions surrounding dissatisfaction, which can range from disappointment to frustration to rage. The results clearly point to the fact that the stronger the negative emotion, the more consumers are motivated to hurt the company in some way. That is, rather than trying to explain their problem to the company in hopes of fixing the situation, angry customers want to "get even." Learning how to avoid situations that would provoke such negative emotions is critical, as is training customer service employees to identify and deal with these strong emotions when they occur.[39]

Obviously, marketers should strive to minimize dissatisfaction *and* to effectively resolve dissatisfaction when it occurs. However, marketers also need to strive to maximize the chances that consumers will complain to their firm rather than engage in negative WOM and brand switching. We discuss these issues next.

Marketing Strategy and Dissatisfied Consumers

Firms need to satisfy consumer expectations by (1) creating reasonable expectations through promotional efforts and (2) maintaining consistent quality so the reasonable expectations are fulfilled. Because dissatisfied consumers tend to engage in negative WOM and because WOM is such a powerful decision influence, one dissatisfied consumer can cause a ripple or multiplier effect in terms of discouraging future sales.[40] Both offline and online WOM are important to consider.

> I feel mad. I put it in my Christmas letter to 62 people across the country. I mean, I told everybody don't buy one of these things because the transmission is bad.[41]

The above example is a marketer's nightmare. Yet the rise of social media has created challenges in this arena that make the above example seem like a minor nuisance. One such incident involved Dave Carroll and United Airlines:

> Dave Carroll is a musician and was travelling with his $3,500 710 Taylor acoustic guitar. From his seat he saw baggage handlers throwing his guitar without regard to its safety. When he reached his destination, he found that the guitar was ruined. United did not take responsibility even though Carroll complained to the company numerous times in numerous ways. So, being a musician, Dave made a music video about this experience and posted it on YouTube. This video has had over 10 million views and within days of being posted, United's stock fell 10 percent![42]

When a consumer is dissatisfied, the most favorable consequence is for the person to communicate this dissatisfaction to the firm but to no one else. In the above example, Dave Carroll made numerous attempts that United did not heed. This is unfortunate because such complaining can alert the firm to problems, enable it to make amends where necessary, and minimize negative word-of-mouth communications. Many firms have discovered that customers whose complaints are resolved to their satisfaction are sometimes even more satisfied than are those who did not experience a problem in the first place, particularly if the problem is minor and not repeated.[43]

Unlike Dave Carroll, consumers often do not complain for a variety of reasons.[44] These include:

- *Demographics.* Lack of resources such as income and education.
- *Personality.* Traits such as introversion and agreeableness.
- *Company.* Makes complaining process difficult and uncomfortable.

A lack of consumer complaining is always a problem, but when the firm contributes to it, it does so at the risk of damaging its reputation and its bottom line. Consider United's stock price drop worth $180 million.

Handling negative consumer comments and complaints generated via online social media can be particularly challenging. AT&T is one company that has gotten serious about dealing with bad press online based on issues with its network, particularly as it was the only option for iPhone users until just recently. Consider the following:

> On a normal day, AT&T has 10,000 mentions on social networks, but during stressful moments . . . they rise precipitously. The marketer is out to calm those twit storms by staffing up its social-media customer-care corps. The team began with five people dedicated to responding to customer dissatisfaction on Twitter and YouTube and has since moved to Facebook and grown to 19 people. To date, 47% of people reached on social media respond to the social team, which results in 32,000 service tickets per month.[45]

Such efforts by AT&T and others are designed to (a) recognize customer problems and utilize their input in the new era of social media, (b) act on the consumer input, and (c) influence the "narrative" by contributing to the conversation (see Consumer Insight 14–1 for more detail on such strategies).

ILLUSTRATION 18-5

This online company is aligning its internal processes toward proactively responding to consumer issues and needs.

Acting on complaints in a timely and effective manner is a key to customer satisfaction.[46] Most consumers who complain want a tangible result. Further, the results desired vary by customer type and the nature of the problem, requiring customized response capabilities.[47] Failure to deal effectively with this expectation can produce increased dissatisfaction. Therefore, firms need to resolve the cause of consumer complaints, not just give the consumers the opportunity to complain.[48]

In fact, for many firms, retaining customers by encouraging and responding effectively to complaints is more economical than attracting new customers through advertising or other promotional activities. It has been estimated that it costs only one-fifth as much to retain an old customer as to obtain a new one.[49] Training *front-line employees* who deal directly with customers to use appropriate communication styles and empowering them to resolve problems as they arise are two ways firms can increase customer satisfaction and retention.[50]

Unfortunately, many corporations are not organized to effectively resolve and learn from consumer complaints. This area represents a major opportunity for many businesses.[51] Consider the following:

> When Sprint's new CEO Gary Forsee joined the company last March, he wanted to know why hundreds of millions of dollars were being spent on bringing in new wireless customers, while existing unsatisfied customers went out the back door. Mr. Forsee, a 30-year veteran of telephone companies including AT&T and BellSouth, wanted Sprint to put customer service in its place, right next to customer acquisition. So, Sprint changed—a lot. In fact, Sprint business units were completely reorganized around a new focus: the customer experience. No longer are customers acquired and then "thrown over the wall" to customer service. Marketing, customer service and sales are no longer three different silos, but reside in a combined unit working together.[52]

Sprint's companywide approach yielded dividends, with customer turnover down since the reorganization. Illustration 18–5 shows another company that is aligning its processes to proactively deal with customer issues and the customer experience in an online context.

CUSTOMER SATISFACTION, REPEAT PURCHASES, AND CUSTOMER COMMITMENT

LO6

Satisfaction is an important driver of customer loyalty and many organizations are investing in programs to enhance customer satisfaction, as shown by the following excerpt about New York–Presbyterian Hospital (NYP):

> NYP has looked very carefully at best practices for improving patient satisfaction across the country. To improve the patient experience, NYP implemented the Commitment to Care philosophy. Commitment to Care is a set of service expectations for all staff to follow in their work and interaction with patients, families and colleagues. The expectations are based on feedback that comes directly from patients and address their key priorities and needs. It was created to give employees clarity about what is expected of them and a clear set of standards by which to evaluate and recognize staff for issues related to service. Metrics [on key service dimensions] are an important tool for both the hospital and for our patients.[53]

Given increasingly sophisticated and value-conscious consumers and multiple brands that perform at satisfactory levels, producing satisfied customers is necessary but not sufficient for many marketers. Instead, the objective is to produce committed or brand-loyal customers.

Figure 18–4 illustrates the composition of the buyers of a particular brand at any point in time. Of the total buyers, some percentage will be satisfied with the purchase. As we have seen, marketers are spending considerable effort to make this percentage as high as possible. The reason is that, while many satisfied customers will switch brands,[54] satisfied customers are much more likely to become or remain repeat purchasers than are dissatisfied customers, particularly when satisfaction perceptions are strong and held with confidence.[55] **Repeat purchasers** continue to buy the same brand though they do not have an emotional attachment to it. They may do so out of habit or because they don't see viable options to their current choice.

As we saw earlier, some dissatisfied customers may also become or remain repeat purchasers. These individuals perceive the **switching costs**—*the costs of finding, evaluating,*

Creating Committed Customers Is Increasingly the Focus of Marketing Strategy FIGURE 

and adopting another solution—to be too high.[56] However, they may engage in negative word-of-mouth and are vulnerable to competitors' actions.

Repeat purchasers are desirable, but *mere* repeat purchasers are vulnerable to competitor actions. That is, they are buying the brand out of habit or because it is readily available where they shop, or because it has the lowest price, or for similar superficial reasons. These customers have no commitment to the brand. They are not brand loyal. **Brand loyalty** is defined as

> a biased (i.e., nonrandom) behavioral response (i.e., purchase/recommend) expressed over time by a decision-making unit with respect to one or more alternative brands out of a set of such brands that is a function of psychological (decision-making, evaluative) processes.[57]

Service and store loyalty are generally defined in the same or a similar manner.[58] Thus, a consumer loyal to a brand (store or service), or a **committed customer,** has an emotional attachment to the brand or firm. The customer likes the brand in a manner somewhat similar to friendship. Consumers use expressions such as "I trust this brand," "I like this outlet," and "I believe in this firm" to describe their commitment, as in the following customer quote:

> I tried it myself one time and eventually adopted a taste for it. Now I drink it all the time. I have it every morning after I come in from my run. I drink it after I clean the house. I always have a glass of it in my hand. That's me. I am very loyal to Gatorade. I would say that I am very loyal to that. I know they have other brands of that now, I see coupons all the time, but I have never even picked up a bottle of them. Never even tried them. Because I like Gatorade a lot. I really do.[59]

In a higher involvement context, NYP Hospital, discussed earlier, goes well beyond having, measuring, and reporting on key metrics to high-touch efforts that deliver personalized and humane service to its patients and treat patients and family with compassion and respect. Such efforts go well beyond mere satisfaction toward building a committed, loyal customer base.

Brand loyalty can arise through a number of processes, including:

- *Brand identification.* This is when a consumer believes the brand reflects and reinforces some aspect of his or her self-concept. This type of commitment is most common for symbolic products such as beer and automobiles. It is also likely in service situations that involve extended interpersonal encounters.[60]
- *Brand comfort.* Research in services has also found that loyalty can arise from *consumer comfort.* Consumer comfort is "a psychological state wherein a customer's anxiety concerning a service has been eased, and he or she enjoys peace of mind and is calm and worry free concerning service encounters with [a specific] provider."[61] Service employees likely play a strong role in developing comfort given the high-contact nature of many services.
- *Brand delight.* Brand loyalty may also arise through performance so far above expected that it delights the customer.[62] Such superior performance can be related to the product, the firm itself, or, as mentioned earlier, the manner in which the firm responds to a complaint or a customer problem. Delight has been demonstrated for high-involvement services as well as for more mundane customer website visits.[63]

Given the above, it is obvious that it is more difficult to develop brand-loyal consumers for some product categories than for others. Indeed, for low-involvement product categories with few opportunities for truly distinct performance or customer service, most firms should focus on creating satisfied repeat purchasers rather than loyal or committed customers.[64]

Committed customers are unlikely to consider additional information when making a purchase. They are also resistant to competitors' marketing efforts—for example, coupons. Even when loyal customers do buy a different brand to take advantage of a promotional deal, they generally return to their original brand for their next purchase.[65] Committed customers are more receptive to line extensions and other new products offered by the same firm. They are also more likely to forgive an occasional product or service failure.[66]

Finally, committed customers are likely to be a source of positive word-of-mouth communications. This is extremely valuable to a firm. Positive WOM communications from a committed customer increase the probability of the recipient's both becoming a customer and sharing the positive comments with other people.[67] Consumer Insight 18–1 shows how some marketers are utilizing a WOM measure to capture customer satisfaction and loyalty and predict future growth.

It is no surprise, therefore, that many marketers attempt to create satisfied customers and then try to convert them to committed customers. Committed customers are much more profitable to the firm than mere repeat purchasers, who in turn are more profitable than occasional buyers.[68]

Repeat Purchasers, Committed Customers, and Profits

Churn is a term used to refer to *turnover in a firm's customer base.* If a firm has a base of 100 customers and 20 leave each year and 20 new ones become customers, it has a churn rate of 20 percent. Churn at Amica, an insurance company dedicated to loyalty, is at an amazingly low 2 percent per year![69] Reducing churn is a major objective of many firms today. Why? It typically costs more to obtain a new customer than to retain an existing one, and new customers generally are not as profitable as longer-term customers. Consider the profits generated by one credit card firm's customers over time:[70]

Year	Profits
Acquisition cost	($51)
Year 1	$30
Year 2	$42
Year 3	$44
Year 4	$49
Year 5	$55

Acquisition costs include such expenses as advertising, establishing the account, mailing the card, and so forth. First-year profits are low because many new customers are acquired as a result of a promotional deal of some type. In addition, their initial usage rate tends to be low and they don't use all the features. This is a common pattern for both consumer and industrial products. Auto service profits per customer increased from $25 the first year to $88 in the fifth year, and an industrial laundry found they went from $144 to $258.

Figure 18–5 shows the sources of the growth of profit per customer over time. *Price premium* refers to the fact that repeat and particularly committed customers tend to buy the brand consistently rather than waiting for a sale or continually negotiating price. *Referrals* refers to profits generated by new customers acquired as a result of recommendations from existing customers. *Lower costs* occur because both the firm and the customer learn how to interact more efficiently over time. Finally, customers tend to use a wider array of a firm's products and services over time.[71]

Although committed customers are most valuable to a firm, reducing churn can have a major impact on profit even if the retained customers are primarily repeat purchasers.

CONSUMER INSIGHT 18-1

Do You Know Your Net Promoter Score?

Companies are always looking for better ways to measure true attitudinal loyalty. A recent approach that has garnered considerable interest is called the **net promoter score** (NPS). It might surprise you to find that NPS does not measure attitudinal loyalty through satisfaction scores or through some direct loyalty measure.[72] Instead, it is an *indirect* measure based on WOM. The technique is based on the following question:

"How likely is it that you would recommend (company X) to a friend or colleague?"

0-----1-----2-----3-----4-----5-----6-----7-----8-----9-----10

Not at All Likely | Neutral | Extremely Likely

Three categories of consumers are created based on their answers to this question, as follows:

Promoters: score 9 or 10
Passively Satisfied: score 7 or 8
Detractors: score 0 to 6

NPS is then calculated by subtracting the proportion of a firm's customers who are detractors from the proportion who are promoters. Passively satisfied customers are seen as essentially neutral in a way that makes them unlikely to engage in any proactive behavior regarding the company, either positive or negative. So, a company with 60 percent promoters, 30 percent passively satisfied, and 10 percent detractors would have an NPS of 50 (= 60% promoters – 10% detractors). Thus, the NPS *measures the percentage of a firm's customer base left after subtracting out the firm's detractors.*

Several points about NPS are worth noting.

1. Higher NPS scores, in many industries, are strongly related to positive firm growth. That is, if a firm's NPS score is going up (growth in promoters relative to detractors), then future growth in revenues is likely. This makes sense when you consider how powerful and trusted WOM is as a source of consumer information and as a basis for consumer choice.
2. NPS, although based on a WOM question, appears to tap into attitudinal loyalty because recommending to a friend or colleague involves social risk and requires proactive behavior on the part of the firm. Such risk taking and effort on behalf of a brand would seem most likely for a consumer who is highly *committed* to that brand.
3. NPS is very simple compared to many satisfaction and loyalty questionnaires that can involve dozens of questions.

NPS is not perfect (doesn't work well in all industries) and is not the only measure out there (other measures exist that are highly correlated with a firm's financial performance). However, the simplicity of NPS and its strong relationship with growth have made it popular with companies such as GE, Intuit, and American Express. The simplicity of NPS can also be a weakness when used inappropriately, and care in its use is important. NPS is a barometer of what's going on with the company. Measuring NPS is useless unless it aids change management at all levels of the organization to align firm and employee actions with customer feedback. As one expert notes:

> If we're going to act, we need more than a number. [Consumer] comments are essential, with driver analysis the next step. What do [consumers] comment about? What leads to being a promoter? To a detractor? And what will get passives off the fence?

Therefore, companies who use NPS often recommend supplementing the "recommend" question with questions that get at underlying reasons for the score. One company follows the "recommend" question with an open-end question that asks, "What is your primary reason for your rating [on the recommend question]?" Such an approach is still quite simple and yet provides the basis for marketing strategies to convert passively satisfied and detractor customers into promoters.

Critical Thinking Questions

1. Why do you think NPS is strongly related to firm growth?
2. Do you think NPS is also related to firm profits?
3. When might NPS not be a good predictor of firm growth?

Sources of Increased Customer Profitability over Time

FIGURE 18-5

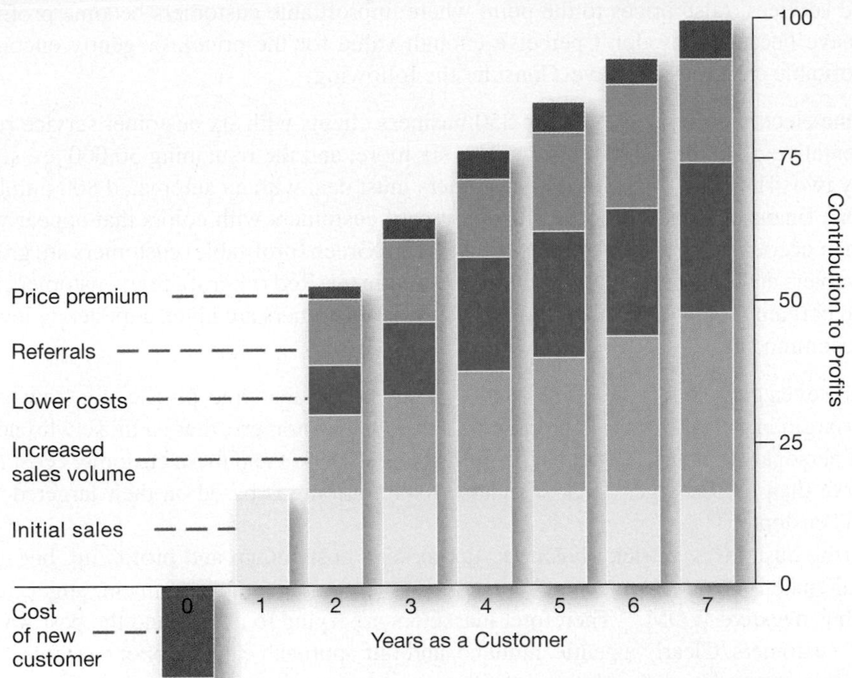

Source: "Sources of Increased Customer Profitability over Time." © 1999 TIME Inc. Reprinted by permission.

Reducing the number of customers who leave a firm in a year increases the average life of the firm's customer base.[73] As we saw earlier, the longer a customer is with a firm, the more profits the firm derives from that customer. Thus, a stable customer base tends to be highly profitable per customer. Reducing the number of customers who leave various types of firms each year by five percent has been found to increase the average profits per customer as follows:[74]

Firm Type	Percent Increase in Average Profits per Customer
Auto service	30%
Branch banks	85
Credit card	75
Credit insurance	25
Insurance brokerage	50
Industrial laundry	45

The motivation for marketers to retain customers is obvious. Phil Bressler, the co-owner of five Domino's Pizza outlets in Maryland, found that a regular customer was worth more than $5,000 over the 10-year life of the franchise agreement. He makes sure that every employee in every store is constantly aware of that number. Poor service or a bad attitude may cost the outlet several thousands of dollars, not just the $10 or $15 that might be lost on the single transaction![75]

However retaining some customers is more profitable than others. For example, at a typical commercial bank, the top 20 percent of customers generate six times more revenue than they cost. In contrast, the bottom 20 percent generate three to four times more costs than they do revenue. Firms increasingly understand the need to either strip out value-added services, raise prices to the point where unprofitable customers become profitable (or leave because they don't perceive enough value for the price), or gently encourage unprofitable customers to leave. Consider the following:

- One electric utility serves its top 350 business clients with six customer service representatives. The next 700 are served by six more, and the remaining 30,000 are served by two. The 300,000 residential customers must deal with an automated 800 number.
- One financial institution codes its credit card customers with colors that appear when their accounts appear on a service rep's screen. Green (profitable) customers are granted waivers and otherwise given white-glove treatment. Red (unprofitable) customers have no bargaining power. Yellow (marginal profit) customers are given a moderate level of accommodation.

ING even goes so far as to "fire" customers that don't match its profile of a "low touch, low margin" financial services provider. High-touch customers, that is, those who need a lot of personal attention, are not part of ING's target market and these customers cost more to serve than ING charges. That's because ING's pricing is based on their targeted "low touch" customer.[76]

Firing customers is tricky business. It can keep costs down and profits up, but it can also alienate former customers and create negative emotions (abandonment, anger, rage), and thus negative WOM.[77] Therefore, marketers are trying to understand the best ways to "fire" customers. Clearly a gentle, humane, and fair approach can help. For example, some companies go so far as to offer suggestions about where the customer might find a better "fit" with his or her needs.

Repeat Purchasers, Committed Customers, and Marketing Strategy

An important step in developing a marketing strategy for a particular segment is to specify the objectives being pursued. Several distinct possibilities exist:

1. Attract new users to the product category.
2. Capture competitors' current customers.
3. Encourage current customers to use more.
4. Encourage current customers to become repeat purchasers.
5. Encourage current customers to become committed customers.

Each of the objectives listed above will require different strategies and marketing mixes. The first two objectives require the marketer to convince potential customers that the marketer's brand will provide superior value to not using the product or to using another brand. Advertisements promising superior benefits, coupons, free trials, and similar strategies are common approaches. While some firms are content to consider the sale the last step, smart firms now realize the critical importance of retaining customers after the initial sale. This is true even for infrequently purchased items—rather than repeat sales, the marketer wants positive, or at least neutral, word-of-mouth communications.

The last three objectives, listed earlier, focus on marketing to the firm's current customers. All require customer satisfaction as a necessary precondition. As Figure 18–6 indicates, this requires that the firm deliver the value expected by the customer. Techniques for

Customer Satisfaction Outcomes FIGURE 18-6

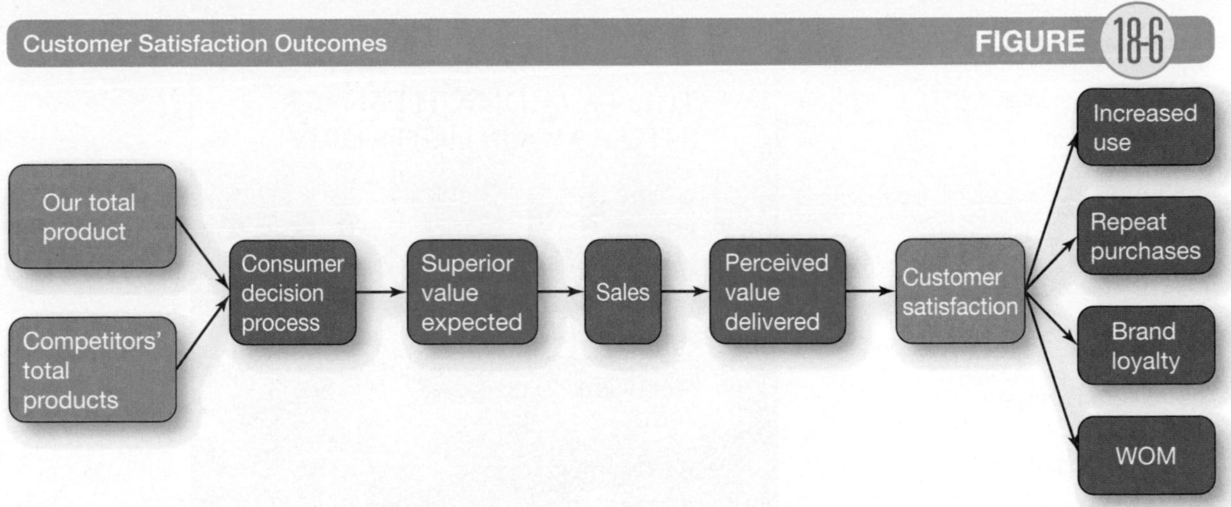

creating satisfied customers were described earlier. Marketing efforts focused on a firm's current customers are generally termed *relationship marketing.*

Relationship Marketing *An attempt to develop an ongoing, expanding exchange relationship with a firm's customers* is called **relationship marketing.**[78] In many ways, it seeks to mimic the relationships that existed between neighborhood stores and their customers many years ago. In those relationships, the store owner knew the customers not only as customers but also as friends and neighbors. The owner could anticipate their needs and provide help and advice when needed. Relationship marketing attempts to accomplish the same results, but because of the large scale of most operations, the firm must use databases, customized mass communications, and advanced employee training and motivation.[79]

Consider the following example:

> Lees Supermarkets, a family-owned and -operated company, started a Shoppers Club that records the purchases of members. Frequent or heavy shoppers are offered special incentives and deals. These offers can be customized on the basis of past purchasing patterns. In addition, last Thanksgiving, 600 regular, high-volume members were rewarded with free turkeys. Such an unexpected reward can produce delight and loyalty among key customers.[80]

Relationship marketing has five key elements:[81]

1. Developing a core service or product around which to build a customer relationship.
2. Customizing the relationship to the individual customer.
3. Augmenting the core service or product with extra benefits.
4. Pricing in a manner to encourage loyalty.
5. Marketing to employees so that they will perform well for customers.

This list of elements makes it clear that relationship marketing is centered on understanding consumer needs at the individual consumer level.[82] Not all customers are equally receptive to relationship marketing efforts. Perceptions that such relationships with the firm will be inconvenient and not yield adequate benefits and concerns over privacy are several factors that reduce consumer propensity to engage with relationship marketing efforts.[83]

ILLUSTRATION 18-6

Successful customer loyalty programs such as Capital One's BuyPower Card, are based on understanding the needs of key customers (in this case GM consumers) and providing benefits of value to them.

A substantial amount of effort is currently being focused on **customer loyalty programs.** In addition to frequent-flier programs offered by most major airlines, programs designed to generate repeat purchases include the following:

- Marriott has Marriott Rewards. Members earn points for staying at Marriott hotels and are classified into Silver, Gold, or Platinum, based on the number of stays per year. This classification system and its large customer database help Marriott customize its amenities and promotions based on each customer's individual profile.
- Sports franchises use card-based reward programs where members earn points for attending events and can redeem those points for team memorabilia, food, and drinks. Teams can also use the member data to create personalized communications and offerings, including season-ticket packages to their most attractive members.[84]

However, it is important to distinguish between programs that simply generate repeat purchases and those that generate committed and loyal customers.[85] Committed customers have a reasonably strong emotional attachment to the product or firm. Generating committed customers requires that the firm consistently meet or exceed customer expectations. Further, customers must believe that the firm is treating them fairly and is, to some extent at least, concerned about their well-being. Thus, *generating committed customers requires a customer-focused attitude in the firm.* It also requires that this attitude be translated into actions that meet customers' needs.[86]

Loyalty programs can be effective in generating committed customers if they understand and fulfill key customer needs (e.g., promotional awards on a favored brand), as shown by the Capital One ad in Illustration 18–6.

Research continues to investigate online loyalty. While differences in type of site and purpose of visit (buying versus browsing) are likely to exist, evidence supports Figure 18–6 in suggesting that perceived value and satisfaction are important determinants of online loyalty just as they are for products, services, and traditional retail outlets.[87] In addition, research has identified factors unique to online settings that drive e-loyalty. For example, one study finds security and privacy to be critical.[88] Other research identifies customization and personalization, interactivity, convenience, and online community as factors that drive e-loyalty, WOM, and willingness to pay.[89]

SUMMARY

SMART BOOK

LO1: Describe the various postpurchase processes engaged in by consumers

Purchase is followed by a number of processes including use, evaluation, and, in some cases, satisfaction, and consumer responses related to satisfaction including repurchase, positive word-of-mouth, and loyalty. Evaluation can also lead to dissatisfaction, which is sometimes associated with complaining, as well as erosion of loyalty, brand switching, and negative word-of-mouth.

LO2: Define and discuss postpurchase dissonance

Following some purchases, consumers experience doubts or anxiety about the wisdom of the purchase. This is known as *postpurchase dissonance.* It is most likely to occur (1) among individuals with a tendency to experience anxiety, (2) after an irrevocable purchase, (3) when the purchase was important to the consumer, and (4) when it involved a difficult choice between two or more alternatives.

LO3: Discuss the issues surrounding product use and nonuse and their importance to marketers

Whether or not the consumer experiences dissonance, most purchases are followed by product use. This use may be by the purchaser or by some other member of the purchasing unit. Monitoring product usage can indicate new uses for existing products, needed product modifications, appropriate advertising themes, and opportunities for new products. Product liability laws have made it increasingly important for marketing managers to be aware of all potential uses of their products.

Product nonuse is also a concern. Both marketers and consumers suffer when consumers buy products that they do not use or use less than they intended. Thus, marketers frequently attempt to influence the decision to use the product as well as the decision to purchase the product.

LO4: Summarize disposition options and their relevance to marketers and public policy

Disposition of the product or its package may occur before, during, or after product use. Understanding disposition behavior is important to marketing managers because of the ecological concerns of many consumers (and resulting green marketing efforts, see Chapter 3), the costs and scarcity of raw materials, and the activities of federal and state legislatures and regulatory agencies. *E-waste* is an emerging area of concern related to disposition.

LO5: Explain the determinants and outcomes of satisfaction and dissatisfaction

Consumer perceptions regarding satisfaction and dissatisfaction are a function of a comparison process between consumer expectations of performance and their perceptions of actual performance. When expectations are met or exceeded, satisfaction is likely to result, and in some cases commitment or loyalty is developed. When expectations are not met, dissatisfaction is the likely result. Service is a major determinant of customer satisfaction even when the core purchase involves a physical product. Service and product failures, failure to adequately address product and service problems, and bad pricing are key factors that lead to dissatisfaction.

Dissatisfaction can lead to many undesirable responses from the perspective of the firm, including erosion of loyalty, negative word-of-mouth, and switching brands. One positive response for the firm is customer complaining, although customers often are reluctant to complain and companies are often not well prepared to act on those complaints when they do occur.

LO6: Describe the relationship between satisfaction, repeat purchase, and customer commitment

Satisfaction results in a number of positive outcomes including repeat purchases, positive word-of-mouth, and, in some cases, loyalty. Not all satisfied customers are loyal. Simply meeting expectations (passive satisfaction in the language of Consumer Insight 18–1) is typically not enough to generate the psychological commitment that is associated with loyalty. *Repeat purchasers* are also not necessarily loyal customers. Repeat purchasing can occur out of habit (it's what I always buy) or necessity (it is the only option out there) and not out of a commitment to the brand. Repeat purchasers who are not *committed customers* are vulnerable to competitor attempts to steal them away. Thus, *brand loyalty* or customer commitment, defined as a willingness to repurchase coupled with a psychological commitment to the brand, is critical to marketers. As online retailing continues to grow, marketers are examining ways in which e-satisfaction and e-loyalty can be bolstered. *Relationship marketing* and loyalty programs are strategic efforts on the part of the firm that can be used to bolster satisfaction, repeat purchases, and, in some cases, loyalty.

KEY TERMS

REVIEW QUESTIONS

1. What are the major postpurchase processes engaged in by consumers?
2. How does the type of decision process affect the postpurchase processes?
3. What is *postpurchase dissonance?*
4. What characteristics of a purchase situation are likely to contribute to postpurchase dissonance?
5. In what ways can a consumer reduce postpurchase dissonance?
6. What is *consumption guilt?*
7. What is *use innovativeness?*
8. What is an *off-label use* and why is it important to companies?
9. Why are surveys not always the most effective way to get at innovative product uses?
10. What is meant by *product nonuse* and why is it a concern of marketers?
11. What is meant by the disposition of products and product packaging and why does it interest governmental regulatory agencies and marketers?
12. What is *e-waste* and why is it a growing concern?
13. What factors influence consumer satisfaction? In what way do they influence consumer satisfaction?
14. What is the difference between *instrumental* and *symbolic performance* and how does each contribute to consumer satisfaction?
15. What is *affective performance?*
16. What courses of action can a consumer take in response to dissatisfaction? Which are used most often?
17. What determines satisfaction for online retailers?
18. What would marketers like consumers to do when dissatisfied? How can marketers encourage this?

19. What is *churn?* How does it affect profits?
20. What are the sources of increased profits from longer-term customers?
21. What is the relationship between customer satisfaction, repeat purchases, and committed customers?
22. What is the difference between *repeat purchasers* and *committed customers?*
23. What are *switching costs?*
24. Why are marketers interested in having committed customers?
25. What is the *net promoter score?*
26. What is *relationship marketing?* What strategies are involved?
27. What are *loyalty programs?* What do most of them actually do?
28. What factors influence e-loyalty?

DISCUSSION QUESTIONS

29. How should retailers deal with consumers immediately after purchase to reduce postpurchase dissonance? What specific action would you recommend, and what effect would you intend it to have on the recent purchaser of (gift of) the following?
    a. PBS donation
    b. A condominium
    c. Dance lessons
    d. A hybrid automobile
    e. Microwave oven
    f. Tropical fish
30. What type of database should your university maintain on its students? In general, what ethical concerns surround the use of such databases by institutions and companies?
31. How should manufacturers deal with consumers immediately after purchase to reduce postpurchase dissonance? What specific action would you recommend and what effect would you intend it to have on the recent purchaser of the following?
    a. Cell phone
    b. Expensive watch
    c. Tablet computer
    d. Corrective eye surgery
32. How do some companies capitalize on the concept of use innovativeness?
33. Discuss how you could determine how consumers actually use the following. How could this information be used to develop marketing strategy?
    a. Microwave
    b. Wrist watches
    c. Online banking services
    d. Movies on demand
    e. Hair color
    f. Hotel reward points
34. How would you go about measuring consumer satisfaction among purchasers of the following? What questions would you ask, what additional information would you collect, and why? How could this information be used for evaluating and planning marketing programs?
    a. Cell phone service
    b. Walmart.com
    c. Car insurance
    d. Six Flags theme parks
    e. Health care services
    f. Exercise bike
35. What level of product dissatisfaction should a marketer be content with in attempting to serve a particular target market? What characteristics contribute to dissatisfaction, regardless of the marketer's efforts?
36. Describe the last time you were dissatisfied with a purchase. What action did you take? Why?
37. Are you a *mere* repeat purchaser of any brand, service, or outlet? Why are you not a committed customer? What, if anything, would make you a committed customer?
38. Respond to the questions in Consumer Insight 18–1.
39. What are some of the possible negative consequences of "firing" customers?

40. Are you a committed customer to any brand, service, or outlet? Why?
41. Design a customer loyalty program for the following:
    a. High-end hotel chain
    b. Grocery store chain
    c. Cosmetics line
    d. Catering service

APPLICATION ACTIVITIES

42. Develop a brief questionnaire to determine product nonuse among college students and the reasons for it. With four other classmates, interview 50 students. What do you conclude?
43. Develop a questionnaire designed to measure consumer satisfaction of a clothing purchase of $100 or more. Include in your questionnaire items that measure the product's instrumental, symbolic, and affective dimensions of performance, as well as what the consumer wanted on these dimensions. Then interview several consumers to obtain information on actual performance, expected performance, and satisfaction. Using this information, determine if consumers received what they expected (i.e., evaluation of performance) and relate any difference to consumer expressions of satisfaction. What are the marketing implications of your results?
44. Develop a survey to measure student dissatisfaction with service purchases. For purchases they were dissatisfied with, determine what action they took to resolve this dissatisfaction and what the end result of their efforts were. What are the marketing implications of your findings?
45. Develop a questionnaire to measure repeat purchase behavior and brand loyalty. Measure the repeat purchase behavior and brand loyalty of 10 students with respect to the following. Determine why the brand-loyal students are brand loyal.
    a. Batteries
    b. Spaghetti sauce
    c. Coffee
    d. Lightbulbs
    e. Clothing stores
    f. Online stores
46. With the cooperation of a durables retailer, assist the retailer in sending a postpurchase letter of thanks to every other customer immediately after purchase. Then, approximately two weeks after purchase, contact the same customers (both those who received the letter and those who did not) and measure their purchase satisfaction. Evaluate the results.
47. Interview a grocery store manager, a department store manager, and a restaurant manager. Determine the types of products their customers are most likely to complain about and the nature of those complaints.
48. Measure 10 students' disposition behaviors with respect to the following. Determine why they use the alternatives they do.
    a. Laptop computer
    b. Cell phones
    c. Mattress
    d. Televisions
    e. Plastic items
49. Interview 20 students to determine which, if any, customer loyalty programs they belong to, what they like and dislike about them, and the impact they have on their attitudes and behaviors. What opportunities do your results suggest?

REFERENCES

1. B. Wansink, *Mindless Eating: Why We Eat More Than We Think* (New York: Bantam Books, 2006).
2. D. M. Mochon, M. I. Norton, and D. Ariely, "Bolstering and Restoring Feelings of Competence via the IKEA Effect," *International Journal of Research in Marketing,* December 2012, pp. 363–69.
3. D. Kahneman, J. L. Knetsch, and R. H. Thaler, "Anomalies: The Endowment Effect, Loss Aversion, and Status Quo Bias," *Journal of Economic Perspectives,* Winter 1991, pp. 193–206.
4. G. J. Thompson, "Interpreting Consumers," *Journal of Marketing Research,* November 1997, p. 444. Published by the American Marketing Association; reprinted with permission.

5. See J. C. Sweeney, D. Hausknecht, and G. N. Soutar, "Cognitive Dissonance after Purchase," *Psychology & Marketing,* May 2000, pp. 369–85.
6. M. F. Luce, "Choosing to Avoid," *Journal of Consumer Research,* March 1998, pp. 409–33.
7. S. J. Gould, "An Interpretative Study of Purposeful, Mood Self-Regulating Consumption," *Psychology & Marketing,* July 1997, pp. 395–426.
8. See, e.g., R. Kivetz and I. Simonson, "Self-Control for the Righteous," *Journal of Consumer Research,* September 2002, pp. 199–217; and J. Xu and N. Schwarz, "Do We Really Need a Reason to Indulge?," *Journal of Marketing Research,* February 2009, pp. 25–36.
9. See S. Ram and H.-S. Jung, "Innovativeness in Product Usage," *Psychology & Marketing,* January 1994, pp. 57–69; N. M. Ridgway and L. L. Price, "Exploration in Product Usage," *Psychology & Marketing,* January 1994, pp. 70–84; and K. Park and C. L. Dyer, "Consumer Use Innovative Behavior," in *Advances in Consumer Research,* vol. 22, ed. F. R. Kardes and M. Sujan (Provo, UT: Association for Consumer Research, 1995), pp. 566–72.
10. M. B. Kemp, *CMOs Must Connect the Dots of the Online Brand* (Cambridge, MA: Forrester Research, Inc., July 27, 2010).
11. V. A. Taylor and A. B. Bower, "Improving Product Instruction Compliance," *Psychology & Marketing,* March 2004, pp. 229–45; and D. Bowman, C. M. Heilman, and P. B. Seetharaman, "Determinants of Product-Use Compliance Behavior," *Journal of Marketing Research,* August 2004, pp. 324–38.
12. A. B. Bower and D. E. Sprott, "The Case of the Dusty Stair-Climber," in *Advances in Consumer Research,* vol. 22, ed. Kardes and Sujan, pp. 582–87. See also B. Wansink and R. Deshpande, *Marketing Letters,* 5, no. 1 (1994), pp. 91–100.
13. Bower and Sprott, "The Case of the Dusty Stair-Climber," p. 585.
14. S. L. Wood, "Remote Purchase Environments," *Journal of Marketing Research,* May 2001, pp. 157–69.
15. For detailed statistics, visit the U.S. Environmental Protection Agency website at www.epa.gov.
16. L. Williams, "Current United States Recycling Statistics," *Green Living,* www.greenliving.lovetoknow.com, accessed June 30, 2011.
17. K. Y. Larkin, "Computer Recycling Statistics," *Green Living,* www.greenliving.lovetoknow.com, accessed June 30, 2011.
18. "Cashing in on Old Gadgets," *CNN.com,* accessed January 17, 2008.
19. K. Hall, "Sony Likes the Yield from Its Junk," *BusinessWeek,* September 17, 2007, p. 40.
20. E. M. Okada, "Trade-ins, Mental Accounting, and Product Replacement Decisions," *Journal of Consumer Research,* March 2001, pp. 433–66.
21. A. Biswas, "The Recycling Cycle," *Journal of Public Policy & Marketing,* Spring 2000, pp. 93–105.
22. See B. G. Goff, J. S. Boles, D. N. Bellenger, and C. Stojack, "The Influence of Salesperson Selling Behaviors on Customer Satisfaction with Products," *Journal of Retailing,* 2 (1997), pp. 171–83.
23. V. Mittal, P. Kumar, and M. Tsiros, "Attribute-Level Performance, Satisfaction, and Behavioral Intentions over Time," *Journal of Marketing,* April 1999, pp. 88–101; and R. J. Slote-Graff and J. J. Inman, "Longitudinal Shifts in the Drivers of Satisfaction with Product Quality," *Journal of Marketing Research,* August 2004, pp. 269–80.
24. See, e.g., A. S. Mattila, "The Impact of Cognitive Inertia on Post-Consumption Evaluation Processes," *Journal of the Academy of Marketing Science,* 31, no. 3 (2003), pp. 287–99.
25. See, e.g., K. E. Clow, D. L. Kurtz, J. Ozment, and B. S. Ong, "The Antecedents of Consumer Expectations of Services," *Journal of Services Marketing,* 11, no. 4 (1997), pp. 230–48.
26. See J. Ozment and E. A. Morash, "The Augmented Service Offering for Perceived and Actual Service Quality," *Journal of the Academy of Marketing Science,* Fall 1994, pp. 352–63; and G. B. Voss, A. Parasuraman, and D. Grewal, "The Roles of Price, Performance, and Expectations in Determining Satisfaction in Service Exchanges," *Journal of Marketing,* October 1998, pp. 48–61.
27. See, e.g., C. P. Bebko, "Service Intangibility and Its Impact on Customer Expectations," *Journal of Services Marketing,* 14, no. 1 (2000), pp. 9–26; B. Bickart and N. Schwartz, "Service Experiences and Satisfaction Judgments," *Journal of Consumer Psychology,* 11, no. 1 (2001), pp. 29–41; D. M. Szymanski and D. H. Henard, "Customer Satisfaction," *Journal of the Academy of Marketing Science,* Winter 2001, pp. 16–35; J. C. Sweeney and G. N. Soutar, "Consumer Perceived Value," *Journal of Retailing,* 77 (2001), pp. 203–20; P. K. Kopalle and D. R. Lehmann, "Strategic Management of Expectations," *Journal of Marketing Research,* August 2001, pp. 386–94; J. Wirtz and A. Mattila, "Exploring the Role of Alternative Perceived Performance Measures and Needs-Congruency in the Customer Satisfaction Process," *Journal of Consumer Psychology,* 11, no. 3 (2001), pp. 181–92; E. Garbarino and M. S. Johnson, "Effects of Consumer Goals on Attribute Weighting, Overall Satisfaction, and Product Usage," *Psychology & Marketing,* September 2001, pp. 929–49; and M. Heitmann, D. R. Lehmann, and A. Herrmann, "Choice Goal Attainment and Decision Consumption Satisfaction," *Journal of Marketing Research,* May 2007, pp. 234–50.
28. S. M. Keaveney, "Customer Switching Behavior in Service Industries," *Journal of Marketing,* April 1995, pp. 71–82. See also D. Grace and A. O'Cass, "Attributions of Service Switching," *Journal of Services Marketing,* 14, no. 4 (2001), pp. 300–21; V. Mittal, J. M. Katrichis, and P. Kumar, "Attribute Performance and Customer Satisfaction over Time," *Journal of Services Marketing,* 15, no. 5 (2001), pp. 343–56; C. de Matos, J. Henrique, and C. Rossi, "Service Recovery Paradox," *Journal of Service Research,* August 2007, pp. 66–77; and S. Anderson, L. K. Pearo, and S. K. Widener, "Drivers of Service Satisfaction," *Journal of Service Research,* May 2008, pp. 365–81.
29. See, e.g., S. Taylor, "The Effects of Filled Waiting Time and Service Provider Control over the Delay on Evaluations of Service," *Journal of the Academy of Marketing Science,* Winter 1995, pp. 38–48; and M. K. Hui, M. V. Thakor, and R. Gill, "The Effect of Delay Type and Service Stage on Consumers' Reactions to Waiting," *Journal of Consumer Research,* March 1998, pp. 469–79.

30. V. Mittal, W. T. Ross Jr., and P. M. Baldsare, "The Asymmetric Impact of Negative and Positive Attribute-Level Performance on Overall Satisfaction and Repurchase Levels," *Journal of Marketing,* January 1998, pp. 33–47. See also G. J. Gaeth et al., "Consumers' Attitude Change across Sequences of Successful and Unsuccessful Product Usage," *Marketing Letters,* 8, no. 1 (1997), pp. 41–53.

31. I. E. Swan and L. J. Combs, "Product Performance and Consumer Satisfaction: A New Concept," *Journal of Marketing,* April 1976, pp. 25–33.

32. See H. Mano and R. L. Oliver, "Assessing the Dimensionality and Structure of the Consumption Experience," *Journal of Consumer Research,* December 1993, pp. 451–66; and L. W. Turley and D. L. Bolton, "Measuring the Affective Evaluations of Retail Service Environments," *Journal of Professional Services Marketing,* 19, no. 1 (1999), pp. 31–44. See also S. M. Nowlis, N. Mandel, and D. B. McCabe, "The Effect of a Delay between Choice and Consumption on Consumption Enjoyment," *Journal of Consumer Research,* December 2004, pp. 502–10; and R. D. Raggio, and J. Folse, "Gratitude Works," *Journal of the Academy of Marketing Science,* 37 (2009), pp. 455–69.

33. B. B. Holloway and S. E. Beatty, "Satisfiers and Dissatisfiers in the Online Environment," *Journal of Service Research,* 10, no. 4 (2008), pp. 347–64.

34. H. Evanschitzky et al., "E-satisfaction," *Journal of Retailing,* 80 (2004), pp. 239–47.

35. R. Sousa and C. A. Voss, "Service Quality in Multichannel Services Employing Virtual Channels," *Journal of Service Research,* May 2006, pp. 356–71.

36. See., e.g., J. Singh, "A Typology of Consumer Dissatisfaction Response Styles," *Journal of Retailing,* Spring 1990, pp. 57–97; J. Singh, "Voice, Exit, and Negative Word-of-Mouth Behaviors," *Journal of the Academy of Marketing Science,* Winter 1990, pp. 1–15; K. Gronhaug and O. Kvitastein, "Purchases and Complaints," *Psychology & Marketing,* Spring 1991, pp. 21–35; S. W. Kelley and M. A. Davis, "Antecedents to Customer Expectations for Service Recovery," *Journal of the Academy of Marketing Science,* Winter 1994, pp. 52–61; M. A. Jones, D. L. Mothersbaugh, and S. E. Beatty, "Switching Barriers and Repurchase Intentions in Services," *Journal of Retailing,* 76, no. 2 (2000), pp. 259–74; M. A. Jones and J. Suh, "Transaction-Specific Satisfaction and Overall Satisfaction," *Journal of Services Marketing,* 14, no. 2 (2000), pp. 147–59; J. Lee, J. Lee, and L. Feick, "The Impact of Switching Costs on the Customer Satisfaction-Loyalty Link," *Journal of Services Marketing,* 15, no. 1 (2001), pp. 35–48; and I. Roos, B. Edvardsson, and A. Gustafsson, "Customer Switching Patterns in Competitive and Noncompetitive Service Industries," *Journal of Service Research,* February 2004, pp. 256–71.

37. See also S. P. Brown and R. F. Beltramini, "Consumer Complaining and Word-of-Mouth Activities," in *Advances in Consumer Research,* vol. 16, ed. T. K. Srull (Provo, UT: Association for Consumer Research, 1989), pp. 9–11; and J. E. Swan and R. L. Oliver, "Postpurchase Communications by Consumers," *Journal of Retailing,* Winter 1989, pp. 516–33.

38. J. Goodman and S. Newman, "Understanding Customer Behavior and Complaints," *Quality Progress,* January 2003, pp. 51–55. For additional research and statistics, visit www.tarp.com.

39. See, e.g., A. K. Smith and R. N. Bolton, "The Effect of Consumers' Emotional Responses to Service Failures on Their Recovery Effort Evaluations and Satisfaction Judgments," *Journal of the Academy of Marketing Science,* Winter 2002, pp. 5–23; N. N. Bechwati and M. Morrin, "Outraged Consumers," *Journal of Consumer Psychology,* 13, no. 4 (2003), pp. 440–53; and R. Bougie, R. Pieters, and M. Zeelenberg, "Angry Customers Don't Come Back, They Get Back," *Journal of the Academy of Marketing Science,* Fall 2003, pp. 377–93.

40. I. M. Wetzer, M. Zeelenberg, and R. Pieters, "'Never Eat in That Restaurant, I Did!,'" *Psychology & Marketing,* August 2007, pp. 661–80.

41. Thompson, "Interpreting Consumers."

42. See, e.g., C. Ayres, "Revenge Is Best Served Cold—on YouTube," *The Times,* July 22, 2009; and R. Sawhney, "Broken Guitar Has United Playing the Blues to the Tune of $180 Million," *Fast Company,* July 28, 2009.

43. See R. A. Spreng, G. D. Harrell, and R. D. Mackoy, "Service Recovery," *Journal of Services Marketing,* 9, no. 1 (1995), pp. 15–23; and L. Dube and M. F. Maute, "Defensive Strategies for Managing Satisfaction and Loyalty in the Service Industry," *Psychology & Marketing,* December 1998, pp. 775–91. For an alternative view, see T. W. Andreassen, "From Disgust to Delight," *Journal of Service Research,* August 2001, pp. 39–49; G. Maxham II and R. G. Netemeyer, "A Longitudinal Study of Complaining Customers' Evaluations of Multiple Service Failures and Recovery Efforts," *Journal of Marketing,* October 2002, pp. 57–71; and S. Weun, S. E. Beatty, and M. A. Jones, "The Impact of Service Failure Severity on Service Recovery Evaluations and Post-Recovery Relationships," *Journal of Services Marketing,* 18, no. 2 (2004), pp. 133–46.

44. A literature review and model are in N. Stephens and K. P. Gwinner, "Why Don't Some People Complain?," *Journal of the Academy of Marketing Science,* Summer 1998, pp. 172–89. See also A. L. Dolinsky et al., "The Role of Psychographic Characteristics as Determinants of Complaint Behavior," *Journal of Hospital Marketing,* 2 (1998), pp. 27–51; E. G. Harris and J. C. Mowen, "The Influence of Cardinal-, Central-, and Surface-Level Personality Traits on Consumers' Bargaining and Complaining Behavior," *Psychology & Marketing,* November 2001, pp. 1115–85; C. Kim et al., "The Effect of Attitude and Perception on Consumer Complaint Intentions," *Journal of Consumer Marketing,* 20, no. 4 (2003), pp. 352–71; J. C. Chebat, M. Davidow, and I. Codjovi, "Silent Voices," *Journal of Service Research,* May 2005, pp. 328–42; K. Bodey and D. Grace, "Contrasting 'Complainers' with 'Non-complainers' on Attitude Toward Complaining, Propensity to Complain, and Key Personality Characteristics," *Psychology & Marketing,* July 2007, pp. 579–94; and C. Orsingher, S. Valentini, and M. de Angelis, "A Meta-Analysis of Satisfaction with Complaint

Handling in Services," *Journal of the Academy of Marketing Science,* 38 (2010), pp. 169–86.

45. K. Patel, "How AT&T Plans to Lift Its Image Via Social Media," *Advertising Age,* June 21, 2010.

46. J. Strauss and D. J. Hill, "Consumer Complaints by E-Mail," *Journal of Interactive Marketing,* Winter 2001, pp. 63–73. See also A. S. Mattila and J. Wirtz, "Consumer Complaining to Firms," *Journal of Services Marketing,* 18, no. 2 (2004), pp. 147–55.

47. See A. K. Smith, R. N. Bolton, and J. Wagner, "A Model of Customer Satisfaction with Service Encounters Involving Failure and Recovery," *Journal of Marketing Research,* August 1999, pp. 356–72; A. Palmer, R. Beggs, and C. Keown-McMullan, "Equity and Repurchase Intention Following Service Failure," *Journal of Services Marketing,* 14, no. 6 (2000), pp. 513–28; A. S. Mattila, "The Effectiveness of Service Recovery in a Multi-Industry Setting," *Journal of Services Marketing,* 15, no. 7 (2001), pp. 583–96; J. G. Maxham III and R. G. Netemeyer, "Modeling Customer Perceptions of Complaint Handling over Time," *Journal of Retailing,* 78 (2002), pp. 239–52; M. Davidow, "Organizational Responses to Customer Complaints," *Journal of Service Research,* February 2003, pp. 225–50; and C. Homburg and A. Furst, "How Organizational Complaint Handling Drives Customer Loyalty," *Journal of Marketing,* July 2005, pp. 95–114.

48. See C. Goodwin and I. Ross, "Consumer Evaluations of Response to Complaints," *Journal of Consumer Marketing,* Spring 1990, pp. 39–47; J. G. Blodgett, D. J. Hill, and S. S. Tax, "The Effects of Distributive, Procedural, and Interactional Justice on Postcomplaint Behavior," *Journal of Retailing,* 2 (1997), pp. 185–210; and C. M. Voorhees, M. K. Brady, and D. M. Horowitz, "A Voice from the Silent Masses," *Journal of the Academy of Marketing Science,* 34, no. 4, (2006), pp. 514–27.

49. P. Sellers, "What Customers Really Want," *Fortune,* June 4, 1990, pp. 58–62.

50. B. A. Sparks, G. L. Bradley, and V. J. Callan, "The Impact of Staff Empowerment and Communication Style on Customer Evaluations," *Psychology & Marketing,* August 1997, pp. 475–93.

51. See F. F. Reichheld, "Learning from Customer Defections," *Harvard Business Review,* March 1996, pp. 56–69. See also H. Estelami, "The Profit Impact of Consumer Complaint Solicitation across Market Conditions," *Journal of Professional Services Marketing,* 20, no. 1 (1999), pp. 165–95; and N. A. Morgan, E. W. Anderson, and V. Mittal, "Understanding Firms' Customer Satisfaction Information Usage," *Journal of Marketing,* July 2005, pp. 131–51.

52. B. S. Bulik, "Brands Spotlight Customer Experience," *Advertising Age,* April 19, 2004, pp. 1, 14.

53. R. Liebowitz, "Putting Patients First," *Healthcare Executive,* July–August 2008, pp. 42–44.

54. T. O. Jones and W. E. Sasser Jr., "Why Satisfied Customers Defect," *Harvard Business Review,* November 1995, pp. 88–95; P. T. L. P. Leszczyc and H. J. P. Timmermans, "Store-Switching Behavior," *Marketing Letters,* 8, no. 2 (1997), pp. 193–204; B. Mittal and W. M. Lassar, "Why Do Customers Switch?," *Journal of Services Marketing,* 12, no. 3 (1998), pp. 177–94; and C. Homburg and A. Giering, "Personal Characteristics as Moderators of the Relationship between Customer Satisfaction and Loyalty," *Psychology & Marketing,* January 2001, pp. 43–66.

55. See V. Mittal and W. Kamakura, "Satisfaction, Repurchase Intent, and Repurchase Behavior," *Journal of Marketing Research,* February 2001, pp. 131–42; and M. Chandrashekaran et al., "Satisfaction Strength and Customer Loyalty," *Journal of Marketing Research,* February 2007, pp. 153–63.

56. For a discussion of switching costs and repurchase intentions, see Jones, Mothersbaugh, and Beatty, "Switching Barriers and Repurchase Intentions in Services"; P. G. Patterson and T. Smith, "A Cross-Cultural Study of Switching Barriers and Propensity to Stay with Service Providers," *Journal of Retailing,* 79 (2003), pp. 107–20; T. A. Burnham, J. K. Frels, and V. Mahajan, "Consumer Switching Costs," *Journal of the Academy of Marketing Science,* Spring 2003, pp. 109–26; and M. A. Jones et al., "The Positive and Negative Effects of Switching Costs on Relational Outcomes," *Journal of Service Research,* May 2007, pp. 335–55.

57. J. Jacoby and D. B. Kyner, "Brand Loyalty versus Repeat Purchasing Behavior," *Journal of Marketing Research,* February 1973, pp. 1–9. See also S. Rundle-Thiele and M. M. Mackay, "Assessing the Performance of Brand Loyalty Measures," *Journal of Services Marketing,* 15, no. 7 (2001), pp. 529–46; A. Chaudhuri and M. B. Holbrook, "The Chain of Effects from Brand Trust and Brand Affect to Brand Performance," *Journal of Marketing,* April 2001, pp. 81–93; C. F. Curasi and K. N. Kennedy, "From Prisoners to Apostles," *Journal of Services Marketing,* 16, no. 4 (2002), pp. 322–41; and V. Liljander and I. Roos, "Customer-Relationship Levels," *Journal of Services Marketing,* 16, no. 7 (2002), pp. 593–614.

58. See, e.g., R. R. G. Javalgi and C. R. Moberg, "Service Loyalty," *Journal of Services Marketing,* 11, no. 3 (1997), pp. 165–79.

59. S. Fournier, "Consumers and Their Brands," *Journal of Consumer Research,* March 1998, p. 355.

60. See E. Garbarino and M. S. Johnson, "The Different Roles of Satisfaction, Trust, and Commitment in Customer Relationships," *Journal of Marketing,* April 1999, pp. 70–87; J. Singh and D. Sirdeshmukh, "Agency and Trust Mechanisms in Consumer Satisfaction and Loyalty Judgments," *Journal of the Academy of Marketing Science,* Winter 2000, pp. 150–67; D. Sirdeshmukh, J. Singh, and B. Sabol, "Consumer Trust, Value, and Loyalty in Relational Exchanges," *Journal of Marketing,* January 2002, pp. 15–37; and C. B. Battacharya and S. Sen, "Consumer–Company Identification," *Journal of Marketing,* April 2003, pp. 76–88.

61. D. F. Spake et al., "Consumer Comfort in Service Relationships," *Journal of Service Research,* May 2003, pp. 316–32.

62. R. L. Oliver, R. T. Rust, and S. Varki, "Customer Delight," *Journal of Retailing,* 73, no. 3 (1997), pp. 311–36; and R. T. Rust and R. L. Oliver, "Should We Delight the Customer?,"

Journal of the Academy of Marketing Science, Winter 2000, pp. 86–94.

63. A. Finn, "Reassessing the Foundations of Customer Delight," *Journal of Service Research,* November 2005, pp. 103–16.

64. R. L. Oliver, "Whence Consumer Loyalty," *Journal of Marketing,* Special Issue 1999, pp. 33–44.

65. See J. Deighton, C. M. Henderson, and S. A. Neslin, "The Effects of Advertising on Brand Switching and Repeat Purchasing," *Journal of Marketing Research,* February 1994, pp. 28–43.

66. See D. Bejou and A. Palmer, "Service Failure and Loyalty," *Journal of Services Marketing,* 12, no. 1 (1998), pp. 7–22; and R. L. Hess Jr., S. Ganesan, and N. M. Klein, "Service Failure and Recovery," *Journal of the Academy of Marketing Science,* Spring 2003, pp. 127–45.

67. M. Johnson, G. M. Zinkhan, and G. S. Ayala, "The Impact of Outcome, Competency, and Affect on Service Referral," *Journal of Services Marketing,* 12, no. 5 (1998), pp. 397–415.

68. E. W. Anderson, C. Fornell, and R. T. Rust, "Customer Satisfaction, Productivity, and Profitability," *Marketing Science,* 16, no. 2 (1997), pp. 129–45.

69. J. McGregor, "Customer Service Champs," *Bloomberg Businessweek,* February 18, 2010.

70. F. F. Reichheld and W. E. Sasser Jr., "Zero Defections," *Harvard Business Review,* September 1990, pp. 105–11; and R. Jacob, "Why Some Customers Are More Equal than Others," *Fortune,* September 19, 1994, pp. 215–24. See also V. A. Zeithaml, "Service Qualilty, Profitablity, and the Economic Worth of Customers," *Journal of the Academy of Marketing Science,* Winter 2000, pp. 67–85.

71. For additional research examining these various outcomes, see T. Hennig-Thurau, K. P. Gwinner, and D. D. Gremler, "Understanding Relationship Marketing Outcomes," *Journal of Service Research,* February 2002, pp. 230–47; P. C. Verhoef, P. H. Franses, and J. C. Hoekstra, "The Effect of Relational Constructs on Customer Referrals and Number of Services Purchased from a Multiservice Provider," *Journal of the Academy of Marketing Science,* 30, no. 3 (2002), pp. 202–16; H. S. Bansal, P. G. Irving, and S. F. Taylor, "A Three-Component Model of Customer Commitment to Service Providers," *Journal of the Academy of Marketing Science,* 32, no. 3 (2004), pp. 234–50; C. Homburg, N. Koschate, and W. D. Hoyer, "Do Satisfied Customers Really Pay More?," *Journal of Marketing,* April 2005, pp. 84–96; and K. Seiders, G. B. Voss, D. Grewal, and A. L. Godfrey, "Do Satisfied Customers Buy More?," *Journal of Marketing,* October 2005, pp. 26–43.

72. This insight is based on F. F. Reichheld, "The One Number You Need to Grow," *Harvard Business Review,* December 2003, pp. 46–54; M. Anstead, "What's Missing When It Comes to Net Promoter," *Credit Union Journal,* March 30, 2009, p. 8; M. Creamer, "Do You Know Your Score?," *Advertising Age,* July 23, 2006, pp. 1 and 24; T. L. Keiningham et al., "A Longitudinal Examination of Net Promoter and Firm Revenue Growth," *Journal of Marketing,* July 2007, pp. 39–51; A. Gigliotto et al., "NPS Not the Only Way," *Marketing News,* September 15, 2007, pp. 48–52; and C. Pasquale, "Closing the Customer Feedback Loop," *Harvard Business Review,* December 2009, pp. 43–47.

73. See S. Li, "Survival Analysis," *Marketing Research,* Fall 1995, pp. 17–23.

74. Reichheld and Sasser, "Zero Defections," p. 110.

75. See also S. Lingle, "How Much Is a Customer Worth?," *Bank Marketing,* August 1995, pp. 13–16.

76. E. Esfahani, "How to . . . Get Tough with Bad Customers," *Business 2.0,* October 2004, p. 52.

77. See, e.g., T. Wagner, T. Hennig-Thurau, and T. Rudolph, "Does Customer Demotion Jeopardize Loyalty?," *Journal of Marketing,* May 2009, pp. 69–85.

78. See G. S. Day, "Managing Market Relationships," *Journal of the Academy of Marketing Science,* Winter 2000, pp. 24–30.

79. See the special issue on relationship marketing, *Journal of the Academy of Marketing Science,* Fall 1995; and G. E. Gengler and P. P. Leszczyc, "Using Customer Satisfaction Research for Relationship Marketing," *Journal of Direct Marketing,* Winter 1997, pp. 23–29.

80. L. Freeman, "Marketing the Market," *Marketing News,* March 2, 1998, p. 1. Other examples are in G. B. Voss and Z. G. Voss, "Implementing a Relationship Marketing Program," *Journal of Services Marketing,* 11, no. 4 (1997), pp. 278–98; B. G. Yovovich, "Scanners Reshape the Grocery Business," *Marketing News,* February 16, 1998, p. 1; and G. Brewer, "The Customer Stops Here," *Sales & Marketing Management,* March 1998, pp. 31–36.

81. L. L. Berry, "Relationship Marketing of Services," *Journal of the Academy of Marketing Science,* Fall 1995, pp. 236–45.

82. See N. Bendapudi and L. L. Berry, "Customers' Motivations for Maintaining Relationships with Service Providers," *Journal of Retailing,* 73, no. 1 (1997), pp. 15–37.

83. C. Ashley et al., "Why Consumers Won't Relate," *Journal of Business Research,* July 2011, pp. 749–56.

84. J. Raymond, "Home Field Advantage," *American Demographics,* April 2001, pp. 34–36.

85. See G. Levin, "Marketers Flock to Loyalty Offers," *Advertising Age,* May 24, 1993, p. 13; C. Miller, "Rewards for the Best Customers," *Marketing News,* July 5, 1993, p. 1; J. Fulkerson, "It's in the Cards," *American Demographics,* July 1996, pp. 38–43; and J. Passingham, "Grocery Retailing and the Loyalty Card," *Journal of the Market Research Society,* January 1998, pp. 55–63. See also L. O'Brien and C. Jones, "Do Rewards Really Create Loyalty?," *Harvard Business Review,* May 1995, pp. 75–82; R. N. Bolton, P. K. Kannan, and M. D. Bramlett, "Implications of Loyalty Programs Membership and Service Experiences for Customer Retention and Value," *Journal of the Academy of Marketing Science,* Winter 2000, pp. 95–108; and A. W. Magi, "Share of Wallet in Retailing," *Journal of Retailing,* 79 (2003), pp. 97–106.

86. See F. Rice, "The New Rules of Superlative Services," *Fortune,* Autumn–Winter 1993, pp. 50–53; P. Sellers, "Keeping the Buyers," *Fortune,* Autumn–Winter 1993, pp. 56–58; and G. A.

Conrad, G. Brown, and H. A. Harmon, "Customer Satisfaction and Corporate Culture," *Psychology & Marketing,* October 1997, pp. 663–74.

87. J. Holland and S. M. Baker, "Customer Participation in Creating Site Brand Loyalty," *Journal of Interactive Marketing,* Autumn 2001, pp. 34–45; R. E. Anderson and S. S. Srinivasan, "E-Satisfaction and E-Loyalty," *Psychology & Marketing,* February 2003, pp. 123–38; L. C. Harris and M. M. H. Goode, "The Four Levels of Loyalty and the Pivotal Role of Trust," *Journal of Retailing,* 80 (2004), pp. 139–58.

88. J. Gummerus et al., "Customer Loyalty to Content-Based Web Sites," *Journal of Services Marketing,* 18, no. 3 (2004), pp. 175–86.

89. S. S. Srinivasan, R. Anderson, and K. Ponnavolu, "Customer Loyalty in E-commerce," *Journal of Retailing,* 78 (2002), pp. 41–50.

Part Four CASES*

4-1 SCENT MARKETING REACHES CONSUMERS' EMOTIONS

Scent Marketing, which is also known as ambient marketing, is known to marketers as branding's final frontier. Some marketers call it the "business of emotional transportation." Retailers have long been manipulating atmospheric variables, such as music, color, and physical layouts. However, scent has received much less attention until recent times. Studies have shown that the power of scent can have tremendous effects on consumers' emotions and subsequent behavior. Scent is able to lift consumers' moods, influence them to linger within retail stores, and increase purchases. According to Professor Eric Spangenberg:

> We've shown that scent can increase the customer's positive shopping behavior. . . . It keeps people in the store longer, they enjoy it more and they express more positive intentions to return.

Retailers using scent marketing can be divided roughly into two groups: those using natural scents and those using technology to implement artificial scents. Consumers are widely aware of the first group, especially with retailers that sell baked goods. Cinnabon and Panera Bread are two examples of retailers that rely heavily on scent to promote their goods. Cinnabon intentionally locates its stores in indoor shopping areas, such as malls and airports, so that smells can linger in the walkways and lure consumers. Cinnabon places its ovens near the front of the stores so that the scent of warm cinnamon rolls will carry even further. A test location that had the oven in the back of the store had significantly lowered sales. The cinnamon treats are baked every half hour so that the smell does not dissipate. Franchisees are instructed to use the weakest oven hood that is allowed so that the maximum amount of aroma possible will infiltrate the surrounding areas. Likewise, Panera Bread reassigned bakers from night shifts to day shifts so that consumers would have more exposure to the scent of baking bread. Both of these retailers also carefully craft their menu of savory items so that the scents do not clash with the smell of baked goods, steering away from ingredients like garlic.

The benefits of scent marketing are not limited to food retailers. Many other types of retail locations have also joined the scent marketing trend. Many retailers are investing in developing their own custom "brand scent." According to Andrew Kindfuller, chief executive officer of ScentAir, a prominent manufacturer of scent diffusers:

> Brands realize now that this is a part of doing business. We're implementing these systems in many different environments—not just hotels and retail, but funeral homes, retirement villages, and medical and dental and law offices.

Singapore Airlines, Westin Hotels, Ritz Carlton, Victoria Secret, Juicy Couture, Bloomingdale's SonyStyle electronics stores, Select Comfort bedding stores, casinos, cruise lines, banks, and even Goodwill Industries are just some of the examples of business cited in popular media as using scent marketing. These companies use scent diffusion systems to consistently and evenly pump their custom aromas through the air.

Arriving at a brand scent is no simple task. Retailers pay anywhere from $5,000 to $50,000 to formulate a signature scent that consumers come to identify with a brand and that will keep the customers in stores longer to drive up sales. The technology has come a long way, from simple fans to cold air diffusion and dry air evaporation that incorporate HVAC systems in the stores. According to Jennifer Dublino, chief operating officer of the Scent Marketing Institute:

> In the old days, they used these cartridges with some sort of material soaked in scented oil and a fan would blow it out. The scent would be really intense at first, but then it would wane.

*Part Four cases are contributed by Carolyn Findley Musgrove, Assistant Professor of Marketing, Indiana University Southeast.

Back then, merchandise in the store would be coated in a fine film of oil. Recent advances solved that issue. According to Ed Burke, marketing director of ScentAir:

> The mist is so fine you can't even see it coming out of the atomizer. You don't have to worry about residue, and you can control the intensity.

Scent marketing works so well because consumers' sense of smell is directly linked to their emotions, more so than any of the other senses. Smells send signals from consumers' odor receptors in their noses directly to the amygdala, which is the emotion processing area of the brain. According to Pam Ellen, a marketing professor at Georgia State University:

> All of the other senses, you think before you respond, but with scent, your brain responds before you think.

According to Steven Semoff, co-president of the Scent Marketing Institute:

> In retail spaces, you're saturated with visual and audio to the point where you've learned to turn them off, but olfactory is a different kettle of fish. Sight and hearing senses go to the left brain, but smell is hardwired to the right brain's limbic system, which is your emotional core. It triggers an emotional response, and the customer builds an emotional connection with the brand.

Unfortunately for retailers, there are some pitfalls associated with scent marketing. Not all consumers respond to various scents in similar ways. Certain scents can trigger allergic reactions and asthmatic episodes in a small proportion of consumers. Also, many consumers may find smells to be offensive, especially if the odor is too strong or they have prior associations between a particular scent and a negative experience. Further, if there is a mismatch between the setting and the scent, then it could have deleterious effects. According to Ladd Smith, the president of the Research Institute for Fragrance Materials:

> One man's pleasure is another's pollution. Involuntary exposure drives us crazy.

Even worse, many people have ethical concerns about the use of scent marketing, particularly when consumers are unaware that it is being used. The Federal Communications Commission says that transmitting information below the consumer's threshold of awareness is unethical. Martin Linstrom, the author *Brand Sense,* discusses scent marketing in the context of real estate:

> "People will make quicker decisions, be willing to pay more for the property and most likely be so emotionally engaged that they are removed from the rational part of their behavior," Lindstrom says. "I don't need to tell you that this is on the ethical line in my opinion, but from a pure behavioral point of view, that is most likely going to happen."

Kevin Bradford, a marketing professor at the University of Notre Dame, echoes this sentiment:

> Scent affects mood and scent affects emotion. It works without you having the opportunity to filter it. To me, that is extremely unethical. . . . Scent could be introduced to the environment at a level lower than what consumers could possibly detect, and it would still affect their emotions. Consumers should be able to detect the things that are influencing them.

Yet, others disagree. For example Alex Hiller, of Nottingham Business Schools, says:

> Yes, changing smells is manipulative—this is the whole point. But it is mild, and I would argue that consumers realize and accept that in all artificial, and especially retail, environments, some mild form of manipulation does take place and it in no way constrains anyone's freedom, autonomy or well-being.

The founder of Nose Knows Design, Tracy Pepe, argues that is it no different than manipulating lighting to create a more pleasant retail environment. She says:

> Scent is very similar to great lighting. Great lighting—as opposed to just a light bulb—can change the mood. It can warm you up. It can invite your guests. Smell is the same thing. . . . We, as a society, are kind of dead, visually. We're on our phones, we are constantly looking at screens. So there's this hole. And what scent does is that it propels you back in time so you remember what it felt like. If you're walking in a mall, for example, and you smell crayons, you're going right to that emotional connection of peeling the paper off. And all of a sudden there's a human aspect to it.

In any case, scent marketing is becoming increasingly prevalent among all types of retailers. Whether ethical or not, it is effective and does not appear to be going anywhere. According to the executive director of marketing at the National Retail Federation, Mike Gatti:

> It is fairly widespread here. . . . A lot of retail companies use it, and its purpose really is to keep customers in your store, to create this welcoming environment—and it works; it does keep people in your store longer. It helps people feel better in their shopping, and in a lot of cases causes them to spend more money.

Discussion Questions

1. Chapter 13 discusses aromas as a situational characteristic that influences consumer behavior. Assemble a small group of consumers and perform a focus group about their impressions of scent marketing. Also, investigate what effects consumers believe these scents have with their behavior. Compare and contrast these conscious reactions with what behavioral effects we know that scents have based on existing research.
2. Chapter 14 discusses the nature of problem recognition. Discuss the role that scent marketing might play in problem recognition in terms of actual state and desired state.
3. Chapter 16 discusses consumer choice processes. Does scent marketing most impact affective choice, attitude-based choice, or attribute-based choice? Justify your answer.
4. Chapter 16 also discusses bounded rationality, which is consumers' limited capacity for processing information. Many retailers who use scent diffuser use such small amounts of scent that consumers may not realize that the retailer's scent is playing a role. Discuss the ethical implications.
5. When it comes to the ethical implications of scent marketing, do you feel that there is a difference in retailers that use natural scents (like food retailers baking in the retail space) versus retailers that use artificially manufactured scents?
6. Brainstorm a short list of brands; make sure that some are typically involved with nominal decision making and others are typically associated with extensive decision making. Then, imagine you are a marketer for those brands and describe the types of aromas that would match with each brand.
7. Visit a local shopping mall and the lobbies of several major hotel chains. Pay attention to the smells that you encounter while in each retail establishment. Prepare a short report that compares and contrasts the scents that you encounter in each location.

Source: J. Caplan, "Scents and Sensibility," *Time,* October 8, 2006, http://content.time.com; J. Vlahos, "Scents and Sensitivity," *New York Times,* September 9, 2007, www.nytimes.com; "N.Y. Grocery Turns to Scent Marketing," *CBS News,* July 18, 2011, www.cbsnews.com; J. Smialek, "Retailers Mix Holiday Tunes, Scents to Spur Christmas Sales," *The Round Table,* December 19, 2012, www.mhsroundtable.com; J. Sutton, "Scent Makers Sweeten the Smell of Commerce," *Reuters,* December 19, 2011, www.reuters.com; "The Smell of Commerce: How Companies Use Scents to Sell Their Products," *The Independent,* August 11, 2011, www.independent.co.uk; A. Kadet, "The New Muzak: Scent Marketing," *Market Watch,* May 15, 2012, www.marketwatch.com; R. Klara, "In a Growing Trend, Retailers Are Perfuming Stores with Near-Subliminal Scents," *Adweek,* March 5, 2012, www.adweek.com; C. Lewis, "When Scent Crosses the Ethical Line," *The Globe and Mail,* September 10, 2014, www.theglobeandmail.com; D. Montaldo, "Retailers Tap into Consumer's Response to Smell," *About.com,* http://couponing.about.com; S. Naussaur, "Using Scent as a Marketing Tool, Stores Hope It—and Shoppers—Will Linger," *The Wall Street Journal,* May 20, 2014, http://online.wsj.com; C. Winter, "What Should a Bank Smell Like?," *Bloomberg Businessweek,* January 9, 2014, www.businessweek.com; and M. Hague, "A Sense of Occasion: How Luxury Hotels and Condos Seduce You with Signature Scents," *The Globe and Mail,* September 10, 2014, www.theglobeandmail.com.

4–2 AMAZON PRIME AIR PREPARES FOR TAKEOFF

In 2013, Amazon's CEO Jeff Bezos, on a *60 Minutes* interview, introduced his company's plans to revolutionize the way that packages are delivered to consumers. The new service is called Amazon Prime Air and it will consist of a fleet of drones that will deliver small packages directly to consumers' doorsteps within a half hour of making a purchase on Amazon.com. According to Mr. Bezos:

> It could be a 10-mile radius from a fulfillment center. So, in urban areas, you could actually cover very significant portions of the population. And so, it won't work for everything; you know, we're not gonna deliver kayaks or table saws this way. These are electric motors, so this is all electric; it's very green, it's better than driving trucks around. This is . . . this is all an R&D project.

Since its inception, Amazon has had a reputation for innovation and its future plans are no different. The online retail giant began with digital media, such as books and music, and evolved to offer a huge variety of products, such as clothing, furniture, toys, electronics, and more, as consumers became increasingly comfortable with online shopping. One consumer barrier for online shopping was shipping costs, so Amazon introduced its subscription-based Amazon Prime program that included free shipping and other consumer benefits. Now, as many other online retailers have followed suit and started to offer free shipping, Amazon's competitive advantage has eroded.

With Amazon Prime Air, Amazon would again offer innovative benefits that would set it apart from its competitors. Also, being able to offer such quick delivery would allow Amazon to better compete with brick-and-mortar retailers that offer consumers more immediate gratification of possessing products at the time of purchase, rather than waiting a number of days for delivery. With Amazon Prime Air, consumers will be able to enjoy their purchases very quickly, while still enjoying the convenience and comfort of shopping in their own homes. According to Mr. Bezos:

> I would define Amazon by our big ideas, which are customer centricity, putting the customer at the center of everything we do, invention. We like to pioneer, we like to explore, we like to go down dark alleys and see what's on the other side. . . . You gotta earn your keep in this world. When you invent something new, if customers come to the party, it's disruptive to the old way.

The public's reception of Amazon's announcement was mixed. Many consumers were excited at the prospect of Amazon Prime Air services. However, others felt that it was simply a cheap publicity stunt to draw headlines on the day before Cyber Monday. Others who resided near Amazon fulfillment centers were concerned about the noise that a fleet of drones would cause while flying overhead 24 hours a day. Some consumers even announced plans to shoot the drones out of the sky, either because they dislike the idea of drones or because they want the packages that they would carry.

Likewise, the business community had mixed perceptions. Many of Amazon's competitors, as well as logistics companies, scoffed at the idea of Amazon Prime Air. The CEO of FedEx called the idea "almost amusing" and the CEO of eBay called it a "long term fantasy"; Groupon answered the announcement with a satirical proposal of its own innovative delivery system—a catapult. Meanwhile, Google announced its own plan, called Project Wing, to utilize drones for other purposes, including delivering disaster relief.

While Amazon's research and development speeds forward, the biggest barrier to launching Amazon Prime Air is legal regulation from the Federal Aviation Administration (FAA). According to Mr. Bezos:

> The hardest challenge in making this happen is going to be demonstrating this to the standards of the FAA that this is a safe thing to do. . . . I know it can't be before 2015, because that's the earliest we could get the rules from the FAA. My guess is that's, that's probably a little optimistic. But could it be, you know, four, five years? I think so. It will work, and it will happen, and it's gonna be a lot of fun.

Amazon has joined a coalition of firms, including 3D Robotics, Parrot, and DJI Innovations, whose purpose is to advocate for the legalization of drone use for commercial purposes and educate the public on the safety and benefits of their use. The coalition has the support of Congress, as the FAA Modernization and Reform Act of 2012 mandated that the FAA open U.S. national airspace to civilian and commercial small drone traffic. However, FAA regulations have not yet been revised. In 2014, Amazon petitioned the FAA for an exemption to their rules that restrict the commercial use of drones and for permission for the company to begin to test its drones in an outdoor setting. So far, the FAA has not approved Amazon's request. In order to continue its research and development on the drones, Amazon plans to carry on by taking its outdoor testing to India, where there is a much more lenient regulatory environment. It is imperative that the research and development continues so that once the regulations in the United States are revised to allow commercial drones, Amazon will be prepared to launch its program.

Discussion Questions

1. Chapters 15 and 17 discuss information search and shopping. If Amazon is successful with its launching of Amazon Prime Air, how could this change the information search in the consumer decision process and could it result in more online purchases?
2. Chapter 16 discusses evaluative criteria and Chapter 18 discusses postpurchase cognitive dissonance. What are some things that Amazon could do to aid consumers in making decisions about a product and the evaluative criteria for the product they are considering purchasing? Could this help make consumers feel more comfortable about purchasing a product online and reduce postpurchase guilt and dissonance?
3. Chapter 17 discusses perceived risks. What perceived risk is Amazon reducing? How?
4. Chapter 17 also discusses characteristics of online shoppers and provides a typology of online shopping segments. Justify your response. (Hint: Multiple segments could be correct depending on your justification.)
   a. Which of these segments would be most likely to adopt Amazon Prime Air?
   b. Which of these segments would be least likely to adopt Amazon Prime Air?

5. Chapter 13 discusses situational characteristics. Which situational characteristics might play a role in a consumer's decision to purchase with Amazon Prime Air? Explain.
6. Chapter 7 discusses types of innovation. Is Amazon Prime Air best described as a continuous, dynamically continuous, or discontinuous innovation?

Source: C. Dillow, "Amazon Aims for Drone Delivery," *Fortune,* December 12, 2013, http://fortune.com; J. Freed, "FedEx CEO Finds Delivery Drones 'Almost Amusing,'" *Huffington Post,* December 18, 2013, www.huffingtonpost.com; D. Gross, "Amazon's Drone Delivery: How Would It Work?," *CNN,* December 2, 2013, www.cnn.com; "Groupon Unveils Their Answer to Amazon's Drone Delivery: Catapults," *Huffington Post,* December 11, 2013, www.huffingtonpost.com; A. Kleinman, "eBay CEO Calls Amazon Drones A 'Long-Term Fantasy,'" *Huffington Post,* www.huffingtonpost.com; D. Nicks, "Amazon's Drone Strike," *Time,* December 2, 2013, http://business.time.com; C. Rose, "Amazon's Jeff Bezos Looks to the Future," *CBS News,* December 1, 2013, www.cbsnews.com; M. Snider, "Amazon Looks to Gain Liftoff for Drone Delivery Testing," *USA Today,* August 17, 2014, www.usatoday.com; T. Mogg, "Bezos Maintains He's Serious about Amazon's Drone Delivery Service, Currently Testing Tech," *Digital Trends,* April 14, 2014, www.digitaltrends.com; G. McNeal, "Six Things You Should Know about Amazon's Drones," *Forbes,* July 11, 2014, www.forbes.com; E. Mack, "Beware! 8 Sinister Consequences of Google and Amazon Drones," *Cnet,* September 2, 2014, www.cnet.com; L. Lorrenzetti, "Amazon May Be Flying to India to Test Drone Deliveries," *Fortune,* August 20, 2014, http://fortune.com; and D. Kravets, "FAA Grounds Amazon's Drone Delivery Plans," *Ars Technica,* June 24, 2014, http://arstechnica.com.

4–3 TARGET RESISTS THE CHRISTMAS CREEP

Christmas Creep is the retail phenomenon in which retail stores set up Christmas displays earlier and earlier every year. Many stores are now beginning their Christmas holiday season around Halloween rather than the more traditional, post-Thanksgiving beginning of the holiday shopping season. For example, Sears ran Black Friday (traditionally the day after Thanksgiving) Door Busters before Halloween. Others use out-of-store methods to engage in Christmas Creep. For example, Pier 1 conducted an e-mail campaign that featured a snowman encouraging consumers to "get an early start on Christmas"—in July of 2010.

Retail stores beginning their holiday season as early as the summer months is becoming more common. Hobby Lobby is another company employing Christmas Creep. In 2008, Christmas décor was in Hobby Lobby stores in August. In 2009, it was available in July. By 2010, Hobby Lobby stocked their shelves with Christmas décor as early as June. According to one shopper:

> I've heard of the Christmas Creep, but this year it's a Christmas Sprint! Today, June 19, 2010 at the Hobby Lobby . . . Christmas merchandise already on SALE at 40% off!!!! It's not even Father's Day, and they are already starting to deck the halls.

During 2010, Target made a deliberate effort to wait closer to the actual traditional holiday season to begin its holiday promotions. It said that this move is in response to consumers becoming burned out by overexposure to Christmas displays, advertising, and other promotions. Thus, Target delayed its holiday advertising campaign until after Thanksgiving. According to Chief Marketing Officer Michael Francis:

> Guests really tire of these messages when they're started too early in the season, and it doesn't align with where they are in their lives. They look at Thanksgiving as family time . . . and aren't yet ready to get into the frenzy that defines the Christmas shopping season.

This decision was not made haphazardly. Target conducted extensive research to find out how consumers really felt about Christmas Creep, through guest surveys and evaluation of point-of-sale data. Besides, Francis has noted that with a slowing economy, consumers are less likely to make purchases earlier in the holiday season.

> The last several years we've seen shoppers shopping much closer to need. The Christmas season, which had been spread over six weeks, is becoming more of a sprint.

Although Target is taking the strategy of delaying its holiday media blitz, it is still paying attention to the segment of consumers who prefer to shop early. Therefore, some Christmas merchandise is stocked in the store earlier and only select customers are targeted with holiday e-mails and direct mail prior to the main holiday media campaign launch.

There are mixed consumer reactions to Christmas Creep. Some consumers view Christmas Creep as a source of frustration and experience "emotional pushback." Other consumers are not bothered by the early holiday promotions. In any case, Christmas Creep stimulates a lot of discussion on consumer blogs. Experts have different views on Christmas Creep. According to Chris Morran, senior editor at Consumerist.com, a webpage dedicated to consumer issues that regularly documents instances of Christmas Creep:

> Our readers are pretty divided on the whole Christmas Creep thing. There are those that find it truly offensive and gaudy and unnecessary. And there are those that don't care at all and those that actually like it. . . . People are, sadly, getting used to it.

According to Wharton marketing professor Stephen Hoch:

> It's like a mini-arms race. The competition among retailers means nobody wants to be second. That moves the shopping season up a little bit more each and every year. Are consumers going to revolt against it? No. Will it get people in a holiday mood? No; people will get in the holiday mood during the holidays. Does it give retailers a chance to set displays up sooner? Sure.

According to Herb Kleinberger, a partner and retail store practice leader at IBM Business Consulting Services:

> Jumping the gun too soon can create an emotional pushback. In a certain sense, the consumer has to be emotionally ready to shop, and that may not happen until the weather [becomes colder].

In an extreme example of emotional pushback, one small town board in upstate New York even blocked Christmas Creep when they denied their local Walmart's proposal for extended holiday hours early in the season, citing traffic noise, night lighting, and the sounds of car doors slamming.

Retailers have incentive to begin their holiday campaigns earlier and earlier in the year. Many retailers take in 20 to 30 percent of their revenue during the holiday season. Meanwhile, research from The National Retail Federation found that 40 percent of consumers planned to start their holiday shopping before Halloween in 2010. However, less than half of shoppers complete their holiday shopping before the second week in December.

Despite mixed opinions from consumers on Christmas Creep, it is a trend that is here to stay. Retailers fall into a cycle in order to keep up same-store sales for a particular month, compared to that month the previous year. If the holiday promotions are extended to an earlier month one year, then they must be extended at least as early the following year in order to maintain similar or better sales figures. According to Mr. Morran:

> It's definitely happening more and more and it isn't just Christmas Creep now. You start seeing Valentines the day after Christmas. At some point there's got to be diminishing returns.

Also, according to Professor Hoch:

> I don't think we'll see a retreat on this one. Comping [comparing this year's sales to the same period last year] is a self-fulfilling prophecy. That will keep on driving this Christmas creep.

Discussion Questions

1. Chapter 13 defines and discusses the role of ritual situations in shopping behavior. What ritual situations play a role in this case?
2. How is Target using a multi-channel strategy to better focus Christmas Creep messages on those customers who they know do their holiday shopping earlier?
3. Chapter 14 focuses on the problem-recognition portion of the consumer decision-making process. By engaging in Christmas Creep, what role do marketers play regarding problem recognition?
4. Chapter 17 discusses how retail managers may manipulate atmospherics to create specific mood responses from customers. Using the text, the case, and your own experiences, how might decorating retail stores in a holiday theme well before Thanksgiving, or even Halloween, affect the atmospherics of the store? Why are atmospherics important?
5. Chapter 3 discusses several cultural values that play a role in consumer behavior. Which value(s) discussed in the text are relevant to Christmas Creep and holiday shopping? Why?

Source: "Christmas Creep: The Shopping Season Is Longer, but Is It Better?," *Knowledge @ Wharton,* March 1, 2006, http://knowledge.wharton.upenn.edu; "Grinch? No, but the 'Christmas Creep' Is Here," *MSNBC,* October 26, 2006, http://msnbc.msn.com; J. Kelly, "It's Not the Eggnog Talking: Christmas Is Starting Earlier," *Washington Post,* November 20, 2008, http://washingtonpost.com; A. Heher, "Black Friday Deals 2009: 'Christmas Creep' Leads to Earlier Deals," *Huffington Post,* November 2, 2009, www.huffingtonpost.com; C. Alexander, "It's June, Time for Hobby Lobby to Kick Off the Christmas Creep Season," *Consumerist.com,* June 20, 2010, www.consumerist.com; N. Zmuda, "Shoppers, Retailers Divided on Timing of Seasonal Onslaught," *Advertising Age,* November 8, 2010, p. 2; N. Zmuda, "Target Takes a Holiday from Early Ad Barrage," *Advertising Age,* November 8, 2010, p. 3; C. Berk, "New York Town Says No to Walmart & 'Christmas Creep,'" *CNBC,* November 17, 2010, http://cnbc.com; and B. Popken, "Pier 1 Kicks Off Christmas Creep Season," *Consumerist.com,* July 13, 2011, http://consumerist.com.

4–4 NETFLIX CONTINUES TO CHANGE THE FACE OF IN-HOME MOVIES AROUND THE GLOBE

Netflix has changed the way consumers rent movies and have reaped the financial reward. Many consumers now use non-television platforms such as Netflix, although at roughly 25 percent penetration, there still seems to be room for growth. Part of Netflix's power is its availability on a wide range of platforms, including Blu-ray players and gaming consoles.

Recently, Netflix decided to split its online-streaming-video and DVDs-by-mail services into separate subscriptions. This change upset many of its customers since it represents a 60 percent increase in the total subscription fee to get both options. Consumers vented their frustrations with this price increase on social media such as Facebook and Twitter and threatened to cancel their subscriptions.

Interestingly, Netflix executives said they expected this reaction but said the increased revenue is required to sustain rising costs of expansion. The negative reaction by customers to this move seems to have emboldened competitors to strike back. Blockbuster, Amazon, and Walmart are now more heavily promoting their own online video-streaming services to compete with Netflix in an effort to attract disgruntled customers. Analysts predict that Netflix will lose over 2 million subscribers as a result of this change.

Such losses may be offset by Netflix's global expansion. Netflix has added instant-streaming video service to numerous countries in Central and South America and the Caribbean, where "pay TV" is very popular. Consider the following statistics:

> Mexico and Brazil are the pay TV powerhouses of Latin America. Brazil has 8.9 million pay TV homes now and will have around 20 million by the end of 2014. Mexico has 9.7 million pay TV homes today and this will grow to 18.7 million pay TV homes by 2014. These are strong markets growing very rapidly, with 26 percent and 40 percent growth respectively during 2010.

Other regions where Netflix plans to expand include Europe and Asia. Tables A and B give financial information about digital movie delivery services globally.

Worldwide Market Potential for Digital Movie Delivery Services TABLE A

Region	US$ Million	% of Globe
Asia	2,694	30.10
Europe	2,327	26.00
North America & the Caribbean	2,288	25.60
Latin America	715	8.00
Middle East	448	5.00
Africa	354	4.00
Oceana	122	1.40
Total	8,948	100.00

Source: Philip N. Parker, INSEAD (2008), www.icongrouponline.com.

Market Potential for Digital Movie Delivery Services in Europe TABLE B

Country	US$ Million	% of Europe
Germany	380.63	16.36
The United Kingdom	288.85	12.41
France	276.72	11.89
Italy	241.08	10.36
Spain	183.98	7.91
Russia	142.91	6.14
The Netherlands	86.19	3.70
Poland	85.39	3.67
Belgium	50.93	2.19
Sweden	44.91	1.93
Greece	44.07	1.89
Ukraine	44.00	1.89
Austria	43.09	1.85
Switzerland	40.43	1.74
Norway	34.94	1.50
Czech Republic	33.93	1.46
Romania	33.64	1.45
Portugal	31.07	1.34
Denmark	27.38	1.18
Hungary	26.03	1.12
Ireland	25.50	1.10
Finland	25.18	1.08
Kazakhstan	22.29	0.96
Slovakia	14.86	0.64
Belarus	14.34	0.62
Other	84.75	3.64
Total	2327.12	100.00

Source: Philip M. Parker, INSEAD (2008), www.icongrouponline.com.

Discussion Questions

1. Chapter 10 discusses how consumers cope with product and service encounters including product and service failures. Describe in what sense Netflix's change in pricing strategy could be seen as a product or service failure and the coping strategies that their customers appear to be utilizing.
2. What factors do you feel contributed to customers' high levels of anger toward Netflix's new pricing policy? How might Netflix have handled this situation better? Explain.
3. Netflix, as well as its competitors, use the Internet as part of a multi-channel strategy. Research the product and service offerings of two or more of Netflix's competitors in the in-home movie industry, such as Blockbuster, Walmart, Amazon Prime, or Redbox. Compare, contrast, and explain how the competitors you chose are using a multi-channel strategy.
4. Chapter 17 describes several segments of Internet shoppers that were identified by Experian based on their attitudes and behaviors. Which of these segments are most likely to fit the target market for digital movie delivery? Multiple segments may be correct. Explain the basis for your answer.
5. Chapter 15 discusses information search in the consumer decision-making process. Explain which of the strategies relating to information search patterns shown in Table 15–3 Netflix's competitors could best use to capture market share in light of Netflix's new pricing?
6. Netflix has begun the process of expanding its online video-streaming service globally. According to the case, Netflix already has a strong presence in the Western Hemisphere and is considering expansion into other countries.
   a. Using Table A and what you've learned about cross-cultural marketing and culture variations, explain why Netflix may be interested in expanding into Europe.
   b. Which of the European countries in Table B would be especially attractive for Netflix to enter? Justify your answer
   c. What considerations should Netflix make when approaching a foreign market?

Source: M. Shaer, "Netflix Goes Global, but Without the Red Envelopes," *CS Monitor,* January 28, 2010, www.csmonitor.com; B. Snyder, "How Netflix Stays Ahead of Shifting Consumer Behavior," *Advertising Age,* February 22, 2010, p. 28; M. Carmichael, "Study Brings New Meaning to the Words 'Media Diet,'" *Advertising Age,* January 24, 2011, p. 2; M. O'Neill, "How Netflix Bankrupted and Destroyed Blockbuster," *Business Insider,* March 1, 2011, www.businessinsider.com; "Netflix Stock Soars on Global Expansion News," *IB Times,* July 5, 2011, http://ibtimes.com; T. O'Brien, "Netflix Bringing Instant Streaming to Latin America, Global Domination Plan on Track," *Engadget,* July 5, 2011, http://engadget.com; S. Ovide, "Blockbuster Attacks Netflix New Prices," *The Wall Street Journal,* July 12, 2011, http://blogs.wsj.com; L. Baker, "Blockbuster Targets Disgruntled Netflix Customers," *Reuters,* July 14, 2011, http://reuters.com; "Blockbuster Offers Deal to Netflix Customers," *Associated Press,* July 15, 2011, http://boston.com; "Netflix Sags as Wal-Mart Video Streaming Service Debuts," *Fox News,* July 26, 2011, http://foxnews.com.

4–5 MACY'S EMBRACES BEACON TECHNOLOGY

Since the advent of online retailing, there has been an inherent tension between it and brick-and-mortar retailers. Consumers are increasingly making their purchases in an online setting as the breadth of options has proliferated and consumers have become less apprehensive about entering financial information on websites. A consumer survey by SmartFocus, a digital marketing company showed that the majority of consumers still prefer to shop and purchase in brick-and-mortar stores, but nearly 60 percent of consumers are increasing their online shopping activities. According to the CEO of SmartFocus, Rob Mullen:

> The US shopper survey shows that consumers are becoming more sophisticated about digital shopping. Using mobile phones and tablets to find bargains is becoming the norm rather than the exception.

Millennials are more likely to shop online than any other generation and are more receptive to sharing their data with online advertisers in exchange for more personalized shopping experiences. Mr. Mullen said:

> In today's digital world, it's about reaching out to shoppers with their preferred technology—their mobile phone—and offering them relevant deals. The survey reinforces that fact that shoppers know the value of their personal data—and are willing to trade some of that for access to discounted offers. Besides the sale in question, shoppers will also benefit when marketers are able to analyze their data. Data analysis enables discovery of previously unrecognized patterns of behavior and allows merchants to put together more relevant offers.

Another concern for brick-and-mortar stores is showrooming. This is the practice of consumers shopping in brick-and-mortar stores in order to inspect products physically, but then actually purchasing the products from online retailers. The SmartFocus survey showed that about 60 percent of consumers engage in showrooming, with the primary motivation of seeking lower prices. Showrooming demonstrates that there is an inherent value of shopping within the physical store and actually coming in contact with products that interest consumers. This is especially true in the apparel context, where consumers gain much more product information from handling clothing and trying it on than from viewing pictures and descriptions online. According to Arnie Gullov-Singh, chief revenue officer for a women's fashion website:

> Women especially still want to try something on. The future for brick-and-mortar is about that instant gratification and solving for that problem, and less about solving for fulfilling demand for things.

Some retailers are finding productive ways to work with digital media to turn showrooming to their advantage. Thomas Husson, a mobile analyst at Forrester Research, said:

> Instead of fearing showrooming, I think retailers can leverage mobile as a bridge between offline and online worlds.

Macy's is partnering with technology companies Apple and Shopkick to engage consumers through their mobile devices during the time while they are shopping in the stores. In 2013, Macy's conducted a pilot test of location-based marketing, called shopBeacon, in their flagship stores in Manhattan and San Francisco. Shopkick installed Apple's iBeacon transmitters throughout the stores that would allow the retailer to track consumers' movements as they shopped different locations throughout the stores. This location-based technology operates through the Bluetooth technology in shoppers' smartphones. As the consumers entered the stores, the Shopkick app would send alerts to the consumers' mobile devices to welcome them. Then, as they walked near certain locations within the stores, more alerts would offer various promotions, such as personalized department-level deals, discounts, recommendations, and rewards for the products in their immediate vicinity. In order to be tracked, shoppers need to download the Shopkick app. Also, the app could tie shoppers' online browsing with the store visits, reminding them of items they liked online when they enter the store. According to Holly Thomas, vice president of national media relations and cause marketing at Macy's, New York:

> [Shopkick] presented a great opportunity to pilot a location-based effort that would allow us to communicate with our customer via the one thing she always has on her—her mobile phone. Once a customer downloads the Shopkick app to her iPhone, we are able to give her special offers, information and rewards just for walking in a Macy's store. We think this is a dynamic and exciting addition to our mobile and digital efforts.

The 2013 pilot test was so successful that Macy's expanded the shopBeacon technology to all of the Macy's retail locations in 2014. At 4,000 new devices, this was the largest-scale expansion of in-store location-based technology by a major retailer to date. In a press release, Macy's chair and chief executive officer said:

> Macy's and Bloomingdale's remain committed to operating at the forefront of innovation, as well as fostering a locally relevant shopping experience in every store. We will continue to test, to learn, and to proceed aggressively with new ideas that excite our customers and that make shopping more convenient and fun. Our goal remains to help our customers shop whenever, wherever and however they prefer, and to use the entire inventory of the company to satisfy demand. We are a multi-faceted retailer with stores, technology, Internet capability and mobile access that come together for our customers. They are at the center of all our decisions, and our ongoing research and development will continue to help us understand how to personally engage with them.

The largest challenge to making shopBeacons in Macy's stores a success is consumer acceptance. Consumers need to proactively download an app to engage with this in-store location-based technology. However, the allure of highly personalized promotions that would enhance their shopping experiences is a motivation for many to download an app and share their personal data, especially if they are already engaged with the retailer.

Discussion Questions

1. Would this shopBeacon technology be best targeted to individuals engaged in the nominal, limited, or extended decision-making process (or more than one)? Justify your response.

2. Chapter 17 discusses omni-channel shoppers. Do you think the benefits of this technology will outweigh the possible nuisance of push notifications as they move through the store and simultaneously receive information on their smartphones?
3. Chapter 15 discusses mobile search and details five segments of mobile phone users. Which of these segments do you feel will be most accepting of shopBeacon technology? Which would be least accepting? Why?
4. Chapter 15 also discusses marketing strategies based on information search patterns. Which of these strategies is best complimented by location-based technology? (Hint: More than one could be correct with a logical explanation.) Explain your answer.
5. Chapter 17 discusses the nature of unplanned purchases. How would Macy's shopBeacon program affect
   a. Planned purchases?
   b. Unplanned purchases?
6. Assemble a small group of consumers and conduct a focus group on their perceptions of location-based technology like shopBeacon. Would they download the app to engage with it? Would they opt in for some retailers and not others? Why? Would it play a role in their selection of retailers to patronize?
7. Chapter 9 discusses brand image and product positioning. Think about Macy's and other department stores' brand images. One axis should be high versus low technology adoption. The other axis could be any bipolar set of adjectives of your choosing. Then, construct a perceptual map that includes several department stores.
8. Chapter 7 discusses types of innovation. Is shopBeacon best described as a continuous, dynamically continuous, or discontinuous innovation?

Source: D. Butcher, "Macy's Exec: Location-Based Mobile Rewards Key Tactic to Drive Foot Traffic," *Mobile Commerce Daily,* August 19, 2010, www.mobilecommercedaily.com; R. Borison, "Macy's, Shopkick up the Ante for Personalized Shopping," *Mobile Commerce Daily,* November 21, 2013, www.mobilecommercedaily.com; H. Bray, "How Location-Based Apps Will Shape the Future of Shopping," *Discover,* April 30, 2014, http://blogs.discovermagazine.com; H. Clancy, "Apple's iBeacon Signals Turning Point for Mobile Engagement," *Fortune,* February 28, 2014, http://fortune.com; S. Cole, "Macy's Begins Pilot Test of Apple's iBeacon in Flagship New York, San Francisco Stores," *Apple Insider,* November 20, 2013, http://appleinsider.com; T. Danova, "Beacons: What They Are, How They Work, and Why Apple's iBeacon Technology Is Ahead of the Pack," *Business Insider,* September 13, 2014, www.businessinsider.com; A. Fiorletta, "Macy's Invests in New Omnichannel Strategies," *Retail Touchpoints,* September 16, 2014, www.retailtouchpoints.com; N. Gagliordi, "Macy's Rolls Out Retail's Largest Beacon Installation," *ZD Net,* September 15, 2014, www.zdnet.com; E. Griffith, "Consumers Hate In-Store Tracking (but Retailers, Startups and Investors Love It)," *Fortune,* March 24, 2014, http://tech.fortune.cnn.com; A. Guesenhues, "Macy's Takes iBeacon Technology Nationwide, Installing More Than 4,000 Devices," *Marketing Land,* September 16, 2014, http://marketingland.com; C. Kern, "New Survey Reveals Brick-and-Mortar Shopping Still Thrives, but Online Shopping Is Growing," *Integrated Solutions for Retailers,* September 17, 2014, www.retailsolutionsonline.com; J. McDermott, "WTF Are In-Store Beacons?," *DigiDay,* January 17, 2014, http://digiday.com; and S. Perlberg, "Retailers Look for Digital Magic as In-Store Sales Decline," *The Wall Street Journal,* September 10, 2014, http://blogs.wsj.com.

4–6 TESLA'S NOVEL AND ENVIRONMENTAL APPROACH DRIVES AMAZING BRAND LOYALTY

Tesla Motors, Inc. is a Palo Alto, California–based automotive company that is shifting paradigms in terms of automotive vehicles themselves and the way that they are marketed. Teslas are priced as luxury vehicles, starting in the range of $70,000 to $120,000 depending on the model. Tesla produces fully electric vehicles that are powered by 7,000 battery cells that are linked to an electric motor. They can drive roughly 250 miles on a single charge, which restricts their use for long road trips. However, Tesla is in the process of building charging stations on the route between New York City and Los Angeles that will be solar-powered. According to the founder of Tesla, Elon Musk:

> You can drive for free, forever, on pure sunlight. That's the, you know, message we're trying to convey. So even if, like, there's a zombie apocalypse and the grid breaks down, you'll still be able to charge your car.

While Tesla is still a young company, it has been wildly successful, even during times of economic recession. The sales per square foot of Tesla showrooms double that of Apple. Tesla's order backlog is roughly 30 weeks long, at a value of over $226 million, while the production rate by the end of 2015 is expected to be 100,000 vehicles per year. Several states, including California, Nevada, Arizona, New Mexico, and Texas, competed for Tesla's new $5 billion Gigafactory that will produce lithium ion batteries and employ up to 6,500 people.

Tesla's customers are extremely loyal to the Tesla brand. Critics draw parallels between the level of fanaticism of Tesla customers and of Apple customers. In *Consumer Reports'* 2013 annual survey, Tesla Motors received the highest owner satisfaction score: 99 out of 100. Tesla customers evangelize the brand to almost anyone who will listen, which is one way that its popularity has spread organically. Tesla meet-up events for brand enthusiasts are quite common and even featured on Tesla's website. Tesla's extreme brand loyalty can be attributed to several factors, including its revolutionary approach that challenges the traditional automotive industry, an emotional connection, and a culture of transparency.

To its customers, Tesla stands for revolution of the automotive industry in terms of new technology and a new way of conducting business that is at odds with the established automotive industry. Tesla eschews traditional advertising and the franchise dealership model that is common among established automotive brands. Instead, Tesla takes a direct marketing approach with very little mainstream advertising and non-negotiable pricing. Tesla primarily sells directly to consumers through its website and operates comparatively tiny retail showrooms that often house a single vehicle. These showrooms are often found within high-end indoor shopping malls where there is much more foot traffic than traditional automobile dealerships enjoy. Much of the awareness of the brand is spread through free positive publicity. According to Jeremy Anwyl, the vice president of an auto consultancy called Edmunds.com:

> They're selling very few cars when you think about it—but they are getting an awful lot of buzz. You have to credit [Musk], who's very Steve Jobs–like in how he deals with the media. A lot of the attention is not generated through what we consider traditional advertising. It's really through social media.

This direct-to-consumers approach has made enemies out of auto dealership associations, which have filed a series of lawsuits against Tesla in various states in order to halt direct sales, claiming that laws requiring consumers to purchase vehicles from franchises encourage healthy price competition. Tesla owners have turned out in droves to protest these lawsuits both online and in places like Missouri and Texas. This controversy only serves to further reinforce brand loyalty and a sense of a bond among Tesla's customers, as it gives them a common enemy to rail against: the mainstream institution of the traditional combustion engine automotive manufacturers.

Another reason behind Tesla's brand loyalty is that Tesla has succeeded in establishing an emotional connection with its customers as well. Tesla's fully electric technology stands for an effort to solve energy problems in environmentally friendly ways. Saving the environment is a cause for which many consumers hold a deep passion. For example, one Tesla enthusiast said:

> That's how cool this car is. You feel like you're part of something bigger, a new age of motor vehicles. . . . Elon Musk is my hero.

Finally, Tesla's culture of transparency is another incredibly attractive feature to consumers. Tesla establishes a relationship of open communication with its customers through social media and its blog. Whenever there has been any negative publicity, the chief executive officer, Elon Musk, has addressed it publicly through Twitter and published internal e-mail correspondences on its website. Recently, in an effort to develop increasingly environmentally friendly technology, Tesla made its designs open source so that they could be improved more quickly with the help of the public. According to Mr. Musk:

> It is impossible for Tesla to build electric cars fast enough to address the carbon crisis.

In sum, Tesla's revolutionary approach disrupts the competitive status quo of the automotive industry and pushes the standards of environmental friendliness. This style, coupled with intense emotional connection and a standard of transparency, has proven to drive a very high level of brand loyalty among consumers and enthusiasm among investors. This is an innovative brand from which the public can expect great things to come.

Discussion Questions

1. Chapter 9 discusses schemas, which are also known as schematic memories and knowledge structures. Construct a schema diagram for Tesla.
2. Describe at least two segments of the market for Tesla electric vehicles. List the different needs, demographics, and psychographics for owning a Tesla for each of these segments.
3. Based on your analysis in the previous question, develop ads for each segment. Be sure to include key positioning statements, key copy points, visuals, and so forth for each and defend your decisions.
4. Evaluate Tesla's website (www.teslamotors.com).
5. With the ever- looming possibility of high gasoline prices and concerns about carbon emission, discuss

how Tesla can be both a utilitarian decision and a value-expressive decision.

6. In general, how do gas prices or fuel costs factor into the decision-making process for consumers in terms of influencing the consideration set and decision-making rule used in selecting a transportation option? In the context of Tesla's high sticker price, does your answer change? If so, how? Detail and explain. (Hint: Consider the marketing strategies based on information search patterns in Chapter 15.)
7. To which of the eight "Shades of Green" segments discussed in Chapter 3 does Tesla appeal most? Explain you answer.
8. Chapter 7 discusses types of innovation. Is a Tesla best described as a continuous, dynamically continuous, or discontinuous innovation? Explain your answer.

Source: S. Reynolds, "Why You Should Copy Tesla's Way of Marketing," *Forbes,* September 1, 2013, www.forbes.com; P. D'Arcy, "Tesla Marketing Strategy," *Science of Revenue,* January 20, 2014, http://scienceofrevenue.com; S. Dechert, "Tesla Scores Again with 'Interactive' Marketing," *Clean Technica,* August 21, 2014, http://cleantechnica.com; M. McCarthy, "Tesla Generates Small Sales, Big Buzz without Paid Ads," *Advertising Age,* June 10, 2013, http://adage.com; M. Niquette, "Consumer Advocates Support Tesla Direct Sales in Dispute," *Bloomberg,* March 20, 2014, www.bloomberg.com; J. Owyang, "Tesla Lets Go, to Gain the Market," *Web-Strategist.com,* June 14, 2014, www.web-strategist.com; S. Pelley, "Tesla and SpaceX: Elon Musk's Industrial Empire," *CBS News,* March 30, 2014, www.cbsnews.com; D. Smith, "How GoPro and Tesla Hacked Digital Marketing," *The Next Web,* May 7, 2014, http://thenextweb.com; A. Taylor, "Is Tesla the Ultimate Momentum Stock?," *Fortune,* August 15, 2014, http://fortune.com; and T. Walsh, "The Cult of Tesla Motors Inc: Why This Automaker Has the Most Loyal Customers," *The Motley Fool,* September 2, 2014, www.fool.com.

4-7 GILT GROUPE'S INNOVATIVE APPROACH TO LOYALTY PROGRAMS

Gilt Groupe is an online fashion retailer that offers luxury fashion brands at substantial discounts. Consumers must become members to view the content and be allowed access to Gilt's frequent flash sales. Gilt Groupe has become wildly popular, as over 6 million members have joined since its inception in 2007. However, as flash sales sites are becoming so popular, the number of such sites is naturally increasing. IBIS World predicts that by 2018 there would be around 150 flash sales sites, which would be a sharp increase from the roughly 90 sites in 2014. Thus, Gilt Groupe is innovating in ways to stand out and keep its customers engaged.

Gilt Groupe has launched a loyalty program called Gilt Insider Program, which takes a novel approach to loyalty programs. Unlike many traditional loyalty programs that only award points to members when they make purchases, Gilt Insider Program awards points, called Insider points, to members for a variety of activities that engage them with the brand. Members still earn points by purchasing products, but they also can earn points through referring friends, visiting flash sales, connecting with the brand through social media, and browsing the website. Gilt Groupe studied its customers' behavior and aligned the program with actions that customers are already doing to reinforce engagement with the brand.

According to Elizabeth Francis, chief marketing officer at Gilt Groupe:

> We wanted to create a loyalty program that rewards our members not just for their purchasing but for all the ways they interact with our brand. Gilt Insider perks are a collection of our member's most requested asks—from having early sale access to a brand they love, to deeper discounts, to the opportunity to attend exclusive events. The rewards program is designed to provide Gilt members with a platform to pick and choose from the rewards they love the most.

The reward structure is somewhat unique, but fits well with Gilt Groupe's business model. Insider points can be redeemed for a variety of rewards, including early access to flash sales, access to exclusive events, additional discounts, and free shipping. Because the Gilt Groupe business model revolves around exclusive access to flash sales of limited quantities of luxury items, early access is incredibly valuable to its customers. Gilt Groupe has used the knowledge of what its customers value most and has formulated the Gilt Insider Program to incentivize consumer engagement. Ms. Francis said:

> It's expensive from a technology perspective. We communicate frequently with our customers. We knew what our members wanted. This is a great way for us to engage.

According to a 2013 global Nielsen survey of Internet users, these incentives should appeal to many consumers. Eighty-four percent of respondents said they are more likely to patronize retailers with loyalty programs. Seventy-five percent of respondents report that discounted and free products are the most appealing reward. Enhanced customer service is an important reward for 44 percent of respondents and free shipping was important to 42 percent of respondents. According to Julie Currie, the senior vice president of global loyalty at Nielsen:

> Savvy retailers are mining the data and looking for new and innovative ways to achieve the benefits most important to their customers. . . . In markets where loyalty programs are long established, customers tend to be savvy about copy-cat promotional offerings that don't offer unique advantages. New and innovative concepts, especially in the online space, that connect with how consumers want to shop are proving to be most effective.

While it is possible for members to accumulate points through many types of engagement other than making purchases, it would take a very long time to earn enough points without purchasing to earn rewards. For example, members earn 25 points for referring a friend and 100 points for visiting the site for five consecutive days. However, lower-level rewards like free shipping start at 3,500 points. In order to reach the lowest denomination of voucher discount ($80) without making a purchase, a member would need to browse a Gilt Groupe sale every weekday for 250 weeks. Purchases that earn five points per dollar spent accumulate points at a much higher rate.

As members of the Gilt Insider Program accumulate points, they achieve access to three tiers of program status: Select, Premier, and Noir. These tiers are accessible at the 5,000-, 10,000-, and 25,000-point thresholds. With advancement to each additional tier, members are offered additional perks, such as waitlist priority and exclusive VIP customer service lines. For wealthier customers, which are a target market for Gilt Groupe, holding exclusive status with special privileges is more of a motivation than discounts. According to Ms. Francis:

> To make it fair we crafted a program that rewarded engagement, i.e. site visitation and social interaction, in addition to purchasing, so that members could advance up tiers as they earned points.

Tiered loyalty programs, which are modeled after airlines' loyalty programs, are a growing trend that is meant to entice consumers in an environment where traditional loyalty programs have become so common that they often are expected and overlooked. According to Jeff Berry, the senior director of knowledge development for LoyaltyOne, a global provider of loyalty programs for retailers:

> When pretty much every retailer is offering a program with points per purchase, tiers offer that extra incentive to choose one over another. It almost has become the overall scorecard for customers, so they understand where they are relative to where they could be.

While the Gilt Insider Program is an innovative way to stand out from other flash sales sites and the proliferation of loyalty programs among retailers, whether it is a sustainable advantage is yet to be seen. The average North American consumer belongs to between 8 and 12 loyalty programs. According to Niraj Dawar, the author of *Tilt: Shifting Your Strategy from Products to Consumers:*

> From a brand manager's perspective, the question is what is a consumer loyal to, are they loyal to the brand that you're selling or are they loyal to the points? If they're loyal to the points the moment you stop those points your product will stop selling. Or the moment a competitor offers an equivalent amount of points on a slightly different program, the consumer will switch.

Customer Insight Group, Inc., a consulting group that specializes in loyalty program marketing, offers the following 10 tips for successful loyalty programs, many of which the Gilt Insider Program incorporates:

1. Only require and gather customer information that you plan on using.
2. Make sure your employees know the benefits of your loyalty program and that they don't keep it a secret.
3. Enrollment in your loyalty program lagging? Create an employee contest to see who can enroll the most new customers.
4. One easy way to entice more customers to join your program is offer them an incentive at enrollment.
5. Don't just focus on adding members. To get results, you need member participation.
6. Make it easy for your staff to talk about the benefits of the loyalty program by giving them a script.
7. Secret shop your loyalty program to see if there are training issues.

8. Consider implementing a minimum loyalty program enrollment requirement for employees and make it a component of their employee evaluation.
9. Customers will carry your loyalty card if your customers see value in the program and if they are engaged in your brand.
10. Tier your loyalty program so customers have a reason to give you a greater share of wallet and loyalty.

Discussion Questions

1. Define loyalty as you understand it from the text. Do you think the Gilt Insider Program at Gilt Groupe helps create loyalty? Explain.
2. Conduct a small focus group of consumers who you think may fit the Gilt Groupe target market. Ask the participants about their perceptions of the Gilt Insider Program. How effective do they think this loyalty program will be in generating engagement and loyalty? What is their opinion of the rewards that are offered as part of the program? Then, repeat this exercise with another group of consumers who you think would not be part of the Gilt Groupe target market.
3. This loyalty program was designed to achieve two goals, namely, increasing consumer engagement with Gilt Groupe and increasing sales from Gilt Groupe.
   a. How well do you think that the Gilt Insider Program will meet each of these goals?
   b. Which of the goals do you think will be best achieved by this loyalty program?
   c. This program was launched in 2013. Because some time has passed since then, perform an Internet search to discover any reports on the Gilt Insider Program's progress. How well did your predictions from parts a and b perform?
4. Many Gilt Groupe members will likely log in to Gilt.com to browse the flash sales daily in order to accumulate points in the Gilt Insider Program. This engagement will expose them to sales and many are likely to make unplanned purchases. Chapter 13 discusses situational influences. What situational characteristics are likely to play a role in these purchase decisions? (Hint: More than one category could apply.)
5. Chapter 17 discusses Internet retailing and provides a typology of online shopping segments.
   a. Which segments are very likely to enroll in the Gilt Insider Program? Why?
   b. Which segments are very unlikely to enroll in the Gilt Insider Program? Why?
6. Chapter 9 discusses schemas, which arc also known as schematic memories and knowledge structures. Construct a schema diagram for Gilt Groupe.

Source: C. Gallarello, "Gilt.com Unveils Gilt Insider Program," *Gilt.com,* July 18, 2013, www.gilt.com; Gilt, "Gilt.com Unveils Gilt Insider Program," *PR Newswire,* July 18, 2013, www.prnewswire.com; K. Grant, "Retail Loyalty Programs Add Tiers to Reward Big Spenders," *CNBC,* August 28, 2013, www.cnbc.com; "Nielsen Survey: 84 Percent of Global Respondents More Likely to Visit Retailers That Offer a Loyalty Program," *Nielsen,* November 12, 2013, www.nielsen.com; T. Novellino, "Taking a Nooner with Gilt.Com Now Pays Points," *Upstart Business Journal,* July 18, 2013, http://upstart.bizjournals.com; H. Ongley, "Seems Like Gilt Wants You to Hack Their New Loyalty Program," *Styleite,* July 18, 2013, www.styleite.com; A. Bosanac, "Customer Loyalty Programs Turn Shameless Amid Intense Competition," *Huffington Post,* August 11, 2014, www.huffingtonpost.com; and S. Burnett, "Customer Loyalty Programs: Stats, Facts and Tips for 2014," *Customer Insight Group, Inc.,* February 14, 2014, www.customerinsightgroup.com;

4–8 ALBERTSONS DITCHES SELF-CHECKOUT IN FAVOR OF HUMAN CONTACT

Albertsons, a major national grocery store chain, is eliminating self-checkout stations in many of their stores because they want to promote more human contact with customers. One hundred Albertsons locations, owned by the independent company Albertsons LLC, are phasing out self-checkout lines and replacing them with more traditional lanes with cashiers. This move is only the start of an effort to increase the employee interaction with customers. Albertsons' executives feel that their shoppers are not getting enough human interaction and there is a lack of relationship building during the shopping experience:

> We just want the opportunity to talk to customers more . . . that's the driving motivation. . . . Our customers are our highest priority, and we want to provide them with an excellent experience from the time they park their car to when they leave.

After their announcement, there was some public concern because many consumers preferred self-service checkout options and were upset at the prospect of losing them. Albertsons' representatives quickly reassured customers that this change is only affecting some of the independently owned Albertsons. In particular,

SUPERVALU, which operates 460 Albertsons in the Pacific Northwest, California, and Nevada, made swift moves to let their shoppers know that this publicized change would not be affecting their stores. According to another Albertsons spokesperson, Lilia Rodriguez:

> Despite many incorrect reports, Albertsons stores owned by SUPERVALU will continue to operate self check-out lanes. Since this story broke last week, our customers have called us and we learned first-hand that they want and appreciate the convenience of self check-out lanes.

As evidenced by the conflicting quotes, there is some disagreement as to how beneficial self-service checkout is for customers. Self-service checkout lanes were originally introduced as a way to reduce retailers' labor costs and speed up shoppers' checkout times. They have quickly spread in popularity. For example, in 1999 only six percent of grocery stores offered self-service checkouts. By 2007, 69 percent of stores offered the stations. Many consumers feel that the machines provide them with valuable convenience. Others feel they are actually less convenient, given that the self-service machines often have error messages that require a cashier to come help anyway. According to David Livingston of DJL Research, whether it is more beneficial to have a human cashier or a self-service checkout may depend on the quality of the employees in terms of customer service.

> I advised many clients not to [install self-checkouts] because they have such excellent cashiers and customer service. The cashiers were friendly, attractive and much faster than self-checkouts. Encountering a friendly cashier was part of the shopping experience. For large sterile retailers, there is no doubt that self checkouts will be better received by customers. How often must we encounter some inept, hideous-looking, slow cashier chewing gum? If this is the best certain retailers can hire, then of course, offer self-checkouts.

Tables A, B, and C provide further information about consumers' perceptions and behaviors in relation to self-service checkout options.

TABLE A Importance of Self-Checkout When Selecting Primary Grocery Store

Not at all important	31%
Not too important	32%
Somewhat important	26%
Very important	14%

Source: Food Marketing Institute, "U.S. Grocery Shopper Trends," 2007 report.

TABLE B Consumer Insights into Self-Checkout: "I Like Self-Checkout . . ."

When I'm only buying a few items	66%
Because I believe it's faster than regular lanes	53%
Because it provides greater privacy	41%
Because I like to bag my own groceries	34%
No matter how many items I buy	32%
As I don't believe a cashier adds customer service to the checkout process	24%

Source: Food Marketing Institute, "U.S. Grocery Shopper Trends," 2007 report.

TABLE C What Percentage of Transactions Did You Conduct Using Self-Service Devices This Past Week?

Location	Average	100%	75%	50%	25%	None
Bank	73	36	21	16	9	18
Grocery store	38	8	11	19	20	42
Retail store	33	6	10	17	24	43
Airline	29	15	8	6	5	66
Hotel/motel	21	8	5	8	8	71
Restaurant	18	4	5	9	13	70
Hospital/clinic/doctor's office	10	2	2	6	9	81
Other location	19	5	5	9	12	68

Source: NRC Corporation, 2008 Self-Service Consumer Survey for North America, "The Self-Service Revolution Is Real."

Discussion Questions

1. The presence of self-service checkout lanes and/or service employees is part of the physical surroundings in Albertsons' store atmosphere, or environment.
   a. Using the Typology of Service Environments in Figure 13–2, describe where Albertsons would be positioned within the grid.
   b. Does having more human contact and less self-checkout lanes influence Albertsons' position?
2. Chapter 17 discusses the relationship between involvement, sales personnel, and the likelihood of self-service. Cashiers are a basic form of sales personnel. Describe Albertsons' service environment in terms of involvement and the appropriateness of sales personnel versus self-service.
3. Interpret the information in Tables A, B, and C.
   a. What are the primary needs that self-service checkouts satisfy for those customers who prefer them?
   b. What other industries present the best opportunities for the self-service checkout industry to grow?
4. Chapter 10 discusses Maslow's hierarchy of needs. What need is Albertsons attempting to fulfill by increasing their human contact with their customers? Explain.
5. Chapter 7 discusses categories of innovations. What type of innovation is self-service checkout technology?

Source: "The Self-Service 'Buy-and-Pay' Market," *Packaged Facts,* June 2008; A. Anand, "Major Grocer Getting Rid of Self-Checkout Lanes," *MSNBC,* July 10, 2011, http://msnbc.msn.com; "Supervalu-Owned Albertsons Stores Maintain Self Check-out Lanes," *Business Wire,* July 11, 2011, www.marketwatch.com; A. Gasparro, "US Supermarkets Look Beyond Standard Self-Checkout Service," *The Wall Street Journal,* July 11, 2011, http://online.wsj.com; C. Moran, "Some Albertsons Ditching Self-Checkout Lanes in Favor of Humans," *Consumerist.com,* July 11, 2011, http://consumerist.com; A. Turano, "Why Self-Checkout Lanes Are Increasingly Getting Checked-off," *Retail Customer Experience,* July 11, 2011, http://retailcustomerexperience.com.

part

V ORGANIZATIONS AS CONSUMERS

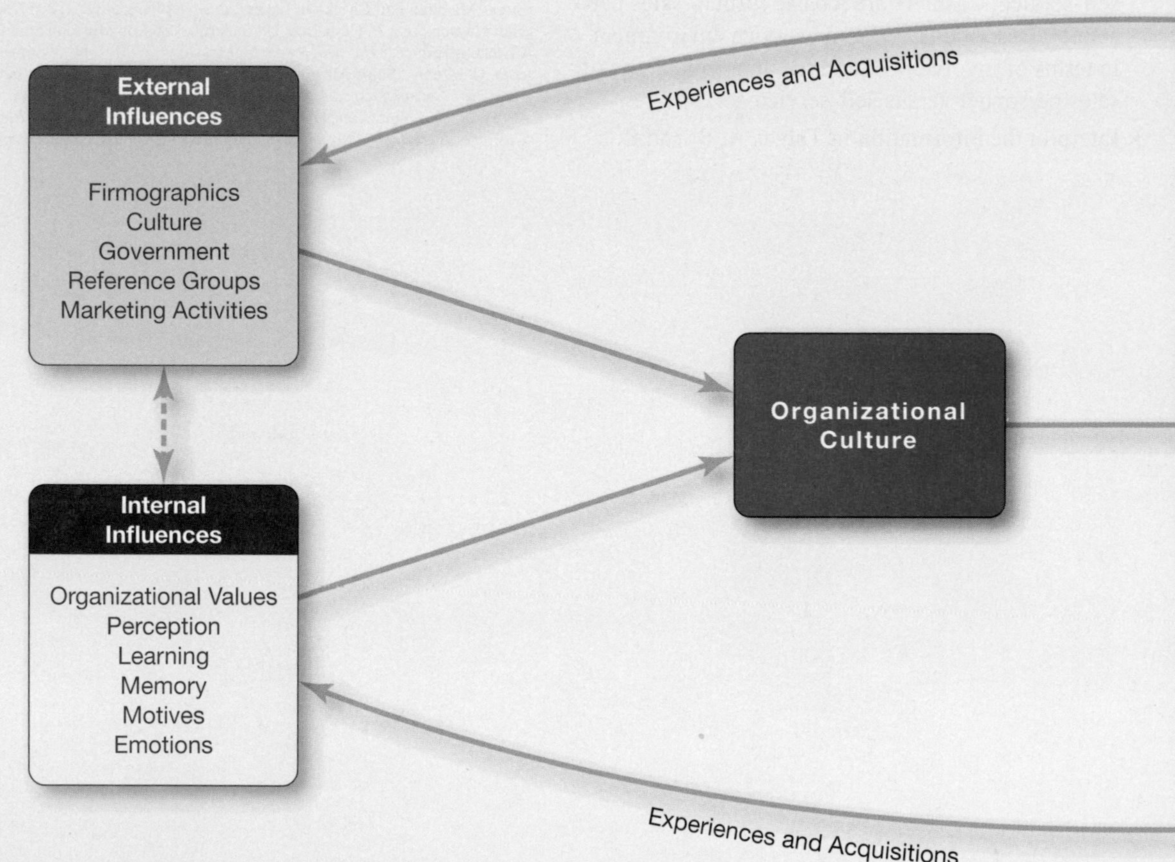

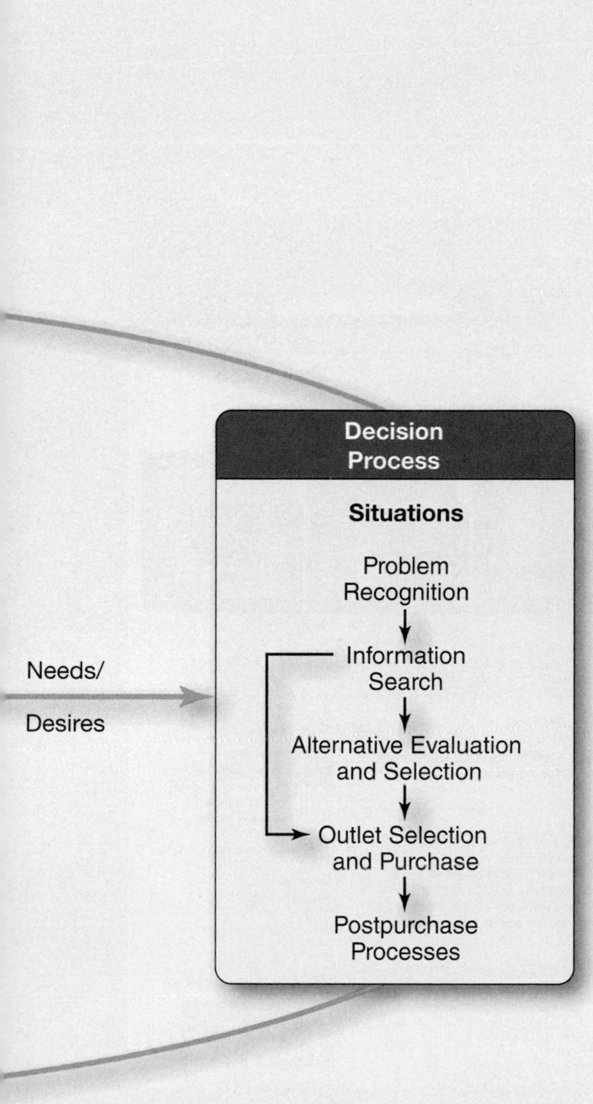

The stereotype of organizational buying behavior is one of a cold, efficient, economically rational process. Computers rather than humans could easily, and perhaps preferably, fulfill this function. In reality, nothing could be further from the truth. In fact, organizational consumer behavior is as human as individual and household consumer behavior.

Organizations pay price premiums for well-known brands and for prestige brands. They avoid risk and fail to properly evaluate products and brands both before and after purchase. Individual members of organizations use the purchasing and consumption process as a political arena and attempt to increase their personal, departmental, or functional power through purchasing. Marketing communications are perceived and misperceived by organization members. Likewise, organizations learn correct and incorrect information about the world in which they operate.

Organizational purchase decisions take place in situations with varying degrees of time pressure, importance, and newness. They typically involve more people and criteria than do individual or household decisions. Thus, the study of organizational buying behavior is a rich and fun-filled activity.

On this and the facing page is a version of our model of consumer behavior modified for organizational buying. Chapter 19 explains these modifications.

chapter

19 Organizational Buyer Behavior

LEARNING OBJECTIVES

LO1 **Describe the organizational purchase process.**

LO2 **Summarize the external factors that influence organizational culture.**

LO3 **Summarize the internal factors that influence organizational culture.**

LO4 **Explain the influence of organizational buyer segments on marketing strategy.**

It may sound funny to say it this way, but businesses are consumers too! They have needs and wants, are influenced by internal factors like values, and are influenced by external factors like reference groups. Relationships matter, as do efforts to build and foster brand image. Understanding what drives businesses, and the people who run them, is critical to marketing success. Consider the following:

Segmentation. While small and moderate-sized businesses often get lost in the shuffle, marketers increasingly realize that this segment has a lot of potential. However, tapping this potential requires adapting to the unique needs and wants of this customer base. For example, in the North American IT industry, slightly more than half of all spending comes from companies with fewer than 1,000 employees. IBM is aggressively courting these customers with a program called IBM Express, which offers flexible and reasonably priced products and services tailored to this market.[1]

Branding. Think brands don't matter in the world of organizational buying? Don't tell that to companies like Dell. Dell has the unenviable task of trying to move into major "enterprise" accounts in terms of hardware and consulting services even while it has moved into the consumer retail market. Major corporate buyers are still finding it difficult to see Dell on the same level in enterprise solutions, as, say, IBM. The irony is that IBM was in a similar situation several decades ago and has managed to emerge as one of the leaders in the industry.[2]

Personal Relationships. Personal relationships matter. A study of how corporations judge their ad agencies found that creativity of the agency was the top factor. This makes sense because creativity is related to the actual "objective" performance of an agency. However, similarity between the agency representative and the client in terms of professional, personal, and social background was also important. The more similar the *people* in the relationship, the more highly the agency was rated.[3]

ILLUSTRATION 19-1

Communicating with organizational buyers often involves many of the same principles used to reach household buyers—in this case, fear appeal.

Purchase decisions by businesses are often described as "rational" or "economic." However, as the chapter opener suggests, various factors beyond functional utility influence organizational decisions. This is not so surprising when you consider that businesses and other organizations are made up of individuals, and that these individuals, not "the organization," make the purchase decisions.

Understanding organizational purchasing requires many of the same concepts used to understand individual consumer or household needs (see Illustration 19–1). Although larger and often more complex than individual consumers and households, organizations too develop preferences, memories, and behaviors through perceptions, information processing, and experience. Likewise, organizations develop cultures that create relatively stable patterns of behaviors over time and across situations.

Like households, organizations make different types of buying decisions. In some instances, these buying decisions are routine replacement decisions for a frequently purchased commodity product or service such as paper or pens. At the other end of the continuum, organizations face new, complex purchase decisions that require careful problem definition, extensive information search, a long and often technical evaluation process, perhaps a negotiated purchase, and a long period of use and postpurchase evaluation.

Because there are many similarities between analyzing consumer behavior and analyzing organizational buyer behavior, our basic conceptual model of buyer behavior still holds. However, organizations are not just a collection of individuals. Organizations do develop unique rules and cultures that influence the behavior of their members. Thus, it is important that we understand the unique characteristics of organizations that relate to their purchasing behavior.

Figure 19–1 shows our basic model of buyer behavior modified to be applicable to an organizational buying context. We will begin our discussion by examining the organization decision process. Then we will examine the internal and external factors that determine organizational culture, the organizational equivalent of household lifestyle.

ORGANIZATIONAL PURCHASE PROCESS

Decision-Making Unit

LO1

Decision-making units (DMUs) are the individuals (representing functional areas and management) within an organization who participate in making a given purchase decision.[4] These often function as **buying centers** when they consist of individuals from various areas of the firm, such as accounting, engineering, manufacturing, and marketing, who meet specifically to make a purchase decision. They are often relatively permanent for recurring decisions and ad hoc for nonroutine ones. Large, highly structured organizations ordinarily involve more individuals in a purchase decision than do smaller, less formal

Overall Model of Organizational Buyer Behavior **FIGURE 19-1**

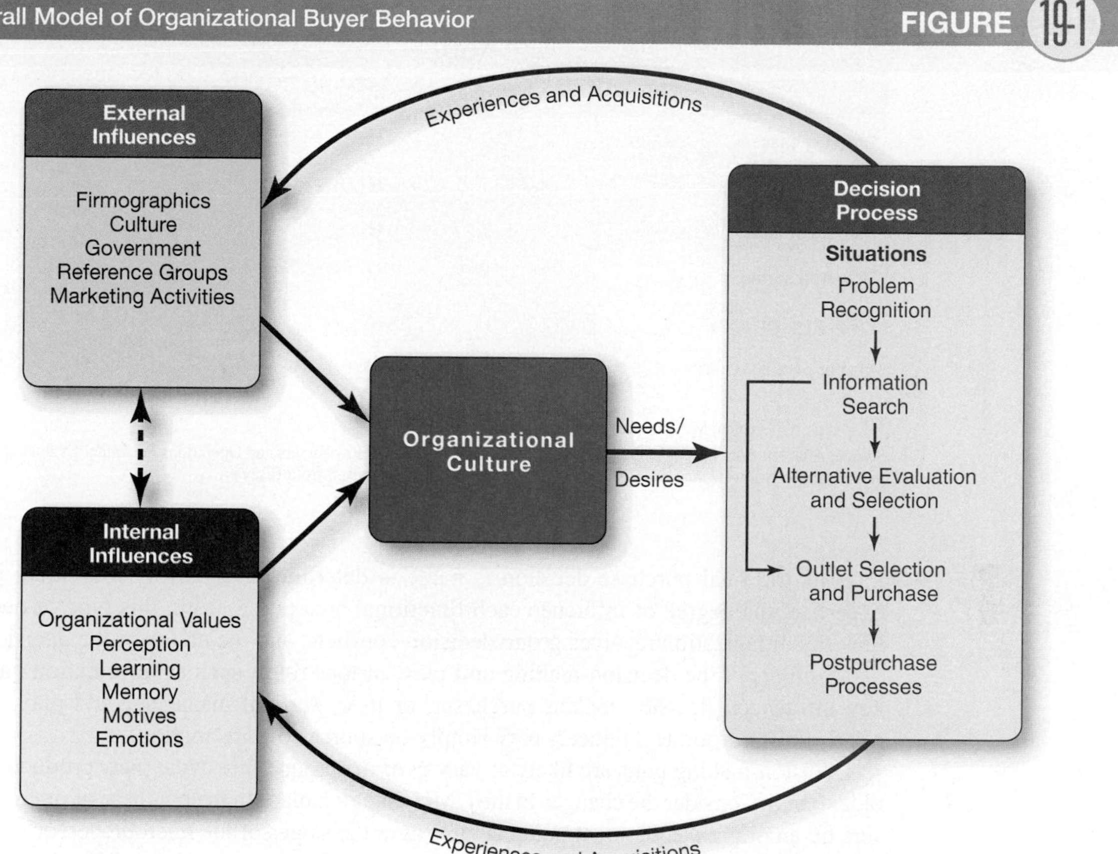

organizations. Important decisions are likely to involve individuals from a wider variety of functional areas and organizational levels than are less important purchase decisions.

The following describes a Hewlett-Packard salesperson's view of the DMU and the buying process for very expensive imaging systems for large hospitals:

> Selling in the hospital market is a two-stage process and the buying cycle ranges from 3 to 12 months. In the first stage, I deal with medical professionals. They are most concerned with image quality, product reliability, and service. I must establish relationships and awareness of our products' functionality and reliability with a number of people, and the product demonstration is critical.
>
> The second stage is negotiations with administrators, who are more driven by price and cost issues. But much depends on the hospital's situation. For example, if a hospital is renowned for cancer treatment, they want the best available systems in that area and are more price sensitive with other equipment.[5]

In Table 19–1, we see that buyers in retail and wholesale firms assign different priorities to the performance of suppliers than do the operations people in those same firms. Organizations marketing to these firms must meet the needs of each group and communicate that to each group. Note that focusing only on the buyers, a common strategy, is not likely to be successful.

Service Attribute Importance for Retail and Wholesale Buyers and Operations Personnel

Attribute*	Buyer Rating	Operations Rating
Ordering ease	**H**	M
Product availability	**H**	M
Delivers on time	**H**	M
Delivered sorted	M	**H**
Palletizing capability	M	**H**
Master package quality	M	**H**

*H = high importance; M = modest importance.

Source: Adapted from M. B. Cooper, C. Droge, and P. J. Daugherty, "How Buyers and Operations Personnel Evaluate Service," *Industrial Marketing Management,* 20, no. 1 (1991), p. 83, with permission from Elsevier.

How the final purchase decision is made is determined in part by individual power, expertise, the degree of influence each functional area possesses in this type of decision, how the organization resolves group decision conflicts, and the nature of the decision.[6]

Members of the decision-making unit play various roles, such as information gatherer, key influencer, decision maker, purchaser, or user. A plant manager could play all five roles, while corporate engineers may simply be sources of information.

Decision-making units are likely to vary over the product life cycle (new products versus older ones). Consider the changes in the DMU that took place in the purchase of microprocessors by an original equipment manufacturer over the stages of the microprocessor's product life cycle. Early stages in the life of the new microprocessor presented a difficult, important decision that required a large DMU. As the product grew in its utilization, a simpler decision evolved, as did a change in the structure of the DMU. Finally, as the microprocessor moved into a mature stage, it became a routine low-priority decision involving primarily the purchasing function. These changes are illustrated below:

Stage of Product Life Cycle	Size of DMU	Key Functions Influencing the Purchase Decision
Introduction	Large	Engineering and R&D
Growth	Medium	Production and top management
Maturity	Small	Purchasing

Purchase Situation

The buying process is influenced by the importance of the purchase and the complexity and difficulty of the choice. Simple, low-risk, routine decisions are generally made by an individual or even an automated process without extensive effort. At the other extreme are decisions that are complex and have major organizational implications. A continuum of purchase situations lies between these two extremes. A useful categorization of organizational purchase situations is provided in Table 19–2 and described in the following paragraphs.[7]

Organizational Purchase Situations and Buying Responses

TABLE 

	Straight Rebuy	Modified Rebuy	New Task
Situational characteristics			
Purchase importance	Low	Moderate	High
Choice complexity	Low	Moderate	High
Purchasing characteristics			
Size of DMU	Very small	Medium	Large, evolving
Level of DMU	Low	Midlevel	Top of organization
Time to decision	Very brief	Moderate	Long
Information search	None/very limited	Moderate	Extensive
Analysis techniques	None/price comparisons	Several	Extensive, complex
Strategic focus	None	Limited	Dominates

Note that this is similar to the purchase involvement construct discussed in Chapter 14. For consumers, we divided the purchase involvement continuum into three categories: nominal, limited, and extended. These correspond closely to the straight rebuy, modified rebuy, and new task purchase situations shown in Table 19–2.

Straight Rebuy This situation occurs when the purchase is of minor importance and is not complex. This is generally the case when reordering basic supplies and component parts. In such cases, the reordering process may be completely automated or done routinely by clerical personnel. Such purchases are often handled under a contract that is reviewed and perhaps rebid periodically. Price or reliability tends to be the dominant evaluative criterion. No consideration is given to strategic issues.

Modified Rebuy This strategy is used when the purchase is moderately important to the firm or the choice is more complex. This typically involves a product or service that the organization is accustomed to purchasing, but the product or the firm's needs have changed. Or because the product is important to the firm (it is simple, but the firm uses a lot of it or it is an important component of the firm's output), the firm may periodically reevaluate brands or suppliers. The DMU is likely to include several representatives, including some midlevel managers. More information is gathered and more evaluative criteria are analyzed. Strategic issues also begin to play a role.

New Task This approach tends to occur when the buying decision is very important and the choice is quite complex. This would involve decisions on such things as an initial sales automation system or a new advertising agency. The buying organization will typically have had little experience with the decision and perhaps with the product or service. The DMU is likely to be large and evolve over time. Top management will be involved in the decision, and strategic issues will be of prime importance. The time involved is frequently quite long, ranging from many months to a year or more.

Clearly, the marketing strategy and tactics for one particular type of purchase situation would be inappropriate for others. Thus, marketers must understand the purchase task confronting their organizational consumers and develop appropriate marketing strategies.

Steps in the Organizational Decision Process

Because organizational decisions typically involve more individuals in more complex decision tasks than do individual or household decisions, marketing efforts to affect this process are much more complex.[8] Shown in Table 19–3 are the likely stages in the decision process and sources of influence at each stage in a large company's decision to acquire a new customer relationship management (CRM) system. Obviously, such decisions won't be made the same way for every organization. However, the key here is recognizing that this is a new task buy situation in which the DMU will involve many sources of influence, with varying criteria, varying levels of power, and varying media habits. The company trying to sell the CRM system must provide relevant information to each source of influence in order to be successful. This is no easy task in such a complex and large DMU.

Problem Recognition In Table 19–3, the sales manager and director of operations play the key roles in recognizing the need. Triggers for this problem recognition could

TABLE 19-3 Decision Process in Purchasing a New CRM System

Stages of the Purchase Decision Process	Key Influences within Decision-Making Unit	Influences Outside the Decision-Making Unit
Problem recognition	Director of operations	Field sales agents
	Sales manager	Administrative staff
		Sales assistants
		CRM sales representative
Information search	Data/CRM specialist	Operations personnel
	Director of operations	CRM sales representative
	Purchasing manager	Other corporate users
		Office systems consultant
Alternative evaluation	Vice president of sales	Office systems consultant
	Data/CRM specialist	CRM sales representative
	Director of operations	
	Sales manager	
	Purchasing manager	
Purchase decision	General management	
	Vice president of sales	
	Purchasing manager	
Product usage	Director of operations	Field sales agents
	Sales manager	Administrative staff
		Sales assistants
		CRM sales representative
Evaluation	Director of operations	Field sales agents
	Sales manager	Administrative staff
	Vice president of sales	Sales assistants
	General management	

Group Involvement in the Decision Process in High-Tech Organizations TABLE 19-4

Stages of Decision Process	Level of Involvement in Each Stage of Decision Process					
	Board of Directors	Top Management	Head of Department	Lab Technician or Operator	Purchasing Manager or Buyer	Finance Manager Accountant
Recognizing the need to purchase	L	M	H	M	L	L
Determining product specifications	L	M	H	M	L	L
Deciding which suppliers to consider	L	M	H	L	M	L
Obtaining quotations and proposals	L	M	H	L	M	L
Evaluating quotations and proposals	L	H	H	L	L	M
Final product or supplier selection	M	H	H	L	L	L

Note: L = low; M = moderate; H = high.
Source: Adapted from R. Abratt, "Industrial Buying in Hi-Tech Markets," *Industrial Marketing Management,* 15 (1986), p. 295, with permission from Elsevier.

be numerous, including conflicts between field sales agents and sales assistants, as well as ongoing customer service problems identified by field sales agents or customers themselves and passed on to the sales manager.

Table 19–4 shows that in high-tech markets, the head of a department is most likely to recognize a problem or need to purchase. Perhaps more important is that purchasing managers are not a source of problem recognition. This points out the danger of salespeople calling on purchasing agents only. As shown in Table 19–4, problem recognition and determining specifications often occur without much involvement of purchasing personnel.

Information Search Information search can be both formal and informal.[9] Site visits to evaluate a potential vendor, laboratory tests of a new product or prototype, and investigation of possible product specifications are part of formal information search. Informal information search can occur during discussions with sales representatives, while attending trade shows, or when reading industry-specific journals. Industrial buyers search for information both to help make the best decision and to support their actions and recommendations within the organization.[10]

For complex technology products, organizational buyers often hire consultants both to provide information and to help evaluate alternatives. Consider the role played by consultants in the purchase of sales automation systems:

> The second step in the buying cycle was to evaluate the potential to automate existing processes. . . . Customers were usually not equipped to do this in-house. It was common for SA consultants to help them. Their deep understanding of the industry, and their skills and experience, made them the best option for this step.
>
> In the third step, the customer decided how the different functions to be automated were related, and determined how data was to be collected, stored, and analyzed. This again was usually done by SA consultants with the support of the customer's information systems department.
>
> The customer decided the type of SA software and hardware to be purchased. . . . Here again, the customer relied heavily on the consultant.[11]

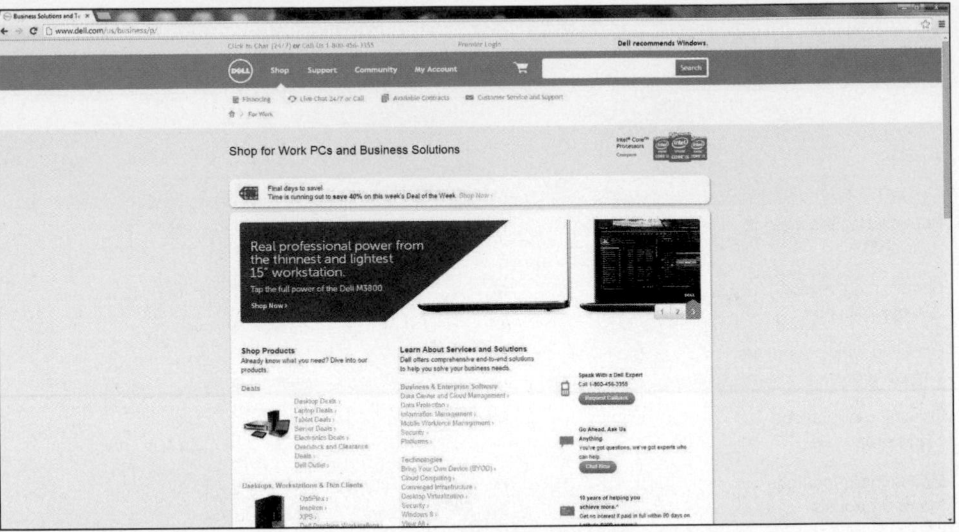

ILLUSTRATION 19-2

Dell Computer capitalizes on the manner in which the web is an invaluable tool for organizational buyers. One of the many functionalities they use is search.

Organizational buyers often search for product and price information on the Internet. The Dell Computer site shown in Illustration 19–2 provides detailed information online to help businesses assess which products are the right fit for the right price.

Evaluation and Selection The evaluation of possible vendors and selection of a given vendor often follow a **two-stage decision process.**[12] The first stage is making the buyer's approved vendor list. A conjunctive decision process is very common. In this manner, the organization can screen out potential vendors that do not meet all its minimum criteria. In a government missile purchase, 41 potential manufacturers of a given missile electronics system were first identified. After site visits to inspect manufacturing capability and resources, the organization pared this list of 41 down to 11 that met the government's minimum criteria.

A second stage of organizational decision making could involve other decision rules, such as disjunctive, lexicographic, compensatory, or elimination-by-aspects. For the government purchase discussed above, a lexicographic decision process was next used, with the most important criterion being price. Using this decision rule, the organization selected two vendors.

The process of evaluation and selection is further complicated by the fact that different members of the decision-making unit have differing evaluative criteria.[13] Recall the difference in criteria for imaging systems between hospital administrators and medical professionals described earlier. Table 19–5 shows that purchasing, management, engineering, and operations use differing sets of performance criteria. For example, purchasing is more concerned with pricing policies, terms and conditions, and order status; engineers are more concerned with product knowledge, product operations, and applications knowledge. A salesperson calling on these accounts would need to understand and respond to the unique as well as the shared criteria of these purchase influencers. A recent study in South Africa similarly found that different criteria were important for different members of the DMU for indoor industrial circuit panels.[14] The SAP site shown in Illustration 19–3 focuses on several key performance criteria of organizational buyers. *To which function or level of the organization is this ad targeted?*

Evaluative Criteria and Organizational Role

TABLE 

Evaluative Criteria Used in Purchase Decision	Functional Role in Organization			
	Purchasing	Management	Engineering	Operations
Vendor offers broad line	X	X		
Many product options available	X	X		
Ease of maintenance of equipment			X	X
Competence of service techniques		X	X	X
Overall quality of service		X	X	
Product warranty	X	X	X	X
Delivery (lead time)				X
Time needed to install equipment	X			X
Construction costs	X		X	X
Vendor has lowest price	X	X	X	
Financial stability of vendor	X		X	X
Vendor willing to negotiate price	X			
Vendor reputation for quality	X	X	X	
Salesperson competence		X	X	X
Compatibility with equipment	X	X		
Available computer interface	X			

Source: Adapted from D. H. McQuiston and R. G. Walters, "The Evaluative Criteria of Industrial Buyers: Implications for Sales Training," *Journal of Business and Industrial Marketing,* Summer–Fall 1989, p. 74.

It is generally assumed that business purchases are strictly economic, with the goal of maximizing the profits of the purchasing organization.[15] However, power, prestige, security, and similar noneconomic criteria also play important roles in business purchase decisions.[16] Research finds that there are organizations that buy "green," similar to the "green consumers" described in Chapter 3. These organizations have policies or individual champions for socially responsible buying behavior by the organization.[17] Firms wishing to do business with these organizations must meet their requirements for products produced in an environmentally sound manner.

Brand image and equity also play roles in the evaluation process for organizations. Obviously, brand can be a surrogate indicator of quality (see Chapter 16). And research suggests that while brand may not always be the most important consideration, it can result in organizational buyers paying a price premium.[18]

Purchase and Decision Implementation Once the decision to buy from a particular organization has been made, the method of purchase must be determined. From the seller's point of view, this means how and when they will get paid. In many purchases, payment is not made until delivery. Others involve progress payments. For a firm working on the construction of a building or highway or developing a new military aircraft that will take several years, payment timing is critical.

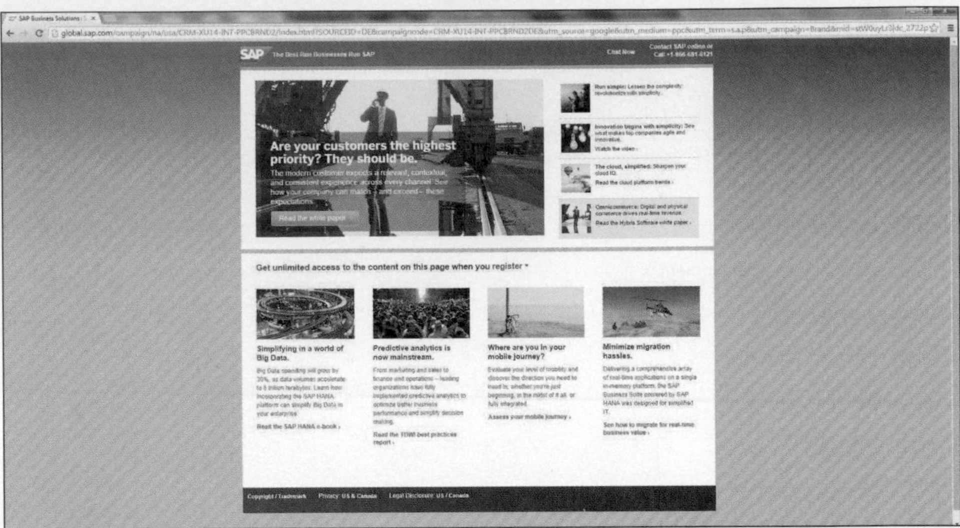

ILLUSTRATION 19-3

Organizations buy for many reasons. The SAP site attempts to persuade based on several key evaluative criteria.

On an international basis, purchase implementation and method of payment are even more critical. Some countries prohibit the removal of capital from their country without an offsetting purchase. This led Caterpillar Tractor Company to sell earthmoving equipment in South America in exchange for raw materials, such as copper, which it could sell or use in its manufacturing operations.

Terms and conditions—payments, warranties, delivery dates, and so forth—are both complex and critical in business-to-business markets. One U.S. manufacturer of steam turbines lost a large order to a foreign manufacturer because its warranty was written too much to the advantage of the seller.

Firms marketing to organizations such as Honeywell increasingly use the Internet to sell their products directly to customers or through online wholesalers (see Illustration 19–4).[19] They also use it to generate leads for telephone or direct sales calls and to solicit orders either on the Internet or via an 800 number.

Usage and Postpurchase Evaluation After-purchase evaluations of products are typically more formal for organizational purchases than are household evaluations of purchases. In mining applications, for example, a product's life is broken down into different components such that total life-cycle cost can be assessed. Many mines will operate different brands of equipment side by side to determine the life-cycle costs of each before repurchasing one in larger quantities.

A major component of postpurchase evaluation is the service the seller provides during and after the sale.[20] Table 19–6 indicates the importance that one group of customers and managers assigned to different aspects of after-sales service. Notice that the managers did not have a very good understanding of what was important to its customers. Clearly, this firm needs a better understanding of its customers' needs.

Similar to households, dissatisfied organizational buyers may switch suppliers or engage in negative word-of-mouth communications.[21] Firms marketing to organizations pursue strategies similar to those followed by consumer marketers in dealing with dissatisfied customers. They seek to minimize dissatisfaction and encourage those who become dissatisfied to complain to them and to no one else.[22]

Otis Elevator uses customer problems and a sophisticated database not only to increase customer satisfaction but to improve the design and functioning of its elevators. The following is an excerpt regarding their OTISLINE service center:

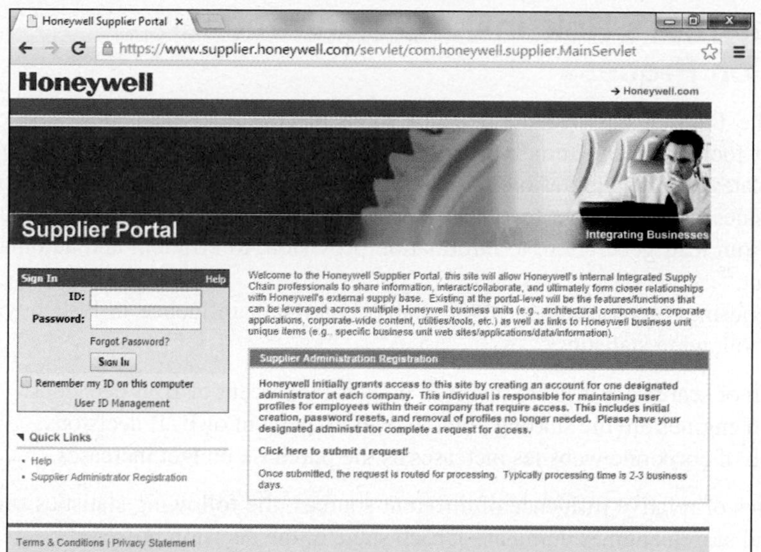

ILLUSTRATION 19-4

Honeywell clearly understands that the Internet is a major source of supply for many organizational buyers.

Imagine you are a building maintenance supervisor. It is 5 o'clock in the morning. You awaken and prepare to go to work. Unbeknownst to you, one of the elevators in your building has had a malfunction. If ignored, it could cause a bigger problem, delaying thousands of people on their way to their office suite. As you make your coffee, the monitoring system on the elevator detects the problem and makes a service call. Even before you get on the road to the office, a mechanic has arrived with the part and fixed the glitch. You enter, board the same elevator and know nothing about the problem until you pass the Otis mechanic on his way out the door.

The preceding scenario could be a true story written by Otis Elevator, thanks to the OTISLINE system. Simply put, OTISLINE is a communications service center for customers. Operators work 24 hours a day, handling emergency calls, dispatching mechanics and entering and updating information on the elevators. Close to 1.35 million elevators are handled by Otis call centers at 325 locations around the globe.[23]

TABLE 19-6 After-Sale Services "GAPS"

	Importance of Service Item			Ratings of Service		
After-Sales Service Item	**Customers**	**Managers**	**Gap**	**Customers**	**Managers**	**Gap**
Attitude and behavior of technician	H	M	+	M	M	0
Availability of technical service staff	H	M	+	M	H	–
Repair time when service needed	M	H	–	M	H	–
Dispatch of breakdown call	H	M	+	M	H	–
Availability of spare parts during call	M	M	0	H	H	0
Service contract options	M	H	–	M	H	–
Price-performance ratio	M	H	–	M	H	–
Response time when service needed	M	H	–	M	H	–

Note: H = high rating; M = moderate rating. Gap is positive (manager higher than customer), negative (customer higher than manager), or zero (manager and customer are the same).

Source: Adapted from H. Kasper and J. Lemmink. "After-Sales Service Quality: Views between Industrial Customers and Service Managers," *Industrial Marketing Management,* 18 (1989), p. 203, with permission from Elsevier.

The Internet's Role in the Organizational Decision Process

Just as the Internet has become a major force in consumer decisions, so too is it an important tool in organizations. In fact, business-to-business (B2B) e-commerce in the United States is estimated at over $6 trillion and represents a substantial proportion of all B2B sales.[24] As we have seen, the Internet can play a variety of roles in the decision process from lead generation, to information provision, to efficient and automated order fulfillment.[25]

As in business-to-consumer (B2C), search is a major influence in B2B buying. Consider the following statistics:[26]

- Search or search engines are involved in over 90 percent of B2B decisions.
- Search engines are the starting point in over 60 percent of B2B decisions.
- Search of corporate websites increases as the purchase budget increases.

In terms of relative influence of different sources, the following statistics suggest that search and search engines dominate at each stage of the decision process:[27]

- Research stage—search used 30 percent more than B2B trade publications.
- Consideration stage—search used 21 percent more than B2B trade publications.
- Choice stage—search used 62 percent more than traditional media.

Perhaps not surprisingly, over 70 percent of the roughly $4 billion that is spent on B2B Internet marketing is devoted to paid search.[28] From a strategic point of view, the increased availability of information from the Internet means there is a need to change the role of salespeople. Salespeople are a dominant part of marketing strategy for B2B, much more so than in B2C. Historically, there was a clear informational role for salespeople. However, given the informational role of the web in today's B2B environment, salespeople need to adopt the role of solution provider rather than information provider.[29]

In terms of website design, recent research suggests that site organization (ease of navigation), customization, privacy/security, information value, and personalization are important drivers of B2B website effectiveness.[30] These characteristics are similar to those found to be important in B2C contexts (see Chapter 17).

Having examined organizational purchasing behavior in some detail, let us now apply the remainder of our revised model to further our understanding of organizations as consumers.

ORGANIZATIONAL CULTURE

LO2

At the hub of our consumer model of buyer behavior are self-concept and lifestyle. Organizations also have a type of self-concept in the beliefs and attitudes the organization members have about the organization and how it operates. Likewise, organizations have a type of lifestyle in that they have distinct ways of operating. We characterize these two aspects of an organization as its **organizational culture** (see Figure 19–1). Organizational culture is much like lifestyle in that organizations vary dramatically in how they make decisions and how they approach problems involving risk, innovation, and change.[31] The term **corporate culture** is often used to refer to the organizational culture of a business firm.

Organizational culture reflects and shapes organizational needs and desires, which in turn influence how organizations make decisions. For example, the Environmental

Protection Agency, the Red Cross, and IBM are three large organizations. Each has a different organizational culture that influences how it gathers information, processes information, and makes decisions.

EXTERNAL FACTORS INFLUENCING ORGANIZATIONAL CULTURE

Firmographics

We discussed earlier the important role of consumer demographics in understanding consumer behavior. Firmographics are equally important. **Firmographics** involve both *organization characteristics*—for example, size, activities, objectives, location, and industry category—*and characteristics of the composition of the organization*—for example, gender, age, education, and income distribution of employees.

Size Large organizations are more likely to have a variety of specialists who attend to purchasing, finance, marketing, and general management; in smaller organizations, one or two individuals may have these same responsibilities. Larger organizations are generally more complex because more individuals participate in managing the organization's operations. That there are often multiple individuals involved in the purchase decision in a large organization means advertising and sales force efforts must be targeted at various functions in the firm. Each message might need to emphasize issues of concern only to that function. The same purchase decision in a smaller firm might involve only the owner or manager. Different media would be required to reach this person, and one message would need to address all the key purchase issues.

Activities and Objectives The activities and objectives of organizations influence their style and behavior. For example, the Navy, in procuring an avionics system for a new fighter plane, operates differently than Boeing does in purchasing a similar system for a commercial aircraft. The Navy is a government organization carrying out a public objective, whereas Boeing seeks a commercial objective at a profit.

Table 19–7 is a matrix that provides examples of the interface between broad organizational objectives and activities. Organizational objectives can be categorized as commercial, governmental, nonprofit, and cooperative. The general nature of organizational activity is described as routine, complex, or technical. For example, a government

Organizational Activities Based on Organizational Objective and Nature of Activity TABLE 19-7

General Organizational Objective	Nature of Organizational Activity: Routine	Complex	Technical
Commercial	Office management	Human resource management	New-product development
Governmental	Highway maintenance	Tax collection	Space exploration
Nonprofit	Fund-raising	Increase number of national parks	Organ donor program
Cooperative	Compile industry statistics	Establish industry standards	Applied research

organization purchasing highway maintenance services would operate differently from a government organization procuring missiles. Likewise, a cooperative wholesale organization set up as a buying cooperative for several retailers would have a different organizational culture from a cooperative research institute set up by firms in the semiconductor industry. And a nonprofit organization involved in organ donations is likely to differ from one organized to gather industry statistics.

Commercial firms can be usefully divided into public firms (stock is widely traded) and private firms (one or a few individuals own a controlling share of the firm). In public firms, management is generally expected to operate the firm in a manner that will maximize the economic gains of the shareholders. These organizations face consistent pressures to make economically sound, if not optimal, decisions.

However, a substantial percentage of business purchases involve privately held firms whose CEO is often the controlling shareholder. In this situation, the firm can and frequently does pursue objectives other than profit maximization. One study found that the following motives drive the management of such firms:[32]

- Building a place for the entire family to work and be involved.
- Having complete, autocratic control over an environment.
- Building a lasting "empire."
- Becoming wealthy.
- Doing what the family expects.
- Avoiding corporations or working for others.
- Obtaining status.
- Improving the world or the environment.

Segmenting these firms according to the motives of the owners is a useful approach for developing sales messages. For example, Micron Electronics targeted the owners and managers of smaller, entrepreneurial firms. Its ads positioned it as understanding and caring about the needs and concerns of these individuals more than the larger firms do. One ad stated, "They wouldn't give you the time of day. They said you weren't a player. . . . They're holding on line three." Merrill Lynch shown in Illustration 19–5 is also clearly targeting this group with an ad designed to appeal to concerns regarding long-term wealth management.

Location As we saw in Chapter 5, there are a number of regional subcultures in the United States. These subcultures influence organizational cultures as well as individual

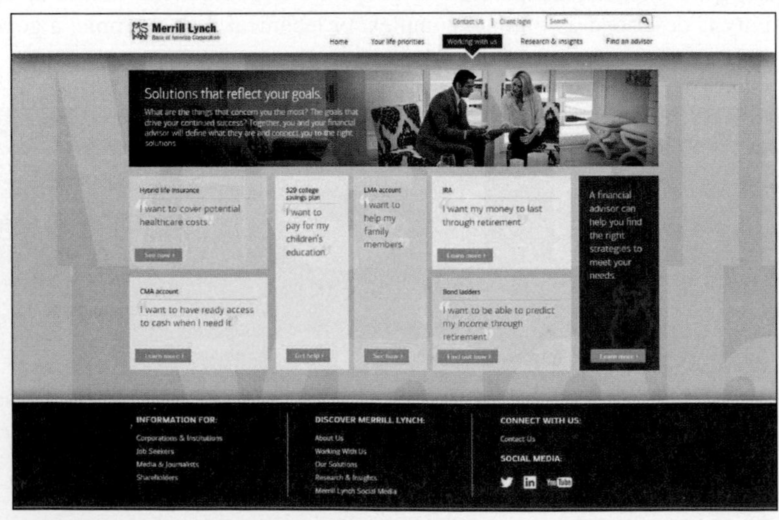

ILLUSTRATION 19-5

Organizations are often privately held and their owners have specific needs and motives that create unique market opportunities for firms such as Merrill Lynch.

lifestyles. For example, firms on the West Coast tend to be more informal in their operations than those on the East Coast. Dress is more casual, relationships are less formalized, and business is on more of a personal level in the West than elsewhere in the country. The Midwest and South also have unique business styles. Marketing communications and sales force training need to reflect these differences.

Location-based differences are magnified when doing business in foreign cultures. Firms that open branches outside their home countries frequently experience some difficulties managing the workforce and operating within the local community. Global B2B selling is as difficult as global B2C selling. Chinese relationships were discussed in Chapter 2, using the term *guanxi.* Recall that *guanxi* is personal connections/relationships on which an individual can draw to secure resources or advantages when doing business as well as in the course of social life.[33] However, firms must be careful to fully understand this and other culturally bound concepts. One Chinese informant indicated that Americans overdo the stereotypical "wine and dine" aspect, which is looked at with suspicion by the Chinese. Consider the following:

> I find that some foreigners come and they try too hard to overly respect Chinese local cultures and China in general. It comes across as almost a bit fake. Chinese sides pick up on that. They will use it. Chinese are good at looking for weakness that they can exploit. Some foreigners come here and are overly respectful. I explain to them that that is not respectful in Chinese cultures.[34]

It appears that the "over-the-top" or "trying too hard" aspect is a problem. Americans react the same way to overeager efforts by marketers in that they see it as a sign of desperation and not genuine or real. Nuance and true understanding are keys to successful ventures cross-culturally.

Industry Category Two firms can be similar in terms of size (large), location (Illinois), activity (manufacturing), objective (profit), and ownership (public), and still have sharply differing cultures due in part to being in differing industries. If one of the two firms described above manufactured heavy equipment and the other, computers, we would expect differing cultures to exist.

Organization Composition Organization cultures influence the behaviors and values of those who work in the organizations. However, the types of individuals who work in the organization also heavily influence organization cultures. An organization composed primarily of young, highly educated, technically oriented people (say, a software engineering firm) will have a different culture from an organization composed primarily of older, highly educated, nontechnical individuals (say, an insurance firm). While the culture of most organizations is influenced more by the characteristics of the founder and top managers, the overall composition of the organizational membership is also important.[35]

Macrosegmentation Organizations with distinguishing firmographics can be grouped into market segments through a process called **macrosegmentation.** These segments, based on differences in needs due to firmographics, are called *macrosegments.*[36] IBM's decision to focus in a special way on midsize businesses, discussed in the opener, is an example. First Chicago Bank stated:

> We've tried too long to be everything to everyone. We're in the process of rolling out a strategy in all our branches where we segment customers and tailor our marketing campaigns to those segments.

Two of the macrosegments the bank is targeting are midsized and small businesses. Each segment will have a marketing team that focuses on that segment.[37]

Culture/Government

Variations in values and behaviors across cultures affect organizations as well as individuals.[38] For example, in most American firms, shareholder or owner wealth is a dominant decision criterion. Corporate downsizing has resulted in hundreds of thousands of workers and managers losing their jobs in order to enhance profitability. These actions have been acceptable in American society. Similar corporate behavior would not be accepted in much of Europe or Japan. In these societies, worker welfare is often on a par with or above concern about corporate profit. Plant closure laws, layoff regulations, and worker benefits tend to be much higher than in America.

In America, Japan, and most of Europe, bribery and similar approaches for making sales are not acceptable, and these governments enforce a wide array of laws prohibiting such behaviors. In America, both the legal and social constraints against bribery are strong enough to make corporate gift giving from a supplier to a buyer difficult or impossible.[39] In other parts of the world, "bribes" are an expected part of many business transactions. This poses a difficult ethical dilemma for firms doing business in these regions. Ignoring any legal constraints imposed by the American government, *should an American firm provide an expensive "gift" to the purchasing agent in a foreign country where it is common knowledge that such gifts are essential to do business with the country's firms?*

In many parts of the world, businesses and governments are partners or at least work closely together. In the United States, an arm's-length or even adversarial relationship is more common. One example of this is the antitrust investigation being launched by the U.S. government against Google. *How do you think this might affect Google's culture over time?*

Reference Groups

Reference groups influence organizational behavior and purchasing decisions. Perhaps the most powerful type of reference group in industrial markets is that of lead users. **Lead users** are *innovative organizations that derive a great deal of their success from leading change.* As a result, their adoption of a new product, service, technology, or manufacturing process is watched and often emulated by the majority.[40] This statement from a Hewlett-Packard salesperson illustrates their role:

> Another aspect of hospital buying behavior is the role of key accounts. A pyramid of influence operates in this market, with smaller and medium-sized hospitals often relying on larger research and teaching hospitals for technology cues. Therefore, maintaining a strong position in influential hospitals is critical.[41]

Other reference groups such as trade associations, financial analysts, and dealer organizations also influence an organization's decision to buy or not buy a given product, or to buy or not buy from a given supplier. **Reference group infrastructure** refers to *the flow of purchase influence within an industry.* As an example, the success of a new technology product depends on how the firm influences the reference groups located along the

Combining Lead-User and Infrastructure Reference Groups

FIGURE 

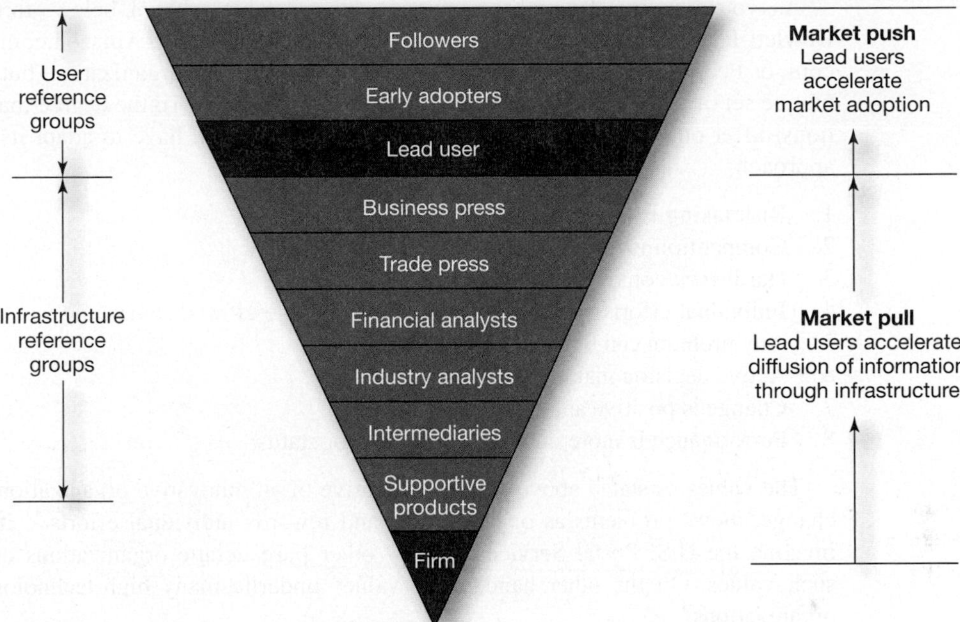

Source: R. Best and R. Angelihard, "Strategies for Leveraging a Technology Advantage," *Handbook of Business Strategy,* 1988.

continuum separating it from its market. The more the firm gains positive endorsement or use throughout this infrastructure, the greater its chances of customers treating it as a preferred source of supply.

If we combine the concept of lead users with reference group infrastructure, as shown in Figure 19–2, we have a more comprehensive picture of organizational reference group systems. Because the lead users play such a critical role, their adoption of a product, technology, or vendor can influence the overall infrastructure in two powerful ways. First, a lead user's decision to adopt a given supplier's innovative product adds credibility to the product and supplier. This in turn has a strong positive impact on the infrastructure that stands between the firm and its remaining target customers. Second, a lead-user decision to purchase will have a direct impact on firms inclined to follow market trends.

The strategy implication of this is clear. Marketers of new industrial products, particularly technology products, should focus initial efforts on securing sales to visible lead users.

INTERNAL FACTORS INFLUENCING ORGANIZATIONAL CULTURE

Organizational Values

Hewlett-Packard and Apple Computer both manufacture and market computers. However, each organization has a distinct organizational culture. Hewlett-Packard is corporate and formal and takes itself seriously. Apple is less formal, is creative, and promotes a more

LO3

open organizational culture. Marketing managers must understand these differences in order to best serve the respective organizational needs.

As you examine the eight common business values shown below, think of how Hewlett-Packard might differ from Apple, Macy's from Target, Amazon.com from Buy.com, or FedEx from the U.S. Postal Service. Each is a large organization, but each has a unique set of values that underlies its organizational culture. To the degree that organizations differ on these values, a firm marketing to them will have to adapt its marketing approach.

1. Risk taking is admired and rewarded.
2. Competition is more important than cooperation.
3. Hard work comes first, leisure second.
4. Individual efforts take precedence over collective efforts.
5. Any problem can be solved.
6. Active decision making is essential.
7. Change is positive and is actively sought.
8. Performance is more important than rank or status.

The values as stated above are representative of an innovative organization that seeks change, views problems as opportunities, and rewards individual efforts.[42] It is hard to imagine the U.S. Postal Service or many other bureaucratic organizations encouraging such values. On the other hand, these values underlie many high-technology start-up organizations.

The ad in Illustration 19–6 would appeal to organizations and individuals with an orientation toward efficiency and active problem solving.

Perception

To process information, a firm must go through the same sequential stages of exposure, attention, and interpretation as consumers. Of course, given the more complex nature of organizations, the processes involved are also more complex.[43] A business customer develops certain images of seller organizations from their products, people, and organizational activities. Like people, organizations have memories and base their decisions on images or memories they have developed. Once an image is formed by an organization, it is very difficult to change. Therefore, it is important for an organization to develop a sound communications strategy to build and reinforce a desired image or brand position.[44]

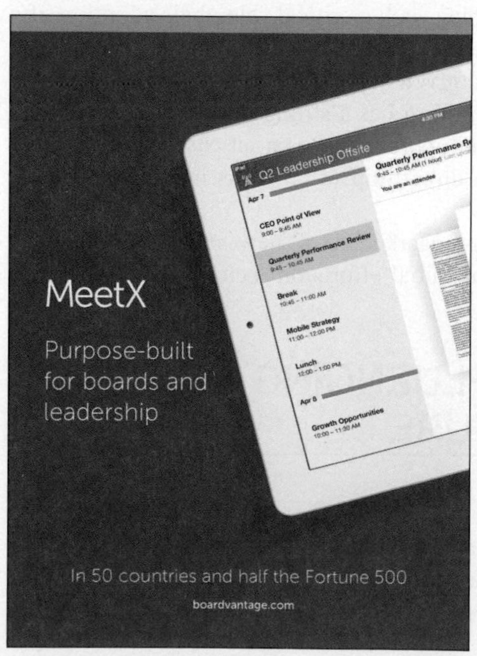

ILLUSTRATION 19-6

Ads should appeal to the values of the organizations they are targeting. This ad will appeal to businesses and individuals that value efficiency and active problem solving.

The Windstream ad in Illustration 19–7 provides a great example of how industrial ads can be designed to work across cultures.[45]

Ad size and repetition have a positive effect on awareness and action. One major study found a 20 percent gain in awareness when two or more ads are placed in the same issue of a specialized business

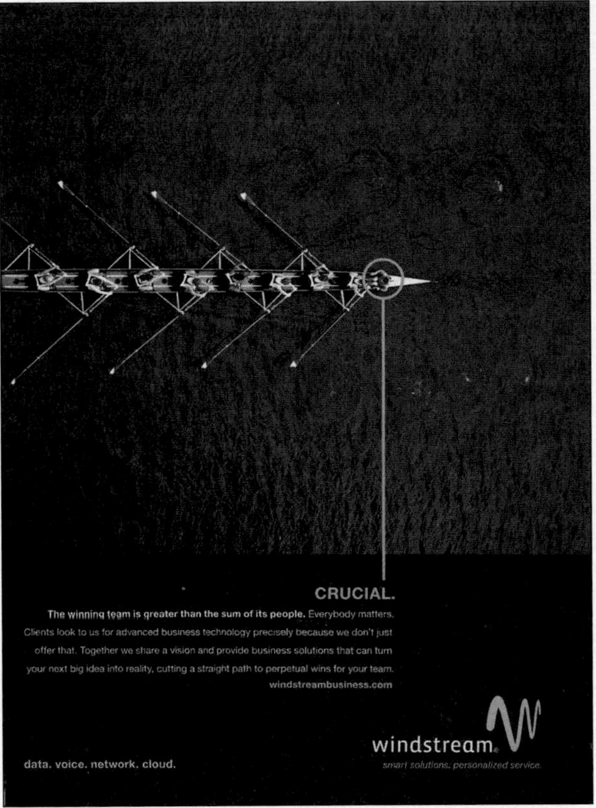

ILLUSTRATION 19-7

Well-done industrial advertising campaigns such as this Windstream ad create and enhance the image of the firm.

magazine compared with only one.[46] The size of the advertisement also affects action in the form of inquiries generated by the advertisement. Research examining B2B magazine advertisements shows that full-page ads are much more effective at generating inquiries than smaller ads.

While advertising (online and traditional) plays an important role in communicating to organizations, direct sales calls are the most important persuasive element of the communications mix in most industrial markets. This is the case despite the high cost of such calls, which is thought to be in the range of $300 per call. One reason for the significant role of salespeople is that businesses are not just economic entities. Business buyers prefer to do business with firms they know, like, and trust. Those relationships are most often formed between members of the firms involved, with sales personnel being the most common representative of the selling organization. As one successful salesperson stated:

> You have to have a great product but you also have to make the customer like you as a salesperson.[47]

Learning

Like individuals, organizations learn through their experiences and perceptions.[48] Positive experiences with vendors are rewarding and tend to be repeated. Purchasing processes and procedures that prove effective tend to be institutionalized in rules and policies. Likewise, negative experiences with vendors produce learning and avoidance behavior, and purchasing procedures that don't work are generally discarded. Developing the capacity to learn efficiently is increasingly a key to organizational success.[49]

Motives and Emotions

Organizational decisions tend to be less emotional than many consumer purchase decisions. However, because humans with psychological needs and emotions influence these decisions, this aspect of marketing to an organizational customer cannot be overlooked or underestimated.

Quite often there is considerable personal or career risk in organizational purchase decisions. The risk of making a bad purchase decision can elicit feelings of self-doubt or psychological discomfort. These are personal emotions that will influence purchase decisions. FedEx appeals to risk avoidance with ads that ask, in essence:

> How do you explain to your boss that the important papers didn't arrive but you saved the company $5 by using a less expensive overnight mail service?

ORGANIZATIONAL BUYER SEGMENTS AND MARKETING STRATEGY

LO4 Each of the factors discussed in this chapter is important for marketing strategy because each contributes to the type of buyer that an organization faces. There are many different ways to characterize or segment organizational buyers. One important way is in terms of transactional versus relational exchanges. Some buyers, due to size, their market position and strategies, and culture are more transactional in their approach to buying, while others are more relational. **Transactional exchanges** *involve single transactions, are short lived, involve few investments by the buyer and seller in the relationship, and involve low loyalty.* Alternatively, **relational exchanges** *involve multiple events, occur over an extended period of time, involve significant investments by the buyer and seller, and involve higher levels of loyalty.*[50] The following excerpt from an industry analyst puts it this way:

> There are two types of buyers: transactional and relational. The transactional buyer, as implied by the name, is focused only on the transaction. What's the cheapest, the best, the fastest for the money. If a distributor [seller] wins one transaction, he earns no loyalty from the transactional customer, only the opportunity to compete again in the next transaction. A relational customer, on the other hand, is focused on finding a distributor he can trust and depend upon. Money [price] is a factor, but the relational customer believes that if he builds a relationship with a trustworthy distributor, he'll be treated fairly on price.[51]

Research suggests that many of the factors we have discussed in this chapter influence whether the relationship will be transactional or relational. These factors are:[52]

- *Industry structure.* When there are only a few buyers, then buyers have power over sellers. In many cases, because the seller threat is reduced, buyers may prefer more relational exchanges to facilitate value creation activities of the partnership.
- *Decision-making culture.* When buying decisions are relegated to the procurement department, a short-term and price-focused decision-making culture is more likely and such buyers should tend to prefer transactional exchanges.

- *Decision-making structure.* When the DMU is larger and cross-functional, this reflects a more complex decision process and buyers facing such a structure should tend to prefer relational exchanges.
- *Risk tolerance.* Buyers with lower risk tolerance should prefer relational exchanges because such an approach reduces uncertainty over access to and quality of the inputs they buy.
- *Nature of the purchase.* Buyers engaged in complex purchases (e.g., new task buy) that require substantial education and after-sale support should tend to prefer relational exchanges that deliver on these important aspects.

The notion of relational exchange relates to *relationship marketing,* which we discussed in Chapter 18. Relationship marketing is at least as important in industrial marketing as it is in consumer marketing.[53] The basic idea at the organizational level is for the seller to work closely with the buyer over time with the objective of enhancing the buyer's profits or operations while also making a profit. Relationships are formed to create value that otherwise wouldn't be possible. That is, a buyer and suppler working together may be able to pool resources, technology, and patents to develop a new product faster and cheaper than either could have done alone.

Healthy business relationships depend on a number of value dimensions.[54] These are:

- *Legitimacy and compatibility.* This dimension deals with actual delivered quality, perceived quality as represented by brand reputation, as well as trust and reliability.
- *Social relations.* This dimension deals with friendship, closeness, and the extent of buyer–seller communication.
- *Economic and shared values.* This dimension deals with the extent to which buyer and seller are integrated through joint manufacturing, information technology, and values.
- *Learning bonds.* This dimension deals with the extent to which buyer and seller cooperate in learning through joint research and development, staff exchanges, and training.

There are often gaps between buyers' and sellers' perceptions of relationship quality, with sellers overrating quality, particularly early in the relationship.

Relationship Length	**Buyer**	**Seller**
Short Term		
Legitimacy/compatibility	4.9	5.7*
Social	4.7	5.2*
Economic/shared values	4.5	4.8
Learning	2.8	3.1
Medium Term		
Legitimacy/compatibility	4.9	5.4*
Social	4.8	4.9
Economic/shared values	4.5	4.7
Learning	3.3	2.9
Long Term		
Legitimacy/compatibility	5.4	5.3
Social	5.2	5.4
Economic/shared values	5.1	5.0
Learning	3.8	3.4

Note: Higher numbers mean higher perceived performance. Asterisk means significant difference.

Source: Adapted from B. R. Barnes et al., "Perceptual Gaps and Similarities in Buyer–Seller Dyadic Relationships," *Industrial Marketing Management,* 36 (2007), p. 667.

CONSUMER INSIGHT 19-1

Loyalty and Relationship Marketing Strategies

Not all relationships are created equal and not all buyers are worth a relational investment. Buyers who want and are willing to pay for value-added services and who desire positive relationship outcomes such as enhanced performance and lower costs of transactions are worth investing in and having relationships with. Those who see the world through a strict price lens and don't want, or won't pay for, value-added services need to be treated in a different manner.[55]

It begins by understanding two things about a buyer:

1. How much does it cost to serve the buyer? This relates to the profitability of a buyer and also how much of an investment in value-added services can be made while still being profitable.
2. Where is the buyer on the "loyalty ladder." Buyers at higher levels of loyalty want to make relationship-specific investments in your firm, want to collaborate on new ventures, are willing to pay premiums, and so on.

Combining these two factors leads to four different organizational buyer segments:

- ***Commodity Buyers*** (Low Cost/Low Loyalty). These customers don't want value-added services and don't want to pay for them. They simply want the basic product (commodity) at the lowest price. These customers, if they are profitable due to their low cost, should be served as a transactional customer.
- ***Underperforming Buyers*** (High Cost/Low Loyalty). Unless the firm can cut costs to make them a profitable commodity buyer, or convince them to pay for the value-added services to make them a profitable partner, they should generally be terminated. While not easy, it can actually be more profitable to NOT sell to a buyer.
- ***Partner Buyers*** (High Cost/High Loyalty). Although expensive to serve, these customers generally are loyal and thus tend to be willing to pay for the value-added services provided. These customers should be managed in a relational manner, with an eye toward increasing the efficiencies of the relationship to lower costs and increase profits.
- ***Most Valuable Customers*** (Low Cost/High Loyalty). These buyers are most profitable because they demand and pay for value-added services but are lower in cost to serve due to economies of scale, experience, and so on. These customers, like partners, should be managed in a relational manner.

Many businesses market and manage to their buyers in the same way. The buyer segments listed above, however, show that some buyers are worth having a relationship with and others are not. One expert estimates that fewer than 10 percent of buyers fall into the most valuable customer category. Because relational or relationship marketing is expensive in terms of both time and effort, only some buyer segments are worthy of having a relationship with.

Critical Thinking Questions

1. What makes some customers more valuable than others?
2. How might you move an underperformer to partner status?
3. Why are commodity buyers worth holding onto?

Clearly, the long-term success of a relationship depends on buyers perceiving high value from the relationship. This is less likely earlier in the relationship and sellers tend to be biased toward more positive perceptions. Such *mis*-perceptions are clearly important to examine and the buyer–seller gaps must be eliminated or substantially reduced for the relationship to remain healthy. This can involve periodic assessments by both parties using so-called relationship performance scorecards and the development of strategies to reduce any value gaps.[56]

Some businesses make the mistake of assuming all buyers are worth developing relational exchanges with. As in the consumer domain (B2C), in the organizational domain (B2B) this is not always true. Some customers are worth having strong relationships with, some should be managed as transactional clients, and some should be terminated. Consumer Insight 19–1 provides insights into these strategic issues and decisions.

SUMMARY

LO1: Describe the organizational purchase process

Like households, organizations make many buying decisions. In some instances, these buying decisions are routine replacement decisions; at other times, they involve new, complex purchase decisions. Three purchase situations are common to organizational buying: *straight rebuy, modified rebuy,* and *new task.* Each of these purchase situations will elicit different organizational behaviors.

The organizational decision process involves problem recognition, information search, evaluation and selection, purchase implementation, and postpurchase evaluation. While functional attributes such as price and quality certainly play a critical role, brand image can also be important, in some cases even increasing the prices that organizational buyers are willing to pay.

Purchase implementation is more complex, and the terms and conditions more important than in household decisions. How payment is made is of major importance. Finally, use and postpurchase evaluation are often quite formal. Many organizations will conduct detailed in-use tests to determine the life-cycle costs of competing products or spend considerable time evaluating a new product before placing large orders. Satisfaction depends on a variety of criteria and on the opinions of many different people. To achieve customer satisfaction, each of these individuals has to be satisfied with the criteria important to him or her.

LO2: Summarize the external factors that influence organizational culture

Organizations have a style or manner of operating that we characterize as organizational culture. *Firmographics* (organization characteristics such as size, activities, objectives, location, and industry category, and characteristics of the composition of the organization such as the gender, age, education, and income distribution of employees) have a major influence on organizational culture. The process of grouping buyer organizations into market segments on the basis of similar firmographics is called *macrosegmentation.*

Reference groups play a key role in business-to-business (B2B) markets. *Reference group infrastructures* exist in most organizational markets. These reference groups often include third-party suppliers, distributors, industry experts, trade publications, financial analysts, and key customers. *Lead users* have been shown to be a key reference group that influences both the reference group infrastructure and other potential users.

Other external influences on organizational culture include the local culture in which the organization operates and the type of government it confronts.

LO3: Summarize the internal factors that influence organizational culture

Internal factors affecting organizational culture include organizational values, perception, learning, memory, motives, and emotions. Organizations hold values that influence the organization's style. Individuals in the organization also hold these values in varying degrees. Organizations also develop images, have motives, and learn. Seller organizations can affect how they are perceived through a variety of communication alternatives. Print advertising, direct mail, sales calls, and the Internet are common. Whereas organizations have rational motives, their decisions are influenced and made by people with emotions. A seller organization has to understand and satisfy both to be successful.

LO4: Explain the influence of organizational buyer segments on marketing strategy

Each of the factors discussed in this chapter is important for marketing strategy because each contributes to the type of buyer that an organization faces. One important way to segment organizational buyers is in terms of transactional versus relational exchanges. *Transactional exchanges* involve single transactions, are short lived, involve few investments by the buyer and seller in the relationship, and involve low loyalty. Alternatively, *relational exchanges* involve multiple events, occur over an extended period of time, involve significant investments by the buyer and seller, and involve higher levels of loyalty. Factors such as industry structure, decision-making culture and structure, risk tolerance, and the nature of the purchase influence whether a buyer takes a relational or transactional approach. Marketers must adjust their strategies, particularly as they regard relationship marketing, depending on the type of buyer they face. Periodic audits can be helpful in ensuring that buyers are getting the value they desire from a relationship.

KEY TERMS

REVIEW QUESTIONS

1. How can an organization have a culture? What factors contribute to different organizational cultures?
2. How would different organizational activities and objectives affect organizational culture?
3. What are *organizational values?* How do they differ from personal values?
4. What are *firmographics* and how do they influence organizational culture?
5. Define *macrosegmentation* and describe the variables used to create a macrosegmentation of an organizational market.
6. What types of reference groups exist in organizational markets?
7. What are *lead users* and how do they influence word-of-mouth communication and the sales of a new product?
8. What is a *decision-making unit?* How does it vary by purchase situation?
9. How can a seller organization influence perceptions of a buyer organization?
10. What are *organizational motives?*
11. What is a *two-stage decision process?*
12. What is the distinction between relational and transactional exchanges?
13. What are the three purchase situations commonly encountered by organizations? How do organizations typically respond to each situation?
14. In what ways does the Internet play a role in the organizational decision process?

DISCUSSION QUESTIONS

15. Describe three organizations with distinctly different organizational cultures. Explain why they have different organizational cultures and the factors that have helped shape the style of each.
16. Respond to the questions in Consumer Insight 19–1
17. Describe how Hewlett-Packard might vary in its organizational culture from the following. Justify your response.
    a. Dell Computer
    b. Lenovo
    c. Apple
18. Discuss how the following pairs differ from each other in terms of organizational activities and objectives. Discuss how these differences influence organizational cultures.
    a. Walmart, Target
    b. DHL, the US Postal Service
    c. Buy.com, Banana Republic
    d. Mercedes Benz, Kraft Foods
19. What role does brand/brand image play in the organizational decision process?
20. Discuss how Acer might use a macrosegmentation strategy to sell computers to businesses.
21. Discuss how a small biotechnology firm could influence the reference group infrastructure and the lead users to accelerate adoption of its products in the market.
22. "Industrial purchases, unlike consumer purchases, do not have an emotional component." Comment.
23. For each of the three purchase situations described in the chapter (Table 19–2), describe a typical purchase for the following:
    a. Wendy's
    b. Mercedes Benz
    c. Target
    d. Your university
    e. Publix

APPLICATION ACTIVITIES

24. Interview an appropriate person at a large and at a small organization, and ask each to identify purchase situations that could be described as straight rebuy, modified rebuy, and new task. For each organization and purchase situation, determine the following:
    a. Size and functional representation of the decision-making unit
    b. The number of choice criteria considered
    c. Length of the decision process
    d. Number of vendors or suppliers considered
25. Review two issues of a magazine targeting organization buyers or purchase influencers. What percent of the ads contain emotional or other noneconomic appeals?
26. Interview a representative from a commercial, a governmental, and a nonprofit organization. For each, determine its firmographics, activities, and objectives. Then relate these differences to differences in the organizational cultures of the organizations.
27. Interview a person responsible for purchasing for a business or government agency. Have that person describe and evaluate any attempts at relationship marketing by its suppliers. What do you conclude?
28. For a given organization, identify its reference groups. Create a hierarchical diagram, as shown in Figure 19–2, and discuss how this organization could influence groups that would in turn create favorable communication concerning this organization.
29. Interview a manager at a business or government agency who has recently been involved in an important purchase decision (e.g., a capital equipment acquisition). Have the manager describe the key influences at each phase of the decision process as shown in Table 19–3. Discuss how this information might be used in developing a marketing strategy for this industry.

REFERENCES

1. J. Gilbert, "Small but Mighty," *Sales & Marketing Management,* January 2004, pp. 30–35.
2. C. Lawton, "A New Dell Dude Looks to Rebuild an Ailing Brand," *The Wall Street Journal,* August 22, 2007, p. B3E; R. Karlgaard, "Michael Reinvents Dell," *Forbes,* May 9, 2011, p. 32; and "Dell's Differentiated Enterprise Solutions and Services Driving Long-Term Value and Growth," *Business Wire,* June 28, 2011.
3. T. Crutchfield et al., "Birds of a Feather Flock Together," *Journal of Advertising Research,* 43, no. 4 (2003), pp. 361–69.
4. See, e.g., T. V. Bonoma, "Major Sales" *Harvard Business Review,* July–August 2006, pp. 2–13.
5. F. V. Cespedes, "Hewlett-Packard Imaging Systems Division," Harvard Business School case 9-593-080, September 6, 1994, p. 4.
6. R. Ventakesh, A. K. Kohli, and G. Zaltman, "Influence Strategies in Buying Centers," *Journal of Marketing,* October 1995, pp. 71–82; and M. A. Farrell and B. Schroder, "Influence Strategies in Organizational Buying Decisions," *Industrial Marketing Management,* 25 (1996), pp. 393–403.
7. See W. J. Johnson and J. E. Lewin, "Organizational Buying Behavior," *Journal of Business Research,* January 1996, pp. 1–15; and E. J. Wilson, R. C. McMurrian, and A. G. Woodside, "How Buyers Frame Problems," *Psychology & Marketing,* June 2001, pp. 617–55. See also L. C. Leonidou, "Industrial Buyers' Influence Strategies," *Journal of Business and Industrial Marketing,* 21, no. 1 (2005), pp. 33–42.
8. S. J. Puri and C. M. Sashi, "Anatomy of a Complex Computer Purchase," *Industrial Marketing Management,* January 1994, pp. 17–27; E. Day and J. C. Barksdale Jr., "Organizational Purchasing of Professional Services," *Journal of Business and Industrial Marketing,* 9, no. 3 (1994), pp. 44–51; and D. Narayandas, "Building Loyalty in Business Markets," *Harvard Business Review,* September 2005, pp. 1–9.
9. See A. M. Weiss and J. B. Heide, "The Nature of Organizational Search in High-Technology Markets," *Journal of Marketing Research,* May 1993, pp. 220–33.
10. P. M. Doney and G. M. Armstrong, "Effects of Accountability on Symbolic Information Search and Information Analysis by Organizational Buyers," *Journal of the Academy of Marketing Science,* Winter 1996, pp. 57–65; and P. L. Dawes, D. Y. Lee, and D. Midgley, "Organizational Learning in High-Technology Purchasing Situations," *Industrial Marketing Management,* 36 (2007), pp. 285–99.
11. D. Narayandas, "SalesSoft, Inc.," Harvard Business School case 9-596-112, March 24, 1998.
12. For a discussion of organizational decision making, see J. B. Heide and W. M. Weiss, "Vendor Consideration and Switching Behavior for Buyers in High-Technology Markets," *Journal of Marketing,* July 1995, pp. 30–43; W. E. Patton III, "Use of Human Judgment Models in Industrial Buyers' Vendor Selection Decisions," *Industrial Marketing Management,* 25 (1996), pp. 135–49; and J. Yu and C Tsai, "A Decision Framework for Supplier Rating and Purchase Allocation," *Computers & Industrial Engineering,* 55 (2008), pp. 634–46.
13. J. E. Stoddard and E. F. Fern, "Buying Group Choice," *Psychology & Marketing,* January 2002, pp. 59–90.
14. M. Bendixen, K. A. Bukasa, and R. Abratt, "Brand Equity in the Business-to-Business Market," *Industrial Marketing Management,* 33 (2004), pp. 371–80.
15. See K. N. Thompson, B. J. Coe, and J. R. Lewis, "Gauging the Value of Suppliers' Products," *Journal of Business and Industrial Marketing,* 9, no. 2 (1994), pp. 29–40.
16. See, e.g., A. Kumar and D. B. Grisaffe, "Effects of Extrinsic Attributes on Perceived Quality, Customer Value, and Behavioral Intentions in B2B Settings," *Journal of Business-to-Business Marketing,* 11, no. 4 (2004), pp. 43–63.
17. M. E. Drumwright, "Socially Responsible Organizational Buying," *Journal of Marketing,* July 1994, pp. 1–19. See also D. Pujari, K. Peattie, and G. Wright, "Organizational Antecedents of Environmental Responsiveness in Industrial New Product Development," *Industrial Marketing Management,* 33 (2004), pp. 381–91.
18. M. Bendixen et al., "Brand Equity in the Business-to-Business Market," *Industrial Marketing Management,* 33 (2004), pp. 371–80. See also P. Michell, J. King, and J. Reast, "Brand Values Related to Industrial Products," *Industrial Marketing Management,* 30 (2001), pp. 415–25; and H. Hansen, B. M. Samuelsen, and P. R. Silseth, "Customer Perceived Value in B-t-B Service Relationships," *Industrial Marketing Management,* April 2008, pp. 206–17.
19. See, e.g., G. S. Lynn et al., "Factors Impacting the Adoption and Effectiveness of the World Wide Web in Marketing," *Industrial Marketing Management,* 31 (2002), pp. 35–49; and H. Min and W. P. Galle, "E-Purchasing," *Industrial Marketing Management,* 32 (2003), pp. 227–33.
20. K. Smith, "Service Aspects of Industrial Products," *Industrial Marketing Management,* 27 (1998), pp. 83–93.
21. S. Y. Lam et al., "Customer Value, Satisfaction, Loyalty, and Switching Costs," *Journal of the Academy of Marketing Science,* 32, no. 3 (2004), pp. 293–311; R. E. Plank and S. J. Newell, "The Effect of Social Conflict on Relationship Loyalty in Business Markets," *Industrial Marketing Management,* 36 (2007), pp. 59–67; and C. Jayawardhena, "Outcomes of Service Encounter Quality in a Business-to-Business Context," *Industrial Marketing Management,* 36 (2007), pp. 575–88.
22. S. W. Hansen, J. E. Swan, and T. L. Powers, "Encouraging 'Friendly' Complaint Behavior in Industrial Markets," *Industrial Marketing Management,* 25 (1996), pp. 271–81.
23. United Technologies, "UTC Products at a Glance: OTISLINE," press release, http://utc.com, accessed July 28, 2008.
24. "B to B E-Commerce," *The Marketing Site,* www.themarketingsite.com.
25. H. H. Bauer, M. Grether, and M. Leach, "Building Customer Relations over the Internet," *Industrial Marketing Management* 31 (2002), pp. 155–63; J. B. MacDonald and K. Smith, "The Effects of Technology-Mediated Communication on Industrial Buyer Behavior," *Industrial Marketing Management,* 33 (2004), pp. 107–16; G. Easton and L. Araujo, "Evaluating the Impact

of B2B E-commerce," *Industrial Marketing Management,* 32 (2003), pp. 431–39; and L. M. Hunter et al., "A Classification of Business-to-Business Buying Decisions," *Industrial Marketing Management,* 33 (2004), pp. 145–54.

26. G. Hotchkiss et al., *The Role of Search in Business to Business Buying Decisions* (Kelowna, BC, Canada: Enquiro, October 27, 2004); and P. Bruemmer, "Search Plays Key Role in B2B Sales," *Search Engine Guide,* www.searchengineguide.com, accessed July 1, 2011.
27. Bruemmer, "Search Plays Key Role in B2B Sales."
28. "Forrester: B2B Interactive Spending to Double by 2014," *BtoB,* March 4, 2010, www.btobonline.com, accessed July 1, 2011.
29. C. Klein, "Death of the Dark Side of Sales," *Sales Bloggers Union,* February 15, 2010, www.salesbloggers.com, accessed July 1, 2011.
30. G. Chakraborty, V. Lala, and D. Warren, "What Do Customers Consider Important in B2B Web Sites?," *Journal of Advertising Research,* March 2003, pp. 50–61; and G. Chakraborty, P. Srivastava, and D. L. Warren, "Understanding Corporate B2B Web Sites' Effectiveness from North American and European Perspective," *Industrial Marketing Management,* 34 (2005), pp. 420–29.
31. See S. Kitchell, "Corporate Culture, Environmental Adaptation, and Innovation Adoption," *Journal of the Academy of Marketing Science,* Summer 1995, pp. 195–205; and P. Berthon, L. F. Pitt, and M. T. Ewing, "Corollaries of the Collective," *Journal of the Academy of Marketing Science,* Spring 2001, pp. 135–50.
32. K. M. File and R. A. Prince, "A Psychographic Segmentation of Industrial Family Businesses," *Industrial Marketing Management,* May 1996, pp. 223–34.
33. M. Ewing, A. Caruana, and H. Wong, "Some Consequences of *Guanxi,*" *Journal of International Consumer Marketing,* 4 (2000), p. 77. See also F. Balfour, "You Say *Guanxi,* I Say Schmoozing," *BusinessWeek,* November 19, 2007, pp. 84–85.
34. H. Gao, D. Ballantyne, and J. G. Knight, "Paradoxes and Guanxi Dilemmas in Emerging Chinese-Western Intercultural Relationships," *Industrial Marketing Management,* February 2010, pp. 264–72.
35. See J. E. Stoddard and E. F. Fern, "Risk-Taking Propensity in Supplier Choice," *Psychology & Marketing,* October 1999, pp. 563–82.
36. See R. L. Griffith and L. G. Pol, "Segmenting Industrial Markets," *Industrial Marketing Management,* January 1994, pp. 39–46.
37. G. Brewer, "Selling an Intangible," *Sales & Marketing Management,* January 1998, pp. 52–58. See also S. P. Kalafatis and V. Cheston, "Normative Models and Practical Applications of Segmentation in Business Markets," *Industrial Marketing Management,* 26 (1997), pp. 519–30.
38. See, e.g., C. Nakata and K. Sivakumar, "Instituting the Marketing Concept in a Multinational Setting," *Journal of the Academy of Marketing Science,* 29, no. 3 (2001), pp. 255–75.
39. See F. Gibb, "To Give or Not to Give," *Sales & Marketing Management,* September 1994, pp. 136–39.
40. A. N. Link and J. Neufeld, "Innovation vs. Imitation: Investigating Alternative R&D Strategies," *Applied Economics,* 18 (1986), pp. 1359–63.
41. Cespedes, "Hewlett-Packard Imaging Systems Division."
42. For a discussion of innovativeness, see G. T. M. Hult, R. F. Hurley, and G. A. Knight, "Innovativeness," *Industrial Marketing Management,* 33 (2004), pp. 429–38.
43. D. I. Gilliland and W. J. Johnston, "Toward a Model of Business-to-Business Marketing Communications Effects," *Industrial Marketing Management,* 26 (1997), pp. 15–29.
44. See S. M. Mudambi, P. Doyle, and V. Wong, "An Exploration of Branding in Industrial Markets," *Industrial Marketing Management,* 26 (1997), pp. 433–46; J. Lapierre, "The Role of Corporate Image in the Evaluation of Business-to-Business Professional Services," *Journal of Professional Services Marketing,* 16 (1998), pp. 21–41; and D. H. McQuiston, "Successful Branding of a Commodity Product," *Industrial Marketing Management,* 33 (2004), pp. 345–54.
45. L. Hochwald, "It's the Sizzle That Sells," *Sales & Marketing Management,* April 1997, p. 51.
46. *CARR Report No. 120.3* (Boston: Cahners Publishing Co., undated).
47. G. Conlon, "A Day in the Life of Sales," *Sales & Marketing Management,* September 1997, pp. 42–63.
48. See J. M. Sinkula, "Market Information Processing and Organizational Learning," *Journal of Marketing,* January 1994, pp. 35–45; G. T. M. Hult and E. L. Nichols Jr., "The Organizational Buyer Behavior Learning Organization," *Industrial Marketing Management,* May 1996, pp. 197–207; and S. J. Bell, G. J. Whitwell, and B. A. Lukas, "Schools of Thought in Organizational Learning," *Journal of the Academy of Marketing Science,* Winter 2002, pp. 70–86.
49. D. A. Garvin, "Building a Learning Organization," *Harvard Business Review,* July 1993, pp. 78–91; S. F. Slater and J. C. Narver, "Market Orientation and the Learning Organization," *Journal of Marketing,* July 1995, pp. 63–74; G. T. M. Hult, "Cultural Competitiveness in Global Sourcing," *Industrial Marketing Management,* 31 (2002), pp. 25–34; and C. Lai et al., "The Effects of Market Orientation on Relationship Learning and Relationship Performance in Industrial Marketing," *Industrial Marketing Management,* February 2009, pp. 166–72.
50. J. N. Sheth and R. H. Shah, "Till Death Do Us Part . . . But Not Always," *Industrial Marketing Management,* 23 (2003), pp. 627–31.
51. M. Dandridge, "Seven Myths Busted," *Electrical Wholesaling,* March 2010.
52. Sheth and Shah, "Till Death Do Us Part . . . But Not Always."
53. See, e.g., A. Walter et al., "Functions of Industrial Supplier Relationships and Their Impact on Relationship Quality," *Industrial Marketing Management,* 32 (2003), pp. 159–69; Sheth and Shah, "Till Death Do Us Part . . . But Not Always"; and T. L. Keiningham, T. Perkins-Munn, and H. Evans, "The Impact of Customer Satisfaction on Share-of-Wallet in a Business-to-Business Environment," *Journal of Service Research,* August 2003, pp. 37–50.
54. B. R. Barnes, P. Naude, and P. Mitchell, "Perceptual Gaps and Similarities in Buyer–Seller Dyadic Relationships," *Industrial Marketing Management,* 36 (2007), pp. 662–75. See also C. Steinman, R. Deshpande, and J. U. Farley, "Beyond Market Orientation," *Journal of the Academy of Marketing Science,* 28,

no. 1 (2000), pp. 109–19; and P. H. Andersen and R. Kumar, "Emotions, Trust and Relationship Development in Business Relationships," *Industrial Marketing Management,* 35 (2006), pp. 522–35.

55. This Consumer Insight is based primarily on D. Narayandas, "Building Loyalty in Business Markets," *Harvard Business Review,* September 2005, pp. 1–9. See also K. A. Richards and E. Jones, "Customer Relationship Management," *Industrial Marketing Management,* April 2008, pp. 120–30; and S. F. King and T. F. Burgess, "Understanding Success and Failure in Customer Relationship Management," *Industrial Marketing Management,* June 2008, pp. 421–31.

56. S. Janda, J. B. Murray, and S. Burton, "Manufacturer–Supplier Relationships," *Industrial Marketing Management,* 31 (2002), pp. 411–20; L. F. Lages, A. Lancastre, and C. Lages, "The B2B-RELPERF Scale and Scorecard," *Industrial Marketing Management,* August 2008, pp. 686–97; and J. M. Whipple, D. F. Lynch, and G. N. Nyaga, "A Buyer's Perspective on Collaborative versus Transactional Relationships," *Industrial Marketing Management,* 39 (2010), pp. 507–18.

Part Five CASES

5–1 RAEX LASER STEEL

The global steel market has been historically plagued with overcapacity and slow growth. This has created fierce competition and a perception among industrial buyers that steel is a commodity. The result has been that, in many cases, the deciding factor in a purchase decision is price, with resulting downward pressure on profitability.

One strategy that some steel manufacturers have used is to cut operating costs in order to help protect profit margins. Another strategy that some manufacturers have been attempting is a product differentiation approach accompanied by a strong brand name around which to build a distinctive image. But is branding useful in an industrial (B-to-B) context? The answer appears to be yes:

> [I]ndustrial firms hold very positive views about the benefits of brand names and feel that branding is valuable to marketing success and is a major corporate asset. In addition, industrial firms perceive a number of competitive differential benefits in the use of manufacturer brands, with quality, reliability, and performance rated as primary factors.

Clearly industrial marketers see value in branding. However, do industrial buyers? The answer here depends on the extent to which the brand (*a*) creates benefits of value to buyers and (*b*) consistently delivers these core benefits. When these two factors are present, brand name becomes the symbol of these benefits and core values and provides for differentiation in the marketplace. In addition, consistent delivery over time results in increased trust, stronger relationships, and enhanced loyalty.

Rautaruukki Ojy (RO) is a steel manufacturer in Finland. It has a strong reputation in Europe but is relatively small. Rather than go the cost-cutting route, it decided to take the differentiation route. Its opportunity came when laser cutting technology became available. After hearing initial grumbling about steel quality problems associated with laser cutting, RO conducted intensive research to understand the nature of the problem/opportunity.

RO found that laser cutting involves preprogrammed computer settings. These settings involve considerable setup time, so users want to be able to save the cutting specs for reuse later on. However, this requires very high consistency in terms of the chemical composition and quality of the steel both within a batch of steel and across batches. The nature of the industry was also one where companies outsourced their laser cutting needs to specialty "job shops." Order quantity from these job shops was highly variable and not predictable. Given the technical nature of laser cutting, an educated customer service department was also critical.

As a result of this research, RO created RAEX LASER brand steel. The value components included:

- Consistent quality steel within and across batches to meet laser cutting specifications.
- Flexibility in order size acceptance through its distributors. The supply chain for RO is one of manufacturer (RO) to distributors, to end users (job shops who do laser cutting). Because the job shops had highly variable order size needs and they were unpredictable, RO had to provide flexibility in order size fulfillment. In managing supply, RO also created a cooperative atmosphere among its distributors whereby it would share inventories if needed in order to keep the supply chain running. Educational seminars and an annual retreat are part of this process.
- Customer service. Because education was critical, RO engaged in extensive training of its internal customer service personnel to provide them with the tools to deliver the highest customer service possible.

The results were very positive. Sales increased with the introduction of the RAEX LASER brand and its value components. Customer loyalty increased and buyers were willing to pay a *price premium* to get RAEX LASER steel and all that goes with it. And their efforts even caught the attention of the largest laser cutter manufacturer, which recommended RAEX to new buyers of its machines!

Discussion Questions

1. Create a diagram linking the value drivers for RAEX LASER steel to buyer satisfaction, trust, relationship quality, and loyalty. Explain how RAEX branding was much more than a promotion-driven process.

2. Should promotion and advertising come first or last in the brand-building process? Does this depend on whether the promotion is targeted at the "external consumers" (in this case, the job shops) or the "internal consumers" (in this case, customer service employees)? Explain.
3. Discuss the importance of "internal marketing efforts" discussed in Question 2 to the success of RAEX's branding strategy.
4. Are buyers of RAEX LASER just "paying more for the name" or is it due to the economic benefits associated with the name? What, if any, economic benefits accrue to buyers of RAEX LASER steel?
5. Does the fact that job shops use brand name in their decision process mean that they are irrational decision makers?
6. Describe the various ways in which reference groups and word-of-mouth might operate in this setting.
7. The RAEX LASER brand was replaced by "Ruuki Laser" workshop-friendly steel. Evaluate this decision in light of the perceptual issues relating to branding.

Source: D. H. McQuiston, "Successful Branding of a Commodity Product," *Industrial Marketing Management*, 33 (2004), pp. 345–54; and www.ruukki.com, accessed July 27, 2011.

5-2 PACCAR—MORE THAN SHINY TRUCKS

Paccar makes two of the most recognizable names in trucking: Kenworth and Peterbilt. These trucks represent the premium end of the over-the-road (OTR) truck market. It sells and leases its products to a large array of businesses with varying needs, wants, and resources. The truck industry is considered a commodity market for the most part, with price generally topping the list of buying criteria. In this market, Paccar and its trucks stand out. It has created a strong brand image for premium trucks, high quality, technology, and intense brand loyalty. Consider the following:

> Herbert J. Schmidt is a truck guy, but not just any truck. It's Kenworth or nothing. For the past 20 years, Contract Freighters Inc. has bought only Kenworth rigs, and the chief executive of the Joplin (Mo.) trucking company intends to stick with Kenworth . . . with plans to order at least 700 new trucks. Sure, these 10-wheel diesels cost 10% more than rivals' trucks. But when Schmidt factors in everything else—reliability, trade-in value, even the plush interiors that attract better drivers—he says they're worth it. "It's not the price," he says, "It's the quality."

Paccar's success can be attributed to a number of factors:

- *Quality.* In a commodity market, these trucks are premium quality, luxury products. Freight-hauling companies love them because of their quality, reliability, and trade-in values. Drivers love them because of the plush and comfortable interiors, among other things (consider that OTR drivers spend days on end in their trucks and often sleep in them). Both Kenworth and Peterbilt recently won the JD Powers Award.
- *Benchmarking.* Paccar is unusual in that it doesn't benchmark its products only against other truck brands. It specifically picks the leader in each area of concern and benchmarks against them. So, in IT it's Microsoft; in custom manufacturing it's Dell.
- *Technology.* Paccar actually considers itself a technology company as much as a trucking company. More accurately, it applies technological expertise to the trucking industry to remain a leader. Examples include its Electronic Fleet Management System, which is a computerized module that can be installed in its trucks and integrated into an owner's IT system to increase efficiency, help with regulatory compliance, and reduce paperwork.
- *Customization.* No "off-the-lot" purchases necessary here. With its custom manufacturing process, buyers can select from thousands of options and within six to eight weeks take delivery of their custom-built truck.
- *Industry reputation.* Paccar and its trucks are recognized throughout the industry as a leader in quality (JD Powers), technology (National Medal of Technology), and computing (Computer World Honors). These awards help to further solidify an already strong reputation.
- *Lease options.* If you are buying 700 trucks like Herbert Schmidt, you have the technology, capital,

and human resources to manage and operate your own fleet. However, smaller carriers have problems in these areas. A growing business for Paccar is its leasing operation, which provides services such as truck maintenance, eliminating the need for the carrier to maintain a staff of trained technicians—a huge overhead expense.

Finally, in response to environmental issues and rising fuel prices, Paccar is taking the lead with hybrid trucks.

Discussion Questions

1. Define *loyalty* as you understand it from the text. Does Paccar with its Kenworth and Peterbilt trucks create loyalty? Explain.
2. What type of buying process (straight rebuy, modified rebuy, new task) is the decision to buy Kenworth for Herbert Schmidt? Would the buying process be the same for all carriers? Explain.
3. Using all possible sources of information including the case, the Internet, and OTR truck dealers, develop what you think the decision-making unit looks like for a truck purchase. Does its size depend on the size of the company or other factors? Explain.
4. Using all possible sources of information including the case, the Internet, OTR truck dealers, complete the following information in Table A. What implications does this have for Paccar and other truck companies in terms of their marketing efforts?
5. Explain the role of reference groups for Paccar and its trucks?
6. Describe the differences you would expect between a company that owned its own trucks versus those that lease. Relate these to the internal and external influences shown in Figure 19–1.
7. How does Paccar's hybrid offering fit into its current brand image?

TABLE A Evaluative Criteria and Organizational Role

Evaluative Criteria Used in Purchase Decision	Functional Role in Organization			
	____	____	____	____
1.				
2.				
3.				
4.				
5.				
.				
.				
.				
.				
.				
.				
.				
.				
.				

Source: M. Arndt, "Built for the Long Haul, *BusinessWeek,* January 30, 2006, p. 66; and information from Paccar's website, www.paccar.com, accessed July 27, 2011.

part

VI CONSUMER BEHAVIOR AND MARKETING REGULATION

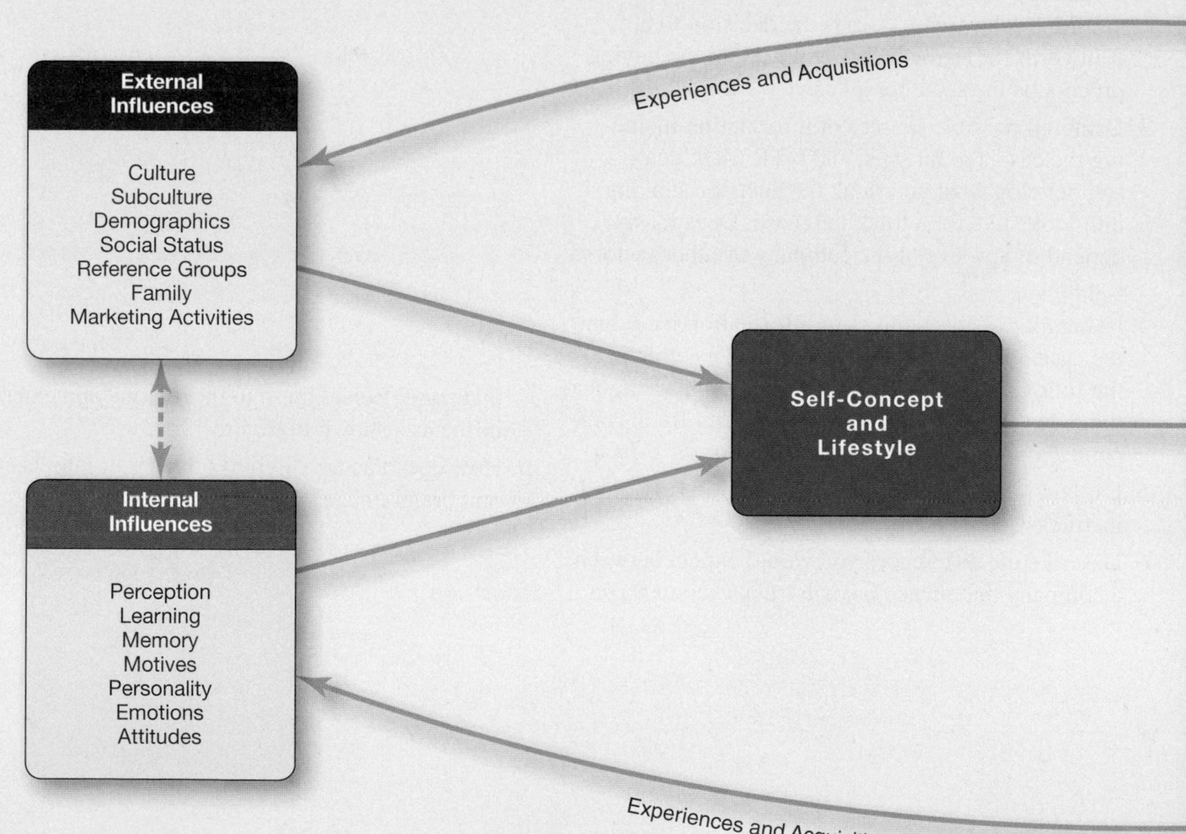

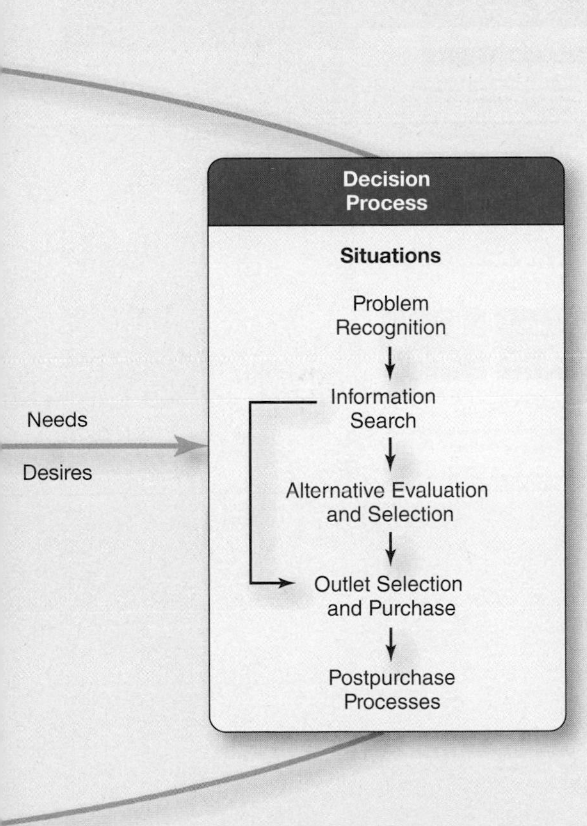

Throughout the text, we have emphasized that knowledge of consumer behavior is as important to those who would regulate consumer behavior as it is to those who engage in marketing activities. Government officials, consumer advocates, and citizens all need to understand consumer behavior to develop, enact, and enforce appropriate rules and regulations for marketing activities. Consumers in particular need to understand their own behaviors and how their purchase and consumption behaviors help determine the type of marketplace and society we have.

In this section, we will analyze the role of consumer behavior principles in regulating marketing practices.

We will pay particular attention to the regulation of marketing activities focused on children. We also discuss regulations covering advertising, product, and pricing practices aimed at adults.

chapter

20 Marketing Regulation and Consumer Behavior

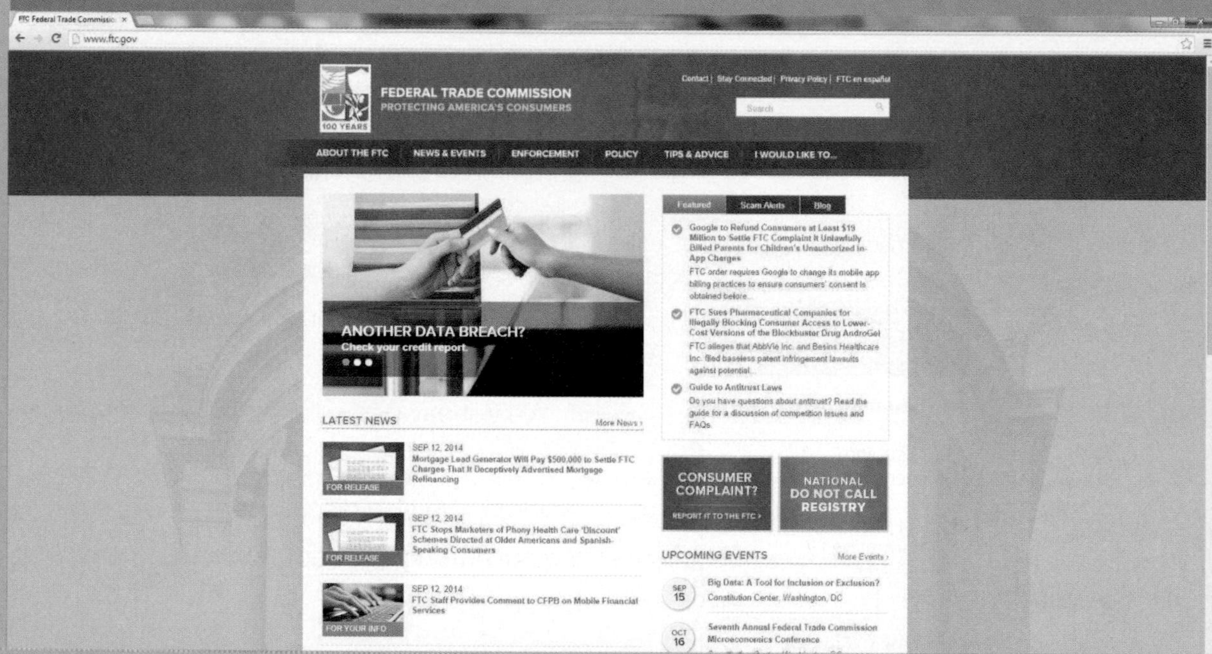

LEARNING OBJECTIVES

LO1 **Explain the two major concerns in marketing to children that CARU deals with.**

LO2 **Describe the various marketing activities aimed at children that are controversial.**

LO3 **Discuss new guidelines by the FTC regarding online privacy protection for adults.**

LO4 **Explain marketing communication issues related to adults including deceptive advertising.**

LO5 **Discuss regulation concerns when marketing to adults as they relate to product and price.**

Agencies such as the FTC, FDA, USDA, and FCC likely spring to mind in relation to government regulation. News media are populated with stories of the need for government regulatory bodies to protect consumers from the hidden dangers in the marketplace. In 2014 Toyota was fined $1.2 billion, the largest payment by an automaker in U.S. history, for safety issues of sudden acceleration from sticky pedal and floor mat entrapment, linked to 37 deaths.[1] Sharing the news space with Toyota was another car maker accused of corporate misconduct. GM must explain its failure to ask for a recall for its Chevy Cobalts and Saturn Ions with defective ignition switches that shut off. The problem, resulting in at least 12 deaths, is one that GM knew of as early as 2001. Two months into 2014, Nestle, USA, issued a massive recall of its Hot Pockets product out of concern that it was made with USDA-recalled "diseased and unsound" beef. In 2012 the nation was shocked by news stories of a nationwide outbreak of fungal meningitis carried in steroid medication produced by New England Compounding Center that killed 64 people and left at least 751 people with lingering and, in some cases, debilitating symptoms.

Consumers have no way to test the safety of cars they are driving, the foods they are eating, or the medications they are taking, and rely on government regulatory bodies for this assurance. From this perspective, governmental regulatory bodies are cast in a mediating role to protect consumers from the actions of companies. The FTC's website shown at the beginning of this chapter, prominently displays its purpose of protecting America's consumers.

Another perspective that may not come as quickly to mind is the need for government regulating bodies to protect companies from consumers, as in the case of counterfeit products. Imitation is not always the sincerest form of flattery. Sometimes it's just counterfeit. Media alerts of the arrest of major producers of fake health and beauty products—Vicks Vaporub, Vaseline, Chapstick, Johnson's Baby Oil—are reminders of the harm that may come to consumers who unknowingly buy counterfeit.

But what about the situation when consumers knowingly seek out and buy counterfeit goods. Consumer demand for counterfeit goods is strong, with an estimated worldwide underground economy that rivals illicit drugs and surpasses that of weapons smuggling and human trafficking. Consumer demand for counterfeits includes not only fake innocuous items that have low performance risk like fashion items—Dr. Dre Beats headphones, Mont Blanc pens, Rolex watches, Gucci purses—but also fakes that have high performance risk—fake alcohol, fake drugs—items that hold the potential to threaten consumer health, safety, and welfare. Consumers knowingly buy fakes with their concomitant lower quality as a means to own brand-image items beyond their economic reach. Ownership of fake goods may also serve as a means to help consumers create or bolster a desired identity. Interestingly, unbeknownst to consumers, part of the identity derived from buying counterfeit goods may be its impact on consumers to engage in subsequent unethical behavior such as cheating.

Consumer complicity is a major reason not only for the strength of counterfeiting, but also for the strength of piracy, a consumer behavior related to counterfeiting. With media—music, movies, e-books, TV programs, video games—now readily available on demand, wait time has been reduced to zero. With the effortless click of a mouse or a swipe across the screen, the media are instantly available for consumption and can be had just as easily whether consumers pay for them or not. Piracy occurs when consumers opt not to pay for them. Recent anti-piracy efforts, including the (2013) "Six Strike Anti-Piracy Scheme," do not seem to have created a noteworthy drop in piracy behavior, but a concomitant rise in anonymity services that hide the identity and location of the user seems to indicate that users would rather hide than quit this behavior.

Government regulation is one leg of a three-legged stool—consumers, business, and government. Each leg is needed to balance the whole.

Marketing is a highly visible, important activity. It affects the lives of individuals, the success of nonprofit groups, and the profits of businesses. As indicated throughout the text, there are many issues where the appropriate ethical action for marketers is not clear-cut. As a marketing manager, you will face many such situations in your career. However, society has declared that some marketing actions are clearly inappropriate. It has done so by enacting laws and regulations that prohibit or require specific marketing actions. In this chapter, we examine the regulation of marketing practices. Regulating marketing activities requires the same level of understanding of consumer behavior as does managing marketing programs. Our consideration of the regulation of marketing practices will separate regulations designed to protect children from those designed to protect adults.

A KEY CAVEAT about the material in this chapter is that consumer regulation is an ongoing and dynamic endeavor, particularly as it relates to technology, e-commerce, and marketing to children. Thus, what may be accurate at one point in time may become incomplete or obsolete at a later time. This is true of the material in this chapter and also true of any organization's knowledge and information and policies relating to various areas of regulation. Thus, it is the responsibility of all involved to ensure that up-to-the-minute information is sought prior to decision making and action in this arena. As you will see, the breadth, complexity, and evolution of the issues involved make regulation, compliance, and enforcement a highly demanding set of activities for both firms and government regulators.

REGULATION AND MARKETING TO CHILDREN

LO1

The regulation of marketing activities aimed at children focuses primarily on product safety, advertising and promotions, and privacy protection. Product safety issues focus on appropriate product design and materials. We will concentrate on privacy protection and advertising and other promotional activities[2] targeting children as consumers. The regulation of these activities rests heavily on theories of children's consumer behavior, particularly their information-processing skills.

There are a variety of state, federal, and voluntary guidelines and rules governing marketing to children. Despite these rules, many feel that some marketers continue to take advantage of children and that the overall marketing system, particularly advertising, is socializing children to value things (products) rather than intangibles such as relationships and integrity.

One basis for the concern over marketing to children is based on *Piaget's stages of cognitive development* (Chapter 6), which indicates that children lack the ability to fully process and understand information, including marketing messages, until around 12 years of age.[3] This and related theories are the basis for most regulation of advertising aimed at children and, according to critics, for some marketing programs that deliberately exploit children.

Concerns about the Ability of Children to Comprehend Commercial Messages

The American advertising industry's primary self-regulatory body, the National Advertising Division (NAD) of the Council of Better Business Bureaus, maintains a special unit to review advertising aimed at children—the **Children's Advertising Review Unit (CARU).** Four of the eight principles that underlie CARU's guidelines for advertising directed to children relate to their ability to comprehend commercial messages:[4]

1. Advertisers have special responsibilities when advertising to children or collecting data from children online. They should take into account the limited knowledge, experience, sophistication, and maturity of the audience to which the message is directed. They should recognize that younger children have a limited capacity to evaluate the credibility of information, may not understand the persuasive intent of advertising, and may not even understand that they are being subjected to advertising.
2. Advertising should be neither deceptive nor unfair, as these terms are applied under the Federal Trade Commission Act, to the children to whom it is directed.
3. Advertisers should have adequate substantiation for objective advertising claims, as those claims are reasonably interpreted by the children to whom they are directed.
4. Advertising should not stimulate children's unreasonable expectations about product quality or performance.

Some of the specific guidelines relating to information processing that guide CARU's policing of children's advertising are shown in Table 20–1.

Information Processing–Related Guidelines of CARU

1. Whether an advertisement leaves a misleading impression should be determined by assessing how reasonable children in the intended audience would interpret the message, taking into account their level of experience, sophistication, and maturity; limits on their cognitive abilities; and their ability to evaluate the advertising claims.
2. Claims should not unduly exploit a child's imagination. While fantasy, using techniques such as animation and computer-generated imagery, is appropriate for both younger and older children, it should not create unattainable performance expectations nor exploit the younger child's difficulty in distinguishing between the real and the fanciful.
3. Advertisements should demonstrate the performance and use of the product in a way that can be duplicated by a child for whom the product is intended.
4. All disclosures and disclaimers material to children should be understandable to the children in the intended audience, taking into account their limited vocabularies and level of language skills. For young audiences, simple words should be chosen, e.g., "You have to put it together." Since children rely more on information presented in pictures than in words, demonstrative disclosures are encouraged.
5. Program personalities, live or animated, should not be used to advertise products, premiums, or services in or adjacent to a television program primarily directed to children under 12 years of age in which the same personality or character appears.

Source: *Self-Regulatory Program for Children's Advertising* (Children's Advertising Review Unit, Council of Better Business Bureaus, Inc., 2009).

CARU and others are interested in the impact that the *content* of children's advertising has, as well as the ability of children to process advertising messages. However, our current focus is limited to children's abilities to *comprehend* advertising messages. There are two main components to this concern: (1) Do children understand the selling intent of commercials? and (2) Can children understand specific aspects of commercials, such as comparisons?

Do Children Understand the Selling Intent of Commercials? Research suggests that younger children have at least some difficulty understanding the selling intent of commercials.[5] Currently, the advertising industry strives to separate children's commercials from the programs by prohibiting overlapping characters and by using *separators,* such as "We will return after these messages."

This problem is growing in intensity, as children's products are often the "stars" of animated children's films and television programs. Increasingly, product lines and television programs (and movies) are being designed jointly with the primary objective being sales of the toy line. Parents have expressed concerns ranging from the effects that toy-based programming has on their children's behaviors and emotional development to the fear that such programming may replace other more creative and child-oriented programs.[6]

This concern has led to a variety of proposals to restrict or eliminate such programs. These proposals have produced an ongoing debate about who controls the television set. One argument is that it is the parent's responsibility to monitor and regulate their children's viewing behaviors. If a sufficient number of parents find such programs inappropriate and refuse to let their children watch them, advertisers will quit sponsoring them and they will no longer be available. Another argument is that today's time-pressured parents do not have time to screen all the shows their children watch. Furthermore, tremendous peer pressure can develop for children to watch a particular show or own the products associated with it. Denying a child the right to watch such a show then causes arguments and resentment. Therefore, society should set appropriate standards within which broadcasters should operate. *Which, if either, of these views matches your own?*

Can Children Understand the Words and Phrases in Commercials? The second aspect of comprehension involves specific words or types of commercials that children might misunderstand. For example, research indicates that disclaimers such as "Part of a nutritious breakfast," "Each sold separately," and "Batteries not included" are ineffective with preschool children.[7] Not only do young children have a difficult time understanding these phrases, the problem is compounded when such disclaimers are presented in a manner that does not meet the Federal Trade Commission's "Clear and Conspicuous" requirements for such disclaimers.[8] For example, consider the following toy ad disclaimer:

> The disclaimer noted that "TV Teddy comes with one tape. Other tapes sold separately." However, it appeared near the bottom of the screen in lettering that measured only 3.5 percent of the screen height against a multicolor background. It was not repeated by an announcer and appeared for less than three seconds. A child would have to read at 200 words per minute to read the message!

In relation to words and phrases, CARU recommends wording and language that are age appropriate (such as simple words for young audiences) and prohibits price minimizations such as "only" and "just." It also suggests specific phrasing for certain situations, such as "you have to put it together," rather than "assembly required." Several cases involving CARU and the information-processing skills of children include the following:

- Nintendo agreed to discontinue advertising in which groups of four people such as a family or young girls at a slumber party are shown playing Mario Party 8 [on the Wii system] each with her or his own separate remote control. Even though a small video super indicated "Game and system sold separately," CARU was concerned that "children watching the advertisement could be confused by what is included in the initial purchase of the Wii game system."[9]

- Nabisco, Inc., agreed to change its advertising for KoolStuf Oreo Toaster Pastries after CARU brought a consumer complaint to its attention. The commercial showed Oreo cookies going into a toaster and popping up as KoolStuf toaster pastries. A four-year-old saw the commercial and tried to do the same thing by putting Oreos into a toaster. When they melted, he tried to remove them with a pair of metal tongs before being stopped by his mother.[10]

Concerns about the Effects of the Content of Commercial Messages on Children

Even if children accurately comprehend television ads, there are concerns about the effects the content of these messages has on children. These concerns stem in part from the substantial amount of time American children spend viewing television. The large amount of time children devote to watching television, including commercials, gives rise to two major areas of concern:

- The impact of commercial messages on children's values.
- The impact of commercial messages on children's health and safety.

Four of the eight basic principles that underline CARU's guidelines for advertising directed at children focus on these concerns (the other four, as we saw, are concerned with children's information-processing capabilities). They are:[11]

1. Products and content inappropriate for children should not be advertised directly to them.
2. Advertisers should avoid social stereotyping and appeals to prejudice, and are encouraged to incorporate minority and other groups in advertisements and to present positive role models whenever possible.
3. Advertisers are encouraged to capitalize on the potential of advertising to serve an educational role and influence positive personal qualities and behaviors in children, for example, being honest and respectful of others, taking safety precautions, and engaging in physical activity.
4. Although there are many influences that affect a child's personal and social development, it remains the prime responsibility of the parents to provide guidance for children. Advertisers should contribute to this parent–child relationship in a constructive manner.

Several of the specific guidelines derived from these principles are provided in Table 20–2.

Health and Safety CARU challenged a television commercial for 4 Wheelers by Skechers, which ran during traditional children's viewing time. The ad featured teens skating and performing a stunt without the use of any safety gear such as helmets or pads. According to CARU, this violates the third guideline in Table 20–2. Skechers appealed the ruling, stating that there are no children shown in the commercial; protective gear while skating or roller-blading is not required by law; it warns purchasers to "always" wear protective gear in the safety pamphlet that comes with the product; and the skates are not being portrayed in an athletic or sporting manner.[12] *What do you think? Was CARU correct or was Skechers?*

In many instances, children and teenagers are exposed to advertising directed at adults. For example, CARU found that Proactiv Solution cleansing system, which is labeled as

Examples of Specific Guidelines of the Children's Advertising Review Unit

1. Advertising should not urge children to ask parents or others to buy products. It should not suggest that a parent or adult who purchases a product or service for a child is better, more intelligent or more generous than one who does not.
2. Advertisers should not convey to children that the possession of a product will result in greater acceptance by peers or lack of a product will result in less acceptance by peers.
3. Advertisements should not portray adults or children in unsafe situations, or in acts harmful to themselves or others. For example, when activities (such as bicycle riding or skateboarding) are shown, proper precautions and safety equipment should be depicted; when an activity would be unsafe without adult supervision, supervision should be depicted.
4. Advertising should not portray or encourage behavior inappropriate for children (e.g., violence or sexuality) or include material that could unduly frighten or provoke anxiety in children; nor should advertisers targeting children display or knowingly link to pages of a website that portray such behaviors or materials.

Source: *Self-Regulatory Program for Children's Advertising* (Children's Advertising Review Unit, Council of Better Business Bureaus, Inc., 2009).

"keep out of reach of children," was being advertised in time slots and locations likely to involve children's programming and viewership. The company responded by removing the ad from those time slots and locations.[13]

Even ads clearly not targeting children can have potentially harmful consequences:

> A television commercial for Calgonite automatic dishwasher detergent showed a woman inside an automatic dishwasher. The commercial was withdrawn voluntarily after CARU received a complaint that a three-year-old child had climbed into a dishwasher shortly after viewing the commercial.[14]

The problem caused by the Calgonite commercial illustrates the difficulty marketers face. This commercial was not aimed at children nor shown during a children's program. The fact that children watch prime-time television extensively places an additional responsibility on marketers.[15]

Ensuring that advertisements portray only safe uses of products is sometimes difficult, but it is not a controversial area. Advertising of health-related products, particularly snack foods and cereals, is much more controversial.

Values Advertising is frequently criticized as fostering overly materialistic, self-focused, and short-term values in children:

> We cannot afford to raise a generation of children that measures its own value by the insignia on their clothes—not by the compassion in their hearts or the knowledge in their minds.[16]

One reason is the magnitude of advertising focused on kids. One estimate is that marketers spend $15 billion per year advertising to children.[17] In addition, estimates of the number of TV ads that children are exposed to ranges from 18,000 to 40,000 per year.[18] Obviously, these numbers are conservative in terms of total ad exposure because they exclude other popular media such as the Internet. Many are concerned that this consistent pressure to buy and own things is producing negative values in children.

Numerous cosmetics companies and day spas are now targeting children at increasingly younger ages with both products and advertisements. Most position the products in terms of fun rather than sensuality. For example, Disney's products are packaged in boxes with pictures of Tinkerbell, Winnie the Pooh, and similar characters.[19] According to an industry expert, girls 8 to 12 are now wearing platform heels and "low-rise jeans, tight miniskirts and midriff-baring T-shirts."[20]

There is also an increase in concern about looking thin and in eating disorders in children as young as six.[21] Many find this apparent shortening of childhood and the related body image problems inappropriate. They assign a large part of the blame to the marketing of products such as cosmetics and personalities such as Lindsay Lohan.

Summary of Advertising and Children Available evidence suggests that the vast majority of ads meet CARU guidelines.[22] CARU reviews thousands of ads every year and has over a 95 percent success rate in resolving issues related to children's advertising.[23] However, given the enormous amount of time children spend with all forms of media, most will see many ads that are in violation of these guidelines. Clearly, CARU does not cover all aspects of advertising. For example, it does not, nor could it, oppose generating desires for products that many families cannot afford. Nonetheless, CARU has greatly enhanced the level of responsibility in advertising aimed at children. Many consumer advocates would like it to expand the areas it covers and increase the stringency of its rules.

Controversial Marketing Activities Aimed at Children

LO2

There are a number of marketing activities targeted at children in addition to television advertising that are controversial and for which various regulatory proposals are being considered. For example, violent entertainment products (movies, videos, and music) labeled for those 17 and older were, until recently, routinely marketed to kids. Highly publicized acts of violence by teenagers produced threats of regulation and improved self-regulation by the industries.[24] However, it remains a problem.

Three additional issues are described in this section, namely, mobile marketing, commercialization of schools, and Internet marketing.

Mobile Marketing and Children Sometimes referred to as the "third screen," cell phones are an increasingly integral part of our lives. And marketers see younger children as the next big growth market. A considerable proportion of those in their teen years and younger have cell phones.[25]

Various types of promotional efforts are being used, including ringtones, mobile games, text-in contests, and mobile advertising. The ability of marketers to infiltrate yet another media domain with promotions and materials that are seen as further blurring the line between advertising and entertainment has many parents and consumer advocate groups worried. Some years back when Disney announced that it would, in a partnership with Sprint, offer cellular phone service targeted specifically at children in the 8- to 12-year range, concerns grew even stronger. Consider an excerpt from a letter to Congress by Commercial Alert, a nonprofit consumer advocate group:

> If Disney Corporation and the others just wanted to give children a way to contact parents in emergencies, that would be one thing. The telecommunications companies—to parents at least—are playing up this angle. Telecommunications lobbyists in Washington will harp on it as well. But despite the industry's rhetoric, Disney and the telecommunications companies really want to use children as conduits to their parents' wallets. And marketers want another way to bypass parents and speak directly to the nation's children.
>
> *Advertising Age* reported on July 11th that many corporations, including McDonald's, Coca-Cola, and Timex, are moving "from small [mobile phone advertising] tests to all-out campaign[s]." Children already are bombarded with too much advertising. They don't need more advertising through their mobile phones, whether it is telemarketing, text message marketing, adver-games, or any other type of commercial messages.[26]

Obviously, the battle lines are being drawn. *Which side of this debate do you come down on more—that of the marketers or of the consumer advocates? Does your answer depend on the age of the children and the nature of the tactics utilized?*

Commercialization of Schools There has been ongoing concern and controversy around the commercialization of elementary and high schools. Schools are often motivated by money as budgets continue to be tight. The issue of commercialization covers a broad sphere of activities. Consumers Union has the following classification system:[27]

- *In-school ads.* Ads in such places as school buses, scoreboards, bulletin boards, as well as coupons and free samples. For example, Sonic Drive-in launched Sonic Invasion, which included in-school ads and e-mail blasts designed to get students to go to a website and vote for their school. Although the call to action wasn't buying burgers, the exposure for Sonic clearly was a positive aspect of the campaign for the company. Other aspects might include schools selling naming rights to companies and distributing ads in student newspapers. For example, advertisers can now get national runs in high school newspapers through Campus Media Group.
- *Ads in classroom.* Ads in classroom magazines and television programs. This also includes ads in magazines distributed in school libraries. Channel One has created substantial controversy in this area. It provides 12 minutes of news to participating schools but contains two minutes of commercials. Research indicates that the commercials have an impact on students.
- *Corporate-sponsored educational materials and programs.* Also called sponsored educational materials, or SEMs. SEMs are teaching materials provided by corporations, usually for free. They come in various forms, including posters, activity sheets, and multimedia teaching aids. While many criteria can be used to evaluate these materials, one of the main criteria is the level of commercialism. Highly commercialized SEMs that are thinly veiled ads with little educational value draw the most scrutiny.
- *Corporate-sponsored contests and incentive programs.* When companies gain access through various contests and incentives, including prizes such as travel and free pizza.

Another area of great concern includes direct sales, usually by food products companies. The major food and beverage companies are working to develop and comply with voluntary guidelines designed to deal with this issue.

Internet Marketing and Children Children are major users of the Internet. Not surprisingly, marketers use the Internet to communicate with kids. Two major concerns have emerged: invading children's privacy and exploitation of children through manipulative sales techniques. We will consider the online privacy issue in the next section.

Concern regarding manipulative Internet practices often revolves around the creation of sites that blur the line between entertainment and advertising. This goes back to concerns touched on earlier in terms of difficulties that children have in discerning selling intent and their ability to distinguish commercial from noncommercial content. Adver-games are just one area of concern. These customized games, which are placed on a company's website, prominently feature or integrate the company's brands and products as part of the game itself. Consider the following excerpt:

> Kraft's Nabiscoworld.com features adver-games for at least 17 brands, plus classic games such as chess, mah-jongg and backgammon. Some games integrate brands into the play. In Ritz Bits Sumo Wrestling, for example, players control either the Creamy Marshmallow or the Chocolatey Fudge cracker in a belly-smacking showdown, which results in the "S'more"-flavored cracker.[28]

As we saw earlier, young children have a difficult time understanding the difference between "content" and "advertising." Adver-games are a little of both and in that sense make it even tougher for younger children, especially, to recognize selling intent.

Children's Online Privacy Issues

Online privacy relates to the collection and use of information from websites. Collecting information from children is a sensitive issue, as well it should be, given all we know about their information-processing deficits relative to those of adults. Concern over the invasion of children's privacy prompted Congress to pass the **Children's Online Privacy Protection Act (COPPA)** in October 1998. It authorizes the FTC to develop specific rules to implement the provisions of the act. In 1999, the FTC issued the *Children's Online Privacy Protection Rule,* also referred to as The Rule. Key provisions of The Rule under COPPA are detailed in Table 20–3.

The Rules became effective in April 2000 and appear to be working, although, clearly, ongoing diligence on the part of the FTC and commercial entities is required.

CARU adopted similar but more detailed rules. Privacy is now a major CARU issue:

- CARU was concerned that the website for the Jonas Brothers (a band popular with children) collected personally identifiable information from children without obtaining verifiable parental consent and that it used "tip-off" language that would alert younger children to enter a false age. The company worked to get its site into compliance.[29]
- Pinkspage, the fan site for the artist Pink, did not contain a privacy statement. In addition, CARU was concerned that a visitor of any age could submit personal identifying information such as an e-mail or street address at the "Fan Club" registration.[30]
- A social network site specifically for kids under 13, fbfkids.com, was found at the time of the CARU review not to have a privacy policy and it was unclear whether verifiable parental consent was being obtained when children were asked to provide personally identifiable information.[31]

Key Provisions of The Rule under COPPA — TABLE 20-3

The Rule applies to (a) operators of commercial websites or online services directed to children under 13 that collect personal information from children, (b) operators of general audience sites that knowingly collect personal information from children under 13, and (c) operators of general audience sites that have a separate children's area and that collect personal information from children. Nonprofits are not covered.
Privacy Policy—Post privacy policy on the homepage of the website and link to the privacy policy everywhere personal information is collected.
Parental Notice—Provide parents notice about the site's information collection practices and, with some exceptions, get verifiable parental consent ***before*** collecting personal information from children.
Parental Consent—Give parents the choice to consent to the collection and use of a child's personal information for internal use by the website, and give them the chance to choose not to have that personal information disclosed to third parties.
Parental Access—Provide parents access to their child's information, and the opportunity to delete the information and opt out of the future collection or use of the information.
Conditional Access—Do NOT condition a child's participation in an activity on the disclosure of more personal information than is reasonably necessary for the activity.
Confidentiality—Maintain the confidentiality, security, and integrity of the personal information collected from children.

Source: *You, Your Privacy Policy and COPPA* (Washington, D.C.: Federal Trade Commission).

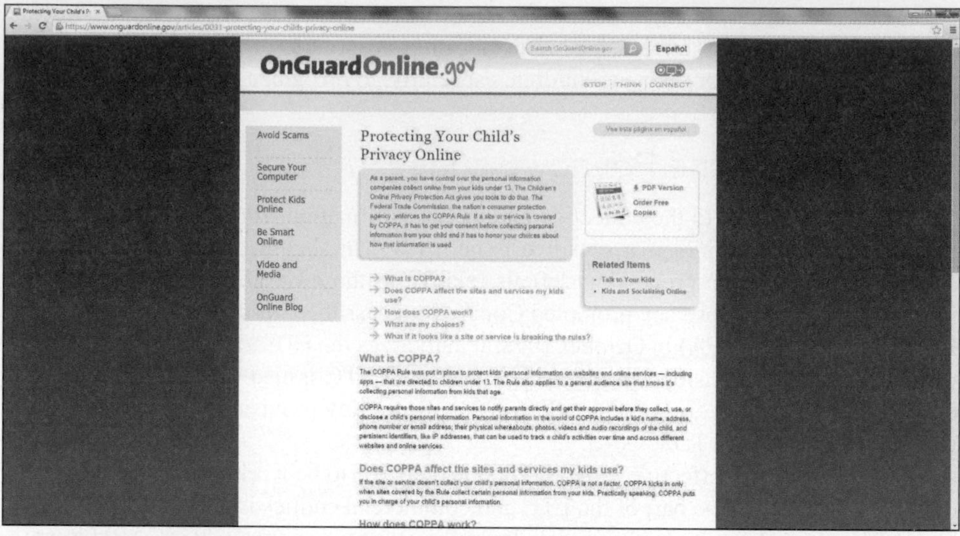

ILLUSTRATION 20-1

Education is an important aspect of the FTC's fight against online privacy invasion among children. OnGuardOnline.gov is designed to help parents protect their children's privacy.

The importance of consumer education also plays a prominent role in the FTC's approach. This can be seen in the fact that it has created an online learning tool on its website dedicated toward helping kids learn to be smarter consumers as part of its fight against online privacy invasion among children (see the OnGuardOnline.gov site shown in Illustration 20–1).

REGULATION AND MARKETING TO ADULTS

Regulation of marketing activities aimed at adults focuses on numerous issues including privacy, marketing communications, product features, and pricing practices. We deal with each of these in this section.

Consumer Privacy

LO3 There is increasing demand for regulation to protect the privacy of adults. Historically, concern was focused on offline issues such as the selling of subscription and customer lists, and the combination of that information with publicly available information to create powerful marketing databases. Today, the major focus of adult online privacy issues relates to the Internet and the way in which those earlier problems and issues are magnified given the speed and ease of information gathering and combination that is now possible. Companies argue that data collection and mining in order to offer a more targeted offering are beneficial to consumers. Consumer advocates often argue that such procedures are invasive. *Which side do you most agree with and why? Does it depend on what types of information are collected?*

With adult privacy issues, the FTC has been hesitant to craft specific legislation. Instead, it offered guidelines under a "notice and choice" approach, indicating that consumer-oriented commercial websites that collect personal identifying information from or about consumers should comply with four standards: (1) notice—of information collection and sharing practices, (2) choice—as to how personally identifying information (PII) is used,

New FTC Privacy Protection Framework

TABLE 20-4

Part 1: Privacy by Design: Companies should promote consumer privacy through their organizations and at every stage of the development of their products and services.

- Companies should incorporate substantive privacy protections into their practices, such as data security, reasonable collection limits, sound retention practices, and data accuracy.
- Companies should maintain comprehensive data management procedures throughout the life cycle of their products and services.

Part 2: Simplified Choice: Companies should simplify consumer choice.

- Companies do not need to provide choice before collecting and using consumers' data for commonly accepted practices such as product fulfillment.
- For practices requiring choice, companies should offer the choice at a time and in a context in which the consumer is making a decision about his or her data.

Part 3: Greater Transparency: Companies should increase the transparency of their data practices.

- Privacy notices should be clearer, shorter, and more standardized, to enable better comprehension and comparison of privacy practices.
- Companies should provide reasonable access to the consumer data they maintain; the extent of access should be proportionate to the sensitivity of the data and the nature of its use.
- Companies must provide prominent disclosures and obtain affirmative express consent before using consumer data in a materially different manner than claimed when the data was collected.
- All stakeholders should work to educate consumers about commercial data privacy practices.

Source: *Protecting Consumer Privacy in an Era of Rapid Change* (Washington, DC: Federal Trade Commission, December 2010).

(3) access—to their information and to correct or delete information, and (4) security—firms should ensure that the collected information is secure.

However, in response to the rapidly changing online environment, and in particular in response to the increased use of "covert" behavioral tracking and targeting of consumers online, the FTC has recently put forth a new framework and guidelines, as detailed in Table 20–4.

A major emerging aspect of privacy relates to consumer choice to have their online searching and browsing behavior tracked. This is dealt with in Part 2 of the FTC's new guidelines. In more specific language, the FTC offered the following comments:

> Most of us at the Commission believe that it's time for a Do Not Track mechanism with respect to third-party ads; that is, consumers should be able to choose whether or not to allow the collection of data about online searching and browsing.[32]

The FTC's new framework and guidelines are currently voluntary. However, the FTC chair made clear the need for companies to be proactive in their approach to this issue, stating:

> Some in the industry support what we're doing, but we know that others will claim that we are going too far. To those highly-paid professional naysayers, I have only one question: What are you for? Because it can't be the status quo on privacy.[33]

Marketing Communications

LO4 There are three major concerns focused on the information that marketers provide to consumers, generally in the form of advertisements: the accuracy of the information provided, the adequacy of the information provided, and the cumulative impact of marketing information on society's values. We will briefly look at advertising's impact on society's values before focusing on the accuracy and adequacy of consumer information.

Advertising and Values We discussed the impact of advertising on values in the previous section on advertising to children. The concern is the same for advertising directed at adults—the long-term effect of a constant flow of messages emphasizing materialistic or narcissistic values may be negative for both individuals and society. Many feel that the ads for Axe body products for men objectify young women. Indeed, major controversy erupted when it was discovered that Dove, the brand that is actively promoting realistic body images and offering resources to women to feel better about their physical appearance, is owned by Unilever, the same company that owns and markets Axe. The contradiction is readily apparent. Bloggers had a field day and even developed an ad that spoofed the original Dove ad in ways that played off the contradiction.[34]

Most ads for women's cosmetics and clothing emphasize beauty or sex appeal as major benefits. Each individual ad is probably harmless. However, critics charge that when people see such themes repeated thousands of times for hundreds of products, they learn to consider a person's looks to be more important than other attributes.[35] This can lead to injurious consumption patterns such as excessive tanning or inappropriate dieting despite knowledge of the associated health hazard.[36] These harmful effects may be most severe in younger women.[37] Further, those who cannot afford such products or who are not "good looking" suffer. Others argue that individuals have been concerned with their looks and possessions in virtually all cultures and times. They argue that advertising does not cause a society's values; it merely reflects them.

Portrayals of beauty and casual attitudes toward sex are not the only ways advertisements are argued to influence values. The portrayal of women in the mass media in general and in advertising in particular often has been limited to stereotypical roles or as decoration.[38] This in turn can influence the concepts girls develop of themselves and their role choices. Of course, many firms now portray females in a more positive, realistic fashion, as shown in Illustration 20–2.

A Nike campaign generated a positive response from many women as well as advertising critics. A television ad in the campaign combined quick camera takes and slow-motion shots of teenage girls on a playground, with images of girls playing on swing sets and monkey bars. The sound portion is a variety of girls' voices describing the long-term benefits of female participation in sports:

> I will like myself more; I will have more self-confidence if you let me play sports. If you let me play, I will be 60 percent less likely to get breast cancer. I will suffer less depression if you let me play sports.
>
> I will be more likely to leave a man who beats me. If you let me play, I will be less likely to get pregnant before I want to; I will learn what it means to be strong.[39]

The manner in which ethnic groups, the elderly, and other social groups are portrayed in ads and the mass media can affect the way members of these groups view themselves as well as the way others see them.[40] Marketers need to ensure that their ads reflect the diversity of the American society in a manner that is realistic and positive for all the many groups involved. These portrayals should involve both the content of the ads and the shows

ILLUSTRATION 20-2

Many firms now portray females in a more positive, realistic fashion.

sponsored by the ads.[41] For example, the relative absence of Hispanic roles and actors on network television has been an ongoing concern among Hispanics, although evidence suggests that this is changing.[42]

Consumer Information Accuracy The salesperson tells you, "My brand is the best there is." Does he or she need scientific proof to make such a statement? At what point does permissible puffery become misleading and illegal? Does it vary by the situation? The consumer group involved?[43]

An ad shows a pair of attractive female legs. The headline reads, "Her legs are insured for $1,000,000. Her policy came with one minor stipulation. Schick Silk Effects." Schick Silk Effects is a women's razor. How do you interpret this ad? Many would assume that the insurance company insisted on her using only this brand as a condition of the policy. This suggests that the insurance company considers this razor to be very good at protecting women's legs while they shave. However, in exceedingly fine print at the very bottom of the ad is this disclaimer: "Policy condition included by insurer at the request of Warner-Lambert Co." Warner-Lambert is the firm that markets Silk Effects. In other words, the firm that owns the razor had the requirement that this razor be used in the insurance policy. This leads to a very different interpretation of the ad. *Should this ad be illegal? Is it unethical?*

Because of such problems, various businesses, consumer groups, and regulatory agencies are deeply concerned with the interpretation of marketing messages and deceptive advertising. However, determining the exact meaning of a marketing message is not a simple process, nor is judging whether an ad is deceptive or not. Consumer Insight 20–1 tries to shed light on consumer deception by using a psychological framework.

Obtaining accurate assignments of meaning is made even more difficult by the variation in information-processing skills and motivations among different population groups.[44] For example, this warning was ruled inadequate in a product liability case involving a worker who was injured while inflating a truck tire:

> Always inflate tire in safety cage or use a portable lock ring guard. Use a clip-on type air chuck with remote valve so that operator can stand clear during tire inflation.

CONSUMER INSIGHT 20-1

Pragmatic Implications: A Psychological View of Deception

The FTC Act requires, among other things, that an advertisement must be truthful and nondeceptive, and advertisers must have evidence to back up their claims. It can be very difficult to understand when a marketing message is deceptive. One way to get a better handle on it is to understand that the FTC doesn't view only what is directly stated by an advertiser, but also what could be reasonably inferred by consumers in the given situation.[45] Specifically, there are direct claims and two types of implications that can be inferred from a claim. We illustrate with examples:

- *Direct claim:* Royal makes tires for the Jeep Liberty. If you have a Jeep Liberty and find that Royal doesn't make tires for the Jeep Liberty, this is a false claim.
- *Logical implication:* Royal makes tires for all SUVs. Because the Jeep Liberty is an SUV, if Royal doesn't make tires for the Jeep Liberty, this is again a false claim.

Direct claims and logical implications are relatively straightforward. If the evidence does not support the claim, the claim is said to be false.

However, another category of implications exists called pragmatic implications. **Pragmatic implications** *are the implied meanings (that are neither directly stated nor logically implied) that consumers derive when interpreting language in a "practical" way.* For example, if a friend tells you, when asked, that they "can" come right over to help you with a project, you might *infer* that this means they *will* come to help. Notice, however, that they didn't actually (directly) say they would help, only that they *could.* Your inference that they *would* help is called a pragmatic implication. Inferences are part of the perceptual process (Chapter 8). Let's go back to the Royal tires example one more time.

- *Pragmatic implication:* Need new tires for your Jeep Liberty? Royal can help.

Many consumers would *infer* from this claim that what Royal meant to say was that they have tires to fit the Jeep Liberty. But again, notice that they never directly made a claim to that effect. The question is, can Royal be held liable for deceptive advertising in this situation? The answer is yes if they don't indeed have tires

The court held that (1) "there is a duty to warn *foreseeable* users of all hidden dangers" and (2) "in view of the unskilled or semiskilled nature of the work and the existence of many in the workforce who do not read English, warnings *in the form of symbols* might have been appropriate since the employee's ability to take care of himself was limited."[46] Thus, marketers must often go to considerable lengths to provide messages that the relevant audience will interpret correctly.

Regulating the verbal content of ads is difficult. Regulating the more subtle meanings implied by the visual content of ads is much more difficult.[47] For example, some are critical of beer advertisements that portray active young adults in groups having fun and consuming beer. These critics contend that the visual message of these ads is that alcohol consumption is the appropriate way for young adults to be popular and have fun.

Both government and business self-regulatory groups have begun regulating visual communications.

- The FTC challenged ads for Beck's beer that featured young adults drinking on a sailing ship. It charged that the ads promoted unsafe marine conduct.
- The NAD required Balance Bar to drop all claims referring to clinical studies and *visuals of physicians* in its advertising after ruling that its formula was not proved to be "clinically effective for the general population."

to fit the Jeep Liberty because the FTC, when judging deception, looks not only at what is directly stated, but also at what a reasonable consumer might infer.

A few categories of pragmatic implications are:

- *Hedge words*—words that pragmatically imply something not literally stated. An example would be "Weedex fights weeds." Many consumers seeing this statement would likely believe that what is being claimed is that Weedex "kills" weeds. Because Weedex never directly claimed this, one might be tempted to say that they did not deceive consumers. But, if the FTC judged that, among other things, a consumer acting reasonably would infer that the claim meant "kill" and that in fact Weedex does not kill weeds (or Weedex doesn't have sufficient evidence to support that claim), it could deem the statement as deceptive advertising.
- *Juxtaposed imperatives*—this is a fancy way of saying that you put two unrelated statements together in a manner that makes them seem related and changes their meaning. Consider the following: "Have a safe winter. Drive on Royal tires." Many consumers seeing this claim would likely infer something to the effect that "using Royal tires will help me drive safer in the winter." However, what was directly stated was simply "Have a safe winter. . . ." and "Drive on Royal tires. . . ." Again, even though the claim was not directly made, the fact that it was indirectly made (through a pragmatic implication) means it could be judged as deceptive.

If this sounds complicated, it is. In some industries, like insurance, there are literally whole units dedicated to "policing" what their marketing materials say in order to ensure compliance in terms of the FTC Act and other state and federal laws that might apply. The bottom line in marketing communication is that "just because you don't state something directly, doesn't mean you didn't state it at all." And the law provides recourse for both false direct claims as well as false implied claims.

Critical Thinking Questions

1. In what way does understanding consumer perception help marketers avoid deceptive advertising?
2. Can you think of other techniques or methods that might generate pragmatic implications and thus put a marketer in danger of deceptive advertising?
3. What effects do you think occur when it is revealed via an FTC settlement that a firm was engaged in deception?

But issues regarding visual aspects can go even deeper. Illustration 20–3 shows a national brand and a competing brand with similar packages. *Are consumers misled by such packages? Or are these legitimate attempts to position competing products as being similar to the brand leaders?*[48]

Corrective advertising is advertising run by a firm to cause consumers to unlearn inaccurate information they acquired as a result of the firm's earlier advertising. Three examples of corrective advertising messages follow:

- "Do you recall some of our past messages saying that Domino sugar gives you strength, energy, and stamina? Actually, Domino is not a special or unique source of strength, energy, and stamina. No sugar is, because what you need is a balanced diet and plenty of rest and exercise."
- "If you've wondered what some of our earlier advertising meant when we said Ocean Spray cranberry juice cocktail has more food energy than orange juice or tomato juice, let us make it clear: we didn't mean vitamins and minerals. Food energy means calories. Nothing more."

  "Food energy is important at breakfast since many of us may not get enough calories, or food energy, to get off to a good start. Ocean Spray cranberry juice cocktail helps because it contains more food energy than most other breakfast drinks."

ILLUSTRATION 20-3

Is imitation the sincerest form of flattery or a source of consumer confusion?

"And Ocean Spray cranberry juice cocktail gives you and your family vitamin C plus a great wake-up taste. It's . . . the other breakfast drink."

- Sugar Information, Inc.: "Do you recall the messages we brought you in the past about sugar? How something with sugar in it before meals could help you curb your appetite? We hope you didn't get the idea that our little diet tip was any magic formula for losing weight. Because there are no tricks or shortcuts; the whole diet subject is very complicated. Research hasn't established that consuming sugar before meals will contribute to weight reduction or even keep you from gaining weight."

Although the effectiveness of corrective advertising has been debated, the FTC considers it a useful tool in protecting the public. Likewise, firms injured by the false claims of competitors often request it as a remedy. Indeed, the threat of lawsuits by competitors can serve as a strong deterrent of comparative advertising. For example, Procter & Gamble is revisiting its aggressive advertising strategy across its various brands in light of all the substantial litigation it has created (e.g., lawsuits by Playtex, J&J-Merck, Kimberly-Clark, and Georgia Pacific).[49]

Adequacy of Consumer Information It is important that consumers have not only accurate information but adequate information as well. To ensure information adequacy, a number of laws have been passed, such as the federal truth-in-lending legislation.

Nutritional labeling has been required for years and was significantly revised in 1990. Research findings on the impact of such labels are mixed, but the labels do provide valuable information to many consumers. A consistent stream of consumer behavior research since these rules were enacted has uncovered a number of potential improvements in the manner in which the information should be presented. Unfortunately, as with many such programs, those who are relatively disadvantaged in terms of education and income are least able to use this type of information.[50]

A more recent FDA labeling rule deals with trans fats. While the Nutritional Labeling and Education Act (NLEA) of 1990 led to the nutrition fact box on food packaging that includes a line for total fat, this rule requires a line for trans fats as well. The logic behind this change, which involves costs to companies in terms of research into trans fat content and label redesign, is explained here:

> The latest health threat is so-called trans fats, which are hydrogenated oils used to make margarine, deep fried foods, cookies, cakes and crackers. They give foods the texture consumers expect, and help foods stay fresh longer than alternative ingredients. Trans fats have an effect similar to saturated fats in the body and raise the level of LDL (bad) cholesterol, but they also lower HDL (good) cholesterol levels. Because of this, the U.S. Food and Drug Administration . . . issued a ruling requiring food manufacturers to modify their package labels to reflect the *total amount* of trans fats used in their products.[51]

ILLUSTRATION 20-4

The trans fat rule requires packaging adaptations by companies and serves as a way for certain brands to differentiate themselves from the competition on an attribute of importance to consumers.

Obviously, this ruling provides opportunities for some food marketers and challenges for others. Given consumer health concerns, marketers of products such as Edy's (Illustration 20–4) can use trans fats as a point of differentiation not just in the nutrition facts box but also in more prominent locations on the container.

Marketers, consumer groups, and public officials would like consumers to have all the information they need to make sound choices. One approach is to provide all potentially relevant information. This approach is frequently recommended by regulatory agencies and is required for some product categories such as drugs.

Problems with this approach can arise, however. The assumption behind full disclosure is that each consumer will utilize those specific information items required for the particular decision. Unfortunately, consumers frequently do not react in this manner. This is true particularly for low-involvement purchases but can also be true of higher-involvement purchases as well. Instead, consumers may experience *information overload* (Chapter 8) and ignore all or most of the available data. The Clarasonic ad shown in Illustration 20–5 was designed to chunk information to help reduce information overload.

In the drug category, relatively simple print ads require attached disclosures, usually printed in small type, telling of dosage, precautions, and warnings in order to comply with federal full-disclosure regulations. Many marketers claim that such ads add to the costs of advertising and therefore reduce the available consumer information without an offset in consumer benefit.[52] Many consumer advocates agree that the current approach is not meeting the needs of consumers.

In the area of online privacy policies, which appear to be increasing in length, there is considerable variation in format that can affect consumer information overload and comprehension.[53] The FTC has made this a part of their new framework (see Table 20–4).

A new issue confronting marketers and regulators is disclosure in Internet advertising. Disclosure involves providing relevant qualifiers to advertising claims such as "limited to stock on hand" or "available at participating outlets only." The FTC requires disclosures to be "clear and conspicuous," and this standard has been translated into clear guidelines for print, television, and radio ads. The FTC provides the following general guidelines to online marketers. *Are these general guidelines enough?*

- Place the disclosure near the claim it is qualifying.
- Make the disclosure prominent.
- Avoid having other aspects distract from the disclosure.
- Repeat the disclosure if ad length warrants it.

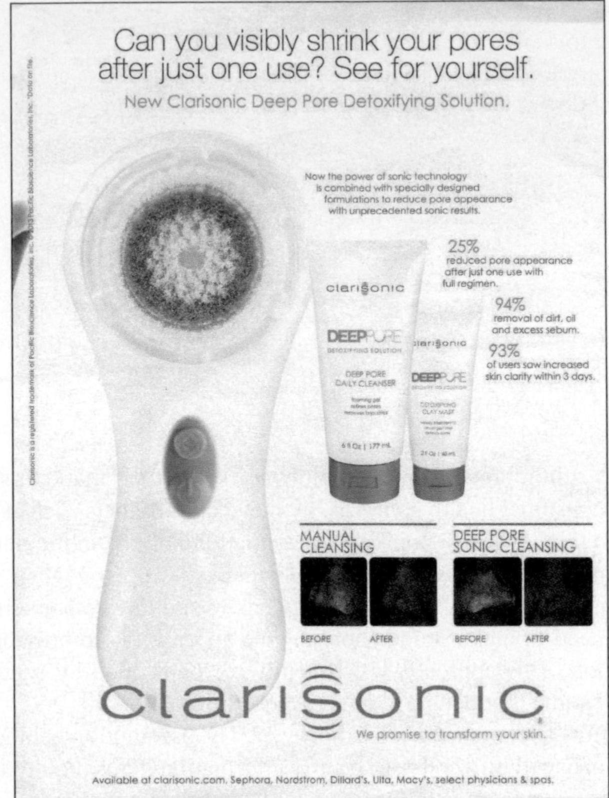

ILLUSTRATION 20-5

This Clarasonic ad is an example of how organizing information in certain ways can reduce information overload.

- Make sure disclosures are adequate in volume, size, and duration.
- Make the language of the disclosure understandable to the intended audience.

Product Issues

LO5 Consumer groups have two major concerns with products: *Are they safe?* and *Are they environmentally sound?* A variety of federal and state agencies are involved in ensuring that products are safe to use. The most important are the Food and Drug Administration and the Consumer Product Safety Commission. Product safety is generally not a controversial issue. However, it is impossible to remove all risk from products.

Should tricycles be banned? Accidents involving tricycles are a major cause of injury to young children. Manufacturers, consumer groups, and individuals differ on where the line should be drawn and who should draw it. Some feel that tricycles should indeed be banned. Others feel that parents should decide if their children should ride tricycles. However, both would agree that information on both the risks of tricycle riding and ways of reducing the risk should be made available to purchasers, though there is disagreement on who should make the information available and how it should be made available. Of course, tricycles represent only one of many products subject to such a debate.

We examined consumers' desires for environmentally sound products in some detail in Chapter 3. As indicated there, many consumers want products whose production, use, and disposition produce minimal environmental harm. Many marketers are striving to produce such products. Nonetheless, consumer groups continue to push for more stringent regulation in this area.

Potentially injurious products such as guns, tobacco products, and alcoholic beverages are subject to a wide variety of regulations at the federal, state, and even city levels. The FDA recently unveiled new package designs for cigarettes to be in place by 2012 in which half of the package must be covered by a verbal warning accompanied by a visual "warning" such as a picture of damaged teeth or lungs.[54]

Pricing Issues

Consumer groups want prices that are fair (generally defined as competitively determined) and accurately stated (contain no hidden charges). The FTC is the primary federal agency involved in regulating pricing activities.

Perhaps the most controversial pricing area today is the use of reference prices. An **external reference price** is *a price provided by the manufacturer or retailer in addition to the actual current price of the product.* Such terms as "compare at $X," "usually $X," "suggested retail price $Y—our price only $X" are common ways of presenting reference prices (see Chapter 17). The concern arises when the reference price is one at which no or few sales actually occur. Most states and the federal government have regulations concerning the use of reference prices, but they are difficult to enforce. Given the history of abuse of reference prices, it is not surprising that many consumers are skeptical of them.

SUMMARY

SMARTBOOK

LO1: Explain the two major concerns in marketing to children that CARU deals with

Marketing to children is a major concern to regulators and consumer groups. One major reason for this concern is evidence based on Piaget's theory of cognitive development that children are not able to fully comprehend commercial messages. Comprehension here has two dimensions. The first is that children often don't understand the persuasive intent of commercials. The second is that children often don't comprehend specific words and phrases. A second reason for concern over marketing to children is the potential effects it has on their safety and values. *CARU (Children's Advertising Review Unit of the Better Business Bureau)* has specific voluntary guidelines by which it evaluates advertisements targeted at children.

LO2: Describe the various marketing activities aimed at children that are controversial

There are a number of marketing activities aimed at children other than television advertising that cause concerns. Marketing to children through mobile devices is an emerging concern. Corporate programs that place strong sales messages in "educational" materials supplied to schools have also come under attack. Children's advocates are now particularly concerned about marketing to children on the Internet. The federal government has passed legislation to protect children's online privacy called *COPPA (Children's Online Privacy Protection Act).* CARU also has guidelines on this topic.

LO3: Discuss new guidelines by the FTC regarding online privacy protection for adults

With adult privacy issues, the FTC has been hesitant to craft specific legislation. However, in response to the rapidly changing online environment, and in particular in response to the increased use of "covert" behavioral tracking and targeting of consumers online, the FTC has recently put forth a new framework and guidelines that deal with designing privacy into organizations, simplifying consumer choice in the area of privacy, and offering greater transparency and simplicity to privacy practices and statements.

A major emerging aspect of privacy relates to consumer choice to have their online searching and browsing behavior tracked. The FTC is supportive of a Do Not Track approach to this issue, which would allow consumers to opt out if they wish.

LO4: Explain marketing communication issues related to adults including deceptive advertising

There is concern about the cumulative effect of advertising on adult values just as there is with children. In addition, regulators and businesses alike are concerned that adults receive accurate and adequate information about products. Accuracy of information relates to deceptive advertising, and it is important to keep in mind that the FTC examines ads in terms of the truthfulness of both direct claims and implications. *Pragmatic implications* are one form of implication and *are the implied meanings (that are neither directly stated nor logically implied) that consumers derive when interpreting language in a "practical" way.*

Regulation is also focused on the amount of information provided. The assumption that appears to underlie much of this legislation is that more or full information is desirable. However, intuition and research suggest that too much information can lead to overload and suboptimal consumer outcomes.

LO5: Discuss regulation concerns when marketing to adults as they relate to product and price

The focus of consumer concern and regulation of products is twofold: (1) Are they safe? and (2) Are they environmentally sound? Concern with pricing is that prices be fair and accurately presented in a manner that allows comparison across brands.

KEY TERMS

Children's Advertising Review Unit (CARU) 709
Children's Online Privacy Protection Act (COPPA) 715
Corrective advertising 721
External reference price 725
Pragmatic implications 720

REVIEW QUESTIONS

1. What are the major concerns in marketing to children?
2. What are the main issues concerning children's ability to comprehend advertising messages?
3. What is *CARU?* What does it do? What are some of its rules?
4. What are the major concerns about the *content* of commercial messages targeting children?
5. What are the issues concerning the impact of advertising on children's health and safety?
6. What are the issues concerning the impact of advertising on children's values?
7. What are the concerns associated with mobile marketing to children?
8. What is meant by "commercialization of schools"? What are the various areas in which commercialization can occur, and what are the major concerns?
9. Why are consumer advocates worried about marketing to kids on the Internet?
10. Describe the key provisions of The Rules under *COPPA.*
11. How would you go about deciding if COPPA has been effective?
12. What are the major concerns with marketing communications targeting adults?
13. What are the issues concerning the impact of advertising on adults' *values?*
14. What is a pragmatic implication and how does it relate to information accuracy and deception?
15. What are the concerns with *consumer information adequacy?*

16. What is *information overload?*
17. What is *corrective advertising?*
18. What are the FTC's general guidelines for "clear and conspicuous" *disclosure* in an online setting?
19. What are the major regulatory issues with respect to products?
20. What are the major regulatory issues with respect to prices?
21. What is a *reference price?* What is the concern with reference prices?

DISCUSSION QUESTIONS

22. A television advertisement for General Mills' Total cereal made the following claim: "It would take 16 ounces of the leading natural cereal to equal the vitamins in 1 ounce of fortified Total." The Center for Science in the Public Interest filed a petition against General Mills claiming that the advertisement is deceptive. It was the center's position that the claim overstated Total's nutritional benefits because the cereal is not 16 times higher in other factors important to nutrition.
    a. Is the claim misleading? Justify your answer.
    b. How should the FTC proceed in cases such as this?
    c. What are the implications of cases such as this for marketing management?
23. Turkey ham looks like ham and tastes like ham but it contains no pork; it is all turkey. A nationwide survey of consumers showed that most believed the meat product contained both turkey and ham. The USDA approved this label based on a dictionary definition for the term *ham:* the thigh cut of meat from the hind leg of any animal. Discuss how consumers processed information concerning this product and used this information in purchasing this product. (One court ruled the label to be misleading but was overruled by a higher court.)
    a. Is the label misleading?
    b. How should the FTC proceed in such cases?
24. How much and what type of (if any) advertising should be allowed on television programs aimed at children of the following ages?
    a. Under 6
    b. 6 to 9
    c. 10 to 12
25. Are the self-regulatory attempts by the food and beverage industry enough in regard to regulating food marketing to children? What, if any, additional actions would you propose? Explain.
26. Does advertising influence children's values? What can the FTC or CARU do to ensure that positive values are promoted? Be precise in your response.
27. What rules, if any, should govern mobile marketing to children?
28. What rules, if any, should govern marketing to kids on the Internet?
29. What rules, if any, should govern advertising and promotional messages presented in the classroom?
30. Does advertising influence or reflect a society's values?
31. Do you agree that beer advertisements portraying groups of active young adults having fun while consuming beer teach people that the way to be popular and have fun is to consume alcohol?
32. Respond to the questions in Consumer Insight 20–1.
33. Do you think corrective advertising works? Evaluate the three corrective messages described in the text.
34. "Because riding tricycles is a major cause of accidental injury to young children, the product should be banned." State and defend your position on this issue (the first part of the statement is true).
35. To what extent, if at all, do you use nutrition labels to guide your purchases? Why?
36. Do you believe reference prices generally reflect prices at which substantial amounts of the product are normally sold? Does this vary by store, season, or other circumstances?

APPLICATION ACTIVITIES

37. Watch two hours of Saturday morning children's programming on a commercial channel (not public broadcasting). Note how many commercials are run. What products are involved? What are the major themes? Would hundreds of hours of viewing these commercials over the course of several years have any impact on children's values or behaviors?
38. With parental consent, interview a child 2 to 4 years of age, one between 5 and 7, and one between 8 and 10. Determine their understanding of the selling intent and techniques of television commercials.
39. Interview two grade-school teachers and get their responses to material provided by corporations and the level of educational versus commercial content.
40. Repeat Question 37 for prime-time television and adults.
41. Find and copy or describe an ad that you feel is misleading. Explain why.
42. Visit a large supermarket. Considering both cost and nutrition, identify the best and worst breakfast cereal focused on children. What do you conclude?

REFERENCES

1. This opener is based on J. Hyde, "Toyota's $1.2 Billion Fine, GM Recall Highlight Defects in U.S. Auto Safety," *Motoramic,* March 19, 2014, http://autos.yahoo.com/blogs/motoramic/toyota-s--1-2-billion-fine--gm-recall-highlight-defects-in-u-s--auto-safety-164518294.html, accessed August 29, 2014; J. Aleccia, "Hot Pockets Included in Massive Meat Recall," *NBC News,* February 18, 2014, www.nbcnews.com/health/health-news/hot-pockets-included-massive-meat-recall-n33241, accessed August 29, 2014; T. W. Martin, "Dangers from Compounding Pharmacies Persist," *The Wall Street Journal,* September 9, 2013, http://online.wsj.com/news/articles/SB10001424127887324324404579041001254487312, accessed August 29, 2014; A. Zulueta, "Massive Fake Health and Beauty Supplies Ring Busted," *CNN,* March 9, 2014, www.cnn.com/2014/03/08/justice/new-york-counterfeit-beauty-supplies/, accessed August 29, 2014; S. Hargreaves, "Counterfeit Goods Becoming More Dangerous, *CNN,* September 27, 2012, http://money.cnn.com/2012/09/27/news/economy/counterfeit-goods/, accessed August 29, 2014; G. McCraken, "Culture and Consumption: A Theoretical Account of the Structure and Movement of the Cultural Meaning of Consumer Goods," *Journal of Consumer Research,* 1986, pp. 71–84; F. Gino, M. I. Norton, and D. Ariely, "The Counterfeit Self: The Deceptive Costs of Faking It," *Psychological Science,* 21 (2010), pp. 712–20; and Ernesto, "Six Strikes Anti-Piracy Scheme Turns One Year, but Does It Work?," *TorrentFreak,* February 25, 2014, http://torrentfreak.com/six-strikes-anti-piracy-scheme-turns-one-year-140225/, accessed August 29, 2014.
2. For an overview of this area, see S. Bandyopadhyay, G. Kindra, and L. Sharp, "Is Television Advertising Good for Children?," *International Journal of Advertising,* 20, no. 1 (2001), pp. 89–116.
3. See D. R. John, "Consumer Socialization of Children," *Journal of Consumer Research,* December 1999, pp. 183–209.
4. *Self-Regulatory Program for Children's Advertising* (New York: Children's Advertising Review Unit (CARU), Council of Better Business Bureaus, 2009).
5. See M. C. Martin, "Children's Understanding of the Intent of Advertising," *Journal of Public Policy & Marketing,* Fall 1997, pp. 205–16.
6. L. Carlson, R. N. Laczniak, and D. D. Muehling, "Understanding Parental Concern about Toy-Based Programming," *Journal of Current Issues and Research in Advertising,* Fall 1994, pp. 59–72.
7. M. A. Stutts and G. G. Hunnicutt, "Can Young Children Understand Disclaimers?," *Journal of Advertising,* 16, no. 1 (1987), pp. 41–46.
8. R. H. Kolbe and D. D. Muehling, "An Investigation of the Fine Print in Children's Television Advertising," *Journal of Current Issues and Research in Advertising,* Fall 1995, pp. 77–95; and D. D. Muehling and R. H. Kolbe, "A Comparison of Children's and Prime-Time Fine-Print Advertising Disclosure Practices," *Journal of Advertising,* Fall 1998, pp. 37–47.
9. CARU, Council of Better Business Bureaus, "CARU Recommends Nintendo Modify Advertising for Wii Game System, Game," January 30, 2008.
10. CARU, Council of Better Business Bureaus, "Nabisco Puts Safety First in TV Ads," October 4, 2000.
11. *Self-Regulatory Program for Children's Advertising.*
12. CARU, Council of Better Business Bureaus, "Skechers USA, Inc. Appeals CARU Decision," April 10, 2002.
13. CARU, Council of Better Business Bureaus, "CARU Recommends Guthy-Renker Discontinue Advertising Proactiv to Children," June 9, 2008.
14. "B-M Drops Spots after Query by NAD," *Advertising Age,* April 20, 1981, p. 10.
15. See C. Preston, "The Unintended Effects of Advertising upon Children," *International Journal of Advertising,* 18, no. 3 (1999), pp. 363–76.
16. H. Clinton, "FTC Action," *Advertising Age,* October 9, 2000, p. 58. For an opposing view, see R. Bergler, "The Effects of Commercial Advertising on Children," *International Journal of Advertising,* 18, no. 4 (1999), pp. 411–25.
17. "Advertising Strategies to Target Kids Raise Questions," *10News.com,* July 11, 2005.
18. See, e.g., *The Role of Media in Childhood Obesity* (Washington, DC: Kaiser Family Foundation); and P. M. Ippolito, *TV*

Advertising to Children 1977 v. 2004 (Washington, DC: Bureau of Economics, FTC, Research Presentation, July 14, 2005).

19. M. M. Cardona, "Young Girls Targeted by Makeup Companies," *Advertising Age,* November 27, 2000, p. 15.
20. M. Scott, "Girls Clamoring for Grown-up Shoe Styles," *Marketing News,* November 19, 2001, p. 25.
21. M. Irvine, "More Young Children Fret over Body Image," *Eugene Register Guard,* July 23, 2001, p. 1.
22. S. W. Colford, "Top Kid TV Offender: Premiums," *Advertising Age,* April 29, 1991, p. 52.
23. *Guidance for Food Advertising Self-Regulation* (New York: National Advertising Review Council, White Paper, May 28, 2004).
24. See K. Anders, "Marketing and Policy Considerations for Violent Video Games," *Journal of Public Policy & Marketing,* Fall 1999, pp. 270–73; I. Teinowitz, "FTC Report Refuels Debate on Violent Entertainment," *Advertising Age,* April 30, 2001, p. 4; I. Teinowitz, "Violence Revisited," *Advertising Age,* December 3, 2001, p. 3; and I. Teinowitz, "Entertainment Gets a Pass," *Advertising Age,* December 10, 2001, p. 16.
25. Y. Noguchi, "Connecting with Kids, Wirelessly," *Washington Post,* July 7, 2005, p. A1.
26. Commercial Alert, "Children's Advocates Ask Congress to Investigate Marketing of Mobile Phones to Kids," press release, July 26, 2005, www.commercialalert.org.
27. Classification scheme and descriptions come from *Captive Kids* (Yonkers, NY: Consumers Union, 1995 Research Report, copyright 1998). Additional content from J. E. Brand and B. S. Greenberg, "Commercials in the Classroom," *Journal of Advertising Research,* January 1994, pp. 18–27; I. Teinowitz, "Marketer Obesity Efforts Get Low Consumer Marks," *AdAge.com,* June 7, 2005; S. Thompson, "Pepsi Hits High Note with Students," *Advertising Age,* October 9, 2000, p. 30; S. Jarvis, "Lesson Plans," *Marketing News,* June 18, 2001, p. 1.; M. M. Cardona, "High School Papers Group to Take Ads," *Advertising Age,* March 29, 2004, p. 13; and A. Enright, "Food, Drink Firms Take New Path to Reach Youths in, out of Class," *Marketing News,* August 15, 2006, pp. 8–10.
28. J. Pereira, "Junk-Food Games," *The Wall Street Journal,* May 3, 2004, pp. B1.
29. CARU, Council of Better Business Bureaus, "Echo Participates in CARU Process," May 21, 2008.
30. CARU, Council of Better Business Bureaus, "CARU Refers Fansite of Singer Pink to Federal Trade Commission," April 10, 2002.
31. CARU, Council of Better Business Bureaus, "CARU Refers fbfkids, fbfkiddies to FTC for Further Review," March 17, 2011.
32. *Preliminary FTC Staff Privacy Report* (Washington, DC: Federal Trade Commission, December 1, 2010).
33. Ibid.
34. See, e.g., M. Gillett, "A Company's Ugly Contradition," *Boston Globe,* November 5, 2007.
35. See B. G. Englis, M. R. Solomon, and R. D. Ashmore, "Beauty *before* the Eyes of Beholders," *Journal of Advertising,* June 1994, pp. 49–64; C. R. Wiles, J. A. Wiles, and A. Tjernlund, "The Ideology of Advertising," *Journal of Advertising Research,* May 1996, pp. 57–66; M. C. Martin and J. W. Gentry, "Stuck in the Model Trap," *Journal of Advertising,* Summer 1997, pp. 19–33; M. K. Hogg, M. Bruce, and K. Hough, "Female Images in Advertising," *International Journal of Advertising,* 18, no. 4 (1999), pp. 445–73; and T. Reichert, "The Prevalence of Sexual Imagery in Ads Targeted to Young Adults," *Journal of Consumer Affairs,* Winter 2003, pp. 403–12.
36. S. Burton, R. G. Netemeyer, and D. R. Lichtenstein, "Gender Differences for Appearance-Related Attitudes and Behaviors," *Journal of Public Policy & Marketing,* Fall 1994, pp. 60–75.
37. R. Gustafson, M. Popovich, and S. Thompson, "Subtle Ad Images Threaten Girls More," *Marketing News,* June 4, 2001, p. 12.
38. For research in these areas, see R. W. Pollay and S. Lysonski, "In the Eye of the Beholder," *Journal of International Consumer Marketing,* 6, no. 2 (1993), pp. 25–43; D. Walsh, "Safe Sex in Advertising," *American Demographics,* April 1994, pp. 24–30; and R. H. Kolbe and D. Muehling, "Gender Roles and Children's Television Advertising," *Journal of Current Issues and Research in Advertising,* Spring 1995, pp. 49–64.
39. C. Rubel, "Marketers Giving Better Treatment to Females," *Marketing News,* April 22, 1996, p. 10.
40. See L. Langmeyer, "Advertising Images of Mature Adults," *Journal of Current Issues and Research in Advertising,* Fall 1993, pp. 81–91; C. R. Taylor and J. Y. Lee, "Not in *Vogue,*" *Journal of Public Policy & Marketing,* Fall 1994, pp. 239–45; T. H. Stevenson and P. E. McIntyre, "A Comparison of the Portrayal and Frequency of Hispanics and Whites in English Language Television Advertising," *Journal of Current Issues and Research in Advertising,* Spring 1995, pp. 65–74; M. T. Elliott, "Differences in the Portrayal of Blacks," *Journal of Current Issues and Research in Advertising,* Spring 1995, pp. 75–86; J. M. Bristor, R. G. Lee, and M. R. Hunt, "Race and Ideology," *Journal of Public Policy & Marketing,* Spring 1995, pp. 48–59; E. J. Wilson and A. Biswas, "The Use of Black Models in Specialty Catalogs," *Journal of Direct Marketing,* Autumn 1995, pp. 47–56; and K. Karande and A. Grbavac, "Acculturation and the Use of Asian Models in Print Advertisements," in *Enhancing Knowledge Development in Marketing,* ed. C. Droge and R. Calantone (Chicago: American Marketing Association, 1996), pp. 347–52.
41. See L. J. Shrum, "Television and Persuasion," *Psychology & Marketing,* March 1999, pp. 119–40.
42. See, e.g., *Fall Colors* (Oakland, CA: Children Now, 2003–04).
43. See A. Simonson and M. B. Holbrook, "Permissible Puffery versus Actionable Warranty in Advertising and Salestalk," *Journal of Public Policy & Marketing,* Fall 1993, pp. 216–33.
44. C. A. Cole and G. J. Gaeth, "Cognitive and Age-Related Differences in the Ability to Use Nutritional Information in a Complex Environment," *Journal of Marketing Research,* May 1990, pp. 175–84; and W. Mueller, "Who Reads the Label?," *American Demographics,* January 1991, pp. 36–40.
45. R. J. Harris, "Comprehension of Pragmatic Implications in Advertising," *Journal of Applied Psychology,* 62, no. 5 (1977), pp. 603–608; G. J. Gaeth and T. B. Heath, "The Cognitive Processing of Misleading Advertising in Young and Old Adults," *Journal of Consumer Research,* June 1987, pp. 43–54; I. L. Preston, *The Tangled Web They Weave* (Madison, WI: University of Wisconsin Press, 1994); and *Advertising FAQ's: A Guide for Small Business* (Washington, DC: Federal Trade Commission, 2001).

46. B. Reid, "Adequacy of Symbolic Warnings," *Marketing News,* October 25, 1985, p. 3.
47. See G. V. Johar, "Consumer Involvement and Deception from Implied Advertising Campaigns," *Journal of Marketing Research,* August 1995, pp. 267–79.
48. See J.-N. Kapferer, "Brand Confusion," *Psychology & Marketing,* September 1995, pp. 551–68; and D. J. Howard, R. A. Kerin, and C. Gengler, "The Effects of Brand Name Similarity on Brand Source Confusion," *Journal of Public Policy & Marketing,* Fall 2000, pp. 250–64.
49. S. Ellison and B. Steinberg, "P&G Is Settling Disputes on Ads as Suits Pile Up," *The Wall Street Journal,* November 26, 2003, pp. B1, B3.
50. See, e.g., A. Mitra et al., "Can the Educationally Disadvantaged Interpret the FDA-Mandated Nutrition Facts Panel?," *Journal of Public Policy & Marketing,* Spring 1999, pp. 106–17; J. A. Garretson and S. Burton, "Effects of Nutrition Facts Panel Values, Nutrition Claims, and Health Claims," *Journal of Public Policy & Marketing,* Fall 2000, pp. 213–27; G. Baltas, "The Effects of Nutrition Information on Consumer Choice," *Journal of Advertising Research,* March 2001, pp. 57–63; and S. K. Balasubramanian and C. Cole, "Consumers' Search and Use of Nutrition Information," *Journal of Marketing,* July 2002, pp. 112–27.
51. D. L. Vence, "The Lowdown on Trans Fats," *Marketing News,* March 15, 2004, pp. 13–14.
52. See M. Wilkie, "Rx Marketers 'Test' FDA Guides on Print DTC Ads," *Advertising Age,* April 6, 1998, p. 18.
53. G. R. Milne, M. J. Culnan, and H. Greene, "A Longitudinal Assessment of Online Privacy Notice Readability," *Journal of Public Policy and Marketing,* Fall 2006, pp. 238–49.
54. S. Young, "FDA Reveals Bigger, Graphic Warning Labels for Cigarette Packages," *CNN.com,* June 21, 2011.

Part Six CASES

6–1 ABERCROMBIE SELLS ASHLEY PUSH-UP TRIANGLE BIKINI TOPS TO TWEENS

Tweens [8–14 years old] make up a large market and possess considerable purchasing power. Not surprisingly then, marketers are paying increasing attention to this segment. However, targeting tweens is not without controversy. Recently, Abercrombie & Fitch introduced padded bikini tops that came in sizes that fit girls as young as eight years old. Parent groups were outraged by the swimsuit tops that were originally marketed as "pushup triangles," and there was an immediate public backlash against Abercrombie. Consider the follow comments posted on Abercrombie's website:

- Shame on you for sexualizing small children.
- In a world where parents work hard to keep their children safe, you go and make little girls look like they have breasts? Perverts.

In response, Abercrombie & Fitch repositioned the bikini tops as "lightly lined" and changed the suggested age range to 12 years or older. Eventually, the particular garment was removed from the website entirely.

Abercrombie & Fitch is no stranger to controversy involving youthful consumers. In the fall of 2010, after a seven-year hiatus, they resumed publication of their *A&F Quarterly,* which features young people in group settings while in various stages of undress. Public reactions compared the publication to soft pornography and suggested that it encourages group sex among teens. In 2002, Abercrombie & Fitch had a similar controversy over their sales of child-sized thong underwear, printed with slogans such as "eye candy" and "wink wink." Abercrombie & Fitch unapologetically declined to recall the underwear:

> The underwear for young girls was created with the intent to be lighthearted and cute. Any misrepresentation of that is purely in the eye of the beholder.

Parents and child advocates worry that marketers and the media are instilling and reinforcing unhealthy gender stereotypes among tweens and teens through their portrayal of all females as sexy fashionistas who obsess over shopping and celebrities, and of all males as constant tough guys who are preoccupied with video games, cars, and sports. Abercrombie & Fitch's stunts routinely spur boycotts and outrage among the media and parents as their brand image suffers.

Estimates of tweens' purchasing power range from \$43 billion to \$51 billion. Tween girls routinely spend personal funds on cosmetic products that are specifically developed for them by firms, including brands such as Lip Smackers and Mary Kate and Ashley. This massive purchasing power comes primarily from allowances and gifts, and provides influence over the way families make spending decisions. Tweens also play an important role in how their parents spend an additional \$170 billion on them each year. They also often influence major family purchases, such as vacations and computers.

The consumer behavior of the tween market is separate and distinct from the child and teen markets. Tweens are image-conscious and are willing to pay a premium for the latest craze. As a way to encourage acceptance among their peers, tweens tend to imitate popular styles and those worn by their favorite pop stars. Tweens want to look like their peers, yet retain their own individual style. For example, clothing brands that offer a variety of colors of the same cool style of clothing are popular among tweens. Tweens are also driven by the desire for higher quantities of similar or same products. Tweens often collect many varieties of the same type of accessory, such as bracelets and necklaces. According to Nita Rollins, the head of marketing intelligence at the digital marketing agency Resource Interactive:

> More is more. Nothing succeeds like excess. . . . [Tweens] aren't aware of social codes of restraint, so they see no reason why they don't need 10 American Girl dolls or several pairs of jeans or sneakers.

Finally, tweens are very socially and environmentally conscious. Consider: All of their short lives, tweens have heard cause-related and green marketing messages and naturally are concerned about the environmental and social impacts of the products they consume.

According to Ken Nisch, the chair of the retail consulting and design firm JGA:

> [Tweens] feel the pain of everybody. They want to know if animals were hurt in making this. They have social consciousness at a very young age. They have great lives, and so they want to give back.

Discussion Questions

1. Marketing to tweens brings some ethical concerns to the forefront. Chapter 6 discusses Piaget's stages of cognitive development.
   a. Which of Piaget's stages covers tweens?
   b. How well are tweens able to comprehend abstract concepts, such as objectification of women?
2. Examine the actions of Abercrombie & Fitch from the perspective of the CARU guidelines presented in Chapter 20. Which guidelines most relate to concerns over their targeting of young girls with products more appropriate for adults?
3. Chapter 3 discusses several key American values. Which of these values are being triggered by critics of Abercrombie & Fitch who react negatively to products such as padded bikini tops for tweens? Why?
4. Chapter 6 discusses the consumer socialization process. Some people feel consumer socialization is a responsibility of the parents, while others feel that marketers help socialize children as consumers by targeting them. What can parents of tweens do to ensure that their children are socialized as consumers in a positive way when they are faced with marketplace options that include risqué clothing for children?
5. Chapter 6 discusses family decision making and family purchase roles. What roles do tweens play in family decision making? How do roles of tweens differ in different purchasing contexts?
6. Using the information in this case and the description of tweens in the text, imagine you are marketing sparkly lip gloss. What ethical issues should be considered when developing persuasive messages targeted at this audience?

Source: "Abercrombie's Sexy Undies 'Slip,'" *CNN Money,* May 28, 2002, http://money.cnn.com; J. O'Donnell, "As Kids Get Savvy, Marketers Move Down the Age Scale," *USA Today,* April 13, 2007, www.usatoday.com; C. Sweene, "Never Too Young for That First Pedicure," *New York Times,* February 28, 2008, www.nytimes.com; K. Reynolds, "Tweens and the Retail Market," *University of Alabama,* 2009, www.ua.edu/ features/tween/economy .html; "Marketing and Consumerism: Special Issue for Teens and Tweens," *Media Awareness Network,* 2010, www.media-awareness.ca; L. Chernicoff, "Exclusive Inside the New Abercrombie & Fitch Quarterly," *Fashionista .com,* June 24, 2010, http://fashionista.com; N. Mandel, "Padded Swimsuits for All? Abercrombie and Fitch Marketing Padded Tops to Young Girls," *NYDailyNews.com,* March 27, 2011, http://articles.nydailynews.com; L. Dishman, "Abercrombie's Padded Bikinis for Tweens Prove There's Nothing New Under the Retail Sun," *CBS Interactive Business Network,* March 28, 2011, www.bnet.com; and J. McCarthy, "Abercrombie Responds to Tween Bikinigate," March 29, 2011, *iVillage.com,* www.ivillage.com.

6–2 CHILDREN'S ONLINE PRIVACY PROTECTION

Table A provides a grid that can be used to evaluate how well various websites targeted toward children under 13 years of age adhere to The Rules under COPPA (Children's Online Privacy Protection Act).* Each row represents one of the key provisions of The Rules under COPPA (for more detail on each provision, see Table 20–3). Each column represents a different company website.

Each company website can be rated in terms of its adherence to each COPPA provision on the following scale: 1 = very poor; 2 = poor; 3 = adequate; 4 = good; 5 = very good. Alternatively, a check-box procedure might be used in which a checkmark is placed in each cell where the provision is met.

Discussion Questions

1. Visit at least three websites designed to appeal to children under 13 (e.g., Nick.com, Disney.com, and so on) and complete the COPPA Evaluation Grid.
2. Prepare a report including the COPPA Evaluation Grid and discuss how well these companies appear to be adhering to the The Rules under COPPA. Are there areas in which you see room for improvement? Explain.
3. Do you feel COPPA is adequate? Detail any areas where COPPA could be strengthened in order to better protect children's online privacy.

*Note: The core categories presented here and in Chapter 20 appear to hold true. However, "The Rules under COPPA" continue to evolve. It is important for every responsible organization to stay current on how those changes affect their efforts to stay compliant with COPPA and to protect the online privacy of children.

The Rules under COPPA—Evaluation Grid

TABLE 

COPPA Provision	Company A	Company B	Company C
Privacy Policy			
Parental Notice			
Parental Consent			
Parental Access			
Conditional Access			
Confidentiality			

Appendix A

Consumer Research Methods

In this appendix, we want to provide you with some general guidelines for conducting research on consumer behavior. While these guidelines will help you get started, a good marketing research text is indispensable if you need to conduct a consumer research project or evaluate a consumer research proposal.

SECONDARY DATA

Secondary data are basically existing information or data. Any research project should begin with a thorough search for existing information relevant to the project at hand. Internal data, such as past studies, sales reports, and accounting records, should be consulted. External data, including reports, magazines, government organizations, trade associations, marketing research firms, advertising agencies, academic journals, trade journals, and books, should be thoroughly researched.

Computer searches are a fast, economical means of conducting such searches. University and large public libraries, as well as companies, often subscribe to various databases that can be invaluable sources of information, reports, and data. These include, but are not limited to, (*a*) ABI Inform—electronic access to trade and academic publications; (*b*) MarketResearch.com—an online source of detailed industry reports; (*c*) Simmons Market Research Bureau data; (*d*) Gfk Mediamark Research and Intelligence, LLC; and (*e*) Standard Rate and Data Service (SRDS). Publicly available demographic information can be found at the U.S. Census (www.census.gov). And a great source for global information is *The World Fact Book* (www.cia.gov/cia/publications/factbook/).

PRIMARY DATA COLLECTION: ISSUES AND METHODS

If the specific information required is not available from secondary sources, we must gather primary data. Primary data are information or data that we collect for the first time in order to answer a specific research question. Thus, we might use the U.S. Census data to better understand the demographics driving gardening (secondary data) but conduct a survey to collect information (primary data) regarding the specific brand name we will use for our new garden tool.

Sampling

Collecting primary data generally involves talking to or observing consumers. However, it could involve asking knowledgeable others, such as sales personnel, about the consumers. In either case, time and cost constraints generally preclude us from contacting every single potential consumer. Therefore, most consumer research projects require a sample—a deliberately selected portion of the larger group. This requires a number of critical decisions, as described below. Mistakes made at this point are difficult to correct later in the study. The key decisions are briefly described below.

Define the Population The first step is to define the consumers in which we are interested. Do we want to talk to current brand users, current product-category users, or potential product-category users? Do we want to talk with the purchasers, the users, or everyone involved in the purchase process? The population as we define it must reflect the behavior on which our marketing decision will be based.

Specify the Sampling Frame A sampling frame is a list or grouping of individuals or households that reflects the population of interest. A phone book and shoppers at a given shopping mall can each serve as a sampling frame. Perfect sampling frames contain every member of the population one time. Phone books do not have households with unlisted numbers or those with no landline; many people do not visit shopping malls, while others visit them frequently. This is an area in which we generally must do the best we can without expecting a perfect frame. However, we must be very alert for biases that may be introduced by imperfections in our sampling frame.

Select a Sampling Method The major decision at this point is between a random (probability) sample and a nonrandom sample. Nonrandom samples, particularly judgment samples, can provide good results. A judgment sample involves the deliberate selection of knowledgeable consumers or individuals. For example, a firm might decide to interview the social activity officers of fraternities and sororities to estimate campus attitudes toward a carbonated wine drink aimed at the campus market. Such a sample might provide useful insights. However, it might also be biased because such individuals are likely to have a higher level of income and be more socially active than the average student.

The most common nonrandom sample, the convenience sample, involves selecting sample members in the manner most convenient for the researcher. It is subject to many types of bias and should generally be avoided.

Random or probability samples allow some form of a random process to select members from a sample frame. It may be every third person who passes a point-of-purchase display, house addresses selected by using a table of random numbers, or telephone numbers generated randomly by a computer. If random procedures are used, we can calculate the likelihood that our sample is not representative within specified limits.

Determine Sample Size Finally, we must determine how large a sample to talk to. If we are using random sampling, there are formulas that can help us make this decision. In general, the more diverse our population is and the more certain we want to be that we have the correct answer, the more people we will need to interview.

DATA COLLECTION METHODS

Depth Interviews

Depth interviews can involve one respondent and one interviewer, or they may involve a small group (8 to 15 respondents) and an interviewer. The latter are called **focus group interviews** and the former are termed **individual depth interviews** or one-on-ones. Groups of four or five are often referred to as minigroup interviews. Depth interviews in general are commonly referred to as qualitative research. Individual depth interviews involve a one-to-one relationship between the interviewer and the respondent. The interviewer does not have a specific set of prespecified questions that must be asked according to the order imposed by a questionnaire. Instead, there is freedom to create questions, to probe those responses that appear relevant, and generally to try to develop the best set of data in any way practical. However, the interviewer must follow one rule: He or she must not consciously try to affect the content of the answers given by the respondent. The respondent must feel free to reply to the various questions, probes, and other, more subtle ways of encouraging responses in the manner deemed most appropriate.

Individual depth interviews are appropriate in six situations:

1. Detailed probing of an individual's behavior, attitudes, or needs is required.
2. The subject matter under discussion is likely to be of a highly confidential nature (e.g., personal investments).
3. The subject matter is of an emotionally charged or embarrassing nature.
4. Certain strong, socially acceptable norms exist (e.g., child care) and the need to conform in a group discussion may influence responses.
5. A highly detailed (step-by-step) understanding of complicated behavior or decision-making patterns (e.g., planning the family holiday) is required.
6. The interviews are with professional people or with people on the subject of their jobs (e.g., finance directors).

Focus group interviews can be applied to (1) basic need studies for product ideas creation, (2) new-product ideas or concept exploration, (3) product-positioning studies, (4) advertising and communications research, (5) background studies on consumers' frames of reference, (6) establishment of consumer vocabulary as a preliminary step in questionnaire development, and (7) determination of attitudes and behaviors.

The standard focus group interview involves 8 to 12 individuals. Normally, the group is designed to reflect the characteristics of a particular market segment. The respondents are selected according to the relevant sampling plan and meet at a central location that generally has facilities for recording the interviews. The discussion itself is led by a moderator. The competent moderator attempts to develop three clear stages in the one- to three-hour interview: (1) establish rapport with the group, structure the rules of group interaction, and set objectives; (2) attempt to provoke intense discussion in the relevant areas; and (3) attempt to summarize the group's responses to determine the extent of agreement. In general, either the moderator or a second person prepares a summary of each session after analyzing the session's transcript.

Observation

Observation can be used when (1) the behaviors of interest are public (or in some way traceable as in behavioral tracking of online patterns via cookies); (2) they are repetitive, frequent, or predictable; and (3) they cover a relatively brief time span. An observational study requires five decisions:

1. *Natural versus contrived situation.* Do we wait for a behavior to occur in its natural environment, or do we create an artificial situation in which it will occur?
2. *Open versus disguised observation.* To what extent are the consumers aware that we are observing their behavior?
3. *Structured versus unstructured observation.* Will we limit our observations to predetermined behaviors, or will we note whatever occurs?
4. *Direct or indirect observations.* Will we observe the behaviors themselves or merely the outcomes of the behaviors?
5. *Human or mechanical observations.* Will the observations be made mechanically or by people?

Physiological Measures

Physiological measures are direct observations of physical responses to a stimulus such as an advertisement. These responses may be controllable, such as eye movements, or uncontrollable, such as the galvanic skin response. Eye-tracking cameras allow researchers to determine how long a consumer looks at each element in a stimulus, such as a point-of-purchase display, ad, or package, and the sequence in which the elements are examined. Galvanic skin response can be measured (via a lie detector) to detect the intensity of emotional responses to ads or packages.

Projective Techniques

Projective techniques are designed to measure feelings, attitudes, and motivations that consumers are unable or unwilling to reveal otherwise. They are based on the theory that the description of vague objects requires interpretation, and this interpretation can be based only on the individual's own attitudes, values, and motives.

Table A–1 provides descriptions and examples of the more common projective techniques.

Surveys

Surveys are systematic ways of gathering information from a large number of people. They generally involve the use of a structured or semi-structured questionnaire. Surveys can be administered by mail, by telephone, in person, or online. Personal interviews

TABLE A-1 Motivation Research Techniques

	I. Association Techniques
Word association	Consumers respond to a list of words with the first word that comes to mind.
Successive word association	Consumers give the series of words that come to mind after hearing each word on the list.
Analysis and use	Responses are analyzed to see if negative associations exist. When the time to respond (response latency) is also measured, the emotionality of the word can be estimated. These techniques tap semantic memory more than motives and are used for brand name and advertising copy tests.
	II. Completion Techniques
Sentence completion	Consumers complete a sentence such as "People who buy a Cadillac ______________________________."
Story completion	Consumers complete a partial story.
Analysis and use	Responses are analyzed to determine what themes are expressed. Content analysis—examining responses for themes and key concepts—is used.
	III. Construction Techniques
Cartoon techniques	Consumers fill in the words or thoughts of one of the characters in a cartoon drawing.
Third-person techniques	Consumers tell why "an average woman," "most doctors," or "people in general" purchase or use a certain product. Shopping lists (describe a person who would go shopping with this list) and lost wallets (describe a person with these items in his or her wallet) are also third-person techniques.
Picture response	Consumers tell a story about a person shown buying or using a product in a picture or line drawing.
Analysis and use	Same as for completion techniques.

generally take place in shopping malls and are referred to as mall intercept interviews. Each approach has advantages and disadvantages.

- **Personal interviews** allow the use of complex questionnaires, product demonstrations, and the collection of large amounts of data. They can be completed in a relatively short period of time. However, they are very expensive and are subject to interviewer bias.
- **Telephone surveys** can be completed rapidly, provide good sample control (who answers the questions), and are relatively inexpensive. Substantial amounts of data can be collected, but it must be relatively simple. Interviewer bias is possible.
- **Mail surveys** take the longest to complete and must generally be rather short. They can be used to collect modestly complex data, and they are very economical. Interviewer bias is not a problem.
- **Online surveys** are increasingly popular because they are highly cost-effective (respondents enter the data), fast, and easy to conduct. A major concern with online survey research historically has been the demographic skew or bias due to income, education, ethnic, and gender gaps. As the online population has become more representative of the general population, such concerns have reduced.

A major concern in survey research is nonresponse bias. In most surveys, fewer than 50 percent of those selected to participate in the study actually do participate. In telephone and personal interviews, many people are not at home or refuse to cooperate. In mail surveys, many people refuse or forget to respond.

We can increase the response rate by callbacks in telephone and home personal surveys. The callbacks should be made at different times and on different days. Monetary inducements (enclosing $1) increase the response rate to mail surveys, as do prenotification (a card saying that a questionnaire is coming) and reminder postcards.

If less than a 100 percent response rate is obtained, we must be concerned that those who did not respond differ from those who did. A variety of techniques are available to help us estimate the likelihood and nature of nonresponse error.

Experimentation

Experimentation involves changing one or more variables (product features, package color, advertising theme) and observing the effect the change has on another variable (consumer attitude, repeat purchase behavior, learning). The variable(s) changed is (are) called the *independent variable(s)*. The "change" is called a "manipulation," which simply means that we are systematically varying a factor at different levels. For example, if we presented different groups of consumers with a product priced at $1.00, $1.50, and $2.00, then we would have manipulated price at three levels.

The variable(s) that may be affected by the manipulation(s) is (are) called the *dependent variable(s)*. The objective in experimental design is to structure the situation so that any change in the dependent variable is very likely to have been caused by a change in the independent variable. The way this is done is through high levels of "control," which generally means that we manipulate variables of interest and hold all other factors constant. Thus, we could present three different product concepts that differed only in terms of price. Everything else, including design, package color, and so on, would be held constant (or remain the same) across the different price levels. The logic is that because only the manipulated variable changed, we have high confidence that it was the reason (cause) for any observed changes in the dependent variable.

There are numerous experimental designs depending on the number and level of independent variables the researcher wishes to investigate. There are different kinds of experiments that reflect the level of control that we can achieve. In a laboratory experiment, we carefully control for all outside influences and can conclude with confidence that our independent variables *caused* the changes in our dependent variable(s). Lab experiments thus yield high levels of *internal validity*.

In a field experiment, we conduct our study in the most relevant environment possible. This generally means giving up the pristine control of a lab setting. However, the reason for doing so is to see how consumers actually react in "real-world" settings. Field experiments are important because they help establish *external validity,* which is the extent to which our results are likely to hold true in real-world settings. This can mean that unusual outside influences may distort our results (that is, reduce internal validity). However, careful planning can often avoid these unusual influences.

Conjoint Analysis: Examining Attribute Importance Using Experimentation

Conjoint analysis is an application of experimentation. In conjoint analysis, the consumer is presented with a set of products or product descriptions in which the potential evaluative criteria vary (are manipulated). For example, consider a laptop manufacturer who is interested in the importance of four different attributes: processor (two levels: Intel Core Duo 2.0 GHz versus Intel Core Duo 2.4 GHz), Energy Star compliant (two levels: yes versus no), weight (two levels: 4 lbs versus 5.1 lbs), and price (three levels: $850, $1,250, and $2,000). This would result in 24 different notebook computer configurations ($2 \times 2 \times 2 \times 3 = 24$) that vary on four criteria. Two might be:

Intel Core Duo 2.4 GHz	Intel Core Duo 2.0 GHz
Energy Star compliant (yes)	Energy Star compliant (no)
5.1 lbs	4 lbs
$1,250	$850

The consumer ranks all 24 such descriptions in terms of his or her preference for those combinations of features. Based on these preference ranks, sophisticated computer programs derive the relative importance consumers assign to each level of each attribute tested.

For example, in Figure A–1, imagine a consumer was asked to rank in terms of overall preference 24 different computer designs featuring different levels of four key evaluative criteria. The preferences were then analyzed in light of the variations in the attributes. The result is a preference curve for each evaluative criterion that reflects the importance of that attribute. On the basis of the data in Figure A–1, processor is a particularly important evaluative criterion for this consumer while weight (at least in the range examined) is of almost no importance.

Conjoint analysis is limited to the attributes listed by the researcher. Thus, a conjoint analysis of soft-drink attributes would not indicate anything about calorie content unless the researcher listed it as a feature. If an important attribute is omitted, incorrect market share predictions are likely to result. In addition, conjoint analysis is not well suited for measuring the importance of emotional or feeling-based product choices. For example, what types of attributes would you use to perform a conjoint analysis of perfumes?

Questionnaire Design

All surveys and many experiments use questionnaires as data collection devices. A questionnaire is simply a formalized set of questions for eliciting information. It can measure (1) behavior—past, present, or intended; (2) demographic characteristics—age, gender, income, education, occupation; (3) level of knowledge; and (4) attitudes and opinions. The process of questionnaire design is outlined in Table A–2.

Using Conjoint Analysis to Determine the Importance of Evaluative Criteria for a Laptop Computer

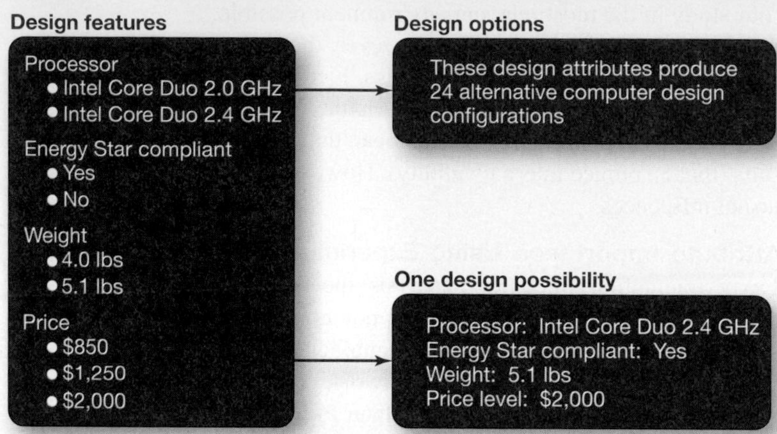

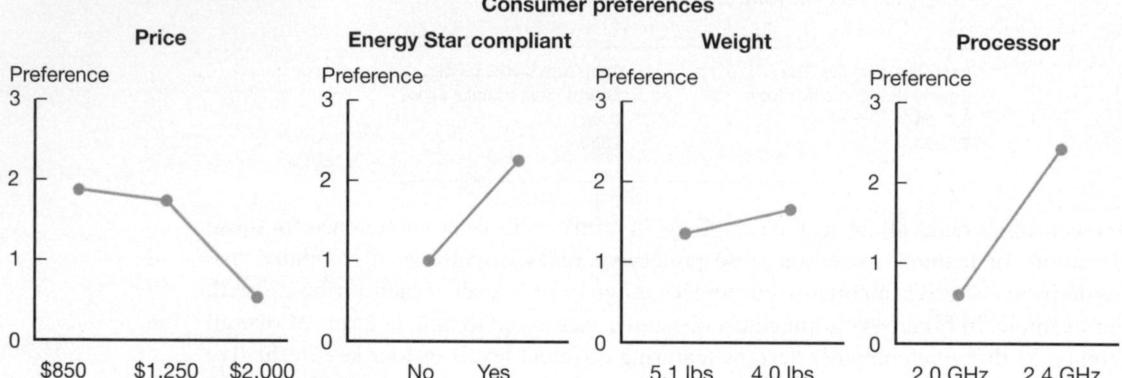

Relative importance

Evaluative criteria	Importance
Processor	45%
Weight	5
Energy Star compliant	25
Price	25

- Processor is the most important feature in this example, and Intel Core Duo 2.4 GHz is the preferred option.
- While price and Energy Star compliance are also important, price becomes important only between $1,250 and $2,000.

Attitude Scales

Attitudes are frequently measured on specialized scales, as detailed next. The instructions indicate that the consumer is to mark the blank that best indicates how accurately one or the other term describes or fits the attitude object.

Questionnaire Design Process — TABLE A-2

1. *Preliminary decisions*
   Exactly what information is required?
   Exactly who are the target respondents?
   What method of communication will be used to reach these respondents?
2. *Decisions about question content*
   Is this question really needed?
   Is this question sufficient to generate the needed information?
   Can the respondent answer the question correctly?
   Will the respondent answer the question correctly?
   Are there any external events that might bias the response to the question?
3. *Decisions about the response format*
   Can this question best be asked as an open-ended, multiple-choice, or dichotomous question?
4. *Decisions concerning question phrasing*
   Do the words used have but one meaning to all the respondents?
   Are any of the words or phrases loaded or leading in any way?
   Are there any implied alternatives in the question?
   Are there any unstated assumptions related to the question?
   Will the respondents approach the question from the frame of reference desired by the researcher?
5. *Decisions concerning the question sequence*
   Are the questions organized in a logical manner that avoids introducing errors?
6. *Decisions on the layout of the questionnaire*
   Is the questionnaire designed in a manner to avoid confusion and minimize recording errors?
7. *Pretest and revise*
   Has the final questionnaire been subjected to a thorough pretest, using respondents similar to those who will be included in the final survey?

Various types of attitude scales exist, including the following:

Noncomparative Rating Scale Noncomparative rating scales require the consumer to evaluate an object or an attribute of the object without directly comparing it to another object. An example would be:

"How do you like the taste of Diet Pepsi?"

Like it very much	Like it	Dislike it	Strongly dislike it
________	________	________	________

Comparative Rating Scale Comparative rating scales provide a direct comparison point (a named competitor, "your favorite brand," "the ideal brand"). An example would be:

"How do you like the taste of Tom's of Maine compared with Ultra Bright?"

Like it much more	Like it more	Like it about the same	Like it less	Like it much less
________	________	________	________	________

Semantic Differential Scale The semantic differential scale requires the consumer to rate an item on a number of scales bounded at each end by one of two bipolar adjectives. For example:

"Rate the Honda Accord on the following attributes."

Fast ________ ________ ________ ________ ________ ________ ________ Slow

Fancy ________ ________ ________ ________ ________ ________ ________ Plain

The end positions indicate "extremely," the next pair in from the ends indicate "very," the middlemost pair indicate "somewhat," and the middle position indicates "neither/nor."

Likert Scale Likert scales ask consumers to indicate a degree of agreement or disagreement with each of a series of statements related to the attitude object, such as the following:

1. *Macy's is one of the most attractive stores in town.*

Strongly agree	Agree	Neither agree nor disagree	Disagree	Strongly disagree
______	______	______	______	______

2. *The service at Macy's is not satisfactory.*

Strongly agree	Agree	Neither agree nor disagree	Disagree	Strongly disagree
______	______	______	______	______

To analyze responses, each response category is assigned a numerical value. For example, in the Likert scales above we could assign values such as 1 (Strongly agree) through 5 (Strongly disagree). Or a +2 through −2 system could be used with 0 representing the neutral point (Neither agree nor disagree).

Measuring the Three Attitude Components

As we discussed in Chapter 11, attitude can be broken into its cognitive, affective, and behavioral components. Table A–3 provides a detailed set of items for each attitude component.

EVALUATING ADVERTISING EFFECTS

A successful advertisement, or any other marketing message, must accomplish four tasks:

1. *Exposure.* It must physically reach the consumer.
2. *Attention.* The consumer must attend to it.
3. *Interpretation.* It must be properly interpreted.
4. *Memory.* It must be stored in memory in a manner that will allow retrieval under the proper circumstances.

Advertising evaluation covers all these tasks. However, most of the effort is focused on attention and, to a lesser extent, memory.

Measures of Exposure

Exposure to print media is most frequently measured in terms of circulation. Data on circulation are provided by a variety of commercial firms. Frequently, however, these data are not broken down in a manner consistent with the firm's target market. Thus, a firm may be targeting the lower-middle social class, but circulation data may be broken down by income rather than social class.

Diary reports, in which respondents record their daily listening patterns, and telephone interviews are the two methods used to measure radio listening. Television viewing is measured primarily by **people meters** (mechanical observation), which are electronic devices

TABLE A-3 Measuring Attitude Components

Cognitive Component (Measuring Beliefs about Specific Attributes Using the Semantic Differential Scale)							
	Diet Coke						
Strong taste	_____	_____	_____	_____	_____	_____	Mild taste
Low priced	_____	_____	_____	_____	_____	_____	High priced
Caffeine free	_____	_____	_____	_____	_____	_____	High in caffeine
Distinctive in taste	_____	_____	_____	_____	_____	_____	Similar in taste to most

Affective Component (Measuring Feelings about Specific Attributes or the Overall Brand Using Likert Scales)					
	Strongly Agree	**Agree**	**Neither Agree nor Disagree**	**Disagree**	**Strongly Disagree**
I like the taste of Diet Coke.	_____	_____	_____	_____	_____
Diet Coke is overpriced.	_____	_____	_____	_____	_____
Caffeine is bad for your health.	_____	_____	_____	_____	_____
I like Diet Coke.	_____	_____	_____	_____	_____

Behavioral Component (Measuring Actions or Intended Actions)	
The last soft drink I consumed was a _____.	
I usually drink _____ soft drinks.	
What is the likelihood you will buy Diet Coke the next time you purchase a soft drink?	_____ Definitely will buy
	_____ Probably will buy
	_____ Might buy
	_____ Probably will not buy
	_____ Definitely will not buy

that automatically determine if a television is turned on and, if so, to which channel. They allow each household member to log on when viewing by punching an identifying button. The demographics of each potential viewer are stored in the central computer so viewer profiles can be developed.

Websites can automatically record (mechanical observation) the number of total and unique (from distinct computers) visits per time period. Banner ads and the sites on which they appear are often evaluated on the *clickthrough rate*—the percentage of site visitors or total number of people who click on the banner ad.

Measures of Attention

The attention-attracting powers of commercials, packages, and websites can be partially measured in a direct manner using **eye tracking** (mechanical observation) or eye fixations. While a consumer looks at images of print ads, billboards, store shelves, packages, or websites, a camera underneath the screen sends an invisible beam of light off the consumer's pupil. The camera indicates exactly what the consumer is attending to. This technology allows marketers to determine (1) what parts of the message were attended to, (2) what sequence was used in viewing the message, and (3) how much time was spent on each part.

Indirect measures of attention, which also tap at least some aspects of memory, include theater tests, day-after recall, recognition tests, and Starch scores. *Theater tests* involve showing commercials along with television programs in a theater. Viewers complete questionnaires designed to measure which commercials, and what aspects of those commercials, attracted their attention. **Day-after recall (DAR)** is the most popular method of measuring the attention-getting power of television commercials. Individuals are interviewed the day after a commercial is aired on a program they watched. Recall of the commercial and recall of specific aspects of the commercial (assessed through questionnaires) are interpreted as a reflection of the amount of attention.

DAR measures of television commercials have been criticized as favoring rational, factual, hard-sell ads and high-involvement products while discriminating against feeling, emotional, soft-sell ads. However, for many product–target market combinations, the latter approach may be superior. In response, substantial work has been done to develop recognition measures for television commercials. In **recognition tests,** the commercial of interest, or key parts of it, along with other commercials are shown to target market members. Recognition of the commercial, or key parts of it, is the measure.

Starch scores are the most popular technique for evaluating the attention-attracting power of print ads. The respondents are shown advertisements from magazine issues they have recently read. For each advertisement, they indicate which parts (headlines, illustrations, copy blocks) they recall reading. Three main scores are computed:

1. *Noted.* The percentage of people who recall seeing the ad in that issue.
2. *Seen-associated.* The percentage of those who recall reading a part of the ad that clearly identifies the brand or advertiser.
3. *Read most.* The percentage of those who recall reading 50 percent or more of the copy.

Starch scores allow an indirect measure of attention to the overall ad and to key components of the ad.

Measures of Interpretation

Marketers investigating *interpretation* can use any number of the research methods we've discussed, including focus groups, surveys, and projective techniques. A critical task for marketers is to move beyond cognitive interpretation and tap emotions and feelings as well. Techniques such as the AdSAM® discussed in Chapter 11 can be quite useful in this regard.

Appendix B

Consumer Behavior Audit*

In this appendix, we provide a list of key questions to guide you in developing marketing strategy from a consumer behavior perspective. This audit is no more than a checklist to minimize the chance of overlooking a critical behavioral dimension. It does not guarantee a successful strategy. However, thorough and insightful answers to these questions should greatly enhance the likelihood of a successful marketing program.

Our audit is organized around the key decisions that marketing managers must make. The first key decision is the selection of the target market(s) to be served. This is followed by the determination of a viable product position for each target market. Finally, the marketing mix elements—product, place, price, and promotion—must be structured in a manner consistent with the desired product position. This process is illustrated in Figure B–1.

Consumer Influences Drive Marketing Decisions FIGURE B-1

Consumer influences

External influences
- Culture, subcultures, values
- Demographics, income, and social class
- Reference groups and households
- Marketing activities

Internal influences
- Needs, motives, and emotions
- Perceptions and memory
- Personality and lifestyle
- Attitudes

Situational influences
- Physical, time, social, task, and antecedent

Decision process influences
- Problem recognition
- Information search
- Alternative evaluation
- Outlet selection
- Purchase
- Postpurchase processes

→

Marketing decisions

Marketing segmentation
- Target segment(s)
- Single or multiple target segments

↓

Product positioning
- Key product differentiation variables
- Position relative to competition

↓

Market mix
- Product features
- Price level
- Promotional appeal
- Place (distribution)
- Services

*Revised by Richard Pomazal of Wheeling College.

MARKET SEGMENTATION

Market segmentation is the process of dividing all possible users of a product into groups that have similar needs the products might satisfy. Market segmentation should be done prior to the final development of a new product. In addition, a complete market segmentation analysis should be performed periodically for existing products. The reason for continuing segmentation analyses is the dynamic nature of consumer needs.

A. External influences
   1. Are there cultures or subcultures whose value system is particularly consistent (or inconsistent) with the consumption of our product?
   2. Is our product appropriate for male or female consumption? Will ongoing gender-role changes affect who consumes our product or how it is consumed?
   3. Do ethnic, social, regional, or religious subcultures have different consumption patterns relevant to our product?
   4. Do various demographic or social-strata groups (age, gender, urban/suburban/rural, occupation, income, education) differ in their consumption of our product?
   5. Is our product particularly appropriate for consumers with relatively high (or low) incomes compared with others in their occupational group?
   6. Can our product be particularly appropriate for specific roles, such as students or professional women?
   7. Would it be useful to focus on specific adopter categories?
   8. Do groups in different stages of the household life cycle have different consumption patterns for our product? Who in the household is involved in the purchase process?

B. Internal influences
   1. Can our product satisfy different needs or motives in different people? What needs are involved? What characterizes individuals with differing motives?
   2. Is our product uniquely suited for particular personality types? Self-concepts?
   3. What emotions, if any, are affected by the purchase and/or consumption of this product?
   4. Is our product appropriate for one or more distinct lifestyles?
   5. Do different groups have different attitudes about an ideal version of our product?

C. Situational influences
   1. Can our product be appropriate for specific types of situations instead of (or in addition to) specific types of people?

D. Decision process influences
   1. Do different individuals use different evaluative criteria in selecting the product?
   2. Do potential customers differ in their loyalty to existing products or brands?

PRODUCT POSITION

A product position is the way the consumer thinks of a given product or brand relative to competing products or brands. A manager must determine what a desirable product position would be for each market segment of interest. This determination is generally based on the answers to the same questions used to segment a market, with the addition of the consumer's perceptions of competing products or brands. Of course, the capabilities and motivations of existing and potential competitors must also be considered.

A. Internal influences
   1. What is the general semantic memory structure for this product category in each market segment?
   2. What is the ideal version of this product in each market segment for the situations the firm wants to serve?
B. Decision process influences
   1. Which evaluative criteria are used in the purchase decision? Which decision rules and importance weights are used?

PRICING

The manager must set a pricing policy that is consistent with the desired product position. Price must be broadly conceived as everything a consumer must surrender to obtain a product. This includes time and psychological costs as well as monetary costs.

A. External influences
   1. Does the segment hold any values relating to any aspect of pricing, such as the use of credit or conspicuous consumption?
   2. Does the segment have sufficient income, after covering living expenses, to afford the product?
   3. Is it necessary to lower price to obtain a sufficient relative advantage to ensure diffusion? Will temporary price reductions induce product trial?
   4. Who in the household evaluates the price of the product?
B. Internal influences
   1. Will price be perceived as an indicator of status?
   2. Is economy in purchasing this type of product relevant to the lifestyle(s) of the segment?
   3. Is price an important aspect of the segment's attitude toward the brands in the product category?
   4. What is the segment's perception of a fair or reasonable price for this product?
C. Situational influences
   1. Does the role of price vary with the type of situation?
D. Decision process factors
   1. Can a low price be used to trigger problem recognition?
   2. Is price an important evaluative criterion? What decision rule is applied to the evaluative criteria used? Is price likely to serve as a surrogate indicator of quality?
   3. Are consumers likely to respond to in-store price reductions?

DISTRIBUTION STRATEGY

The manager must develop a distribution strategy that is consistent with the selected product position. This involves the selection of outlets if the item is a physical product, or the location of the outlets if the product is a service.

A. External influences
   1. What values do the segments have that relate to distribution?
   2. Do the male and female members of the segments have differing requirements of the distribution system? Do working couples, single individuals, or single parents within the segment have unique needs relating to product distribution?

3. Can the distribution system capitalize on reference groups by serving as a means for individuals with common interests to get together?
4. Is the product complex such that a high-service channel is required to ensure its diffusion?

B. Internal influences
1. Will the selected outlets be perceived in a manner that enhances the desired product position?
2. What type of distribution system is consistent with the lifestyle(s) of each segment?
3. What attitudes does each segment hold with respect to the various distribution alternatives?

C. Situational influences
1. Do the desired features of the distribution system vary with the situation?

D. Decision process factors
1. What outlets are in the segment's evoked set? Will consumers in this segment seek information in this type of outlet?
2. Which evaluative criteria does this segment use to evaluate outlets? Which decision rule?
3. To what extent are product decisions made in the retail outlet?

PROMOTION STRATEGY

The manager must develop a promotion strategy, including advertising, nonfunctional package design features, publicity, promotions, and sales force activities that are consistent with the product position.

A. External factors
1. What values does the segment hold that can be used in our communications? Which should be avoided?
2. How can we communicate to our chosen segments in a manner consistent with the emerging gender-role perceptions of each segment?
3. What is the nonverbal communication system of each segment?
4. How, if at all, can we use reference groups in our advertisements?
5. Can our advertisements help make the product part of one or more role-related product clusters?
6. Can we reach and influence opinion leaders?
7. If our product is an innovation, are there diffusion inhibitors that can be overcome by promotion?
8. Who in the household should receive what types of information concerning our product?

B. Internal factors
1. Have we structured our promotional campaign such that each segment will be exposed to it, attend to it, and interpret it in the manner we desire?
2. Have we made use of the appropriate learning principles so that our meaning will be remembered?
3. Do our messages relate to the purchase motives held by the segment? Do they help reduce motivational conflict if necessary?
4. Are we considering the emotional implications of the ad and/or the use of our product?

5. Is the lifestyle portrayed in our advertisements consistent with the desired lifestyle of the selected segments?
6. If we need to change attitudes via our promotion mix, have we selected and properly used the most appropriate attitude-change techniques?

C. Situational influences
   1. Does our campaign illustrate the full range of appropriate usage situations for the product?

D. Decision process influences
   1. Will problem recognition occur naturally, or must it be activated by advertising? Should generic or selective problem recognition be generated?
   2. Will the segment seek out or attend to information on the product prior to problem recognition, or must we reach them when they are not seeking our information? Can we use low-involvement learning processes effectively? What information sources are used?
   3. After problem recognition, will the segment seek out information on the product or brand, or will we need to intervene in the purchase decision process? If they do seek information, what sources do they use?
   4. What types of information are used to make a decision?
   5. How much and what types of information are acquired at the point of purchase?
   6. Is postpurchase dissonance likely? Can we reduce it through our promotional campaign?
   7. Have we given sufficient information to ensure proper product use?
   8. Are the expectations generated by our promotional campaign consistent with the product's performance?
   9. Are our messages designed to encourage repeat purchases, brand-loyal purchases, or neither?

PRODUCT

The marketing manager must be certain that the physical product, service, or idea has the characteristics required to achieve the desired product position in each market segment.

A. External influences
   1. Is the product designed appropriately for all members of the segment under consideration, including males, females, and various age groups?
   2. If the product is an innovation, does it have the required relative advantage and lack of complexity to diffuse rapidly?
   3. Is the product designed to meet the varying needs of different household members?

B. Internal influences
   1. Will the product be perceived in a manner consistent with the desired image?
   2. Will the product satisfy the key purchase motives of the segment?
   3. Is the product consistent with the segment's attitude toward an ideal product?

C. Situational influences
   1. Is the product appropriate for the various potential usage situations?

D. Decision process influences
   1. Does the product or brand perform better than the alternatives on the key set of evaluative criteria used by this segment?
   2. Will the product perform effectively in the foreseeable uses to which this segment may subject it?
   3. Will the product perform as well as or better than expected by this segment?

CUSTOMER SATISFACTION AND COMMITMENT

Marketers must produce satisfied customers to be successful in the long run. It is often to a firm's advantage to go beyond satisfaction and create committed or loyal customers.

1. What factors lead to satisfaction with our product?
2. What factors could cause customer commitment to our brand or firm?

Photo Credits

Ch. 1

Page 4, Photo by Gilbert Carrasquillo/Getty Images. P. 7, Used with permission of Maryland Office of Tourism. P. 7, Used with permission of Jim Gallop/North Dakota Tourism. P. 9, ©2014 Oakley, Inc. All Rights Reserved. P. 11, ©Richard Levine/Alamy. P. 14, ©Luminox USA. P. 14, ©Tudor. P. 19, Used with permission of Zippo Manufacturing Company. P. 21, Used with Permission of Alpargatas USA. P. 26, ©Lars A. Niki.

Ch. 2

Page 36, ©Rosalrene Betancourt 5/Alamy. P. 36, ©Richard Levine/Alamy. P. 39, ©Andry A/Alamsyah/Alamy. P. 42, ©vario images GMbH& Co. KG/Alamy. P. 46, ©Marie Hornbein. P. 48, Photo by Sankei via Getty Images. P. 52, Agency: JayGrey/Sydney; Art Director: Jay Furby; Photography: Zena Holloway. P. 57, Courtesy of Junwu Dong. P. 62, NetPhotos/Alamy. P. 63, © McGraw-Hill Education. Barry Barker, photographer. P. 65, AP Photo/Hasan Jamali.

Ch. 3

Page 76, Stockbyte/Getty Images. P. 80, Equibal Inc. TBP4®. www.thebodyperfect.com. P. 83, ©Club Mediterranee S.A. P. 84, CLOROX® is a registered trademark of The Clorox Company. Used with permission. ©2011 The Clorox Company. Reprinted with permission. P. 87, PRNewsFoto/The Estee Lauder Companies Inc. P. 89, Audi of America. All rights reserved. ©Copyright 2015. P. 90, (C) TakeTheWalk.net. All Rights Reserved. P. 90, ©2014 Procter & Gamble. All claims valid only in the U.S. P. 95, ©McNEIL-PPC, Inc. 1998–2014. All rights reserved. P. 97, PRNewsFoto/Resam/AP Images. P. 97, PRNewsFoto/Alikay Naturals/AP Images. P. 99, Courtesy of Tyson Foods, Inc. P. 100, ©2015 Georgia-Pacific. All rights reserved.

Ch. 4

Page 108, ©ZUMA Press, Inc./Alamy. P. 116, PRNewsFoto/WallFlower Jeans/AP Images. P. 119, Courtesy Campbell Soup Company. P. 121, ©The Procter & Gamble Company. Used by permission. P. 123, © McGraw-Hill Education. Jill Braaten, photographer. P. 126, ©2015 PVH Corp. P. 127, Courtesy Betweentalk.com. P. 131, ©Lars A. Niki. P. 132, PRNewsFoto/LAGOS/AP Images. P. 133, PRNewsFoto/LG Electronics USA, Inc./AP Images. P. 133, ©2014 Homer TLC, Inc. All rights reserved. P. 134, ©2014 Homer TLC, Inc. All rights reserved.

Ch. 5

Page 146, Photo by Brad Barket/Getty Images for Essence. P. 149, PRNewsFoto/MetLife/AP Images. P. 156, Used with permission of CanyonRanch License, LLC. P. 156, PRNewsFoto/U R Curly/AP Images. P. 160, ©2015 S. C. Johnson & Son, Inc. All rights reserved. P. 161, ©2014 ESPN, Inc. P. 163, ©Singapore Press Holdings Limited. P. 166, ©2015 Wal-Mart Stores, Inc. P. 170, Courtesy C28.com. P. 173, © Doctor's Associates, Inc.

Ch. 6

Page 182, ©Image Source/Alamy. P. 186, ©2014 CSC Brands, LP. All Rights Reserved. P. 190, Copyright ©2015 CALVIN KLEIN. ALL RIGHTS RESERVED. P. 191, Courtesy Le Petite Retreat Spa. P. 193, PRNewsFoto/Hotels.com/AP Images. P. 194, PrNewsFoto/Princess Cruises/AP Images. P. 196, Used with Permission of Winnebago Industries, Inc. P. 199, PRNewsFoto/American Beverage Corporation/AP Images. P. 203, PRNewsFoto/Hormel Foods/AP Images. P. 205, Used with permission of Capital One Financial Corporation.

Ch. 7

Page 214, ©ZUMA Press Inc./Alamy. P. 220, Used with permission of Sneakerhead.com. P. 222, COPYRIGHT ©2015 CARE2.COM, INC. AND ITS LICENSORS. ALL RIGHTS RESERVED. P. 225, Used with permission of SRAM LLC. P. 229, Used with permission of Destination DC. P. 232, PRNewsFoto/Anheuser-Busch/AP Images. P. 236, PRNewsFoto/got chocolate?/AP Images. P. 240, ©2015 Procter & Gamble. All rights reserved. P. 240, ©2015 S.C. JOHNSON & SON, INC. ALL RIGHTS RESERVED. P. 241, Kyodo via AP Images. P. 247, Used with permission of Xeros, Inc.

Ch. 8

Page 272, Kimball Stock Collection. P. 278, AP Photo/Christof Stache. P. 280, PRNewsFoto/Travel Oregon/AP Images. P. 283, *Both ads* Courtesy of Konica Business Machines, U.S.A. P. 284, ©2015 Volkswagen of America. P. 285, Courtesy the Libman Company. P. 290, PRNewsFoto/Hotels.com/AP Images. P. 292, PRNewsFoto/Brown Shoe Company/AP Images. P. 294, ®2014 Link Snacks Inc. All Rights Reserved. P. 295, Courtesy PUMA. P. 297, PRNewsFoto/Hyundai Motor America/AP Images. P. 300, PEPSI, the Pepsi Globe, MOUNTAIN DEW and CODE RED are registered trademarks of PepsiCo, Inc. Used with permission. P. 300, Used with permission of Reebok. P. 300, Used with permission of BP p.l.c. P. 300, Used with permission of Belk. P. 303, Courtesy Integrated Solutions, UC.

Ch. 9

Page 312, ©Sparky2000/iStockphoto LP. P. 316, PRNewsFoto/S&T Bank/AP Images. P. 321, Used with permission of Fel-Pro Gaskets/Federal-Mogul Motorparts. P. 321, Courtesy Campbell Soup Company. P. 325, Courtesy CIBA VISION Corporation. P. 326, Courtesy of iRobot Corp. Produced by BPL Marketing, London. Photography by Chris Biggs, London. P. 330, Courtesy KitchenAid. P. 334, CLOROX® is a registered trademark of The Clorox Company. Used with permission. ©2005 The Clorox Company. Reprinted with permission. P. 337, Courtesy Lee Jeans Co., Inc. P. 340, Courtesy of Riviana Foods, Inc. P. 343, ©2015 Procter & Gamble. All rights reserved. P. 343, ®, ™, ©2015 Kellogg NA Co.

Ch. 10

Page 352, Tomohiro Ohsumi/ Bloomberg via Getty Images. P. 356, Courtesy of The United States Marine Corps and the advertising agency of record, JWT. P. 357, PRNewsFoto/ USANA Health Sciences, Inc./ AP Images. P. 358, PRNewsFoto/ PANDORA Jewelry/AP Images. P. 359, Used with permission of Quaker Pet Group. P. 360, PRNewsFoto/ Rexam/AP Images. P. 362, Courtesy The Gillette Company/Procter & Gamble. P. 370, PRNewsFoto/Deckers Outdoor Corporation/AP Images. P. 374, PRNewsFoto/ASICS/AP Images. P. 375, PRNewsFoto/Jockey International, Inc./AP Images.

Ch. 11

Page 382, Doug Meszier/Splash News/ Newscom. P. 388, PRNewsFoto/ Brizo®/AP Images. P. 389, ©2014 CSC Brands LP. All Rights Reserved. P. 393, PRNewsFoto/Deckers Brands/ AP Images. P. 394, PRNewsFoto/ Bulbs.com/AP Images. P. 399, PRNewsFoto/COTY Fragrances/AP Images. P. 401, Used with permission of American Family Life Assurance Company of Columbus. P. 403, Courtesy Talent/Brazil. P. 404, PRNewsFoto/Disney Parks/AP Images. P. 404, Used with permission of Paramount Farms International LLC. P. 405, Courtesy The Humane Society of the United States. P. 406, COPYRIGHT ©2015 COTY INC. ALL RIGHTS RESERVED. P. 406, Ballistic Wallet™.

Ch. 12

Page 418, ©2015 Delta Air Lines, Inc. P. 421, PRNewsFoto/TAG Heuer/ AP Images. P. 425, PRNewsFoto/ Long Tall Sally/AP Images. P. 428, Used with permission of EAS Brand/ Abbott Laboratories-Nutrition. P. 430, Courtesy of Dunlop Manufacturing, Inc. P. 433, Used with permission of Jaguar Land Rover North America LLC. P. 433, Copyright ©2015 TomTom International BV. All rights reserved. P. 434, Copyright New Mexico Tourism Department ©2013-Present. All Rights Reserved. P. 435, Used with permission of CPG Building Products. P. 438, Courtesy GM Archives.PRNewsFoto/Glamour-Sales/AP Images.

Ch. 13

Page 470, ©2014 CSC Brands, LP. All Rights Reserved. P. 475, ©Materne. All Rights Reserved. P. 477, Purestock/Getty Images. P. 477, Purestock/Getty Images. P. 481, Used with permission of Reebok. P. 482, ©Zappos Development, Inc. P. 484, PRNewsFoto/Rexam/AP Images. P. 485, Designed by Joseph Zunner; ©2015 All Rights Reserved. Property of The Gorilla Glue Company. P. 486, Used with permission of Huhtamaki, Inc. ©2011. Design by The Burin Group. P. 488, ©Arla Foods Inc.

Ch. 14

Page 496, ©2015 The Procter & Gamble Company. Swiffer® is a registered trademark of Procter & Gamble. P. 502, Courtesy of VIRBAC. P. 505, Courtesy US Department of Homeland Security/FEMA. P. 505, ©The Procter & Gamble Company. Used by permission. P. 507, ©2009 The City of New York, Department of Health and Mental Hygiene. All Rights Reserved. Ad agency: Rivet New York. P. 509, © McGraw-Hill Education. Jill Braaten, photographer. P. 511, PRNewsFoto/MilkPEP/ AP Images. P. 511, PRNewsFoto/ Biota International, LLC/AP Images. P. 512, ©2015 Maui Jim, Inc. Lahaina, Hawaii. P. 513, Courtesy of TropiClean; Designers: John Williams, Brian Collier.

Ch. 15

Page 518, ©Beamly 2015. P. 522, PRNewsFoto/Method/AP Images. P. 527, Used with permission of Orbitz Worldwide. P. 529, ©NetPhotos/Alamy. P. 540, ®/™ Trademarks ©Mars, Incorporated 2015 EMPTATIONS® Cat and Cloud designs are ® trademarks. P. 540, PRNewsFoto/ Kellogg Company/AP Images. P. 541, Used with permission of Sunstar Americas, Inc. P. 542, Courtesy American Honda Motor Co., Inc.

Ch. 16

Page 550, ™Stitch Fix, Inc. P. 554, Used with Permission of Huntsman Springs. P. 554, ©The Procter & Gamble Company. P. 555, PRNewsFoto/ SNO™/AP Images. P. 556, ©2015 Viviscal. All Rights Reserved. P. 556, PRNewsFoto/Yvolution/AP Images. P. 557, PRNewsFoto/Bugaboo/AP Images. P. 558, ©2015 Blue Buffalo Co. Ltd. P. 558, PRNewsFoto/Nestle Purina/AP Images. P. 562 , Courtesy Grana Padano Cheese. P. 566, Used with permission The Honest Kitchen. P. 568, PRNewsFoto/Texas Instruments/ AP Images. P. 569, PRNewsFoto/ BlueCross BlueShield Western NY/AP Images. P. 570, ©2015 Frito-Lay North America, Inc.

Ch. 17

Page 580, ©Tom Salyer/Alamy. P. 583, ©2014 Homer TLC, Inc. All rights reserved. P. 585, PRNewsFoto/Jambu Footwear/AP Images. P. 587, Courtesy The Bloomington Convention and Visitors Bureau-Home of Mall of America. P. 589, Used with permission of Orbix Hot Glass. P. 594, ©Lars Niki. P. 597, ©M. Hruby. P. 600, Used with Permission of L.L.Bean. P. 604, Courtesy STI Group/Germany; Nestlé S.A. and Nestlé S.A. P. 605, Courtesy of Gardener's Supply.

Ch. 18

Page 620, ©Inter IKEA Systems B.V. 1999–2015. P. 624, PRNewsFoto/Hyundai Motor America/AP Images. P. 625, ©2014 Procter & Gamble. All rights reserved. P. 626, ®, ™, ©2015 Kellogg NA Co. P. 628, Image courtesy American Cleaning Institute; www.cleanininginstitute.org. P. 636, PRNewsFoto/Clayton Homes/AP Images. P. 644, ©2015 Capital One.

Ch. 19

Page 672, Used with permission of IBM Corporation. P. 674, Used with permission of Brenthaven. P. 680, ©2015 Dell. P. 682, ©2014 SAP SE or an SAP affiliate company. All rights reserved. P. 683, ©2015 Honeywell International Inc. P. 686, ©Ira Roberts. P. 690, Used with permission of Board Vantage. P. 691, Copyright ©2015 Windstream Communications. All rights reserved.

Ch. 20

Page 706, Courtesy of Federal Trade Commission. P. 716, Courtesy of Federal Trade Commission. P. 719, PRNewsFoto/lucy/AP Images. P. 722, © McGraw-Hill Education. / Bob Coyle, photographer. P. 722, © McGraw-Hill Education. Jacques Cornell photographer. P. 723, © McGraw-Hill Education. Jill Braaten, photographer. P. 724, ©2014 Pacific Bioscience Laboratories Inc. All rights reserved.

Name Index

Page numbers followed by n refer to notes.

a

b

C

d

e

f

g

h

i

j

k

m

q

r

S

t

U

V

W

x

y

z

Case Index

Subject Index

a

d

e

j

k

l

m

n

o

P

t

u

v

W

Y

Z